THE SECOND
BARNHART DICTIONARY
OF NEW ENGLISH

Clarence L. Barnhart
Sol Steinmetz
Robert K. Barnhart

BARNHART/HARPER & ROW, *Publishers*

*Bronxville, New York, Cambridge, Hagerstown, Philadelphia,
San Francisco, London, Mexico City, São Paulo, Sydney*

FIRST EDITION

ISBN: 0-06-010154-7

LIBRARY OF CONGRESS CATALOG CARD NUMBER: 80-65573

TABLE OF CONTENTS

Preface v

Editorial Advisory Committee vii

Editorial Staff ix

Explanatory Notes xi

Pronunciation Key xiv

Dictionary A-Z 1-520

Language Notes

Abbreviations 1

Abstracted Forms 3

Acronyms 6

Back Formations 50

Blends 72

Borrowings 79

Clipped Forms 107

Code Words 109

Coinages 111

Combining Forms 113

Compounds 115

Derivatives 141

Euphemisms 181

Functional Shifts 210

Idioms 251

Meanings 298

Nonce Words 323

Patterned Forms 346

Proper Names 373

Technical Terms 462

Trademarks 475

Usages 490

PREFACE

This dictionary is a continuation of the first *Barnhart Dictionary of New English* issued in 1973. It is the outgrowth of files so burgeoning with new words and new meanings and new applications of old words to fit new situations that we are publishing this material three years ahead of our scheduled time for a second book.

English is in nearly universal use; it is also growing and changing rapidly so that users of English throughout the world need a dictionary that contains the important new words and meanings. Unabridged dictionaries are issued infrequently and standard desk dictionaries have scant space for new entries and almost none at all for citations showing the new words in use, or for discussions relating the new words to the standard vocabulary. Therefore it is not surprising that the first Dictionary of New English (1973) and the second Dictionary of New English (1980) contain more than 10,000 words and meanings not entered or inadequately explained in standard dictionaries. Together or separately these two books supplement the current dictionaries of the English language.

In making the second Dictionary of New English, we have largely followed the principles and the editorial practices of the first dictionary by 1) giving enough context in the citations to indicate the environment in which a word is used, 2) providing ample identification of sources and their dates to show the type of writing, 3) marking the level or area of usage in usage labels, 4) writing usage notes to give editorial judgment, 5) pronouncing difficult words in an IPA-based key, and 6) providing etymologies wherever appropriate.

Following our usual practice, we asked a committee of distinguished scholars to review our editorial principles. As a result of conferring with members of this committee, we have greatly expanded the number of usage notes and also included a new type of usage note, such as those under *abortion* and *developing*, which lists and correlates terms connecting them with the new practices of our changing world. Such long notes of usage are particularly helpful in explaining new words. In addition, we have introduced a series of articles, such as those under *Acronyms* and *Back Formations*, which discuss processes of word formation with numerous examples drawn from entries in this dictionary.

Another innovation strongly urged on the editors by the Advisory Committee is to supply the year of our earliest available evidence for use of a word or meaning. This date in brackets, usually in an etymology, should provide a fair approximation of the time when a word or meaning achieved widespread use in the language.

This dictionary is the result of the cooperation of the Editorial Advisory Committee, our editorial staff, the outside readers of the manuscript, and the research staff that reads for new words year by year. The group has worked to produce a dictionary that provides information not easily available elsewhere and has participated in developing innovations in dictionary-making.

All sampling processes are plagued with inadequacies. No doubt this dictionary suffers from them by omission and, regrettably, by commission. We will gratefully welcome comments and suggestions for their correction. Our design is to make an up-to-date and accurate record of standard English and we invite your help in doing this.

Clarence L. Barnhart
Sol Steinmetz
Robert K. Barnhart

EDITORIAL ADVISORY COMMITTEE

YUTAKA MATSUDA

Professor of English, Kwansei Gakuin University, Nishinomiya, Japan.
Author of *The American Impact on British Empire*, 1975, and *Aspects of English Usage*, 1977.

ANGUS McINTOSH

Professor of English and Director, Middle English Dialect Project, University of Edinburgh, Edinburgh, Scotland.
Author of *Introduction to a Survey of Scottish Dialects*; co-author of *Patterns of English*.

LADISLAS ORSZÁGH

Chairman of the Lexicographical Committee of the Hungarian Academy of Sciences; formerly Professor of English at the University of Debrecen, Hungary.
General Editor of *Angol-Magyar Szótár: Magyar-Angol Szótár* [English-Hungarian and Hungarian-English Dictionary].

I. WILLIS RUSSELL

Professor Emeritus of English, University of Alabama.
Chairman of the Research Committee on New Words of the American Dialect Society.
Co-editor of "Among the New Words" department in *American Speech*.

MATTHEW H. SCARGILL

Professor of Linguistics and Department Head, University of Victoria, Canada.
Director of Lexicographical Centre for Canadian English.
Co-editor of *Dictionary of Canadian English* series, and *A Dictionary of Canadianisms on Historical Principles*.
Author of *An English Handbook* and *Modern Canadian English Usage*.

EDITORIAL STAFF

EXPLANATORY NOTES

The Second Barnhart Dictionary of New English is a supplement to existing general purpose, English-language dictionaries. As such it closely follows the style of current dictionaries, which makes the framework of this dictionary a familiar one that is easy to use. It will be doubly familiar to users of the first *Barnhart Dictionary of New English* (1973), as the new book serves to continue the record of changing English found in the previous work.

However, there are some innovations in style and departures from traditional dictionary content that deserve explanation.

Usage Notes and Articles

Editorial comments and related information about usage, word formation, cultural or historical facts, etc., are provided in notes and articles. They describe changing fashions in current English usage, based on evidence from our files. This departure from the traditional dictionary practices includes usage notes such as those listed under *dingbat, prioritize, fulsome,* and general articles at *abortion, acupuncture, developing, death, person,* etc., when it seems appropriate to give the user much of the contemporary information available from an editorial reading of our files.

Another source of information about the present-day direction of the language is the series of articles discussing processes and types of word formation and usage, such as *Abbreviations, Borrowings, Coinages, Euphemisms, Nonce Words,* and *Technical Terms*. These Language Notes contain examples derived from entries in this book.

The usage notes appear at the end of entries, following the date or the etymology and are indicated by the sign (►); the articles generally appear at the end of entries but the Language Notes form separate entries. A list of these Language Notes will be found in the Table of Contents.

Arrangement of Entries

1) Many derivative forms of main-entry words are listed in smaller boldface type directly under the entries to which they are related, as **psychobiographer** and **psychobiographical** under the main entry **psychobiography.** Although these subentries have citations they are not defined, because, like the run-on entries in standard dictionaries, the meaning is easily derived from the main entry. The grouping may also serve to unlock their function by showing that their relationship to the head word is more a grammatical than a semantic shift. Moreover, grouping related entries explains subtle elements of development of the language.

2) Derivatives and compounds are entered separately whenever they cannot be satisfactorily explained by a combination of the prefix, suffix, or combining form with the root word. New affixes (as in *-aholic*) and new meanings of affixes and com-

bining forms (as *petro-*) are recorded under the affix or combining form. Unusually active affixes and combining forms are entered and examples of their use and productivity are given. The user should look first under the affix or combining form. If the word is not given there, it may have a specialized meaning or be unusually frequent and the user should consult the proper alphabetical order of the main entries.

3) Variant spellings appear as entries only if they are very common; normally only the most frequent spelling is given because of the great variation found in the spelling of new words. Thus, the spellings *Parti Québécois* and *Parti Quebecois*, which appear in the quotations under *Parti Québecois*, are not listed as variants.

4) The names of popular new products and services that are known to be registered trademarks are capitalized and described as trademarks in this book. Variant spellings of trademarks that occur very frequently are also recorded, but they should not be regarded as indications of the legal status of a trademark (that is, as to whether it is becoming a generic term).

Dating of Entries and Definitions

1) Every main entry in this dictionary has the year of its earliest appearance in our files or in other sources as far as the editors could ascertain. The year is in brackets at the end of the main entry, but before subentries and usage notes, or at the beginning of an etymology.

> **blow·back**. . . . [1975 for def. 1; 1978 for def. 2]
> **bullhorn,** *v.t.* . . . . [1970, verb use of the noun (1955)]
> **Chis·an·bop**. . . . [1976, from Korean . . .]
> **displaced homemaker**. . . . [1978]

While the date supplied should provide some idea about when a word or meaning became current, it is not necessarily the earliest attestation and serves only as a rough guide to the word's appearance in the language. In most cases an example can probably be found that antedates the year cited here, for the usage predominant at any given time has usually been nurtured in an earlier decade or an even longer period of time.

Sometimes a word or meaning exists for a long time in isolation among the members of a particular group or within a specialized field of activity or in use restricted to its coiner, before it comes into general currency. Whenever our files disclose such a fact, two dates are provided: the first is the year of our earliest quotation for the term; the second date is the year the term begins to be frequently recorded, indicating its probable emergence into the mainstream of the language as indicated by appearance in popular sources.

> **cluster headache**. . . . [1953, 1972]
> **lacto-ovo-vegetarian**. . . . [1952, 1975 . . .]
> **layering**. . . . [1971, coined in 1950 by Bonny Cashin,
> born 1915, an American fashion designer]
> **biorheology**. . . . [1969, coined in 1948 by A. L. Copley
> from *bio-* of biology + *rheology* (1931) . . .]

2) In many instances the original meaning or root form of an entry is given a date. This date serves to explain the relationship between the new formation and the older established form and to show the gradual change in form and meaning that occurs in the language.

> **carpool** or **car-pool**, *v.i.* . . . . [1966, verb use of *car pool* (1940's)]
>
> **ban**, *v.t.* . . . . [1966, specialized sense of *ban* to forbid, prohibit (OED 1816)]
>
> **senior citizenship**. . . . [1972, from *senior citizen* (1955) + -*ship*]
>
> **back-to-basics**. . . . [1975, from the phrase *back to (the) basics;* the phrase *the basics* is an Americanism (1950's) meaning the fundamentals or elementary principles]

3) To confirm or establish information about the chronology of English vocabulary the editors consulted various well-known historical dictionaries, including *The Oxford English Dictionary* (OED), the first two volumes of *A Supplement to the Oxford English Dictionary* (OEDS), *The Century Dictionary and Encyclopedia* (OC) and its supplement (OCS), the *Dictionary of Americanisms* (DA), *A Dictionary of American English* (DAE), *A Dictionary of Canadianisms on Historical Principles*, the *Middle English Dictionary*, *The Stanford Dictionary of Anglicised Words and Phrases*, *A Dictionary of Australian Colloquialisms*, *A Dictionary of South African English*, and the *Dictionary of Jamaican English*.

Pronunciation

1) The pronunciation of a hard or unfamiliar word is given in parentheses immediately after the entry word; no pronunciation is given for well-known words. Entries with pronunciations are syllabicated for the convenience of the user.

Usually only one pronunciation is provided despite the possibility of variants except in the case of loanwords where the foreign pronunciation is often accompanied by an Anglicized form. The pronunciation we provide is the one most likely to be heard in the United States but does not preclude the use of other pronunciations equally acceptable in various parts of the English-speaking world.

2) The pronunciation key, given in full on the following pages, is composed of symbols in a broad adaptation of the International Phonetic Alphabet. The letter *y*, however, is an exception which we use to represent what in English is spelled with *y* in *yes* and *you* and *yarn* (for IPA *y*, a non-English vowel sound, we use Y).

In indicating the pronunciation of *vowels and diphthongs* we have chosen, at points of difference, to represent "American" rather than "British" speech. Thus although the key contains (ɔ) to represent an "aw"-type of "British" pronunciation of the *o* in *hot*, we use the (a) which represents an "ah"-type vowel that is preponderant in America.

PRONUNCIATION KEY

A. Vowels and Diphthongs

æ   a in *hat* (hæt)

ɑ   o in American *hot* (hɑt)
ɑː   a in *father* ('fɑ: ðər)
ai   i in *nice* (nais)
au   ou in *out* (aut)

e   e in *set* (set)
ei   a in *gate* (geit)

i   i in *hit* (hit)
iː   ee in *feet* (fiːt)

ɔ   o in British *hot* (hɔt)
ɔː   aw in *raw* (rɔː)
ɔi   oi in *oil* (ɔil)

ou   o in *go* (gou)
u   oo in *book* (buk)
uː   oo in *boot* (buːt)

ə   u in *cup* (kəp), a in *ago* (ə'gou)

B. Accented Vowels with R

ar   ar in *part* (pɑrt)
er   ar in *care* (ker)
ir   ear in *hear* (hir)

ɔr   or in *lord* (lɔrd)
ur   oor in *poor* (pur)
ər   ir in *bird* (bərd)

C. Syllabic Consonants

əl   le in *little* ('lit əl)
əm   m in *prism* ('priz əm)

ən   on in *prison* ('priz ən)
ər   ar in *altar* ('ɔːl tər)

D. Consonants

(1) Ordinary Letter Values

b   in *bed*
d   in *did*
f   in *fat*
g   in *go*
h   in *had*
k   in *kit*
l   in *leg*
m   in *man*

n   in *not*
p   in *pig*
r   in *run*
s   in *sad*
t   in *tan*
v   in *vat*
w   in *wet*
y   in *yes*

z   in *zoo*

(2) Special Symbols

∫   sh in *she* (ʃiː)
tʃ   ch in *chin* (tʃin)
ŋ   ng in *sing* (siŋ)
θ   th in *thin* (θin)

ð   th in *then* (ðen)
ʒ   s in *measure* ('meʒ ər)
dʒ   j in *join* (dʒɔin)

E. Foreign Sounds

Foreign words are for the most part pronounced with the nearest equivalents in English sounds. For example, the close *e* of a French word such as *né* is represented by *ei* as in English *nay* (nei). The following symbols, however, are used for some specifically foreign sounds:

a   a in French *patte* (pat)
œ   eu in French *heure* (œr)
x   ch in German *ach* (ɑːx)

ʏ   u in French *du* (dʏ)

~   over a vowel letter, nasal vowel, as in French *sans* (sɑ̃), *vin* (vɛ̃), *bon* (bɔ̃), *un* (œ̃), Portuguese *são* (sɑ̃u)

F. Accents

'   primary stress, as in bə'luːn *(balloon)*

ˌ   secondary stress, as in 'el əˌvei tər *(elevator)*

*A Dictionary of
New English*

A

A, a symbol used in Great Britain to designate motion pictures that are unrestricted for showing to adult audiences but may not be suitable for showing to children under 14, and therefore require parental discretion and guidance. The approximate U.S. equivalent symbol is *PG.*

At the Paris Pullman, Ravi Shankar is being lionised in Raga (A). *Russell Davies, "Cinema," The Observer (London), March 31, 1974, p 36*

[1970] ► This symbol was used in Great Britain from about 1914 for motion pictures designated by the Board of Film Censors as suitable only for adults, as distinguished from *U* — suitable for universal exhibition. In the current system the symbol has been given a less restrictive meaning. See G for another usage note.

AA, a symbol used in Great Britain to designate motion pictures to which persons under 14 are not admitted unless accompanied by an adult. The approximate U.S. equivalent symbol is *R.*

The committee recommends acceptance of the British Board of Film Censors' four new categories of U, A, AA and X. *The Times (London), May 15, 1970, p 4*

Being a fantasy about a fantasy, *Westworld* (Universal, AA) could well catch on. *Russell Davies, "Cinema," The Observer (London), March 17, 1974, p 34*

[1970, probably from *A*ccompanied by *A*dult]

Abbreviations. ► As space-saving and time-saving devices, abbreviations have become commonplace in current English writing and speech. The types of words or phrases most frequently abbreviated are technical terms and the names of groups and organizations. Often the abbreviations are more commonly used than the terms or names themselves. Scientists, for example, invariably use the abbreviation *DNA* in place of the long and hard-to-pronounce *deoxyribonucleic acid,* and the abbreviations of government organizations, such as *CIA* and *FBI,* are far more frequent, even in formal writing and speech, than the names they stand for. The usual style or practice is to give the standard term or name when it is first mentioned and follow it with the abbreviation in parentheses: exclusive economic zone (EEZ), transcendental meditation (TM), videocassette recorder (VCR); thereafter only the abbreviation is used.

As a rule, abbreviations are pronounced letter by letter: *ERA* (for Equal Rights Amendment) is pronounced 'i:'ar'ei, *IV* (for intravenous) is likewise pronounced 'ai'vi: When the abbreviation occurs only in writing (as *b.y.* for billion years and *mg* for milligram) the abbreviation is usually read as the words it stands for: "billion years, milligram." However, when the abbreviation is for a technical non-English term (as *q.i.d.* for Latin *quater in die*) it is usually translated into English in its full form "four times a day." Other common abbreviations follow a variety of rules, such as *i.e.,* pronounced 'ai'i: or translated "that is" and *viz.,* pronounced viz or translated "namely." Other abbreviations (known as ACRONYMS) are pronounced as words: *NOW* (for National Organization for Women) is pronounced nau. Some forms can be treated as either ordinary abbreviations or acronyms: *VAT* (for value-added tax) can be prounounced as 'vi:ei'ti: or as the word (væt).

The tendency today is to omit periods after abbreviations of technical terms and organizations: CPR (for cardiopulmonary resuscitation) rather than *C.P.R.;* EPA (for Environmental Protection Agency), not *E.P.A.* Some abbreviations, though, appear both with and without periods with equal frequency: *CB* or *C.B.* (for citizens band), *UPC* or *U.P.C.* (for Universal Product Code).

Abbreviations can be used as nouns, verbs, and other parts of speech (AC/DC, ETS), can produce derivatives (CBer, TMer) and variants (CJD, C-J DISEASE), and can form new words (GRASER).

Symbols are similar in appearance and sometimes in function to abbreviations, but need not be shortened forms of the words, phrases, or notions they represent. Thus Y functions as a symbol for *upsilon,* a subatomic particle, and AA is a symbol used in Britain to designate certain motion pictures.

The frequency with which abbreviations are used instead of the full forms has led to care in choosing names whose abbreviations are not misleading. When the *Federation of British Industry* found that their abbreviation was *FBI,* they promptly renamed themselves the *Confederation of British Industry (CBI).*

ABC or **A.B.C.,** abbreviation of *Advance Booking Charter,* a type of low-cost air fare available to passengers booking flights a definite length of time before the date of departure. *Often used attributively.*

Air travel also registered substantial gains in 1977, stimulated by the continuing popularity of "alphabet fares," such

1

as the OTC (one-stop tour charter), and the ABC (advanced booking charter). *William A. Davis, "Travel," The Americana Annual 1978, p 506*

The A.B.C. passenger would not be required to be a member of any pre-formed group and would merely have to purchase his round-trip charter transportation from an independent tour operator or travel agent sufficiently far in advance. *"Air Charter Plan Offered by C.A.B.," The New York Times, Feb. 12, 1976, p 61*

[1972] Compare APEX, OTC, SUPER SAVER. See also AFFINITY GROUP.

ABD, abbreviation of *All But Dissertation* (applied to a doctoral candidate who has the necessary credits for a Ph.D. degree but has not written the dissertation).

Last month, 50 carefully selected PH.D.'s and A.B.D.'s (all but dissertation) completed the Careers in Business project, a unique, tuition-free program sponsored by the New York State Department of Education. *Time, Aug. 14, 1978, p 76*

Ph.D./DBA preferred. ABD's considered, less than ABD will be considered for a one-year temporary appointment only. *Advertisement by University of Southern Maine, The New York Times, April 15, 1979, p E11*

[1963]

Ab·gren·zung (Anglicized 'ab gren,tsuŋ; *German* 'ap gren tsuŋ), *n.* a policy of total separation of East Germany from West Germany.

While Willy Brandt, the West German Chancellor, talks of "two states in one German nation," Erich Honecker talks of *Abgrenzung*—a strict separation. *Time, Oct. 1, 1973, p 35*

While I was there in the winter the word on every official lip was *abgrenzung*. It means demarcation or separation, and is the label attached to the policy of deepening the division between the two Germanies, and banishing forever all hope of reunification. *Richard Davy, "Bridges Over a Troubled Border," The Times (London), May 3, 1972, p 16*

[1972, from German, literally, demarcation]

abortion, *n.* ► Johnson (1755) gives only two meanings: (1) "the act of bringing forth untimely" and (2) "the produce of untimely birth." The first meaning in Johnson is also the first meaning in the OED, as shown in the 1547 quotation from Andrew Boorde, *The Breviary of Healthe:* "Abhorsion is when a woman is delivered of her chylde before her tyme." Included under the first OED definition is a quotation from William Robertson's *The History of America* I, iv. 297 (1778) adding the idea of deliberate destruction of the fetus: "The women by the use of certain herbs procure frequent abortions."

This term is now used chiefly to mean the deliberate expulsion of a fetus at a pregnant woman's request with the intent of destroying it. This act has long been considered criminal or illegal in many countries, and was so considered in Great Britain until 1967 (when Parliament legalized it during the first 28 weeks of pregnancy within certain guidelines) and in the United States until 1973 (when the Supreme Court ruled that no state may prevent a woman from having an abortion during the first six months of pregnancy). Methods of legal abortion now include MENSTRUAL EXTRACTION, SALINE, VACU-UM ASPIRATION and the older *D and C.* ANTIABORTION groups continue to oppose the legalization of abortion on the grounds that it violates the right of fetuses to life; their movement is called PRO-LIFE or RIGHT-TO-LIFE and they are often referred to as RIGHT-TO-LIFERS. The more moderate ANTIABORTIONISTS are willing to allow abortions under some specific circumstances (as when continued pregnancy endangers a woman's health) but all are opposed to ABORTION-ON-DEMAND. Advocates of legislation permitting abortion are the PROABORTION groups, or PROABORTIONISTS (sometimes also simply called ABORTIONISTS), who insist on abortion-on-demand on the ground that a woman has the right to privacy and to choose what happens to her own body. Some proabortion groups wish to do away with all legal restrictions on induced abortions, though even the most liberal governments, as that of Sweden, are committed to the belief that fully developed fetuses must be protected, since the induced abortion of such "viable" fetuses may amount to the taking of a human life. See also PERSON and TEST-TUBE BABY.

Both in this country [Great Britain] and abroad, the overwhelming weight of evidence and opinion is that women who are refused an abortion are more likely to become emotionally disturbed than those who are aborted. A degree of remorse after abortion is not uncommon, as with any unwelcome event involving personal responsibility, but it is usually transient and mild and psychiatric assistance is rarely sought. *Colin Brewer, "Assessing the Psychiatric Factors in Abortion," The Times (London), Jan. 31, 1975, p 11*

Soviet gynecologists frown on abortion as a method of birth control for medical reasons and also because the state wants to increase the birth rate to develop a larger work force. "We do not consider abortion a good method of birth control," said the tall, silver-haired doctor. "We prefer other methods — the pill, the loop, diaphragms, condoms, rhythm. But if a woman wants an abortion during her first three months of pregnancy, that is her choice. After that, she can have an abortion only for medical reasons." *Hedrick Smith, "Abortion in the Soviet Union: Legal, Common, but Frowned Upon," The New York Times, Nov. 27, 1974, p 32*

abortionism, *n.* the support or advocacy of abortion-on-demand.

First, abortion foes must point out that abortionism is indeed an "ism," a creed quite as specific and aggressive as any creed its proponents denounce, demanding not only tolerance but legitimization, complete with tax dollars to pay for human death. *M. J. Sobran Jr., "Abortion: The Class Religion," National Review, Jan. 23, 1976, p 31*

[1976, from *abortion* + *-ism*] ► This term is chiefly used by antiabortionists. See also the note under RIGHT-TO-LIFE.

abortionist, *n.* a person who supports or advocates abortion-on-demand.

Marxist vocabulary has spread into all political nooks and crannies. Ecologists as well as abortionists envision "revolution." Whatever or whoever has position and power is termed "imperialist" and "fascist," and recently also "chauvinist." *Gerhart Niemeyer, "Days and Works," National Review, Feb. 20, 1976, p 157*

[1976, from *abortion* + *-ist*] Compare ANTIABORTIONIST and PROABORTIONIST.

► This term is chiefly used by antiabortionists. Its earlier meaning (recorded since 1872) is a person who induces illegal abortions.

abortion-on-demand, *n.* the right of a pregnant woman to have an abortion at any time during pregnancy.

Abortion-on-demand after the first six or seven months of fetal existence has been effected by the Court through its denial of personhood to the viable fetus, on the one hand, and through its broad definition of health, on the other. *John T. Noonan, Jr., "The Right to Life: Raw Judicial Power," National Review, March 2, 1973, p 261*

In some other countries, legislatures were also concerned with the matter of abortion. The Italian Chamber of Deputies legalized abortion on demand but the law was defeated in the Senate in June. *William D. Hawkland, "Law," Britannica Book of the Year 1978, p 485*

[1973]

Abstracted Forms. ► *Abstracted* means the use of a part of a word or phrase in what seems to be the meaning it contributes to the expression, as when *-gate* acquires a meaning from appearance in *Watergate*, then *Koreagate*, etc. In this way a linguistic form that is identical to all or part of an older form but is used in a different or broader range of contexts is described in this book as having been "abstracted from" the older form. For example, the combining forms -AHOLIC, -HOLIC, and -OHOLIC have all been drawn from *workaholic* (itself patterned on *alcoholic*) in order to extend this word's specific meaning of being compulsive about work to the general idea of being compulsive about anything. Most abstracted forms are combining forms: -GATE abstracted from WATERGATE, PORN- or PORNO- abstracted from the clipped forms *porn* or *porno* (*adj.* and *n.*). Sometimes the reverse occurs and a noun or adjective is abstracted from a combining form, as MAXI, *n.*, meaning "something very large," abstracted from *maxi-*, a combining form meaning "very large." Some words are abstracted from phrases and compounds: the slang word CITY in the sense of "person or thing of a specified character" was abstracted from the slang phrase FAT CITY; and phrases and compounds are often the bases of abstraction: RUN-OF-THE- was abstracted from *run-of-the-mill;* DIAL-A-, apparently from *Dialaphone;* FLEXI-, from such compound trademarks as *Flexi-Van.* See COMBINING FORMS.

A·ca·pul·co gold (ˌɑ: kəˈpuːl kou), a strong variety of Mexican marijuana.

American users seek out 'Acapulco Gold' as the strongest variety of Mexican marihuana, but no one knows whether Acapulco Gold is really obtained from a special variety of Cannabis, whether it is simply any marihuana with a high proportion of flowering tops as opposed to lower leaves . . . or whether it is just any marihuana a dealer can get a high price for. *Andrew T. Weil, Science Journal, Sept. 1969, p 38*

If you plan to grow your own backyard vegetable garden — a prudent idea these days, with onions the price of Acapulco Gold — you really should know that it's not nearly enough to douse your little herbaceous, photosynthetic friends with fish emulsion, blood meal, liquid humus, and kelp concentrate. *F. P. Tullius, "Talking to Your Veggies," The New Yorker, Aug. 13, 1973, p 26*

[1967, so called because it is grown near Acapulco, Mexico and because of the plant's golden color] Compare COLOMBIAN GOLD.

A·cas (ˈeiˌkæs), *n. British.* acronym for *Advisory, Conciliation and Arbitration Service*, a QUANGO of the Department of Industry consisting of some permanent civil servants and some co-opted members, the purpose of which is to arbitrate (at the request of both sides of an industrial dispute) when the ordinary process of conciliation has failed.

Acas completed conciliation in 2,595 disputes, and settlements were reached or arrangements to move towards a settlement were agreed in 2,123 of those, representing 82 per cent of the cases. *"Conciliation Service Settles 82% of Cases," The Times (London), April 13, 1976, p 4*

[1976]

accelerogram, *n.* a record or graph of the acceleration of tremors occurring in an earthquake.

Synthetic accelerograms were constructed on a computer by the author and William B. Joyner of the U.S. Geological Survey in order to determine experimentally how an earthquake generated observed ground shaking. *Illustration legend, "The Motion of the Ground in Earthquakes," Scientific American, Dec. 1977, p 78*

[1973, from *accelerate* + connecting *-o-* + *-gram*, derived from *accelerograph* (1954), instrument producing such a record]

acceptable, *adj.* capable of being tolerated; bearable.

DDT is eaten by Americans at only 10 per cent of the rate recommended by the WHO [World Health Organization] as a maximum acceptable daily intake. *Jon Tinker, "Cleaning Up America," New Scientist and Science Journal, Sept. 23, 1971, p 681*

In the light of what is now known about the almost unmatched toxicity of dioxin — and of what is *not* known about its precise mode of action and its long-term effects on human beings — should the government accept the assurances of herbicide manufacturers that a little dioxin is "acceptable" to people, just because the dioxin contaminant is being spread and sprayed around over large, rather than small, areas? *The New Yorker, July 25, 1977, p 54*

[1969, extended from the original (OED *c*1386) meaning "worthy or sure of being accepted"] See also ADI and ACTION LEVEL.

accepted pairing, advertising in which some advantageous feature of a competitor is conceded, especially to contrast that feature with a more desirable one of the advertised product or service.

At the same time, smart agencies were playing around with concepts like "accepted pairing" and "pre-emption." Avis was lagging behind Hertz. Doyle Dane realized that the simple negation of an unfavorable image doesn't pay. You don't deny the image, you make it work in your favor. The "We Try Harder" campaign was an example of "accepted pairing." *Ted Morgan, The New York Times Magazine, Jan. 25, 1976, p 53*

[1976] Compare COMPARATIVE ADVERTISING.

ac·cess[1] ('æk səs *or* æk'ses), *v.t.* **1** to obtain access to; reach.

Users can access the European Space Agency's system at Frascati, near Rome, by dialling an Orpington telephone number (a local call for most users in the Home Counties) and a telephone call to a London number gives users access to U.S. computers via a Post Office network at a cost of about £15 per hour. *New Scientist, Sept. 14, 1978, p 790*

Massive racks of "live storage" allow pallets to run for yards away into their insides. The pallets run on gentle slopes in open, parallel passageways, which can only be accessed from each end. *Tim Eiloart, New Scientist, Dec. 13, 1973, p 798*

2 to retrieve (data) from a computer storage unit or device.

DCS, MERIT, and TSS have dynamic file access, the ability of a program to access a remote data set as if it were local with no special planning. *David J. Farber, "Computer Networks," McGraw-Hill Yearbook of Science and Technology 1973, p 157*

[1970, def. 1, verb use of the noun (OED 1382) meaning "entrance" or "admission"; 1973 def. 2, verb use of noun (1950) used in computer technology]

access[2], *n. British.* the temporary release of programming by a radio or television station in order to allow an independent group to use the broadcasting facilities.

For purposes of our discussion, 'access' was defined roughly in terms of BBC 2's *Open Door* programmes of last winter, i.e. in the words of the working-committee's report, 'access involves temporary abdication of programme management by a broadcasting organisation, in order that an organisation or group might broadcast messages, subject only to the laws of the land.' *The Listener, Sept. 19, 1974, p 35*

Attributive use.

access channel: But I see nothing inconsistent in supporting the idea of a third and quite different force in broadcasting, designed from the outset to accommodate independent contributions and provide a public service in the fullest sense. It must be ten years since some of us first proposed an accommodation of 'access' channel. *Philip Purser, The Listener, Dec. 25, 1976, p 848*

access television: Access television is the term used for letting various minority and pressure groups, like one-parent families, black immigrants, people who want to stop black immigrants, old soldiers who feel they have been robbed of pensions, vegetarians, Vegans, even transvestites, into the studio to do their own thing. *Stanley Reynolds, "Open Door/BBC 2," The Times (London), May 31, 1976, p 7*

[1974]

access program, 1 *U.S.* a television program shown by a network affiliate during specified hours each week.

An analysis published in Broadcasting concluded that on the whole, the most successful "access programs" — those bought or produced by the stations for these periods — usually were updated versions of former network hits, such as "The Lawrence Welk Show" and "Hee-Haw." *Rufus W. Crater, et al., "Television and Radio," Britannica Book of the Year 1973, p 664*

2 *British.* a radio or television program designed for use by independent groups. See ACCESS[2].

Nevertheless, it was recognised that access programmes did present real problems for many existing broadcasting organizations. *The Listener, Sept. 19, 1974, p 357*

[1973 for def. 1; 1974 for def. 2]

accommodationist, *adj. U.S.* favoring accommodation or compromise, especially with the white establishment.

It was extremely easy for Randolph and Owen to dismiss the genuine conservatives, those protectors of Booker T. Washington's accommodationist legacy, who had counselled "first your country, then your rights." *Jervis Anderson, "Profiles: A. Philip Randolph—I," The New Yorker, Dec. 2, 1972, p 99*

[1970, from *accommodation* + *-ist*]

accommodation payment, a payment in which a customer is knowingly overcharged and later secretly given back the extra money, thus concealing the bribe.

A-T-O said it also found about $400,000 of previously undisclosed "accommodation payments," or kickbacks, to foreign customers, relating to sales of about $4.5 million. *"A-T-O Inc. Disclose Additional $400,000 In Dubious Payments," The Wall Street Journal, Nov. 12, 1976, p 14*

[1976]

accountability, *n. U.S. Education.* the holding of schools and teachers accountable for student performance by allocating school funds or teachers' salaries on the basis of the test scores of students.

Volume Three deals with the fundamental concern of productivity — or how to get a more effective performance out of teachers for less money; and with its corollary, accountability — or how to arrange the relationship between schools and parents so that the parents can be sure they are getting what they want for the taxes they are paying. *William K. Stevens, The New York Times, Oct. 22, 1972, p 9*

[1972, specialized sense of the noun (OED 1794) meaning the state of being held accountable or responsible]

accounting package, a computer program or routine that keeps account of the day-to-day use and operation of a computer, used especially in scheduling the workload and in analyzing the amount of time the equipment is used.

Recent innovations in the use of accounting packages include the development of commercial products that accept data collected by the accounting package and produce special reports in simplified formats that facilitate the use of the information in the operation and management of the computer installation. *Michael F. Morris, "Digital Computer Usage," McGraw-Hill Yearbook of Science and Technology 1975, p 156*

[1975]

accretion disk, a disk of gases or other interstellar matter around a black hole, neutron star, or other celestial body, formed by the gravitational attraction of the interstellar matter to the celestial body.

This formation, called an accretion disk, may be very important in some stellar birth sequences. In our own solar system . . . the planets and asteroids formed from the accretion disk as the sun grew in the embryo core. *Stephen P. Maran, "The Birth of a Star," The World Book Science Annual 1979 (1978), p 66*

The rate of flow of gas into the black hole may vary, perhaps because the accretion disc is not uniform in composition, or because the accretion disc as a whole is disturbed in some way. *The Times (London), May 12, 1976, p 9*

Exerting its gravitation attraction on its huge visible neighbor, the black hole apparently stretches the star into an egg shape and pulls off large amounts of gases. As the particles of gas spiral inward, orbiting the black hole in ever tighter circles before entering the event horizon, they collide, compress and heat up. Temperatures within this so-called accretion disk of gases surrounding the black hole reach 10 million degrees C., sending streams of intense X rays into space. *Time, Sept. 4, 1978, p 59*

[1976]

AC/DC or **AC-DC** ('ei,si:'di:,si:), *adj. Slang,* **1** capable of being sexually involved with either sex; attracted to both sexes; bisexual.

This is not just the look-alike, dress-alike unisex of Rolling Stone Mick Jagger and wife Bianca; AC-DC sexuality has jumped out of the closet and into the dinner party. *Newsweek, Aug. 27, 1973, p 56*

2 fluctuating between opposites; indecisive, ambivalent, or nonaligned.

The fact that the politically A.C.-D.C. Moynihan should be thought of as having a chance of becoming the Democratic senatorial nominee has much to do with the Democrats' eagerness not to make another mess of things. *Andy Logan, "Around City Hall," The New Yorker, June 7, 1976, p 109*

[1971; the term, however, is much older although it is recorded only in Wentworth and Flexner's *Dictionary of American Slang* (1960) with this note: "Some jocular use c1940." *AC/DC* and *AC-DC* are from the abbreviation of *Alternating Current/Direct Current.*]

ACD solution, a substance used to prevent coagulation of whole blood stored in blood banks.

Using current technology, whole blood can now be preserved for three weeks or more. A popular formulation was and still is the so-called ACD solution (dextrose-citric acid-sodium citrate), which permits a refrigerated shelf life of 21 days. By adding adenine or inosine to ACD, it has become possible to extend this period, although the medical properties of these modified solutions require further study. *William J. Kuhns and Louanne Kennedy, "Blood," 1975 Collier's Encyclopedia Year Book (1974), p 67*

[1974, *ACD* abbreviation of *acid citrate dextrose*]

ace, *v.t.* Often, **ace out.** *U.S. College Slang.* to get a high or the highest grade in (a test or course).

The dramatic device that gives *The Paper Chase* its unity and tension is the question of whether Hart will get his grades, whether he will ace-out Kingsfield's course. *Jay Cocks, "Cinema," Time, Oct. 29, 1973, p 98*

[1970, extended from the earlier (1920's) sports meaning "to score an ace" against an opponent (in tennis, golf, etc.); influenced by the fact that *A* is both the highest grade and the letter that appears on the ace in a deck of playing cards]

ac·e·ta·min·o·phen (,æs ə tə'min ə fən), *n.* a crystalline drug used against pain or fever instead of aspirin in cases of hemorrhagic, sinus, or asthmatic disorders. *Formula:* $C_8H_9NO_2$

Acetaminophen, another tongue-twister, though about

equivalent to aspirin offers a few advantages. It is less irritating to the stomach (good for ulcer victims) and can be substituted for aspirin by patients who have an allergy to salicylates. Unfortunately, it does not possess the antiinflammatory properties of aspirin and so is not very effective for arthritis patients. It does work for headache, menstrual cramps, and muscle aches. *Joe Graedon, The People's Pharmacy, 1976, p 67*

The medical profession's concern about the use of analgesics has been heightened by the aggressive introduction of aspirin substitutes such as Tylenol and Datril, which contain the drug acetaminophen. Though this drug has the advantage of not causing the stomach irritation associated with aspirin and though it can be taken by the few people sensitive to aspirin, it also has drawbacks: in large doses it can cause liver damage. In addition, since it is not an anti-inflammatory agent it does not work against the swollen joints characteristic of arthritis. *"Relieving the Analgesic Headache," Time, Aug. 1, 1977, p 70*

[1968, from *acetic* + *amino* + *phenol*]

A·ché (a:'tʃei), *n.* a member of a nomadic hunting tribe of South American Indians living like Stone Age people in the jungles of eastern Paraguay.

The Achés . . . subsist on honey, insects, fish and any animals they can reach with seven-foot bows and arrows. *"A Stone Age Culture is Threatened," The New York Times, Jan. 27, 1974, Sec. 4, p 2*

[1974] Compare TASADAY and YANOMAMA.

A chromosome, any one of the set of chromosomes characteristic of a species.

The designation B indicates a supernumerary chromosome, in contrast to the A chromosomes, the representatives of the normal complement. *John Bishop, "B Chromosomes in Grasshoppers," Nature, Jan. 22, 1976, p 174*

[1976]

acid dust, dust particles with a high concentration of acidity.

But in addition to acid rain and smog, blamed for most of the deleterious effects of the Los Angeles basin's notorious air pollution, the researchers discovered that acid dust was also to blame. *"Science Watch," The New York Times, Dec. 12, 1979, p C2*

[1979] Compare ACID PRECIPITATION, ACID RAIN.

acid flush, a run-off of precipitation with a high concentration of acidity.

Snow in Norway accumulates for half a year and then the acidic content thaws out first, so in early spring there is an "acid flush" that can kill fish. *The Times (London), July 19, 1977, p 18*

[1977] Compare ACID PRECIPITATION.

acid mist, fog with a high concentration of fine particles of a toxic chemical.

Man is stricken by "acid mist" in Chicago, caused by the leakage of silicon tetrachloride from a chemical storage tank on April 26. *Picture legend, "The Natural Environment," Britannica Book of the Year 1975, p 286*

[1975] Compare ACID RAIN.

acid precipitation, precipitation (such as rain or snow) of high acidity (rated on the pH scale as 5.6 or even less) resulting from the emission into the atmosphere of pollutants.

Some experts fear that acid precipitation could lead to a

5

acid rain

15 percent reduction in timber yields in the next 20 years. That eventually could increase housing costs, since white pine, often used in home construction, is particularly vulnerable. *"The Growing Furor Over Acid Rain," U.S. News & World Report, Nov. 19, 1979, p 66*

[1978] Compare ACID RAIN.

acid rain, rain containing a high concentration of acidity, resulting from the emission into the atmosphere of pollutants, primarily sulfur and nitrogen oxides, which form sulfuric and nitric acid in raindrops.

Scandinavian and American researchers suspect that acid rains have killed fish in many lakes in both regions. Several high-altitude lakes in the Adirondacks are now devoid of fish. There is also evidence that acid rain may be damaging trees and other plants. *Boyce Rensberger, The New York Times, May 23, 1975, p 76*

It dissolves concrete, rusts cars, kills fish and stunts tree growth by up to 60%. And it comes disguised in gently falling rain. Academics have been fighting over it and businessmen have been suing because of it. *It* is acid rain, the latest environmental shocker, an ecological time bomb on a short fuse that can't be ignored. *Maclean's, July 11, 1977, p 17*

[1975] Compare ACID MIST and ACID PRECIPITATION.

ac·ne·i·gen·ic (ˌæk ni: əˈdʒen ik), *adj.* causing or producing acne.

The acneigenic potential of a chemical appears to be directly related to its overall toxicity. The importance of this fact is the implication that chloracne in an experimental animal can provide a very important screening test for systemic (not only skin) toxicity. *New Scientist, April 13, 1978, p 79*

[1978, from *acne* + connecting -*i-* + -*genic*, combining form meaning "producing" (ultimately from Greek *genés* born + English -*ic*)]

acoustic microscope, a microscope in which the object being studied is scanned with sound waves and its image is reconstructed with light waves.

Acoustic microscopes have several advantages over their optical counterparts in certain fields. This is because the image depends on the object's structural and mechanical properties, as opposed to its reflective and refractive properties. Thus the instruments have potential in electronics for revealing surface stresses in microcircuits which would be hidden from an optical microscope. Also the structure of living cells can be studied without damaging them by the "staining" that is required with an optical microscope. *New Scientist, Nov. 16, 1978, p 80*

The actual and potential applications of high-resolution acoustic microscopes range from fine-scale materials analysis to the study of biological tissues and organs. *Scientific American, July 1978, p 80*

[1976]

acoustic microscopy: The single British research group working on acoustic microscopy, based at University College London, has hailed as a "significant advance" the development in the US of the first acoustic microscope that can "see" objects as sharply as a conventional optical microscope. *New Scientist, Nov. 16, 1978, p 523*

acoustooptics, *n.* a branch of physics dealing with the generation of light waves by means of ultrahigh-frequency sound waves.

Practical applications of acoustooptics are showing up in many areas where laser light may be used to gain or transmit information . . . An example is the manufacture of integrated optics (similar to integrated circuits in electronics) for transmission of information. *"Future Ahead for Acoustooptic Technology," Science News, Dec. 9, 1972, p 381*

[1972, from *acousto-* acoustic + *optics*]

ACP, abbreviation of *African, Caribbean, and Pacific Associables,* an organization of 46 Third World countries formed for purposes of trading as a group with the European Economic Community and other nations of Europe, North America, etc.

The fact that Lomé [the Lomé Convention] involved all of black Africa, not just former British and French colonies, gave a new dimension to Europe's relations with developing countries as a whole, involving as it did virtual free access for all ACP products to the European market without reciprocity, and a $4,000 million development fund. The ACP considered it important enough to institutionalize themselves as a grouping complete with secretariat and regular ministerial meetings (the three held during the year were in Ghana, Guyana and Malawi). *O. E. Wilton-Marshall, "African Conferences and Institutions," The Annual Register of World Events in 1975 (1976), p 339*

[1974]

ac·ri·tarch (ˈæk rəˌtɑrk), *n.* an oceanic one-celled fossil organism of unknown classification.

H. Tappan recently suggested that quantitative and qualitative changes in the oceanic phytoplankton are indicated by its fossil record. In Fig. 1 blue-green algae, green algae, acritarchs . . . , dinoflagellates, and euglenids are represented as fossils by their highly resistant organic walls. *Helen Tappan, "Faunal Extinction," McGraw-Hill Yearbook of Science and Technology 1972, p 215*

[1963, from Greek *ákritos* indistinguishable + *arché* beginning]

ac·ro·lect (ˈæk rəˌlekt), *n. Linguistics.* the dialect that has most prestige among the speakers of a language, usually the standard dialect.

ACROLECT . . . is used for the collection of linguistic features of most prestige among a given community of speakers. *J. L. Dillard, Black English, 1972, p 299*

[1964, coined by the American linguist William A. Stewart from *acro-* highest (part) + dia*lect*] Compare BASILECT.

acronym, *v.t.* to make an acronym of; designate by an acronym.

Nitrogen oxide, acronymed NO_x, is another of the plant's noxious by-products, emitted at the rate of 240 tons per day. *Anthony Wolff, "Showdown at Four Corners," Saturday Review, June 3, 1972, p 30*

[1967, verb use of the noun]

Acronyms. ▶ These are words formed from the initial letters or syllables of other words. ANZAM (from the initials of Australia, New Zealand, and Malaysia) and SALT (from Strategic Arms Limitation Talks) are typical acronyms. They differ from abbreviations in that they are pronounced as words rather than as sequences of letters and often share the grammar of standard words, taking on plurals (*WASP*s, *MIRV*s), shifting to new parts of speech, etc.

6

act

Acronyms became popular during World War II, when words like *JATO* or *jato* (jet-assisted take-off), *WAC* or *Wac* (Women's Army Corps), *SHAEF* (Supreme Headquarters, Allied Expeditionary Force), and *radar* (*ra*dio *d*etecting *a*nd *r*anging) began to proliferate. The word *acronym* itself was coined in the 1940's to describe these new words (from *acro-* end, tip + *-onym* name, ultimately from Greek *ákros* and *ónyma*).

Most acronyms are spelled with capital letters like abbreviations, but they rarely appear with periods (see ABBREVIATIONS). When they become very common, they are frequently spelled in lower case: *quasar* (*quasi*-stell*ar*), *laser* (*l*ight *a*mplification by the *s*timulated *e*mission of *r*adiation). If they are proper names they usually retain the initial capital: *Anzam*, *Soweto* (*So*uth *We*stern *To*wnships), MARISAT (*Mari*time *sat*ellite), AMESLAN (*Ame*rican *S*ign *Lan*guage).

Acronyms are coined in English in almost all fields of activity. For example, computer technology has produced GIGO (garbage in, garbage out), MIPS (millions instructions per second), RAM (random-access memory), and ROM (read-only memory); law enforcement, PINS (Persons In Need of Supervision) and SWAT (Special Weapons and Tactics); aerospace, DOMSAT (*dom*estic *sat*ellite) and GUIDO (*guid*ance *o*fficer); medicine, MEDLARS (*Med*ical *L*iterature *A*nalysis and *R*etrieval *S*ystem) and its successor, MEDLINE; education, TEFL (teaching English as a foreign language) and TESOL (Teachers of English to Speakers of Other Languages); the military, COMINT (*com*munications *int*elligence), ELINT (*el*ectronic *int*elligence), MARV (*ma*neuverable *r*eentry *v*ehicle); environmentalism, ADAPTS (*A*ir *D*eliverable *A*ntipollution *T*ransfer *S*ystem) and UNEP (United Nations Environment Program); the government, CETA (Comprehensive Employment and Training Act), ERDA (Energy Research and Development Administration).

Politics has provided some of the quaintest and most suggestive examples of how acronyms can be coined or distorted for humorous or other effects: CREEP (*C*ommittee to *Ree*lect the *P*resident), GINNIE MAE (Government National Mortgage Association), MAD (mutual assured destruction), MEOW (moral equivalent of war), QUANGO (*qua*si-autonomous *n*ational *g*overnmental *o*rganization), WIN (Whip Inflation Now). The acronyms of foreign political and economic organizations often have an exotic ring: CARICOM, OPEC, SWAPO, ZANU, ZAPU. Some acronyms were formed in a foreign language and taken into English without a change: FRELIMO, GULAG.

Acronyms are sometimes deliberately modeled on older acronyms. Thus GRASER (gamma-ray amplification by stimulated emission of radiation) was clearly patterned after *laser* and the latter's own predecessor, the acronym *maser*. While the form of TASER (Tele-Active Shock Electronic Repulsion) also shows the influence of *laser*, its meaning (a kind of electronic gun) suggests that it may be modeled on *phaser*, the name of a futuristic gun

used in the popular science-fiction television series "Star Trek."

Acronyms have become so popular that new organizations seeking a name often seem to think first of a catchy and relevant short word to present to the public, and only then of a name for it to be the acronym of. One of the most popular acronyms in recent years has been GASP, adopted for obvious reasons by a number of antismoke and antipollution groups. Each group claimed it as its own coinage by providing a name for which the acronym supposedly stands: Group Against Smoke and Pollution, Gals Against Smoke and Pollution, Greater Washington Alliance to Stop Pollution, etc. But opting for originality, another group chose to call itself *ASH* (Action on Smoking and Health).

While an acronym can serve as a convenient code for a particularly long or cumbersome phrase, the indiscriminate use and coinage of acronyms is often deplored by literate people. An article in *New Scientist* (Feb. 29, 1968, p 473), entitled "Acronymania — A Modern Contagion," after decrying the unhealthy proliferation of acronyms, lists a glossary of proscribed forms, including DOTEL (Defenders of the English Language). The article ends: "Applications to join DOTEL will be forwarded on request."

acrylic, *n.* **1** a paint made with an acrylic resin as the vehicle, used especially in art.

Many artists abandoned the traditional media for environments and happenings and other new technologies. The painterly manner of abstraction, so widespread in the 1950s, changed to the hard-edged manner, with its dry, flat surfaces, usually painted in acrylic. *Paul C. Mills, "Richard Diebenkorn: Painting Against the Tide," Saturday Review, Nov. 4, 1972, p 55*

2 a painting done with acrylics.

Byron Burford—Acrylics on paper, some portraying carnival and circus life. Starts Saturday, March 1. *"Goings On About Town: Art," The New Yorker, March 3, 1975, p 10*

It's doubtful, however, that secretaries will ever reach the collecting level of Bob Billingsley who, to reach his presidential suite at Reed Paper, passes a $2,800 Jean McEwen oil, a $2,500 Gordon Smith acrylic (Fraser River Flats). *Valerie Ross, "A Thing of Beauty Is a Joy Forever, and/or a Tax Write-Off," Maclean's, March 22, 1976, p 54*

[1972, noun use of the adjective (as in *acrylic resin*, 1930's)]

act, *n.* **get one's act together,** *U.S. Slang.* to get organized; eliminate differences, inconsistencies, etc.; plan or work systematically.

There is no great battle crying to be fought over refugee policy reform. It merely requires that the administration get its act together and the legislators bargain out their differing emphases, so that the country can remain true to values it has long held dear. *The Manchester Guardian Weekly (The Washington Post section), April 9, 1978, p 16*

There I was, . . . weeping, feeling like a miserable, self-indulgent, neurotic, middle-aged woman who couldn't get her act together. *Eleanor Coppola, "Diary of a Director's Wife," The New York Times Magazine, Aug. 5, 1979, p 40*

[1978, apparently from show-business usage, referring to the need to harmonize diverse elements to produce a cohesive performance]

ac·ti·graph or **ac·to·graph** ('æk tǝ,græf), *n.* any device which records changes in the activity of a substance, organism, etc.

The presence of . . . isotopic methylmercury was established . . . by scanning the chromatographic sheets in an actigraph. *T. Edwards and B. C. McBride, "Biosynthesis and Degradation of Methylmercury in Human Faeces," Nature, Feb. 5, 1975, p 463*

Single crabs are placed in plastic boxes. . . . The boxes are balanced on a knife-edge fulcrum, and as the incarcerated crab moves between ends of this improvised actograph the box teeters, closing a microswitch that causes a deflection of a pen on a chart recorder. *John D. Palmer, "Biological Clocks of the Tidal Zone," Scientific American, Feb. 1975, p 70*

[1975, probably from *act* or *activity* + connecting *-i-* or *-o-* + *-graph* instrument that records]

ac·tin·in ('æk tǝ nin), *n.* a protein forming part of the complex of actin and myosin in muscle tissue.

The other proteins are not so well understood, but it is quite possible that the small proteins found in association with the active part of myosin, like troponin, regulate its movement. Another kind of function may be illustrated by actinin, which may help to maintain the regular architecture of the myofibrils. *Dennis Bray, "How Movements Evolved," New Scientist, Jan. 27, 1972, p 199*

[1972, from *actin* + *-in*]

action level, the level of concentration at which a toxic or other unwanted substance in a food in the United States is considered hazardous enough to public health to warrant government action to prevent the sale of the food.

In Washington, a spokesman for the Food and Drug Administration said that last May the agency established an "action level" of 0.1 part per million for Mirex in fish. Fish containing that level or more will be seized if shipped in interstate commerce. *Richard Severo, "Albany Plans Hatchery on a Contaminated Lake," The New York Times, Sept. 2, 1976, p 64*

[1976] Also called DEFECT ACTION LEVEL. See also ACCEPTABLE and ADI.

action replay, *British.* a videotape playback of a highlight of a sports event or the like.

To see only the action replays of the Royal Wedding, that long-drawn-out Match of the Day, was no doubt to miss the cumulative effect of an occasion. *Stuart Hood, "Television: Match of the Day," The Listener, Nov. 22, 1973, p 720*

[1973] The corresponding U.S. term is INSTANT REPLAY.

activator RNA, a form of ribonucleic acid believed to carry information used to activate the genes.

In either case the RNA transcribed from the integrator genes is designated activator RNA, since it bears information used for gene activation. *Roy J. Britten, "Gene Action," McGraw-Hill Yearbook of Science and Technology 1973, p 204*

[1970]

active euthanasia, the killing of a person who is incurably ill or injured, especially by the administration of a drug or other treatment that causes or hastens death.

As an adviser of the Euthanasia Council, Van Dusen . . .

supported explicitly only the right to die without being kept alive by heroic measures—a view that Pope Pius XII held. This is called "passive" euthanasia, which in law and morality is treated totally differently from active euthanasia, or "mercy killing." *"Religion: Good Death?" Time, March 10, 1975, p 84*

[1975] Also called POSITIVE EUTHANASIA.

► When the term *euthanasia* is used without a preceding modifier it usually means active euthanasia. See EUTHANASIA.

active site, the site on the surface of an enzyme at which its catalytic action takes place.

Although chemical methods alone had suggested the probable location of the active site, only the structure of the molecule could explain the specificity of the enzymes. *Robert M. Stroud, "A Family of Protein-Cutting Proteins," Scientific American, July 1974, p 78*

[1963]

active transport, the movement of a substance across a cell membrane by means of chemical energy. Active transport is always in a direction opposite to that of diffusion.

The transmission of nerve pulses, heart function, and kidney processes are coupled to a process known as active transport—the movement of sodium and potassium ions across cell membranes. *John G. Lepp, "Zoology," 1972 Britannica Yearbook of Science and the Future (1971), p 340*

[1963]

actualize, *v.t.* to fulfill the potentials of.

Society Schooling is based on the premise that human beings actualize themselves through work, that positive self-concepts are formed as individuals respond positively and successfully to stimuli in their immediate environment, and that learning to initiate, to lead, and to organize work is a vital form of education. *George Richmond, Saturday Review, June 24, 1972, p 45*

—*v.i.* to fulfill one's potential.

The professionals, she found, were a ludicrously earnest lot. "I come across as a human being," one of them soberly assured her. Their jargon was tiresome—they were always "resonating," "actualizing," "peaking," or having "gut reactions." *Time, July 27, 1970, p 74*

[1970; original meaning (1810) is "to make actual"]

actualizer, *n.:* In regard to comments about our leaders practicing TM, I would prefer seeing some actualizers in managerial positions attempting to effect changes in a similar direction (thus benefiting us all) than some stressed-up person who can't make decisions because, essentially, he doesn't know who he is! *Jon Jackman, Psychology Today, July 1974, p 8*

ac·u·pres·sure ('æk yǝ,preʃ ǝr), *n.* a method of relieving pain by applying pressure with the fingers on various points where major nerves are close to the skin; the use of finger pressure instead of needles to relieve pain.

The advantages of diagnosis by way of acupressure are obvious, a probing finger on the outside of the body as compared, for example, to opening up the body to see what's wrong. One of the new alternative medical centers . . . reports considerable success in diagnosing otherwise inexplicable complaints with acupressure. *Stephen A. Applebaum, Out In Inner Space, 1979, p 117*

Batja Cates . . . is really a foot magician. Her foot massage is based on some of the same principles as acupressure—that certain parts of the body carry life energy, and each energy line is related to the function of the body. *Nona Cleland, "There's the Rub," Sunday News (New York), June 3, 1979, p 43*

[1977, extended meaning of "a method of arresting surgical hemorrhage by pressure" (OED 1859), ultimately from Latin *acū* with a needle + English *pressure*] Compare SHIATSU.

acupuncture, *v.t.* to treat or anesthetize by inserting fine needles into specific parts of the body.

According to police findings, the two quack herb doctors acupunctured Chong Pyong-Chon, first daughter of Mrs. Park Okrye, 31. The girl died of heart failure one hour after the therapy Saturday. *Korea Times, Feb. 13, 1973, p 4*

[1972, verb use of the noun] ▶ Although the noun *acupuncture* first entered English in the late 1600's (the date of the OED quotation is 1684), it then referred only to medical practice in far-off China; thus it did not attain widespread currency until its expanded use in the 1970's. In the 1960's Chinese doctors used acupuncture as an anesthetic in performing major surgery. In the 1970's the American medical profession became interested in the anesthetic qualities of acupuncture and the term attained widespread currency in the language.

Derived from Latin *acus* needle + English *puncture*, the term designates the ancient Chinese practice of inserting fine needles into specific points of the body to relieve pain and treat disease. The method spread in ancient times from China to Japan and other parts of the Orient, but it was not widely practiced in Europe until the 1950's. Reports of its use in France, appearing in the English-language press, produced the first derivative of the term, *acupuncturist* (1952). The following early quotation refers to Vietnamese practitioners of the art.

Among recent exceptional meetings in France have been the first congress, in Paris, of acupuncturists (doctors who stick needles into you in the Chinese fashion). *The New Yorker, Sept. 15, 1956, p 88*

While acupuncture was vigorously promoted by the Communist Chinese government in the 1960's, for both the treatment of disease and surgical anesthesia, Americans were generally unfamiliar with its use until direct contact with the mainland Chinese was established in 1971. Then the method began to gain adherents and practitioners in the United States and Canada, where the term *acupuncturist* was applied to both physicians and nonphysicians who tried or experimented with acupuncture along with standard biomedical techniques. A recent quotation illustrates this use.

The best technically trained acupuncturist in the world with no medical training, who accepts patients, guesses at what is wrong and treats them, is a disaster looking for some place to happen. *D. A. Geekie, "Your View: Getting the Point," Maclean's, Aug. 1974, p 12*

Two other derivative terms have appeared: *acupunctural* (of or relating to acupuncture, 1971), and *acupunctured* (treated or anesthetized by acupuncture, 1972).

Surgeons are now so confident about the effects of acupunctural anaesthesia that they begin by the clock, without testing to check whether the operational area is numbed. *Neville Maxwell, "The Laughing Man With a Hole in His Chest," The Sunday Times (London), Oct. 3, 1971, p 5*

As American doctors verified that Chinese doctors were doing lung and other major surgery on acupunctured awake patients, some scientists became intensely curious about the wonders of the ancient practice. *Lawrence K. Altman, "Review of the Year: Health and Disease," Encyclopedia Science Supplement (Grolier) 1972, p 237*

Various theories as to how acupuncture works have been proposed. One widely cited explanation is the GATE-CONTROL THEORY, according to which acupuncture activates a pain-reducing mechanism by stimulating large neural fibers that inhibit the action of pain fibers. This inhibition occurs at any GATE of the nervous sytem at which pain signals are modulated before being carried off to the brain. Other scientists claim, however, that acupuncture has no neurological basis but rather is related to hypnosis and other psychological states.

Some experiments have tended to support the assumption that acupuncture is a form of psychosomatic treatment which may relieve pain and the symptoms of some diseases because of the patients' faith in its effectiveness. The Journal of the American Medical Association (June 16, 1975) reported that several experiments showed acupuncture to have about the same level of effectiveness in reducing chronic pain as placebos, sugar pills, or water injection whose beneficial effects are psychologically induced. See ELECTROACUPUNCTURE, NEEDLE THERAPY, QUACKUPUNCTURE, STAPLEPUNCTURE, and TEH CH'I.

acute-care, *adj. U.S.* designated or designed for the care and treatment of patients with diseases of relatively short duration; equipped to treat nonchronic diseases.

Citing a "drastically eroded" financial situation, the head of the city's Health and Hospitals Corporation has recommended reducing from 15 to 11 the number of acute-care municipal hospitals. *David Bird, The New York Times, Jan. 21, 1976, p 1*

[1976]

A/D, abbreviation of *analog-to-digital* (conversion in computers).

The terminal also performs important associated functions such as "companding." This function is a quasi-logarithmic compression of the analogue signal before or concurrent with A/D conversion and a corresponding expansion after or concurrent with D/A conversion; its purpose is the handling of the large dynamic range of diverse speakers without sacrificing the overall signal-to-noise ratio for those who speak softly. *Ernest R. Kretzmer, "Communication Terminals," Scientific American, Sept. 1972, p 138*

[1972] Compare D/A.

adaptor, *n. Molecular Biology.* a molecule of RNA (ribonucleic acid) that binds amino acids to their correct positions on messenger RNA templates during protein synthesis.

The DNA unfolds when it replicates, and each single strand is free to pick up a complementary partner. The information is carried in a "code" contained in the order of these bases. Three sequential bases constitute a "word," and it is this word that is read by the ribosomes, which do the hooking up of the molecules in the cell to make the proteins. The concept of such a ribosome "adaptor" is also largely due to Crick. *Jeremy Bernstein, Review of "The Eighth Day of Creation," by Horace Freeland Judson, The New York Times Book Review, April 8, 1979, p 34*

[1963]

ADAPTS (ə'dæpts), *n.* acronym for *Air Deliverable Antipollution Transfer System*, a system used by the U.S. Coast Guard for cleaning up oil spills along coastlines with inflated nylon bags coated with rubber, special pumps, and other devices deliverable by air.

The pumps that were put onto the crumbling tanker and lost in violent seas were the Coast Guard's air-deliverable anti-pollution control systems, known as ADAPTS, designed for the Coast Guard by Ocean Science and Engineering Inc., Long Beach, Calif. *Victor K. McElheny, "Storm Termed Block to Salvaging of Oil," The New York Times, Dec. 24, 1976, p A-8*

[1976]

added value, the value or cost increase added to a commodity at each stage of its production and distribution. It forms the basis of the *added-value tax* or *value-added tax* (abbreviated *VAT*) that is ultimately passed on to the consumer. *Often used attributively.*

For food and materials generally, and for substitute sources of energy like nuclear and solar power, the early prospect was one not of definite exhaustion but rather of steadily rising marginal cost. In short, the price of food, materials and energy, in terms of manufactured products or 'added value', would be bound to rise. *H. V. Hodson, "Editorial," The Annual Register of World Events in 1974 (1975), p 4*

The international division of labour is speeding up, and unless Europe acts now, it will be left with only a few high added-value industries and a few small subcontractors. *Jacques Attali, "Crisis Versus Change," The Manchester Guardian Weekly (Le Monde section), Jan. 18, 1975, p 12*

[1974, abstracted from earlier (1968) *added-value tax*] See ZERO-RATE.

add·on, *n U.S.* **1** an attachment that extends the usefulness, power, or application of a device

Attachments to the color television receiver which provide the capability of screening taped material, whether homegrown or rented, will be the consumer's prime demand. These sophisticated television "add-ons," known in the industry as electronic video recording and playback equipment . . . *Allan Yale Brooks, "Electronics," 1973 Collier's Encyclopedia Year Book, p 274*

2 *Figurative use.*

Finally, literature and philosophy are assigned the role of add-ons — intellectual adornments that have nothing to do with "genuine" education. *Norman Cousins, "How to Make People Smaller Than They Are," Saturday Review, Dec. 1978, p 15*

[1973, from the verb phrase *add on*]

address, *v.t.* to indicate or find (the location of a

piece of stored information) in a computer.

Now, instead of the hardware for a given control application being relatively expensive and roughly proportional to the size of the task, the hardware is amazingly cheap — and the size of control task is limited only by the amount of memory which can be addressed (a 10 bit address handles 1024 program steps). *Fred Heath, New Scientist, Jan. 15, 1976, p 120*

[1976, verb use of *address, n.* (OEDS 1951) the location of a piece of information in a computer memory; see also ADDRESSABLE, *adj.* (1963) just below]

addressable, *adj.:* The past year represents a milestone in demonstrating the practical feasibility of electron beam addressable memory systems (EBAM systems). *Dennis E. Speliotis, "Computer Memory," McGraw-Hill Yearbook of Science and Technology 1976, p 146*

a·den·yl·ate (ə'den ə,leit), *v.t.* to convert (a substance, as messenger RNA) to adenylic acid (a constituent of many coenzymes important in muscle contraction and sugar metabolism).

The NIH [National Institute of Health] workers conclude that the maternal mRNA in the unfertilized egg is unadenylated or partially adenylated. *New Scientist, Dec. 14, 1972, p 623*

[1972, from *adenyl* substance derived from adenine + *-ate* verb suffix meaning to cause to become]

adenylation, *n.:* The longevity of the latent messages in the unfertilized egg implies that adenylation of a genetic message can occur well before its translation. *D. W. Slater, et al., Nature, Dec. 8, 1972, p 334*

ad·e·nyl·ate cyc·lase (,æd ə'nil it 'sai,kleis), another name for ADENYLYL CYCLASE.

The enzyme in membrane fractions responsible for converting ATP to cyclic AMP was named adenyl cyclase. (It is now referred to as adenylyl cyclase or adenylate cyclase.) *G. Allan Robison, "Cyclic AMP," 1974 Britannica Yearbook of Science and the Future (1973), p 382*

[1973]

ad·e·nyl·yl cyc·lase (,æd ə'nil il 'sai,kleis), an enzyme located in the membrane of the cell wall responsible for converting ATP (the substance that supplies the energy needed for muscle contraction) to cyclic AMP (a regulatory agent in many cellular processes).

Many tissues contain membrane-bound adenylyl cyclases, which are activated only by specific hormones. Kidney tubules contain one which responds to antidiuretic hormone; heart muscle contains one which is activated by glucagon; and thyroid tissue contains one which is activated by the thyroid-stimulating hormone. *Irwin Fridovich, "Molecular Biology: Biochemistry," Britannica Book of the Year 1976, p 471*

[1972]

ADI, abbreviation of *acceptable daily intake.*

The scientific component involves two disciplines: firstly, physical chemistry to determine quantitatively the migrants into the food; second biological medicine to determine their ADI (acceptable daily intake — the maximum amount that can safely be ingested by humans). Provided the migration is below the ADI for each migrant there is no toxic hazard. *New Scientist, Dec. 18, 1975, p 732*

[1969] See ACTION LEVEL.

A·di·das (ə'di: dəz), *n.* a trademark for athletic equipment, especially footwear and garments. *Also used attributively.*

We triple-tied our Adidas at the Staten Island staging area — Fort Wadsworth, alongside the approach to the bridge, and prepared to report on the marathon by joining it and going the classic distance. *The New Yorker, Nov. 6, 1978, p 35*

The athlete has his Adidas bag, the pilot his flight bag, the hiker his backpack — why not let the city guy have his purse? *Duncan G. Steck, "Fashion," 1976 Collier's Encyclopedia Year Book, p 249*

[1975, named for *Adi Dass*ler, German manufacturer who in 1948 founded the company that produces them]

► The trademark is spelled in lower-case, as *adidas*, but in common usage it is written with an initial capital. Adidas are usually recognized by three parallel stripes contrasting with the ground color of the shoe upper, clothing, etc.

ad·i·po·ki·net·ic hormone (ˌæd ə pou ki'net ik), a hormone secreted by the nerve cells of insects that controls the release of fatty substances from the adipose cells for use by the flight muscle cells.

The case of adipokinetic hormone and RPCH means that two arthropod groups have evolved the same hormone, but different kinds of tissue cells have developed the receptors for them. This is quite a common evolutionary occurrence in vertebrates. *New Scientist, Dec. 9, 1976, p 587*

[1976, from *adipo*se fatty + *kinetic* setting into motion]

adjustment center, *U.S.* a part of a prison where intractable and often mentally deranged inmates are kept in solitary confinement.

In the world of prisons notable advances have also been made recently in prettying-up the nomenclature. Guards are now "correctional officers"; solitary confinement punishment cells, "adjustment centers"; prisons, "therapeutic correctional communities"; convicts, "clients of the Department of Corrections." *Jessica Mitford, "Prisons and Funerals," The New York Times, Sept. 5, 1973, p 41*

[1973]

adjuvant therapy, treatment of disease involving the use of substances that enhance the action of drugs, especially drugs that stimulate the production of antibodies.

A procedure becoming known as the "extended simple" mastectomy is being done in some medical centers. This procedure is actually a modified radical mastectomy, with the removal of fewer nodes. If cancer is found in any, some kind of adjuvant therapy is begun immediately. *Rose Kushner, New York Post, Feb. 3, 1979, p 14*

[1976]

adopt, *v.* adopt out, *U.S.* to give up for adoption.

My husband said he would let me decide whether I wanted to keep the baby or adopt it out. I first decided to adopt it out, but at the very last minute I changed my mind and kept it. *Letter to "Dear Abby," Louisville Courier Journal, April 21, 1971 (page not known)*

[1970] ► The preposition *out* in this verb phrase serves to reverse the meaning of *adopt* (to take a child and bring up as one's own), perhaps on the

pattern of *rent* to pay for the use of, *rent out* to receive payment for the use of, and others.

adperson, *n.* a person who is in the advertising business, such as a copywriter, agent, or executive.

Actually, advertising isn't one of those "what do you want to be when you grow up" professions. It's something most adpersons fall into, for one reason or another, like flunking out of dental school. *Ted Morgan, "New! Improved! Advertising!" The New York Times Magazine, Jan. 25, 1976, p 52*

[1976, from *ad* advertisement + -PERSON]

► For the plural, the form *adpeople* also occurs, as in the following quotation.

Perhaps adpeople harbor an unconscious combination of dissatisfaction, foolishness and guilt about their jobs which must be compensated by awards and high salaries. *Joseph F. Regele Jr., Water Mill, N.Y., in a Letter to the Editor, The New York Times Magazine, Feb. 15, 1976, p 42*

adrenalin or **adrenaline,** *n. Figurative.* something that stirs to action; a stimulant; stimulus.

A cheap and plentiful supply of money is adrenalin for the stock market. *Charles J. Rolo, The New York Times Magazine, Feb. 22, 1976, p 28*

[1964, from *adrenalin(e)*, a hormone that speeds up the heartbeat; *Adrenalin* is a trademark in the United States for the synthetic hormone epinephrine]

adrenalize, *v.t.* to stir up; stimulate; excite.

On the evening of April 25th, 1972, 18 miles north of Eureka, in Arcata, the home of Humboldt State University, an adrenalized SRO crowd jammed into a college auditorium to hear America's most renowned Marxist. *"William Smith 1934-1972," Rolling Stone, May 24, 1973, p 44*

[1966, from ADRENALIN + -*ize* (verb suffix)]

ad·re·no·dox·in (əˌdren ə'dak sən), *n.* a protein containing iron that takes part in the transfer of electrons within animal cells; a proteinlike ferredoxin produced by the adrenal glands.

A number of animal proteins have properties similar to those of plant ferredoxins — for example, adrenodoxin from adrenal glands — so we have included them as "honorary ferredoxins." *Richard Cammack, et al., New Scientist and Science Journal, Sept. 23, 1971, p 697*

[1971, from *adreno*- adrenal (gland) + ferre*doxin*]

a·dri·a·my·cin (ˌei dri: ə'mai sən), *n.* an antibiotic derived from daunomycin and used experimentally as an anticancer drug. *Formula:* $C_{27}H_{29}NO_{11}$

The all-out therapy involves simultaneous use of three highly toxic drugs — Cytoxan, adriamycin and vincristine — and radiation to the tumor in the chest and to the brain, where lung cancers commonly spread. *Jane Brody, "New Findings on Lung Cancer Show Early Promise," The New York Times, March 27, 1976, p 20*

[1973, from Italian *adriamicina*, from *Adriàtico* Adriatic + -*micina* -mycin (ultimately from Greek *mýkēs* fungus)]

adult, *adj. Especially U.S.* euphemism for dealing in sex, pornography, etc.

Officials in a few cities, including Las Vegas and Oklahoma City, have proposed creation of special "adult business districts" patterned after Boston's so-called "combat zone," a neighborhood of adult book stores, strip-tease establishments and pornographic movie theaters. *Robert Lindsey, The New York Times, Nov. 28, 1976, Sec. 1, p 1*

The governor of California could be seen emerging from a restaurant in the middle of one of the gaudier blocks of strip shows, massage parlors and "adult" entertainments in this city. For 15 minutes or so, Brown led members of his staff on a slow stroll past bookstores of the sort your old English teacher never recommended. *The Manchester Guardian Weekly (The Washington Post section), July 10, 1977, p 17*

[1972, abstracted from such phrases as "for adults only" and "restricted to adults" in reference to pornographic motion pictures] Compare X-RATED. See also EUPHEMISMS.

advantage law or **advantage rule,** a rule in rugby under which play may not, at the discretion of the referee, be stopped for an infraction if stopping the play may cause a disadvantage to the team not guilty of the offense.

For the last half-hour—the French referee, André Cuny, whose ideas of the advantage law had not always coincided with those of Wales, was operating with a torn calf muscle, by remote control. *Peter West, The Times (London), Feb. 9, 1976, p 8*

[1969, *advantage rule*]

adversarial, *adj. British.* of, involving, or as if opponents in a legal contest; adversary.

There is no suggestion that the magistrates acted in any way improperly; but this only casts a stronger doubt on the system under which juvenile courts have to reach their decisions—the adversarial system of plaintiff and defendant. *John MacDonald, London, "Reaching Decisions on Child Custody," in a Letter to the Editor, The Times (London), Nov. 2, 1976, p 13*

[1967] ► In the U.S., *adversary* is the standard adjective used in legal and judicial contexts: *the adversary system of justice, adversary hearings, adversary proceedings. Adversarial* occurs only in British citations in our file.

advocacy, *n.* Often used attributively in referring to the advocacy of a highly personal, partisan, or activist point of view or policy.

advocacy advertising: It also argues for media access for people who want to counter the so-called "advocacy advertising" of such companies as Imperial Oil, which has flooded the country with commercials telling Canadians about "the big, tough expensive job of developing petroleum." *Maclean's, May 15, 1978, p 60*

advocacy journalism: "Reflections on Joan Little" by Mark Pinsky depicted rather graphically how advocacy journalism has turned reporting into show biz and made a mockery of the public's right to know. *Diane Ravitch, Columbia University, in a Letter to the Editor, Columbia Journalism Review, May/June 1976, p 54*

Compare NEW JOURNALISM.

advocacy journalist: Advocacy journalists claim derivative constitutional legitimacy from a reading of the First Amendment which stretches liberty into license. In the constant, natural struggle for power, they must be seen as combatants, as distinct from neutral observers of the battle. *Gordon Liddy, "Gordon Liddy: A Patriot Speaks," Harper's, Oct. 1974, p 47*

advocacy planning: Robert Goodman's *After the Plan-*

ners (75p) rejects even the modern philosophy of advocacy planning, only recently emerging on the British scene, for planning by the small community for the small community, in other words a return to Greek-type democracy. *Judy Hillman, The Manchester Guardian Weekly, Sept. 30, 1972, p 23*

[1967]

aeon, *n. Geology and Astronomy.* one billion years.

You are correct about the "indefinite-period" definition in dictionaries, but "aeon" is being increasingly used by earth and planetary scientists as a convenient short synonym for "billion years." *Kendrick Frazier, Science News, Aug. 26, 1972, p 130*

[1972, specialized meaning of *aeon* (1647) "an immeasurable period of time"]

aeroacoustic, *adj.* of or relating to aeroacoustics.

Extensive acoustic treatment alone may not provide sufficient noise reduction in some situations, and thus a coordinated aeroacoustic approach is needed. *H. H. Hubbard and D. J. Maglieri, "Aircraft Noise," McGraw-Hill Yearbook of Science and Technology 1976, p 98*

[1966]

aeroacoustics, *n.* the study of sound propagation in the air and its effect on the environment.

Aero-acoustics Expert William Meecham of the U.C.L.A. School of Engineering and Applied Science reports that people who reside within a 3-mile radius of Los Angeles International Airport have a 19% higher death rate than people who live six miles away. Most of the difference was in stress-related disease. *Time, Sept. 18, 1978, p 104*

[1966, from *aero-* combining form meaning air + *acoustics*]

aerobic, *adj.* **1** of or relating to aerobics (a system of building up physical fitness, developed by Kenneth H. Cooper, an American physician, by correlating oxygen consumption and pulse rate with various exercises).

The cardinal requirement of aerobic exercise is that it must tax the person's capacity, to the point where he is breathing hard and his heart is pounding at 130 beats per minute or more. *Time, March 8, 1971, p 30*

Then dropping the medical jargon, she said, "Aerobic dancing is jogging, calisthenics, and jazz dancing to music, in that order." *Nancy Adinolfi, Review-Press Reporter (Bronxville, N.Y.), Aug. 2, 1979, p 3*

2 of, relating to, or improving the body's consumption or use of oxygen.

Doctors look on aerobic capacity as a critical guide to fitness. *Trevor Fishlock, The Times (London), March 6, 1976, p 14*

[1971, back formation from *aerobics* (1968)]

aerobody, *n.* a lighter-than-air aircraft; an airship or any similar flying vehicle.

Miller—a gentle bit of a nag—reminded the group as a whole that they were to refer to the aircraft as an aerobody. He said, "I'm very anxious that we preserve this semantic thing. This is not an airplane. We consider 'aerobody' to be a generic description we have coined. That's well understood, isn't it?" *John McPhee, "Profiles," The New Yorker, Feb. 10, 1973, p 43*

The Pentagon is also stepping up research on a new advanced ICBM and is even looking into the possibility of basing them on zeppelins called "aerobodies." *Newsweek, April 22, 1974, p 53*

[1973, from *aero-* air + *body*]

aerograph, *v.i.* to create a painting or design by using an airbrush.

. . . acid-etched gilding to hand-enamelling and ground-laying to aerographing — all executed by hand skills which few firms in the world today (outside Crown Derby, Doulton, Spode, Wedgwood, Worcester) can call upon. *Arthur Bryan, The Times (London), Oct. 12, 1970, p II*

[1970, verb use of noun *aerograph* (1898) airbrush]

aeromodeller, *n. British.* a person who makes model airplanes.

Aeromodellers will be delighted to know that, as with all the aircraft in the museum, the Hurricane's camouflage markings and paint-scheme are exactly representative of the aircraft as it would have looked in its heyday — in this case 1940 — even to the thickness of the strokes of the serial numbers. *J. M. Ramsden, The Times (London), Nov. 18, 1972, p III*

[1965]

aerophobe, *n.* a person with an abnormal fear of flying.

An organization, Scoff, the Society for the Conquest of Flight Fear, has been formed in London. . . . Scoffers may eventually wear Scoff badges and use Scoff luggage labels. This way the airlines staff would recognize that they were dealing with fragile human cargo, and aerophobes would also recognize each other and give mutual support. *The Auckland Star, New Zealand, Feb. 17, 1973, p 14*

[1966, from *aero-* air + *-phobe* one who fears or has an aversion to, ultimately from Greek *phóbos* fear]

aerophobia, *n. Biology.* movement of an organism or part of an organism away from oxygen or air.

Some bacteria swim toward molecules of food, a process called chemotaxis. Some that require oxygen for growth migrate toward oxygen (aerotaxis), while bacteria to which oxygen is toxic migrate away from it (aerophobia). *Jerald C. Ensign, "Microbiology," The World Book Science Annual 1977 (1976), p 309*

[1976, from *aero-* air + *-phobia* fear of]

► The earlier sense (since 1775) of this term is that of an abnormal fear of air or gases, especially drafts.

aeroshell, *n.* a protective metallic shell equipped with small thrusters, used for decelerating a spacecraft for a soft landing.

When it reaches an altitude of about eight hundred thousand feet, the lander, inside a sort of pod called an aeroshell, should enter the Martian atmosphere. *Henry S. F. Cooper, Jr., The New Yorker, June 28, 1976, p 30*

Physical characteristics of the atmosphere will be measured during the landing phase by sensors located on the aeroshell and within the lander. *New Scientist, Aug. 7, 1975, p 314*

[1966, from *aero-* air + *shell*]

aerosol, *n.* ► *Aerosol* meaning "very fine colloidal particles of a solid or liquid substance, such as fog or smoke, suspended in the air or in some other gas" came into the language in the 1920's. In the 1940's it acquired the meaning of a substance packed under pressure. In the early 1970's this term

acquired the connotation of a substance dangerous to the environment and public health because of the possibly hazardous CHLOROFLUOROCARBON or CHLOROFLUOROMETHANE used in many aerosol containers as gas propellants. These propellants (commonly known as fluorocarbons and widely sold under the trademark *Freon*) were shown to accumulate in the upper regions of the atmosphere, where they are broken down by ultraviolet sunlight, releasing chlorine atoms whose reactions are believed to deplete the OZONE SHIELD which protects the earth from dangerous ultraviolet radiation. Alerted to a possible government ban on the use of such propellants, manufacturers began to produce and advertise NONAEROSOL spray cans, thereby reinforcing the public's distrust of the word *aerosol*. This new usage implied that all such cans used the dangerous fluorocarbon gas, whereas actually only about half of all aerosol cans on the market used it.

To protect those companies whose aerosol products are not propelled by fluorocarbons, the study group recommended a requirement that cans containing such propellants be so labeled. . . . About 4,000 workers participate directly in producing fluorocarbons in the 15 American plants where aerosols are made. *Walter Sullivan, "Federal Study Urges Ban on Aerosol Sprays," The New York Times, June 13, 1975, p 44*

The term was further discredited when a U.S. government ban was imposed in 1974 on aerosol cans of paints, solvents, and degreasers using vinyl chloride as a propellant, this compound having been proved to be cancer-producing.

Robert Abplanalp, the inventor of the original aerosol spray-can valve, announced the invention of a new valve that used butane, isobutane, or propane gas as a propellant in place of chlorofluorocarbons. *Michael Allaby, "Environment," Britannica Book of the Year 1978, p 369*

aerosolic, *adj.:* The oxygen isotopic ratio of the tracer mineral quartz has been used by R. N. Clayton and associates to identify the global distribution of long-range aerosolic dusts carried by winds. *Marion L. Jackson, "Atmospheric Pollution," McGraw-Hill Yearbook of Science and Technology 1975, p 112*

Af (æf), *n.* a derogatory name for a black African in Zimbabwe (Rhodesia) and South Africa.

A common feature of the conversation with whites was the use of pejoratives to refer to blacks. . . . In English-speaking households, the word "natives," or "Afs" were common. *John F. Burns, The New York Times, June 22, 1976, p 13*

[1976, shortened from *African*] Compare HOUTIE.

A·far triangle ('ɑ: fɑr), an extensive, lava-covered triangular region in northeastern Ethiopia, at the juncture of the Red Sea and the Gulf of Aden. It is regarded by some geologists as evidence of continuing continental drift and as a focal point about which new oceans may form.

If we suppose that the Afar triangle is a part of the Red Sea, the coast of Arabia matches very well the contour of the "coastline" of the part of the African continent from which it is assumed to be separating. *Haroun Taziett, Scientific American, Feb. 1970, p 32*

[1969, from *Afar*, another name of the Danakil, a

Hamitic people of northeastern Ethiopia and the adjacent Djibouti (the former Territory of Afars and Issas)]

affinity group, a group, such as a club, church, union, or other organization, authorized to take charter flights at reduced fares.

The change, approved in September, allows the vacationer to choose between dozens of destinations at a price that includes air fare, hotel room, ground transport, taxes and tips. And no longer does the traveler have to belong to a so-called affinity group, such as a club or union, to qualify for the reduced rates. The new package is often less than the price of a scheduled-airline ticket. *Time, Jan. 19, 1976, p 62*

[1971]

affirm, *adj. U.S. Informal.* affirmative; correct (used especially in replies).

"You think Main Bus B is good, don't you?" Swigert asked anxiously. Brand answered, "That's affirm. We think it is, but we want to check it out anyway." *Henry S. F. Cooper, Jr., "Annals of Exploration: An Accident in Space — I," The New Yorker, Nov. 11, 1972, p 129*

[1971, short for *affirmative*]

affirmative action, 1 *U.S.* a positive program designed to combat the effects of discrimination against minorities, women, the elderly, etc., in contrast to a policy statement merely decrying such discrimination. *Often used attributively.*

. . . a proposed "affirmative action" plan to assure fair representation for women, youths and racial minorities at national conventions. *St. Petersburg Times, Nov. 29, 1974, p 19-A*

"Affirmative action" includes a whole range of special steps. . . . These include compensatory and remedial training, expanded recruitment, validation of tests and criteria for jobs or university admission and related measures to help the disadvantaged realize their potentials and provide equal opportunity for all. *Samuel Rabinove, New York, in a Letter to the Editor, The New York Times, Sept. 13, 1977, p 32*

Those who do not support affirmative action in general will rejoice in a negative decision by the Supreme Court. I believe that the Court is, in essence, ruling on the whole issue of whether minorities in our society can be given special consideration as we try to remove the obstacles and scars of hundreds of years of racism. *Coretta Scott King, "Counterpoints," The Atlantic, Jan. 1978, p 76*

2 any action taken to improve past performance or eliminate grievances.

Once again under fire for its lack of affirmative action, the Federal Trade Commission strove this year to demonstrate the range of its powers. FTC Chairman Lewis A. Engman announced on February 19 that the agency was adopting new policies to open itself to "greater public scrutiny." *Janet M. Knight, "Consumer Affairs," 1975 Collier's Encyclopedia Year Book (1974), p 199*

[1965] ▶ This term spread in the mid-1970's and quickly established itself as a key phrase in the vocabulary of the civil-rights movement. It appeared at first mostly in business letterheads and advertisements (e.g., "an equal opportunity/affirmative action employer") as firms sought to comply with government-mandated programs to compensate for past discrimination in employment, education, and housing. See EQUAL OPPORTUNITY. The phrase originated in a series of Presidential directives (1961, 1965, 1972), where it appeared typically in contexts such as this one (from Executive Order 11246 of September 24, 1965): "The contractor will take affirmative action to ensure that applicants are employed, and that employees are treated during employment, without regard to their race, creed, color, or national origin."

As pressure to implement affirmative action mounted, the concept itself became the center of controversy. *Affirmative action* quickly came to mean more than merely deliberate recruitment, training, and promotion of blacks and women; specific numerical standards or percentages to be achieved according to set timetables were established. The issue debated was whether any particular group or class of people, even one that has suffered from past discrimination, could constitutionally be given preferential treatment at the expense of other groups. Opponents of affirmative action, calling it a QUOTA SYSTEM which discriminated against the majority, raised the charge of REVERSE DISCRIMINATION. Supporters argued that only through firm reparatory steps can minorities and women overcome the discriminatory practices of the past; a quota system was therefore essential to any plan of affirmative action.

The constitutionality of *affirmative action* was tested before the Supreme Court in two historic cases: the DeFunis case (1974) and the Bakke case (1978); both dealt with white applicants who were denied admission to, respectively, a law school and a medical school, although their scholastic records were superior to those of the minority applicants who were admitted. Whereas in 1974 the court declared the DeFunis case moot on a technicality, in the Bakke case the court's decision was a compromise that satisfied neither side of the argument. The court, while ruling in Bakke's favor on the grounds that a quota based solely on race was unacceptable, maintained that racially oriented admissions policies to overcome past discrimination were not in themselves unconstitutional, thus upholding the principle of *affirmative action.*

Afghanistanism, *n.* undue emphasis on things happening in remote foreign places, to the neglect of important domestic affairs.

Afghanistanism (also a recurring disease in journalism) is a malady that encourages pontification on problems far distant while conveniently ignoring the home front. *Allan Fotheringham, Maclean's, June 28, 1976, p 52*

[1966, from *Afghanistan,* the country in southwestern Asia (used as an example of a distant place) + *-ism*] ▶ When this term was used to comment on reporting in the 1950's, Russian interests were active in Afghanistan. Again these activities and the word *Afghanistanism* are reemerging.

AFP, abbreviation of ALPHAFETOPROTEIN.

Others had shown that AFP was the only protein in amniotic fluid produced just by the fetus and not also by the mother. With this knowledge, Dr. Brock, a biochemist, developed a theory that high levels of AFP would be present in cases of neural tube defects because more AFP would leak from the malformed fetus into the amniotic fluid. *Lawrence K. Altman, "U.S. Researchers Are Beginning Use of British Testing for Birth Defects," The New York Times, Sept. 11, 1977, Sec. 1, p 26*

[1973]

Afro-beat, *n.* a form of popular music combining elements of highlife (West African jazz), calypso, and American jazz.

Westerners first hearing Fela's Afro-beat music find it an acquired taste. The numbers seem too long, often lasting 20 minutes or more, with the brief snatches of lyrics in pidgin English, the lingua franca of the lower classes. *The New York Times Magazine, July 24, 1977, p 11*

[1974]

Afro-Latin, *adj.* of, based on, or combining African and Latin American music.

Soul music again experienced a strong year, owing largely to the success of such Motown artists as the Temptations, the Jackson Five, and Stevie Wonder. If there were any major musical developments in this style, they were those which were Afro-Latin in general sound. *Carman Moore, "Music," 1971 Collier's Encyclopedia Year Book, p 362*

[1967] ► This term is used generically to describe the class of dance music that includes the 1940's Afro-Cuban (mambo, conga, etc.), the Brazilian samba, and the more recent SALSA.

Afro-rock, *n.* modern African music incorporating much of the style of traditional rock music.

Afro-rock is a term frequently used in contemporary African music. Manu Dibango, Osibisa, Fela Anikulapo-Kuti, and Victor Uwaifor are internationally famous in this new brand of African soul music. *Laz Nnanyelu Ekwueme, "Music: The Pulse of Life," The Times (London), Jan. 18, 1977, p II*

[1977]

a·gar·ose ('ɑ: gəˌrous), *n.* a polysaccharide carbohydrate that is the main constituent of agar, the solid medium used for bacterial cultures.

Insulin does not enter the cells which it affects. This has been dramatically demonstrated by experiments in which hormone effects are produced by insulin attached to beads of agarose, which certainly cannot penetrate the cell membrane. *Robert Freedman, New Scientist and Science Journal, Sept. 30, 1971, p 739*

[1971, from *agar* + *-ose* suffix used in names of types of sugar, as in *sucrose, glucose,* and *fructose*]

age-date, *v.t., v.i.* to determine scientifically the age of archaeological or geological materials.

A new age-dating method, using the elements samarium and neodymium, was successfully applied to lunar rocks. The results suggest that a major melting and chemical separation of the moon was going on about 4.4 billion years ago. *Bevan M. French, "What the Moon Tells Us," Encyclopedia Science Supplement (Grolier) 1977/1978 (1977), p 345*

— *n.* a specimen's age obtained by scientific dating.

The dark material has been distributed to scientists, and the age-dates may be available in time for the Fourth Lunar Science Conference, March 5-8 at Houston. *"Did Lunar Volcanism End 3 Billion Years Ago?" Science News, Feb. 24, 1973, p 117*

[1966] Compare AMINO-ACID DATING, IODINE-XENON DATING, RUBIDIUM-STRONTIUM DATING, THERMOLUMINESCENT DATING.

ageist or **age-ist,** *adj.* prejudiced or discriminating against older people as a group.

She called him "a sexist, age-ist pig . . ." *"Patty: Words From a 'Recruit'," Newsweek, May 6, 1974, p 24*

Our ageist society usually lumps all old people into one great, gray mass without differentiating them. Yet there are several subgroups that should be taken into account. *Maggie Kuhn, "New Life for the Elderly: Liberation from 'Ageism'," The New Old: Struggling for Decent Aging, edited by Ronald Gross, et al., 1978, p 302*

[1974, from earlier (1970) *ageism* prejudice or discrimination against the aged, coined by Robert N. Butler, an American gerontologist] See GERONTOPHOBIA, GRAY POWER.

a·gen·bite of in·wit (ə'gen,bait əv 'in,wit), *Especially British,* remorse of conscience.

[Malcolm] Muggeridge is haunted (so he intimates) by plastic grass, the possibility that dawn will be photographed as though it were dusk. What agenbite of inwit must seize the old gentleman as they lard him with make-up prior to committing him to the arms of his camera. *Robert Robinson, The Times (London), April 17, 1972, p 14*

[1967] ► This is an archaism and a literary term revived in the 1960's. It was used earlier in *Ulysses* (1922) by James Joyce, who adapted it from the title of a Middle English (1340) manuscript, *Ayenbite of Inwyte* meaning "The Remorse of Conscience." *Ayenbite* (the components mean "again-bite") is a calque or loan translation of the Latin source of *remorse* and *inwit* is a calque of the Latin source of *conscience.*

Agent Blue, Agent Orange, Agent Purple, Agent White, the names of four herbicidal spraying materials having great toxicity, used especially for purposes of defoliation and crop destruction, especially during the Vietnam war.

On another front it was reported by the Washington Post that more than a million gallons of Agent Orange (the most powerful defoliant used in Vietnam and banned since April, 1970) was being shipped back to the United States. . . . This move still leaves the less toxic Agent White and Agent Blue at the disposal of United States and South Vietnam forces. *"Environmental Encounters," New Scientist, Jan. 6, 1972, p 36*

As a component of the American military defoliant known as Agent Orange, 2,4,5-T had been rained down by the tens of thousands of tons, and over some five million acres, in herbicidal warfare operations in South Vietnam in the nineteen-sixties. *The New Yorker, Sept. 4, 1978, p 35*

[1970, so called from the color of the code stripe of each of the herbicides on their containers]

age pigment, an aggregate of fluorescent brown compounds of proteins, lipids, and carbohydrates that become concentrated in some cells as a person or animal grows old.

Highly insoluble particles accumulate in some cells as a function of age. These particles, often referred to as "age pigment," may occupy as much as 30% of the space inside an old cell. *Nathan W. Shock, "Will You Live to Be 100," 1972 Britannica Yearbook of Science and the Future (1971), p 83*

[1962]

age-specific, *adj.* limited in action or effect to a definite age group.

Fig. 1 shows the age-specific death rates from carcinoma of the cervix in England and Wales, and this clearly shows the importance of using our resources on women over thirty-five, especially those who have not yet been tested. *Arthur I. Spriggs, Nature, July 21, 1972, p 137*

[1963]

AGI, abbreviation of *adjusted gross income.*

Surrey contended the Treasury distorts its reports by computing the tax rates paid by the rich on their "adjusted gross income" (AGI) and not their actual income, often far higher. *"Congress Told Wealthy Escaping Bulk of Taxes," Honolulu Star-Bulletin, Feb. 5, 1973, p 2*

[1972]

ag·no·sic (æg'nou sik), *adj.* unable to recognize familiar objects because of brain damage.

He sees faces, figures, objects around him: he sees them clearly, yet is unable to recognise them. They too have lost their meaning: he has become 'mentally blind'—agnosic. *Oliver Sachs, The Listener, June 28, 1973, p 872*

[1973, derivative of *agnosia* (1900), from New Latin, from Greek *agnōsia,* from *a-* without + *gnôsis* knowledge or recognition]

agoraphobia, *n.* ▶ This term, defined in dictionaries as "an abnormal fear of open spaces," has been redefined in the past few years as a major psychological disorder that comprises a complex of different fears, all involving panicking in unfamiliar circumstances and situations. The following quotations describe the symptoms of this phobia:

Agoraphobia once meant "fear of the marketplace," but it has come to mean fear of the marketplace of life. It includes the fear of both open and closed spaces—elevators, bridges, ball parks, bank lines—as well as a sort of floating dread that travels as far as the imagination can reach. *Julie Baumgold, "Agoraphobia: Life Ruled by Panic," The New York Times Magazine, Dec. 4, 1977, p 46*

Agoraphobia is the commonest phobia. It covers a cluster of fears that involves being away from home: the fear of open spaces, of lakes and oceans, of bridges and tunnels, of crowds, of stores and theaters, of being lost, and so on. The term generally refers to various groupings of these fears as well as to any one of them alone. *Fraser Kent, "Agoraphobia," Encyclopedia Science Supplement (Grolier) 1979 (1978), p 58*

The causes of agoraphobia are not known, but many psychologists consider it a habit or learned behavior. According to this theory, the condition may be sparked by a single experience of sudden panic which proves to be extremely traumatic, leaving the patient in a constant state of fear and anxiety over a possible recurrence of the original experience. To break this pattern of behavior, a common treatment is BEHAVIOR MODIFICATION through de-

sensitization, in which the patient is gradually exposed to the feared situations until the anxiety attacks diminish and eventually disappear. This treatment has worked with some patients. Other methods, called IMPLOSION and FLOODING, bring the patient face-to-face with the object or situation feared, on the theory that a direct confrontation will remove the source of anxiety.

The term *agoraphobia* was coined in 1871 by the German psychiatrist Carl Westphal (1833-1890) as *Agoraphobie,* from the Greek words *agorá* "marketplace" and *-phobíā* "fear." The word first appeared in English in 1873, and the derivative *agoraphobic,* meaning (one) having agoraphobia, in 1884. Quotations for another derivative, the noun *agoraphobe,* have been in our files since 1955:

The inmates include suicidal types, agoraphobes, and plain nervous people. *The New Yorker, Aug. 13, 1955, p 47*

a·grav·ic (‚ei'græv ik), *adj.* having zero gravity; characterized by an absence of gravitational pull.

Theoretically, absolute agravic conditions in the true sense of the word do not exist in the universe. *US Air Force Glossary of Standardized Terms, Department of the Air Force, Washington, Vol. 1, Jan. 2, 1976, p 2*

[1965, from *a-* not, without + *grav*ity + *-ic*]

agri-, a combining form meaning "of or involving agriculture; agricultural," abstracted from *agriculture* (ultimately from Latin *ager* field). The first term in the group was *agri-horticultural* (1912). However, the appearance of *agribusiness* (1955) was the source of the present growth in *agri-* as a word element. In current usage the combining form tends to overlap or become interchangeable with the earlier *agro-* (from Greek), so that one may find *agrobusiness* as well as *agribusiness, agrichemical* as well as *agrochemical,* and so on. Below are some examples of terms using the new form.

agri-argument, *n.:* This convoluted agri-argument comes out in a volume issued this weekend, in time for the Labour party conference next week. *Nicholas Faith, The Sunday Times (London), Oct. 3, 1971, p 72*

agribiz, *n.:* Take my advice, kid. Forget about show biz and go back to agribiz. *Cartoon legend by W. Miller, The New Yorker, Nov. 22, 1976, p 49*

agribusinessman, *n.:* As for being a peanut farmer, Carter is actually a wealthy agribusinessman, whose income comes from warehousing and shelling other farmers' peanuts and from commodities trading. He does own and live on a peanut farm, but it is run by his brother. *Steven Brill, Harper's, March 1976, p 80*

agrichemical, *adj.:* As a result, while the agrichemical giants stick with their profitable poisons, the few smaller companies that have taken a chance on the third-generation insecticides complain that the E.P.A. regulation is driving them out of the business. *Anthony Wolff, The New York Times Magazine, Nov. 28, 1976, p 53*

agri-corporation, *n.:* Hutterites control only about one per cent of the province's arable land—but other farmers still resent, envy and fear the sect, partly because its frugal, communal lifestyle finances efficient, modern, prosperous, expansionist agri-corporations. Therefore Hutterites find themselves derided on the one hand for their home-made, traditional clothing, their German dialect and their strict morals, and on the other for their large-scale wholesale purchases of farming equipment (the Wilson colony alone boasts nine combines, six of them two-year-old, top-of-the-line machines worth $45,000 each). *Maclean's, Dec. 25, 1978, p 22*

agricrime, *n.:* Farm machinery is being engraved with identification numbers to discourage gangs of highly organized thieves from stealing and then fencing such heavy booty. . . . Agricrime has become so bad in the state of California that the annual loss in crops and machinery is estimated at $30 million. *Time, Oct. 3, 1977, p 27*

agri-industrial, *adj.:* Agriculturalists would continually "redesign" the fruit to suit the packers' specific need. Our "green ripe" tomatoes are the latest results of agri-industrial improvement. *Richard W. Langer, "Weekend Gardening: Terrace Tomatoes," The New York Times, May 14, 1976, p C22*

agrindustry, *n.:* Then there are crop and orchard wastes, food-processing wastes, wastes from forestry, pulp and paper production textiles, tanneries, and a host of "agrindustries." *William E. Small, "Agriculture: The Seeds of a Problem," Encyclopedia Science Supplement (Grolier), 1972, p 208*

agripower, *n.:* Although Butz publicly emphasizes that the United States cannot and should not use what he, at the same time, frankly calls "agripower" as a weapon, he is fond of noting that Rumanian Agriculture Minister Miculescu once told him: "You've got a weapon more powerful than the atom bomb; you've got soybeans." *James Risser and George Anthan, The New York Times Magazine, June 13, 1976, p 53*

agriproduct, *n.:* . . . with the pre-tax contribution from that part of the world up by £3m to just under £11m — and that despite a sizable setback in the big agriproducts subsidiary Seacoast which, as expected, suffered from lower prices although volume was steady. *The Times (London), Dec. 9, 1976, p 21*

agri-proletariat, *n.:* "Secondly they use unorganised, cheap and migratory labour. Those are not farmworkers down there. It's an agri-proletariat, just like the nineteenth century industrial proletariat." *Pearson Phillips, quoting Jane Fonda, The Manchester Guardian Weekly, Oct. 31, 1976, p 19*

agrobusiness, *n.* the coordination or relation of business techniques and methods of farm production and distribution; agriculture treated as a business.

In his recent book on the *Agrobusiness* Gerard Garreau claimed that "the real power of the cereal companies does not only derive from agreements on prices, but sometimes takes on a political dimension." He recalls that the French firm Dreyfus, whose "dynastic founder was but 17 years old when he did his first deal, buying a cartload of wheat from a farmer in Alsace and selling it in Basle," refused to sell wheat to Chile, thereby dealing a severe blow to the regime of President Allende, *Times (London), March 7, 1978, p II*

[1971, variant of earlier (1955) *agribusiness*]

agrochemical, *adj.* of or involving both agriculture and chemistry.

Amid the loud and often outrageous claims being made in the United States by the organic school of farming on the one hand, and the agrochemical businesses on the other, it is refreshing to come across a group of people (where else but in England?) who for the past thirty-four years have been calmly and quietly studying the soil-plant-animal cycle and the effect of different agricultural methods on this cycle. *Lisa Alther, "Organic Farming on Trial," Natural History, Nov. 1972, p 16*

[1963]

agroecological, *adj.* of or involving both agriculture and ecology.

Every agroecological milieu has its own problems, and new ones keep appearing. For example, during the southwest monsoon period in India, many soil nutrients are lost because of leaching. *Indira Gandhi, "A World Without Want: The Need for Modern Agricultural Programs," Britannica Book of the Year 1975, p 11*

[1975, from *agro-* agricultural + *ecological*]

agroecosystem, *n.* the system of ecological relationships existing in agriculture; an agricultural ecosystem.

Ecological accounting of energy inputs and outputs of an agroecosystem provides greater understanding of the interrelations and mechanisms underlying various crop production alternatives. *David Pimentel, Science, Feb. 14, 1975, p 561*

By this process, agroecosystems characteristically have higher herbivore loads and a lower diversity of herbivore species than natural communities. *Simon A. Levin and Richard B. Root, McGraw-Hill Yearbook of Science and Technology 1978, p 128*

[1970, from *agro-* agricultural + *ecosystem*]

agrometeorological, *adj.* of or relating to the effects of weather and climate on agriculture.

Four noteworthy contributions deserve special attention, namely those . . . on the organisational details of any agrometeorological forecasting and information service, and those . . . on agricultural management. *Harry Jessop, New Scientist, Feb. 1, 1973, p 263*

[1973]

agro-politics, *n.* politics concerned with agriculture, such as the distribution of farm products, especially food crops, etc.

It is quite another [thing] to get Mrs Smith, Frau Schmidt or Madame Dubois to serve meat dishes containing a lot of vegetable substitute unless it has the same familiar taste of pork or chicken or whatever. This is where the flavour makers bring world agro-politics right into the ordinary kitchen. They can make a pork sausage made with one-third of meat substitute taste at least like your average pub sausage. *Gwen Nuttall, The Sunday Times (London), March 16, 1975, p 72*

[1975]

agrotechnician, *n.* a specialist in the technology of agriculture.

Since 1961, Nestlé agrotechnicians, veterinary specialists and agronomists have been hard at work, creating, with the farmer, a modern milk-producing district in this region. *The Times (London), April 8, 1976, p III*

[1976]

agrotechnology, *n.* the tools, machines, and techniques used in modern agriculture to increase production; the technology of agriculture.

The importance of efforts to import foreign agrotechnology is apparent in Peking's recent decision to increase its allocations of foreign currency funds to local production units to buy equipment from abroad. *The Times (London), Sept. 29, 1978, p III*

[1973]

agrotechnologist, *n.:* The beauty of our country paths is that they are an organic and continually evolving part of the countryside, not a blueprint by recreational planners, agro-technologists or, for that matter, ramblers. *Christopher Hall, London, in a Letter to the Editor, The Times (London), July 6, 1973, p 17*

AGS, abbreviation of *abort guidance system* (for use when the primary guidance system of a spacecraft fails to function properly).

And to cap it off, minutes after liftoff from the moon, the secondary guidance and navigation system called AGS (Abort Guidance System) went out. *Science News, Feb. 13, 1971, p 111*

[1969]

aha reaction, *Psychology.* the sudden achievement of insight or illumination, especially in creative thinking.

He had been studying that sudden insight into the solution of a problem that psychologists sometimes call the "Aha" reaction. Great turning points in science often hinge on these mysterious intuitive leaps. *Martin Gardner, "Mathematical Games," Scientific American, Oct. 1977, p 18*

What goes on in a person's mind when he or she solves an important problem with a single flash of insight? How does somebody come up with a short, elegant solution to a seemingly difficult problem? Psychologists call these hunches *aha!* reactions. They have no relationship to general intelligence, but they are closely connected to creativity in science, business, and everyday activity. *Science News, Dec. 23-30, 1978, p 434*

[1977] ► This term has apparently replaced the earlier phrases *aha experience* (1958) and *ah-ah experience* (1947), used by psychologists, especially of the Gestalt school, to designate the moment of revelation or discovery when one exclaims "aha!" or, as Archimedes is reputed to have done, "eureka!" Variant current expressions are *aha phenomenon* and *aha process.*

a·her·ma·type (ei'hər mə,taip), *n.* a coral that does not form reefs.

The exchange of such nutrients as phosphates between corals and the surrounding medium is much less in herma-typic corals than ahermatypes, and less in hermatypes with zooxanthellae [algae living in the coral] than in those from which the algae were removed. *Peter W. Glynn, "The Coral Reef Community," 1977 Britannica Yearbook of Science and the Future (1976), p 208*

[1976, back formation from earlier (1950's) *ahermatypic* not reef-building, from *a-* not + *hermatypic* (from Greek *hérma* reef + *týptein* to strike, form)] Compare HERMATYPE.

AHH, abbreviation of *aryl hydrocarbon hydroxylase,* an enzyme that converts the cancer-producing chemicals in tobacco smoke and in polluted air into their active form within the lungs.

Study after study has linked cigarette smoking to lung cancer, but just why one smoker succumbs to lung cancer and another escapes has been a scientific mystery. Researchers have not discovered the answer, but they have come up with an experimental blood test that, by measuring an enzyme called aryl hydrocarbon hydroxylase (AHH), seems to distinguish cigarette smokers whose hereditary makeup makes them prone to develop lung cancer from those resistant to developing cancer. *Lawrence K. Altman,*

"Health and Disease," Encyclopedia Science Supplement (Grolier) 1974, p 251*

[1973]

Ah·ma·diy·ya or **Ah·ma·diy·yah** (*Anglicized* ɑ:-mɑː'di: yə), *n.* an Islamic missionary sect of India and Pakistan, whose members are active in many countries. *Often used attributively.*

Riots erupted in Pakistan in June between adherents of the Ahmadiyya sect, said to number over 300,000, and other Muslims. The Ahmadiyya's claim that their founder ... was a prophet, offended orthodox Muslims who believe prophecy terminated with Muhammad. *Kenneth J. Perkins, "Islam," The Americana Annual 1975, p 485*

[1970, from Arabic, from the name of the founder Mirza Ghulam *Ahmad,* 1839-1908]

-a·hol·ic (-ə'hɔ: lik), a combining form meaning "one addicted to, obsessed with, or having a compulsive need of or for (something specified or a specified activity)." The following examples illustrate its use:

beefaholic, *n.:* More people, it seems, are joining with Los Angeles housewife Anne Brone. "We've cut way down on our beef," she said last week. "We used to be 'beefaholics.' ... Well, I tell you something: we discovered we can live without beef. The hell with it." *Newsweek, Sept. 24, 1973, p 98*

bookaholic, *n.:* It's a disease that affects an untold number of Americans: that uplifting feeling that somewhere around the corner is a bookstore and waiting inside are at least three or four volumes that just have to be had. For a bookaholic, life without plenty of books lying around the house is like a day without orange juice. *"Another Social Disease Is Isolated—Bookaholism," The Tuscaloosa News (Alabama), July 10, 1977, p 3C*

footballaholic, *n.:* Until Thanksgiving Day, I had considered myself just another enthusiastic fan of pro football, not an abuser, a footballaholic. *William Raspberry, The Washington Post, Dec. 2, 1974, p 25*

golfaholic, *n.:* One is Bernie Porter, the excellent club craftsman from Augusta, Georgia, who has studied the methods, and offered his own, in nearly every golf manufacturing facility east of the Mississippi.

The other is Donald Goldstein, a sleek, mod insurance man from Birmingham, who probably knows more manufacturers personally than Porter and other club craftsmen. Goldstein, you see, is a "golfaholic." *Southern Living, May 1971, p 29*

hashaholic, *n.:* The U.S. Army hospital in Wurzburg, West Germany, had an "accessible, defined population" of 36,000 G.I.s, ... 16,000 of these had used hash at least once. The drug was more readily available than marijuana, and thousands of men were on it consistently enough to be dubbed "hashaholics" by their buddies. *"Medicine: Hashaholics," Time, July 24, 1972, p 53*

spend-aholic, *n.:* With the Christmas gift season bringing out the latent spend-aholic in the most sober of budget-watchers, credit crises are as commonplace as holiday hangovers. *Ralph Blumenthal, "Holiday Epidemic: Credit Abuse," The New York Times, Dec. 20, 1978, p C1*

sweetaholic, *n.:* Though a svelte 5 feet 8 inches and 119 pounds Kim admits to being a "sweetaholic" who dieted resolutely before winning the beauty pageant in Charleston, S.C., then "pigged out" on pecan pie a la mode. *Newsweek, May 30, 1977, p 53*

wheataholic, *n.:* "I am a wheataholic. Other people dream of whisky. I dream of hot bread." *Arnold Hano, TV Guide, May 12, 1973, p 20*

wordaholic, *n.:* Only by tracking bromides can word-aholics impose any kind of constraints and make our excellent lingo vogueword free. *The New York Times Magazine, July 23, 1978, p 23*

[1972, abstracted from *workaholic* a person with a compulsive desire to work, coined in 1971 by Wayne Oates, an American pastoral counselor, from *work* + connecting *-a-* + alco*holic;* see WORKAHOLISM] See also the variants -HOLIC and -OHOLIC.

AI¹, abbreviation of ARTIFICIAL INTELLIGENCE.

The effort to get machines to learn, see, hear, deduce, and intuit — to achieve what is called "Artificial Intelligence," or AI — has received little popular attention, presumably, at least in part, because of this conviction that AI is already a fact. Who, except for the handful of professionals involved, has even a vague sense of why artificial intelligence has proven to be so difficult a task, what the problems are, how they are being attacked, and what theories have been proposed and abandoned? *The Atlantic, Aug. 1974, p 40*

[1971]

AI², abbreviation of AMNESTY INTERNATIONAL.

Amnesty International (AI) was founded in 1961 by Peter Benenson, a London lawyer. Sean MacBride, a recipient of the 1974 Nobel Prize for Peace, was chairman of AI from 1961 to 1975. The organization, which now has 170,000 members in 107 nations, works for the release of any prisoner who has been jailed for political or religious reasons. "Nobel Prizes: Prize for Peace," *Britannica Book of the Year 1978, p 114*

[1975]

AID, abbreviation of *artificial insemination by donor.*

The BMA is expected to set up an inquiry into AID — artificial insemination by donor — after hearing evidence that the increasing number of abortions is depriving childless couples of children to adopt. *John Windsor, "Doctors Reject Statutory Euthanasia," The Manchester Guardian Weekly, July 31, 1971, p 8*

[1966] Compare AIH.

AIH, abbreviation of *artificial insemination by husband.*

Eventually our gynaecologist . . . decided we should try AIH. This involved Heather in repeated trips to the gynaecologist's various clinics at the likely time of ovulation. *Keith Diggle, "Birth Pangs," The Manchester Guardian Weekly, Feb. 3, 1973, p 21*

[1966] Compare AID.

AIM, abbreviation of *American Indian Movement,* a militant American Indian civil-rights organization in the U.S. and Canada, founded in 1968, that seeks the restoration of property and other rights granted by treaties.

The move into Custer did not induce the local prosecutor to change his mind and the battle between the police and the Indians followed. Since then, the AIM has mounted forays into several of the towns in the area and it has had a certain success. In Sturgis, for instance, it was agreed that the Indian charged with murder should be given $15,000 bail. *The Times (London), Feb. 20, 1973, p 6*

Pronouncing the state [North Dakota] "a zone of war," the AIM urged Indians who plan to visit the area to bring along "gas masks, first aid kits, and self-defense equip-ment." "The Week," *National Review, May 24, 1974, p 568*

[1972] See NATIVE AMERICAN.

ai·o·li (ei′ou liː; *French* a yɔ′liː), *n.* a kind of mayonnaise heavily seasoned with garlic, usually served with fish.

They make a sauce called Polonaise which somewhat resembles aioli and is worth trying ($2 a pint). *'Good Food Guide," The Times (London), Sept. 23, 1972, p 9*

[1965, from Provençal, from *ai* garlic + *oli* oil]

airborne soccer, *U.S.* a game similar to soccer in which a Frisbee is substituted for the ball by two teams of seven players.

There are well-developed games like Guts, where teams of five, 15 yards apart, engage in an all-out, 100 m.p.h., flying disk war. The Ultimate game, airborne soccer, boasts an intercollegiate league of 52 schools. *Stancil E. D. Johnson, "Frisbee Imperiled," The New York Times Magazine, July 18, 1976, p 47*

[1976] Compare FRISBEE GOLF.

air bridge, 1 a closed passageway connecting two buildings above the ground.

But even in the partial model of Arcosanti, one can see Soleri's architectural intent. Air bridges connect units. Roof gardens spread on top of truss systems into which residences are fitted. *Robert B. Kaiser, Saturday Review, Feb. 12, 1972, p 39*

2 a closed movable passageway used to allow direct access from a passenger terminal to an aircraft.

The original passenger terminal, called the beehive because of its shape, was connected by a tunnel to the station. . . . Access to the aircraft from the beehive was through canvas tunnels, the forerunners of today's movable air bridges. *Arthur Reed, Special Report: Gatwick, The Times (London), May 17, 1976, p 12*

[1965] ► An earlier meaning of this term is a link or passage formed between two or more distant points by aircraft.

air broker, *British.* a person who arranges charter flights for the transport of cargo.

There is still another sector of the air chartering market, one that goes hand in hand with the Baltic Exchange. Without doubt the exchange came into air broking as adjunct to its shipbroking, many of the leading air brokers being in fact subsidiaries of shipping companies. For them the exchange is almost a captive market. *Craig Howard, "Too Wide for the City Alone," The Times (London), April 22, 1976, p III*

[1972, patterned on earlier (OED 1816) *ship broker*]

air-cushion or **air-cushioned,** *adj.* supported above the ground or water by a cushion of air produced by propellers or fans.

Air-cushion landing devices for large aircraft have passed their first demonstration trials. *"Technology: State of the Art," Science News, Jan. 31, 1976, p 73*

Among the alternatives are air-cushioned transport, attractive magnetic levitation and repulsive magnetic levitation. *Henry H. Kolm, and Richard D. Thronton, "Electromagnetic Flight," Scientific American, Oct. 1973, p 17*

[1963]

air dam, a device that reduces air resistance, increases stability, or otherwise improves the performance of an automobile, aircraft, or other vehicle moving through the air.

The car is six inches longer than the other Escorts, thanks to its streamlined nose, which has an integral air dam and has been fitted to cut drag and front-end lift. *Peter Waymark, "Motoring: Road Test: Ford Escort RS 2000," The Times (London), Feb. 5, 1976, p 27*

The top face [of the kite] is described as spanned by a novel aerodynamic surface called an air dam, which operates to stabilize the flight while greatly increasing the lift. *Stacy V. Jones, "Modular Kite System," The New York Times, April 10, 1976, p 41*

[1974]

airdash, *v.i.* to rush by airplane; fly quickly or in a rush.

Governor B. K. Nehru, who airdashed to Shillong yesterday, flew back to Imphal today and had his final round of discussions with the persons concerned at the political and administrative levels. *Sachin Barooah, The Hindustan Times Weekly, March 25, 1973, p 1*

[1973] ► The term appears to have originated in and be used chiefly in India.

air gun, another name for AQUAPULSE GUN.

Much mapping of ocean topography today is done with sound impulses. One quite useful device is the "air gun," a compressed-air cylinder that is towed submerged behind a ship. It sends out low-frequency sound waves by means of explosions set off at regular intervals. *Igor Lobanov-Rostovsky, Encyclopedia Science Supplement (Grolier) 1973, p 185*

[1970] ► The earlier meanings of *air gun* are an air rifle or air pistol, an airbrush, and an air hammer.

air hall, *British.* a large collapsible plastic dome used especially to enclose outdoor swimming pools, tennis courts, or other athletic grounds.

They stress the value of air halls ("balloon" courts), which can permit play in bad weather and, at £4,000, are relatively cheap compared with permanent structures. *Rex Bellamy, The Times (London), Nov. 14, 1970, p 12*

[1969] Compare AIR STRUCTURE, BUBBLE².

airlock module, an airtight compartment in a space station where the atmospheric pressure, temperature, and electrical power of the station are controlled and adjusted for various activities.

When the three astronauts of the third crew came aboard, they floated headfirst out of the conical command-and-service module; through the docking adapter . . . through a hatch into the airlock module; through another hatch . . . and finally on into the cavernous workshop. *Henry S. F. Cooper, Jr., The New Yorker, Aug. 30, 1976, p 35*

[1971] *Abbreviation:* AM

airplay, *n.* the broadcasting of a phonograph record.

The "underground" promotion man for the record company knew that reviews influenced FM airplay and availability in stores. *Ed Ward, "The Bootleg Blues," Harper's, Jan. 1974, p 35*

The singer seems quite at home on 'Mr. Bojangles' as on Bob Marley's 'Stir it up' and all tracks, with perhaps the exception of a terrible arrangement of 'Only You,' deserve wide airplay. *Week-end Star (Kingston), Sept. 7, 1973, p 18*

[1973]

air structure, 1 an experimental or temporary structure supported by jets or cushions of air.

Other institutions exploring the growing field of air-structures included Harvard, the University of Minnesota, La-Verne (Calif.) College, and South Dakota State University. *Sandra Millikin, "Architecture," Britannica Book of the Year 1974, p 95*

2 another name for BUBBLE².

Not that indoor tennis is on the wane. The new Murray Hill Racquet Club with its bubble or air structure atop the old East Side Airlines Terminal building at 320 East 38th Street, is one of the latest of some 25 commercial tennis clubs, the majority of them in bubbles, that have opened in and near Manhattan alone. *Eleanor Blau, The New York Times, Jan. 2, 1977, Sec. 8, p 1*

[1967] Compare AIR HALL.

a.k.a. or **a/k/a** or **AKA,** *Especially U.S.* abbreviation of *also known as.*

The Russian Embassy, a.k.a. the Little Kremlin, had nothing to do with the Soviets. It was a big ol' house on West Avenue in Austin, rented for a couple of sessions in the late 1950s by a group of madcap liberal House members. *Molly Ivins, The Atlantic, March 1975, p 54*

"The Last Testament of Lucky Luciano" begins on Nov. 23, 1897, and ends on Jan. 6, 1962, the dates when Salvatore Lucania (a/k/a Lucky Luciano) was born, and when he died. *Thomas Plate, The New York Times Book Review, March 23, 1975, p 4*

Now, with a style as gawky and loose as disco is poised and pent up, New Wave music (aka Punk) challenges the mindless complacency of an era in which both René Simard and Joe Clark have won followers. *Maclean's, Nov. 13, 1978, p 78*

[1971] ► The abbreviation *a.k.a.* has long been used in law and business and especially by police departments in the United States in place of *alias,* which denotes a false or assumed name, whereas a.k.a. merely indicates another name which may or may not be used by someone to conceal his identity. The abbreviation became widespread in American English in the early 1970's and from the beginning was applied to variant names of all people and things. In *The Underground Dictionary* edited by Eugene E. Landy (1971), *a.k.a.* is used to indicate a cross reference from one word to a synonymous word or words, e.g. **"leave,** *v.* Depart. **a.k.a.** blow, cut, cut out, . . . split, slide, splurge, take off, walk."

ALA·de·hy·dra·tase (ˌei elˌei di'hai drəˌteis), *n.* an enzyme important in the synthesis of heme (the nonprotein part of hemoglobin).

Dr Hernberg found that lead affected the functioning of an enzyme involved in haem synthesis, and called, for short, ALA-dehydratase. *Bryan Silcock, The Sunday Times (London), April 25, 1971, p 13*

[1970, *ALA* abbreviation of *aminolevulinic acid*]

alarm reaction, the initial reaction of the body to stress, characterized by the production of hormones that quicken the pulse, raise the blood sugar level, dilate the pupils, and increase perspiration.

Whether stress leads to disease or to increased energy and achievement depends on how the body takes it. The physiological process is what Dr. Selye calls the general adaptation syndrome. There are three stages: alarm reaction, resistance and exhaustion. During the first stage, the body acknowledges the stressor, which might be the news of a raise or of getting fired. The body's response is immediate. The pituitary-adrenal-cortical system produces arousal hormones necessary for either "flight or fight." *Kathy Slobogin, "Stress," The New York Times Magazine, Nov. 20, 1977, p 50*

[1972] See GENERAL ADAPTATION SYNDROME.·

albatross¹, *n.* a heavy burden, as of debt, responsibility, guilt, etc. (often in the phrase *an albatross around one's neck*).

What was hailed as the biggest breakthrough for Rolls-Royce in March 1968, has become an albatross around the company's neck. *Victor Keegan, The Manchester Guardian Weekly, Nov. 21, 1970, p 22*

[1963, in allusion to the albatross in Coleridge's *The Rime of the Ancient Mariner*]

albatross², *n. British.* a hole in golf played in three holes less than par.

An albatross is a rare bird in golf—probably even rarer than a hole in one—and today one was achieved by Harnett, of Portmarnock, who holed his second shot to the 12th with a brassie, winning the hole but losing the match. *Peter Ryde, The Times (London), June 2, 1970, p 13*

[1965, patterned on *eagle, birdie*]

al·bo·my·cin (‚æl bou'mɑi sən), *n.* an iron-containing antibiotic derived from a species of actinomycetes and used against bacteria that are resistant to penicillin.

At least two antibiotics are known to be absorbed into bacteria via enzyme transport systems that evolved for other purposes. Thus albomycin contains ferrichrome, a material normally used by bacteria as a source of iron, and is conveniently taken into the cell via the ferrichrome uptake system. *New Scientist, March 15, 1973, p 590*

[1973, apparently from Latin *albus* white + *-mycin* (from Greek *mýkēs* fungus), as in *actinomycin*]

ALCM, abbreviation of *air-launched cruise missile.*

If the new B-1's are not built, the Air Force has a less dramatic option with the development of a nuclear armed ALCM . . . which could be carried aboard the current B-52 bomber force. *Robert M. Lawrence, The Americana Annual 1976, p 384*

[1975] Compare SLCM. See CRUISE MISSILE.

Aleutian disease, a viral disease of mink noted for its similarity to various human diseases of connective tissue.

In Aleutian disease of mink, for example, there is a marked host response to the presence of the virus; indeed, the proliferation of certain cells and proteins (plasma cells and γ-globulins) of the immunological systems is one of the main problems in the progress of the disease. *Richard Kimberlin, New Scientist, March 15, 1973, p 602*

[1966, from the *Aleutian* Islands]

Al·ex·bow ('æl iks‚bou), *n.* the trademark for a device that breaks arctic sea ice upward and throws it clear on each side.

Early in 1970 the Canadian federal government decided to spend an additional Can$500,000 on the further development of the "Alexbow," a Canadian-designed ice plow that would lift ice out of a ship's path rather than crushing it. *Kenneth de la Barre, Britannica Book of the Year 1971, p 103*

[1968, from Scott *Alex*ander, the Canadian inventor of the device + *bow* (from its shape)]

al·fa·foe·to·pro·tein (‚æl fə‚fi: tou'prou ti:n), *n. British.* variant of ALPHAFETOPROTEIN.

David Brock of the Western General Hospital, Edinburgh, works on alfafoetoprotein, an α-globulin formed in the unborn child from the age of six weeks. *"In The Wake of Thalidomide Come the Teratogenists," New Scientist, Jan. 18, 1973, p 121*

[1973]

Al Fa·tah (‚ɑ:l fɑ:'tɑ:), the largest guerrilla group in the Palestine Liberation Organization (PLO).

The publication said the main guerrilla group, Al Fatah, had been making contact with other groups to rally them around the new program, which will be introduced in the Palestinian legislature in exile, known as the National Council. *The New York Times, March 1, 1976, p 4*

[1966, from Arabic, literally, the conquest; *Fatah* is also an acronym in reverse for *Harakat Tahrir Filastin* Palestine Liberation Movement] Also shortened to FATAH. Compare BLACK SEPTEMBER.

Alf Gar·nett ('ælf'gɑr nit), *British.* a type of working class British man who often reacts to social pressures in a bigoted and self-righteous manner.

Beneath that veneer, presumably, lie dark and hideous passions: Lord Hunt worries that "the Alf Garnetts" may become the decisive voice in our society. *Lewis Chester, The Sunday Times (London), Jan. 25, 1970, p 11*

[1968, from the name of a television character created by the English actor Warren Mitchell in Johnny Spealght's BBC comedy series "Till Death Us Do Part" (1967)] Compare ARCHIE BUNKER, OCKER.

Al·fi·sol ('æl fə‚sɔ:l). *n.* (in U.S. soil taxonomy) any of a group of soils which are usually moist and are characterized by an iron-rich surface layer.

This time-related variation is exhibited as horizontal variability in most localities. Alfisols on glaciated land surfaces 20,000 years old, for example, are commonly associated with Entisols a few hundred years old on floodplains. *Paul F. Smith, "Soil," McGraw-Hill Yearbook of Science and Technology 1976, p 367*

[1972, probably from *Alfa* (variant of *alpha* the first of a series) + connecting *-i-* + *-sol* (from Latin *solum* soil)] Compare ARIDISOL, HISTOSOL, INCEPTISOL, MOLLISOL, OXISOL, SPODOSOL, ULTISOL, VERTISOL.

Al·fvén wave (ɑ:l'vein), *Physics.* a wave propagated within plasma as it interacts with a magnetic field.

Alfvén is credited with opening the whole field of magnetohydrodynamics, which is the study of electrically conductive gases, called plasma, in a magnetic field, and with the discovery of Alfvén waves. *Caroline G. Dudley, 1971 Collier's Encyclopedia Year Book (1970), p 380*

[1963, named after Hannes O. *Alfvén*, born 1908, Swedish physicist]

al·ga·tron ('æl gə‚trɑn), *n.* a laboratory structure in which algae are grown under controlled climatic conditions.

The system involves both photosynthetic algae and non-photosynthetic bacterial components cultured in spin-type reactors (algatrons). *"Isolated Environment Cleans Its Air and Water," New Scientist and Science Journal, Aug. 26, 1971, p 469*

[1967, from *alga* + *-tron* an instrument or device, as in *cyclotron*]

al·go·lag·ni·ac (ˌæl gəˈlæg ni: æk), *n.* a person who gets sexual pleasure from inflicting or experiencing pain; a sadomasochist.

Readings in continental decadent literature of the *fin de siècle:* among others, a model esthete and satanist from France (Huysmans), a hair-fetishist from Belgium (Rodenbach), a senile satyr from Holland (Couperus), some algolagniacs from Denmark (Jacobsen, Bang). *"Dark Days in the Groves of Academe," The New Yorker, March 29, 1976, p 61*

[1976, derivative of *algolagnia* (1901) sadomasochism, from Greek *álgos* pain + *lagneíā* lust]

al·go·lag·ni·a·phile (ˌæl gəˈlæg ni: əˌfail), *n.* another name for ALGOLAGNIAC.

The dazzlingly literate personal ads have launched at least three marriages and countless friendships through such entreaties as "couple seek avid algolagniaphile [a sado-masochist], female, 30s, to complete harmonious ménage à trois." *Elizabeth Peer, Newsweek, Oct. 29, 1973, p 70*

[1973, from *algolagnia* + *-phile* lover of]

alimony, *n.* ► Legal and general reference books still define this term traditionally in terms of a wife's support. However, many states redefined alimony to allow either spouse to sue for support, depending on the circumstances. A significant legal change in the use of the term occurred in March, 1979, when the Supreme Court ruled (in Orr *vs.* Orr) that state laws under which only husbands could be required to pay alimony, were unconstitutional. This ruling will change the definition of alimony as the following quotation suggests:

Theoretically, the Court's ruling could be interpreted as wiping out the New York alimony law altogether, leaving the courts with no authority to order anyone, male or female, to pay alimony until the Legislature enacts a substitute alimony law.

However, it is likely, several lawyers said yesterday, that the courts will instead simply reinterpret the current law, reading it as permitting alimony payments to "spouses" and not merely to "wives." *Lesley Oelsner, "No Sudden Boon for New York Men Seen in High Court Alimony Ruling," The New York Times, March 7, 1979, p B3*

See MARRIAGE, PALIMONY.

alimony drone, *U.S. (usually used disparagingly).* a divorced woman who chooses not to remarry in order to continue receiving alimony.

There are rules, decisions, and statutes instructing the judge that wives should not be permitted to become "alimony drones"—self-indulgent, indolent parasites. *Norman Sheresky and Marya Mannes, Saturday Review, July 29, 1972, p 34*

Alimony drone is an indolent divorcee living on alimony. *Sylvia Porter, New York Post, Feb. 26, 1975, p (not known)*

[1972]

al·la·tec·to·my (ˌæl əˈtek tə mi:), *n.* removal of an insect's corpus allatum (gland that secretes various

hormones) in experiments on molting, metamorphosis, etc.

Allatectomy of the treated fifth instar larvae reversed the effects of the prior treatment with juvenile hormone. *Lynn M. Riddiford, et al., "Delayed Effects of Juvenile Hormone on Insect Metamorphosis Are Mediated by the Corpus Allatum," Nature, June 23, 1972, p 458*

[1968, from corpus *allatum* + *-ectomy* surgical removal (from Greek *ektomé* a cutting out)]

allatectomize, *v.t.:* Our results, however, do not entirely rule out the possibility that some JHA might have some intrinsic hormone activity. The fact that various compounds have been reported to produce juvenile hormone activity in allatectomized insects, has been put forward in support of this contention. *Michael Slade and C. F. Wilkinson, "Juvenile Hormone Analogs: A Possible Case of Mistaken Identity?" Science, Aug. 17, 1973, p 673*

Allen charge, *U.S. Law.* a charge or instruction to a hung jury in which the judge urges dissenting jurors to reconsider their views in deference to the majority and do their utmost to reach a verdict.

To many laymen the Allen charge may seem innocuous —an attempt to balance the defendant's right to a hung jury, if the jurors cannot agree, against the judicial system's need to dispose of cases on the docket. But seasoned criminal lawyers feel that its use almost invariably leads to a conviction. *Martin Garbus, "Law: Juries: The Problem of the 'Dynamite' Charge," The New York Times, Oct. 8, 1972, Sec. 4, p 6*

[1967 (but cf. *Black's Law Dictionary,* 1951), after the case of *Allen* vs. United States (1897) in which the charge was first used] Also called DYNAMITE CHARGE.

al·lo·ge·ne·ic (ˌæl ə dʒəˈni: ik), *adj.* genetically different.

Glands cultured for 4 weeks have survived for more than 40 days in allogeneic recipients. *Barbara B. Jacobs, McGraw-Hill Yearbook of Science and Technology 1976, p 108*

The cells, taken either from the patient himself (autologous cells) or from a similar case (allogeneic cells), are first killed and treated in various ways to enhance their immunogenic power. *Lucien Israel, Conquering Cancer, 1978, p 118*

[1965, from *allo-* other + *geneic*, as in *syngeneic*] Compare XENOGENEIC.

al·lo·type (ˈæl əˌtaip), *n.* a variant genetic trait that produces antibodies in an individual when tissue is introduced from another individual having another variation of the trait.

In the rabbit there are several separate genetic markers, called allotypes, which are the characteristics manifested by inheritable amino acid sequence differences at various positions on both light and heavy polypeptide chains. *Hugh O. McDevitt, "Medicine," 1971 Britannica Yearbook of Science and the Future (1970), p 266*

[1970, from *allo-* other + *type*]

► An older meaning of this term in biology is that of a specimen having the opposite sex of the specimen on which a description of the species is based.

al·lo·zyme (ˈæl əˌzaim), *n.* an enzyme that varies genetically from one group or species to another.

A further area of present interest is the existence of certain pairs of species which show only very slight genetic difference as measured by allozymes. These cases may represent pairs of newly formed species. *Hampton L. Carson, Nature, Feb. 5, 1976, p 359*

[1976, from *allo-* other + *-zyme* enzyme]

all-play-all, *n. British.* a tournament in which every contestant plays every other contestant. The equivalent U.S. term is *round robin. Often used attributively.*

There is still the feeling, in many people's minds, that a genuine international tournament is one played on the all-play-all principle, with the further notion that such a system lends itself least to the strokes of luck which can occur in events held on the Swiss system. *The Times (London), May 21, 1977, p 9*

[1968]

al·pha-en·dor·phin (,æl fə en'dɔr fin), *n.* a pain-suppressing hormone produced in the pituitary gland.

Roger Guillemin of the Salk Institute went on to isolate two other peptides, as well as beta-endorphin itself, from a mixture of hypothalamus and pituitary tissue from pigs. One of them, named alpha-endorphin, has a sequence corresponding to amino acids 61 through 76 of beta-lipotropin, and it has analgesic and tranquilizing effects in animals. *Solomon H. Snyder, "Opiate Receptors and Internal Opiates," Scientific American, March 1977, p 55*

[1976, from *alpha-* first of a series + ENDORPHIN]

al·pha·fe·to·pro·tein (,æl fə,fi: tə'prou ti:n), *n.* a glycoprotein abundant in the blood serum of fetuses. Its presence in high concentrations in the blood of an adult indicates pregnancy or certain kinds of cancer; higher concentrations than normal for pregnancy indicate a birth defect in the fetus.

A study in 19 centres in Britain has shown that a blood test for alphafetoprotein (AFP) can indicate with considerable accuracy if a pregnant woman is carrying a foetus affected by spina bifida or anencephaly (absence of most of the brain). *New Scientist, June 30, 1977, p 759*

[1973, from *alpha* first of a series + FETOPROTEIN]
See CARCINOEMBRYONIC ANTIGEN.

al·pha·ga·lac·to·si·dase (,æl fə gə,læk tə'sai deis), *n.* a form of galactosidase, an enzyme that metabolizes fat. The abnormal function of alphagalactosidase is believed to be responsible for FABRY'S DISEASE.

Testing skin cells from a Fabry's patient, the investigators found them deficient in activity of a specific enzyme called alphagalactosidase. *Science News, Oct. 17, 1970, p 312*

[1970, from *alpha* first of a series + *galactosidase*]

al·pha₁-an·ti·tryp·sin (,æl fə,wən,æn ti'trip sin), *n.* a protein of human blood serum that normally inhibits the action of the enzyme trypsin. A deficiency of alpha₁-antitrypsin is believed to indicate a predisposition to emphysema and other lung disorders.

Much of the literature on alpha₁-antitrypsin argues the need for the identification of deficient individuals so they can be warned that they are at unusually high risk and should modify their surroundings accordingly. *Tabitha Powledge, "Can Genetic Screening Prevent Occupational Disease?", New Scientist, Sept. 2, 1976, p 486*

[1976, from *alpha* first of a series + the number *1* + *anti-* against + *trypsin*]

alpha receptor, a site or structure in a cell at which the stimulus of certain adrenergic (adrenaline-producing) agents elicits a usually excitatory response.

Stimulation of the alpha-receptors produced a stimulation of the associated muscles: the lungs worked harder to get more oxygen or the blood vessels expanded to increase circulation. Stimulation of the beta-receptors had the opposite effect, of slowing down activity. *The Times (London), March 19, 1973, p 3*

[1963, shortened from *alpha-adrenergic receptor*]

Alpine or **alpine,** *adj.* of or designating ski races that include downhill, slalom, and giant slalom events.

None of the men Alpine skiers was able to come close to matching Mittermaier's combination of Olympic and World Cup dominance. *Roger Allaway, "Sports: Skiing," 1976 Collier's Encyclopedia Year Book (1975), p 524*

With training techniques and equipment ever more sophisticated and timing more exact, alpine skiing today resembles Formula One auto racing: runs get faster and the risks bigger. *Time, Feb. 2, 1976, p 64*

[1973, so called from these events having originated in the Alps] Compare NORDIC.

Alpinist or **alpinist,** *n.* a skier who takes part in Alpine competition; an Alpine skier.

Cindy Nelson, 20, is the only American alpinist given much chance to win a medal. But the favorite in Cindy's best event, the downhill, will probably be Austrian Brigitte Totschnig. *Time, Feb. 2, 1976, p 64*

[1976, from ALPINE + *-ist*]

▶ The original meaning of *Alpinist* (1880's) is a person devoted to the climbing of high mountains.

also-runner, *n.* an unsuccessful participant in any competition.

The luck of the nonseeding put into practice this fall brought Yale to Brown at the very start of the League program, and Brown, an also-runner for so many seasons, is something else these days, in part because of the current coach and in part because Michalko is its first-string quarterback. *"Football," The New Yorker, Sept. 27, 1976, p 79*

[1965, variant of *also-ran* (1890's)]

altered state of consciousness, any state of mind that differs from the normal mental state of a conscious person.

Other cultures have long had techniques for arriving at altered states of consciousness—through such means as chanting, whirling, fasting, breathing exercises, and flagellation. Now such procedures are recognized to have dramatic effects on body chemicals which contribute to the achievement of the desired state. *Constance Holden, "Altered States of Consciousness," Science, March 9, 1973, p 983*

It is beginning to be thought that telepathy, clairvoyance, mystical transports, and other altered states of consciousness may be latent in most, if not all, of us, along with psychic powers and dominions not demonstrated. *Calvin Tomkins, The New Yorker, Jan. 5, 1976, p 30*

[1972] *Abbreviation:* ASC

23

alternative or **alternate,** *adj.* being or representing an alternative to established or conventional institutions, values, ideas, etc.

Which is not to say that Durham does not have its pockets of "alternative" behaviour. There is a beleaguered minority of self-conscious radicals, of "hairies" and "politicos"—as I now and then heard them called—and the Students' Union bookshop seemed to be aiming many of its wares in their direction. *"The State of English—2: University of Durham," The Times Literary Supplement, Feb. 18, 1972, p 183*

The so-called alternate theater made a tremendous contribution to the variety of the season. Andrei Serban's La Mama Equity Theater Company fashioned a brilliant interpretation of Brecht's *The Good Woman of Setzuan. Henry Hewes, "Theater," 1976 Collier's Encyclopedia Year Book (1975), p 544*

[1970]

alternative birthing, any of various methods of childbirth in which the delivery is performed at home or in a homelike setting, usually without the use of obstetric instruments or strong sedating drugs.

Illinois Masonic's alternative birthing center is a small, completely independent unit with two bedrooms, a nurses' station with rolltop desk, and a small lounge where family and friends can wait. Because no instruments or heavy drugs are used, only women who appear headed for normal births are admitted. *Time, April 24, 1978, p 60*

The "alternative birthing" movement continued to spread. . . . More women declined to have their babies under sterile, technologically sophisticated hospital conditions. *Martha Roth, The Americana Annual 1979, p 321*

[1978] See LEBOYER.

alternative energy or **alternate energy,** power and heat derived from sources other than fossil fuels (petroleum, coal, natural gas) or nuclear fission.

The institute's work will cover four general areas of research: a survey of existing energy resources, including an assessment of alternative (renewable) energy sources such as solar energy, geothermal energy, bio-gas, and wind power. *Don Hinrichsen, "Energy Meets Ecology in Sweden," New Scientist, March 24, 1977, p 687*

It seems that while there are many committed to alternate energy, and particularly to wind power, the state of technology is not very healthy and both funds and expertise for research are severely limited. *Susan Soucoup, "An Ill Wind that Blows No Power," Maclean's, Dec. 4, 1978, p 14*

[1975]

alternative school, any school that differs from conventional schools in organization, purpose, and teaching methods, formed because of dissatisfaction with the existing educational system.

The two most controversial of these "alternative schools," financed with $3.6 million in federal funds, are Black House, a high school staffed by blacks for blacks only, and Casa de la Raza, a kindergarten-through-high school, the walls of which are decorated with Cuban posters lauding the NLF and such homilies as "All Power Comes from the Barrel of a Gun." *Michael Grant, National Review, March 16, 1973, p 310*

[1972] Compare FREE SCHOOL, STREET ACADEMY.

alternative technology, technology that uses small-scale, inexpensive tools that are simple to use and methods which conserve natural resources and protect the environment from exploitation and destruction.

The 'alternative technology' movement in industrially advanced societies is struggling to recover some of the self-sufficient technology of an earlier generation. In Africa the crops, cultivation practices, crafts and medicines that support a largely self-sufficient way of life are still part of a living tradition, but a major research effort is now required to establish and preserve this knowledge and skill in permanent form. *Paul Richards, "What Environmental Crisis Means in Africa," Nature, Jan. 29, 1976, p 258*

[1973] *Abbreviation:* AT Compare APPROPRIATE TECHNOLOGY, INTERMEDIATE TECHNOLOGY.

altruism, *n.* instinctive cooperation or self-sacrificing behavior among animals; animal behavior that seems analogous to human altruism.

The weirdest aspect of the behavior of social animals, beyond scientific understanding, is their ceaseless giving away of things. They carry food to each other all day long, they shelter and protect each other, and on occasion they drop dead for each other. The trait seems to be genetically determined, and the biologists have already made up a technical term, borrowed from an old word, now part of the professional jargon: *altruism. Lewis Thomas, "Altruism," The New York Times Magazine, July 4, 1976, p 109*

In sociobiology, altruism . . . is what happens when a predator breaks into a nest of termites or ants. Members of the colony's "soldier caste" instinctively rush to place themselves between the intruder and the rest of the colony. Like almost all insect behavior, this act is believed to be governed by instinct. *Boyce Rensberger, "Sociobiology," Encyclopedia Science Supplement (Grolier) 1976, p 46*

[1975] See SOCIOBIOLOGY.

altruistic, *adj.:* Dolphin society provides examples of altruistic behavior. The drawing depicts an observed incident in which a harpooned dolphin . . . was supported by companions at the sea surface so that it could breathe. *Picture legend, "Sociobiology," Encyclopedia Science Supplement (Grolier) 1976, p 46*

altruistically, *adv.:* Harry Power of the University of Michigan reported that one way to measure the frequency of true altruism was to give bluebirds the choice of behaving altruistically or selfishly toward the offspring of other bluebirds. *John G. Lepp, "Zoology," 1977 Britannica Yearbook of Science and the Future (1976), p 347*

AM, abbreviation of AIRLOCK MODULE.

The workshop, AM and MDA [multiple docking adapter] combined provide 12,763 cubic feet of space, about four times larger than the Salyut station and equivalent to a well organized three-bedroom house with a lot of closet and storage space. *Everly Driscoll, "SKYLAB: Focus on Earth, the Sun, the Stars and Man," Science News, May 5, 1973, p 293*

[1973]

am·a·ret·to (ˌæm əˈret tou), *n.* an Italian liqueur with an almond taste.

After establishing that White House aide Hamilton Jordan had eaten a steak and salad, the lawyer asked: "What was Hamilton drinking?" "Amaretto and cream," replied the bartender, "because he wanted something sweet which is. . . ." His voice trailed off. He started again. "The Amaretto we use is only 40 proof so with the cream it is not

exactly like putting martinis down." *The New York Times,
Feb. 23, 1978, p 31*

[1978, from Italian, originally a cake or macaroon
made from bitter almonds, from *amaro* bitter]

ambient air standard, the maximum concentration
of an air pollutant considered tolerable for human
beings in the outdoor air of a particular area.

EPA Acting Administrator Robert Fri said . . . only four
cities would probably have trouble meeting ambient air
standards for nitrogen dioxide: Los Angeles, Chicago, Salt
Lake City and Metropolitan New York. "*EPA Briefs: NO₂
and New Source Pollution*," *Science News, June 16, 1973, p
387*

[1973] Compare POLLUTANT STANDARDS INDEX.

am·bi·sex·u·al (ˌæm bi'sek ʃu əl), *n.* a bisexual person.

. . . populating his hotel with football rowdies, ambisex-
uals and couples on their second honeymoon. *Ned Chaillet,
The Times (London), Aug. 19, 1976, p 5*

[1976]

am·bi·son·ics (ˌæm bi'san iks), *n.* high-fidelity sound
reproduction that simulates electronically the directional qualities of the sound waves which it reproduces.

The new concept, called "ambisonics," aims at giving
the listener the experience not only of the spacial positioning of the performers, but also of the directional qualities of
the reverberant sound—the quality that adds the atmosphere and realism of a live performance. "*Technology
Review: After Quadraphonic Comes Ambisonic*," *New Scientist, Dec. 20, 1973, p 843*

[1973, from Latin *ambi-* around + English *sonics*]
Compare SURROUND-SOUND.

a·mel·i·a (ə'mel i: ə), *n.* a congenital absence of the
arms or legs.

Dr. McBride had acknowledged to the committee that his
original statement about Imipramine was incorrect in relation to two of three cases of birth defects originally cited by
him. The one that was correct was a case of amelia (total
absence of arms). "*Doubt on Relation of Drug to Deformities*," *The Times (London), March 9, 1972, p 7*

[1967, from New Latin, from *a-* without + Greek
mélos limb]

▶ Although this term has long been used in medicine, it has only recently appeared in popular writing as a result of the interest generated by this and
similar conditions caused by various drugs taken
during pregnancy, such as thalidomide.

Am·er·Eng·lish (ˌæm ər'iŋ gliʃ), *n. British.* American English.

One of the glories of the English language is that it wel-
comes in and naturalizes its vocabulary from every other
tongue. It combines and adopts useful words from Anglo-
Saxon and Teutonic roots alongside Latin, French, Greek,
Hindi, Australian, AmerEnglish, and anything else that
comes to tongue, with majestic disinterestedness. *Philip
Howard, "Deciding Whether a Word Gets a Work Permit,"
The Times (London), May 20, 1976, p 18*

[1976, from *Amer*(ican) + *English*, patterned on
Amerasian (1965) and *Amerindian* (OEDS 1900)]
Also, AMERO-ENGLISH.

American Sign Language, a system of communication by manual signs used by the deaf in North
America. It is considered by some linguists to
possess most of the range of morphological and syntactic processes found in natural languages.

What we see on these two dozen close-ups of Mary Beth
and a couple of friends are formal words of signing, or
American Sign Language (what a few bright chimpanzees
such as Washoe have been learning lately, by the way).
*Philip and Phylis Morrison, "Books," Review of "Hand-
talk: An ABC of Finger Spelling and Sign Language" by
Remy Charlip and Mary Beth, Scientific American, Dec.
1974, p 148*

[1965; cf. *A Dictionary of American Sign Language
on Linguistic Principles*, 1965, by William Stokoe,
Jr. and others] *Abbreviation:* ASL Also called
AMESLAN.

Am·er·o·Eng·lish (ˌæm er ou'iŋ liʃ), *n.* a variant of
AMERENGLISH.

The impingement of "franglais," or more precisely,
Amero-English, into French cultural life is still a thorn in
the side of French science authorities. "*More Language
Problems in Space*," *New Scientist, June 14, 1973, p 702*

[1973, from *American* + connecting *-o-* + *English*]

A·mes·lan ('æm əs ˌlæn), *n.* acronym for AMERICAN
SIGN LANGUAGE.

Among the sign languages, the deaf in the United States
use two principal means of communication, Ameslan and
finger spelling. Finger spelling is not a language but rather
a means of transposing any alphabetized language such as
English into a gestural mode. Ameslan is a language, and it
is the primary means of communication for deaf people in
North America. Although Ameslan is more efficient, the
deaf who know how to read and write seem to prefer finger
spelling—it has more cachet. *Eugene Linden, Apes, Men,
and Language, 1974, p 18*

The next research step involves placing chimps with
Ameslan competence alongside others unaware of this
method of communication—to see whether the first group
will try to teach sign language to the second. Preliminary
indications are positive. There are also indications that female chimps versed in Ameslan automatically teach it to
their young, beginning almost immediately after birth.
Terence Dickinson, Maclean's, March 21, 1977, p 68

[1974]

Ames test, a test for detecting cancer-producing substances by measuring their relative ability to cause
a mutation.

At present, there are two ways to prevent cancer. The
first is to try—with the help of the Ames test, for example—
to eliminate mutagenic agents from everything that can be
ingested or breathed in. No effort should be spared to accomplish this. *Lucien Israel, Conquering Cancer, 1978, p 53*

Because of the mutation/virus-intrusion assumption, the
hunt for industrial carcinogens has settled upon substances
that cause mutations among laboratory organisms. The
most recently developed method is the "Ames test," . . .
which uses a highly specialized strain of bacteria that is
very susceptible to mutations to measure mutagenic effect.
DDT and other chlorinated hydrocarbons have been subjected to the Ames test, and the results show that they do
not cause mutations. The only exception is toxaphene,
which—ironically—is the only chlorinated hydrocarbon
pesticide still in use. *William Tucker, "Of Mites and Men,"
Harper's, Aug. 1978, p 57*

25

aminazin

[1976, named after Bruce *Ames*, an American biochemist]

a·min·a·zin (ə'min ə zin), *n.* the Russian name for chlorpromazine (Thorazine), a sedative used especially in the treatment of mental illness.

Fainberg was given injections of aminazin, known in English as Thorazine, another antipsychotic drug, which makes a normal person feel sleepy and groggy, practically turning him into a vegetable if administered in sufficient quantities. *Ludmilla Thorne, The New York Times Magazine, June 12, 1977, p 30*

One of the neuroleptic drugs which is most widely applied to political inmates is aminazin. *Harvey Fireside, Soviet Psychoprisons, 1979, p 146*

[1970, from the Russian trademark for this substance] Compare SULFAZIN.

amino-acid dating, a method of dating geological or archaeological specimens of organic origin by measuring the proportion of the two different forms of an amino acid in a specimen.

Barraco is also investigating a new method of establishing the date of death of the mummified bodies. The new method, called amino-acid dating, not only may prove more accurate than radiocarbon dating, but also requires much smaller samples of tissue and wrappings. Amino acids are small protein units found in equal amounts as d- and l-forms in the living body. After death, however, the d- form slowly but constantly changes to the l- form. The amount of change is proportionate to the time the person has been dead. *Theodore A. Reyman, "Dead Men Do Tell Tales," The World Book Science Annual 1977 (1976), p 93*

[1972] Compare IODINE-XENON DATING, RUBIDIUM-STRONTIUM DATING, THERMOLUMINESCENT DATING. See also AGE-DATE.

am·i·trip·ty·line or **am·i·trip·ty·lene** (ˌæm ə'trip tə-li:n), *n.* an antidepressant drug used especially to treat nonpsychotic depression, marketed under the trademark Elavil. *Formula:* $C_{20}H_{23}N$

Drugs such as amitriptyline and chlorpromazine, as well as electroshock treatment (ECT), also suppress REM sleep, but there is no rebound following their termination and these drugs are not addictive. *John R. Smythies, "Drug Addiction," McGraw-Hill Yearbook of Science and Technology 1971, p 171*

She was placed on probation after being found not guilty of administering a noxious dose of amitriptylene in her baby's medicine so as to endanger her life but admitted giving doses to the baby while in hospital. *The Times (London), July 21, 1976, p 2*

[1964, from *amino* + altered form of *trypt*amine, a substance in nerve tissue + meth*yl* + *-ine* or *-ene* (chemical suffixes)]

am·i·trole ('æm ə ˌtroul), *n.* a highly toxic herbicide used especially against poison ivy. *Formula:* $C_2H_4N_4$

Herbicides are used to kill or inhibit the growth of brushy plants which compete with more desirable trees for light, water, nutrients, and growing space. The phenoxy herbicides (2,4-D and 2,4,5-T), aminotriazole (amitrole), and picloram are frequently used in forestry. *Logan A. Norris, "Pesticide," McGraw-Hill Yearbook of Science and Technology 1974, p 330*

[1963, contraction of *aminotriazole* (1950's)]

Amnesty International, an independent international organization that investigates violations of human rights by governments and works for the release of persons imprisoned for political or religious reasons.

It is one of the grim truths of the second half of the 20th century that rarely before in history has torture been in such widespread use. Amnesty International, the widely respected human rights organization headquartered in London, estimates that in the last decade torture has been officially practiced in 60 countries; last year alone there were more than 40 violating states. *"Human Rights: Torture As Policy: The Network of Evil," Time, Aug. 16, 1976, p 31*

The death roll in Uganda now is reckoned to be "anywhere around 300,000 or above" according to a detailed report — Human Rights Violations in Uganda — published in London by Amnesty International. *Patrick Keatley, "Genocide in Uganda," The Manchester Guardian Weekly, Oct. 29, 1978, p 8*

The West German branch of Amnesty International Friday called for an investigation into what is described as the inhuman torture of political prisoners in Turkey. *Athens News, April 1-2, 1973, p 3*

[1961] *Abbreviation:* AI See HUMAN RIGHTS.

► The organization became widely known in the early 1970's and in 1977 was awarded the Nobel Peace Prize. It was founded in 1961 by Peter Benenson, an English lawyer.

a·mo·ti·va·tion·al (ˌei mou tə'vei ʃə nəl), *adj.* characterized by a lack of motivation; unmotivated.

The topic, known to psychologists as the amotivational syndrome, refers to general apathy, mental confusion and lack of goals among college students that often led to the student's dropping out. *Bayard Webster, The New York Times, Jan. 28, 1976, p 25*

[1969, from *a-* not + *motivational*]

a·mour fou (ə'mu:r 'fu:), *French.* an insanely obsessive passion or infatuation; (literally) insane love.

The story concerns a teenage girl . . . who falls for her mother's married tenant, has a child by him and drowns it, follows him everywhere until she learns he has remarried for money, and ends up as a prostitute. Borowczyk invests this tale of *amour fou* with a sense of doom. *Derek Malcolm, Film review of "Story of Sin," The Manchester Guardian Weekly, March 14, 1976, p 21*

[1963]

am·ox·y·cil·lin or **am·ox·i·cil·lin** (əˌmɑk sə 'sil in), *n.* an oral penicillin effective against a large variety of bacteria, introduced into the United States from Great Britain in 1975. *Formula:* $C_{16}H_{19}N_3O_5S$

A newer antibiotic in the family is beginning to take over the running. Amoxycillin has been sold on the Continent only during the past two years. Its patents will in turn run out between 1981 and 1983, but meanwhile it is a drug unique to Beecham with no licensed competitors to worry about. *James Poole, The Sunday Times (London), May 4, 1975, p 63*

[1971, from *amino*-hydr*oxy*phenyl (part of its chemical name) + penic*illin*]

am·phi·path·ic (ˌæm fə'pæθ ik) or **am·phi·path** ('æm fəˌpæθ), *adj.* variants of AMPHIPHILIC.

Amphipath molecules, as the Greek derivation implies, are those in which one part of the molecule has an affinity for water and the other part has a greater affinity for itself than for water. *Alec Bangham, New Scientist, Jan. 14, 1971, p 63*

A membrane can be disrupted by a high concentration of a detergent, which is an amphipathic molecule that forms the small droplets called micelles. The detergent dissolves the components of the membrane by enveloping the hydrophobic portions of both lipids and proteins in micelles, where they are protected from contact with water. *Harvey F. Lodish and James E. Rothman, "The Assembly of Cell Membranes," Scientific American, Jan. 1979, p 53*

[1971, from *amphi-* both + *-pathic* affected by]

am·phi·phile ('æm fəˌfail), *n.* an amphiphilic compound.

Phospholipids are amphiphiles, and amphiphiles are known to form lyotropic liquid crystals with water. *Glenn H. Brown, "Liquid Crystal," McGraw-Hill Yearbook of Science and Technology 1971, p 259*

[1971, back formation from *amphiphilic*]

am·phi·phil·ic (ˌæm fə'fil ik), *adj.* having or showing two different affinities (as for water and fat).

Some molecules, such as fatty acids and phospholipids, have a long hydrophobic tail and a hydrophilic head group, and are known as amphiphilic molecules. *J. N. Israelachvili, "Van der Waals Forces," McGraw-Hill Yearbook of Science and Technology 1976, p 26*

[1971, from *amphi-* both + *-philic* liking]

anabolic, *n.* short for ANABOLIC STEROID.

Anabolics are supposed to be used for sick cases, where there is some body-wasting disease, and I suppose it led to the belief that they had the effect of producing extra muscle. *The Cape Times, April 7, 1973, p 5*

[1965, noun use of the adjective]

anabolic steroid, any of a group of synthetic hormones that increase the size and strength of muscles, often used by athletes during training.

Earlier in the year the IOC [International Olympic Committee] added anabolic steroids, the so-called body-building drugs, to the list of prohibited substances at the Olympic Games. *D. K. R. Phillips, "Sporting Record," Britannica Book of the Year 1975, p 636*

The East Germans are suspected of feeding strength-building anabolic steroids to their athletes like so much Wiener schnitzel. Three weeks before the Olympics, the pill-taking stops; no traces are ever discovered in the now routine urine sampling. *Michael Posner, "Let the Games Begin," Maclean's, July 1976, p 32*

[1967, from *anabolic* increasing constructive metabolism, and *steroid* any of a class of compounds including the primary sex hormones] Also called MUSCLE PILL.

analogue, *n.* **1** a synthetic chemical substance that is similar in function to a natural chemical.

Fourteen prostaglandins occur naturally in human tissues of the lung, liver, uterus, and gastrointestinal tract, and chemists have synthesized hundreds of similar molecules called analogues. *Earl A. Evans, Jr., "Biochemistry," The 1975 World Book Year Book, p 232*

2 a synthetic substance used as a substitute for meat, fish, and other foods.

And they're tinkering with analogues of scallops, prawns, and, one gets the impression, a good many other products

that they're not yet willing to talk about publicly. *Dan Greenberg, "Forum: America's Meat Crisis," New Scientist, Aug. 2, 1973, p 277*

[1973, extended from the earlier meaning of an analogous word, thing, or situation]

anchor, *n.* *U.S.* the newscaster who coordinates a television or radio broadcast or program; anchorperson. The approximate British equivalent is PRESENTER.

In the fall, NBC moved David Brinkley to Washington, as permanent anchor there for the news of the nation's capital. *John M. Gunn, "Television and Radio," The Americana Annual 1978, p 482*

—*v.t., v.i.* to serve as anchor (of).

When Barbara Walters joins ABC's Evening News next fall, she will be the highest-paid woman ever to anchor a national news program—but not the first in the world. *Time, May 31, 1976, p 39*

On Sundays, she [Deanna Lawrence] anchors the six- and eleven-o'clock news for Channel 13. Her ambition is simple and straightforward— "to anchor in a top-ten market." *The New Yorker, April 11, 1977, p 104*

[1974, shortened from *anchorman* (1956) to eliminate the supposed reference to gender, perhaps by analogy with *chair* for *chairman* or *chairwoman*] See also CO-ANCHOR.

anchorperson, *n.* another name for ANCHOR.

Many stations, in their fierce fights for local-news rating supremacy, have placed more importance on importing young and beautiful "anchorpersons"—who know little of their new communities—than on the content of the news itself. *TV Guide, Aug. 14, 1976, p A-2*

Help Wanted M/F
Anchorperson for CBC National News.
Must be neat, articulate and willing to read other people's words. *Jack McIver, "The National, With Uhh . . .?" Maclean's, Oct. 4, 1976, p 77*

[1973, replacement of *anchorman* (1956) to eliminate the supposed reference to gender] See -PERSON.

anchorwoman, *n.* *U.S.* a female ANCHOR.

"Hi, people! This is Patty Smith, anchorwoman for Eliot Hendron, who, as you may not know, has been overwhelmed by the events of the last half hour." *John Cheever, Falconer, 1975, p 187*

Miss Walters was recently hired away by ABC-TV for $5 million to become the first permanent anchorwoman on a network evening newscast. *The New York Times, May 5, 1976, p 83*

[1974, patterned on *anchorman* (1956) to counter the supposed reference to gender]

Andean Group, a free-trade association formed in 1969 by Bolivia, Chile, Colombia, Ecuador, and Peru, and joined in 1973 by Venezuela.

The increasing cohesion of the Andean group is the most remarkable and heartening development in South America during the past decade. *The New York Times, Nov. 19, 1979, p A26*

[1972, because the *Andes* Mountains run through these countries]

an·dro·cen·trism (ˌæn drə'sen triz əm), *n.* emphasis on the male sex or the male role; concentration on males to the exclusion of females.

Even if the Christian tradition has largely been as andro-centric as Aristotle, it has not been entirely so, not by any means. And, whatever Professor Mascall says, androcentrism of the kind he expresses is now no more morally tolerable than racial discrimination or slavery. *"Reverend Madam," Review of·"Women Priests?" by E. L. Mascall, The Times Literary Supplement, Nov. 17, 1972, p 1399*

[1972, from *androcentric, adj.* (OEDS 1903) + *-ism*]

an·drog·en·ize (æn'drɑdʒ ə,naiz), *v.t.* to strengthen the male characteristics of, especially through the injection of male hormones.

But genetic females can be virilised by giving them male hormones, androgens, during foetal development. These androgenised females show rates of rough and tumble play and mounting comparable to normal males. *"Monitor: Androgens Burn Masculinity Onto the Brain," New Scientist, Sept. 16, 1976, p 591*

[1970, from *androgen* male sex hormone + *-ize*]

androgenization, *n.:* The feminizing treatment is successful if the male rats were castrated at birth. The early androgenization has permanent effects. *A.D. Jost, Science Journal, June 1970, p 72*

androgynous, *adj.* not distinguishable as to sex in appearance, behavior, etc.; having the roles or characteristics of both sexes.

Traditional personality tests, like the society they were developed in, often draw a firm line between "masculinity" and "femininity." Stanford University psychologist Sandra Bem argues that these labels may not apply in today's changing world. She has adopted the term "androgynous" to refer to people who freely cross sex-role barriers. Using a questionnaire she developed, Bem found that about half of the 1,500 students she tested conformed to the traditional sex roles. Another 35 per cent were androgynous, and the remaining 15 per cent were "cross-sex typed"—that is, feminine men or masculine women. *James Hassett, "Behavioral Sciences," Encyclopedia Science Supplement (Grolier) 1976, p 31*

For beneath the clothing that symbolizes the new woman lies the new body. This is jogged, Jacuzzi-bathed, exercised, and dieted to the point of looking androgynous. *Kennedy Fraser, The New Yorker, June 19, 1978, p 65*

[1962, extended from the original (OED 1651) sense of "being both male and female; hermaphrodite," from Latin *androgynus*, ultimately from Greek *anér, andrós* man + *gyné* woman]

► The term in popular usage is generally synonymous with *unisex* and *unisexual* (1968).

an·drol·o·gy (æn'drɑl ə dʒi:), *n.* the study of diseases of the male sex, especially disorders of the male reproductive system.

Another measure of the field's growing importance: emergence of the new medical specialty of andrology. Though still in its infancy, andrology is concerned with male fertility problems in much the same way that gynecology has treated disorders of the female reproductive system. *Joann S. Lubin, "The Man's Turn: Scientists Foresee Likely Development of Male Contraceptive," The Wall Street Journal, Sept. 1, 1975, p 1*

[1975, from Greek *anér, andrós* man + English *-logy* study of]

Andromeda strain, any strain of bacteria, viruses, or other microorganisms whose accidental release

from a laboratory might have catastrophic effects because of its unknown biochemical makeup.

Molecular biologists called for an historic temporary ban on research such as . . . combining animal, viral and bacterial DNA, fearing that it might lead to the creation of uncontrollable "Andromeda strains," or biological warfare agents. *"Science News of the Year: Biology," Science News, Dec. 21-28, 1974, p 402*

He [Bernard Davis, a Harvard Medical School microbiologist] insists that those who worry about infections are totally ignorant of medicine's long history of safely handling highly contagious bacteria and viruses. Nor, he says, do they understand how difficult it is for a microbe to become pathogenic. He adds: "Those who claim we are letting loose an Andromeda strain are either hysterics or are trying to wreck a whole new field of research." *Time, April 16, 1977, p 33*

[1971, from *The Andromeda Strain,* a science fiction novel (1969) by the American author Michael Crichton, born 1942, in which an unknown type of bacteria picked up in outer space escapes accidentally from a returning space probe, killing the population of a town and threatening to contaminate the world] See RECOMBINANT DNA RESEARCH.

an·dro·stene·di·one (,æn drə, sti:n'dai oun), *n.* a hormone that promotes male secondary characteristics, produced by the testes, ovaries, and adrenal glands.

Recently [B.J.] Everitt and his colleagues have learned that when the female monkey's adrenals—the principal secretors of the male hormone androstenedione—are removed, her sexual receptivity is greatly reduced. *"Science and the Citizen: Petite Différence," Scientific American, Aug. 1972, p 46*

[1972, derived from *androsterone* (1930's) an androgenic steroid (male sex hormone)]

An·ec·tine ('æn ek ti:n), *n.* the trademark of a derivative of curare, used as a muscle relaxant.

Dr. Arthur Nugent is particularly quotable on aversion therapy with Anectine, a curare derivative: 'Even the toughest inmates have come to fear and hate the drug. I don't blame them. I wouldn't have one treatment myself for the world.' *Malcolm Deas, Review of the "The American Prison Business" by Jessica Mitford, The Listener, Feb. 20, 1975, p 250*

[1973]

angel dust, *Slang.* a potent depressant drug, phencyclidine or PCP, used as a narcotic, especially when mixed with a barbiturate or when sprinkled on marijuana, mint leaves, or parsley and smoked.

Angel dust goes by dozens of street names, some of them indicating the form in which it is sold and others as trade names coined by individual street sellers. Peace pills, white powder, superjoint, busy bee, hog elephant tranquilizer, crystal, and green tea are some of the more popular names.

It also is called killer weed because it causes numbness in the arms and legs and because it makes some users feel "dead." *Marcia Kramer, "Angel Dust," the New Killer in Town," Daily News (New York), Feb. 23, 1978, p 5*

[1971]

an·gi·o·ker·a·to·ma (,æn dʒi: ou,ker ə'tou mə), *n.; pl.* **-mas, -ma·ta** (-mə tə). a small vascular tumor on the skin.

Fabry's disease . . . can give rise to a characteristic skin lesion, angiokeratoma, and the patients may die in middle age of a cerebral artery hemorrhage or renal failure. *John C. Crawhall and Marianne Banfalvi, "Fabry's Disease . . ." Science, Aug. 11, 1972, p 527*

[1970, from *angio-* vessel, vascular (from Greek *angeion*) + *keratoma* a callus (from Greek *kéras, -atos* horn + New Latin *-oma* growth, tumor)]

Anglo or **anglo,** *n., pl.* **-glos.** **1** *Canadian.* a Canadian of English descent; an English-speaking Canadian.

Some Anglos still insult the French by telling them to "speak white." Throughout Quebec, as well as in "English Canada," economic tradition identifies the Anglos as the businessmen and bankers and the French as the laborers and small shopkeepers. *Valerie Miner Johnson, "O Canada!" Saturday Review, Oct. 1972, p 61*

2 *British.* an Englishman, especially as distinguished from someone who is Scottish, Welsh, or Irish.

He [Sean O'Casey] was more completely Irish than many of those who built the first fame of the dramatic renaissance — most of them tended to have a touch of the Anglo about them. *Gerard Fay, The Manchester Guardian Weekly, Sept. 24, 1964, p 14*

For quite small outlays the French were printing up all their advanced poetry, their surrealist texts polemical and pornographic, their Dada manifestoes. It is only natural that the Anglos should follow. In London, by 1922 small presses were getting busy about T. S. Eliot . . . *Virgil Thomson, The New York Review of Books, Feb. 19, 1976, p 42*

3 an English-speaking person.

He wanted them to know where he stood, and started ridiculing my explanation, condescending to me as a representative of capitalism and the Pentagon. "Of course, you *would* believe that!" The Eritreans threw each other an amused glanced, to find us Anglos disagreeing. *Edward Hoagland, Harper's, July 1978, p 52*

The birds remain Dominica's property. Holly's great enjoyment for the company of captive parrots makes her painfully sensitive to the dead Dreads' accusation that she is just one more *Anglo* come to exploit Dominica. *David R. Zimmerman, "The Jungle Crusade of 'Holly Parrot'," The New York Times Magazine, Aug. 6, 1978, p 45*

— *adj.* **1** *Canadian.* English-speaking.

I was oblivious at the time, as were most of my Anglo classmates, as was the community in general. . . . If the French Fact had emerged then I doubt we'd have handled it less clumsily than it is being handled now. *John Gault, Maclean's, Jan. 1974, p 58*

2 *British.* of or for Englishmen.

The Anglo view nevertheless needs its spokesman. *Eric Earnshaw, "Plight of the Anglos Among the Celtos," The Times (London), Jan. 8, 1972, p 14*

[1959 for noun def. 1, abstracted from *Anglo-Canadian,* probably by influence of *Anglophone* (English-speaking); 1964 for noun def. 2, abstracted from the combining form *Anglo-*] Compare FRANCO.

▶ In the U.S. *Anglo* has been long used, especially in the Southwest, for a non-Hispanic white American.

A·nik ('ɑ: nik), *n.* any of a group of communications satellites launched by Canada to provide television, radio, and telephone services to the country.

The Canadians have established a trio of spacecraft, called Aniks, for their own use. These spacecraft have brought telephone and television service to remote sections of Canada. *J. Kelly Beatty, "Communications Satellites," Encyclopedia Science Supplement (Grolier) 1977/1978 (1977), p 332*

[1972, from the Eskimo word for "brother"; the name was proposed by a Montreal girl in a nationwide contest]

animal liberation or **animal lib,** a militant movement seeking to protect animals from abuse and exploitation.

A group called Animal Liberation Front . . . sneaked into the hospital the night before and rescued five animals they said were being used in cruel and inhumane experiments. *New York Post, March 16, 1979, p 12*

From that struggle alone, we could never deduce so much more that has since happened — all the other "liberations" that nobody saw coming, even as recently as a decade ago. Women's lib, men's lib, gay lib, gray lib, . . . even animal lib. *Theodore Roszak, Person/Planet, 1978, p 67*

[1978] See ANIMAL RIGHTS, SPECIESISM.

animal park, *U.S.* a large park designed for the display of wild animals in which the settings resemble the natural environment of wildlife.

William Conway of the Bronx Zoo thinks some of the animal parks in this country are badly managed. "They don't know how to take care of the animals," he maintains. *Barbara Ford, Encyclopedia Science Supplement (Grolier) 1973, p 91*

[1972] Also called SAFARI PARK, especially in Great Britain.

animal rights, the fair treatment of animals on ethical or moral grounds; protection from abuse and exploitation sought for or extended to animals.

The thinking of researchers is also beginning to be affected by the growing movement for animal rights. The rising concern for the welfare of animals is seen by some people as a natural extension of contemporary movements promoting civil rights, women's rights, homosexual rights, human rights and children's rights. *Patricia Curtis, "New Debate Over Experimenting With Animals," The New York Times Magazine, Dec. 31, 1978, p 20*

[1978] See SPECIESISM.

animal rightser: Although the new Animal Welfare Act is promulgating minimum standards for the physical well-being of laboratory animals, little attention is being paid to what one animal rightser calls their "social, emotional, and behavioral" needs. *Constance Holden, "Briefing — Assertion of Dolphin Rights Fails in Court," Science, Jan. 6, 1978, p 37*

a·ni·ma·teur (ˌa ni ma'tœr), *n.* a prime mover; the creative or animating agent behind any enterprise or undertaking.

The Church at every period of its history needs gadflies, for all too easily the Church militant can become the Church dormant or the Church complacent. Indeed the Holy Spirit, the Church's Lord and Lifegiver, is called by the writer of the Fourth Gospel the *Paraclete.* It is an untranslatable word. "Comforter" will not do, not in the modern sense of that word. "Stimulator" would be nearer at least to some of its original *nuances.* The French have a

29

word for it—*Animateur. Donald Cantuar, The Times (London), Feb. 5, 1976, p 10*

[1965, from French, literally, animator] ▶ Often italicized, the term is chiefly literary and used mainly in contexts that deal with or refer to the French.

an·i·so·my·cin (ˌæn ai sə'mai sin), *n.* an antibiotic related to streptomycin, used against various pathogenic fungi in plants, and in medicine against the disease-producing parasitic flagellate trichomonad. *Formula:* $C_{14}H_{19}NO_4$

To investigate the role of protein synthesis . . . one group of reserpine culture ganglia was maintained for 48 h in the presence of anisomycin, a specific blocker of peptide bond formation. *R. E. Zigmond and A. V. P. Mackay, Nature, Jan. 11, 1974, p 113*

[1968, from *aniso-* unlike + *-mycin*, as in *streptomycin*]

anneal, *v.t., v.i. Molecular Biology.* to link up or reconnect complementary sequences of (DNA or RNA molecules).

The DNA from SV40 virions was also separated into single strands by heating, and the resulting single strands were then "annealed" with the cellular DNA at a lower temperature. *Scientific American, Feb. 1978, p 121*

[1967, extended sense of the term meaning to temper glass or metals] Compare SPLICE. See also RECOMBINANT DNA RESEARCH.

an·o·dyn·in (ˌæn ə'dai nin), *n.* a hormonelike substance that relieves pain.

Last summer, other scientists isolated two more analgesic chemicals in the bloodstreams of animal species; one was named anodynin, from anodyne, or medicine to relieve pain; it has pain-killing properties as potent as enkephalin and beta-endorphin. *Laurence Cherry, "Solving the Mysteries of Pain," The New York Times Magazine, Jan. 30, 1977, p 52*

[1976, from *anodyne* + *-in* (chemical suffix)]

anointing of the sick, (in the Roman Catholic Church) a new name for the sacrament of extreme unction.

Extreme Unction suggests that the person to be anointed is indeed *in extremis*, while *Anointing of the Sick* has a more soothing, perhaps euphemistic, quality. *Henry R. Stern, "The Changing Language of American Catholicism," American Speech, Summer 1979, p 84*

[1963] See RITE OF RECONCILIATION.

anoretic or **anorectic,** *n.* variant of ANOREXIC.

Records at Toronto's Hospital for Sick Children, for example, show that in 1965 only one anoretic was treated; in 1974, the last year for which figures are available, 20 were admitted. *Bill Dampier, "Medicine: Dying to Be Thin: The Strange Case of the Terminal Diet," Maclean's, Feb. 23, 1976, p 46*

The full-blown anorectic has totally rejected this fatness, together with the biological and reproductive maturity that it heralds. To say that anorexia nervosa has arisen on this account is, apart from being teleological, an over-simplified view. *The Times (London), Nov. 29, 1977, p 20*

[1965, noun use of the adjective (early 1900's) meaning "causing a loss of appetite," from *anorexia*; see ANOREXIC]

▶ An earlier and related meaning of *anoretic* is "an appetite-suppressing drug."

an·o·rex·ic (ˌæn ə'rek sik), *adj.* suffering from anorexia; lacking appetite; avoiding food, especially from emotional stress.

For both neurotic and normal women, being an ideal weight is a vital component of sexual attractiveness. In a recent case study an anorexic girl saw herself as emaciated, introverted, unsociable and unhappy—the very opposite of being sexually attractive. *The Times (London), Sept. 7, 1978, p 18*

—*n.* an anorexic person.

Anorexics tend to sleep fitfully, and when they awake, they experience naturally occurring trancelike periods; it is on these periods that the therapist builds. *E. C. Zeeman, Scientific American, April 1976, p 81*

[1974, from *anorexia* an abnormal lack or loss of appetite (from Greek *anorexiā*) + *-ic*] See BULIMAREXIA.

an·or·gas·tic (ˌæn ɔr'gæs tik), *adj.* unable to attain orgasm.

Almost all anorgastic women can be taught to respond and revalue themselves to their good. *Alex Comfort, Review of "The Female Orgasm" by Seymour Fisher, The Listener, April 26, 1973, p 550*

[1973, from *an-* not + *orgastic*] Compare NONORGASMIC.

an·o·vu·la·tion (ænˌɑv yə'lei ʃən), *n.* stoppage or suppression of ovulation.

Exposure of newborn female rats to exogenous estrogens or androgens induces permanent sterility with polycystic ovaries, anovulation, persistent vaginal estrus, and absence of female mating behavior. *A. H. Conney and J. J. Burns, Science, Nov. 10, 1972, p 582*

[1963, from *an-* without + *ovulation*]

answer, *n.* someone or something that corresponds (to another); counterpart; equivalent.

Poles have long thrilled to the heroics of Captain Klos, Warsaw's answer to James Bond, who consistently traps West German agents. *Time, Nov. 30, 1970, p 22*

Calling a magazine Success doesn't necessarily make it one, either. At last report, Canada's answer to Playboy and Penthouse was close to folding. *Maclean's, April 1974, p 94*

[1966, extended meaning of "a gesture or act done in return"]

antenna chlorophyll, a group of chlorophyll molecules that collect light energy and convert it into electronic energy in photosynthesis.

Although many questions remain to be answered, these models . . . for antenna chlorophyll are sufficiently explicit to provide a working basis for current developments of biomimetic systems for the conversion and utilization of solar energy for chemical purposes. *J. J. Katz and L. L. Shipman, "Photosynthesis," McGraw-Hill Yearbook of Science and Technology 1977, p 338*

[1976, so called from its receiving light waves the way a radio antenna receives radio waves]

an·te·o·saur ('æn ti: əˌsɔr), *n.* a carnivorous mammalian reptile of the Permian period; a therapsid or theriodont.

Because skull length/body length ratios are fairly constant in primitive mammal-like reptiles, body weight for the smaller genera can be estimated by comparing the cube of the skull length to the cube of the skull length of an anteosaur (taken as 1,000 kg). *Robert Bakker, "Anatomical and Ecological Evidence of Endothermy in Dinosaurs," Nature, July 14, 1972, p 82*

By the late Permian, the ice sheets had receded. But in what is now the Karroo region of South Africa the winters were still cold. Here, on a late winter morning, two carnivorous, or meat-eating male anteosaurs battle for the control of a pack of females by banging bony snouts and brows. *Picture legend, "A New Image for Dinosaurs," The World Book Science Annual 1977 (1976), p 64c*

[1972, from New Latin *Anteosaurus*, the genus name, probably from *ante-* before + connecting *-o-* + *-saurus* lizard (from Greek *saûros*)]

Anthony dollar, a one-dollar coin with raised inner borders, made of copper and nickel and bearing a likeness of the American suffragist leader, Susan B. Anthony (1820-1906), first issued in July, 1979.

Will the Anthony dollar go the way of the pocket-sagging Eisenhower "silver" dollar or the recently resuscitated two-dollar bill? Is it another Edsel in the world of cash? *Brad Knickerbocker, "Anthony Dollar: Edsel of Coins?" The Christian Science Monitor, Aug. 3, 1979, p 2*

The Anthony dollar, they say, looks and feels too much like a quarter. *People Weekly, Sept. 17, 1979, p 96*

[1979]

anthropozoology, *n.* the study of man as a member of the animal kingdom; the zoology of man.

The two big bookstalls in Trastevere go in for porn and fladge, modulating through books of Nazi atrocities to the anthropozoology of Desmond Morris; but British fiction means a reprint of *Crome Yellow*, with a picture of Edith Sitwell on the cover. *Anthony Burgess, "Viewpoint," The Times Literary Supplement, Aug. 4, 1972, p 916*

[1972, from *anthropo-* man + *zoology*]

antiabortion, *adj.* opposed to or prohibiting induced abortions, especially abortion-on-demand.

The antiabortion movement, making its case for the fetus, and hence for the family, does not have bright prospects. It is arguing for the obligations of the family at a time when the family is a declining American institution. *Russell Baker, The New York Times Magazine, March 28, 1976, p 9*

[1966] Compare PRO-LIFE, RIGHT-TO-LIFE. See also ABORTION.

antiabortionism, *n.*: Mr. Sobran says that sex is "essentially procreative." I don't know what he means by that and suspect that he doesn't either. Furthermore, I think it is a mistake to tie antiabortionism too closely to sex-is-for-procreation. *Antony C. Wells, in a Letter to the Editor, National Review, Feb. 6, 1976, p 64*

antiabortionist, *n.*: . . . a Washington lawyer, quoted in the *Lifeletter* of The Ad Hoc Committee in Defense of Life, . . . "The biggest point anti-abortionists have won is that here, for the first time, an ordinary citizens' jury has been forced to face up to what abortion actually involves, and all that it means—and they didn't like it. *That* lesson won't be lost on the average congressman." *"Edelin Abortion Verdict: III. The Cultural Context," National Review, March 14, 1975, p 262*

His [Edward J. Golden's] program moved into high gear

in January 1972, when busloads of antiabortionists began rolling into Albany, heavily laden with sensational literature. *Marion K. Sanders, Harper's, March 1974, p 27*

Compare ABORTIONIST, PROABORTIONIST.

anti-antibody, *n.* an antibody that attacks other antibodies, especially antibodies produced by injected lymph cells.

Perhaps part of the viral DNA becomes incorporated into the white cell's DNA and subsequently proteins are made upon the instructions of the viral DNA. This would mean that, when such a white cell makes antibodies, the antibodies would have an abnormal structure which would itself provoke the production of "anti-antibodies," causing a chain reaction, inflammation and damage to the joint. *"Arthritis Research Spotlights Virus," New Scientist, Oct. 5, 1978, p 9*

[1972]

antiatom, *n.* counterpart of any atom in antimatter.

Symmetry between matter and antimatter is one of the basic principles of particle physics. To every particle there corresponds an antiparticle. . . . It is possible to build up antiatoms, and a certain poem went so far as to conjure up antiworlds in which Professor Edward Teller met his opposite, Professor Edward Antiteller. *Dietrick E. Thomsen, Science News, March 31, 1973, p 211*

[1967]

antiauthority, *adj.* opposed to or rejecting authority; hostile to the officials or government of a country, state, etc.

Though today's terrorists have comparable anti-authority aims, their motivations are by no means uniform. *E. J. Kahn, "Profiles: How Do We Explain Them?" The New Yorker, June 12, 1978, p 38*

The Irish are a teen-age vogue in Germany now, as cowboys and Indians used to be. To be "antiauthority" is chic, and somehow the I.R.A. has captured the imagination of youths who haven't the slightest idea of the gray horror of Belfast. *Flora Lewis, "The Trouble With Europe," The New York Times Magazine, April 2, 1978, p 49*

[1967] ► A similar term, *antiauthoritarian*, meaning "opposed to authoritarianism" has been in use since the 1930's.

antibusing, *adj. U.S.* opposed to the busing of students to achieve a racial balance in schools.

As chairman of an education subcommittee, [Walter] Mondale stayed with his position in favor of busing ("as one constitutional tool") right through the worst of the antibusing furor. *Brock Brower, "The Remaking of the Vice President," The New York Times Magazine, June 5, 1977, p 44*

[1969, from *anti-* opposed to + BUSING]

antibuser, *n.*: Conventional-minded political reporters are indignant when voters hesitate between [George] McGovern and George Wallace or describe themselves as hawks and antibusers and then vote for McGovern. *Arthur Schlesinger, Jr., The New York Times Magazine, July 30, 1972, p 11*

anticharm, *n.* the counterpart of charm in antimatter.

Theory says the psi's contain both charm and anticharm, since they are made of a charmed quark and an anticharmed antiquark. (Quarks are the building blocks out of which particles are constructed according to the most widely accepted theory.) *"Charm at Last: How Sweet It Is,"*

anticharmed

Science News, June 5 and 12, 1976, p 356

[1974]

anticharmed, *adj.:* The new particle found at Fermilab appeared to be an anticharmed antibaryon of 2.26 GeV mass. *Dietrick E. Thomsen, "Physics," 1977 Collier's Encyclopedia Yearbook (1976), p 444*

anti-Confucian, *adj.* (in Communist China) of or relating to criticism of the teachings of Confucius which are considered backward-looking and reactionary.

In China another anti-Confucian campaign early in the year was . . . linked with the disgraced Lin Piao, so that 'Confucius and Lin Piao were like two cucumbers on the same root.' A new edition of the *Analects* of Confucius criticized him as a 'forefather of all reactionaries.' *Geoffrey Parrinder, "Religion," The Annual Register of World Events in 1974 (1975), p 388*

Behind the Cultural Revolution and the "Criticize Confucius" Campaign was Mao's hope that vital links to the past would not die with him. . . . For people in both societies [China and the United States], the past comes alive only when there is some kind of personal connection, an emotional entry point that gives history relevance. Occasionally that connection occurs on a national level, such as the Anti-Confucian campaign in China or the television series "Roots" in America. *Robert Oxnnam, "The Past Is Still Present" in The China Difference, edited by Ross Terrill, 1979, p 69*

[1974] Compare CONFUCIAN. See also CAPITALIST ROADER and GANG OF FOUR.

anti-Confucianism, *n.:* The unended open season on Confucius provides an arena for veiled controversy over the successions of Chou and Mao; and, in fact, sputterings against power holders who "continue to take the capitalist road" (the great crime in the Cultural Revolution) have lately been heard . . . Yet Professor [Merle] Goldman, at least, sees some grounds for optimism. She points out that the recent anti-Confucianism has brought back a number of old writings that the regime had cast aside. *"The Talk of the Town: Notes and Comment," The New Yorker, March 8, 1976, p 28*

antidrug, *adj.* opposed to the use of narcotics.

Secretary of State William Rogers . . . as chairman of a Cabinet-level International Narcotics Control Committee is the top man in the U.S. anti-drug effort. *"Search and Destroy—The War on Drugs," Time, Sept. 4, 1972, p 30*

[1967]

an·ti·feed·ant (ˌæn ti'fi: dənt), *n.* a chemical substance that repels plant-eating insects.

Antifeedants may be especially advantageous because they control plant-eating insects indirectly through starvation while leaving parasites, predators, and insect pollinators unharmed. If crops were sprayed with efficient, synthetic antifeedants, the pests might turn from crops to weeds. *George B. Kauffman, "Applied Chemistry," 1979 Britannica Yearbook of Science and the Future (1978), p 281*

Attibutive use.

Recently . . . they have isolated several "anti-feedant" compounds that appear to dull an insect's taste nerves so that it stops eating and dies. *William Tucker, "Of Mites and Men," Harper's, Aug. 1978, p 47*

[1972, from *anti* + *feed* + *-ant* (noun suffix)]

antifemale, *adj.* antagonistic or hostile to all women.

According to the complaint by the National Organization of Women, the station not only discriminates against women in employment practices but is antifemale in its basic approach, from programming to commercials. *"Show Business & Television: The Challengers," Time, May 29, 1972, p 57*

[1966]

antifeminism, *n.* opposition to the beliefs and practices of feminists.

Los Angeles's Ballance, who refers to all women as "fillies," or "chicklets" and who calls fat women "porkers" and "lardos," has stirred controversy because of the frank sex talk he provides and because of his alleged antifeminism. One Los Angeles women's libber refers to him as "the complete pig." But Ballance contends that he helps people. *"The Media: Sex on the Dial," Newsweek, Sept. 4, 1972, p 90*

[1972]

antifeminist, *n.:* The antifeminist today, as well as yesterday, holds that the physiological and psychological differences between the sexes determine the roles they play—and prefer to play—as well as their condition in society. *Clare Boothe Luce, "Woman: A Technological Castaway," Britannica Book of the Year 1973, p 25*

antilymphocytic serum or **antilymphocyte serum,** a substance consisting of antibodies against lymphocytes, used for preventing rejection of transplanted tissue.

It seems that if other immunosuppressive drugs are used without antilymphocytic serums, the normal regulatory mechanisms that keep latent viruses suppressed may be upset and the viruses may be activated. *The Times (London), Feb. 6, 1973, p 16*

Clarke and coworkers have speculated whether antidonor gamma globulin, consisting of many antibodies including human antilymphocyte serum, might prevent the formation of immune antibodies to a skin or organ graft. *C. A. Clarke, "Blood Groups," McGraw-Hill Yearbook of Science and Technology 1970, p 128*

[1965]

antinatalism, *n.* limitation of the population by controlling the birth rate.

If the introduction of shifts in social institutions had some advantages in addition to antinatalism—for instance, greater freedom for women, a value in its own right—these could be taken as offsetting some other, possibly harmful, consequences. *Daniel Callahan, "Ethics and Population Limitation," Science, Feb. 4, 1972, p 492*

[1972, from *anti-* against + *natal*ity birth rate + *-ism*] Compare PRONATALISM.

antinatalist, *adj.:* "Although lip service was paid to the idea that the rate of population growth was not sufficiently high, in fact the actual consequences of much Soviet legislation were then anti-natalist." A liberalized abortion law adopted in 1955, for example, was of major importance in reducing the birthrate. *"Science and the Citizen: The Population of the U.S.S.R.," Scientific American, Jan. 1973, p 46*

an·ti·ne·o·plas·ton (ˌæn tiˌni: ə'plæs tɑn), *n.* a substance that inhibits the growth or spread of tumors, especially cancerous ones.

One protein inhibited growth of all three types. The other three were more specific, inhibiting the growth of a specific type of cancer. The researchers dubbed the proteins "antineoplastons," since "neoplasm" means tumor. *"Proteins*

that Halt Cancer Cells," Science News, April 24, 1976, p 260
[1976, from *antineoplastic* (1954), from *anti- + neoplastic* of tumors, from *neoplasm* (1860's) a tumor; form influenced by Greek *plastón, plastós* molded]

antinuclear, *adj.* opposed to the use of nuclear energy.

Members of the congressional Joint Committee have referred to the environmentalists as "anti-nuclear." *Richard Lewis, "Citizens v. Atomic Power," New Scientist, Nov. 23, 1972, p 450*

Demonstrations by the Clamshell Alliance, a coalition of antinuclear groups, stopped construction of the controversial Seabrook nuclear power plant in New Hampshire several times. *Andrew L. Newman, "Environment," The 1979 World Book Year Book, p 315*

— *n.* an opponent of the use of nuclear energy.

At present the AEC [Atomic Energy Commission] seems convinced that those who oppose its natural predilection for nuclear energy are, as one high AEC official said, the "arch-antinuclears." *Paul Jacobs, "The Mail," The Atlantic, April 1971, p 34*

[1971, extended from the original (1957) sense of "opposed to nuclear weapons"]

► As the ENERGY CRISIS of the early 1970's gave impetus to the building of nuclear reactors to generate low-cost electric power, antinuclear groups began to stage protest demonstrations against these "peaceful" uses of nuclear energy, which they claimed posed a serious threat to public health because of the difficulty of dealing with radioactive waste safely and because of the other forms of radioactivity the nuclear power plants poured into the environment. Their cause gained dramatic support in March, 1979, when an accident in a nuclear reactor on Three Mile Island, in southern Pennsylvania, caused the discharge of radioactivity and threatened to trigger a MELTDOWN of the reactor core. See CHINA SYNDROME.

antinuke, *adj., n. Informal.* variant of ANTINUCLEAR.

Last year voters in Ohio, California, Oregon, Colorado, Washington, Arizona and Montana rejected propositions to curb nuclear power. But the anti-nukes have won some fights too. *Time, March 21, 1977, p 73*

[1977, shortened and altered from *antinuclear,* on the pattern of *nuke* (1959) a nuclear weapon or nuclear power plant]

antinuker, *n.:* When actress-activist *Jane Fonda* took centre stage recently and trooped her political colors before 90,000 anti-nukers on Washington's Capitol Hill, the impact registered on everyone from a 70-year-old lady dressed as a mushroom to U.S. President *Jimmy Carter. Jane O'Hara, "People," Maclean's, June 18, 1979, p 35*

anti-object art, another name for POST-OBJECT ART.

The most spectacular exhibition of anti-object art was Earth, Air, Fire, Water: Elements of Art at the Boston Museum of Fine Arts. It presented 50 artists, who created burning fires, falling waters, and moving air. *Victor H. Miesel, "Art," The Americana Annual 1972, p 113*

[1970]

antipsychiatry, *n.* a movement within psychiatry that rejects the conventional concepts and practices of the field, especially the concept of mental illness whereby patients are treated medically to the exclusion of other methods.

[Gregory] Bateson saw schizophrenia as a special strategy that a person invents to survive a "double bind" or "can't win" situation. With the publication of the double-bind theory in 1956, Bateson was hailed as the father of antipsychiatry, a controversial movement that holds that the medical model is not applicable to mental illness. *Ted Morgan, The New York Times Magazine, Feb. 29, 1976, p 32*

[1967] Compare LAINGIAN.

antipsychiatrist, *n.:* He [Peter Breggin] is a good example of the kind of antipsychiatrist who is especially common in the United States and increasingly vocal in Britain, who is unwilling to admit that any patient should be protected against his own impulses, or hospitalised or treated against his will. *Henry Miller, New Scientist, July 27, 1972, p 190*

antisickling, *adj.* counteracting or inhibiting the sickling of red blood cells characteristic of sickle cell anemia.

The investigators then injected DBA into mice and found that it had no acute effects. In view of this discovery, and DBA's antisickling ability, they conclude that it might well be an effective and safe sickle cell drug. *Science News, Jan. 10, 1976, p 22*

[1976]

an·ti·smok·ing (ˌæn ti'smou kiŋ), *adj.* seeking to stop or curb the smoking of tobacco.

Countries with an investment in tobacco as a cash crop are hardly likely to enthuse about anti-smoking programmes. *Lawrence McGinty, New Scientist, March 23, 1978, p 779*

[1962]

antitail, *n.* a small spikelike part of a comet's tail that, unlike the main tail, appears to be pointing toward the sun.

The view of the comet from the Earth shows how the anomalous "anti-tail" is explained by a perspective generated view of the tail's large dust particles. Comet Kohoutek also showed an anti-tail, first detected by the Skylab astronauts and later photographed at many observatories, but here the theory has been abundantly confirmed by infrared work. *Keith Hindley, "Comets in Perspective," New Scientist, April 17, 1975, p 122*

[1968] See DUST TAIL, GAS TAIL.

antitechnology, *n.* opposition to technological research and development, especially when pursued at the expense of humanitarian interests and values.

The second prominent figure to unfurl the banner of antitechnology was Lewis Mumford. His conversion was particularly significant since for many years he had been known and respected as the leading historian of technology. *Samuel C. Florman, "In Praise of Technology," Harper's, Nov. 1975, p 53*

[1967]

antitechnological, *adj.:* Quite aware of the strong antitechnological sentiments within the art world, Tuchman and his associates wisely chose a limited number of entries from some of the biggest names in the American art world: Roy Lichtenstein, Claes Oldenburg, Robert Rauschenberg,

Tony Smith, and Andy Warhol. *Jack W. Burnham, "Art and Technology," 1973 Britannica Yearbook of Science and the Future (1972), p 350*

antitechnologist, *n.:* The risk of nuclear accident is sufficient justification in his view not to proceed with nuclear power plants. The risk of producing lethal bacteria is sufficient reason to stop DNA research. Mr. Rompler supports the antitechnologists because they can name the risk. He seems to see a risk and draws the line. *Peter McCabe, "Letters: The Risk of Progress," Harper's, April 1978, p 7*

antiterrorist or **antiterrorism,** *adj.* designed to combat terrorists or terrorism.

The opposition Christian Democratic Party also unveiled a legislative package of new antiterrorist measures that would ban forced feeding of prisoners on hunger strikes, simplify identity checks on suspects, widen the legal definition of terrorists and speed up court trials. *Royal Gazette (Bermuda), May 28, 1973, p 6*

According to an American source, a British antiterrorist expert has also gone to Italy where he, and a liaison man from a similar West German unit, are helping the Italians develop their own antiterrorism teams. *The New York Times, May 7, 1978, Sec. 4, p 1*

[1964; 1967] ► The synonymous terms *counterterrorist* and *counterterrorism* have been used chiefly as nouns, originally (1950's) in the context of the Algerian revolt against France.

An·tu·rane ('æn təˌrein), *n.* a trademark for a drug that stimulates the excretion of uric acid, used to treat gout and experimentally to prevent the formation of blood clots. *Formula:* $C_{23}H_{20}N_2O_3S$

A drug used to relieve gout apprently reduces by almost one-half the risk of dying from a second heart attack in the months following the first. Patients who began using the antigout drug Anturane (sulfinpyrazone) four to five weeks after their first heart attack had a death rate of 4.9 percent a year compared with 9.5 percent a year for patients taking a placebo. Reports that Anturane prevented blood platelets from clumping together to form clots led to speculation that this drug could be beneficial in combatting recurrent heart attacks. *Science News, Feb. 18, 1978, p 101*

[1968, probably from *ant-* (variant of *anti-* against) + *uric* acid + *-ane* (chemical suffix)]

anx·i·o·lyt·ic (æŋˌzɑi ə'lit ik), *n.* a drug used to relieve anxiety; a tranquilizer.

Physicians no less than patients, says Dr. Shapiro, have always been, and still are, subject to fads and fashions in medicines, and the anxiolytics are today's "in" drugs. *Gilbert Cant, "Valiumania," The New York Times Magazine, Feb. 1, 1976, p 2*

—*adj.* used or tending to relieve anxiety; tranquilizing.

In their letter, the doctors point out that big cash savings could be made by prescribing meditation rather than anxiolytic, hypotensive and antidepressant drugs and sleeping pills. *The Times (London), Aug. 31, 1978, p 1*

[1976, from *anxiety* + connecting *-o-* + *-lytic* dissolving, as in *hydrolytic*]

ANZAM or **An·zam** ('æn zæm), *n.* acronym for *Australia, New Zealand, and Malaysia.*

ANZAM joins Australia and New Zealand with Britain to defend Malaysia. *C. L. Sulzberger, The New York Times, July 15, 1970, p 38*

[1965] ► The pattern for this acronym was set by *Anzac* (for *A*ustralian and *N*ew *Z*ealand *A*rmy *C*orps), which came into use in World War I (about 1915), especially as a generic name for any Australian soldier. The form *ANZUS* or *Anzus* (for *A*ustralia, *N*ew *Z*ealand, and the *U*nited States) was created in 1951 to designate a tripartite mutual-defense pact in the Pacific formed by these countries.

ANZUK ('æn zək), *n.* acronym for *Australia, New Zealand and United Kingdom.*

Military aid to South Vietnam and Cambodia ceased. The infantry battalion stationed in Singapore as part of the ANZUK (Australia-New Zealand-U.K.) forces was brought home, although air squadrons in Malaysia—fulfilling a need that country could not meet—remained. *Thomas B. Millar, "Australia's Defense Reappraised," Britannica Book of the Year 1976, p 155*

[1972] ► See the note under ANZAM.

AONB or **A.O.N.B.**, *British.* abbreviation of *Area of Outstanding Natural Beauty*, a scenic area under national protection.

Both the national parks and the AONBs receive substantial exchequer grants for carparks and lavatories, and the main difference between them is that the AONBs are not subject to even the minimal national control that is exercised in the national parks. There are 32 AONBs at present, with another 10 in the pipeline. *Jon Tinker, "The Protected Quarter," New Scientist, Sept. 27, 1973, p 731*

[1970]

A-1 protein, a protein found in the myelin of people with multiple sclerosis, believed to contribute to the onset of the disease.

He [E. H. Eylar] and his colleagues found that protein taken from the brains of multiple sclerosis patients, a so-called A-1 protein, and injected into experimental animals, sensitized the animals' lymphocytes (immune cells). *"Biomedicine: New Treatment for Multiple Sclerosis," Science News, Oct. 16, 1976, p 250*

[1970]

a·pa·min ('ei pə min), *n.* a polypeptide, derived from bee venom, that is destructive of nervous tissue, used experimentally in neurology and medicine.

Apamin is the smallest neurotoxic polypeptide known, and it is the only one whose interaction with the spinal cord is well established. *E. Habermann, "Bee and Wasp Venoms," Science, July 28, 1972, p 317*

[1972, from Latin *apis* bee + English *amino* acid]

a·part·ho·tel (əˌpart hou'tel), *n. British.* a building with furnished apartments which are sold to individuals as investors but which are rented and serviced as hotel suites when the owners are away.

Melia was the first hotel group to use the aparthotel system for the 1,000-room luxury Castilla Hotel in Madrid. *Patricia Tisdall, The Times (London), Sept. 13, 1976, p 21*

[1972, from *apartment* + *hotel*]

► This type of building differs from an *apartment hotel* (known since the early 1900's) in that the units of the latter are rented to the permanent residents, not sold as investments.

aperture card, a key-punch card with an opening to

hold a microfilm frame or frames, used in data processing, documentation, and the like.

The microfilm copies of patents offered to the public and for examiners' use will be stored in the form of aperture cards, which have space for eight images each. *Science News, July 23, 1966, p 57*

Microfiche is a postcard-size piece of film containing the images of the original documents in a grid pattern. Aperture cards are mainly used in the engineering department and are basically an 80 column card holding one 35mm frame of the original drawing. *The Times (London), Sept. 14, 1977, p 15*

[1966]

aperture synthesis, (in radio astronomy) a method of detecting signals by combining the reception of several small antennas.

One of the most powerful techniques radioastronomers use is that of "aperture synthesis." They take two receiving aerials and make simultaneous observations of one source while varying their separation. From the results they obtain they can build up an effective signal equivalent to that which would be produced by one large aerial as big as their widest separation. *New Scientist, Feb. 12, 1970, p 296*

The energy received by the antenna must be phase-coherent to allow the synthesis to be accomplished. Thus synthetic apertures are usually used in high resolution radar systems. Alternatively, the antenna may be fixed and the source of energy moving, as in aperture synthesis used in radio astronomy. *R. C. Hansen, "Radar," McGraw-Hill Yearbook of Science and Technology 1976, p 337*

[1965] Compare VLBI. See also SYNTHETIC-APER-TURE RADAR.

a·per·tu·ris·mo (aː‚per tuːˈriːs mou), *n.* the opening of the political process in Spain after Francoism.

Which is the real Spain—the Spain of the future? Is it Franco's surviving State apparatus, with the attached political lobby known as the "Bunker," which still meets for lunch at the Madrid Jockey Club, shaking its head at all this rampant "aperturismo?" *Walter Schwarz, "Can Spain Avoid Another Civil War?" The Manchester Guardian Weekly, Feb. 29, 1976, p 9*

[1975, from Spanish, from *apertura* opening]

► In the early 1960's *aperturismo* was borrowed from Italian in the sense of an opening of Catholic thinking to new trends in ecumenical and political relations. The term was short-lived, however, as the word *aggiornamento*, used in a similar sense, gained currency and replaced it.

APEX or **A·pex** (ˈeiˌpeks), *n.* acronym for *Advance purchase excursion*, a system of low-cost air fares for reservations paid in advance made for travel abroad of several weeks' duration (usually from 22 to 45 days).

Apex fares have been in force on the North Atlantic routes for the past two years and have been a great success. To book for the European version passengers will have to commit themselves a month before travel and stay at their destinations not less than two weeks (one week in the case of Greece) and not more than three months. *Arthur Reed, "Advance Air Tickets at Half Fare," The Times (London), Jan. 14, 1977, p 4*

[1971] Compare ABC, OTC, SUPER SAVER.

apocalypticist or **apocalyptician,** *n.* one who fore-sees or warns of imminent catastrophe.

The parallel thought among many apocalypticists, then, runs like this: Why bother with efforts to do away with poverty and war? Of course, one should be personally moral and humane, but he or she should do this apart from politics. Human engineering will not bring progress or paradise. God will intervene and then all will be well. *Martin E. Marty, "That Old-Time Religion Again," The Americana Annual 1973, p 18*

You might be taken to task for writing that Enoch Powell has a 'hang-up' about race, but you would probably get away with calling him an 'apocalyptician' (i.e. one who predicts devastating calamities), though both expressions are American and of recent origin. *Tony Cash, "Very American. Very Stiff Upper Lip," The Listener, Jan. 15, 1976, p 45*

[1973] Also called DOOMSDAYER.

► The older, related term *apocalyptist* (early 1800's) means a writer of an apocalyptic work.

ap·o·di·za·tion (‚æp ə dəˈzei ʃən), *n.* **1** *Optics.* a method of controlling the overlap between adjacent images by modifying the amplitude of the aperture.

Apodization to correct for line shape distortions introduced by truncation of the input signals. *E. D. Becker and T. C. Farrar, "Fourier Transform Spectroscopy," Science, Oct. 27, 1972, p 365*

2 *Electronics.* a method of varying the overlap between adjacent electrodes in an electric filter.

A popular method of achieving this [alteration of the amplitude-frequency response], due to ease of design and relative insensitivity to fabrication errors, has been apodization of the input IDT [interdigital transducer]. *J. H. Collins, "Filter, Electric," McGraw-Hill Yearbook of Science and Technology 1975, p 190*

[1971, probably from *aperture* perio*dization*]

Apollo asteroid, any one of a group of asteroids whose paths cross the orbit of the earth.

In the initial excitement of the study of a newly discovered object, such as the unique Apollo asteroid 1976AA, some confusion and contradictory conclusions are likely to appear. *David Morrison, Science News, Feb. 28, 1976, p 131*

[1971, from the name of the first of these asteroids, discovered by the German astronomer Karl Reinmuth at the Heidelberg Observatory in 1932 and named by him Apollo]

apple, *n.* *U.S. Slang.* **1** a derogatory name for an American Indian who is part of or cooperates with the white establishment.

In the surging tide of Indian militancy, the most outspoken group is the American Indian Movement, leaders of last November's occupation of the BIA [Bureau of Indian Affairs] building in Washington, as well as the Wounded Knee takeover. The group's tactics enrage more conservative Indians, whom AIM refers to as "apples"—red on the outside, white on the inside. *"Behind the Second Battle of Wounded Knee," Time, March 19, 1973, p 18*

Also called UNCLE TOMAHAWK.

2 a citizens band radio operator.

Because of overcrowding, many a CB enthusiast (called an "apple") is strapping an illegal linear amplifier ("boots") on to his transceiver ("ears") which is limited by the Federal Communications Commission ("Big Daddy" in the US) to an output power of no more than five watts. *Nicholas*

apple-pie

Valéry, "Big Daddy and the Barefoot Apples," New Scientist, June 30, 1977, p 764

See also EARS and note under CBer.
[1971 for def. 1; 1975 for def. 2]

apple-pie, *adj.* having or showing traditional American values and traits.

Could the Cuban vision of life, as reflected in these films, be so appealing that it would corrupt and endanger apple-pie America? *Marjorie Rosen, Saturday Review, June 17, 1972, p 50*

[H. Ross] Perot also has mounted a million-dollar-plus ad campaign that trades frankly on the appeal of his Horatio Alger career and apple-pie patriotism. "For 38 years of my life I was a 'little guy,' " reads one ad. "There are so many of us. We are America. We make this big engine go. That's why duPont is interested in the individual investor." *"Wall Street: Perot the Evangelist," Time, June 4, 1973, p 84*

Loose Change: Three Women of the Sixties, by Sara Davidson . . . The three California women that this book is about were apple-pie sorority sisters at Berkeley who were more or less radicalized by the spirit of the times. *The New Yorker, July 11, 1977, p 89*

[1963, from the notion that apple pie is an old-fashioned, characteristically American food]

applications satellite, an artificial satellite used for some specific purpose, such as communications, meteorology, air traffic control, or navigation.

Despite an increasing tendency to think in terms of applications satellites, the European Space Research Organisation is still maintaining a viable scientific programme. Recently ESRO has opted for two new scientific satellites to fly, respectively, in 1977 and 1979. *"ESRO Decides on a Pair of Scientific Satellites," New Scientist, May 10, 1973, p 327*

[1970]

appropriate technology, a form of technology that uses methods and devices suited to particular circumstances and conditions, such as the lack of capital and abundance of labor in developing countries or the energy shortage and depletion of natural resources in developed countries.

The technology produced within that value system fails the basic criteria of appropriate technology—that it must address the area of greatest need, must promote self-reliance on the part of those for whom it is designed, and must be environmentally sound. *Constance Holden, "Pioneering Rural Technology in India," Science, Jan. 11, 1980, p 159*

Soap making has become an appropriate technology classic. The oil is locally produced, technology for small scale soap making already exists, the market is local, and soap can be produced for half the price of the nationally advertised brands. *Joseph Hanlon, "Does AT Walk on Plastic Sandals?" New Scientist, May 26, 1977, p 468*

[1973] *Abbreviation:* AT Also called SOFT TECHNOLOGY. Compare ALTERNATIVE TECHNOLOGY, INTERMEDIATE TECHNOLOGY. See also NEW ALCHEMIST.

▶ *Appropriate technology* is used principally by environmentalists and ecologists to designate the kind of technology that relies on human or animal labor, solar power, windmills, and other sources of energy that do not harm the environment and are compatible with decentralization, instead of on large, centralized machinery that is costly to install and operate. The term may be viewed as a broadening of the concept of INTERMEDIATE TECHNOLOGY to emphasize its applicability to developed as well as developing countries. It was first used by the British economist E. F. Schumacher in his influential book *Small Is Beautiful: Economics as if People Mattered,* published in 1973.

appropriate technologist: John Todd, who, as founder of the New Alchemy Institute on Cape Cod, ranks with Brand as a leading appropriate technologist, says, "My impression is that his understanding of human society and phenomena within it operates in a slightly different time frame from most people's." *Wade Greene, Psychology Today, Nov. 1978, p 74*

a·près- (ɑːˈprei-), a combining form meaning "after or following some (specified) activity" (used usually before a noun, often to form a phrase functioning as an adjective), as in:

après-film: Kissinger, who was holding court next to the lobster souffle at an après-film party in the German embassy here, was buttonholed by Washington Post reporter Bob Woodward . . . *Susan Watters, "Eye," Women's Wear Daily, Feb. 6-13, 1976, p 4*

après-40: So what if you're après-40 or even more. There are advantages to everything. *Advertisement for a book by Anita Porter, "Polly's Principles," Harper's, Nov. 1974, p 88*

après-game: Frequently, this budget also includes weekly après-game libations . . . J. Walter Thompson, for instance, allots $1,100 for its team. *Pamela Jablons, "The Corporate Pitch: Play Ball!" The New York Times, Aug. 31, 1977, p 19*

après-sun: The sun also dries you: Skin care après-sun. *Advertisement by Helena Rubinstein, Harper's Bazaar, May 1974, p 39*

après-surgery: With the subject of mastectomy no longer discussed in guarded whispers, help has come for problems après-surgery. *"Beauty Journal: After A Mastectomy," Ladies' Home Journal, Feb. 1976, p 42*

après-swim: In bikinis and *après*-swim wrappers, the poolside lollers gather at midday. *Horace Sutton, Saturday Review, Oct. 24, 1970, p 38*

après-tennis: An entire fashion industry was springing up for après-tennis, with matching ankle-length skirts, color-coordinated separates and hats. *Newsweek, April 21, 1975, p 58*

[1963, abstracted from *après-ski* (1958), from French, literally, after-ski]

aq·ua·ki·net·ics (ˌæk wə ki'net iks), *n.* a system of training infants and young children to remain afloat in deep water.

"Understand, aquakinetics is purely a survival program for babies at risk," Dr. [John] Schieffelin stressed. "The children float; they do not learn to propel themselves through water. When they grow older, these same children will have to be taught to swim." *Claire Berman, "Learning to Swim: The How and When," The New York Times, June 27, 1975, p 43*

[1975, from *aqua* water + *kinetics* motion (of bodies)]

aq·ua·nau·tics (ˌæk wə'nɔː tiks), *n.* underwater exploration and research using scuba diving and its equipment.

Finally, recognizing the growing importance of such research, the University of California at Berkeley has just approved the country's first full-credit "aquanautics" course. *"Diving for Knowledge of the Ocean's Life," Science News, April 7, 1973, p 222*

[1973, from *aquanaut* (1964) a person who engages in underwater exploration or research + *-ics*]

Aq·ua·pulse gun ('æk wə,pəls), the trademark for a compressed-air device used in undersea exploration to measure shock waves reflected off the ocean bottom as an indicator of rock structures beneath the surface.

The ship also tows four rubber-walled Aquapulse guns, two on each side of the ship. Shock waves are produced by exploding a mixture of propane and oxygen inside the Aquapulse guns. *Carl H. Savit, "Refining the Search for Oil," The World Book Science Annual 1976, p 18*

[1976] Also called AIR GUN.

ar·a-A ('ær ə'ei), *n.* a drug derived from arabinose and adenine, used against viral infections, especially those causing encephalitis, hepatitis, and influenza. *Formula:* $C_{10}H_{13}N_5O_4 \cdot H_2O$

The successful use of the drug . . . ara-A not only destroys the herpes virus without affecting the host cell, but is low enough in toxicity to permit internal application. *Joan Arehart-Treichel, "Medicine," 1978 Collier's Encyclopedia Year Book (1977) p 350*

Agents which interfere with viral metabolism are also likely to injure host cells. It is this fact which is the primary obstacle to the development of selective antiviral agents, and which makes the apparent efficacy of ara-A so remarkable. *Science News, Oct. 15, 1977, p 243*

[1975, from *arabi*nose + *A*denine] Also called VIDARABINE.

Arabist, *n.* a supporter of Arab interests and aspirations.

The Ambassador, who is a career Foreign Service officer but not an Arabist, has made a special point of meeting many Israeli politicians and journalists, and he has conveyed an impression of genuine interest, concern and sympathy. *Marvin Kalb, "A Journey Through a Land of Doubts," The New York Times Magazine, July 17, 1977, p 40*

[1970, extended meaning of "a student of Arabic language and literature" (OED 1847)]

ar·chae·bac·te·ri·a (,ar ki: bæk'tir i: ə), *n.pl.* a group of microorganisms genetically distinct both from bacteria and from plant and animal cells, that are believed to have evolved before bacteria. They ingest carbon dioxide and hydrogen and emit methane, thriving in a warm, oxygen-free environment.

One of the oldest known forms of life, which developed between three and a half and four billion years ago — the earth and Mars originated four and a half billion years ago — are . . . archaebacteria, which are neither plant nor animal but are ancestral to both, and which inhabit such anaerobic spots as the mud beneath deep hot springs in Yellowstone National Park; they die when they are exposed to oxygen. *The New Yorker, Feb. 5, 1979, p 52*

[1977, coined by Carl R. Woese, an American biophysicist, from *archae-* ancient (ultimately from Greek *arché* beginning) + *bacteria*] Also called (individually) METHANOGEN. See THIRD KINGDOM.

ar·chae·o·as·tron·o·my or **ar·che·o·as·tron·o·my** (,ar ki: ou ə'stran ə mi:), *n.* the study of the astronomical beliefs and practices of ancient civilizations.

Archeoastronomy has become a "growth science" in the last few years. Prehistoric arrangements of stones with astronomical significance, such as Britain's famous Stonehenge, have now been more or less firmly identified in many parts of both the Old and New Worlds. Now two archeologists have located what they believe is the first astronomical monument in Africa, near Lake Turkana in northwestern Kenya. *The New York Times, May 21, 1978, Sec. 4, p 7*

[1972, from *archaeo-* ancient + *astronomy*] Also called ASTROARCHAEOLOGY.

archaeoastronomer, *n.:* In the Old World the debate over Stonehenge still rages but there is now fairly wide agreement that this 4,000-year-old arrangement of massive hewn stones was intended, at least, to sight the summer solstice sunrise. Some archeoastronomers believe the complex monument also was used to reckon lunar movements. The most hotly debated claim for Stonehenge is that it was used to predict lunar eclipses. *The New York Times, Feb. 19, 1978, Sec. 4, p 9*

archaeoastronomical, *adj.:* Nineteen basalt pillars at a megalithic site in northwestern Kenya are aligned towards the 300 BC rising directions of seven star formations of significance in the Cushitic calendar still used in the area today. This is the first archaeoastronomical site in sub-Saharan Africa and implies that a prehistoric calendar based on astronomical observations was in use in eastern Africa 2300 years ago. *New Scientist, June 22, 1978, p 825*

ar·chae·o·mag·net·ism or **ar·che·o·mag·net·ism** (,ar ki: ə'mæg nə,tiz əm), *n.* the magnetism remaining in archaeological or geological specimens, used especially as a means of determining the age of a specimen and the location of the earth's magnetic poles in antiquity.

Archaeomagnetism as a dating method was also used effectively for the first time. The method is based on the fact that while the earth behaves like a magnet, the poles of its magnetic fields constantly shift. When clay is heated to about 1100°F., as it is in baking pots in a kiln or in burning a fire in a clay-lined hearth, the electrons in the clay particles begin to move in a direction that reflects the orientation of the earth's magnetic field. The clay thus becomes magnetized, and its poles align with the magnetic field of the earth. This polarization is maintained after the clay cools. *Leslie G. Freeman, Jr., The 1968 World Book Year Book, p 207*

M. J. Aitken and G. H. Weaver . . . have deduced approximate declinations from the magnetic field "frozen" into pottery kilns of known age (archaeomagnetism). *Sidney Searle, New Scientist, Jan. 3, 1974, p 13*

[1964, from *archaeo-* ancient + *magnetism*]

archaeomagnetic, *adj.:* The same archaeomagnetic analyses also yielded fairly precise estimates of the strength of the prevailing Earth's magnetic field at the time of firing for two of the artifacts. *Michael Barbetti, The Times (London), July 1, 1976, p 18*

ar·chae·om·e·try or **ar·che·om·e·try** (,ar ki: 'am ə-tri:), *n.* the science of dating archaeological specimens, as by carbon dating or archaeomagnetism.

But the new UC experiments confirm that the timber came from a tree that was chopped down around A.D. 700, UCLA archaeologist Rainer Berger reported last week at a symposium on archaeometry and archaeological prospection at the University of Pennsylvania Museum in Philadelphia. *Science News, March 26, 1977, p 198*

[1965, from *archaeo-* ancient + *metry* measurement] See AGE-DATE.

archaeometrist, *n.:* It would appear that there is a hard core of "archeometrists" with a drifting satellite of scientists dabbling in archeology and archeologists dabbling in science. *James E. Fitting, Science, March 3, 1972, p 976*

Ar·chie Bun·ker ('ɑr tʃi: 'bəŋ kər), *U.S. and Canadian.* a type of working-class man who often reacts to social pressures in a bigoted and self-righteous manner.

Our cities would lead us to believe that apartment buildings should be very high and as predictable as Archie Bunker's prejudices. *Harvey Cowan, Maclean's, March 1974, p 34*

My answer was that it must be precisely my kind of person who must gladly give it all away for the sake of his country if his country is to survive. We can count on Archie Bunker, God bless him. But Archie isn't MacArthur, he isn't a cryptanalyst, he isn't a journalist writing to the millions of Archies. *William F. Rickenbacker, "Land of the Free," National Review, Feb. 6, 1976, p 96*

Attributive use.

A self-employed iron worker with a self-described "Archie Bunker" perception of the world, Mr. Lambiase is described by Democrats as one of the most effective political leaders in the city. *Ronald Sullivan, The New York Times, June 5, 1976, p 12*

[1972, from the name of a television character played by the American actor Carroll O'Connor in the comedy series *All in the Family* (modeled on the British comedy series *Till Death Us Do Part* and first shown on CBS in January 1971)] Compare ALF GARNETT, OCKER.

Archie Bunkerism, *U.S.* an inept or illiterate expression used by an Archie Bunker (or the television character of that name).

There has never been a grandfather figure quite like Senator Sam Ervin. . . . His apt biblical allusions, his dropped g's and regionalisms ("Yo' thinkin' . . . *Yew*nited States") are a happy antidote to Archie Bunkerisms. *Stefan Kanfer, Time, June 25, 1973, p 15*

[1972] Shortened form, BUNKERISM.

Archipelago, *n.* short for GULAG ARCHIPELAGO.

Leningrad is a colder, more imperious city than Moscow. Literary trials are more frequent there (just last year Vladimir Marazim was on his way to the Archipelago—and now, thanks to a humane solution, he is in Paris, working for the new magazine *Continent*). *Carl R. Proffer, The New York Review of Books, Feb. 19, 1976, p 8*

[1976]

architectural barrier, any feature of a building or other construction that prevents or hinders access or use by physically handicapped people.

"Architectural barriers" can be curbs which are too high for a person in a wheelchair to negotiate by himself, steps leading into a building, light switches too high for him to reach, restrooms without handrails, base-plug electrical outlets—the list could go on and on. *Betty West, The Tuscaloosa News (Alabama), May 20, 1976, Sec. 1, p 1*

The accelerated program to eliminate architectural barriers for the handicapped is another manifestation of increasing sensitivity to the needs of others. *Ron Wiedenhoeft, "Architecture," 1979 Collier's Year Book (1978), p 131*

[1963] ► The U.S. *Architectural Barriers Act* of 1968 ruled that "All government buildings designed, constructed, altered or leased by the Federal government and supported financially, wholly or in part with Federal funds must be barrier-free."

ar·cho·saur ('ɑr kə,sɔr), *n.* a prehistoric reptile that was the ancestor of the dinosaurs, pterosaurs (flying reptiles), and crocodilians.

Not only is there no evidence for dinosaurs having sustained speed capability, there is no need to postulate such a thing. Living archosaurs, the crocodiles and their allies, have an astonishing turn of speed in short bursts, which seems to suffice very well indeed for their needs. *Dr. Beverly Halstead, University of Reading, "Temperatures Rise Over Hot-blooded Dinosaurs," Sunday Times (London), Dec. 7, 1975, p 13*

[1969, from New Latin *Archosauria* the class of such reptiles, from Greek *árchōn* ruler + *saûros* lizard]

A·ri·ca (ə'ri: kə), *n.* a system of consciousness-raising and self-realization, originally developed in Chile. *Often used attributively.*

In 70 hours over two marathon weekends, est aims at "transforming your ability to experience living" through techniques apparently derived from Scientology, psychoanalysis, humanistic psychology, Arica, Gestalt, transactional analysis and various Eastern religions. *"Behavior: Est: 'There Is Nothing to Get'," Time, June 7, 1976, p 53*

Christmas has too deep a draft to find a comfortable berth in our neighborhood; in our neighborhood, as in lots of others in the city, shoals of unbelievers, reefs of Arica converts, riptides of Sun Myung Moonies, and dozens of partly submerged late-afternoon drinkers make navigation risky. *"The Talk of the Town," The New Yorker, Dec. 26, 1977, p 19*

[1973, named for the city in northern Chile where the first institute using this system was established]

A·rid·i·sol (ə'rid ə,sɔ:l), *n.* (in U.S. soil taxonomy) any of the group of soils of the world's desert regions, characterized by accumulations of calcium carbonate, magnesium, and soluble salts.

Similar to Mollisols in losses of nutrient elements during formation are the Aridisols, Inceptisols of cold or dry regions, and Vertisols. If anything, losses from these soils are smaller than from Mollisols. Collectively these broad groups and the Mollisols occupy 40% of the land surface of the Earth. *Roy W. Simonson, "Soil," McGraw-Hill Yearbook of Science and Technology 1972, p 374*

[1972, from *arid* + connecting *-i-* + *-sol* (from Latin *solum* soil)] Compare ALFISOL, ENTISOL, HISTOSOL, SPODOSOL, ULTISOL.

ark, *n.* a structure resembling a greenhouse built over several connected ponds, forming a self-sufficient food-producing system, which may be used as an alternative to conventional agriculture.

One ark is under construction on Cape Cod. It is a good deal larger than the other buildings, more dramatic and more futuristic looking, mainly because of its long concave panels of reinforced fiberglass which are designed to capture the low-angle rays of the morning and late-afternoon sun. *Wade Greene, "The New Alchemists," The New York Times Magazine, Aug. 8, 1976, p 38*

[1975, so called in allusion to Noah's *ark*, because of the large variety of life forms grown in it and because it is regarded as a means of survival if conventional agriculture should fail] See NEW ALCHEMIST.

ar·mal·co·lite (ˌɑr'mæl kə̩lait), *n.* a lunar mineral composed of iron, magnesium, and titanium, found in lunar rocks brought back to earth by the crew of Apollo 11.

A new mineral discovered on the Moon by the Apollo 11 mission has been identified for the first time on Earth also in a sample found in a diamond-bearing pipe at Kimberley earlier this year, it was disclosed here today. The mineral is known as armalcolite. *The Times (London), Sept. 28, 1973, p 7*

[1971, from Neil *Arm*strong, Edwin *Al*drin, and Michael *Col*lins, the Apollo 11 astronauts + *-ite,* suffix for a mineral or rock substance]

armpit, *n. U.S. Slang.* an unpleasant, grimy, or undesirable place.

She [Sally Quinn] is an amateur, of considerable intelligence and charm, but still an amateur, with no real notion of who might be out there in the armpit of America, grunting at what she says. *The New York Times, Aug. 19, 1973, p 15*

I am a sophomore at Ball State University. We have a saying around here that sums it up in one sentence. Muncie is the armpit of Indiana. Case closed. *Lori Yeater, in "Letters to the Editor," Time, Nov. 13, 1978, p K3*

[1973, from the notion that the armpit is a fetid or unpleasant part of the body] Compare PIT.

a·ro·ma·to·ther·a·py (ə̩rou mə tə'θer ə piː), *n.* treatment of the skin by the application of oils, essences, resins and other fragrant substances extracted from herbs and fruits.

Starting at 18 with a nose job by Sir Archibald McIndoe (no less) the Princess has undergone hypnosis, cell implants . . . silicone injections, an eyelid lift, aromatotherapy, yoga and gymnastics. *Philippa Toomey, Review of "The Beautiful People's Beauty Book" by Princess Luciana Pignatelli, The Times (London), Feb. 22, 1973, p 11*

[1973, from *aromatic* + connecting *-o-* + *therapy*]

arp or **Arp,** *n.* short for ARP SYNTHESIZER.

The traditional conflict between engineering excellence and artistic spontaneity has been decided in the engineer's favor. The new jargon is Vu-meters and equalizers, moogs, arps, decibels, phasing, pan-podding, dolby and de-dolby. A recording booth looks like a rocket-launch control panel. *Peter Moscoso-Gongora, "Performing Arts: Woodstock Was," Harper's, Sept. 1972, p 40*

[1972]

Arp synthesizer or **ARP synthesizer,** the trademark for an electronic device for generating a large variety of musical sounds, used in producing electronic music.

Shortly afterward, he found the technical direction he wanted his music to take in the Arp and Moog synthesizers, machines which can electronically produce any sound

desired. . . . He didn't sacrifice the emotional content of his music, but the Arp and Moog did offer him the dimension he wanted. *Jack Salter, "A Sense of Wonder," The New York Times Magazine, Feb. 23, 1975, p 26*

[1972] Often shortened to ARP or ARP.

ar·riére-garde (*Anglicized* ˌær i'er 'gɑrd; *French* a-ryer 'gɑrd), *n.* the group of intellectuals who follow conventional trends or ideas, especially in the arts; those who are behind the avant-garde.

For the arrière-garde there appears this week an agreeably readable first novel by Peter Prince called *Play Things,* which records the misadventures of a timid young man in charge of an adventure playground in a tough area. *J. G. Farrell, "Books," The Listener, Sept. 7, 1972, p 312*

—*adj.* of or relating to the arrière-garde.

On other scores as well, this contemporary composition has certain arrière-garde characteristics, its most obvious antecedent being Schoenberg's Pierrot Lunaire. *Jon Darius, "Music: Percussive Sculptures," New Scientist, Aug. 16, 1973, p 407*

[1962 for noun, from French, literally, rear guard; 1966 for adj.] Also called DERRIÈRE-GARDE.

arrow of time, the direction in which time flows, considered as the continuity or sequence of events from past to future, or in some theories from future to past, as in explaining time in relation to black holes in the universe.

The "Arrow of Time" has been much discussed by philosophers and by some scientists, and various manifestations, which have also been offered as explanations of this directionality, are to be noted in the world around us. *F. D. Peat, Ottawa, Canada, "Letters to Nature: Black Holes and Temporal Ordering," Nature, Oct. 13, 1972, p 387*

Time-travel stories . . . force the reader into contemplations of the nature of causality and the arrow of time. *Carl Sagan, "Growing Up with Science Fiction," The New York Times Magazine, May 28, 1978, p 28*

The most provocative predictions concerning the future of the universe relate to the arrow of time. From our lifelong observations we are so convinced that time always flows in the same direction that it becomes very difficult to conceive of any other situation. Yet every physicist knows that, on the atomic level, a sequence of events can flow with equal ease in either direction. *Walter Sullivan, Black Holes, 1979, p 225*

[1972] Compare TIME-SYMMETRIC, TIME WARP.

ar·te pov·e·ra ('ɑr tei 'pɑv ər ə), a form of art in which the work itself is not viewed or exhibited directly but presented at second hand through photographs, maps, drawings, or descriptive language.

Artists working under the various labels of conceptual art, antiform art, process art, software, earthworks, and *arte povera* have rejected the object in favor of the environment. They are concerned with space, time, and change, with man's needs, with natural forces, and with the way things relate to each other. Their work deals with ideas that can only be annotated in exhibitions, with events that defy direct viewing, and with processes which are not subject to duration, solidity, or salability. *Benjamin de Brie Taylor, "Art," 1971 Collier's Encyclopedia Year Book (1970), p 112*

[1970, from Italian, literally, impoverished art]

ar·thro·trop·ic (ˌɑr θrə'trɑp ik), *adj.* tending to cause disease of the joints.

Animal models indicate that a variety of known microorganisms, including bacteria or their cell walls, mycoplasma, and viruses are arthrotropic and can induce acute and chronic arthritis. *David Hamerman, "Arthritis," McGraw-Hill Yearbook of Science and Technology 1975, p 109*

[1974, from *arthro-* joint (from Greek *árthron*) + *-tropic* tending toward (from Greek *tropé* a turn)]

article, *v.i. Canadian.* to work or train as an articled clerk (*in, with,* or *for* a professional firm).

He went to law school, worked hard enough to graduate in the top third of his class, and articled with the Halifax law firm of Rutledge, McKeigan, Craig and Downie. *Michael Enright, Maclean's, March 22, 1976, p 30*

[1974] ► In British (and less commonly American) usage this verb is used only as a transitive: *to article someone* (literally, to bind a person by articles of apprenticeship) *to an attorney; to be articled to an accounting firm.* The Canadian usage was not recorded until the early 1970's.

artificial blood, a chemical substance used as a substitute for natural blood, especially a mixture of fluorocarbons that can carry large amounts of oxygen.

More than a quart of artificial blood was used for a surgical patient who could not accept a normal blood transfusion because he had a rare blood type.... The chemical solution used as artificial blood can keep patients alive by carrying oxygen to the body's cells and carrying away carbon dioxide, the waste product of metabolism. *Edward Edelson, "First U.S. Use of Artificial Blood Saves a Life," Daily News (New York), Nov. 21, 1979, p 2*

[1975] See PERFLUOROCHEMICAL.

artificial gene, a chemically synthesized copy of a gene made by joining specific sequences of nucleotides (compounds that determine the structure of genes).

The first wholly artificial gene with the potential for functioning inside a living cell has been synthesized by Nobel laureate Har Gobind Khorana and his associates at the Massachusetts Institute of Technology, Cambridge. *Thomas H. Maugh II, "Molecular Biology: A Better Artificial Gene," Science, Sept. 28, 1973, p 1235*

Geneticists also passed two landmarks in the creation of artificial genes. Harvard biologist Argiris Efstratiadis and his colleagues announced in January that they had completely synthesized a mammalian gene for the first time. The gene is one that controls hemoglobin production in rabbits. *John H. Douglas, "Science and Research," The 1977 World Book Year Book, p 483*

[1973] Compare RECOMBINANT.

artificial intelligence, 1 the means by which computers, robots, and other automatic devices perform tasks which normally require human intelligence, such as solving problems, making fine distinctions, playing games, and the like.

Mathematicians and engineers at the Massachusetts Institute of Technology Artificial Intelligence laboratory have combined a computer, a television camera and a mechanical arm into a system with enough artificial intelligence to recognize blocks of various sizes, colors and shapes, and to assemble them into structures without step-by-step instructions from an operator. *Robert J. Trotter, "Robots Make Intelligent Teachers," Science News, Aug. 4, 1973, p 76*

2 the field of science which studies and develops these means.

Asked to say what artificial intelligence has to show for its first fifteen years, any practitioner is bound to say "Terry Winograd's program." *Max Clowes, "Talking to Machines," Review of "Understanding Natural Language" by Terry Winograd, Nature, Nov. 10, 1972, p 112*

[1966] *Abbreviation:* AI Also called MACHINE INTELLIGENCE. See also INTELLIGENT.

artificial sight or **artificial vision,** the ability of a blind person to perceive objects by electrical stimulation of the visual cortex.

A team of researchers at the University of Utah and the University of Western Ontario reported that artificial sight had been electrically stimulated in two blind patients, one of whom had been blind for 28 years. *Allan Yale Brooks, "Electronics," 1975 Collier's Encyclopedia Year Book (1974), p 228*

In 1974, a team of electronic and medical researchers ... demonstrated that electrical stimulation of the cortex of the brain could produce light pulses, known as phosphenes, which might be the basis of artificial vision for the blind. *Samuel Weber, "Electronics," The World Book Science Annual 1977 (1976), p 272*

[1974] See BRAILLE CELL, CORTICAL BRAILLE.

artificial skin, a substance made from carbohydrates reinforced with the protein fiber of cattle or other animals, used in medicine as a substitute for human skin.

Artificial skin designed and constructed from animal tissue by Boston engineers and surgeons offers hope of new treatment for thousands of persons who suffer from burns each year. *The New York Times, Jan. 3, 1976, p 35*

[1976]

art rock, a form of rock music that uses elements of traditional or classical music, especially in the style of instrumentation.

Ever since that group recorded "Sergeant Pepper" in 1967, there have been many excursions into art-rock, the fusion of conservatoire style in instrumentation with the electronics and idioms of pop. *Robert Shelton, "Barclay James Harvest: Rainbow," The Times (London), Dec. 5, 1972, p 14*

[1972] Compare PROGRESSIVE ROCK.

ASAT ('ei,sæt), *n.* a type of hunter-killer satellite that is designed to track an orbiting satellite and explode near it, spraying the satellite with metal-piercing fragments.

ASAT ... has a parabolic "dish" antenna that homes in on the target satellite and gets the ASAT—actually a space bomb—close to the target, where it detonates. The ASAT goes off like a super hand grenade. *"Targeting a Hunter-Killer," Time, Oct. 17, 1977, p 10*

[1977, from *A*nti-*Sat*ellite interceptor]

asbestos cancer, cancer of the lungs or of some other organs, caused by long-term exposure to asbestos fibers found in many household products and in emissions from factories, mines, etc.

The increasing use of asbestos and the many years' delay between exposure and development of cancer suggests that the incidence of "asbestos cancer" in workers outside the industry may be increasing. *"British Medical Journal Sci-*

ence Report," The Times (London), March 18, 1977, p 21

[1976] ► This is a newly identified disease, unrelated to *asbestosis* (1920's), a lung disease of workers caused by extensive inhalation of asbestos particles.

as·bes·tot·ic (ˌæs bes'tɑt ik), *adj.* affected by or showing asbestosis (chronic congestion of the lungs caused by inhaling asbestos particles).

They then reported to the committee, that among these employees they had found only eight whose X-rays could be diagnosed as asbestotic. *Paul Brodeur, "Annals of Industry: Casualties of the Workplace," The New Yorker, Nov. 19, 1973, p 120*

[1973]

ASC, abbreviation of ALTERED STATE OF CONSCIOUSNESS.

Experiences of ecstasy, mystical union, other "dimensions," rapture, beauty, space-and-time transcendence, and transpersonal knowledge, all common in ASC's, are simply not treated adequately in conventional scientific approaches. *Charles T. Tart, Science, June 16, 1972, p 1203*

[1972]

ASEAN or **A·se·an** ('ɑ: si: ən), *n.* acronym for *Association of South East Asian Nations,* an organization for economic and cultural cooperation between Indonesia, Malaysia, the Philippines, Singapore, and Thailand, formed in Bangkok on August 8, 1967.

With Thailand's fertile rice bowl and Indonesia's developing oil resources (not to mention the unexploited offshore petroleum fields in the area) Tokyo has long realized, and Moscow, Peking and Washington are beginning to realize, that the ASEAN countries now provide perhaps the greatest new potential for profitable partnership with the industrial nations. *James Reston, "Carter Turns to Asia," The New York Times, April 30, 1978, Sec. 4, p 19*

[1967] ► *ASEAN* gained new importance after the 23-year old SEATO (Southeast Asia Treaty Organization) was formally dissolved on June 30, 1977.

a·sea·son·al (ei'si: zə nəl), *adj.* not seasonal; readily adapting to different seasons of the year.

In addition to being more responsive to fertilizer, the new strains are aseasonal, that is, not very sensitive to daylength (photoperiod). . . . The aseasonality and early maturity of new strains are opening new possibilities for multiple cropping and year-round farming. *Gail W. Finsterbush, "Food," McGraw-Hill Yearbook of Science and Technology 1972, p 221*

[1964, from *a-* not + *seasonal*]

Asiadollar, *n.* a United States dollar deposited in Asian banks and used in various money markets of Asia.

The Singapore market in Asiadollars is now said to total some $US 3,000m. *The Times (London), May 8, 1973, p II*

Attributive use.

U.S. companies flock to buy Asiadollar CDs. *Business Week, April 10, 1978, p 82*

[1973, patterned on *Eurodollar* (1960)]

ASL, abbreviation of AMERICAN SIGN LANGUAGE.

ASL is a system of communication developed for deaf people and used extensively throughout North America. It is a set of hand gestures that corresponds to individual words. (The other system for the deaf, finger spelling, is not

used in this research.) *Joyce Dudney Fleming, "The State of the Apes," Encyclopedia Science Supplement (Grolier) 1974, p 42*

[1969]

as·pa·rag·i·nase (ˌæs pə'rædʒ əˌneis), *n.* a bacterial enzyme that breaks down the amino acid asparagine, obtained chiefly from sewage bacteria and used to treat certain types of leukemia.

Chad was now also supposed to begin series of injections of a fifth drug, asparaginase, which kills leukemic cells by starving them of an essential amino acid. Asparaginase is used in leukemia chemotherapy to "consolidate" remissions induced by vincristine and prednisone. *Marion Steinmann, "A Child's Fight for Life: Parents vs. Doctors," The New York Times Magazine, Dec. 10, 1978, p 167*

[1964, from *asparagine* + *-ase* (suffix meaning enzyme)]

as·par·tame (æs'pɑr teim), *n.* an artificial sweetener, about 200 times as sweet as sugar, containing 4 calories a gram. *Formula:* $C_{14}H_{18}N_2O_5$

Since cyclamates were banned nearly five years ago, researchers have worked diligently to find an artificial sweetener that is both safe and free of saccharin's bitter aftertaste. And last week the U.S. Food and Drug Administration announced approval of such a substance: a synthetic product known chemically as aspartame. *"How Sweet It Is," Newsweek, Aug. 5, 1974, p 73*

[1973, from *aspar*tic acid + phenyl*a*lanine *m*ethyl *e*ster, the chemical constituents of the substance]

aspherics, *n.pl.* lenses whose polished surfaces are not spherical, used especially in television and film cameras; aspheric lenses.

Among the top quality lenses introduced in 1975 were many zooms and ultra-wide focal lengths. Light in weight, their compact design was made possible by incorporating lenses varying slightly from sphericity (aspherics) in the Canon lenses and solid catadioptric design (combining lenses and mirrors) in the Vivitar series I. *Barbara L. Lobron, "Photography," The Americana Annual 1976, p 449*

[1969, from *aspheric* (1920's) *adj.,* not spherical + *-s,* plural suffix]

assertiveness training, a method of training submissive individuals to behave with confidence, often by assuming an aggressive attitude.

Corrective devices, plastic surgery, cosmetic treatments, charm schools, assertiveness training—nothing helped make her anything except more gimmicked up and more self-conscious. *Howland Barber, "Is Emmy Ready for TV?" TV Guide, May 15, 1976, p 4*

Talking to people about the purposes of the group, showing them how assertiveness training can be personally advantageous, and taking the initiative to see that things run relatively smoothly—all these are highly assertive behaviors. *Spencer A. Rathus and Jeffrey S. Nevid, BT: Behavior Therapy, 1977, p 126*

[1975] Also, **assertive** or **assertion training.**

asset stripping, *British.* the use of a company's assets or resources by a parent company to finance other enterprises, such as the purchase of a company.

The firm proposals in the Government paper reflect . . .

41

public and political pressure on the Government to stamp out "asset-stripping," the practice by which financiers take over companies and merely sell off their assets, sometimes creating unemployment. *Stewart Fleming, The Manchester Guardian Weekly, Aug. 4, 1973, p 9*

[1972]

asset stripper: So, too, in the Government's view, do certain members of what has been called the British school of asset strippers. It would be perfectly possible to defend most asset stripping on the basis that it is concerned with taking over badly run companies, slimming them down, realizing unused assets and injecting new management. The Government, however, has largely accepted the general view that it is often inhuman and has unacceptable social side-effects. *The Times (London), Jan. 2, 1973, p 15*

associable, *adj.* belonging to a cooperative economic or trade association of several countries.

Moves toward closer relations with Cuba and a number of African nations continued, and Kingston was the venue for the meeting in July between the ACP (Africa, Caribbean, and Pacific) . . . associable states and the EEC. *Sheila Patterson, "Jamaica," Britannica Book of the Year 1975, p 418*

—*n.* an associable country or state.

Not only are some of the associables from the Caribbean and the Pacific but the African states, since independence, have tended to divide along Francophone and Anglophone lines. *The Times (London), July 25, 1973, p 16*

[1973, extended sense of the adjective meaning "capable of being associated" (OED 1855)] Compare ASSOCIATE.

► This term was adopted to avoid confusion with *associated* as applied to a state or nation. An associated (or associate) state is a former protectorate that retains economic or political association with the country that once governed it (as for example the members of the French Community). An associable state is a member of an economic association of small, usually underdeveloped, countries.

associate, *n.* a former colony or protectorate that has attained partial independence, as by gaining control of its domestic affairs, but is bound politically or economically to the former colonial power, especially in international relations; an associated state.

A referendum in Sikkim gave preponderant support to these changes and New Delhi accepted them, even though it had earlier agreed to the protectorate's enjoying the status of "an associate." *Kuldip Nayar, "India," The Annual Register of World Events in 1975 (1976), p 253*

[1967, noun use of the adjective (1953) as applied to a state] ► See ASSOCIABLE.

associated gas, natural gas found in conjunction with petroleum.

Every oil reservoir is, in fact, a gas reservoir as well. Gas that is found with oil is known as "associated gas." *Joel Legunn, "Natural Gas," Encyclopedia Science Supplement (Grolier) 1975, p 182*

[1972] Compare DISSOLVED GAS.

astigmatic, *n.* a person having astigmatism.

People with good eyesight can see lines in the vertical and horizontal planes with equal clarity. But when astigmatics were tested, it was found that the acuity of horizon-

tal or vertical lines corresponded to the nature and the degree of the astigmatism, in spite of the fact that all of them wore correcting lenses. *The Times (London), April 7, 1972, p 16*

[1972, noun use of the adjective (OED 1849)]

as·tra·tion (ə'strei ʃən), *n.* the formation of new stars.

All in all, it's a large observational scheme. . . . And it may show how details of star formation ("astration," to use the newly coined word) and chemical changes affect progress along the line. *Dietrick E. Thomsen, "Astration and Galactic Evolution," Science News, Nov. 6, 1976, p 300*

[1976, from *astro-* star + form*ation*]

as·tro·ar·chae·ol·o·gy (ˌæs trou ɑr ki: 'al ə dʒi:), *n.* another name for ARCHAEOASTRONOMY.

The sheer volume of new evidence is fostering a widening interest in the astronomy of the ancients. Investigation of these matters, a field called archaeoastronomy by many and astroarcheology by a few, is emerging as a legitimate activity in science. *Boyce Rensberger, "Prehistoric Astronomy Was Pretty Good Science," The New York Times, Feb. 19, 1978, Sec. 4, p 9*

[1973, from *astro-* star + *archaeology*]

astrochemistry, *n.* the study of the chemical composition of heavenly bodies and the regions of outer space.

Now that astronomers have shown for certain that complex molecules do exist deep in space, it is interesting to consider the range of chemical reactions that may start up inside cosmic gas clouds. The occurrence of the vast clouds of molecules in the Milky Way has thus opened up a new science—astrochemistry. *"Monitor: A Negative Way to Build Organic Molecules in Space," New Scientist, May 3, 1973, p 262*

[1973, patterned after *astrobiology, astrobotany,* and *astrogeology*]

As·tro·Turf ('æs trou,tərf), *n.* the trademark of an artificial surface for lawns and playing fields, made of a green, grasslike nylon material backed with vinyl.

The outfielders . . . are wonderfully fast afoot, an essential attribute on Candlestick's slick AstroTurf, which now covers the whole infield except for dirt cutouts around the mound and the bases. *Roger Angell, "The Sporting Scene: Baseball," The New Yorker, June 19, 1971, p 75*

Putting, however, is primitive: the player must move to an Astroturf green and aim at a real hole. *"Modern Living: Golf by Illusion," Time, April 30, 1973, p 83*

[1966, from *Astro*dome, an indoor ball park in Houston, Texas where this surface was first used + *turf*] Also spelled **Astroturf.** Compare GRASS-TEX, HAR-TRU, TARTAN TURF.

as·ymp·to·pi·a (ˌæs im'tou pi: ə), *n. Nuclear Physics.* a hypothetical region of the electromagnetic spectrum characterized by extremely high energies at which the forces of certain particles and their antiparticles asymptotically approach constant values or equality.

Such fantastic power could finally bring experimenters to that wonderland of high-energy physics that . . . S. J. Lindenbaum calls "asymptopia": the far-out region on the energy scale where all the complex events inside the atom —and hence the very nature of matter—comes within reach of man's understanding. *"Toward Asymptopia," Time, Jan. 10, 1972, p 46*

On the basis of recent research it appeared that this high-energy realm, dubbed "asymptopia," must either lie at a yet higher energy than particle accelerators now achieve or indeed may not exist at all. *Lawrence W. Jones, "High-Energy Physics," 1975 Britannica Yearbook of Science and the Future (1974), p 310*

[1969, blend of *asymptote* (line which continually approaches a given curve without meeting it) and *utopia* ideal place]

AT, abbreviation of: **1** ALTERNATIVE TECHNOLOGY.

In essence, Alternative Technology (AT) is trying to re-create the freedom, togetherness, and rugged self-suf-ficiency of the best 19th-century American homesteading communities. *Gerald Leach, "Technology Tunes to Nature," The World Book Science Annual 1975 (1974), p 207*

2 APPROPRIATE TECHNOLOGY.

The U.S. government has established the National Center for Appropriate Technology in Butte, Montana, with $3.3 million to research and disseminate AT information. *Wade Greene, "The Selling of Soft Tech," Psychology Today, Nov. 1978, p 70*

[1974 for def. 1; 1976 for def. 2]

-a·thon (-ə,θɑn), a combining form meaning "mara-thon" (applied to any prolonged or extended activ-ity, event, etc., of a specified kind, usually involving endurance), as in:

Bachathon, *n.:* Rosalyn Tureck first performed the com-plete Preludes and Fugues of Bach's "Well-Tempered Clavier," along with the Goldberg Variations, in six con-certs at Town Hall, in 1937. . . . She is commemorating the fortieth anniversary of this "Bach-athon" in a repeat per-formance this autumn. *"The Talk of the Town: Rosalyn Tureck," The New Yorker, Oct. 10, 1977, p 36*

begathon, *n.:* Turner broadcast a weekend telethon . . . which his competitors derisively rechristened . . . "begathon"; the tactic brought in more than $25,000, in amounts ranging from 25 cents to $200. *J. S. Maynor, TV Guide, June 12, 1976, p 15*

bikeathon, *n.:* The Calgary and District International De-velopment Society hopes to raise between $30,000 and $40,000 with the 72-mile "bike-a-thon" May 6. *The Province (Vancouver), April 14, 1973, p 54*

jigathon, *n.:* A Celtic bumpkin can be enticed by his local wood spirits into a jigathon that makes years seem like min-utes. In America, a Catskill rube like Rip Van Winkle loses himself in the revels of a dwarf bowling league. *Time, Oct. 9, 1978, p 108*

killathon, *n.:* Here we are in the all too near future, when pollution is so thick that skywriters engrave their words with hammer and chisel. Population is so dense that the au-thorities sponsor a killathon, in which patriotic citizens dispatch themselves in diverse ways. *Laurence I. Barrett, Review of "Mother Earth," Time, Nov. 6, 1972, p 83*

space-athon, *n.:* Half a year away from earth is hard to imagine, let alone accomplish, but now the Soviets in their latest space-athon have done it. *Rosalind Ellis, in a Letter to the Editor, New York Post, Aug. 24, 1979, p 22*

workathon, *n.:* Their performance was a workathon of sweaty energy in which the drama of male-female en-counter was inflated to cartoon scale. *Don McDonagh, "Zany Couple Caricature Dance Style," The New York Times, Aug. 30, 1977, p 35*

[1972] ▶ This form has previously appeared in only

three widely-established terms: *walkathon* (1932), *talkathon* (1948), and *telethon* (1952), all from *mara-thon* (OEDS *exten.* 1908). It has lately become productive, influenced probably by the popularity of telethons. The form *-athon* is used after a con-sonant-final root, while *-thon* follows a vowel (as in *telethon*). Another example of *-thon* is:

The event at the Manhattan Center Saturday night was billed as a "disco-thon"—a competition among local free-lance discotheque disk jockeys. *Richard J. Meislin, The New York Times, Aug. 16, 1976, p 35*

atmospherics, *n.pl.* atmosphere or ambiance espe-cially created to stimulate optimism, confidence, etc., in order to achieve some desired result.

[Henry] Kissinger frequently stage-manages negotiations to produce the right kind of "atmospherics." *"Superstar Statecraft: How Henry Does It," Time, April 1, 1974, p 28*

These people keep in touch with one another and with the press, and while they do not have tangible power, they can affect others' decisions about whom to back and can af-fect the press's view of what's going on. They supply some of the atmospherics that influence events and fill the air of an election. *Elizabeth Drew, "A Reporter in Washington, D.C.: Winter Notes—II," The New Yorker, May 24, 1976, p 120*

"Open communication and travel across national bor-ders, trade, commerce, tourism, cultural exchanges and free passage of transportation"—was designed to reassure the American Jewish leaders with whom he [President Carter] was meeting. But the Israelis, who have bitter expe-rience of diplomacy, must ask themselves how much of this is pre-conference atmospherics. *William E. Farrell, "Hawk on a Mission of Peace," The New York Times Maga-zine, July 17, 1977, p 49*

[1963]

ATPase (,ei,ti:'pi:,eis), *n.* an enzyme that breaks down adenosine triphosphate (ATP), the substance that supplies the energy needed for muscle contrac-tion, sugar metabolism, etc.

As the amino acid passes through the cell membrane, it may stimulate ATPase. ATPase in turn splits a molecule of ATP just inside the cell, in the cytoplasm. *Joan Arehart-Treichel, "Getting Protein Into the Mammalian Cell," Sci-ence News, Jan. 20, 1973, p 44*

[1961, from *ATP* + *-ase* (suffix meaning enzyme)]

attack dog, *U.S.* a dog trained to attack on command in order to assist police or soldiers in their duty or to protect individuals against thieves, muggers, etc.

Policemen with attack dogs ordered the students into a fleet of trucks after a crowd of about 1,500—a number equal to the university's entire enrollment—gathered on the campus for a memorial meeting. *John F. Burns, The New York Times, Sept. 16, 1977, p A1*

[1970]

attendance teacher, *U.S.* an official charged with finding and returning truants and other absentee students to school.

They used to be called truant officers, and the cartoonists always depicted them snagging youthful hookey players with butterfly nets or long hooks and then dragging them off to school. In those days, most children skipped school as a lark. Today, they are called attendance teachers, and they do not use butterfly nets or hooks and insist they never did.

attosecond

Judy Klemesrud, The New York Times, June 7, 1976, p 34
[1972]

at·to·sec·ond ('æt ou‚sek ənd), *n.* one quintillionth of
a second.

They habitually think in terms of microseconds or nano-
seconds—millionths or billionths of a second. And, though
they do not often have occasion to work with attoseconds,
they are unblinkingly aware of them. *E. J. Kahn, Jr., "Our
Far-flung Correspondents: The Leap Second," The New
Yorker, Aug. 27, 1973, p 50*

[1973, from *atto-* prefix for one quintillionth (10^{-18})
(from Danish *atten* eighteen) + *second*]

attrition, *v.t.* Usually, **attrition out.** *U.S.* to reduce
the number of (jobs or workers) by not hiring people
to fill positions made vacant by retirement, transfer,
etc.

No legislature was going to allow ninety thousand city
employees to be laid off, or even, in the union phrase, "at-
tritioned out." *Andy Logan, "Around City Hall," The New
Yorker, May 15, 1971, p 121*

[1971, verb use of the noun (1963)]

Au·brey hole ('ɔ: bri:), any one of the 56 equally
spaced holes which form the outermost ring of the
Stonehenge circle.

[Gerald S.] Hawkins has suggested that the Aubrey holes
at Stonehenge were used to count the years of a 56-year
cycle, important in the motion of the Moon and the occurrence of eclipses. . . . We suggest also that the Aubrey
holes, if they were used as counters at all, were used to
count intervals of 56 months rather than 56 years. *R. R.
Newton and R. E. Jenkins, Silver Springs, Md., Nature, Oct.
27, 1972, p 511*

[1959, named for John *Aubrey*, 1626-97, an English
antiquary, and author of *Brief Lives*, who discovered
the holes]

audible, *n. U.S. Football.* a play called out by the
quarterback at the line of scrimmage to replace the
play called in the huddle or to execute a play
without a huddle when time is about to run out.

"There are times when I can see myself standing behind
the Baltimore Colts' offensive line, calling audibles to pick
up a blitz." *Vida Blue, quoted in Time, Aug. 23, 1971, p 44*

[1967, noun use of the adjective]

au·di·o·don·tics (‚ɔ: di: ou'dɑn tiks), *n.* the study of
the relationship of teeth to hearing.

Elsewhere, researchers in audiodontics had an explanation for the curious habit of Beethoven's of holding one end
of a drumstick in his mouth and pressing the other end
against the piano frame. He was listening with his teeth.
*"Ariadne's Year: September," New Scientist, Jan. 3, 1974, p
26*

[1973, from *audio-* sound, hearing + *-odontics* study
or treatment of the teeth]

audio pollution, a name for SOUND POLLUTION.

Traffic noise is man's most widespread form of audio
pollution, and year by year the problem is becoming more
acute. Schools, recreational areas, and even homes are subjected to this irritating invasion. *D. I. Cook and D. F. Van
Haverbeke, "Noise Control," McGraw-Hill Yearbook of Science and Technology 1975, p 282*

[1975]

audiovisuals, *n.pl.* teaching materials involving the
use of both sounds and pictures; audiovisual material or equipment.

The curriculum has begun to draw fire, mainly because
of the realistic audio-visuals. *Edward B. Fiske, The New
York Times, Jan. 9, 1972, Sec. 4, p 7*

[1972, noun use of the adjective *audiovisual*]

audit trail, a record of the passage of data in a computer or data processing machine from one step to
the next, used especially to trace data from a final
output or report back to the original or source items.

Another barrier that the computer criminal or unauthorized user of a computer system has to cope with is that of
the computer's audit trail—the internal monitoring system
that can record all significant actions of the users and is
supposed to provide means of detecting and tracing unauthorized attempts to gain entry. *Thomas Whiteside,
"Annals of Crime: Dead Souls in the Computer—II," The
New Yorker, Aug. 29, 1977, p 60*

[1970, so called from its original use in computerized accounting systems as the means by which
auditors can trace transactions backward and for-
ward]

au·la·co·gen (ɔ:'læk ə dʒən), *n. Geology,* a narrow
rift valley filled with sediment, associated with plate
tectonics as an early fracture of a protocontinent.

Aulacogens can now be recognized as failed arms of
three-armed rift systems. When the two successful arms
opened to form an ocean, the failed arm remained as a rift
valley running inland from the new seacoast. The rift
became a feature of the drainage pattern of the continent,
accumulating a thick deposit of sediments. *Kevin C. Burke
and J. Tuzo Wilson, "Hot Spots on the Earth's Surface,"
Scientific American, Aug. 1976, p 56*

[1972, from Russian *aulakogen,* coined by the Soviet geologist Nicholas S. Shatsky from Greek
aulákos furrow + *-genēs* born]

Auntie, *n. British.* a nickname for the B.B.C. (British
Broadcasting Corporation).

Vintage Years is essentially a delightful collage of anecdotes recounted by two men who were working for Auntie
when so many of the fabled BBC events occurred. *Chris
Dunkley, The Times (London), Nov. 16, 1972, p 11*

[1963, chiefly (and originally) in reference to its supposedly strait-laced and conservative outlook] Compare BEEB.

Aunt Tom, *Slang (derogatory use).* **1** a black woman
with a servile attitude toward whites; a female
Uncle Tom.

Because Imogene seems to be something of an Aunt Tom
in involuntary servitude, the part might draw protests from
some black groups—even though Imogene manages to escape her situation near the end. *Sunday Post-Herald
(Hongkong), May 20, 1973, p 28*

2 a woman who does not support the cause of
Women's Liberation.

In a radio debate, Women's Libber Betty Friedan told
anti-libber Phyllis Schlafly, "I consider you a traitor to your
sex, an Aunt Tom." *"The Week," National Review, May 25,
1973, p 564*

[1968, patterned on *Uncle Tom*]

44

► *Aunt Tom* appears to be the longest-lived of various related terms of disparagement from the 1960's for women who do not support the activists who oppose racial or sexual prejudices. Included among the terms are *Aunt Jane* (1964), *Aunt Jemima* (1967), *Aunt Tabby* (1969), and *Aunt Thomasina* (1964).

au·ral·ize ('ɔr ə ˌlɑiz), *v.t.* to hear mentally; imagine the sound of.

If you can imagine the kind of sound produced by Dietrich Fischer-Dieskau and Hermann Prey in the same cast, then you can also auralize the comparable efforts of Gundula Janowitz and Tatiana Troyanos. *Irving Kolodin, Saturday Review, Nov. 4, 1972, p 68*

[1972, patterned on *visualize*]

Aus·sie ('ɔː siː), *n. Informal.* an Australian terrier.

"It hurts me so much to realize there is antagonism among those who profess to care deeply for our breed," her letter adds. "I have tried desperately to promote good will. Our Aussies are so full of loving good spirits—why can't their owners measure up to them?" *Lis Harris, The New Yorker, Jan. 26, 1976, p 63*

[1976, by shortening and alteration]

► The earlier meanings of *Aussie*, "an Australian," "of or from Australia," and "Australia," have been used since World War I.

au·then·ti·fi·ca·tion (ɔːˌθen tə fəˈkei ʃən), *n.* confirmation; ratification.

You know about the black briefcase, don't you? Inside are the Emergency War Order (EWO) authentification codes, which are changed frequently and are supposed to ensure that only the President, their possessor, can authorize a thermonuclear missile or bomber launch. *Ron Rosenbaum, "The Subterranean World of the Bomb," Harper's, March 1978, p 86*

[1970, altered from earlier *authentication*, probably by influence of *verification, certification, ratification*, etc.]

autistic, *n.* a person, usually a child, suffering from autism (a pathological condition characterized by self-absorption and lack of contact with reality).

Thanks to the relentless lobbying of the National Society for Autistic Children in Albany, N.Y.—composed largely of parents—more than 30 states have passed laws providing special education for autistics in the last four years. *Matt Clark, "Troubled Children: The Quest for Help," Newsweek, April 8, 1974, p 52*

[1968, noun use of the adjective (1912)]

autocross, *n.* an automobile competition to test driving skill and speed.

With the local autocross schedule for the winter months decidedly on the lean side, five Northern California autocross drivers slipped across the border to enter the final Southern California Championship Slalom (their name for autocross). *Gordon Martin, San Francisco Chronicle, Dec. 19, 1963, p 54*

Almost every weekend a special attraction must be organized—a gymkhana, autocross meeting, boxer dog show, camping meeting, steam fair or circus. *Victoria Brittain, The Times (London), July 8, 1972, p 14*

[1963, from *auto-* automobile + *cross* (as in *motocross* a motorcycle race)]

autogenic training, 1 a method similar to autosuggestion or self-hypnosis, by which a person learns to induce physiological changes, such as raising or lowering the temperature, in his own body.

Well, what are we to do about the stress that kills and cripples? Dr Malcolm Carruthers, of the Maudsley Hospital, London, advocated the use of autogenic training. This is a highly disciplined form of thought control, which the individual practices upon himself. *Donald Gould, "It's All in the Mind," New Scientist, Dec. 14, 1978, p 841*

2 another name for BIOFEEDBACK TRAINING.

Autogenic training . . . involves detecting the variable to be controlled, displaying information about it on a dial or with a light or sound, and then letting the subject practice controlling it. The procedure has been used experimentally in treating high blood pressure and migraine headaches. *Samuel Moffat, 1973 Britannica Yearbook of Science and the Future (1972), p 78*

[1964, from *auto-* self + *-genic* producing]

autoinjector, *n.* a small hypodermic syringe containing a dose of medicine for self-administration, especially such a syringe containing an antidote for nerve gas.

At present, there is no prophylactic treatment against the nerve gas poisoning, and medical countermeasures are restricted to therapy with the drug atropine. . . . Autoinjectors containing doses of atropine or atropine/oxime mixtures are available or on standard issue in a number of armed forces. *"Monitor: When Do Antidotes Provoke?" New Scientist, Sept. 20, 1973, p 673*

[1968]

autoland, *n.* the automatic landing of an aircraft by means of electronic devices.

Only when the experts were satisfied was the aircraft cleared for autoland on a normal line service. *The Times (London), Sept. 4, 1972, p VI*

[1963, from *automatic land*ing]

► This is more often called *instrument landing* in the United States, and *blind landing* in Great Britain.

autopen, *n.* a device that automatically produces a facsimile of a signature.

For three weeks, starting in late July, Caroline [Kennedy] will be a "go-fer," sorting mail and operating the autopen that prints Uncle Ted's signature on routine letters. *Time, June 10, 1974, p 59*

[1974, from *automatic + pen*]

autoregulation, *n.* the self-regulation or automatic adjustment of an organ, ecological system, etc., to changing conditions.

G. Wesley Hatfield, microbiologist at the University of California at Irvine, received the 1975 Eli Lilly and Company Award in Microbiology and Immunology . . . for research on the autoregulation of gene expression. *The World Book Science Annual 1976 (1975), p 389*

[1970, from *auto-* self + *regulation*]

autoregulative, *adj.:* The particles are large aggregates of molecules, many of which are not therefore accessible to the other reactants. The surfaces of such large particles show special properties: they adsorb ions, double electrical layers form around them, they often function in catalysis. Their "autoregulative properties" were attributed to "the

45

surface field around the particle." *Robert Olby, The Path to the Double Helix, 1974, p 7*

autoshape, *v.i. Behavioral Psychology.* to respond to a stimulus without the normal pattern of conditioning.

In the present experiment, we assessed the effects of initial treatments by measuring resistance to the powerful autoshaping procedure. If noncontingent food delivery produces a helplessness-like effect, then subjects so treated should autoshape slower than controls not given this treatment. *Larry A. Engberg, et al., Science, Dec. 1, 1972, p 1003*

[1972, from *auto-* self + *shape, v.*]

auto-train, *n.* **1** a train equipped to transport passengers and their automobiles between designated locations.

Each year millions of Northeasterners solve the paramount vacation question (WHERE TO GO) by opting for Florida, only to face the second (HOW TO GET THERE). The problem is compounded by the multiplicity of choices: private car, bus, rail, auto-train, plane. *Paul Grimes, The New York Times, Jan. 25, 1976, Sec. 10, p 1*

2 Auto-Train, *U.S.* the trademark of a rail service using such trains.

The successful operations of Auto-Train Corp., which hauls family automobiles in special cars while the riders sit, eat, sleep, and are entertained in lounge cars, were given another boost by the introduction of new tri-level auto carriers, each of which carried 12 cars instead of the 8 on the bi-level carriers. *Frank A. Smith, "Transportation," 1976 Britannica Yearbook of Science and the Future (1975), p 411*

[1964, from *auto* automobile + *train*]

autotransfusion, *n.* a method of blood transfusion in which a surgical patient's blood is collected in a reservoir and returned to his body during surgery.

The objections of some religious sects to blood transfusions were being overcome by perfection of the technique of autotransfusion. Hundreds of U.S. hospitals had the equipment to collect blood as it was lost, filter and process it, then return it to the body after corrective measures had been taken. *Donald W. Gould and Byron T. Scott, Britannica Book of the Year 1975, p 345*

[1963, from *auto-* self + *transfusion*]

av·a·lan·chine (ˌæv əˈlæn tʃiːn), *adj.* like an avalanche; huge; torrential; overpowering.

On top of the avalanchine sums of money it consumes in exchange for little tangible reward, the land speed record is a hobby involving risks that grow all the more prohibitive as the speeds inch higher. *Sonny Kleinfield, Harper's, July, 1974, p 68*

[1973, from *avalanche* + *-ine*, a suffix forming adjectives from nouns; possibly a revival as *avalanchine* is recorded in the OED with one quotation (*c*1860)]

av·go·lem·o·no (ˌæv gouˈlem ə nou), *n.* **1** a chicken soup made with eggs and lemon, introduced from Greece.

Lunch one day was artichoke fritters . . .; dinner was avgolemono, then veal. *The Times (London), Jan. 1, 1972, p 12*

2 a sauce made with eggs and lemon, used in various Greek dishes.

Before the pineapple there had been sole cooked with

grapes, avgolemono. *Sylvia Townsend Warner, The New Yorker, Nov. 12, 1973, p 45*

[1966, from Modern Greek *avgolémono*, from *avgó* egg + *lemóni* lemon]

aviator glasses or **aviators,** *n.pl.* wide, metal-rimmed eyeglasses, often tinted, with lenses that curve downwards.

Dick wears silver aviator glasses and flared jeans and cowboy boots of black tooled leather. *"The Talk of the Town," The New Yorker, June 20, 1977, p 28*

Kathy Lingg breaks out her old wire-rimmed aviators and goes instantly incognito. *Jesse Kornbluth, "The Red-Glasses Look: Anatomy of a Fad," The New York Times Magazine, Sept. 23, 1979, p 101*

[1972]

A Victoria, a virulent strain of the influenza virus, first identified in 1975 in Victoria, Australia.

A vaccine against A-Victoria flu virus was made available to Americans at the same time a swine flu vaccine was, and the A-Victoria strain did strike. Thus, if a swine flu epidemic had also occurred, the vaccines might well have saved millions of lives. *Science News, May 21, 1977, p 324*

[1975] See INFLUENZA A, B, C

AWACS or **A·wacs** (ˈei wæks), *n.* acronym for *Airborne Warning and Control System*, a system of the U.S. Air Force for the early detection of enemy bombers that utilizes aircraft with special radar equipment.

The major effort at NATO for the last year has been to get European allies to agree to buy the system, known by its initials, AWACS, to give the Europeans a longer time—15 minutes instead of 3—to detect a Soviet aerial strike. *Bernard Gwertzman, "Nato Defers Buying U.S. Warning System," The New York Times, Dec. 9, 1976, p 5*

[1970]

ax·i·on (ˈæk siːˌɑn), *n.* a hypothetical subatomic particle with neutral charge and zero spin, and a mass of less than one-thousandth of a proton.

The postulated new particle is called the axion and its existence has been deduced independently by Professor S. Weinberg of Harvard University and Professor F. Wilczek of Columbia University, New York. If the axion is found not to exist then the theory of quantum chromodynamics will lose much of its attractiveness. *The Times (London), Feb. 16, 1978, p 14*

[1978, perhaps from Greek *áxios* worthy + English *-on* elementary unit or particle; for a possible semantic connection, see the etymology of CHARM] Compare INSTANTON.

ax·ot·o·my (ækˈsɑt ə miː), *n.* microsurgery performed on the axon of a nerve cell.

Axotomy, or section of a nerve cell axon, induces anatomical as well as biochemical changes in the soma of neurons, especially those connected with the periphery. *Guillermo Pilar and Lynn Landmesser, Science, Sept. 22, 1972, p 1116*

[1972, from *axon* + *-tomy* a cutting]

a·ya·tol·lah (ˌɑː yəˈtou lə), *n.* a religious leader of the Shiite sect of Islam in Iran.

Among the Shiites in Iran, religious leaders carry doctrine down to the grass roots. First, there are the ayatollahs, like Khomeini, about 1,200 of them in the Shiite world, who serve as all-purpose father figures — as collectors and distributors of funds, as confessors, spiritual counselors, legal advisers, teachers and even as marriage counselors. . . . Ayatollahs reach the populace through a network of about 180,000 mullahs, who, in effect, serve as field officers in the Shiite setup. These mullahs can spread the word to every one of Iran's 35 million people. *Judson Hand, "Iran: the Politics of Faith," Daily News (New York), Feb. 4, 1979, p 41*

[1963, from Arabic *āyatollāh*, literally, sign of God] Also spelled **ayatullah.**

► The term has become widely known since January, 1979, through the name of Ayatollah Ruholla Khomeini, the Shiite leader who rose to power in Iran after the deposition of the Shah. *Ayatollah* is commonly used as a capitalized title before the name or preceded by *the*, as in:

The campaign against the government was orchestrated largely by the exiled religious leader Ayatollah Ruholla Khomeini. *Arthur C. Turner, "Iran," The Americana Annual 1979, p 262*

Those who know the Ayatullah expect that eventually he will settle in the Shi'ite holy city of Qum and resume a life of teaching and prayer. *"The Khomeini Era Begins," Time, Feb. 12, 1979, p 39*

A·za·ni·a (ə'zei ni: ə), *n.* the name given to South Africa by African nationalists.

It has become pretty obvious to us that these are crucial years in the history of Azania. The winds of liberation which have been sweeping down the face of Africa have reached our very borders. There is no more doubt about the inevitability of change — the only questions now remaining are how and when. *Steven Biko, "In Black and White," The New York Times, Sept. 18, 1977, Sec. 4, p 1t*

[1976, from the name of an Iron Age civilization that flourished in southern Africa from about A.D. 500 to about 1500] Compare ZIMBABWE.

Azanian, *n.:* Representative [Charles C.] Diggs sometimes refers to South Africa by the name its indigenous would-be liberationists have given it — "Azania" — and he . . . began to take the somewhat softer position that it might be all right for American companies already in South Africa to remain there, provided they share their profits with the majority of the South African people — which was, of course, black Azanians. *E.J. Kahn, Jr., "Annals of International Trade," The New Yorker, May 14, 1979, p 133*

Aztec two-step, another name for MEXICALI REVENGE.

South of the border, it is *turista* or "the Aztec two-step." In Asia, visitors from the West call it "Delhi belly." By any name, traveler's diarrhea, a debilitating digestive upset caused by a change in the system's bacterial population, is a synonym for misery that can spoil a trip and jeopardize the victim's health. *"Medicine: Back to Basics," Time, May 22, 1972, p 104*

[1970] ► See the note under DELHI BELLY.

B

Baath·ism or **Ba'ath·ism** ('bɑːˌθiz əm), *n*. principles of the Baath political party of Syria and Iraq, promoting socialism and Arab nationalism.

Baathism, the ideological driving force for the regime, might win an appeal in an area which will undoubtedly suffer a series of political traumas in the coming years. *Paul Martin, The Times (London), April 3, 1970, p X*

[1963, from *Baath* or *Ba'ath* (name of the party, literally, Renaissance) and *Baathist, adj., n.,* both 1955]

Ba·ba ('bɑː bɑː), *n.* **1** the title of a Hindu spiritual guide or guru.

After Nityananda died, in 1961, Muktananda began to let a few disciples live with him. "There were no special activities in those days," one of them told me. "We spent hours sitting with Baba, or helping him in the garden. In the afternoons he let us chant a little and we meditated on a porch outside his room." *Paul Zweig, "The Master of Ganeshpuri," Harper's, May 1977, p 86*

2 Often spelled **baba,** any guru or spiritual guide.

With the meditation melange has come a plethora of practitioners: experimental psychologists, mind researchers, masters, swamis, priestesses, gurus, babas and lamas. *Russell Chandler, "They Still Search for Inner Peace," New York Post, Feb. 26, 1977, p 23*

[1967, from Hindi *bābā* (literally) father]

baboonery, *n.* a place where baboons are kept.

I found that, in addition to the baboonery in Texas, there are, among other things, . . . seven large Primate Centers under the auspices of the National Institutes of Health. *Emily Hahn, "A Reporter At Large, On the Side of the Apes—I," The New Yorker, April 17, 1971, p 48*

[1971] ► An earlier meaning "a collection or colony of baboons," is given in the OED with a citation dated 1613. The usual meaning of this word since the 19th century is "baboonish condition or behavior."

baby-battering, *n.* the act or practice of inflicting harmful physical abuse on an infant or small child, usually by a parent.

Baby-battering claims the lives of six children every week in England and Wales, and leaves 3,000 a year severely injured. A further 40,000 children suffer mild or moderate damage, but 400 every year suffer injuries causing chronic brain damage. *Pat Healy, The Times (London), June 16, 1977, p 4*

[1972] Compare CHILD BATTERING. See also CHILD ABUSE.

baby batterer: But "just the other night I screamed and screamed at him maybe for ten minutes without stopping. I

shook him real hard and chucked him down in his cot and that made him cry all the more." . . . This is the stuff of which baby-batterers are made. *"Mothers without fathers," Review of "In No Man's Land" by Tony Parker, Times Literary Supplement, June 30, 1972, p 742*

baby boom, 1 the sudden great increase in the U.S. birth rate following World War II, especially between 1947 and 1961 (used chiefly in reference to the generation that came of age and joined the work force in the 1970's).

People who were born in the baby boom that started in the late forties and were educated in the late sixties are moving in a self-contained lump through American society, like a rat moving through the body of a python. *The New Yorker, April 10, 1978, p 120*

What was abnormal was a quarter-century of stable or declining crime rates between the end of Prohibition and 1960, an era that ended when the baby boom produced a huge generation of 14- to 24-year-olds, the prime age for crime. *Time, Nov. 6, 1978, p 76*

2 any great increase in a population's birth rate.

The Nazis encouraged a baby boom; Zero Population Growthers champion a baby bust. The philosophies of control underlying the goals of both groups are identical—and identically odious. *Ellen N. Langston, New Orleans, La., in a Letter to the Editor, Saturday Review, April 8, 1972, p 16*

The labour force is being pushed up by the baby boom of the 1960s to such an extent that an extra 680,000 jobs would be needed between now and 1981 just to keep unemployment at its present level. *The Times (London), July 25, 1977, p 1*

[1967; *boom* a sudden increase of activity, rapid growth or expansion (OED 1879)]

► Although historically the United States baby boom occurred in the late 1940's, the term *baby boom* became current during the 1970's according to the data in our files.

baby boomer, a person born in a baby boom; member of a baby-boom generation.

We accept as normal the gross and permanent depletion of our oil and natural gas, diminished research in agriculture, an unemployable body of baby boomers, inner cities in decay. *The Manchester Guardian Weekly (The Washington Post section), May 15, 1977, p 17*

Some think the baby-boomers will soon sire a mini-boom of their own; others, that changing roles for women and economic stress will combine to keep the birth rate down. *Jane Bryant Quinn, "Baby-Boom Economics," Newsweek, June 18, 1979, p 70*

[1974] Also called BOOM BABY.

baby bust, a sudden decline in the birth rate.

48

The aging of the U.S. population is partly a result of the "baby bust" of the 1970's. Very low levels of fertility persisted during 1977, but the rates have begun to climb slightly. For the year ending June 30, 1978, the general fertility rate (the number of births per 1,000 women of childbearing age) was projected at 66.1, compared to 65.3 in 1976-1977. *Teresa A. Sullivan, "Population," 1978 Collier's Encyclopedia Year Book (1977), p. 453*

[1972, patterned on BABY BOOM]

BAC, abbreviation of *blood alcohol concentration.*

In each sex, the highest BAC's were found in the 45- to 65-age groups. *"Behavioral sciences: Social characteristics of alcoholics," Science News, March 18, 1972, p 186*

[1964]

BACAT (bæ'kæt), *n.* acronym for *barge aboard catamaran.*

The British Waterways Board was becoming heavily involved with Denmark in the development of a new barge-carrying vessel, designed largely for the European system. Known as the BACAT (barge aboard catamaran), it was to carry 18 450-ton barges designed for the European waterway system or, alternatively, 10 European barges and 3 of the larger 850-ton barges built under U.S. patents. *Guy Hawtin, "Transportation: Water Transportation," Britannica Book of the Year 1974, p 690*

[1973]

bachelorette, *n.* an unmarried girl or woman who lives independently.

Articles now offer tips on housework for the woman who hates housework, and describe the delights open to the "bachelorette" who has left her family and is in no hurry to get married. *Wendy Michener, Saturday Night (Canada), Nov. 1965, p 35*

Writing a poem all by yourself is something that nobody can do with you, and this is a special problem for people who are already panicked about being alone, such as so-called singles. I say "so-called" because the words "single," "bachelorette," etc., may be thought to apply to people's *imaginations,* and they do not. *Veronica Geng, "Teaching Poetry Writing to Singles," The New Yorker, June 12, 1978, p 29*

[1961, from *bachelor* + -*ette* (feminine suffix)]

back burner, on the back burner, in a secondary place; postponed as subordinate.

The first of the High Energy Astronomy Observatory satellites . . . resumed development earlier this year after being put on the back burner by NASA in January 1973. *Science News, Aug. 10, 1974, p 88*

—*adj.* secondary; subordinate.

Integration has become a back-burner issue, by choice or hard political realism. The up-front concern now is to improve economic and social conditions for blacks in the urban ghettos and the rural backwaters—where most blacks are. *Peter Goldman, "Black Power at Work," Newsweek, Feb. 19, 1973, p 33*

[1973] Compare FRONT BURNER.

back·cast ('bæk,kæst), *v.t., v.i.* to describe something or some time in the past without having seen or experienced it, especially to reconstruct (past events) on the basis of study or other evidence.

Thus our present ills, Mr Johnson is sure, are the nemesis that hubris—here, principally late-nineteenth-century hubris—inevitably brings. He is even bold enough to back-

cast how things would have gone had we acted rightly. *Marghanita Laski, "Books," Review of "The Offshore Islanders" by Paul Johnson, The Times (London), Sept. 7, 1972, p 9*

If a model that is shown to be an adequate representation of a given historical period then cannot "backcast" that period, Meadows says, very reasonably, that testing by backcasting cannot then be judged significant. *Guy Streatfield, "No Limit to the Growth Debate," New Scientist, March 8, 1973, p 533*

[1961, patterned on *forecast*]

back channel, *U.S.* a secret, clandestine, or irregular means of communicating.

The United States SALT delegation . . . didn't know that Nixon's national security adviser had set up a "back channel" and was making a deal or two on his own with the Russians. *Marilyn Berger, "Vance and Brzezinski: Peaceful Coexistence or Guerrilla War?" The New York Times Magazine, Feb. 13, 1977, p 23*

There are clear signs that the Israelis and Egyptians, perceiving that movement toward Geneva had stalled, set up their own "back-channel" diplomatic operation that cleared the way for the week's public rush toward a Sadat appearance in Jerusalem. *Jim Hoagland, The Manchester Guardian Weekly (The Washington Post section), Nov. 27, 1977, p 15*

[1975] ► The use derives from diplomatic jargon, in which the reference is to channels other than the normal official diplomatic channels.

backcourtman, *n.* a basketball player who plays the backcourt and brings the ball out into the offensive zone.

Archibald also became the first guard to score more than 1,000 field goals—he had 1,028—and the first backcourtman in 17 years to lead the league in minutes played, with a total of 3,681. *B. Peter Carry, "Sports: Basketball," 1974 Collier's Encyclopedia Year Book, p 491*

[1967, from *backcourt* + *man*]

back end, that part of the fuel cycle of a nuclear reactor in which the used fuel is reprocessed to separate usable uranium and plutonium from radioactive waste.

The Government has planned . . . a system for recycling plutonium fuel, and so put into effect a commercially operable breeder-reactor program that would produce fuel as it generates power—the so-called "back end" of the fuel cycle. *Barry Commoner, "A Reporter at Large: Energy—II," The New Yorker, Feb. 9, 1976, p 48*

The danger of nuclear weapons proliferation already has led President Carter to halt nuclear fuel reprocessing. . . . But that only increased the spent-fuel storage problem, part of the less publicized but perhaps more threatening "back-end" dilemma of the nuclear process—nuclear waste disposal and the decommissioning of nuclear facilities that have already outlived their usefulness. *Tom Wicker, "Paying the Nuclear Piper," The New York Times, Sept. 27, 1977, p 39*

[1976]

Backfire, *n.* or **Backfire bomber,** a supersonic intercontinental warplane developed by the Soviet Union, officially known as the Tupolev V-G (after Andrei N. Tupolev, 1888-1972, Soviet aircraft designer).

The first 25 long-range bombers known in the West as

Back Formations

Backfires, swing-wing, Mach 2 aircraft capable of attacking targets anywhere in the United States, have been delivered to the Soviet Air Force. *Drew Middleton, "Soviet Edge Seen in Nuclear Arms," The New York Times, April 19, 1976, p 7*

The problem is that weapons such as the new Soviet mobile medium-range missile, the SS-20, and the Backfire bomber do not fit into either the SALT talks, which deal with U.S. and Soviet strategic weapons, or the troop reduction talks, which deal mostly with conventional weapons. *The Manchester Guardian Weekly (The Washington Post section), Oct. 8, 1978, p 15*

[1975, from the NATO code name of this bomber]

Back Formations. ► These are new words formed by dropping parts of existing words. For example: the verb *housekeep*, formed from the noun *housekeeper* by dropping the suffix *-er* or from *housekeeping* by dropping *-ing*, or EPT formed from *inept* by dropping the prefix *in-*. Back formations reverse the more frequent process of affixation; instead of DERIVATIVES that are formed by the addition of an affix, they are formed by clipping a word-forming element.

Many back formations are created by analogy. A word such as *escalator* may be assumed to derive from the verb *escalate* on analogy of known derivatives; for instance *elevator* from *elevate* and *decorator* from *decorate*. The hypothetical form *escalate* appears to be an established formation; so the original user was probably quite unconscious of the fact that *escalate* was at that time a new coinage.

Some back formations are created by subtracting a supposed rather than a traditionally analyzed suffix from a word: for example, DISGRUNT from *disgruntled* by dropping the supposed suffix *-led* and perhaps by influence of the verb *grunt;* (dropping the traditional suffix would have produced the verb form *disgruntle*).

This device is also used to produce NONCE WORDS, such as *pensable* (from *indispensable*) and *gainly* (from *ungainly*). Such back formations suggest a play on words.

Back formations created in the 1970's seemed particularly frequent in the formation of verbs, such as HOUSE-SIT from HOUSE-SITTER, MITOSE from *mitosis* (on analogy with *diagnose*, from *diagnosis*), and SAFEKEEP from *safekeeping*. Verbs were formed from either a noun or an adjective, as TUMESCE from *tumescence* or *tumescent*. On the other hand, nouns created from adjectives include SLEAZE from *sleazy* and RAUNCH from *raunchy*, or from other nouns.

Science and technology often have an apparent need for verbs changed from nouns by the process of back formation. For example, ELECTROPHORESE from *electrophoresis*, IMMUNOSUPPRESS from *immunosuppression*, THERMOREGULATE from *thermoregulation*, TRANSAMINATE from *transamination*, TRANSFECT from *transfection*, VASOLIGATE from *vasoligation*.

The back formation has long and recognized standing as one of the traditional sources of new coinages. A careful examination of entries in this book will show that back formations continue to make needed and substantial contributions to English vocabulary. See also CLIPPED FORMS.

back-mu·tate (ˌbæk'myu: teit; -myu:'teit), *v.i. Genetics.* to mutate back to the original form.

. . . of all the mutations studied by Yanofsky it is the only one not to back-mutate or revert to "wild type." *F.H.C. Crick, Scientific American, Oct. 1966, p 59*

The first category comprises mutator genes which do not appear to be unidirectional in preference. Auxotrophs of various types are more abundant than in the normal strain, and the auxotrophs back-mutate at a higher frequency. *Kaare Jyssum, "Bacterial genetics," McGraw-Hill Yearbook of Science and Technology 1970, p 120*

[1964, back formation from *back mutation* (1914)]

back-of-the-book, *adj. U.S.* of or relating to printed or broadcast material of general interest, such as developments in science, the arts, and education, as opposed to current world or national events.

The second major area of departure for ABC news is in so-called "back-of-the-book" stories: features, essays and interviews that focus on areas apart from the "official" hard news of press conferences, statistics and catastrophes. *Jeff Greenfield, "The Showdown at ABC News," The New York Times Magazine, Feb. 13, 1977, p 34*

[1968]

back-of-the-envelope or **back-of-an-envelope,** *adj.* quickly and easily determined; not requiring elaborate calculations.

But recycling has little to do with the problem I was raising, which is how one provides the capital stock of metals that would be required for cars in use. A simple back-of-the-envelope sum illustrates the problem. *Gerald Leach, London, in a Letter to the Editor, New Scientist, Dec. 6, 1973, p 727*

The calculations themselves, Levine says, are easy. Back-of-an-envelope stuff. Thus it's a little strange, but apparently true, he says, that they've never before been published. *Jonathan Eberhart, "Sunny Days on Other Worlds," Science News, June 11, 1977, p 380*

[1973]

backstroke, *v.i.* to swim lying on one's back.

The '40s collage includes . . . a likeable fantasy of America's post-war dreams—Esther Williams bathing beauties backstroking across the dry stage. *Lance Morrow, "The Theater," Review of "Over Here," Time, March 18, 1974, p 66*

[1970, verb use of noun]

backstroker, *n.:* The American men won eight of their 15 swimming events, and they did it even though two of their stars—breast-stroker John Hencken of Santa Clara, Calif., and backstroker John Naber of Menlo Park, Calif.—passed up the meet. *Frank Litsky, "Swimming," The 1976 World Book Year Book, p 478*

back-to-basics, *adj. Especially U.S.* of, characterized by, or advocating a return to the basic principles of religion, education, etc.

As the national mood has changed, the style and tone of the churches have undergone a major adjustment as well, gradually turning toward a "back-to-basics" approach that stresses the need for sound beliefs and personal faith. *Kenneth A. Briggs, "Protestant Churches Returning to Basic*

Beliefs," The New York Times, March 9, 1975, p 1

Disappointing test results have intensified the back-to-basics movement in education, which stresses reading, writing, and math in the lower grades. At the high school level, the movement concentrates on basic-knowledge and vocationally-oriented courses. *Edward Alvey, Jr., "Education," The Americana Annual 1976, p 221*

Frank Freed and his daughter, Dolly, are advocates of a back-to-basics lifestyle that cost them less than $1,500 last year—total. *Today (New York), June 12, 1979, p B3*

[1975, from the phrase *back to (the) basics;* the phrase *the basics* is an Americanism (1950's) meaning the fundamentals or elementary principles]

bac·te·ri·o·cin (bæk₁tir i:'ou sən), *n.* any antibiotic effective against the same or closely related bacteria from which it is derived.

For example, the killing effects of certain bacteriocins on bacteria . . . may involve transmission and amplification of localized events over the entire surface of a membrane. *S. J. Singer and Garth L. Nicolson, "The Fluid Mosaic Model of the Structure of Cell Membranes," Science, Feb. 18, 1972, p 729*

[1967, from *bacterio-* bacteria + *colicin,* a substance of this kind]

bac·te·ri·o·pho·bi·a (bæk₁tir i: ə'fou bi: ə), *n.* an abnormal fear of contamination by bacteria.

Many theories were advanced for his [Howard Hughes] being a recluse who had shunned all public appearances for nearly two decades. Some said that his bacteriophobia allowed him no contact with the "diseased" outside world. *"Obituary: Mr. Howard Hughes," The Times (London), April 7, 1976, p 16*

[1976, from *bacterio-* bacteria + *phobia* fear]

bac·te·ri·o·rho·dop·sin (bæk₁tir i: ou rou'dɑp sən), *n.* a protein capable of converting light energy into a useful form of cellular energy, found in the bacterium *Halobacterium halobium.* Other than the chlorophyll-based photosynthesis of plants, this is the only known cellular system that converts light to life-sustaining energy.

Walther Stoeckenius and colleagues discovered a purple, light-absorbing pigment protein similar in structure to rhodopsin, the visual pigment in animal retinas. They named the protein "bacteriorhodopsin." This membrane pigment can capture light energy, store it chemically, and use it to drive metabolic processes. This finding may shed light on the evolution of vision and provide a harnessable system for large-scale energy production. *Janet L. Hopson, "Biochemistry," The Americana Annual 1977, p 117*

[1976, from *bacterio-* bacteria + *rhodopsin* visual purple (from Greek *rhódon* rose + *ópsis* sight + English *-in*)]

bad, *adj. U.S. Slang, Chiefly (and originally) Black English.* good; admirable; excellent.

"Our differences are complementary. Bullins is a bad dude. There's no better playwright in the American theatre today." *Jervis Anderson, "Profiles: Ed Bullins, Dramatist," The New Yorker, June 16, 1973, p 52*

Last year, some students prepared their own black dictionary. "I found some words I'd never heard of," says Monro, "and some I hadn't understood, like why the word 'bad' in black slang means 'good'." *"Education: The Man from Harvard," Newsweek, Sept. 24, 1973, p 88*

It was, said the "baddest" heavyweight champion of the world, "like being in the middle of a rainbow knowing that at the end there's a pot of money waiting." The irony, added Larry Holmes, was he thought the waiting was over when he won the World Boxing Council version of the title last June from Ken Norton. *Michael Katz, "Is Holmes Too Good a Boxer?" The New York Times, Jan. 26, 1979, p A11*

[1973] ► The use of *bad* (and of its usual superlative *baddest*) to mean "good" surfaced about 1970, although it was fairly common among black jazzmen during the 1950's (See Robert S. Gold, *A Jazz Lexicon,* 1964). The impetus behind the usage was probably a wish to defy the conventional expression of approval and to conceal the intended meaning from outsiders, either nonblacks or nonjazzmen. Clarence Major, in his *Dictionary of Afro-American Slang* (1970), defines *bad* as "a simple reversal of the white standard, the very best." However, the Africanist David Dalby tentatively traces the usage back to an African origin, citing the frequent use of negative terms to describe positive extremes in various African languages. (See "The African Element in American English" by David Dalby, in *Rappin' and Stylin' Out,* ed. Thomas Kochman, 1972, p. 170). Whatever its origins, the usage entered the mainstream of general American slang, and in *The Underground Dictionary* (1971), Eugene E. Landy states (without reference to blacks) that it "Can be either positive or negative—e.g. A *bad* scene can mean an unfortunate experience or a very good experience."

bad actor, *U.S.* a chemical, plant, etc. found or thought to be harmful.

In addition to desirable nutrients, the sludge contains some "bad actors"—heavy metals like chromium and nickel that could accumulate to levels toxic to plants, and elements like arsenic, mercury and cadmium that are potentially toxic to man and animals. *Jane Brody, The New York Times, July 9, 1976, p A9*

Bad actors in the pea family (Fabaceae) include the rosary pea (Abrus precatorius), one of the most poisonous plants known. *Guy Hartman, "Poisonous Garden Plants," Encyclopedia Science Supplement (Grolier) 1979 (1978), p 85*

[1976, extended sense of the U.S. slang term (1940's) for a mean, troublesome person or animal]

bag lady, *U.S.* short for SHOPPING BAG LADY.

In truth, bag ladies have a great deal of pride and dignity in spite of their disarray. They have chosen the agony of doorway life rather than the far worse agony of being forced to beg and grovel on their knees for assistance from city agencies supposedly designed to help people in trouble, but which in fact destroy them. *Wendy Walton, New York Post, Feb. 5, 1979, p 22*

[1977]

bagman, *n. Canadian Slang.* a person who directs finances in a political campaign.

A confidential memo from the party's chief bagman, Toronto lawyer Patrick Vernon, indicated the PCs [Progressive Conservatives] will have to somehow find a way eventually to pay off a further $400,000 still owing on old loans. *Julianne Labreche, "Ottawa: To the Aid of the Party," Maclean's, Feb. 23, 1976, p 17*

[1976, probably transferred from the U.S. Slang

sense of a person who collects and distributes graft or protection money]

Ba·ha·sa Malay or **Ba·ha·sa Malaysia** (bɑ:'hɑ: sə), the Malay dialect adopted as the official language of Malaysia.

In response to demands for increased special concessions to Malaysians, the Malay Chinese Association (MCA) finally agreed to accept Bahasa Malay as the national language. *John N. Stalker, "Malaysia," The 1972 World Book Year Book, p 422*

These are the two points Malaysia's education and language authorities have continually to bear in mind in effecting the change from English to Bahasa Malaysia (modern Malay) as the main medium of instruction. *The Times (London), Aug. 31, 1977, p VI*

[1972, from Malay *bahasa* language, from Sanskrit *bhāṣā*]

bak·kie ('bɑ: ki:), *n.* (in South Africa) a small, light van with an open back, used especially by farmers.

Another nasty moment came between Jamestown and Sterkspruit when the "bakkie" had a puncture and it seemed to take us ages to change the wheel. *The New York Times, Jan. 8, 1978, Sec. 4, p 19*

[1973, from Afrikaans, from *bak* container + *-kie* (diminutive suffix)]

BAL, abbreviation of *blood alcohol level.*

A person of Prefontaine's slight build would have his "driving impaired" if his BAL was in the range of .05 to .07 per cent. He would have reached that low level of intoxication by drinking either three shots of liquor or three glasses of beer within a 2-hour period. *Belle Cannon, "Olympic Lesson for Drinking Drivers," The Manchester Guardian Weekly (The Washington Post section), Aug. 15, 1976, p 16*

[1976]

balance of terror, 1 distribution of nuclear power among nations, serving as a deterrent to the use of nuclear weapons.

To achieve a more stable balance of terror at existing nuclear levels, the negotiators at Moscow signed two nuclear arms pacts, one limiting the installation of antiballistic missiles to two locations in each country, the other freezing offensive weapons at current levels for five years, ensuring numerical superiority for Soviet missiles. *Norman A. Graebner, "United States: Foreign Relations," 1973 Collier's Encyclopedia Year Book, p 588*

2 the ability of a group to exert a dominant influence through the use of brute power.

By "a healthy atmosphere" they [teachers] seemed to mean a balance of terror, with unruly students held in check by the spectre of paddles stockpiled in the principal's office. *"The Talk of the Town," The New Yorker, May 30, 1977, p 27*

The sheer weight of the peacekeeping forces in Lebanon seems sufficient to keep the country from exploding again. The Syrian troops bear most of the burden. Intervening first on the side of the Moslems and Palestinians, then on the side of the Christians, they brought under control and finally ended the civil war. "They hold the balance of terror," commented one Lebanese editor. *The New York Times, July 2, 1978, Sec. 4, p 4*

[1955] ▶ In the sense of definition 1, this term first appeared in the 1950's as the atomic-age analogue of the much earlier (1701) military-political term *bal-*

ance of power, though the mere fact of distribution seems to have overshadowed the older concept of "parity" associated with *balance of power.*

Balance of terror was only sporadically used until the mid-1960's, when nuclear armament became a matter of stockpiling weapons and developing sophisticated missile delivery systems, and atomic bombs began to proliferate among smaller nations. In the following early quotation, the attribution of the term to Churchill is erroneous; the phrase he used in his famous "Iron Curtain" speech of 1946 was "balance of power," which he described as precarious unless security was achieved through U.S.-British cooperation.

Even without any system of international control whatsoever, the danger of nuclear weapons being used is not very great, because of the risk involved for the aggressor in attempting a total knockout blow. But this kind of security—was it Churchill who first called it a "balance of terror"?—is not likely to appeal to mankind indefinitely. *William R. Frye, Bulletin of the Atomic Scientists, Dec. 1955, p 359*

ba·la·tik or **ba·la·tic** (bɑ:'lɑ: tik), *n.* a trap for wild game used in the Philippines.

We checked three balatiks and four deadfall monkey traps, all empty. No one seemed surprised. Animal kills obviously, were rare, and meat no more than a luxury. *National Geographic Magazine, Aug. 1972, p 245*

The *balatic,* which is known to probably all Filipino peoples, is without question the most effective trap for obtaining wild pigs and deer; it is a bow device that shoots an arrow across the paths of pigs and deer when they have struck a trip cord. *Manuel Elizalde, Jr. (in collaboration with Robert B. Fox), "The Tasaday Forest People," Encyclopedia Science Supplement (Grolier) 1972, p 303*

[1972, from the native name]

ball¹, *n.* **run with the ball,** *U.S. Informal,* to take up and carry forward an enterprise, venture, or the like.

A 5-year federally funded American FPC [fish protein concentrate] program in Washington State recently ended when Congress declined to extend the experimental period. Even so, the technology developed has not been wasted, says Dr. Bruce Stillings of the National Marine Fisheries Service. Federal approval may still be forthcoming at a later date, and "private industry might choose to run with the ball," he says. *Peter Tonge, Encyclopedia Science Supplement (Grolier) 1973, p 111*

[1971, figurative use of the sports term (especially in U.S. football) meaning to advance in an attempt to score]

ball², *v.t., v.i. U.S. Slang (vulgar use).* to have sexual intercourse (with).

Its [the book's] tone is True Romance, with pulpish purple passages such as "the two of us were in love with, and occasionally balling the same silver-tongued devil of a man." *Dan Wakefield, "Kozmic Blues," Review of "Going Down With Janis" by Peggy Caserta and Dan Knapp, The Atlantic, Sept. 1973, p 108*

[1969 (but used in jazz circles since the 1950's), extended sense of *ball, v.,* to have a ball, have a good time (1940's), probably influenced by *ball, n.,* vulgar slang for testis (used since the 1300's)]

balloon pump, a device consisting of a balloon and

a synchronizing pump that is attached to the line connecting a heart-lung machine and the aorta, used to convert the continuous flow of blood from the machine to a pulsating flow.

In 1975, Dr. David Bregman of Columbia-Presbyterian Medical Center in New York City reported having developed an external balloon pump which avoids the risks inherent in placing the balloon in the aorta. . . . As a result, the body is better supplied with blood while the patient is on the pump. *Frank E. Gump, "Medicine: Surgery," The World Book Science Annual 1977 (1976), p 304*

[1976; the device has been in use since 1967]

bal·lo·ti·ni (ˌbæl əˈti: ni:), *n.pl.* tiny particles or beads of glass, used in industry as a grinding medium and for other purposes.

The difficulties of using foreign cullet for making bottles has prompted what may be the most profitable line of thought—using ground-up glass in "secondary products." In the US especially, experiments using cullet in the manufacture of road surfaces (glasphalt), tiles, ballotini (reflective glass beads in paints for road signs), and glass reinforced plastics have been reasonably successful. *"Technology review: Spiritual ideas stir the building industry," New Scientist, Nov. 29, 1973, p 627*

[1965, probably from Italian *ballottini*, plural of *ballottino*, diminutive of *ballotta* small ball, from *balla* ball]

ball park, *U.S.* the general or approximate area of an estimate (usually in the phrase **in the ball park**).

Dr. Henry C. Huntley, director of the U.S. Public Health Service's Division of Emergency Health Services, emphasizes that "We *can* save lives with adequately equipped ambulances and properly trained personnel. It may be 50,000 or 75,000, but a figure of 60,000 is in the right ball park." *Arthur S. Freese, "Trauma: The Neglected Epidemic," Saturday Review, May 13, 1972, p 59*

The committee could conclude only that the apparent monetary benefits of less pollution and the apparent costs of emission control lie in the same ballpark (a factor of two or three, one way or the other). *"NAS study backs pollution limits," Science News, Sept. 14, 1974, p 166*

[1962, transferred use of the term for a baseball field]

ball-park figure, *U.S.* a rough estimate; an approximate figure.

Some ball-park figures on two-year leases: up to $250 monthly for a full-size luxury car, $80 to $90 for a compact. *"New Cars for Hire—By the Day, Month or Year," Woman's Day, July 1973, p 80*

"If you recall, I didn't give you an 'estimate.' I gave you a 'ballpark figure.' " *Cartoon legend by Joe Mirachi, The New Yorker, April 10, 1978, p 33*

[1972; see BALL PARK]

ball·sy (ˈbɔːl ziː), *adj. U.S. Slang.* cockily aggressive; robust; tough.

But [Gordon] Parks insists that Shaft—"a ballsy guy, to hell with everybody, he goes out and does his thing"—was an important symbol for the black community. *"Show Business: Black Market," Time, April 10, 1972, p 53*

Jane [Fonda]. Dressed à la chinoise. Still, a star. The only star they have. But it's wrong: The ballsy, broad voice seems hesitant and confused. "And so I think . . . and so I think . . ." *D. Keith Mano, "Arts and Manners: The Gimlet Eye: Atrocity Jane," National Review, Nov. 23, 1973, p 1303*

[1971, from *balls, n.pl.*, vulgar slang for testes]

Bal·mer lines (ˈbɑːl mər), *Physics.* lines of hydrogen in the visible region of the spectrum.

Balmer lines in the visible portion of the hydrogen spectrum indicate that the principal constituent of the interstellar medium is hydrogen. The lines are produced when the single electron of the hydrogen atom cascades down to the second energy level of the atom. *Illustration legend, "The Birth of Stars," Scientific American, Aug. 1972, p 53*

[1965, named after Johann *Balmer*, 1825-1898, a Swiss physicist, who in 1885 worked out a formula by which the wavelength of any of these lines may be calculated. This term has largely replaced the earlier *Balmer series*.]

ban, in South Africa: *—v.t.* to bar from writing or speaking publicly or engaging in political activity (applied to any person or organization officially regarded as a threat to law and order, especially under the Internal Security Act of 1977).

A person who is banned cannot meet with more than one person at a time except for his immediate family. He cannot write anything for publication and he cannot be quoted, publicly or in print, even after he is dead. *John Darnton, "Banning: Unique South African Punishment," The New York Times, Oct. 27, 1977, p A8*

—n. an act of banning or the condition of being banned.

Woods now has time, lots of time. He is forbidden to write at all, even in a private diary. The government is watching: as part of the ban, the Woodses have been informed that their home, their phones, even their two cars are bugged. Plainclothesmen keep their house under surveillance. *Time, Nov. 7, 1977, p 38*

[1966, specialized sense of *ban* to forbid, prohibit (OED 1816)]

banning, *n.*: The death in detention of the black activist, Steven Biko, in September 1977 brought an outraged international response to which the authorities reacted with widespread banning and detentions on October 19. *The Manchester Guardian Weekly, Oct. 1, 1978, p 8*

Ba·na·ban (ˈbɑː nə bən), *n.* a native or inhabitant of Ocean Island, an atoll in the western Pacific noted for its rich phosphate deposits. It is one of the Gilbert Islands.

The Banabans have not accepted a £6.5 millions offer from the British Government in compensation for exploitation of their Pacific island and are preparing for a new fight. They will continue to fight both for higher compensation and the independence of their island. *Christopher Sweeney, The Manchester Guardian Weekly, June 5, 1977, p 4*

—adj. of or relating to these people or their island.

The British government announced an exgratia payment of U.S. $11 million to the 2,500 Banabans now living on Rabi Island, in Fiji, as a final settlement of Banaban claims. The Australian government increased aid to nine countries. Priority was to be accorded projects strengthening the islanders' sense of self-reliance. *R. M. Younger, "Oceania," The Americana Annual 1978, p 383*

[1967, from the original name of the atoll]

Ba·nach space (ˈbɑː nɑːx), *Mathematics.* a geometric configuration of space, used in function analysis to show varying relationships among interdependent values.

Specialists in the field of Banach spaces were gratified by the solution of one of the oldest problems in the subject. These spaces had been invented by the Polish mathematician S. Banach as a vehicle for the study of functional analysis. *Irving Kaplansky, "Mathematics," Britannica Book of the Year 1972, p 447*

[1963, named after Stefan *Banach*, 1892-1945, a Polish mathematician who devised an algebra of such spaces] Compare HILBERT SPACE.

banalization, *n.* the act of making banal; reduction of something to the trite or ordinary.

Surely, the most serious trivialization and banalization of the Third is Test Match Special, which next week once again forces adult interests off the air in favour of schoolboy stuff. *F. A. Sowan, South Croydon, in a Letter to the Editor, The Times (London), June 5, 1972, p 15*

[1968, from *banalize* (1963) + *-ation*]

banana, *adj.* denoting or belonging to any small country, especially in Central America, whose entire economy is based on the export of a single agricultural commodity, such as bananas or other fruit.

If we didn't get into the Common Market, I think that, try as we might, we would sink into the state of a third-rate banana country. *Kenneth Harris, Interview of Don Ryder, The Listener, May 18, 1972, p 652*

The CIA began by handing out bribes to tropical politicians and banana generals in the Fifties. *Andrew St. George, "The Cold War Comes Home," Harper's, Nov. 1973, p 78*

[1971, abstracted from *banana republic* (1935)]

banana belt, *U.S. Slang.* a winter resort whose climate is considered comparatively mild.

Skiers enjoying the sport at some of the giant-sized areas in New England and upper New York have cause to thank this southern Catskill Mountain country—often joshingly referred to as "The Banana Belt." For it was in this Sullivan County region that machine-made snow was first produced on a practical basis. *Michael Strauss, The New York Times, Jan. 6, 1977, p 34*

[1963 (originally applied on Baffin Island to mainland North America), because the region *(belt)* is considered warm enough to grow *bananas*]

banana seat, a kind of long, upward-curving seat on a child's bicycle.

"High-rise" handlebars, which force a small child to steer with elbows at chinlevel, and the long, narrow "banana" seats, which invite additional passengers, are major contributors to instability—and may cause additional accidents. *"Safety-First for Cyclists," The Reader's Digest, Aug. 1974 (page unknown)*

[1972]

band, *v.t. British, Education.* to group (pupils) according to level of their scholastic ability to achieve distribution in enrollment.

The Inner London Education Authority's system of "banding" children being transferred from primary to secondary school, may be made illegal under the Education Bill. Children are "banded" as above average, average and below average. *The Times (London), Jan. 31, 1976, p 1*

[1976, back formation from *banding* (1970)]

banding, *n.:* Banding is a form of selection used in some

areas to ensure an even spread of abilities in the intake of comprehensive schools ... but the amendment does not permit the introduction of any new banding arrangements. *George Clark, The Times (London), Nov. 23, 1976, p 2*

band·gap ('bænd₁gæp), *n. Physics.* a difference between two allowed bands of electron energy; an energy range of electrons over which no quantum states are allowed.

Depending on the magnitude of the bandgaps ..., a solid may be an insulator, semiconductor, or metal. For a solid to exhibit the properties of a semiconductor or an insulator, bandgaps must exist in all directions of electron motion. *W. E. Spicer, "Solid-State Physics," 1978 Britannica Yearbook of Science and the Future (1977), p 387*

[1962, from electron *band* + *gap*]

Ban·gla·desh·i (₁bæŋ gləˈdeʃ iː), *n.; pl.* **-desh·is** or **-desh·i,** a native of Bangladesh, formerly the province of East Pakistan, and since 1971 an independent nation.

There are also 1,600 Pakistanis, who earn a basic £14.69 a month and 1,000 Bangladeshi, earning £16.73 a month. *The Times (London), May 9, 1973, p 2*

Such predictions, of course, are almost timeless, too. Bangladeshis made them themselves a decade ago—protesting against Pakistani domination. *Peter Preston, The Manchester Guardian Weekly, Nov. 9, 1974, p 5*

—*adj.* of Bangladesh or its people.

Pakistan returned the Bangladeshi civilians who had been detained in Pakistan after the war. *Sir Percival Griffiths, "Bangladesh," The Annual Register of World Events in 1974 (1975), p 296*

[1971, from Bengali *Bangla Desh*, Bengal Nation]

bang stick, a weapon used by a diver against an attacking shark or other marine animal. It consists of a stick loaded at the end with an explosive charge that fires on impact.

"Suddenly five or six huge grey sharks came churning up from the bottom and several more raced in from the shallows," recalls Alan Emery, a marine scientist. . . . "I really thought my time was up because the guy riding shotgun for me panicked and took off. And he took the bang stick (a weapon with a magnum shell at the end which explodes when poked broadside into a shark). *Maclean's, Jan. 22, 1979, p 39*

[1976]

ban·jax ('bæn dʒæks), *v.t. Slang.* to hit, beat, or overcome.

Ha-ha, so she ups and banjaxed the old man one night with a broken spade handle, and robbed him of his four rattling pennies in a tin and made off out of the clutter. *Ted Walker, "The Third Person," The New Yorker, Oct. 28, 1972, p 40*

O'Toole brought with him a new, free "version" of the play which translates it verbally from Czarist Russia to the Ireland of Brendan Behan. "Well, I'm banjaxed!" cries Vanya on learning that his monstrous brother-in-law plans to sell the family estate from under the family. *Maclean's, Oct. 9, 1978, p 70*

[1970, apparently from dialectal Irish; origin uncertain]

bankable, *adj.* certain to produce box-office success and profits.

At 37, Pacino has become a "bankable" superstar, whose commitment to a project means that a film will be made and will be guaranteed a certain success. *Mel Gussow, "The Basic Training of Al Pacino," The New York Times Magazine, June 5, 1977, p 21*

[1964, extended from the earlier sense (OEDS 1818) of acceptable at or by a bank; influenced by the requirement of some banks that filmmakers include a famous star in any film venture to be financially backed by them]

bankability, *n.:* In the secret and all-powerful Q Ratings that are researched for TV networks to determine a performer's appeal — and ultimately his bankability in a series — Rich Little . . . calibrated right up there in third spot. *Marci McDonald, Maclean's, Feb. 9, 1976, p 32*

barb, *n. U.S. Informal.* short for *barbiturate.*

But there is no question that "barbs" are reaching the very young — in high school, junior high and even earlier. Several reasons are given. Barbs are cheaper than heroin — only $1 for five pills in most places — and not as detectable as marijuana, the smell of which is known to most school teachers. *Dana Adams Schmidt, "Medicine: Seconal: Higher and Higher On the Downers," The New York Times, June 4, 1972, Sec. 4, p 7*

[1972]

Barcelona chair, a stainless steel chair with leather cushions and usually without arms.

The furniture, simple and usually entirely machine made, ranges from the modern classics — the Barcelona chair, the Wassily chair, the Eames lounge chair and ottoman — to inexpensive, down-to-earth pieces such as the director's chair, some of the bentwood styles, and cubes and cylinders in place of small tables. *Helen W. Harris, "Interior Design," 1974 Collier's Encyclopedia Year Book, p 294*

[1965, originally exhibited in *Barcelona* in 1929 by Ludwig Mies van der Rohe, its designer] Compare EAMES CHAIR.

bar code, 1 a code of lines and numbers printed on a packaged product for identification by an optical scanner.

Large bar code labels — like the one shown here — will soon be appearing on nearly all supermarket items as part of an attempt to speed the changeover to electronic cash registers. With the labels, the shop assistant simply passes a handheld scanner over the code and the price of the item is automatically pulled out of a minicomputer memory. *"New Code to Speed Supermarket Checkout," New Scientist, May 24, 1973, p 498*

2 Also, **bar-code,** *v.* to furnish with such a code.

The Council of Periodical Distributors has asked mass market publishers to . . . "bar code" their books, so that distributors will be able to provide sales and returns information to publishers with greater speed. *Sandra K. Paul, Publishers Weekly, April 10, 1978, p 36*

[1973] Compare UNIVERSAL PRODUCT CODE.

bar-coded, *adj.:* By using a series of "light pens" (similar to those already used in retail outlets) bar-coded information on labels attached to pathology specimens and, later, on X-ray details can all be read into the machine without any additional work. *A. E. Phillips, "Telecommunications: Patient Care," The Times (London), June 8, 1976, p 11*

bare, *adj.* **go bare,** *U.S.* to carry no insurance against claims of malpractice, product liability, etc.

Although the average cost of product liability insurance is now 1% of sales, the rate is more than ten times higher for some small manufacturers of high-risk products, such as trampolines, air rifles and football equipment. An increasing number of companies are "going bare," dropping coverage altogether. *Time, Feb. 20, 1978, p 65*

So absurd has the situation become that some doctors are opting out, transferring all their assets to their wives and "going bare," that is stating that there is no point in sueing them because they have neither insurance nor personal assets. *"The 100,000 Dollar Doctor," The Manchester Guardian Weekly, Feb. 26, 1978, p 19*

[1976]

barefoot, *adv. U.S. Slang.* within legal limits of CB (citizens band) radio transmission power.

"While a lot of people like to use linear amplifiers . . . I run as 'barefoot' as they come," said Gary. "Let's face it, anyone can blast out by using 500 to 1000 watts of power, but as far as I can see, when you 'walk all over' everybody, you're destroying their right to talk." *"Personal Comment on Linears," CB Guide, May 1976, p 69*

[1976, so called because BOOTS is CB slang for an illegal linear amplifier that boosts transmission power, hence *barefoot* without such an amplifier] Compare APPLE, def. 2.

barefoot doctor, a worker trained as a medical auxiliary and sent to rural areas to perform services such as assisting at childbirth, dispensing medication, and administering first aid.

The October 1974 issue of the CHINESE MEDICAL JOURNAL reports that a million "barefoot doctors" — that is, doctors' assistants — have been sent into China's rural areas. "Most of the barefoot doctors," the issue explains "can now diagnose and treat with traditional and Western medicine commonly seen diseases, and some can perform minor operations under commune hospitals' doctor supervision. Most women barefoot doctors have mastered midwifery, and some can manage difficult labor and sterilization operations. *Joan Arehart-Treichel, "Off the Beat: What we can learn from Chinese medicine," Science News, March 1, 1975, p 141*

The World Health Organisation has pioneered experiments in many countries with health structures based on the primary health worker, better known as the barefoot doctor. Unesco has been busy canvassing the notion of functional education related to the "felt needs" of the community. *The Manchester Guardian Weekly, Jan. 1, 1978, p 9*

[1970, translation of Chinese *chijiao yisheng*] Also (officially translated) PRIMARY HEALTH WORKER. Compare RED GUARD DOCTOR. ▶ The term referred originally to Chinese medical auxiliaries and derives from the fact that many of them were peasants trained during the slack farming season under an expanded rural health program; peasants trained for other services were referred to as *barefoot specialists,* as in the following early quotation:

Specialists were put to work on improving seed strains and treating plant diseases. One important feature of these activities was that urban specialists were used not only to perform tasks but also to train farmers in basic skills. These semitrained personnel, or "barefoot specialists," then played a central role in implementing the rural development programs. *Ellis Joffe, "China," 1971 Collier's Encyclopedia Year Book, p 169*

bargaining chip, something that can be used to gain an advantage or bring about a concession.

Hitherto the revenue-sharing proposals have helped the U.S. in its role as purported world leader; moreover, they are a bargaining chip in dealing with some developing countries who, under revenue sharing, would stand to benefit. *Deborah Shapley, Science, Jan. 25, 1974, p 292*

One side has argued that we should proceed to develop weapons that could be used as "bargaining chips" in negotiations, and it cites the antiballistic-missile treaty as a successful example of this approach. *Andy Logan, The New Yorker, April 4, 1977, p 102*

[1972] Also shortened to CHIP.

▶ The use became prominent during the SALT I negotiations in which various details of the arms programs of the superpowers served as bargaining chips. The phrase derives from gambling chips, used in counting points or to represent money. See DÉTENTE.

bar·gel·lo (bar'dʒel ou), *n., pl.* **-loes;** *v.,* **-loed, -lo·ing,** — *n.* an upright stitch used in needlework to produce zigzag or oblique lines.

The store also sells material for bargello, an Italian geometric pattern, and crewel embroidery material will be added. *Melody Cornett, The News (Mexico City) (Supplement), Week ending April 28, 1973, p 1-C*

— *v.i., v.t.* to use this stitch; make such stitches on canvas.

To demonstrate his find, he opened a desk drawer and pulled out a canvas that was in the midst of being bargelloed; it was attached to a smooth birch easel that seemed to have its leg folded beneath it. *"Nice for Needlework. Tools for Living," Harper's, March 1974, p 99*

[1972, named for *Bargello*, a museum of sculpture in Florence, Italy]

barotolerance, *n.* the ability to withstand high pressure.

Compared with the elaborate food-finding and gathering capabilities developed in highly evolved organisms, the bacteria's only way of adapting to the environmental conditions of the deep sea appears to be their acquisition of psychrotolerance [tolerance of cold] and barotolerance. *Holger W. Jannasch and Carl O. Wirsen, "Microbial Life in the Deep Sea," Scientific American, June 1977, p 52*

[1977, from *baro-* pressure + *tolerance*]

Barr body, a darkly staining piece of chromatin found in the cell nuclei of females, especially female mammals.

Female tissues all yield cells with two X chromosomes, of course, but only one of these chromosomes is active; the other condenses into a strongly staining region, the "Barr body." It was shown 10 years ago that single cells from skin samples of women who had only one gene on the X chromosome for a particular enzyme (judged by their having borne several male children without the enzyme) gave rise to clones of which half possessed the enzyme and half lacked it. Every woman is thus a mosaic of clones, in each of which only one of the two X chromosomes functions. *Philip Morrison, "Books," Review of "The Mammalian Cell As a Microorganism: Genetic and Biochemical Studies in Vitro" by Theodore T. Puck, Scientific American, Feb. 1973, p 121*

[1963, named after Murray L. *Barr*, born 1908, a Canadian anatomist who discovered it]

bar·y·on·i·um (,bær i:'ou ni: əm), *n.* a short-lived hypothetical elementary particle composed of two quarks and two antiquarks.

A recent experiment at CERN, Geneva, has shown that there is a candidate for such a meson with a mass of 2·6 GeV.... All of these experiments concern the annihilation of protons by their antiparticles, antiprotons, and it is in just this type of reaction that physicists believed baryonium states would be most clearly seen. *New Scientist, March 24, 1977, p 698*

[1977, from *baryon* a heavy elementary particle + *-ium* (suffix for chemical elements)] Compare CHARMONIUM. See also QUARK.

base, *n.* **touch base with,** *U.S. Informal.* to get in touch with; contact.

He moves easily and surely in the wild arena of the Jesus freaks, with a wary eye for phonies, hustlers, and thrill seekers. He seems to have touched base with every active group and is not hesitant about judging the sincerity and effectiveness of each. *David Poling, Review of "Berkeley Journal: Jesus and the Street People—A Firsthand Report" by Clay Ford, Saturday Review, July 22, 1972, p 58*

[He] quickly outraged White House staffers by choosing his top assistants without touching base with the President. *"A Bureaucratic Surprise," Time, June 17, 1974, p 89*

[1966]

baseload, *n. British.* the minimum amount of goods, services, etc. needed or produced to stay in business.

British Shipbuilders, the recently formed state shipbuilding organization, has secured a useful baseload of orders in the course of this year but is anxious to extend this. *The Times (London), Sept. 27, 1977, p 19*

[1976, transferred sense of the term for the quantity of electric power that a power plant must produce to satisfy ordinary or minimum needs]

-bashing, a combining form added to nouns and meaning "attacking," "abusing," as in:

bureaucrat-bashing: As issues, immigration and welfare are out, balanced budgets and bureaucrat-bashing are in. *Maclean's, April 3, 1978, p 24*

dissident-bashing: But now, through a convergence of circumstances, the issue has again been raised, and there is a better-than-ever possibility that Soviet dissident-bashing may evoke a serious response from the American scientific community. *The Manchester Guardian Weekly (The Washington Post section), Jan. 22, 1978, p 15*

Republican-bashing: The America he sprang from, the America of a small town drug store in South Dakota, somehow sustained him in the worst moments. So did his sheer pleasure in Republican-bashing. He kept after Richard Nixon — Brand X, he would call him. *The New York Times, Jan. 15, 1978, Sec. 4, p 5*

union-bashing: We must get away from the idea that every time you disagree with the trade unions it is union-bashing or being tough. *The Times (London), Oct. 11, 1977, p 5*

[1966, from *bashing* a beating, gerund of *bash* to strike hard, beat]

ba·sho ('ba: ʃou), *n. sing.* or *pl.* a fifteen-match tournament in sumo wrestling.

Kitanoumi's growing dominance of the sport was strikingly evident when he won both the March and September *basho* with perfect 15-0 records. Wajima won the opening Hatsu *basho* in January (12-3). *Andrew M. Adams, "Combat Sports," Britannica Book of the Year 1978, p 255*

[1976, from Japanese, matches, tournament]

ba·si·lect ('bei sə,lekt), *n. Linguistics.* a speech variety or dialect that has least prestige among speakers of a language.

In the American Black community where prestige language still involves the adaptation toward white norms, Black children are the principal speakers of basilect. A sentence like *We don't suppose to go* is more nearly basilect than *We ain't supposed to go* and is more characteristic of younger speakers, even though the second sentence would not be called Standard English by most Americans. *J. L. Dillard, Black English, 1972, p 299*

[1964, coined by the American linguist William A. Stewart from *basi-* lowest part, base + dia*lect*] Compare ACROLECT.

basket, *n.* **1** a group of related issues, especially ones for discussion in a negotiation or conference; package.

"Experts" from the same 35 governments will meet in Geneva this September to try to work out practical ways to put the principles of Helsinki into effect.... Their work will be broken down into four clusters of issues that have come to be called "baskets." *"The Geneva Follow-up: Four Baskets Full of Problems," Newsweek, July 16, 1973, p 39*

In negotiating 'basket three', the highly controversial package which dealt with co-operation in humanitarian and other fields, Western states pressed hard to force concessions from the Russians. *John C. Garnett, "Defence Negotiations and Organizations," The Annual Register of World Events in 1974 (1975), p 358*

2 any set, grouping, or collection of things.

The main alternative to the dollar before the ministers is a switch of oil pricing to the average of a "basket" of currencies. The economics department of OPEC headquarters in Geneva has prepared a study of four alternative baskets, based on combinations of four to 15 different currencies — excluding the dollar and OPEC's own currencies. Payment itself would remain in dollars whichever new pricing system was adopted. The switch would effectively increase crude oil prices, for each of the four alternative baskets would bring higher rates per barrel. *The Manchester Guardian Weekly, May 14, 1978, p 7*

[1973, translation of French *corbeille*] ► The sense of definition 1 arose during the 34-nation Conference on European Security and Cooperation which opened in Helsinki in November, 1972 and ended with the Helsinki Agreement of August 1, 1975, which incorporated four baskets: Basket I, dealing with security issues and containing ten principles to guide relations between states; Basket II, dealing with cooperation in economics, science, technology, and the environment; Basket III, the most controversial package, which dealt with cooperation in humanitarian and other fields, including the free movement of people and information, family reunification, education, and culture; and Basket IV, dealing with follow-up of the agreement in terms of improving international security and cooperation in Europe and the further development of the process of détente. See DÉTENTE, HUMAN RIGHTS.

basket case, *U.S. Slang.* **1** a person in an extremely nervous condition; one incapable of functioning normally because of nervous strain; a nervous wreck.

"Still, I think the great distances of this country are a deterrent to long drives," [Harold] Graham went on. "Dad's a basket case by the time he gets out to Yellowstone from the East." *David Butwin, "Booked for Travel," Saturday Review, Jan. 22, 1972, p 16*

There are various degrees of mental illness and a person needn't be a basket case before he decides he should talk things over with a professional. *Ann Landers, "Your Problems," Graphic, July 25, 1974, p 6*

2 anyone or anything reduced to an extremely helpless or weakened condition.

Country-by-country investigations, even of the so-called basket cases like Bangladesh, led us to believe that in fact there may well be no country without adequate agricultural resources to feed its population. *Frances M. Lappe and Joseph Collins, "Four Myths About World Hunger," The Manchester Guardian Weekly (Washington Post Section), May 22, 1977, p 16*

[1967, figurative and transferred senses of the term (c. 1919) for a person who has lost both arms and both legs]

basse cou·ture (bɑːs kuːˈtYr), women's fashions below the standards of high-fashion designers.

Runners-up were such alleged exemplars of *basse couture* as Princess Anne, Raquel Welch, Tennis Champ Billie Jean King, Jacqueline Onassis . . . Elke Sommer, Sarah Miles, the Andrews Sisters and Liv Ullmann. *Time, Jan. 14, 1974, p 27*

[1965, from French *basse* low + *couture* sewing; a facetious usage on the model of *haute couture*, probably coined in English]

batch-process, *v.t., v.i.* to process as a single unit or batch in automatic data processing.

Imperial College, London, has about 150 schools using its IBM 7090 computer, with punched cards as the input method. A simple type of punch is used to code the cards, and the cards are batch-processed as part of the normal work of the college's Centre for Computing and Automation. *Kenneth Owen, "Strange Tale of the Automaton Chessplayer," The Times (London), March 17, 1972, p 19*

[1972, back formation from *batch processing* (1966)]

batch processor: Because the central computer is used as a batch processor, the limitations, costs, and complications of time sharing are avoided. *M. V. Mathews, Science, July 5, 1968, p 26*

bath, *n.* **take a bath,** *U.S. Slang.* to take a loss; suffer a reversal.

"The people who put up the money for the festival are going to take a big bath. . . . But your welfare is a hell of a lot more important, and the music, than a dollar." *Penelope Gilliatt, The New Yorker, April 11, 1970, p 161*

In a lifetime of betting, Martin has made his share of mistakes. "In the 1970 World Series," he concedes, "I picked Cincinnati as six to five favorites over Baltimore. We took a bath on that." *"The Betting Bowl," Time, Jan. 14, 1974, p 36*

[1970]

baton-charge, *v.t., v.i. British.* to attack with drawn truncheon.

The children of Trafalgar were standing on the playground watching tear gas being fired in the city below. A police car stopped in the road outside and a policeman jumped out and baton-charged a boy of nine or ten. *Two Schoolteachers, Cape Town, South Africa, "The Riots in South Africa," in a Letter to the Editor, The Manchester Guardian Weekly, Nov. 14, 1976, p 2*

The police and troops baton-charged, and running battles with the demonstrators took place over a wide area. *"60 Injured in Riot Outside Irish Prison," The Times (London), April 4, 1977, p 1*

[1976, verb use of *baton charge* (1890's)]

ba·tra·cho·tox·in (bəˌtrei kə'tɑk sən), *n.* a very toxic substance extracted from the skin secretion of a species of frog common in Colombia, used in toxicology and medical research.

Studies of tetrodotoxin stimulated the use of various other chemicals as tools. They include tetraethylammonium, DDT, batrachotoxin, scorpion venoms, and saxitoxin. *Toshio Narahashi, "Biopotentials and Electrophysiology," McGraw-Hill Yearbook of Science and Technology 1971, p 130*

[1965, from Greek *bátrachos* frog + English *toxin*]

Bau·dot code (bɔ:'dou), a code for transmitting data in which five or six bits (binary digits) of equal length represent one character.

Even a four-letter word could take up a million bits in a high-resolution photograph. At the other extreme a simple, nonredundant, two-level Baudot code can be used to represent the same four-letter word in only 24 bits. *Myron Tribus and Edward C. McIrvine, "Energy and Information," Scientific American, Sept. 1971, p 186*

[1970, originally a telegraph and teletype code for transmitting data along five-channel lines, named after J. M. E. *Baudot*, 1845-1903, a French inventor]

Bayes·i·an ('bei zi: ən), *adj.* of or relating to a method of calculating probabilities from individual samples with known characteristics rather than from frequency-distribution data and other empirical evidence.

Each day, the central computer uses Bayesian statistics to do a forward projection and calculates the probability that each of the input numbers is not merely a random fluctuation but stands for a change in slope or a step function. *New Scientist, Feb. 15, 1973, p 363*

—*n.* a follower or adherent of Bayesian statistics.

The basic rift between Bayesians and non-Bayesians, which goes right to the bottom of the discussion on scientific truth and statistical method, is not given the importance it deserves, and Ramsey's work is nowhere mentioned. *A. W. F. Edwards, "Book Review: Probability in Science," Review of "Scientific Truth and Statistical Method" by Marcello Boldrini, Nature, Aug. 18, 1972, p 417*

[1965, from Thomas *Bayes*, 1702-1761, an English mathematician, who devised a famous theorem (known as *Bayes' theorem* or *principle*) which introduced the concept of inverse probability, i.e. probability derived from a given sample by inductive reasoning]

Bav·is·ter's medium ('bæv ə stərz), a culture medium in which egg cells undergo fertilization in the laboratory.

The oöcytes would be ready for fertilization three or four hours after aspiration. The eggs were placed in Bavister's medium, and sperm were added to reach a concentration of from one to two million per milliliter. *R. G. Edwards and Ruth E. Fowler, Scientific American, Dec. 1970, p 51*

[1970, named after B. D. *Bavister*, a British biologist, who devised it in 1970 at the University of Cambridge] See EXTERNAL FERTILIZATION.

ba·zaa·ri (bə'zɑː riː), *n.* an Iranian merchant or shop owner.

He went on, "The merchants of the bazaars worked hand and glove with the mullahs. They were the two most conservative elements in the cities. The bazaaris usually rented land from the religious foundations and made the foundations big gifts. But both the bazaaris and the foundations have been outmoded by recent developments." *Joseph Kraft, "Letter from Iran," The New Yorker, Dec. 18, 1978, p 142*

[1978, from Persian *bāzārī*, from *bāzār* market, bazaar]

▶ This term became current during the revolution of 1978-79, in which the bazaaris played a major role by uniting with the mullahs or religious leaders against the Shah. See AYATOLLAH.

BCD, abbreviation of *binary coded decimal,* a system used in automatic data processing to represent digits of a decimal number by binary numerals.

Covvey has also developed a binary coded decimal (BCD) to binary converter to make counts of blood flow after a radioactive substance has been injected into the blood. *Science Journal, June 1970, p 21*

[1965]

B cell or **B-cell,** *n.* a lymph cell that secretes antibodies against most infectious bacteria.

These proliferate so as to manufacture antibodies, circulating substances capable of recognizing and neutralizing— or at least attaching themselves to—the particular antigen and that antigen only. Thereafter, B cells with a memory will remain on the alert throughout the life of the organism, ready to start proliferating immediately if the same antigen appears again. *Lucien Israel, Conquering Cancer, 1978, p 19*

[1970, originally from *B*(ursa of Fabricius), an organ of chickens in which the cell was discovered + *cell;* later, when applied to mammals, from *b*one-derived + *cell*] Also called B LYMPHOCYTE. Compare T CELL.

B chromosome, an extra chromosome that appears in some members of a species.

B chromosomes occur in many species of animals and plants. They are heterochromatic, do not pair with A chromosomes, and have no simple Mendelian effects upon the phenotype. They have been observed, however, to have very sharp clinal distributions which suggests a greater tolerance of B chromosomes under more favourable environmental conditions. *John Bishop, "B Chromosomes In Grasshoppers," Nature, Jan. 22, 1976, p 174*

[1976] Compare A CHROMOSOME.

beachball, *n.* a compact sealed sphere designed to enclose an astronaut during an emergency transfer from an orbiting spacecraft to a rescue vehicle.

The beachballs are nothing if not cramped. The user must step through the zippered opening, tuck into a near-fetal position and close himself into a sphere only 34 inches in diameter, broken only by a single, tiny, plastic porthole. Someone outside the beachball plugs the sealed container into the shuttle's oxygen supply while transfer preparations are being completed. *"Beachballs to the Space-Shuttle Rescue," Science News, May 22, 1976, p 327*

[1976] Also called PERSONAL RESCUE ENCLOSURE.

beam weapon, a weapon that fires particle beams or laser beams, especially against nuclear missiles.

The first [question] is whether it is possible to develop a beam weapon powerful and accurate enough to neutralize fleets of attacking missiles on land or at sea. The second and more urgent question is whether the Russians are already close to achieving such a weapon. *Malcolm W. Browne, "Weapon That Fights Missiles Could Alter World Defense Focus," The New York Times, Dec. 4, 1978, p D11*

[1977] Compare ENHANCED RADIATION WEAPON. Also called DIRECTED-ENERGY WEAPON.

beam weaponry: The whole intention of beam weaponry would be to destroy or disrupt the electronics and guidance systems of incoming missiles, triggering self-destruction before they arrived anywhere near their original target area. *The Manchester Guardian Weekly, May 8, 1977, p 6*

beanbag chair or **beanbag,** *n.* a chair filled with pellets that takes on the shape of the person sitting on it.

To get more height, the Detrichs used all low furniture—beanbag chairs in the living room and a legless sofa in the den. *"New Designs for Living," Newsweek, Jan. 22, 1973, p 77*

Trevor Baxter's gay Bishop, reclining on a beanbag while oozing appreciation of Simon and Garfunkel, and executing a sumptuous return to episcopal protocol, is as hilarious as ever. *The Times (London), July 25, 1977, p 9*

[1972, from its supposed resemblance to the small bag of dried beans used for throwing in children's games]

beatout, *n. Baseball.* a play in which a batter makes a base hit by outrunning the throw of an infielder to first base.

Yankees finished road segment of schedule by drawing 1,427,000, that's largest in 10 years . . . Bladt's second-inning beatout in opener ended zip for 12 at plate for him. *Red Foley, "Tribe (3-2), Yankees (11-5) Split; Margin Still 3 1/2," New York Daily News, Sept. 22, 1975, p 53*

[1975, from the verb phrase *beat out*]

beautiful, *adj.* fashionable; elegant.

At a Washington party the other night, a party jam-packed with beautiful men and interesting women, I learned that the I.R.S. is planning to issue, more or less immediately, revised Form 1040s for 1976. *"The Talk of the Town: Notes and Comment," The New Yorker, Jan. 19, 1976, p 21*

[1973, abstracted from *beautiful people*]

—*interj.* Used as a general term of admiration or approval.

The control room is full of young women in blue jeans, and the steady flow of conversation includes many (sometimes too many) explosions of "Wow! Beautiful! Far out!" and "Too much!" *Thelma Dickman, "Women: Liberated Radio: No Chicks, Broads or Girls Allowed," Maclean's, April 1974, p 16*

But one day, without warning, it worked. I had the Secret

of the Saw, and like all good secrets it was simple: don't fight it; let the saw follow itself down the pencil line. Beautiful. *Jack McClintok, "The Pleasures of Construction," Harper's, Aug. 1974, p 38*

[1966] ► Although *beautiful* has been applied for centuries in informal usage to anything that one likes or admires ("a beautiful argument," "a beautiful incision"), during the late 1960's it became very common as a replacement of a variety of adjectives such as "simple," "easy," "nice," "friendly," "charming," and the like. For example in the phrase *Beautiful People* it has the meaning "fashionable" and in such catch phrases as *black is beautiful, small is beautiful* it means "of high quality or worth." Its use as an exclamation or interjection parallels the use of "wonderful," "great," and other words of approval to express a pleasurable emotion rather than to describe something that gives pleasure.

beau·til·i·ty (byu:'til ə ti:), *n.* the combined qualities of beauty and utility.

The best new word that fills a gap in the language was minted by architectural writer Ada Louise Huxtable to describe a happy marriage of form and function: "beautility." *William Safire, "Webster's Birthday," The New York Times, Oct. 15, 1973, p 37*

. . . a survey of what Lewis Carroll called portmanteaus—words created by a kind of linguistic dialectic from two other words, like the now accepted *beautility. Bernard Levin, "Literally, the Writing on the Wall," The Times (London), April 20, 1977, p 16*

Indeed what better word expresses Alessi's striking talent for combining function with beauty than "Beautility." *Advertisement by Alessi Fratelli, The New Yorker, Nov. 27, 1978, p 137*

[1973, blend of *beauty* and *utility*]

beauty, *n. Nuclear Physics.* the property of a type of quark called BOTTOM QUARK.

Now that there is an upsilon-prime (and there may yet be other members of the family) studies of the spectroscopy of beauty may begin. The difference in mass between the upsilon and the upsilon-prime gives some information about the force between beauty and antibeauty; a more numerous group would help even more. *Science News, Sept. 16, 1978, p 196*

[1977, named on the model of CHARM]

bec·lo·meth·a·sone (ˌbek lou'meθ ə soun), *n.* a steroid compound used as an inhalant in the treatment of asthma. *Formula:* $C_{28}H_{37}ClO_7$.

Beclomethasone, a cortisonelike compound marketed in England in 1972, was immediately recognized as a significant advance in the treatment of asthma, for it can be delivered directly to the lungs, thereby eliminating the deleterious side effects . . . that occurred when cortisone was swallowed in tablet form and distributed throughout the body. In 1976, four years after Beclomethasone was introduced in England, it was approved by the United States. *Richard Spark, The New York Times Magazine, March 20, 1977, p 70*

[1972, short for the pharmaceutical name *beclomethasone dipropionate*]

bec·que·rel (ˌbek ə'rel or ˌbek'rel), *n.* the international unit of radioactivity, equal to one disintegration per second. It is intended to replace the *curie*.

Among the SI's [Système International] derived units with special names are those for . . . radioactivity (the becquerel, or spontaneous nuclear transitions per second) and absorbed dose of radiation (the gray, or joules per kilogram). *"Science and the Citizen," Scientific American, March 1976, p 60A*

[1976, named for Antoine H. *Becquerel*, 1852-1908, French physicist]

bed of nails, *British.* an extremely difficult or uncomfortable position or situation.

He sets a lot of store by his new organization, already backed by a "task force" of 11 civil servants – shortly to be supplemented by an advisory council of people from all walks of life involved in the North Sea oil discoveries in Scotland. . . . I asked him whether he thought he had been given a bed of nails in his job. He said: "No. It appeals to me as a challenge." *The Times (London), June 8, 1973, p 18*

But the famous Government-union compact might just emerge from the economic furnace on one condition: that the Chancellor can find a way of producing a socially just Budget. Mr. Healey had drawn the real bed of nails this time. *The Manchester Guardian Weekly, March 9, 1974, p 12*

[1966, originally used by Ray Gunter, born 1909, British government official, in describing the Ministry of Labour soon after he became its head in the Labour government of Harold Wilson; patterned on *bed of roses* (OED 1806, from the nail-studded bed fakirs lie on]

bed·so·ni·a (bed'sou ni: ə), *n., pl.* **-ni·as, -ni·ae** (-ni:-i:). an intracellular parasitic microorganism that causes trachoma and various other diseases.

Certainly the resemblance that the smaller elements of mycoplasmas and bedsonias bear to true viruses is close enough for them to have been confused on many occasions. *Kenneth Bisset, New Scientist, Feb. 8, 1973, p 298*

[1964, New Latin, from Samuel Phillips *Bedson*, 1886-1969, a British virologist]

Beeb (bi:b), *n. British.* a nickname for the British Broadcasting Corporation.

The Beeb is to be congratulated on this new venture, and for making available through the SBC [School Broadcasting Council] at this early stage films and tapes of some of the programmes for groups of teachers to inspect. *Richard Fifield, "Media: BBC to Launch New Science Education Series," New Scientist, Feb. 6, 1975, p 338*

[1971, from the pronunciation of *BB* in *BBC*, abbreviation of British Broadcasting Corporation] Compare AUNTIE.

bee·die or **bee·di** ('bi: di:), *n.* (in India) a small cigarette rolled by hand and tied with thread.

Beedi rollers usually work at home for one of a few large employers. But in this village, the rollers began to sell their *beedies* at nearby markets. By holding out against the landlords, these peasants had become a major talking point in other villages. The *beedies* were marketed partly as a form of public support for the struggle. *Joseph Hanlon, "India: back to the villages: What prospects for appropriate technology?," New Scientist, June 9, 1977, p 594*

[1974, from Hindi]

beef·a·lo ('bi: fə,lou), *n.* any of a breed of beef cattle

developed in the United States by crossbreeding domestic cattle and buffaloes.

This, uh, beefalo, a cow-and-buffalo hybrid, shuffled into a Manhattan parking lot, where its California developer proclaimed the beige beauty's virtue: protein-rich meat, low feeding cost (it grazes), high fertility rate, fast maturation. *Picture legend, "Agriculture," 1976 Collier's Encyclopedia Year Book (1975), p 111*

[1974, blend of *beef* (cattle) and *buffalo*] Compare YAKOW.

▶ This hybrid, developed by D. C. Basolo, a rancher in Tracy, California, represents the second successful attempt to cross the buffalo with domestic beef cattle. The first was the *cattalo* (from *cat*tle + buff*alo*) developed in the 1880's by a Texas rancher, Colonel Charles Goodnight. In 1958, researchers of the Canadian Department of Agriculture produced an experimental cross-breed which they also named *cattalo*. The beefalo, according to its breeder, is three-eighths buffalo, three-eighths Charolais cow, and one-quarter Hereford.

bee·fish ('bi: ,fiʃ), *n.* a mixture of ground beef and minced fish, used for making hamburgers, etc.

Beefish is just one product involving minced fish that is starting on the long path to the market. Researchers in the Fishery Service's Pacific Fishery Products Technology Center in Seattle not only have made a preliminary effort to incorporate the product into hot dogs, but have also managed to lose its fish taste . . . *New Scientist, March 21, 1974, p 763*

[1974, blend of *beef* and *fish*]

beef Wellington, a roasted filet of beef covered with pâté de foie gras and baked in a pastry crust.

Writing, for example, of the beef Wellington served in a restaurant he is surveying, Mr. Britchky pauses to observe that "filet mignon, wrapped in pâté and pastry, and served in a brown sauce flavored with a deglazing of beef" is "really a silly dish." *"On and Off the Avenue: Wise Men Bearing Gifts," The New Yorker, Dec. 16, 1972, p 105*

[1965, probably named for the Duke of *Wellington*]

bee's knees, *U. S.* a cocktail made with lemon juice and gin and sweetened with honey. See the quotation for the etymology.

The definite comment on the subject seems to have come from a cerebral and resourceful acquaintance, also from Washington, D.C., who notes that, "Besides being the name of a cocktail invented at the Savoy Hotel in London, 'the bee's knees' was a slang expression of the 20's meaning something like 'super' or 'smashing'. According to H. L. Mencken's 'The American Language,' the expression was coined by Tad Dorgan, the cartoonist, who also originated 'the cat's pajamas,' 'the snake's hips' and similar absurd superlatives." *Craig Claiborne, "On the Techniques for Roasting Beef, Readers Still Remember Old Recipe," The New York Times, March 10, 1975, p 33*

[1975]

behavioralism, *n.* the principles and methods of sociology, psychology, anthropology, and other social sciences that study human behavior.

Anglo-American political scientists have been anxious to become, so to speak, the natural scientists of the political; they have learnt from writers such as R. K. Merton and T. S. Kuhn that the natural sciences progress under the domination of paradigms, beliefs held by the scientific community about what it is they are, at bottom, investigating, and how it is to be uncovered. But "behavioralism" was never within striking distance of being such a paradigm, for, while a paradigm does dictate to a considerable extent the methodology we can intelligibly adopt, the converse does not hold. *Review of "Power and Community" by Philip Green and Sanford Levinson, The Times Literary Supplement, Feb. 4, 1972, p 115*

[1963, from *behavioral* (science) + *-ism*] ► *Behavioralism* should not be confused with *behaviorism*, which is psychological study by investigation and analysis of objective acts of behavior.

behavioralist, *n., adj.:* The old guard are, for example, variously described as institutional, descriptive, historical, philosophical, empirical, theoretical; the Essex school as behavioralist and post-behavioralist, statistical, quantitative, analytical, theoretical . . . *PHS, The Times (London), April 14, 1970, p 12*

behavior mod, short for BEHAVIOR MODIFICATION.

The heart of behavior mod lies in correct use of positive reinforcement, simply because this most closely approximates normal human behavior. *Henry L. Govert, in a Letter to the Editor, Time, April 1, 1974, p 5*

BT is often equated with behavior modification—"Behavior Mod"—and criticized as a tool for behavior control. *Spencer A. Rathus and Jeffrey S. Nevid, "BT: Behavior Therapy," 1977, p 301*

[1974]

behavior modification, the modification of habits and patterns of behavior by psychological methods such as reinforcement therapy (the use of rewards to reinforce normal responses), aversion therapy (inducing an aversion to harmful habits), the use of teaching machines to facilitate learning, and the like. *Often used attributively.*

Behavior modification is now widely employed in mental hospitals, and during 1969-70 it was extended to use with brain-damaged children, in whom it was found to reduce inattentiveness and restlessness. Unlike Freudian psychoanalysis, which probes into the life history of the individual and requires hundreds of hours of patient-therapist interaction, behavior modification seeks to change responses and symptoms at the time they occur. *Austin E. Grigg, "Psychology," The Americana Annual 1971, p 562*

[He] feels the behavior-modification process is misunderstood by the public. "They see salivating dogs, shocks, clockwork oranges. They misunderstand the process." *Sharland Trotter and Jim Warren, "The Carrot, the Stick and the Prisoner," Science News, March 16, 1974, p 181*

[1971] See SKINNERISM.

behavior modifier: Leading behavior modifiers may be surprised to find Gesell [Institute] people with at least one foot in their camp. *Louise Bates Ames, with Joan Ames Chase, "How to Improve Your Child's Behavior," Family Circle, June 1972, p 2*

Be·liz·e·an or **Be·liz·i·an** (bi'li: zi: ən), *adj.* of or relating to Belize (since 1973 the official name of the Central American country formerly known as British Honduras).

The Mexicans have made it clear that they . . . support Belizean independence. *The Times (London), Nov. 1, 1978, p 6*

The Belizian problem will not go away. Guatemala will continue with its threats. Britain may soon be forced to end its defense treaty without solving the problem. Understandably, the Belizians do not want to fall under the authoritarian right-wing Guatemalan rule. *Maclean's, August 22, 1977, p 38*

—*n.* a native or inhabitant of Belize.

The Belizeans, a proud and friendly race of English-speaking creoles, want the British out too, but they want the military protection only Britain can give. *Simon Winchester, the Manchester Guardian Weekly, Oct. 12, 1974, p 9*

[1973, from *Belize*, name of the capital of British Honduras until 1970, from Maya *beliz* muddy water, in reference to the river of that name, supposed to be muddy in the rainy season]

bell lap, the final lap of a race, signaled by the sounding of a bell.

As the race got under way, [Dave] Wottle ran dead last for 500 meters, but was finally inspired by the sight of the favorite, Russia's Yevgeny Arzhanov, beginning his furious kick on the bell lap. *"Sport: Dampening the Olympic Torch," Time, Sept. 18, 1972, p 58*

[1972, originally (about 1960) used in bicycle races]

belly up, *Slang, chiefly figurative.* **1** to fall down flat; collapse; drop dead.

The feed-lot operators are moaning too, because a consumer rebellion against beef and soaring costs of fattening cattle threaten to trim their profits to the bone. Says an official of the Colorado Cattlemen's Association: "A lot of boys are going to belly up." *"Price Squeeze on the Feed-Lots," Time, March 18, 1974, p 78*

2 flattened out; collapsed; dead (often in the phrase *go belly up*).

As the oxygen in the service module was what the astronauts were breathing, it had already crossed Liebergot's mind that the astronauts could be what he called "belly up" in a matter of hours. *Henry S. F. Cooper, Jr., "Annals of Exploration: An Accident in Space—I," The New Yorker, Nov. 11, 1972, p 62*

If New York can go belly-up, why not any city in the nation? *Hobart Rowen, "Risky Road To A New York City Default," The Manchester Guardian Weekly (The Washington Post section), Oct. 11, 1975, p 17*

[1968]

bench scientist, a scientist who works in a laboratory; research scientist.

. . . there is no longer any talk of 'wasting your education' or 'prostituting your science' if you prefer not to be a bench scientist. *A. W. Selwyn, Science Journal, Feb. 1970, p 73*

"Bench scientist" is the term used by higher echelon administrators in USDA [U.S. Dept. of Agriculture] to refer to active scientists—by whom the term is generally much resented. *Footnote, Nicholas Wade, "Robert W. Long: The Banker Who Heads Agricultural Research," Science, Jan. 17, 1975, p 150*

[1970]

benign neglect, the deliberate disregard of a bad situation presumably in order to avoid tensions or provocations that might make the situation worse.

1976, for racial and other minorities, and women, was a year during which their needs were on the back burner of benign neglect. Affirmative action programs were at best slowing down the process of hiring those who had previously been favored. *Martin Gruberg, "Civil Liberties and Civil Rights," The Americana Annual, 1977, p 167*

The United States government continued its policy of "benign neglect" towards Latin America throughout the year, even abandoning the efforts made earlier to seek a new treaty governing the future of the Panama Canal Zone. *Richard Gott, The Manchester Guardian Weekly, Jan. 2, 1977, p 13*

[1971] ► The usage arose in 1970 from a memorandum sent by Daniel Patrick Moynihan, then serving as a Presidential counselor, suggesting that "the issue of race could benefit from a period of 'benign neglect'." Although Moynihan's stated intention in the memo had been to emphasize the progress made on the racial front ("We may need a period in which Negro progress continues and racial rhetoric fades"), the memo was widely attacked and the provocative phrase "benign neglect" taken up as an anti-Administration slogan.

According to *Time* (March 16, 1970, p 26), the phrase was "first used in 1839 by the Earl of Durham, Governor General of Canada; in a report to Parliament he praised the Whiggish policy of "benign neglect" toward Canada, which had helped, he said, move that country toward self-government."

During the 1970's, *benign neglect* has been frequently used in contexts free from any allusion to its political origin, as the following quotations illustrate:

Black composers and women composers share a heritage of musical subjugation—of malign as well as benign neglect. *Paul Elliott, New York, "Music Mailbag," The New York Times, June 27, 1971, p 31*

How we do, and at the same time, do not, think about our children's books, is best reflected by that infuriating form of benign neglect, the roundup review. *John Goldthwaite, "Notes on the Children's Book Trade," Harper's, Jan. 1977, p 85*

Be·nin·ese (bə ni:'ni:z), *n.* a native or inhabitant of Benin (country in western Africa called, until 1975, Dahomey).

The most recent in a series of decrees restricting foreign input to Benin came from the Ministry of Information and National Orientation. Henceforth, all Beninese are prohibited from visiting foreign embassies in Cotonou without written Ministry permission. *Karen Deyoung, "Blight of Benin," The Manchester Guardian Weekly, April 4, 1976, p 17*

[1976]

Ben·i·off zone ('ben i: af), a region beneath the earth's surface associated with volcanic activity, deep earthquakes, and tectonic plate margins.

Inclined earthquake zones, called Benioff zones, underlie active volcanic chains and have a variety of complex shapes. *John F. Dewey, "Plate Tectonics," Scientific American, May 1972, p 51*

[1968, named after (Victor) Hugo *Benioff*, born 1899, an American seismologist]

Ben·late ('ben ˌleit), *n.* trademark for BENOMYL.

The fungicide used is a solution of Benlate in lactic acid which is injected through holes half an inch in diameter in the trunk near ground level; the best dose appears to be about 15 grams to the foot circumference. *"Trials show fungicide can check Dutch elm disease," The Times (London), Nov. 20, 1972, p 5*

[1969]

Benn·er·y ('ben ər i:) or **Benn·ism** ('ben iz əm), *n. British.* the policy of extending state ownership and intervention in private industry.

In practice, "Bennery" might be taken to imply a commitment to nationalization and state intervention, plus worker participation in management, or outright worker control that went further than the government's declared program. *Harford Thomas, Britannica Book of the Year 1975, p 112*

Three desperate problems beset Labour when this year began. The problem of Europe and splitting in two; the problem of an incomes policy, and splitting in two; the problem of Bennism, petrified industry, rampant trades unionism, and splitting in two. *"Comment: Harold Wilson —the Best Prime Minister We've Got?" The Manchester Guardian Weekly, Jan. 4, 1976, p 6*

[1975, from Anthony Neil Wedgwood *Benn*, born 1925, Britain's secretary of state for industry in 1974 + *-ery* or *-ism*, noun suffixes]

ben·o·myl ('ben əˌmil), *n.* a fungicide used to control diseases of flowers, fruits, vegetables, and lawn grass. It is related to thiobendazole. *Formula:* $C_{14}H_{18}N_4O_3$

Hope of curing elm trees infected with Dutch elm disease fungus (DED) was raised by two developments: a pressure technique for injecting mature trees with liquids containing chemicals and a water-soluble form of the fungicide benomyl that inhibits the disease without damaging the tree. *Marcella M. Memolo, "Agriculture," 1974 Britannica Yearbook of Science and the Future (1973), p 160*

[1970, from *benzomethyl*, part of the chemical name]

Ben·tley compound ('ben tli:), one of a group of chemicals with extremely potent narcotic effects, used especially to incapacitate wild animals.

. . . drugs known as the Bentley compounds which, although difficult to isolate, are ten thousand times as powerful as heroin. Some Government scientists, fearing that the Bentley compounds would replace heroin, suggested growing the *bracteatum* on Air Force bases surrounded by barbed wire and guard dogs. *Ed Epstein, The Sunday Times Magazine (London), March 9, 1975, p 17*

[1966, named for K. W. *Bentley*, a British chemist who synthesized the compounds in the early 1960's]

ben·zo·di·az·e·pine (ˌben zou dai 'æz əˌpi:n), *n.* the chemical substance that is the source of various widely used tranquilizing drugs such as Valium (diazepam) and Librium (chlordiazepoxide).

When researchers demonstrated binding of opium drugs to specific sites on brain cell membranes, the race was on to discover natural substances that would also bind and suppress pain. Enkephalins and endorphins were soon identified. Now Danish biochemists Richard F. Squires and Claus Braestrup report in the April 21 *Nature* specific binding for another important group of drugs. These psychoactive drugs, called benzodiazepines, which include antianxiety medicines and hypnotics, seem to attach to receptors on rat brain cell membranes. *"Coming Next: The Brain's Own Valium," Science News, May 21, 1977, p 332*

[1972, from *benzo-* benzene + *di-* two + *-az-* nitrogen + *ep-*, *epi-* besides + *-ine* (chemical suffix)]

be·rim·bau (bə'rim bɑu), *n.* a stringed musical instrument of Brazil. It usually has one metal string.

Facing each other in the circle are two Brazilians, Purple Shirt No. 5 and Breaker-of-Iron, both rhythmically undulating while a *berimbau* quavers. Suddenly, Purple Shirt drops on his hands and kicks one foot out in the *bencao*, aiming at Breaker's ribs. Breaker fades into a *negativa*, slumping smoothly backward onto one hand and one foot as the blow whistles harmlessly past, then lashes out in the hammer, his foot aimed at Purple Shirt's groin. . . . At about this point, any non-Brazilian begins to wonder what in the world is going on. The answer: *capoeira* . . . a combination of folk dancing and self-defense that has become a national craze. *"Modern Living," Time, May 1, 1972, p 84*

[1967, from Brazilian Portuguese, perhaps from an African language]

Berlin Wall, a barrier preventing communication, especially the free flow of information.

A significant call to demolish the "Berlin walls" that have divided Christians over the centuries was issued by Léon Josef Cardinal Suenens. *Alfred Paul Klausler, "Religion," Britannica Book of the Year 1972, p 600*

This insider considers it conceivable, though unlikely, that Nixon was so isolated by his Berlin Wall of Ehrlichman and Haldeman that he did not know about either the espionage plans or the later concealment. *"Guerrilla Warfare at Credibility Gap," Time, July 2, 1973, p 16*

[1968, from the name of the 26-mile long wall dividing East and West Berlin, built in 1961 by the East Germans]

Bermuda Triangle, an area of the North Atlantic in which disappearances of airplanes and ships have been popularly attributed to mysterious forces.

There have been about half a dozen successful books on the Bermuda Triangle, some of them going high in the best-seller lists. Although they all tell basically the same stories, they advocate different solutions: the missing craft have been carried off by unidentified flying objects (presumably so the extra-terrestrials can check on how well mankind is faring on the long road to civilisation); they have been sucked under the sea by an erratic laser-power source from the lost civilisation of Atlantis; they have encountered a time-space warp and been carried into another dimension. *Graham Massey, "The Case of the Bermuda Triangle," The Listener, Feb. 19, 1976, p 199*

[1975, so called from the triangle formed by the points between Florida, Bermuda, and Puerto Rico comprising this area; popularized in the book *The Bermuda Triangle* (1974), by Charles Berlitz] Also called DEVIL'S TRIANGLE.

Be·rufs·ver·bot (bə'ru:fs vər,bout), *n., pl.* -bo·te (-,bou te). the West German policy of prohibiting anyone suspected of radical political tendencies from employment in the civil service.

Literally a prohibition against engaging in one's profession, *Berufsverbot* is the popular term given to procedures designed to screen out applicants for public-sector jobs if they advocate the destruction of the constitution. It does not differ in intent from the loyalty oath requirements for government employees in many democratic countries. *Harper's, Aug. 1978, p 5*

[1976, from German *Berufs* (genitive of) vocation + *Verbot* prohibition]

best-case, *adj.* designed to include or provide for the most favorable conditions or circumstances possible.

Research with recombinant DNA may provide major new social benefits of uncertain magnitude: more effective and cheaper pharmaceutical products; better understanding of the causes of cancer; more abundant food crops, even new approaches to the energy problem. These and other possible outcomes are envisioned in "best-case scenarios" for the future application of recombinant-DNA technology. *Clifford Grobstein, Scientific American, July 1977, p 22*

[1977, patterned on WORST-CASE]

be·ta-ad·ren·er·gic (,bei tə,æd rə'nər dʒik), *adj.* of or relating to beta receptors; BETA-BLOCKING.

New uses for the beta-adrenergic drug propranolol continue to be reported. The drug is already in established use for preventing certain cardiac arrhythmias, treating hypertension, and slowing the heart rate in hyperthyroidism. *Frank P. Mathews, "Medicine," 1974 Collier's Encyclopedia Year Book (1973), p. 348*

Dr. K. M. Fox and his associates in Hull, England, reported . . . that beta-adrenergic blocking drugs widely used to relieve angina—the pain associated with coronary artery disease—may also reduce the likelihood of a heart attack. *Michael H. Alderman, "Medicine: Internal Medicine," The World Book Science Annual 1976 (1975), p 298*

[1969, from *beta (receptor) + adrenergic* producing or activated by adrenalin (from *adren*aline + Greek *érgon* work + English *-ic*)]

beta-blocking, *adj.* (of a drug) preventing or inhibiting the absorption of adrenalin in heart and blood vessel cells by blocking the cells' beta receptors.

Recent experience with the beta-blocking drug practolol confirms that the surveillance of patients undergoing novel therapy leaves much to be desired. Indeed, the authors of the paper recommending registered release cite beta-blocking agents as one area in which the new scheme should be tried out. *Bernard Dixon, "Comment: Monitoring Medicines," New Scientist, Jan. 13, 1977, p 59*

[1966]

beta-blocker: The doctors said their results "might be related to the type of treatment." A majority of the treated men got a "beta-blocker," a kind of drug known to reduce the incidence of sudden death in heart-attack patients. American doctors have only recently begun to use beta-blockers. That might help explain why studies in the United States have not so far found any significant link between treating hypertension and reduced heart attacks. *The New York Times, Jan. 29, 1978, Sec. 4, p 18*

be·ta-en·dor·phin (,bei tə en'dər fin), *n.* a pain-suppressing hormone produced in the pituitary gland.

The substance is beta-endorphin classed as a hormone, tested by medical researchers as a painkiller and hailed as "the brain's own opiate." Actually it originates in the pituitary gland but seems to exert its effects in the brain. Because camels have a notoriously high tolerance for pain, the University of California's master hormonologist, Choh Hao Li, imported more than 500 camel pituitaries from Iraq and identified and synthesized the active segment—beta-endorphin—of a larger molecule he had identified in 1965. *Time, Jan. 23, 1978, p 98*

beta-lipotropin

[1976, from *beta-* second of a series + ENDORPHIN]
Compare ALPHA-ENDORPHIN.

beta-lipotropin, *n.* a form of the pituitary hormone lipotropin that contains 91 amino acids, sequences of which include various endorphins and enkephalins.

Opiatelike proteins in the brain that relieve pain and that alter various mental states and behaviors have been exciting medical researchers recently. Called enkephalins and endorphins, they all derive from a larger parent protein—beta-lipotropin. *"A New Class of Neurotransmitters?" Science News, July 23, 1977, p 58*

[1976, from *beta-* second in a series + LIPOTROPIN]

beta receptor, a site or structure in a cell at which the stimulus of certain adrenalin-producing agents elicits a usually inhibitory response.

Stimulation of the alpha-receptors produced a stimulation of the associated muscles; the lungs worked harder to get more oxygen or the blood vessels expanded to increase circulation. Stimulation of the beta-receptors had the opposite effect, of slowing down activity. *The Times (London), March 19, 1973, p 3*

[1963] Compare ALPHA RECEPTOR.

bête blanche (‚bet 'blɑ̃ʃ), a slight cause of aversion; minor irritation or nuisance.

No doubt the South African Communist Party, the author's special *bête noire* (or, as he makes it appear, *bête blanche*) has often made an ass of itself, and at no times more egregiously than when dancing to Moscow's tune. *Review of "African Liberation Movements" by Richard Gibson, Times Literary Supplement, May 26, 1972, p 598*

[1967, from French, literally, white beast, patterned on *bête noire*]

BFT, abbreviation of BIOFEEDBACK TRAINING.

Many researchers contributed to the discovery of BFT, and physiologist Dr. Barbara Brown is perhaps foremost among them. While other researchers in the early 1960s were still experimenting with rats and rabbits, Brown explored BFT techniques with human subjects. *Newsweek, Oct. 14, 1974, p 76*

[1971]

Bi·af·ran (bi:'æf rən *or* bai'æf rən), *adj.* of or having to do with Biafra, the eastern region of Nigeria which was an independent republic of the Ibo people between 1967 and 1970.

The crime wave is linked to high unemployment, especially in the East-central State, where thousands of demobilized former Biafran soldiers roam the streets with firearms secured during and after the civil war. *Franklin Parker, "Nigeria: Public Execution," 1972 Collier's Encyclopedia Year Book, p 387*

—*n.* a native or inhabitant of Biafra.

Nevertheless, in spite of these setbacks and strong rumours that their money is running out and food is getting short, surrender by the Biafrans remains unlikely. *William Norris, The Times (London), March 23, 1968, p 5*

[1967; the secessionist region was named after the Bight of *Biafra* (since 1975 called the Bight of Bonny), a part of the Gulf of Guinea]

Bible-thump, *v.i. Slang.* to act like a preacher; evangelize.

The Defenders [a television series] may bible-thump a bit in an all-American way, but . . . never refuses a fence. *Monica Furlong, Punch, June 29, 1966, p 963*

. . . the Bible-thumping gospeller Aimee Semple McPherson. *The Times (London), April 28, 1970, p 12*

[1965, back formation from *Bible-thumper* (1920's)]

bicommunal, *adj.* composed of two national communities.

Under the proposed formula, Cyprus would become a bicommunal and (effectively) federal republic—independent, sovereign, integral and, if so desired, non-aligned—to consist of two constituent regions, inhabited predominantly by Greek Cypriots, the other predominantly by Turkish Cypriots. *The Times (London), Nov. 22, 1978, p 8*

[1977, from *bi-* two + *communal*]

bicycle kick, *Soccer.* a kick made with both feet off the ground and moving the legs as if pedaling a bicycle.

Kidd's bicycle kick just on half-time was a rare challenge for the Bristol goalkeeper. *The Times (London), Feb. 18, 1978, p 6*

[1965]

bicycle-kick, *v.i.:* McGrath nodded it to Gabriel and Gabriel with his back to goal bicycle-kicked over his own blond head. *Malcolm Winton, The Sunday Times (London), Sept. 5, 1971, p 23*

bidialectal, *adj.* using or able to use two dialects of a language.

The public schools continue to vacillate between the old line, "Talk American, boy, American," and the more cosmopolitan line, "Are our er um Black students ahh bilingual or um bidialectal?" *Toni Cade Bambara, Review of "Black English: Its History and Usage in the United States" by J. L. Dillard, The New York Times Book Review, Sept. 3, 1972, p 16*

[1969, from *bi-* two + *dialectal;* patterned on *bilingual*]

bidialectalism, *n.:* The purpose of this study [Bi-Dialectalism: A Policy Analysis] is to examine bidialectalism as an educational policy. The study is in two major sections: the first portion is concerned with the problems inherent in the policy process itself, with those aspects of educational decision-making which combine to make reasonable policy outcomes difficult to achieve; the second section reviews in detail the development of bidialectal language arts policies, studying not so much their success or failure as their value content. *Newsletter of the American Dialect Society, Vol. 6, No. 3, Nov. 1974, p 35*

bidialectalist, *n.:* Since there are clearly millions and millions of Americans, both children and adults, who will live and die as nonstandard speakers, the bidialectalists are in fact assuming the permanent existence of a social system which rewards and punishes, not according to merit (no dialect is better than another—remember?), but according to the observance or nonobservance of the superficialities of linguistic decorum. *James Sledd, "Bidialectalism: A New Book and Some Old Issues," American Speech, Fall-Winter 1973, vol. 48 (1976)*

bifunctional, *adj.* having two distinct functions.

The two hormones share the same bifunctional physiological action in that they both promote bodily growth and stimulate mammary development and milk secretion, as well as have similar immunological responses. *William J.*

Bailey, *"Chemistry: Structural Chemistry," 1973 Britannica Yearbook of Science and the Future (1972), p 214*

[1968, from *bi-* two + *functional*]

big, *adj.* **be big on,** *Slang.* to be enthusiastic about; be a great fan or admirer of.

"I'm very big on [Goldwater]," the New Nelse [Nelson Rockefeller] has been saying. "We have been good friends over the years—with a few unfortunate hiatuses." *National Review, May 23, 1975, p 544*

She said, "I have just been to Macy's. I have been going to Macy's every day for the last two weeks. I am very big on Macy's." *The New Yorker, May 16, 1977, p 36*

[1968]

Big Apple, 1 a nickname for New York City.

All of them are well aware of the negative aspects of life in New York. They are familiar with the pits in the Big Apple. *Women's Wear Daily, March 23, 1973, p 21*

Her first trip to the Big Apple culminated in an eventful romance . . . Now she's back in New York to stay. *"The Happy Life of Margaux Hemingway," Town and Country, March 1975, p 41*

2 big apple, the most important part; focus; chief concern.

When you are this way you do not care much how a woman works, sex being peripheral to your life, and you think that your own heavings and gruntings are sufficient unto themselves. They are not, but when the big apple in your life is yourself you never get to know it. *John Corry, Harper's, July 1970, p 65*

[1970] ▶ **Big Apple** replaced in the 1970s the earlier nickname for New York City, *Fun City*, much used during the 1960's. The term *Big Apple* was originally used by U.S. jazzmen in the 1930's to refer to any big city, especially a big northern city. Around 1937 the *Big Apple* became the name of a popular jazz dance. The derivation of the term is uncertain. The possible origin is suggested in *Dan Burley's Original Handbook of Harlem Jive* (1944), which defines *apple* as "the earth, the universe, this planet. Any place that's large."

big C, *Informal,* cancer.

Critics of the US government's efforts to combat cancer have castigated its failure to spend more money on investigating possible links between diet and the "big C". *New Scientist, Oct. 19, 1978, p 156*

John Wayne . . . whose cancerous left lung was removed in 1964, accepted the news with true grit. "I've licked the Big C before," he said. *Time, Jan. 29, 1979, p 69*

[1977]

big dress, a wide, loose, flowing dress, made in the style of the Big Look.

One "big dress," for example, was adored for its color (which was copper and looked good with her red hair), but rejected for its voluminousness, which she [Julie Harris] found overwhelmed her small frame. *Mary Ann Crenshaw, "Fashion: Untheatrical," The New York Times Magazine, March 30, 1975, p 56*

[1975] Also called DROOP.

bi·gem·o·ny ('bɑi'dʒem ə ni:), *n.* predominant influence or authority of two nations over the others in a group.

Bigemony . . . generally refers to the condominium exercised by the two superpowers, but inside the Nato camp, too, there are signs of a bigemony of sorts emerging, based on a Bonn-Washington axis. *David Rudnick, "Why Nato Must Not Allow the Germans to Dominate," The Times (London), Dec. 14, 1976, p 14*

This new "bigemony" was not to be with decrepit Britain, but with reborn West Germany. *The New York Times, May 21, 1978, Sec. 4, p 21*

[1976, from *bi-* two + he*gemony*] Compare HEGEMONY.

big enchilada, *U.S. Slang.* a very important or influential person; bigwig.

The evening began with Missouri Congressman James Symington quipping, "We have been brought together by the big enchilada of the Democratic Party [W. Averell Harriman]." *"People," Time, May 27, 1974, p 52*

Finally, there were so many complaints that the California Department of Motor Vehicles was given real teeth by the Legislature to crack down on the hucksters. As a result, most of the big enchiladas of the used-car business in those days ended up broke. *Bill Davidson, "King of the Iron Merchants," The New York Times Magazine, March 2, 1975, p 34*

[1974] See ENCHILADA.

▶ This phrase became popular during the Watergate affair when the White House tapes revealed a reference by H. R. Haldeman to the then Attorney General John Mitchell as "the big enchilada."

Bigfoot, *n.* another name for SASQUATCH.

A recent book had listed 800 sightings of Bigfoot, . . . the bear/ape/man whose existence has been persisted in by Californians for a century at least. *New Scientist, Jan. 3, 1974, p 26*

[1972]

Big Look or **big look,** a fashion in women's clothes introduced in 1974, characterized by loose, broad, voluminous designs.

The Big Look differed from the midi in that it brought the fabric flowing in immense yardages about the body. It meant very little inner construction, very few seams. Linings, interfacings, and even turned-under hems were practically eliminated. As a result, the clothes could be piled on top of each other in layers without making the wearer look enormous. *Kathryn Z. Livingston, "Fashion," The 1975 World Book Year Book, p 328*

The big look, properly proportioned, can work on a small woman. *Picture legend, "Fashion: Untheatrical," The New York Times Magazine, March 30, 1975, p 57*

[1974] Compare LAYERED LOOK.

Big Mac (mæk), a nickname for MAC (the *Municipal Assistance Corporation*, created in 1975 to alleviate New York City's fiscal crisis).

Empowered to borrow up to $3 billion on behalf of the city, and backed by its sales and stock-transfer taxes, "Big Mac," a variant on the moral-commitment authority, was depicted as a temporary "bridge" to provide funds to the city until it straightened out its books and could return to the market on its own. *M. J. Rossant, "How Rockefeller Destroyed New York," Harper's, Jan. 1976, p 70*

[1975, from the name of a popular hamburger sold by the *McDonald's* chain of fast-food stores]

bik·ie ('bɑi ki:), *n. Especially Australian Slang.* a motorcyclist, especially one belonging to a motorcycle gang; biker.

More than 30 "bikies" were taken into custody last night four miles south of Feilding after police swooped on an old farmhouse. *"Police Hold 30 Bikies After Swoop," The Auckland Star (New Zealand), April 21, 1973, p 2*

[1970, from *bike* motorcycle + *-ie* diminutive suffix]

bilayer, *n.* a biological structure consisting of two layers each of the thickness of one molecule.

The phospholipid bilayer, now confirmed as the basic molecular arrangement in membranes, may also be the structural basis of the low density lipoproteins in human blood serum. *"Biological Chemistry: Bilayers in Blood Serum," Nature, Nov. 3, 1972, p 10*

[1968, from *bi-* two + *layer*; patterned on *monolayer* (1933)]

bilevel, *adj.* having two levels.

Inside the deceptively simple brick house, with a stunning bilevel addition done in exposed rough beams with vaulted ceiling, Gini Johnson is preparing wild rice and peas and loins of pork and beef. *Paul Wilkes, The Atlantic, Dec. 1970, p 90*

— *n.* a structure or vehicle with two levels, especially a house with a bilevel ground floor.

Part of a sample spiel: "Look at what the Lions from Leo [a local real estate company] have this week! This lovely Georgian bi-level on a sprawling treed lot! The price for all this? Much less than you think! Call the Lions from Leo!" *"An Hour Commercial?", Time, Dec. 4, 1972, p 45*

[1970, from *bi-* two + *level*]

binary weapon or **binary nerve gas,** also shortened to **binary,** a nerve gas consisting of two comparatively nontoxic chemicals that become lethal when mixed in a projectile fired at a target.

The US's current obsession with chemical weapons produced by reacting two agents (binary weapons) is based largely upon environmental considerations. The final product agents in a binary reaction are not necessarily more toxic than VX—indeed some are less. If and when such chemical munitions are developed and deployed, many are likely to be binary VX. *New Scientist, Oct. 12, 1978, p 101*

[1974]

bind·in ('bɑin din), *n.* a protein in the sperm cells of sea urchins that binds to receptor sites of eggs.

In the sequence of events that make up fertilization, bindin may do more than glue sperm to eggs. It may also signal the sperm and egg membranes to merge so that genetic material can pass from the sperm into the egg. "Bindin is at the proper place at the proper time." *Science News, Nov. 26, 1977, p 356*

[1977, from *bind, v.* + *-in* (chemical suffix)]

bioaccumulation, *n.* the accumulation of toxic chemicals in living things.

There were signs of outright sabotage of certain scientific programs that had been undertaken to measure the possible bioaccumulation of dioxin in the Seveso environment. *The New Yorker, Sept. 4, 1978, p 62*

[1975] Compare BIOMAGNIFICATION.

bioaccumulative, *adj.:* Perhaps most worrisome: PCBs are bio-accumulative, increasing in concentration as they move up nature's food chain. *Bill Dampier, "Environment," Maclean's, Feb. 9, 1976, p 55*

bioacoustics, *n.* the study of sounds produced by or affecting living organisms.

It is a marginal comfort to know that the relatively new science of bioacoustics must deal with similar problems in the sounds made by other animals to each other. No matter what sound-making device is placed at their disposal, creatures in general do a great deal of gabbling, and it requires long patience and observation to edit out the parts lacking syntax and sense. *Lewis Thomas, "Notes of a Biology Watcher," Harper's, Feb. 1973, p 98*

[1964]

bioacoustic or **bioacoustical,** *adj.:* Brough goes on to explain his "bioacoustic" method, in which a starling's taped "distress call" is broadcast over loudspeakers at a roost. If broadcast early in the roosting season over many evenings, the distress call will keep the birds from landing, but if introduced too late or into well-established roosts, the piercing sound, like that of a drill on metal, has no more effect on starlings than the sound of truck motors or jet engines. *Natural History, Aug. 1975, p 44*

Particularly outstanding is the paper by Tandy and Keith on African *Bufo,* including a wealth of biological and bioacoustical data, and the study of the mechanisms of vocalization. *Jay M. Savage, "Book Reviews," Science, Feb. 9, 1973, p 559*

bioactive, *adj.* having an effect on living matter.

By making the ceramic porous enough, the bone can be induced to dissolve the ceramic so that it can be replaced by newly growing bone . . . Bioactive ceramics have been used to plug and bridge bone defects, close surgical skull openings and to implant artificial-tooth roots that later bind to the jaw as bone tissue grows into the ceramic's pores. *Science News, March 18, 1978, p 168*

[1974]

bioactivity, *n.:* The bioactivity of the drugs correlates with their ability to reach this metastable conformation. *New Scientist, Nov. 21, 1974, p 561*

bioavailability, *n.* the extent to which a drug or nutrient is absorbed and made available at its point of action in the body.

One assumes that, if 20 companies manufacture the same drug, each of those 20 products contains exactly the same amount of active ingredient and that each is made under equally rigorous and sanitary manufacturing processes. One also assumes that each is the same as far as bioavailability or therapeutic equivalence is concerned. *Barbara J. Culliton, Science, Jan. 25, 1974, p 284*

Dietary fiber may decrease the bioavailability of certain essential nutrients. Continued ingestion of fiber-rich foods or of individual components of fiber can result in decreased absorption and reduced blood levels of calcium, magnesium, iron, and zinc. *David Kritchevsky, "Food," McGraw-Hill Yearbook of Science and Technology 1978, p 175*

[1970] Compare PHARMACOKINETICS.

bioceramic, *n.* a ceramic substance implanted to help promote the regrowth of missing bone.

A team at the College of Engineering at Clemson University, South Carolina, is using porous calcium aluminate, titania and porcelain implants to provide a matrix for bone ingrowth. The team . . . has found that these "bioceramics" are well tolerated by various body tissues when implanted in dogs and man. *"Technology Review: Ceramics Make*

Inroads into Bone Growth," New Scientist, March 30, 1972, p 692

[1972] Compare BIOGLASS.

biochemistry, *n.* biochemical composition or characteristics.

The virus has developed the capacity to change its biochemistry, thus guaranteeing a fresh crop of victims every time a change occurs. *Paul Ferris, "The Flu: Sure Nuisance, Possible Disaster," The New York Times Magazine, Jan. 11, 1976, p 13*

The biochemistry of nucleic acids in which Watson put so little trust that winter in Copenhagen was yielding facts in Paris, New York, and elsewhere that profoundly affected the search for the nature of the gene. *The New Yorker, Dec. 4, 1978, p 132*

[1967, extended sense of the term (1880's) for the science dealing with biochemical processes]

biocompatible, *adj.* being biologically compatible; not causing rejection.

Thin films and thin-film technology constitute another obvious field of application which includes many different subjects ranging from superconductivity . . . to biocompatible coatings, dry batteries, printing, and others. *Science, Sept. 8, 1972, p 849*

[1972] See BIOMATERIAL.

biocompatibility, *n.:* A new class of polymer with remarkable biocompatibility and high permeability to oxygen was employed successfully in experimental lung-support systems. *John F. Henahan, "Applied chemistry," 1977 Britannica Yearbook of Science and the Future (1976), p 278*

bioconversion, *n.* the use of biological materials and processes to convert a compound, waste material, solar energy, etc. to a new form.

Eventually the direct conversion of solar radiation to electricity by means of photovoltaic cells or its bioconversion to wood, methane, or other fuels on a large scale may become economically feasible. *Allen L. Hammond, "Solar Energy: The Largest Resource," Science, Sept. 22, 1972, p 1088*

[1969]

bioenvironmental, *adj.* of, relating to, or involving the interaction between living things and the environment.

His main plea is for greater use of bioenvironmental controls such as rotation and intercropping, which have been replaced by continuous monocultures, susceptible to pest outbreaks. *Jon Tinker, "Pesticides still the Exception on US Farms," New Scientist, May 31, 1973, p 531*

[1965]

bioethical, *adj.* of or relating to the ethical problems arising in biological research and experimentation.

By whatever name, bioethical questions have always troubled us—but perceptions of them change. Today, because the new medicine has made them so much more visible, bioethical questions are being examined more carefully, more extensively, and under a number of broad rubrics. *Harper's, Aug. 1978, p 21*

[1974]

biofeedback training, a method of training people to alter or control processes of their bodies, such as blood pressure, heart rate, or muscle tension.

Biofeedback training enables a patient to become aware of muscle tension and to learn to control it. A therapist places electrodes on the patient's forehead and connects them to a gauge that indicates the extent of muscle contraction or relaxation. A temperature-registering device on the fingers is connected to a visual temperature gauge. *David R. Coddon, "Help for the Headache," The 1978 World Book Year Book, p 103*

[1971] *Abbreviation:* BFT. Also called AUTOGENIC TRAINING.

biofuel, *n.* a fuel composed of material that was once living matter, such as coal.

New alchemist Richard Merrill is the coeditor of *Energy Primer,* a do-it-yourself guide to renewable forms of energy such as solar, wind, water, and biofuels. *Nicholas Wade, "New Alchemy Institute: Search for an Alternative Agriculture," Science, Feb. 28, 1975, p 729*

[1975]

biogas, *n.* gas that is a mixture of methane and carbon dioxide, produced for use as fuel by bacterial action on organic waste matter.

Some countries faced with fuel shortages, notably India, built bio-gas plants to convert sewage and animal wastes to fertilizer and methane, a fuel gas. *Eugenia Keller, "Chemistry: Fuel," The Americana Annual 1974, p 166*

Biogas burns in a slightly modified methane burner with a sufficiently hot flame for cooking. *Gerald Leach, "Technology Tunes To Nature," The World Book Science Annual 1976 (1975), p 209*

[1974] Compare SYNGAS.

biogasification, *n.* the production of biogas.

Biogasification, which is "perhaps the most important technology for converting biological material to more useful forms of fuel," should be vigorously pursued. *New Scientist, July 24, 1975, p 219*

[1975]

bi·o·ge·o·coe·nol·o·gy (ˌbaɪ ou ˌdʒiː ou siː ˈnɑl ə·dʒiː), *n.* the study of ecosystems.

The publication in 1968 of an English translation of *Fundamentals of Forest Biogeocoenology* brought to the West a new insight into Soviet conservation activities. *Herbert L. Edlin, Britannica Book of the Year 1969, p 227*

[1968, from Russian *biogeotsenologiya,* from *biogeotsenoz* biogeocoenose + *-logiya* -logy]

bi·o·ge·o·coe·nose (ˌbaɪ ou ˌdʒiː ou siˈnouz), *n.* any ecological community and its environment viewed as a unit; ecosystem.

Chapters two to six take in turn various components of forest biogeocoenoses—the atmosphere; a phytocoenose; animal life; microorganisms; soil. *J. N. Black, New Scientist, Aug. 22, 1968, p 398*

[1968, from Russian *biogeotsenoz*]

bioglass, *n.* a calcium and phosphorous biomaterial similar to window glass, used in medicine.

Bioglass has been used successfully to fuse living bone to artificial hip joints in sheep, leg bones in dogs, teeth and jawbones in baboons and middle ears in cats. Human trials are underway in Europe, and U.S. trials will start soon. *"Chemistry: Ceramic bones and glass 'glue'," Science News, June 19, 1976, p 392*

[1976] Compare BIOCERAMIC.

biohazardous, *adj.* of or relating to danger, risk, or harm resulting from biological research.

The committee was to assess the advisability and need for life scientists at Princeton to participate in such potentially biohazardous work. The possible dangers of this research had to be considered in terms of its effect on the campus and the community. *Robert M. May, "Adapting the Guidelines," The World Book Science Annual 1978 (1977), p 43*

[1977, from *biohazard* (1965) danger or peril resulting from biological research + *-ous*] Compare BIOSAFETY.

bioinorganic, *adj.* of or having to do with inorganic processes in biochemistry.

This book would seem to represent required reading for anyone professionally interested in bioinorganic chemistry, but biochemists and coordination chemists generally would gain much from it. *C. A. McAuliffe, Review of "Inorganic Chemistry of Vitamin B_{12}" by J. M. Pratt, Nature, Sept. 15, 1972, p 177*

[1972] Compare BIOORGANIC.

bioinstrumentation, *n.* the use and development of measuring and monitoring instruments for transmission of data about life processes.

So far, space biology has resulted in a multitude of unpublicized spin-offs such as bio-instrumentation and miniaturization now in use in hospitals and research laboratories across the nation. *Everly Driscoll, "Man's Response to Zero-G," Science News, Sept. 9, 1972, p 174*

[1964]

biological magnification, another name for BIOMAGNIFICATION.

A process called biological magnification contributed to the ospreys' decline. Chemicals spilled into rivers, for example, are often concentrated in algae. In the operation of a food chain, each successive predator absorbs — and further concentrates — the poisons contained in its prey. After being passed from algae to worms or other small water animals to fish to ospreys, for instance, the chemicals are so concentrated that they may damage reproductive mechanisms. *David R. Zimmerman, "Reprieve for the Dwindling Ospreys," The World Book Science Annual 1973 (1972), p 52*

[1973]

biomagnification, *n.* the progressive concentration of toxic chemicals with each new link in the food chain.

As far as damage to aquatic life is concerned, for example, Mr. Edmund M. Sweeney, the public hearing examiner, finds that as a "finding of fact," DDT "can have a deleterious effect on freshwater fish and marine organisms when applied directly to water" and that "the theory of biomagnification would seem to be adequately demonstrated in the case of fish, giving rise to concern over use of pesticides with a persistence such as DDT." *"New World: DDT Condemned," Nature, June 23, 1972, p 423*

[1972] Compare BIOACCUMULATION.

biomagnify, *v.i.:* Probably the best news is that arsenic residues from soil and water do not biomagnify in the food chain. *"Chemistry: Arsenic and Environment: Good Score," Science News, Sept. 21, 1974, p 184*

biomass, *n.* plant material used as a source of energy.

The process by which vegetable material or "biomass" as it is technically known is transformed into alcohol fuel is simple. Brazilians have been converting sugar cane into alcohol by fermentation since colonial days, and ethyl alcohol was mixed with gas as early as the 1930s. . . . "Biomass energy just may be the wave of the future," said the U.S. official. *The Manchester Guardian Weekly (The Washington Post section), Sept. 10, 1978, p 15*

[1977, extended from the original (1930's) sense of the total mass or weight of living material in a unit of area]

biomaterial, *n.* biocompatible fabric, plastic, or other material used to replace natural tissue or to construct artificial organs.

Drugs influencing these mechanisms, such as anticoagulants, are widely used to delay or limit thrombus formation in the presence of a biomaterial. That they are still necessary to achieve acceptable haemocompatibility shows just how far we are from the ideal solution. *Alain Carpentier, "A Bloody Sticky Problem," New Scientist, Dec. 2, 1976, p 526*

[1972]

bionic, *adj.* **1** consisting of electronic or mechanical components that replace or augment anatomical structures and thereby supposedly produce extraordinary strength, powers, and abilities.

The Steve Austin doll seems to offer more opportunity for adventure. He has a "bionic eye" with a lens that offers a wide-angle view of the world when you look through a hole in the back of his head; a "bionic grip" that can be closed to grasp a girder (supplied with the doll); and a "bionic arm" . . . that can be raised and lowered. *"Dolls," Consumer Reports, Nov. 1977, p 638*

2 *Figurative.* having extraordinary strength or ability; extremely powerful.

His awed colleagues in the federal Liberal caucus call Jamieson "the bionic mouth" in tribute to his oratorial skills, and to spend some time with him is to realize that this Newfie jokester is a raconteur without peer in Canadian public life. *Robert Miller, Maclean's, Dec. 12, 1977, p 41*

Some lawyers have described Sun's purchase of Becton Dickinson's stock earlier this year as a "bionic bear hug," suggesting that Becton was not left with a great deal of time or flexibility to oppose the move by Sun. *Tom Goldstein, "Business and the Law," The New York Times, Dec. 1, 1978, p D4*

[1976, from the earlier meaning (1970) of or relating to *bionics* the study of the anatomy of animals as a basis for improvements on electronic devices or methods (OEDS 1960), made popular by the television hero known as the *bionic man* whose electronic and mechanical components give him extraordinary strength and powers; ultimately from *bio-* + *electronic*]

bionically, *adv.:* Horror-stricken, I watched last night as the perfect housewife cleaned house bionically . . . in less time than it takes to tell. *Alan Coren, "The Bionic Woman —ITV," The Times (London), July 2, 1976, p 11*

bioorganic, *adj.* of or having to do with organic processes in biochemistry.

One area of bioorganic research focused on the molecular changes wrought by enzymes on small organic substrates. *David S. Watt, "Organic Chemistry," 1978 Britannica Yearbook of Science and the Future (1977), p 274*

[1972] Compare BIOINORGANIC.

biophilia, *n.* love of life as a natural human instinct.

Biophilia and necrophilia are in many ways similar to Freud's concept of the life instinct and the death instinct. There is, however, an essential difference. For Freud, both tendencies are normal parts of the biological equipment of man, while in the view presented here, this holds true only for biophilia. *Erich Fromm, "The Erich Fromm Theory of Aggression," The New York Times Magazine, Feb. 27, 1972, p 84*

[1968, from *bio-* + *-philia* love of, patterned on *necrophilia*]

biophilic, *adj.*: MacCoby, an ardent McCarthy supporter, runs an intensely biophilic household — interviews with him tend to be punctuated by rousing nursery rhymes for the benefit of the children. *Lewis Chester, The Sunday Times (London), July 21, 1968, p 10*

biophilosophy, *n.* the approach to philosophy through biology.

The final unit contains a discussion of animal behaviour and the evolution of man, language and race. The whole is rounded off with a chapter entitled "Biophilosophy." *Andrew Miller, Review of "From Cell to Philosopher" by Michael D. Nicklanovich, New Scientist, July 26, 1973, p 217*

[1966]

biophilosopher, *n.*: As a biologist, he [Dr. Salk] believes that his science is on the frontier of tremendous new discoveries; and as a philosopher, he is convinced that humanists and artists have joined the scientists to achieve an understanding of man in all his physical, mental and spiritual complexity. Such interchanges might lead, he would hope, to a new and important school of thinkers he would designate as biophilosophers. *Howard Taubman, The New York Times, Nov. 11, 1966, p 73*

bioplasma, *n.* See the quotation for the meaning.

The concept of bioplasma is a key to the understanding of Soviet parapsychology. Bioplasma is presumed by the Russians to be a fourth state of matter that constantly interacts with other states of matter, perhaps transforming itself into them from time to time, just as water becomes steam or ice. It is bioplasma that explains the workings of acupuncture and other aspects of Soviet parapsychology. *Stanley Krippner and Richard Davidson, "Parapsychology in the U.S.S.R.," Saturday Review, March 18, 1972, p 59*

[1972, from Russian *bioplazma*]

biopolymer, *n.* a protein, nucleic acid, steroid, or other biological polymer.

It has been established in the past several years that many biopolymers can behave as transducers in that they exhibit electric potentials when deformed mechanically. These biological transducers comprise collagen, keratin, elastin, dentin, and cellulose and include, as well, many polycrystalline organic materials such as polypeptides and amino acid crystals. *Robert J. Pawluk, "Connective Tissue," McGraw-Hill Yearbook of Science and Technology 1974, p 136*

[1966]

biopsy, *v.t.* to perform a biopsy on.

Howard Jones and his colleagues at Baltimore searched the notes of known cases of cervical carcinoma in an attempt to find any whose cervix had been biopsied in the past. They found twenty-four such cases, and were able to review stored histological material going back as far as twenty years. *Arthur I. Spriggs, "Population Screening by the Cervical Smear," Nature, July 21, 1972, p 135*

[1964, verb use of the noun]

bi·o·res·me·thrin (‚baɪ ou rez'mi: θrin *or* ‚baɪ ou‑rez'meθ rin), *n.* variant of RESMETHRIN.

One of these compounds, bioresmethrin . . . has the highest selectivity ratio known for any insecticide chemical; it is 32,000 times more toxic (on a milligram per kilogram basis) to houseflies when applied topically than to rats when given orally. *Science, March 23, 1973, p 1235*

[1971]

bi·o·rhe·ol·o·gy (‚baɪ ou ri:'ɑl ə dʒi:), *n.* the study of the flow and deformation of blood, mucus, and other fluids in animals and plants.

The author [Elementary Rheology] . . . gives a brief history of the subject, an account of the main lines of work, definitions of terms used, and short chapters on topical subjects such as haemorheology, aspects of biorheology, and psychorheology. *Science Journal, April 1969, p 85*

[1969, coined in 1948 by A. L. Copley from *bio-* of biology + *rheology* (1931) science dealing with flow and deformation of matter, ultimately from Greek *rheós* a flowing]

biorheologist, *n.*: In addition to the efforts of manufacturers to optimize the design of their units by reducing shear stress and turbulence, two approaches are receiving the attention of biorheologists. *Henry L. Gabelnick, "Biorheology," McGraw-Hill Yearbook of Science and Technology 1973, p 72*

biorhythmic, *adj.* of or involving rhythmical or cyclic changes in the functions or activities of organs and organisms.

Biorhythms are physical, emotional and mental elements, all cyclical, that are said to determine, or at least play a large role in a person's behavior and performance at a given time. The biorhythmic forecast is determined by date of birth. *Neil Amdur, The New York Times, Sept. 10, 1977, p 19*

[1966, from *biorhythm* (1964) + *-ic*]

biorhythmicist, *n.*: Although there has been no rational explanation so far for the claims of biorhythmicists, variations of the concept have been put to practical use in at least two countries. *"Moonstruck Scientists," Time, Jan. 10, 1972, p 48*

biorhythmicity, *n.*: Put another way, one function of the central nervous system may be to order the activity of the organism in time. This is clearly apparent in the massive shifts of bodily activity that accompany the sleep-waking cycle known to be controlled by the brain. Thus the study of sleep is, among other things, the study of biorhythmicity. *J. Allan Hobson, "Body Rhythms," McGraw-Hill Yearbook of Science and Technology 1977, p 147*

biosafety, *n.* safety in biological research. *Often used attributively.*

"There is a growing sentiment that the burden of proof is shifting toward those who would restrict recombinant DNA research." And to further make the point about a significant change in attitude in the Administration, the name of the local groups designated to oversee the way research is carried out has been switched through 180 degrees from biohazard committees to biosafety committees. *New Scientist, Sept. 7, 1978, p 674*

[1977] Compare BIOHAZARDOUS.

bioshield, *n.* a protective device encasing a spacecraft during and after its sterilization with a heat cycle prior to launch.

Last summer, the two Viking landers were baked for eighty hours, at a peak heat of two hundred and thirty-three degrees Fahrenheit, inside containers called "bioshields," which were not removed until the two craft were safely on their way toward Mars. *Henry S. F. Cooper, Jr., "Profiles," The New Yorker, June 21, 1976, p 60*

[1976]

biosonar, *n.* the use of sonarlike impulses by an animal to facilitate movement without harm through its surroundings.

Dr. Griffin's book, *Listening in the Dark*, is the most complete treatise on biosonar to be found in current literature, and his work on bats has been the basis for much of the work today. *Thomas C. Poulter, "Biosonar," McGraw-Hill Yearbook of Science and Technology 1966, p 13*

[1963]

biotechnology, *n.* the use of microorganisms as catalytic agents to produce useful materials or facilitate industrial processes.

The term biotechnology is unfortunately ambivalent, and is confused further by the widespread use of synonyms like "biochemical engineering," "microbial technology" and "fermentation technology." But the meaning that is most widely accepted is that it is the industrial processing of materials by microorganisms and other biological agents to provide desirable products and services. It incorporates fermentation and enzyme technology, water and waste treatment, and some aspects of food technology. *Allan Bull and John Bu'Lock, "The Living Micro Revolution," New Scientist, June 7, 1979, p 808*

[1976, specialized sense of the term meaning originally (1940's) the area of technology dealing with the relation between people and machines]

biotoxic, *adj.* relating to or consisting of poisons produced by animals and plants.

In the case of man, painful experience rather than instinct has taught him to respect biotoxic substances. *Bruce W. Halstead, "Biotoxins: The Poisons of Life," 1977 Britannica Yearbook of Science and the Future (1976), p 223*

[1972, from *biotoxin* (1959), from *bio-* biological + *toxin* poison]

biotoxicity, *n.*: The considerable biotoxicity of copper waste obviates any chance of proper restoration at a feasible cost. *Peter Stubbs, "Two Sorts of Longing," New Scientist, Nov. 30, 1972, p 491*

biotoxicology, *n.* the study of poisons produced by animals and plants.

This fragment of Shakespearean dialogue summarizes the thinking of those involved in directing the present and future efforts of modern biotoxicology. Drug companies are showing progressive interest in poisonous organisms as sources of pharmaceuticals. *Bruce W. Halstead, "Biotoxins: The Poisons of Life," 1977 Britannica Yearbook of Science and the Future (1976), p 231*

[1976, blend of *biotoxic* and *toxicology*] See CRINO-TOXIN, ZOOTOXIN.

biotransformation, *n.* chemical transformation of a compound through biological action.

Biotransformation of mercury in association with microorganisms has been observed in at least three other species; the bacterium *Pseudomonas* K-62 strain transformed some organo-mercury compounds to the free metal; inorganic or phenylmercury was methylated by bacteria in natural sediments; and *Neurospora crassa* is able to methylate inorganic mercury through a different metabolic pathway. *David Ben-Bassat, et al., Jerusalem, "Letters to Nature: Growth of Chlamydomonas in a Medium Containing Mercury," Nature, Nov. 3, 1972, p 44*

[1969]

biowarfare, *n.* biological warfare.

In the event he [Mike Gaze] wrote to the director of Porton, saying that biowarfare was not his thing. Once in the Army, he applied for a job doing physiological research on environmental topics. *Graham Chedd, "How Do Nerves Know Where to Go?" New Scientist, Oct. 12, 1972, p 93*

[1966]

birr (bir), *n. pl. and sing.* the monetary unit of Ethiopia that replaced the Ethiopian dollar in 1976.

The Ethiopian *birr*, divided into 100 cents, is the unit of currency; it is based on 5·52 grains of fine gold. It consists of notes of [various] denominations, and bronze 1-, 5-, 10-, and 25-cent coins. *The Statesman's Year-Book 1977-78, p 916*

Budget (1975-76 est.): revenue 1,175,000,000 birr; expenditure 1,331,000,000 birr. Money supply (April 1977) 996.7 million birr. *"Ethiopia," Britannica Book of the Year 1978, p 378*

[1977, probably from Amharic]

birth pill, an oral contraceptive in pill form.

David Moreau yesterday announced his resignation as managing director of Syntax Pharmaceuticals, the British end of the birth-pill company. *The Times (London), June 16, 1970, p 25*

[1965, short for *birth-control pill*]

bi·stat·ic radar (,bai'stæt ik), a system of radar used in astronomy and space sciences.

The conclusion is drawn from studies by bistatic radar—using a sender and receiver in different locations. The sender in this case was the lunar orbiter Explorer 35; the receiver was Stanford's 150-foot radio antenna. *Science News, Aug. 31, 1968, p 213*

[1963]

Bitter coil, an electric coil for the generation of a strong magnetic field in a fusion reactor.

It is possible that the reactor will incorporate elements of the "Bitter coil" that has enabled the Alcator of the Massachusetts Institute of Technology to produce extremely powerful magnetic fields. *Walter Sullivan, "New Fusion Reactor Likely to Break Even in Fuel Use," The New York Times, March 22, 1976, p 38*

[1968, named after Francis *Bitter*, an American physicist]

bi·u·nique·ness (,bai yu'ni:k nis), *n. Linguistics.* the principle of one-to-one correspondence between phonemic and phonetic representations.

The principle of bi-uniqueness forces the inventor of writing to practice a kind of economy of symbols, so that if he can't *hear* a distinction between some class of utterance-pairs, he can't *write* one, and if he *does* consistently hear a distinction, he must write it or fail the read-back test. *Fred W. Householder, Linguistic Speculations, 1971, p 148*

[1971, from *bi-* two + *uniqueness*]

black[1], *adj., n.* ► As a label of racial identity, *black* was revived in the late 1960's by the American civil-rights movement and so successfully popularized in the following years that it virtually removed from circulation the formerly standard label *Negro*. However, as late as 1967 a new encyclopedic reference book dealing with black history and culture was entitled *The Negro Almanac* and used the label Negro throughout.

Historically, *black* and *negro* were used interchangeably, e.g. "He noticed the approach of the black . . . with a smile of contempt" (James Fenimore Cooper, *The Spy*, 1821). It was chiefly during the twentieth century that *negro* was capitalized (*Negro*), and *black* went out of fashion among whites, as it was considered an insult to refer to the color of a black person's skin. Thus *Negro* became the accepted label and standard spelling, though a number of old and new euphemisms, e.g. "colored" (DAE 1780), "Afro-American" (DA 1853), and "nonwhite" (OEDS 1921), were used until the 1960's.

The revival of *black* probably succeeded in part because black leaders promoted the label, using it in slogans emphasizing pride in being black (*Black Power, Black is Beautiful*), and in designating concepts intended to raise the consciousness of blacks (*black nationalism, black culture*).

black[2], *n. British*. Usually, **the black,** an instance or policy of boycotting by trade unions.

Mr. Bernie Steer, one of their [Transport and General Workers' Union] leaders, told me after yesterday's meeting: "The black is there, it stays there, it will be extended. Nothing this meeting has decided will alter that. If the black is going to be lifted the Government will have to see us and accept our arguments." " '*Blacking' Goes On, Steward Says," The Times (London), May 5, 1972, p 1*

[1968, noun use of *black, adj.* (1956) applied to work boycotted by trade unions, short for *blackleg, adj.* (1800's) of or relating to work done against the rules of a trade or other group]

black advance, *U.S.* the practice of following a political candidate's scheduled appearances for disruptive purposes.

More likely to last, but in a technical rather than general vocabulary, are locutions like "plumbers" (to plug the leaks of news) or "black advance," (to disrupt a political opposition's rallies). *William Safire, "The Word-Watchers," The New York Times, Aug. 15, 1974, p 33*

[1974, so called in reference to the candidate's *advance*, or travel arrangements during a campaign] Compare DIRTY TRICKS.

black art, art produced by blacks or dealing with black culture, especially in the United States.

Except in certain picturesque aspects, black art is not distinct from majority art; the complaint is that it has been insufficiently incorporated in the national tradition. Mr. Driskell makes the point that his show is devoted to "documenting the quality of a body of work that should never have been set apart as a separate entity." But if black art had not been "set apart" (save for its exclusion through prejudice), how could it have represented black experience? *Harold Rosenberg, "The Art World," The New Yorker, Aug. 22, 1977, p 84*

[1968]

black-bag job, illegal entry by a Federal law-enforcement agent to obtain information.

People also feared that the FBI-controlled system would encourage the growth of a national police force complete with shades of 1984 and gestapo tactics. So-called "black bag" jobs, wiretapping, and other misdeeds committed by FBI agents in the past and only recently revealed by Congressional committees have justified that fear in the hearts of many Americans. *Nancy French, "US May Abandon Police Computer," New Scientist, Sept. 23, 1976, p 649*

[1976, variant of earlier (1971) *bag job*]

black caucus or **Black Caucus,** *U.S.* a group of black civil rights advocates, especially at a national political convention or in Congress.

Five years ago, the Congressional Black Caucus held its first fund-raising event here — a well-attended dinner, the proceeds of which were used to establish and operate a caucus office . . . The caucas is the organization of all black members of the House of Representatives, all of whom are Democrats. *Charlayne Hunter, "Black Caucus Fund Dinner Becomes 2-Day Affair," The New York Times, Sept. 29, 1975, p 20*

[1967]

black consciousness, a political movement in South Africa that stresses the common cultural heritage and destiny of blacks in their struggle against apartheid. *Also used attributively.*

The white authorities have been alert to the dangers, for them, of the development of black consciousness, which quickly won more popularity at black schools and universities than militant left-wing ideologies. *Nicholas Ashford, "Leaders' Arrests Aid Black Militancy," The Times (London), Aug. 24, 1976, p 4*

With one exception all of the banned organisations are part of the black consciousness movement. They include the Black Peoples' Convention, the South African Students' Organisation, the Union of Black Journalists, the Black Woman's Federation and several regionally based black youth movements. *The Manchester Guardian Weekly, Oct. 30, 1977, p 7*

[1976] ► The name of this movement was adopted from the phrase frequently used in the 1960's in reference to the growing self-awareness of black Americans.

Adult Negroes have tried to erase their blackness by dressing, thinking and living "white," an approach that is giving way to the new black-consciousness that says "black is beautiful." *George Gent, The New York Times, July 3, 1968, p 71*

black-flag, *v.t.* to signal (a racing-car driver) to leave the course.

Another drama near the end of the race surrounded Jean-Pierre Beltoise, winner at Monaco earlier in the season. . . .

71

In what looked like a secure sixth place, he was black-flagged to lap 12 for a trifling fault on his car. *Eric Dymock, The Manchester Guardian Weekly, Aug. 5, 1972, p 24*

[1963, so called from the black flag waved for this purpose]

black mist, (in Japan) corrupt or scandalous business or political practices.

Opposition-party politicians, whose leverage is now much greater than it was, are determined to get to the bottom of all these matters—"black mist" affairs, they are called—and the continuing American investigations may help them. *The New Yorker, Jan. 23, 1978, p 55*

[1966, translation of Japanese *kuro kiri* black mist or fog (that obscures the vision); so called from the intentional cover-up often practiced in such cases]

Black September, a terrorist group of Palestinian Arabs.

The highest cash ransom, $5 million, was paid by Lufthansa German Airways to five Arab terrorists who hijacked a Boeing 747 on a New Delhi-Athens flight on February 21. The money probably went to finance the extremist Black September arm of the Palestinian liberation guerrilla army. *Robert H. Lindsey, "Skyjacking: A New Tool Of Terrorists," The Americana Annual 1973, p 47*

[1972, named to commemorate the month in 1970 when Jordan launched an offensive military operation against Palestinian commandos] Compare AL FATAH, PLO.

Black Septembrist: These same Chileans and their Swiss friends, who were so loud in their denunciation of the Black Septembrists in Munich and Paris, apparently saw no parallel with terrorists in Chile. *Nena Ossa, "Letter from Rome: Fact, Fiction, and Agitprop," National Review, Dec. 21, 1973, p 1409*

Also called SEPTEMBRIST.

blacks·ploi·ta·tion (ˌblæk sploi'tei ʃən), *n.* variant spelling of BLAXPLOITATION.

. . . the black glistening giants of blacksploitation films. On all sides, these larger- and simpler-than-life figures are at play, and their play hypnotizes us. *Paul Zweig, "The Hero in Literature," Saturday Review, Dec. 1978, p 35*

[1974]

black theater, plays written, directed and produced by blacks and using the black community as their reference.

Nor is he [Ed Bullins] likely to be friendly toward anyone who disparages black theatre—to which he is passionately devoted—or the work of any playwright he admires. *Jervis Anderson, "Profiles: Ed Bullins, Dramatist," The New Yorker, June 16, 1973, p 40*

[1970]

blade·lette or **blade·let** ('bleid ˌlet), *n.* a small piece of stone chipped to form a sharp edge, used as a weapon during the Stone Age.

Late in the Upper Paleolithic and during the ensuing Mesolithic, it became the fashion to make smaller and smaller bladelettes. Commonly inserted as "side blades" into lateral grooves in antler and bone projectile points, such "microblades" lacerated the flesh of wounded game animals and thus promoted free bleeding and rapid death. *Charles E. Borden, Britannica Book of the Year 1969, p 101*

[1964, from *blade* + *-lette, -let* (diminutive suffixes)]

blast, *n. Slang.* a good time; great fun.

And Meyer himself had a blast. An entirely unpretentious man, whose major contribution to a scheduled discussion of "Art and Pornography" was the statement that the former "was a very broad subject" and that he didn't "know anything about pornography," he had dreaded this confrontation with sophisticated, distinguished Yale. *Richard Schickel, Harper's, July 1970, p 37*

[1966, extended from earlier (1959) sense of "a party"]

blax·ploi·ta·tion (ˌblæk sploi'tei ʃən), *n. U.S.* the exploitation of interest in blacks by making movies and plays with black actors, especially for black audiences. *Often used attributively.*

We must come to understand that all the "violence" in the "blaxploitation" films only serves to create another form of escapism. *Henry Louis Gates, Jr., "Portraits in Black," Harper's, June 1976, p 24*

[1972, blend of *black* and *exploitation*] Also spelled BLACKSPLOITATION.

bleeper, *n.* an electronic device to generate electronic telephone signals.

Because many countries have their own sets of tones, the international phone phreak will need a set of bleepers. One presented in evidence at the trial was very elaborate, being capable of simulating seven different signalling systems. *Duncan Campbell, New Scientist, Dec. 13, 1973, p 757*

[1966, from *bleep* (1953) + *-er*] See BLUE BOX.

Blends. ► These are special types of COMPOUNDS. In the analysis of blends, this book considers them as formations that combine two words and include any letters or sounds they have in common. The two words are literally blended or fitted into each other; *smog* was coined by blending *sm(o)ke* and *f(o)g*, *motel*, by blending *m(ot)or* and *h(ot)el*. Blends are sometimes called portmanteau words, after Lewis Carroll's explanation in *Through the Looking Glass:* "You see it's like a portmanteau—there are two meanings packed into one word."

Blends can fuse words together so that the original forms are no longer easily recognized, as in FACTION (*fact* and *fiction*), and sometimes blends can be so complete that there is some doubt about their components: SCUZZY is perhaps a blend of *scummy* and *fuzzy*; EXTENCISOR is apparently an irregular blend of *extensor* (muscle) and *exercise*; JARGONAUT is a blend of *jargon* and *argonaut*, probably by influence of *argot*.

Blends shorten a long and perhaps awkward phrase: EXERCYCLE for the phrase *exercise bicycle*, MOTOWN, a natural contraction of *Motor Town*, and BLAXPLOITATION, an ingenious blend of *black exploitation*.

The form of a blend often embodies the ideas or meanings the two words are intended to convey. There is a special fitness to blends formed to give a name to something that is itself a blend: YAKOW (blend of *yak* and *cow* in pronunciation represented by *k* and *c*), BEEFALO (blend of *beef* (cattle) and *buffalo*), or FRENGLISH (blend of *French* and English), YINGLISH (blend of *Yiddish* and *English*). Two separate concepts combined may also be represented by the blending of two words as in BEAUTILITY, to join *beauty* and *utility*.

Other examples of blends in this book are SCRAP-NEL (blend of *scrap* and *shrapnel*), INFLUMP (blend of *inflation* and *slump*), HAPPENSTANTIAL (blend of *happenstance* and *circumstantial*), SLIMNASTICS (blend of *slim* and *gymnastics*), and SWINGLE (blend of *swinging* and *single*).

According to the American linguist Margaret M. Bryant (in "Blends Are Increasing." *American Speech* 49, 3-4, 1976), before the mid-19th century the formation of blends was somewhat rare, but today the process is frequently used, especially to form trademarks in such diverse fields as fashion, sports, technology, politics, education, and art. Many blends are NONCE WORDS, and a good many are journalistic coinages. *Time* magazine is noted for its coinage of blends, such as *cinemactress*. The frequent use of blends by newspapers and magazines, especially in headlines, has probably contributed to the popularization of this type of word formation.

ble·o·my·cin (,bli: ou'mai sən), *n.* any of a group of antibiotics derived from a species of soil bacteria (*Streptomyces verticillus*), used in treating cancers of the skin, tongue, and lungs.

One of the newest drugs is an antibiotic, bleomycin, which has had early success in treating some heretofore resistant forms of cancer. It has produced improvement in patients in the terminal stage of Hodgkin's disease, and has been called the best drug so far for some highly resistant solid tumors, such as squamous cell carcinoma. *Ronald Kotulak, "Cancer Under Attack," 1973 Britannica Yearbook of Science and the Future, (1972), p 89*

[1970, from *bleo-* (of uncertain origin) + *-mycin*, as in *streptomycin* (from Greek *mýkēs* fungus)]

bleph·a·ro·plas·ty ('blef ə rou,plæs ti:), *n.* cosmetic surgery to remove the excess fat and skin from the lower eyelids that cause bags under the eyes, crow's-feet, etc.

How did Senator William Proxmire (D., Wis.) get two black eyes? Gossips ruled out a barroom brawl (he doesn't drink) or a domestic disagreement . . . The most likely explanation was blepharoplasty — plastic surgery to remove bags under the eyes. *"People," Time, Feb. 21, 1972, p. 44.*

[1971, from Greek *blépharon* eyelid + *-plastia* a molding] Popularly called EYELIFT. Compare RHY-TIDECTOMY.

▶ This term was recorded in 19th-century dictionaries in the sense of "the operation of making a new eyelid from a piece of skin transplanted from an adjacent part" (*Century Dictionary*, 1889) and "the operation of supplying any deficiency caused by wound or lesion of the eyelid" (OED, 1882). In recent years, with the increasing use of cosmetic surgery, the term has been revived with a new sense.

blind·side ('blaind,said), *v.t.* **1** to hit (a player) on his unguarded or blind side.

That great sportsman Mike Curtis ("The Beasts of Baltimore," January issue) took the cheapest shot of all time when he slammed into (blindsided, as these brave gladiators say) an overexuberant spectator who ran onto the field in a recent Baltimore-Miami game. *Thomas F. Cleary, in a Letter to the Editor, The Atlantic, March 1972, p. 28*

2 *Figurative use.* to deal an unexpected blow.

At one point, Oregon's Tom McCall asked a question most of his colleagues were thinking — whether those Republicans who stand with the President [Nixon] were going to be "blindsided by any more bombs," *"National Affairs: A New Tale of the Tapes," Newsweek, Dec. 3, 1973, p. 33*

[1972] Compare CHEAP SHOT.

blind trust, a trust that manages the financial holdings of an individual, usually to prevent possible conflict of interest between the person's duties in some public office and his business interests.

On Jan. 20, 1977, the day he became President, Mr. Carter's 62 percent interest in the business was transferred to a "blind trust" administered by . . . an Atlanta lawyer and confidant of Mr. Carter's. The White House has said that the trust buffers Mr. Carter from direct knowledge or control over the business. *Nicholas M. Horrock, The New York Times, Jan. 18, 1979, p. A1*

[1969]

bliss out, *U.S. Slang.* to experience or fill with intense bliss; become or make ecstatic.

Initiates learn to see a dazzling white light, hear celestial music, feel ecstatic vibrations. . . . The process is called "blissing out." *Newsweek, Nov. 19, 1973, p. 157*

Davis displayed the nonstop, glowing smile and the glazed eyes of one who is "blissed out." *The New Yorker, April 8, 1974, p. 32*

His Peninsula neighbors are too blissed out on tranquillity to know or care what he does for a living. *"The Best Places to Live in L.A.; Palos Verdes Peninsula," Town and Country, May 1974, p. 124*

[1973, verb use of *bliss, n.*, apparently patterned on *freak out*; a term popularized by followers of the Hindu guru, Maharaj Ji]

blissout, *n. U.S. Slang.* a thoroughly blissful state; rapturous or ecstatic condition.

At the end of the week, she wins something like the Academy Award, except it's at a ceremony where she is the only one being honored, and her girl friends and boy friends are all there, gathered round, to be happy for her. This blissout is the movie every actress must at some point have dreamed of making. *Pauline Kael, "The Current Cinema," The New Yorker, Dec. 20, 1976, p. 117*

[1974, noun use of BLISS OUT]

BL La·cer·tae object ('bi:'el lə'sər ti:), any of a group of compact celestial bodies that are the sources of intense radiation but lack clearly defined emission lines in their spectra.

In the past few years still another class of objects has been added to this catalogue of astronomical prodigies: the BL Lacertae objects. The first of them was discovered less than 10 years ago, and about 30 more are known today. Like the quasars they are apparently distant and unaccountably bright, but they have spectral peculiarities all their own. As in quasars and Seyfert galaxies, their intense radiation seems to come from a comparatively small volume. *Scientific American, Aug. 1977, p. 32*

[1970, so called because the first such object discovered (in 1929) was identified as a variable star in the constellation *Lacerta* (the Lizard)]

block association, *U.S.* an organization formed by residents of a city block or other small area to protect and promote their interests.

New York City has 39,000 blocks and about 10,000 block associations, many active and some dormant.... Block associations have been responsible for organizing a whole range of activities from cleaning up garbage-strewn lots to organizing street fairs and block parties. *John Lewis, Daily News (New York), May 27, 1979, p MB1*

[1972]

block grant, *U.S.* a fixed grant of money made by the Federal Government to the states.

The President ... would also consolidate 59 specific Federal programs into four so-called "block grants" to the states for health, education, child nutrition and social services for the poor, disabled and elderly. The states would no longer be required to add their own funds for these purposes. *"President and Candidate Ford Says 'Retrench'," The New York Times, Jan. 25, 1976, Sec. 4, p 1*

[1975] ► The term has been used in Great Britain since the turn of the century for a fixed grant made by the Exchequer to local authorities.

blood-CSF barrier, a selective impermeability of the capillaries in the central nervous system that prevents most harmful substances in the blood from reaching the cerebrospinal fluid (CSF).

In summary, all the proteins tested, with the exception of lysozyme, have been found in foetal CSF in concentrations much higher than those detected in CSF from normal adult subjects. These results, therefore, support the suggestion that the human blood-CSF barrier is not fully developed during foetal life. *M. Adinolfi, et al., London, "Letters to Nature: Permeability of the Blood-Cerebrospinal Fluid Barrier to Plasma Proteins During Foetal and Perinatal Life," Nature, Jan. 15, 1976, p 140*

[1976] ► *Blood-brain barrier* (1952) was the first of these body-defense systems to be recognized.

The blood-brain barrier is a mechanism which screens substances passing from the blood vessels into the brain. *"Biochemistry," Science News, Feb. 7, 1953, p 88*

Bloody Maria, *U.S.* an alcoholic drink made with tequila and tomato juice.

Though a few diehards still down tequila the traditional way—straight, with a lick of salt and a wedge of lime—most gringos prefer cocktail variations like the Margarita, made with lime juice and triple sec. Other Aztec ¡Oles!: T'n'T (with tonic); Bloody Maria or Mexican Mary (substituting tequila for vodka). *"Modern Living: Aztec ¡Ole!," Time, Jan. 26, 1976, p 62*

[1976, patterned on earlier (1950's) *Bloody Mary,* a drink of vodka and tomato juice]

blowback, *n.* **1** the enlargement of an image that has been reduced to a microscopic size.

Figure 4 shows three blowbacks from laser-machined frames. The original document in each case was an 8.5 × 11 in. (216 × 279 mm) page which was scanned in raster fashion, with 2000 lines from the top of the page to the bottom. *H. A. Watson, "Laser Machining," McGraw-Hill Yearbook of Science and Technology, 1976, p 233*

2 false or misleading information that is spread in a foreign country by intelligence agents but that unexpectedly circulates back to the country of origin.

Everyone was especially concerned that American *officials* had sometimes fallen victim to blowback, and one witness, who had formerly been on the staff of the C.I.A., described efforts he had made on several occasions to apprise policymakers that they had been taken in by their own government. *The New Yorker, Feb. 27, 1978, p 26*

[1975, for def. 1; 1978, for def. 2]

blowdown, *n.* the sudden, forceful rupture of a cooling pipe in a nuclear reactor, especially in a power plant.

In nuclear parlance, "blow-down" is synonymous with catastrophe, as it signifies loss of coolant with the nuclear reactor continuing to produce heat with nothing to carry it away. *New Scientist, June 22, 1978, p 828*

Last week, near snow-swept Mud Lake, Idaho, the Nuclear Regulatory Commission undertook to allay fears. It staged a nuclear accident in miniature, deliberately sabotaging a small test reactor's primary cooling system to see if the back-up system would avert a blowdown. *Time, Dec. 25, 1978, p 47*

[1978, extended sense of the earlier term for a device to let off steam or gas] Compare MELTDOWN.

blow-dry, *v.t.* **1** to dry or style (the hair) with a BLOW DRYER.

Where hairstylists once painstakingly set hair in curlers or rollers, they now, as often as not, simply cut and briskly blow-dry a breezy new style. *"Blow Dryers: Basic Weapon for the Revolution in Hairstyles," Consumer Reports, Nov. 1977, p 626*

2 to blow-dry the hair of.

A bevy of bobbed, permed, blow-dried and finger-teased models paraded to popular songs. *The Times (London), Feb. 6, 1976, p 14*

—*adj.* dried or styled by blow-drying.

The blow-dry hairdo placed more emphasis than ever on a good haircut and on hair that was in good condition. *Kenneth E. Battelle, "Hairstyles," 1971 Collier's Encyclopedia Year Book (1970), p 234*

—*n.* an act or instance of blow-drying.

Staff benefits include having your hair baked set (only horrids like me would clamour for a blow-dry). *Prudence Glynn, "Fashion," The Times (London), Jan. 27, 1977, p 11*

[1969]

blow dryer, a hand-held hairdryer that blows and directs warmed air, used for drying and styling the hair.

Normal hair probably does not need shampooing more than twice or three times a week under regular conditions, and even that much might be excessive for some people. Even the latest fad of hair-styling blow-dryers may dry hair too much and promote breakage and splitting. *Joe Graedon, The People's Pharmacy, 1976, p 104*

The notion that styling one's hair should require a minimum of time and effort has caught on with women and men alike, and using a blow dryer has become a unisex morning ritual. The results are natural and uncontrived—though not unstyled. *"Blow Dryers," Consumer Reports, Nov. 1977, p 626*

[1969]

blowout, *n.* an abnormal swelling of a blood vessel; aneurysm.

Only decades later, after a deceptively quiet lull, does syphilis kill by causing a blowout of the aorta, the main artery leading from the heart, among other ways. *Lawrence K. Altman, "Syphilis Vaccine Is Tested After Bacterium Is Grown," The New York Times, March 13, 1976, p 49*

[1974]

blue box, a device attached to a telephone to generate electronic impulses that circumvent operator assistance and a record of the call. It is used by PHONE PHREAKS.

The blue box—which can actually be any color, but was christened after the first one found—beeps electronic imitations of Bell signals so that users can "seize" lines to make free calls all over the world. *Lynn Langway with Jeff B. Copeland, Washington, "Telephones: Listening In," Newsweek, Feb. 17, 1975, p 79*

[1975]

blue-eyed, *adj.* **1** *U.S. (especially Black English) Slang.* white; Caucasian.

"Blue-eyed soul brother" or "blue-eyed soul sister" is used to label whites who understand and appreciate black culture, and whose actions toward black people are without the reservation, strangeness, and racism that characterize the actions of many white people. *Ken Johnson, "The Vocabulary of Race," in Rappin' and Stylin' Out, edited by Thomas Kochman, 1972, p 145*

2 *Canadian Slang.* of English extraction; Anglo-Saxon.

Canadian poetry, too, is being pulled apart by regional interests . . . Recently, anthologies of West Coast, Montreal English, Maritime, and practically everything but blue-eyed poets have been published. A book full of Italo-Canadian poets, many of whom were born in Canada, write of their longing "to roam on the hills of Tuscany." *Barbara Amiel, "Poetry: Capsule Comments on Canada," Maclean's, Jan. 15, 1979, p 51*

[1968, from def. 1; 1976, for def. 2]

blue-eyed devil, *U.S. Slang.* a derogatory name for a white person.

Blue-eyed devils or *Devils* . . . is usually used in a collective sense and is usually pluralized . . . The adjective "blue-eyed" clarifies to whom "devil" is applied. This label for white people was first used by the Muslim leaders Elijah Muhammed and Malcolm X. *Ken Johnson, "The Vocabulary of Race," in Rappin' and Stylin' Out, edited by Thomas Kochman, 1972, p 142*

[1972] Compare PADDY.

blue flu, *U.S.* an organized absence of policemen or firemen from work on the pretext of sickness, to influence contract negotiations or to protest working conditions.

City dwellers have learned recently about the "blue flu" that often afflicts police officers who are suspicious of proposed changes. *James Vorenberg, "The War on Crime: The First Five Years," The Atlantic, May 1972, p 67*

He and Samuel DeMilla, the P.B.A. [Patrolmen's Benevolent Association] president, warn of strikes or "blue flu" if demands aren't met, while other union leaders complain such demands are unrealistic and by misleading the patrolmen may trigger just the troubles that the police union predicts. *The New York Times, March 26, 1978, Sec. 4, p 6*

[1968, so called from the blue color of police and fire uniforms] Compare YELLOW FLU.

blue-rinse or **blue-rinsed,** *adj. Especially U.S.* consisting of or typified by elderly women who are carefully groomed and socially active.

He also goes traipsing across the United States . . . reciting poems to the blue-rinsed brigade. *Geoffrey Moorhouse, The Manchester Guardian Weekly, Aug. 1, 1970, p 16*

. . . an unlikely coalition of affluent communities, led by embattled suburban matrons known as "the blue rinse set." *Shirley Hazzard, "Letter from Australia," The New Yorker, Jan. 3, 1977, p 46*

[1964, so called from the frequently blue-rinsed gray hair of such women]

blue shift, a shift of the light in a celestial body towards the blue end of the spectrum, indicating movement of the light source towards the observer.

During the collapse, the Doppler effect which, in our present universe, gives rise to a red shift would be reversed and any radiation produced would have been amplified by a blue shift. Now, shift the spectrum of any radiation to the blue and in effect you raise its associated temperature, so the state of maximum density could have been very hot. This heat would have survived the bounce into the expansion phase, and so the big bang would have been a hot big bang. *Dennis Sciama, "Cosmology Now: Cosmological Models," The Listener, May 25, 1972, p 682*

[1965, patterned on *red shift* (1931)]

blue-shift, *v.t.:* In the switchback universe, however, the divisions are quite clear. Even better, the background radiation is a necessary feature of the universe. During the contracting phase of each cycle, starlight and other radiation is blueshifted to an ever-increasing degree, eventually being scrambled up in the fireball between cycles. *"Monitor: Times Are Changing in the Switchback Universe," New Scientist, Nov. 9, 1972, p 318*

► Blue shifts are rare phenomena and remain largely theoretical; almost all extragalactic objects show the red shift. In 1978, however, an object (designated SS433) was discovered in or on the fringes of the Milky Way simultaneously flying toward and away from the earth at very high speeds—that is, exhibiting alternately a red shift and a blue shift. Since the motion toward the earth was estimated to be as fast as 20,000 miles a second, this was regarded as the largest blue shift ever observed.

The blue shift and red shift variations seem to occur in tandem, as though on opposite sides of a central energy source. Yet they appear to be too far apart for such coordinated behavior.

The cyclic variations do not apply to the dominant emission of light from the "star" itself. Also an examination of old photographs has shown no significant variation in its brightness over the last 50 years. In this respect, it differs from quasars, which tend to be highly variable. *Walter Sullivan, "Astronomy Is Puzzled by Oddity in the Sky," The New York Times, April 24, 1979, p C1*

blues rock, a blend of the blues and rock music.

Although it can hardly be said to have pushed blues rock, country rock or good old rhythm and blues into the background, classical rock's success has been an immense surprise to the U.S. record industry, which has yet to produce an American model. *"Rock Goes to College," Time, Sept. 23, 1974, p 90*

. . . Commander Cody and His Lost Planet Airmen perform some earthy (despite their name) blues-rock and country-rock. *"Goings On About Town," The New Yorker, March 10, 1975, p 6*

[1974]

blue straggler, any of a group of blue stars somewhat to the left of the top of the main sequence.

Perhaps the most puzzling stars to explain are the "blue stragglers," a small number of stars that seemingly refuse to turn off the main sequence. Actually they may represent a brief transitional stage between the red-giant and horizontal-branch phases. *Icko Iben, Jr., Scientific American, July 1970, p 33*

[1970]

B lymphocyte, another name for B CELL.

The lymphocytes involved in immunity are of two quite distinct classes. The first of these, the so-called B lymphocytes, are those that mature into cells that actually manufacture antibodies. But they cannot do so without the help of the second lymphocyte class, known as T cells. *Graham Chedd, "Genetics, Immunity and Disease," New Scientist, May 25, 1972, p 432*

[1972]

boa, *n.* a proposed system of jointly floated currencies whose exchange rates are allowed to fluctuate against each other within limits that are wider than in the SNAKE.

Members of the boa arrangement would place part of their reserves in such a fund and in return receive drawing rights on the assets of the fund which could be used to settle debts incurred . . . *The Times (London), June 13, 1978 (page not known)*

[1978, patterned on SNAKE]

boarder baby, *U.S.* an infant or young child who is kept indefinitely in a hospital because the parents are not able or legally permitted to assume custody.

The problem of the so-called boarder babies—children stuck in hospitals for months and sometimes years after the medical reasons for their hospitalization have disappeared—is said by municipal administrators to have resulted from a "bureaucratic morass." . . . A good example of a boarder baby would be a child born addicted to drugs as a result of his or her mother's addiction. *"Boarder Babies," The New York Times, Dec. 7, 1976, p 40*

[1976] Compare HEROIN BABY.

boat people, refugees from southeastern Asia, especially Vietnam, who emigrate in boats for any country that will allow them to enter.

Department spokeswoman Jill Schuker said there has been a sizable increase recently in the number of "boat people" fleeing Vietnam. *"U.S. Assails Viet Abuses Forcing People to Flee," Los Angeles Times, Nov. 17, 1978, p 1*

The 25,000 people whose entry was authorized last June, . . . include many of the 3,500 Vietnamese on board the cargo ship Hai Hong, which was turned away by the Malaysians, as well as 15,000 other boat people who have been given temporary refuge in such countries as Malaysia, Indonesia and Thailand. *The Times (London), Nov. 30, 1978, p 7*

[1977]

bodh·ran ('baθ ræn), *n.* an Irish drum.

Apart from the violin, traditional Irish instruments include a small flute, the "tin whistle," a goatskin drum called a bodhran, the pipes and of course the small Irish harp. *Barbara Crossette, "It's a Great Time to Be Irish," The New York Times, Oct. 28, 1977, p C17*

[1976, from Irish *bodhrán* a deaf person, from *bodhar* deaf]

body art, a form of art in which the body of the artist or another person is decorated or used in other ways for some aesthetic effect, and often recorded photographically.

Painting, declared obsolete by '60s pundits, spurned outright by conceptualists who turned to film, video, earth works and body art—how could Snow, a role model for the upwardly modern, revert to such a *retardataire* medium? "It might be more radical now to be conservative," muses Snow . . . in his downtown Toronto studio. *Maclean's, Dec. 11, 1978, p 4*

[1971]

body artist: Like the art and language group, body artists are disinterested in and despairing of the traditional formal concerns of abstract art. *Victor H. Miesel, "Art," The Americana Annual 1975, p 104*

body bag, a rubberized, zippered sack for holding and transporting a corpse.

They dragged him down the stairs and put him in a body bag. It's like a straight jacket. *Studs Terkel, Harper's, Feb. 1974, p 64*

[1967]

body dancing, another name for TOUCH DANCING.

Reporters of social doings now tell us that "body-dancing" is back, and that They are doing it.

Since I never seem to be where They are, I can only testify to what we did from the age of 18 onward during the '30s, '40s, and late '50s of this century. We never called it "body-dancing"; it was just a delicious way for males and females to move together on any smooth public or private floor large enough for a small band and free movement. *Marya Mannes, "Dancing Cheek to Cheek," Newsweek, Dec. 10, 1973, p 16*

[1973]

body scanner, a CAT scanner used to diagnose abnormalities of the body.

The body scanner took large numbers of low-dosage pictures from different angles, processed the results in a computer, and fed them out as detailed three-dimensional pictures of organs such as the lungs, pancreas, kidneys and other internal structures 'seen' from any required angle. Besides being three-dimensional, these pictures were far clearer and more detailed than those taken either with conventional X-ray machines or by any other means. Doctors confirmed that the body scanner would revolutionize diagnosis. *John Newell, "Science, Medicine and Technology," The Annual Register of World Events in 1975 (1976), p 356*

[1975] Compare BRAIN SCANNER.

body scanning: "In diagnosing disease," Dr. Cooper points out, "total body scanning machines are probably the biggest breakthrough in radiology since the invention of the X-ray tube." *T. K. Irwin, Family Weekly, April 4, 1978, p 4*

bodyshell, *n.* the outer shell or frame of a motor vehicle.

The derby is a two-door saloon version of the Polo, sharing virtually the same mechanical specification and layout but offering a "three-box" bodyshell, with separate boot, in place of the two-box hatchback. *The Times (London), Jan. 19, 1978, p 29*

[1976]

body shirt, a tight-fitting shirt or blouse, especially one which is snapped or sewn between the legs.

For those ladies who want their tattoos only temporarily, and without pain, there are Lyle Tuttle-designed body shirts which can be worn when desired, and removed at will. *The Bangkok Post, March 18, 1973, p 14*

[1970]

body-shirted, *adj.:* One of the body-shirted pretty young women came up to Mr. White and said she was going to Macy's to buy some candles. *"The Talk of The Town," The New Yorker, Aug. 28, 1971, p 20*

body shop, *U.S. Slang.* **1** a place of prostitution.

I found your article on the body shops [Dec. 15] disheartening. It seems ludicrous for law enforcement officers to devote so much effort to cracking down on a harmless exercise the prostitutes and their clients have been pursuing for thousands of years. It would seem more sensible merely to tax these operations at a fairly high rate. *John S. Connolly III, Washington, D.C., "Forum: Body Shops," Time, Jan. 5, 1976, p 4*

2 a business firm that provides people needed for such purposes as filling a hall, staging a demonstration, etc.

Not all consultants are consulting firms. . . . Others are employees of concerns known in the trade as "body shops," suppliers of a phantom work force in an era of mandatory Federal personnel ceilings. *The New York Times, Dec. 5, 1977, p 32*

[1975, specialized use of the term for an automobile body repair ship]

Bok globule (bɑk), any of a class of interstellar dust clouds that are compact, opaque, and regular in form, thought to be the precursor of stars.

Lacking an internal energy source, Bok globules are among the coldest objects in interstellar space: most are only about 10 degrees Kelvin (10 degrees Celsius above absolute zero). Hence they are nearly ideal subjects for comparison with theoretical cloud models, the highly simplified representations of essential cloud physics that astrophysicists construct to test their understanding of interstellar processes. *Robert L. Dickman, "Bok Globules," Scientific American, June 1977, p 67*

[1977, named after Bart J. *Bok,* a Dutch-American astronomer who first suggested their importance in 1947]

bo·lo tie ('bou lou) or **bo·la tie** ('bou lə), a cord or leather necktie with a decorative clasp, worn in the western United States.

The attorney in Las Vegas, a young chap in a fancy office, wearing a bolo tie and expensive boots, said right away that Earl C. had a case. *Patricia Zelver, The Atlantic, Dec. 1970, p 79*

The state legislature passed 208 bills during the first session, ranging from the significant (establishment of state kindergartens) to the innocuous (recognizing the bola tie as the official state neckware). *Clyde Andrew Murray, "Arizona," 1972 Collier's Encyclopedia Year Book (1971), p 122*

Wesley Bolin, whose death Saturday thrust the governor-

ship on Mr. Babbitt, had an affinity for sport shirts and Western-style string ties called bolos. *The New York Times, March 8, 1978, p 15*

[1964, probably from its resemblance to the *bola,* a weapon used by South American cowboys] Also shortened to **bolo.**

bong (bɔŋ), *n.* a pipe for smoking marijuana or hashish.

A bong is a long, vertical pipe with a large smoke chamber and a hole that creates a carburetor effect, enabling you to draw cool air in on top of the hot smoke. According to the theory, the heavier, colder air sinks and presses the smoke down in your lungs, thereby giving a more intense high. Upper Berks County Grain Company, (the third of the paraphernalia Big Three after Adams Apple and Ripps) has come up with the fanciest bong of all: a gold-plated number two feet high that retails for $800 to $1,000. *Anthony Astrachan, "Pot Luck," The New York Times Magazine, March 21, 1976, p 21*

[1976, of uncertain origin]

boog·ie or **boog·ey** ('bug i: *or* 'bu: gi:), *n.* **1** a very fast and lively form of rock'n'roll based on the blues.

"Hip Shake" is a simple Slim Harpo boogie, spotlighting effective mantric guitar and clattering percussion. "Casino Boogie" slows it down, with rolling electric piano (Nicky Hopkins, sessionman supreme), and Richard effectively adding an occasional second part to Jagger's lead vocal. *Richard Williams, "The Stones 9 Years on and Still at the Top," The Times (London), May 25, 1972, p 12*

2 *Slang.* another name for DISCO.

Bianca's Boogie is so exhausting that few can follow. John Travolta can, of course. The 25-year-old slick-hipped star of Saturday Night Fever and Grease couldn't do even a disco kneesbend until he hired Jimmy Gabina. *"Can Jogging Ruin Your Health?" Australasian Post, Jan. 25, 1979, p 6*

—*v.i. Slang.* to dance uninhibitedly, especially to disco music.

Says Cleveland Promoter Jules Belkin, "They are up on the seats boogieing and running around the hall." *"Faces in the Crowd," Time, June 24, 1974, p 83*

Billy . . . is torn between going to college or going boogeying with friends at the local disco. *John J. O'Connor, The New York Times, Feb. 1, 1979, p C24*

[1972, extended sense of *boogie* (1941) a style of playing blues on the piano]

bookteller, *n. U.S.* a person who reads books aloud for phonograph or tape recordings.

The actors he hires as booktellers are, he says, "highly skilled pros, who are not superstars." They include Jerry Orbach, Moses Gunn, Leonard Frey, John McGiver. "We bend over backward to select the right voice, one that will enhance the text." *Lewis Grossberger, "90-Minute Novels Switch On Cassette Set," New York Post, April 23, 1974, p 4*

[1974]

boom baby, *U.S.* Usually plural. **boom babies.** a person born during a BABY BOOM.

The boom babies provide a strong core readership within what is sometimes called "the upper half of the eighteen-to-thirty-five market" not just because of their numbers but also because of their habits. *The New Yorker, April 10, 1978, p 120*

The fervent cry of many of the boom babies in the '60s was "Don't trust anyone over 30." Now that so many of them have crossed that barrier, into the golden twilight of their 30s, they are apt to glamorize their new estate just as they did their former. *Time, April 24, 1978, p 100*

[1973] Also called BABY BOOMER.

boom carpet, the area affected by a sonic boom.

Of those who have been asked [their opinion of Concorde] in a Government-sponsored survey, as residents of the so-called boom carpet, many will only have experienced a minor boom such as is felt when one is several miles away from the flight path. *Monica Vincent, Truro, Cornwall, in a Letter to the Editor, The Times (London), May 31, 1972, p 20*

[1966] Also called BOOM PATH.

boom corridor, a restricted route for supersonic aircraft.

BOAC would like to operate Concorde with only one stop — at Lagos, West Africa. The most efficient way of doing this would be to establish a "boom corridor" through the sparsely-populated deserts and jungles of Morocco, the Spanish Sahara, Mauritania, and Mali, then, after crossing the Gulf of Guinea, through Angola and Botswana. *David Fairhall, "More Concorde Tests," The Manchester Guardian Weekly, Jan. 6, 1973, p 8*

[1972]

boom path, another name for BOOM CARPET.

The aircraft is inefficient at subsonic speeds, and inordinately noisy as a result. During normal supersonic flight, which the airlines promise, would not occur over U.S. territory, the plane lays down a "boom path" 50 miles wide. *Patrick Dineen and Bill Lowther, Maclean's, Jan. 1976, p 55*

[1976]

boomy, *adj. U.S.* growing vigorously; prosperous.

At home, the company's business is not nearly so boomy. Bob Fluor blames federal fumbling. "We expect little or no refinery work here until we get some kind of energy policy," he says. *"Corporations: Flourishing Fluor," Time, Jan. 5, 1976, p 75*

[1976, from *boom* a sudden or rapid growth in business]

bootleg turn, an abrupt turning around of an automobile by using the emergency brake to lock the rear wheels and spinning the steering wheel in a sharp turn.

To offset the added weight, which brings the total up to some 4,500 lbs., he equips the car with a high-powered engine (400 h.p. or more) and an especially strong, road-hugging suspension system. The result: an auto that can absorb considerable punishment and still execute bootleg turns and high-speed escapes. *Time, July 10, 1978, p 55*

[1978]

boots, *n.pl. U.S. Slang.* an illegal linear amplifier connected to a citizens band radio to boost transmission.

Because of overcrowding, many a CB enthusiast (called an "apple") is strapping an illegal linear amplifier ("boots") on to his transceiver ("ears") which is limited by the Federal Communications Commission ("Big Daddy" in the US) to an output power of no more than five watts. *Nicholas Valéry, New Scientist, June 30, 1977, p 764*

[1977]

bootstrap, *n.* a theory in particle physics which holds that all nuclear particles are composed of each other, as distinguished from the theory that all particles are built out of a limited number of elementary particles, such as the quark.

Interdependence is the core of Chew's thinking. The simple fact that all particles are related should be enough to determine everything. If we study hard enough, Chew maintains, we will find that the masses and electric charges of all particles, and the strengths of the forces between them, are exactly what they are because no other arrangement would be logically and mathematically self-consistent. This theory is known as the bootstrap, because it suggests that physics can pull itself up by its bootstraps. Assume nothing, prove everything. *Robert H. March, "The Quandary Over Quarks," The World Book Science Annual 1975 (1974), p 92*

[1966] See QUARK.

born-again, *adj. Especially U.S.* **1** of or having to do with personal conversion and renewed commitment to Christ as the way to salvation; evangelical; revivalistic.

I worried that the Carters' born-again religion came dangerously close to fanaticism. It didn't seem wise or prudent for a candidate to speak so often of Christ and Christianity. *Harriet Van Horne, "Things to Come," New York Post, Nov. 5, 1976, p 36*

The Born Again movement expressed itself chiefly in efforts to win other people to personal salvation, and measured progress by the degree of success it tended to see. The most flamboyant and aggressive effort at such conversion came from the Campus Crusade organization, headed by evangelist Bill Bright. *Martin E. Marty, "Protestantism," The 1978 World Book Year Book, p 450*

2 *Figurative.* marked by a rebirth or renewal (as of interest, freshness, or youth); resurgent.

On their way to *gourmandise*, a curious thing has happened to born-again American cooks: they have rediscovered the glorious raw ingredients and inimitable provincial dishes of their own country. *"Living: Love in the Kitchen," Time, Dec. 19, 1977, p 56*

Gross, Joy. The 30-Day Way to a Born-Again Body: a total regimen plus the new natural carbohydrate diet that can make you stay thinner, look younger, live longer. *Library Journal, Nov. 15, 1978, p 2342*

3 born again, *Especially U.S.* converted through a personal renewed commitment to Christ as savior.

Speaking or singing in tongues — messages transmitted via an unknown language — is a regular event for the "born again" — people who have welcomed Jesus into their hearts. *Suzanne Zwarun, "Religion: The Holy Roman Rollers," Maclean's, Nov. 15, 1976, p 74*

A devout Baptist, [Anita] Bryant claims she was "born again" at the age of eight. *Time, June 13, 1977, p 20*

[1976] ► The phrase *born again*, though familiar to evangelists and many Christians, became popular in 1976 when Presidential candidate Jimmy Carter openly described himself as "a born-again Christian." The source of the phrase is in the Gospel of John (3:3 and 3:7): "Jesus answered and said ... Except a man be born again, he cannot see the kingdom of God. ... Marvel not that I said unto thee, Ye must be born again."

Borrowings. ▶ English borrows words liberally from other languages; it has, so far as we know, throughout its history. Though the purposes and conditions of borrowing vary greatly, the appearance of a foreign word in English often means the writer is using a native name for an unfamiliar thing or idea. Expanding global contacts are accompanied by more and more borrowings from languages, especially those of Asia and Africa, at one time considered exotic because they were not generally familiar.

French and Latin, traditional sources of much of our vocabulary, continue to play an active role in the borrowing process. Some of the borrowings from French in this book—such as PÉQUISTE and INDÉPENDANTISTE are cultural and of a familiar type; but DÉJÀ ENTENDU and DÉJÀ LU are new creations from French words on the model of the long established *déjà vu;* and HAUT and APRÉS- were "abstracted" in English from French phrases. OBDUCT is, in a sense, a borrowing from Latin that follows the familiar pattern of taking a word from the Latin stock when needed; but this particular example is also a *reborrowing,* for it was once used in English but abandoned. Even though Latin is no longer the lingua franca of the intellectual community, English is still subject to recurring vestiges of its influence, evident in a writer's use of FUROR COLLIGENDI, an uncontrollable urge or rage to collect things, on the model of the older *furor loquendi* (rage for speaking) and *furor scribendi* (rage for writing).

Other languages that were significant contributors in the past continue to provide new borrowings:

German BÜROLANDSCHAFT, GANZFELD, GLEIT-ZEIT
Italian CALZONE, CONSIGLIERE, GONZO
Russian GULAG, SAMBO, ZEK
Spanish APERTURISMO, HUAYCO, SALSA
Yiddish NUDZH, TCHOTCHKE, ZETS

The growing influx of African and Asian words is illustrated by:

Bantu languages
  (Shona) CHIMURENGA
  (Setswana) PULA
  (siSwati) LILANGENI
  (Swahili) KHANGA, KWANZA, UJAMAA
Amharic (Ethiopia) KEBELE, DIRGUE, BIRR
Arabic KHOUM, OUGIYA, SAHRAWI
Pashto (Afghanistan) BUZKASHI
Persian BAZAARI, KOMITEH
Chinese DAZIBAO, HEI JEN, HOISIN
Japanese HAYASHI, IPPON, KUROMAKU
Korean CHISANBOP, TAEKWONDO

Borrowings sometimes enter English in the form of loan translations. The new senses of HEGEMONY and REEDUCATION are each a translation of a Chinese and a Vietnamese term. Other loan translations include GLIDING TIME from the German GLEITZEIT and DIALOGUE OF THE DEAF, from the French DIA-LOGUE DES SOURDS. In several instances, the foreign term and the loan translation enjoy currency in English, a situation which is becoming commoner as cultural contacts expand.

The degree to which new borrowings become naturalized in English varies considerably. The verb OBDUCT (from Latin *obductus*) and the noun PEREN-NITY (from French *pérennité*) are Anglicized forms, adapted by analogy with many standard words derived from Latin or French; hence they cannot visually be distinguished from native or naturalized words and so can hardly be considered foreign, despite the fact that they are recent borrowings. Least "assimilated" are those borrowings which retain their original spellings and an approximation of their original pronunciations, such as CUISINE MIN-CEUR and BERUFSVERBOT. Even such clearly foreign loanwords can remain in English for a very long time (for example *à la carte*, in English since 1826, and *coup d'état*, in English since 1646), and though they retain their foreign appearance, they become fully established (though not wholly integrated) words in English.

For a discussion of borrowings in English, see the Introduction (pp. 1-61) to *A Dictionary of Foreign Words and Phrases in Current English* by A. J. Bliss (Routledge and Kegan Paul, London, 1966).

Bos·ny·wash ('bɑs nə‚waʃ), *n.* a thickly populated region of the eastern United States extending from New England to the nation's capital.

There is no question but that a period of intense development took place after the Second World War (after my birth) which radically altered not just my corner of the world but the entire region, creating the Eastern megalopolis, the Boston-New York-Washington axis sometimes referred to as Bosnywash. *Suzannah Lessard, The New Yorker, Oct. 11, 1976, p 54*

[1969, from *Bos*ton + *New York* City + *Wash*ington, D.C.]

▶ Similar names have been proposed for other regions comprising several large metropolitan areas: *Chipitts* (*Chi*cago to *Pitts*burgh) and *Sansan* (*San* Francisco to *San* Diego).

BOSS (bɔ:s *or* bɑs), *n.* the secret intelligence organization of South Africa.

The group is convinced that there have been between eight and 20 BOSS agents working in Britain. *Peter Harvey, "South African Secret Police and British Security," The Manchester Guardian Weekly, Nov. 27, 1971, p 9*

[1969, acronym for *Bureau of State Security*]

Botswanian or **Botswanan,** *n.* a native or inhabitant of Botswana, a country in southern Africa (the former Bechuanaland), independent since 1966.

He hopes that the school's target of 250 pupils will eventually comprise a majority of Botswanians. *The Times (London), May 9, 1970, p 8*

—*adj.* of Botswana or its people.

The Botswanan Government has said the cattle were slaughtered by veterinary officers to prevent the spread of foot and mouth disease. *The Times (London), May 27, 1977, p 9*

[1967]

bottleneck, *n. U.S.* a style of guitar playing in which a piece of glass, metal, etc., is used to press down on the strings to produce a gliding sound.

Otherwise they might feel it's kind of freaky for a girl who looks like Bonnie to be singing and playing the country blues of the black man. But she draws gasps from the crowd when she lets herself go on the guitar—bottleneck, slide, funky, chords overlapping, notes ringing out of solitary confinement, bending them like•one to the delta born, evoking that rare vintage whine of train whistles, lost love and dusty lament. *Hubert Saal, "Music: Bonnie and Blue," Newsweek, Nov. 6, 1972, p 66*

[1966, from the use of the broken neck of a bottle for this purpose]

bottleneck inflation, *Economics.* a rise in prices without an increase in the aggregate demand for goods.

The Japanese, who buy about nine-tenths of their oil from the Middle East, are understandably the gloomiest. They have even coined a new phrase—"bottleneck inflation"—to describe the 17 per cent rise in wholesale prices and 13 per cent in consumer prices officially expected in the six months to the end of March. *The Manchester Guardian Weekly, Dec. 8, 1973, p 1*

[1970] Compare HESIFLATION, SLUMPFLATION.

bottomless, *adj.* **1** completely naked; nude.

The court decided that state liquor authorities had the power to withhold liquor licenses from places that featured bottomless dancers or erotic films. *"The Law: The Court Moves Against Porn," Time, June 25, 1973, p 72*

2 featuring naked dancers or performers.

It is a piece of ethnocentrism to assume that Saturday night is the night all Americans go out on the town—movies, plays, ballet, bottomless bars and the like. *Arnold Hano, "Can Archie Bunker Give Bigotry A Bad Name?", The New York Times Magazine, March 12, 1972, p 32*

[1972, patterned on *topless*]

bottom line, usually, **the bottom line. 1** the line that summarizes the net profit or loss of a company or organization; the last line of a financial statement.

His only interest is in the bottom line. He doesn't know or care about books or art or music or even his own wife—only about the bottom line. *Harper's Bazaar, Oct. 1972, p 105*

These three are competing with other airlines for passengers and with each other for performance on the bottom line. *"How United Airlines Pulled Out of Its Dive," Business Week, June 29, 1974, p 66*

2 *Figurative.* the main point; gist; summary.

And the bottom line of the lesson is simple: Throw away your analysts, your figures, and your chart board—get yourself a dart board. *Cleveland Amory, "Curmudgeon-at-Large," Saturday Review, Dec. 18, 1973, p 13*

The bottom line is that Patrick Buchanan wants to have news broadcasts subservient to advertisers. *Leonard Spinrad, New York, N.Y., in a Letter to the Editor, TV Guide, Aug. 24, 1974, p A-6*

I think Jackson was right (but for the wrong reason). Once the Court identifies the police action as unconstitutional, that ought to be the end of the matter. There should be no "degrees" of "offensiveness" among different varieties of *unconstitutional* police conduct. A violation of the

Constitution ought to be the "bottom line." This is where the *Weeks* and *Mapp* Courts drew the line. This is where it ought to stay. *Yale Kamisar, Judicature, Aug. 1978, p 84*

3 *Figurative.* the chief quality; basic characteristic.

In his new play, *Seascape,* Edward Albee seems drained of almost all vitality—theatrical, intellectual, artistic. And vitality was always Albee's bottom line, the one quality that even his detractors admitted he possessed. *Jack Kroll, "Theater: Leapin' Lizards," Newsweek, Feb. 10, 1975, p 75*

Also used attributively.

What came after was bottom-line architectural pragmatism and the city as setting for social tragedy rather than a brave new world. *Ada Louise Huxtable, "Looking Back at the World of Tomorrow," The New York Times Magazine, Jan. 26, 1975, p 41*

At the net level the difference is even more marked, as Thomson should experience a net, bottom-line effect on only 0.66 per cent against an estimated figure of 5.8 per cent. *"Alternatives for North Sea Financing," The Times (London), Feb. 5, 1976, p 21*

[1970] ► This term became widespread in the United States during the early 1970's, although it is said to have been used as far back as the 1930's in the New York financial district. The phrase may be a translation of the old Yiddish expression *di untershte shure,* whose figurative meaning is also identical with that of the English phrase.

bottom quark, a quark that has three times the mass of a charmed quark.

The upsilon, formed of a bottom quark and a bottom antiquark, is 10 times more massive than the proton. *Walter Sullivan, "New Quarks Stir Debate On Basic Laws of Nature," The New York Times, Feb. 13, 1979, p C2*

[1977] Compare TOP QUARK. See also QUARK.

bowhunt *v.i., v.t.* to hunt game with a bow and arrow.

I had finally done what I was beginning to believe was impossible—I'd killed a groundhog with a bow!

That episode took place only a few years ago. Since then I have bowhunted chucks at every opportunity. *Outdoor Life, March 1971, p 211*

[1968]

bow shock, or **bowshock,** *n.* a shock wave caused by the interaction of solar wind with a planet's magnetic field.

The real-time surprise of the mission occurred when the spacecraft, traveling inside the bow shock that is the junction between the magnetic field and the solar wind, passed back out of the bow shock and more than 10 hours later popped back in. *"Jupiter Revisited: The Rosetta Stone," Science News, April 13, 1974, p 237*

About 5 million miles (8 million kilometers) from Jupiter, Pioneer detected a major change in the solar wind as the spacecraft passed through an interplanetary shock wave, or bowshock, caused by the planet. *Michael J. S. Belton, "Astronomy: Planetary," The World Book Science Annual 1975, p 246*

[1970, so called from the resemblance of the planetary phenomenon to the wave produced by the bow of a ship] See SHOCK FRONT.

bow wave, another name for BOW SHOCK.

One of the most striking discoveries is that the upper atmosphere of Mars ends in a region of ions that forms a kind of bow wave like that of the earth. This is interpreted as a shock front caused by the interaction of the Martian atmosphere and the solar wind. *Dietrick E. Thomsen, "Mars 2 and 3 Early Results," Science News, June 30, 1973, p 420*

[1972, extended sense of *bow wave* (1877)]

box¹, *n. British.* short for BOX JUNCTION.

Do not enter box, runs the injunction, unless your exit is clear. *The Times (London), May 5, 1970, p 11*

[1970]

box², *n. U.S.* a large, portable radio, often combined with a cassette stereo system.

Up at Crazy Eddie's off Fordham Road . . . they have 40 different kinds of boxes on display—cacophony to go, at prices better than $300 a box. Even children buy. Jon Wettingfeld, one of Crazy Eddie's salesmen, explains the selling technique, zooming up both antennas on a Sanyo box, boosting the bass and treble to maximum, getting the stereo dial needles bouncing like Groucho's eyebrows, and zit-zutting across the FM dial to 92, WKTU, where the disco throbs all day. *Francis X. Clines, "Music from the 'Box' Is Their Forte—or Triple Forte," The New York Times, Aug. 14, 1979, p B3*

[1979]

box junction, *British.* a road intersection that may not be crossed by a vehicle, even if the lights are in its favor, unless the exit is clear of traffic.

Bradford police have temporarily stopped prosecuting motorists for breaches of the box junction regulations, it was stated today. *"Doubts on Box Junctions," The Times (London), Nov. 9, 1972, p 3*

[1965, so called from the boxlike grid of yellow lines painted on the road surface at such an intersection, introduced in Great Britain in 1963]

boy·chik or **boy·chick** ('bɔɪ̯tʃik), *n. U.S. Slang.* boy; kid; young fellow.

The Allen persona—the urban boychik as social misfit— is, of course, an act, a put-on, no more the real performer than Chaplin's tramp or Jack Benny's miser. *"Show Business and TV: Woody Allen," Time, July 3, 1972, p 58*

We get the idea that Francine, a beauty operator, has left Reggie because he'll always be a kid. This is a cheat; Newman deserved the chance to take a bigger bite out of the character—Reggie shouldn't have had to be the bouncing boychick even in his dealings with his wife. *Pauline Kael, "The Current Cinema," The New Yorker, March 7, 1977, p 94*

[1965, from American Yiddish *boytshik* (literally) little boy, from English *boy* + Yiddish diminutive suffix *-tshik* (from Russian *-chik*)]

B particle, a hypothetical elementary particle that is the unit particle of the NEUTRAL CURRENT.

The B particle is the electrically neutral counterpart of the W particles and with them it forms a triplet of the same mass. *Dietrick E. Thomsen, "Weak Interaction: Puzzle of the Fourth Force," Science News, Oct. 9, 1971, p 253*

[1969, perhaps from *boson particle*]

bpi, abbreviation of *bits* (or *bytes*) *per inch*, a unit of measure for memory capacity in databanks.

Developments in peripheral equipment included almost simultaneous announcements by IBM and Storage Technology Corp. of magnetic-tape systems with data stored at 6,250 bits per linear inch of tape (bpi). *Wallace B. Riley, "Computers," Britannica Book of the Year 1974, p 204*

[1974]

bps, abbreviation of *bits* (or *bytes*) *per second.*

Speech is transmitted at a rate measured in "bits-per-second" (bps). Most modern telephone systems operate at 64,000 bps, which is extremely wasteful. Military communication systems work on only 16,000 bps, but only by accepting a lower quality of voice reproduction. *The Times (London), July 20, 1978, p 4*

[1972] See BPI.

b quark, short for BOTTOM QUARK.

The b quark is the fifth in order of search. . . . Evidence for the b was first found in the upsilon particles discovered about two years ago. The upsilons are examples of what is called hidden beauty. They are made of a b quark and an anti-b quark, and therefore in a sense they are subject to internal cancellation. *"Bare Bottom; Naked Charm: Booms-a-Daisy Physics," Science News, Sept. 22, 1979, p 196*

[1978]

bra burner, *Slang.* a derogatory term for a militant feminist or Women's Liberationist.

Barbara Frum [Barbara Frum's article *Great Dames* appeared in the April issue of *Maclean's*] has done more for women than a hundred bra-burners could achieve in a century! *Ann Koyich, Edmonton, in a Letter to the Editor, Maclean's, June 1973, p 20*

The young girl with the nonassertive mother may have learned from television and schoolmates that women as well as men can behave assertively, and home influences may have placed her in conflict by leading her to believe that assertive women are "women's libbers," "bra burners," "commies," or "sluts." *Spencer A. Rathus and Jeffrey S. Nevid, BT: Behavior Therapy, 1977, p 86*

[1972, so called from the practice of feminists burning brassieres in the Women's Liberation movement]

braille cell, a group of phosphenes (luminous rings of the visual cortex) forming a unit of perception in experiments in which a blind person's cortex is electrically stimulated to enable him to perceive braille symbols without touching them.

The number and spatial distribution of phosphenes is inadequate for presentation of 26 ordinary letters. Consequently, as indicated in Fig. 2, six non-interacting phosphenes were selected to form a 'braille cell.' *Wm. H. Dobelle, Michael G. Mladejovsky, and Jerald R. Evans, Salt Lake City, Utah, et al., "Letters to Nature: 'Braille' Reading by a Blind Volunteer by Visual Cortex Stimulation," Nature, Jan. 15, 1976, p 111*

[1976] See CORTICAL BRAILLE.

brain box, *Informal.* an electronic computer.

But then someone plugged the brainbox in, and $18,000-a-month worth of Hewlitt-Packard 21-MX and associated software revealed that it didn't work. As the end of September approached and the value of lost trading edged over $19 million, exchange information, so necessary for business, still wasn't reaching the public. *Maclean's, Oct. 2, 1978, p 43*

[1966]

brain dead, showing a final cessation of electrical

81

activity in the brain, as evidenced by flat tracings on an electroencephalograph.

Her mother believed that God had kept Karen alive "so that others could be helped" by a ruling on when life may become death. But because Karen was not "brain dead," few lawyers were surprised when Judge Robert Muir ruled against any "pulling of the plug." *"The Law: Karen's Precedent," Time, April 12, 1976, p 50*

Laura Schwed came home from a Nassau County day camp last Thursday with a slight sore throat. By the next afternoon, she was "brain dead." *Lindsay Miller, New York Post, July 21, 1977 [page not known]*

[1976, patterned on *brain death* (1968)] See DEATH.

brain gain, an increase in a country's professional and skilled work force resulting from the immigration of foreign scientists, scholars, etc., seeking better job opportunities.

The United States remains the most popular destination, drawing almost half the annual total, or 2,684 last year. An estimated 620,000 Japanese and their descendants live there. Latin America takes the next largest total, as a result of emigration treaties with Japan and the ties of family members already there. For the recipient countries the emigrants produce the opposite of the brain drain, a brain gain. *Andrew H. Malcolm, "The Japanese Emigrant," The New York Times, Nov. 7, 1977, p 12*

[1966, patterned on *brain drain* (1963)]

brain hormone, any of various hormones produced in the hypothalamic region of the brain, such as LRF, TRF, and somatostatin, especially hormones that act upon the pituitary gland to cause release of various factors or hormones.

Before the discovery of brain hormones, the pituitary, a small gland nestled at the base of the brain, was commonly called the body's "master gland." *Edward Edelson, "Discovery of Brain Hormones a Giant Step for Doctors," Sunday News (New York), June 22, 1975, p 74*

Enkephalin is composed of a string of five amino acids, the building blocks of proteins. The particular string that comprises one form of enkephalin is also found in a string of 91 amino acids that comprise the brain hormone known as betalipotropin. *Nature-Times News Service, "Science Report: Pharmacology: Replacing Morphine," The Times (London), Sept. 18, 1976, p 14*

[1975]

brain life, the capacity of the brain or central nervous system to function, as shown by neurobiological tests.

Scientists and physicians should accept "brain life" as a definition for the beginning of human life just as they have accepted "brain death" — complete absence of detectable brain waves — as the leading indicator of death, [Dr. Dominick] Purpura told a symposium held on the fifth anniversary of the Rose F. Kennedy Center for Research in Mental Retardation and Human Development. *Edward Edelson, "Fetus Has No Brain Life Until 8 Months: Doc," New York Daily News, May 9, 1975, p 14*

[1975, patterned on *brain death* (1968)]

brain scan, an X-ray picture made by a BRAIN SCANNER.

They also propose . . . that boxers should be compelled to go to hospital for a brain-scan after being knocked out. Regular brain-scanner checks should also be carried out, they

say. *The Times (London), Aug. 19, 1978, p 6*

[1975]

brain scanner, a CAT scanner used to diagnose abnormalities in the brain.

At many hospitals, brain scanners are running 10 and 12 hours a day, six days a week, and there are still long waiting lists of patients. *Jonathan Spivak, "Super X Rays: A 'Glamour Machine' Is Hailed by Doctors as a Boon to Diagnosis," The Wall Street Journal, Dec. 10, 1975, p 1*

[1975] Compare BODY SCANNER, CAT SCANNER.

Brand X, an unidentified item serving as a foil to show the comparative superiority of another item.

Once it [ego] has achieved righteousness, it is ready to sign up for holy war and to kill all who remain confused or who have developed a sort of righteousness (Brand X) that varies in any detail (or only in nomenclature) from the one, true Eternal Verity brand label. *John Ciardi, "Manner of Speaking," Saturday Review, Jan. 22, 1972, p 25*

Republican prospects of unity contrast with Brand X, which is likely to hold primaries for Comptroller and Attorney General; even Governor Carey may face a primary contest. *The New York Times, May 28, 1978, Sec. 4, p 7*

[1970, from the practice in advertisements of referring to a competing product as "brand X"]

Brayton engine, an engine that utilizes a gas turbine to generate mechanical power.

A Brayton engine uses high-speed rotating turbine instead of pistons to compress its working fluid. A diesel uses the heat of compression to ignite the fuel-air mixture. *Illustration legend, "Engines for the Eighties," The World Book Science Annual 1978 (1977), p 97*

[1977, named after G. B. *Brayton*, an American engineer who invented it in the 1800's]

break, *n. U.S.* **1** access to a radio channel by a citizens band radio operator.

"Sometimes it drives me up a wall," Barbara said. "We have the base station here in the house and I'll be trying to call Gene when he's on the way home in his car, and I just won't be able to get a break — I just can't get on the air." *Marshall Schuon, "Using Citizens Band on Vacation," Family Circle, Aug. 1976, p 20*

2 *Also used as an interjection:*

We heard a driver call a passing truck: "Break, Channel 10. I'm calling that blue truck with Ohio plates, westbound. I am eastbound. What's ahead?" *E. D. Fales Jr., "Two-Way Radio for Your Home and Car," Parade, Nov. 16, 1975, p 27*

[1975, from *break* interruption]

breaker, *n. U.S.* **1** a citizens band radio operator requesting the use of a channel.

You get in on the conversation by picking up your microphone, pressing the send-button and asking for a "break," as: "Breaker 19, breaker 19." Usually someone will respond, "Go ahead, breaker," and you're on the air. Simple as that. *Michael Harwood, "America With Its Ears On," The New York Times Magazine, April 25, 1976, p 28*

2 *Also used as an interjection:*

"I'm on the truck's CB all the time," he tells CB Guide. "It seems as soon as I say 'Breaker, breaker, this is Sonny Pruitt,' I'm never at a loss for someone to chat with." *David J. Anderson, CB Guide, May 1976, p 21*

[1963, from *break (in)* to interrupt + -*er*]

breath·hold diving ('breθ₁hould), underwater diving without the use of breathing apparatus, especially a form of diving used by seals, dolphins, etc., in which the breath is held underwater for regular periods, during which the heart rate and brain waves slow down markedly.

The adaptation to breathhold diving of marine animals is probably an especially well developed instance of a very general asphyxial defence mechanism common to all vertebrates from fish to man. *R. W. Elsner, Science Journal, April 1970, p 72*

[1966]

bri·co·lage (bri:kou 'lɑ:ʒ), *n.* the use of ready-made tools or other objects for a variety of purposes.

Thank You Hide, 1970, is a fair example of Wiley's [the artist William T. Wiley] *bricolage*, with its rusty pickax snagged, like an unwanted anchor, on a knotted line from an improvised fishing pole, its ragged sheet of ox hide . . . *"Art: Quirky Angler," Time, Jan. 17, 1972, p 38*

[1964, from French, puttering around, doing odd jobs; originally, the act or skill of causing a ball (as in tennis or billiards) to rebound; see BRICOLEUR]

bri·co·leur (bri: kou 'lœr), *n.* a person who makes use of ready-made tools or other objects for a variety of purposes.

Two years ago several graduate students in related fields made a five-year commitment to launch something called the Bricoleur Association. According to Claude Lévi-Strauss, the *bricoleur*'s "universe of instruments is closed and rules of his game are always to make do with 'whatever is at hand,' that is to say with a set of tools and materials which is always finite and is also heterogeneous because what it contains bears no relation to the current project." *"Opportunity: How to Be a Bricoleur," Harper's, Sept. 1974, p 87*

[1974, from French, putterer, handyman, from *bricoler* to do odd jobs, from *bricole* an odd job; originally, the rebound or ricochet of a ball]

bri·ga·tis·ti (₁bri: gɑ:'ti:s ti:), *n.pl.* members of the RED BRIGADES.

The Communists, in the organization's view, had sold out; the aim of the *brigatisti*, much like that of 19th century anarchists, was to purify society by overthrowing all existing institutions. But the Red Brigades seem to have no coherent vision of what would replace them. *Time, March 27, 1978, p 43*

[1978, from Italian, from *Brigate (Rosse)* Red Brigades + *-isti*, plural of *-ista* -ist]

Bril·louin scattering (bri: yə'wæ), *Physics.* the scattering of light by phonons (units of sound or vibration in crystals).

Krishnan brings the book to a close with a very lucid account of Brillouin scattering, which is an excellent introduction to this subject. *N. Sheppard, "Book Review: Raman Principles," Review of "The Raman Effect," edited by A. Anderson, Nature, July 28, 1972, p 234*

[1965, named after Louis Marcel *Brillouin*, 1880?-1948, a French physicist who described it in 1922]

broadcast journalism, the gathering, editing, and reporting of news for radio and television.

Some powerful broadcasters want the Government to-

tally out of broadcast journalism, and they cite the 1974 landmark First Amendment case that applies to newspapers — *Tornillo v. The Miami Herald*, in which the Supreme Court decided "it has yet to be demonstrated how Government regulation in this crucial [editing] process can be exercised consistent with First Amendment guarantees of a free press." *Fred W. Friendly, "What's Fair On The Air?," The New York Times Magazine, March 30, 1975, p 48*

[1968] Compare ELECTRONIC JOURNALISM, PRINT JOURNALISM.

broadcast journalist: The Shadow in the Cave bears the mark of these years — witness his definition of the broadcast journalist as "a eunuch in the harem of ideas." *Stuart Hood, "Broadcasting on a Leash," Review of "The Shadow in the Cave" by Anthony Smith, The Manchester Guardian Weekly, Nov. 17, 1973, p 23*

broadcast satellite, an artificial satellite designed to receive and transmit television signals.

Broadcast satellites are expected to provide both developed and less-developed countries with further means of transmitting their own television programs and setting up both medical and educational consulting services in sparsely settled areas or regions where lines of microwave towers would be expensive to establish and maintain, as in India or the Canadian arctic. *Victor K. McElheny, "Powerful Broadcast Satellite Placed Over Equator," The New York Times, Jan. 30, 1976, p 11*

[1970]

broe·der·bond ('bru: dər₁band), *n.* a secret fraternity, especially one formed for some unsavory or evil purpose.

These people don't all know each other. It's not as though there were some sinister, trans-Canada *broederbond* pulling it all together. But they all know *about* each other, which sometimes amounts to the same thing. *Alexander Ross, Maclean's, March 1974, p 56*

One gathered how deep in the Cabinet, Government and even the powerful but shadowy *Broederbond*, were the divisions between those who wanted radical and swift change and those who wanted to conserve. *The Times (London), Sept. 24, 1977, p 10*

[1974, transferred sense of *Broederbond* (1953) the name of a secret society of Afrikaners organized in 1938 to maintain white supremacy in South Africa, from Afrikaans *broederbond* brotherhood]

bro·mo·crip·tine or **bro·mo·cryp·tine** (₁broumə'krip ti:n), *n.* a drug that inhibits excessive secretion of the pituitary hormone prolactin, used especially in the treatment of acromegaly and of infertility in women and men. *Formula:* $C_{32}H_{40}BrN_5O_5$

Bromocriptine, a drug derived from the fungus ergot that has proved useful in treating some rare cases of infertility in women, may also help women who fail to conceive as a side-effect of the oral contraceptive pill. *"Science Report: The Pill: Drug May Counter Side-Effects," The Times (London), Mar. 12, 1977, p 4*

In one report, . . . bromocryptine increased sexual libido and restored spermatogenesis and sexual potency in seven male patients. *"Biomedicine: A Drug to Soup-Up Sex," Science News, Aug. 13, 1977, p 105*

[1976, shortened from *bromoergocryptine*, from *bromo-* bromide + *ergot* + *crypt* small tubular gland (a reference to the pituitary gland) + *-ine* (chemical suffix)]

83

Brompton cocktail

Brompton cocktail or **Brompton mixture,** a preparation of narcotics used to relieve pain caused by cancer.

Heroin is thought to be better than other narcotics for treating some cases of cancer pain. The so-called Brompton cocktail, which can include both heroin and cocaine, is valuable in treating nausea and other symptoms. *The New York Times, Feb. 26, 1978, Sec. 4, p 7*

In order to ease the physical pain of our cancer patients, we used an American version of the English Brompton mixture. This liquid analgesic that makes use of morphine, instead of heroin (which is illegal in the United States) enabled us to give pain medication orally rather than by injections . . . With the help of G. Humma, a pharmacist at the Indianapolis Methodist Hospital, a handbook of the Brompton mixture was developed and became available to any physician who was willing to try this marvelous cocktail . . . In all the years that we have used the Brompton mixture, our patients have been able to be comfortable, alert, and conscious, and we have never had an overdose or a drug addiction. *Elizabeth Kübler-Ross, To Live Until We Say Good-Bye, 1978, p 23*

[1978, named after the *Brompton* Chest Hospital, where it was apparently first used]

Brøn·sted acid or **Brön·sted acid** ('brœn sted), an acid that can yield a proton (hydrogen ion) to another substance.

It has recently become possible to determine the acidities of a variety of Brønsted acids in the gas phase and, thus, in the absence of solvent. *John I. Brauman, "Acid and Base," McGraw-Hill Yearbook of Science and Technology 1975, p 89*

[1967, named after J. N. *Brønsted*, a Danish chemist who in 1923-24 defined acids and bases in terms of proton transfer]

broomball, *n.* a game similar to ice hockey in which a volleyball is propelled over the ice with brooms.

This year (January 28 to February 6) the carnival's main event will be the seventh annual 500-mile snowmobile race from Winnipeg to St. Paul. There will also be speed skating, curling, sports car racing and slow-pitch softball on ice, broomball, chess, ski jumping, and the country's oldest hot-air balloon race. *David Butwin, "In the Days of the Ice Palace," Saturday Review, Jan. 29, 1972, p 55*

[1972] ▶ This game is well-known in Canada and the *Dictionary of Canadianisms on Historical Principles* (1967) attests the use of the term since 1933. The game became known outside Canada in the early 1970's.

Brown Book, an annual report on Great Britain's petroleum reserves, explorations, requirements, etc., published by the British Department of Energy since 1974.

What should have been a good week for Britain's North Sea oil business, with publication of this year's "Brown Book" showing yet another rise in the region's estimated reserves, was marred by the blow-out on Phillips Petroleum's Bravo oil production platform in the Norwegian Ekofisk field. *New Scientist, April 28, 1977, p 79*

[1974, from the *brown* color of its cover]

brownie, *n. U.S. Slang.* a chocolate brownie made with marijuana as an ingredient.

An extract of orange peel — which produced an odor so

powerful that Department of Agriculture researchers were driven from their laboratory — is being tested. If it is used, the State Department believes it will give marijuana smokers "the foulest smelling joint or brownie they ever had." *The New York Times Magazine, Nov. 19, 1978, p 60*

[1969, popularized by the film "I Love You, Alice B. Toklas" (1968), in which eating such cakes is shown to have the same effect as smoking marijuana]

brownie point or **Brownie point,** *Especially U.S. Informal.* credit earned by a person for doing the proper or expected thing.

TV station managers realize that the Federal Communications Commission regards full news coverage as a part of the price of a ticket to ride the public airwaves. At license-renewal time, stations discover that such brownie points count more than Nielsen numbers with the FCC. *Harry F. Waters, Newsweek, Dec. 10, 1973, p 78*

Even though you may be untanned and chubby, you gain considerable points if you can yell at your old pal the massage lady, "Got myself all beefed up on the safari, Miss Lois. You'd better slap me back into shape." You win another Brownie point if your children go to boarding school. *Sondra Gotlieb, "Slimming in Arizona With the Very Rich," Maclean's, Oct. 1974, p 54*

[1972, figurative use of *Brownie point*, a supposed point earned by a Girl Scout Brownie for a good deed]

brown sugar, *Especially U.S. Slang.* a grainy, low-grade variety of heroin made in southeastern Asia.

They turned to Asia, where opium is cultivated by hill tribesmen in the lush "golden triangle" formed by the borders of Burma, Thailand and Laos. The product is inferior to the French variety, which was 90 percent pure opium and looked like fine confectioner's sugar. The Asian heroin is coarser — hence its nickname "brown sugar" — and is only 35 to 65 percent pure. It has been known to contain caffeine or even strychnine. *Christopher S. Wren, "The Moscow Connection," The New York Times Magazine, Jan. 9, 1977, p 16*

[1976] Compare MEXICAN BROWN.

brown thumb, *U.S.* 1 lack of ability or success in making plants grow.

The Gardener's Catalogue, by Tom Riker and Harvey Rottenberg. (Morrow, $6.95) How to find what you need to turn a brown thumb into a green one. *Advertisement of Best Sellers, Trade Paperbacks, The New York Times Book Review, Feb. 16, 1975, p 29*

2 someone with a brown thumb.

Traditionally, drying flowers and leaves has been an autumn activity, but now most brown-thumbs go picking all year round. *Susan Cheever Cowley with Lisa Whitman, and Joseph B. Cumming, Jr., "Life Style: The Dry Look," Newsweek, March 10, 1975, p 39*

[1975, patterned on *green thumb* (1943)] Compare WET THUMB.

BSA, abbreviation of *bovine serum albumin.* See the quotation.

BSA is a protein derived from the blood of cattle and is a common substance for experimental use in laboratory experiments in biology. *Dietrick E. Thomsen, "Proteins and Metals Stick Together," Science News, May 18, 1974, p 324*

[1968]

bubble¹, *n.* short for MAGNETIC BUBBLE.

NASA has developed a solid-state data recorder with no mechanical moving parts at all. The device is based on tiny magnetic domains, called "bubbles," which exist in specially prepared garnet chips. With the aid of a magnetic film, applied in a precise pattern on the chips' surfaces, these bubbles can be controlled in such a way as to perform logic functions. *"Aerospace: Recorder Uses No Moving Parts," Science News, Dec. 7, 1974, p 362*

[1970]

bubble², *U.S.* a domelike structure used to enclose a tennis court, swimming pool, etc., to protect it from bad weather.

Plastic bubbles and other indoor facilities have gone up by the hundred, transforming tennis into a year-round game even in the northern stretches of the country. *Herbert Warren Wind, "The Sporting Scene," The New Yorker, Oct. 7, 1972, p 116*

[1971] Also called AIR STRUCTURE. Compare AIR HALL.

bubble domain, another name for a MAGNETIC BUBBLE.

Thousands of bubble domains can be generated in a square inch of material. They can also be made to move around in the material. These two properties give them a high potential for application in computer memories and similar devices. *Dietrick E. Thomsen, "The Magnetic World of Bubble Domains," Science News, May 8, 1971, p 318*

[1971]

bubble-gummer, *n.* a performer of BUBBLE-GUM MUSIC.

You've got some nerve calling the Osmonds bubble-gummers (MUSIC, Sept. 3)! *Renée Marie, "Osmondmania," in a Letter to the Editor, Newsweek, Sept. 24, 1973, p 17*

[1973]

bubble-gum music, rock music with simple, repetitive lyrics.

Older rock fans dismiss the stuff as "bubble gum music," but Micky Dolenz, one of the Monkees, the pre-packaged group who capitalized on subteens in the sixties, defends the genre as "first-grade music for kids in first grade." *Sara Davidson, "Feeding on Dreams in a Bubble Gum Culture," The Atlantic, Oct. 1973, p 64*

[1968, so called from the popularity of bubble gum among children who usually make up the audience for this type of music]

bubbleheaded, *adj. U.S. Slang.* silly; flighty; lightheaded.

Who would have expected the Swiss director Alain Tanner and his co-writer, John Berger, to turn out a bubbleheaded political comedy? *Pauline Kael, "The Current Cinema," The New Yorker, Oct. 18, 1976, p 75*

He is making love to his wife (a porky and bubbleheaded blonde played delightfully by Andréa Ferréol) . . . *Time, Nov. 6, 1978, p 88*

[1966, from earlier slang (1950's) *bubblehead* a silly or stupid person]

bubble memory, a computer memory that stores data in magnetic bubbles.

Bubble memories are inherently serial in organization, so that access time depends on the number of storage loca-

tions in a serial path and on the maximum shifting rate. In present devices serial paths range in length from about 10 locations to 1,000 or more; shifting rates range from a fraction of a microsecond to several microseconds. *Scientific American, Sept. 1977, p 140*

[1973]

bubble umbrella, a dome-shaped transparent umbrella.

She is a sartorial contrast to the local Puerto Rican women: belted raincoat, stockings, high heels. She is carrying a book, a newspaper, a pocketbook, and a bubble umbrella. *"The Talk of the Town," The New Yorker, Sept. 23, 1972, p 29*

[1972]

buckwheat braid, *U.S.* a short braid or pigtail, often tied with a ribbon.

But no successor to the Afro coiffure has caught on more rapidly than the corn-row-tight, Topsylike plaits that until recently were worn by women. Now a growing number of soul brothers are sporting buckwheat braids in as many variations as there are African nations, where the style is traditional. *"Modern Living: The Masculine Twist," Time, Dec. 24, 1973, p 84*

[1971]

bu·fa·di·en·o·lide (ˌbyuː fəˌdaɪ'en ə laɪd), *n.* any of a group of physiologically active steroid hormones that includes bufalin.

The bufadienolides [are] a closely related family of steroids found in both toad venoms and in many plants, and potentially of great importance in the therapy of heart disease and cancer. Bufadienolides (from *bufo*, the Latin for toad) have been widely used in primitive medical practice for thousands of years. *New Scientist, Aug. 6, 1970, p 272*

[1970, from *bufa*lin + *di-* double + *-ene* hydrocarbon + *-ol* alcohol or phenol + *-ide* chemical compound]

bu·fa·lin ('byuː fə lin), *n.* a steroid compound derived from the venom of toads, used in the treatment of heart disease.

The cardiac action of bufalin, for example, has been found about equal to digitoxigenin (from digitalis), and in terms of local anesthetic potency is about 90 times more active than cocaine. *George R. Pettit, "Chemistry: Chemical Synthesis," 1975 Britannica Yearbook of Science and the Future, 1974, p 209*

[1970, from *Bufo* genus of toads + *-alin*, as in *digitalin*]

bu·lim·a·rex·i·a (byuːˌlim ə 'rek siː ə), *n.* a psychological disorder in which a person alternates between an abnormal craving and an aversion to food, found especially among young women.

Recently, we have encountered a related syndrome that we call *bulimarexia.* . . . Women suffering from bulimarexia alternately gorge themselves with food and then empty themselves, whether by fasting, vomiting, or through self-induced diarrhea. The resemblance to anorexia is plain. Anorexic women also usually break off their harsh fasting with an eating binge. But the distinguishing feature of bulimarexia is its *regular* binges, its orgies of eating followed by ritual purifications, over and over again. *Marlene Boskind-Lodahl and Joyce Sirlin, "The Gorging-Purging Syndrome," Psychology Today, March 1977, p 50*

[1976, from *bulim*ia insatiable appetite + connecting -*a*- + ano*rexia* abnormal aversion to food]

bulk buy club, *British.* a club formed to save its members money by buying goods in bulk rather than in normal sizes and packages.

Where a full time post office, shop or garage cannot be sustained, we need combined or part time services. If it really is not possible to run a commercial service then there should be consumer cooperatives or bulk buy clubs operating perhaps in village halls. *The Times (London), Sept. 19, 1978, p 17*

[1977]

bullhorn, *v.t. U.S.* **1** to address or announce over a loudspeaker.

The casualty list of world revolution is endlessly varied, and as S. I. Hayakawa said while bullhorning protesters off the San Francisco State campus "There are no innocent bystanders." *R. Z. Sheppard, Time, Nov. 16, 1970, p 100*

Glick at last bullhorned the request to guards not ten feet from him, through the wire. *Garry Wills, "Love on Trial: The Berrigan Case Reconsidered," Harper's, July 1972, p 63*

2 *Figurative use.*

While this message of preventive medicine is being bullhorned into one ear, there is a steady muttering of dissent going into the other. It is not clear if the dissent is widespread. It has certainly been well publicized. *Harold M. Schmeck Jr., "Dissent Surrounds Flu Shot Program," The New York Times, Oct. 7, 1976, p 19*

[1970, verb use of the noun (1955)]

Bu·mi·pu·tra or **bu·mi·pu·tra** (ˌbuː miˈpuː trə), *n.* a member of the indigenous or native people of Malaysia; a Malay, as distinguished from an ethnic Chinese of Malaysia. *Often used attributively.*

The New Economic Policy . . . promised that the Government's eventual aim was to take care of all the country's poor but the policy orientation for the next five years was concentrated almost totally on the Bumiputras. *M. G. G. Pillai, "Malaysia: Shrewd Changes to Keep Political Popularity," The Times (London), Aug. 31, 1976, p 1*

[1972, from Malay, literally, sons of the soil] See BUMIPUTRAIZATION.

bu·mi·pu·tra·i·za·tion (ˌbuː miˌpuː trə aiˈzei ʃən), *n.* government policy in Malaysia to give preferential treatment to Malays in business, education, language, etc., to compensate for former discrimination by the economically dominant Chinese.

Government officials maintain that bumiputraization — which is clearly a code word for discrimination — is designed to redress the balance. In recent years, and particularly this year, there have been a number of changes openly designed to hold back the Chinese and advance the Malays. *David A. Andelman, "Ethnic Chinese Flee Malay Pressure," The New York Times, July 18, 1976, Sec. 1, p 2*

[1976, from *Bumiputra* + -IZATION]

bump, *n.* Usually **the bump,** a rock 'n' roll dance. See the quotation for details.

Instead of the Twist, hipsters nowadays prefer such contemporary contortions as the Puerto Rican Hustle . . . and, of course, the Bump, where partners bump each other back to back, belly to belly. *Elizabeth Peer with Lisa Whitman, "Entertainment: Bump in the Night," Newsweek, March 24, 1975, p 89*

—*v.i.* to dance the bump.

There is no shortage here of glittering clubs in which to hustle, walk, bump or samba the night away. *Shawn G. Kennedy, "The New Discotheque Scene," The New York Times, Jan. 3, 1976, p 10*

[1975]

bumper strip, *U.S.* a sticker bearing a printed slogan for display on an automobile bumper.

Many Texans are bitter over the Sooners' recruiting forays into their state. A bumper strip seen often around Austin in recent years reads "O.U., The Best Texas Money Can Buy," as if U.T., whose athletic facilities are better than those of most European countries, were lacking in that commodity. *The New York Times Magazine, Jan. 1, 1978, p 20*

[1961, variant of *bumper sticker* (1960)]

BUN, abbreviation of *blood urea nitrogen* (nitrogen in the form of urea found in the blood).

In principle, an artificial kidney is simply a device that leads the blood outside the body and past a cellophanelike membrane. On the other side of the membrane is a briny solution resembling blood — clean blood. Impelled by osmotic pressure, excess water, BUN, sodium, potassium and other wastes sneak through the membrane from the blood into the briny solution. Thus purified, the blood then flows back into the body. *Alan Anderson Jr., "Dialysis or Death," The New York Times Magazine, March 7, 1976, p 42*

[1976]

bun·ga·ro·tox·in (ˌbəŋ gə rouˈtak sən), *n.* a nerve poison, isolated from a snake venom, which blocks the action on muscle tissue of the chemical that transmits nerve impulses (acetylcholine). It is used especially to identify acetylcholine receptors.

Using radioactive bungarotoxin (which binds specifically to ACh [acetylcholine] receptor sites), Nirenberg is able to count the number of receptors in the clusters; it turns out that there are in the region of 9000 per sq. m — this figure is very close to that for receptor concentration in "mature" synapses. *"A Molecular Guiding Hand Helps Nerves and Muscles Get Together," New Scientist, March 1, 1973, p 471*

[1971, from New Latin *Bungarus* (*mueticinctus*) the banded krait, a snake from Taiwan producing the venom + English connecting -*o*- + *toxin*]

Bunker, *n.* Usually, **the Bunker,** a nickname for the coalition of ultra-conservative politicians and government officials of the regime of Francisco Franco (1892-1975); Francoist loyalists as a group.

The reactionary right, the "Bunker," was admittedly still a force to be reckoned with, but many of its members were also shareholders and beneficiaries of *desarrollo* (economic development). *David Rudnick, "Spain: The Post-Franco Era," Britannica Book of the Year 1977, p 627*

[1976, from Spanish (*el*) *Bunker*, from English *bunker* in allusion to the group's entrenched position in government] Compare FRANQUISTA.

Bunkerism, *n, U.S.* short for ARCHIE BUNKERISM.

Besides the song, the album (Atlantic Records) contains excerpts from a dozen shows, a litany of the Bunkerisms that have won *All in the Family* the respect of rednecks and the laughter of liberals. *"Scorn Along with Archie," Time, Jan. 17, 1972, p 47*

[1972]

bu·ra·ku·min ('bur ə ku,min), *n.pl.* (in Japan) people living in small villages or their descendants, long treated as an inferior caste, although officially granted equality in the 1860's.

He considers the Japanese minority known as the Burakumin an encouraging example of what can happen when caste barriers fall. In ancient times, the Burakumin ranked as subhuman, and they are still outcasts in many respects. But the gap in achievement disappears when Burakumin move to the United States, where Americans treat them exactly like other Japanese immigrants. *The New York Times, March 12, 1978, Sec. 4, p 7*

[1967, from Japanese, from *buraku* village, hamlet]

burn bag, *U.S.* a receptacle for secret documents to be officially destroyed by burning.

The most explosive testimony came from Yeoman First Class Charles E. Radford, a clerk who had been assigned to Kissinger's National Security Council staff. In a 23-page statement, Radford admitted rifling White House "burn bags" and briefcases in search of top-secret memos meant only for Kissinger and President Nixon. *Newsweek, March 4, 1974, p 20*

[1973] ► Though this term has long been used in intelligence work, it became current in 1973 in connection with the Watergate investigations.

burn-bag, *v.t. U.S.* to put in a burn bag.

Sen. Edward M. Kennedy pointedly asked what Kelley would do if he were approached with a pitch to stump or gumshoe for the President or to burn-bag evidence in a case that might embarrass the White House ("I would refuse," he said). *"The FBI: Kelley on the Grill," Newsweek, July 2, 1973, p 21*

[1973]

burnout, *n. Drag Racing Slang.* a ride at very high speed.

"Titanium skid plates on the rear of the car, and he'll make a real loud burnout for you. Those long smoky burnouts are to heat up the tires, you know. And when he raises up, oh, Tom is going to raise up for you! White hot sparks come out of those titanium plates, and it's got to be the greatest show in drag racing." *Alan Harrington, "Deus ex Machina," Harper's, Jan. 1976, p 28*

[1976]

Bü·ro·land·schaft ('bʏ rou,la:nt ʃa:ft), *n.* Also Anglicized as **burolandschaft.** a style of interior decoration for offices, in which functional dividers, such as screens or plants, replace walls and work units are arranged to allow for flexibility in the use of space. *Often used attributively.*

Plants play an important part in the open office-landscape concept (*Bürolandschaft*), which developed in Germany and has become widely influential. *Jeanne G. Weeks, "Interior Design," The Americana Annual 1973, p 358*

As an exercise in international architecture this . . . burolandschaft interior will win acclaim, maybe even affection. *Robert Waterhouse, "People and Places: High Society," The Manchester Guardian Weekly, Oct. 13, 1973, p 18*

The open-plan use of a large, unpartitioned office floor . . . is the antithesis of true *Burolandschaft. The Times (London), Sept. 15, 1977 (page unknown)*

[1968, from German, literally, office landscape]

bur·ri·to (bə'ri: tou), *n.* a flour tortilla rolled around a spicy mixture of beef, cheese, and refried beans.

Even the drive-in Dairy Queen offers tacos, enchiladas, and burritos along with its standard shakes, burgers, and fries. *Berton Roueché, "Profiles: Zavala [County, Texas]," The New Yorker, Dec. 4, 1978, p 59*

[1971, from Mexican Spanish, literally, little burro]

bursectomize, *v.t.* to subject to a bursectomy.

We used this approach to obtain information on the relative sensitivity of IgA development to bursectomy. Fifteen chick embryos were bursectomized at 1-day intervals beginning on day 16 of incubation. *Science, Jan. 26, 1973, p 399*

[1973]

bur·sec·to·my (bər'sek tə mi:), *n.* removal of a bursa (lubricating sac) of the body by surgery or hormone injection.

A small portion of chicks subjected to this "hormonal bursectomy," however, are tolerant of foreign skin, an anomaly first noted by Noel L. Warner and Aleksander Szenberg of the Walter and Eliza Hall Institute of Medical Research in Melbourne. *Max. D. Cooper and Alexander R. Lawton III, "The Development of the Immune System," Scientific American, Nov. 1974, p 60*

[1968, from *bursa* + *-ectomy* surgical removal]

burster, *n.* another name for X-RAY BURSTER.

Most of the bursters are located within the galactic disk and are concentrated toward the galactic center. Three slow bursters have been found, however, to lie in globular clusters that were previously known to contain persistent X-ray stars. The single rapid burster lies in the direction of a previously unknown globular cluster that is nearly hidden by interstellar dust. *George W. Clark, "X-Ray Stars in Globular Clusters," Scientific American, Oct. 1977, p 42*

[1976]

bus, *n.* a spacecraft that carries one or more detachable craft or vehicles.

The cluster of probes, making the trip from earth mounted on a single, cylindrical "bus," includes one large probe and three small ones (plus the bus itself, which is also instrumented). The large probe, carrying the atmospheric-composition experiments, will separate from the bus 24 days before reaching the planet and head for a planned entry near the day-side equator. *Science News, Aug. 12, 1978, p 100*

[1968]

businesspeak, *n.* commercial jargon.

While they got on with their day to day job as "medical managers," they saw the Department of Health in its efforts to reorganise NHS administration, produce document after document written in almost unintelligible businesspeak. *Michael O'Donnel, "Voyeur," New Scientist, April 13, 1972, p 94*

[1971, blend of *business* and *speak*, patterned on *Newspeak* and *doublespeak*, the artificial languages in George Orwell's novel *1984*]

bus·ing ('bəs iŋ), *n. U.S.* the transportation of students by buses to schools outside their neighborhoods to achieve a racial balance in schools.

The studies suggest that *on the average* busing probably increases black students' test scores, but that there are plenty of exceptions. *Mary Bane and Christopher Jencks, "Five Myths about Your IQ," Harper's, Feb. 1973, p 40*

Busing is mandatory in San Francisco, but the latest survey showed that the schools had "lost" 3000 white students during the past year. The Berkeley school system, one of the first to begin busing, has more white students than when integration began, but Berkeley does not seem to have inspired nearby school districts. *Carl Irving, "Education in the San Francisco Bay Area," Science, Jan. 25, 1974, p 341*

Also, *especially British,* **bussing.**

The issue which won Wallace much support in this state [Florida] was bussing, which was the transporting of children from their home neighbourhood to schools in other districts to promote racial integration. *James Bishop, "The Americas and the Caribbean: The United States of America," The Annual Register of World Events in 1972 (1973), p 50*

[1964, from gerund of *bus, v.* (1950's) to transport by bus] Also called CROSS-BUSING. Compare ANTIBUSING.

bu·sul·fan (byu:ˈsəl fən), *n.* a highly toxic white, crystalline substance, used in medicine to destroy certain leukemic cells or tumors and in agriculture as a chemical sterilant. *Formula:* $C_6H_{14}O_6S_2$.

A major step toward integrating several control procedures for eradicating the boll weevil, a cotton pest, has been made with the discovery of a chemosterilant. Busulfan makes male boll weevils sexually sterile with little or no other damage to the weevil. *Robert B. Rathbone, "Agriculture," The Americana Annual 1973, p 73*

[1968, from the chemical constituents *bu*tanediol dimethane *sulf*onate + *-an*]

busway, *n.* a road, or lane of a road, set aside for buses.

Ninety per cent of commuters who travel by road come in by buses running on special 'busways' that give the vehicle complete priority over all others from garage to terminus. *Jeremy Bugler, "The Death of the Urban Motorway," The Listener, June 14, 1973, p 785*

[1963, patterned on *motorway, bikeway,* etc.]

Bu·ta·zo·lid·in (ˌbyu: təˈzou lə din), *n.* a trademark for phenylbutazone, an anti-inflammatory and pain-killing drug with no stimulating side effects. *Formula:* $C_{19}H_{20}N_2O_2$.

Since the start of the season in California, the state's Horse Racing Board has lifted restrictions on the use of Butazolidin, an analgesic medication that gives sore-going, bad-legged horses a little help. *Audax Minor, The New Yorker, Feb. 6, 1971, p 75*

The Blazers team physician once suggested treatment with cortisone and Butazolidin, anti-inflammatory analgesics regularly used by athletes. *Pete Axthelm and Gerald Lubenow, "Sports: The Great White Enigma," Newsweek, March 31, 1975, p 74*

[1966] Also shortened to BUTE or Bute.

butcher-block, *adj.* made or designed like a butcher's chopping block, usually with thick strips of laminated maple.

The kitchen has white cabinets, butcher-block counters and dining table. *Picture legend, "International Style Revisited," The New York Times Magazine, Feb. 23, 1975, p 64*

An upper West Side restaurant that is positively prospering and that features hanging plants, butcher-block tables,

directors' chairs, and an enclosed sidewalk gallery. *"Goings on About Town," The New Yorker, Feb. 3, 1975, p 8*

[1967]

Bute or **bute** (byu:t), *n.* short for BUTAZOLIDIN.

The crisis over the use of phenylbutazone, known as "Bute" after the trade name Butazolidin, came to a head last week when news leaked out that traces of "Bute" had been found in the saliva of Rock Roi, winner of the Ascot Gold Cup. *"Legal Horse Drug Crisis Hits British Racing," The Sunday Times (London), July 11, 1971, p 1*

"Bute" does not by itself, make a horse run faster—or slower—but by relieving pain it allows an afflicted horse to perform at its best. The most famous case involving "bute" occurred in the 1969 Kentucky Derby, when Dancer's Image finished first and had his purse taken away.... Kentucky has since legalized Phenylbutazone. *Michael Katz, The New York Times, March 10, 1976, p 29*

[1968]

butt-end, *v.i. Ice Hockey.* to jab an opponent with the end of the handle of a hockey stick.

Henderson and Esposito became virtuosos, and ultimately managed to save the series. But others fell back on the NHL way of doing things: punch, elbow, slash, butt-end, charge and otherwise mangle. *John Gault, Maclean's, Sept. 1974, p 70*

[1974, verb use of earlier noun (1963)]

butt·leg·ger (ˈbət‚leg ər), *n. U.S.* a person who engages in the illegal transportation and sale of cigarettes on which no cigarette tax has been paid.

A triple combination of greed is the basic element in buttlegging. Racketeers are making millions by spiriting low-tax cigarets bought in tobacco-happy North Carolina into New York, where taxes are high. New York State gathers in $325 million a year in cigaret taxes, despite the losses to the buttleggers, and doesn't want to lose that. *"Greed Feeds Buttlegger," Herald Statesman (Yonkers, N.Y.), Oct. 13, 1973, p 6*

[1973, from *butt* (U.S. slang term for a cigarette) + *boot*legger]

bu·tut (ˈbu: tu:t *or* bu'tu:t), *n.* a unit of money of Gambia, equal to 1/100 of a dalasi.

A new decimal currency became effective on July 1. The dalasi, which was divided into 100 bututs, replaced the Gambian pound; it was pegged at four former Gambian shillings. The move did not involve devaluation. *Philip M. Allen, "Gambia," 1972 Collier's Encyclopedia Year Book, p 254*

[1971, from the Gambian name of the coin]

butyl nitrite, variant of ISOBUTYL NITRITE.

Inhaling butyl nitrite is said to induce a warm feeling, giddiness, flushing of the skin and a "rush" as the blood vessels dilate, the heartbeat quickens and blood rushes to the brain. *"Feds Weighing Ban on Dangerous Disco Drug," New York Post, Aug. 22, 1979, p 3*

[1979]

buyback, *adj.* of or involving an oil company's purchase of oil it has produced but that is claimed by the government of an oil-producing country as its share of the total amount obtained from its resources.

But "it is the Arabs" who are forcing up prices with their takeovers of foreign oil companies and buy-back arrangements. *"Pondering the Tasks Ahead," Time, May 27, 1974, p 66*

Senator Birch Bayh made public today a Mobil Oil Corporation letter and memorandum that sought to persuade the Treasury to let oil companies take tax credits for the "buyback" oil they purchase from foreign governments, such as Iran and Saudi Arabia. *The New York Times, Oct. 28, 1976, p 74*

—*n.* the purchase of something the buyer has produced or previously owned or had a share in.

Calling . . . a conglomerate, "perhaps the most successful practitioner of the art of blotting up excess shares and raising per-share earnings," *The Advisor* pointed out that the company began buybacks in 1972 at $20 a share. *Robert Metz, "Market Place," The New York Times, Sept. 13, 1977, p 44*

[1973 for adj., specialized use of earlier (1954) sense "of buying back, repurchasing;" 1963 for noun] See DOWNSTREAM, POSTED PRICE.

buy-off, *n. U.S.* **1** the act of purchasing all rights to a product or service.

The Bendix engineers at last developed a sort of enlarged screwdriver, which went through several different phases of production and was almost "finalized," Mr. Micocci says, when NASA "gave it the buy-off"—that is, bought it but didn't use it. *Henry S. F. Cooper, Jr., The New Yorker, April 12, 1969, p 106*

2 one whose service is or has been paid up in full.

[Jack] Aaron's and other principal actors' pay is based on the number of times the commercials are shown on national networks in successive 13-week cycles. The first time the spot is shown, the principal actor receives $136 (supporting actors—those who do not speak on camera—are sometimes referred to as "buy-offs" because they accept a flat fee). *James Conway, "They Tried It," The New York Times Magazine, May 21, 1972, p 50*

[1969, from the verb phrase *buy off*]

buz·ka·shi ('bu:z'ka: ʃi:), *n.*, or **buz kashi,** the national sport of Afghanistan, involving competitive riding on horses for the possession of a dead goat.

Grab the goat and ride, Omar! sport known as *buzkashi. R. H. Boyle, Sports Illustrated, May 17, 1971, p 58*

The players in the game of Buz Kashi do not form teams. The object of the game is not to prove one group better than another, but to find a champion. There are famous champions from the past, and they are remembered. *J. Bronowski,*

"The Harvest of the Seasons: War Games," The Listener, May 17, 1973, p 647

[1968, from Pashto, literally, goat snatching]

b.y., abbreviation of *billion years.*

The Cobalt Beds of Canada, which are thought to be 2.2 b.y. old. *Patrick Echlin, New Scientist, May 8, 1969, p 287*

The Earth is nowadays considered to be about 4.6 billion years (b.y.) old, although no terrestrial rocks closely approaching this age have yet been found. Indeed, it is most unlikely that they ever will be. *S. Moorbath, "Age of Earth," McGraw-Hill Yearbook of Science and Technology 1974, p 156*

[1969]

b.y.o.b., abbreviation of *bring your own booze* (or *bottle*).

The dance was held in the game room of the rec center— where else? Music was provided by a local group called the Mixed Bag, admission was $1 per person, b.y.o.b. *Mary Alice Kellogg, "Singles in the Suburbs, or, You Can Go Home Again," Saturday Review, June 24, 1972, p 18*

[1972]

bypass, *n.* a natural or artificial canal introduced to provide an alternate passage or pathway for circulation, digestion, etc.

The DeBakey bypass, a spherical plastic chamber the size of an apple, skirts the heart's left ventricle, through which blood is normally pumped, and offers a parallel route. *Science News Yearbook 1970, p 84*

—*v.t.* to replace by means of a bypass.

Wu and his colleagues were particularly impressed by a new operation developed here for treating coronary disease. At Montefiore, he looked on while Dr. George Robinson bypassed a clogged coronary artery in a 33-year-old man with a section of vein taken from the patient's leg. *"Medicine: The Doctors from China," Newsweek, Nov. 6, 1972, p 80*

[1970, extended from earlier noun sense (1961)]

byr, abbreviation of *billion years.*

Liquid water first appeared on our planet around 3.8 Byr ago, so this particular ecological niche seems to have been relatively stable for a very long time. *Ann Henderson-Sellers, "The Evolution of the Earth's Atmosphere," New Scientist, Oct. 26, 1978, p 287*

[1976]

C

c, abbreviation of CHARMED.

James D. Bjorken . . . proposed that the new quantum number be called charm, and the fourth quark is now labeled the *c,* or charmed, quark. *David B. Cline, Alfred K. Mann and Carlo Rubbia, "The Search for New Families of Elementary Particles," Scientific American, Jan. 1976, p 53*

[1976]

cable, *n.* short for *cable television.*

According to Diane Martin: "The variety available on cable today is already astounding – six hundred programs a week in New York seen only on cable." *"The Talk of the Town: First Days of J.," The New Yorker, March 15, 1976, p 26*

We're the fastest growing cable country in the world. Seventy percent of Canadian households have access to cable now. I think it's about 8% in the States. Surely the survival of the CBC grows more precarious as cable increases. *Maclean's, Feb. 7, 1977, p 9*

[1972] See CABLEVISION.

cablecast, *n.* a telecast by cablevision.

Shuey also helped develop and produce a series of cablecasts to acquaint Kansas voters with the candidates during the 1974 primary and general elections. *News Release of the National Cable Television Association, Washington, D.C., April 14, 1975*

—*v.i.* to telecast by cablevision.

Subscription cablecasting of sports is not permitted within two years of the sports event telecast live on a regular basis on a Grade A . . . signal in the system community, or within two years of the specific sports event telecast in the community when it occurred. *Mary Alice Mayer Phillips, "Cable Communications – A Springboard to Tomorrow," Britannica Book of the Year 1973, p 656*

[1968, from *cable* (television) + tele*cast*]

cablecaster, *n.:* The FCC decided . . . that cablecasters can bring in up to two additional channels from beyond normal reception range. *"Look and Listen," Popular Science, April 1972, p 34*

cablecasting, *n.* telecasting by cablevision.

From everybody's standpoint, the best thing in the franchise is a requirement that the two companies keep abreast of current developments in the art of cablecasting. *TV Guide, April 10, 1971, p 39*

[1968] Also called NARROWCASTING.

cablevision, *n.* cable television, a system for transmitting television programs by coaxial cable to individual subscribers.

"A consortium of local cablevision interests could, theoretically at all events, raise enough cash to buy and preempt certain programme material (I have in mind, for example, great sporting occasions) and by so doing deny them to the general public," he said. "Cablevision is a system which, to put the matter bluntly, contains possibilities of discrimination against sections of the population." *The Times (London), Sept. 8, 1973, p 14*

[1972, from *cable* tele*vision*]

cabtrack, *n.* a proposed automatic taxicab, consisting of an electrically powered car shuttling around an elevated loop track.

Cabtracks have the potential to bring most city destinations within three minutes walk of a station, but they would have to be threaded through the structure of London with great care. *Timothy Johnson, "Science and the Paymasters," New Scientist, July 27, 1972, p 206*

[1971]

CAD, abbreviation of *computer-aided design.*

CAD is generally a matter of entering design information into the memory of a computer whose output is linked with a CRT display which can present human operators with graphical portrayals of a part's shape or plotted parametric performance. *W. T. Gunston, Science Journal, May 1970, p 43*

[1968] Compare CAI, CAP.

café coronary, a condition resembling coronary thrombosis, caused by choking on food.

The stricken woman was a victim of "food inhalation," an often fatal accident that is so often misdiagnosed as a heart attack that it has come to be called the café coronary. *"Medicine: Death at Dinner," Time, Oct. 22, 1973, p 68*

[1973] See HEIMLICH MANEUVER.

ca·fé thé·â·tre (kαˌfei tei'α: trə), a cafe where lectures and theatrical presentations, often of a controversial nature, are given.

Besides its teaching activities, the institute has a library of 60,000 books and a large modern auditorium where M. Zavriew presents new French films and plays – he introduced Parisian *café-théâtre* to London – and invites lecturers as diverse as M Jean-Louis Barrault and M Claude Lévi-Strauss. *John Ardagh, The Times (London), Feb. 11, 1976, p 13*

[1972, from French] Compare DINNER THEATER.

CAI, abbreviation of *computer-assisted instruction.*

Although computer-assisted instruction, or C.A.I. varies in purpose and capability, the operative word is "interactive" – the student, through a keyboard, in effect carries on a dialogue with the machine as he performs its programmed exercises. *Evan Jenkins, "Education: Classroom Revolution: Computer Interaction," The New York Times, June 13, 1976, Sec. 4, p 9*

[1967] Compare CAD, CAP.

Californicate or **Californiate**, *v.t.* to disfigure or ravage the landscape of (a state, scenic area, etc.) by urbanization and industrialization.

In Utah we see no bumper stickers reading DON'T CALIFORNICATE UTAH. Utah is busy Californicating itself. *Wallace and Page Stegner, "Rocky Mountain Country," The Atlantic, April 1978, p 76*

Whether . . . "the region is none.the worse for that," visitors to the ziggurats beside the Var or road travellers on the same, now Californiated route from Cannes to Grasse, may question; but Nice remains totally, and traditionally, French. *Michael Ratcliffe, The Times (London), Sept. 1, 1977, p 11*

[1972, blend of *California* and *fornicate,* in allusion to uncontrolled development of southern California]

Californication, *n.:* Legislators, scientists and citizens are now openly concerned about the threat of "Californication"—the haphazard, mindless development that has already gobbled up most of Southern California. *"The Nation: American Scene: The Great Wild Californicated West," Time, Aug. 21, 1972, p 15*

ca·ló (ka:'lou), *n.* a variety of Mexican Spanish containing many slang expressions and English words, spoken by Chicano youths in the southwestern United States.

A lot of articles and letters are written in *caló,* a cholo slang that combines Spanish and English, or in Chicano rhetoric left over from the movement of the late sixties. *Calvin Trillin, The New Yorker, July 10, 1978, p 72*

To espouse the terminology of *Zoot Suit* (a lengthy glossary of *caló* is provided by the program), I can describe the cheap set . . . only as *¡Que desmadre!,* though the costumes of Peter J. Hall rate a guarded *¡Orale!,* whereas the staging by Luis Valdez is as *pinche* as his dramaturgy. *John Simon, "Theater: West Coast Story," New York Magazine, April 9, 1979, p 93*

[1975, from Mexican Spanish *Caló* the argot of the Mexican underworld; see *El Lenguaje de los Chicanos,* Center for Applied Linguistics, 1975, pp xiv, 191]

cal·zone (kæ 'zou ni: *or* kæl'zoun), *n.* a dome-shaped baked pie filled usually with cheese.

I went partway down into the valley and stopped at a pizzeria called the Capri, where I had a calzone. Two boys on skateboards were slaloming down the steeply graded sidewalk. *Alex Shoumatoff, "Profiles: Westchester (N.Y.)," The New Yorker, Nov. 13, 1978, p 117*

[1976, from Italian, from dialectal *calisoni* a kind of dumpling or patty, influenced in form by Italian *calzoni* trousers]

camel's nose, *U.S.* a small or superficial part of something very large, especially something difficult or unpleasant to deal with.

Even this amount, the authors of the study . . . contend, "represents merely the camel's nose of the modernization program planned for the Aerospace Defense Command (ADC)." *"Science and the Citizen: Flying Circus," Scientific American, June, 1973, p 39*

The tightly drawn Carter proposal, limiting transfers to years in which unemployment averaged more than 6 percent, would be retroactive to 1975-76 and almost certainly would include 1977. The "camel's nose" worriers fear that Congress will be tempted to lower the 6 percent figure and

increase the Treasury withdrawals. *Edward A. Cowan, "Carter's Social Security Proposal Raises Funding and Benefit Issues," The New York Times, May 16, 1977, p 49*

[1965, abstracted from the metaphorical phrase *to let the camel's nose into the tent*]

camp·to·the·cin (ˌkæmp touˈθi: sən), *n.* an extract from a tree in China long used there in treating cancer, or a synthetic chemical identical to it.

Information about new drugs or new ways to exploit tried and tested drugs, which allow experimentalists to probe further into the metabolic processes of eukaryotic cells, is always welcome and no doubt the suppliers of camptothecin can look forward to a boom in demand as a result of what Abelson and Pentman have to say in *Nature New Biology* next Wednesday (May 31). *"Selective Inhibition of RNA Synthesis," Nature, May 26, 1972, p 195*

[1966, from New Latin *Camptotheca (acuminata)* the species of tree + English *-in* (chemical suffix)]

Ca·nut·ism (kəˈnu: tiz əm), *n. British.* stubborn resolve to resist change.

Mr. Edward Heath's proposal to cut Bank rate by 2 per cent was . . . not so much conservatism as Canutism. Mr. Heath could not insulate Britain from the world trend in interest rates without comprehensive exchange controls, . . . *Alfred Morris, The Manchester Guardian Weekly, April 10, 1969, p 24*

[1969, from King *Canute,* 994?-1035 (whose court believed that he could hold back the tide on command) + *-ism*]

CAP¹, abbreviation of *computer-aided production.*

But the logical extension of CAD is into the field of general industrial manufacturing, so that CAD can become CAP—computer aided production. *W. T. Gunston, Science Journal, May 1970, p 44*

[1968] Compare CAD, CAI.

CAP², abbreviation of *Common Agricultural Policy,* a program of price supports for agricultural products of members of the European Community.

By means of variable import duties, CAP penalizes the sale of American farm products except those items that Europe does not produce at all. *Arnaud de Borchgrave, Newsweek, Feb. 12, 1973, p 39*

If the CAP goes (with its butter and beef mountains and milk and wine lakes), what is left? Free internal trade perhaps? But even that will not likely survive the economic splintering of the EEC. *John Palmer, The Manchester Guardian Weekly, Jan. 2, 1977, p 6*

[1967]

cap, *n. U.S.* an upper limit on increases in cost; ceiling.

To make these escalation clauses more palatable, some landlords offered abatement or "caps" on how much rent could be increased above the base figure, which itself is a critical point of negotiation. *Carter B. Horsley, "Escalation: Office Tenants and Landlords Vie," The New York Times, June 16, 1976, p 65*

Edward F. King [is] founder of an organization that wants to put a cap on state spending. *Time, Oct. 2, 1978, p 34*

[1976]

capitalist road, the policies and objectives of capitalist roaders.

In a message broadcast through loudspeakers, he [Peking's Mayor] charged that the riots were aimed at Chairman Mao Tse-tung and the Central Committee of the Chinese Communist Party and that behind them were persons who supported the "capitalist road." *The New York Times, April 6, 1976, p 1*

[1976, loan translation from Chinese]

capitalist roader, a Chinese communist accused of promoting capitalistic methods of production.

The underlying theme of the power struggle known as the Cultural Revolution was Mao's attacks on "capitalist roaders" who introduced an incentive system in the early 1960's. *Sunday Post-Herald (Hongkong), June 24, 1973, p 19*

It was in the 1960s that Mao, complaining that his former comrades, Teng among them, were treating him like a "dead ancestor," ... Teng, at that time secretary-general of the Communist Party and Mao's designated successor, Liu Shao-chi, were swept from power as "capitalist roaders," *Maclean's, Aug. 8, 1977, p 43*

[1967, loan translation from Chinese] Compare CONFUCIANIST. See also CODE WORD.

capital transfer tax, *British.* a government tax imposed on money or property transferred from one person to another, especially by inheritance.

Now comes the new squirearchy: the bowler-hatted money managers from the City, eased into landed power with the help of capital transfer tax and the inexorable demise of the wealthy owner-farmer. *The Listener, June 8, 1978, p 718*

[1975] *Abbreviation:* CTT

cap·o di (tut·ti) cap·i ('ka:p ou di: 'tu: ti: 'ka:p i:), **1** a Mafia overlord.

The death last fall of New York Don Carlo Gambino, who as *capo di tutti capi* had brought a measure of peace to the nation's Mafia families through guile, diplomacy and strong-arm discipline ... *Time, May 16, 1977, p 32*

2 *Figurative use.*

At 7:25 on a warm evening in August, Jean-Pierre Rampal, *capo di capi* of flutists the world over, is looking down at the stage of Avery Fisher Hall from the private Green Room to the right above it. *Peter Hellman, "The Most Magic Flute," The New York Times Magazine, Feb. 22, 1976, p 30*

[1972, from Italian]

ca·po·ei·ra (ˌka: pə 'wei rə), *n.* a Brazilian dance of African origin, combining elements of folk dancing and self-defense.

African traditions still survive, like the *capoeira*, an intricate dance/fight routine rather like a graceful karate, which men practise in the market place. *Joe Beresford, "Brazil: Special Report," The Times (London), May 3, 1976, p XIII*

[1967, from Portuguese, literally, coop for capons, fortification]

cap·sid ('kæp sid), *n.* the protein shell surrounding the core of a virus particle.

In the virus particle, DNA occurs associated with two or three arginine-rich (basic) proteins. This nucleoprotein complex forms the core of the virus particle and is surrounded by a shell (capsid) which has the strict symmetrical shape of an icosahedron. *Erling Norrby, "Adenovi-*

ruses," McGraw-Hill Yearbook of Science and Technology 1971, p 89

[1963, from French *capside*, from Latin *capsa* box + French *-ide* -id (suffix meaning structure, body)] Compare NUCLEOCAPSID. See also ENCAPSIDATE.

cap·so·mere ('kæp sə₍mir), *n.* one of the identical units that make up a capsid.

J. T. Finch and A. Klug examined single crystals of poliovirus by x-ray diffraction and concluded that the virion had icosahedral (5:3:2) symmetry, and that the capsid was therefore likely to be composed of 60 *n* asymmetric structural units ("capsomeres"). *Douglas G. Scraba, "Animal Virus," McGraw-Hill Yearbook of Science and Technology 1972, p 116*

[1961, from French *capsomère*, from *capsid*e + connecting *-o-* + *mère* (from Greek *méros* part)]

capture, *n.* retrieval of information stored in a computer memory bank.

... the credit card holder can be replaced with a document holder or a roll of paper tape, for other data capture purposes. *"Technology Review: Electronics to Reduce Bad Credit Cards Impression," New Scientist, Jan. 27, 1972, p 207*

[1972]

car·bar·yl ('kar bə₍ril), *n.* an insecticide having a wide range of applications, used as a substitute for DDT. It is a carbamate compound with a short period of toxicity. *Formula:* $C_{12}H_{11}O_2N$

The death of bees in enormous numbers is the result of a recent switch by canning companies, who are the largest vegetable growers, from DDT to an insecticide thought more benign, carbaryl. *Science News, Oct. 31, 1970, p 349*

[1964, from *carba*mate + *aryl* an aromatic hydrocarbon radical]

car·ben·i·cil·lin (karˌben ə'sil in), *n.* a type of penicillin effective against various gram-negative bacteria. *Formula:* $C_{17}H_{18}N_2O_6S$

Pfizer's J. B. Roerig Division and the British-owned Beecham Pharmaceuticals ... announced they were in the market with carbenicillin, a new antibiotic effective against *Pseudomonas aeruginosa*, a bacterium looming with new importance in human disease.... Carbenicillin has "little or no toxicity even in very high dosage." *Science News, Aug. 22, 1970, p 164*

[1968, contraction of *carb*oxy*b*enzyl*p*en*icillin*, its chemical name]

car·be·nox·o·lone (ˌkar bə'nak sə loun), *n.* a drug that reduces inflammation, used in the treatment of gastric ulcer. *Formula:* $C_{34}H_{50}O_7$

Synthesized from glycyrrhizic acid, a derivative of licorice root, carbenoxolone increases the ability of cells to bind protein, thus, it is believed, increasing the secretion of protective mucus. *Frank P. Mathews, "Medicine," 1974 Collier's Encyclopedia Year Book (1973), p 336*

[1965, from *carbon* + *-ene* hydrocarbon + *oxygen* + *-ol* alcohol or phenol + ket*one*]

car bomb, an explosive device concealed in a motor vehicle that is set off as an act of terrorism.

A full-scale resumption of the Provisional IRA's bombing campaign may have been temporarily averted by the capture on Saturday of the largest quantity of bomb-making materials ever found in the province. If it had got through, the haul would have enabled terrorists to make up to 60 car bombs. *Christopher Walker, The Times (London), Jan. 19, 1976, p 1*

[1972]

car bombing: After a ten-week trial at Winchester, eight young men and women were found guilty of complicity in the London car-bombings. *James Margach, "United Kingdom," The Annual Register of World Events in 1973 (1974), p 29*

car·cin·o·em·bry·on·ic antigen (ˌkɑr sə nouˌembri:'ɑn ik), a protein substance causing the body to produce antibodies against it (antigen), found in the cells of certain cancer tumors as well as in the normal cells of a fetus.

Whatever progress has been made toward developing biochemical tests [for early detection of cancer] is based on the findings that tumors and embryonic tissues share, for some unknown reason, several enzymes and structural proteins not found in mature healthy tissues. The two most important of these substances are carcinoembryonic antigen, which was first found in colon tumors, and alpha-fetoprotein, which was first discovered in liver tumors. *Thomas H. Maugh II, "Cancer: The Long War," 1976 Collier's Encyclopedia Yearbook (1975), p 61*

[1967, from *carcino-* tumor, cancer + *embryonic*] *Abbreviation:* CEA

card¹, *v.t. U.S. Slang.* to require an identification card of (someone) to prove legal age (often used as a way of excluding someone from entering a night club, etc.).

Blacks are not the only people who are particularly likely to be carded by disco doormen. Discos in Boston started as a sort of refuge for homosexuals, and as gay discos became increasingly invaded by straight couples homosexuals began to feel that keeping out straight voyeurs was a matter of protection rather than discrimination. *Calvin Trillin, "U.S. Journal: Boston," The New Yorker, Dec. 13, 1976, p 145*

[1976, verb use of noun *card*, short for *identification card*]

card², *n.* **play the** (or **one's** _____ **card**, to use a (particular) gambit or tactic so as to gain an advantage or attain a goal.

He plays the human rights card by noting that violaters such as Argentina, Chile, Haiti, Nicaragua and Ethiopia were recipients of some $600 millions in the last year. *The Manchester Guardian Weekly, July 9, 1978, p 7*

To make matters worse, in Soviet eyes, the Administration has recently appeared to be courting Peking in order, as Brezhnev angrily put it, to "play the 'Chinese card' " against Moscow. *Time, July 24, 1978, p 8*

During his visit, Teng had played his "U.S. card" six different ways. He left conservatives at odds and the Soviets fretful. *William Ringle, "Teng Departs After Playing His U.S. Card," The Burlington Free Press (Vermont), Feb. 6, 1979, p 1*

[1973] ► This is a new version or variant of several older figurative expressions derived from cardplaying, such as *play one's cards* (*right, well,* etc.), *play one's cards close to the vest* (or *the chest*), *play one's best card,* etc.

car·di·o·gen·ic shock (ˌkɑr di: ou'dʒen ik), shock due to an impairment in the output of blood by the heart.

Today heart muscle or pump failure is the leading cause of death in CCUs. Cardiogenic shock due to pump failure is related to the size of the myocardial infarction, or heart muscle death, and despite heroic measures, the mortality rate remains formidable. *Ralph C. Scott, "Medicine: Heart and Vascular Disease," The Americana Annual 1974, p 376*

[1968, from *cardio-* the heart + *-genic* originating in]

car·di·o·pul·mo·nar·y resuscitation (ˌkɑr di:-ou'pul məˌner i:), the full form of CPR.

Cardiopulmonary resuscitation . . . is "a psychomotor skill that needs practice," a New York Heart Association spokesman said. "A person can do mouth-to-mouth resuscitation without special training. It's the chest compression that can be dangerous. Done incorrectly, it can crack ribs and possibly puncture internal organs." *Hope MacLeod, "Heart Attack: You May Save a Life," New York Post, Jan. 30, 1979, p 28*

[1973]

care, *v.* **could care less,** *U.S. Informal.* not to care at all; be completely indifferent (to).

I realize that some people care about seeing those kinds of things, but I think the majority of people could care less. *The Tuscaloosa News (Alabama), Jan. 30, 1973, p 4*

But wearing a baggy, pinstriped '40s suit, Mitchum looks as if he could care less what the film is going to do for his career. *Karin Winner, Women's Wear Daily, April 18, 1975, p 14*

Asked if she would vote this year, [she] said, "I never have and I never will. I didn't watch the debates, and I could care less." *Barbara Trecker, New York Post, Oct. 27, 1976, p 35*

What they had in sight was the behemoth of sport, No. 1 in the world with a global audience of more than a billion: soccer. Never mind that Americans could have cared less about the game. Americans loved sport, and once exposed to the beauties and excitement, they would become hooked. How could a billion soccer fans be wrong? *The New York Times Magazine, Aug. 28, 1977, p 20*

[1966, alteration of *(I) couldn't care less,* an expression that became popular in the 1940's, probably by influence of the earlier (1930's) *I couldn't agree more;* see the derivations in Eric Partridge's *A Dictionary of Catch Phrases,* 1977]

► The widespread use of this expression in American English during the 1970's prompted considerable discussion both in the popular press and in scholarly journals. According to a note in *American Speech* (45, 1-2, 1973, p 29), its use by the columnist Abigail ("Dear Abby") Van Buren was promptly corrected by several of her readers, and Theodore M. Bernstein, the late style editor of *The New York Times,* called it a "degenerated" expression that "makes no sense." The following exchange about the usage appeared in an Ann Landers column.

My husband's favorite expression is "I could care less." I say it should be, "I couldn't care less." Who is right?
Waiting for the Verdict
Dear Waiting: You are. The Harper Dictionary of Contemporary Usage calls the increasing use of the expression "I could care less" an "ignorant debasement of the lan-

guage." But I'll bet when you tell your husband, he'll say, "I could care less." *Ann Landers, Daily News (New York), Nov. 1, 1976, p 66*

Various explanations for the origin of, or motivation for, the expression have been suggested. Roger W. Wescott wrote in the language quarterly *Verbatim* (III, 1, May 1976, p 13): "I interpret *I could care less* as elliptical: add . . . *but it would be difficult!"* Atcheson L. Hench proposed in *American Speech* (48, 1-2, 1975, p 159) that the cause of the change from *couldn't care* to *could care* "lies in the act of slurring or of careless hearing. A listener has not heard the whole phrase; he has heard a slurred form. *Couldn't care* has two dental stops practically together, *dnt*. This is heard only as *d* and slurring results."

In addition, James B. McMillan cites in *American Speech* (53, 3, Fall 1978, pp 233-35) the following factors:

Redundancy of *-n't*. Comparable phrases like *couldn't eat less* and *could eat less* are common and antonymic, hence ellipsis of *-n't* doesn't occur. But since *He could care less* is rarely if ever used to mean "His concern could be smaller," the presence or absence of the affix *-n't* fails to make a meaningful contrast; hence the affix becomes redundant and ellipsis ensues.

Influence of suffix *-less*. The negation in many words like *lifeless*, *speechless*, and especially *careless* may have been extended to the collocation *could care less* so that it has become an idiom with a negative sense.

Frequency of the idiom. The accelerated frequency of *couldn't care less* since the 1940's has led to its alteration. "Frequency begets redundancy, in the sense that in a familiar collocation less than the whole may effectively carry the semantic burden (hence such shortenings as syncope, clipping, and nicknaming)."

care label, a label on a garment or fabric providing instructions for its cleaning.

The office thought the industry should consider whether . . . all clothing should have non-detachable care labels. *"Complaints by 41,800 on Clothing," The Times (London), Feb. 17, 1977, p 3*

[1967]

Car·i·com or **CARICOM** (ˌkær ə'kɑm), *n.* acronym for *Caribbean Community* or *Caribbean Common Market*, a common market established in 1974 by ten countries of the eastern Caribbean which comprised the earlier Caribbean Free Trade Association from 1968 to 1973.

Haiti and Surinam applied to join Caricom, and diplomatic relations were established between Caricom countries and Cuba. *Philippe Decraene, "Dependent States: Caribbean," Britannica Book of the Year 1975, p 230*

[1974]

carousel, *n.* a circular tray for a slide projector, having slots from which each slide is dropped or pushed in front of the lens and then returned to its slot.

Houziaux has invented a teaching machine to remove

some of the load from lecturers. His automatic tutor is based on a carousel of 35-mm slides, a magnetic tape recorder, and a small computer that handles the logic decisions on what to ask the pupil next. *Simon Mitton, "Education: Astronomy for Schools," New Scientist, Nov. 29, 1973, p 654*

[1971]

car·pool or **car-pool** ('kɑrˌpuːl), *v.i. U.S.* to join a car pool; take turns in driving each other to work, shop, etc.

In Houston, Texas, five friends and neighbors car-pool daily to their jobs at Shell Oil Company's headquarters. *Julie Candler, "Woman at the Wheel," Woman's Day, Oct. 1974, p 4*

If we won't car-pool, and if we won't or can't use mass transportation, can we at least get more mileage from the gallon? *Donald E. Carr, "The Lost Art of Conservation," The Atlantic, Dec. 1975, p 65*

[1966, verb use of *car pool* (1940's)] Compare VANPOOL.

carpooling or **car-pooling,** *n.:* The Senate commanded Zarb to promulgate, within 90 days, precise standards of energy conservation covering everything from decorative lighting to carpooling and mass transit use. *David S. Broder, The Tuscaloosa News (Alabama), April 24, 1975, p 4*

cartoon, *n.* a computer printout forming a pictorial display or image. *Also used attributively.*

QUANTIZED IMAGE, or cartoon, is formed by the computer. It selects three levels of optical density corresponding to the average red-cell absorption, minimum nuclear absorption and average nuclear absorption respectively. *Marylou Ingram and Kendall Preston, Jr., Scientific American, Nov. 1970, p 75*

A geological cartoon representation of gross geological relationships in the Eastern Alps. That part of the section above the line 1-1 is well established, that below the line is inferred. *Illustration Legend, "Plate Tectonics and Continental Collision," Nature, Sept. 22, 1972, p 203*

[1970]

car-top, *v.t., v.i. U.S.* to transport on top of an automobile.

Transportability (it can't be car-topped, needs a special trailer) and ease of construction were secondary. *Paul Wahl, "Hang Gliders," Popular Science, May 1974, p 100*

[1968]

cash bar, *U.S.* a bar at a party or reception at which alcoholic drinks are sold.

The twentieth reunion of the class of '52 was to consist principally of a daylong gathering at the Myopia Hunt Club in Hamilton, Massachusetts. There were to be seminars, and lunch, followed by golf and swimming, then a cash bar and dinner. *Ralph Maloney, "One's Twenty-fifth," Atlantic, July 1972, p 80*

[1972]

cashless society, a society in which transactions of payment or other exchange of funds are made by credit card, computer, or other electronic technology.

Computerized checking accounts—the electronic transfer of funds from the consumers' checking accounts to the merchants' accounts—have brought six Long Island, New York, communities closer to the "cashless society."

Jane Samz, Encyclopedia Science Supplement (Grolier) 1979 (1978), p 98

[1972] Also called CHECKLESS SOCIETY. See DEBIT CARD and ELECTRONIC FUNDS TRANSFER (SYSTEM).

cassette, *v.t.* to record (on tape, film, or videotape) for replay from a cassette.

The most recent programmes have been in the entertainment field—EVR has cassetted 150 films. *"Technology Review: Moving Picture With EVR's Cassette TV," New Scientist, Jan. 13, 1972, p 84*

Education, especially, might be better served with cassetted specialized lessons and a financed or subsidized library of lessons and of culture. *The Times (London), Sept. 25, 1973, p 9*

[1972, verb use of the noun]

Castle Catholic, a derogatory term in Northern Ireland for a Catholic who supports British rule of Northern Ireland.

The SDLP [Social Democratic Labour Party] can no more choose who should lead the Unionist Party than the Unionists can—as they used to pipe-dream—select Castle Catholics (Uncle Toms) for power-sharing. *"Comment: Ulster's New Bargain," The Manchester Guardian Weekly, July 28, 1973, p 10*

[1973]

Castlerobin bomb, a complicated home-made bomb fitted with booby traps to prevent defusing.

Bomb technology has also declined in other ways. There has been a sharp fall-off in the incidence of sophisticated arming circuits and an absence for some months of the complex "Castlerobin" bombs with anti-handling devices. *"Technology Review: IRA Bombers Switch to Dangerous Chemicals," New Scientist, Sept. 21, 1972, p 487*

[1971, perhaps from *Castle* (Catholic) + (round) *robin*]

CAT, *n.* acronym for COMPUTERIZED AXIAL TOMOGRAPHY.

In CAT the patient is put on a revolving table and X-rays are shot from all angles to get information so that the computer can construct a two-dimensional picture of a slice through the patient's brain, for example. In this case the 360° scans of CAT are not possible. The angles are limited by the depth of the holes and reflections from the surface. *Science News, Nov. 18, 1978, p 348*

[1975] See also CAT SCAN, CAT SCANNER.

catastrophe, *n.* any of the sharp discontinuities treated by catastrophe theory.

Dr. Zeeman suggested that many real events—a sudden change in a chemical reaction, the sudden buckling of a steel girder, the sudden decision of a dog to attack, the sudden differentiation of growing cells into an embryo—could be represented as "catastrophes" on suitable mathematical surfaces. *Malcolm W. Browne, "Catastrophe Theory," Encyclopedia Science Supplement (Grolier) 1979 (1978), p 101*

[1973]

catastrophe theory, a system in mathematics proposed for describing a discontinuity or phenomenon of sudden change in a continuous process, such as behavior, financial cycles, or some other state, by fitting the attributes of the change into a geometric model consisting of dimensional planes that describe the change.

Catastrophe theory has been particularly interesting in its applications to the biological and social sciences, perhaps because discontinuous and divergent phenomena abound there. For example, Thom suggests applications not only in embryology but also in the theory of evolution, in reproduction, in the process of thought and in the generation of speech. *Scientific American, March 1976, p 60D*

[1972, proposed by René Thom]

Catch-22, n. **1** a hidden difficulty involving a puzzling paradox.

The present series of international conferences suffers from a universal Catch-22, which states that any problem we can solve is part of a larger problem which we cannot. *New Scientist, Nov. 7, 1974, p 393*

The Catch-22 of [movie] sequels goes something like this: In order to sell, stress has to be laid on the original success; but the more sharply focused these earlier memories, the more pallid the successor. *Jaws 2* is a case in point. *Maclean's, July 10, 1978, p 59*

2 *attributive use.*

There is a "Catch-22" aspect to the story. Because discrimination prevented many women and minority workers from getting jobs in the past, they have no seniority; because they have no seniority, they are the first to be laid off. *Newsweek, Dec. 2, 1974, p 72*

[1971, from *Catch-22*, title of a novel (1961) by the American writer Joseph Heller, born 1923. The title refers to a paradoxical Air Force rule by which a pilot is considered insane if he keeps flying combat missions without formally asking to be relieved; if, however, he does put in such a formal request, he is adjudged sane and may not be relieved.] Compare DOUBLE-BIND.

Catch-23, *n. U.S.* variant of CATCH-22.

The speech showed that Kissinger . . . has come to accept what Washington insiders call the "Catch-23" of the oil business. Put simply, the idea is that to escape the political clutches of the cartel, the West will have to develop vast new sources of energy . . . The catch is that the very act of producing all this new energy may lead to a glut of oil and a sharp drop in its price, thus undercutting the price of the new energy. *"Henry the K and Catch-23," Newsweek, Feb. 17, 1975, p 25*

[1973; see the etymology of CATCH-22]

catch-up, *n.* **play catch-up,** *U.S.* **1** *Sports,* to try to overtake an opposing team by playing unconventionally, taking risks, etc.

Leading Oakland in the American League's Western Division by 7 games, the Royals bask in the front-runner's knowledge that this year playing catch-up is for other guys. *"Sport: Royal Flush in K.C.," Time, Aug. 23, 1976, p 63*

2 *Figurative use:*

The demonstrated existence of the necessary technologies can, in fact, serve as a deterrent to cutoffs or a restraint against drastic price increases. There is yet time to develop the requisite technologies for a number of vulnerable materials before such situations arise, rather than playing catch-up as in the case of energy technologies alternative to oil. *Philip H. Abelson and Allen L. Hammond, "The New World of Materials," Science, Feb. 20, 1976, p 633*

[1971]

cat·e·cho·la·min·er·gic (ˌkæt əˌkou lə məˈnər dʒik),

adj. activated by or producing catecholamine, a hormone acting upon nerve cells.

The regions of catecholaminergic neurons (caudate nucleus, substantia nigra, hypothalamus, and locus coeruleus) were dissected out under a microscope from frozen sections of the brain. *Toshiharu Nagatsu, et al., Science, Jan. 23, 1976, p 290*

[1973, from *catecholamine* + Greek *érgo*n work + English *-ic*] Compare DOPAMINERGIC, NORADREN-ERGIC, SEROTONERGIC.

ca·te·nac·ci·o (ˌkaː təˈnaːt tʃiː ou), *n.* a formation in soccer using four defenders in the defensive line, three players in midfield, and three on the attack.

Juventus, winner of 15 national titles ... represents the conservative, traditional style known as *catenaccio* (literally, door bolt). The emphasis is on tight defense, with the opponent's attacks being used as springboards for counterthrusts and breakaway strikes, by swift forwards. *"Europe: The Toes That Bind," Time, June 4, 1973, p 40*

[1964, from Italian]

CAT scan, an X-ray picture made by a CAT SCANNER.

The CAT scan can detect certain abnormalities that ordinarily can be diagnosed only through surgery, including hematoma of the liver (a blood mass caused by injury) and tumors of the pancreas. *Jane E. Brody, "Popular New X-Ray Unit Could Raise Cost of Care," The New York Times, May 8, 1976, p 9*

[1976]

CAT scanner, a machine which produces three-dimensional X-ray pictures by COMPUTERIZED AXIAL TOMOGRAPHY (CAT).

Although Mrs. Hancock is thankful to her doctors, she especially praises the new machine that diagnosed the growth in the right hemisphere of her brain. The machine, known as a CAT scanner, produced in minutes an X-ray picture revealing the deadly tumor that had escaped her physicians' notice and conventional diagnostic efforts, apparently for 13 years. *Jonathan Spivak, "Super X Rays: A 'Glamour Machine' Is Hailed by Doctors As a Boon to Diagnosis," The Wall Street Journal, Dec. 10, 1975, p 1*

[1975] Also called CT SCANNER.

CAT scanning, the act or process of producing X-ray pictures with a CAT SCANNER.

CAT scanning came of age in 1976. The abbreviation CAT stands for computerized axial tomography. This is a technique that makes possible precise diagnosis in many cases where the abnormality is unclear or undetectable by conventional X-ray or radioactive scans. *Irwin J. Polk, "Medicine," The Americana Annual 1977, p 322*

[1976] Also called CT SCANNING.

Cay·ley ('kei liː), *n.* the material that fills large highland depressions on the moon creating a smooth undulating terrain. It is typically a breccia type of rock with light color and smooth surface.

The Cayley is the plains-forming fill unit that is scattered throughout the entire Central Highlands. It is characterized by mostly smooth to undulating terrain. "The Cayley must be volcanic, because it fills in like bathtub rings," says Muehlberger. *Everly Driscoll, "Journey to the Descartes Highlands," Science News, April 8, 1972, p 236*

[1972, from *Cayley Plain*, where it was first encoun-

tered, named for Sir George *Cayley,* 1773-1857, a British pioneer of aviation]

CBer or **C.B.er** (ˌsiːˈbiː ər), *n. U.S.* an owner or operator of a CB radio.

The first is the practice of many CBers to spend hours in their parked autos enthusiastically modulating with anyone who can hear them. *Jerry Schmetterer, "CB Roundup," Daily News (New York), June 5, 1977, p 16*

[1963] ▶ Although CB radio was introduced in the United States in 1945 with the establishment of the Citizens Radio Service, it was used mainly by sportsmen and professional people until the early 1960's, when it attracted the interest of the general public. Its popularity rose especially in the 1970's, when the energy crisis made CB radio useful for finding fuel sources when gas stations closed as well as for communicating warnings of speed traps after the national speed limit dropped to 55 (the "double nickel").

Though CB radios exist in other English-speaking countries, they are called by different names. The abbreviation *CB* is the popular name both in the United States and Canada. The official Canadian equivalent is General Radio Service or *GRS.*

See APPLE (def. 2), BAREFOOT, BOOTS, BREAK, DOUBLE NICKEL, EARS, GOOD BUDDY, HAMMER, MODULATE, RATCHET JAW, SMOKEY, 10-4, common expressions used by CB radio operators.

CCD, abbreviation of CHARGE-COUPLED DEVICE.

The CCD can also function as an image sensor. A silicon CCD is an excellent optical detector throughout the visible spectrum—potential wells can be created by shining a light on it. Thus a completely solid state version of a television camera pickup tube, or vidicon, can be made of a CCD array. *Samuel Weber, "Electronics," The World Book Science Annual 1973, p 304*

[1970]

CCU, abbreviation of *coronary care unit.*

It has been estimated that at least two-thirds of sudden deaths are due to unrecognized and untreated disorders of the cardiac rhythm. To prevent such disasters, it seemed logical to bring the trained personnel and equipment of the CCU to the patient outside the hospital as quickly as possible. *Henry I. Russek, "Medicine: Cardiology," 1975 Britannica Yearbook of Science and the Future (1974), p 276*

[1974] Compare ICU.

CEA, abbreviation of CARCINOEMBRYONIC ANTIGEN.

The researchers have found that if CEA is present in the blood of a person above a specified amount, he or she very likely has cancer. If the protein recedes in the blood of a person being treated for cancer, the recession is a good sign that treatment is working. And if the protein increases in the blood during treatment, that is a sign that treatment is probably not working. *"Promising Tests for Cancer," Science News, June 9, 1973, p 367*

[1970]

celiac, *n.* a person who has celiac disease, a digestive disorder chiefly of young children, characterized by diarrhea and abdominal swelling.

Wheat, or more specifically wheat gluten, is known to be

especially toxic to celiacs. Gluten is the sticky plant protein found in cereal grains. When it is removed from the diets of celiacs, their psychotic behavior diminishes. *Science News, Jan. 31, 1976, p 69*

[1976, noun use of *celiac, adj.*]

cell fusion, a method of producing new cells in the laboratory by placing together cells of different types or from different species until two cells fuse their nuclei.

The scientists collected some of these cells and used a process called cell fusion to join them with a type of cell that grows easily in the test tube. From the new combination cells, the scientists isolated and established a line of combination cells that constantly synthesize antibodies against the sheep red blood cell antigen. *Jacques M. Chiller, "Immunology," The World Book Science Annual 1978 (1977), p 299*

[1975]

cell-mediated immunity, a defense mechanism of the body which acts against bacteria, toxins, or other foreign agents by increasing the production of antibodies that adhere to cell membranes.

Scientists at the Georgetown University School of Medicine have found that women's natural cell-mediated immunity against German measles is lowered during pregnancy. Cell-mediated immunity constitutes an important defense against viral infections. *"Biomedical Sciences: Pregnant Women Vulnerable to Disease," Science News, Oct. 20, 1973, p 253*

[1972]

cellular engineering, the scientific alteration of cell structure or substitution of cells as medical treatment for certain conditions and as basic research into biological phenomena. It is similar to and overlaps with genetic engineering.

Since it is extremely difficult to find an unrelated marrow donor whose tissues are suitably matched to the patient's, doctors have turned to other means of treating such children.

The new techniques, as well as marrow grafts represent an attempt at "cellular engineering" to correct the life-threatening effects of birth defects. *Jane E. Brody, "New Treatment Reported for Immune Deficiencies," The New York Times, May 14, 1976, p D12*

[1972]

cel·lu·lite (sel yə'lait *or* 'sel yə li:t), *n.* a substance made up of fat, water, and wastes that is supposed to form unsightly lumpy pockets beneath the skin.

The book speaks directly to women who worry about having dimpled flesh, "jodhpur thighs," "saddlebag buttocks" and other imperfections. These are caused, says Mme. Ronsard, by cellulite. . . . Cellulite cannot be burned off by conventional diets, says Ronsard: even when poundage is pared away, this "superfat" remains. *"Medicine: Battle of the Bulges," Time, March 10, 1975, p 76*

The Society argues not only that cellulite does not exist, but also that the diets designed to diminish it are potentially harmful over the long term. "To present 'cellulite' as a disorder of the liver, and by confused association of the kidneys, intestine and skin, is a distortion of science and shows total ignorance of pathophysiology," states the position paper, *"This Week: Growing Fat on Cellulite?", New Scientist, Jan. 1, 1976, p 4*

[1971, from French, coined by Nicole Ronsard, a French dietitian, from *cellule* cell]

cen·o·sphere ('sen ə,sfir), *n.* a thin-walled, glassy ball of calcined clay in which gases have been trapped during cooling, found in fly ash.

The balls, called cenospheres, can withstand extremely high pressure. They can be used to provide buoyancy in deep-ocean operations, as a closed-pore insulation in a space shuttle design, and for making light-weight floating concrete. *Frederick C. Price, "Chemical Technology," The World Book Science Annual 1974, (1973), p 273*

[1971, from *ceno-* empty (from Greek *kenós*) + *sphere*]

cents-off, *adj. U.S. and Canada.* having to do with a promotion of a product in which its price is reduced a few cents when a shopper presents a coupon with the purchase. The coupon is an obligation under which the manufacturer reimburses the retailer for the cents the latter takes off the price of the product.

"Cents off" specials . . . are in reality the regular price. *Walter Stewart, "The Games Supermarkets Play," Maclean's, Aug. 1974, p 64*

Cents-off coupons continued to show growth and widespread consumer acceptance. The First National Bank of Chicago released a study showing that 88% of those interviewed said they redeemed coupons and 56% said they used coupons weekly. *John Calascione and Edward Mark Mazze, "Consumerism," Britannica Book of the Year 1976, p 209*

[1963]

ceph·a·lo·cide ('sef ə lə,said), *n.* the murder of intellectuals as a group.

It was not genocide, as some have called it, but cephalocide, the cutting off of the head, the planned elimination of the intellectual leadership. It was carefully plotted; lists were drawn up; and it was ruthless. *James A. Michener, "A Lament For Pakistan," The New York Times Magazine, Jan. 9, 1972, p 48*

[1972, from *cephalo-* head + *-cide* killing]

CETA ('si: tə), *n. U.S.* a revenue-sharing program in which state and local governments receive federal funds to provide job training and public-service jobs for the unemployed.

Founded in 1973 and instructed by Congress to decentralize the federal manpower training programs, CETA has grown rapidly and is now the Government's chief program for fighting unemployment. The agency's 1978 budget is about $12 billion — almost three times the amount spent for the War on Poverty at its peak in the 1960s. *Time, July 24, 1978, p 18*

Federal funds — chiefly CETA — that once helped the libraries to pay staff are now drying up. Worn-out reference books are not being replaced. Fewer books are available for borrowing, and loan time has been reduced. *Harriet Van Horne, "Lament for the Vanishing Library," New York Post, Dec. 1, 1978, p 20*

[1976, acronym for *Comprehensive Employment and Training Act*, an act passed in 1973 which established this program]

CETI, abbreviation of *communication with extraterrestrial intelligence.*

At a September CETI meeting, participants felt that the best way of determining whether thinking beings indeed lived in outer space lay in analyzing radio waves of extraterrestrial origin for possible information content. *"Science," The 1972 Compton Yearbook, p 430*

[1971] Compare SETI.

CFC, abbreviation of CHLOROFLUOROCARBON.

It was no joke to think that an innocent squirt from a shaving cream container or armpit dryer could be harming the world—there has been a steady search for substitutes for the CFCs. If you recall, CFCs, according to Rowland and Molina, were getting up into the ozone layer and destroying our protection against ultraviolet from the Sun. *New Scientist, Oct. 19, 1978, p 248*

[1977]

CFM, abbreviation of CHLOROFLUOROMETHANE.

Chlorofluorocarbons F-11 and F-12 (otherwise known as chlorofluoromethanes or CFMs) rise into the lower stratosphere where they produce chlorine atoms that deplete the ozone thus increasing human exposure to harmful ultraviolet rays and causing extra cases of skin cancer. *"This Week: Aerosols Lost in the Ozone," New Scientist, Sept. 23, 1976, p 627*

[1976]

cGMP, abbreviation for CYCLIC GMP.

Michel Simon, working at Gif sur Yvette in France, claims that cGMP is converted directly into cAMP [cyclic AMP] at each beat of a frog's heart. *"Monitor: Frog Heartbeat Triggers Chemical Conversions," New Scientist, May 27, 1976, p 465*

[1974]

channeling, *n. Physics.* the ability of accelerated nuclear particles or ions to pass through the atomic rows and planes of a crystal or similar solid.

Channeling takes place in extremely perfect crystals, which have a precisely regular array of atoms. This regular array leaves unobstructed channels between planes of atoms. Particles that enter the channels in the right way are constrained to move along them by the forces exerted on them by the atoms in the walls of the channels. And so the particles go right out the other side of the crystal. *Science News, Jan. 5, 1980, p 5*

[1967]

charge-coupled device, a semiconductor chip with an array of cells in which electrical charges can be stored or shifted between cells by means of electrical pulses applied to a pair of external terminals, used chiefly to store visual or binary information. *Abbreviation:* CCD

Charge-coupled devices store data at densities perhaps ten times as great as those of conventional semiconductor arrays and are easier and cheaper to build because they require no internal connections. *Wallace B. Riley, "Computers," Britannica Book of the Year 1973, p 191*

A prototype television camera the size of a man's hand and weighing less than a pound has been made using a charge-coupled device as the image sensor. *William C. Hittinger, "Metal-Oxide-Semiconductor Technology," Scientific American, Aug. 1973, p 57*

[1972]

charged particle beam, another name for PARTICLE BEAM (def. 2).

Dr de Geer notes that in the past two years some Americans have said that the Russians have been building a new military device, a charged particle beam. Such a beam would be directed at incoming nuclear missiles. *The Times (London), Dec. 7, 1977, p 20*

[1977]

charismatic, *n. U.S.* a Christian who believes in charismatic gifts (such as the gift of speaking in tongues and healing by the laying on of hands), especially a member of a church practicing the teachings and methods of American pentecostalism.

Among Pentecostal Christians, both Roman Catholic and Protestant, exorcism through "deliverance" prayers has become as common as speaking in tongues. Many of these "charismatics" believe that they have already been filled by an outside force—the Holy Spirit—and have received the Pentecostal "gift" for discerning other spirits, which enable them to spot any poor sinner who has let a demon get inside. *Newsweek, Feb. 11, 1974, p 66*

In the troubled '60s there began to appear the "neo-Pentecostalists," most of whom prefer to be known as Charismatics. They share Parham's belief in baptism by the Holy Spirit, but they prefer to remain in their own churches rather than join a Pentecostal church. They are predominantly white and middle class, and they are growing rapidly. Starting with one parish in California in 1960, the Charismatics now number about 5 million. *Time, Aug. 8, 1977, p 43*

[1970, noun use of the adjective] Compare NEO-PENTECOSTAL. See also EXORCISM.

charm, *n.* the property of a fourth type of quark (hypothetical nuclear particle) whose existence eliminates certain particle decays predicted by the three-quark theory.

The case for *charm*—or the fourth quark—became much firmer when it was realized that there was a serious flaw in the familiar three-quark theory, which predicted that strange particles would sometimes decay in ways that they did not. In an almost magical way, the existence of the charmed quark prohibits these unwanted and unseen decays, and brings the theory into agreement with experiment. *Sheldon L. Glashow, "The Hunting of the Quark," The New York Times Magazine, July 18, 1976, p 36*

Of the several different quarks thought to exist, one was differentiated by the property known as charm, a quantum number that must be conserved during any interaction among particles. The year was notable for a series of experimental results that all tended to confirm the existence of charm. *S. B. Palmer, "Physics," Britannica Book of the Year 1978, p 584*

[1974, named by the American physicists Sheldon L. Glashow and James Bjorken "for we were fascinated and pleased by the symmetry it brought to the subnuclear world"] See QUARK.

charmed, *adj.* possessing or exhibiting the property of charm.

Not to be outdone by Gell-Mann, Glashow named his new quark c for charmed. Charmed quarks added whole new families of hadrons. *Robert H. March, "A Subatomic Surprise," The World Book Science Annual 1976 (1975), p 115*

The main significance of the discovery of the psi particle was that it provided compelling evidence for the existence of a fourth kind of quark, which had earlier been named the "charmed" quark. According to the revised quark picture, the psi particle is a hadron consisting of a charmed quark and a charmed antiquark. *Scientific American, March 1978, p 50*

[1975, from *charm + -ed*]

charm·o·ni·um (tʃɑːrˈmou niː əm), *n*. any particle, such as the psi particle, composed of a charmed quark and a charmed antiquark.

The discovery of the charmonium was an event of the utmost importance in elementary-particle physics. Nothing so exciting had happened in many years. For believers in quarks the new particle was the first experimental indication that a fourth quark existed. *Sheldon L. Glashow, "The Hunting of the Quark," The New York Times Magazine, July 18, 1976, p 36*

[1975, from *charm + -onium*, as in *muonium, pionium*] Compare ORTHOCHARMONIUM, PARACHARMONIUM.

Charter 77, 1 a petition circulated privately in Czechoslovakia and published in the West in 1977, calling on the Czechoslovak government to respect political and civil rights and remove restrictions on freedom of expression.

The large number of signatories—by now more than 300—of Charter 77 in Czechoslovakia has taken the Husak regime and the outside world by surprise. The charter leaders insist that they represent a "citizens' initiative" and do not want to be interpreted as an organised opposition to existing authority. Yet they are once again being seen as the manifestation of a move inside the Communist block to achieve communism "with a human face." *Hella Pick, "Caught by a War of Dissent," The Manchester Guardian Weekly, Jan. 23, 1977, p 8*

2 the group or movement of dissidents who issued this petition.

During the first nine months of 1977, the spokesmen for Charter 77 issued 13 documents dealing with various shortcomings in different areas of Czechoslovak life. Some were concerned with immediate issues, like lists of signatories (in excess of 700 by the middle of the year) and details of repressive measures taken by the authorities against charter activists. Others were analyses of violations of human rights in specific areas. *George Schöpflin, "Czechoslovakia," Britannica Book of the Year 1978, p 277*

[1977, from the year 1977 in which the document appeared] See HUMAN RIGHTS.

chartist, *n*. a signatory or supporter of CHARTER 77.

In addition to the Kohouts, the chartists include former Foreign Minister Jiří Hájek, former Politburo Member František Kriegel, former Party Secretary Zdenek Mlynar, Student Leader Jiří Mueller, Dramatist Váelav Havel and the widow and son of Rudolf Slánský, the Czechoslovak Communist Party secretary-general who was executed in 1952 during Stalinist-style purges, *"Human Rights: Spirit of Helsinki, Where Are You?" Time, Jan. 24, 1977, p 38*

[1977]

charts (tʃɑrts), *n.pl.* Usually, **the charts**, a list of the best-selling or most popular items of a kind (in a particular week, month, etc.).

Freud gives us the psycho-analytical insights without

which no deserving American novel could possibly hit the charts. *Emma Tennant, Review of "Ragtime" by E. L. Doctorow, The Listener, Jan. 22, 1976, p 92*

"I've also discovered in doing this film that people really do respect me. In rock-and-roll you don't feel that so much because in popular music, if you're not on the charts every minute of the day, you really feel you're a failure, and it's not like that in acting." *Warren Hoge, "Bette Midler Goes Hollywood," The New York Times Magazine, Dec. 10, 1978, p 100*

[1965, used originally in reference to recordings of popular songs]

chauvinism, *n*. exaggerated loyalty to members of one's own sex; a superior attitude toward the opposite sex.

Israeli society does not discourage a woman, once she has married and had children, from having a career and equal financial status with men—if she can manage it. The married women I met concurred in this view—or felt impelled, out of chauvinism, to pretend that they did. *Barbara Gelb, "Journey to Israel and Egypt," The New York Times Magazine, Nov. 26, 1978, p 114*

[1972, abstracted from *male chauvinism* (1970) and *female chauvinism* (1972)]

chauvinist, *n*.: Chauvinist [Michael] Caine prefers his wife to be at home. "She's not going to make a career out of this," he predicted confidently. "She's going to have lots of kids." *"People," Time, March 3, 1975, p 49*

chauvinistic, *adj*.: Linda Wolfe's new book, Playing Around: Women and Extramarital Sex (244 pages. Morrow. $7.95) may cause some chauvinistic husbands of the old school to sit bolt upright in their easy chairs and howl with rage and alarm. *Judson Hand, "A Feminist View of Women's Role in the Sexual Revolution," New York Sunday News, June 29, 1975, p 18*

cheap shot, *U.S. and Canada.* an unfair and contemptible action or statement directed at an easy target.

Bruce Porter's article . . . about Utica's political aberration—[Mayor] Ed Hanna—contains one omission and two cheap shots which call for a response. *John O. Lindell, Oneonta, N.Y., in a Letter to the Editor, The New York Times Magazine, Oct. 10, 1976, p 82*

"The whole thing is cutting edge: you can't worry too much about being loved; at some time, you have to decide, 'Let's go! Bang!' If the others know that it's not a cheap shot, that often you might be right, they'll still respect you." *The New Yorker, Sept. 18, 1978, p 46*

[1967] Compare BLINDSIDE.

cheap-shot artist, *U.S. and Canada.* a person who takes cheap shots at opponents.

"Who Is Attacking the Teamsters Union?" The ad supplied its own answer: "An unholy alliance of political midgets, some lying media gossip peddlers and a few self-appointed labor 'reformers' whose secret motives are destructive and un-American." It termed Fox "a cheapshot artist." *A. H. Raskin, The New York Times Magazine, Nov. 7, 1976, p 92*

[1967]

checkbook journalism, the payment of large sums to public figures for exclusive journalistic interviews.

In 1965, the Press Council, after investigating all aspects

of chequebook journalism, condemned as immoral the practice of rewarding criminals for their disclosures for public entertainment. *The Times (London), June 6, 1973, p 18*

The Frost-Nixon deal carries Watergate checkbook journalism to its greatest extreme to date.... Frost argues that since Nixon is out of office, the interviews are not news but a memoir and therefore immune to the checkbook charge. *"The Press: Frost's Big Deal," Time, Aug. 25, 1975, p 58*
[1963]

checkless society, another name for CASHLESS SOCIETY.

It is projected that in the 1980s the "cashless" or, more appropriately, "checkless" society will come into being. The means for this new financial system will be the debit card, which is planned to replace the credit card of today. The debit card will be used to initiate a transaction at the bank itself, at a retail outlet, or at a remote unattended location where money can be deposited or withdrawn around the clock. *Rod N. Thorpe, "Electrical Communications," McGraw-Hill Yearbook of Science and Technology 1977, p 173*
[1965]

checkoff, *n. U.S.* the opportunity of making a contribution from a part of one's refund or dividends or of adding an additional amount to one's payment for use in a specific program, such as political campaign funding.

According to a sampling of early returns, an average 13% of taxpayers are choosing the checkoff. *"Choosing the Checkoff," Time, Feb. 18, 1974, p 8*

Rep. Frederick Richmond of New York, an arts activist, is coming to the rescue with a bill, H.R. 1042. This is a proposal to establish an "income-tax checkoff" on tax returns. A box on tax forms would enable taxpayers to add to the taxes they owe, or subtract from the amount the government owes them, by a stated amount. Thus the proposal is not quite the same as the checkoff for Presidential campaigns, since it would add to government revenues—or perhaps it would only seem to. *Harper's, Aug. 1977, p 19*
[1973, originally (since the early 1900's) applied to the system of withholding union dues from workers' wages]

Checkpoint Charlie, a crossing point between two hostile forces or territories.

Governments, it appears, are watching not only world affairs and their Checkpoint Charlies but also football. *Geoffrey Green, The Times (London), June 5, 1970, p 16*

"We take our copy to Checkpoint Charlie" a reporter for Al Anwar explained, referring to the dividing line between Christian and Moslem quarters of the City, "and Christian taxi-drivers take it up to Hazmiyeh." *James M. Markham, "A Day in Beirut: Death Begins in Afternoon," The New York Times, May 3, 1976, p 3*
[1970, from the name of the checkpoint between East and West Berlin where foreigners may cross over] Compare BERLIN WALL.

che·mo·im·mu·no·ther·a·py (ˌkiː mou iˌmyuː nou-ˈθer ə piː), *n.* a medical treatment combining immunotherapy with chemotherapy.

There were indications that immunotherapy (stimulation of the body's immune system) combined with other treatments might be of value. For example, chemoimmu-

notherapy with anticancer drugs and BCG (attenuated tubercle bacillus) might induce definite increases in the remission rate in malignant melanoma. *Diane J. Fink, "Health and Disease," Britannica Book of the Year 1976, p 384*
[1976, from *chemo-* chemical + *immuno-* immunological + *therapy*]

che·mo·sens·ing (ˌkiː mouˈsen siŋ), *n.* the detection of a chemical by a living cell or cells.

But the extremely important ecological and behavioral roles of chemosensing are just beginning to be appreciated and understood by science. *Richard H. Gilluly, "Taste, Smell, and Ecology," Science News, Aug. 7, 1971, p 98*
[1971]

chemosensor, *n.:* Just as bacteria detect attractants by means of chemosensors rather than indirectly through some secondary benefit, so the bacteria are equipped with other chemosensors that detect repellents directly; they do not simply sense the repellents by experiencing some harm they do. *Julius Adler, "The Sensing of Chemicals by Bacteria," Scientific American, April 1976, p 43*

che·mo·tax·on·o·my (ˌkiː mou tækˈsɑn ə miː), *n.* the classification of plant and animal organisms by their chemical constituents rather than by their appearance.

Chemotaxonomy has really gotten started only in the past several years, and even less is known about the chemotaxonomy of marine organisms than about that of land animals. Marine organisms are exceedingly difficult to classify chemically, because of the plethora of organisms to be found in the vast marine environment. *Joan Lynn Arehart, "Drugs From the Sea," Encyclopedia Science Supplement (Grolier) 1972, p 174*

He established an internationally known research school, which has produced a vigorous stream of papers on natural products chemistry—biogenesis of terpenes and steroids, chemotaxonomy, synthesis of steroid hormone analogues. *New Scientist, Oct. 17, 1974, p 190*
[1963, from *chemo-* chemical + *taxonomy*]

cher·eme (ˈker iːm), *n.* a basic signal unit in AMERICAN SIGN LANGUAGE.

Ameslan has fifty-five cheremes. Nineteen identify the configuration of the hand or hands making the sign; twelve, the place where the sign is made; and twenty-four, the action of the hand or hands. *Eugene Linden, Apes, Men, and Language, 1974, p 18*
[1974, from Greek *cheir* hand + English *-eme* unit of language (as in *phoneme* basic unit of speech)]

Chi·ca·na (tʃiˈka: nə), *n.* a Mexican-American woman or girl; a female Chicano. *Often used attributively.*

Says Chicana Leader Cecilia Suarez: "Our issues are bread-and-butter ones; Women's Lib is trying to get equal job opportunities, but we are still trying to get our women into school. *"Women's Liberation Revisited," Time, March 20, 1972, p 31*

The big change is for the term *chicano*. . . . A sense of pride is shown in the answers to the question about self-classification. Of the forty-seven informants, thirty-one wrote *chicano* or *chicana*. *Lurline H. Coltharp, "Pachuco, Tirilon, and Chicano," American Speech, 1975, p 29*
[1972, from Mexican Spanish, feminine of *Chicano*]

chicken, *n. U.S. Slang.* a young or adolescent male prostitute.

Along Selma Avenue and Sunset Boulevard, male and female teen-agers, many of them runaways, line up under the guise of hitchhiking. Grandfatherly "chicken hawks," men in their 50s and 60s, haggle with "chickens," teen-age boy hustlers, through the windows of Cadillacs. *Time, Aug. 15, 1977, p 23*

[1973]

chicken hawk, *U.S. Slang.* a man who preys on boys for sexual purposes, especially one who solicits young male prostitutes.

Most of his time now is devoted to tracking down molesters of young girls and "chicken hawks," street parlance for men with a sexual preference for boys. *Barbara Ascher, "Crime," People, Oct. 9, 1978, p 99*

[1973]

chicken run, a derisive term used in Rhodesia (now Zimbabwe Rhodesia) for the route or flight taken by whites out of the country in anticipation of black rule.

Others are deciding to cut their losses and leave. "Yes, we're taking the chicken run," says a Scottish automobile worker, "but nobody wants to admit it publicly. If the word gets out, the revenue office will be breathing down your neck to see if you're not fiddling some extra cash out." *Time, Aug. 1, 1977, p 27*

More than 1,700 white Rhodesians joined the exodus from the country last month, setting a record for any month since Rhodesia broke away from Britain in 1965. The previous record for those taking "the chicken run" as whites call it, was in May 1977 when there was a net loss of 1,339. *The Manchester Guardian Weekly, Nov. 5, 1978, p 6*

[1977, from *chicken* coward + *run* trip, flight (as in *milk run*)]

chicken soup, *U.S. Aerospace Slang.* a solution of amino acids, vitamins, and other nutrients used in experiments to detect the presence of metabolic activity on Mars.

A sample of Martian soil will be loaded into a test chamber, then moistened with a substance scientists have named "chicken soup," a nutrient broth . . . containing radioactive carbon 14. The sample will then be incubated at a temperature of 47°F. for up to eleven days. During the experiment, any organism that functions by metabolism is likely to consume the nutrient and release gases that contain radioactively labeled wastes. Viking's sensors are capable of detecting them. "*Space: Mars: The Riddle of the Red Planet," Time, Aug. 2, 1976, p 23*

[1976]

child abuse, deliberately harmful treatment of a child by a parent or other adult, including physical, psychological, and verbal abuse.

"Child abuse occurs in all walks of life," Dr. Horowitz said. "Doctors and lawyers, too, batter their kids. Ten per cent of children under 5 years of age who come in with trauma are cases of child abuse. The parent may say a child slipped when it was really thrown down the stairs. Physicians and nurses tend to buy the story. Either they don't want to believe the parents did it or they don't want to think about it." *The New York Times, Jan. 6, 1974, p 36*

Child abuse can be defined as any act, not necessarily physical, that causes a child needless pain. Of course, the occasional and not-too-hard spanking given for a good reason by an otherwise loving parent does not add up to abuse. Nor do occasional hostile feelings. After all, most parents have likely thought at one time or another, "I'm going to whip that kid." The real difference between the abuser and the nonabuser is that the former lets those spankings or feelings get out of hand. *Abby Alvin Belson, "Child Abuse," Encyclopedia Science Supplement (Grolier) 1976, p 37*

[1972] Compare BABY-BATTERING, CHILD-BATTERING.

child-battering, *n.* the act or practice of inflicting harmful physical abuse on a child by an adult.

Child-battering is an unspeakable act that can never be justified, leaving unerasable scars on the child's mind as well as body. Still, to help deal with the problem, researchers must ask whether the victims play a role in evoking parental violence. The evidence increasingly indicates that, in fact, they do. *Julius Segal and Herbert Yahraes, "Bringing up Mother," Psychology Today, Nov. 1978, p 96*

[1972] Compare BABY-BATTERING.

child-batterer, *n.:* Not all the cases are in deprived areas: there are child-batterers in middle-class districts, but they are not easy to detect. In a multi-storey block of flats, a child in pain will be heard screaming and someone may complain. Even so, a case of child-battering is very often difficult to prove. *David Tindall, The Listener, Nov. 22, 1973, p 690*

child-resistant, *adj.* that is difficult for a child to open or tamper with and endanger himself; safe for children.

The commission has now proposed a standard for book matches calling for a matchbook that is child-resistant in that it requires two or more sequential motions to open, or more than a certain amount of strength. *Frances Cerra, "Consumer Notes: New Matches," The New York Times, April 21, 1976, p 28*

The introduction of child-resistant packaging for children's aspirin in 1976 has reduced the number of children accidentally poisoned to less than half the 1975 figure. *The Times (London), Aug. 12, 1977, p 14*

[1975]

chil·i·dog ('tʃil i:ˌdɔːg), *n.* a frankfurter roll with chili con carne on it.

"What is for chow?" "Chilidogs." "He'll be back. Daumier does love his chilidog." *Donald Barthelme, "Daumier," The New Yorker, April 1, 1972, p 31*

[1971, from *chili* + *(hot) dog*] Compare CORNDOG.

chillout, *n. U.S.* a period of uncomfortably cold indoor temperatures caused by the shortage of fuel for heating.

There is one major hitch: if refineries produce enough gasoline to meet peak demand this summer, they may have to curtail heating-oil output enough to threaten more chillouts next winter. "*Economy & Business: Oil: The Growing Gasoline Gap," Time, April 16, 1973, p 88*

[1973, patterned after *blackout* and *brownout* in the supply of electricity]

chi·mu·ren·ga (ˌtʃi muːˈreŋ gə), *n.* a war of liberation in Africa, especially a war to establish black rule.

China syndrome

The broadcasts from Mozambique, which call upon the young men to cross the border and join the guerrillas in their camps, talk of the *chimurenga*. . . . in the *chimurenga* of 1976, the blacks are using Kalashnikov Ak-47 assault rifles, grenade launchers and 60-mm. mortars. *Richard Hall, "Black Victory in Rhodesia: How Bloody Will It Be?" The New York Times Magazine, July 11, 1976, p 31*

[1967, from Shona (a Bantu language), literally, strife, rebellion]

China syndrome, a catastrophic nuclear accident resulting from an uncontrollable MELTDOWN.

And without an adequate pool of water, the cladding on the fuel rods would melt, and fuel pellets would soon begin to melt together to form a concentrated lump. Such a meltdown, some fear, would lead to the so-called China Syndrome— a nuclear lava flow of such intense heat that it would burn its way through its thick steel capsule, through the nine- or 10-foot thick reinforced concrete slab, and down deep into the soil beneath the plant, in a manner that would recall the childhood fantasy of digging through the earth to China. *Don G. Meigham, "How Safe is Safe Enough?", The New York Times Magazine, June 20, 1976, p 41*

[1973] ► This term became widely publicized in March, 1979, when an accident at a nuclear power plant on Three Mile Island, in Middletown, Pennsylvania (10 miles south of Harrisburg), caused a temporary release of dangerous radioactivity, triggering fears of a meltdown. The incident coincided with the release of a motion picture entitled "The China Syndrome," which dealt with a massive meltdown in a nuclear power plant.

chi·nois (ʃiː'nwaː), *n.* a fine-meshed metal strainer for kitchen use.

The British housewives who attend the cookery courses . . . are all sent in search of two utensils vital to the tips they are taught—a conical metal sieve called a *chinois*, and a pan with a rounded copper bottom for making the perfect omelette. *Robin Young, "Shopping," The Times (London), June 1, 1976, p 6*

[1972, from French]

chip, *n.* short for BARGAINING CHIP.

If Turner had been able to report the real state of affairs that the Soviet crop was poor, . . . the President could have used the need for grain as a chip in the ongoing SALT negotiations. *Maclean's, March 6, 1978, p 59*

[1973]

chip-kick, *British.* —*n.* (in rugby, soccer, etc.) a short, often lofted, kick aimed to gain a more advantageous position by repossession after chasing the ball or by a throw-in after kicking the ball so it goes out of bounds.

Barry John, from fly-half, put in the most delicate and perfect of chip-kicks to bamboozle the defence. *Vivian Jenkins, The Sunday Times (London), May 23, 1971, p 22*

—*v.t., v.i.* to kick with a chip-kick.

An aberration by the lively Burton, chip-kicking good loose ball away in the Australian 25, happily led up to a five yard scrummage and try No. 2. *Peter West, The Times (London), Jan. 5, 1976, p 5*

[1969, probably from *chip* short, lofted shot (in golf) + *kick*] Compare GARRYOWEN.

Chiron, *n.* another name for OBJECT KOWAL.

Chiron travels around the Sun in an eccentric orbit which takes it from inside the orbit of Saturn out to the orbit of Uranus. *Charles T. Kowal, "Asteroid," McGraw-Hill Yearbook of Science and Technology 1979, p 102*

[1978, named by its discoverer after the centaur *Chiron* in Greek legend, who was a descendant of the gods Saturn and Uranus]

Chis·an·bop ('tʃiz ən,bɑp), *n.* trademark for a system of calculating arithmetically with the fingers and thumbs, invented by Sung Jin Pai, a Korean mathematician. It is used especially to teach elementary arithmetic.

With Chisanbop, the fingers are used to count to 99, with larger numbers being carried over by memory or written down. On the right hand the thumb stands for one unit with a place value of five, while each finger represents one additional unit. On the left hand the thumb stands for 50, with each finger representing 10. *Peter Carlyle-Gordge, "Education: Let Your Fingers Do the Counting," Maclean's, Jan. 8, 1979, p 37*

[1976, from Korean, literally, finger counting]

chlor·de·cone ('klɔr də koun), *n.* the generic name of KEPONE.

Chlordecone is the common chemical name of Kepone, which was originally developed by the Allied Chemical Corporation and manufactured, until last summer, by its subcontractor, the Science Products Company of Hopewell, Va., which is now insolvent. *Harold M. Schmeck, Jr., "Pesticide Is Linked to Animal Cancer," The New York Times, April 8, 1976, p 28*

[1972, from *chlor-* chlorine + *dec-* ten + *-one* ketone]

chlo·ro·flu·o·ro·car·bon (,klɔr ə,flu: ə rə'kɑr bən), *n.* any of various compounds of carbon, chlorine, fluorine, and hydrogen, used especially as refrigerants and aerosol propellants but restricted in use during the 1970's because of their suspected depletion of the ozone shield of the atmosphere.

In America, where aerosols have been used to dispense everything from toothpaste to chocolate whip and chantilly cream, the suggestion that the Earth might literally be scorched to death as a result caused profound alarm. In 1975 there was a 15 per cent drop in the manufacture of chlorofluorocarbons, largely due to lost aerosol sales. In Europe there was reaction too, but the authorities have not followed the American rush to ban chlorofluorocarbons. *The Times (London), Nov. 1, 1977, p 10*

[1959, from *chloro-* chlorine +*fluoro-* fluorine + *carbon*] *Abbreviation:* CFC. Compare HALOCARBON. See also AEROSOL.

chlo·ro·flu·o·ro·meth·ane (,klɔr ə,flu: ə rə'meθ ein), *n.* any of various chlorofluorocarbons used especially as refrigerants and aerosol propellants.

Every day, millions of aerosol cans of cleansers, deodorants, shaving cream, and other household items release chlorofluoromethanes, propellant gases that may be reducing the atmosphere's ozone layer, which protects the earth from the sun's ultraviolet radiation. *Joseph Eigner, "Shattering the Ozone Shield," The World Book Science Annual 1976 (1975), p 280*

[1970, from *chloro-* chlorine + *fluoro-* fluorine +

methane] Abbreviation: CFM. Compare HALOMETH-ANE. See also AEROSOL.

choke point or **chokepoint,** *n.* any route that cannot be easily bypassed; a geographic point for which there is no immediate alternative in travel or communication.

To quote from the *Survey,* "(the Soviet) access to the open seas passes through a number of choke points (such as the Bosphorus, Gibraltar, and the Greenland-Iceland-United Kingdom gap) and her freedom to deploy outside the range of her land-based fighter cover is limited whereas Nato ship-borne air power is considerable." *Raymond Fletcher, The Times (London), May 31, 1976, p 8*

[1966]

cho·lin·o·mi·met·ic (ˌkou lə nou miˈmet ik), *adj.* similar to or imitating acetylcholine (chemical which transmits nerve impulses), especially in its ability to affect the flow of impulses in the nervous system.

The direct effects of the cholinomimetic agents on transmission in bladder ganglia underscore the complexity of drug actions at ganglionic synapses. *William R. Saum and William C. De Groat, "Parasympathetic Ganglia: Activation of an Adrenergic Inhibitory Mechanism by Cholinomimetic Agents," Science, Feb. 11, 1972, p 661*

—*n.* a cholinomimetic agent.

The scientists implanted tubes into the appropriate point in the hypothalamus of the pacifist rats and fed in small doses of a chemical that promoted the flow of "messages" along the pathway of neurons, or nerve cells, involved in the killing behavior. Such substances, known as cholinomimetics, work by mimicking the action of chemicals found normally in the nervous sytem. *Time, March 30, 1970, p 47*

[1968, from acetyl*choline* + connecting *-o-* + *mimetic* mimicking]

chopper, *n. Slang.* **1** a motorcycle, especially one that is custom-built with the front suspension extended to place the front wheel farther forward than is customary.

My wheel or chopper is a light pistachio-coloured two-stroke *motorino,* that cost in lire the equivalent of £60. *Germaine Greer, The Sunday Times (London), Aug. 8, 1971, p 22*

2 Also called **chopper bike** or **bicycle,** a bicycle with high handlebars and tall back support.

"Chopper" bicycles have already been criticised on safety grounds. Now a group of researchers at the Royal Victoria Infirmary, Newcastle, has found that children riding choppers have a greater chance of ending up in hospital if they have an accident than children on other bicycles. *"Technology Review: Chopper Bike Accidents Cause More Serious Injuries," New Scientist, Nov. 1, 1973, p 338*

[1969]

chor·e·ol·o·gy (ˌkɔr iːˈal ə dʒiː), *n.* the study or writing of dance notations.

If you want to know how to choose a good teacher, or the best age to start dancing classes, the answers are here, but so too are more recondite subjects, such as a discussion of choreology, the art of writing down dances, in which the aims and merits of the two leading systems are more clearly and fairly assessed than in many longer accounts. *The Times (London), Nov. 20, 1978, p 15*

[1970, from *choreo*graphy + *-logy* study of]

choreologist, *n.:* Sitting on a chair by the piano . . . is the company's official notator, or choreologist, as he is titled—a man named Jurg Lanzrein, who is jotting down symbols on a large pad as he takes note of this or that bit of action. *Bernard Taper, "Profiles: George Balanchine," The New Yorker, Oct. 22, 1973, p 51*

chor·e·o·po·em (ˈkɔr iː ouˌpou əm), *n.* a poetic drama that includes dancing.

[Ntozake] Shange's choreopoem presents seven brightly dressed black women, including the author herself, on a barren stage. Barefoot, they weave and bob around like sisters at a revival meeting. Each one has a tale to tell . . . *Time, July 19, 1976, p 44*

[1976, from *choreo-* dancing, dance + *poem*]

choz·rim (xɔːzˈriːm), *n.pl.* Israelis who return to Israel after having emigrated.

The Government also makes attractive loans to returnees, including housing loans, and permits a range of exemptions for the stiff customs levies. "From April 1976, when our budget year began, until last October," said Yoram Shachal, Zarankin's boss, "the *chozrim* numbered 3,400." *James Feron, "The Israelis of New York," The New York Times Magazine, Jan. 16, 1977, p 24*

[1977, from Hebrew, literally, returnees] Compare YORDIM.

Christ·in·gle service (ˈkris ˌtiŋ gəl), a Christmas service in the Church of England at which purses of money are brought forward by children for the Children's Society, and in return each donor receives an orange tied with a red ribbon and pierced with a candle surrounded by raisins and jellies on sticks.

A Christingle service is to be held in Canterbury Cathedral, with Dr. Ramsey receiving the purses from children, on December 28 at 3 pm. *"Christingle Service Is Popular," The Times (London), Dec. 22, 1972, p 15*

[1972, probably from *Christ*mas + *ingle* fire, flame (from Scottish Gaelic *aingeal* fire, light)]

► In informal usage, the decorated orange is called a *Christingle.* It symbolizes the world, while the candle is a symbol of the light of the world, the raisins and jellies represent the fruits of the earth, and the red ribbon symbolizes the life of Christ.

Christmas tree (bill), *U.S.* a legislative bill that provides benefits for various special-interest groups, especially because of numerous amendments not directly related to the main part of the proposed law.

Next came what members called the "Christmas Tree," wherein they traded amendments to help their friends and screw their enemies. Hung on the tree were guarantees of fuel to buses, truckers, the tour business, farmers, the building trades, schoolteachers. *Arthur Hadley, "The Agony and the Energy Bill," New Times, Feb. 22, 1974, p 22*

Mr. Nessen said that the President regarded the proposal as "a Christmas tree bill" and an "ineffective way to create jobs" because public works projects take time to get started. *Richard L. Madden, "$6.2 Billion Voted for Public Works by Defiant House," The New York Times, Jan. 30, 1976, p 1*

[1971] ► This term was originally applied to a tax

103

bill affecting foreign investors that was passed in 1966 and signed "with reservations" by President Lyndon B. Johnson, who noted that it would "confer special tax windfalls and benefits upon certain groups."

Christmas tree effect, *Astronomy.* the hypothesis that the change in frequency of light emissions from some quasars is not due to their motion but to internal changes.

Detailed radioastronomical studies of a number of quasars indicate that each of those objects is composed of several components that appear to be moving swiftly apart from each other. In some cases the apparent velocities are greater than that of light.

In order to save modern physics from such forbidden speeds some very ingenious models have been devised, such as the Christmas tree effect, which says that the apparent motions are really a series of well-timed blinks of a string of stationary components. *Science News, April 24, 1976, p 267*

[1973]

chro·mo·dy·nam·ics (ˌkrou mou dai'næm iks), *n.* the theory dealing with the COLOR FORCE.

An essential requirement of chromodynamics is that each species of quark possess three aspects called colors, which have to do with the way it combines with other quarks to form a larger particle. *Sheldon L. Glashow, "The Hunting of the Quark," The New York Times Magazine, July 18, 1976, p 29*

The differentiation by "color" refers to the fact that quarks seem to behave as if they carried three different kinds of charge — not electrical charge, but something analogous to it. The study of the "color" of both matter and antimatter suggested the name "chromodynamics," which has nothing to do with real, visible color. *Malcolm W. Browne, "Detection of the Elusive 'Gluon' Exciting Scientists," The New York Times, Sept. 2, 1979, p 28*

[1976, from *chromo-* color + *dynamics*] Also called QUANTUM CHROMODYNAMICS. See QUARK.

chron·o·bi·ol·o·gy (ˌkran ou bai 'al ə dʒi:), *n.* the study of rhythmical or cyclical changes in living organisms.

Many other areas of classical agricultural phenology, intensive phenological ecosystems studies, and medical phenology (chronobiology and allergies caused by seasonal discharge of pollen and spores) are under investigation in many parts of the world. *Helmut Lieth, "Phenology," McGraw-Hill Yearbook of Science and Technology 1976, p 323*

[1976, from *chrono-* time + *biology*]

chronobiologist, *n.*: Chronobiologists are not completely sure why humans have seasonal or "circannual" rhythms, but according to Halberg, these changes are not just psychological. Blood pressure, cholesterol levels and hormones are all implicated. *Science News, April 10, 1976, p 233*

chro·non ('krouˌnan), *n. Physics.* a hypothetical quantum of time.

In 1976 Dr [Robert] Ehrlich found that the lifetimes of all known elementary particles were consistent with being an integral number of "chronons." He put the magnitude of the chronon at 2×10^{-23} s. *New Scientist, May 4, 1978, p 291*

[1978, from Greek *chrónos* time + English *-on* elementary unit]

churn, *v.t., v.i. Slang.* to increase unnecessarily the amount of business transacted in a brokerage account, the number of return visits in a professional practice, etc., in order to generate more income.

Churning: Unnecessarily requiring patients to report or to return to a health center for additional treatment. *The New York Times, Aug. 31, 1976, p 54*

Stories abound of customers' accounts being "churned," traded recklessly to generate commissions. *Maclean's, May 16, 1977, p 70*

Churning: legal research and motions that have marginal (or no) relevance or usefulness but add to billable hours. Also known as "running up the meter." *Time, April 10, 1978, p 65*

[1968]

chy·mo·pa·pa·in (ˌkai mou pə'pai ən), *n.* a protein-digesting enzyme of the tropical papaya plant, used as a meat tenderizer and experimentally as a drug to relieve pressure and pain on nerve roots.

The FDA [Food and Drug Administration] sometimes criticized for not allowing new drugs on the market, has allowed 15,302 persons to be injected with chymopapain, a nonsurgical treatment for damaged spinal discs. Even if few of the patients were cured, few of them died. Papain, an enzyme extracted from the papaya, is widely sold in groceries as a meat tenderizer. *National Review, Oct. 24, 1975, p 1156*

[1973, from Greek *chȳmós* juice + English *papain* an enzyme in papaya juice]

Cigarette, *n.* or **Cigarette hull,** a type of large inboard motorboat with an open cockpit, used for offshore racing.

Driving a deep-vee Cigarette hull to vie with *Kudo* was Betty Cook, Paul's wife, who became the first woman in the sport's history to compete in the open class. She joined the class late in the season, after a year of racing in the production class; her boat was the 36-ft Cigarette *Kaama. Robin Herman, "Sports: Powerboating," 1976 Collier's Encyclopedia Year Book (1975), p 513*

[1974, so called for its shape]

ci·gar·let (sə'gar lit), *n.* a short, thin cigar.

Hitherto a cigar filler crop has been produced in sufficient volume for internal commercial purposes, and a variety of Rhodesian-made cigars and cigarlets has been on the market for some years. *The Rhodesia Herald, Feb. 16, 1973, p 14*

[1968, from *cigar* + *-let* small, short]

cig·gy or **cig·gie** ('sig i:), *n. Informal.* a cigarette.

Tobacco is also very cheap. A Monte Christo cigar — costing in London up to £2 in a restaurant — amounts to about 45p. Local ciggies are cheap — say 12p a packet. But British brands are about the same as at home. *Brian Jackman, "Spain," The Sunday Times (London), Dec. 28, 1975, p 34*

[1962, by shortening]

ci·lan·tro (sə'læn trou), *n.* coriander, especially in reference to its use in Mexican cooking.

The vegetable section burst with feathery bunches of parsley and pungent fresh cilantro, enough tropical fruits to suggest a headdress for Carmen Miranda, tiny emerald-green tomatoes, prickly cactus leaves, and at least eight kinds of chili peppers. *Mimi Sheraton, "Ethnic Escape From the Quick and the Frozen," The New York Times, June 5, 1976, p 13*

[1965, from Spanish, ultimately from Latin *coriandrum*]

ci·met·i·dine (sai'met ə₁di:n), *n.* a drug that inhibits the secretion of acid in the stomach, introduced into the United States and Canada from Great Britain in 1977 for use in the treatment of peptic ulcers and various gastrointestinal diseases. *Formula:* $C_{10}H_{16}N_6S$

The drug is called cimetidine. So far it has been shown that it can cure ulcers quickly and effectively. Eight studies involving over 650 patients were recently completed in the United States. They showed that 70 per cent of the patients on cimetidine were healed after only four to six weeks. Significant numbers, in fact, were healed after two weeks. Cimetidine works because it blocks the action of histamine, which stimulates the secretion of gastric acid. *Maclean's, Dec. 25, 1978, p 39*

[1977, from cyano-imidazol-methyl-guanidine, chemical constituents of the drug]

cin·e·an·gi·o·gram (₁sin i:'æn dʒi: ə græm), *n.* a motion-picture record of a fluoroscope showing the passage of a radiopaque substance through the blood vessels.

The raw material for the image analysis is a cineangiogram—an X-ray cine film taken of the heart after the injection of a radio-opaque dye. The dye absorbs X-rays, so the film follows its progress through the heart. *"Technology: A Closer Look at the Heart in Motion," New Scientist, March 25, 1976, p 680*

[1976, from *cine-* motion picture + *angiogram*]

cin·e·fluor·os·co·py (₁sin i: flur'ɑs kə pi:), *n.* motion-picture photography of a fluoroscopic examination.

The crocodile's heart is analogous to a mammal's. Both direct measurements and cinefluoroscopy confirm that its four chambers can pump blood from the body to the lungs and from the lungs to the body without mixing. *Anthony C. Pooley and Carl Gans, "The Nile Crocodile," Scientific American, April 1976, p 117*

[1976, from *cine-* motion picture + *fluoroscopy*]

cinema novo or **cinema nôvo,** a movement of radical film-makers of Brazil, noted especially for the combination of fantasy and melodrama in their work.

Brazil had released Glauber Rocha's early films *Barravento* and *Terra em Transe,* Ruy Guerra's *Os Fuzis,* and Carlos Diegues's *Ganga Zumba,* all 'guerrilla' films representing the *cinema nôvo. Roger Manvell, "The Arts: The Cinema," The Annual Register of World Events in 1972 (1973), p 441*

[1970, from Portuguese *cinema nôvo* new cinema]

cin·gu·lot·o·my (₁siŋ gyə'lɑt ə mi:), *n.* a form of psychosurgery in which incisions are made into the cingulum (bundle of association fibers) of the brain.

The MIT study . . . examined 34 adult patients who had undergone surgical lesions in the brain's anterior cingulate region. (Psychosurgery has progressed from the gross severing of frontal lobes some 30 years ago to smaller, more lo-

calized cuts in various regions of the brain.) The patients had problems ranging from pain to depression to obsessive-compulsive behavior to schizophrenia and other emotional problems. Ten of the subjects had experienced more than one psychosurgical operation, including four who had three cingulotomies. *Science News, May 14, 1977, p 315*

[1972, from *cingul*um + connecting *-o-* + *-tomy* surgical incision]

cingulotomist, *n.:* H. T. Ballantine of Massachusetts General Hospital is probably the most prolific cingulotomist, and he does it for alleviation of intractable pain as well as for various "neuropsychiatric illnesses" such as depression, anxiety states, and obsessional neuroses that have not proved amenable to other kinds of treatment. *Science, March 16, 1973, p 1110*

CINS (sinz), *n. U.S.* acronym for *Child(ren) In Need of Supervision.*

These children, who are variously labelled Persons in Need of Supervision (PINS), Children in Need of Supervision (CINS), Juveniles in Need of Supervision (JINS), or Wayward Minors, depending on the state they live in, will be guilty of nothing more serious than being a burden or a nuisance. They are not juvenile criminals—they have committed no act for which an adult could be prosecuted. *The New Yorker, Aug. 14, 1978, p 55*

[1972]

cir·ca·lu·na·di·an (₁sər kə lu:'nɑ: di: ən), *adj.* characterized by or occurring in the 24-hour, 50-minute cycles of the lunar day.

This change in periodicity when an organism is placed in constant conditions is a property of almost all clock-controlled biological rhythms. Since tidal rhythms follow the lunar day, they are called circalunadian (about a lunar day). *John D. Palmer, "Biological Clocks of the Tidal Zone," Scientific American, Feb. 1975, p 70*

[1975, from Latin *circā* around + *lūna* moon + *diēs* day + English *-an*]

circular file, *U.S. Slang.* the wastepaper basket (especially of an office).

A petition to amend the tax law was sent to Governor Carey's office in April but Mr. Bourke said "it probably went into the circular file somewhere." *The New York Times, Sept. 19, 1976, Sec. 1, p 20*

[1967]

circumgalactic, *adj.* surrounding or revolving about a galaxy.

Because the permitted galactic source distributions lead to a soft X-ray flux which peaks at low galactic latitudes, . . . the observed increase in flux at high latitudes must arise from an extragalactic or circumgalactic component. *R. M. Gaze and M. J. Keating, "The Visual System and 'Neuronal Specificity'," Nature, June 16, 1972, p 380*

[1970]

circumglobal, *adj.* revolving or traveling about the earth; circumterrestrial.

These big balloons are also bearing payloads for Project Boomerang, the "poor man's satellite," on circumglobal missions. *New Scientist, Jan. 10, 1974, p 55*

circumglobally, *adv.:* "Because they are distributed circum-globally . . . : peregrines provide an ideal focus for international cooperation," said Dr. Ward, who is chief of the Ecological Research Office. *"Soviet Study U.S. Data on*

Falcons," The New York Times, Feb. 15, 1976, Sec. 1, p 73

[1974]

circumplanetary, *adj,* surrounding or revolving about a planet.

Mariner 10 will conduct a search for dwarf satellites, nevertheless, but if W. R. Ward and M. J. Reid are on the right track, the search will be more fruitful on the surface than in circumplanetary space. *Jon Darius, New Scientist, Nov. 1, 1973, p 353*

[1973]

city, *n. U.S. and Canadian Slang.* someone or something of a specified character; a (specified) condition, situation, person, prospect, etc.

In a CBS-TV special called *Funny Papers.* . . . It turned out that Daddy Warbucks is straight city, but Carroll O'Connor is pretty sexy. *"People," Time, Jan. 17, 1972, p 32*

"All my life I'm taught by my family to *keep it going,* don't get boring at the dinner table. When I learned I could do that by just being honest, whole vistas of trouble opened up. I get on a talk show, I get talking and *whoa!* Trouble city!" *Richard Dreyfuss, quoted to Cameron Crowe, Rolling Stone, Jan. 11, 1979, p 86*

[1972, abstracted from FAT CITY]

► *City* is now more popular than *-ville,* the slang suffix extensively applied in the 1960's, which generated such concoctions as *dullsville, nowheresville,* and *weirdsville.*

civ·ex ('siv eks), *n.* a system for reprocessing nuclear fuel in a breeder reactor in such a way as to avoid production of pure plutonium, which can be used to make nuclear weapons.

The United States cannot prevent a nation from going nuclear—peacefully or militarily—if it wants to, he said, even with civex. Civex is only designed to prevent subnational groups and terrorists from misusing it for military aims, he said. It also permits the United States to export, to those nations committed to developing a fast breeder reactor, a safer reprocessing technology. *Science News, March 4, 1978, p 132*

[1978, apparently from *civ*ilian (i.e., nonmilitary) + *ex*traction]

CJD, abbreviation of CREUTZFELDT-JAKOB DISEASE.

All three natural diseases, scrapie, kuru and CJD are caused primarily by rather unusual types of viral agent, although it is recognised that genetic factors may considerably affect the length of incubation. *Richard Kimberlin, "Viral Origins for Chronic Brain Disease," New Scientist, Nov. 18, 1976, p 381*

[1972]

C-J disease, short for CREUTZFELDT-JAKOB DISEASE.

Scrapie, kuru, and C-J disease will all "take" if inoculated into the brain of a chimpanzee. *Steven Ashley, Harper's, Jan. 1977, p 29*

[1972]

clad·o·gram (,klæd ə,græm), *n.* a diagram of sequences in an evolutionary tree.

Immunological distances are . . . apportionable along derived cladograms and thus serve as reliable indicators of phylogenetic affinities among the taxa being compared. *John E. Cronin and Vincent M. Sarich, Nature, April 22, 1976, p 700*

Given the acceptance of a particular cladogram for a group of species taxa, there may be a number of evolutionary trees consistent with that cladogram. *Joel Cracraft, "Animal Systematics," McGraw-Hill Yearbook of Science and Technology 1979, p 98*

[1966, from *clado-* (from Greek *kládos* branch)+ *-gram* diagram]

clambake, *n.* a group of marine animals living in areas of the ocean floor heated by a hot spring.

Leading the observers to the hot water veins was the unusual presence—for these 2,700-meter depths—of large groups of animals clustered around them, apparently thriving in the 9°C-warmer-than-usual water. Though well-known in shallow water, this is the first known occurrence of such clusters in the deep sea. The scientists have taken to calling these clusters of animal communities "clambakes." *Science News, March 19, 1977, p 183*

[1977, transferred sense of the earlier (1830's) meaning "a gathering at which clams are baked"]

clam diggers, *U.S.* trousers cut off at midcalf.

Clam diggers or pedal pushers, this midcalf length is very fashionable. This pair is styled in white cotton after sailor's pants. *Patricia Peterson, "Fashion: Lengthwise," The New York Times Magazine, March 21, 1976, p 75*

[1976, so called from their original use in digging for clams] ► The term was applied to such pants in the 1940's and revived in recent years.

clap·om·e·ter (klæ'pam ə tər), *n.* a meter for measuring the applause of an audience.

"You're easily tops, lad." Hughie Green was enthusing, putting an arm round his shoulder. The applause and the laughter gave off warmth, like a fire. The clapometer was bursting itself, registering 98, a record. "You're bringing the house down," Hughie Green said. *William Trevor, The Times (London), June 12, 1976, p 8*

[1972, from *clap* to applaud + connecting *-o-* + *-meter*]

clap track, prerecorded applause added to a sound track.

John played rhythm guitar, George the lead, and afterward, when a "clap track" (the sound of people clapping) was dubbed over, everyone except Lennon's wife, Yoko Ono, rushed into the studio to join in the applause. *Newsweek, March 26, 1973, p 100*

[1973, patterned on *laugh track* (1962)]

clast (klæst), *n. Geology.* a rock fragment; piece of broken rock.

In 1971 H. A. Lee pointed out that the most commonly used methods in glaciated terrain include sampling of heavy clasts, basal till, and eskers. *Stephen E. Kesler, "Geochemical Prospecting," McGraw-Hill Yearbook of Science and Technology 1973, p 205*

[1972, back formation from *clastic, adj.,* consisting of broken pieces of older rock]

Cle·o·cin (kli:'ou sən), *n.* a trademark for CLINDAMYCIN.

Cleocin . . . appears especially useful in treating infections caused by anaerobic bacteria, those that thrive without oxygen, such as *Bacteroides* most commonly found in patients after surgery or during drug or radiation therapy that impairs their normal defense mechanisms against infection. *Arthur Hull Hayes, Jr., "Drugs," The World Book Science Annual 1974 (1973), p 283*

[1970]

client, *n.* a person viewed euphemistically as a subject of regulation by a government agency or public authority.

In the world of prisons notable advances have also been made recently in prettying-up the nomenclature. Guards are now "correctional officers"; solitary confinement punishment cells, "adjustment centers"; prisons, "therapeutic correctional communities"; convicts, "clients of the Department of Corrections." *Jessica Mitford, "Prisons and Funerals," The New York Times, Sept. 5, 1973, p 41*

They're trying to change their image. An end to fear and loathing; they call us "clients" now, and they take video tape courses in courtesy. But basically a tax collector is just that, and they haven't changed a great deal in the last 2,000 years. *Grattan Gray, "Cheating on Your Income Tax?" Maclean's, April 1974, p 41*

[1973, originally (1920's) applied to a social worker's case]

clin·da·my·cin (ˌklin dəˈmai sən), *n.* a semisynthetic antibiotic used against respiratory infections caused by certain bacteria. *Formula:* $C_{18}H_{33}ClN_2O_5S$

The study was useful medically since it showed that one of the drugs, clindamycin, reached the fetus in sufficient amounts to control syphilis. *Newsweek, June 24, 1974, p 74*

[1970]

cli·o·met·ric (ˌkli: ouˈmet rik), *adj.* of or relating to CLIOMETRICS.

Genovese finds no source alien to his needs. He is the first historian to combine such traditional sources as government records and slaveholder diaries with extensive use of the slaves' own narratives in a picture of slavery as a whole—and with at least a few cliometric citations as well. *Anthony Astrachan, Saturday Review, Jan. 11, 1975, p 23*

[1970, from *Clio*, the Greek muse of history + *metric* of or involving measurement]

cliometrically, *adv.:* Dr. Fogel of the University of Chicago has cliometrically calculated that railroads were not so crucial to industrial growth as the traditional wisdom has pictured them. *Encyclopedia Science Supplement (Grolier) 1970, p 290*

cli·o·met·rics (ˌkli: ouˈmet riks), *n.* the study of history by the use of advanced methods of mathematical analysis, particularly the processing of large quantities of historical data through computers.

The book [*Time on the Cross*, by Robert W. Fogel and Stanley L. Engerman] is sure to produce new interest in the burgeoning science of cliometrics, the manner of applying computers to the reconsideration of social and economic phenomena, and in that sense alone it is a remarkable document. *Simon Winchester, The Manchester Guardian Weekly, April 27, 1974, p 5*

[1970, from CLIOMETRIC]

cliometrician, *n.:* Together they are the leading edge of a new wing of historians known as cliometricians because their methods marry Clio, the muse of history, to the practice of quantifying the past with the help of computers. *Timothy Foote, Time, June 17, 1974, p 98*

Clipped Forms. ► New words are sometimes formed in English by dropping syllables or "clipping" older words. *Bus, taxi, gym, plane,* and *phone* are now generally accepted in formal English and most people are no longer aware that *bus* was clipped from *omnibus* and *taxi* from *taxicab.* The clipped form is not always acceptable usage and many, such as the nouns *ad, dorm,* and *vet,* are still considered informal by some writers and speakers.

A number of clipped forms appeared in the 1960's: *deli, limo, mayo, mod, narc.* Some recent examples, recorded in this book, are MESC (*mescaline*), MUNI (*municipal*), QUAD (*quadraphonic* and *quadrillion*), SCHIZ (*schizophrenic* or *schizophrenia*).

Clipping often alters spelling. Based on the pronunciation, *tranquilizer* is changed to TRANK and *flagellation* becomes FLADGE, a shift to the spelling pattern *-adge* in order to represent the fact that the sound of the first vowel is carried over in both words. Some clipped forms are altered by the addition of a diminutive or other ending: TEENY from *teen-ager,* TRANNIE from *transistor,* VEGGIES from *vegetables.*

For another type, see BACK FORMATIONS.

clockwork orange, someone deprived of his individuality by scientific conditioning and made into an automaton.

[Albert] Bandura feels the behavior-modification process is misunderstood by the public. "They see salivating dogs, shocks, clockwork oranges. They misunderstand the process," he says. *Sharland Trotter and Jim Warren, Science News, March 16, 1974, p 181*

[1972, from *A Clockwork Orange*, title of a novel (1962) by the British author Anthony Burgess, born 1917, about transformation of a deviant and violent personality by exposure to a form of aversion therapy. The phrase is from the Cockney expression "queer as a clockwork orange."]

clone, *n.* **1** a person or thing that is an exact duplicate, or appears to be an exact duplicate, of another; a carbon copy; replica.

Both blond and blue-eyed, Mr. Driver and Mr. Haddow agree that they are clones, then fall to squabbling over who is the original. *Leslie Bennetts, "The Clones of 'Scrambled Feet'," The New York Times, July 20, 1979, p C3*

2 a person who acts in a mindless, mechanical fashion; automaton; android; robot.

One of his most cutting inventions—or adaptations—is the urban guerrilla seen as Mickey Mouse. In *Six Terrorists,* 1971, a file of them strut across the page, in aviator jackets and miniskirts, equipped with flick knife and carbine: young bourgeois clones of affectless violence. *Time, April 17, 1978, p 94*

Elsewhere, they suggest the possibility of using clones for work involving radiation or dangerous chemicals, or for fighting wars. *The Manchester Guardian Weekly (The Washington Post section), Sept. 24, 1978, p 17*

—*v.t.* to produce an identical, or nearly identical, copy or copies of (a person or thing) from a model or blueprint.

Since it costs about $2 billion to design and tool up for an all-new plane and engines, most of the new generation will be cloned from present models, scaled down in size and outfitted with the latest technology. *Time, Aug. 14, 1978, p 57*

[1978, figurative senses of the noun *clone*, meaning two or more individuals duplicated or propagated asexually from a single (sexually produced) ancestor, and the verb meaning to reproduce or propagate a clone]

cloning, *n.:* Added to these possibilities is the often-dreaded question of cloning. This has turned out to be the subject that catches the imagination, that titillates movie audiences and shows up so often in science fiction. The movie scenario generally involves some demented dictator — or mad scientist — who clones up a whole army of perfectly obedient, tenacious soldiers who mindlessly obey his every command. Or, in an alternative approach, the dictator who, to ensure his continued reign, clones up a few copies of himself to keep ready in case of the worst. *Robert Cooke, Improving on Nature, 1977, p 10*

clo·ni·dine ('klou nə ˌdɑin *or* 'klou nə ˌdiːn), *n.* a drug that lowers high blood pressure, found also to block and reverse the effects of withdrawal from heroin and other narcotics. *Formula:* $C_9H_9Cl_2N_3$

The scientists suggest that clonidine and naltrexone may be used in sequence to first effect a nearly painless withdrawal from heroin and then to maintain the ex-addict in a prevention program. Neither of the substances is addictive — giving them a significant advantage over methadone maintenance, say the researchers. *Science News, Aug. 5, 1978, p 85*

[1972, probably irregular from cy*clo*- cyclic + an*ilide* + -*ine* (chemical suffix)]

closed caption, a caption to aid the deaf and hard of hearing, used in a system of restricted transmission of television-program captioning.

The programs are to be encoded with what are called "closed" captions — subtitles that are invisible on all television sets except those specially equipped to make them appear. *The New York Times, Oct. 5, 1976, p 89*

[1976, shortened from *closed-circuit caption*]

closed captioning: The closed captioning system operates through the imposition of encoded visual subtitles on Line 21 of the TV vertical blanking interval — a portion of the screen that does not ordinarily contain video information. *"Closed Captioning: A Glossary of Terms," The Deaf American, April 1979, p 7*

close-look satellite, an earth satellite used for detailed military photo reconnaissance.

With their shorter lifetime in orbit, the close-look satellites had less stringent reliability requirements than the area-surveillance models and were therefore able to reach full operational status more quickly. *Ted Greenwood, "Reconnaissance and Arms Control," Scientific American, Feb. 1973, p 19*

[1972]

closet, *adj.* hidden; covert; secret.

But for the G.I.s in the rear areas, there was another enemy to fight: hard drugs. To find out why, I invited a "closet" addict from Army headquarters in Saigon to come over and talk. *Jon Larsen, Time, Feb. 5, 1973, p 23*

Mr. Fairlie . . . swings into step with the revisionist transmogrification of Dwight D. Eisenhower into a closet dove who would have abandoned the nation's commitments in Southeast Asia and elsewhere. *Robert D. Novak, "Revisionism, Ltd.," Review of "The Kennedy Promise: The Politics of Expectation" by Henry Fairlie, National Review, March 2, 1973, p 269*

[1968, extended from earlier (1600's) sense of "private; secluded"]

Club of Rome, an international group of businessmen, economists, and scientists who periodically issue reports and predictions about global problems of food, population, industry, environment, and other factors of survival.

In its famous doomsday treatise four years ago, the Club of Rome depicted a world consuming its resources and polluting itself at a rate that — if continued — would ensure its early destruction. The only hope for global salvation was suggested in the report's title: *The Limits to Growth.* *"American Notes," Time, April 26, 1976, p 12*

Mr. Lapham dismisses the warnings of the Club of Rome because they are the product of research that was conceived in a villa — as though he expected better advice on the world's energy situation from people who had lived all their lives in a ghetto. *Harper's, Oct. 1977, p 4*

[1972, so called because the group was founded in Rome]

cluster bomb, a bomb consisting of a number of small fragmentation bombs or several explosive canisters.

The new US Administration has embargoed the sale of cluster bombs using fuel/air explosives (FAE) to Israel. *"US Arms Sales Embargoes," New Scientist, Feb. 24, 1977, p 443*

[1965]

cluster-bombed, *adj.:* A better measure of the peace process is to be found in the collapse of Israeli-Egyptian negotiations, and in the cluster-bombed villages of south Lebanon. *Harper's, Aug. 1978, p 75*

cluster bombing: The majority of the population actually live in the areas serviced by ERA [Eritrean Relief Association], where there are over 600,000 displaced persons and where daily napalm and cluster bombing causes an ever-increasing number of civilian casualties. *The Manchester Guardian Weekly, Nov. 19, 1978, p 2*

cluster headache, a type of severe, disabling headache occurring several times daily or every two or three days, usually for a period of time and then recurring later.

Cluster headache is an exquisitely painful type of migraine. Its victims are primarily middle aged men, although women and people as young as 20 years of age may be affected. The headaches come in blindingly painful bunches over a period of hours, days, or weeks, and then vanish for months or even years before recurring. Occasionally, a cluster appears once and never recurs. *Vita West-Muir, "Migraine," Encyclopedia Science Supplement (Grolier) 1979 (1978), p 243*

[1953, 1972]

CNC, abbreviation for *computer numerical control.*

Development of the CNC systems, each of which has its own built-in minicomputer to run a machine tool, was held back because of relatively high costs. *George J. Berkwitt,*

"Manufacturing," The 1973 World Book Year Book, p 411 [1972] Compare DNC.

co-anchor, *U.S. −v.t., v.i.* to anchor (a television or radio program) jointly with another or others.

Barbara Walters was brought from the "Today" show to co-anchor ABC's evening news with Harry Reasoner. Then NBC, not to be outdone in on-camera personality, brought up David Brinkley from Washington to co-anchor with John Chancellor. *The New Yorker, Oct. 31, 1977, p 123*

−*n.* a person who co-anchors.

The drop in the "Today" show ratings over the last year might perhaps be attributed to her NBC co-anchor Jim Hartz. *John J. O'Connor, The New York Times, April 24, 1976, p 55*

[1969]

coat gene, the viral gene that codes for coat protein.

The second gene is the coat gene. This gene codes for a protein that makes a coat around the virus. The third gene is known to be the polymerase gene. *Joan Arehart-Treichel, Science News, Jan. 6, 1973, p 12*

[1973]

coat protein, a protein that acts as a protective sheath for a virus, making it resistant to antibodies of the host organism.

The putative coat proteins prepared from different clones of one strain of *T. brucei* differed in composition. This supported the view that coat protein is the variant antigen, an idea now further strengthened by Cross's latest discovery that mice immunised with purified coat glycoprotein (molecular weight 65,000 ±3,000) are protected against subsequent infection with living trypanosomes of the same, but not of other, clones. *J. R. Baker, Nature, Jan. 1 and 8, 1976, p 15*

[1976]

cochair, *v.t.* to chair jointly; share the chairmanship of.

The occasion was a press conference to announce a forthcoming backgammon tournament in Las Vegas that was being co-chaired by Magriel and the venerable jack-of-all-games Oswald Jacoby. *"The Talk of the Town," The New Yorker, Dec. 5, 1977, p 40*

[1968]

cockpit, *n. Geology.* an enclosed depression with no evidence of a dry valley. It is a feature of the limestone topography of Jamaica.

To the south of the fault there are well developed cockpits whilst to the north the landscape is physically disarmingly similar to the chalk downlands of southern England. *D. I. Smith, "Where Limestone Fashions Landscape," Geographical Magazine, Oct. 1972, p 35*

[1972]

code dating, the practice of placing coded information on perishable products to indicate date of manufacture, expiration of shelf life, or time limit for sale.

Consumerism is not about to fade away; rather, it is begetting a spate of legislation to regulate retailers' conduct, including unit and dual pricing and code dating. *Theodore D. Ellsworth, "Retail Business," 1971 Collier's Encyclopedia Year Book, p 460*

[1971] See BAR CODE.

code word or **codeword,** *n.* **1** a seemingly inoffensive word or expression which conceals an offensive meaning or message.

Those who advise us that "law and order" is a codeword for racism will have a bit of difficulty pinning the racist tag on Coleman Young, first black mayor of Detroit. *"The Week," National Review, Feb. 1, 1974, p 120*

Initially, the Arabs were stunned when Carter endorsed "defensible borders" for Israel (code word for no return to the 1967 frontiers). *"Middle East: Code Words from an Oracle," Time, March 28, 1977, p 27*

2 any group of three nucleotides in the genetic code; a codon.

Information for the synthesis of protein molecules is stored as a sequence of code words in the DNA of the cell nucleus and is transcribed as a similar sequence onto RNA messenger molecules. Each code word is made up of nucleotides taken in groups of three and represents one of the 20 amino acids shown in the chart (opposite); in the code words depicted, A = adenine, C = cytosine, G = guanine, T = thymine, and U = uracil. Carried to the site of protein synthesis in the cytoplasm, the sequence of RNA code words directs the proper placement of amino acids in the growing protein chain. *Illustration legend, "The Living Cell," 1976 Britannica Yearbook of Science and the Future (1975), p 62*

[1968 for def. 1, transferred sense of the military term *code name*, as in "the operation went by the code name (or code word) Skyrocket"; 1964 for def. 2, probably short for *genetic code word*] Compare WORD.

► *Code word* in the sense of definition 1 is now used to attack opponents or to question motives by ascribing a concealed ("code") meaning to a slogan or other expression. This usage developed during the 1960's in the civil-rights movement, when politicians calling for "law and order" were accused by civil-rights leaders of using the phrase as a "code word" for suppressing the struggle for civil rights. Likewise in 1970, BENIGN NEGLECT was widely regarded as a code word for deliberately ignoring the civil-rights struggle. And in 1976, the alleged code word was ETHNIC PURITY, used by Jimmy Carter during his campaign for the Presidency:

Says one Midwestern liberal leader: "The question is whether or not 'ethnic purity' is a code word, and if so, is it calculated to lose 5% of the black vote and pick up 12% of Wallace's support? . . ." *Time, April 26, 1976, p 16*

Frequently *code word* is applied to various veiled references that attack ideology. A Chinese code word is HEGEMONY, meaning Soviet expansionism, and before the elimination of the GANG OF FOUR (referring to Mao Tse-tung's widow and three associates) a typical "reactionary" in the Communist Party was usually charged with CONFUCIANISM and with being a CAPITALIST ROADER. Other code words or phrases are evident in the following quotation:

The Western European leaders formally rejected the "dictatorship of the proletariat" and "proletarian internationalism," the code word for party discipline under Russian leadership. *John Holmes, "Focus on the World," The 1977 World Book Year Book, p 20*

The difference between *code* *word* and

euphemism becomes blurred in many cases; whereas *euphemism* often implies good intention by the user, as in the phrase "senior citizen" instead of "old person" to avoid offending, *code word* often suggests that the user has a harmfully deceptive purpose in concealing his meaning by substituting an innocent-sounding word for one that is likely to meet with disfavor. (See EUPHEMISMS.) In the following two quotations, the first uses *code word* almost as though it meant "euphemism," while the second uses the term with the meaning of "deceptive motive."

Whether the end of the war comes by negotiation or by unilateral withdrawal—for which the code word is "Vietnamization"—it will be accompanied or followed by large changes in American foreign policy. *Richard H. Rovere, The New Yorker, Nov. 1, 1969, p 174*

The term "law and order" has become, for many whites, a code word for enforcing separation between the races—or worse, a means of justifying brutal suppression and disregard of civil liberties. *Lyndon B. Johnson, Britannica Book of the Year 1969, p 35*

co-edition, *n.* one of several editions of the same book published by two or more companies at the same time, usually in different countries.

Italian publishers are in unison in complaining about rising costs, but with sales depressed, they do not feel they can raise prices. . . . One way out of the problem that several publishers have found is "co-editions," books with a lot of art work utilizing Italians' graphic skills. They are printed in Italy under the name of a foreign publisher with a translation of the text provided by the foreign house and sold in both countries. *The New York Times, Jan. 25, 1976, Sec. 3, p 40*

[1969]

coevolution, *n.* the simultaneous evolution of two or more unrelated, but often mutually dependent, forms or organisms.

They conclude that the prime function of these ubiquitous plant substances is as ultraviolet pigments. They have probably played an important part in the coevolution of flowers with ultraviolet-sensitive insects. *New Scientist, Aug. 24, 1972, p 375*

[1967]

coevolutionary, *adj.:* Gilbert draws attention to . . . the coevolutionary advantages of pollen feeding not only to the *Heliconius* butterflies but also to the plants from which they are able to collect limited but continuous amounts of pollen. *Nature, July 14, 1972, p 76*

coevolve, *v.i.* to undergo coevolution; evolve simultaneously, especially in response to one another.

They found that the eaters and the eaten progressively evolved in close response to each other—coevolved. (Some plants developed defensive alkaloid poisons. Some caterpillars acquired a taste for alkaloids. The plants diversified wildly. The caterpillars diversified with them. What evolved really was the relationship, stably dynamic, unpredictable and sure.) *"The CoEvolution Quarterly," Harper's, April 1974, p 105*

[1972]

Cogas, *n.* acronym for *coal-oil-gas,* applied to the gasification of coal or oil.

A consortium of companies is developing the Cogas (coal-oil-gas) process, in which carbonization is accomplished in a fluidized bed of coal at comparatively low temperature. *Neal P. Cochran, "Oil and Gas from Coal," Scientific American, May 1976, p 27*

[1973]

co·gen·er·a·tion or **co·gen·er·a·tion** (ˌkou dʒenəˈrei ʃən), *n.* the production of heat and electricity from the same facility, especially by using the steam left over from industrial processes to generate electric power.

Many industries examined the feasibility of co-generation—simultaneously producing process steam for manufacturing and electricity. The Administration considered offering new incentives to encourage industry to try this system. Among the items being considered were a 30 per cent tax credit for co-generation investment. *James J. O'Connor, "Energy," The 1978 World Book Year Book, p 312*

Beguiling arguments are made . . . for do-it-yourself power, which usually involves "co-generation"—using surplus heat from electricity generation to heat and cool buildings. That yields more total energy from every barrel of oil and that is why President Carter has endorsed co-generation as a conservation measure. *Editorial in The New York Times, April 18, 1979, p A18*

[1976, coined by the American physicist Amory B. Lovins, born 1948]

cognitive dissonance, *Psychology.* the holding of contradictory attitudes at the same time or the performing of acts that conflict with one's beliefs.

Cognitive Dissonance Theory . . . holds that people cannot easily entertain two ideas at once, if these ideas are basically at odds with each other. One way out of such a dilemma, should it arise circumstantially, is to come down heavily on one side. With rationalisations, counterarguments and, if possible, outside support, the other side of the dilemma is routed. *Mallory Wober, The Listener, Sept. 6, 1973, p 298*

[1968] Compare DOUBLE-BIND.

cohabitee, cohabitant or **cohabitor,** *n.* a person who lives with another without being married to him or her.

The burden of their message is that a full and meaningful and ever-deepening relationship between cohabitants can only be achieved if each cohabitee continually strives to discover more and more about the nature of him/herself and his/her mate. *Donald Gould, "Forum: Cohabitation," New Scientist, Oct. 4, 1973, p 51*

Staff at the Lord Chancellor's office and parliamentary draftsmen had helped in drawing it up "and we had always intended it to give co-habitee couples the same rights as married couples." *Philip Jordan, "Women Hail 'Mistresses' Charter'," The Manchester Guardian Weekly, Dec. 4, 1977, p 3*

Cohabitors frequently draw up a contract for themselves outlining their respective duties and areas of ownership. It is in your best interest if the two of you have something in writing about your relationship. A written letter of agreement, notarized and stating whatever you want to say about the division of your property, is a document a court will try to honor. *Ruth Rejnis, Her Home, 1980, p 137*

[1973, from *cohabit* to live together as husband and

wife without being legally married (*c*1530) + *-ee* or *-ant* or *-or*; *cohabitant* in the general sense of one who dwells together with others has been in use since the 1500's] Compare LIVE-IN and ROOMMATE. See also MARRIAGE, PALIMONY.

Coinages. ► *Coinage* refers broadly to the creation of a new word or phrase or a new meaning.

In most cases it is difficult or impossible to ascribe the invention of new words and phrases to specific individuals. Words enter the mainstream of language generally after they have been used for a considerable time in some specialized area, and after such a time the circumstances of their creation are forgotten. Even names of new products or services are hard to trace; usually new products and services are named anonymously by the firms that produce or provide them. This category of coinage includes trademarks such as ASPARTAME, GRANOLA, INSTAMATIC, KEPONE, LAETRILE, and TASER, entered in this book; see also the separate note under the heading TRADEMARKS.

Words invented to name new concepts and discoveries are, however, often closely associated with the persons who created or invented them. The creator or discoverer is usually also the coiner of the word. A partial list of such coinages entered in this book is ACROLECT, BASILECT, CELLULITE, ECOTECTURE, ENKEPHALIN, FACTOID, HOLON, ME DECADE, SPECIESISM, TARDYON, X-OGEN, and ZOOSEMIOTICS.

The names of the coiners, when they are known, are given in the etymologies in this book. Sometimes two or more names are coined independently for the same thing. The first of a new family of elementary particles was named J PARTICLE by Samuel C. C. Ting and PSI PARTICLE by Burton Richter. Some physicists took to referring to it as the J/PSI PARTICLE, but others coined still another synonym, PSION. Similarly, a microscopic form of life discovered in 1977 was simultaneously christened ARCHAEBACTERIA and METHANOGEN.

The use of an older word with a new meaning to name a new thing or idea is also a type of coinage. Examples of this are CATASTROPHE as a new mathematical concept, LAYERING to describe a new fashion in clothes, and CAYLEY as the name for a material found on the moon. Such coinages are often associated with the names of people who first used these words in a special way.

A special type of attributable coinage that is just now popular is the book title, such as CATCH-22, CLOCKWORK ORANGE, GODFATHER, GULAG (ARCHIPELAGO), and LAST HURRAH. The readers have turned these titles, by allusion, into common words.

New terms may be coined, of course, by any of the processes discussed in separate notes elsewhere in the book, such as blending (BEAUTILITY), compounding (DECIDOPHOBIA), derivation (EPHEMERALIZATION), acronym (MAD), borrowing (HOLON), and others.

Cointelpro (ˌkou in'tel prou), *n.* acronym for *counterintelligence program*, a program of the U.S. Federal Bureau of Investigation to disrupt by secret actions the activities of individuals or groups regarded as a threat to domestic security.

Mr. Kelley has stated that Cointelpro is a thing of the past which has been "purged" from bureau operations, but events conspire to contradict him. Early last month, for example, the F.B.I. withheld for two weeks from Denver police information about yet another Socialist Workers Party burglary carried out by one of its informants. *"Editorial: Cointelpro Taint," The New York Times, Aug. 3, 1976, p 28*

[1975]

COLA, *n. U.S.* acronym for *cost of living adjustment.*

The last U.R.W. [United Rubber Workers] contract included no COLA at all, and as a result the average hourly wage for rubber workers has fallen $1.35 behind that of automobile workers (who have been getting a cost of living increase). The union is demanding parity with auto workers' wages in addition to a "meaningful" further wage increase, a COLA clause and improvements in pension and insurance plans. *Time, March 8, 1976, p 52*

[1976]

cold, *n.* **in from the cold,** back into favor; no longer in a condition of isolation or neglect.

No writer has been more harshly excluded from public life than Biermann since he wrote an extraordinary poem, "The Wire Harp," which had the ghost of Francois Villon drunkenly haunting the Wall and teasing the murderously trigger-happy Vopos. But now he too might be brought in from the cold—on probation no doubt. *W. L. Webb, The Manchester Guardian Weekly, April 20, 1974, p 18*

While Reagan and Gianotti were moles, they were debriefed once a week by another agent dressed in street people's sloppy garb and then would dictate a long report to an FBI stenographer. After the arrests were made, they at first wanted to keep their cover, but now, after a month of enjoying the real world again, they are happy to be in from the cold. *Time, Jan. 9, 1978, p 14*

[1972, abstracted from *come in from the cold*, phrase popularized by *The Spy Who Came in From the Cold*, title of a novel (1964) by John Le Carré]

cold-turkey, *v.i., v.t. U.S.* to quit a habit or addiction abruptly.

If you are not cold-turkeying, try to figure out which cigarettes are most important to you. After breakfast? After dinner? Some people find they can cut down to just four or five a day this way. *"The Smoking Habit," Harper's Bazaar, April 1974, p 124B*

What all this means, of course, is that taking leave of your local club for foreign destinations no longer obliges you to "cold turkey" tennis entirely, and it may even provide you with the chance to play more than you might have been able to if you'd stayed at home. *Barry Tarshis, "International," Town and Country, April 1975, p 114*

[1974, from the noun phrase *cold turkey* (1920's) addict's sudden deprivation of his habit]

collectibles or **collectables,** *n.pl.* items suitable for collecting, especially rare or outdated objects of little intrinsic value.

One finds Art Deco restaurants, shops with plants and baskets, shops with secondhand clothes (now called "antiques" and viewed as high fashion), and shops filled with the less-than-antiques that used to be called "junk" and are now called "collectibles." *"On and Off the Avenue: Christmas Gifts for Women," The New Yorker, Nov. 22, 1976, p 127*

The popularity of collectables from the past — such as a vogue for items of the 1930s and 1940s — may be a measure of the times. Dr. Simon Conrad, a Beverly Hills, Calif., psychiatrist who has written on collecting, says: "Collectors turn to the past more seriously in time of national crisis. Today, this country is going through a period of unrest and discontent. It is not surprising to find that an increasing number of people are showing interest in what has gone before." *Charles and Bonnie Remsberg, "The Anatomy of Collecting," The 1971 World Book Year Book, p 125*

Each collectible has a history or use that evokes the life-styles of other places, other periods. *Advertisement for "The Encyclopedia of Collectibles," Time, May 14, 1979, p 66*

[1952, 1963, noun use of the adjective (1600's)]

collector, *n.* short for SOLAR COLLECTOR.

The temperature that can be achieved when solar radiation is absorbed in a collector — the absorbing device — depends on how intensely the collector concentrates the energy. The simplest type of collector does not concentrate the radiation at all. Such a collector is a flat plate painted black and encased in an insulated, glass-covered box. *Barry Commoner, "A Reporter at Large: Energy—II," The New Yorker, Feb. 9, 1976, p 63*

[1976]

Colombian gold, a potent South American variety of marijuana.

They loiter on the sidewalk, trying to buy marijuana from the storklike black youth who can say, "Colombian gold" in a carrying whisper without moving his lips. *Tom Buckley, The New York Times Magazine, Jan. 23, 1977, p 30*

The Bottom Line is adrip with hip: denim and silk, Heineken Dark on the tables and Colombian Gold in the air. *Dave Hirshey, Daily News (New York), Leisure section, April 1, 1979, p 3*

[1976, so called from its frequent place of origin and bright yellow color] Compare ACAPULCO GOLD. See also THAI STICK.

color, *n.* any of three hypothetical quantum states which combine to produce the strong force that binds quarks.

More complex versions of this theory have been proposed since its introduction in 1963, including the idea that the three basic quarks are subdivided still further by quantum properties called colors. This embellishment is believed necessary because the quarks, having half-integer spins, are fermions and therefore must obey the Pauli exclusion principle. In many of the baryon and meson configurations constructed of quarks, sometimes two and even three identical quarks must be set in the same quantum alignment — an arrangement forbidden by the exclusion principle. By assuming three colors — red, yellow and blue — for each of the basic quarks, nine quarks become available, and it is then possible to construct all the known hadrons without violations. *Henry T. Simmons, "Particle Physics: A Realm of Charm, Strangeness, and Symmetry," 1977 Britannica Yearbook of Science and the Future (1976), p 157*

[1975, so called because when the colors red, yellow, and blue combine the result is white, suggestive of the neutralized state in which combined quarks should be] Compare FLAVOR. See also COLOR FORCE, GLUON, QUARK.

Color Abstraction, the style of color-field paintings.

Taken together, the Olitski retrospective at the Whitney, the Kelly at the Museum of Modern Art, and the Hamilton at the Guggenheim evoke the dominant avant-garde styles of the nineteen-sixties: Color Abstraction and Pop Art. *Harold Rosenberg, "The Art World," The New Yorker, Oct. 15, 1973, p 113*

[1973]

color-field, *adj.* of or designating a form of abstract art that relies more on color than on form.

Also showing are . . . four large color-field paintings from the late Morris Louis's "Omega" series. *Time, May 4, 1970, p NY3*

A number of exhibitions were devoted to artists who had worked in the 20th century. Works by the colour-field abstractionist Jules Olitski were shown at the Pasadena (Calif.) Museum of Modern Art in a show organized by the Boston Museum of Fine Arts and first seen there. *Sandra Millikin, "Art Exhibitions," Britannica Book of the Year 1975, p 87*

[1967]

color force, the strong force which binds quarks.

Today, we think that both mesons and nucleons are composite systems made of quarks. The nuclear force is regarded as a mere indirect manifestation of a more basic *color force* responsible for the permanent entrapment of quarks. *Color* is used in this new technical sense with no relation to the ordinary meaning of the word. *Sheldon L. Glashow, "The Hunting of the Quark," The New York Times Magazine, July 18, 1976, p 29*

[1976] See CHROMODYNAMICS, GLUON.

color man, *U.S.* a radio or television announcer who adds color or variety to the broadcast of a public event by providing background information on the participants, describing or analyzing their actions, etc.

He [Wally Schirra] also signed on to be Walter Cronkite's color man on CBS's play-by-play coverage of the Apollo space shots. *Esquire, Jan. 1973, p 182*

What [Bill] Russell is, according to the pros both on the court and in the control booth, is simply the wisest, wittiest and most forthright basketball analyst in broadcasting — if not the best "color man" (a phrase rarely used to his face) in any sport. *Newsweek, March 12, 1973, p 61*

[1971, from *color* meaning "interest, vividness"] ► The following variants of *color man* have also been recorded:

color announcer: The Second Annual Unofficial Miss Las Vegas Showgirl Pageant, with host Steve Allen, color announcer Phyllis Diller and judges Louis Nye, Rip Taylor and Jane Meadows. *TV Guide, Feb. 1, 1975, p A-78*

color babbler: There is one short scene in which Dick Button, playing a TV color babbler, describes the moves of a Japanese wrestler in terms of figure skating, the only sport his character knows anything about. *Time, Aug. 21, 1978, p 53*

COM or **com,** abbreviation for *computer output microfilm,* a computer printout made directly on microfilm.

Microfilm may thus take some of the load off computer memories. At the same time, it may also help break the bottleneck of computer printout through a great new range of systems known as computer-output-microfilm, or COM for short. *Lawrence Lessing, "Microfilm Emerges from its Dusty Corner," Encyclopedia Science Supplement (Grolier) 1973, p 412*

There are now about 40 com machines in Britain, some owned by bureaux and serving several firms, but the total number of com users cannot number more than 200. It is, however, growing at 25 per cent per year. *Clare Smythe, "Try Microfiche Instead of Computer Terminals," New Scientist, May 3, 1973, p 277*

[1970]

comanagement, *n.* another name for WORKER PARTICIPATION.

"Let each one choose quite freely the type of society he wants . . . but we must reject with the utmost vigour formulas which under diverse labels aim through comanagement at unionizing and paralysing the management of firms." *Charles Hargrove, "French Employers Reject Comanagement," quoting Ambroise Roux, The Times (London), Jan. 14, 1976, p 18*

[1976] Also called COSUPERVISION.

com·bi ('kɔm bi:), *n. British, Informal.* combination.

When business is slack at weekends, the aircraft are turned into "combis" — with half the cabin carrying passengers and the other half cargo. *Arthur Reed, The Times (London), Nov. 4, 1976, p VII*

[1969, by shortening]

combined immunodeficiency disease, a disease characterized by the absence of both T cells and B cells in the body. It is usually fatal and occurs among the young who die of such secondary conditions as pneumonia and sepsis.

In 1972 Hilaire Meuwissen of the Albany (N.Y.) Medical Center and his colleagues identified three infants who had serious combined immunodeficiency disease and who also lacked a particular enzyme in their red blood cells. *"Children Without Immunity: Causes Probed," Science News, Feb. 28, 1976, p 138*

[1973] *Abbreviation:* CID

Combining Forms. ▶ This term is usually restricted to forms that occur in COMPOUNDS and DERIVATIVES, such as *semi-* and *-naut;* sometimes, of course, the form coincides with a free-standing word, such as *graph* as contrasted with *telegraph;* and even a free-standing word may be used as a combining form, such as -PERSON in place of *-man.*

Many of our combining forms are BORROWINGS from Latin or Greek and are so well established in English that they are freely used to form new words. Even the simplest list of words beginning with AGRI-, *bio-,* INDUSTRIO-, *micro-,* astro-, PETRO-, SEXO-, illustrates the range and productivity of such forms. Combining forms are particularly frequent and important in the creation of new TECHNICAL TERMS.

Like other linguistic forms, these word components are subject to change and extension of meaning. For instance, the development of astronautics in the 1960's expanded the meanings of the old combining forms of *astro-* and *cosmo-* to include outer space and space travel. More recently, the energy crisis has caused the form PETRO- to take on an extended meaning related to the oil industry, while -ATHON was applied to any prolonged activity resembling a marathon. Similar changes are noted under the entries SYN-, FLEXI-, -ORIENTED, and -WATCHER. Other examples of the use of combining forms taken out of older words, such as -GATE in WATERGATE, are cited in the separate notes on ABSTRACTED FORMS and NONCE WORDS.

come, *v. U.S. Slang* **1 come down,** to happen; occur.

The depth of insight that *Roots* inspired was always within these men — usually shown only in small asides or jokes. *Roots* brought it all up front.

"It makes me proud. That's me I am watching. That's my roots," someone would say.

"We would be better off if this [slavery] hadn't come down — if we were left alone," a young man commented. *Time, March 7, 1977, p K-2*

And what's the government doing for all those families; is it telling anybody what really came down there? There's nothing being done and it will never be finished for me until something is done. *Jeffrey A. Jay, "After Vietnam: I. In Pursuit of Scapegoats," Harper's, July 1978, p 15*

2 where one is coming from, what one feels or experiences.

The book is a record of what the natives are into, what they have going, . . . whom they are getting it on with, where they're coming from, and what's coming down. *Susan Lardner, "Books," The New Yorker, April 24, 1978, p 157*

[1977 for defs. 1 and 2]

comint or **COMINT** ('kɑm int), *n.* the system or process of gathering intelligence by intercepting communications.

Comint organizations . . . endeavour to intercept as much enemy signal traffic as possible. This may mean establishing listening stations close to an enemy border (or in the air) to intercept frequencies which travel over line of sight paths such as VHF, UHF and microwave, or in good receiving sites at strategic points around the world to intercept high frequency communications. *John Marriott, "No Break in the Code War," New Scientist, March 2, 1972, p 466*

[1969, acronym for *communications intelligence*] Compare ELINT, HUMINT, SIGINT.

com·ix ('kɑm iks), *n.pl.* comic strips of the underground press, characterized by disorganized and purposely offensive subjects and characters.

It is the feeling of freedom and the knowledge that most obscenity laws are mushy, and thus vulnerable to legal attack, that enables many printer-distributors and originators of comix to operate with what they consider impunity. . . . *Walt Kelly, "The Funnies Are Relevant," The 1972 Compton Yearbook, p 59*

The advertisement continued: "The largest selection of your favourite comix along with searing pungent coverage of up-to-the-minute topics and dirty small ads." *The Times (London), Jan. 18, 1973, p 2*

[1972, humorous alteration of *comics* (influenced by *mix*)]

commerciogenic, *adj.* having commercial appeal.

Progress in the separation of the major components of

113

foodstuffs, namely proteins, fats, and carbohydrates, and their subsequent recombination made possible the introduction of many new foods tailored for convenience, novelty, and economy. Such "commerciogenic" foods were criticized by some U.S. nutritionists on the grounds that they tend to impair the nutritional status of those in greatest need by diverting limited resources from the purchase of staple foodstuffs to those with high acceptability and convenience. *H. B. Hawley, "Food Processing," Britannica Book of the Year 1975, p 306*

[1974, from *commerci*al + connecting *-o-* + *-genic*, as in *photogenic, mediagenic*]

common-area charge, *U.S.* money paid in addition to the rent to cover the costs of maintaining areas and services that everyone uses.

Rents will be $8.50 a year per square foot, plus a common-area charge. *Alan S. Oser, " 'Speculative' Office Construction in Jersey," The New York Times, May 26, 1976, p 67*

[1976]

Common Cause, an independent political organization, founded in the United States in 1970, devoted to reform of governmental practices that are not responsive to the needs or wishes of the people.

The post-Watergate reforms—many of them brought about by the zeal of Common Cause and other agitators for righteousness—have led to disclosure of political and moral as well as financial assets and liabilities. *Richard Rovere, "Affairs of State," The New Yorker, May 8, 1978, p 145*

[1971]

Common Causer: The sampling here . . . ranges from cynical wheeler-dealer to idealistic Common Causer. *David Sheridan, "The Lobbyist: Out of the Shadows," Saturday Review, April 8, 1972, p 49*

common-site picketing or **common-situs picketing,** *U.S.* the picketing of a subcontractor at a construction site by members of a union.

Blacks are said to be upset that they are not represented in the Carter policy-making apparatus; organized labor is disenchanted because of his conservative approach to two crucial issues—higher minimum wages and common-site picketing. *Maclean's, April 18, 1977, p 61*

Ford said collective bargaining provisions of the bill have great merit, but "it is to the common situs picketing title that I address my objections." *The Tuscaloosa News (Alabama), Jan. 3, 1976, p 1*

[1976] Also called SITUS PICKETING.

Communicare, *n. British.* a community center which provides a wide range of social welfare services.

At Killingworth the people have been 'given' a lot—Communicare, for example. This is a complex of health, pastoral, youth and sports centres, and a good library. It is a fine idea, and well-used. *Bel Mooney, New Statesman, Jan. 3, 1975, p 8*

[1968, from *community care*, probably patterned on *Medicare* (U.S.), *denticare* (Canada)]

community home, *British.* a reform school.

One of the most controversial innovations of the 1969 Act was the care order under which the local authority can put children into community homes. *Brian Harris, The Times (London), Jan. 2, 1976, p 9*

[1972] ▶ This term has replaced *approved school*, which in the 1930's replaced the older *reformatory* in Great Britain.

community medicine, general practice medicine for families and individuals.

There were no general practitioner models in the teaching hospital, nor did the hospital exhibit any interest in what is now called community medicine (a new term for general practice). *Robert H. Ebert, "The Medical School," Scientific American, Sept. 1973, p 141*

[1971] Also called FAMILY MEDICINE or FAMILY PRACTICE.

Com·o·ran ('kɑm ə rən) or **Co·mo·ri·an** (kə'mɔr i:-ən), *adj.* of or relating to Comoros Islands, an island country in the Indian Ocean, independent (except for Mayotte) since 1975.

Only weeks after the mercenary takeover of the Comoros, black African statesmen . . . expelled the Comoran delegation from the annual Organization of African Unity conference in Khartoum, the Sudan. *"Mercs Rule African Nation," High Times, Jan. 1979, p 112*

—*n.* a native or inhabitant of Comoros.

The Comorians have competed for some time with the Malagasy for jobs as dock workers, guards and municipal employees, reports from the area, which was calm, today said. *"Comoro Aide in Talks on Madagascar Clashes," The New York Times, Dec. 24, 1976, p A-7*

[1973, from *Comoro* + *-an* or *-ian* (adjective and noun suffixes)]

comp, *U.S. Informal.* —*v.i.* to compensate.

The group was flown free from New York by the Las Vegas Hilton, is being comped for rooms, meals and beverages at that hotel; but after the first two days—this is their fourth and last—the junketeers have felt free to gamble elsewhere. *Robert Alan Aurthur, "Hanging Out," Esquire, March 1974, p 44*

—*n.* compensation.

Willis's company-paid supplemental unemployment benefits ran out three weeks ago. "I've been coming down here for about five weeks," said the soft-spoken bachelor. "I'm still drawing [state] comp, but that doesn't make it." *Lynn Langway with Jon Lowell and Rich Thomas, "Unemployment: Last Resort," Newsweek, March 3, 1975, p 58*

[1974, by shortening]

com·pan·der or **com·pan·dor** (kəm'pæn dər), *n.* a device used for companding.

Unlike the Dolby B system now in use for tapes, or the DBX companders (compressor/expander), the Burwen filter can remove noise from existing program material. *John R. Free, "Look and Listen," Popular Science, July 1974, p 12*

[1967, blend of *compressor* and *expander*]

com·pand·ing (kəm'pæn diŋ), *n.* the process of compressing transmission signals over a communications channel and expanding them upon reception; use of a COMPANDER.

The terminal also performs important associated functions such as "companding." This function is a quasi-logarithmic compression of the analogue signal before or concurrent with A/D [analog-to-digital] conversion and a corresponding expansion after or concurrent with D/A [digital-to-analog] conversion. *R. Kretzmer, "Communication Terminals," Scientific American, Sept. 1972, p 138*

[1969, from *compand*er + -*ing* (noun suffix)]

company, *n.* **the Company,** *U.S. Slang.* the Central Intelligence Agency.

The congressional hearings came after Journalist Carl Bernstein's charges in the Oct. 20 issue of *Rolling Stone* magazine that at least 400 employees of American news organizations have worked directly for or informally aided the CIA over the past 25 years. . . . Most of the relationships had ended, Bernstein added, but as of 1976 some 50 American journalists were still bound by secret agreements with "the Company." *Time, Jan. 9, 1978, p 12*

[1975]

comparative advertising, advertising in which a competing product is named and compared unfavorably with the advertised product.

Controversy continued among advertising industry leaders on the effectiveness of comparative advertising. Some spokesmen contended that the approach only served to create confusion in the minds of prospective purchasers. Others argued that comparative advertising made messages more pointed and informative by allowing them to stress specific product attributes instead of emphasizing such intangibles as the glamour or romance associated with the product. *Robert V. Zacher, "Retail Business: Advertising," 1978 Collier's Encyclopedia Year Book (1977), p 478*

[1975] Compare ACCEPTED PAIRING. ► The British equivalent is *knocking copy* (1950's).

complementary, *adj.* (of a DNA or RNA molecule) having two strands that are specific for each other, so that each strand can serve as a template for synthesizing new molecules.

It is known that the genetic information within a cell—those instructions received from its precursor cells—is coded into the sequence of molecules that make up the long strands of DNA (deoxyribonucleic acid). As necessary, the message is transcribed into complementary RNA (ribonucleic acids), which in turn translate the information into a sequence of amino acids (proteins) that carry out the instructions. *Alexander Leaf, "Why People Age," 1978 Collier's Encyclopedia Year Book (1977), p 89*

[1966]

Compounds. ► A compound, formed by putting together two or more words, may appear in various forms: RACQUETBALL, PLATEGLASS, TALL SHIP, DIALOGUE OF THE DEAF, MAN-PORTABLE, HIP-SHOOTING. Compounds can also be made from one or more combining forms such as -ATHON, FLEXI-, and -AHOLIC. Often the same compound will appear as open and closed in form, for example, LAID-BACK, LAIDBACK, and LAID BACK. Only the most frequent form is given in this dictionary; the variants are confined to the illustrative quotations. Other kinds of compounds are discussed in the articles on DERIVATIVES, ABSTRACTED FORMS, and BLENDS.

Compounds may be formed from various parts of speech. Some of the commonest consist of noun + noun (ROADMAN, EVENT TREE), noun + adjective (MEDIA-SHY), adjective + noun (SOLAR POND), adverb + noun (DOWNLINK), and noun + participle (LEARNING-DISABLED). The compound often differs in part of speech from its components (see FUNCTIONAL SHIFTS). For example, the compound PASS-ALONG is a noun made up of a verb and adverb, RIP-STOP is an adjective made up of a noun and verb, and the verb STONEWALL is made up of an adjective and noun.

Many recent compounds show a great variety of combinations, including such forms as GIVEBACK, RIGHT-BRAIN, TEACHWARE, HANDS-ON, FREE-FREE, HOUSE-SIT, RIGHT-TO-LIFE, and FREEZE-FRACTURE. Such compounds require definitions to unlock their special meaning that is more than the sum of its parts (e.g. MAGNET SCHOOL, EYE-IN-THE-SKY, and GREEN POUND). There are numerous simple constructions that appear to be self-explanatory but the specialized application of the words reveals that they are a true semantic compound and that they function as a syntactic unit in special or technical writing; for example, APPROPRIATE TECHNOLOGY, EXECUTIVE PRIVILEGE, LANGUAGE PLANNING, FREEDOM OF INFORMATION.

Conversely, there are compounds whose parts are no longer separated: the closed compounds, DOCUDRAMA (*docu*mentary + *drama*), PLANTIMAL (*plant* + an*imal*), ZEDONK (*zeb*ra + *donk*ey), and the compounds of BLENDS that have letters or sounds in common, BEAUTILITY (bea*uty* and *ut*ility), SLIMNASTICS (*slim* and gym*nastics*), and MOTOWN (*mo*tor and *town*).

Like all words, compounds develop or acquire new meanings. Some old compounds with new senses are AIR GUN, BLUE-EYED, SLINGSHOT, and WISHBONE.

comprehensivist, *n.* **1** a person who advocates general or broad knowledge and study; one who opposes specialization.

R. Buckminster Fuller is a rarity in this age of science—a practicing natural philosopher. A self-described comprehensivist, he has been urging us for decades to realize that human societies, like biological species, court extinction when they become overspecialized. *Harper's, April 1972, p 58*

2 *British.* a supporter or advocate of COMPREHENSIVIZATION.

The NFER [National Foundation for Educational Research] report revives hopes that good education is a likely product of good comprehensive schools, especially those which enjoy long-term stability, a characteristic of all the schools surveyed. . . . Its use as ammunition by die-hard comprehensivists intent on shot-gun marriages between schools could result in rather less contented bedfellows. *John Delin, "Comment: Comprehensives Cleared," New Scientist, June 15, 1972, p 605*

[1970]

comprehensivization or **comprehensivisation,** *n. British.* the process of making a school or schools comprehensive by providing a curriculum for students of all levels of ability.

"We are going to face a time of very great change. Nobody can say what the total comprehensivization of the schools system is going to bring about because it hasn't happened yet. It's on the point of happening and we won't

115

see the results for a few years, so it's a brave person who makes a prediction." *Lord Annan, quoted by Brian Connell, The Times (London), Aug. 9, 1976, p 5*

So, 30 years on, we seem to have come back to the position we were in about secondary education, when our predecessors were concerned with creating some attempt at equality in secondary education. Now the same arguments are going to be brought forward about the comprehensivisation of higher education. *The Listener, May 23, 1974, p 661*

[1965]

compulsory, *n.* a required demonstration of skills in figure skating, gymnastics, and the like.

All nine judges have placed Miss Linichuk and her partner in first place after the compulsories and as a generalization, have invited the Minenkovs ... to outscore Miss Linichuk and Karponosov by about 0.2 of a mark in tomorrow night's climax if they are to retain the gold medal. *The Times (London), March 11, 1978, p 15*

[1968, noun use of the adjective]

computer crime, a crime committed by obtaining illegal access to a computer and manipulating records stored in it with transactions that transfer funds in bank accounts or possession of other assets.

While some reported computer crimes involve the theft or embezzlement of only thousands of dollars, quite a few involve very large sums; a million dollars from a computer crime is considered a respectable but not an extraordinary score. *Thomas Whiteside, "Annals of Crime: Dead Souls in the Computer—1," The New Yorker, Aug. 22, 1977, p 38*

[1972]

computer criminal: He made another point which helps explain why the computer criminal does not bear the social stigma of other kinds of thief: "Computer crime, to those who engage in it, is not like stealing a purse from an old lady; it imparts to theft a nice, clean quality." *The Times (London), July 10, 1978, p 12*

computer-enhanced, *adj.* (of a photograph) improved in distinctness, clarity or intensity by the use of a computer to control developing.

Computer-enhanced photography is nothing new to astronomers, but its use has now expanded to bring out very faint features on photographic plates taken by earth-bound telescopes. *Jane Samz, "Computers and Mathematics: Review of the Year," Encyclopedia Science Supplement (Grolier) 1979 (1978), p 99*

[1976]

computer enhancement, improvement in the quality of a photograph, especially one taken at great distance, by programming a computer to lighten lighter segments and darken darker segments of the original image.

Images of 185-kilometre squares of ground recorded by the Landsat Earth resources satellite with computer enhancement have shown that up to 30 per cent more of the state of Maryland is involved in strip coal mining than had previously been recognised. *"This Week: Landsat Locates More Mines in Maryland," New Scientist, Aug. 26, 1976, p 428*

[1976]

computer game, any of various games that use

electronic circuitry programmed to rules of play, often showing progressive steps of the game with flashing lights or a display screen.

Simon, an electronic computer game ... challenges one's ability to remember its seemingly random flashes of colored lights and gives the raspberry to any player who forgets the sequence.... Comp IV, a computer game that has become the next big winner in the Milton Bradley line-up ... challenges the player to find out which three numbers have been programmed into the unit by the other player. *John Mariani, "Playing the Games," Saturday Review, Dec. 1979, p 40*

[1979] Compare VIDEO GAME.

computerized axial tomography, X-ray photography in which images of an internal part of the body are combined by computer into a single cross-sectional picture.

Computerized axial tomography consists of passing a fan-shaped beam of X-rays through a patient's body to radiation detectors on the opposite side as the patient or X-ray apparatus is rotated stepwise around a single axis. By measuring the X-ray density along each diameter of the complete rotation, data is acquired for each plane of the body being studied. *C. Frederick Kittle, "General Medicine," 1978 Britannica Yearbook of Science and the Future (1977), p 363*

[1976] *Abbreviation:* CAT

computer model, a description constructed by a computer program that is designed to describe a system, project, etc., and is capable of showing the effects of variations applied to it.

Mr. Michael Noble, Minister of State for Trade and Industry, said that "the age of the computer model is now with us and, from the heated debates about such models, as applied recently to the environment, it is evident that the institute is being born at an auspicious moment when there is as evident a need for a great deal of sound scientific research in the methodology and application of systems analysis." *Nature, Oct. 13, 1972, p 361*

[1972]

computer modeling: Computer modeling could save NASA considerable time and money in designing the new space shuttle, narrowing down design possibilities from perhaps a hundred at the outset to less than a dozen, which would require the precision of wind tunnel testing to choose between them. *John H. Douglas, "The Computer Gang Called Illiac IV," Science News, Oct. 13, 1973, p 236*

com·pu·tis·ti·cal (ˌkʌm pyəˈtis tə kəl), *adj.* statistically computed; having to do with statistical computations.

... manuscript 54, a complicated collection of computistical texts, many of which are accompanied by diagrams. *Review of "Catalogue of the Collection of Medieval Manuscripts Bequeathed to the Bodleian Library ...," The Times Literary Supplement, Nov. 3, 1972, p 1348*

[1972, from *compu-* (combining form for "computer") + sta*tistical*]

con·cer·ta·tion (kɔ̃ ser taˈsy ɔ̃; *Anglicized* ˌkɑn sərˈtei ʃən), *n.* (in French politics) cooperation and coordination of activities between groups having divergent interests.

President Giscard spoke of the "concertation" already under way. He said in a passage not amenable to precise translation, that concertation "in no way excluded there being a prior harmonization of positions (on the oil price question) within each of the major interested parties." *The Times (London), Dec. 15, 1974, p 1*

[1969, from French, from *(se) concerter* to act in concert, collaborate]

con·do ('kɑn dou), *n. Especially U.S.* short for *condominium* (in two senses): **1** an apartment house in which each unit is owned individually.

Semiretired attorney William Heiberger, for instance, was told that the myriad rec facilities at Century 21, his North Miami Beach condo, would cost him a mere $25 a month. *Newsweek, March 25, 1974, p 78*

2 a unit in such an apartment house.

The going market value for these opulent condos is between $80,000 and $90,000. *Advertisement, Town & Country Nov. 1972, p 196*

[1970]

confluence model, a theory which relates intellectual growth to family size and the years between the birth of children. It holds that as the number of young children increases the intellectual level of the family unit drops.

The confluence model also addresses the question of differences in intellectual test performance among different national, regional and ethnic groups. *"Families and Intellect," Science News, April 17, 1976, p 246*

[1976]

confrontation state, a country that is hostile to a neighbor or bordering country.

The *New York Times* conceded that the sale to the Saudis of sixty F-15s would "alter the balance of forces in the Middle East." The Israelis issued a statement suggesting that the Saudis might "transfer the planes to confrontation states engaged in active fighting with Israel, or employ mercenaries, probably Americans, to fly the planes." *Harper's, May 1978, p 19*

[1976] Compare FRONT-LINE. See also REJECTIONIST.

Confucian, *adj.* (in Communist China) of or associated with the traditional teachings of Confucius and therefore backward-looking; reactionary.

A new attack today in the official daily, Jenmin Jih Pao, equated unidentified "capitalist roaders" in the party with "Confucian disciples" who favored a restoration of the revisionist line. *Fox Butterfield, The New York Times, Feb. 14, 1976, p 6*

High-powered research stopped because it was "elitist"; advanced training for promising graduate students, who might carry the flame of discovery for the next generation, was prohibited as "Confucian"; a large fraction of agricultural colleges and research stations were shut down altogether for a couple of years. *Nick Eberstadt, "Has China Failed?" The New York Review of Books, April 5, 1979, p 39*

[1974] Compare ANTI-CONFUCIAN.

Confucianist, *n.*: This year's campaign against Confucianists and rightists was only the latest in a long series of rectification efforts in Chinese Communist Party history. *Jonathan D. Pollack, "China," 1975 Collier's Encyclopedia Year Book (1974), p 177*

congressperson or **Congressperson,** *n. Especially U.S.* a member of the United States Congress.

Now, the pool's locker room is being partitioned and hair driers are being installed for the convenience of female congresspersons. *Newsweek, April 21, 1975, p 47*

"Ignore anything addressed to Congressperson." *D. Reilly, Cartoon Legend, The New Yorker, May 12, 1973, p 46*

[1972, from *Congress* + -PERSON]

connection, *n.* **1** a place through which narcotics or other illegal goods are smuggled.

At least 15 other foreigners have been detained in the Soviet Union on narcotics charges in the last year, reflecting a growing concern of the Soviet authorities about the "Moscow connection," as some Westerners here have nicknamed the Moscow transit route. *Christopher S. Wren, "3 Americans on Trial in Soviet Plead Guilty to Heroin Charge," The New York Times, Aug. 25, 1976, p 10*

2 any secret or conspiratorial relationship.

Lyndon Johnson used to tell intimates that he blamed Cubans for Kennedy's death. Last week, the Castro connection was the chief topic of testimony before the House Select Committee on Assassinations. *Time, Oct. 2, 1978, p 22*

[1972, probably extended from earlier sense (1930's) of "a narcotics drug dealer or supplier," and more lately reinforced by *The French Connection*, the movie version (1971) of a book (1969) by Robin Moore]

Con·rail ('kɑn,reil), *n. U.S.* acronym for *Consolidated Rail (Corporation)*, a federally subsidized private operator of several northeastern railroads, formed in 1976.

Unlike Amtrak, Conrail is a private corporation, formed by congressional mandate from the ruins of half a dozen bankrupt carriers; but like Amtrak, Conrail is federally funded, the difference being that Amtrak's funds are grants, while Conrail's funds are, in effect, loans, *Luther S. Miller, "Transportation," The Americana Annual 1978, p 504*

[1976]

conscientization or **conscientisation,** *n.* a movement in Latin America to raise the consciousness of the uneducated and underprivileged.

Paolo Freire, a prominent Brazilian educator . . . has claimed that he could teach fifteen million illiterate Brazilians to read in six weeks if the government would allow all its teachers to use his method—a method based on what Freire calls the principle of "conscientization," or "awakening the political conscience of the deprived." *Francine DuPlessix Gray, The New Yorker, April 25, 1970, p 68*

It may be objected—and often is—that the Latin American hierarchies . . . do not bother to make a stand when the people who are being tortured or killed or put in prison are mere members of the laity. This objection, however, can be met by pointing to the evidence of *conscientisation*, of a becoming aware of one's own potentialities, that is spreading throughout the church in Latin America and joining hierarchy and people together in the fight for special justice in an unprecedented way. *John Horgan, "Storm on the Holy See," Saturday Review, March 28, 1970, p 73*

[1970, from Portuguese and Spanish]

consciousness, *n.* **raise one's consciousness.** to develop or increase one's political, social, or personal

117

awareness, especially in behalf of a cause.

The ideas of Greer, Millett and Firestone have been used as fuel for 'consciousness-raising' . . . and the consciousness that was raised was more than the sum of the books. *Germaine Greer, The Listener, Nov. 15, 1973, p 671*

But we know what they're doing in the movie: they illustrate the various humiliations to which aging women are subject, and they spell things out—loss of self-esteem, problems of identity. They're in the movie to raise *our* consciousness. *Pauline Kael, "The Current Cinema: Empathy, and Its Limits," The New Yorker, March 6, 1978, p 99*

[1970]

consciousness-raiser, *n.* **1** a person involved in or devoted to consciousness-raising.

During the last federal election in the fall of 1972 left-nationalist consciousness-raisers succeeded in persuading only 5 per cent of voters to worry about American economic domination. *John Muggeridge, "Letter From Canada: North of the Border Radical Chic," National Review, April 12, 1974, p 428*

2 something designed or intended to raise one's consciousness.

Varda One, editor of *Everywoman*, says that words like manglish, as she calls the English language, and herstory are "reality-violators and consciousness-raisers." *Casey Miller and Kate Swift, Words and Women, 1976, p 135*

[1974]

conspecific, *n.* an animal or plant of the same species as another.

The honeypot is thus much more vulnerable than other ant species to the crushing jaws of its conspecifics, and when death is so likely to result from combat, slavery becomes preferable. *"Monitor: The First Example of Ritual Combat in Ants," New Scientist, June 10, 1976, p 580*

[1972, noun use of the adjective (OED 1859) meaning "of the same species"]

construct, *n.* an object produced by a constructivist painter or sculptor.

There is no sense of precariousness in Camargo's geometry. The calculations are precise and cool, and, because of the seeming absence of all chance, his constructs are as reposeful as the interior of a church. *Robert Weale, "Art— Sergio de Camargo," New Scientist, Jan. 24, 1974, p 218*

[1974]

consumerization, *n.* the act or practice of promoting or emphasizing the consumption of goods, especially as the basis of a sound economy.

Mindful of the Western Pop artists who had played on the consumerization of U.S. life just as they themselves were playing on the propagandism of life in the U.S.S.R., they gave their art the acronym SOTS, a transliteration of the Russian first letters for "Social Socialism" and "Soviet Realism." *Grace Glueck, "Dissidence as a Way of Art," The New York Times Magazine, May 8, 1977, p 34*

[1976, from *consumer* + *-ization*]

contact-inhibited, *adj.* governed by contact inhibition, a process in which contact between the surfaces of cells stops cell division.

Probably the most widely studied phenomenon in cell culture is that of contact inhibition of division. This occurs when normal cells are grown until they form a layer a single

cell thick over the surface of the culture vessel, at which point (the saturation density), cell division decreases dramatically and the cells are said to be contact-inhibited *Robert Shields, "The Medium is the Message," Nature, Feb 27, 1975, p 689*

[1972, from *contact inhibition* (1966)]

contact-inhibitable, *adj.*: The study of surafce differences between cells that are contact-inhibitable and cells that are not is being hotly pursued because one key to the governance of the cell cycle may be found here. *Daniel Mazia, "The Cell Cycle," Scientific American, Jan. 1974, p 64*

contact visit, a prison visit during which a prisoner is permitted to have physical contact with visitors.

Following the ruling Spenkelink was allowed "contact" visits with his 67-year-old mother, Lois, and his fiancee Carla Key of Jacksonville. *New York Post, May 25, 1979, p 2*

[1976]

contact visiting: Currently, in city facilities where contact visiting is not yet in effect, inmates are separated from their visitors by Plexiglas windows and they must speak to each other by telephone. Contact visiting would allow them to speak with a table between them, and would enable them to kiss, hug or hold hands. *Leslie Maitland, "Commission Delays Jail Contact Visits," The New York Times, Sept. 28 1976, p 76*

containerport, *n.* a seaport with facilities to load and unload containerized cargo.

A containerport at Port Newark at a standstill as a result of strike. *Picture legend, "New Jersey Piers Are Quiet as Longshoremen Stay Out," The New York Times, Oct. 4 1977, p 26*

[1976, from *container*ship + *port*, by analogy with *seaport*]

containment boom, a floating barrier used to encircle an oil spill and prevent its spread.

The high-seas containment booms, rated effective in 5 foot seas and 20-knot winds, and seaworthy in 20-foot sea and 40-knot winds, lose their effectiveness in rougher weather. *David F. White, "Controls for Large Oil Spill Lag," The New York Times, Dec. 30, 1976, p 10*

[1976] Compare CYCLONET.

content-addressable memory, a computer memory whose storage locations are made accessible by identifying any part of their contents (rather than by identifying the position of specific contents).

Content-addressable memories, in which partial knowledge of a stored word is sufficient to find the complete word, would be extremely useful in some applications. Electronic content-addressable memories have never been common because the cost per bit is far higher than it is for location-addressable memories. *David A. Hodges, "Micro electronic Memories," Scientific American, Sept. 1977, p 135*

[1970]

contextualize, *v.t.* to place in context, especially one that is appropriate.

Aretha's Greatest Hits, an album so well contextualized that it stands solidly on its own as a fabulous musical experience, marks off intervals in a celebrated recording career *Ellen Sander, Saturday Review, Jan. 29, 1972, p 49*

The search for gifts, like group dynamics and other less mentionable personality games, must be contextualized sociologically and theologically. *Douglas Davies, Lecturer in Theology, Nottingham, "Gift of Tongues," in a Letter to the Editor, The Times (London), July 29, 1976, p 15*

[1972, from *contextual* + *-ize*]

contingency management, a method of treatment used in behavior modification that controls events or other things that cause a reaction in order to reinforce desired behavior.

Briefly, contingency management procedures rest on the notion that behavior is controlled by its reinforcing consequences. There are positive and negative reinforcers, which refer to stimuli or events that an individual desires or avoids, respectively. *Ralph Barocas and William G. Johnson, "Behavior Modification," McGraw-Hill Yearbook of Science and Technology 1976, p 52*

[1976]

contract, *n. Underworld Slang.* an assignment to kill someone for pay.

"There's one thing I haven't told you," Jones says, cupping his hands around a cigarette. "I don't know if it should be in the story. . . . I've done some hits—you know, a contract. It was right after I got out of prison, and I needed some bread." *James Willwerth, "Portrait of a Mugger," Harper's, Nov. 1974, p 92*

Some policemen believe that a West End mobster named "Lucky" has put a contract out for Savard. Inspector Jean-Claude Rondou, in charge of the Montreal Urban Community police force's criminal investigation bureau, doubts it. *Steve Kowch, "Canada: Montreal: The Roaring Seventies," Maclean's, May 31, 1976, p 24*

Federal officials . . . revealed talk among mobsters about the contract on Galante. *Time, Nov. 13, 1978, p 37*

[1972] Compare HIT, OPEN CONTRACT.

▶ Although this term became widely known during the 1970's, its use in the underworld has been attested since the early 1960's.

contract marriage, a marriage in which a man and woman agree to be married for a specified period.

Another alternative is the contract or renewable marriage, in which both partners agree to live with each other monogamously for a stated length of time, say four years. *Paul Nowack, "Till Divorce Do Us Part," Maclean's, April 19, 1976, p 30*

[1976] Compare OPEN MARRIAGE, SERIAL MARRIAGE. See also MARRIAGE.

controlled substance, *U.S.* any drug that has the capacity to modify behavior and whose possession and use is regulated by law.

A stroll down the corridors of the courthouse revealed a parade of crime listings to make the blood run cold—Murder, Burglary, Criminal Possession of a Controlled Substance, Criminal Sale of a Controlled Substance, Assault, Rape, Possession of Illegal Weapons. *Dorothy Gallagher, "A Murder in Morningside Park," The New York Times Magazine, Aug. 28, 1977, p 26*

Lasco had [been] convicted at 17 of aggravated assault, breaking and entering, and possession of controlled substances. *New York Post, Oct. 10, 1979, p 18*

[1972] ▶ The term derives from the *Controlled Substances Act,* passed in 1970, which specified as potentially harmful or dangerous certain drugs ranging from amphetamines and barbiturates to heroin, marijuana, and LSD. It imposed a penalty for illegal possession of any controlled substance.

convergence, *n.* a reduction of differences between Communist and non-Communist societies.

Party ideologists . . . denounce Western scholars who suggest that convergence is underway. They try to persuade their people that, while great powers with differing social systems can live side by side in peace, the ideological battle must go on with undiminished fury. *Mark Gayn, "Russia Today: Reality and the Fading Dream," The 1976 World Book Year Book, p 152*

[1970] See DÉTENTE.

cook-off, *n. U.S.* a competition of creativity in food preparation and cooking ability.

Given the apparent eagerness of notables to display their culinary prowess, celebrity cook-offs could become the biggest thing in fund raising since Girl Scout cookies. *Time, Oct. 18, 1976, p 112*

[1973, patterned on *bake-off* (1952); compare FLY-OFF]

cook-up, *n.* something improvisational; something concocted.

These disputed pictures are different. They are cook-ups. And on top of the absurdity of ascribing them to Palmer, their pedigree leaves me in doubt. *Geoffrey Grigson, Trôo, France, "Samuel Palmer's Works," in a Letter to the Editor, The Times (London), Aug. 7, 1976, p 13*

[1971, from the verb phrase *cook up*]

coolie jacket or **coolie coat,** a jacket, usually quilted, resembling that formerly worn by laborers in China.

Quilted "coolie" jackets and vests, frog closings, mandarin collars, and other classic oriental touches found their way into sportswear fashions. *Ann Elkins, "Fashion," The Americana Annual 1976, p 247*

[1972]

co·op·é·rant (kou ɔ pei'rã), *Anglicized* **co·op·e·rant** (kou'ɑp ə rənt), *n.* a participant in the program of French assistance to underdeveloped countries.

Claustre was captured in the spring of 1974 while exploring pre-Islamic tombs with a young French *coopérant*—roughly the equivalent of a U.S. Peace Corpsman—and a West German doctor and his wife. *Time, Feb. 14, 1977, p 38*

There are more than 200 "cooperants" doing jobs roughly equivalent to Peace Corps jobs. Nearly a hundred Frenchmen are already working in various capacities along the banks of the Suez Canal. *Jean-Pierre Peroncel-Hugoz, "A Special Role," The Manchester Guardian Weekly (Le Monde section), June 6, 1976, p 14*

[1973, from French, literally, cooperator]

cooperativity, *n.* the tendency of the first in a series of molecular bindings to promote the binding of the second **(positive cooperativity)** or to retard the binding of the second **(negative cooperativity).**

An interesting and important feature is that the iron sites can interact, so that when some of them have bound oxygen the others acquire it more readily. The mechanism is thought to involve strains transmitted through the intervening protein structure, and the resulting cooperativity serves to promote efficient oxygen uptake and release in the circulating blood. *George Lang, "Mössbauer Effect," Mc-*

Graw-Hill Yearbook of Science and Technology 1977, p 306

[1972, from *cooperative* + *-ity*]

cooperativize, *v.t.* to make or turn into cooperatives.

All the old trades have been "cooperativized" — tinkers, tailors, cobblers, blacksmiths, carpenters, etc. *Neville Maxwell, "Workers' Groups Change Life of Tibetans," The New York Times, July 10, 1976, p 3*

[1972]

cooperativization, *n.:* The outcome of the manysided development of the national economy in the conditions of industrialization and agricultural cooperativization, has been the continuous expansion of the country's resources. *Ion Mitran, "The New Social Experience of Romania," The Times (London), Dec. 29, 1972, p 1*

Coordinated Universal Time, another name for UNIVERSAL COORDINATED TIME.

In their article Cannon and Jensen compared the Coordinated Universal Time (UTC) time scales during 1972 of seven laboratories and concluded that "the scale of the Royal Greenwich Observatory (RGO) was running at an anomalous rate," even though they recognized that it was "the most stable clock of all." *C. J. A. Penny, H. M. Smith, and G. A. Wilkins, "Report: Acceleration and Clocks," Science, Feb. 6, 1976, p 489*

[1972]

Cope's rule, the theory that among animals that do not fly, body size increases with evolutionary development.

Another intriguing feature about Lucy is her diminutive stature: she stood at around three and a half feet tall. . . . It is difficult to say much about the third individual. The chances are, however, that this one too was a somewhat miniature version of the large individuals common a million years later. The pressures of evolution may have enhanced the statures of them all. A gradual increase in body size of this sort is a common, and repeated, feature of evolution in groups of species and is known as Cope's rule. *Roger Lewin, "The Most Complete Three-Million-Year-Old Near-Human Skeleton Found by US/French Team in Ethiopia," New Scientist, April 8, 1976, p 72*

[1976, named after Edward Drinker *Cope,* 1840-1897, an American paleontologist]

copilot, *n. U.S. Slang.* an amphetamine.

"Go Ask Alice," records the entry of 15-year-old Alice into the world of drugs . . . of taking "Dexie," marijuana, "copilots," LSD, heroin, everything. *Webster Schott, The New York Times Book Review, May 7, 1972, Part II, p 1*

[1972, from its popularity with truck drivers to ward off sleep]

co-president, *n.* an executive who shares the position of president with another.

As for Richard Cooke, he was also co-president of the Hawaiian Electric Company and of the Hawaiian Agricultural Company. *Francine du Plessix Gray, "Profiles: The Sugar-Coated Fortress — II," The New Yorker, March 11, 1972, p 39*

[1965]

cop·u·lin ('kɑp yə lin), *n.* the sex attractant of female monkeys.

Monkeys produce a collection of simple volatile fatty

acids — "pheromones" — called copulins, . . . whose function is to lure the male. The female's sexual activity parallels the levels of copulins, being highest at midpoint and falling off towards the end of the menstrual cycle. *New Scientist, Feb. 6, 1975, p 302*

[1972, from *copul*ate + *-in* (chemical suffix)]

Co·re·per (kɔ re'pei), *n.* a French acronym for *la Commission de Représentants Permanents,* or Committee of Permanent Representatives, the liaison of the European Economic Community, which effectively directs the daily operations of the EEC. *Often used attributively.*

Coreper meets twice a week. It prepares the ground for meetings of the Council of Ministers, filtering out many Commission proposals before they even reach the Council table. Many decisions, formally endorsed later by the Council, are effectively taken by Coreper. *Michael Hornsby, The Times (London), April 27, 1976, p 14*

[1970]

corequake, *n.* a violent structural disruption in a planet, star, etc., originating in its core.

Stimulated by the plausible suggestion that heavier neutron stars might possess a solid inner neutron core, M. Ruderman, J. Shaham and I have suggested that these giant speed-ups might arise as a result of corequakes which represent the sudden release of elastic energy stored in a *solid* neutron lattice deep in the stellar interior. *David Pines, "Starquakes," New Scientist, May 30, 1974, p 546*

[1972] Compare CRUSTQUAKE.

co-residence, *n. British.* residence at a university by members of both sexes.

While agreeing that more places should be made available for women undergraduates at Oxford, many dons fear that uncontrolled moves towards co-residence would mean that the women's colleges would be relegated to a second-class status. *Diana Geddes, "Women's Colleges at Oxford Fear Second-class Status," The Times (London), March 15, 1977, p 4*

It is rather sad that, just at the moment when women might begin to think it fun to go to a women's college, they're being tempted away by the glamour of men's colleges.

This whole question of co-residence, as it's called at Oxford and Cambridge, may be thought to be a matter of very little importance. *Mary Warnock, "Statutory Women," The Listener, June 8, 1972, p 754*

[1972]

core time, the part of a working day when most or all employees are present, especially when starting and quitting times are staggered.

Core times in a typical U.S. plan might stretch from 9:30 a.m. to noon and from 1:30 to 4 p.m. Employees may arrive as early as 7 a.m. and stay as late as 6:30 p.m. The only requirement, aside from being present at core time, is that at week's end an employee's total hours meet the company requirement of, say, 40 hours. *Jourdan Houston, "Flexible Work Time Punches In," The Reader's Digest, Oct. 1978, p 210*

[1972] Compare FLEXTIME.

corn·dog ('kɔrn,dɔ:g), *n. U.S.* a frankfurter dipped in hot cornbread batter and eaten on a stick.

Some junk food richly deserves that name, although it

must be remembered that one man's meat is another man's corndog. *Time, July 4, 1977, p 45*

[1977, from *corn* + hot *dog*] Compare CHILIDOG.

corner reflector, an arrangement of prismatic mirrors that is used to reflect laser light directly back towards its source. It is used in interplanetary measurements.

Another promising technique is measuring the round-trip travel time of ultrashort laser pulses beamed to earth satellites and particularly to the special mirrors, known as corner reflectors, placed on the moon by American astronauts and by unmanned Russian spacecraft. *William G. Melbourne, "Navigation Between the Planets," Scientific American, June 1976, p 71*

[1965, from its resemblance to the corner of a room where floor and walls meet]

cor·ni·chon (kɔr niːˈʃɔ̃), *n.* a gherkin or any other small sour pickle.

The food at the party was exceptionally good: pâté and tiny sour cornichons, two whole Scotch salmon with mustard-and-dill sauce, wheels of Brie, and other first-rate items. *"The Talk of the Town," The New Yorker, Oct. 24, 1977, p 33*

[1966, from French, ultimately from *corne* horn]

coronal hole, a dark portion in the corona of the sun characterized by low density of matter.

Surprisingly, bright points were also found within the dark "coronal holes" at the sun's poles. Each of the coronal holes measures more than three hundred thousand miles across, and is a good deal cooler and less dense than the corona. They are thought to be the major source of the solar wind—a stream of electrons and protons which radiates continuously from the sun. The presence of bright points at the coronal holes was an added mystery, which solar scientists are still thinking about. *Henry S. F. Cooper, Jr., "A Reporter at Large: Life in a Space Station—II," The New Yorker, Sept. 6, 1976, p 40*

[1975]

co·ro·na·vi·rus (kəˌrou nəˈvai rəs), *n.* any of a group of spherical viruses with many minute projections which suggest the solar corona. The coronavirus group includes those for the common cold, avian infectious bronchitis, and mouse hepatitis.

The human coronaviruses, however, were initially only capable of growth in organ culture, but after a period of adaptation by this means they could be grown on standard continuous cell cultures. *Nature, March 10, 1972, p 81*

[1968, from *corona* + *virus*] Compare ONCOR-NAVIRUS.

corotate, *v.i.* to rotate with, or at the same time or rate as, another body.

The Jovian satellites, and probably the Saturnian satellites, offer obstacles to corotating plasma fields as the inner planets offer obstacles to the solar wind. Voyager will investigate the interactions of satellites with the planetary plasmas during the mission. *New Scientist, Aug. 18, 1977, p 401*

[1965]

corotation, *n.:* How far out do you go before corotation of the sun and corona changes; that is, before the corona starts to drag behind. *Dietrick E. Thomsen, Science News, Feb. 28, 1970, p 227*

correctional facility or **correction facility,** *U.S.* a prison.

Having got permission to land, we started to come in low over the Green Haven Correctional Facility. The last thing we saw from the air was some of the inmates out in the yard, playing basketball. *Alex Shoumatoff, The New Yorker, Nov. 13, 1978, p 56*

[1972]

correctional officer or **correction officer,** *U.S.* a prison guard.

The first fruit of the committee's report was the outbreak of renomenclaturing in 1970, under which guards became "correction officers," prisons metamorphosed into "correctional facilities," and other euphemisms banished other unpleasantnesses. *Susan Sheehan, The New Yorker, Oct. 31, 1977, p 95*

[1972]

correspondent bank, *U.S.* a large bank that provides banking services to smaller banks, such as holding their deposits, clearing their checks, and acting as their agent or consultant in large transactions.

Few bankers thought Lance was wrong to seek personal loans from correspondent banks, which provided services for the banks he ran in exchange for interest-free accounts. Said one Florida banker: "He's going to go to a bank where he does business. It's as simple as that." *Time, Sept. 19, 1977, p 18*

[1963]

correspondent account: Correspondent accounts, which are non-interest-bearing pools of money that small banks deposit in larger banks in another city to expand services to their customers there, are described by bankers as a standard and very beneficial practice. *Judith Miller, The New York Times, Sept. 25, 1977, Sec. 1, p 30*

corset, *n. British.* a restriction placed on banks in order to control the money supply by reducing profits from interest-bearing deposits.

The Government has chosen the so-called "corset," which holds back the growth of bank deposits, as its main weapon in bringing the growth of the money supply under control. The measure immediately hits back at the sharp growth in lending to consumers and the service industries revealed in banking figures published earlier last week and their contribution to the money supply. *Alex Brummer, "Healey Squeezes Banks to Curb Jitters," The Manchester Guardian Weekly, June 18, 1978, p 5*

[1976, so called from its constricting effect]

cortical braille, a system of stimulating the visual cortex to produce braille cells (a group of phosphenes forming a unit of perception) so that a blind person can perceive braille symbols without touching them.

The patient who has a high-school education is a very poor braille reader, averaging about 1 word min^{-1} on high school level, grade 11 (contracted) braille; consequently, he rarely uses tactile braille. He believes, and we concur, that he will become considerably faster at 'cortical braille' with practice, particularly when he can control the rate of presentation through a modified tablet now being interfaced with the computer. *Wm. H. Dobelle, et al., Salt Lake City, "Letters to Nature: 'Braille' Reading by a Blind Vol-*

unteer by Visual Cortex Stimulation," Nature, Jan. 15, 1976, p 112

[1976] Compare OPTACON, TEXT-TO-SPEECH. See also BRAILLE CELL.

cor·ti·co·pon·tine cell (ˌkɔr tə kouˈpɑn ti:n), one of a group of cells in the cortex of the brain that transmits visual stimuli to the pons Varolii which connects the two hemispheres of the brain.

The technique calls for electrically stimulating the axons of corticopontine cells . . . at their far end, so that a spike is conducted along the fiber and invades the cell body. Mitchell Glickstein and Alan R. Gibson, "Visual Cells in the Pons of the Brain," Scientific American, Nov. 1976, p 97

[1976, from cortico- cortex + pontine of the pons Varolii]

cost-cut, v.t. to cut the cost of (an operation, enterprise, etc.)

The reason is that the stockpile may be cost-cut right out of existence. "JPL has said in a letter to the NSF [which sponsors the U.S. Antarctic Research Program] that they can no longer afford to maintain the Antarctic Simulator after July 1," "Antarctic Bacteria Survive Millennia," Science News, May 4, 1974, p 285

[1971, back formation from cost-cutting, adj.]

cosupervision, n. another name for WORKER PARTICIPATION.

M Ambroise Roux, . . . president of the Compagnie Générale d'électricité, said that joint works committees had become an "organ of challenge much more than an organ of cooperation." Cosupervision presented grave dangers. Charles Hargrove, "French Employers Reject Comanagement," The Times (London), Jan. 14, 1976, p 18

[1976]

co-surveillance, n. another name for WORKER PARTICIPATION.

The committee's report, issued in February, proposed a whole series of reforms, including the idea of "co-surveillance" (co-supervision) by up to one-third representation of worker members, sitting with shareholder representatives on supervisory boards or boards of directors exercising supervisory functions. R.O. Clarke, "Industrial Relations," Britannica Book of the Year 1976, p 407

[1976]

counteradvertising, n. U.S. advertising which refutes the claims of other advertisements.

The FTC also advocated that broadcasters allow "counteradvertising" by groups that oppose a product or a message that regular advertisers are trying to push. Under the proposal, for example, antipollution forces would be entitled to free time to rebut auto-company commercials. "Consumerism: Shift at the FTC," Time, Jan. 22, 1973, p 70

[1972] ▶ Synonymous terms which have appeared in recent years have been counterad, countercommercial, countermessage, and counterspot.

counter drug, a drug sold without a doctor's prescription.

Then, at the age of 70, he [Sir Derrick Dunlop] retired . . . to become a director of the Sterling-Winthrop Group Limited, the wholly owned British subsidiary of an American pharmaceutical company selling ethical and counter drugs. Donald Gould, Review of "Medicines in our Time" by Sir

Derrick Dunlop, New Scientist, Jan. 17, 1974, p 151

[1974, short for over-the-counter drug]

counterdrug, n. a drug that creates a distaste for heroin, alcohol, or some other habit-forming substance.

Antabuse is a counterdrug that produces an aversion to alcohol. Amitai Etzioni and Richard Remp, Science, Jan. 7, 1972, p 32

[1972, from counter- opposing + drug]

counterphobic, adj. relating to or expressing a preference for something feared.

Just as with the alcohol drinker, his drug of choice contains the counterphobic anticipation of more total dissolution, here of psychic boundaries rather than inhibitions. It is not accidental that adverse reactions to marijuana sharply diminish when the effects of the drug are thoroughly familiar to potential users. Norman E. Zinberg and John A. Robertson, Drugs and the Public, 1972, p 76

[1970, from counter- opposing + phobic]

counterphobically, adv.: "Please come right over," said the Playwright, in a fragment of forthright dialogue counterphobically opposed to his usual ambiguous and allusive circumlocutions. Herbert Gold, Saturday Review, Oct. 21, 1972, p 54

country, n. short for country music or country-and-western (music derived from or imitating folk music, especially of the southern and western United States).

The records noticed here are worth more than a listen, but they are not the creations of people conscious of living in great days. Gospel, country, heavy rock, Sweet Baby James-ish vocalizing: the musical styles are mixed and remixed. Dennis Duffy, "Music," Maclean's, April 1973, p 94

Austin's musicians . . . have made the city the fastest-growing country-music center in the U.S. Nashville, still the capital of country, may provide more regular work. "Groover's Paradise," Time, Sept. 9, 1974, p 70

— adj. of or relating to such music.

Eleven straight years in which her records have been on the top of the country hit charts have allowed her to buy 2,300 acres in Tennessee — a spread that includes the entire town of Hurricane Mills. "Country Queen," Newsweek, Dec. 4, 1972, p 67

[1968]

covert action or **covert operation,** a secret and often illegal operation conducted by a police force or intelligence branch of government.

Veteran agency operatives often say that without covert action the C.I.A. would be nothing but a collection of sophisticated professors with mounds of intelligence, and the agency itself would be only a more specialized version of the State Department. Taylor Branch, "The Trial of the C.I.A.," The New York Times Magazine, Sept. 12, 1976, p 115

Colby also said that this eight million dollars' worth of covert operations in Chile had been approved beforehand by the National Security Council's 40 Committee, which was assigned the responsibility for authorizing all such operations. Richard Harris, The New Yorker, April 10, 1978, p 45

[1975]

cowboy, *v.i. U.S.* to work or live as a ranch hand.

Ten children survived, and seven of them were boys, and they all cowboyed — except one who roughnecked in the oil fields near Houston and one who took up pentecostalism and died from shock while caressing a prairie rattler at a revival meeting. *Jane Kramer, "Profiles: Cowboy — II," The New Yorker, June 6, 1977, p 47*

[1968, verb use of the noun (1860's)]

CPR, abbreviation of CARDIOPULMONARY RESUSCITATION (a combination of mouth-to-mouth breathing, or other ventilation techniques, and chest compression, used to provide emergency life support).

CPR consists of hard pressure on the lower breastbone 60 to 70 times a minute (to force blood out of the heart) alternating with mouth-to-mouth ventilation. *"Medicine: Award of the Heart," Time, Nov. 26, 1973, p 71*

[1973]

CPU, abbreviation of *central processing unit* (of a computer).

The central processing unit (CPU) provides the computer with arithmetic, logical and control capabilities. The arithmetic unit of a CPU provides for the simplest of arithmetic operations; namely, nothing more than addition, subtraction, multiplication and division. . . . Together the primary storage and the CPU are the heart of the computer. *R. Clay Sprowls, "Computers," Encyclopedia Science Supplement (Grolier) 1971, p 138*

[1967]

CR, abbreviation of *consciousness-raising.*

But the makeup of what are popularly called "CR" groups has not changed perceptibly since those early days of the women's rights movement. Now, as then, the consciousnesses being raised are overwhelmingly white, middle class and college-educated. *Georgia Dullea, "A Decade Old, Consciousness-Raising Develops a New Look," The New York Times, Nov. 27, 1976, p 17*

[1976]

crackback, *n. U.S. Football.* a block at knee level on a linebacker or defensive back by a pass receiver coming from the blind side of the field. The crackback is a major cause of knee injuries.

But it is also legal and effective, and as O.J. says happily, "J.D.'s got himself such a reputation for the crackback that guys are always looking for him out of the corner of their eye." *Newsweek, Nov. 26, 1973, p 68*

[1972, from *crack, n.* a blow + *back* player behind the line of scrimmage]

craftsperson, *n.* a person who is skilled at a craft or crafts.

About 100 craftspersons from all parts of the state will have booths to demonstrate their work and their wares, including glassblowing, batik and leather work. *Harold Faber, The New York Times, Oct. 7, 1977, p C10*

[1974] See -PERSON.

crater, *v.i. U.S. Slang.* to die (literally and figuratively).

"Don't let him crater on me!" "Crater" is Ben Taub slang. It means die. *Life, Nov. 6, 1970, p 29*

Thirty seconds later a young woman is apologizing for being tardy: her car has cratered; she's been detained by

repairs. *Larry L. King, The Atlantic, Jan. 1972, p 72*

[1970, probably extended from the earlier (OEDS 1917) transitive sense "to destroy with crater-forming artillery shells"]

crawl, *n.* a list of credits, titles, announcements, etc., shown on television.

The crawl, or credit list, of the show, which usually appears (it is omitted when the show runs long) at the end of every program, includes the names of the Producer (John Gilroy), the Creative Consultant (the television term for idea man — in this case, Marshall Brickman), the Director, one or more Writers, two Associate Producers, one Musical Director, four Talent Coördinators/Interviewers . . . *L. E. Sissman, "Profiles: Dick Cavett," The New Yorker, May 6, 1972, p 43*

[1962]

CREEP or **Creep,** *n.* a derisive acronym for *Committee to Reelect the President,* the campaign committee whose activities led to the Watergate scandal.

The officials in charge of CREEP apparently shared the illusions that lie at the heart of the Agency — that the politics of a country can be guided by tapping the phone of a Larry O'Brien or a Spencer Oliver, or by employing someone like Donald Segretti to write fake letters. *Taylor Branch, Harper's, Jan. 1974, p 56*

[1972] Compare CRP.

Creutz·feldt·Ja·kob disease (ˈkrɔits felt ˈyɑː kɔp, Anglicized ˈkrɔits felt ˈdʒei kəb), a rare, degenerative disease of the human nervous system that causes mental deterioration and death. This disease is important in the study of viruses with a long incubation period (slow viruses) because of its similarity to certain other diseases caused by such viruses.

The first neuropathological studies of kuru brain in 1967 immediately suggested a close similarity between kuru and Creutzfeldt-Jakob disease (CJD) of man, first described in early 1920. This is a rare disease, but unlike kuru, it has a world wide distribution. In 1968 Gajdusek and his colleagues established that CJD could be transmitted to primates and later studies confirmed a viral aetiology for this disease as well. *Richard Kimberlin, "Viral Origins for Chronic Brain Diseases," New Scientist, Nov. 18, 1976, p 381*

[1971, named after Hans Gerard *Creutzfeldt* (1883-?) and Alfons M. *Jakob* (1884-1931), who first described it] Also called JAKOB-CREUTZFELDT DISEASE. See SLOW INFECTION.

crib, *n.* a trench lined on the sides and covered with concrete to dump atomic waste so that the radioactive contents can gradually seep into the soil through the dirt bottom.

One crib already rests on so intense a concentration of plutonium that the dump could conceivably explode and spew the toxic plutonium into the air. *"Science: Ultimate Garbage Crisis," Newsweek, Aug. 20, 1973, p 80*

[1973]

crib crime or **crib job,** *U.S. Slang.* the mugging of an old person.

. . . "crib" crimes — muggings in which old people are accosted at their own front doors and pushed into their apartments, where they not only lose their belongings but suffer physical abuse as well. *Richard Severo, "How Twins Came to Prey on Aged," The New York Times, Dec. 14, 1976, p 42*

The young hoods . . . plan what they call a "crib job," because it is as easy as taking money from a baby. *"Cities: The Elderly: Prisoners of Fear," Time, Nov. 29, 1976, p 22*

[1976] Compare PUSH-IN CRIME.

criminal chromosome, an extra Y chromosome present in the genetic makeup of a small percentage of men. It occurs in addition to the normal presence of a single X and Y chromosome.

When Richard Speck murdered eight nurses in Chicago, his defense argued that he couldn't help it because he bore an extra Y chromosome. . . . This revelation inspired a rash of speculation; articles on the "criminal chromosome" inundated our popular magazines. The naïvely determinist argument had little going for it beyond the following: Males tend to be more aggressive than females; this may be genetic. If genetic, it must reside on the Y chromosome: anyone possessing two Y chromosomes has a double dose of aggressiveness and might incline to violence and criminality. *Stephen Jay Gould, "Criminal Man Revived," Natural History, March 1976, p 18*

[1976]

crin·o·tox·in (ˌkrin əˈtɑk sən); *n.* an animal poison produced by a specialized gland and released through pores of the skin.

Little is known about the biological or chemical properties of most crinotoxins, although much recent research has concentrated on the structure and synthesis of certain frog and toad crinotoxins. *Bruce W. Halstead, "Biotoxins: The Poisons of Life," 1977 Britannica Yearbook of Science and the Future (1976), p 229*

[1976, from *crin*in substance that stimulates secretion of certain glands (from Greek *krínein* to separate) + connecting *-o-* + *toxin*] See ZOOTOXIN.

crisis center, a place established as a headquarters or other center of operations from which a disaster is monitored, emergency relief is controlled, psychological counseling is available, or other assistance is given during a time of difficulty.

Mrs. Washington describes Poe as a kind of crisis center where pregnant teen-agers can count on support from their classmates and teachers in an informal atmosphere. *Courtenay Cannady, The Tuscaloosa News (Alabama), Jan. 8, 1973, p 5*

[1972]

crisis of capitalism, a fiscal crisis attributed, especially by Marxists, to structural flaws or weaknesses in the capitalist system.

Another worldwide crisis of capitalism is upon us. Why it has appeared and what consequences it portends for the economic system in which we live are the questions I wish to consider here. But first we should take note that it is *another* crisis of capitalism. From its earliest days, capitalism has always been as critically ill as it has been intensely alive. *Robert L. Heilbroner, "Reflections: Boom and Crash," The New Yorker, Aug. 28, 1978, p 52*

[1976]

critical mass, a sufficient number or amount to bring about a desired result efficiently.

A few thought more liberals would help (four percent)

and a few thought more conservatives (five percent). But the critical mass (a plurality of over forty percent) grouped itself around a nonpartisan, nonideological solution: throw all the rascals out. *William Greider, "Aftergate," Esquire, Sept. 1975, p 100*

[1972, figurative use of the physics term meaning "the minimum amount of fissionable material needed to achieve a chain reaction"]

cro·mo·lyn sodium (ˈkrou mə lin), a drug for preventing attacks of bronchial asthma. *Formula:* $C_{23}H_{14}Na_2O_{11}$

There is, however, a relatively new development in the management of asthma which holds some light for real scientific benefit. *Cromolyn Sodium* . . . offers a fresh approach for asthma treatment. It is a powder-type medication administered through an aerosol inhalator directly into the lungs much the same way the previously mentioned nebulizers are used. *Joe Graedon, The People's Pharmacy, 1976, p 180*

[1973, from the chemical name (*disodium*) *cromogly*cate + *-in* (chemical suffix)]

cross-busing, *n. U.S.* another name for BUSING.

Charlotte supports the forty-third largest school system in the United States, and is the first of such size to implement extensive cross-busing. *Frank Barrows, "School Busing: Charlotte, N. C.," The Atlantic, Nov. 1972, p 18*

[1964]

cross-frontier, *adj.* occurring between two or more unrelated businesses, professions, or other interests and activities not generally associated with one another.

British companies have shown most interest in the activities of the European Community's "Marriage Bureau," set up two and a half years ago to foster cross-frontier cooperation between medium and small companies. *David Cross, "EEC 'Marriage Bureau' Attracts British Companies," The Times (London), Jan. 10, 1976, p 17*

[1970]

cross-holdings, *n.pl. British.* reciprocal holdings of shares by two or more companies.

Through a series of cross-holdings, Dunlop has, broadly speaking, a 49 per cent interest in Pirelli operations in Italy and other countries in the EEC, and 40 per cent elsewhere, while Pirelli has similar interests in Dunlop's operations. *John Earle, "EEC Companies: Multinationals, Pirelli-Dunlop," The Times (London), Dec. 15, 1972, p XII*

[1966]

crossover, *n.* **1** (of music) the act or process of crossing over in style or appeal.

The ability of a few artists to effect a "reverse crossover" —moving from white audiences to black audiences—was reflected in the energetic and soulful singing of Leo Sayer. His singles, such as "How Much Love," enjoyed popularity on both black- and white-oriented radio stations. *Leonard Feather, "Popular Music," The 1978 World Book Year Book, p 413*

2 music which crosses over in style or appeal. *Often used attributively.*

The latest trend is crossovers—songs that make the country charts while also getting on the pop or the middle-of-the-road listings. In fact, a song stands a poor chance of reaching the top spot on one chart without at least appearing on another. *"Lefty Frizzell Hard to Match," The Tuscaloosa News (Alabama), June 11, 1975, p 8*

[1972, from CROSS OVER] Compare FUSION.

cross over, 1 to shift from one style of music to another, as from jazz to rock.

Billy Cobham, the drummer, and George Duke, the pianist, are two jazz musicians who have "crossed over," as the saying goes, about as far as one can cross. Mr. Cobham, who was a charter member of the Mahavishnu Orchestra jazz/rock group, usually applies his awesome technique to thunderous, rock-style drumming while Mr. Duke, who graduated from various jobs as a jazz sideman to a lengthy stint with the rock satirist Frank Zappa, manipulates an arsenal of electronic keyboards and sings. *Robert Palmer, "Cobham-Duke Band Plays a Restrained Jazz-Rock," The New York Times, June 28, 1976, p 23*

2 (of music) to transcend limits of style or appeal.

This Wednesday, Kal is, as usual, trying to find out which records are about to "break" (become hits) in the popular market, which regional hits are about to become national hits, which black records and country records are about to "cross over" to the mass pop market. *George W. S. Trow, "Profiles: Kal Rudman," The New Yorker, Dec. 23, 1972, p 32*

Fusion enjoys a crucial advantage over mainstream and avant-garde jazz: it "crosses over" a wide range of radio formats, a key element to selling any music today. *Michael Segell, Rolling Stone, Jan. 11, 1979, p 43*

[1972]

cross-ownership, n. U.S. ownership by a company of one or more newspapers and radio or television stations.

Today, 104 TV outlets are owned by newspaper publishers, many in the papers' hometowns. This practice, known as "cross-ownership," has been criticized by some liberals and conservatives alike, and last week the Justice Department took steps to deprive three major publishers of their hometown interests. *Newsweek, Jan. 14, 1974, p 43*

[1973]

cross-reactive, adj. likely to undergo an immunological cross-reaction.

This phenomenon is also referred to as cross-reactivity between various HL-A antigens. . . . if this nonreactive cell suspension has an HL-A antigen which is cross-reactive with the stimulating antigen, it may absorb out all antibody activity from the antiserum, which becomes nonreactive even against cells from the stimulating donor. *F. Kissmeyer-Nielsen, "Transplantation Biology," McGraw-Hill Yearbook of Science and Technology 1972, p 399*

[1972, from earlier (1959) *cross-reaction* reaction between an antibody and nonspecific antigen]

cross-reactivity, n.: Quantitative assay of immunological cross-reactivity between antigens on foetal and tumour cells is particularly important as it was demonstrated recently that the common antigen of foetal and tumour cells is distinct from the tumour-specific transplantation antigen, at least in chemically induced rat tumours. *F. A. Salinas, et al., Nature, Nov. 3, 1972, p 41*

cross-subsidize, v.i., v.t. to support an unprofitable operation out of the profits of another operation.

Another source of waste may have been the practice of cross-subsidizing, by which the federal government in effect forces transportation companies to pay for losing

tracks, bus routes, and air routes by charging rates for the more frequently used lines that are higher than they would be if they were determined independently. *Thaddeus F. Tuleja, "Transportation," 1976 Collier's Encyclopedia Year Book (1975), p 549*

[1972]

cross-subsidization, n.: Cross-subsidization occurs when some users of a facility are charged less than the costs of providing for them, and the resulting losses are financed by other users, who pay more than their costs. *Peter Mackie, "Cross-Subsidizing Ferry Fares on the Channel Routes," The Times (London), April 14, 1976, p 24*

cross-trading, n. the business of a shipping line in which it conveys cargo between foreign ports.

Cross-trading, as it is called, still represents probably about 40 per cent of the total earnings of British liner shipping after more than a decade of growing nationalism on world trade routes in which developing countries have demanded substantial new carrying rights in many trades. *Michael Baily, The Times (London), Jan. 16, 1976, p 19*

[1976]

crown ether, Chemistry. a combination of ethers whose atoms are arranged in a closed chain.

Many-atom ring systems (crown ethers and cryptates) containing oxygen, nitrogen, or sulfur were shown to have high affinity for inorganic cations, and an anion-complexing cryptate also was reported. *Frederick D. Greene, "Organic Chemistry," Britannica Book of the Year 1978, p 245*

[1973, from the crownlike shape of the arrangement]

CRP, abbreviation of *Committee to Reelect the President.*

Mitchell's admission that he had known about some of the dirty work going on in the C.R.P. while he was its director and his claim that he had kept the President in the dark about it to insure his reëlection implied that this demonstrated the President's innocence of any malfeasance. *"The Talk of the Town," The New Yorker, Aug. 13, 1973, p 21*

[1973] Compare CREEP.

cruise missile, a guided missile directed by a computerized navigational system.

Complicating the task of international control is the fact that the cruise missile exists in two versions, with nuclear or conventional warheads, and that there is no way at present of distinguishing one from the other at a distance. *Andre Fontaine, The Manchester Guardian Weekly (Le Monde section), Feb. 1, 1976, p 12*

A cruise missile can be defined as a dispensable, pilotless, self-guided, continuously powered, air-breathing warhead-delivery vehicle that flies just like an airplane, supported by aerodynamic surfaces. Unlike a ballistic missile, which is powered and hence usually guided for only a brief initial part of its flight, after which it follows a free-fall trajectory governed only by the local gravitational field, a cruise missile requires continuous guidance, since both the velocity and the direction of its flight can be unpredictably altered by local weather conditions or changes in the performance of the propulsion system. *Kosta Tsipis, "Cruise Missiles," Scientific American, Feb. 1977, p 20*

[1968] See TERCOM.

cruiseway, n. British. a stream or canal that has been improved to accommodate pleasure boating.

It is not only uneconomic to enlarge the cruiseways, it is

125

undesirable. Their chief attractions — human scale, as an open museum of industrial archaeology with historic canal-side buildings and canal "plant," the segregated pedestrian towpath system, the fact they are hedged in by buildings to form a strange secret world in the towns and pass through unspoilt remote countryside — are precisely the factors that make them so expensive to enlarge. *Lewis Braithwaite, Leamington Spa, "Using Waterways," in a Letter to the Editor, New Scientist, July 19, 1973, p 163*

[1967]

crustquake, *n.* a violent structural disruption in a planet, star, etc., originating in its crust rather than its core.

Two especially large speed-ups, corresponding to a relative frequency jump of a few parts in a million, separated by a period of 29 months, have been observed for the Vela pulsar. Both the magnitude and frequency of these speed-ups pose a severe problem for crustquake theory; interpreted as crustquakes, the fractional change in the oblateness of the star in a 'quake' of this magnitude would be almost 10 per cent. *David Pines, "Starquakes," New Scientist, May 30, 1974, p 546*

[1972] Compare COREQUAKE.

cry·o·ca·ble (ˈkrɑi ouˌkei bəl), *n.* an underground electric cable supercooled to increase its conductive quality.

By economising on materials, GE hopes to bring cryocables within commercial practicability. It envisages an underground cryocable system capable of carrying 3500 MVA or more, with three cables to a 20 in. diameter steel pipe. *New Scientist, June 15, 1972, p 623*

[1972, from *cryo-* freezing + *cable*]

cryoelectronics, *n.* a branch of electronics dealing with the effects of supercooling in transmitting electric power.

Concise treatment of the whole range of cryoelectronics which includes low temperature effects of conductors, insulators and semiconductors, superconduction in machines, magnets and cables, microwave effects, cryotrons and memories. *"Books of the Week: Cryoelectronics" by W. P. Jolly, Science News, Sept. 8, 1973, p 146*

[1973, from *cryo-* freezing + *electronics*]

cryopreservation, *n.* the preservation of living tissues by supercooling.

Currently, doctors at Downstate Medical Center in Brooklyn, N.Y., are perfecting a technique of preserving corneas in human-tissue culture, thereby circumventing the potential hazards of cryo-preservation. *"Medicine: Eyes on Ice," Newsweek, Aug. 27, 1973, p 62*

[1972, from *cryo-* freezing + *preservation*]

cryoprotectant, *adj., n.* variant of CRYOPROTECTIVE.

Offerijns has actually frozen them ["pacemaker" cells of the heart], using a cryoprotectant agent called dimethyl sulfoxide (DMSO), and revived 80 percent of them successfully. *Joan Arehart-Treichel, "The Icy World of Organ Freezing," Science News, Aug. 19, 1972, p 125*

[1972, from *cryo-* freezing + *protectant*]

cryoprotective, *adj.* providing protection against supercooling.

They found that embryos exposed to dimethylsulphoxide, a cryoprotective (antifreeze) agent and cooled at 0.3 to 2.0 degrees C. per minute gave the best chances of survival. *"Frozen Embryo Grows to Healthy Calf," Science News, June 30, 1973, p 419*

— *n.* a cryoprotective agent.

Of particular importance is the influence of cryoprotectives on the degree of concentration of salts, especially sodium chloride and potassium chloride, in the remaining liquid phase during initial freezing. *Franklin H. Cocks, "Cryobiology," McGraw-Hill Yearbook of Science and Technology 1975, p 151*

[1971, from *cryo-* + *protective*]

cryoresistive, *adj.* supercooled to reduce resistance.

Transmission cables insulated with compressed gas, cables cooled to the temperatures of liquid nitrogen (called cryoresistive transmission lines), and cables cooled even more so that they become superconducting are all being developed as options to the conventional underground power lines. *William D. Metz, Science, Dec. 1, 1972, p 968*

[1970, from *cryo-* + *resistive*]

cryp·tate (ˈkripˌteit), *n. Chemistry.* compound in which atoms with unbonded electrons cluster around a metal ion in a symmetrical arrangement.

A novel type of complex has recently been prepared, in which the metal ion is quite literally surrounded by its coordinating groups: it is, in effect, trapped within a tiny organic cage. Called *cryptates,* these complex ions were first made by J. M. Lehn, J. P. Sauvage and B. Dietrich of the Institut de Chemie, Strasbourg. *New Scientist, July 16, 1970, p 121*

[1970, from *crypt-* hidden, latent (from Greek *kryptós*) + *-ate* (chemical suffix)]

cryp·to·bi·ote (ˌkrip touˈbɑi out), *n.* an organism that survives in a state of metabolic inactivity.

Cryptobiotes could be revived after exposure to a temperature close to absolute zero; at this temperature metabolic processes, if they proceed at all, must be extremely slow and the destructive effects of oxygen must be minimal. *John H. Crowe and Alan F. Cooper, Jr., "Cryptobiosis," Scientific American, Dec. 1971, p 33*

[1971, back formation from earlier (1965) *cryptobiotic* surviving in a state of metabolic inactivity, characterized by *cryptobiosis* (1959)]

cryptoexplosion structure, a crater or similar geologic feature formed by a sudden explosion, as that caused by the impact of very large meteorites, and characterized by a circular depression, uplifted bedrock in the center, shatter cones, and often rock deformations unrelated to volcanic activity.

Both Mars and the moon are dotted with surface craters, mostly created by impact. Some scientists believe the terrestrial craters that most closely resemble lunar and Martian craters are a class called cryptoexplosion structures. *"Earth Sciences: Origins of Terrestrial Craters," Science News, April 1, 1972, p 218*

[1967, from *crypto-* hidden + *explosion;* so called because of the lack of precise evidence for the cause of the explosion]

cryp·to·sys·tem (ˈkrip touˌsis təm), *n.* a system for using or deciphering a secret code; a cryptographic system.

The major powers . . . use machines to generate ciphers

so strong that, even given a cryptogram and its plaintext, and all the world's computers of this and the next generation, a cryptanalyst would need centuries to reconstruct the cryptosystem and use the reconstruction to read the next message. *David Kahn, "Big Ear or Big Brother?" The New York Times Magazine, May 16, 1976, p 67*

[1968, from *crypto*graphic + *system*] See PUBLIC KEY.

CT scanner, variant of CAT SCANNER.

The CT scanner . . . produces television-like pictures of the inside of the body and can detect a minute cancerous growth. *Warren Gerard, "Health," Maclean's, May 14, 1979, p 42*

[1976, *CT*, abbreviation of *computerized tomography*]

CT scanning, variant of CAT SCANNING.

CT scanning—the X-ray technique pioneered by EMI for photographing "slices" of the body—has swept the US medical scene so rapidly that there has been no time for a proper evaluation, according to the report. *New Scientist, May 19, 1977, p 380*

[1976]

CTT, *British.* abbreviation of CAPITAL TRANSFER TAX.

Those who choose life in the Channel Islands or the Isle of Man as the answer to our tax evils will find this does not work at all for CTT, because they are deemed to have a United Kingdom domicile for all time. *Vera Di Palma, The Times (London), Jan. 29, 1977, p 18*

[1977]

C-type virus, a virus containing RNA (ribonucleic acid) that causes leukemia in animals and is thought also to cause cancer in humans.

Biologists have . . . known for years, in fact, that some viruses—and especially a few that cause cancer in birds and mammals—carry no DNA of their own. They carry *no* doublestranded genetic codebook of their own at all. Instead, these viruses, known as the C-type viruses, merely carry a simple singlestrand bit of RNA that contains all of their own virus-building instructions. *Robert Cooke, Improving on Nature, 1977, p 61*

[1970, probably from *C*ancer-*type*] Also called TYPE C VIRUS.

Cuban sandwich, *U.S.* See the quotations for the meaning.

What Tampa calls "Cuban sandwiches" are made of Cuban bread, sliced open and filled overpoweringly with ham, pork, sausage, cheese and dill pickles. *Waverley Root and Richard de Rochemont, "Foreign Influences," The New York Times Magazine, Oct. 17, 1976, p 82*

That familiar long sandwich crammed with a meal's worth of edibles—what is it called? In New York it is a hero sandwich; in the South, it is known, unheroically, as a poor boy. Pennsylvanians call it a hoagie, New Englanders a grinder and Floridians a Cuban sandwich. *Time, Dec. 4, 1978, p 81*

[1976]

cued speech, a method of communication for the deaf which combines lip reading with manual signs by associating particular sounds with certain hand positions.

The Gallaudet schools also are experimenting with a method known as "cued speech," developed in 1966 by R. Orin Cornett, vice-president of Gallaudet College. Cues consist of 12 hand signals that, when used with lip reading, allow a deaf person to see clearly any word that is spoken. *William J. Cromie, "Learning for Living in a Silent World," The 1975 World Book Year Book, p 162*

[1973]

cui·sine min·ceur (kwiːˌziːn mæˈsœr), French cooking which curtails the use of starch, sugar, butter, and cream traditionally associated with French cuisine.

Les Prés is run by Michel Guérard, high priest of the cuisine minceur, the technique of low calory cooking that appeals to slimmers as well a lovers of good food. *"Tito Overlooks French Hotel Bill," The New York Times, Oct. 23, 1977, p 16*

[1975, from French, literally, slimness cooking]

cu·mecs (ˈkyuː meks), *n.* acronym for *cubic meters per second.*

The flood flow in Woolwich Reach moving upriver during a surge tide is some 4000 cumecs, whereas a high flow over Teddington Weir following heavy rains or snow melt could be of the order of 300 cumecs. *R. W. Horner, London, "Flood Problem," in a Letter to the Editor, New Scientist, Jan. 4, 1973, p 44*

[1970]

curl, *n. Surfing Slang.* the curve of water formed on top of a breaking wave.

The transition from the smooth to the broken part of the wave occurs, in a good surfing wave, with water springing from the wave crest in a sheet—a "curl" in surfers' terminology—which covers a pocket of air, the "tube." *Howell Peregrine, "Surfing Brought to Rest, New Scientist, July 6, 1978, p 8*

[1969]

currency snake, another name for SNAKE.

Chancellor Schmidt and President Giscard . . . still hope that an enlarged and improved currency snake will be an important step in the direction of eventual economic and monetary union within the Community. *Peter Jenkins, "Callaghan Rejects Eurocash under Labour Pressure," The Manchester Guardian Weekly, Oct. 29, 1978, p 1*

[1976]

current sheet, another name for MAGNETODISK.

One of the most impressive characteristics is the enormous distance to which the current sheet extends into space. *Edward J. Smith, "Solar Magnetic Field," McGraw-Hill Yearbook of Science and Technology 1978, p 335*

[1976]

cursor, *n.* a flashing square of light that can be moved to any position on the display screen of an electronic typesetter, computer, etc., to indicate where a change is to be made.

"Now, suppose you want to get a little color into this," Butsikares said, and he began tapping keys—marked with arrows pointing up, pointing down, pointing sideways—around the word "HOME." A tiny square of light known as the "cursor" began to move up the face of the tube. It was something like the bouncing ball that used to hop from word to word in song lyrics on movie screens. *"The Talk of the Town," The New Yorker, Feb. 10, 1975, p 31*

[1972, extended sense of the earlier term for a sliding part of any instrument (such as a slide rule or a filter placed on a radar screen) that facilitates computing or sighting, from Latin *cursor* runner]

cutout, *n. Slang.* a person or business used to conceal contact or connection between members of a clandestine operation, as in espionage.

The firm [U.S. Recording Company] operated as a "cutout," or front, for the FBI's purchase of eavesdropping equipment; the idea was to prevent targets of wiretapping — such as gangsters or spies — from learning the bureau's capabilities simply by examining government purchasing records. *"The FBI: Just How Incorruptible?" Time, April 5, 1976, p 23*

Nader keeps his own movements secret and his sources ignorant of one another. He communicates with his *apparat* through a system of "cutouts" (a suburban housewife receives some of his sensitive calls on her home telephone) and "dead-drops" (the newsstand of the National Press Building). *Charles McCarry, "The Public Ways of the Private Nader," Saturday Review, Feb. 12, 1972, p 35*

[1966]

CVI, abbreviation for *common variable immunodeficiency,* a condition marked by decreased numbers of antibodies (immunoglobulins).

People with CVI have normal numbers of B lymphocytes — the cells that make antibodies — but the cells fail either to synthesize or to secrete antibodies. *Jacques M. Chiller, "Immunology," The World Book Science Annual 1976 (1975), p 296*

[1975]

cy·an·o·bac·te·ri·um (ˌsai ə nou bæk'tir i: əm), *n., pl.* **-te·ri·a** (-'tir i: ə). any of a group of blue-green algae lacking a distinct nucleus.

The modern chloroplast, for example, may be derived from a cyanobacterium that was engulfed by another cell and that later established a symbiotic relationship with it. *J. William Schopf, "The Evolution of the Earliest Cells," Scientific American, Sept. 1978, p 116*

[1978, from *cyano-* blue + *bacterium*]

cycleway, *n. British.* a road or lane reserved for cyclists.

A scheme to provide cycleways through Central London's parks has been suggested. *The Listener, Feb. 7, 1974, p 179*

[1963, from *cycle* (OED 1881, short for *bicycle* or *tricycle*) + *way*]

cyclic GMP, a chemical compound that functions as a messenger to stimulate the action of hormones and that interacts with the related chemical cyclic AMP in cellular metabolism.

A second cyclic nucleotide, guanosine 3', 5' monophosphate (cyclic GMP), is also present in all living systems, but until recently few investigators have studied the relation of this compound to regulatory processes. It has now been proposed that cellular regulations may be influenced by the interaction of cyclic AMP and cyclic GMP. *Gina Bari Kolata, "Cyclic GMP: Cellular Regulatory Agent?" Science, Oct. 12, 1973, p 149*

[1970, *GMP,* abbreviation of *guanosine monophosphate,* a compound of guanosine (a constituent of nucleic acid) and one phosphate group]

cy·clo·net (ˌsai klou'net), *n.* a mechanical device for separating oil and water in an oil spill, which relies on the affinity of substances of different weights for different vortices a cyclonet creates.

Now a French company, Alsthom, has developed a device for clearing oil slicks — the cyclonet which it claims meets the two fundamental requirements of speed and simplicity. *"Technology Review: French Cyclone to Clear Oil Slicks," New Scientist, Nov. 15, 1973, p 481*

[1973, from French, from *cyclo-* circular, rotating + *net* clean] Compare CONTAINMENT BOOM.

cy·clo·phos·pha·mide (ˌsai klə'fas fəˌmaid), *n.* a drug derived from nitrogen mustard, used especially to control leukemia. *Formula:* $C_7H_{15}Cl_2N_2O_2P$

Modern drugs such as methotrexate and cyclophosphamide are extremely valuable in the treatment of many cancers and especially leukaemias where, in most cases, an increase in survival time has been achieved. *Science Journal, March 1970, p 63*

[1962, from *cyclo-* cyclic compound + *phosph*orus + *amide*]

cy·pro·ter·one acetate (sai'prou təˌroun), a drug which suppresses the hormone testosterone, used to control sexual hyperactivity in males. *Formula:* $C_{24}H_{29}ClO_4$

Cyproterone acetate was used to treat female patients suffering from severe premenstrual tension, depression and irritability. Daily dosages of the hormone were administered beginning seven days before the onset of menstruation. A marked improvement was noted in 80 percent of the women. *"Behavior: Sex Hormones and Depression," Science News, Feb. 7, 1976, p 88*

[1968, from *cyclo-* cyclic compound + *propyl* univalent radical of propane + *testos*terone]

cy·to·cha·las·in (ˌsai tou kə'læs ən), *n.* any of a group of structurally related fungal by-products that inhibit the activity of contractile elements in cells, causing the arrest of cytoplasmic division, the migration of cell nuclei, and other effects on cellular processes.

The great value of the cytochalasins as research tools, in spite of present ignorance of their precise mode of action, is that they appear to achieve their reversible impact on cell behavior with a minimum of undesirable side effects such as inhibition of respiration or protein synthesis. *Donovan Des S. Thomas, "Cytochalasins," McGraw-Hill Yearbook of Science and Technology 1975, p 155*

[1966, from *cyto-* cell (from Greek *kýtos*) + Greek *chálasis* loosening]

cy·to·meg·a·lo·vi·rus (ˌsai touˌmeg ə lou'vai rəs), *n.* a virus which causes a disease of the central nervous system similar to infectious mononucleosis, attacking and enlarging cells, and is characterized by inclusion bodies in the cell nucleus.

Cytomegalovirus and herpes simplex virus have led to brain damage, deafness, blindness and other malformations of the central nervous system. *"Four Viruses Vindicated from Causing Birth Defects," Science News, Jan. 12, 1974, p 20*

[1968, from *cyto-* cell + *megalo-* enlarged + *virus*]

cy·to·sol ('sai təˌsɔ:l), *n.* the liquid component of cytoplasm; cytoplasm without other cellular components that are associated and usually suspended in it.

Although long-chain fatty acids are at best poorly soluble in aqueous media, a mechanism to account for the apparent facility with which they traverse the cytosol (aqueous cytoplasm) has not been identified. *Robert K. Ockner, et al., "A Binding Protein for Fatty Acids in Cytosol . . . ," Science, July 7, 1972, p 56*

[1972, from *cytoplasm* + *solution*]

cytosolic, *adj.*: Homogenisation of a tissue *in vitro* also gives dilution of the cytosolic GSP [glutathione peroxidase] . . . to concentrations that are less inhibitory than those *in vivo, H.W. Cook and W. E. M. Lands, Ann Arbor, Mich., "Letters to Nature: Mechanism for Suppression of Cellular Biosynthesis of Prostaglandins," Nature, April 15, 1976 p 632*

cy·to·stat·ic (‚sai tə'stæt ik), *n.* any drug or combination of drugs that inhibits the multiplication of cells, used especially in the treatment of cancer.

If we set aside hormones, which, as we have seen have equally wide scope but limited effectiveness, the cytostatics are the first really general treatment of the disease of cancer, the first means of reaching—of controlling or preventing—lesions that are spread throughout the organism. *Lucien Israel, Conquering Cancer, 1978, p 97*

[1976, noun use of the adjective (1957), from *cyto-* cell + *static* (from Greek *statikós* causing to stand)]

Cy·trel (‚sai'trel), *n.* British trademark for a tobacco substitute made from cellulose, used in cigarettes.

Supplements like Cytrel reduce tar and nicotine in cigarette smoke to very low levels, firmly anchoring synthetic/tobacco mix smokes at the foot of the tar league tables. Equally important is that Cytrel adds nothing to tobacco smoke. *"Technology: Tobacco's Supplementary Benefits," New Scientist, July 29, 1976, p 228*

[1975] Compare NEW SMOKING MATERIAL.

D

D/A, abbreviation of *digital-to-analog.*

The processing includes the analogue-to-digital (A/D) conversion before transmission and the inverse digital-to-analogue (D/A) conversion after transmission. *Ernest R. Kretzmer, "Communication Terminals," Scientific American, Sept. 1972, p 138*

[1972]

da·la·si (dɑ:'lɑ: si:), *n.* monetary unit introduced into Gambia in 1971 to replace the Gambian pound.

There had also been a record peanut crop (accounting for over 90% of exports) at unprecedented world prices, averaging 747 dalasis per ton (and reaching over 1,000 dalasis) as against 491 dalasis in 1973. *Molly Mortimer, "The Gambia," Britannica Book of the Year 1975, p 317*

[1971, from the Gambian name of a coin worth originally 4 shillings] See BUTUT.

Da·lek or **da·lek** ('dɑ: lek), *n. British.* a robot that talks with a rasping, monotonous voice.

It is, of course, inconceivable that a Party numbering many millions of adherents can consist entirely of official Daleks, even in a culture which is quite remarkably constrained from independent commentary. *Ken Coates, The Manchester Guardian Weekly, Aug. 16, 1975, p 22*

The Brothers have returned (BBC 1, Sunday) a bit dusty from their absence. Chairman Merroney still betrays all the emotion of a Dalek. *The Listener, Feb. 12, 1976, p 180*

So, like programmed daleks, the French military planners proceed to their "second generation." This consists of 18 intermediate range ballistic missiles . . . each in an underground silo on the ironically named Plateau d'Albion. *The Times (London), July 26, 1973, p 16*

[1965, said to have been coined by one of the writers of the "Dr. Who" B.B.C. science-fiction television series from an encyclopedia volume DA-LEK]

damageability, *n.* the capacity to inflict or sustain damage.

Perhaps the first guide is to do with damageability. The child has to learn to recognize two classes of object he might unwittingly spoil. *Jane Adrian, The Times (London), Oct. 21, 1970, p 14*

In an effort to cut the costs of highway accidents, insurers accelerated their studies of the damageability and reparability of automobiles. *Kenneth Black, Jr., "Insurance," The Americana Annual 1974, p 296*

[1970, from *damage* + *-ability*]

dance language, the series of patterned movements by which honeybees communicate.

He [Karl von Frisch] proved conclusively for the first time that fish can hear, and bees, he deduced, can distinguish between odours and communicate with each other through a dance language. *Philip Kopper, "Nobel Prizes," Britannica Book of the Year 1974, p 510*

[1968]

D & D, abbreviation of *Death and Dying.*

Study courses for nurses, nuns, priests, and ordinary folk —all these have sprung up within the last few years. Thanatology, the "science" of D&D, is here fullblown. *Malachi B. Martin, "Out of This World: Death at Sunset," National Review, Nov. 22, 1974, p 1356*

[1974] ► The abbreviated phrase derives from the title of a pioneering book, "On Death and Dying" (1969) by Elisabeth Kübler Ross. See DEATH.

Dane particle

Dane particle, a large spheroidal virus particle found in the blood of a person infected with serum hepatitis.

When a serum containing antibody against hepatitis *B* was reacted with a serum containing the various antigenic particles, all three particle forms were agglutinated: the 22-nanometer spheres, the filamentous forms, and the 42-nanometer "Dane particles." If the blood samples were treated with a detergent to remove the outer shell of the Dane particle, however, the naked core was not agglutinated with the other particles. In other words, the envelope of the Dane particle was antigenically related to the 22-nanometer spheres and the filaments but the core of the Dane particle was antigenically distinct from those forms. *Joseph L. Melnick, et al., "Viral Hepatitis," Scientific American, July 1977, p 46*

[1971, named after David M. S. *Dane*, a British medical scientist who led the research team that first detected the particle in 1970]

DAP, abbreviation of *Draw-a-Person*, a psychological test in which the subject draws a picture of a person, which is then analyzed for indications of personality characteristics of the subject.

Our recent research suggests that the Rorschach and DAP may be projective tests in more ways than one. In interpreting the results of these tests, the average clinician may project his own preconceptions and assumptions into his description of the patient. *Loren J. and Jean Chapman, Encyclopedia Science Supplement (Grolier) 1972, p 40*

[1972]

dap·sone ('dæp,soun), *n.* a drug that inhibits the growth of the bacteria that causes leprosy, used also in treating some forms of dermatitis. *Formula:* $C_{12}H_{12}N_2O_2S$

The well-established anti-leprosy drug Dapsone . . . has been found to reduce inflammation pain and swelling without the side effects of cortisone-type drugs. *New Scientist, Sept. 29, 1977, p 799*

[1966, from *di*aminodiphenyl *sulf*one, the chemical name]

Da·ri ('dɑ: ri:), *n.* a variety of modern Persian spoken chiefly by the Tadzhik ethnic group.

The lower house of the Shura, or parliament, seldom had a quorum and spent most of its session on a linguistic issue —whether civil servants should know both Pushtu and Dari (Persian), Afghanistan's two official languages. *Louis and Nancy Hatch Dupree, "Afghanistan," The Americana Annual 1973, p 65*

[1972]

dark repair, the repair of a damaged or broken strand of a molecule of DNA with the help of special enzymes but without the use of light.

The second system excises radiation-induced damage from one strand of DNA and resynthesizes the missing segment by using the opposite, complementary strand of DNA as the template. *Jeremy Baptist, 1973 Britannica Yearbook of Science and the Future (1972), p 303*

[1969] Compare EXCISION REPAIR, RECOMBINATIONAL REPAIR.

dartist, *n.* a person who plays the game of darts.

In the U.K. Unicorn world championships, dartists from

16 nations competed for top honours. *Edmund Carl Hady, "Darts," Britannica Book of the Year 1977, p 648*

[1971, from *dart* + *-ist*; perhaps humorously influenced by harmony in *dart* and *artist*]

dart tag, a small metal dart with a plastic streamer attached, inserted into the back of a fish as an identifying tag.

For small fish, small dart tags that were fired from a "pistol" also came along, as did dart tags that were inserted in an incision cavity. *Nelson Bryant, "Wood, Field and Stream: Laser Beam for Fish Branding," The New York Times, Jan. 13, 1976, p 27*

[1976]

da·ru·ma (dɑ:'ru: mɑ:), *n.* a Japanese doll used as a good-luck symbol. See the quotation for details.

Some three weeks earlier, one member of the Lockheed staff had brought a large *daruma*—a papiermâché figure of a famous Buddhist monk of that name—to the room. Traditionally, in Japan, when a wish is made, the left eye of a daruma is painted in, and if the wish comes true the right eye is also painted in. During the party, Kotchian painted in the right eye. *Robert Shaplen, "Annals of Crime: The Lockheed Incident—I," The New Yorker, Jan. 23, 1978, p 74*

[1963, from Japanese, after *Daruma*, the Japanese name of Bodhi*dharma*, the legendary founder of Zen Buddhism]

Dash·a·vey·or ('dæʃ ə,vei ər), *n.* a trademark for a transportation system. See the quotation for details.

The next system, the Dashaveyor, is already in operation though at very slow speeds in a mine experiment. This uses small, electrically powered, self-propelled units which would operate at speeds up to 80 mph on fixed guideways with wheels both above and below the rails. *The Manchester Guardian Weekly, April 4, 1970, p 7*

[1970, from Stanley E. *Dashe*w its designer + connecting *-a-* + con*veyor*]

data, *v.t. U.S.* to compile or possess detailed information about (a person or group).

By the mid-Fifties the FBI not only had all "card-carrying" Communists in the U.S. identified and "dataed," but had the Soviet intelligence services, the KGB and the military GRU, so thoroughly penetrated that it could actually influence their direction. *Miles Copeland, "Dirty Tricks and All: The Unmentionable Uses of a CIA," National Review, Sept. 14, 1973, p 993*

[1973, verb use of *data, n.*]

data buoy, a buoy equipped with weather sensors and transmitters, used especially to obtain early warnings of storms and other meteorological events.

The inability to obtain regular meteorological data from a variety of fixed points in the oceans has long posed a problem to weather forecasters. A network of sophisticated data buoys was seen as a good way to solve the problem. *"Oh (Scientific) Buoy! First One Placed in Gulf," Science News, June 24, 1972, p 407*

[1972]

data capture, the simultaneous automatic recording and processing of data, as by means of equipment connecting distant locations with a central computer or processing unit.

A brief review of this type must unfortunately pay scant

attention to many sectors of even the hardware market. These include . . . the development in data capture, one of the most vital areas of computing. *J. H. Bonnett, The Times (London), Dec. 4, 1972, p II*

[1969]

data link, a communications link for direct transmission of data from one or more distant points to a central computer or processing unit.

Digital communication systems, often called "data-links," are beginning to appear in increasing numbers. The data-link is bound to proliferate. It is the natural communication medium for the pulse trains that pass between digital electronic devices. *The Times (London), May 26, 1977, p 18*

[1963]

data logger, an instrument that receives data in the form of electrical signals and records them in digital form.

The output is primarily via data loggers and a computer, and consists in part of a digitised continuous body heat map from which the experimenters can study the body's heat patterns. *"Technology Review: Computer Maps Fat People's Heat," New Scientist, Dec. 21, 1972, p 703*

[1963]

da·ta·ma·tion (ˌdei təˈmei ʃən), *n.* the automatic processing of data, especially as a branch of commerce and industry.

In the field of computer technology the distinction between *hardware* and *software* has lately been blurred by the introduction of the term *firmware*. At the same time, *datamation* has been adopted as the new term for computer processing. *Simeon Potter, "New Words and Meanings in Current English," Language Teaching Abstracts, Jan. 1972, p 72*

[1963, from *data* + auto*mation*]

Dataroute, *n.* a Canadian telecommunications system for the transmission of data in digital form.

Canada's new Dataroute system is designed to provide low rates for a digital data transmission service that is needed because of the increasing flow of business information and the increasing use of computers in Canada. . . . The new system utilizes a type of transmission called data under voice. *Paul Weiner, "Telecommunications: Trans-Canadian Digital Data Network," The Americana Annual 1974, p 578*

[1974]

data set, an analog-to-digital or digital-to-analog converter used in data communications.

"Modem" is a contraction of modulator-demodulator. Modems, also known as data sets, adapt alphanumeric information (letters and numerals) for transmission over standard voice channels. Questions and answers, or requests and acknowledgements, flow in rapid message bursts from agents' terminals to the central computer and back again. *Ernest R. Kretzmer, "Communication Terminals," Scientific American, Sept. 1972, p 136*

[1972]

data-undervoice, *n.* Also spelled **data under voice,** a method of digital data transmission in which the data signals and voice signals are sent simultaneously over a microwave radio relay system by using different frequency bands for the data signals and the voice signals.

The new development achieved during 1971 that would eventually link machines in most cities of the U.S. was a technological breakthrough known as data-undervoice (or DUV). What made DUV so significant and its potential impact so far-reaching was that it could be used on the existing microwave radio relay network, a transmission facility that reaches almost every corner of the U.S. *Irwin Welber, "Communications," 1973 Britannica Yearbook of Science and the Future (1972), p 215*

[1972]

Da·tel or **da·tel** (deiˈtel *or* ˈdei tel), *n.* a service of the British postal system, providing high-speed transmission of data by computer for subscribing business firms.

An extension of Telex is Datel, the provision of high speed data links for computers. *Peter Laurie, "The Power of the Post Office," The Sunday Times (London), June 20, 1971, Magazine Sec. p 23*

[1967, from *data* + *Telex*] Compare PRESTEL.

daycare, *v.t.* to place (a preschool child) in a daycare center.

Marcy, the wife, discovers the women's lib movement, retains her teaching job at Harvard, daycares her children, and dabbles in New Left causes. *Patricia S. Coyne, Review of "Black Conceit" by John Leonard, National Review, Jan. 18, 1974, p 97*

[1974, verb use of DAY CARE]

daylight, *v.i.* to work at a regular daytime job.

When [Lily] Tomlin isn't working before the cameras or a concert audience she's likely to be working on new characters. Recently she turned up without make-up and with hair piled atop her head at a Burbank supermarket, where she daylighted for four days perfecting her "Dot, the checkout lady." *Newsweek, April 21, 1975, p 90*

[1975, verb use of the noun, on the pattern of *moonlight, v.* (1957)]

daylighting, *n.:* These are just two instances of the irregular employment practices—"black labour" the trade unions call it—which have always been part of the Italian way of life. They go well beyond moonlighting, which presupposes daylighting or a regular daytime job in the first place. *John Earle, The Times (London), Oct. 24, 1977, p 27*

Day 1 or **Day One,** *Informal.* the first day of any period of time; the very beginning.

From Day 1, fashion has dictated that women's tender toes be squeezed into a pointed-toe shoe that ignores the realities of human anatomy. *Betty Vaughn, The New York Times Magazine, Sept. 2, 1979, p 47*

[1976]

day-sailer, *n. Especially British.* a small sailboat used for short pleasure trips.

In the following years he [Uffa Fox] designed dozens of boats from dinghies and day-sailers to cruisers and ocean-racers, and achieved a high place among the world's leading marine architects. *The Times (London), Oct. 27, 1972, p 16*

[1964, from *daytime* + *sail, v.* + *-er*]

da·zi·bao (ˈdɑː dziːˈbɑu), *n., pl.* **-baos.** another name for WALLPOSTER.

Li Chun-kuang, a young teacher at the Conservatory of Music, in August 1975 posted up a *dazibao* criticising the leadership of the Ministry of Culture for its dead hand on China's cultural life and specifically for suppressing "The Pioneers," a film extolling China's oilfield workers. Li was imprisoned. *David Crook, in a Letter to the Editor, The Manchester Guardian Weekly, Jan. 30, 1977, p 2*

[1972, from Chinese (Pinyin) *dazubao*, literally, big-character poster]

DBA, abbreviation of *dihydro-dimethyl-benzopyran-butyric acid,* a compound that reverses the sickling of cells characteristic of sickle-cell anemia.

Ekong and his team modified xanthoxylol to DBA and tested it for antisickling activity. They incubated DBA with suspensions of sickle cells and found that it completely inhibited sickling. *"A New Antisickling Agent," Science News, Jan. 10, 1976, p 22*

[1976]

DBCP, abbreviation of *dibromochloropropane,* a widely used pesticide, used to kill roundworms that destroy root crops. It is believed to cause sterility in farm workers.

More recently, the National Cancer Institute reported in 1973 that DBCP was carcinogenic in test animals, and in recent months the Environmental Protection Agency (EPA) has kept the pesticide on a list of chemicals suspected of causing hazards to human health. *New Scientist, Sept. 1, 1977, p 516*

[1977]

DCE, *Economics.* abbreviation of *domestic credit expansion,* a British measure of changes in the money supply that now excludes foreign exchange reserves and overseas government borrowing.

Statistically, the DCE approximates to the rise in the money supply plus the balance of payments deficit, although the purity of this equation is marred by such tiresome conventions as that changes in the non-deposit liabilities of the banking sector are excluded from the money supply, but included in DCE. *Peter Jay, "The Chancellor Bids Safely and Plays Boldly," The Times (London), Jan. 15, 1976, p 19*

[1970]

DCS or **D.C.S.,** abbreviation of *Dorsal Column Stimulator,* a small electrical device that supplies impulses to stimulate the spinal nerves and relieve pain.

During a brief operation, the D.C.S. is implanted in the skin, . . . with the source of the pain determining its position; for example, if the patient suffers from leg pain, the D.C.S. is implanted just above the point at which the nerves from the leg reach the spinal column. *Laurence Cherry, "Solving the Mysteries of Pain," The New York Times Magazine, Jan. 30, 1977, p 50*

[1973]

de-accession, *v.t., v.i.* to sell or exchange pieces of a museum's collection or any other formal collection.

Last September, the Met revealed that it had de-accessioned a major work from the De Groot bequest, Henri Rousseau's *The Tropics,* and secretly sold it, along with Vincent Van Gogh's *The Olive Pickers,* to Marlborough Fine Art galleries. *"Art: The Met: Beleaguered But Defiant," Time, Feb. 26, 1973, p 43*

A good number of paintings in the original donation, none

of them fakes, did turn out to be wrongly attributed, and were deaccessioned by the university as we began to rebuild the collection. *William B. Jordan, "The Mail," The Atlantic, May 1975, p 28*

—*n.* the act or practice of de-accessioning a part of an art or other collection.

Richard F. Brown, director of Fort Worth's Kimbell Museum of Art, felt that . . . the "principle" of de-accession is right although he might "disagree with the particular object chosen for de-accession." *"Picture Puzzle at the Met," Newsweek, Jan. 29, 1973, p 76*

[1972, from *de-* do the opposite of + *accession*]

de-acquisition, *n.* **1** a piece to be de-accessioned from a collection.

When it was announced seven months ago that museum director Thomas Pearsall Field Hoving's de-acquisitions would include Picasso's "Women in White" and Manet's "Boy with a Sword," it aroused the kind of reaction that has made Hoving a controversial figure ever since he was Mayor Lindsay's parks commissioner. *"Art: Wheeling and De-Dealing," Newsweek, Oct. 16, 1972, p 117*

2 the act or process of de-accessioning.

After much public debate and recrimination because of alleged secrecy and disregard of the public interest in handling several *de-acquisitions* (selling or exchanging works), the Metropolitan Museum of Art presented its own guideline for future transactions: Public notice will be given for the sale or exchange of works valued at more than $25,000, and any sale, other than to another museum, will be made at public auction. *Joshua B. Kind, "Visual Arts: New Forms," The 1974 World Book Year Book (1973), p 527*

[1972]

dead letter box or **dead letter drop,** a place for depositing secret messages and other material without having to come in direct contact with the recipient.

It was said that ever since coming to West Germany Guillaume had been collecting intelligence material and dispatching it to his masters—either by radio, by courier or through 'dead letter' boxes. *H. N. Crossland, "Germany," The Annual Register of World Events in 1974 (1975), p 156*

The Soviet newspaper *Izvestia* published details of a year-old case in which they had discreetly expelled an attractive young American woman, obviously a CIA operative, caught planting money, poison and cameras at what the thriller books call a "dead letter drop" for another agent to pick up. *Maclean's, July 10, 1978, p 47*

[1971, so called in reference to a post-office dead letter, which cannot be delivered or returned]

de·af·fer·ent·ed (di:ˈæf ər ən tid), *adj.* having the afferent or sensory nerve fibers (which convey impulses to the central nervous system) severed or otherwise interrupted.

Monkeys can even learn to perform new conditioned responses with deafferented extremities with vision occluded. *Robert Cohn, et al., "Summated Cortical Evoked Response Testing in the Deafferented Primate," Science, Dec. 8, 1972, p 1114*

[1972]

deal, *v.* **deal up,** *U.S.* to promise a defendant who is a minor figure in a criminal case a degree of immunity from prosecution in return for information that will help convict someone who is more important or charged with a greater crime.

But the plea bargaining has its own controlling strategy — "dealing up" for testimony ever closer to the top — and [Charles] Colson by that measure was the biggest catch yet. *Newsweek, June 17, 1974, p 17*

[1974]

death, *n.* ▶ The traditional definition of death as "the final cessation of the vital functions of an individual" (OED) has been challenged in recent years by medical developments. LIFE-SUPPORT equipment can prolong the vital functions of the lungs and heart even after the brain has ceased to function and a patient is BRAIN DEAD. As long as a person's life is being supported by a mechanical respirator, switching off the respirator (pulling the PLUG) raises the moral issue of causing the patient's death.

The concept of *brain death*, originally formulated by a group of Harvard University surgeons in 1968, has gained acceptance in two states, Kansas and Maryland, which adopted statutes in the early 1970's that recognize the absence of spontaneous brain function in defining death.

However, many physicians believe it is their duty to prolong a patient's life and contend that disconnecting life-support equipment amounts to EUTHANASIA. Many others, represented by the RIGHT-TO-DIE movement, make a distinction between ACTIVE EUTHANASIA and PASSIVE EUTHANASIA that amounts to letting death occur naturally after withdrawing life-support equipment.

Although a patient has the legal right to refuse life-support treatment, a comatose or brain-damaged patient cannot exercise this right and a LIVING WILL is often prepared in advance instructing physicians to discontinue life-prolonging treatment if the testator becomes permanently brain-damaged so that the patient may be permitted "death with dignity."

Some states of the United States are considering legislation that would permit active euthanasia by administration of death-hastening drugs if an incurable patient wishes to be put to death painlessly.

Concern with death and dying (D & D) has become the subject of many popular books and articles. Scholarly journals are published by specialists in the field called THANATOLOGISTS. These experts also give courses in DEATH EDUCATION, provide DEATH THERAPY and GRIEF THERAPY, and have pioneered in the creation of HOSPICES, institutions devoted to the care of the dying where suffering is eased by the use of the BROMPTON COCKTAIL and other pain-relieving measures.

death education, a program of courses that provides information about death and the problems and needs of the dying.

Many critically ill patients suffered greatly from loneliness. To help solve this problem, a number of medical schools, hospitals, colleges, and even high schools and churches began to give courses in death education. *Robert Fulton, "Death," The World Book Encyclopedia (1979), Vol. 5, p 53*

[1979] Compare D & D.

death squad, any of various unofficial vigilante groups in Latin America whose members murder petty criminals, suspected leftists, etc.

What causes alarm in the serried ranks of the Latin American diaspora — exiles spread over several continents — is that the victims of the assassination schemes are for the most part political moderates, and there seems to be no geographical limit to the operations of the death squads. *Richard Gott, The Manchester Guardian Weekly, Oct. 3, 1976, p 8*

Military regimes in Argentina, Brazil, Uruguay, Paraguay, Bolivia and Chile, augmented by plainclothes "death squads," have killed many guerrilla leaders and followers; some survivors have gone into exile. *The New York Times, June 25, 1978, Sec. 4, p 6*

[1969]

death therapy, supportive therapy for patients suffering from terminal diseases; advice, reassurance, and other guidance given to help a patient and his family cope with his imminent death.

John Parkins: "I've heard of death therapy, death counseling, and I think it's a good idea. Not for me, because I found out about my sickness early, and I provided my own therapy." *Bill Cameron, Maclean's, April 1973, p 24*

[1973] Compare GRIEF THERAPY.

debit card, a card enabling a bank customer to withdraw cash at any time from any of the bank's automatic teller machines and to charge purchases of goods and services directly to funds on deposit in the bank.

It is projected that in the 1980s the "cashless" or, more appropriately, "checkless" society will come into being. The means for this new financial system will be the debit card, which is planned to replace the credit card of today. The debit card will be used to initiate a transaction at the bank itself, at a retail outlet, or at a remote unattended location where money can be deposited or withdrawn around the clock. *Rod N. Thorpe, "Electrical Communications," McGraw-Hill Yearbook of Science and Technology 1977, p 173*

[1977, patterned on *credit card* (1956), from which it differs by effecting a debit in the bearer's bank account instead of entitling the bearer to credit with a business firm]

de·ca·rock ('dek ə₁rɑk), *n.* another name for GLITTER ROCK.

Wedged between the regression of nostalgia and the perversity of deca-rock is the real core of the pop product — the myriad soft and hard rock bands, and the individual singer-songwriters, both black and white. *Maureen Orth, "Pop: Messiah Coming?" Newsweek, Dec. 24, 1973, p 48*

[1973, short for *decadent rock*]

dec·et ('des ət), *n.* another name for DECIMET.

Gell-Mann's quarks explain the elementary-particle families in his Eightfold Way classification system. They combine by threes to form a 10-member family, the baryon decet. *Robert H. March, "The Quandary Over Quarks," The World Book Science Annual 1975 (1974), p 85*

decidophobe

[1974, from *dec-* ten (from Greek *déka*) + *-et*, as in *octet, sextet,* etc.]

decidophobia, *n.* a fear or avoidance of deciding something, especially something important.

Without Guilt and Justice. Walter Kaufmann. Wyden. An influential scholar of Nietzsche unsparingly attacks the American disease of "decidophobia"—an unwillingness to make fateful decisions—proposing "moral autonomy" as a cure. *"Books in Review," 1974 Collier's Encyclopedia Year Book (1973), p 109*

[1972, coined from *decide* + connective *-o-* + *phobia*]

decidophobe, *n.:* The decidophobe often restricts himself, Kaufmann says, by making one of ten major choices that automatically eliminates the need for many future decisions. *"Avoiding Decisions," Time, March 6, 1972, p 52*

dec·i·met ('des ə met), *n.* a group of ten nuclear particles with approximately the same mass, hypercharge, and isotopic spin.

The grouping of these families of elementary particles into superfamilies (octets, decimets and so on) was proposed independently in the early 1960's by Murray Gell-Mann and Yuval Ne'eman. *Illustration legend, "Unified Theories of Elementary-Particle Interaction," Scientific American, July 1974, p 55*

[1965, from Latin *decimus* of ten + English *-et*, as in *octet, sextet,* etc.] Also called DECET.

decimetric, *adj.* of or having to do with radio waves ranging from 0.1 to 1 meter in length, or a frequency of 300 to 3000 megahertz.

Trapped particle species will be the object of a University of California experiment—the Jovian trapped radiation detector, which will endeavour to relate these particles to the decimetric radio emissions. *Peter Stubbs, "Pioneering Further Afield in Space," New Scientist, March 9, 1972, p 537*

[1966, derivative of *decimeter* unit of length equal to a 10th of a meter] Compare DEKAMETRIC.

decision tree, a graphic representation of alternative courses of action, risks, and possible results, used as an aid in decision-making.

The fourth channel questions facing Sir John Eden, the Minister of Posts and Telecommunications, can be laid out in the form of a relatively simple decision tree. First, he must decide whether to allocate the fourth channel now or postpone the decision. . . . Second, he must decide who should be responsible for the fourth channel. And finally, he must decide how this responsibility, once assigned, should be discharged. *Julian Critchley, "Views," The Listener, Oct. 25, 1973, p 543*

[1968] Compare EVENT TREE.

decompress, *v.i.* to pass from a state of stress and become less tense; relax.

"If you grew up in Georgia, you know how to decompress," Rusk recently told an acquaintance who wondered how he had adjusted to his comparatively tranquil post-government life. "My mother would decompress by sitting down in a rocking chair and taking a five-minute nap." *E. J. Kahn, The New Yorker, Feb. 6, 1978, p 62*

[1971, figurative sense of the term meaning to reduce or relieve pressure (as of air or gas)]

decompression, *n.:* Each morning the finance minister awoke, determined to leave public life and end the 15 years of grueling, 12-hour days to spend more time with his family. By midafternoon he would waver, recalling his nine years in cabinet as a power in national affairs and anticipating a difficult decompression to private citizen. *Robert Lewis, Maclean's, Sept. 19, 1977, p 63*

deconvolution, *n.* the unfolding or unwinding of a convoluted line or form, especially one produced by a computer; act or process of deconvolving.

Close examination and comparison of the red absorption band of chlorophyll oligomers, $(Chl_2)_n$, and a variety of photosynthetic organisms by computer deconvolution techniques give considerable support to the thesis that antenna chlorophyll in green plants and in blue-green algae has spectral properties and a structure very similar to those of chlorophyll oligomers, $(Chl_2)_n$. *Joseph J. Katz, "Chlorophyll," McGraw-Hill Yearbook of Science and Technology 1974, p 128*

[1972]

deconvolve, *v.t.* to unfold or unwind (a convoluted line or form, especially one produced by a computer).

Theoretically, photographs from a single moving observation site such as an aircraft can be deconvolved by a computer to obtain neutral wind speed. *D. Rees, et al., London, "Letters to Nature: Neutral Wind Measurement During Daytime in the Thermosphere," Nature, Nov. 3, 1972, p 32*

[1972]

decriminalize, *v.t.* **1** to remove from the category of a crime; declare to be noncriminal.

Glasser would decriminalize heroin and make it available in pharmacies for addicts. *James M. Markham, "What's All This Talk of Heroin Maintenance?" The New York Times Magazine, July 2, 1972, p 8*

The Alaska state bar voted Saturday to support legislation to decriminalize use of marijuana. By a vote of 54-30 at their annual convention, the state bar members urged that legislation be drafted to eliminate all criminal penalties for possession, sale and possession with intent to sell marijuana. *"Flash," The News (Mexico City), June 17, 1973, p 2*

2 to free (a person or activity) from liability to criminal prosecution or penalty.

The recommended removal of all penalties for the private possession of marihuana would do much to decriminalize a large number of those involved with this drug. *Lester Grinspoon, "Half a Loaf: A Reaction to the Marihuana Report," Saturday Review, April 15, 1972, p 21*

Homosexuality was decriminalised, and homosexuals came to be treated with unprecedented tolerance. *The Listener, Dec. 18, 1975, p 8*

[1972, back formation from earlier (1968) *decriminalization;* also 1963 as *v.i.* in the sense of "rehabilitate criminals through psychiatric treatment"]

▶ This term is not strictly synonymous with "legalize," although some writers have used the two terms interchangeably. To *decriminalize* marijuana means to remove its use or possession from the category of a crime, but it does not necessarily mean to make its manufacture, distribution, and sale legal. Its use may still be regulated, the way certain drugs are. To

134

legalize it means to allow it to become available, the way cigarettes and alcohol are at present.

de·cruit (di:'kru:t), *v.t. U.S.* to try to place (an older or unneeded employee) in another firm or in a less critical position with his present employer.

"Decruiting" is a term that developed during the recession . . . It had limited success at that time, since the whole economy was stagnant. Under today's conditions, in which many industries are actively recruiting, the decruiting effort can be more effective . . . The main problem is bringing together companies releasing people and companies which may be able to employ those being let go. *(Newsletter of) Edward Gottlieb & Associates, New York City, Feb. 15, 1974*

[1974, from *de-* do the opposite of + re*cruit*]

decruitment, *n.:* Co-Op Denmark is processing the decruitment program, and a survey of 1285 Danish managers over 50 showed that 70% preferred downgrading to retirement. *Time, May 15, 1978, p 77*

deep cover, 1 concealment of a person's identity as an informant or secret agent, or his location, by use of elaborate security or protective guises.

The author . . . readily admits to having served briefly as a deep cover agent in the CIA after leaving college. *William F. Buckley, Jr., "Books in Brief," National Review, Feb. 20, 1976, p 169*

Wolf says other CIA agents in Canada are disguised under "deep cover," working as professors, businessmen and journalists. *Maclean's, Oct. 9, 1978, p 28*

2 *Transferred use.*

Student records . . . often bulge with personal information — much of it unsubstantiated — such as the political and sexual leanings not only of the student but also of his parents. Ever since the Family Educational Rights and Privacy Act went into effect in late 1974, these records have been kept under deep cover. *Time, Feb. 2, 1976, p 44*

[1963] See SAFE HOUSE.

deep-think, *n. U.S. Slang.* extreme bookishness; academic, pedantic, or esoteric thought. *Often used attributively.*

Though the *[Arizona] Republic* still competently covers Indian life and culture, "We have started to come back from deep-think," says [Jeanne Tro] Williams now. *"The Press: Flight from Fluff," Time, March 20, 1972, p 53*

A plague of deep-think pseudosociology has presented American Big Sports as a model, a metaphor, a paradigm and a proof for American Big Imperialism, American Big Oppression, American Big Sexism, and all the other U.S. Bigs including Infantilism. *Jack Kroll, "Team of Destiny," Review of "The Changing Room," Newsweek, Dec. 11, 1972, p 71*

[1963, back formation from *deep thinker*]

deep throat, *U.S. and Canadian.* a highly placed anonymous informer on criminal activities in government.

Experience has taught, for example, that the media must be able to protect the identity of confidential sources, "deep throats," in order to maintain access to crucial information; neither General Motors nor A & P has that problem. *The New York Times, May 14, 1978, Sec. 4, p 18*

This time, the new Deep Throat of the Natural Governing Party revealed the astounding news that the election will be won in Ontario and B.C. and that the Liberals are solid in Quebec. Any more national scoops like that and the entire press gallery may have to resign in shame and take up chicken-farming. *Allan Fotheringham, Maclean's, Oct. 2, 1978, p 72*

[1973, from the nickname of an informer (or several informers) who, according to the American journalist Bob Woodward, provided him with "deep background" on the Watergate affair (1972-74); originally the title of a pornographic motion picture which was widely exhibited in 1972]

deexcitation, *n.* a lowering or being lowered from an excited or high-energy state.

When an extremely energetic proton collided with a target nucleon, a highly excited and complex state would be generated. Most of the time this state would lose energy with the emission of such strongly interacting particles as pions and kaons. Occasionally, however, deexcitation would result in part from the emanation of virtual photons that would decay immediately into lepton pairs. *Leon M. Lederman, "The Upsilon Particle," Scientific American, Oct. 1978, p 73*

[1964, from *de-* do the opposite of +*excitation* a raising to a higher energy level]

de·ex·cite (,di: ek'sait), *v.t.* to diminish the high-energy level of (an atom, electron, etc.).

The density of the corona is so low that the atoms are not deexcited by collisions before they have a chance to radiate the energy. *Jay M. Pasachoff, "The Solar Corona," Scientific American, Oct. 1973, p 72*

—*v.i.* to be deexcited.

The excited state then de-excites down through lower excited levels until finally it reaches the ground, or stable, state of the nucleus. *H. E. Wegner, 1970 Britannica Yearbook of Science and the Future (1969), p 378*

[1965, from *de-* do the opposite of +*excite* raise to a higher energy level] See EXCIMER.

defect action level, another name for ACTION LEVEL.

CU [Consumers Union] urged the Food and Drug Administration to establish and enforce a sound Defect Action Level for meat and poultry pot pies. A Defect Action Level sets limits on the extraneous matter — commonly known as filth — permissible in food products before the FDA may take regulatory action without further evidence of a health hazard. Only the FDA is authorized to establish Defect Action Levels. *"The FDA and USDA Play Catch 22," Consumer Reports, Feb. 1976, p 67*

[1976]

defective virus, see the quotation for the meaning.

Defective viruses arise naturally when viruses are grown in cells in a laboratory. These agents consist of the same protein coat as a normal virus, but they contain only a fraction of the genetic material. This defect prevents them from successfully infecting cells alone, but they can reproduce in the presence of a normal virus. *Science News, May 14, 1977, p 308*

[1974]

defensive medicine, the practice by physicians of ordering an unusual number of laboratory tests and diagnostic consultations in order to protect themselves from possible malpractice suits.

The practice of "defensive medicine" is increasing among California physicians, surgeons and hospitals in the face of a rising volume of malpractice lawsuits. . . . The practice also includes the refusal to treat high-risk patients. *Everett R. Holler, The New York Times, Jan. 27, 1974, p 20*

[1970]

degear, *v.i. British, Finance.* to reduce the amount of a company's fixed-interest debt and replace it with equity capital.

Whittingham acquired a significant proportion of its land bank near the top of the market. And, while it may be of sparse comfort to shareholders who have ridden the shares from 1973's 170p to yesterday's 19p, the group has now cleared its books of unrealistically valued land and has begun the uphill struggle to degear. *The Times (London), Feb. 18, 1976, p 25*

[1976, from *de-* do the opposite of + *gear* (1930's) to borrow money so as to increase the amount of total capital in relation to equity capital]

degender, *v.t.* to remove reference to gender in.

Among the ideas: degendering language; letting men wear modes of clothing that were equivalent to skirts (caftans, togas and such); giving children nonsex-identification names; having unisex public bathrooms and taking sex off application forms. *Lisa Hammel, "Men's Lib," The New York Times, June 11, 1974, p 46*

[1974, from *de-* remove + *gender*] Compare DESEX. See also HE/SHE.

deinstitutionalize, *v.t.* **1** to divest or free (a church, hospital, or other institution) of its institutional character.

As the function of *teacher* becomes despecialized, so (from our perspective) the process of education becomes deinstitutionalized and is freed to be reconfigured with the "other" processes of our integral lives — perhaps in forms hard to recognize. *Michael Rossman, "How We Learn Today in America," Saturday Review, Aug. 19, 1972, p 31*

2 to enable (an inmate, patient, etc.) to live away from an institution; remove from an institution.

It is a really visionary little organization, anxious to deinstitutionalize the disabled and to encourage young people especially to lead normal, independent lives. *Ann Hales-Tooke, The Times (London), Jan. 5, 1972, p 5*

"We're institutionalizing everybody," [Governor] Brown tells a group of hospital workers to whom he is extolling the virtues of limited growth. "And I'd like to deinstitutionalize everybody. I'd like to have a community that has a more human spirit to it." *The Manchester Guardian Weekly (The Washington Post section), July 2, 1978, p 18*

[1967]

deinstitutionalization, *n.:* Does "deinstitutionalization" represent an enlightened revolution or an abdication of responsibility? It is probably too early for a definitive judgment, but it is not too soon to review the issues raised by this aspect of the community mental health movement and to consider how such a well-intentioned reform as deinstitutionalization could have created so many problems. *Ellen L. Bassuk and Samuel Gerson, "Deinstitutionalization and Mental Health Services," Scientific American, Feb. 1978, p 46*

dé·jà en·ten·du (dei₃ɑ: ã tã'dY), recognition of something already understood or something heard or seen before.

Lindsay may also have a sense of *déjà entendu* about the current judgment, popular in some circles, that it is hope-

less for him even to consider entering the national race. *Andy Logan, "Around City Hall," The New Yorker, Aug. 21, 1971, p 68*

Around *To the Shores of the Polar Sea* (Radio 4), for instance, there hung an air of *déjà entendu* that stereophony could not dispel nor radiophonic cold winds blow away. *Neil Hepburn, The Listener, Feb. 26, 1976, p 246*

[1965, from French] ► See the note under DÉJÀ LU.

dé·jà lu (dei ₃ɑ: 'lY), recognition of something already read or already encountered.

Her first book suffers inevitably from a sense of *déjà lu*. It not only draws heavily on those earlier articles, it trades on childhood experiences shared to some extent by every reader. *"Books," Review of "Looking Back" by Joyce Maynard, Time, May 21, 1973, p 102*

[1966, from French] ► The use of *déjà lu* and the preceding phrase, *déjà entendu*, in English appears to be due to the influence of *déjà vu*, originally adopted from French (1903) by psychologists as a purely technical term for a form of paramnesia. *Déjà lu* and *déjá entendu* are, however, nontechnical, and are used mainly for stylistic or literary effect. See also JAMAIS VU.

dekametric, *adj.* of or having to do with radio waves ranging from 10 to 100 meters in length, or a frequency of 3 to 30 megahertz.

This magnetosphere is believed to be the source of the decimetric (not to be confused with the dekametric) radio emanations that come from the planet. *"Astronomy: Jupiter's Decimetric Radiation," Science News, Sept. 30, 1972, p 216*

[1970, alteration of earlier *decametric* (1966), from *decameter* unit of length equal to 10 meters] Compare DECIMETRIC.

deke (di:k), *n. Especially Canadian.* a maneuver in ice hockey and some other sports that deceives an opponent and draws him away from a defensive position.

He gave them such a fantastic series of dekes, you know what happened? They crashed into each other and knocked each other down. *Herbert Warren Wind, "The Sporting Scene: Orr Country," The New Yorker, March 27, 1971, p 114*

[1966 (1960 *A Dictionary of Canadianisms*), alteration of *decoy.* Spelled also *deek* and used both as a noun and a verb, the term became current in Canada in the early 1960's.]

Delaney amendment or **Delaney clause,** an amendment of the U.S. Food, Drug and Cosmetic Act which forbids the use of any food additive or other substance that is shown to cause cancer in animals or people, regardless of the amount.

If the suspect tumors can indeed be linked to saccharin (rather than to impurities in the drug or to other factors), the FDA [Food and Drug Administration] will once again invoke the Delaney amendment. *"The Bitter and Sweet of Saccharin Research," Science News, March 3, 1973, p 134*

These facts might seem to indicate that at normal levels of consumption, saccharin is safe for humans. Because of the Delaney clause, however, the FDA had no option but to ban the use of saccharin as a food additive, when the results of the Canadian tests were made known. *Romaine*

Bamford, "The Saccharin Ban," Encyclopedia Science Supplement (Grolier) 1977/1978 (1977), p 248

[1970, named after James J. *Delaney*, born 1901, U.S. Congressman from Long Island City, N.Y., author of the amendment]

► Although twenty years old, the Delaney amendment became the focus of intense controversy during the 1970's. The following background was given to the editors by Richard L. Arkin, spokesman on consumer affairs for the then U.S. Department of Health, Education, and Welfare.

In the late 1940's Congress established a committee to investigate "chemicals in foods." Congressman Delaney was named chairman of the committee. The hearings held by the Delaney committee led to the Pesticides Chemical Act of 1954 and the Food Additives Amendment of 1958.

During the hearings, there was testimony concerning tragedies from the use of toxic chemicals as food additives. At the same time, testimony showed that food additives were vital in modern food manufacturing.

When the legislation was finally submitted to Congress, it recognized the need for additives; however, Congressman Delaney inserted a proviso that "no additive shall be deemed to be safe if it is found, after tests which are appropriate for the evaluation of food additives, to induce cancer in man and animals."

The amendment became extremely controversial as scientific analysis became more sophisticated and it became possible to detect extremely minute quantities of substances. In 1970, the Food and Drug Administration banned the use of cyclamates as artificial sweeteners, showing that bladder tumors had developed in rats receiving cyclamates. The "inflexibility" of the Delaney amendment was criticized because the dose that produced the malignant tumors in rats was equivalent to fifty times that recommended for adult human consumption. The controversy was renewed in 1976 with a ban on RED NO. 2, a widely used food coloring, followed in 1977 by the announcement that SACCHARIN is a potential human carcinogen. Other recent studies suggest that nitrates and nitrites as preservatives may also be carcinogenic.

Many scientists believe there is no need to ban a useful substance if the amount used is safe, asserting the proper role of the investigator is to make an analysis of the RISK-BENEFIT RATIO, in which the hazards of using a substance are balanced against the benefits. Other scientists believe the Delaney clause is necessary for the protection of the consumer.

delawyer, *v.t. U.S.* to eliminate the need for a lawyer's services in (a legal proceeding).

Procedural reforms such as no-fault insurance offer ways to "delawyer" particular problems. In New Zealand, virtually all lawsuits for personal injuries (not just auto accidents) have been abolished; these injuries are now handled through a nationwide insurance system. *Thomas*

Ehrlich, "Legal Pollution," The New York Times Magazine, Feb. 8, 1976, p 21

[1976, from *de-* remove + *lawyer*]

delawyerization, *n.*: Group legal service plans, extensive use of paralegal aides for routine functions, ... "delawyerization" through arbitration, no-fault systems of compensation, and encouragement of less expensive lay alternatives —such reforms would improve access to services and reduce costs for the vast majority who are neither wealthy nor impoverished. *Peter H. Schuck, "Legal Poverty," Harper's, Feb. 1976, p 86*

deletion, *n.* the removal or loss of a section of genetic material from a chromosome.

The first mutation was a deletion that removed a "letter" from the genetic message; the second mutation inserted an extraneous letter. Such mutations are called "frame-shift" mutations since they cause succeeding bases to be "read" in incorrect groups of three. *"Science and The Citizen," Scientific American, Jan. 1971, p 46*

[1970] ► A similar earlier (1920's) sense of *deletion*, used in cytology, is "the loss or breaking off of a piece of chromosome in a cell."

Delhi belly, *Slang.* traveler's diarrhea acquired in India.

Lomotil is an "anti-diarrhoeal" creeping into common usage in the rich world. Salesmen on missions abroad take it in their emergency medication packs, lest they succumb to "Delhi belly." *Mike Muller, "Lomotil: A Case of Moral Incontinence?" New Scientist, March 31, 1977, p 786*

[1964, named after *Delhi*, a city in northern India] Compare MEXICALI REVENGE, TOURISTE.

► This widely experienced intestinal ailment has received many names besides the ones listed above: *gyppy tummy*, when contracted in Egypt, *Aden gut* and *Basra belly* when in the Middle East, and *turista* when in Mexico. In this book we have entered only the most recent and commonest of the names.

For years the precise cause has eluded medical scientists, but in May of 1975 researchers reported in the New England Journal of Medicine that the illness appears to be caused by a toxin-producing strain of the bacterium *Escherichia coli.* The particular strain can be found in food and drink and on many unsuspected objects, such as coins and menus. It enters the intestinal tract causing an abnormal discharge of salt and water.

de·lir (di'lir), *v.i.* to be delirious; experience delirium; hallucinate.

Ten years before, in Serbia, the only woman he had ever loved—another man's wife—had become pregnant by him. She suffered a miscarriage, and died the next night, deliring and praying. He would have had a son, a little fellow about David's age. *Vladimir Nabokov, "Perfection," The New Yorker, May 19, 1973, p 36*

[1973, back formation from *delirium*]

deliverance, *n.* the freeing of a person from the influence or control of evil spirits.

Seldom do all the church members accept the practice of deliverance and sometimes the church splits. But in many cases, exorcism leads to increases in church attendance

137

Delphi

and financial support. *"Controversy on Exorcism Grows as Practice Spreads," The New York Times, Nov. 29, 1974, p 33*

[1974] See EXORCISM.

Delphi, *n.* a method of forecasting future developments, especially in an area of technology or science, by collating and summarizing the ideas of a group of experts.

Delphi is a class of routines for getting panels of experts to work anonymously together, perhaps by way of consoles, with feedback from a controlling group that compares and contrasts the answers and the relative expertise. *Philip Morrison, Scientific American, May 1970, p 146*

Often used attributively:

Delphi method: He intends to apply the so-called Delphi method in backing future productions—a kind of consensus forecasting technique in which panels of different experts are called in. *The Times (London), March 9, 1972, p 19*

Delphi process: Such a consensus is sought through the participation of 12 to 15 qualified experts whose judgments will be obtained, combined, and refined in a systematic way—a variant of the Delphi process that has been used extensively to apply expertise to important issues not yet open to analysis. *Paul Brodeur, "Annals of Industry: Casualties of the Workplace," The New Yorker, Nov. 12, 1973, p 171*

Delphi technique: Clearly, what we need is a way of utilising the advantages of a meeting while at the same time also avoiding its many disadvantages. An approach which claims to achieve this aim is the Delphi technique, pioneered by Dr Olaf Helmer at the United States Airforce, RAND Corporation. It has been used in the development of weapons systems and some leading British firms have used the method in developing both production techniques and the products themselves. *Mike Smith, "When Psychology Grows Up," New Scientist, Oct. 10, 1974, p 90*

[1970, after *Delphi*, ancient site in Greece of the Delphic oracle]

Delphology, *n.* the study of methods for making accurate forecasts of future developments, especially in technology and science.

Today's futurologists have elaborated the procedures. They draw data from more disciplines and process them with computers. They talk of Delphology, of model-building, of scenarios. *Jack Williamson, "H. G. Wells: The Man Who Discovered Tomorrow," Saturday Review, Jan. 1, 1972, p 15*

[1969, from *Delphi* (the site of the Delphic oracle) + *-ology* study of] Compare FUTURISTICS.

Delta blues, country music influenced by the blues.

Muddy Waters is the king of dirty blues, down-home blues, funky blues or straight blues—most properly known as Delta or country blues. *"Down Home and Dirty," Time, Aug. 9, 1971, p 40*

[1970, named for the Mississippi *delta* region in southern Louisiana]

demagnify, *v.t.* to reduce to microscopic size, especially for storage; miniaturize.

These systems are really transmission electron microscopes working in reverse. Instead of a specimen there is a mask, and instead of magnifying the object formed by the specimen the object formed by the mask is demagnified. Such a system has been built at the University of Tübingen.

A. N. Broers and M. Hatzakis, "Microcircuits by Electron Beam," Scientific American, Nov. 1972, p 41

[1968]

de-man, *v.i., v.t.* **1** *British.* to reduce the manpower of a plant, industry, etc.; remove from a job or employment.

One expert estimated recently that one employee in three was surplus in British airlines. But de-manning at this scale would cause great disruption to industrial relations. *Campbell Balfour and Ian George Smith, "How Real Are the Pilot's Problems," New Scientist, March 22, 1973, p 673*

2 *U.S.* to deprive of manhood or virility; emasculate.

The girl here is a prototypical Woman as seen by the Male Chauvinist Pig—brainy, too alert, de-manning; and the man in the film is women's lib's prototypical Man—expecting working women to do their jobs without talking about them and to get on with the cooking in good time. *"Goings On About Town," The New Yorker, July 9, 1973, p 19*

[1971]

de·man·deur (də mɑːnˈdœr), *n.* one who makes a request, as before a court of law; petitioner.

As things worked out, SALT did not begin in the summer, as the President suggested. Both sides wanted talks, but neither would be pushed. The Nixon Administration began by feeling pushed, and refused to be rushed. Now Moscow, having been cast in the role of *demandeur* by Washington, would not be hurried. *John Newhouse, "Annals of Diplomacy: SALT," The New Yorker, May 19, 1973, p 112*

[1966, from French]

de-Maoification, *n.* another name for DE-MAOIZATION.

While Teng has not directly attacked the memory of the Great Helmsman, a gradual process of de-Maoification is under way in China. *Time, Nov. 27, 1978, p 40*

[1977]

de-Maoify, *v.t.:* The real question in Peking at the end of the year, with the Central Committee meeting in the Great Hall of the People, and purple ink on the wallposters outside, was not whether Mao should be de-Maoified two years after his death. *The Manchester Guardian Weekly, Jan. 1 1979, p 10*

de-Maoization, *n.* the repudiation or reversal of the policies of the Chinese Communist leader Mao Tse-tung (Mao Zedong), 1893-1976.

Just as the de-Stalinisation debate in Russia was part of the struggle for power between Stalin's successors, so the de-Maoisation debate is a sign of a similar struggle now going on in Peking. *Victor Zorza, "The de-Maoisation of China," The Manchester Guardian Weekly, May 7, 1978, p 9*

[1969]

de-marketing, *n.* the allocation of scarce goods to meet demand.

De-marketing is fast becoming one of the more unpopular words in our lexicon. We hope it disappears along with the gas station advertising's effectiveness and credibility, such as it is.

The word popped up like a pothole with the arrival of the fuel and energy crunch. Some companies, hurt by short

138

ages, found that they had to scurry to satisfy demand rather than increase demand, and that process became known as de-marketing, i.e., undoing, backing off, holding the line. At best, it is a negative word, a *non sequitur. "No Delight in De-Marketing," Advertising Age, April 8, 1974, p 14*

[1974]

Demochristian, *n.* a member of one of the Christian Democratic political parties of Europe.

Both of Italy's main parties, the Christian Democrats and the Communists, face this in somewhat flabby condition. The Demochristians are in far the worse shape. They have ruled almost since World War II, first by themselves and then in varying coalitions. *C. L. Sulzberger, "The Merry Month of May," The New York Times, April 23, 1972, p 15*

[1966, from *Democ*ratic + *Christian*]

demographics, *n.pl. Especially U.S.* statistics of populations, including size, distribution, economic status, etc.; demographic data.

Who bought the first 125,000 mopeds? The demographics are unsettled: Ed Kaufman, M.B.A. director of communications, says that more women than men are buying, but mopeder Gloria Alvarez . . . says she has yet to see another woman mopeder. *Tony Hiss and Jeff Lewis, "The Moped Revolution," The New York Times Magazine, May 15, 1977, p 97*

To the surprise of no one, the demographics of today's jazz consumer reveal an older, more mature fan: mostly male, college-educated and between the ages of twenty and thirty. *Michael Segell, Rolling Stone, Jan. 11, 1979, p 43*

[1967, from *demographic, adj.* (OED 1882)]

demographic transition, a major change in the patterns of fertility and mortality of a population.

Three stages of the demographic transition can usually be detected in every population. The first stage is characterized by high and almost equal birth and death rates and by a low rate of growth. That pattern has existed in most populations throughout most of history. In the second stage mortality declines and is followed by a lagging decline in fertility, so that the rate of population growth is high. The third stage is characterized by low birth and death rates and therefore by a rate of growth that declines gradually. *Tomas Frejka, "The Prospects for a Stationary World Population," Scientific American, March 1973, p 15*

[1971]

demonetarize, *v.t.* to withdraw from use as a monetary standard.

The ban on private ownership is being lifted as one step in a longterm U.S. effort to demonetarize gold — that is, unlink it from currency values and turn it into just another commodity the price of which can go down as well as up without affecting — or afflicting — the international monetary system. *Time, Jan. 6, 1975, p 84*

[1973, alteration (influenced by *monetary*) of *demonetize* (1852)]

demonetarization, *n.:* The Italians' tactics, it is felt in Paris, have been to divert attention from their own monetary waywardness by going over to the attack, and insisting on a demonetarization of gold and the creation of a fully institutionalized monetary union, with a central intervention fund. *Charles Hargrove, The Times (London), July 28, 1972, p 7*

demotivate, *v.t.* to cause to lose motivation or incentive.

The fact was that tax today in Britain started at too low a level and increased at too fast a rate. The present tax levels demotivated people and drove them out of the country. *The Times (London), Nov. 7, 1978, p 4*

[1974]

demotivation, *n.:* A study in managerial demotivation is provided by a survey of over 500 executives published yesterday. It shows that 51 per cent of the respondents believe themselves to be less keen to obtain promotion than they were five years ago. *Rodney Cowton, The Times (London), June 1, 1977, p 21*

demultiplexer, *n.* a device for separating electronic signals transmitted in combined form over a multiplexer.

The audio entertainment is multiplexed before transmission along this centre conductor and each receiver (usually in the aircraft seat side armrest) includes a demultiplexer and a shift register. *Adrian Hope, "Patents Review: Single Line to Concorde Entertainment," New Scientist, March 15, 1973, p 609*

[1968]

demythify, *v.t.* to remove the myths from; strip or rid of mythical aspects.

They are equally convinced of the need for provoking rebellion through a school play. But while Franc considers the play as a chance to demythify the politico-religious system oppressing their comrades, Angelo wants to incite a trauma which will allow him to "take over." *Jean de Baroncelli, "Technocrat versus Idealist," The Manchester Guardian Weekly (Le Monde section), Feb. 24, 1973, p 19*

[1965, variant of *demythicize* (1951); perhaps influenced by *demystify* (1959)]

demythification, *n.:* Then there is that class of film that doesn't quite make it into the Top Ten, but which has given pleasure all the same: Peter Bogdanovitch's *Paper Moon; The Long Goodbye*, Robert Altman's demythification of Raymond Chandler. *The Times (London), Dec. 28, 1973, p 7*

denasserization, *n.* the repudiation or reversal of the policies of Gamal Abdel Nasser, 1918-1970, the president of Egypt from 1956 until his death.

Before the October 1973 war, the great slogan of the initial cautious phase of denasserisation was the "correction" (of the arbitrary, repressive excesses of the great man's rule), and few people — Communists, Moslem brothers, or anyone else — could quarrel with that. But since October 1973, the so-called "Infitah," the "opening," has become the touchstone of everything that Sadat says or does. *The Manchester Guardian Weekly, June 28, 1975, p 9*

[1971, from *de-* opposite of, removal of + *Nasser* + *-ization*]

dendroclimatic, *adj.* of or relating to dendroclimatology.

Dating climatic change. — The great age of these trees makes them of enormous scientific interest. They are important in dendro-climatic research — the study of climatic change as revealed by tree-ring data — and for the study of past fluctuations in the concentration of radiocarbon in the atmosphere. *P. H. Armstrong, "Bristlecone Pines Tell an 8000-Year Story," Geographical Magazine, June 1972, p 639*

[1972, from *dendro-* of trees (from Greek *déndron* tree) + *climatic*]

dendroclimatology, *n.* the study of past climates

139

and climatic conditions by analysis of the annual growth rings of trees.

Dendroclimatology is a subdiscipline of dendrochronology in which the annual variations in climate are reconstructed from variations in characteristics of dated rings. Tree-ring evidence for past climatic variation is unique in that the climatic information is precisely dated to the year. *Harold C. Fritts, "Paleoclimatology," McGraw-Hill Yearbook of Science and Technology 1973, p 311*

[1972]

dendroclimatologist, *n.*: A dendroclimatologist, seeking to reconstruct variations in past climate, tries to exclude or minimize the effects of as many nonclimatic factors as possible by choosing extreme sites where climate is almost always the limiting factor in the growth of trees. *Harold C. Fritts, "Tree Rings and Climate," Scientific American, May 1972, p 93*

deniability, *n. U.S.* the ability of the President or other high government official to deny having any knowledge or connection with an illegal or improper activity.

Brzezinski is known to believe that the President should have broad flexibility, including "deniability"—that is, that it should be possible to carry out operations in a way that would enable the President to deny he knew about them. The question of accountability for such operations was one of the basic issues raised in the recent examination of our intelligence activities. *Elizabeth Drew, "A Reporter at Large: Brzezinski," The New Yorker, May 1, 1978, p 112*

[1973, from *deny* + *-ability*]

► This term first appeared during the Watergate affair in reference to claims that the President was unaware of the wrongdoings of his subordinates.

den·imed ('den əmd), *adj.* wearing denim clothing.

By 7:30 the East and South cellblocks finish breakfast. The yard fills with denimed convicts streaming from the messhalls. *Edward Bunker, Harper's, Feb. 1972, p 40*

In front of the stage the denimed crowd drew into a solid mass after darkness. *The Times (London), Aug. 25, 1973, p 3*

[1968]

denturist, *n.* a dental technician who sells and fits false teeth, as distinguished from a licensed dentist.

In spite of major public support for denturists, on April 24 the provincial legislature voted 21-20 against legislation that would have granted them the right, which they hold in three provinces, to fit dentures for the public. *Andrew S. Harvey, "Nova Scotia," The Americana Annual 1973, p 508*

[1964, from *denture* + *-ist*]

denturism, *n.*: Bootleg dentistry—a dental laboratory technician illegally selling low-cost dentures directly to the public—had occurred sporadically in the U.S. for decades. Although these bootleg technicians had generally been kept under close surveillance, there were indications that denturism, as this activity was often called, might be expanding. *Lou Joseph, "Medicine: Dentistry," Britannica Book of the Year 1974, p 464*

de·ox·y·ri·bo·nu·cle·o·side (di:,ak sə,rai bou'nu:-kli: ə,said), *n.* a compound formed by the pentose sugar deoxyribose and a purine or pyrimidine base. It results from the removal of the phosphate group from a deoxyribonucleotide.

A communication by Berger, Tarien and Eichorn . . . describes proton magnetic resonance and optical spectroscopic studies of the interaction of the copper (II) acetate dimer with various ribonucleosides and deoxyribonucleosides. *"Metal Ions and Nucleic Acids," Nature, Oct. 20, 1972, p 429*

[1968, from *deoxyribo*se + *nucleoside*]

de·ox·y·ri·bo·nu·cle·o·tide (di:,ak sə,rai bou'nu:-kli: ə,taid), *n.* a nucleotide (compound that is the main constituent of nucleic acid) containing the pentose sugar deoxyribose.

As lability to alkali is a characteristic of ribonucleotides as opposed to deoxyribonucleotides, the next step was to see whether ribonucleases had the same effect, and so indeed it proved. *"Nucleic Acids: Finer Structure," Nature, Oct. 20, 1972, p 428*

[1964, from *deoxyribo*se + *nucleotide*]

Department D, the branch of the KGB (Soviet intelligence agency) that creates and disseminates distorted or false information to mislead foreign intelligence agents.

The document shows a number of similarities with other such forgeries, which are usually planted on foreign newspapers and are then given worldwide publicity, through the Soviet propaganda network. The KGB's Department "D" (for "disinformation") has nothing to learn from the CIA's department of dirty tricks, which has in the past distributed similarly crude political forgeries. *Victor Zorza, The Manchester Guardian Weekly, Feb. 22, 1976, p 1*

[1976, from Russian *dezinformatsiya* disinformation (used in the full name of the department)] See DISINFORM.

dependency-prone, *adj.* tending or likely to become psychologically dependent on a drug or drugs.

Drug users may be grouped into three categories. The first consists of dependency-prone persons who, because of psychological and personality problems, have become heavily immersed in drug use and drug subcultures. . . . The ghetto dweller, suffering the shock of cultural displacement and the hopelessness of a filthy slum, is in this category. *Norman E. Zinberg and John A. Robertson, Drugs and the Public, 1972, p 12*

[1969]

deprivation dwarfism, a condition of stunted physical growth in children due to the lack of affection or to other forms of emotional deprivation.

Furthermore, when these children are removed from their stressful surroundings, their growth hormone switches on again and they show typical catch-up growth. This phenomenon was first described under the name of deprivation dwarfism by Lytt I. Gardner of the Upstate Medical Center of the University of New York and by Robert M. Blizzard and his colleagues at the Johns Hopkins Hospital. *J. M. Tanner, "Growing Up," Scientific American, Sept. 1973, p 42*

[1969]

deprofessionalize, *v.t.* to make less oriented toward a profession or professions.

A Yale spokesman denied that the dismissal signalled a change in policy, but Mr. Brustein . . . saw it as part of a plan, supported by Yale's new president, A. Bartlett Giamatti, to "deprofessionalize" the school, opening it up to students not interested in theater careers and introducing academic courses in addition to dramatic skills. *The New York Times, June 25, 1978, Sec. 4, p 9*

[1978, back formation from *deprofessionalization*]

deprofessionalization, *n.:* For to Illich the barefoot doctors represent the brightest jewel in the crown of the "deprofessionalisation" of medicine. *John Loraine, Review of "The Expropriation of Health" by Ivan Illich, New Scientist, Dec. 12, 1974, p 835*

deprogram, *v.t.* to change the beliefs or convictions of (a person, especially a youth, who is thought to have been misled into joining a sect or cult), chiefly by forceful preaching and attempts at persuasion.

Joe Alexander Jr. had been scheduled to deprogram Mike. But he was delayed on another case and the initial task was left to a group of ex-Moonies. *John Cotter, "Moonism: There Isn't an Easy Way Out," Daily News (New York), Dec. 3, 1975, p 54*

Vigilantes have engaged in kidnaping and "deprogramming" U.S. members of oddball religious groups for years. *Time, Dec. 18, 1978, p 52*

[1973, from *de-* do the opposite of + *program, v.*]

deprogrammer, *n.:* Ted Patrick, who calls himself a "deprogrammer" of wayward young people, was found guilty last night of falsely imprisoning two young Denver women. *"De-Programmer of Youth Guilty," The New York Times, May 3, 1974*

deprogramming, *n.:* In an interview Mr Heys told me that he has trained about four deprogrammers through the use of the POWER [Peoples Organized Workgroup on Ersatz Religions] manual and said that "several" successful deprogrammings have been carried out. *Michael Horsnell, "Yard's interest in Anti-cult body," The Times (London), April 4, 1977, p 4*

deradicalize, *v.t.* to cause to abandon or retreat from an extreme position in politics.

Today [David] Obst's [a literary agent] cigars are longer than his hair, and he admits that hobnobbing with publishing fat cats has tended to deradicalize him. *"Agent for Disaster," Newsweek, Jan. 6, 1975, p 60*

[1971]

deradicalization, *n.:* The New York Review, citadel of New Left politics, had gone too far for too long. Somebody somewhere had to expose this intellectually treasonous, anti-American publication and the new tough-minded *Commentary* was the appropriate site.... As another chapter in *Commentary*'s de-radicalization process, there was not a shadow of a doubt about the eventual outcome of "The Case." *Esquire, April 1972, p 112*

derecognize, *v.t.* to withdraw recognition or formal acknowledgment of (a country, etc.).

The nervousness stems primarily from the fact that the United States, the Taiwanese government's staunchest ally and protector, will probably extend full diplomatic recognition, either this year or next, to the Chinese Communist government in Peking and will simultaneously "derecognize" Taiwan. *Robert Shaplen, "Letter from Taiwan," The New Yorker, June 13, 1977, p 72*

[1972, from *de-* do the opposite of + *recognize*]

derecognition, *n.:* How many of these pacts could or should survive "derecognition"? ... How could the U.S. continue to supply arms to a government whose legitimacy it no longer formally recognizes? Government lawyers have been preparing briefs on these and other questions, and the State Department has retained some private law firms, including Lord, Day & Lord in New York City, as "consul-

tants" to study the legal ramifications of derecognition. *Time, Nov. 6, 1978, p 48*

deregulate, *v.t.* to remove controls from; free from regulation or control.

Dr Whitehead suggested 'de-regulating radio'—that is, to impose no requirements at all for community service as a condition for licence-holding on a long-term basis. *Brenda Maddox, "The Quarrel Between Government and Television in America," The Listener, March 9, 1972, p 296*

The White House also sought to persuade Congress and the courts to deregulate the price of gas. *James Ridgeway, "The U.S. Energy Crisis," Britannica Book of the Year 1974, p 289*

[1963, back formation from *deregulation*]

deregulator, *n.:* The deregulators are not uncaring or unthinking. To them, the choice is between excessive, strangling regulation and something less. *Jay Palmer, "Time Essay: The Rising Risks of Regulation," Time, Nov. 27, 1978, p 87*

deregulatory, *adj.:* They ran up against a team of American negotiators in full deregulatory flight, adamant that they were not going to be deflected from their main demand to have cheap fares at once, whatever the effect might be on the airlines. *The Times (London), March 22, 1978, p 23*

Dergue (dərg), *n.* Usually **the Dergue.** the socialist ruling council of Ethiopia, established as the provisional government after the overthrow of Emperor Haile Selassie in 1974.

The military administration, the Dergue, has ... announced a jargon-heavy political programme which included the rights to form political parties and to demonstrate (provided such activities were "anti-feudal, anti-bureaucratic, anti-capitalistic and anti-imperialistic"). *"Ethiopia—the Revolution Yet to Come," The Manchester Guardian Weekly, May 2, 1976, p 10*

[1975, from Amharic, literally, committee] Also spelled DIRGUE.

Derivatives. ► A frequently-used method of creating words is by derivation. The process of derivation forms new words by the addition of a word element, such as a prefix, suffix, or combining form, to an already-existing word, as in DELAWYER, the verb (from the prefix *de-* added to the noun *lawyer*) and DELAWYERIZATION (from the further addition of the suffix *-ization*). Such words are classified as derivatives as distinguished from COMPOUNDS, which are formed by *combining* separate words.

Many derivatives are included because their meanings differ considerably from the words on which they are formed. The noun DESERTIFICATION was derived from *desert* and the suffixal word element *-ification* (probably on the model of such words as *fructification* and *ossification*). The verb DEMYTHIFY was derived from the noun *myth* by the addition of *de-* and the suffixal word element *-ify*. Often a derivative spawns new derivatives: the verb DEREGULATE, a back formation from DEREGULATION (derived from *de-* + *regulation*) gave rise to the noun DEREGULATOR and the adjective DEREGULATORY. In this book many derivatives are listed without a definition below the main entry but have a quotation appended to show their use.

Many established word elements in English continue to be active in producing new derivatives, although some seem to be currently more productive than others. Among these are *anti-*, *co-*, *de-*, *non-*, *post-*, *pre-*, *re-*, *sub-*, and *un-*. The form *eco-*, popular during the 1960's in the special sense "of the environment; ecological," continued during the 1970's to be a source of such formations as ECODOOM, ECOFREAK, ECOMONE, ECOTAGE, and ECOTECTURE. Similarly, the form *mini-*, meaning "small; miniature," continued to be used in derivatives such as MINIBUDGET, MINICALCULATOR, MINICOURSE, MINIFESTIVAL, MININUKE, and MINI-SERIES.

Some current formations of derivatives as nouns include *-al* (RECUSAL), *-ation* (INDEXATION), *-ee* (COHABITEE), *-eer* (LEAFLETEER), *-er* (STOCKER), *-ism* (HEIGHTISM), *-ie* (TRANNIE), *-ity* (COOPERATIVITY), *-ization* (CONSUMERIZATION), *-ship* (RIDERSHIP), *-y* (TEENY). Combining forms used to form nouns include *-gram* (LEXIGRAM, MAILGRAM), *-ectomy* (LUMPECTOMY, VESTIBULECTOMY), and *-ologist* (CHOREOLOGIST, HAIROLOGIST, VATICANOLOGIST). The noun suffix *-IZATION* acquired a new meaning (the transfer of power to an ethnic or national group, as in MOROCCANIZATION) along with its corresponding verb form *-IZE*.

Suffixes and other word elements forming adjectives include *-able* (IMAGEABLE), *-al* (HADAL), *-esque* (FANONESQUE), *-ian* (STRANGELOVIAN), *-ic* (CYTOSOLIC), *-ish* (FUELISH), *-less* (VICTIMLESS), *-proof* (LEAKPROOF), *-y* (SPACY). Other examples of derivative elements are the verb suffixes *-fy* (GENTRIFY, INSONIFY, TECHNIFY), and *-ize* (PRIORITIZE, STRATEGIZE, SUBOPTIMIZE), and the adverbial suffix *-ally* (CLIOMETRICALLY, COUNTERPHOBICALLY).

Derivatives were especially prominent contributors to the language in the fields of physics and biology. The technical suffix *-on*, meaning "elementary unit or particle," was used to produce AXION, GLUON, INSTANTON, LUXON, POMERON, PSION, and TARDYON. The discovery of many new enzymes stimulated use of the suffix *-ase*, meaning "enzyme" (originally abstracted from *diastase*, the enzyme that helps change starch to sugar), as in EXCISIONASE, GYRASE, PRONASE, and ATPASE. Soil taxonomy established the suffix *-sol* (from Latin *solum* "soil") specifically to coin names for ten of the common types of soils, such as ARIDISOL, HISTOSOL, INCEPTISOL, and VERTISOL.

der·mal·op·ti·cal vision (dər mə'lɑp tə kəl), technical name for EYELESS SIGHT.

It is not clear from this paper just which parapsychological phenomena "obviously do happen"; the only ones which the authors unambiguously support as authentic, such as Kirlian photography and Rosa Kuleshova's "dermaloptical vision"—the alleged ability to "see" colours by touching them—are explicitly stated not to be parapsychological. *Anita Gregory, "Forum: Soviet Notebook: Crackdown on Parapsychology," New Scientist, Feb. 13, 1975, p 398*

[1972, from *dermal* + *optical*]

der·ma·to·glyph ('dər mə tə‚glif *or* dər'mæt ə‚glif), *n.* one of the surface lines, markings, or patterns of the skin.

Besides uncovering factors that contribute to the molding of individual dermatoglyphs, Green hopes studies of skin cells in culture will provide clues to greater mysteries of control of cell movement and of local influences on development. *Science News, July 8, 1978, p 24*

[1970, back formation from *dermatoglyphics* the study of skin markings, from Greek *dérmatos* skin + *glyphikós* of carving]

der·ri·ère-garde (‚de ri'er'gɑrd), *n.* another name for ARRIÈRE-GARDE.

[Alec] Wilder has steadily applied these principles to his own work, which comprises an astonishing canon. He has with amusement, called himself "the president of the derrière-garde," but he is a unique and adventurous composer who has written a huge body of music, both popular and formal, most of it nearly unknown. *Whitney Balliett, "Profiles: Alec Wilder, The President of the Derrière-Garde," The New Yorker, July 9, 1973, p 37*

[1963, from French *derrière* behind + *garde* guard (as in *avant-garde*); probably formed in English]

DES, abbreviation of *diethylstilbestrol*.

Several women told the panel that cancer had claimed the lives of their "DES daughters" and another woman whose mother had taken DES during pregnancy, blamed the drug for the cancer operation last year that left her unable to bear children. *"New Birth Pill: A Limited Use?" New York Post, Feb. 28, 1975, p 21*

DES has been wrapped in controversy for years. Just last month an administrative law judge recommended that the Food and Drug Administration order an end to its use as a growth stimulant in beef cattle, where it is widely used to add extra pounds before slaughter. *Michael J. Conlon, "Cancer Link in Daughters of DES Users," City News (New York), Oct. 5, 1978, p 20*

[1972]

de·school·er (di:'sku:l ər), *n.* a person who advocates the elimination of compulsory schools and their replacement with voluntary learning centers.

Unless the deschoolers were exceedingly skillful their efforts would be dysfunctional because the resulting society would be even less able to deal with oppressive authoritarianism. *Michael Cooper, Forres, Morayshire, "Letters: Ivan Illich," The Listener, Dec. 30, 1971, p 907*

From deschoolers and free schoolers, from the radical right and the radical left, the education system is under attack, and so are the teachers who work in it. *Stephen Jessel, "Growing Point," The Times (London), Oct. 11, 1972, p 12*

[1970, from *deschool*, v. (1970) + *-er*]

des·er·ti·fi·ca·tion (‚dez ər tə fə'kei ʃən), *n.* the process of turning into arid land or desert, especially by the encroachment of a neighboring desert or through excessive grazing or cultivation.

The creation of deserts or desert-like conditions is termed desertification. Generally thought of as the degradation of lands by natural and human means, desertification results in the diminution or destruction of the land's biological productivity. The process of desertification is at least as old as civilization but only recently has it been recognized as a serious global problem. *Science News, Oct. 29 1977, p 282*

The single worst problem in developing countries is the destruction of forests and agricultural land. This is the same pattern that led to the "desertification" of Africa's Sahel region and a conservatively estimated 100,000 deaths. *William J. Holstein, "Ecological Time Bomb Ticking in Third World," Athens News, Nov. 12/13, 1978, p 7*

[1973, from *desert* + *-ification* a making or causing to become] See GREEN BELT.

desex, *v.t. U.S.* to remove sexual or sexist references from.

Firemen will be fire fighters and kennelmen will become kennel attendants in the latest round of official "desexing." The city Civil Service Commission Wednesday approved the "desexing" of 170 job titles in an effort to eliminate sex discrimination. *"Job Titles 'Desexed' by City," The Tuscaloosa News (Alabama), Sept. 15, 1974, p 5c*

On a printed form not yet completely desexed, all plebes [at West Point] were asked: "What was the highest rank you attained in the Boy Scouts?" Women have been integrated into the barracks, but the Army has built separate lavatories, and both sexes will be required to wear bathrobes in the hallways. *"The Sexes: Beauties and the Beast," Time, July 19, 1976, p 74*

[1974, from *de-* remove + *sex*, or extended from earlier senses: a. to castrate or spay (OEDS 1911); b. to deprive of sexual characteristics or appeal (1962)] Compare DEGENDER.

des·i ('dez i:), *n. U.S.* short for DESIGNATED HITTER.

(No one has yet suggested an effective estoppage or cease-and-desist for the sportswriters who have begun to refer to the tenth man as the "desi.") This year, the American League bashed 1,552 homers, as against its 1971 total of 1,484 — the designated hitters again making the difference. *Roger Angell, "The Sporting Scene," The New Yorker, Nov. 19, 1973, p 184*

[1973]

designated hitter, *U.S. Baseball.* a tenth player who may be named in the lineup to bat for the pitcher anywhere in the batting order.

In his first winning move, Robinson entered his own name in the Indians' line-up as designated hitter — then stepped up to the plate in his first turn at bat and belted one of those home runs that will live in legend and in the memories of the 56,000 roaring fans who saw it. *Newsweek, April 21, 1975, p 57*

[1973] *Abbreviation:* DH

▶ The use of a designated hitter was introduced by the American League early in 1973. Since its adoption, sportswriters have suggested that other specialists, such as a designated runner (who would run for the catcher) and a second designated hitter, also be added to the traditional nine-player baseball team.

designer, *adj.* designed by and bearing the signature of a noted fashion designer.

Neither will you refer to your pants as slacks, trousers or cut-offs. But *jeans* are OK. Especially *designer jeans*. *Liz Rittersporn, "Fashion Vocabulary," Daily News (New York), Jan. 21, 1979, p 5*

"About 26 percent of the total Mark V's in 1979 are designer cars," said Thomas Green, Ford's custom-car marketing manager. "The image of the designers has been a tremendously successful marketing approach." *Pamela G. Hollie, "Fashion Designers Find a New Market," The New York Times, Jan. 28, 1979, Sec. 12, p 14*

[1978]

des·mo·sine ('dez mə sain), *n.* an amino acid formed in elastic tissue as the linking medium that gives the tissue its elasticity and stability.

Elastin incorporated two previously unrecognized amino acids, which they named desmosine and isodesmosine (from an original Greek root word meaning "bond"). These two amino acids were found to perform cross-linking functions in elastin. *Russell Ross and Paul Bornstein, "Elastic Fibers in the Body," Scientific American, June 1971, p 49*

[1968, from Greek *desmós* band, bond + English *-ine* (chemical suffix)]

des·mo·some ('dez mə soum), *n.* a thickened part of the cell membrane by which epithelial cells are attached to each other.

The first suggestion that cells were linked by special channels came from electro-physiological experiments. Lanthanum staining and electron microscopy then demonstrated that definite structures, classified morphologically as either tight junctions, desmosomes, or gap junctions, existed between cells. *New Scientist, July 11, 1974, p 62*

[1968, from Greek *desmós* band, bond + English *-some* body]

destabilize, *v.t.* to render (a government) unstable or incapable of functioning.

There was little ideological difference between the two parties, but the BLP was reportedly somewhat more to the right . . . and less concerned about allegations of U.S. Central Intelligence Agency plots to "destabilize" Barbados and other governments in the region. *Sheila Patterson, "Barbados," Britannica Book of the Year 1977, p 163*

[1974, specialized sense of the verb "to make (anything) unstable, deprive (something) of stability"]

destabilization, *n.:* Between 1970 and 1973 the C.I.A. had spent five million dollars in Chile on "destabilization" (a euphemism for making it impossible for a government to govern). *Richard Harris, "Reflections: Secrets," The New Yorker, April 10, 1978, p 45*

desublimate, *v.t.* to divest of the ability to sublimate one's instinctive or primitive impulses.

For Rico is persistently, irremediably desublimated: weakwilled, anxious to please, full of doubts and scruples, and inevitably "underneath" in relation to the assorted sublimates with whom he comes in contact. *Giuliano Dego, "The Monday Book," Review of "The Two of Us" by Alberto Moravia, The Times (London), May 1, 1972, p 8*

[1969]

desynchronized sleep, see the quotation for the meaning.

The two distinct states of sleep that we all experience differ in so many ways that they are usually given two separate names. The state characterized by eye movements, dreams, and irregular, desynchronized brain waves is called D-sleep for dreaming or desynchronized sleep. Such sleep is also called rapid eye movement (REM) sleep, or paradoxical sleep, because it is very light in some ways and very deep in others. *Ernest L. Hartmann, "The Way We Sleep," The 1977 World Book Year Book, p 112*

[1974] Compare SYNCHRONIZED SLEEP.

dé·tente (dei'tant), *n.* the improvement of relations between countries, political groups, etc., that have opposing views or interests.

Kissinger's solution was detente (he wasn't the first to

come up with the idea, but he was the one to get it implemented). Detente, as the French writer Andre Fontaine neatly put it, was not the same as peace or else it would have been called peace. It was an arrangement whereby a combination of political, military, technical and commercial agreements were reached for the expressed purpose of preventing the sort of confrontation that would end in mutual annihilation. For a time, roughly between the summers of 1972 and 1975, the process was working. *The Manchester Guardian Weekly (The Washington Post section), July 10, 1977, p 17*

Working harder for détente than any other statesman, Tito this year visited Moscow, Peking and Washington. His formula for détente is a balance of forces between the Soviet Union and the United States, relative political stability within their alliances, progress toward disarmament and freedom for all nations to develop independently. *The New York Times Magazine, Dec. 3, 1978, p 182*

[1973, extended use from early 1900's sense of easing of tensions between nations, from French, literally, slackening]

▶ Since the mid-1960's, *détente* has been used chiefly in the sense of a positive and long-range policy of improving relations between competing nuclear powers especially through the negotiation of various agreements and treaties, the maintenance of open channels of communication, and the fostering of cultural and economic cooperation. Thus *détente* connotes the pursuit of a policy of amicable relations between countries at opposite ends of the political spectrum, rather than its original application to attempts that ease tensions between enemy nations.

During the 1970's the concept of *détente* became virtually the keystone of American foreign policy. To the United States, it was a goal to be achieved through meetings such as SALT I and SALT II. Détente with its agreements and treaties between the contending superpowers was intended as the new instrument to achieve security.

To the Soviet Union, détente meant essentially what a decade earlier went by the name of "peaceful coexistence," that is, the absence of open hostility and the maintenance of formal, bilateral relations between ideological adversaries for mutually advantageous purposes.

Despite the controversy over its meaning, détente as a policy has been pursued by the United States and the Soviet Union for a decade. Those who favor it predict that it will produce a CONVERGENCE (between the Communist and non-Communist societies); its opponents warn that détente will enable the Soviet Union to FINLANDIZE Western Europe. To prevent this and other fears from becoming reality, there was talk of LINKAGE of issues, including the issue of HUMAN RIGHTS, in the SALT negotiations, using the best BARGAINING CHIP available.

The reaction of the United States to the Soviet Union's invasion of Afghanistan in 1980 seemed to signal a temporary displacement of the policy of détente. Compare BALANCE OF TERROR. See CODE WORD.

de·tox ('di:ˌtɑks), *U.S.* —*n.* short for *detoxication* or

144

detoxification (used especially in reference to the part of a hospital or a clinic where alcoholics or drug addicts are treated).

"I went to detox again . . . and it's been five years since I came out and I haven't had a drink or pill since." *William Stockton, "Dual Addiction," The New York Times Magazine, Aug. 6, 1978, p 11*

—Sometimes I hear them howling from the hospital.
—The detox ward.
—Tied to the bed with beige clothes. *Donald Barthelme, "Momma," The New Yorker, Oct. 2, 1978, p 33*

—*v.t.* short for *detoxicate* or *detoxify*.

"They did get me detoxed and clean. They told me I was an alcoholic . . ." *William Stockton, "Dual Addiction," The New York Times Magazine, Aug. 6, 1978, p 38*

[1973 for verb; 1978 for noun]

developed, *adj.* having high industrial and commercial production; economically and technologically advanced or self-sufficient.

A company which wants to make money should not invest in a developed country. It should head for the Third World. *Frances Cairncross, The Manchester Guardian Weekly, Feb. 29, 1976, p 5*

The world's so-called "developed" section—Europe, Russia, North America, temperate South America, Australia, New Zealand, and Japan—had a total population of about 1.2 billion. *Robert C. Cook, "World Population," The 1978 World Book Year Book, p 443*

In the modern and developed economy there is a certain choice as to how resources—labor, land, capital, natural resources—will be organized for productive purposes. *John Kenneth Galbraith, Economic Development in Perspective, 1962, p 31*

[1962, from past participle of *develop*] Compare LESS DEVELOPED. See DEVELOPING.

developing, *adj.* not yet developed; lacking in technology or in capital, resources, etc., and often dependent on economic aid.

At stake was the critical issue of future economic cooperation between the OPEC countries, 14 developing states, and the industrial nations which included Canada, the U.S., Japan and the nine European Common Market countries. *Bernard Kaplan, "The World," Maclean's, Feb. 9, 1976, p 41*

Largely rural developing nations—like India, Brazil and Tunisia—realize that computers can speed the time it takes them to develop into industrialized powerbrokers. *Science News, Sept. 23, 1978, p 214*

Developing countries, I have suggested, can be thought of rather as beads being moved along a string. *John Kenneth Galbraith, Economic Development in Perspective, 1962, p 17*

[1962, from present participle of *develop*] Compare EMERGING.

▶ It is no longer fashionable to describe countries as simply rich or poor. The standards of description have gradually shifted during the 1960's and 70's from a dollars-and-cents evaluation of status to one that also considers technological advantage and achievement. It is thought less accurate to use the old terms *rich* and *poor*. It is decidedly less emotional to use the substitutes *developed, underdeveloped,* or *developing* if they are defined carefully. But they are, in effect, often confusing to many readers. An *underdeveloped* country is one having a low per-capita income and therefore a low standard of living with little or no accompanying technological and industrial development. Typically many countries of the THIRD WORLD are considered underdeveloped, and some of those with the greatest privation are grouped in a designation known as the FOURTH WORLD. However, a few of these countries are now oil-rich but industrially still underdeveloped. Some writers designate such countries as EMERGING or *developing*. The following quotations distinguish between *underdeveloped* and *developing*:

The basic need of the underdeveloped and developing countries is reflected in their struggle against poverty, ignorance and disease. *T. T. Solaru, "Publishing and the Developing Countries," The Times Literary Supplement, May 12, 1972, p 555*

Another fund was to be created by the end of 1973 to aid the underdeveloped regions of the Community, especially the south of Italy. Aid to developing nations was to be increased. *F. Roy Willis, "Europe," The Americana Annual 1973, p 286*

Current usage favors *developing* and *underdeveloped*, but some writers now dispense with both of these terms, using instead the designations *less developed country* (LDC) and *more developed country* (MDC).

All of these characterizations have their own deficiencies as is recognized by at least one writer who had a hand in initiating the new terminology:

How are we to define the "poor" nations? The phrase "under-developed" is not very satisfactory for it groups together very different types of under-development. India and Pakistan, for instance, are heirs of a great and ancient civilization and have many of the other attributes — in art, literature, and administration — of developed states, even though they are very poor. Other areas — one thinks of the Congo — are developed in virtually no sense at all. *Barbara Ward, The Rich Nations and the Poor Nations, 1962, p 37*

A more recent grouping of the disparity among nations is in the designations NORTH and SOUTH, but for the most part the concept of a changing economic evaluation of nations has escaped the dictionary maker's notice. Sometimes a word or two is entered but the range of vocabulary with its parallel terms is omitted.

Development Decade, a ten-year program sponsored by the United Nations to promote the economic and social development of Third World countries. The first Development Decade was from 1961-70.

On the economic and social side, by contrast, the responsible heads of the main UN programmes laboured unceasingly throughout the year to put their machinery in good shape to meet the challenge of the Second Development Decade. *Leslie Aldous, "The United Nations and Its Specialized Agencies," The Annual Register of World Events in 1970 (1971), p 332*

[1970] See the note under DEVELOPING.

Devil's Triangle, another name for BERMUDA TRIANGLE.

Ships and planes disappear, time skips a beat, and earthlings board extraterrestrial craft, all in the Atlantic region known as the Bermuda, or Devil's Triangle — or so a continuing stream of books insists. *Illustration legend, "Triangle Books in Winner's Circle," 1976 Collier's Encyclopedia Year Book (1975), p 161*

[1975]

devolatilize, *v.t., v.i.* to make or become free of volatile matter.

The CO_2 acceptor process uses lignite rather than coal. The moisture content of the lignite is removed by flash drying, and the lignite is devolatilized and transferred into the gasifier unit. *Hubert E. Risser, "Coal Gasification," McGraw-Hill Yearbook of Science and Technology 1970, p 151*

[1965, back formation from *devolatilization* (1963), *de-* opposite of + *volatilization* (1600's)]

devolatilization, *n.:* Complete devolatilization of the coal was not achieved, the amount of volatile matter remaining being equivalent to 20 to 70% of the original volatile matter content. *R. Nicholson and K. Littlewood, Sheffield, England, "Letters to Nature: Plasma Pyrolysis of Coal," Nature, April 21, 1972, p 398*

devolution, *n.* an increased degree of self-government granted to the elected legislative assembly of any element of the United Kingdom, especially Scotland and Wales.

The demand for devolution — the transfer of limited powers from Westminster to elected assemblies in Scotland and Wales — was conceded by the Labour Government not out of conviction but to stem the threatening tide of nationalism, and the legislation that will permit the two assemblies to be set up is therefore viewed with some cynicism even by its intended beneficiaries. *James Lewis, The Manchester Guardian Weekly, Sept. 17, 1978, p 3*

[1976] Compare POWER-SHARING.

► This term was originally used at the turn of the century in the context of Irish politics as an alternative to Home Rule.

devolve, *v.t.* (in British politics) to grant under a policy of devolution.

Most of those who want complete "devolution," and many of those who want more powers than Mr. Wilson is proposing to devolve, have joined the Scottish Nationalist Party. *Robert B. Semple, Jr., "Separatism Posing Challenges for Wilson," The New York Times, Jan. 24, 1976, p 6*

[1976]

devolver, *n.:* "It is hardly possible to proceed with the present proposals," Mr Mackintosh says, "when there are prominent opponents in the Cabinet and among English backbench MPs on both sides of the House, when the devolvers among Scottish Labour and Liberal MPs can scarcely bear to commend the proposals, and the Secretary of State almost breaks into tears every time he has to defend the project. *Ronald Faux, "Scots Labour Chiefs Decide Not to Meet 'Rebel' Group," The Times (London), Jan. 12, 1976, p 2*

dex, *n. Slang.* a tablet of dextroamphetamine, a stimulant. Also called DEXIE.

Gets drunk once a month on 3.2 beer. Pops a dex or a bennie occasionally, especially during exam week. Tried marijuana at a be-in last summer and would do it again if someone had it lying around. Likewise, peyote. *Sherman B. Chickering, "Staying Hip: 1966, Age and Academic Status: 18; College Freshman," Harper's, Sept. 1971, p 63*

dexed

[1966, short for *Dexedrine*, a trademark for *dextroamphetamine*]

dexed, *adj. Slang.* stimulated by dextroamphetamine pills; high on dexes.

Thus, your basic Tequila Sunrise is not merely one of those chic, absurdly yin, innocuously thirst-quenching drinks (so prized by dehydrated athletes, entertainers, and heavily dexed writers working against viciously unfair deadlines), it is also Bombsville-oh-roonie. *Terry Southern, "The Rolling Stones' U.S. Tour: Riding the Lapping Tongue," Saturday Review, Aug. 12, 1972, p 25*

[1972]

dexie or **Dexie,** *n. Slang.* another name for DEX.

"Go Ask Alice," records the entry of 15-year-old Alice into the world of drugs and sex . . . and finally death (perhaps murder, possibly self-induced) after several months of taking "Dexie," marijuana, "copilots," LSD, heroin, everything. *Webster Schott, "What Do YA's Read?," The New York Times Book Review, May 7, 1972, Part II, p 1*

[1967, short for *Dexedrine;* see DEX]

DH, abbreviation of DESIGNATED HITTER.

The New York Yankees and Kansas City Royals have each tried a half-dozen men as DH (although the Yanks may have found their No. 1 in newly acquired Jim Hart). *Jim Hackleman, Honolulu Star-Bulletin, April 23, 1973, p C-1*

[1973]

diabetologist, *n.* a specialist in diabetes or diabetic disorders.

Meeting recently in Boston, 34 of the nation's leading diabetologists joined forces to denounce the FDA warning [against the use of tolbutamide, an antidiuretic drug] and question the study upon which it was based. *Time, Dec. 21, 1970, p 41*

[1965, from *diabetes* + *-ologist* specialist in]

Dial-A- or **dial-a-,** a combining form used, often as part of a trademark, to designate a service obtained by dialing a particular telephone number.

dial-a-bus: Dial-a-bus, an innovation of London transport operates in Hampstead Garden Suburb. The 16-seat vehicles, which run every 15 minutes, pick up customers at their homes and at several fixed stops, and the driver will also stop when hailed if it is safe to do so. *Picture legend, "Transportation," 1976 Britannica Yearbook of Science and the Future (1975), p 408*

Dial-a-Busy: In Virginia, the Chesapeake and Potomac Telephone Co. is testing for 90 days a service named "Dial-a-Busy." A patron who wants no calls dials a number which activates equipment that sounds a fake busy signal if someone phones. *Time, Oct. 10, 1977, p 36*

Dial-A-Joke: The telephone company sponsors Dial-A-Joke and about a dozen other such service announcements. What is its newest? *Dial-a-Trivia. New York Post, Jan. 5, 1979, p 18*

Dial-A-Meal: Dial-A-Meal operates from kitchens in Knightsbridge but when John Hildreth expands it will be into restaurants rather than to buy more kitchen premises. *Mirabel Walker, "Takeaway Meals Take Off," The Times (London), April 10, 1972, p 14*

dial-a-park: When visiting the greater Washington metropolitan area, you can call for up-to-date information about activities in National Capitol Parks. The dial-a-park number is 426-6975. *Southern Living, May 1973, p 18*

dial-a-programme: Who would pay? Commercial interests might, if they were allowed to link up a whole city, so that Rediffusion, for example, installed its dial-a-programme system in Liverpool or a comparable area. *The Listener, Sept. 20, 1973, p 365*

dial-a-ride: To accommodate the new commuting patterns Altschuler foresees the need for much more flexible modes of transportation—he mentions car pools, buses, dial-a-ride. *National Review, Aug. 15, 1975, p 810*

Dial-A-Shrink: "In San Francisco one has been able to buy conversation—more or less sensitively tuned instant friendship—as reported in *Psychiatric News* previously. Now New York . . . not to be outdone, has a new service for the emotionally forlorn—'Dial-A-Shrink'." *Thomas Szasz, The Myth of Psychotherapy, 1979, p 209*

[1961, apparently abstracted from earlier (1957) trademark *Dialaphone*, a machine dialing a telephone automatically]

dia·logue des sourds (dya'lɔ:g de 'sur), a discussion in which the participants pay no attention to each other's arguments.

Steering the discussion back to Minuteman, the Americans sought to explain that all elements of each side's strategic forces must be "survivable"; for one element—Minuteman, say—to become vulnerable would create dangerous anxieties, hence instability. The Russians replied, in effect, Why are you so worried about Minuteman when your sea-based forces will always remain intact and available for the second-strike role? It was a *dialogue des sourds. John Newhouse, "Annals of Diplomacy: SALT," The New Yorker, May 26, 1973, p 86*

[1963, from French, DIALOGUE OF THE DEAF]

dialogue of the deaf, translation of DIALOGUE DES SOURDS.

Better communication is no panacea for every industrial dispute. . . . But English reserve does seem to lead, all too often, to a muted dialogue of the deaf. *The Times (London), Feb. 15, 1974, p 14*

[1974]

dial-up, *adj.* of or relating to access by telephone lines to a computer terminal or other electronic equipment.

The Post Office's involvement includes the holding of the pages of information at a computer centre, and the provision of the dial-up service, which enables users to call up the information they want via their telephones. *The Times (London), July 28, 1978, p 17*

[1972, originally referring to the use of a dial telephone to initiate a station-to-station telephone call]

diamond ring, a great ring of sunlight that appears briefly when the moon covers the solar disk during an eclipse.

There is a considerable drop in temperature, and, about half a minute before totality, things become much darker, the air seems to be very still, the famous "diamond ring" appears followed by Baily's Beads, and just at the instant of totality the light fades completely, the corona appears, and the eclipse is total. The diamond ring and Baily's Beads are caused by the Sun shining through the valleys on the limb of the Moon. *Peter Macdonald, "Eclipse of the Century," New Scientist, July 12, 1973, p 91*

[1963]

di·az·o·troph (dai'æz ə,traf), *n.* any nitrogen-fixing bacterium that converts diazo compounds (compounds having two nitrogen atoms, N_2, united with carbon) into nitrates.

The term "diazotroph" refers to an N_2-fixing organism. Two well-known and much-studied diazotrophs are *Clostridium*, a strict anaerobe (grows and fixes N_2 only in the absence of O_2), and *Azotobacter*, an aerobe (grows and fixes N_2 only in presence of O_2); both are widely distributed in soils. *Ralph W. F. Hardy, "Nitrogen Fixation," McGraw-Hill Yearbook of Science and Technology 1977, p 17*

[1977, from *diazo* + *-troph* one that nourishes (from Greek *trophê* nourishment)]

di·cho·phase ('dai kou,feiz), *n. Biology.* a stage during the interphase following cell division when the cell may either differentiate or proceed toward another division.

After mitosis the new daughter cells have to decide whether to go through the whole cycle again producing more daughter cells, or to become specialised and perform a specific tissue function, ultimately to die as the nucleus degenerates. This time of decision is known as the dichophase. *David Moreau and William Bullough, "A Cellular Switch to Stop Cancer," New Scientist, Oct. 4, 1973, p 28*

[1964, from Greek *dicho-* in two, separate + English *phase*]

dictabelt, *n.* a plastic belt on which dictation is recorded in a dictating machine.

Special prosecutor Jaworski states that the dictabelts the White House finally surrendered likewise have blanks at the most important spots. *Between the Lines—The Wells News Service (Newtown, Pa.), Feb. 15, 1974*

My secretaries in New York, Los Angeles, Washington, and San Francisco . . . get dicta-belts from me every day. *New Statesman, Sept. 5, 1975, p 284*

[1967, from *dicta*tion + *belt*]

did·dly-bop ('did li:,bap), *Especially U.S. Slang.* —*n.* a light, rhythmic sound.

Smiling thinly, he sabotages each phrase; sometimes by putting small diddly-bops into the accompaniment, sometimes by asking her sharply not to touch the piano. *Richard Eder, "Stage: Keyboard Fun With Borge," The New York Times, Oct. 5, 1977, p 28*

—*adj.* light; bland; dull.

I want to have coke up my nose, not this diddly-bop candy. *B. Deneshaw, Canton, N.Y., in a Letter to the Editor, High Times, Jan. 1979, p 8*

[1965, perhaps from *diddle* to trifle away + *bop*, as in *bebop*]

did·dy-bop ('did i,bap), *v.i. U.S. Slang.* to walk with a light, rhythmic motion, as if dancing.

To top off the show, Smith's 19-year-old sister Doris diddy-bopped out in a 1972 bridal outfit: a strapless white Lurex gown worn with a white fake-fur jacket and a gauzy veil with a feather stuck in the side. *"Modern Living: Soul on Seventh Avenue," Time, Aug. 7, 1972, p 52*

[1968, probably imitative]

die-in, *n.* a public demonstration in which participants lie as if dead, imitating the effects of a lethal weapon.

About 100 members of PANG (People Against Nerve Gas) stage a "die-in" on a street in downtown Seattle, Wash., May 17, 1970, to protest the shipment of nerve gas through the area. *Picture legend, "United States," Britannica Book of the Year 1971, p 766*

[1970, patterned on earlier (1960's) *sit-in*, etc.]

di·e·lec·tro·pho·re·sis (,dai i,lek trou fə'ri: sis), *n.* a process that forces uncharged particles in a liquid to move toward the charged area of a nonuniform electric field, used for separating mixtures, such as a suspension of living and dead cells.

Dipolar molecules experience a net force in a strongly inhomogeneous electric field and migrate toward the region of maximum absolute field strength. This migration, called dielectrophoresis, will continue until a concentration gradient reflecting equilibrium with diffusion is attained. *Maurice Eisenstadt and I. Herbert Scheinberg, "Dielectrophoresis of Macromolecules," Science, June 23, 1972, p 1335*

[1968, probably blend of *dielectric* conducting across, nonconducting + *electrophoresis*]

diesel, *v.i. U.S.* (of an internal-combustion engine) to continue firing after the ignition has been shut off.

We also found that when hot, the engine would often diesel (run on) after the ignition was switched off. *Popular Science, Jan. 1971, p 16*

[1971, verb use of *diesel* or *Diesel, n.* (OEDS 1894), a type of internal-combustion engine in which such brief idling occurs]

dieseling, *n.:* And my wife's car is a grade-A gasser. She comes home from the supermarket, parks in the garage, . . . remembers that she left her pocketbook in the car, walks back to the garage—and finds the engine still gasping, chugging, and slobbering like one of the bulldogs after a run at a squirrel. Around Motown, they call that phenomenon "dieseling." If we wanted a diesel, we'd buy one. *"Business and Finance: The Costs of Cleanliness," Newsweek, Dec. 4, 1972, p 99*

die·so·hol ('di: zə,hɔ:l), *n.* a mixture of diesel oil and ethyl alcohol, used as fuel for diesel engines.

As prices for petroleum products rise the economics should become favorable for gasohol and for the diesel fuel-ethanol combination, called diesohol. *John Patrick Jordan, "Agriculture," 1979 Britannica Yearbook of Science and the Future (1978), p 313*

[1978, from *diesel* + alc*ohol*] Compare GASOHOL.

dietary fiber, roughage in vegetables and fruits, eaten to promote health.

Dietary fiber was the latest dietary component to be hailed as the one that does it all. Dietary fiber should not be confused with crude fiber; it includes structural polymers of cell walls, celluloses, hemicelluloses, pectin, lignin, and undigested polysaccharides, and may be three to seven times more plentiful in a diet than the crude fiber included in food composition tables. *Mina W. Lamb, "Nutrition," 1978 Britannica Yearbook of Science and the Future (1977), p 319*

The researchers gave one group of rats a cholesterol-free, chemically defined liquid diet, another group of rats the same diet with cholesterol and still a third group of rats a standard formula diet (in order to serve as a control to the other two groups). By design all three diets were fiber-free, since dietary fiber may protect against colon cancer, and provided equivalent caloric intakes. *Science News, Jan. 20, 1979, p 37*

digital

[1976] Often shortened to FIBER.

digital, *adj.* displaying information electronically in the form of numerical figures.

Advances in microelectronics technology have greatly reduced the cost of solid-state digital watches. These watches, which use electronic number displays rather than the conventional dial face, were primarily a luxury item until 1974. *"Technology," Encyclopedia Science Supplement (Grolier) 1975, p 388*

As we passed through Times Square bound for the IRT [subway], a digital thermometer informed us with a twinkle that it was ninety degrees. *"The Talk of the Town," The New Yorker, Aug. 2, 1976, p 21*

—*n.* a digital device, especially a timepiece, thermometer, or gauge.

Everyone is now sobering up as to the projections for digitals. Of 50 million watches of all kinds sold in the United States this year, perhaps 1.5 million will be digitals. *Isadore Barmash, "Upsurge in Digital Watches," The New York Times, July 20, 1975, Sec. 3, p 1*

[1964, extended from the sense of "using digits" (as in *digital computer*)] See LIGHT-EMITTING DIODE.

digitization, *n.* the conversion of data into numerals or numerical form.

There are two distinct processes: one involves the digitization of contours (using a D-Mac electronic digitizing table) to convert a pre-existing contour map into machine-readable form; the contours can then be re-created at a different scale or on a different projection or in conjunction with different secondary information, using computer-driven draughting devices. *F. Hackman, "Scaling the Heights," Geographical Magazine, Aug. 1972, p 778*

[1966, from *digitize* (1953) to convert into digits + -*ation*]

di·hy·dro·tes·tos·ter·one (dai₁hai drou tes'tas tə-roun), *n.* the biologically active form of the male sex hormone testosterone, produced by addition of two hydrogen atoms, and considered to be responsible for enlargement of the prostate gland.

In the time of "the sere, the yellow leaf," the testicles send decreasing amounts of testosterone to the prostate. But testosterone is metabolized, along the way, to another form of male hormone, dihydrotestosterone (DHT). *Gilbert Cant, The New York Times Magazine, Feb. 16, 1975, p 65*

[1970, from *dihydro-* combined with two atoms of hydrogen + *testosterone*]

dilatancy, *n.* the expansion of rocks under increasing groundwater pressure, believed to be a precursor of earthquakes. *Often used attributively.*

The onset of dilatancy can . . . be detected from observations of ground surface level changes, inclination changes, density changes (through gravitational effects), and magnetic changes, all of which stem from the slight volume change of the dilatant rock mass. *James Brander, "When Do Earthquakes Occur?" New Scientist, Feb. 12, 1976, p 342*

How do scientists explain these precursory changes? The dilatancy model, or theory, has offered the best explanation to date. . . . William F. Brace and his associates at the Massachusetts Institute of Technology (M.I.T.) in Cambridge showed in laboratory studies in the mid-1960s that tiny cracks open in a rock and it swells when forces squeeze it or pull it apart. Brace also showed that dilatancy

slows down the seismic waves passing through rocks, just as it presumably does in the earth's crust. Dilatancy also changes the electric resistance of rocks, another effect noted to occur just before the earthquake. *William J. Cromie, "Earthquake Early Warning," The World Book Science Annual 1976 (1975), p 157*

[1973, extended sense of the geological term (OED 1885) meaning the expansion of granular material, such as sand, caused by rearrangement of the particles]

Dillon's Rule, *U.S.* the rule that if a state contests the powers of a municipal corporation, the judicial decision will always favor the state.

The rule is named after the legal commentator John F. Dillon, and it grows out of the fact that this nation's Constitution does not mention the powers of cities but only the powers of states. The states establish cities as their own creatures, granting them, as Dillon's Rule has it, no powers other than those clearly implicit in the establishing statutes. *"The Talk of the Town," The New Yorker, March 17 1973, p 29*

[1973]

di·meth·yl·ni·tros·a·mine (dai'meθ əl nai'trou sə-mi:n), *n.* a cancer-producing chemical found in certain foods and in tobacco smoke.

Most German beers, and perhaps American brews too, contain trace quantities of dimethyl nitrosamine—a known animal carcinogen. The German Cancer Research Center in Heidelberg announced last week that it had tested 158 beers in a two-year study. *Science News, Jan. 20, 1979, p 40*

Then in August, 1971, a scientist at USDA's Eastern Regional Research Laboratory in Wyndmoor, Pennsylvania, made a shattering discovery. In two of ten samples of hot dogs obtained from a local supermarket, he discovered dimethylnitrosamine (DMN) at eighty parts per billion and forty-eight parts per billion, respectively, the highest levels of DMN ever found in meat up to that time. *Harrison Wellford, "Behind the Meat Counter," The Atlantic, Oct. 1972, p 90*

[1968, from *dimethyl* having two methyl radicals + *nitrosamine* an organic compound] *Abbreviation:* DMN or DMNA

di·mu·on ('dai₁myu: an), *n. Nuclear Physics.* a pair of muons (heavy nuclear particles) that may result from the decay of particles governed by the interactions of neutrinos at high energy.

Several explanations that involve only conventional processes and particles might be invoked to account for the dimuon events. One of the most obvious is the hypothesis that the second muon is created by the decay of a charged pion or kaon produced in the initial neutrino interaction. Because of the different densities of the two targets, however, muons from meson decays would be expected to originate in the liquid scintillator about four times more often than in the iron barrier. Actually the same number of dimuons was observed in the iron as in the liquid, and that ratio excludes the pion and kaon mechanisms. *David B. Cline, et al., "The Search for New Families of Elementary Particles," Scientific American, Jan. 1976, p 53*

[1975, from *di-* two + *muon*] Compare TRIMUON.

dingbat, *n. U.S. Slang.* a stupid or silly person. *Also used attributively.*

I must have the kind of face that builds instant confidence because four times out of five, some dingbat man-

148

ages to sit next to me and I find myself listening to a life story. *Ann Landers, The News (Mexico City), June 24, 1973, p 18*

[1971, extended sense of a slang word apparently related to *dingus* gadget, contraption, ultimately from Dutch or German *ding* thing]

▶ The earliest meaning of this word (mid-1800's) is roughly equivalent to "thingamajig" or "whatchamacallit." In the 1920's it was also applied occasionally to a tramp or hobo. The current sense was popularized, in part, by the American television character ARCHIE BUNKER and is reminiscent of earlier *ding-a-ling* (1960's), "a crazy person," which came from the idea "a person who hears imaginary bells". In Australian slang, *to be dingbats* means to be crazy or stupid. This may have significance because Archie Bunker is said to have been patterned after the British television character Alf Garnett and a similar character, Ocker, on Australian television.

dinner theater, a restaurant where a theatrical production is presented during or following dinner.

Some years ago, store owners discovered the lure of one-stop shopping. Today showmen are making the same discovery. In a converted pancake house in San Diego, a former laundry in Kansas City, a onetime illegal gambling casino in New Orleans and countless other locations, they are drawing packed houses to dinner theaters. *"Neil Simon for Supper," Time, June 3, 1974, p 52*

[1973] Compare CAFÉ THÉÂTRE.

di·ox·i·rane (dai'ak sə,rein), *n. Chemistry.* any of a new class of organic compounds consisting of two hydrogen, one carbon, and two oxygen atoms, believed to be important intermediaries in reactions that produce photochemical smog.

Richard Suenram and Frank Lovas of the US National Bureau of Standards detected dioxirane, the simplest member of the new family, using low temperature microwave spectroscopy during studies of the reaction between ethylene and ozone. *"Dioxirane Implicated in Photochemical Smog," New Scientist, June 22, 1978, p 325*

[1977, probably from *di-* two + *ox-* oxygen + *ring* +-*ane* (suffix used in names of hydrogenated carbon compounds)]

DI particle, another name for DEFECTIVE VIRUS.

Marcus and Sekellick studied DI particles that arise from vesicular stomatitis virus, which causes a cattle disease. The genetic material in that virus is a single strand of RNA, and most of the DI particles contain shorter pieces of that RNA. One set of DI particles, however, contains RNA consisting of two regions that can bind together into a double-stranded structure. *Science News, May 14, 1977, p 308*

[1977, abbreviation of *defective interfering particle*]

diploma tax, a tax imposed on Soviet citizens with academic training who wish to emigrate.

The large number of requests for "family reunion" through the Dutch Embassy, which handles Israeli affairs in Moscow, only increases. All pay an exit tax of 900 rubles, about $1000. The committee helps with this head tax. The ransom—the so called "diploma tax"—is another matter and cannot be paid abroad. It is based on the applicant's education (education belongs to the People), and has been

set as high as $60,000 in the case of one prizewinning scientist. The committee cannot help pay the diploma tax. It is too much like buying slaves. The precedent would be to stimulate extortion. *Herbert Gold, "The Soviet Jews Come Forward," The Atlantic, May 1973, p 92*

[1973] Also called EDUCATION TAX, EMIGRATION TAX, EXIT TAX.

diplomatic shuttle, an act or instance of engaging in SHUTTLE DIPLOMACY.

It was a diplomatic shuttle, but not exactly in the Kissinger mode: no custom-fitted Air Force jet, no phalanx of aides, bodyguards and reporters. British Envoy Ivor Richard last week hopped from capital to capital in southern and eastern Africa in a modest chartered twin-engined Hawker Siddeley executive jet. *"Rhodesia: Richard's Safari of Salvation," Time, Jan. 17, 1977, p 30*

[1976] Often shortened to SHUTTLE.

directed-energy weapon, another name for BEAM WEAPON.

There are a couple of hundred (overtrained) blue-eyed boys in Los Alamos, New Mexico, working on hunter-killer satellites and directed energy weapons like satellite-launched high-energy lasers. *Michael Thomas, "The Shroud of Turin," Rolling Stone, Jan. 11, 1979, p 78*

[1977]

Dirgue (dərg), *n.* a variant of DERGUE.

The crucial victim executed was General Aman Andom, until recently the chairman of the provisional military government or Dirgue. *"Executions in Ethiopia," The Manchester Guardian Weekly (The Washington Post section), Nov. 30, 1974, p 15*

[1974]

dirty, *adj.* (of a floating rate of exchange) manipulated by a country to influence the exchange rate of its currency in its own favor on the money markets.

As it is now the present system is a "dirty," or controlled, float. The Common Market countries which have agreed to a joint float intend to hold their currencies within a 2 1/4% band around the par values compared with a margin of 4 1/2% allowed for other world currencies. *The Auckland Star (N.Z.), March 31, 1973, p 10*

−*v.t.* to manipulate (a floating rate of exchange).

But the "hot money" men merely sat on the sidelines watching the action last week, and as a result there was precious little of it. Because trading was light, central bankers rarely had to "dirty" the float by intervening in the market to maintain the float's new relationships. *"Currency: Safely Floating," Newsweek, April 2, 1973, p 74*

[1973]

dirty tricks, underhanded actions or activity by government agents or political hirelings, designed to disrupt or subvert the machinery of an electoral campaign, a political convention, an established government, etc.

To my mind, the dirty tricks campaign run by the Committee to Reelect the President was far more sinister than the Watergate break-in and wiretapping. After all, those were illegal acts which, once discovered, could be dealt with; the dirty tricks campaign represented something more; it reflected an attitude, an unethical and odious attitude, toward the whole of political life. You could not bring the dirty tricks to a halt by arresting someone; you had to change the state of mind of almost everyone in the top ech-

149

elons of the campaign. *Stephen S. Leopold, "Inside the Watergate Hearings," Maclean's, Dec. 1973, p 66*

The dirty tricks more recently revealed—experimenting with LSD for use on enemies, or with potions to make Fidel Castro's beard fall out—have a long tradition in the secret police of colonizing forces. *Garry Wills, "The CIA From Beginning to End," The New York Review of Books, Jan. 22, 1976, p 28*

[1973] Compare BLACK ADVANCE.

▶ This usage attained wide currency during the Watergate hearings of 1973. However, the term's use in a political context is older. The following pre-Watergate quotation suggests that the term was established in U.S. government circles well before the date (1966) of the quotation itself:

Whether or not political control is being exercised, the more serious question is whether the very existence of an efficient C.I.A. causes the United States Government to rely too much on clandestine and illicit activities, back-alley tactics, subversion, and what is known in official jargon as "dirty tricks." *The Times (London), April 26, 1966, p 9*

The phrase *dirty trick* in the sense of a despicable or malicious act has been known since the 1600's. Used in the plural by CIA agents it became a euphemism and possibly a CODE WORD for sinister activities whose disclosure would have seriously tarnished the CIA's and the government's image.

dirty trickster: Is Charles Colson, famous dirty trickster and convert, a feigning Christian? I don't think so. I believe he may be the truest American Christian since Andrew Carnegie—the man Mark Twain took as the perfect specimen. *Gary Wills, " 'Born Again' Politics," The New York Times Magazine, Aug. 1, 1976, p 8*

disaggregative, *adj.* **1** broken down or separated into component parts.

Some of the differences between neoclassical economics and ecology . . . may be conveyed to the economist if he is asked to envision a disaggregative economics built *ab initio* around the existence of market imperfections. *Scott A. Boorman, "Mathematical Ecology and Its Place Among the Sciences," Review of "Geographical Ecology" by Robert H. MacArthur, Science, Oct. 27, 1972, p 393*

2 of or involving separate or discrete units.

In demonstrating the usefulness of a "system dynamics" approach to specific problems considered at a disaggregative level—as is done effectively in the papers on "DDT Movement in the Global Environment"; on "Mercury Contamination"; and on "The Eutrophication of Lakes"—this objective may have been achieved. *Michael Lloyd, Review of "Towards Global Equilibrium," edited by Dennis L. Meadows and Donella H. Meadows, New Scientist, March 22, 1973, p 680*

[1972, from *dis-* opposite of + *aggregative* collective (1600's)]

disaster film or **disaster movie,** a motion picture whose plot revolves around a catastrophic event.

It's not every disaster film that will cause audiences to long for the realism of *The Towering Inferno* . . . or the convincing effects of *Earthquake*. This movie [*City on Fire*] makes even *The Swarm* look good. *People Weekly, Oct. 22, 1979, p 26*

Danger can be presented in hundreds of ways that are not objectionable, without gore or sadism. The great success of the disaster movies proves this point. [*Mrs.*] *Ben Austin, Farmington, N.M., "Viewers on Violence," in "Letters," TV Guide, July 2, 1977, p A-7*

[1975]

dis·ci·pling (dəˈsai pliŋ), *n.* the practice in the neo-Pentecostal movement of grouping followers into small units under the guidance of a leader whom the disciples obey and are expected to give one tenth of their income to.

Leaders of the charismatic movement who oppose the teaching about discipling say that the seeds of a new denomination have already been planted. *The New York Times, Sept. 16, 1975, p 31*

Attributive use:

The two went to the nation's highest corrections officer and asked to take 12 prisoners out of confinement for two-week "discipling" sessions at Fellowship House, in Washington. *Gary Wills, "Born Again' Politics," The New York Times Magazine, Aug. 1, 1976, p 48*

[1975] ▶ The OED records *discipling* as a verbal noun and participial adjective with several obsolete senses derived from the obsolete verb *disciple*]

dis·cli·na·tion (ˌdis kləˈnei ʃən), *n.* (in the geometric model of a solid) displacement by rotation rather than by linear motion (translation).

The study of disclinations has its origins in the physics of crystalline solids, but as it happens disclinations are seldom observed in ordinary three-dimensional crystals such as those of metals. They do appear in the arrays of oriented molecules called liquid crystals. What is more, they are important structural elements in many ordered materials other than conventional crystals, such as the protein coats of viruses. Disclinations can even be observed in the pattern of fingerprints, in the pelts of striped animals such as zebras and in basketwork. *William F. Harris, "Disclinations," Scientific American, Dec. 1977, p 130*

[1972, from *dis-* (as in *dislocation*) + in*clination*] Compare DISPIRATION.

disclosing agent or **disclosing tablet,** a vegetable dye that is absorbed by plaque adhering to the teeth.

A sure-fire way to detect plaque is to use a "disclosing agent" (tablet or liquid) before or after brushing and flossing. When chewed or swished in the mouth, these agents stain the plaque, making it readily apparent . . . Dentists advise using a disclosing agent, at first, every time you clean your teeth, to detect hard-to-get areas. *Jean Carper, "A New and Better Way to Keep Your Teeth," The Reader's Digest, Feb. 1974, p 221*

[1972]

disco, *n.* music played in discotheques, especially such music with a strong bass rhythm and simple melody. *Often used attributively.*

The hustle, which is believed to have had its origins five years ago in the black and Puerto Rican bars of Queens, is danced to "disco," a black-based rhythm and blues characterized by a strong, rhythmic bass guitar, that in itself is achieving wide popularity. *Dena Kleiman, "The 'Hustle' Restores Old Touch to Dancing," The New York Times, July 12, 1975, p 27*

—*v.i.* to dance to disco music.

It was a hot night the following Spring and she was at Studio 54 and she was discoing with a kid who looked like Bruce Jenner. *James Brady, "Tales of New York," New York Post, Jan. 12, 1979, p 18*

[1975 for noun, abstracted from the combining form *disco-* (as in *disco-beat, disco-band*) itself from *disco,* short for *discotheque;* 1978 for verb] See ROLLER DISCO.

disco jockey, *U.S.* an announcer or master of ceremonies at a ballroom where disco is played. Compare TALK JOCKEY.

They [the musical pieces] are cunningly selected by the all-important disco jockeys who keep a hawk's eye on the floor and choreograph the dancers by changing the pace and style of the records and tapes. *"Living: Hotspots of the Urban Night," Time, June 27, 1977, p 56*

[1977, influenced by *disc jockey* (1940's) a radio announcer of recorded popular music]

discoverist, *adj.* favoring or advocating the DISCOVERY METHOD.

The "discoverist" school owes much to the Swiss psychologist Jean Piaget who said that a child's capacity to learn increasingly complex tasks must develop at its own speed over a period of time. He emphasized the need for exploration and organizing activities on the part of the student. *John H. Douglas, "Science Education: The New Humanity?", Science News, March 24, 1973, p 187*

[1973]

discovery method, a method of instruction in which students pursue knowledge on their own and work out their own solutions to problems under the guidance of a teacher.

Lectures by the teacher and textbooks have been a good deal replaced by "discovery methods" — groups working on joint activities that may bring aspects of traditional subjects together in various ways, with each of the children pursuing his own strongest interests. *Anthony Bailey, The New Yorker, Oct. 29, 1973, p 134*

The report outlines four within-school factors which have brought about the decline in writing skills and SAT [Scholastic Aptitude Test] scores: (1) The proliferation of course options, enabling students to select less demanding courses than the traditional English, math, science and social studies regimen. (2) Confusion about the role of teachers and the appropriate teaching methods, about "traditional" instruction, "open classrooms," "the discovery method," "team teaching" and other "in" terminology. *Albert Shanker, Advertisement by the United Federation of Teachers, The New York Times, April 23, 1978, Sec. 4, p 9*

[1973]

discovery procedure, *Linguistics.* a theoretical procedure by which analysis of a corpus leads to discovery of basic units making up particular structural aspects of a language.

Chapters 4-7 describe the development of Chomsky's transformational grammar. . . . The principal stress is on the rejection of 'discovery procedures' in favor of an evaluation procedure, and on the creativity (or 'open-endedness') of human language as setting a goal for grammatical theory that requires going beyond a corpus. *Dell Hymes, Review of "Noam Chomsky" by John Lyons, Language, June 1972, p 420*

[1965]

diseconomics, *n.pl.* harmful economic policy or inefficient economic growth.

We may be impoverishing the land and forests, exhausting the mines and quarries and strata of oil or natural gas . . . yet still showing apparently healthy economic growth. For the only yardstick by which we measure it is the value of the products we get out, plus paid-for services, or the incomes of those who produce or render them. These are the diseconomics of growth, not accounted for by conventional methods of reckoning. *Tony Aldous, Review of "The Diseconomics of Growth," The Times (London), May 2, 1972, p 21*

Diseconomics of scale appear frequently in complexity theory. *Scientific American, June 1978, p 116*

[1972, from *dis-* opposite of + *economics*]

disfluency, *n.* **1** inability to speak fluently, often in reference to a condition of stuttering.

Himself a stutterer who simply seemed to outgrow his problem, he "found the Iowa approach to 'disfluency' faintly depressing . . . As a theory it seemed too much of a patchwork — a psychological insight here, a contribution from sociology there, a little neurology, a little anthropology, a leavening of old-fashioned common sense." *Christopher Lehmann-Haupt, "Trippingly on the Tongue," The New York Times, Sept. 27, 1977, p 43*

2 an instance of this.

According to a study conducted by one of Johnson's graduate students, these normal childhood "disfluencies" occur on the average of fifty times for every thousand words spoken. For instance, a child may come running into the house shouting, "I-I-I-I want some ice cream." *Gerald Jonas, "A Reporter at Large: The Disorder of Many Theories," The New Yorker, Nov. 15, 1976, p 142*

[1976, from *dis-* lack of + *fluency*]

disgrunt, *v.t.* to say or remark with disgust; express displeasure.

The other two jurors went on to give the prize to Stewart Brand, the collator, leading one critic to disgrunt that next year they'll give it to a Xerox machine. *John Leonard, The New York Times Book Review, April 30, 1972, p 47*

[1972, back formation from *disgruntled;* form influenced by the verb *grunt*]

disinform, *v.t.* to provide with distorted or false information.

Advocates of the change say, in justifying it, that foreign intelligence services today are increasingly using so-called influencing agents for subverting, deceiving and disinforming French public opinion, that they receive their training, instructions and remuneration from abroad. *The Manchester Guardian Weekly (Le Monde section), July 30, 1978, p 13*

[1978, back formation from earlier (1955) *disinformation,* translation of Russian *dezinformatsiya*] See DEPARTMENT D.

disintermediate, *v.i.* *U.S.* to withdraw one's money from intermediate institutions (as savings and commercial banks) for direct investment at higher interest rates in the securities market.

In my very next column it will be my duty to inform NEWSWEEK readers how they can successfully "disintermediate" — i.e., pull their money out of the banking system and get a higher short-term yield with safety. *Paul A. Samuelson, Newsweek, May 6, 1974, p 75*

diskette

[1974, back formation from earlier (1968) *disinter-mediation*]

disk·ette ('dis₁ket *or* dis'ket), *n.* another name for FLOPPY DISK.

Some 442 million information documents of all types, ranging from W-2 forms listing wages to 1099 forms listing dividends and interest earned by corporations as well as by individuals, are filed with the I.R.S. each year by employers, corporations and banks. About 42 percent of these documents are furnished in the form of magnetic tape, disk or diskette, and the rest are provided on paper slips similar to the forms individual taxpayers receive through the mail. *The New York Times, Jan. 17, 1978, p 51*

[1975, from *disk* + *-ette* (diminutive suffix)]

disk pack or **disc pack,** a stack of magnetic disks for recording and storing computer data.

Another way to provide input data that can be read by the computer is to use machine-prepared data files in the form of magnetic tapes or removable disk packs. *Louis Robinson, "Data Processing Systems," Encyclopedia Science Supplement (Grolier) 1969, p 361*

How many magnetic drums or disc-packs are needed to hold 10^{12} bits? *A. C. Larman, Science, Jan. 1971, p 28*

[1969]

dis·par·lure ('dis par₁lur), *n.* a synthetic sex attractant for the female gypsy moth, more persistent than the natural attractant.

Our experiments clearly showed that disparlure is a more potent sex lure than any of the related compounds. The two compounds that elicited the next-largest responses are 20 and 100 times less effective. *Dietrich Schneider, "The Sex-Attractant Receptor of Moths," Scientific American, July 1974, p 34*

[1972, from New Latin *(Porthetria) dispar,* the gypsy moth + English *lure*] Compare GOSSYPLURE.

dis·pi·ra·tion (₁dis pai'rei ʃən), *n.* (in the geometric model of a solid) displacement by spiral or helical motion.

Dispirations constitute a third class of lattice defects; they are based on screw symmetry, which combines translational and rotational components. Screw symmetry can exist in a periodic structure made up of units that are not spherical, such as the small cones here. In a perfect lattice all the cones in a layer point in the same direction, but the direction rotates in passing from one layer to the next. *Illustration legend, "Disclinations," Scientific American, Dec. 1977, p 136*

[1972, from *dis-* (as in *dislocation*) + Latin *spīra* coil, spiral + English *-tion*] Compare DISCLINATION.

displaced homemaker, *U.S.* a married woman who has lost her means of support by divorce, separation, or the death or disability of her husband.

The term displaced homemaker was invented by another Californian, Tish Sommers, 64, who was divorced at 57 and "discovered I was part of an invisible problem, one of the women who had fallen through the cracks, too young for social security, too old to be hired, not eligible for unemployment insurance because homemaking is not considered work." *Time, Jan. 1, 1979, p 64*

[1978]

dissolved gas, natural gas found in a dissolved state in petroleum.

152

A third type of accumulation is also found, in which the natural gas is dissolved in the oil. This is known as "dissolved gas." *Joel Legunn, "Natural Gas," Encyclopedia Science Supplement (Grolier) 1975, p 183*

[1975] Compare ASSOCIATED GAS.

distribution satellite, a communications satellite of relatively low power, that retransmits signals to small geographical areas.

These distribution satellites would be largely supplemental, adding to the facilities now available through land lines and microwave relays. *Sig Mickelson, Saturday Review, Oct. 24, 1970, p 23*

[1968]

diving reflex, a physiological response found in human beings and other mammals, in which submersion of the head in cold water immediately slows the heartbeat and diverts oxygen-rich blood to the brain, heart, and lungs, delaying suffocation and the possibility of brain damage.

Now a number of other survivals from what might have been cold-water drownings are reported in the Aug. 22 NEWSWEEK by Martin J. Nemiroff, a University of Michigan physiologist. He reports that the survivals are primarily due to a mechanism that he calls the "diving reflex." . . . The diving reflex, Nemiroff continues, is especially strong in younger persons. He believes that it is a physiological vestige of the birth process from earlier times, when the transition from placental oxygen to the earth's atmosphere was a more hazardous affair than it is today. *Science News, Sept. 24, 1977, p 200*

[1975, so called because it is the means by which diving mammals, like the porpoise and seal, remain submerged without breathing for long periods]

di·zy·gous (dai'zai gəs), *adj.* derived from two separate zygotes and therefore genetically different; fraternal.

One of the best ways of throwing light on problems like these is by the study of pairs of monozygous and dizygous twins reared together. *"How Much of IQ Is Inherited?", Nature, Nov. 10, 1972, p 69*

[1970, from *di-* two + *zygote* + *-ous;* synonymous with *dizygotic* (1930)] *Abbreviation:* DZ

DMBA, abbreviation of *dimethylbenzanthracene,* a cancer-producing chemical used experimentally to determine resistance to cancer, especially on the skin of rodents.

DMBA induced cancers (papillomas) in 60 per cent of the "old" grafts compared with only 25 per cent in the "young." *"Monitor: Ageing Transplants Take Their Cancer With Them," New Scientist, Feb. 1, 1973, p 230*

[1965]

DMN or **DMNA,** abbreviation of DIMETHYLNITROSAMINE.

In two of ten samples of hot dogs obtained from a local supermarket, he discovered . . . the highest levels of DMN ever found in meat up to that time. No safe level of DMN has been established. *Harrison Wellford, "Behind the Meat Counter," The Atlantic, Oct. 1972, p 90*

[1970]

DMSO, abbreviation of *dimethyl sulfoxide,* a colorless liquid extracted from paper-pulp wastes, used as an industrial solvent, and in medicine chiefly to relieve pain and inflammation.

DMSO hemolyzes or breaks red cells. *Science News, May 30, 1970, p 530*

Doctors commonly prescribe DMSO in Australia, Canada and some European and South American countries, but it can be used legally in the U.S. only on animals. *"The Disputed Drugs," Time, June 20, 1977, p 53*

[1963]

DN·ase (ˌdiː‚enˈeis), *n.* an enzyme that promotes the hydrolysis of DNA (the genetic material in cells).

The smallpox virus is known to make several enzymes. Two of these enzymes are known as DNases. Their function has not been known. What the New York City cytobiologists have found is that one of these DNases is released after the smallpox virus enters a host cell. The DNase then switches off the synthesis of the host cell's DNA. *Science News, July 7, 1973, p 3*

[1967, short for *deoxyribonuclease* (OEDS 1946)]

DNC, abbreviation of *direct numerical control.*

In DNC, the computer with overall control passes information to the machine tools which otherwise would have to read-in their instructions from tapes. The DNC computer thus performs more of a production control and data management function rather than just simple system control. *Nicholas Valéry, "The Only Way for Machine Tools Is Up," New Scientist, Jan. 27, 1972, p 196*

[1971] Compare CNC.

docking adapter, a tunnel-like passage formed by the joining of orbiting spacecraft.

In spite of the grumbling, the clothing was quite versatile: if the astronauts planned to spend much time in the docking adapter, which was usually chilly, they could pull on golden-brown jackets. *Henry S. F. Cooper, Jr., "A Reporter at Large: Life in a Space Station—1," The New Yorker, Aug. 30, 1976, p 37*

One experiment was of an applied science nature. It consisted of melting various metals and semiconductor materials by Slayton and Kubasov in the zero-gravity of space inside a furnace in the docking adapter. *Mitchell R. Sharpe, "Space Exploration," Britannica Book of the Year 1976, p 625*

[1973] Compare AIRLOCK MODULE.

doc·u·dra·ma (ˈdɑk yəˌdrɑː mə), *n.* a television dramatization based on facts, often presented in the style of a documentary to impart a sense of authenticity.

Described as "fact-based," this is the story of Caryl Chessman, who spent 12 years in San Quentin before being excuted in May 1960. Like all fact-based television, whether it be labeled true story or docudrama, this dramatization is not without a point of view or, if you will, a strong bias. *John J. O'Connor, "TV Weekend," The New York Times, Sept. 23, 1977, p C24*

There isn't a shred of new evidence in the docudrama, according to Peter Pearson who co-authored and directed *The Tar Sands.* Larry Pratt, who has seen the final script, agrees. *Sandra Martin, "Television," Maclean's, Feb. 21, 1977, p 59*

Viewers here will be able to pass judgment on these matters of opinion when the docu-drama appears on BBC 1. *The Times (London), Aug. 31, 1978, p 16*

[1976, from *documentary* + *drama*]

docudramatist, *n.:* There ought to be a truth-in-labeling law to separate truth and fiction. But who could write it, and who would pass it? Since there won't be any such law, everybody concerned — and TV docu-dramatists most of all — should be held more accountable for fat content and fact content, properly labeled. *Time, Sept. 19, 1977, p 93*

DOE¹, abbreviation of *Department of Energy* (of the United States, formed in 1977).

"The existence of DOE means 17,000 hungry cunning people in this town depend on OPEC for their livelihood." *William F. Buckley, New York Post, Feb. 3, 1979, p 9*

Both the Senate Energy Committee and DOE predict that by 1985 greater production of natural gas will save the nation 1.4 million bbl. a day in imported oil. *Time, Oct. 9, 1978, p 24*

[1978]

▶ The DOE was created by Congress to integrate the energy-related functions of various government agencies (see ENERGY CRISIS).

Though Great Britain was first to create a Department of Energy, in 1974, the abbreviation DOE has been more generally applied to the Department of the Environment which was created earlier.

DOE², abbreviation of *Department of the Environment* (of Great Britain, formed in 1971).

The DOE — as it has come to be called — swallowed and quickly set about digesting three other independent and quite powerful ministries: Transport, Public Building and Works and Housing and Local Government, which had responsibility for town and country planning. *Tony Aldous, "Great Britain: The Times," The Times (London), April 12, 1972, p V*

[1972] ▶ See the note under DOE¹.

Dol·by or **dol·by** (ˈdoul biː: *or* ˈdɔːl biː), *adj.* of, relating to, or produced by any of various electronic devices that reduce or eliminate noise in recording sound for tapes and in radio broadcasting, especially of recorded music.

Dolby noise reduction plus a simple electronic trick could mean much better reception for people listening to stereo broadcasts. Noise reduction on cassette tape recorders to reduce "tape hiss" is now a well-known technique. *New Scientist, July 18, 1974, p 130*

Cimino's talent is for breadth and movement and detail, and the superlative mix of the Dolby sound gives a sense of scale to the crowd noises and the voices and the music; we feel we're hearing a whole world. *Pauline Kael, "The Current Cinema," The New Yorker, Dec. 18, 1978, p 71*

[1969, abstracted from *Dolby System,* the trademark for such devices, named after Ray *Dolby,* born 1933, their American inventor]

Dolbyized, *adj.* made or provided with a Dolby device or equipment.

Speaking of cassette recorders, with the exception of "Dolbyized" models, you can count on one finger the number of models that have a hi-fi signal-to-noise ratio of 50 db. *"Sound," Popular Photography, Aug. 1971, p 99*

[1971]

doll, *n. Especially U.S. Slang.* a stimulant or depressant drug in pill form.

Jacqueline Susann . . . has made the word "doll" a synonym for pill. *Sara Davidson, Harper's, Oct. 1969, p 65*

dolly

Snow, junk, smack (heroin); cough medicine (codeine); sleeping pills, dolls (barbiturates); downers (tranquilizers); drink, booze (alcohol). *"Table of Drug Abuse: Popular Names," Encyclopedia Science Supplement (Grolier) 1974, p 281*

[1966; see VALLEY OF THE DOLLS]

dolly, *n. Slang.* a tablet of methadone (narcotic used as a substitute for heroin).

Methadone [is] known on the street as "dollies" (Dolophine is the trade name of methadone in tablet form). *Marion K. Sanders, Harper's, June 1970, p 76*

[1970]

do·lo·rol·o·gy (ˌdou ləˈral ə dʒi:), *n. U.S.* the scientific study of pain.

Not until the specialty of dolorology began to emerge did the study of pain itself gain a new emphasis and respectability. *Laurence Cherry, "Solving the Mysteries of Pain," The New York Times Magazine, Jan. 30, 1977, p 13*

[1977, from Latin *dolor* pain + *-ology* study of]

do·los·se (dəˈlas ə), *n. pl. -ses* or *-se.* a tetrapod; a concrete casting used in large numbers that diminishes the force of waves on a beach or dike by breaking them up.

Public Service engineers estimate that 69,000 *dolosse,* each weighing anywhere from 6 1/2 to 42 tons, will be needed. The *dolosse* will interlock with one another, providing thousands of spaces into which sea water can slosh, spending its energy. *Ralph E. Lapp, The New York Times Magazine, June 4, 1972, p 80*

[1972, probably from Afrikaans, from the Setswana word for an animal knucklebone used in witch doctors' rites]

dominance hierarchy, an order of dominance among animals, in which members of a group establish rank by aggressiveness, size, etc.

Lacking language, and dependent for communication on a repertoire of about two dozen sounds and gestures, baboon troops are held together by a dominance hierarchy headed by three or four central males that cooperate to keep order in the troop, control access to females, and provide defense against predators. *Peter B. Dow, Natural History, April 1972, p 25*

Among the females there is generally a simple dominance hierarchy, with larger (older) individuals dominating smaller ones. The dominant female is therefore able to move freely throughout the male's territory and roughly superimposes her territory and feeding area on his. *Ross Robertson, "Sex Changes Under the Waves," New Scientist, May 31, 1973, p 538*

[1972]

dom·sat (ˈdamˌsæt), *n.* a communications satellite restricted in operation to a particular country.

RCA managed to be the first with domsat service by hooking up with Canada's Anik II communications satellite, launched last April, and by building four ground relay stations near New York, San Francisco, Juneau and Anchorage, Alaska. *Newsweek, Jan. 21, 1974, p 83*

[1972, acronym for *domestic satellite,* on the model of *comsat* (communications satellite), *Intelsat* (International telecommunications satellite), etc.] Compare LANDSAT, MARISAT, SEASAT.

don, *n.* a leader in the Mafia.

154

Of the dons of the golden age who had children, only a few seem to have followed their fathers into the rackets. Most law-enforcement officials agree with Puzo: men like Colombo are hardly the equal of their predecessors. *Tom Buckley, "The Mafia Tries a New Tune," Harper's, Aug. 1971, p 56*

[1963, from Italian *don* a form of address for noblemen, priests, and wealthy gentlemen; (literally) master, from Latin *dominus* lord]

do-nothinger, *n.* one who adopts or is committed to a do-nothing policy.

Mr Ford is not a do-nothing President for lack of thrust; he is a do-nothinger from conviction. *Peter Jenkins, The Manchester Guardian Weekly, Dec. 7, 1974, p 1*

[1970] ► The older noun *do-nothing* (1500's) has the general meaning of "one who does nothing; a lazy person; idler."

doomsdayer, *n.* one who predicts or warns of imminent catastrophe; alarmist; doomsayer.

Miller assails the conservationists and doomsdayers of "spaceship earth" who fail to see how the price mechanism and changing technology can keep us from running out of scarce resources. *Alan Miller, "Books in Brief," Review of "The Economics of Energy, What Went Wrong and How We Can Fix It" by Leroy Miller, National Review, Nov. 22, 1974, p 1369*

[1974] Also called APOCALYPTICIST or APOCALYPTICIAN.

doomster, *n.* another word for DOOMSDAYER.

Mr Colin Robinson . . . begins by pooh-poohing the prophecies of doom, repeats all the facts and estimates we know only too well as though they were something new, and ends by reaching the same conclusions as the doomsters. *The Times (London), Jan. 8, 1973, p 16*

[1972, either from *doom* + *-ster* or extended from the old Scottish law term (1600's) meaning "one who dooms or pronounces sentence; a judge or executioner"] See ECODOOMSTER.

doomwatch, *n.* a watching for or warning of impending doom; alarmism. *Also used attributively.*

Dear Bernard Levin! His maverick messianic urge is drawing him deeper and deeper into ideological difficulties. In his latest piece of political doomwatch (directed against Mr Heath, for a change), he . . . forecasts an upsurge of bloody revolt against what Harold Macmillan, no less, once castigated as the "casino society" . . . *The Times (London), July 3, 1973, p 17*

[1972]

doomwatcher, *n.:* Of course the excesses of the doomwatchers need to be pinpointed, but by the same token of scientific caution it is appropriate to criticize with equal rigour the optimistic view that science can solve everything; and here *Nature* has been silent. *Ian Vine, Bristol, "Doomwatching," in a Letter to the Editor, Nature, Oct. 6, 1972, p 353*

doomwatching, *n.:* The road forward does not lie through the despair of doomwatching nor through the easy optimism of successive technological fixes. *Jon Tinker, "Cocoyoc Revisited," New Scientist, Aug. 28, 1975, p 483*

doorstep, *British. —adj.* of or having to do with door-to-door solicitation of sales, contributions, political support, etc.

Mr Pat Duffy (Attercliffe), chairman of the Motor Industry Select Committee, criticised the lack of consultation by Ministers. Mr Riccardo, chairman of the Chrysler Corporation, had behaved like a hustling doorstep salesman. *Adam Raphael, The Manchester Guardian Weekly, Dec. 28, 1975, p 3*

The Conservatives' doorstep organization will no doubt be exemplary tomorrow but will it be good enough to save face for the party? *The Times (London), Aug. 15, 1963, p 5*

—*v.i.* **1** to go from door to door in order to solicit sales, canvass for political support, make an investigation, etc.

For those who lived and sweated through these Watergate summers and winters the report . . . brings back the familiar smell of John Sirica's courtroom, the pudgy face of that inoperative liar Ronald Ziegler, the endless door-stepping on the trail of John Ehrlichman and Archibald Cox and John Dean. *Simon Winchester, The Manchester Guardian Weekly, Oct. 26, 1975, p 10*

2 to wait on, or as if on, a doorstep.

As our crisis stretches from weeks into months, it seemed time to learn how the other half of the journalistic world lives. There they are, nearly every day staked out in wet and windy streets waiting for endless crunch meetings to come to a crunch, or at least an end. Door-stepping, we call it in the trade. *The Times (London), Jan. 29, 1974, p 12*

[1962 for adj.; 1974 for verb]

doorstepper, *n.:* It seemed to owe a lot to his [Roy Hattersley] own experience of workaday life in Yorkshire as the only child of a local government officer, adolescent deviller and doorstepper for the local Labour Party machine, graduate of Hull University and then a Sheffield city councillor. *Derek Harris, "Prices Minister Puts Profits in Perspective," The Times (London), Oct. 23, 1976, p 18*

doorway state, *Nuclear Physics.* a theoretical intermediate state between a simple and a more complex nuclear interaction.

According to quantum theory the underlying sharp compound resonance states into which the doorway state can dissolve must all have the same spin and parity (intrinsic symmetry) as the molecular doorway state, since the total spin and parity are conserved. *D. Allan Bromley, "Nuclear Molecules," Scientific American, Dec. 1978, p 68*

[1968, so called from the figurative doorway through which the initial simple reaction must pass to become a complex system]

do·pa·min·er·gic (ˌdou pə məˈnər dʒik), *adj.* producing or activated by the adrenal hormone dopamine.

Results of recent research in the most common type of idiopathic Parkinsonism—a disorder of the central nervous system—appear to indicate that the disease is related to degenerative changes in the corpus striatum, substantia nigra, and related dopaminergic neurons. *McChesney Goodall, "Parkinson's Disease," McGraw-Hill Yearbook of Science and Technology 1972, p 307*

[1971, from *dopamine* + Greek *érgon* work + English *-ic*] Compare CATECHOLAMINERGIC, NORADRENERGIC, SEROTONERGIC.

Doppler-shift or **Dopplershift,** *v.t.* to cause an apparent shift in (the wave frequency or spectral lines of a source).

Direct information about the constitution, location and velocity of interstellar clouds can be gained by detecting molecules and measuring their position and the amount by which their spectral features are Dopplershifted. *Barry E. Turner, "Interstellar Molecules: Molecules as Interstellar Probes," Scientific American, March 1973, p 56*

[1969, verb use of *Doppler shift* the apparent change in wave frequency as the source or the observer moves towards or away from the other]

dor·mo·bile (ˈdɔr məˌbiːl), *n. British.* a small van equipped as a dwelling and often having a roof that raises to accommodate space for a bunk; camper.

As the horse-drawn carriage declined in use, so we lost the need and hence the ability to refer to the differences which 80 years ago were freely expressed by words like *phaeton, brougham* or *landau.* But, of course, we've balanced such losses with words which avoid crunch meaning *convertibles, fastbacks, dormobiles* and *minibuses. Randolph Quirk, "Watch It, Mate," The Listener, Aug. 2, 1973, p 151*

[1969, from earlier (1963) *Dormobile*, trademark for a vehicle of this kind, apparently from *dormi*tory + auto*mobile*]

dose-response curve, a curve graphed to show the relationship of dosage (of a drug, a gas, radiation, etc.) to the physiological effects produced.

This complex of committees is an attempt to make decisions about the acceptability of risks more democratic. But they face severe problems. First is the hidden complexity of the dose-response curve. Committee members will often find it difficult to know what the response ordinate actually means in human terms. For example, in Jacobsen's study of pneumoconiosis, "response" is expressed in terms of an index of disease progression derived, subjectively, from X-ray films of miners' lungs. *Lawrence McGinty and Gordon Atherley, "Acceptability versus Democracy," New Scientist, May 12, 1977, p 234*

[1972] See PHARMACOKINETICS.

DOT, abbreviation of *Department of Transportation* (of the United States).

This means that about another $50 million . . . will become available for the controversial airliner. The total is considerably short of the $290 million DOT wanted for the current fiscal year. *"Supersonic Transport," Science News, Jan. 9, 1971, p 23*

[1967]

double-bind, *n.* Also, **double bind. 1** a situation of crisis in behavior resulting from repeated subjection to conflicting pressures.

There are times, says R. D. Laing, when people *need* to go mad. Reminding us that schizophrenia literally means "broken hearted," he suggests that feelings of terror and despair are often the result of " 'double-binds,' in which, without conscious malice, one person is repeatedly subjected to simultaneous, absolutely contradictory injunctions and attributions about who he is, or how he feels or what he thinks, until he can no longer tell who he is, or what he feels or thinks." *Anatole Broyard, "On the Need to Go Mad," The New York Times, Jan. 19, 1976, p 27*

2 *Transferred use.* dilemma.

The act of writing autobiographical fiction contains a double-bind of which most writers, probably, are aware. To give fictitious form to a personal experience means that the writer is hiding behind his characters; and yet to come clean, to say, "this is me, and this is how I behaved," immediately removes one of the essential props of fiction: the illusion that the reader is being told all that the author knows. *Jeremy Brooks, "Dance to Disaster," Review of "The Bright Day" by Mary Hocking, The Sunday Times (London), June 22, 1975, p 34*

[1962, coined by the American anthropologist Gregory Bateson in 1956] Compare CATCH-22, COGNITIVE DISSONANCE.

double-digit, *adj.* Especially U.S. equaling or exceeding a rate of 10 per cent (up to a possible 99 per cent).

The runaway economy, beset by 14% inflation and double-digit interest rates, continues to race beyond . . . control. *James Wieghart, Daily News (New York), May 27, 1979, p 5*

Double-digit inflation and steadily rising unemployment do not admit of bromides about 'men of goodwill' and 'getting round the table' unless they are accompanied by some hard policy proposals and some intelligible discussion of priorities. *"Mr Asquith Rides Again," New Statesman, May 16, 1975, p 645*

[1974] Also, TWO-DIGIT and, especially British, DOUBLE-FIGURE.

▶ Although *double-digit* in its current sense became widespread in mid-1974 (probably influenced by the earlier British *double-figure*), the compound may have appeared on occasion in special contexts, as in the following 1959 quotation:

The editors boasted: "Although these three books were written by Shulman at the age of eight, critics have pointed out that they show the insight and penetration of a man of nine." Now Humorist Shulman, 40, has advanced into the double-digit years. *Time, Aug. 31, 1959, p 68*

double dipping, *U.S.* the practice or policy of allowing a retired soldier or civil servant to earn a salary from a new government job while receiving a pension or other benefits from the first job.

The critics, including many Congressmen, consider "double dipping" typical of the ways in which the military pension system has become overly generous and helped to inflate military manpower costs. *Caroline Rand Herron and R. V. Denenberg, "The Nation: The Critics of Double-Dipping," The New York Times, April 10, 1977, p 3*

Passing into verb.

Controller Harrison J. Goldin will move next week to break a deadlock that has stymied attempts to identify retired cops who have been "double-dipping"—earning excess amounts of money from city jobs while receiving disability pensions. *William Federici and Donald Singleton, "Goldin Aims to End Double-Dipping by Ex-Cops," Daily News (New York), Feb. 24, 1978, p 5*

[1975, alteration of earlier (1965) *double dip*]

double dipper: If the panel has its way, there would also be an end to double-dippers, those who draw two Federal paychecks because they have "retired" from the military and later found a place for themselves in the civilian bureaucracy. *The New York Times, April 16, 1978, Sec. 4, p 2*

double-figure, *adj.* Especially British. variant of DOUBLE-DIGIT.

Earlier controls and tariffs on imports had proved largely ineffective in dealing with double-figure inflation which had been accelerating over the past two years reaching more than 40 per cent during September alone. *Michael French-*

man, *"Mexico and Argentina: Measures Fail to Take Pressure Off Prices," Annual Financial Review, The Times (London), Oct. 4, 1976, Sec. X, p 5*

[1966, probably transferred from *double figures* (occasionally *double-figure*) a score of 10 or more, especially in cricket (OEDS 1860)]

double nickel, *U.S. Slang.* the nationwide highway speed limit of fifty-five miles per hour (established in 1973).

"Drive 55" would probably have disappeared with the gas lines had it not been for the discovery that the limit reduced fatal accidents; Washington estimates the saving at 4,500 lives a year. Hence the "double nickel" has won the support of the National Highway Traffic Safety Administration as well as consumer groups. *Peter Passell, "What Price the Double Nickel?" The New York Times, Feb. 5, 1979, p A18*

[1976, originally citizens band radio slang for 55 (two fives = two nickels)]

Douglas bag, a plastic bag for collecting exhaled air or for administering respiratory mixtures.

The inspired air is fed from cylinders so that the gas mixture can be varied, and a reservoir and sampling tubes enable the gas that the athlete breathes to be sampled. Then from the expired air another sample is taken and the total expired air can be collected in a Douglas bag. *Roger Bannister, Science Journal, Nov. 1970, p 37*

[1963, named after C. G. *Douglas,* 1882-1963, an English physiologist]

down, *Especially U.S. Slang. —adj.* depressing; gloomy; downbeat.

. . . there was plenty of talk about "Fat City."
"Very authentic."
"A beautiful picture."
"It's too down. I don't like down movies. I like up movies." *"The Talk of the Town," The New Yorker, Aug. 5, 1972, p 21*

Primarily, a down week with a couple of lighter spots, specifically the lunches with two of our professors. *Scott Turow, "One L: An Inside Account of Life in the First Year at Harvard Law School," The New Yorker, March 20, 1978, p 90*

—v.i. to take downers (depressant drugs).

Amphetamines and barbiturates also have two faces. They are a familiar item in the doctor's armamentarium and, as such, reassuring. And yet excessive "upping" or "downing" can cause severe psychic dislocation, certainly as damaging as any of the effects of LSD. *Norman E. Zinberg and John A. Robertson, Drugs and the Public, 1972, p 49*

[1967 for adj.; 1972 for verb]

downcycle, *n.* a downward or declining cycle in business or the economy.

Mr Charles Baker, the IISI secretary, told a press conference that a survey among its 27 members gave reason to believe that "the downcycle is at an end and that a turnaround has come for all countries." *Peter Hill, "Rise of 10pc Forecast for This Year in Western Steel Output," The Times (London), Jan. 22, 1976, p 20*

[1976]

downlink, *n.* transmission of data signals, etc. from

a spacecraft or satellite to the ground. *Often used attributively.*

Oscar 6 contained a translator that received signals in the 145.9-146.0 MHz range (uplink) and retransmitted them at 29.45-29.55 MHz (downlink). In this manner more than 1,000 amateurs on all continents successfully conducted two-way communications via the satellite. *Morgan W. Godwin, "Television and Radio," Britannica Book of the Year 1974, p 661*

On September 13 ESA also attempted to achieve this capability at 14 and 11 GHz with its *OTS 1* "bird." (The apparently reversed numerical sequence is due to the convention of giving the uplink frequency ahead of the downlink.) *John F. Clark, "Space Flight," McGraw-Hill Yearbook of Science and Technology 1978, p 342*

[1969]

down-looking, *adj.* (of radar) transmitting signals downward, used to detect low-flying aircraft or missiles and to direct the guidance system of a missile.

Given the American decision to deploy cruise missiles aboard B-52 bombers, it was not surprising to learn that the Soviet Union was constructing towers along the Russian borders several hundred feet high to house "down-looking" radar. *Robert M. Lawrence, "Military Affairs," The Annual Register of World Events in 1977 (1978), p 338*

The missile is also provided with a downlooking radar altimeter capable of resolving objects on the ground smaller than the map squares from a height of several kilometers. *Kosta Tsipis, "Cruise Missiles," Scientific American, Feb. 1977, p 22*

[1972] Compare SIDE-LOOKING.

down-market, *Especially British.* —*adj.* of or for the lower-income consumer; of lower grade or quality.

Not so very long ago, for instance, Harold Macmillan's staid and dynastic publishing house might have disdained anything so down-market as the biography of a sex-pot. But they have just bid £12,000 for a potential 'breast-seller'—the life story of Raquel Welch. *Mark Goulden, The Sunday Times (London), June 1, 1975, p 28*

They still make first class cutlery in Sheffield. But down-market imports are threatening to flood the market, some of which gets a Yorkshire coating of silver plate and a 'Sheffield' stamp. *"Knife in the Back?" The Manchester Guardian Weekly, Aug. 13, 1978, p 20*

—*adv.* in or into the down-market field.

Readers who have asked about the matter can be told that there is no reason to believe the paper will move 'down-market' in search of popularity. *Karl Miller, "Views," The Listener, Dec. 27, 1973, p 875*

[1975 for adj.; 1973 for adv.] Compare UP-MARKET.

downpress, *v.t.* to oppress; keep in a state of subjugation (a word used by Rastafarians about the Jamaican government, especially in the lyrics of reggae music).

By 1970 or so the Rastas were saying... something quite specific about Jamaican politics: The System was downpressing the people, capitalism was the plague, and the Hugh Shearer government—as the current embodiment of Babylon—was going to burn. *Frances FitzGerald, "Jamaican Limbo," Harper's, July, 1977, p 12*

[1977]

downpressor, *n.:* Despite the growing popularity of reggae (pronounced REGgay) music, it is most odd that this Caribbean wild man [singer Bob Marley], with his dreadlocks, his ganja-inspired revelations, has attracted such a hysterical following. A gospel of death to the "downpressors" does not seem in keeping with these tame times. *Jon Bradshaw, "The Reggae Way to 'Salvation'," The New York Times Magazine, Aug. 14, 1977, p 24*

down quark, a type of quark (hypothetical nuclear particle) possessing a charge of $-1/3$ and a spin of $+1/2$.

To explain the common, well-behaved particles such as neutrons or protons requires two quarks (and their corresponding antiquarks) designated "up quark" and "down quark" or "neutron quark" and "proton quark" depending on whether one uses California or eastern American terminology. *Science News, May 8, 1976, p 293*

[1976, so called in reference to the downward spin it is supposed to exhibit] Also called D QUARK. See QUARK.

downsize, *v.t. U.S.* to reduce the overall size and weight of (an automobile).

All the automakers are already at work down-sizing their cars for 1978 and later years. *Time, Sept. 13, 1976, p 47*

For the 1978 model year, GM [General Motors] downsized its four intermediate cars... trimming their length by about 8 inches and their weight by up to 825 pounds. *David L. Lewis, "Automobile Industry," 1978 Collier's Encyclopedia Year Book (1977), p 143*

[1976, from *down, adv.* + *size, v.*]

► Technically to *downsize* means to reduce the exterior dimensions of an automobile while the passenger area and trunk remain the same or are increased. Car manufacturers and others in the industry prefer the older word *resized* to describe the new generation of smaller cars, claiming that *downsized* suggests a degrading of the product's appearance or quality.

downstream, *adj., adv.* of or for the refining and distribution of oil; relating to marketing of oil.

BNOC is one of the biggest crude-oil trading companies in the United Kingdom sector of the North Sea.... But with no "downstream" or refining operations of its own it has been selling its share to other companies, many of whom also have no British refineries. *The Manchester Guardian Weekly, July 1, 1979, p 7*

The Saudis are determined to build or buy their own "downstream" facilities—which, in the language of the oilmen, means oil refineries and even chains of service stations in Western Europe and the U.S. *Time, April 2, 1973, p 25*

Oil countries, notably Iran, are also showing a growing interest in investing "downstream." *The Auckland Star (N.Z.), Feb. 10, 1973, p 18*

[1973] Compare UPSTREAM. See also BUY-BACK, POSTED PRICE.

downwelling, *n.* the lowering or depressing of the ocean under the pressure of tectonic plates.

One of the puzzles of the gravity interpretation is that both upwellings (plumes) and downwellings (trenches) lead to gravity highs. This can be rationalized in a density-stratified Earth because plumes and trenches are both places where material is injected into a layer. *K. S. Deffeyes, Nature, Dec. 29, 1972, p 540*

doxycycline

[1968, patterned on *upwelling*] See SEA-FLOOR SPREADING.

dox·y·cy·cline (ˌdɑk səˈsɑi kliːn), *n.* a broad-spectrum antibiotic derived from tetracycline. *Formula:* $C_{22}H_{24}N_2O_8$

The drug is doxycycline, a synthetic form of tetracycline that, in larger doses, is also used to treat gonorrhea. *Newsweek, Dec. 9, 1974, p 71*

A drug to prevent traveler's diarrhea—an antibiotic called doxycycline—was found. *Science News, Dec. 23-30, 1978, p 451*

[1968, from *deoxy-* containing less oxygen than (from *de-* less, fewer + *oxy*gen) + tetra*cycline*]

dozen, *n.* **the dozens,** *U.S. Slang.* a contest of exchanging insults directed against relatives, particularly against the mothers, of those engaged in the exchange.

Playin' the dozens in inner-city schools may cause more fights and disruptions than any other activity. The dozens or playin' the dozens has many names, but most youngsters probably refer to the game as "talkin' about moms"—making derogatory allegations about mothers. *Herbert L. Foster, Today's Education, Sept./Oct. 1975, p 54*

In their study of white American boys' adaptations of the "dozens," Millicent Ayoub and Stephen Barnett suggest that insults against mothers enable adolescents to show that they are loyal to friends rather than to familial values; such abuse is a means of breaking free from the parental household into a wider social world. *Donald Brenneis, "Fighting Words," New Scientist, May 4, 1978, p 281*

[1972] See SHUCKING AND JIVING, SIGNIFYING, SOUNDING, WOOFING.

► This phrase emerged in the 1970s as linguists and social scientists began to investigate Black English and Afro-American culture in general. Among blacks the term is known to have been used at least from the 1920's when a jazz song called "The Dirty Dozens" was composed. The origin of *the dozens* is, however, obscure.

D particle, an elementary particle believed to be composed of a charmed quark and an ordinary antiquark.

Physicists from SLAC and the University of California, Berkeley, reported the discovery of a genuinely charmed particle. Large numbers of them appeared in experiments at SLAC. The new particle is called the D particle. It is electrically neutral [and] is about twice as heavy as the proton. *Thomas O. White, "Physics," The 1977 World Book Year Book, p 453*

[1977]

d quark, short for DOWN QUARK.

Strangeness is among these approximately conserved quantum numbers; as a result weak interactions can convert an *s* quark into a *u* or a *d* quark and strange particles can decay through weak interactions into lighter nonstrange hadrons or into leptons. *Roy F. Schwitters, "Fundamental Particles With Charm," Scientific American, Oct. 1977, p 59*

[1976]

dragon, *n.* **chase the dragon,** to take or use an opiate, especially heroin.

All around me were burning candles the addicts use to light their silver papers to chase the dragon. *Sunday Post-Herald (Hongkong), July 1, 1973, p 1*

Out of the conflict, which has distinct political overtones, one immediate issue has emerged—what to do about White House and Congressional proposals for involuntary, random urinalysis tests for hard drugs, especially in Europe and aboard ships, where opiate use is referred to as "chasing the dragon." *Bernard Weinraub, "A Fog and a Furor Over G.I. Drug Use," The New York Times, July 30, 1978, Sec. 4, p 4*

[1966]

dragway, *n. U.S.* a road or course used for drag races; the paved racing area of a drag strip.

Then, with a blast and crackle of its jets, *Kiss of Death* comes out of the gate, and seven seconds later we watch it spitting and sparking at the dark end of the dragway. Fumes drift over the drag strip. *Alan Harrington, "Deus ex Machina," Harper's, Jan. 1976, p 22*

[1976]

drained weight. See the quotation for the meaning.

And unit price based on net weight is at best misleading. A better way, CU [Consumers Union] believes, would be to state "drained weight" on the labels of cans. Drained weight is the actual weight of the solid food — or net weight minus liquid weight. *"FDA Moves Toward Drained-Weight Labeling," Consumer Reports, Jan. 1976, p 6*

[1976]

dreadlocks, *n.pl.* hair which has formed matted clumps from lack of grooming, worn especially by Rastafarians.

The communal group's life-style soon brought objections from neighbors. Members refuse to bathe with soap, and many wear their hair in unkempt dreadlocks. *Time, Aug. 14, 1978, p 16*

[1975, from *dread* fear + *locks*, so called from the supposed fear by non-Rastafarians of the *dread*ful power of faithful Rastafarians]

dream factory, 1 a motion-picture studio.

What with Hollywood and Disneyland, the Los Angeles metropolitan area is the home of American fantasy. But last week saw an event for which sheer unreality had even the dream factories beaten. *Graham Chedd, New Scientist, Feb. 8, 1973, p 290*

2 the motion-picture industry.

Old Nick making money for the front-office men: another potboiler about the Devil is rampant in the dream factory. . . . a thing called "Exorcist II: The Heretic." *Penelope Gilliatt, "The Current Cinema: The Devil Abroad in Hollywood," The New Yorker, July 18, 1977, p 70*

[1966]

dream machine, the television industry.

Back in the dream machine, BBC 1's *Barlow* continues on whatever, at his level, a beat is called. He has been given smart new surroundings (a flat with two telephones), and reports to various smooth operators of the manipulative mandarin class. *Richard North, "The Arts," The Listener, Jan. 16, 1975, p 83*

[1971, from *The Great American Dream Machine*, a program of topical satire on the public television network in the United States]

Dr. Feelgood, 1 a physician who regularly prescribes amphetamines or other stimulants for his patients.

Was there a "Dr. Feelgood" in the White House, dispensing chemical happiness to his co-workers? . . . The doctor denied it. *Maclean's, Aug. 21, 1978, p 22*

2 *Attributive and transferred use.*

The Carter Administration has responded with a Dr. Feelgood litany that the dollar's health is sound. . . . But the world's money traders are not buying that happy talk. *Time, Oct. 9, 1978, p 45*

[1972] Also called FEELGOOD.

dri·og·ra·phy (drai'ag rə fi:), *n.* a printing process using a flat-surfaced plate and special inks, making unnecessary the use of water to keep nonprinting areas free of ink.

With an attractive combination of wit and clarity, Mr. [James] Moran singles out some of the more portentous exhibits, notably those which indicated improvements in photogravure and driography; and the emergence of optical character recognition devices. *The Times Literary Supplement, May 12, 1972, p 556*

[1970, from *dry* + lith*ography*]

driographic, *adj.*: A necessary adjunct of the driographic system is that the printing ink be optimized for use with the Dry Plate. *John L. Curtin, "Printing Plate," McGraw-Hill Yearbook of Science and Technology 1972, p 340*

drip irrigation, another name for TRICKLE IRRIGATION.

Probably the principal benefit, which is not matched in other techniques, is that drip irrigation supplies plants with the precise amount of water they need. Just enough water is delivered to the root zone of a plant to replenish the amount consumed in evapotranspiration (the water evaporated from the soil and transpired by the plant), and an additional amount to leach salts from the region of the soil close to the roots. *Kobe Shoji, "Drip Irrigation," Scientific American, Nov. 1977, p 65*

[1971]

driveability or **drivability,** *n.* the quality or characteristics of design that make an automobile easy to drive.

These substantial reductions in emissions were accomplished . . . at relatively small cost, although penalties were incurred in both fuel efficiency and driveability. *William G. Agnew, Science, Jan. 25, 1974, p 254*

The car I used was a Volvo 144 fitted with Michelin M + S winter tyres, each studded with 120 tungsten carbide spikes. These project only a millimetre or two from the tread, but totally transform a car's drivability. *The Times (London), Feb. 8, 1973, p 31*

[1972]

drive-through, *adj.* designed or arranged to be seen while riding in one's automobile.

Shuster had been impressed by the large number of people who traveled to Africa primarily to visit the game parks and believed that a drive-through zoo would appeal to the American public. *Robert Scott Milne, "Theme Amusement Parks," The Americana Annual 1975, p 52*

[1973]

droog, *n.* a member of a lawless gang; gangster.

Trotskyist, in Labour terminology, is virtually synony-

mous with hooligan, hoodlum, ruffian, droog. *The Times (London), Jan. 27, 1972, p 16*

[1971, from the word for a young gangster in Nadsat, an artificial language used in the novel *A Clockwork Orange* (1962), by Anthony Burgess, British author, born 1917]

droogie, *n.* a young droog; juvenile delinquent.

Dad came to the new town for a job and a house; and other people came; and more buildings went up; so that subways and walkways replace the fields and paths. Now he waits with the KAB to pick a fight with the lads from Longbenton. He hates it. . . . But what does he *expect?* That, my little droogies, is different. *Bel Mooney, New Statesman, Jan. 3, 1975, p 8*

[1975]

droop, *n.* Often, **the droop.** another name for BIG DRESS.

On a recent sunny day on Fifth Avenue, the droops were out in droves, completely concealing even the shapeliest woman's protrusions and inversions. *Judy Klemesrud, The New York Times, Aug. 27, 1975, p 29*

[1975]

drop, *v.t. Slang.* to swallow or ingest (a drug, especially a narcotic).

For every pain or problem we take a drink, smoke a cigarette of one type or another, or drop a pill. *Joel Fort, The New York Times Book Review, Feb. 13, 1972, Part II, p 22*

He [Ken Kesey] was dropping tabs of acid when most others were still getting high on root beer, and the "Acid Tests" he began on the West Coast of America all but turned-on an entire generation. *The Times Literary Supplement, Feb. 25, 1972, p 209*

[1968]

drop-in, *n.* a dropout who rejoins conventional society without giving up unconventional ideas and ways of living.

Howard Bannister (Ryan O'Neil) . . . is pursued by a madcap young thing, Judy Maxwell, a drop-in who has majored in everything and remembered it all, and who is determined to prise Howard away from Eunice. *Gavin Millar, The Listener, June 29, 1972, p 878*

Montreal sociologists have come up with a new term: they no longer speak of "dropouts" but of "drop-ins." The term is used to describe young people who live outside the ordinary social framework but continue to live parasitically off the same society. *Yves Agnes, The Manchester Guardian Weekly (Le Monde section), Nov. 24, 1973, p 15*

[1967, patterned on *dropout*, but influenced by earlier *drop-in* (1963) a person who drops in; casual visitor]

dropout, *n.* a Jewish emigrant from the Soviet Union who is supposedly going to Israel but emigrates to another country, especially the United States.

An early Israeli attempt to stop the dropouts involved trying to establish an air link between Moscow and Tel Aviv. In that way, Russian Jews might be flown directly to Israel, thus eliminating the Vienna stopover and the refugees' option to go elsewhere. *Time, Nov. 22, 1976, p 37*

[1976]

Dr. Strangelove, variant of STRANGELOVE.

The anti-nuclear lobby would have us believe that the

nuclear industry is run by an army of Dr Strangeloves motivated by nothing more than a desire for personal glory and profit. *New Scientist, Aug. 29, 1974, p 498*

[1966]

drug·o·la (drə'gou lə), *n. U.S. Slang.* illicit payments made by narcotics dealers to secure protection from police or other legal interference.

In an unusual move, the Justice Department has authorized the U.S. Attorney's office in Newark to coordinate a nationwide investigation, and Federal investigators throughout the country are looking for friendly witnesses who will be granted immunity for telling what they know about payola and drugola. *"Payola and the Mob," Newsweek, July 30, 1973, p 62*

[1973, patterned on *payola, gayola*, etc.]

drummer, *n.* **march to** (or **hear**) **a different drummer,** *U.S.* to be different from others; act unconventionally.

Massachusetts voters march to a very different drummer indeed. For many of the independent-minded Yankees, the situation was a source of pride rather than puzzlement—"the other 49 states are all wrong" was the unastonished explanation of Marty Kelly who delivers beer in the Boston area. *"A Different Drummer," Newsweek, Nov. 20, 1972, p 32*

In the new world of the tour, one man, who came to the circuit as recently as 1967, obviously hears a much different drummer. That is Trevino, a throwback not to the nineteen-fifties but practically to the nineteen-thirties. He is an anachronism: the last of the ex-caddies to become a great champion. *Herbert Warren Wind, "The Sporting Scene," The New Yorker, April 28, 1973, p 120*

[1972, abstracted from an epigram in Thoreau's *Walden:* "If a man does not keep pace with his companions, perhaps it is because he hears a different drummer."]

dry, *v.* **dry out,** to receive treatment for alcoholism or drug addiction; be free of dependence on alcohol or drugs.

Elizabeth dried out for a while and then had a relapse, drinking more heavily than before. *"The Price of Alcoholism: Five Case Histories," Time, April 22, 1974, p 80*

[1963] See DETOX.

D sleep, short for DESYNCHRONIZED SLEEP.

Though there is no assurance that cats dream in D Sleep, the psychiatrists acknowledge, the very fact that the animal brains undergo human-like electrical patterns during sleep justifies the cat as "a reasonable subject for our study of the brain as a dream process generator." *Science News, Dec. 17, 1977, p 405*

[1974] Compare S SLEEP.

dual displacement engine, *U.S.* an internal-combustion engine fitted with a device to reduce fuel consumption by turning off the flow of fuel to some of the cylinders.

As long ago as 1917, drivers of Enger autos with V-12 engines could shut off fuel to six of the cylinders by moving a lever protruding through the dashboard under the steering column. Ford has substituted electronic for human control in its "dual displacement engine" (DDE). A small (6 in. by 6 in. by 1 1/2 in.) black box mounted on the fire wall is fed information from five strategically placed sensors. *"Sci-*

ence: Ford's Better Idea," Time, Oct. 4, 1976, p 88*

[1976]

dual pricing, pricing of packaged goods to show both the actual price and the price per pound or other unit.

Consumerism is not about to fade away; rather, it is begetting a spate of legislation to regulate retailers' conduct, including unit and dual pricing and code dating. *Theodore D. Ellsworth, "Retail Business," 1971 Collier's Encyclopedia Year Book, p 460*

[1970]

dual slalom, another name for PARALLEL SLALOM.

The final race was the first dual slalom in World Cup history. In a format borrowed from the professional tour, the skiers raced side by side down parallel courses in direct eliminations. *Frank Litsky, "Skiing," The 1976 World Book Year Book, p 459*

[1976]

duck hook, a deviation of a golf ball from its intended course, usually in the path of an erratic curve.

Too many of the tee shots, at least half, developed a bend about 150 yards down the fairway and disappeared to the left in a sudden, ugly, discouraging curve. Duck hooks, as the professional golfers call them, miserable duck hooks. *Jack Batten, "The Ecstasy of Long Drives," Maclean's, July 1973, p 35*

[1967]

dude, *n. U.S. Slang.* any male; a man or boy; fellow.

"Compared to the Tombs, you know, it was okay.... Every time I went there dudes in the receiving line would be sick ... There was so many dudes in the 'A' pen once that I couldn't sit down. Some of them getting sick on the floor; the dude next to me was moaning about his bust." *James Willwerth, "Portrait of a Mugger," Harper's, Nov. 1974, p 89*

Each time I suggest a program of self-development, they respond with overwhelming enthusiasm. Black teen-agers —some of the roughest, most street-wise dudes you will ever meet—respond to that appeal. *Jesse L. Jackson, The New York Times Magazine, April 18, 1976, p 71*

[1970, extended from the original sense of a city slicker, a dandy (1880's)]

duke, *v.i., v.t. Especially U.S. Slang.* **1** to fight or hit with the fists.

While the book is most certainly addressed to educators, we are not mistreated with stuff about "pattern of errors" or "interference of home tongue" or "mainstream demands," terms which hallmark the language-arts battles when folks be duking in the faculty lounge about the speech of black students. *Toni Cade Bambara, Review of "Black English: Its History and Usage in the United States" by J. L. Dillard, The New York Times Book Review, Sept. 3, 1972, p 3*

"If the cat didn't have a gun available when he got into an argument, he'd probably just duke (punch) the other person," says ghetto-bred Sgt. Fred Williams. "The other guy might end up with a busted lip, but he'd still be alive." *"Crime: The Deadliest City," Newsweek, Jan. 1, 1973, p 21*

2 duke it out, to fight, especially until someone wins.

There is nobody in our organization that takes second place when it comes to getting up and duking it out. Just because we wear suits and ties doesn't mean we're afraid to get into that kind of thing. *Tom Metzger quoted in Maclean's, Jan. 8, 1979, p 8*

[1972, verb use (and back formation) of the slang noun *dukes* the fists (1874), especially in the phrase *put up one's dukes*]

duke-out, *n. Especially U.S. Slang.* a fistfight.

Take the last all-House duke-out. It was, distressingly enough, over ten years ago. Although there have been a fair number of fistfights in the capitol since, none has qualified as total Fist City. *Molly Ivins, "Inside the Austin Fun House," The Atlantic, March 1975, p 48*

[1975, probably from *duke*, verb, on the pattern of *shoot-out* and *breakout*]

dukes-up, *adj. Especially U.S. Slang.* ready to fight; pugnacious.

Aside from a dukes-up debut as official opposition, for two months the party had stood as still as the slate-gray autumn that hung on here almost supernaturally long. *Glen Allen, Maclean's, March 1974, p 10*

Did the blame for that lie with the Communists, who bickered endlessly with their Socialist allies during the campaign? Not to hear Marchais tell it. "We bear no responsibility," he said in a dukes-up, three-hour speech. The cause, he asserted, was purely the Socialists' "obstinacy." *Time, May 8, 1978, p 37*

[1974, abstracted from *put one's dukes up*]

du·met ('du: met), *n.* wire made of an iron and nickel alloy covered with copper, used in incandescent lamps and vacuum tubes.

The new Ragen machine automatically feeds two pieces of dumet—the copper covered leads that go into a light bulb through the glass envelope—which it trims to the proper length and then drops a bead over the filament. Next, it tacks the bead to the dumet at the proper height and then melts and moulds the bead. The filament is then wound, cut to length, formed and transferred and staked to the dumet. A complete mount is then formed. *"Technology Review: Heated Rivalry in Light Bulb Market," New Scientist, Jan. 27, 1972, p 209*

[1972, from *Dumet*, a trademark for such wire]

dummy head, a device resembling a human head with a microphone in each ear, used to receive sound for binaural and quadraphonic sound reproduction and transmission.

The new QB-phonic system makes a recording using two conventional dummy heads, one in front of and one behind a baffle, to capture front and rear sounds and transmit them in four channels via a conventional CD-4 quadraphonic disc. The four channels are processed by introducing delays and frequency filtering, to compensate for the path in air which the sound must take when reproduced by loudspeakers instead of headphones. *New Scientist, March 24, 1977, p 701*

[1976]

dunemobile, *n.* a vehicle for riding on sand dunes.

The foolhardy adventurer may even use his "toboggan" to descend the leeward side of a dune in the summer. A popular sport in the area of the mammoth Sleeping Bear Dune, west of Traverse City, Michigan, is to ride the dunemobiles at high speed over the shifting sands. *John M. Roberts, "The Wandering Sands," Encyclopedia Science Supplement (Grolier) 1972, p 181*

[1972, from *dune* + auto*mobile*]

du·o·plas·ma·tron (,du: ou'plæz mə tran), *n.* an apparatus that produces a stream of ions, as of argon or oxygen.

The ions used for sample bombardment are generated in a hollow-cathode duoplasmatron ion source that is capable of producing ions of a wide variety of gases, including those of a highly electronegative character. *C. A. Andersen and J. R. Hinthorne, "Ion Microprobe Mass Analyzer," Science, Feb. 25, 1972, p 853*

[1964, from *duo-* double + *plasma* highly ionized gas + *-tron* an accelerating device, as a *cyclotron*]

duplex, *n.* a double-stranded DNA or RNA molecule.

Another method of repair occurs in the dark and in cells containing certain repair enzymes. In this process, known as excision repair, a damaged strand on the DNA duplex is removed and replaced by undamaged DNA replicated from the other strand of the duplex. *H. E. Kubitschek, "Life Sciences: Biophysics," Britannica Book of the Year 1975, p 444*

[1963, from the adjective, meaning "twofold" (OED 1817)]

dustbinman, *n. British.* a garbage collector.

"I'll talk with anybody. The dustbinman, or Prince Philip if he wants, as long as he's interested." *Norman Harris, The Sunday Times (London), May 9, 1971, p 55*

The first major confrontation over inflationary wage demands came when local authority workers employed in what were called 'the dirty jobs'—dustbinmen, sewage workers, and street sweepers—began a series of selective strikes. *Ian Waller, "History of the United Kingdom," The Annual Register of World Events in 1970 (1971), p 40*

[1970] ► This term seems to be competing with the earlier Briticism, *dustman* (1700's).

dust cloud, a mass of interstellar matter made up of gases, molecules, and other particles; cloud of cosmic dust.

A typical dust cloud with a diameter of one light-year and a density of 1,000 molecules of hydrogen per cubic centimeter will attenuate light by about four magnitudes and ultraviolet radiation by a factor perhaps as large as 10^{24}. *Barry E. Turner, "Interstellar Molecules: Molecular Life Cycles," Scientific American, March 1973, p 62*

[1965] ► The nebular hypothesis in astronomy holds that stars arise from the condensation of dust clouds.

dust head, *U.S. Slang.* a habitual user of ANGEL DUST.

"Dust heads," as users are called, say that $3 for a marijuana cigaret laced with the hallucinogenic-like drug is a pretty cheap high. *Marcia Kramer, "Angel Dust—Not A Heavenly High," Daily News (New York), Feb. 24, 1978, p 29*

[1978, from angel *dust* + *head*, slang for "drug addict"]

dust tail, the part of a comet's tail consisting of dust particles blown away from the coma by pressure of the sun's radiation.

The observations from Skylab just after Comet Kohoutek swung past the Sun suggest that particles up to 1 mm in diameter were ejected from the nucleus. This is 100 times larger than particles that usually form the dust tails of comets. *William C. Schneider, "Skylab," McGraw-Hill*

duty solicitor

Yearbook of Science and Technology 1975, p 51

[1975] Compare GAS TAIL. See also ANTITAIL.

duty solicitor, a government-appointed solicitor in Great Britain, charged with representing indigents.

The duty solicitor, apart from giving advice to a defendant, would have the advantage of being able to talk to court officials on an informal basis where he finds this desirable. *Marcel Berlins, " 'Duty Solicitor' Experiment Starts Today," The Times (London), May 1, 1972, p 2*

[1972]

DUV, abbreviation of DATA-UNDERVOICE.

DUV, part of the Bell System's Dataphone Digital Service, allows 1.5 million bits of information to be transmitted per second. *R. H. Klie, "Communications," The 1975 World Book Year Book, p 269*

[1975]

du·vay (du:ʹvei), *n. British.* a quilt stuffed with down or feathers; down comforter.

Leena Skoog was scheduled today to spend six hours in a giant deep freeze in a temperature of 25 degrees F below freezing, covered only by a newly-developed quilt. The unlikely event is regarded as the "focal point" of research being carried out in 30 major towns and cities on Thursday and Friday in the now-celebrated attempt to find out how many people sleep in the nude, and so—hopefully—raise sales of duvays. *"Business Diary," The Times (London), March 15, 1972, p 19*

[1972, Anglicized form (based on the pronunciation) of earlier *duvet* (OED 1758) a Continental type of quilt, from French, literally, down]

D.W.I., abbreviation of *driving while intoxicated.*

The D.W.I. offender is generally an individual under pressure, anxious about financial or domestic troubles. *"D.W.I.s Anonymous," Time, Jan. 5, 1970, p 28*

[1968]

dynamic positioning, a system to automatically control the position of a ship by computer.

The ship maintains its position by a process called "dynamic positioning." . . . If the ship begins to drift, the computer automatically activates the appropriate screws (propellers) to hold the ship in position. *N. Terence Edgar, "Drilling Into The Ocean Floor," The World Book Science Annual 1972 (1971), p 122*

[1967]

dynamic scattering, a process in which transparent liquid crystals become opaque and scatter light by application of a charge of electricity, used especially in producing display screens for computers.

In 1968, the RCA laboratories discovered the so-called "dynamic scattering" effect by enclosing a thin film (a few microns thick) of nematic material between transparent conducting plates and applying several tens of volts. *Martin Tobias, "The Fluid State of Liquid-Crystals," New Scientist, Dec. 14, 1972, p 652*

[1968]

dynamite or *sometimes* **dynomite,** *adj. (restricted to an attributive position before nouns) U.S. and Canadian Slang.* superlative; extraordinarily good.

Conceded an Arledge aide last week: "CBS ought to be congratulated. It was dynamite TV." *Time, Nov. 28, 1977, p 47*

She is no longer a dynomite mom. They used to talk these things over, share enthusiasms. *Paul W. Wales, "Mom Gets Lost," The New Yorker, Jan. 23, 1978, p 25*

After a dynamite opening . . . at the Palladium last night, Elton John went up to 54th Street's Studio 54 and ran into —of all people—Goldie Hawn. *New York Post, Oct. 19, 1979, p 7*

[1976, popularized by the character "J.J." in the television situation comedy series *Good Times*]

dynamite charge, another name for ALLEN CHARGE.

Because hung juries are becoming common in political and complicated criminal cases, prosecutors argue that the dynamite charge is necessary to push juries along—that it is difficult to get 12 people to agree on anything and that the criminal process would get stalled if jurors were not told they must decide cases. *Martin Garbus, "Juries: The Problem of the 'Dynamite' Charge," The New York Times, Oct. 8, 1972, Sec. 4, p 6*

[1972]

dyne·in (ʹdain in), *n.* a form of the enzyme ATPase whose action provides the energy for the movement of cilia.

The microtubules of cilia are associated with a protein of high molecular weight. This protein, which Gibbons named "dynein," is an adenosine triphosphatase. Dynein forms arms or projections that are attached to one tubule (the A tubule) of the outer doublets. *Science, Sept. 28, 1973, p 1237*

[1968, coined by Ian Gibbons, an American molecular biologist, from *dyne* the unit of force (from Greek *dýnamis* power) + -*in* (chemical suffix)]

dysautonomic, *adj.* of, relating to, or affected with dysautonomia, an inherited disorder of the autonomic nervous system in which sensory perception and many automatic functions are impaired.

Mercifully, not every dysautonomic child has all the symptoms, but some of them have so many that they cannot attend regular school and require constant care. *"Children Who Cannot Cry," Newsweek, March 19, 1973, p 56*

—*n.* a person affected with dysautonomia.

When NGF [nerve-growth factor] levels were determined . . . the results showed a striking discrepancy: dysautonomics, compared with normal subjects, had a threefold increase in blood-serum levels of a substance immunologically equivalent to NGF. *"Science and the Citizen," Scientific American, Dec. 1976, p 53*

[1973, from *dysautonomia* (1954, from *dys-* abnormal + *autonomic* + -*ia* disorder) + -*ic*]

dys·me·li·a (disʹmi: li: ə *or* disʹmel i: ə), *n.* a deformed condition or development of the limbs.

The deformities are usually severe, and the upper limbs are more severely affected than the lower limbs. This variation in the degree of the defect is also observed in human cases of thalidomide dysmelia. *D. E. Poswillo, et al., London, "Letters to Nature: The Marmoset as an Animal Model for Teratological Research," Nature, Oct. 20, 1972, p 461*

[1972, from New Latin, from *dys-* bad + Greek *mélos* limb]

E

eagle freak, *U.S. Slang (often disparaging).* a person who advocates the protection of wildlife; conservationist.

He is sensitive to criticism of the coal companies and of miners. The concerns of ranchers and environmentalists—"eagle freaks," as they are sometimes called —annoy Sopher. *James Conaway, The Atlantic, Sept. 1973, p 98*

[1973, from bald *eagle* the national bird of the U.S. taken as the representative of endangered species + *freak*] Compare ECOFREAK.

Eames chair (i:mz), a plywood or molded plastic chair shaped to fit the contours of the body.

The Eames chair is hardly a pure work of art; it is a utilitarian object, produced by impulses both sacred and profane. Considered even as a practical chair, it has flaws. But as an object of contemplation, as an instant replay of social change during the past twenty years, the Eames chair is invaluable. *Douglas Davis, "Art: Have a Seat," Newsweek, May 14, 1973, p 81*

[1964, named after Charles *Eames*, 1907-1978, an American designer, who introduced it in the 1940's] Compare BARCELONA CHAIR.

early warning system, anything that detects danger early.

Sixth, the UN would be asked to set up an international early warning system for the ill-effects of man-made pollutants. *Jon Tinker, "A Shopping List For Stockholm," New Scientist, June 1, 1972, p 489*

Essentially the committee has two roles in respect of drugs: it licenses the release of new products and it maintains an early warning system for the detection of unexpected adverse effects from drugs. *The Times (London), Jan. 24, 1973, p 11*

[1966, extended sense of the term originally (1946) used for a system of early warning of aerial attack]

ears, *n.pl. U.S. Slang.* a citizens band radio set.

Because of overcrowding, many a CB enthusiast (called an "apple") is strapping an illegal linear amplifier ("boots") on to his transceiver ("ears") which is limited by the Federal Communications Commission ("Big Daddy" in the US) to an output power of no more than five watts. *Nicholas Valéry, "Big Daddy and the Barefoot Apples," New Scientist, June 30, 1977, p 764*

[1977]

earth art, a form of art that changes some natural object or scenery to fit a concept of the artist.

"When I get discouraged," says [Michael] Heizer, "I go back to painting," but the core of his work—by now the most extensive accomplishment in what has come to be called "earth art"—is out-of-doors, dug, blasted and chiseled into sections of the land in Nevada and California. *Douglas Davis, "The Earth Mover," Newsweek, Nov. 18, 1974, p 113*

[1970] Also called LAND ART.

earth artist: Peter Hutchinson, a British earth artist, has cultivated bread molds on the lip of an active volcano in Mexico. *Calvin Tomkins, "Onward and Upward With the Arts," The New Yorker, Feb. 5, 1972, p 42*

earthlubber, *n.* a person who stays on earth and has not traveled in outer space; one who is not a space traveler.

The applied version, probably no sooner than the 1990s, could provide direct power in space to space stations, spacecraft and other recipients using its own, self-generated laser beam. But efficient, high-powered lasers have also been a long-sought goal of weapons developers, so earthlubbers will be watching too. *Science News, May 15, 1976, p 309*

[1973, from *earth* + *lubber*, patterned on *landlubber*]

earthquake lights or **earthquake lightning,** flashes of bright light occurring during an earthquake, believed to be caused by electric discharges from the earth's crust.

The subject of earthquake lights is fascinating. Few scientists have worked on the question because observations are rare and are usually made by untrained persons. Nevertheless, observations have been made for many years, and the existence of earthquake lights is well established. One hypothesized explanation is linked to the piezoelectric effect in quartz-bearing rock. *Science News, Jan. 7, 1978, p 3*

A puzzling but rare phenomenon known as earthquake lightning—flashes of lightning caused by an earthquake. *The Times (London), Nov. 23, 1970, p 10*

[1970]

earth resources satellite, an artificial satellite that gathers data on the earth's natural resources.

Somewhat of a dark horse in space has been the earth resources satellite. Such vehicles were not even included in early planning. But when astronauts returned with stories of how well they could see the earth below, geologists conceived the idea of the Landsat series of multispectral scanning satellites. *John Noble Wilford, "The Spinoff from Space," The New York Times Magazine, Jan. 29, 1978, p 22*

[1968]

Earth Shoes, a trademark for square-toed shoes with thicker soles in front than in back, designed to lower the heel below the rest of the foot for greater comfort.

She got rid of the demure blue patent pumps she had been wearing and substituted earth shoes, supremely comfortable but odd-looking with their lowered heel. "I hadn't worn them before because I thought people would think them ugly," she explained. *June Callwood, "Margaret's First Hurrah," Maclean's, Aug. 1974, p 7*

The people are your usual mixture of ages, etc. Some are wearing Earth Shoes, some are wearing Gucci loafers. *"The Talk of the Town," The New Yorker, Feb. 3, 1975, p 22*

[1973, so called because they were introduced into the United States from Denmark (where they originated) on Earth Day (April 22) of 1970] Also popularly spelled **earth shoes.**

earth time, time measured by the 24-hour rotation of the earth, especially as a measure of time on other celestial bodies.

The General Conference's 1967 redefinition of the second did not resolve a conflict that had long been going on between proponents of atomic time and proponents of earth time. Astronomers had, naturally, been partial to earth time, and, indeed, *all* time had for centuries been considered their province. But even the astronomers had their differences. *E. J. Kahn, Jr., "Our Far-Flung Correspondents: The Leap Second," The New Yorker, Aug. 27, 1973, p 55*

[1968] Compare EARTH-YEAR.

Earthwatch or **earthwatch,** *n.* a proposed network of stations to monitor world-wide environmental pollution.

We will have an "earthwatch" to monitor and measure the growing sickness of the planet, and perhaps not too late, to have its warnings respected. *Raymond F. Dasmann, "The Aftermath of Stockholm," Natural History, Oct. 1972, p 103*

The difference between the Center and Earthwatch is fundamental: the Center's mission is to observe and report; Earthwatch's will be not only to act as an early-alert system but to take that information and use it to assess the world environment in all facets and make suggestions for changes. *Skip Rozin, "Long live the Center for Short-Lived Phenomena!" Harper's, March 1973, p 51*

[1972] See UNEP. Compare DOOMWATCH.

Earth-year or **earth-year,** *n.* time measured by the 365-day year of the earth, especially as a measure of time on other celestial bodies.

As Pluto moves in its orbit, the pole points farther away from the Earth each year.

The effect of having the pole in the orbital plane is to make a season at one of the poles last for about half the time that Pluto takes to revolve around the Sun. Thus, there would be roughly 124 Earth-years of summer with constant sunlight, followed by 124 Earth-years of winter with constant darkness. *Laura P. Bautz, "Atomic Energy: Pluto's Rotation Axis," The 1974 World Book Year Book, p 203*

[1967] Compare EARTH TIME.

Eb·la·ite ('eb lə‚ait *or* 'i: blə‚ait), *n.* an ancient Semitic language discovered in cuneiform inscriptions on several thousand clay tablets excavated in northern Syria between 1975 and 1979.

Scholars have been electrified by the parallels between the language of the tablets and the language of ancient Hebrews. Eblaite, as the language is referred to, seems to be a West Semitic form unlike Sumerian, Akkadian or any

of the other ancient languages known to modern science. *George Alexander and John Dart, "Origins of Israel Seen in Tablets of 2600 B.C.," New York Post, June 9, 1976, p 60*

The second important aspect of the discovery is the previously unknown language in which many of the tablets were written. Now called Eblaite, it is one of the Semitic family of languages, similar to Phoenician and Hebrew. It is the oldest written Semitic language, as texts in the other languages appear only 1,300 years later. *Patricia Clough, "Clay Tablets Will Revolutionize Early History of Mankind," The Times (London), Jan. 15, 1977, p 1*

— *adj.* of or relating to Eblaite or to the kingdom of Ebla. Also, EBLAN.

The language of the tablets, unknown until now, has been named Eblaite by the researchers. It is related to the Biblical Hebrew that was used about one thousand years later. One of the most important tablets is one containing a vocabulary of Eblaite and Sumeric words. *"Cuneiform Tablets Tell of Ancient Empire," Science News, Aug. 21, 1976, p 118*

Names of Eblaite citizens translate into such biblical names as Abraham, David and Saul, and tablets mention a place called "Urusalima," possibly Ebla's name for Jerusalem. *Steven V. Roberts, "Myth Proves a Factual Guide to Archeology," The New York Times, Dec. 12, 1976, Sec. 4, p 8*

[1976] ► Excavations at Tel Mardikh, site of ancient Ebla, begun in 1964 by Paolo Matthiae, led to the discovery of over 15,000 tablets between 1975 and 1979. The tablets provide a record of a state that apparently flourished during the 2000's B.C. Knowledge of the tablets' contents came as they were deciphered by Giovanni Pettinato. However, the secrecy surrounding the tablets imposed by the Syrian government who suppressed publication of photographs caused many archaeologists to reserve opinion on the findings until full documentation is available to the scholarly community.

Eb·lan ('eb lən *or* 'i: blən), *adj.* variant of EBLAITE.

The existence of the Eblan kingdom was not unknown; ancient Sumerian, Akkadian and Egyptian texts refer to it. However, Paolo Matthiae, 36, and Giovanni Pettinato, 41 . . . were the first to explore Ebla's ruins, which they located some 30 miles south of modern Aleppo. *"Science: A New 'Third World,'" Time, Oct. 18, 1976, p 63*

[1976]

E·bo·la virus (i'bou lə), a virus that causes very high fever and internal hemorrhaging. It was first identified in Zaire and Sudan in 1976.

Another hitherto unknown tropical virus, named Ebola virus . . . joins a growing list of fatal haemorrhagic fever viruses found in Africa, of which Lassa fever and Marburg disease (the so-called green monkey disease) are the most notorious. *Nature-Times News Service, "Science Report," The Times (London), March 21, 1977, p 17*

The Ebola virus that in 1977 caused a severe human epidemic and claimed many lives in Sudan and Zaire was shown to be similar but not identical to the Marburg virus that ten years earlier had caused deaths in Uganda and Europe. *J. R. Porter, "Microbiology," The Americana Annual 1978, p 331*

[1976, named after a river in northern Zaire]

ECCM, abbreviation of *electronic counter-countermeasure.*

Electronic Counter Measures against such missiles

might include sending out scrambling radio signals to distort the beam. . . . Needless to say, most of this equipment is highly classified. It also becomes obsolete very quickly as opponents learn their own ECCM. *Orville Schell, "The Subculture Spawned by Electronic Warfare," Harper's, Oct. 1972, p 74*

[1968] Compare ECM.

ec·dy·ste·rone (ˌek də 'ster oun), *n.* a hormone, related to the molting hormone ecdysone, isolated from crustacea and insects and also from some plants.

One technical problem that has hindered research related to ecdysterone is the lack of a precise physicochemical technique for quantifying tissue and circulating titers of this hormone. *David W. Borst and John D. O'Connor, "Arthropod Molting Hormone: Radioimmune Assay," Science, Oct. 27, 1972, p 418*

[1967, from earlier (1956) *ecdysone* (from *ecdysis* molting) + *sterol* + *-one*, as in *hormone*]

echocardiogram, *n.* the record of an echocardiograph.

The ultrasound technique involves bouncing sound waves off the heart. The sound waves are of such high frequency that they cannot be detected by human ears. Using equipment that costs $20,000, cardiologists can view the anatomical features of the heart in a form called an echocardiogram. *Lawrence K. Altman, "Health and Disease," Encyclopedia Science Supplement (Grolier) 1975, p 234*

[1975, from *echocardio*graphy (1965) + *-gram* tracing, record]

echo effect, a delayed consequence or repetition of an event.

It is possible, indeed, that births will temporarily continue to rise slightly in an "echo effect" of the postwar baby boom, now that women born after World War II, many of whom apparently delayed the birth of their first child, are bearing children. *Teresa A. Sullivan, "Population," 1978 Collier's Encyclopedia Year Book (1977), p 453*

[1971] Compare RIPPLE EFFECT.

ECM, abbreviation of *electronic countermeasure* (a device to confuse the guidance system of an enemy missile).

All the Nato programmes on which the successes and failures in the recent Middle East fighting obviously have a bearing—ECMs, SAMs, anti-tank guided weapons, tank gunnery and armour—will now be critically reviewed. *David Fairhall, "Middle East Lessons for NATO," The Manchester Guardian Weekly, Nov. 24, 1973, p 5*

[1963] Compare ECCM.

ecodevelopment, *n.* development which balances economic and ecological factors.

Rich nations should atone for years of economic exploitation by paying appropriate reparations to the developing countries. For the Third World itself the policy for the future should be one of ecodevelopment, this representing a synthesis of the conflicting needs of the environment and economic growth. *John A. Loraine, "The State of the Planet, 1975: Third World's Voice," New Statesman, Dec. 26, 1975, p 808*

[1975, from *economic* and *ecological* + *development*]

ecodoom, *n.* large-scale ecological destruction; obliteration of a balanced natural environment.

In his presidential address to the British Association for the Advancement of Science Sir Kingsley Dunham had posed the question: "Can our species survive the next few hundred years?" As can be gathered from the extract quoted from the end of his address he was unable to return a confident Yes. But his doubt is not that of the prophets of ecodoom, who predict early disaster unless men achieve a radical revision of their collective goals and behaviour. *The Times (London), Aug. 21, 1973, p 13*

[1972, from *eco-* ecological + *doom*] Compare DOOMWATCH.

ecodoomster, *n.* one who predicts or warns of ecodoom.

Men of goodwill can defend humanity from technological doom, granted an extension of scientific training . . . and of British-style social democracy. A soothing conclusion for those who attended the lectures at Stanford, on which this book is based, but words which are scarcely likely to carry much conviction with the ecodoomsters committed to a cataclysmic view of the world's fate. *Steven Rose, Books: Review of "Reconciling Man With the Environment" by Eric Ashby, The Manchester Guardian Weekly, Oct. 8, 1978, p 20*

[1973] See DOOMSTER.

ecofallow, *n.* a method of farming that combines reduced tillage and crop rotation to control weeds and conserve soil moisture.

Ecofallow markedly increased the grain yields of wheat and sorghum. In this connection, wheat yields increased 6% and 8% and grain sorghum yields 31% and 47% with minimum and no tillage, respectively, above the 10-year average yields of these two crops obtained with conventional tillage. *M. G. Boosalis and Benjamin Doupnik, Jr., "Plant Disease Control," McGraw-Hill Yearbook of Science and Technology 1977, p 341*

[1977, from *eco-* ecological + *fallow*]

ecofreak, *n. Slang (often disparaging).* a fervent conservationist or environmentalist.

Sierra Club members, taunted as "ecofreaks," report that they are being subjected to the most severe criticism they have ever encountered. *Mary Ellen Leary, "California," The Atlantic, Nov. 1973, p 24*

The presenter, Malcolm MacEwen, said that 'some people tend to dismiss Friends of the Earth as doomsters or ecofreaks, but I have found that responsible scientists don't share this view.' *The Listener, March 14, 1974, p 339*

[1972, from *eco-* ecological + *freak*] Also called ECONUT. Compare EAGLE FREAK.

ec·o·mone ('ek ou moun), *n.* a hormone associated with or affecting the balance of nature; ecological hormone.

A consideration of the role of ecomones in the establishment of relations between organisms in the networks of the biochemical continuum is also lacking. *Marcel Florkin, "Book Review: Evolution of Nutrition," Review of "Biology of Nutrition," edited by Richard N. T. W. Fiennes, Nature, Sept. 15, 1972, p 177*

[1972, from *eco-* ecological + hor*mone*]

econiche, *n.* protected habitat in which an organism or species can survive.

But if these unnatural recombinants escaped from the laboratory, particularly during the experimental stages, they might tuck into some econiche where naturally evolved control mechanisms couldn't touch them. *Janet L.*

economic crime

Hopson, "Genetic Sabotage in the Public Interest," *Science News, March 20, 1976, p 188*

[1976, from *eco-* ecological + *niche*]

economic crime, a crime involving the illegal use of money or acquisition of wealth, especially in Communist and Third World countries.

A March 25 decree increased penalties for a number of "economic crimes" and imposed the death penalty for embezzlement, smuggling, corruption, and unauthorized disposal of foreign currency. *William F. Gutteridge, "Uganda," 1976 Collier's Encyclopedia Year Book (1975), p 553*

Two Soviet officials were executed for economic crimes. Mikhail Y. Leviyev, the manager of a Moscow state store and a Jew, had embezzled $2.7 million worth of goods, while Yuri S. Sosnovski, the director of a division of the Timber and Wood Processing Ministry, had accepted bribes of $140,000 from a Swiss businessman. *Ellsworth Raymond, "USSR," The Americana Annual 1976, p 564*

[1975]

economic zone, short for EXCLUSIVE ECONOMIC ZONE.

But they point to a middle level of threats and problems that include . . . friction with neighbouring States over fishing grounds, oil, or other ocean resources, and illegal immigration, as well as the general role of maintaining sovereignty over Australian territories including coastal waters and the adjacent "economic zone," if this becomes international law. *Martin Woollacott, "Australia's Forces Seek New Role," The Manchester Guardian Weekly, Jan. 11, 1976, p 8*

[1973]

econut, *n. Slang (usually disparaging).* an enthusiast about ecology; an ecofreak.

Current delays must now be laid at the door of the "econuts" who are opposing the . . . plans to drill into the granite rocks, for example, even when the authority makes it clear that this would be a purely scientific exercise that does not imply later use of the site as a waste disposal facility. *"This Week: Britain's Energy Debate Goes Critical," New Scientist, Oct. 20, 1977, p 132*

[1972, from *eco-* ecological + *nut* enthusiast]

ecopolitics, *n.* **1** the study of politics in terms of economic factors.

Though Americans tend to think of West Germany and Japan as the economic giants now, and suppose their own strength is poised on the tip of missile launchers, that perception itself is a reflection of the new dominance of ecopolitics. Neither Germany nor Japan owns a warhead, and both rely on the United States for defense. Yet they are powers of recognized importance in the modern world. *Flora Lewis, "As 1978 Closes, Ecopolitics Motivates the Powers," The New York Times, Dec. 31, 1978, Sec. 4, p E3*

2 the study of politics as affected by ecological issues.

A bimonthly *New Ecologist* (no relation) will concentrate on more topical material, including "ecopolitics" and the more practical aspects of living in a "post-industrial" society. *"This Week: A Blueprint for Eco-Publishing," New Scientist, Dec. 8, 1977, p 623*

[1973, def. 1, from *economic* + *politics*; 1971, def. 2, from *ecological* + *politics*]

eco-pornography, *n.* advertising or publicity that exploits and profits from public interest in ecology and pollution control.

Environmentalist groups still abound, the advertising industry is still cashing in on the bandwagon by presenting companies and products as ecology-conscious (eco-pornography is the word that has been coined for such practices) and politicians still pay plenty of lip service to the issue. *"New World—Power and Pollution: Fuel for a Backlash," Nature, April 28, 1972, p 422*

[1971]

eco-pornographer, *n.:* Drag the favorite whipping boy, DDT, around the stage for an exemplary flogging. A tip of the hat to *Silent Spring*, and a pox of the throat to the eco-pornographers of Madison Avenue. *Thomas H. Jukes, "Disasters by Oil and in Print," National Review, July 20, 1973, p 799*

ec·o·tage ('ek ə₁taːʒ), *n.* sabotage of polluters of the environment, especially to dramatize the need for pollution control and conservation programs.

Ecotage, or sabotage for ecological reasons, was used increasingly by some conservation activists in 1971. Ecotage activities ranged from dumping dye into sewage-treatment tanks to show how pollution travels down waterways, to sawing down roadside billboards. *Andrew L. Newman, "Conservation," The 1972 World Book Year Book, p 298*

[1972, from *eco-* ecological + *sabotage*]

ec·o·tec·ture ('ek ə₁tek tʃər), *n.* architectural design that subordinates immediate and practical needs to environmental factors.

Architect Sim Van der Ryn . . . has already coined a phrase for the new style of building: "ecotecture." At a Berkeley conference he once termed the practitioners "outlaw builders." Whatever the label, the craftsmen were individualists who apparently do their best work alone. *"Modern Living: Karma Yes, Toilets No," Time, Nov. 5, 1973, p 75*

[1972, from *eco-* ecological + *architecture*]

ECR, abbreviation of *electronic cash register.*

The long predicted ECR invasion . . . hit Europe five weeks earlier when the giant German Kaufhof chain installed three different ECR systems in three different stores. *"Technology Review: Electronic Cash Register Gets to Work," New Scientist, Nov. 2, 1972, p 273*

[1972]

ecu or **ECU** (ei'ku:, *sometimes* 'i:'si:'yu:), *n.* acronym for *European Currency Unit,* a money of account in the European Common Market, created to settle debts among members and to act as a standard in floating currencies within a narrow range.

In the longer term, however, members of a united Europe might increase trade more with themselves than with the U.S., and a strong, viable ecu ultimately might rival the dollar as a real reserve currency. If that ever happens, Arab and other foreign governments might be tempted to sell dollars in order to invest in that odd new creature that has six parents—the ecu. *Time, Dec. 18, 1978, p 69*

The annexe suggested that ECUs would be used to support the system and implied that they would have a hybrid character. An initial supply would be created against the deposits of a certain percentage of central bank gold and dollar reserves. *The Times (London), Sept. 6, 1978, p 21*

[1972, influenced by French *écu,* a coin] See SNAKE.

EDB, abbreviation of *ethylene dibromide,* a pesticide and antiknock agent in gasoline, linked with sterility and suspected of causing cancer in humans.

There are questions about how much EDB is actually used; the effectiveness of vapor recovery devices and the extent to which they are used; how much people actually use self-service pumps; and on and on. *Luther J. Carter, "Yearly Report on Carcinogens Could Be a Potent Weapon in the War on Cancer," Science, Feb. 9, 1979, p 527*

[1963]

Eddington limit, *Astronomy,* the maximum brightness attainable by a celestial object of a given mass.

If A0620-00 were indeed this far away, the implied x-ray luminosity would be . . . much larger than the Eddington limit for a star. *R. H. Becker, "X-ray Nova," McGraw-Hill Yearbook of Science and Technology 1977, p 427*

[1972, named after Sir Arthur Stanley *Eddington,* 1882-1944, who discovered the relationship between the mass and luminosity of stars] Also spelled **Eddington's limit.**

edifice complex, *U.S.* infatuation with large and costly building projects.

Continued the Ambassador: "If we could turn it [an apartment-dining complex in India] over to the Smithsonian it would make a marvelous memorial to a certain kind of mentality. But that isn't really practical, is it? . . . Let this sad ending be a lesson to the next U.S. Administration tempted by an edifice complex." *Time, Aug. 6, 1973, p 8*

[1973, a play on *Oedipus complex;* perhaps first applied to Gov. Nelson Rockefeller's enthusiasm for building the New York State Mall in Albany, N.Y.]

education tax, another name for DIPLOMA TAX.

But in August, Moscow began levying its now celebrated "education tax" on would-be emigrants. It is a tough measure; a younger Russian who has benefited from training at a state university might be required to pay an exit fee of as much as $30,000. *"Diplomacy: A New Threat to the Détente," Time, March 26, 1973, p 38*

[1972]

EER, abbreviation of *energy efficiency ratio* (the cooling power of an air conditioner in relation to electric power used).

Many brands of air conditioners now come with a number called the energy efficiency ratio (EER). The EER is derived by dividing the number of BTUs of cooling capacity by the unit's wattage. You can do it yourself if the dealer doesn't have the number available. A 10,000 BTU unit that draws 1,000 watts would have an EER of 10, which is good. If it draws 2,000 watts, the EER is 5 and that is terrible. *James K. Page, Jr., and John P. Wiley, Jr., "Cutting Your Home Energy Budget," Encyclopedia Science Supplement (Grolier) 1975, p 196*

[1975]

EEZ, abbreviation of EXCLUSIVE ECONOMIC ZONE.

There was an almost universal extension of fishery limits to 200 mi (as a partial EEZ) or claims of a full EEZ over 200 mi. *Neville March Hunnings, "Law," Britannica Book of the Year 1978, p 488*

[1978]

Effie, *n. U.S.* an award presented annually by the advertising industry for effective advertising.

Fifteen Effies were awarded yesterday morning in the Starlight Roof of the Waldorf-Astoria at the seventh annual presentation. And for the first time an agency got more than three. As a matter of fact two did. Thompson took five and Batten, Barton, Durstine & Osborn, four. *Philip H. Dougherty, "Advertising: Effies Focus on the Bottom Line," The New York Times, June 17, 1976, p 59*

[1970, from the feminine name *Effie,* chosen for its resemblance to the word *effective*]

EFTS or **EFT,** abbreviation of ELECTRONIC FUNDS TRANSFER SYSTEM.

E.F.T.S. (also referred to in some circles as the "checkless society") is a plan to eliminate paper by moving money among major financial institutions via computer. *Steven Rattner, "Social Security Recipients Find 'Checkless Society' Has Problems," The New York Times, Oct. 5, 1976, p 65*

[1973]

egg, *n.* **(with) egg on one's face.** embarrassed and humiliated.

In one masterstroke, he unravelled the mystery contained in the following newspaper account, and so expertly that my department was left with egg on its face. *S. J. Perelman, "Hail, Hail, The Ganglia's All Here," The New Yorker, Sept. 23, 1972, p 32*

There is something reassuringly changeless about the capacity of the highest military authorities for getting egg on their faces. *Lord Chalfont, "An Army of Our Times," The Times (London), Feb. 19, 1972, p 7*

Bob Strauss, for the first time during exemplary service for an Administration conditioned to ineptitude, "got egg on his face" (in the words of one long-time political associate). *Rowland Evans and Robert Novak, "Strauss: Miracle Man With Egg on His Face," New York Post, Aug. 24, 1979, p 23*

[1964]

egg transfer, the surgical transfer of an ovum from the uterus of one female to that of another.

Another reason for an egg transfer (from a donor) might be the patient's serious genetic defects. Or if she is unable to interrupt her career outside the home in order to complete a pregnancy, as may become the case more often in these days of women's liberation, she could have her baby by surrogation. *Joseph Fletcher, The Ethics of Genetic Control, 1974, p 67*

[1974] Compare EMBRYO TRANSFER. See also TEST-TUBE BABY.

ego-state, *n.* one of three states of consciousness, identified as Parent, Adult, and Child according to transactional analysis that typifies how one will interact with people in different situations.

The three ego-states of T.A. do, of course, parallel the Freudian description of the psychic apparatus, but whereas the emphasis in classical psychoanalysis is on the sexual experience of the growing child, the emphasis in T.A. is on the growing child's sense of his or her own worth or lack of worth. *Kenneth Lamott, "The Four Possible Life Positions . . .", The New York Times Magazine, Nov. 19, 1972, p 43*

[1967, coined by Eric Berne, 1910-1970, Canadian-born psychiatrist who founded the transactional analysis method of psychotherapy] See P-A-C.

167

ego trip, something done to boost one's ego, often characterized by self-indulgent behavior.

The speeches, generally addressed directly to the camera, become uncomfortably hortatory, or somewhat smug and self-righteous ego trips. *Arthur Knight, "The Filmed Play," Saturday Review, July 1, 1972, p 63*

Every actor is supposed to have a two-fold dream — to play Hamlet and to have his own one-man show. Few achieve this gigantic ego-trip. *The Times (London), May 2, 1972, p 14*

[1969]

ego-tripper, *n.:* "Public access could become the first electronic soapbox," says Global Village co-director John Reilly, "if it can only survive its ego-trippers." *Cyclops, "Talking Heads," Newsweek, April 9, 1973, p 86*

ego-tripping, *n., adj.:* What is overlooked in the inevitable discussion of the alleged ego-tripping in Mailer's writing is that these more "modest" selves are often at work in the sounds and turns of his sentences — questioning the assertive, the heroic, the outrageous self. *Richard Poirier, "Norman Mailer: A Self-Creation," The Atlantic, Oct. 1972, p 80*

Maybe I can save time by saying what Tate's poems are not. They are not bardic, political, populist, confessional, ego-tripping, hash-inspired or full of fine sentiments and derivative techniques. *Julian Moynahan, Review of "Absences" by James Tate, The New York Times Book Review, Nov. 12, 1972, p 63*

ejaculatorium, *n.* a room in a sperm bank set aside for donors to discharge semen.

Some bank. The bankbook is called *The Semen Depositor's Handbook.* . . . Home collection, the booklet notes, is preferred, but the bank also maintains its own ejaculatorium in Manhattan. *"Modern Living: Frozen Assets," Time, Jan. 3, 1972, p 52*

[1972, from *ejaculate* + *-orium,* as in *sanatorium*]

ek·pwe·le (‚ek pwe'lei), *n. sing. and pl.* the monetary unit of Equatorial Guinea (a country in western Africa) since 1973.

African place names were also substituted for Spanish ones in other areas, and the name of the currency unit was changed from the peseta to the ekpwele. *George Lamson, "Equatorial Guinea," 1974 Collier's Encyclopedia Year Book (1973), p 253*

[1973, from the local name in Equatorial Guinea]

eldercare, *n. U.S.* any program of low-cost medical care for elderly people, especially one providing regular preventive care to supplement Medicare.

In addition, many members of Prosser's eldercare program look forward to the monthly hospital outings as social occasions that give them a chance to see friends. *"Eldercare," Time, Feb. 11, 1974, p 60*

[1965, from *elderly* + *care*]

► This term first appeared for the American Medical Association's plan proposed as an alternative to Medicare which was adopted by Congress in the same year. Since then, *eldercare* has been applied to other private medical-care plans for the aged.

electroacupuncture, *n.* a form of acupuncture using electrically vibrating needles.

Much more striking and immediately verifiable was our observation of four simultaneous major operations performed at the Affiliated Hospital. The only anesthetic was electroacupuncture — a new application of the ancient technique. *Ethan Signer and Arthur W. Galston, "Education and Science in China," Science, Jan. 7, 1972, p 21*

[1972] Compare STAPLEPUNCTURE.

electrogenic, *adj.* capable of producing electricity in living cells and tissues.

Research by several authors suggests that this concentration gradient is brought about by an electrogenic pump situated on the luminal membrane. *D. M. Ensor, "Salt Gland," McGraw-Hill Yearbook of Science and Technology 1974, p 367*

[1970, from *electro-* electricity + *-genic* producing, generating]

electronhole drop or **electronhole droplet,** a liquid form of electrical energy produced by a laser beam in a semiconductor crystal.

The object of the photograph is called an "electronhole drop." It contains an equal number of negatively charged electrons and positively charged "holes" from which electrons have been dislodged by a beam of laser light. *John Noble Wilford, "Photo Shows First Evidence of Electricity in Form of Fluid Droplet," The New York Times, May 19, 1975, p 18*

[1975]

electronic funds transfer system, a system to transfer money from one account or location to another by computer.

"The elimination of what is now known as money could be achieved with the implementation of an electronic funds-transfer system . . . Its future implementation seems assured because of its inherent economies and convenience and because of the increasing pressure to find means of coping with the growing volume of paper surrounding the present debt settlement process." *The Times (London), Feb. 10, 1973, p 22*

Recent developments in autotransaction systems as they apply to electronic funds transfer (EFT) reflect efforts toward implementation of local and regional projects as opposed to research and development and the pilot tests of a few years ago. EFT systems face no real technological barriers. *Robert J. Duffy and Helene Duffy, "Autotransaction Systems," McGraw-Hill Yearbook of Science and Technology 1977, p 142*

[1973] *Abbreviation:* EFTS or EFT. Also called **Electronic Funds Transfer.**

electronic journalism, *Especially U.S.* coverage of news by television.

All three networks emphasized citizenship and the tireless high-mindedness of electronic journalism. None mentioned the high-pricedness. This year the combined coverage cost some $10 million, roughly what the presidential candidates together spent on TV commercials — with about the same results. *Time, Nov. 20, 1972, p 61*

[1971] Compare BROADCAST JOURNALISM, PRINT JOURNALISM.

electronic journalist: Television journalists are probably more subtly manipulated by the people in the street than by corporate public relations directors. This is a terrible dilemma for the electronic journalist. How can he decide when an event is real or merely the concoction of a radical public relations expert? *M. Dallas Burnett, "News and Views," The 1971 Compton Yearbook, p 454*

electronic smog, nonionizing radiation (such as radio and television waves or radar) emitted into the environment in such quantities as to constitute a potential health danger.

In the United States alone, radio waves are emitted not merely by the 10,000 or so commercial radio and television stations but also by some 250,000 relay towers for telephone, teletype, and TV hookups; 15 million Citizen's Band radios; millions of microwave ovens; communications satellites and the immensely powerful transmitters that link us to them; radar at airports and in planes; diathermy machines; burglar alarms; and automatic garage door openers. . . . The result is a pervasive "electronic smog" whose biologic effects we are just beginning to understand. *Robert Claiborne, "Electronic Pollution," Review of "The Zapping of America: Microwaves, Their Deadly Risk, and the Cover-Up" by Paul Brodeur, Saturday Review, Jan. 7, 1978, p 35*

[1978]

electronic warfare, the use of electronic devices for military purposes, such as the interruption of enemy communications by electronic interference.

Electronic warfare, or EW as it is referred to by military-industrial insiders, is a rapidly expanding field of pushbutton defense technology that has already revolutionized modern air warfare. It has also spawned a subculture of EW buffs in the military and electronics industries. *Orville Schell, "The Subculture Spawned by Electronic Warfare," Harper's, Oct. 1972, p 74*

In order to warn against attacking missiles, hostile aircraft, and ships, the Nimitz is bristling with radar and electronic warfare (EW) antennae. *"Technology Review: Shadowing a $600 Million Gunboat," New Scientist, Sept. 18, 1975, p 647*

[1972]

electron spin resonance, reversal of the spin of unpaired electrons by an electromagnetic field, used especially in spectroscopic analysis.

Electron spin resonance (ESR) spectroscopy of free radicals can detect the order and structure of biological membranes, the binding of drugs and other small molecules to proteins, the presence of drugs in biological specimens, translational diffusion within biological membranes, and the properties of the enclosed volume of cells and spheroidal model membranes. *Gerald E. Cohn, "Free Radical," McGraw-Hill Yearbook of Science and Technology 1976, p 191*

[1962]

electropaint, *v.t., v.i.* to deposit paint on (a metal surface) by an electrolytic process.

Ford's tests consisted of driving sets of cars (some with galvanised bodyworks, others electropainted) through salt water fast enough for spray to penetrate every crevice in the bodywork. *"More to Rust Prevention Than You, Zinc?" New Scientist, Nov. 9, 1972, p 334*

—*n.* the paint used in electropainting.

Pollution consciousness stimulated interest in water-based and powder coatings, and water-based electropaints were being used throughout the world to prime automobile bodies. *Lionel Bilefield, "Industrial Review: Paints and Varnishes," 1973 Collier's Encyclopedia Year Book (1972), p 366*

[1966, from *electrolytic* + *paint*]

e·lec·tro·pho·rese (i,lek trə fə'ri:z), *v.t.* to subject to electrophoresis (a method of separating molecules of a substance, such as blood plasma).

A second method has been used by Gitlin . . . in which blood cells are gently lysed and their contents electrophoresed in the presence of antihaemoglobin antisera. *"Proteins and Fused Cells," Nature, Oct. 27, 1972, p 488*

[1968, back formation from *electrophoresis*]

electrophotograph, *n.* an image produced on film by Kirlian photography.

The Kirlians report that their electrophotographs show certain points on the human body radiating light flares more forcibly than the areas around them and that these points correspond exactly to the 741 acupuncture points mapped out by the ancient Chinese. It is also reported that they have produced photographs showing that a plant is diseased before the physical symptoms of the disease appear. *Lisa J. Shawver, "Science Focuses on a 'Light of Life'," Science News, Sept. 29, 1973, p 202*

[1973] Also called KIRLIAN PHOTOGRAPH.

electrosensitivity, *n.* the ability of an animal to sense or detect some object from naturally occurring electric signals; biological sensitivity or responsiveness to electricity.

Aspects of electrosensitivity in which the fish senses its own electric organ discharge will not be treated here except to say that weakly electric fish can locate prey and other objects, can maneuver in the environment, and can even control their posture by utilizing their own electric organ discharge. *Rocco A. Bombardieri, "Electroreception," McGraw-Hill Yearbook of Science and Technology 1977, p 205*

[1972]

electrosleep, *n.* a state of deep sleep induced by passing a mild electric current through the brain.

In a dark, quiet room electrodes are attached to the relaxing patient's eyes and mastoids (the protruding bone behind the ear). A very low-amplitude, pulsating direct current is then passed through the patient's head for up to two hours. The procedure is repeated daily for at least 10 days. The technique, known as cerebral electrotherapy (CET or electro-sleep), is supposed to induce and enhance a state of natural sleep. *"Behavioral Sciences: The Electric Sleeping Machine," Science News, Jan. 12, 1974, p 29*

[1967]

element 106, a radioactive chemical element with atomic number 106 in the periodic table and the 14th of the synthetic transuranium elements. It was synthesized independently by American and Soviet scientists in 1974.

On the basis of its projected position in the periodic table, element 106 is expected to have chemical properties similar to those of tungsten (atomic number 74). *Glenn T. Seaborg, "Element 106," McGraw-Hill Yearbook of Science and Technology 1976, p 175*

[1974]

element 107, a radioactive chemical element with atomic number 107 in the periodic table. Soviet physicists claimed to have synthesized it in 1977 by bombarding bismuth with nuclei of chromium.

During the year a group of Soviet physicists, working at the Joint Institute for Nuclear Research at Dubna under Georgi N. Flerov, announced creation of element 107 as the heaviest transuranic species yet found. *D. Allan Bromley, "Nuclear Physics," 1978 Britannica Yearbook of Science and the Future (1977), p 383*

169

Scientists have predicted the positions of element 107 through 168 in the periodic table. From these positions, the scientists figure that there are several "islands of stability" at the unstable high end of the table. *Samuel F. O'Gorman, "Superheavy Elements," Encyclopedia Science Supplement (Grolier) 1977/1978 (1977), p 302*

[1976]

element 126, a superheavy chemical element believed to exist in nature and the subject of intense research especially during the late 1970's.

Great excitement was caused by the announcement last June that a group of physicists had found evidence for the existence of element 126 and some other ultraheavy elements in samples of monazite, an ancient mineral from Africa. Skepticism and controversy were generated when various experiments could find no such evidence in other pieces of monazite. *Science News, Feb. 5, 1977, p 85*

The elements were observed by bombarding small inclusions in a mineral sample and detecting the X-rays emitted. The X-ray energies agreed with those predicted for several superheavy elements, and the strongest confidence was in element 126. *Gary Mitchell, "Physics," The Americana Annual 1978, p 401*

[1976]

ELF or **elf,** abbreviation of *extremely low frequency,* a frequency range between 30 and 300 hertz in the radio spectrum.

Research projects should take advantage of the opportunity to learn of the effects of weak ELF fields, knowledge also relevant to life under ordinary power lines and among electrical appliances. *Science News, Aug. 13, 1977, p 102*

[1962]

el·int ('el int), *n.* **1** Also **Elint** or **ELINT,** the act or process of gathering intelligence by electronic monitoring, especially from ships, aircraft, or other listening posts.

The first requirement of electronic intelligence, or Elint, is to be able to recognise what is hostile (or potentially hostile) and what is not. The only way to do this is to intercept every possible transmission and identify as much as is practicable, thus building up a library of known transmissions. *John Marriott, "No Break in the Code War," New Scientist, March 2, 1972, p 467*

2 a ship, aircraft, or other listening post that uses electronic equipment to gather intelligence. *Often used attributively.*

"How would we feel if a Russian 'elint' suddenly showed up four miles off our Polaris base of Charleston, S.C., in company with three Soviet destroyers?" one official asked. *William Beecher, The New York Times, June 12, 1968, p 6*

[1968, acronym for *el*ectronic *int*elligence] Compare COMINT, HUMINT, SIGINT.

elliptical, *n.* a galaxy of elliptical shape and without spiral arms.

Ellipticals, by contrast, seem to possess little gas or dust, usually contain late-type dwarf stars and exhibit scant rotation. *Martin J. Rees and Joseph Silk, Scientific American, June 1970, p 26*

[1963, short for *elliptical galaxy*]

ELT, abbreviation of English Language Teaching.

"Experimental summer school on ELT methods in northern Nigeria," *A. M. Shaw, English Language Teaching, Oct. 1969, p 63*

[1969]

El Tor (el 'tɔr), a strain of the bacillus that causes cholera, widely prevalent in Asia, Africa, and Europe since the early 1960's. It causes a mild form of the disease and so spreads undetected in areas where hygiene is poor.

The tests revealed the first known case of El Tor in Britain. *"Cholera May Reach Britain," The Sunday Times (London), July 25, 1971, p 1*

Exactly ten years after its appearance in Indonesia the El Tor variety of cholera reached Western Europe and was reported in the Saragossa area of Spain in July. *Alexander Paton, "Medicine," Britannica Book of the Year 1972, p 449*

[1963, from the name of the Egyptian quarantine station on the Sinai Peninsula where it was first isolated in 1905]

EM, abbreviation of *electron microscope* or *electron microscopy.*

The EM tissue samples after therapy showed the formation of the collagen and new bone in the former defect. *"Electricity Enhances Leg Bone Healing," Science News, March 18, 1972, p 184*

Most EM studies show a very restricted extracellular system of 150-200 angstrom gaps, ... *"Tight Packing May Protect Brain Cells from Poisons," New Scientist, Nov. 28, 1968, p 513*

[1968]

e·ma·lan·ge·ni (ˌei ma: la:ŋ'gei ni:), *n.* the plural of LILANGENI.

The Umbuluzi dam scheme, which would irrigate 8,000 ha, was allotted a further 3 million emalangeni. *Molly Mortimer, "Swaziland," Britannica Book of the Year 1977, p 638*

[1977, from siSwati (a Bantu language) *ema-* plural prefix + *-langeni* root form for "money"]

em·bour·geoi·si·fi·ca·tion (emˌbur ʒwa: sə fə'keiʃən), *n.* the adoption of bourgeois or middle-class practices and values.

I heard a great deal about the Circle 333 Trust: and no one spoke of it as the philanthropic institution which Miss Pickering describes. Many people I spoke to did fear being evicted by the Trust; they were frightened, too, that they would not be able to afford the 'fair rents' which would be charged after conversion, and saw the Trust as yet another agent of creeping, expensive embourgeoisification. *Jonathan Raban, London, in a Letter to the Editor, The Listener, March 8, 1973, p 311*

[1973, blend of earlier *embourgeoisement* (1965) and *bourgeoisification* (1937)] Compare GENTRIFICATION.

embryo transfer, surgical transfer of an embryo to another female, a technique used especially to increase the birth rate of a specific strain of animal.

"Embryo transfer" ... involves (1) injecting a cow with a "follicle stimulating hormone" (a serum, for instance, from pregnant mares) which causes her reproductive system to release five, six or even as many as a dozen ova instead of a single egg; (2) inseminating her artificially; (3) removing the resultant embryos by surgery; and (4) implanting each in an ordinary cow, which then assumes the task of bringing it to term and delivering it to the expectant world of cattle buyers. *Paul O'Neil, "How Now World's Greatest Cow?" The Atlantic, Sept. 1973, p 51*

Last March, the government's Ethics Advisory Board concluded that research on in-vitro fertilization and embryo transfer was "acceptable" in hospitals that receive Federal money. *Susan Jacoby, "Should Parents Play God?" The Reader's Digest, June 1979, p 112*

[1973] Compare EGG TRANSFER.

emerging, *adj.* recently created; newly independent.

The white racist attitudes that are part of the problem at home have also been an often unconscious element in the policy failures of the white political leadership vis-à-vis the emerging nations, most recently in Africa. *Jesse L. Jackson, The New York Times Magazine, April 18, 1976, p 13*

[1975, from present participle of *emerge*] Compare DEVELOPING.

EMG, abbreviation of *electromyograph* (instrument for recording differences in the electric potential of muscles).

Surface EMG recordings were made from both arms during sleep. *Elliot D. Weitzman, Review of "Normal Sleep in Man" by Uroš J. Jovanović, Science, July 14, 1972, p 159*

[1967]

emigration tax, another name for EXIT TAX.

In August, a Soviet measure that awakened international interest was the imposition of a high emigration tax on educated and professional persons seeking to leave that country—a measure that primarily affected Jews who wished to go to Israel. *Robert L. Canfield, "Ethnic Groups," The Americana Annual 1973, p 284*

[1972]

em·i·o·cy·to·sis (ˌem iː ou saiˈtou sis), *n. Biology.* a process of cellular excretion by which the membrane of a granule fuses with the cell membrane and the granule is discharged through an opening in the fused membranes.

The newly formed insulin, proinsulin, and C-peptide are subsequently transferred from the Golgi apparatus to storage granules which discharge by fusing with the plasma membrane in a process known as emiocytosis. *Donald F. Steiner, "Insulin," McGraw-Hill Yearbook of Science and Technology 1973, p 233*

[1973, from New Latin, from Greek *emein* to vomit + New Latin *cyt-* cell + *-osis* process or condition]

emiocytotic, *adj.:* In summary, the present findings suggest that the emiocytotic release of insulin is coupled with an endocytotic process, leading to the relocation of membranous material from the cell membrane into an intracellular vacuolar system. *L. Orci, et al., "Exocytosis-Endocytosis Coupling in the Pancreatic Beta Cell," Science, Aug. 10, 1973, p 562*

EMP, abbreviation of *electromagnetic pulse* (pulse of radiation produced by a nuclear explosion).

It is known that EMPs can erase the memory tapes in computers which form vital parts of present and future aircraft subsystems. Without these tapes such aircraft as the presidential airborne command post (a converted Boeing 747) and the North American Rockwell B-1 strategic bomber would be rendered ineffective. *"Technology Re-*

view: Jumbo Project to Foil EMPs," New Science, March 16, 1972, p 601

[1963]

empty nester, a person whose children have grown up and left home.

"Empty nesters," ready to sell their homes after their children have left, have a strong incentive through capital gains tax laws to reinvest quickly in home ownership. *Carter B. Horsley, " 'Condos' Break the Housing Mold," The New York Times, Feb. 1, 1976, Sec. 8, p 8*

Like their grown children, the empty-nesters are intent on living well. *Angela Ferrante and Eleanor Ward, Maclean's, July 1976, p 52*

[1966]

empty nest syndrome, a form of depression supposedly common among women whose children have grown up and left home.

We knew, of course, about the empty-nest syndrome but were not perceptive enough to recognize it in ourselves. It did not occur to us that to grow gracefully into a new kind of life required an affectionate search for the neglected, unused parts of ourselves. *McCall's, Jan. 1973, p 138*

While depression will not be absent for some women, under the most ideal of conditions, the fact remains that among modern women the "empty nest" syndrome is likely to be more and more of an anachronism. *Estelle Fuchs, The Second Season, 1977, p 70*

[1972; see EMPTY NESTER]

EMR, abbreviation of *educable mentally retarded*.

Children diagnosed as educationally retarded (EMR) . . . were assigned to special small classes offering a different instructional program from that in the regular classes. To qualify for this special treatment, children had to have IQ below 75 as well as lagging far behind their age-mates in scholastic performance. *Arthur R. Jensen, Genetics and Education, 1972, p 5*

Likewise, there is little dispute that the education offered in EMR classes is academically far inferior to that in regular classes. Among other things, witnesses testified that EMR students aren't expected to progress beyond the third to fifth grade level (while peers continue on to the twelfth grade). *New Scientist, Aug. 3, 1978, p 337*

[1970] Compare LEARNING-DISABLED.

emulate, *v.t.* to do the work of (another computer) without requiring extensive modification of the program or routine worked on.

The 1400 series was so popular that many newer computers were emulating them—that is, running 1400-series programs unmodified. The 9700 incorporated the capability of emulating the 1400-series machines much more flexibly than before, taking another step toward what might eventually become basically incompatible lines of computers from various manufacturers that can nevertheless run one another's programs through emulation. *Wallace B. Riley, "Computers," Britannica Book of the Year 1973, p 192*

[1967]

emulation, *n.:* Counterfeiting became possible because an IBM 370/145, for example, could be made to look like an ICL 1904A by replacing the IBM microprogramming with a new set that makes the machine language look like an ICL machine. Quite basic conventions vary between IBM and ICL; during a sorting operation whether the numbers are listed before or after the letters must be accounted for in the microprogramming. This form of mimicry is sometimes known as emulation. *"Technology Review: Counterfeit Computers Better Than Originals," New Scientist, June 22, 1972, p 690*

emulator, *n.:* In general, an emulator consists of special logic . . . which simulates the most frequently used instructions of the emulated computer. *I. Auerbach and J. R. Hillegass, McGraw-Hill Yearbook of Science and Technology 1967, p 155*

en·cap·si·date (en'kæp sə,deit), *v.t.* to enclose (a virus particle) in a protein coat, which makes the particle stable and transmissible.

Conventional viruses are made up of nucleic acid encapsidated in protein, whereas viroids are characterized by the absence of encapsided proteins. In spite of their small size, viroid ribonucleic acids (RNAs) can replicate and produce the characteristic disease syndromes when introduced into cells. *R. K. Horst, "Viroid," McGraw-Hill Yearbook of Science and Technology 1977, p 417*

[1972, from *en-* to put in + *capsid* + *-ate* verb suffix]

encapsidation, *n.:* Only when enough coat protein has accumulated to permit the formation of "disk" aggregates can the assembly of virus particles begin. This would delay the encapsidation of virion RNA thereby allowing time for synthesis of early proteins and (-) strands. *Tony R. Hunter and Tim Hunt, "Messenger RNA for the Coat Protein of Tobacco Mosaic Virus," Nature, April 29, 1976, p 763*

en·ceph·a·li·to·gen (en,sef ə'lai tə dʒən), *n.* a virus or other substance that causes encephalitis.

This basic polymer is not encephalitogenic and is not a general non-specific immunosuppressive agent (our unpublished results). Whereas it efficiently suppresses the disease when administered after the basic encephalitogen, it cannot prevent the disease when injected intravenously in saline before the basic brain protein. *Drorca Teitelbaum, et al., Rehovot, Israel, "Letters to Nature: Protection Against Experimental Allergic Encephalomyelitis," Nature, Dec. 29, 1972, p 565*

[1964, back formation from earlier *encephalitogenic* (OEDS 1923) causing or able to cause encephalitis]

encephalization, *n.* the development and specialization of the brain as the center of the nervous system of animals.

Progressive evolution of encephalization within the mammals came late in their history, in the last 50 million years of a time span of about 200 million years. That evolution transformed the archaic mammalian map into the map of living mammals by another four- or fivefold increase in relative brain size for the average mammal. *Harry J. Jerison, "Paleoneurology and the Evolution of Mind," Scientific American, Jan. 1976, p 95*

[1973, from New Latin *encephalon* the vertebrate brain + English *-ization*]

encephalization quotient, index to a ratio of body weight to brain weight, used to describe animal development. It is computed as a comparison of actual brain weight of any given specimen to average brain weight for animals of the same class and size.

Until the Isthmus of Panama rose just a couple of million years ago. South America was an isolated island continent . . . Here the herbivores display no increase in brain size through time. Their average encephalization quotient remained below 0.5 throughout the Tertiary, and they were quickly eliminated when advanced carnivores crossed the isthmus from North America. *Stephen Jay Gould, "Evolu-*

tion of the Brain," *Natural History, Jan. 1975, p 26*
[1973]

en·ceph·a·lo·my·o·car·di·tis (en,sef ə lou,mai ə-kar'dai tis), *n.* a virus disease, especially of children, characterized by inflammation of the brain and the heart muscle.

Although the ribosomes readily translated globin mRNA and poly U at normal rates, they were unable to translate encephalomyocarditis virus RNA. *"At Last, An Answer to How Interferon Attacks Viruses," New Scientist, Aug. 31, 1972, p 422*

[1964, from *encephalitis* inflammation of the brain + *myocarditis* inflammation of the heart muscle]

enchilada, *n.* **the whole enchilada,** *U.S. Slang.* the complete or entire affair; the whole matter or thing.

Villa readjusted his sunglasses against the blazing Mexican noon and stared out across the vast expanse. "So this is it," he murmured. "The whole enchilada." *Cartoon legend by Jack Ziegler, The New Yorker, June 6, 1977, p 39*

[1977] Compare BIG ENCHILADA.

encounter grouper or **encounter groupie,** a member of an encounter group.

[John] le Carré's set-painting and weather reports are, as ever, top of the line. He reveals himself as a talented parodist, especially receptive to the counterfeit yelps of lovers and the cheapjack philosophy of encounter groupers wasting away with their terminal cases of Kahlil Gibran. *Geoffrey Wolf, Review of "The Naive and Sentimental Lover" by John le Carré, The New York Times Book Review, Jan. 9, 1972, p 7*

It is powerful stuff . . . ending with the same character in the throes of what encounter groupies call a 'primal'. *The Listener, Nov. 6, 1975, p 622*

[1972]

en·cryp·tion (en'krip ʃən), *n.* the act or process of putting information into a cipher or code.

"Encryption" is in and "encoding" is out. . . . Mr. Carter used both the old word and the new in explaining SALT verification: he claimed that the treaty "forbids the encryption or the encoding of crucial missile-test information." *William Safire, "On Language," The New York Times Magazine, Nov. 18, 1979, p 18*

[1964, from *encrypt* (1958) to encipher (from *en-* put into + *crypt*ogram) + *-ion*]

encryptor, *n.:* The . . . encryptor will have two applications in this new financial network. The first application will be for authentication. Each cardholder will have some form of personal identification number as a requirement for access to the network. To provide added security, this number may be encrypted. *Rod N. Thorpe, "Electrical Communications," McGraw-Hill Yearbook of Science and Technology 1977, p 174*

endocast, *n.* an internal cast of a primitive cranium or other hollow bodily structure.

Endocasts, casts of the inside of the cranial cavity, are displayed for four fossil animals. These endocasts, each drawn about one and a quarter times actual size, are natural ones: mineralized remains of sand or other deposits that replaced the soft tissues in the fossil skulls. *Illustration legend, "Paleoneurology and the Evolution of Mind," Scientific American, Jan. 1976, p 91*

A plaster endocast . . . was made by Mr R. J. Clarke and

its volume was determined by water displacement by Mrs Margaret Leakey and Dr A. Walker. *Philip V. Tobias, Johannesburg "Letters to Nature,' Nature, Oct 20, 1972, p 468*

[1972, from *endo-* within, internal + *cast*]

en·do·cy·tose (ˌen dou sai'touz), *v.t.* to absorb or incorporate by endocytosis.

One particularly important role is in endocytosis. In this process, damaged portions of the cell surface and even potentially damaging substances that bind to it are sucked, or endocytosed, into the cell. *Garth L. Nicolson, "Cancer Clues at the Cell's Surface," The World Book Science Annual 1975 (1974), p 119*

[1975, back formation from ENDOCYTOSIS]

en·do·cy·to·sis (ˌen dou sai'tou sis), *n. Biology.* a process of cellular ingestion by which the cell membrane folds inward to enclose and incorporate foreign substances.

Macrophages' role in life is to roam the body and scavenge foreign material they come across. By a process known as endocytosis, macrophages can engulf particles of substantial size. *"Scavengers Can Be Vehicles for Missing Enzymes," New Scientist, Jan. 11, 1973, p 64*

[1963, from New Latin, from *endo-* within, internal + *cyt-* cell + *-osis* process or condition] Compare EMIOCYTOSIS.

endocytotic, *adj.:* The uptake is thought to occur by engulfment of bacteria into vesicles formed by invagination of the plasmalemma during plasmolysis and concomitant degradation of the cell wall, rather than by a strictly endocytotic process. *M. R. Davey and E. C. Cocking, Nottingham, "Letters to Nature," Nature, Oct. 20, 1972, p 455*

en·do·per·ox·ide (ˌen dou pə'rɑk said), *n.* any of a group of highly oxygenated compounds that are precursors of prostaglandins (modified fatty acids with hormonelike functions) and convert naturally to THROMBOXANE and PROSTACYCLIN.

Endoperoxides can be changed by enzyme action into various prostaglandins, including those that produce fever, pain and inflammation. *The New York Times, Oct. 30, 1979, p C1*

[1974, from *endo-* internal (as in a ring rather than a side chain) + *peroxide*]

en·dor·phin (en'dɔr fin), *n.* one of a group of amino acids present in the brain that includes enkephalin and controls various physiological responses. Each endorphin has certain properties of morphine and acts as a natural pain suppressant or opiate of the body.

It now seems possible that the endorphins, discovered only last year, may also play an important and complicated part in maintaining normal behaviours. The endorphins were discovered as a result of research on morphine addiction. *The Times (London), Nov. 4, 1976, p 14*

Research . . . suggests that the acupuncture needles stimulate nerves deep in muscles, causing the pituitary and other brain structures to release endorphin. That chemical then inhibits the cells in the brain that fire in response to pain. *Science News, Nov. 20, 1976, p 324*

This past October, Dr. Roger Guillemin of the Salk Institute reported on several other endorphins, all produced by the brain, that seem to play important roles in a host of bodily activities. "Alpha-endorphin" seems to be a natural

tranquilizer; "gamma-endorphin" makes even timid rats angry and aggressive; other endorphins appear to turn the nightly switch of sleep on and off. *Laurence Cherry, "Solving the Mysteries of Pain," The New York Times Magazine, Jan. 30, 1977, p 52*

Injected into animals, in laboratory tests, the endorphins (a chain of up to 31 amino acids) acted as pain-killers. The shorter-lived enkephalins, which consist of only five amino acids, were destroyed by enzymes before they could kill pain. *Constance Mungall, "On the Pain Threshold," Maclean's, Dec. 13, 1976, p 76*

[1975, from *endogenous* within + m*orphine*] Compare ENKEPHALIN.

end-stopped, *adj.* marked by stops or pauses at the end of a movement.

Ballet has accustomed us to phrases that congeal into moments our eye can seize on; modern dance has accustomed us to big, emphatic changes of the whole body's shape. But Tharp-dancing is rarely end-stopped: The dancers seem almost constantly on the move—sliding and twisting and jabbing their feet through the music, executing small, fluid shrugs and circles with God knows how many parts of their bodies simultaneously. *Deborah Jowitt, "Twyla Tharp's New Kick," The New York Times Magazine, Jan. 4, 1976, p 12*

[1976, extended sense of the term applied in poetry to lines that end with a stop or pause]

enemies list, a list of people regarded as one's enemies and therefore liable to reprisal.

Whatever the propriety of putting a distinguished man of science on an enemies list, it must be acknowledged that the list makers followed the custom of treating the learned with some decorum. *Dan Greenberg, "Forum: Richard Nixon's Scientific 'Enemies'," New Scientist, July 19, 1973, p 152*

At our final stop I get off the bus and look up. Binoculars at the face of a boy in an East German uniform look back at me from the tower. He lowers them, writes something down with his free hand, then raises them again as I move off. Have I finally made an Enemies List? *Joseph A. Rehyansky, "Letter from the Edge of Détente," National Review, Feb. 20, 1976, p 141*

[1973] Compare HIT LIST.

▶ This term became current in 1973 with the disclosure growing out of the Watergate investigations that the White House kept such a list during the Nixon administration.

energy, *n.* Often used attributively in such phrases as **energy accounting** and **energy gap** in referring to the supply or sources of energy or of energy-producing substances such as petroleum, coal, and natural gas.

energy accounting: By now, most people working on energy questions have heard of energy accounting. This extension of the accountant's art adds up all the energy required for components of a system in order to determine the overall energy requirement. For example, a coal-burning electricity plant needs X kilowatt-hours of energy to mine each tonne of coal, Y to lay each kilometre of track to transport it, Z to construct each turbine, and so on. By summing the required energy inputs, we can compare the result to the output. *Herbert Inhaber, "Is Solar Power More Dangerous Than Nuclear?" New Scientist, May 18, 1978, p 444*

energy bush: Land that marginally produces food crops, forage, or trees for lumber would be used to grow "energy bushes," fast-growing trees or other plants raised expressly to fuel nearby electric power plants. *John F. Henahan, "Plants: The Renewable Resource," The World Book Science Annual 1977 (1976), p 167*

energy company: The legislation might also break up "energy companies," requiring a firm to participate in only one energy source, such as coal or oil, but not both. Supporters of this legislation believed lower energy prices could result. *Ragaei El Mallakh, "Energy," The Americana Annual 1977, p 196*

energy gap: Energy conservation seems much too modest a method to take seriously for a problem like the energy gap. People scoff. "America," they say, "did not become great by conserving." *Daniel Yergin, "The Real Meaning of the Energy Crunch," The New York Times Magazine, June 4, 1978, p 110*

energy industry: Specialist banks have been established to serve the energy industry. *William Hall, "Big Emphasis on Specializing," The Times (London), April 1, 1976, p 25*

energy plantation: The Energy Research and Development Administration (ERDA) has recently written several large contracts for the study of biomass energy systems, which would have trees, grasses or other crops grown on "energy plantations" as a source of either electric power or synthetic fuels. *"Science and the Citizen," Scientific American, March 1976, p 60B*

energy tax: Arizona and New Mexico are engaged in a bitter legal and legislative battle on the question of whether one state has the constitutional right to levy an energy tax on the citizens of another. *"Arizona Asks High Court Relief from New Mexico Energy Tax," The New York Times, Jan. 19, 1976, p 8*

[1970] See also ENERGY AUDIT, ENERGY CRISIS, ENERGY PARK.

energy audit, a systematic check of the use of energy within an establishment to determine where savings in the output of energy can be achieved.

His mission: to convince them that outside experts should do "energy audits" of schools and hospitals to see what forms of insulation and heating devices would make them more energy efficient. *Time, June 20, 1977, p 75*

[1977]

energy auditor: Healthy savings can be achieved by some of the big things energy auditors look for, such as attic insulation. *"Had Your Energy Audit Yet?" The Christian Science Monitor, Jan. 8, 1980, p 24*

energy crisis, an acute shortage in the supply of energy-producing fuels, especially oil and natural gas.

In one sense, the term energy crisis means simply that the supplies of fuels and power are less than we want, or that they might cost much more in the future.

In another sense, an enlargement of the first, it refers to a tangled web of problems concerning the quality of the environment and the availability, marketing, and growing demand for energy resources. *Duane Chapman, et al., "Electricity Demand Growth and the Energy Crisis," Science, Nov. 17, 1972, p 703*

The energy crisis hasn't yet hit Boise with anything like an instructive impact. Gas is not only plentiful but a good deal cheaper than it is in the East, even though the nearest refinery is on the coast, 400 miles away. *L. J. Davis, "Tearing Down Boise," Harper's, Nov. 1974, p 40*

On January 31, in his first post-inaugural speech to the nation, he [President Carter] appeared before a glowing fire in the White House library, dressed informally in a gray cardigan sweater, to warn that "the energy crisis is permanent." *Robert Shogan, "United States," The Americana Annual 1978, p 519*

[1970]

▶ In 1970-72, public interest in ENVIRONMENTALISM was at its height, and the "crisis" was deterioration of the environment on SPACESHIP EARTH by overuse and misuse of the planet's resources.

Emphasis shifted in the summer of 1973, when the public faced shortages in heating oil, electric power, and gasoline. In October, the crisis worsened with the fourth Arab-Israeli war and the eleven Arab countries of OPEC instituted an oil embargo, making it clear that unlimited supply of cheap energy was over.

Every oil-producing MAJOR was affected by this cartel, which decreed the POSTED PRICE on crude oil. In turn, oil-producing countries made BUY-BACK arrangements with the oil companies and tried to RECYCLE their oil revenues, often by purchasing DOWNSTREAM facilities with the PETRODOLLARS they accumulated.

To counteract the effects of the crisis, the United States reassessed PROVED RESERVES, studied development of alternative sources of energy, such as SOLAR POWER and GASOHOL, and instituted the reduction of highway speed limits to the DOUBLE NICKEL to conserve gas, gradual elimination of the GAS GUZZLER from the nation's roads (a step which caused auto manufacturers to DOWNSIZE the automobile of the Seventies), establishment of ERDA (for energy research and development), and creation by Congress in 1977 of DOE (to develop and coordinate new energy programs). In addition local and state governments temporarily imposed ODD-EVEN sales of a MINIMUM PURCHASE of gasoline as a form of rationing motorists who TOP OFF their gas tanks and are willing to MISFUEL their cars. See also COGENERATION, RETROFIT, WEATHERIZE.

energy-intensive, *adj.* requiring great expenditure of energy for production.

In the case of copper, feasible new sources may indeed be found: high-copper-content manganese nodules on the ocean floor, for instance (energy-intensive aluminum being a bad example). *"Ecology, Survival and Society," Science News, Feb. 12, 1972, p 101*

[1967, patterned on *capital-intensive, labor-intensive,* etc.]

energy park, *U.S.* a large tract of land on which a number of power-generating facilities are concentrated in order to share resources and thereby save on the cost of separate installations.

These days, however . . . thousands of other Americans here and elsewhere in the country are rapidly finding out that an "energy park" is the latest and most ambitious concept to emerge from the continuing pursuit of more electricity for less money. *James T. Wooten, "Ecologists and Economists Divided on Energy Parks," The New York Times, Aug. 23, 1975, p 23*

[1975, patterned after *industrial park* (1955) and *executive park* (1969)]

enforcer, *n. Ice Hockey.* a very strong and aggressive player used by a team to intimidate or fight opposing players.

Every team employs swashbuckling . . . "enforcers." Chicago Black Hawk defenseman Keith Magnuson has taken boxing lessons from a former world bantamweight champion and knocks out many an opponent with one blow. Philadelphia Flyers' Dave "Hammer" Schultz is called a "star" . . . even though he rarely scores or blocks a puck. He excels at another job: ferocious attacks on opposing teams' stars. *Bill Surface, The Reader's Digest, March 1976, p 34*

[1976, extended from the underworld sense of one employed to enforce discipline by violence]

engineered food, food treated or prepared scientifically to increase its nutritional value and storage life or to replace or supplement other conventional food.

Nutritional research has added two new terms to the food vocabulary: fabricated food and engineered food. Fabricated food covers all kinds of imitation foods, chiefly meat (beef, pork, and poultry), milk, and egg products. The meat substitutes are chiefly made from soybean fibers and most dairy analogs from different types of soybean protein. Engineered food, although now used interchangeably for fabricated food, is a term which indicates that food has been fortified or supplemented and shows evidence of improved nutrition. *George Borgstrom, "Food: Innovations in Nutrition," 1972 Collier's Encyclopedia Year Book (1971), p 247*

[1971] Compare FABRICATED FOOD.

enhance, *v.t.* to improve the quality of (a photograph) by computer.

Once more, in a complex, time-consuming process, the computer is used to enhance the images by altering the contrast and adding "cosmetics" and by filling gaps caused by the loss of data bits on the trail between the camera in the spacecraft and the computer on earth. *Nicholas Panagakos, "Startling Images from Space," 1975 Collier's Encyclopedia Year Book (1974), p 45*

[1974] See COMPUTER-ENHANCED.

enhanced radiation, a large amount of radiation in the form of high-energy neutrons and gamma rays, capable of contaminating almost instantly all living things exposed to it when released in a nuclear explosion that produces relatively little heat and blast.

The neutron warhead is a refinement of nuclear technology that could, according to its proponents, devastate by "enhanced radiation" (what an adjective to modify a noun synonymous with death) invading columns of infantry and artillery but cause little damage to the territory being invaded. *Richard Rovere, The New Yorker, Aug. 1, 1977, p 58*

Attributive use.

It might also be said in favor of enhanced-radiation devices that, as the systems of this new generation of tactical nuclear weapons are currently planned, they incorporate features other than enhanced radiation. *Fred M. Kaplan, Scientific American, May 1978, p 50*

[1976]

enhanced radiation weapon, a nuclear device designed to release enhanced radiation.

The neutron bomb releases most of its energy in the form of instant radiation, particularly neutrons, instead of doing so in the form of blast and heat like the fission weapons which Nato already has. This is why scientists like to call it the enhanced radiation weapon . . . and journalists opt for the neutron bomb—which fits more easily into the single column headline in a newspaper. *The Times (London), April 8, 1978, p 4*

[1976] *Abbreviation:* ERW Compare BEAM WEAPON, MININUKE.

enhanced recovery, another name for TERTIARY RECOVERY.

For the long-term, new sources for gas must be found, but development of them will also depend on the price people are willing to pay for this clean, convenient fuel. So-called "enhanced recovery" techniques can squeeze new gas out of old fields at a cost of $1.50 to $2.50 per Mcf. *Science News, Feb. 26, 1977, p 135*

[1976]

en·keph·a·lin (en'kef ə lin), *n.* an amino acid that is a natural pain suppressant or opiate of the body. It is one of two amino-acid chains in endorphin that is produced in the pituitary.

Outside the brain enkephalin has been detected throughout the gastrointestinal tract in many species, but it has not been demonstrated in substantial amounts in any other tissues. Its striking localization in the intestines and the brain resembles the disposition of other peptides that appear to serve hormonelike roles in the intestines and to act as neurotransmitters in the brain, such as somatostatin, gastrin, vasoactive intestinal peptide and substance P. *Scientific American, March 1977, p 51*

A variety of evidence suggests that the enkephalins are neurotransmitters for specific neuronal systems in the brain which mediate the integration of sensory information pertaining to pain and emotional behavior. *John W. Phillis, "Neurophysiology," McGraw-Hill Yearbook of Science and Technology 1978, p 271*

[1975, coined by John Hughes and Hans Kosterlitz, University of Aberdeen, from Greek *enképhalos* brain + English -*in* (chemical suffix)] Compare ENDORPHIN. See also LEU-ENKEPHALIN, MET-ENKEPHALIN.

enriched, *adj.* containing many stimuli, especially more than usual in a standard laboratory environment.

The team found that rats placed in "enriched" environments—cages holding toys, mazes and other rats—developed, among other things, thicker cerebral cortices than those isolated in bare, or "impoverished," cages. *"Birth Pill Hormones Found to Affect Rat Brains," The New York Times, May 22, 1976, p 11*

[1972]

en·thal·pi·met·ry (en₁θæl pə'met ri: *or* en₁θæl 'pim ə-tri:), *n.* the measurement of total heat content generated or absorbed by a substance, used especially to follow the progress of a chemical reaction.

Enthalpimetry depends on the fact that almost all reactions are associated with the evolution or absorption of heat. *H. J. V. Tyrrell, New Scientist, Feb. 8, 1968, p 300*

Peak enthalpimetry is a novel approach that is applicable to biochemical and clinical analysis. The salient feature is rapid mixing of a reagent stream with an isothermal solvent stream into which discrete samples are intermittently injected. The temperature versus time of the resulting product stream is recorded with the aid of a thermistor circuit that has a sensitivity of 0.00001°. *Joseph Jordan, "Thermoanalysis," McGraw-Hill Yearbook of Science and Technology 1975, p 397*

[1968, from *enthalpy* total heat content + *-metry* measurement]

enthalpimetric, *adj.:* Another reason may well be that many of the analytical problems to which the enthalpimetric method has been applied had earlier been solved in other ways, and the particular virtues of this technique were not made apparent. *H. J. V. Tyrrell, New Scientist, Feb. 8, 1968, p 300*

En·ti·sol ('en tɑi,sɔ:l), *n.* (in U.S. soil taxonomy) any of a group of soils lacking distinct soil horizons, found in all parts of the world and under a wide variety of vegetation.

Soil taxonomy identifies taxa called soil orders that require greatly different amounts of time for development. Entisols, for example, are found on recent deposits, whereas Oxisols may require millions of years to form from unweathered material. *Paul F. Smith, "Soil," McGraw-Hill Yearbook of Science and Technology 1976, p 367*

[1972, probably from *entire* + *-sol* (from Latin *solum* soil)] Compare ALFISOL, ARIDISOL, HISTOSOL, INCEPTISOL, MOLLISOL, SPODOSOL, ULTISOL, VERTISOL.

entrain, *v.t., v.i. Biology.* to alter (the circadian rhythm of an organism) so that it adjusts to or synchronizes with a different 24-hour cycle.

Circadian rhythms are so widespread among animals that we were not surprised to find them in the house sparrow. Its locomotor rhythm is readily entrained by artificial light cycles. If the phase of the entraining cycle is shifted, there are three to six transient, or intermediate, cycles before the bird reorients its activity to the new regime. *Michael Menaker, "Nonvisual Light Reception," Scientific American, March 1972, p 24*

[1972, specialized sense of the term meaning "to draw away; bring on as a consequence" (OED 1568)]

entrainment, *n.:* Through their entrainment feature, circadian clocks would adjust daily to the natural 24-hour cycle of earth rotation, regardless of the rhythm's natural frequency. *Karl C. Hamner, "Biological Clocks," The 1972 Compton Yearbook, p 547*

en·ven·om·ate (en'ven ə,meit), *v.t.* to inject with a venom.

Envenomated rabbits do not show any significant prolongation of clotting time; there are, however, still unconfirmed claims concerning the decrease of oxidative phosphorylation in mitochondria of mice intoxicated with cobra venom. *E. Habermann, "Bee and Wasp Venoms," Science, July 28, 1972, p 321*

[1972] ▶ Coined to distinguish from verb *envenom* (1200's) meaning "to put poison on" or "fill with bitterness."

environmental biology, the branch of biology dealing with the interrelationships of organisms and their environment; ecology.

According to Dr Rene Dubos, professor Emeritus of environmental biology at Rockefeller Institute in New York . . . "All over the globe and at all times in the past, men have pillaged nature and disturbed the ecological equilibrium, usually out of ignorance, but also because they have always

been more concerned with immediate advantages than with long range goals." *Buenos Aires Herald, March 3, 1973, p III*

[1972]

environmental engineer, a specialist in the reduction of pollution and contamination of the environment.

The environmental engineer, a direct descendant of the civil (sanitary) engineer, now uses the scientific and technological advances contributed by applied chemists, chemical engineers, industrial engineers, hydrologists, hydraulic engineers, biologists, statisticians, and aerospace engineers, to achieve a balance . . . *Miguel A. Medina, Jr., "Environmental Engineering: Technology, Ecology Link," Engineering Special (University of Alabama), April 11, 1972, p 9*

[1972]

environmental impact statement, a review of the possible consequences that a proposed idea or project may have on the environment.

A group of middle-class whites in Newark had been able to block a highly controversial low-income housing project by bringing a long series of challenges to the project's environmental impact statements. *William Tucker, "Environmentalism and the Leisure Class," Harper's, Dec. 1977, p 50*

[1973] See IMPACT STATEMENT.

environmentalism, *n.* the interests and activities of environmentalists; concern with the quality of the environment, especially with the effects of uncontrolled pollution of the atmosphere.

The arguments in the United States over environmental problems have not yet reached these basic levels, even though environmentalism got its first major impetus here. *Science News, Feb. 12, 1972, p 101*

The movement of which the New Alchemists are a part brings together many of the cultural and countercultural strains of the last decade, including elements of political anarchism, anti-institutionalism, libertarianism, Zen Buddhism, organic agriculture, environmentalism, antiurbanism. *Wade Green, "The New Alchemists," The New York Times Magazine, Aug. 8, 1976, p 40*

[1972, derivative of *environmentalist* (1970)] ▶ The term *environmentalism* was originally used in the 1920's in the sense of "the tendency to stress the importance of the environment in influencing behavior."

en·vi·ron·men·tol·o·gy (en,vai rən,men'tal ə dʒi:), *n.* the study of environmental problems; science concerned with the quality of the environment.

In creating an executive committee on environmentology with past president E. W. Tucker as chairman, the American Veterinary Medical Association (AVMA) recognized the interrelationship of the environment with most activities engaged in by practitioners. *J. F. Smithcors, "Veterinary Medicine: Environmental Veterinary Medicine," 1974 Britannica Yearbook of Science and the Future (1973), p 336*

[1973]

enzyme engineering, the use of enzymes in technology; application of enzymes or enzymatic processes to agriculture, industry, etc.

Chromosomal material that controls the enzymatic synthesis of fruit-fly protein or silkworm protein can be transferred to bacteria in such a way that the progeny synthesize these proteins. Likewise, the genes that are responsible for skin proteins in frogs can be transferred to bacteria in such a way that the progeny synthesize the proteins. Such methods have led to the expansion of a field called "enzyme engineering," which has great scientific and technical potentials. *J. R. Porter, "Microbiology," The Americana Annual 1975, p 382*

[1972]

:PA, abbreviation of *Environmental Protection Agency* (of the United States, established in 1970).

Not the least of these involves a major "redirection" of the EPA's research program that tends to shift the agency away from development of pollution control technology and toward a narrower mission of supporting the agency's regulatory functions. *Robert Gillette, "The Budget of the U.S. Government, 1974: Environment," Science, Feb. 9, 1973, p 550*

The recall is doubly irritating for Chrysler because the part causing the trouble was modified on the assembly line at the insistence of the EPA in the first place. *"The Wax-Ball Recall," Time, March 18, 1974, p 79*

[1970]

phemeralization, *n.* the practice or process of producing goods that are for temporary use or that are to last for only a short time.

"Ephemeralization" is the key word in Buckminster Fuller's bulging lexicon. To him it means increasing the obsolescence rate of all goods in order to speed up the recycling of elements. The corollary is "regenerative" or inflamed consumerism. *Paul Shepard, Review of Books by Buckminster Fuller, The New York Times Book Review, Jan. 16, 1972, p 4*

[1967, coined by R. Buckminster Fuller from *ephemeral* + *-ization*]

p·i·der·min (‚ep ə'dər min), *n.* a fibrous protein that is the main constituent of the epidermis.

Considerable uncertainty exists about the structure of the fibrinogen molecule. It was classified by Astbury with α-keratin, epidermin, and myosin because it gave an X-ray diffraction pattern which indicated a molecular structure similar to these α-proteins. *"News and Views: Molecular Mechanisms of Blood Clotting," Nature, May 5, 1972, p 9*

[1966, from *epidermis* + *-in*]

p·i·tope ('ep ə‚toup), *n.* the part of an antigen that determines or influences the specific antibody which will react with the antigen.

The specific patterns that are recognized by antibody molecules are epitopes: patches on the surface of large molecules such as proteins, polysaccharides and nucleic acids. Molecules that display epitopes are called antigens. *Niels Kaj Jerne, "The Immune System," Scientific American, July 1973, p 52*

The antibody response to most antigens is chemically heterogeneous, reflecting clonal heterogeneity of the responding cells. This heterogeneity may arise in part from the number of different epitopes present in the structure of complex antigens. *William Lee, Humberto Cosenza, Heinz Köhler, "Letters to Nature: Clonal Restriction of the Immune Response to Phosphorycholine," Nature, Jan. 4, 1974, p 55*

[1973, from *epi-* on, upon + *-tope* place (from Greek *tópos*)]

EPNdB, abbreviation of *effective perceived noise decibels,* a unit of measure of the effects of noise on the hearing, based on the type of sound and its intensity and duration.

Anyone familiar with EPNdB figures will appreciate that these values are literally fantastic. It means that the QTOL's [quiet takeoff and landing (airplane)] "90 EPNdB footprint," the plot of noise forming a contour at 90 effective perceived decibels, lies almost wholly within the boundary of most airports. In practice, it would mean that people living even near the airport would seldom hear the aircraft above the general background of urban noise, whether indoors or out. *Bill Gunston, "A Big Jet for the Environment," New Scientist, July 19, 1973, p 138*

[1971]

ept, *adj.* able; clever; effective.

It is different because it is inept, and those other businesses are very ept indeed. They are eptest at getting what they want from the Administration and fighting for what they want until they get it. *Zoltan Sarfathy, "No Business Like News Business," The Atlantic, Sept. 1973, p 114*

The obvious answer is summed up by a White House official's sardonic crack: "Politically, we're not very ept." *James M. Naughton, The New York Times Magazine, June 6, 1976, p 15*

[1966, back formation of *inept*] See EPTITUDE.

▶ Since a number of words with the prefixes *in-*, *un-*, *dis-*, etc., have no counterparts of opposite meaning with the same base form, there has been a tendency, especially since the 19th century, to create such equivalents, usually for humorous effect. An example of this from the 1600's is *scrutable*, derived from the then 150-year-old *inscrutable*. Although the words *ept* and *eptitude* seem to have become fairly current in recent years (perhaps in part by influence of *apt* and *aptitude*), similar words are sometimes created by writers for the nonce, occasionally by the whimsical dropping of what is not a negative prefix or not even a real prefix, without expecting them to catch on. For example: *armingly, consolate, delible, defatigable, ertia, gainly, gruntled, pensable, sipid, trepid.*

eptitude, *n.* fitness; ability; effectiveness.

What makes Huntford's Anglo-Saxon hackles rise is less the cleverness and thoroughgoing eptitude of the Social Democratic persuasion-*cum*-administration machine . . . than the supine attitude of the Swede-in-the-street. *Paul Britten Austin, "Is Sweden a Land of One-Dimensional Men?" Review of "The New Totalitarians" by Roland Huntford, The New York Times Book Review, Feb. 27, 1972, p 6*

[1967, back formation of *ineptitude*]

E.Q., abbreviation of ENCEPHALIZATION QUOTIENT.

In order to analyze the progressive evolution of encephalization in the mammals, I have computed average E.Q.'s and standard deviations for samples of fossil and living ungulates and carnivores and plotted them as a set of normal curves. *Harry J. Jerison, "Paleoneurology and the Evolution of Mind," Scientific American, Jan. 1976, p 95*

[1973]

equal opportunity, equality in employment regardless of color, race, religion, sex, etc.; nondiscriminatory practices in hiring employees.

Equal Rights Amendment

The last revenue-sharing funds impounded by the federal courts in a legal dispute over equal opportunity in Chicago's police department were released to the city on June 21. *James M. Banovetz, "Chicago," The 1978 World Book Year Book, p 249*

Attributive use.

From now on, Zumwalt declared, Navy commanders will be graded on their own performance in handling racial problems under their command. "The Navy has made unacceptable progress in the equal opportunity area," the CNO warned sternly. "Response which lacks commitment from the heart is obstructionist." *Newsweek, Nov. 20, 1972, p. 35*

[1963] Compare AFFIRMATIVE ACTION.

Equal Rights Amendment, a proposed amendment to the United States Constitution providing for equal rights of both sexes.

The Equal Rights Amendment . . . , which provides that "equality of rights under the law shall not be denied or abridged by the United States or by any State on account of sex," cannot go into effect until 38 states have ratified it. *Milton Greenberg, "Civil Liberties and Civil Rights," 1976 Collier's Encyclopedia Year Book (1975), p 198*

The polls . . . showed that 60 to 70 percent of the people favored an Equal Rights Amendment. People always favor rights. *Martha Weinman Lear, The New York Times Magazine, April 11, 1976, p 31*

[1972] *Abbreviation:* ERA

► In the United States the Equal Rights Amendment, popularly known as *ERA* (pronounced 'i:'ar'ei), was first proposed over half a century ago and introduced in Congress in 1923, just three years after passage of the 19th Amendment, giving women the right to vote. For 48 years women's-rights groups continued to propose the amendment without success, until October 12, 1971, when the House of Representatives approved the amendment followed by the Senate on March 22, 1972.

Congressional approval required ratification within seven years by three-fourths of the states though no time limit is specified in the Constitution. The campaign for the state ratifications touched off a bitter national debate on the merits of the amendment which continued throughout the decade. Due to expire in March, 1979, the amendment was still three states short of ratification when Congress extended the deadline for ratification by 39 months, to June 30, 1982. The extension gave supporters of ERA new hope and its critics further opportunity to defeat the amendment by attempts to rescind approval in several states.

ER, abbreviation of *emergency room.*

Deborah Scher is waiting in the ER. A huddle of nurses moves to the side as Basil wheels the stretcher in and pushes it up alongside one of the beds in a row equipped with respirators and machinery designed for use in cardiac arrests. *Joyce Maynard, The New York Times Magazine, May 23, 1976, p 80*

[1971]

ERA or **E.R.A.,** abbreviation of EQUAL RIGHTS AMENDMENT.

Yet the problems of the ERA could not be entirely in-terpreted as a rebuke to women's rights. The sweeping sim-plicity of the amendment—"Equality of rights under law shall not be denied or abridged on account of sex"—mad many voters, especially women, nervous. The anti-ERA lobby, led by Phyllis Schlafly . . . conjured up the prospec of unisex public toilets, an end to alimony, women force into duty as combat soldiers. *"Women of the Year: Grea Changes, New Chances, Tough Choices," Time, Jan. 5 1976, p 7*

[1972]

ERDA ('ər də), *n.* acronym for *Energy Research an Development Administration* (of the United States 1974-1977).

By bringing together the energy research activities o several different departments and agencies, ERDA is de signed to encourage development of many diverse energ sources without the nuclear bias of AEC's programs "Energy Research Agency Replaces AEC," Science News Oct. 19, 1974, p 248

[1974] ► See the note under DOE[1].

eroticist, *n. Especially British.* 1 a person who ex hibits or is subject to strong sexual desire..

The fully aware eroticist, by the same token, must alway subscribe to the code which he transgresses, otherwise hi pleasure will lose its edge. *"Taboos and Transgressions, Review of "Oeuvres Complètes" by Georges Bataille, Th Times Literary Supplement, March 3, 1972, p 234*

2 a person who produces or distributes erotic mate rial; pornographer.

The most popular adult film, he [Charles Roarty, the ho tel's director of marketing] says, is *Vixen*, directed by Rus Meyer, the master eroticist. *The Times (London), Sept. 2 1972, p 12*

[1972, derived from *eroticism* (1885) erotic charac ter, quality, or condition]

e·rot·o·pho·bic (i,rat ə'fou bik), *adj.* fearing or hat ing sexual expression or activity.

. . . 'we live in what some of the sociologists call an ero ophobic environment', in which the mention of sex is 'de tested' and 'taboo'. *"Out of the Air: Trendies," The Lis tener, April 13, 1972, p 485*

[1972, from *erotic* + connecting -o- + *phobic*]

error box, *Astronomy.* a quadrilateral represen tation of an area in the sky delimiting the approxi mate location of a celestial object or event.

One of the important tasks in X-ray astronomy at th present time is the identification of X-ray sources with vis ble objects so as to see what sort of known objects—if an —emit X-rays. The work involved is to narrow down th locations of the X-ray sources. X-ray observing equipmen characteristically locates a source within a certain "erro box" that may contain several candidates for visual ider tification, and the task is to make the error box smaller c pick the likeliest candidate. *Science News, Aug. 5, 197 p 88*

[1971]

error catastrophe, a theory of aging in which a increase in defective protein causes cell functionin to break down.

These results provide evidence for Orgel's theory of age ing, which suggests that one cause of ageing could be th accumulation of errors in protein synthesis, leading to gradual but irreversible breakdown in the accuracy of the protein synthesizing machinery and finally to a lethal "error catastrophe." *R. Holliday and G. M. Tarrant, "Altered Enzymes in Ageing Human Fibroblasts," Nature, July 7, 1972, p 26*

[1972, perhaps coined by Leslie Orgel in the early 1960's]

ERW, abbreviation of ENHANCED RADIATION WEAPON.

Those who fear that the introduction of the neutron bomb would lower the nuclear threshold believe that the greater military utility of ERWs will lead corps commanders to resort earlier to requests to use tactical nuclear weapons than they would with larger yield nuclear weapons. The supporters of ERWs believe that the greater military utility makes the deterrence value of these tactical nuclear weapons greater than weapons which cause large scale collateral damage, which NATO would be very reluctant to use. *Farooq Hussain, "The Nuclear Threshold—Up or Down," New Scientist, Feb. 23, 1978, p 499*

[1976]

ESB, abbreviation of *electrical stimulation of the brain* (the stimulation of specific areas of the brain by the insertion of electrodes).

But the technique was not designed to stop charging bulls. Delgado and his co-workers at the Yale School of Medicine worked with cats and monkeys and learned to produce definite changes in eating, sleeping, fighting, playing and sex behavior. When applied to humans, ESB was able to evoke such feelings as fear and friendliness, pain and pleasure. *Robert J. Trotter, Science News, April 13, 1974, p 245*

[1970] Compare PACEMAKER, STIMOCEIVER.

Es·ky ('es ki:), *n. Australian.* a trademark for a portable container for keeping drinks cold.

"I knew there was an Esky full of lemonade for the pilot when he got thirsty and I thought I might get it." *The Australian Women's Weekly, Feb. 7, 1979, p 14*

No less popular is Rugby League football, where raucous fans with well-stocked "eskies"—beer coolers—scream and swill and brawl with Sydneyesque abandon. *Picture legend, "Sydney," National Geographic Magazine, Feb. 1979, p 228*

[1974, probably shortened and altered form of *Eskimo*] Popularly spelled, **esky.**

ESL ('es əl), *n.* acronym for *English as a second language.*

This text . . . is intended for beginning and intermediate students of English as a second language and is designed to teach the student skills essential to success in an English speaking community, but which are not normally presented in the ESL classroom. *"New TESOL Texts," Advertisement by UCIS Publications, Pittsburgh, Pa., 1976, p 4*

[1967] Compare TEFL.

ESOL ('es əl), *n. Especially U.S. and Canadian.* acronym for *English for Speakers of Other Languages.*

Learning to omit a distinction is just as hard, often even harder, than learning to make one; Spanish-speaking learners of ESOL have that kind of problem when they have to learn to say *they* in English where Spanish would have *ellos* or *ellas. J. L. Dillard, Black English, 1972, p 272*

[1969]

ESOP ('i: sɑp), *n.* acronym for *Employee Stock Ownership Plan* (any of various plans that promote stock ownership among company employees).

ESOP's have become increasingly popular . . . as a combination of an employee bonus plan and as a source of inexpensive capital for the company. In other cases, employee stock ownership has become a way for workers to buy plants or divisions of companies in danger of being closed by the parent company. *Steven Rattner, "Management: Congressional Encouragement for ESOP's " The New York Times, Sept. 3, 1976, p D1*

Although a recent idea, the ESOP experiment deserves to be followed closely and could be adapted to other countries, especially in circumstances where there is a need to ensure the survival of family businesses or industrial plants located in depressed areas. *Jay McCulley, "ESOP: Between Fable and Reality," The Times (London), April 5, 1977, p III*

[1976]

ESR, abbreviation of ELECTRON SPIN RESONANCE.

In . . . ESR, a strong magnetic field is applied to the sample and the energy absorption is measured when the odd electrons flip their spins from being aligned in the same direction as the field to being aligned in the opposite direction. *William A. Pryor, "Free Radicals in Biological Systems," Scientific American, Aug. 1970, p 72*

[1962]

est, *n.* a system of consciousness-raising and self-realization.

With a dollop of almost every Eastern and Western discipline from Zen Buddhism to Dale Carnegie, "est" promises self-realization in a shiny new package—a 60-hour feel-it-don't-think-it training session developed by Erhard. *Linda Bird Francke, et al., "Life Style: Getting It," Newsweek, Feb. 17, 1975, p 46*

Est's route to increased potential is a Zen-like one: you are perfect as you are; since you cannot be other than what you are, it's okay not to be okay. *Morris B. Parloff, "How Werner Got It," Psychology Today, Nov. 1978, p 136*

[1974, from acronym of *Erhard Seminars Training,* founded in 1971 by Werner Erhard, American entrepreneur]

estian, *adj.:* If somebody tells me he will phone me at 3:00 with, say, some information I need, I know he will phone. If he calls instead at 3:20, we will have an *estian* conversation "acknowledging" that "he broke an agreement," "getting clear about it," "cleaning it up" and "taking responsibility" for it. *New Times, Oct. 18, 1974, p 49*

estie, *n.:* It was the concluding session of the training, and the factorylike positioning of the tables and chairs, the beaming, interchangeable "esties," the steady handclapping, made me feel as if I were being processed on an assembly line. *Leo Litwak, "Pay Attention, Turkeys!" The New York Times Magazine, May 2, 1976, p 56*

eta meson, an elementary particle of zero spin and neutral electric charge, with a mass 1072 times that of an electron.

The particular experiment involves the decay of the eta meson into 3 pi mesons (one with positive charge, one with negative charge and the other neutral). *New Scientist, July 9, 1970, p 64*

[1962, from *eta* the 7th letter of the Greek alphabet; patterned on *pi meson,* etc.]

etch pit, any one of numerous depressions found on

the planet Mars, similar to the depressions found on earth where melting and evaporating permafrost has caused the surface to cave in.

In the region of Novus Mons a smooth finely striated area covers a rough terrain to a uniform depth like a thick layer of syrup. The layer has etch pits and could be water ice—a martian glacier—since it and others similar surround a high land area. *Eric Burgess, "Mars Since the Dust Settled," New Scientist, Feb. 24, 1972, p 423*

[1963, extended sense of the term used for tiny pits in the surface of metal or crystal]

eth·a·cryn·ic acid (ˌeθ əˈkrin ik), a powerful synthetic diuretic substance, used to treat acute pulmonary edema, congestive heart failure, and other conditions. *Formula:* $C_{13}H_{12}Cl_2O_4$

Before they undertook their research, they knew that a chemical inhibitor of sodium ion reabsorption into the kidney cell, ethacrynic acid, also inhibits calcium ion reabsorption into the kidney cell. *"How Sodium Helps Calcium Into the Bloodstream," Science News, April 22, 1972, p 263*

[1965, from ethyl*ene* + ac*etic* + but*yryl* + phen*olic* acid]

eth·e·phon ('eθ ə fan), *n.* a synthetic chemical used to regulate growth of various plants.

Ethephon . . . was used by growers to regulate the maturity of walnuts so that they would all be ready for harvesting at the same time. The chemical was also used to induce flowering in pineapples, and to regulate the harvesting of sour and sweet cherries. *Sylvan H. Wittwer, "Agriculture," The World Book Science Annual 1973 (1972), p 255*

[1972, from chloro*ethyl* phos*phonic* acid]

e·thid·i·um (i'θid i: əm *or* e'θid i: əm), *n.* Often, **ethidium bromide.** a chemical substance that binds differentially to adjacent bases of DNA, used in biochemical research.

Several properties of plasmids support the idea that they are ancestral to the mitochondrial genome. They are similar in size to mitochondrial DNA's, and share the property of being supercoiled circles and of being subject to elimination by acridines and ethidium. *Rudolf A. Raff and Henry R. Mahler, "The Non Symbiotic Origin of Mitochondria," Science, Aug. 18, 1972, p 580*

[1967, from eth*yl* + -*id* + -*ium* (chemical suffixes)]

eth·ni·cism ('eθ nə‚siz əm), *n.* emphasis on ethnic identity; separation into ethnic groups.

In a fever of ethnicism, Italians, Jews, Orientals, Blacks, Hispanics and others have withdrawn into themselves, causing still unmeasured social damage. *Stefan Kanfer, "Candid in New York," The New York Times Magazine, Sept. 24, 1972, p 68*

[1972] ► The now archaic meaning of this term was paganism (1600's). The related term *ethnicity* (1950's) means ethnic quality and ethnic separatism.

ethnic purity, *U.S.* racial, cultural, or national homogeneity within a neighborhood or community.

White liberals appeared to be more put off by Carter's remarks than the blacks. Says one Midwestern liberal leader: "The question is whether or not 'ethnic purity' is a code word, and if so, is it calculated to lose 5% of the black vote and pick up 12% of Wallace's support? Or was it just a blunder?" *Time, April 26, 1976, p 16*

[1976] ► The phrase, used by Jimmy Carter in the 1976 Presidential campaign, was probably an attempt to show sympathy for ethnic feeling, but it was widely interpreted as a veiled reference to support of segregation in housing. See CODE WORD.

ethnoarcheology, *n.* a branch of archeology that studies the culture of a particular group.

Ethnoarcheology . . . is another new endeavor based largely on the new paradigm, one in which archeologists in increasing numbers are doing fieldwork in living societies. . . . Here the guiding question is not only how does technology reflect other subsystems but "how does it reinforce, enforce, and even determine the tasks and functions that it is involved with?" It is in pursuit of this problem that ethnoarcheology has developed. *Science, May 11, 1973, p 617*

Explorations in Ethnoarchaeology, edited by Richard A. Gould. University of New Mexico Press. *"Books," Scientific American, Aug. 1978, p 27*

[1973, from *ethno-* of cultural groups + *archeology*] See GARBAGEOLOGY.

ethnocide, *n.* the willful destruction of the culture of an ethnic group, especially as a government policy of acculturation or assimilation.

I do not believe that Mr. Stolz would be particularly concerned to defend himself from inclusion in the category of those missionaries who, by the verdict of Bishop Alejo Ovelar, "are implicated in the grave crime of ethnocide," because he would see nothing wrong in the destruction of the racial identity of Indians for which he feels little but contempt. *Norman Lewis, "Manhunt," The Sunday Times Magazine (London), Jan. 26, 1975, p 47*

[1972, from *ethno-* cultural group + -*cide* a killing, patterned on *genocide* (1944)]

ethnogenesis, *n.* the formation or evolution of an ethnic group.

It is but natural that such a long-standing ethnogenesis, comprising a great variety of components, bequeathed to us an extremely rich spiritual dowry in Neolithic, Thraco-Dacian and Latin traditions. *Iulian Antonescu and Vasile Drăguţ, "An Historical Journey Through Romania," The Times (London), Dec. 29, 1972, p VIII*

[1972]

ethnogenetic, *adj.:* One would have to study, in some quantitative way, the effects of anesthetic drugs on native-born Chinese living in China, on first- or second-generation Orientals living in Hawaii or California, on transplanted third-generation subjects in whom the ethnogenetic lines have remained unmixed, and finally on hybrids in order to determine the possible effect of intermarriage between races. *Emanuel M. Papper, "Acupuncture: Medicine or Magic?" 1974 Britannica Yearbook of Science and the Future (1973), p 57*

ethogram, *n.* a detailed description of the behavior of an animal.

This book is an expression of an emerging trend to look at human behaviour in much the same way as ethologists of the early 'thirties began to look at animal behaviour. In particular, it is a step in the process of constructing an "ethogram" of our own species; the step characterized by pinpointing, in the seemingly bewildering variety of movements that constitute "behaviour," a core of relatively simple "elements" which can be seen with fair regularity and constancy in all individuals of a species or population. *N. Tinbergen, Review of "An Ethological Study of Chil-*

dren's Behaviour" by W. C. McGrew, Nature, Aug. 25, 1972, p 471

[1968, from *etho-* behavior (from Greek *éthos* character) + *-gram* tracing, record]

Etrog, *n.* an award presented annually since 1967 by the Canadian Film Awards Committee for filmmaking achievements in Canada. The Etrog is a 12-inch gold-finished statuette mounted on a marble base.

The Etrogs will be awarded on the last evening of the festival and most Canadians can assess the judges' decisions after-the-fact when the films are generally released. Among the unseen nominees are George Kaczender's *In Praise of Older Women* starring Karen Black and Etrog nominees Helen Shaver (best actress), Marilyn Lightstone and Alberta Watson. *Maclean's, Sept. 4, 1978, p 13*

[1977, named for Sorel *Etrog,* a Canadian sculptor who designed the statuette]

▶ A new and as yet undetermined name was proposed for this award in 1979 with the establishment of the Academy of Canadian Cinema, into which the Canadian Film Awards Committee has been incorporated.

ETS (,i:,ti:'es), *v.i. U.S. Military Slang.* to be discharged from service, especially on completion of one's tour of duty.

He summarized life since his discharge: "Remember you guys gave me a giant banana split the day I ETSed [got out on schedule]? Well, it's been downhill since then. I came back to Cleveland; stayed with my dad, who was unemployed. Man, was that ever a downer. But I figured things would pick up if I got wheels, so I got a car." *Barbara Garson, "Luddites in Lordstown," Harper's, June 1972, p 69*

[1970, from abbreviation of *Estimated Time of Separation,* patterned on *ETA,* estimated time of arrival]

•u·gle·nid (yu:'gli: nid), *n.* any one-celled flagellate organism related to or resembling the euglena.

Mitotic cell division was the crucial genetic step toward further evolutionary advance. One would not expect it to have developed in a straight-line manner, starting with no mitosis and concluding with perfect mitosis. There must have been numerous dead ends, variations and byways. Evidence of just such uncertain gradualism is found today among the lower eukaryotes, for example the slime molds, the yellow-green and golden-yellow algae, the euglenids, the slime-net amoebas and others. *Lynn Margulis, "Symbiosis and Evolution," Scientific American, Aug. 1971, p 56*

[1968, from New Latin *Euglenida* the order of organisms including the euglena and related forms]

Euphemisms. ▶ New words and expressions are often coined to replace ones that are felt to be too direct, harsh, unpleasant, or offensive. Such euphemisms are usually motivated by a desire to avoid giving offense, as by the use of various circumlocutions for "black" to avoid reference to the color of a black person's skin: "colored," "nonwhite," "member of a minority group," "Afro-American," "Negro." (See BLACK.)

But euphemisms are also created from fear rooted in superstition, exemplified by a word such as MOONCHILD, coined to describe a person born under the sign of Cancer in order to avoid mentioning the name of the dreaded disease; by the use of

the word HOSPICE, originally meaning a guest house for the poor, the sick, etc., as the name of an institution for the care of the dying; by such metaphoric phrases as BUY THE FARM for "to die." To ameliorate the fear associated with death, Catholic churches have replaced the sacramental term *extreme unction,* with its suggestion of being *in extremis* or on the point of death, with the more acceptable name ANOINTING OF THE SICK. Likewise, the sacrament of penance has been renamed RITE OF RECONCILIATION, and the confessional has been supplemented by a ROOM OF RECONCILIATION.

A sense of delicacy or of prudishness has always been a prime motive for employing euphemisms. Despite today's liberalizing trends in sexual matters, direct reference to sexual activities and functions are still frowned upon in polite society. Thus pornographic theaters, sex shops, etc. are often referred to as ADULT (a usage popularized by purveyors of pornography), a sexual affair is called a RELATIONSHIP, and unmarried lovers living together are LIVE-IN friends, ROOMMATES, or COHABITEES.

The desire to upgrade or raise the worth of a position, occupation, or institution by changing its common name to one felt to confer greater dignity or importance is another motive for creating euphemisms. A prison guard is renamed a CORRECTIONAL OFFICER and a place of solitary confinement in a prison is made to seem less dehumanizing by calling it an ADJUSTMENT CENTER. In Great Britain a reform school is now called a COMMUNITY HOME. During the 1960's "garbage collector" was upgraded to *sanitationman,* but even this title was found wanting and so the higher-sounding one of SANITATION ENGINEER was invented. Some barbers who at first were satisfied with calling themselves "hair stylists" later chose HAIROLOGIST as a more appropriate descriptive title. And airline stewards and stewardesses (or "hostesses," as they were once called) became FLIGHT ATTENDANTS, although this was in part contrived to abolish sex discrimination in a job title. The low esteem in which aging is held in a youth-oriented society has necessitated the coinage of SENIOR CITIZENSHIP and THIRD AGE for the old and MIDDLESCENCE for the middle-aged (on the models of *adolescence* and *senescence*).

In modern times, euphemisms became important manipulative devices in political and military propaganda. The Nazis put euphemisms to diabolical use when they coined such terms as "final solution" for the mass extermination of the Jews. The Vietnam War produced such euphemisms as "body count" for the numbers killed in combat and "pacification" for the destruction of an area to eliminate guerrilla activity. Similar to "pacification" was PROTECTIVE REACTION, meaning a bombing raid or attack about which there was nothing protective or defensive.

Governments and their agencies have found it convenient to conceal the true nature of various policies and activities by the use of euphemisms. The emotionally appealing word HOMELAND was chosen by the white government of South Africa to

181

replace the racially-tainted term *Bantustan* for the separate Bantu territories it created. In the United States, underhanded political activities of serious consequences were casually referred to as DIRTY TRICKS. In the jargon of secret intelligence, to cause a foreign government to topple by various covert activities was merely to DESTABILIZE it; and shameful secrets that might embarrass the government if revealed, gave a new definition to FAMILY JEWELS. Some of these euphemisms were originally CODE WORDS, used to convey meaning to insiders.

A paradoxical feature of euphemisms is that when the character or meaning of what they describe catches up with the euphemism itself they lose their character as substitutes and come to denote the very same unpleasant fact or reality they were meant to disguise. At that point they must be replaced by new euphemisms. However, what at first may appear to be a new euphemism, as when poor people become "disadvantaged" and backward students "underachievers," and the retarded "handicapped" and "learning-disabled," is sometimes an outgrowth of a deeper shift in terminology. Many new terms come from an effort to be more accurate or to provide a better description or a description based on more refined information. Such a motivation is evident in the new definitions in psychiatry where an attempt is being made now to replace so-called blanket categories (e.g. hysterical neurosis) with more particular terms (e.g. psychogenic amnesia, psychogenic fugue, somnambulism, multiple personality).

eu·pho·bi·a (yu: 'fou bi: ə), *n. Humorous.* fear of good news (thought of as a prelude to bad news).

Euphobia—the fear of good news—was the useful word coined to describe this kind of reaction. We could hardly have got through the year without it. Never did silver linings adorn so many dark clouds. Mr Callaghan, announcing a "booming Britain" early in the year, was worrying about slump in the very same speech. *The Manchester Guardian Weekly, Jan. 1, 1979, p 3*

[1977, from *eu-* good + *phobia* fear] See GOOD NEWS.

Euro, *adj.* European.

Another suggestion is that the elections could be held on the same day as the general elections, and some of the MPs elected in Westminster could also be Euro MPs with seats in Westminster, as well as being directly elected to Strasbourg. *Eric Heffer, The Times (London), March 11, 1977, p 18*

—*n.* a proposed European monetary unit.

The day of a truly unified Eurocurrency—or "Euro" as moneymen call it—is still far away. *"The Economy: Money: Nearer to Eurocurrency," Time, April 17, 1972, p 82*

[1972, abstracted from the combining form *Euro-*]

Eurobank, *n.* a European bank, especially one holding deposits from various European and other countries.

It is not only American companies which obtain finance from Eurobanks: many European concerns in the high-interest countries also have recourse to this "fountain of short-term money." *Alfred Tholen, Die Welt, "Banking in*

Europe: Where the Streams of Capital Meet," The Time (London), May 24, 1972, p XII

As the recycling goes forward, Eurobanks may face li quidity problems, given the current lightness of mos money markets. *Monthly Economic Letter, First Nationa City Bank, "Paying for the Oil," Forbes, Sept. 1, 1974, p 23*

[1966, from *Euro-* European + *bank*]

Eurobanker, *n.* **1** a banker in a Eurobank.

A prominent newcomer is Stanislas Yassukovich, a American with French and Russian parents who in a coupl of years has made the European Banking company, one o the consortium banks, one of the market's strongest new comers. The press calls such men Eurobankers. *Peter T Kilborn, "Eurodollar Market Booming in London," Th New York Times, Dec. 25, 1976, p 21*

2 a bank which is part of the Eurobank system.

You would think the currency settlement and the queue of borrowers would be good for number one Eurobanker Germany's *Deutsche Bank*. Deutsche Bank will be a gaine from multinational companies extending their German business in a bigger EEC. *The Sunday Times (London) Dec. 19, 1971, p 42*

[1971]

Eurocentric, *adj.* having Europe as its center; prin cipally concerned with Europe or Europeans.

Mr Callaghan . . . had begun to make his moves, notabl to plan a pre-Easter trip to Washington, before he discov ered that the Federal German Chancellor, Helmut Sch midt, and the French President, Valery Giscard d'Estaing were preparing their own Eurocentric response to wha they also had begun to fear might turn into the complete collapse of the dollar as the world's reserve currency. *Pete Jenkins, "Stability in the World's Currency Markets—o Bust," The Manchester Guardian Weekly, Nov. 26, 1978, p 6*

[1972] ▶ A variant, *Europocentric*, has been current since about 1966.

Euroclear, *n.* the clearing house for transactions o Eurobanks.

Euroclear is based in Brussels and already has some 16 members. *Frank Vogl, The Times (London), June 1, 1970 p 22*

[1970] See EUROBANK.

Eurocommunism, *n.* a form of Communism adopted by some Western European Communis parties that emphasizes working within the existing democratic political systems to achieve social change.

The word "Eurocommunism," I am informed by Flora Lewis of The New York Times—who learned this from Ar rigo Levi of Italy's La Stampa—was coined by a Yugoslav named Franj Barberi, who invented the phrase in one of his articles in Milan's Il Giornale. *William Safire, "In France. 'The New Philosophers,' " The New York Times, Oct. 10 1977, p 27*

Eurocommunism is a mouthful of a word which both the Soviet Union and the United States are finding difficult t swallow. It is an in-word, invented to describe a new ver sion of Marxism which preaches obedience to the Western law of the ballot box and independence from Moscow *David North, "Eurocommunism: The 'Threat' That Simply Isn't," Maclean's, July 25, 1977, p 37*

[1976, from *Euro-* European + *communism*]

Eurocommunist, *n., adj.:* There are now three very dif

ferent schools within the European Communist camp. The summit avoided a formal break between the loyalists, and Tito's non-alignment, and the Eurocommunists. *Hella Pick, "Three Ways to European Communism," The Manchester Guardian Weekly, July 11, 1976, p 9*

Santiago Carrillo's 218-page *Eurocommunism and the State* is the strongest written argument for Eurocommunism yet made by one of its leading proponents. The book sounds all the familiar Eurocommunist themes: independence from Moscow, democratic plurality, universal suffrage, respect for human rights. *Time, July 11, 1977, p 32*

Eurocredit, *n.* financial credit in the Eurobank system.

Until now the Eurocredit market has been completely uncontrolled, and recently some leading German banks have been urging cautious lending policies on market participants to keep it this way. *Peter Norman, The Times (London), March 4, 1976, p 18*

[1976]

Eurogroup, *n.* a group formed by the European defense ministers within NATO, with the exception of those of France and Iceland, to promote measures of European defense cooperation.

Some kind of European Defence Community is an almost essential prerequisite of European unity and security. The existing Eurogroup is a useful device, but it excludes France — an indispensable thread in the pattern of European security. *The Times (London), June 15, 1973, p 18*

[1972]

Euronet, *n.* a scientific and technical data communications network linked by computers, operated by the European Economic Community.

The international aspect is important because data networks will ultimately transcend all national boundaries. Euronet, the EEC packet-switched network, is due to start early next year and several similar systems are already operating in the US to which it and existing European system will be connected. *"Technology: DoI Steps Into the Protocol Problem," New Scientist, June 29, 1978, p 918*

[1976, from *Euro-* European + *net*work]

Europatent, *n.* a patent for inventions, valid in all or most European countries.

The first convention provides for a so-called Europatent. The Europatent scheme will be open to all European countries and a single granted Europatent will in many respects function effectively as a national patent in each of the separate European countries belonging to the convention (around 20 so far). Thus any one Europatent will for most practical purposes serve as some 20 separate national patents. *Adrian Hope, "Untrodden Ground of EEC Patents," The Times (London), June 2, 1972, p 21*

[1972]

European Parliament, the popular name of the Assembly of the European Community, the legislative and advisory branch of the European Economic Community. Since 1979 it has consisted of 410 deputies elected by the voters of member nations.

British Ministers are becoming concerned at the increasing demands of the European Parliament to have more influence over Common Market decisions. Leaders of the European Parliament have been applying more pressure recently on the EEC Council of Ministers to consult them over a wide range of policy questions. *John Palmer, "Euro-*

parliament's Demands Worry UK Ministers," The Manchester Guardian Weekly, Nov. 5, 1978, p 4

The European parliament . . . will advise the European Commission and Council of Ministers, the two administrative bodies of the Common Market, formally known as the European Economic Community. *Bernard Valery, Sunday News (New York), June 10, 1979, p 8*

[1977] See MEP.

Europlug, *n.* an electric plug with flexible prongs designed to fit any of the different types of sockets used in European countries.

From the outset of discussions, the Dutch wanted to keep . . . the Euro-plug, which the British bitterly opposed on safety grounds. It is possible to insert the Euro-plug into both round and square pin UK sockets between the Earth and live holes, reversing polarity and making the body of any connected appliance live. *New Scientist, July 8, 1976, p 77*

[1965] ► Related to the Europlug is the proposal to introduce standardized voltage in the nations of the European Economic Community.

eu·so·cial (yu:'sou ʃəl), *adj.* completely or perfectly social.

It is both intrinsically interesting and particularly well written, although lovers of the old, romantic, anthropomorphic style will be both shocked and disappointed to find that Dr Wilson the honeybee is "just one more eusocial apoid." *Mary Jane West Eberhard, "The Social Insects," Review of "The Insect Societies" by Edward O. Wilson, Natural History, Feb. 1972, p 87*

[1972, from *eu-* good, true, truly + *social*]

eusociality, *n.:* There are three levels of increasingly complex behavior on the way to eusociality. The lowest level, communal behavior, is characterized by an aggregation of female insects, all belonging to the same generation; once the females have aggregated they build a communal nest for their young. *J. Wesley Burgess, "Social Spiders," Scientific American, March 1976, p 101*

euthanasia, *n.* ► The development of artificial means to keep dying patients alive by drugs, organ transplants, and respirators has led to a renewed interest in euthanasia, a term traditionally defined as painlessly putting to death the incurably and painfully diseased. This definition has been criticized by those who hold that euthanasia no longer means "putting to death painlessly" but rather "letting die with dignity."

The new definition is based on the distinction between ACTIVE (or POSITIVE) EUTHANASIA, where treatment is *administered* to hasten death, and PASSIVE (or NEGATIVE) EUTHANASIA, in which treatment is *withheld* to hasten death. Both forms are illegal in most countries, but while RIGHT-TO-DIE groups may condemn active euthanasia or "mercy killing" (a popular term since the 1930's), most support or advocate passive euthanasia on the grounds that prolonging life in the terminal stage of incurable illness disregards the rights or will of the patient (see LIVING WILL, INFORMED CONSENT), causes needless deterioration, dependence, and pain, and amounts to a prolongation of dying rather than of life. See DEATH.

eu·tha·nize ('yu: θə,naiz), *v.t.* to put to death painlessly; perform euthanasia on.

At its five New York shelters—one in each of the five
boroughs—the A.S.P.C.A. will be able only to find adoptive
homes for 10 per cent of the animals that will be brought in
next year. The rest will be "euthanized." *Roger Wilkins,
The New York Times, Dec. 29, 1978, p B5*

[1969, from *euthan*asia + *-ize*]

EVA, abbreviation of *extravehicular activity* (activity
outside a space vehicle).

The crew expected therefore to find a lot of fine-grained
material but after the first seven hours stay (EVA) outside
the lunar module, Schmitt could only report seeing coarse
grained material similar to mare basalts but with a high percentage of plagioclase. *"The Last Apollo Landing," Science
News, Dec. 16, 1972, p 388*

[1965]

event, *n.* **1** *Nuclear Physics.* the production of a
nuclear particle by causing other particles to collide.

If interpretations of "events" (particle physicists often
use this word instead of "results," which they apparently
feel is a touch overweening) now taking place in super-
cyclotrons hold up it will be possible to have public television specials on a subject that has not been so treated since
the search for fundamentality went beyond the neat mini-
solar-system model of proton, neutron, and electron. *Fred
Hapgood, "Quarks," The Atlantic, Nov. 1975, p 106*

After analyzing thousands of collisions researchers came
up with about 200 "events" in which charmed particles
seem to have been produced. *R. James Turner, "Science:
Small, Smaller, Smallest," Maclean's, Jan. 10, 1977, p 48*

2 an accidental failure or breakdown, especially in a
nuclear reactor or power plant.

That same month, there was another nuclear event. It
happened at the Hanford reactor, in Richland, Washington.
This nuclear plant spewed 60,000 gallons of radioactive
water into the Columbia River, forcing the reactor to shut
down. It happened accidentally—although the nuclear industry would probably prefer to say it happened eventfully.
Esquire, May 22, 1979, p 80

See BLOWDOWN, EXCURSION, MELTDOWN.

[1962 for def. 1; 1968 for def. 2]

event horizon, *Astronomy.* the boundary of a black
hole (the remains of a collapsed star).

If we drop things radially into a black hole we shall never
quite see them penetrate the event horizon; they will
endlessly spiral around it at a rate given by the angular velocity of the black hole. Someone falling in however would
pass through the event horizon in what to him would be a
perfectly finite time. *Garry Gibbons, "Black Holes Are
Hot," New Scientist, Jan. 8, 1976, p 54*

If two black holes collide and merge to form a single
black hole, the area of the event horizon around the resulting black hole is greater than the sum of the areas of the
event horizons around the original black holes. *S. W. Hawking, "The Quantum Mechanics of Black Holes," Scientific
American, Jan. 1977, p 35*

[1972]

eventing, *n. Especially British.* equestrian competition including dressage, cross-country riding, and
show jumping, usually lasting three days.

Eventing is a comparatively new sport, but in 1976 it is

estimated that 250,000 people went to the Badminton Horse
Trials, and the number of people watching show jumping
on television is second only to soccer. *Philippa Toomey,
The Times (London), Nov. 19, 1976, p 14*

Passing into verb.

Interviewer: Would you like to cook Captain Phillips's
breakfast before he goes off to work, for example?
Anne: I can manage that. It's easy. Especially when he's
eventing, because he's not going to get more than a cup of
coffee. *Interview of Her Royal Highness Princess Anne and
Captain Mark Phillips by Alastair Burnet and Andrew
Gardner, The Listener, Nov. 15, 1973, p 661*

[1971, from *event* + *-ing* action or process connected
with]

eventer, *n.:* The only rider to be hurt was Sarah Glyn, a
three-day eventer and the owner and rider of The-Wheeler-
Dealer. She broke her collarbone in a fall from another
horse during the dressage. *Pamela Macgregor-Morris, The
Times (London), April 9, 1977, p 5*

event tree, a diagram with labeled branches designed to show all the possible consequences of a
particular event, especially an accident or failure in
a system.

Event tree for pipe failure. An event tree can be constructed showing the initial failure of a pipe break and
showing all possible choices of success (up) and failure
(down) of the functions shown. *Saul Levine, "Nuclear Reactor Safety," McGraw-Hill Yearbook of Science and Technology 1976, p 61*

An "event tree" defines an initial failure somewhere
within a system. It then traces, like a genealogy—hence the
name "tree"—the consequences of that failure down
through related equipments and procedures. *Don G.
Meighan, "How Safe Is Safe Enough?" Encyclopedia Science Supplement (Grolier) 1977-1978 (1977), p 181*

[1976] Compare FAULT TREE.

Everywoman, *n.* a typical woman; the prototype of
womanhood.

A political wife, in a sense, is a contradiction in terms. . . .
She must be the model of purity and probity at home, but
she must be Everywoman outside, with a ready smile and a
cheerful word for all the importuning bores on the campaign trail. *"The Relentless Ordeal of Political Wives,"
Time, Oct. 7, 1974, p 15*

[1968, patterned on *Everyman* interpreted as the
typical man, after the name of the hero of an English
morality play of the early 1500's]

evoked potential, the electrical response arising
from the cortex of the brain upon stimulation of a
sense organ.

With human subjects it is possible to measure these signals by recording evoked potentials: small changes in the
electrical properties of the scalp produced as a result of activity of the brain. Because they are objective indicators of
certain brain functions evoked potentials have clinical
applications. For example, in cases of possible hysterical
blindness evoked potentials from the scalp above the oc-
cipital lobes can determine whether or not the brain is
receiving visual information. Similarly, evoked potentials
can be used to detect deafness in infants, which is otherwise quite difficult to diagnose. *Gerald Oster, "Auditory
Beats in the Brain," Scientific American, Oct. 1973, p 99*

[1968]

EW, abbreviation of ELECTRONIC WARFARE.

A whole range of EW equipment has been developed to gather and coordinate as much data as possible about the adversary's radar (land, sea, air, surveillance, weapon control, navigation, etc.), command and control, and communication systems, a form of EW known as Elint (electronic intelligence), *Frank Barnaby, "Towards Tactical Infallibility," New Scientist, May 10, 1973, p 351*

[1972]

ex·a- ('ek sə-), a prefix meaning one quintillion (10^{18}) of any standard unit in the international meter-kilogram-second system of measurements.

One discovery was the development of an analytical technique to identify the presence or absence of a single atom among 10 exa — that is, 10 quintillion (10,000,000,000,-000,000,000) — other atoms. . . . The method uses an intense laser beam to excite a single atom, if it is present among the others, and a sensitive device similar to a Geiger counter to detect the excited atom. *Jay A. Young, "Physical Sciences," Encyclopedia Science Supplement (Grolier) 1977, p 299*

[1976, perhaps alteration of *exo-* outer, from Greek *exō-* out of, outside] Compare PETA-.

ex·cess (ek'ses), *v.t. U.S.* to suspend the assignment of (a public school teacher or other civil servant) because a particular kind of job has been eliminated or declared overstaffed. Excessed employees usually continue on the payroll until they are dismissed.

According to a spokesman for the Board of Education, 243 supervisors were "excessed" last November and transferred out of their districts, although subsidized funds enabled some of them to return. The spokesman said that 165 of the 243 were due to be laid off next month unless additional funds were found. *Arnold H. Lubasch, "Race Quota for Principals Voided by U.S. Court Here," The New York Times, Jan. 20, 1976, p 28*

[1976, verb use (OED 1888) of noun and adjective (OED *a*1400)]

ex·ci·mer ('ek sə mər), *n.* a substance (dimer) formed by the union of atoms in an excited state.

A new form of laser that uses two gases has been developed at the Lawrence Livermore Laboratory in California. It is called a two-excimer laser. The term excimer means that atoms that are energetically excited come together and form molecules, and the molecules then emit the laser light. "Two excimer" means that molecules of two different elements are involved. *"Physical Sciences: A Laser With Two Gases," Science News, June 16, 1973, p 391*

Asbestos adsorbs benzo(a)pyrene molecules, holding them apart in a monomeric form and preventing the formation of excimers. *New Scientist, Oct. 12, 1978, p 111*

[1961, from *excit*ed "raised to a higher level of energy" + di*mer*; stress and articulation modeled on *polymer*]

ex·ci·sion·ase (ek'siʒ ə,neis), *n.* a viral enzyme that promotes the excision of the DNA of the virus from the genetic material of the bacterial host cell.

Similar studies of the reverse process — the excision of viral DNA from the bacterial chromosome . . . have shown that excision requires in addition to integrase the product of a second viral gene (called excisionase). The virus thus introduces into the host cell enzymatic machinery for cut-ting and joining the viral and host DNA at specific sites to bring about the insertion and excision of the provirus. *Allan M. Campbell, "How Viruses Insert Their DNA Into the DNA of the Host Cell," Scientific American, Dec. 1976, p 111*

[1976, from *excision* + *-ase*, a suffix meaning enzyme] Compare RESTRICTION ENZYME.

excision repair, the removal of damaged or mutant base sequences in a molecule of DNA and their replacement by correct ones.

Another method of repair occurs in the dark and in cells containing certain repair enzymes. In this process, known as excision repair, a damaged strand on the DNA duplex is removed and replaced by undamaged DNA replicated from the other strand of the duplex. *H. E. Kubitschek, "Life Sciences: Biophysics," Britannica Book of the Year 1975, p 444*

[1971] Compare DARK REPAIR, RECOMBINATIONAL REPAIR.

exclusionary rule, a rule established by the U.S. Supreme Court that evidence obtained by methods which violate the constitutional rights of the accused cannot be introduced in the trial of a criminal case.

Especially galling are those who escape because of legal rules: drug pushers caught dirty but without proper search warrant, Mafiosi discovered through an illegal wiretap, thugs whose car was stopped by cops acting without probable cause. In such cases, the catchall — or lose-all — complication is the exclusionary rule, which provides that evidence seized illegally may not be used in court. *"The Law: I: Catchall-22," Time, March 8, 1976, p 44*

The primary purpose of the exclusionary rule is to deter police misbehavior. Without the rule, the U.S. Supreme Court has held, lawmen could violate — with impunity — citizens' Fourth Amendment rights to be free of unreasonable searches and seizures. The rule against illegally obtained evidence has applied in Federal courts since 1914, and in 1961, the Court extended it to the states. The decision outraged law-enforcement officials, but it did force them to train policemen in the niceties of constitutional rights. *"A Rule Police Can Live With," Newsweek, June 4, 1979, p 86*

[1959] ► Also known in legal circles as the *Weeks Doctrine* (after the case of *Weeks v. the U.S.*, 1914) or the *Suppression Doctrine*. Before the 1970s references to the rule were infrequent and appeared mostly in legal journals. In recent years, criticism of what is presumed to be leniency of the courts toward suspected or known criminals has led to efforts to persuade the Supreme Court to revise or abolish the exclusionary rule. This has been partially satisfied by several rulings of the Court, as in 1974 (*U.S. v. Calandra*) and 1976 (*U.S. v. Janis*).

exclusive economic zone, the area of coastal waters and their undersea beds whose fishing and mineral resources a country claims exclusive rights to exploit or license others to make use of.

Another unresolved issue is an exclusive economic zone stretching from the new 12-mile limit of the territorial sea, an area where each coastal nation has full jurisdiction, to a limit of 200 or more miles if the continental shelf is particularly broad. Coastal countries would enjoy sovereign rights to prospect and exploit such natural resources as fisheries and off-shore oil and gas fields in their exclusive economic zones. *Paul Hofmann, The New York Times, Aug. 1, 1976, p 19*

excursion

[1975] *Abbreviation:* EEZ. Also shortened to ECO-NOMIC ZONE.

excursion, *n.* an uncontrolled chain reaction in a nuclear reactor that uses high-energy neutrons to produce fissionable material (fast-breeder reactor).

If the temperature of the core rose and gas bubbles of sodium were to form in the coolant, less neutrons would be captured by the sodium than before, thus the reaction would tend to increase. This can lead to the hypothetical "excursion." *John Chesshire, et al., "Negative Reactions to the UK's Fast Reactor Programme," New Scientist, Dec. 9, 1976, p 574*

[1963, extended sense of the original meaning "escape from confinement" (OED 1579)] Compare MELTDOWN.

executive, *n. attrib.* suitable to or befitting the rank or station of an executive, especially in regard to size, quality, design, or use.

I have accepted—I think—the prevalence of *hopefully* and *viable*, and even *executive* used as an adjective indicating an extreme degree of desirability ('executive housing'), though that last has been a severe strain on my patience. *Alasdair Maclean, "Views," The Listener, Feb. 8, 1973, p 170*

Looking and sounding like a confident winner, Tory leader Margaret Thatcher . . . traveled in her own executive bus, which was followed by others filled with dozens of journalists. *Time, May 7, 1979, p 28*

[1961, attributive use of the noun (OEDS 1902) meaning an important administrative officer of a business]

► In the 1950s *executive* was used to suggest various perquisites and privileges that executives had as status symbols, such as elegantly furnished and functional suites of offices *(executive suite)*, vehicles for their special use *(executive airplane, executive jet)* and automobiles *(executive-class car).* Eventually *executive* has come to be applied to anything sophisticated and expensive.

executive clemency, reduction in the penalty of a convicted criminal by the chief executive of a government, such as the President of the United States or the governor of a State. Executive clemency is not a pardon.

Mr. Nixon also denied . . . that he had offered executive clemency to McCord in exchange for his silence. *Peter Jenkins, The Manchester Guardian Weekly, May 26, 1973, p 3*

There is no practical difference between commutation of sentence and Executive clemency. *Time, June 17, 1974, p 3*

[1973]

executive privilege, *U.S.* the privilege claimed for the executive branch of the U.S. government by the President of withholding information from the legislative and judicial branches.

Obviously executive privilege is essential to protect the inner working of Government. Obviously also it is liable to grave abuse. A decade ago President Kennedy tried to end the practice by which lesser officials in the executive branch assumed this authority on their own cognizance. "Executive privilege," he wrote Representative Moss in 1962, "can be invoked only by the President and will not be used without specific Presidential approval." *Arthur Schlesinger Jr., "The Secrecy Dilemma," The New York Times Magazine, Feb. 6, 1972, p 50*

Sparked by the Pentagon Papers affair, charges of excessive secrecy, of improperly concealing information, were leveled at the executive branch. In response, administration spokesmen argued that withholding information deemed by the President or his delegates not in the public interest was a proper exercise of executive privilege, a right intrinsic in the doctrine of separation of powers. *Paul Fisher, "The Pentagon Papers," The Americana Annual 1972, p 185*

Attorney General Richard G. Kleindienst had asserted unlimited executive privilege for all two and a half million employees of the executive branch, and had just told the senators that if they had any objections they could impeach the President. *"The Talk of the Town," The New Yorker, April 28, 1973, p 30*

[1954] ► Although the concept of executive privilege goes back to the very beginnings of American Constitutional history, the term itself first appeared in the 1950's and did not attain widespread currency until the 1970's. According to the American Constitutional expert, Raoul Berger, "The very words 'executive privilege' were conjoined only yesterday, in 1958" (Raoul Berger, *Executive Privilege: A Constitutional Myth,* 1974, p 1). The 1958 reference is to a court case, Kaiser Aluminum & Chem. Co. *v.* United States, in which the term was used by Assistant Attorney General Doub. However, our file reveals a slightly earlier use in a general publication:

Administration officials claim the right under "executive privilege" to decline to tell Congressional investigators about executive department exchanges preliminary to official actions. *The Wall Street Journal, May 28, 1957, p 26*

The words "executive" and "privilege" first appeared together in a relevant context (though not in combination) in a sentence uttered in a Senate speech by Charles Pinckney (1757-1824), the South Carolina delegate to the Constitutional Convention of 1787: "No privilege of this kind was intended for your executive, nor any except that which I have mentioned for your legislature." For an excellent file of quotations giving a record of the use of *executive privilege* see the column "Among the New Words" by I. Willis Russell and Mary Gray Porter in *American Speech,* 48, 3-4, 1976, p 254-5. See also FREEDOM OF INFORMATION.

Exercycle, *n.* a trademark for a stationary bicycle used for exercising indoors.

Fischer passed part of every day swimming, playing tennis, lifting weights, skipping rope, riding an Exercycle, doing sit-ups and pummeling a 300-lb. bag. "You gotta stay in shape," he says, "or it's all over." *"Sport: Cover Story: The Battle of the Brains," Time, July 31, 1972, p 34*

She [Isabel Perón] eats sparingly, pedals an exercycle, watches TV, . . . and plays canasta with a maid. *"People," Daily News (New York), April 16, 1979, p 7*

[1967, blend of *exercise* and *cycle* bicycle] Also popularly spelled **exercycle.**

exit tax, a tax paid by Soviet citizens wishing to emigrate.

Some 13,000 Soviet Jews had emigrated to Israel in 1971.

But their emigration was hampered in 1972 by the Soviet Union's decree requiring that all educated persons wishing to leave the country pay an exit tax graduated according to their level of education and going up to some $25,000 for a holder of a doctorate. *Arthur Campbell Turner, "Israel," The Americana Annual 1973, p 371*

[1972] Also called EMIGRATION TAX. Compare DIPLOMA TAX. See also OVIR, REFUSENIK.

Ex·ner's center ('eks nərz). See the quotation for the meaning.

Exner's center is a motor association area for the part of the primary motor cortex which controls the hand and thus it is part of the structures underlying writing. *Dale W. McAdam and Harry A. Whitaker, "Speech," McGraw-Hill Yearbook of Science and Technology 1972, p 391*

[1970, named after Siegmund *Exner*, 1846-1926, an Austrian physiologist, who first described Exner's plexus, the layer of nerve fibers in this area of the brain]

exoelectron, *n.* an electron emitted from a surface atom of a metal, especially under conditions associated with stress.

Since such processes are exothermal, or heat-emitting, Kramer called the electrons exoelectrons. Although his explanation for the mechanism of electron emission is not accepted today (for example, the exoelectron emission in solidification is believed to be associated with changes in volume and the accompanying breakup of surface layers), the term exoelectron has survived. *Ernest Rabinowicz, "Exoelectrons," Scientific American, Jan. 1977, p 76*

[1963, from *exo-* outer + *electron*; but see quotation for origin of term]

ex·o·nym ('ek sə‚nim), *n.* any of the names given in different countries or languages to the same geographical feature or area (for example, the river *Vistula* in English, a transfer from Latin, has the exonyms *Wisła* in Polish, *Visla* in Russian, and *Weichsel* in German).

The crusade against exonyms will continue in New York until the next conference in five years time of the United Nations group of experts on geographical names. *Philip Howard, "Cartographic Spelling Bee Makes Progress," The Times (London), June 1, 1972, p 4*

[1972, from *exo-* outside + top*onym* place-name]

exorcism, *n.* ► The ancient practice of expelling evil spirits by conjurations and religious or magical ceremonies has been revived in recent years, especially among CHARISMATICS of the NEO-PENTECOSTAL movement. Many of the churches, disliking the term exorcism, prefer to use the word DELIVERANCE in its place.

The popularity of exorcism has grown in proportion to the increasing interest in the occult and the appearance of many books and films dealing with the existence of demons. Probably the most widely read of these books was *The Exorcist* (1971), a novel by William Peter Blatty about a teen-age girl possessed by a demon; an extremely successful motion picture based on it was released in 1973.

For hundreds of thousands of people — housewives, engineers, ministers, businessmen, doctors — the idea of casting demons out of people is no longer strange, though it is relatively new to them. They have seen exorcisms, they say, and some say they have experienced the sudden departure of alien spirits residing in them.

The often frenzied interest surrounding the movie [*The Exorcist*] has come and gone, but the phenomenon of exorcism, which was practiced widely before the movie, continues to spread vigorously. *"Controversy on Exorcism Grows as Practice Spreads," The New York Times, Nov. 29, 1974, p 33*

expansion, *n. U.S. and Canadian.* Often used attributively in such phrases as **expansion club** and **expansion pool** in referring to a sports team formed by buying a franchise from a professional league that expands and allows the new team to draft players from established teams in the league.

expansion city: Even ice hockey has been absorbed. Seven of the eight expansion cities are American. Canadians cannot buy a franchise. Consequently, many Canadian hockey players are living rather ingrown expatriate lives in Oakland and L.A. *Rick Salutin, Harper's, July 1971, p 30*

expansion club: The Philadelphia Flyers, 1974 Stanley Cup winners, believe in the violent approach to the game. Although a relatively young team, they became the first of the expansion clubs to win the championship last year. *Jack Savercool, The New York Times Book Review, March 23, 1975, p 36*

expansion draft: Each NBA team froze seven players on its roster and Klein was then allowed to select two of the remaining men from each team in a special expansion draft. *Jerome Holtzman, Britannica Book of the Year 1967, p 140*

expansion pool: The new look in the league came when six additional franchises were created in an expansion pool. The six clubs were lumped together in the newly formed Western Division, and the six existing clubs played in the Eastern Division. *George Versey, "Sports: Ice Hockey," 1969 Collier's Encyclopedia Year Book (1968), p 523*

expansion team: Expansion teams, such as the Caps and the Kansas City Scouts (who also changed coaches last month after more than a dozen straight losses), are typically launched with fourth-class flotsam — arthritic veterans and immature, unskilled rookies. *Bill Lowther, "Sports," Maclean's, Feb. 9, 1976, p 45*

[1966]

expletive deleted, *U.S.* an expression indicating the omission from print of an obscene word or phrase.

What I really dug was that blues singers were so loose and I was so uptight and inhibited. I was the original [expletive deleted] of the universe. *Stephen E. Rubin, "Forecast: SNOW," The New York Times Magazine, Feb. 15, 1976, p 47*

To an outsider to the field of astronomy, the range of reactions to the term "Janus," listed in many references as the 10th moon of Saturn, is often a bit of a shock. Responses range from acceptance to tolerant smiles to expletive deleted. *"A New Moon of Saturn, and an Old One," Science News, Jan. 29, 1977, p 69*

[1974] ► This term became current, often as a humorous catch phrase, from its frequent use in the version of the transcripts of the Watergate tapes released by the White House in 1975:

The transcripts themselves, which recorded endlessly rambling, disjointed and inconclusive conversations with many gaps punctuated with explanatory brackets such as '(expletive deleted)', '(characterization omitted)', and '(in-

Expo

audible)', raised a good many doubts about the manner in which the nation's business was being conducted in the White House. *James Bishop, "The United States," The Annual Register of World Events in 1974 (1975), p 76*

See the note under WATERGATE for a list of other terms generated by this affair.

Expo, *n.* **1** a large national or international exposition.

There was some talk at first that Fairmount Park, the site of the Philadelphia Centennial Exposition of 1876, be used for the Bicentennial Expo, but park lovers and environmentalists quickly killed that idea. *Julius Duscha, "An American Tragicomedy: Planning the Big Bash for 1976," Saturday Review, July 1, 1972, p 30*

2 Also, **expo.** any large exhibition.

There are now hundreds of stores specializing in personal computers. This thing has taken off like a skyrocket. This expo [a three-day exhibition of personal computers] had five thousand people in here yesterday. *"The Talk of the Town," The New Yorker, Nov. 14, 1977, p 40*

3 Used in combination.

At the Oceanexpo meeting at Bordeaux, France was revealing a potential second generation mining system. *New Scientist, Oct. 13, 1977, p 20*

[1967, short for *Exposition*] ► *Expo* was first used as the name of the international fair held in Montreal in 1967. It was then applied to fairs such as the one in Japan in 1970 and in Spokane, Washington in 1974, and finally to any large-scale exhibition.

exposure age, the length of time a meteorite is exposed to cosmic radiation before falling into the earth's atmosphere.

Measured exposure ages range from some tens of thousands of years up to two billion years. The most obvious way to arrive at an exposure age is simply to measure the concentration of some stable spallation product and then to divide this value by any rate at which the nucleus is produced. *I. R. Cameron, "Meteorites and Cosmic Radiation," Scientific American, July 1973, p 67*

[1973]

express, *v.t.* Usually (*passive*) **be expressed** or (*reflexive*) **express oneself,** to cause (a gene) to synthesize the specific protein it codes for by the processes of transcription (producing messenger RNA) and translation (making the protein from the information encoded in messenger RNA).

Whether the gene would express itself (start making insulin) is not known. But bacterial genes have already been introduced into human cell cultures and have expressed themselves in those cells. *Joan Arehart-Treichel, "Molecular Biology's Flower Child," Science News, Jan. 6, 1973, p 13*

A cell makes mRNA when a gene, which is a section of a DNA strand, is to be expressed. In most cases, genes express themselves by causing specific proteins to be made. Using the gene's structure as a template, or pattern, a cell forms an mRNA strand whose bases carry the gene's message for protein construction. The mRNA strand then interacts with a cell particle called a ribosome, which reads the message and helps assemble the protein. *Julian Davies, "Biochemistry," The World Book Science Annual 1977 (1976), p 248*

[They] announced that they had inserted into *Escherichia coli* bacteria a gene that codes for production

188

of the hormone somatostatin and had induced the bacteria to express the gene—that is, to produce the hormone from it. *Thomas H. Maugh II, "Biochemistry," 1979 Collier's Encyclopedia Year Book (1978), p 157*

[1968, extended from an older sense used in genetics, "(of a gene or genetic character or effect) to be manifested in the observable character or phenotype of an organism"] See RECOMBINANT DNA RESEARCH.

expression, *n.* the process by which a gene synthesizes a specific protein; manner in which a particular gene expresses itself.

The expression of certain genes can be experimentally controlled in bacteria. *Jerald C. Ensign, "Microbiology," The World Book Science Annual 1972 (1971), p 338*

The recent advances in understanding gene function and expression stem largely from the new and sometimes controversial scientific technology called recombinant DNA research. *Harold M. Schmeck, Jr., "Study Alters View of Gene Structure," The New York Times, May 22, 1979, p C1*

[1968] See SENTENCE, SYNONYM, WORD.

ex·ten·ci·sor (ek'sten,sai zər), *n.* a mechanical device for exercising and strengthening the fingers and wrist.

Dr. Robert P. Nirschl of Arlington, Va., recommends squeezing a rubber ball and doing forearm curls with a five-pound weight; he also advises the use of an extencisor. *Rex Lardner, The New York Times Magazine, Nov. 12, 1972, p 32*

[1972, apparently irregular blend of *extensor* and *exerciser*]

external fertilization, the fertilization of an egg, especially a human ovum, outside the body by introduction of sperm into an egg cell surgically removed from an ovary.

Another, potentially more vexing, argument is that external fertilization constitutes "interference with nature." . . . Some observers fear that external fertilization experiments will lead to a science fiction nightmare—a "brave new world" in which procreation will be moved from the bedroom to the laboratory. . . . Counterbalancing the possible problems of external fertilization are substantial potential benefits. *Thomas H. Maugh, "Test-Tube Babies," 1979 Collier's Encyclopedia Year Book (1978), p 341*

[1974, extended from an earlier zoological usage (c1943) describing normal fertilization in certain invertebrates, fish, and amphibians that takes place after eggs have left the female body] Also called IN-VITRO FERTILIZATION. See TEST-TUBE BABY.

externalization, *n.* *U.S.* the method of transacting sales of stock by transmitting orders to buy and sell to the floor of a stock exchange.

Internalization refers to two separate types of securities transactions that now are prevented by the regulations of the New York Stock Exchange but may be permitted if the S.E.C. issues specific rules. As opposed to externalization, where orders to buy and sell stock are transmitted to the floor of an exchange, internalized orders would be handled completely within the confines of a broker's office. *Leonard Sloane, "'Internalization,' a Different Way to Trade Stock," The New York Times, Jan. 17, 1977, p 37*

[1977]

extracurricular, *n.* an extracurricular activity.

Besides attending nightly cheerleader practices, she's [Judy Bell] Tracy's representative to Girls State, one of eight girls who represent the school at a statewide leadership conference, on the yearbook staff, and in enough extracurriculars that she'll be listed in the high school *Who's Who. Diane Divoky and Peter Schrag, "Football and Cheers," Saturday Review, Nov. 11, 1972, p 64*

[1965, noun use of the adjective (OEDS 1925)]

eye contact, a meeting of eyes; direct look at the eyes, exchanged with another.

Bruce Kramer, Harry Reems's lawyer, recalls: "For seven weeks I saw a jury that was friendly and receptive. We maintained eye contact. After the film was shown they wouldn't look us in the eye." *Ted Morgan, The New York Times Magazine, March 6, 1977, p 36*

The eyes of the wolf also communicate a great deal (as in the domesticated dog, but perhaps more so). Subordinates are constantly attentive to the leader, and as soon as eye contact is made, they submissively avert their eyes. *The New Yorker, April 24, 1978, p 57*

[1967]

eye-in-the-sky, *n., pl.* **eyes-in-the-sky.** electronic ground surveillance apparatus used in aircraft or artificial satellites.

Police are also deploying night vision equipment on their helicopters. Lockheed's Airborne Night Observation Device and similar equipment manufactured by RCA and International Telephone and Telegraph give the police a nocturnal eye-in-the-sky, peeking in on unsuspecting persons. *Robert Barkan, New Scientist, June 15, 1972, p 620*

The CIA . . . has been trying to keep tabs on Soviet agriculture with eye-in-the-sky photo satellites, and its findings have been reasonably accurate in the past. *Time, Nov. 28, 1977, p 88*

[1966, patterned on earlier *spy-in-the-sky* (1960); perhaps influenced by *pie in the sky,* a pleasant prospect (c1918), from the IWW song of Joe Hill *Pie in the Sky* (c1912), which contained the refrain, "You will eat, bye and bye, In that glorious land above the sky, Work and pray, live on hay, You'll get pie in the sky when you die."] Compare SPY SATELLITE.

eyeless sight, the ability to sense the colors of objects, and sometimes further developed to sense printed matter, through sensitivity of the skin, especially in the fingertips.

Certain investigators believe that another manifestation of radiesthesia may be involved in such psychic phenomena as reading print or identifying colors with the hands (eyeless sight), a medium's communication with someone by other than the five senses while utilizing some object associated with that person (object reading, or psychometry), and dowsing. *Samuel Moffat, "The Psychic Boom," 1973 Britannica Yearbook of Science and the Future (1972), p 80*

Also called SKIN VISION. Technical name, DERMAL-OPTICAL VISION.

[1972] ▶ The term was first used in a more general sense in 1924 in a book entitled *Eyeless Sight; a Study of Extra-Retinal Vision and the Paroptic Sense,* translated from the French by C. K. Ogden. In the original work, *Vision Extra-Retinienne* (1920) by the French Nobel Prize-winning novelist Jules Romains, there was an account of his research concerning the faculty of seeing without the use of the eyes. When the book was ridiculed by many scientists Romains abandoned his research, but it was taken up again in the 1960's in connection with the field of parapsychology. However, there are much earlier accounts of eyeless sight by Robert Boyle, the English chemist, followed by occasional accounts in the 1800's. In the 1930's there was research in this field in Brazil. See the article "Eyeless Sight" in the *Encyclopedia of Occultism and Parapsychology* by Leslie Shepard, Gale Research Company.

eyes-only, *adj.* U.S. (of confidential information) intended to be read only by the recipient and not passed along to others; top-secret.

[J. Edgar] Hoover sent the Rowley letter to six senior bureau officials on an "eyes-only" basis. There is no record of FBI meetings or discussions of those allegations. *Ronald Kessler and Laurence Stern, The Manchester Guardian Weekly (The Washington Post section), Oct. 10, 1976, p 15*

In February, Walker received an "eyes only" message from an old friend, Army Chief of Staff General Bernard W. Rogers. The communication assured him that Rogers was working to line up another "four-star slot" for him and implied that there would be no problem in finding one. *Time, Oct. 9, 1978, p 37*

[1972, abstracted from the phrase *for your eyes only,* a heading put on intelligence reports; *For Your Eyes Only* is a collection of espionage stories (1960) by British author Ian Fleming]

F

fabricated food, food mixed with cheaper substitutes, such as vegetable fiber, as part of the ingredients to replace traditional varieties of meat, milk, eggs, etc.

Scientists and industry analysts predict a surge in the use of so-called fabricated foods — items that are not in the form or shape we're used to or contain ingredients not usually associated with the products. *Louise Cook, The Tuscaloosa News (Alabama), Aug. 21, 1975, p 11*

[1970] Compare ENGINEERED FOOD.

fabric sculpture, a sculptured work made of pieces of cloth.

And perhaps some nostalgia for literalism is expressed in the newly fashionable mode of fabric sculpture, which painstakingly scissors, pieces, and pokes into being illustrations as rich and nappy as Pyle's and as broadly luminous as Maxfield Parrish's. *John Updike, "Books," The New Yorker, Aug. 14, 1978, p 96*

[1971] Compare FIBER ART.

Fa·bry's disease ('fɑ: bri:z), an inherited metabolic disorder caused by the deficiency of a galactoside enzyme, allowing accumulation of a fatty acid in body tissue.

Fabry's disease . . . can give rise to a characteristic skin lesion, angiokeratoma, and the patients may die in middle age of a cerebral artery hemorrhage or renal failure. *John C. Crawhall and Marianne Banfalvi, "Fabry's Disease: Differentiation between Two Forms of α-Galactosidase by Myoinositol," Science, Aug. 11, 1972, p 527*

[1967, named after Johannes *Fabry*, 1860-1930, a German dermatologist who first described (in 1898) the skin rash caused by the disease] See ALPHAGALACTOSIDASE.

FAC, abbreviation of *forward air controller.*

The FACs — forward air controllers who spot targets from tiny two-engine Cessnas for the fighter-bombers — were also forced to fly dangerously lower. During one four-hour mission, FAC Captain Conrad Pekkola, 32, dodged 15 SAMs as he circled the area between Khe Sanh and the DMZ. *David DeVoss, "The Air War: To See Is to Destroy," Time, April 17, 1972, p 39*

[1965]

facility trip, *British.* a trip taken at the expense of a government, business, etc., often to promote its interests; junket.

But what about those shadowy areas where perks are part of the public relations world in which a journalist cannot avoid existing: the facility trip, the publisher's party, the Christmas drinks, the lunch at the Savoy? *Peter Black, "Views," The Listener, May 31, 1973, p 713*

[1973, so called from the hotel, car, and other facilities usually provided on such trips]

faction, *n.* a book based on or consisting of facts but written in the form of a novel and published as fiction.

He promises his publisher a "faction" — one of the mixtures of fact and fiction craved by the present age. *"Books," Review of "Henry In A Silver Frame" by James Eastwood, The New Yorker, Sept. 2, 1972, p 71*

Alex Haley called *Roots* a work of "faction," blending fact and fiction, but the distinction wasn't made all that clear on TV, embarrassing Haley deeply. *Time, Sept. 19, 1977, p 93*

[1966, blend of *fact* and *fiction*]

factionalize, *v.t. U.S.* to divide into opposing groups; separate into factions; make factional.

The Republicans plan to push hard for more than a year to put it over. And with the Democrats certain to be factionalized in at least some areas, the GOP'ers feel they'll have a good chance. *"Dave Donnelly's Hawaii," Honolulu Star-Bulletin, April 2, 1973, p A-4*

[1971, from *factional* involving factions, partisan (OED 1650) + *-ize*]

factoid, *n.* a published statement taken to be a fact by virtue of its appearance in print; some account or event that is unsubstantiated but widely accepted.

He [Norman Mailer] speculates at length on fictionalizing biography, treating the actual person much as a novelist treats an imagined one. What this amounts to in *Marilyn* is . . . juggling facts, guesses, and factoids as suits his fancy, with the result that he loses authority as both biographer and novelist. *George P. Elliott, Review of "Marilyn" by Norman Mailer, Harper's, Oct. 1973, p 108*

[1973, coined by the American novelist Norman Mailer from *fact* + *-oid* resembling]

factoidal, *adj.:* Also from Farrar, Straus: Tom Wolfe's "The Right Stuff," probably factoidal, too, about . . . the early astronauts. *Herbert Mitgang, The New York Times, June 25, 1979, p C13*

FAE, abbreviation of FUEL AIR EXPLOSIVE.

FAE bombs were first used in combat in 1967, by the US Marines in Vietnam. One-hundred-pound BLU-73 FAEs — containing the highly volatile ethylene oxide, which burns spontaneously without oxygen — were used to detonate mines and defoliate trees across areas of over 700 sq.m. *Frank Barnaby, "Crossing the Nuclear Threshold," New Scientist, Jan. 19, 1978, p 151*

[1973]

fag hag, *U.S. Slang.* a woman who consorts habitually or exclusively with male homosexuals.

Homosexuals who felt socially isolated would sit together at mealtime, as much to escape the careless insults of faggot jokes as to ward off the loneliness. Girls who stop to talk to them still risk being called "fag-hags." *Grace and Fred M. Hechinger, "Homosexuality on Campus," The New York Times Magazine, March 12, 1978, p 16*

[1972, from *fag* homosexual + *hag* ugly old woman or witch]

fail, *n. U.S.* the failure of a broker or brokerage firm to deliver securities by a given time.

The main measuring device for the seriousness of back-office trouble was the amount of what Wall Street calls "fails." Fails, which might more bluntly be called defaults, occur when on the normal settlement date for any stock trade—five business days after the transaction itself—the seller's broker for some reason does not physically deliver the actual sold stock certificates to the buyer's broker, or the buyer's broker for some reason doesn't receive them. *John Brooks, "Annals of Finance: The Go-Go Years," The New Yorker, July 3, 1973, p 50*

[1968, noun use of the verb]

fall, *v.* **fall about,** *British, Informal.* to be overwhelmed with laughter; to break up laughing.

"The thought of producing a book in that time is enough to make us fall about," chortled Bodley. Yes, but hold on a minute, the book is only 16 pages long and we here on *The Times* produce similar miracles nightly, except Saturdays. *The Times (London), Jan. 19, 1973, p 14*

[1972]

FALN or **F.A.L.N.,** abbreviation of *Fuerzas Armadas de Liberación Nacional,* Spanish for Armed Forces of National Liberation, the name of a Puerto Rican terrorist group demanding independence for Puerto Rico.

"WE DON'T DESERVE THIS" was the headline over an editorial in the *News* on August 4th, the day after the F.A.L.N., a fanatical group advocating Puerto Rican independence, had planted several bombs in Manhattan office buildings, killing one person. *The New Yorker, Sept. 5, 1977, p 74*

[1975] Compare INDEPENDENTISTA. ▶ The same name and abbreviation were earlier (1963) used by a Venezuelan terrorist organization.

false color, a photographic process using infrared film, on which images of highly contrasting colors differentiate temperatures of sources of heat by variations of infrared radiation to detect camouflage and environmental pollution, to survey crops, forests, and other natural features of the earth's surface, and to aid in the study of other planets.

Earth crater in Saskatchewan was photographed in false color by Skylab astronauts. It is Deep Bay Crater at south end of Reindeer Lake. It is nine kilometers across and 100 million years old. *Picture legend, "Cratering in the Solar System," Scientific American, Jan. 1977, p 85*

[1968]

false-color, *adj.:* Global color variations on Mars are shown in this "false-color" composite assembled from photographs taken by Viking I shortly before it entered its circum-Martian orbit. *Picture legend, Science News, Nov. 12, 1977, p 327*

family, *n.* a group of hippies living together, as in a commune.

He [Elia Katz] also repeatedly encountered hypocrisy: *e.g.,* among the health food faddists in Pennsylvania and, most notably, in the bosom of the "Family" in Taos, New Mexico. *H. L. Van Brunt, Review of "Armed Love" by Elia Katz, Saturday Review, Jan. 22, 1972, p 78*

The term "snuff film" itself dates to the days of Charles Manson and his family. It was Manson who frequently used the word "snuff" to mean "murder." *Dick Brass, New York Post, Oct. 1, 1975, p 28*

[1972]

family ganging, *U.S.* the practice of giving medical treatment to several members of a family covered by medical insurance when only one member has requested or needs care.

Abuses such as "ping-ponging," in which patients who come to the clinic with a single complaint are referred to a string of different specialists, and "family ganging," in which a physician treats all accompanying family members whether or not they are sick, were documented earlier this year by Senator Frank Moss, a Utah Democrat who posed as a Medicaid patient during his own investigation of the facilities. *Linda Greenhouse, "Curbs Imposed on Medicaid Mills in Carey Plan to Save $50 Million," The New York Times, Oct. 6, 1976, p 1*

[1975]

familygram, *n. U.S.* a brief radio message transmitted by relatives to a sailor at sea.

Crewmen also begin to worry inordinately about friends and relatives on shore. The Navy tries to soothe their fears with "familygrams"—radioed messages received when the sub surfaces. *"Behavior: The Limits of Astronauts," Time, Sept. 17, 1973, p 65*

[1962, from *family* + *-gram,* as in *telegram*]

family hour, *U.S.* a television viewing period, usually from 7 to 9 p.m., when programs containing excessive violence or sexual material are barred and only programs regarded as suitable for viewing by parents and children together are shown.

It was the protests against television violence and other elements, particularly at times when children might be watching, that had much to do with the networks' decision to institute the family hour, relegating all possibly objectionable programs to the hours after nine o'clock, when children would be in bed. *"On and Off the Avenue: Under the Children's Christmas Tree," The New Yorker, Dec. 12, 1977, p 114*

The family hour is still in effect at the three networks, spokesmen there say, though the term "family hour" is not officially used anymore. "There is," as one network put it, "a greater sensitivity exercised during the 8-9 p.m. hour." *Michael Shain, "'Family Hour', 4 Years Later," New York Post, March 28, 1979, p 45*

[1975] Compare FRINGE TIME, PRIME TIME.

family jewels, *U.S. Slang.* shameful secrets; skeletons in the closet, applied to various underhanded activities or operations engaged in especially by members of the U.S. Central Intelligence Agency.

A turncoat . . . gave up to congressional investigating committees delicious CIA secrets, among them the notorious 693-page list of the "family jewels"—such tricks as the surveillance of journalists, interception of mail, drugging of unknowing CIA employees, assassination attempts against Fidel Castro, Patrice Lumumba, Rafael Trujillo.

family medicine

This, he says, is where the mole business probably got started. *The Manchester Guardian Weekly (The Washington Post section), June 11, 1978, p 17*

[1978] See DIRTY TRICKS.

▶ The term is also recorded in various slang dictionaries as an old taboo phrase meaning "testicles." The term *jewels* was already used in this sense before 1500 (see the *Middle English Dictionary*).

family medicine, another name for COMMUNITY MEDICINE.

My 14 years at the Steiner School . . . provided a solid, deeply humanistic basis for the pursuit of my M.D.-Ph.D. program and a career in family medicine—a "newly emerging" medical discipline devoted to the holistic approach to the patient. *Daniel R. Szekely, in a Letter to the Editor, The New York Times Magazine, Oct. 30, 1977, p 78*

[1966]

family practice, another name for COMMUNITY MEDICINE.

A new specialty, known variously as community medicine or family practice and stressing a general and person-oriented approach to medicine, was gaining in popularity. *Peter Stoler, "Medicine," Britannica Book of the Year 1973, p 456*

[1973]

family practitioner: Family practitioners, formerly known as "GPs" (for general practitioners), were the clinicians consulted in some 40%, or about 258 million, of those patient visits. This illustrates the continued pressure on a branch of medicine where a continued shortage of personnel has been acknowledged. *Byron T. Scott, "General Medicine," 1977 Britannica Yearbook of Science and the Future (1976), p 365*

family therapy, a form of psychotherapy in which the therapist involves a family group (especially parents and children) in treating one member of the family.

[Mel] Roman, a professor of psychiatry at Albert Einstein College of Medicine, sees family therapy as the wave of the future. "Family therapy says we're all in this together. No one's at fault. Everybody is responsible." *Beverly Stephen, "Seeds of Discontent," Daily News (New York), April 17, 1979, p 43*

[1977]

family therapist: For an hour a week over a period of eight weeks, I had sat behind a one-way mirror in an observation room in a psychiatric clinic and watched and listened to their sessions with a new breed of healer called a family therapist. *Janet Malcolm, "A Reporter at Large: The One-Way Mirror," The New Yorker, May 15, 1978, p 39*

Fanonesque or **Fanonist** or **Fanonian,** *adj.* characteristic of the radical political ideas of Frantz Fanon, 1925-1961, a revolutionary leader in Algeria, who believed in a world-wide peasants' revolution against colonial oppression.

A young West Indian named Errol improbably arrives to rent a room, and Mr. Didcot eventually takes him into his confidence. The plot unfolds in a sort of Fanonesque parable. *John W. Hughes, Review of "A Dark Corner" by Celia Dale, Saturday Review, April 22, 1972, p 87*

His simple answer to this very large and difficult question is given in what have become familiar Fanonist terms, though stated in his own peculiar language. *Thomas Hodgkin, "Back to Africa," The Manchester Guardian Weekly, July 10, 1971, p 18*

BURN! (1970)—Gillo Pontecorvo's passionate, controversial epic about a slave uprising on a Caribbean island, told from a neo-Marxist, Frantz Fanonian point of view. *"Goings On About Town," The New Yorker, March 11, 1972, p 18*

[1970]

fan·tas·mo (fæn'tæz mou), *adj. Informal.* supremely fantastic: **a** most strange or fanciful.

The figures that populate his [Richard Condon's] books are, instead, fantasmo embodiments of various sorts of foaming mania. *"Books," Review of "Arigato" by Richard Condon, Time, Oct. 23, 1972, p 106*

b that is so good, quick, high, just, etc., as to be unbelievable.

Antioch College, Yellow Springs, Ohio, the absolute fantasmo super-pinnacle of academic liberalism, has been completely wiped out for the last six weeks by a student strike and the occupation of key buildings. *National Review, June 22, 1973, p 671*

[1972, from *fantastic* + *-mo*, as in *supremo* (from Spanish, supreme)]

Faraday cup, a device that captures charged particles and determines their type, charge, and direction.

Large numbers of projectiles are required in nuclear-reaction studies. The projectiles that do not strike a nucleus simply joggle their way through the electron clouds of the atoms in the target and continue on in a well-defined beam. They are caught in a Faraday cup, where their accumulated charge is used as a measure of the beam's intensity. *Chris D. Zafiratos, "The Texture of the Nuclear Surface," Scientific American, Oct. 1972, p 105*

[1967, named after Michael *Faraday*, 1791-1867, English physicist and chemist]

farm, *n.* **buy the farm,** *U.S. Military Slang.* to be killed in action; die while in service.

Schwarzkopf needed to know what was going on. "Are you sure you need a jungle penetrator?" he said. "You know they're risky even in the daylight."

"Sir," Cameron answered, "the only thing I can tell you is that two of my people have bought the farm, and if I don't get it two more will." *C. D. B. Bryan, "Annals of War: Friendly Fire—III," The New Yorker, March 15, 1976, p 95*

[1967, alteration of earlier Air Force slang *to buy a farm,* meaning to crash, recorded in *The United States Air Force Dictionary* (by W. A. Heflin, 1956)]

fastback, *n.* a racing boat with a stern that slopes down in an unbroken curve.

When preliminary Cup races began in Newport, *Mariner* continued to lose embarrassingly to *Courageous* and *Intrepid.* Working 20 hours a day back at the drawing board and test tank, Chance designed a modified fastback. *Time, July 29, 1974, p 63*

[1974, transferred use of *fastback* (1962) an automobile with a sloping rear roof]

Fa·tah (fɑ: 'tɑ:), *n.* variant of AL FATAH.

"Fatah therefore decided to send guerrilla cadres into Israel," he reported. It was the border from which the

192

Israelis least expected any trouble. *Egyptian Mail, Feb. 17, 1973, p 4*

[1968]

fat city, *U.S. Slang.* 1 an excellent condition, situation, or prospect.

"Mr. Huston, just what does the expression 'fat city' mean?"

"It's a jazz musician's term," Huston said. "It's a dreamer's term, meaning no boundaries to the possibilities. It's the pot of gold at the end of the rainbow." *"The Talk of the Town," The New Yorker, Aug. 5, 1972, p 21*

"I've put it behind me," Stockdale says of his long ordeal. "I think of it as just another tour of duty. In so many ways, I'm in fat city." *"The POW's: What a Difference a Year Makes," Newsweek, February 25, 1974, p 68*

2 a poor or undesirable condition, situation, or prospect.

Furthermore, since the novel [Leonard Gardner's "Fat City"] fails to show how or why its principal characters wind up in "fat city" (argot for "out of condition" as well as for a loser's vain dreams), it appeared destined to benefit from filming, because documentation is an effect more convincing in film than in fiction, as well as being more appropriate to the form. *Charles Thomas Samuels, "Sightings: How Not to Film a Novel," American Scholar, Winter 1972, p 148*

[1965, def. 1 from *fat*, yielding much, fertile, plentiful; def. 2 from *fat*, overweight, obese; the use of *city* probably influenced by the slang suffix *-ville* (as in *dullsville*), literally, town, village]

fat-mouth, *v.i. U.S. Slang.* to talk excessively, especially without taking action.

They have to do something, have to move, where they can no longer sit back and fat-mouth about it, because the country will be on fire. *Don A. Schanche, "Panthers Against the Wall," quoting Eldridge Cleaver, The Atlantic, May 1970, p 61*

"Steve Adubato figured he would establish himself as Defender of the Italians," Baraka told me. "But he didn't realize that he would have to out-fatmouth Imperiale." *Calvin Trillin, "U.S. Journal: Newark," The New Yorker, Dec. 30, 1972, p 64*

[1970]

fault tree, a diagram with labeled branches that show all the possible consequences of accident or failure in a system.

One group of nuclear critics is . . . especially critical of the particular analytical methods used for risk projections (called fault tree analysis). The method concentrates on minor design comparisons and does not reveal gross design errors. *"Nuclear Safety: Study Finds Risks Small," Science News, Aug. 24 and 31, 1974, p 117*

[1974] Compare EVENT TREE.

fave rave, *British, Slang.* an infatuation with a popular performer, especially a singer.

He [David Cassidy] was hired, therefore, as an actor, but as soon as he was seen on screen he was snatched by the American fan magazine market, always at the ready to replace a current fave rave. *The Times (London), July 30, 1973, p 15*

[1969, from *fave* (short for *favorite*) and *rave* infatuation, craze]

FBS, abbreviation of *forward-based system.*

Primary components of the FBS are aircraft carriers and shorter-range aircraft and missiles, which are based in several countries of Western Europe as well as in South Korea. *Robert M. Lawrence, "Military Forces," The Americana Annual 1977, p 336*

[1971]

FEA, abbreviation of *Federal Energy Administration* (of the United States, 1974-1977).

The FEA figures that a 25% tax credit for such purchases as storm windows and doors, and insulation for unfinished attics could lead to a reduction of 50,000 to 100,000 bbl. a day. *"Some Ways to Cut the Waste," Time, Oct. 14, 1974, p 34*

[1974] ► See the note under DOE[1].

feasibility study, a study to determine the desirability and practicability of adopting a plan or system.

An essential ingredient of the sensible feasibility study on which Mintech has embarked, therefore, is an assessment of the value which the main categories of intercity traveller put on different aspects of the journey. *Angela Croome, Science Journal, March 1970, p 5*

A feasibility study must consider many factors, one of the most important being the assurance that the industrial plant can at all times utilize all, or practically all, of the steam generated from processes such as the fuel gas processes for the contracted quantities of solid waste to be accepted. *Douglas R. Nichols, "Combustion," McGraw-Hill Yearbook of Science and Technology 1978, p 126*

[1963]

Fe·de·ral·es (ˌfei dei'rɑː leis; *Anglicized* ˌfe də'ræleiz), *n.pl.* Mexican federal troops. *Sometimes used in the singular.*

Died. Lucio Cabañas, 37, Mexican guerrilla and folk hero; of wounds suffered in a gun battle with Federales; in the Sierra Madre del Sur above Acapulco. *"Milestones," Time, Dec. 16, 1974, p 69*

At the Palace, she said she was strapped to a table while a *Federal* interrogated her with applications of an electric cattle prod . . . until she passed out. *David Harris, "Busted in Mexico," The New York Times Magazine, May 1, 1977, p 50*

[1967, from Mexican Spanish, short for Spanish *Fuerzas Federales* Federal Forces]

feederliner, *n.* a passenger aircraft serving to link outlying areas with the main airline.

The first new airliner of any size to be built in Britain for more than a decade, the 70-100 seat Hawker Siddeley 146 jet feederliner, was announced last week as a joint project with the Government. *David Fairhall, "New UK Jetliner," The Manchester Guardian Weekly, Sept. 8, 1973, p 9*

[1966, from *feeder line* (1920's) a branch airline + *-er*; patterned on *airliner, jetliner,* etc.]

fee-for-service, *n.* separate payment for each medical service received by a patient. *Often attributive.*

Prepaid groups . . . had earned good reputations for giving high quality care more cheaply than did the traditional fee-for-service system. The groups worked on a fixed budget and had an incentive to keep people well and out of the hospital where care is very expensive. *Nancy Hicks, The New York Times, May 17, 1976, p 16*

[1973]

feelgood, *n.* **1** Usually spelled **Feelgood.** variant of DR. FEELGOOD.

The best way to guard against Feelgoods and charlatans is for the medical profession to keep its own house in order. We ought not to ask doctors to make the ethical decisions that are the responsibility of all society. But conversely, only physicians can protect us from quacks. If the doctors will monitor other doctors, we the people will look out for the politicians. *Shana Alexander, "Vigilantism in High Places," Newsweek, Dec. 25, 1972, p 29*

2 (*used disparagingly*) a carefree, blissful state; perfect contentment.

The chief exponents of psychic feelgood tend to come from Asia, California and the psychological sciences, no one of which has an impressive record at making people feel good. *Russell Baker, "The Pursuit of Unhappiness," The New York Times Magazine, May 15, 1977, p 12*

Attributive use.

Some critics, especially those who dislike Neil Simon (with whom Ross has collaborated closely), dismiss him as a "feel-good" director whose style reeks of old fashioned 1950's-style seamless sleekness. *Leo Janos, "That Hollywood Touch," The New York Times Magazine, Nov. 12, 1978, p 17*

[1972] Compare BLISSOUT.

feet, *n.pl.* **find one's feet,** *British.* to become firmly established or settled.

Mali went through its third year under military rule with the soldiers still trying to find their feet. *Kaye Whiteman, "French-Speaking West and Equatorial Africa," The Annual Register of World Events in 1971 (1972), p 251*

We look in satisfied bemusement at the rise of the working classes since 1970. We have not yet proved more responsible than the middle-class supremacy of a hundred years but we have only had four years to find our feet in. *J. J. Fookes, "View from the Pit," New Statesman, June 27, 1975, p 824*

[1961]

fel·late (fə'leit), *v.i., v.t.* to perform fellatio (on).

Linda Peabody is small shakes as Lois Angeles, and Coffin settles down to a life of routine acid-toking and zestful fellating. *New Statesman, June 27, 1975, p 833*

The blow she had struck was with an ice pick and for the recipient, a jailer named Clarence Alligood, it was fatal. On August 15, 1975, she was acquitted in a North Carolina courthouse; her defense of self-defense—Alligood had forced her to fellate him, so she killed him—stood up. *Maclean's, May 16, 1977, p 64*

[1968, back formation from *fellatio*]

FeLV, abbreviation of *feline leukemia virus* (causing lymphosarcoma, a kind of cancer, in cats and shown to be spread by contagion).

Hardy and Old find that overt infection with FeLV and incidence of leukaemia is highest in cats living in communities. Blood relationships between the animals has no influence. *"Monitor: Cats Lead the Way to Vaccination Against Cancer," New Scientist, Aug. 9, 1973, p 308*

[1973]

female chauvinism, exaggerated pride in, or loyalty to, the female sex.

Now for a notorious example of female chauvinism: **Notable American Women,** *1607-1850* . . . edited by Edward T. James (traitor!) and sponsored by (naturally) Radcliffe College. Just what are the qualifications of these 1,359 women? Judge for yourself: There are actresses like Laurette Taylor and Alma Gluck, artists like Helen Hokinson and Mary Cassatt, heroines like Pocahontas. *David M. Glixon, Saturday Review, May 6, 1972, p 70*

[1972, patterned on *male chauvinism* (1970)]

female chauvinist: You know, there are a lot of women I know in the music business that like to say, "Oh, well I just couldn't make it because, you know, the men held me back," and all this sort of female chauvinist bull. And it just seems to me that the better I got at what I did, the less trouble I had from that kind of attitude. *"Frontlines: Rock's Queen at 32," Maclean's, Oct. 2, 1978, p 4*

female chauvinist pig, *Humorous.* a woman who regards herself or all women as superior to men.

On the one hand, . . . there were male chauvinist pigs like myself, while, on the other, there were female chauvinist pigs like one of my best friends amongst extra-musical production staff. *Hans Keller, The Listener, Sept. 27, 1973, p 428*

[1973]

fem·to·me·ter ('fem tou ˌmi: tər), *n.* one quadrillionth of a meter.

Although the [gold atom] nucleus is 10^{15} times denser then the remainder of the atom, even in it there is a great deal of "empty space." Each nucleon has a diameter of approximately one femtometer (10^{-15} meter); the center-to-center distance between neighboring nucleons is some two femtometers. *Illustration legend, "The Texture of the Nuclear Surface," Scientific American, Oct. 1972, p 101*

Metres and kilometres won't upset the Establishment but there would certainly be disgruntled mutterings if the solar distance were reported as 150 gigametres, or the classical electron radius as 2.8 femtometres. *"Feedback: Astronomers drowning in numerical data," New Scientist, June 1, 1972, p 516*

[1972, from *femto-* one quadrillionth (10^{-15}) (from Danish *femten* fifteen) + *-meter* or *-metre*]

fender-bender, *n.* *U.S. and Canadian Slang.* **1** a collision between automobiles.

An automobile accident is unpleasant anywhere, but it would be hard to top the hassle of a Moscow fender-bender as I discovered recently when my little Russian-made Zhiguli (modeled after the Italian Fiat 124) slid into a bread truck at an intersection. *Peter Osnos, "Auto Repairs, Moscow-Style," The Manchester Guardian Weekly (The Washington Post section), Nov. 16, 1975, p 20*

2 a driver involved in such a collision.

This system of compensating those who have suffered injuries in car accidents—by trying to figure out which fender-bender was at fault—is about the most chaotic one that could have been devised. *Fred P. Graham, The New York Times, Feb. 18, 1968, Sec. 4, p 4E*

[1966]

fen·flur·a·mine (fen 'flur əˌmi:n), *n.* a drug used as an appetite depressant in the treatment of obesity. *Formula:* $C_{12}H_{16}F_3N$

Our Medical Correspondent writes: Ponderax (fenfluramine) is widely used to reduce appetite in overweight patients and is generally regarded as very safe. In contrast with other slimming pills, such as amphetamines, it has no stimulant effect and is not addictive. *The Times (London), March 15, 1973, p 3*

[1970, from *fen-* (variant of *phen-* phenyl) + *fluor-* fluorine + *amine*]

fe·nit·ro·thi·on (fə‚nit rou'θai ən), *n.* a highly toxic yellow oil that contains phosphorus and inhibits the enzyme cholinesterase, used to kill insects and other pests. *Formula:* $C_9H_{12}NO_5PS$

The codling moth that is responsible among other pests for maggoty apples is on the wing, and if you can reach your apple trees a spraying with a good insecticide such as fenitrothion (Fentro) would be worth while, especially if you have only a light crop. *The Times (London), July 9, 1977, p 11*

[1965, from *fen-* (variant of *phen-* phenyl) + *nitro-* nitric (acid) + *-thion* containing sulfur (from Greek *theîon* sulfur)]

fen·thi·on (fen 'θai ən), *n.* a highly toxic brown liquid that contains phosphorus and inhibits the enzyme cholinesterase, used to kill insects and other pests. *Formula:* $C_{10}H_{15}O_3PS_2$

At a park 40 miles south of Nashville, a contact poison called Fenthion, mixed with diesel fuel, was sprayed on roosting birds. Fenthion kills by attacking the birds' nervous system. *Wayne King, "Blackbirds, Roosting by the Millions, Damaging Farms in South," The New York Times, Feb. 29, 1976, p 33*

[1968, from *fen-* (variant of *phen-* phenyl) + *-thion* containing sulfur (from Greek *theîon* sulfur)]

Fermiology, *n.* the study of physical phenomena based on the quantum-mechanical concepts and theories of Enrico Fermi.

While the "Fermiology" of matter is extensively explained in textbooks, the understanding of non-Fermi electrons is another matter entirely. *William D. Metz, Science, July 14, 1972, p 156*

The gradient from momentum space representations ("Fermiology") to real space representations (clustering, localization) crosses the frontier between physics and chemistry. *Nature, July 21, 1972, p 130*

[1972, from Enrico *Fermi*, 1901-1954, Italian-born American physicist + *-ology* study of]

fer·re·dox·in (‚fer ə'dak sən), *n.* a plant and bacterial protein containing iron and sulfur, whose function is to transfer electrons from one enzyme or group of enzymes to another.

Ferredoxins . . . have no enzymic activity themselves, but nevertheless have a wide variety of applications. . . . Because of the simplicity and efficiency of ferredoxin, advocates of the chemical evolution theory of the origin of life have proposed that it was among the first proteins to be synthesized on earth. *Richard Cammack, "Protein," McGraw-Hill Yearbook of Science and Technology 1977, p 354*

[1962, coined by the American biochemists Leonard E. Mortenson, Raymond C. Valentine, and James E. Carnahan, from Latin *ferrum* iron + English *redox* oxidation-reduction + *-in* (chemical suffix)]

fetal alcohol syndrome, a group of defects in a newborn, including mental retardation and abnormally small head size, resulting from an excessive consumption of alcohol by the mother during pregnancy.

Seventy-four percent of the babies born to women who drank 10 ounces or more daily during pregnancy suffered . . . abnormalities associated with the fetal alcohol syndrome, compared with some 35 percent of the babies born to women who drank less than 10 ounces daily or none at all. *Science News, March 26, 1977, p 205*

A group of French researchers first recognised what has come to be called the "fetal alcohol syndrome" (malformations and behavioural damage) after a study of 9000 mothers in 1963. In the same study they also noticed the lesser, but still important, effects of more restrained drinking. *New Scientist, Jan. 11, 1979, p 76*

[1977]

fe·to·pro·tein (‚fi tə'prou ti:n), *n.* a protein found normally in significant amount in the blood serum of a fetus, especially ALPHAFETOPROTEIN.

Other cancers are associated with the reappearance of fetoproteins, for example, carcinoembryonic antigens, found in colonic cancer. *R. Harris, "Leukemia," McGraw-Hill Yearbook of Science and Technology 1974, p 263*

[1973, from *feto-* fetus + *protein*]

fe·to·scope ('fi: tə‚skoup), *n.* an optical instrument for direct observation of the fetus in the womb.

Another instrument that is becoming useful in diagnosing genetic and birth defect problems afflicting the unborn child is the fetoscope, a device which actually allows the doctor to look inside the womb. The fetoscope uses thin optical fibers — which themselves are still being developed and improved — to pipe light into the uterus and then carry the image of the fetus out. *Robert Cooke, Improving on Nature, 1977, p 93*

[1971, from *feto-* fetus + *-scope* instrument for viewing]

fe·tos·co·py (fi:'tas kə pi:), *n.:* The fetus can also be examined by ultrasound waves or, still as an experimental procedure, by fetoscopy (direct visual inspection) or by sampling the fetal blood. The optimum time for such prenatal tests is about the 16th week of gestation, and additional time may be required for tissue culture, bringing the fetus close to the period of viability. *Christopher Tietze and Sarah Lewit, "Legal Abortion," Scientific American, Jan. 1977, p 24*

fettucine Alfredo, a dish made with fettucine (Italian noodles), butter, Parmesan cheese, black pepper, and often heavy cream.

Kelly was addressing an audience over a luncheon of fettuccine Alfredo at Toronto's crusty La Scala restaurant. *Ian Brown, Maclean's, Dec. 11, 1978, p 41*

[1966, from Italian *fettucine all' Alfredo,* named after *Alfredo,* the owner of a restaurant in Rome noted for this dish]

Feyn·man diagram ('fein mən), a graphic representation of various interactions of elementary particles, such as electrons, positrons, and photons.

Electromagnetic and weak processes exhibit striking similarities when depicted in the form of Feynman diagrams. Such diagrams symbolize the interactions that underlie subnuclear phenomena, for example the collision between two particles, which physicists refer to as a scattering event. *Steven Weinberg, "Unified Theories of Elementary-Particle Interaction" (Illustration legend), Scientific American, July 1974, p 53*

[1968, named after Richard P. *Feynman,* born 1918, an American nuclear physicist who devised it]

F factor, a genetic factor that enables bacteria either to donate genetic material to other bacteria or to become the recipient of such material.

The F factor, which determines sexuality and conjugation in *E. coli* . . . is infectious, can transmit itself sequentially by conjugation and is an intact duplex DNA loop (of about 62 megadaltons), and there is about one of these F plasmids for every chromosome. *Royston C. Clowes, "The Molecule of Infectious Drug Resistance," Scientific American, April 1973, pp 22, 23*

[1972, from *Fertility factor*]

fiber, *n.* short for DIETARY FIBER.

Read the modern literature on nutrition written for the public to see how little space is devoted to the need for fiber or, as grandmother used to call it, roughage. *Marian Burros, "Nutritionists Cool Fight Against Fiber Diets," The Tuscaloosa News (Alabama) from The Washington Post, April 27, 1975, p 6C*

The aspect of diet that has received the most attention and the widest publicity in the past year has been its nonnutritive content, which is identified by the all-inclusive designation "fiber." *David Kritchevsky, "Food," McGraw-Hill Yearbook of Science and Technology 1978, p 174*

[1975]

fiber art, the art of producing three-dimensional structures by weaving, winding, or otherwise shaping fibers on special frames to form artistic designs.

Most fiber art exploits the expressive potential of the fiber itself, playing up the hairiness of rope, emphasizing the sleekness of plastic yarns, or revealing unexpected qualities in wool. *Mimi Shorr, "Fiber Sculpture," Saturday Review, May 20, 1972, p 58*

[1972] Compare FABRIC SCULPTURE.

fibre-tip pen, *British.* a pen with a tip made of fibers pressed together; felt-tip pen.

The directors wear short grey overall jackets, their breast pockets charged with fibre-tip pens. *The Sunday Times Magazine (London), May 18, 1975, p 17*

[1971; *felt-tip pen* has been used since the 1950's]

fi·brin·bi·o·plast (ˌfai brin 'bai ə ˌplæst), *n.* a synthetic fibrous material used to replace human tissue.

Known as the Euroamerican Technocorporation, it will produce and market the Hungarian biochemical invention "fibrinbioplast," a human tissue substitute, usable in 30 different kinds of surgical operations. *Jan Karski, "Hungary," The Americana Annual 1973, p 340*

[1973, from *fibrin* fibrous protein + *bio-* living + *-plast* formed matter]

fi·bro·gen·e·sis (ˌfai brə 'dʒen ə sis), *n.* the production or proliferation of fibrous tissue.

Inhalation of the various fibre types results in pulmonary fibrogenesis and an increased incidence of bronchogenic tumours in animals. *"Asbestos: Biological Effects," Nature, Dec. 1, 1972, p 256*

[1969, from *fibro-* fiber + *genesis*]

FIDO or **Fi·do** ('fai dou), *n. U.S. Aerospace.* an engineer concerned with the dynamics of a space flight, such as velocity, elevation, and changes in attitude and direction.

In the front row . . . sat three Flight Dynamics Engineers,

the men responsible for the ship's trajectory: from right to left, the Guidance Officer, or GUIDO, who was the chief navigation officer, the Flight Dynamics Officer, or FIDO who plotted the trajectory and made sure the spacecraft followed it; and the Retrofire Officer, or RETRO, who was in charge of the spacecraft's reëntry into the earth's atmosphere. *Henry S. F. Cooper, Jr., "Annals of Exploration: A Accident in Space—I," The New Yorker, Nov. 11, 1972, p 49*

[1969, probably from *Flight Dynamics Officer*]

field-effect, *adj.* relating to or using the effect produced by a varying electric field.

Field-Effect Electronics. . . . covers the theory and applications of field effect transistors. Both junction and insulated gate transistors are given intensive coverage *"Books of the Week," Science News, March 11, 1972, p 176*

The alternative is the liquid crystal display (LCD), which takes only a fraction of the power of an LED display and therefore can be left on all the time. But despite improvements made lately with so-called field-effect liquid crystals, which use polarising filters over the display and back ground reflecting surface, these are still difficult to read in dim light or the dark. *Nicholas Valéry, "Electronics in Search of Temps Perdu," New Scientist, Oct. 30, 1975, p 285*

[1972]

filamentous virus, a virus consisting of clusters of fine filaments.

Viruses can be readily observed in experimentally infected sensitive (indicator) strains that are lysed by viral infection. The filamentous virus . . . (about 10 nm in diameter) is first observed in the nucleus and, later, after lysis of the nuclear membrane, in the cytoplasm. *L. S. Diamond and C. F. T. Mattern, "Virus," McGraw-Hill Yearbook of Science and Technology 1975, p 411*

[1971]

fil·iale (fil'yal), *n.* a subsidiary company in France.

This could mean that such outstanding problems as the present Westinghouse-EDF imbroglio may go on for some time yet, although it is unlikely that the new government will veto the Creusot-Loiret-Westinghouse nuclear filiale *Henry Kahn, "Paris Notebook," New Scientist, July 27, 1972, p 204*

[1971, from French]

Finlandize, *v.t.* to cause (a country or political area) to adopt a policy of neutrality or accommodation in its relations with the Soviet Union.

Direct confrontations are unnecessary. The Russians can succeed better by indirection. They hope to Finlandize Western Europe. *Saul Bellow, "Reflections," The New Yorker, July 19, 1976, p 43*

Beyond its political significance, the conference drew new attention to the Finnish role of neutrality. This attention brought to mind for many the term "Finlandization." Urho Kekkonen said that "Generally speaking, Finlandization should also be taken to refer to political conciliation with the Soviet Union, and I have noticed with satisfaction that there are many others who want to be Finlandized in this sense. In this sense it seems that only China and Albania do not want to be Finlandized." *Erik J. Friis, "Finland," The Americana Annual 1976, p 250*

[1972, back formation from *Finlandization* (1969) the adoption of a neutral policy like that of Finland in its relations with the Soviet Union]

firebreak, *n.* a check in the escalation from conventional wars or weapons to all-out nuclear wars or weapons.

NATO says it needs neutron bombs to counter large concentrations of Warsaw Pact tanks. But conventional anti-tank missiles would probably do the job better at much less cost. They would also be less risky. Neutron warheads are likely to erode the gap between conventional and nuclear weapons—the so-called "firebreak"—and thus increase the probability of nuclear war. *Frank Barnaby, "Comment: An Extraordinary Decision," New Scientist, Oct. 26, 1978, p 250*

[1962, transferred sense of the term (DAE 1884) for a strip of cleared land used to check the spread of a forest or prairie fire]

firestorm, *n. U.S.* a violent, devastating outburst; explosion; storm.

Following the "Saturday Night Massacre" of Cox, Richardson, and Ruckelshaus, the White House was inundated by a "firestorm" of indignation (the figure employed by General Alexander Haig). The subsequent fortnight brought demands from a variety of sources that the President resign. *"The Week: Deliberate Sense," National Review, Nov. 23, 1973, p 1281*

The announcement that Sergeant Major Lymo Hascarni . . . had tied up the coveted big game (against, it is rumored, keen bidding from Liechtenstein and Bolivia) created an initial firestorm of protest from American basketball fans. *The New Yorker, Oct. 21, 1974, p 36*

[1967, figurative sense of the term (1940's) meaning the windstorm accompanying the explosion of incendiary or atomic bombs]

first cousin, something or someone closely connected with another; a close relation.

On November 6, on the island of Amchitka in the Aleutians, a seismic event occurred that, though not an earthquake, was a first cousin to one. *J. Joseph Lynch, S. J., "Earthquakes," The Americana Annual 1972, p 247*

Herr Alfred Tetzlaff is the hero of West Germany's hottest new situation comedy. He is a first cousin to both *All in the Family's* Archie Bunker and his relative, Alf Garnett of the BBC comedy series *Till Death Us Do Part. "Television Transplants," Time, May 13, 1974, p 96*

[1968, figurative use of the term for a child of one's uncle or aunt]

First World, the chief industrialized countries within the political power bloc of the world, including many of the countries of Western Europe, the United States, Japan, and the Soviet Union. *Often used attributively.*

At times he [Dom Helder] has used his foreign platforms for stinging denunciations of terror and torture in Brazil; more often he tries to prick the conscience of the First World for its complicity in the Third World's troubles. *"Pastor of the Poor," Time, June 24, 1974, p 61*

I was dismayed to read Dr. Hanlon's column, which is libellous and has obviously been printed because of the knowledge that it is difficult for Third World Scientists to take legal action against a "First World" journal. *Anand Kumar, Hyderabad, India, in a Letter to the Editor, New Scientist, Feb. 6, 1975, p 339*

[1974, patterned on *Third World* (1965) the underdeveloped countries of the world] Compare SECOND WORLD, THIRD WORLD, FOURTH WORLD. See also NORTH.

FIS, *British.* abbreviation of *Family Income Supplement.*

Even FIS families, who receive a supplement because of their low wages, sometimes have to pay income tax. *Pat Healy, "Parity for the Single Parent Families," The Times (London), Jan. 27, 1972, p 16*

If Mr. Millin asks his boss not to pay him the second stage of the deal, the family will, by next week, be marginally better off because they will be entitled to claim FIS again, as the eligibility threshold is going up. *John Cunningham, "Harsh Life Down on the Farm," The Manchester Guardian Weekly, July 26, 1975, p 4*

[1972]

fiscal drag, *Economics.* the depressing effect on economic growth of an excess of tax collections over government expenditures.

In France, the newly re-elected conservative Government has just promised a two-year tax freeze, after decisively beating a left-wing alliance committed to big tax increases for business and the rich. Even in places where taxes seem most onerous, among them Scandinavia and Britain, there is an increasing drive towards adjustments intended to eliminate fiscal drag and taxation of the purely paper capital gains that inflation brings. *Paul Lewis, "As in America, Europeans Want Benefits, Not the Taxes," The New York Times, July 30, 1978, Sec. 4, p 3*

[1972]

fishkill, *n.* a large-scale destruction of fish by water pollution.

He was at Escambia Bay talking about "fishkills"— that's three or four acres of pollution-poisoned fish piled 15-feet high, and the kills happen 300 times a year. *Richard Reeves, The New York Times Magazine, March 12, 1972, p 112*

[1962]

five, *n.* **take five,** *Slang.* to take a rest; relax.

Being a peripatetic President is tiring, so Cuba's Fidel Castro decided to take five—on a reviewing stand in Ethiopia's Revolution Square. As Colonel Mengistu Haile Mariam, Ethiopia's head of state, chatted away, Castro slumped in his chair and watched a parade. *Time, Oct. 2, 1978, p 89*

[1965, extended sense of the phrase meaning "take a five-minute break," used (since the 1930's) especially during rehearsals for a play, concert, etc.]

fix, *n. Informal.* something whose supply becomes continually necessary or greatly desired.

Some viewers, of course, outraged at the loss of their favorite soap operas and talk shows, would have preferred it canceled before it had even started. "Is this [televising of House of Commons session] going to happen *every* day?" was a repeated bleat from those deprived of their Monday soap fix. *David Cobb, "Canada: All in The Commons," Maclean's, Oct. 31, 1977, p 20*

I wondered, too, why he, a serious writer, even did these shows year in and year out, and whether or not he was gearing up for another round of publicity not to promote the book, because the book still wasn't finished, but to convince himself, meanwhile that he was alive, to get a fix. *Anne Taylor Fleming, "The Private World of Truman Capote," The New York Times Magazine, July 9, 1978, p 23*

[1976, figurative use of the slang term for a shot of a narcotic]

fladge (flædʒ), *n. Especially British Slang.* flagellation as a form of sexual perversion; flogging.

The two big bookstalls in Trastevere go in for porn and fladge, modulating through books of Nazi atrocities to the anthropozoology of Desmond Morris. *Anthony Burgess, "Viewpoint," The Times (London) Literary Supplement, Aug. 4, 1972, p 916*

[1972, altered and shortened form of *flagellation*]

flag of necessity, *U.S.* a foreign flag under which a ship is registered and sailed to avoid strict regulation, paying certain taxes, etc.

In the United States the flag of convenience is bluntly called the flag of necessity, for without it owners would not be able to operate in what is a very competitive market. *Digby Brindle-Wood-Williams, The Times (London), March 19, 1970, p V*

[1967]

flagship, *n.* the chief or leading item of a group or collection.

Located in the city's plush southeastern section, Myers Park High School has long been the flagship of Charlotte's educational system, known for its legions of National Merit Scholars and All-State quarterbacks. *Frank Barrows, The Atlantic, Nov. 1972, p 20*

The patents, Bunker Ramo claimed, cover crucial components used in IBM's 360 and 370 computer series—the "flagships" of its computer line. *Newsweek, March 11, 1974, p 74*

Attributive use.

Although the *Beacon* was the first Copley newspaper . . . the editorial tone of the fiercely conservative chain is set by the flagship paper, the *San Diego Union. Joseph Goulden, Harper's, April 1970, p 77*

[1963, figurative use of the naval term]

flak·ey ('flei ki:), *adj. Slang.* very unconventional; eccentric or crazy.

An officer might handle vast sums of money, the temptations were enormous, and there was some flakey behaviour. *Terry Coleman, "Honor Blight," The Manchester Guardian Weekly, Oct. 13, 1973, p 19*

[1972, variant form of earlier *flaky* (1969)]

flame-out, *n. U.S.* **1** the act or fact of being destroyed or crushed; destruction or extinction.

But now the great surge that carried racial justice briefly to the top of the nation's domestic agenda in the 1960s has been stalemated—by war, economics, the flame-out of the old civil-rights coalition. *"Black America Now," Newsweek, Feb. 19, 1973, p 29*

2 some person crushed by a sense of defeat or something destroyed by the loss of an exciting or fascinating quality.

A man often faces the jolting realization that he cannot accomplish all his early dreams, and, more important, begins to think seriously for the first time about the inevitability of death. Some flameouts simply sink into depression, others start to drink heavily. *Time, April 13, 1970, p 90*

[1970, figurative use of an earlier meaning (1950) the extinction of flame in the combustion chamber of a jet engine]

flame stitch, another name for BARGELLO.

You will look for bargello or "flame stitch" in vain in the "Dictionary." I could find nothing in any of the illustrations under that or any other name that looked like it. Bargello means, literally, police headquarters in Italian. Bargello (also called "Florentine stitch" today) obviously takes its name from the great museum of sculpture in Florence. *Russell Lynes, "The Needlepoint Boom," The New York Times Magazine, June 11, 1972, p 57*

[1965]

flan·ken ('flɑːŋ kən), *n.pl. U.S.* cooked ribs of beef cut from the flank.

I picked out flanken in horseradish with boiled potatoes and lima beans, a cup of noodle soup, a large roll, a cup of coffee, and a piece of cake—all for sixty cents. *Isaac Bashevis Singer, "A Day at Coney Island," The New Yorker, July 31, 1971, p 35*

[1966, from Yiddish, from German *Flanken* sides, flanks (of beef, etc.)]

flare, *n.* short for FLARE PASS.

No self-respecting football fan would dare to offer advice without couching it in jargon: red dogs, crack-back blitz . . . flares, and loops. *Jeff Greenfield, "Hockey Fanatics," Harper's, Jan. 1972, p 22*

[1972]

flare pass, a quick pass in U.S. football to a back heading toward the sideline.

We will miss watching men like Humm throw flare passes with such a low trajectory that only defense men six inches high could intercept. *J.W.L., "Football," The New Yorker, Sept. 30, 1972, p 106*

[1965]

flash, *n. U.S. Slang.* the initial effect of a narcotic.

Many speed freaks still prefer to inject speed with particular impurities because amphetamine laced with other substances, such as ether, is thought to produce a heavier flash or more intense rush than pure methamphetamine does. *Lester Grinspoon, M.D., and Peter Hedblom, "Amphetamines Reconsidered," Saturday Review, July 8, 1972, p 38*

[1972] Compare RUSH.

flasher, *n. Slang.* a person who exposes himself indecently.

Sara never rides the subway. She fears—not necessarily in the following order—murderers, rapists, purse-snatchers, flashers and all of the seamy types who take advantage of rush-hour crowds to rub up against women. *Susan Jacoby, The New York Times, Jan. 12, 1978, p 18*

[1974, from *flash* to display + *-er*] Compare STREAKER.

flashlight fish, any of a family of fishes, especially *Photoblepharon palpebratus*, that emit light from special luminescent organs.

The Atlantic flashlight fish lives in more than 500 feet of water and only enters lesser depths to feed during darkness. Its light organs, which may be seen by divers as far as 50 feet away, contain glowing bacteria and can be covered with a lid. Nealson plans to study the relationship between the fish and its bacteria. *Science News, March 4, 1978, p 135*

[1975]

flash pack, *British.* a product displaying a reduced price on the package.

"Flash-packs," as they are called in the trade, are largely responsible for housewives' confusion over grocery prices.

It is hard to remember the "real" price of an article if you hardly ever pay it. There can be 40 or 50 flash-packs on show in a big supermarket at any one time. *The Times (London), Sept. 8, 1972, p 12*

[1970]

flat pack, a thin, sealed package of semiconductors with leads connecting the unit to microelectronic circuits.

The Chinese diode-transistor logic element uses a method of packaging (developed in the U.S.) called the TO-5 package; the transistor-transistor element uses what is called flat pack. *Raphael Tsu, "High Technology in China," Scientific American, Dec. 1972, p 14*

[1968]

flat-plate collector, a group of flat metal-and-glass plates to absorb solar radiation, mounted over air ducts or tubes carrying liquid that are heated from the energy absorbed from the plates.

Flat-plate collectors sloped toward the south in Madison, with a slope equal to the latitude, will have incident on them an average daily radiation of 3.4 kw-h/m² in January and 5.6 kw-h/m² in July. These data illustrate the gains to be obtained by orienting a collector in a favorable manner. *John A. Duffie and William A. Beckman, "Solar Heating and Cooling," Science, Jan. 16, 1976, p 144*

[1976]

flat time sentence, *U.S.* a prison sentence specified by law and that cannot be reduced by judiciary discretion or parole.

The legislatures in Maine, California and Indiana have already adopted "flat time" sentences, which have a specific number of years. These sentences are usually shorter than "indeterminate" terms, where the maximum is high and a judge has broad discretion to sentence a defendant to, say, five to 15 years. *Tom Goldstein, "Inequities Common in Jail Sentences," The New York Times, Dec. 19, 1976, Sec. 4, p 8*

[1961]

fla·vo·dox·in (flei vou'dɑk sən), *n.* an electron-carrying protein containing riboflavin and associated with oxidation-reduction reactions in bacterial cells.

Consistent with their reductive character, ferredoxins and flavodoxins, proteins otherwise typical of anaerobes, have been implicated in nitrogen fixation by *Azotobacter* and also by the aerobic root nodule system. *John R. Postgate, "Nitrogen Fixation," McGraw-Hill Yearbook of Science and Technology 1974, p 308*

[1971, from *flavo-* flavin, flavoprotein (literally, yellow) + re*dox* oxidation-reduction + *-in* (chemical suffix)] Compare RUBREDOXIN.

fla·vo·my·cin (ˌflei vou'mɑi sən), *n.* an antibiotic derived from soil bacteria and related to streptomycin.

Regulations will also be made so that from 1 March, 1971, flavomycin and virginiamycin can be used as feed antibiotics available without prescription though subject to some conditions, including the extent and method of use. *Tam Dalyell, New Scientist and Science Journal, Feb. 25, 1971, p 433*

[1970, from *flavo-* yellow + *-mycin* fungal substance (ultimately from Greek *mýkēs* fungus)]

flavor, *n.* a specific type or variety of quark (subatomic particle proposed as a constituent of known particles).

The different kinds of quarks . . . are known technically as flavors. They follow the universal rule that each particle of matter is matched by a companion antiparticle that is equal in mass but opposite in electrical charge. *Robert H. March, "Physics," The World Book Science Annual 1978 (1977), p 324*

Experiments of recent years led to the grouping of different quarks in terms of at least five "flavors" and three "colors." Such names are merely conveniences, and have no more meaning than numbers. *Malcolm W. Browne, "Detection of the Elusive 'Gluon' Exciting Scientists," The New York Times, Sept. 2, 1979, p 28*

[1976] See QUARK.

flea collar, a collar for dogs and cats, containing a substance to kill fleas and ticks.

The message, complete with merry jingle, was a commercial for flea collars for dogs and cats. *The Times (London), Nov. 4, 1978, p 11*

[1972]

flesh, *n.* **press (the) flesh,** *Especially U.S.* to shake hands.

[Pete V.] Domenici is a breathless, ebullient crowd pleaser, while strong, low-key Jack Daniels, in contrast, is a diffident public speaker who prefers to press the flesh with individual voters in a kind of Western one-on-one campaign. *Time, Nov. 6, 1972, p 58*

The state assemblymen . . . stayed at the rear of the crowd for a while to clap shoulders, press flesh, show off their memory for names, and often mention, incidentally, next week's fund-raiser. *Andy Logan, "Around City Hall: But Not for Love," The New Yorker, Sept. 4, 1978, p 86*

[1972] ► According to William Safire (*Safire's Political Dictionary*, 1978), the phrase was first used by Lyndon B. Johnson in 1960. The expression may have originated in black jazz slang.

flex·i- ('flek si:-), a combining form meaning "flexible," used originally (1960's) in various trademarks (*Flexi-Van, Flexiprene*) but now freely used to form compounds such as the following:

flexibacteria, *n.pl.:* Some researchers studying the growth of filamentous bacteria, called flexibacteria, in Yellowstone National Park geyser pools, believed that the formation of stromatolites by flexibacteria may have taken place in the Precambrian. *Albert Smith, "Botany: Fossil Plants," 1974 Britannica Yearbook of Science and the Future (1973), p 202*

flexi-cover, *n.:* One is left wondering whether, for it to survive and quench the thirst of the further education students rather than just the academics, Copley's *Camden* may not have to become more workaday: go into flexi-covers and on to less beautiful paper. *Tony Aldous, The Times (London), May 27, 1977, p III*

flexinomics, *n.* [*flexi-* + economics]: Vice President Spiro Agnew sounded off in Las Vegas about "the strange, new 'flexinomics' being tested and scrapped by a desperate candidate" whom he did not have to name. *"The Campaign: Reverse Coattails," Newsweek, Sept. 25, 1972, p 33*

flexi-roof, *n.:* On television, meanwhile, they showed a lovely flexi-roof, called a Gridshell, which inscrutably reverses the effect of a draped fisherman's net, and by imitating that sort of lattice-work, becomes convex rather than

flexible time

concave. Clever stuff. *Richard North, The Listener, March 27, 1975, p 415*

[1972] See FLEXITIME.

flexible time, another name for FLEXTIME.

The company working day is lengthened, normally in Germany from seven in the morning till seven in the evening. And two quite different types of working time are introduced—"flexible" time, during which employees have the choice of being in or not, and "core" time, when everybody should be present at desk or workbench. *Brian Hammond, "Gliding Time Comes to Britain," New Scientist, March 16, 1972, p 602*

[1972]

flexitime, *n.* variant of FLEXTIME.

In the search for improving the work environment, flexitime has become a legitimate option. What began as an experiment is no longer a novelty, and most of its users are convinced that its benefits far outweigh any shortcomings. *Jourdan Houston, "Flexible Work Time Punches In," The Reader's Digest, Oct. 1978, p 210*

[1973]

flextime, *n.* the staggering of working hours to enable each employee to work the full quota of time but at periods most convenient for the individual.

Flextime is especially appreciated by working parents, who can choose either to see their children off to school in the morning or to pick them up after classes, and sports enthusiasts, who can play golf or tennis in the early morning or late afternoon. Supervisors report that productivity generally improves under Flextime—since employees can work at the hours when they feel most alert—and that absenteeism drops. *Time, Jan. 10, 1977, p 52*

[1972, from *flexible* + *time*] Also called FLEXITIME, FLEXIBLE TIME, GLIDING TIME. Compare CORE TIME.

flight attendant, a person who attends passengers in an airplane.

A few of the new words will give the flavour of their enervating bowdlerisation. Salesmen become sales persons. Maids become house workers. Airline stewardesses become airplane flight attendants. Foremen become supervisors, jury foremen become jury forepersons. *Harold Evans, "Person to Person," The Sunday Times (London), May 4, 1975, p 18*

American Airlines agreed today to rehire 300 flight attendants who were dismissed between 1965 and 1970 because they became pregnant and to pay them a total of $2.7 million. *The New York Times, Oct. 4, 1977, p 40*

[1974] ▶ This term has replaced *stewardess* and *hostess*, both used since the 1930's. It was adopted by the airlines to eliminate reference to gender in job titles. See DEGENDER, PERSON.

flight capital, funds transferred from one country to another, usually to avoid impounding or losses resulting from taxation, inflation, devaluation, etc.

Swiss officials are considering a variety of measures aimed at toughening the regulation of the country's 553 banks. . . . Many of the possible reforms affect the way the banks handle funds from abroad—including stolen funds, flight capital, tax-dodge money and other unsavory negotiables that have found their way into the Swiss system, no questions asked. *"Banking: Less Go-Go in Switzerland," Time, July 18, 1977, p 74*

[1962, from the phrase *flight of capital*, long used in economics to designate the movement of capital out of a country]

flight capitalist: Judging from the financial statistics of Swiss banks, it is more the exception than the rule for the flight capitalists to be caught. *Clyde H. Farnsworth, "Flood of Smuggled Cash Is Enriching Swiss Banks," The New York Times, May 11, 1976, p 52*

flip chart, a chart to display information in sequence, consisting of large sheets attached at the top that can be turned over one after the other.

The apparently dreaded flip-charts that were mentioned are quite simply one of the many methods used to help experts in highly technical areas communicate graphically in the course of lectures, etc. *The Times (London), Nov. 10, 1974, p 20*

[1963]

flip-flops, *n.pl.* or **flip-flop sandals,** flat sandals, made of composition rubber, held on the foot by a thong that goes between the toes and over the instep.

A woman in Tampa said that her daughter had left home on October 28th—wearing a white blouse, pink pants, and green "flip-flops"—and had not been in touch since. *Calvin Trillin, "U.S. Journal: St. Petersburg, Florida," The New Yorker, April 15, 1972, p 132*

We have passed whole families climbing up in wellington boots and flip flops, and people climbing Striding Edge at Hellvelyn without maps or compasses. *The Times (London), Aug. 23, 1977, p 11*

[1969, so called from the flip-flopping motion of the sole hitting against the foot]

flipping, *n. U.S. Slang.* See the quotation for the meaning.

The bill contained other provisions which Wallace contends never would have passed on their own merits: abolition of garnishments on the first $80 of a worker's pay; outlawing "flipping," or charging interest on interest, a common loan-sharking practice. *Stephan Lesher, The New York Times Magazine, Jan. 2, 1972, p 33*

[1969]

FLIR, *n.* acronym for *forward-looking infrared,* an electronic device to detect objects in the dark, used by the military in night fighting.

The FLIR . . . heat-sensitive system is like a television camera that can see at night. Objects show up on a screen, defined by the heat they are giving off, which is picked up by the camera. FLIR was initially developed for use in aircraft but now can be used by ground troops as well. *Lee Lescaze, The Manchester Guardian Weekly (The Washington Post sec.), Oct. 24, 1976, p 15*

[1976, so called because it was originally intended for use in the nose of an airplane]

float, *v.i.* to fluctuate in value on the international monetary market in response to supply and demand rather than by government support or regulation.

Overseas, the currency fluctuations caused by the high price of oil forced France to stop supporting the price of the franc—allowing it to float against other currencies. *Newsweek, Jan. 28, 1974, p 56*

—*v.t.* to allow (a currency) to float.

The Germans are angry with the French for floating the

200

franc and thus trying to underprice German exports. *William Rademaekers, Time, Feb. 11, 1974, p 38*

—*n.* the act or process of floating a currency or currencies.

According to West German officials, the collective float against the dollar by six of the nine Common Market countries would be a "dirty" one. *The Cape Times, March 17, 1973, p 4*

[1965 for v.i.; 1970 for v.t. and noun]

float·fishing, *n.* **1** fishing in which a float is used on the line to suspend or carry along the bait.

Float fishing, though it can easily be used in still waters, is the best method that exists of covering a lot of ground in rivers. *Nicholas Evans, The Sunday Times (London), June 20, 1971, p 20*

2 fishing while floating down a river in a boat.

After an unsuccessful effort to find a school of small bluefish that we hoped to catch for bait we anchored off the mouth of Lookout Bight and Barden Inlet. . . . The latter named species [pinfish] are most commonly used in the area when floatfishing for kings, but Earnhardt believes the young blues are much better. *Nelson Bryant, The New York Times, Oct. 24, 1976, Sec. 5, p 8*

[1963]

floating decimal point, a decimal point that is automatically moved into place as each operation is performed on an electronic calculator.

On top of that, the machine has a minus sign indicator. A floating decimal point.
True underflow for calculations beyond 8 digits. *Calculator advertisement by J. Montgomery Ltd., London, England, New Scientist, May 3, 1973, p 285*

[1973] ► The concept of the *floating decimal point* (OEDS 1948) was introduced with the early calculating machines, but it did not enter the general vocabulary until development of the inexpensive electronic pocket calculator.

o·ka·ti (flou'ka: ti:), *n.sing.* or *pl.* an inexpensive shaggy rug made in Greece.

Personally, I would still choose wood which does not show signs of wear on the main traffic routes, is not ruined if somebody drops a bottle of ink over it, and improves rather than deteriorates with age. It helps even cheap rugs such as goatskin, Greek flokati, and Italian . . . druggets look expensive. *Jose Manser, The Times (London), June 26, 1976, p 22*

[1966, from Modern Greek *phlokátē*]

flooding, *n. Psychology.* a method of treating a phobia by controlled exposure of the patient to the cause.

Flooding consists of directly confronting the patient with the situation or object that is feared. Instead of simply imagining the stimulus (as in desensitization), the phobic is safely exposed to it. As with desensitization, the stimuli are carefully graded and presented in a systematic way, with the patient relaxing between encounters. *Fraser Kent, "Agoraphobia," Encyclopedia Science Supplement (Grolier) 1979 (1978), p 62*

[1969, from gerund of *flood, v.,* to deluge, overwhelm] Compare IMPLOSION. See also AGORAPHOBIA.

floor-crossing, *n.* the act or practice of voting with members of the opposing party in a legislative body, especially in a parliament modeled after the British parliament.

Maclean's: Is the two-party system here to stay? Will Congress MPs now defect to Janata?
Desae: We will stop defections by law. We certainly do not approve of floor crossing. We will probably have three parties rather than two, but the plethora of parties will disappear. *"Prime Minister Morarji Desai, in His Own Words," Maclean's, April 4, 1977, p 59*

[1967]

floor-crosser, *n.:* That well-known floor-crosser Reg Prentice . . . made his debut on the Conservative back benches last week. *The Times (London), Nov. 11, 1977, p 14*

floppy disk or **floppy disc,** a flexible magnetic disk on which to store data in a digital computer memory.

A one-ounce "floppy" disk can contain as much information as 3,000 punch cards. It can also be reused and is read much faster than cards by a computer. *Picture legend, "Information Sciences," 1976 Britannica Yearbook of Science and the Future (1975), p 322*

The BBC is now working towards the storage of word data on floppy discs to control the electronic generation of characters in synchronisation with the transmission of a feature film. This provides ideal source of English language sub-titles for foreign movies. *"Technology: Broadcasters See Range of New Video Technique," New Scientist, Sept. 30, 1976, p 696*

[1975] Also called DISKETTE.

Flo·ry temperature ('flɔr i:), a temperature at which a particular polymer dissolved in a suitable solvent exhibits properties that differentiate it from other polymers.

Dr. Flory called this the "theta temperature." He found that when any polymer was studied at its "theta temperature," the measurements of its properties could be compared to those of different polymers. Polymer chemists now know it as the Flory temperature. *The New York Times, Oct. 16, 1974, p 31*

The Flory temperature . . . became the basis for the development of hundreds of different plastics and synthetics. *Time, Oct. 28, 1974, p 52*

[1974, named after the American chemist Paul J. Flory, born 1910, who discovered it]

floss, *v.i.* to clean the teeth with dental floss.

Effective brushing, flossing, and irrigation of the teeth pry loose the colonies referred to as dental plaque. *Simon W. Rosenberg, "A Vaccine Against Tooth Decay," The Americana Annual 1978, p 174*

[1973, verb use of the noun]

flower bond, a United States Treasury bond purchased below face value and, until 1976, redeemable at face value if used to pay Federal estate taxes. Now return on the bond is partly taxable as a capital gain.

"Flower bonds," Federal Government issues that can be purchased at discounts and later cashed in at face value to pay a deceased owner's Federal estate taxes, are not subject to capital gains taxes. *Robert Metz, The New York Times, May 22, 1976, p 32*

fluidized-bed combustion

[1975, thought to be so called from the association of *flowers* with the deceased bond holder and his estate]

fluidized-bed combustion, the burning of fuel, especially coal, in a hot, fluidized bed of fine particles to reduce nitrous-oxide fumes and increase heating efficiency.

The Energy Research and Development Administration (ERDA) worked to improve the technology of coal utilization. The ERDA program concentrated on coal liquefaction and gasification and fluidized-bed combustion (FBC). *James J. O'Connor, "Coal," The 1978 World Book Year Book, p 259*

[1977]

fluidized-bed combustor: A fluidized-bed combustor is a furnace chamber whose floor is slotted, perforated, or fitted with nozzles. Air is forced through the floor and upward through the chamber. When the chamber is partially filled with particles of either reactive or inert material, this material will "fluidize" at an appropriate air flow rate. At fluidization, the bed of material expands (bulk density decreases) and exhibits the properties of a liquid. *Michael Pope, "Combustion," McGraw-Hill Yearbook of Science and Technology 1978, p 123*

fluoroplastic or **fluorplastic**, *n.* any of a group of plastics made from fluoropolymers.

The real problem comes from burning: some plastics (eg, polystyrene and ABS) give off dense, sooty smoke; others (eg, PVC and chlorinated polythene) give off hydrochloride acid gas; the fluorplastics (eg, Teflon) give off fluorine; and all the thermoplastics melt and clog up grates and burners. *Jon Tinker, "Must We Waste Rubbish?" New Scientist, May 18, 1972, p 390*

[1971, from *fluoro*polymer + *plastic*]

flu·o·ro·pol·y·mer (ˌflu: ə rə'pal ə mər), *n.* any of various polymers made by replacing the hydrogen atoms in hydrocarbon molecules with fluorine.

Substitution of fluorine on a carbon will induce a chemical shift of approximately 0.3 eV on the adjacent carbon. This information allows chemical characterization of fluoropolymer systems that formerly could not be analyzed by conventional techniques. *William M. Riggs, "Electron Spectroscopy," McGraw-Hill Yearbook of Science and Technology 1974, p 168*

[1964, from *fluoro-* fluorine + *polymer*]

flux·oid ('flək sɔid), *n.* a form or quantum of magnetic flux associated with the passage of a current in high magnetic fields.

Fluxoids participate in two types of interaction of special importance. First, they interact with the current and are driven in a direction mutually perpendicular to the direction of current flow and to the direction of the magnetic field. Therefore fluxoids created by the self-magnetic field of a current are driven from the surface to the interior of the conductor. *Donald P. Snowden, "Superconductors for Power Transmission," Scientific American, April 1972, p 89*

[1965, from *flux* + *-oid*]

fly-drive, *n.* travel in which a tour provides air transportation and car rental. *Often used attributively.*

Canvas Holidays . . . has 35 camps, with fly-drive holidays tied in, and with choices of fishing, tennis, boules, water-skiing, or just exploring. *Sheila Black, "Shopping," The Times (London), Jan. 4, 1977, p 7*

—*v.i.* to travel in this way.

I have read Roland Gelatt's "Ups and Downs of a Fly Drive" . . . and would like to add some pointers based on my own experiences "fly-driving" in England, Holland and Belgium. *Harry M. Matthews Jr., Brooklyn, N.Y., "Fly Drive," in a Letter to the Editor, The New York Times, Jan 9, 1977, Sec. 8, p 31*

[1976]

fly-driver, *n.:* I shudder at the thought, suggested by M Gelatt's itinerary, of a novice "fly-driver," weary with jet lag, jumping from his airplane into a strange car and as tempting the treacherous and unfamiliar climb to Ronda *Marsha Mittman, Roslyn, N.Y., "Fly-Drive," in a Letter t the Editor, The New York Times, Jan. 9, 1977, Sec. 8, p 3*

fly-off, *n.* U.S. a competitive demonstration of flight capability between two or more aircraft.

The contract is the first under the Pentagon's new "fly before-you-buy" policy—and was won by Fairchild after it prototype competed in a "fly-off" with one made b Northrop Corp. *"Aviation: Whither the TriStar?" New week, Jan. 29, 1973, p 55*

Attributive use.

A flyoff competition between the two prototypes is tent tively scheduled for 1976; the winner will become th army's new attack helicopter. *William Kyer West, "Aer space," 1974 Collier's Encyclopedia Year Book (1973), 121*

[1967, probably patterned on *bake-off* (1952); com pare COOK-OFF]

FOI, abbreviation of FREEDOM OF INFORMATION.

Last month Convicted Felon Gary Bowdach told a Senat subcommittee that he had filed "scores" of FOI request with the FBI for himself and fellow inmates at the feder penitentiary in Atlanta "to try to identify informants Why? "To eradicate them," Bowdach replied. *Time, Sep 25, 1978, p 27*

[1976]

fo·li·vore ('fou lə vɔr), *n.* an animal, especially primate, that feeds on leaves.

The three-toed sloth is a primitive mammal that . . hangs in the forest canopy, and reaches out occasionally t pluck leaves from three favorite tree species, and is the classified an "arboreal folivore" (a tree-dwelling leaf eater *Science News, July 24, 1976, p 58*

[1972, from Latin *folium* leaf + English *-vore*, as i *carnivore*] Compare FRUGIVORE.

folivorous, *adj.:* Presbytis entellus and Gorilla gorilla as the only folivorous primates that do forage extensively o the ground. *J. F. Eisenberg, et al., "The Relation Betwee Ecology and Social Structure in Primates," Science, Ma 26, 1972, p 871*

folk mass, a mass using folk music, often with aud ence participation in the singing.

When his wife-to-be, Joan Bruder, the daughter of a apartment-house superintendent, had come down fro Mount Holyoke to visit him on weekends . . . she ha worshipped at St. Thomas More Church, the Roman Cath lic chapel where Richard Herrin now played guitar at fol masses. *Jesse Kornbluth, "A Fatal Romance at Yale," Th New York Times Magazine, May 7, 1978, p 82*

[1965]

folk-pop, *n.* popular music with elements of fol

song melody and lyrics. *Often used attributively.*

Not content with hyphenated forms, such as folk-pop or jazz-rock, the group attempts an ambitious fusion of folk, pop, or jazz and with classical and contemporary music and various ethnic strains. *Robert Palmer, "Later Influences Enrich Jazz of New Orleans Band," The New York Times, April 13, 1976, p 28*

In the past two months, East Germany has arrested dozens of intellectuals, harassed citizens seeking to emigrate to the West, and exiled its leading folk-pop hero, Balladeer Wolf Biermann. *"Human Rights: Spirit of Helsinki, Where Are You?" Time, Jan. 24, 1977, p 38*

[1965]

folkster, *n. U.S.* a folk singer.

An outfit known as Orphan will share the stage with a group called Travis Shook and the Club Wow through Monday, Jan. 15. In addition, some folksters named Patchwork will be here Wednesday and Thursday, Jan. 10-11. *"Goings On About Town," The New Yorker, Jan. 13, 1973, p 5*

[1963, from *folk* (*singer*) + -*ster,* as in *hipster, mobster,* etc.]

foodaholic, *n.* a person having an uncontrollable desire for food; person obsessed with eating.

Lynn [Redgrave] admits that she once had a weight problem. "At 23, when I made 'Georgy Girl,' I was a foodaholic," she said. She dieted and trimmed her 5-foot-10 frame to a slim 135 pounds soon afterward and successfully maintains that weight. *Ann Guarino, Sunday News (New York), March 23, 1975, p 11*

[1975, alteration of earlier (1965) *foodoholic,* from *food* + alco*holic*] See -AHOLIC.

▶ The earlier spelling *foodoholic* was recorded by Margaret M. Bryant in "Blends are Increasing," *American Speech,* Fall-Winter 1974:

Are you a foodoholic suffering from creeping overweight? *New York World Telegram and Sun, March 30, 1965, p 19*

food processor, an electric appliance that cuts, slices, chops, shreds, minces, and otherwise processes food at high speed.

A food processor may be less expensive to manufacture than a blender, but the Cuisinart food processor does not come cheap. *Isabel Forgang, Daily News (New York), Aug. 19, 1979, "You" section, p 10*

[1977]

footprint, *n.* **1** the area within which debris from a spacecraft, satellite, etc., is predicted to land.

The so-called "footprint" of debris could be as large as 4,000 miles long and 100 miles wide, but its size will be affected by a variety of factors, including whether the spacecraft "skips" slightly when it first encounters the earth's atmosphere. *Richard D. Lyons, "Skylab's Fall to Earth Is Predicted For Noon Today, and Over Oceans," The New York Times, July 11, 1979, p A18*

2 any area marked or affected by a force.

The "scanning/spot beam" approach calls for a narrow microwave beam that would rapidly sweep the entire United States much as an electron beam scans a television screen. The beam's "foot-print" would cover about 1 percent of the country's area, sweeping the contiguous 48 states in 0.01 second. *Science News, Jan. 7, 1978, p 8*

Engine manufacturers have been working for the past four years to develop hush kits and claim to have had a large degree of technical success. Fitted to new BAC 1-11 airliners, the Rolls kits have reduced the 90-decibel noise "footprint" produced on the ground by the two Spey engines from 25 to 12 1/2 square miles. *Arthur Reed, "Cost Rules Out the Silencing of Older Aircraft," The Times (London), March 19, 1976, p 5*

[1965, transferred from the original sense (1500's) of "a mark made by a foot"]

Formula 5000, a racing car powered by an engine of up to 5000 cubic centimeters displacement.

In the seven-race Formula 5000 series, the Lola-Chevrolets driven by Brian Redman of England and Mario Andretti of Nazareth, Pa., won three races each, and Redman won the series. These cars looked like Indianapolis cars, but their stock-block engines were much cheaper. *Frank Litsky, "Automobile Racing," The 1975 World Book Year Book, p 215*

[1973]

▶ *Formula* refers to the engine and design specifications to which the car is built for a particular race.

Formula One or **Formula I,** a racing car powered by an engine of from 1500 up to 3000 cubic centimeters displacement.

The drivers' championship was raced in Formula One cars with single seat, open cockpit, and open wheels. The engines were limited to 3 liters, and most were Cosworth-Ford V8's. *Frank Litsky, "Sports: Auto Racing," 1974 Collier's Encyclopedia Year Book (1973), p 485*

These are the élite, and they are no more a conspiracy than are the Continental circus of Formula I drivers—they are simply self-selecting. *Clive James, "Viewpoint," The Times Literary Supplement, June 2, 1972, p 630*

[1965] ▶ See the note under FORMULA 5000.

forward-based, *adj.* (of missiles or other weapons) based or situated close to the target; short-range.

The chief purpose of the forward-based aircraft is to counter the seven hundred-odd Soviet medium- and intermediate-range ballistic missiles (MR/IRBMs) targeted on the cities of America's European allies. *John Newhouse, "Annals of Diplomacy: SALT," The New Yorker, May 26, 1973, p 86*

Negotiations toward a second agreement, SALT II, were started in late 1972 with a view toward exploring further limitations on strategic arms and securing some reduction in forward-based systems. *Robert J. Ranger, "Defense," Britannica Book of the Year 1973, p 213*

[1971] *Abbreviation:* FB, as in FBS (forward-based system).

Fos·bur·y flop ('faz bər i:), Also shortened to **Fosbury.** a style of high jumping in which the jumper goes over the bar headfirst and stretched out faceup to land on his back.

Eighteen months ago he had the experience every Fosbury Flop jumper dreads when he jumped in training, missed the pit, and landed on his head. *"Athletics Round-Up," The Sunday Times (London), Aug. 10, 1975, p 19*

—*v.i.* to use the Fosbury flop.

He watches the high-jumper carefully as he hurls himself into space *backward*—what must it *feel* like to that Fosbury-flopping guy? *James Dickey, The New York Times Book Review, Sept. 24, 1972, p 4*

[1968, named after Dick *Fosbury*, an American athlete who, as an Oregon State University student, originated it at the Olympic Games of 1968]

four-channel, *adj.* another name for QUADRAPHONIC.

> Last November RCA dropped one shoe in the path of Columbia's advancing four-channel record band wagon. *Ivan Berger, "The Quad Quandary," Saturday Review, April 22, 1972, p 41*

[1970]

four-color conjecture, the hypothesis that only four colors are needed to color any map on a plane surface so that no adjacent regions will be the same color.

> The normally restrained world of higher mathematics was jolted in the summer of 1976 when news from the University of Illinois indicated that a team of mathematicians had resolved the century-old four-colour conjecture. *Lynn Arthur Steen, "Mathematics," Britannica Book of the Year 1977, p 505*

[1963, variant of earlier *four-color problem* (OEDS 1879)]

fourplex, *n. U.S.* a house or building containing four separately owned apartments; a four-family condominium.

> At their best, fourplexes combine the economics of scale (common walls, roofs and plumbing) with the land-use advantages of cluster housing. *"Housing: Four on the Floor," Newsweek, Nov. 20, 1972, p 106*

[1972, from *four* + *-plex*, as in *duplex, triplex*] Also called QUADROMINIUM.

Fourth Revolution, the introduction of electronic and computerized instruction in schools.

> The first of [Sir Eric] Ashby's revolutions was the shift from home instruction to the school; the second, the adoption of the written word as a tool of education; the third, the invention of printing and the use of the book. The Fourth Revolution lies in the future with the electronic media. *Garry Pownall, New Scientist, June 22, 1972, p 705*
>
> At the same time, a "Fourth Revolution" is taking place throughout the educational world, with sophisticated electronics beginning to replace the teacher in providing information guidance and the inevitable testing to students. *John H. Douglas, "Science Education: The New Humanity?" Science News, March 24, 1973, p 186*

[1972, coined by British biologist and educator Eric Ashby in a 1967 report for the Carnegie Commission on Higher Education entitled "The Fourth Revolution: Instructional Technology in Higher Education"]

Fourth World, the world's poorest and most underdeveloped countries in Africa, Asia, and Latin America.

> The Shah of Iran has promised the World Bank a billion dollars; the ruler of Abu Dhabi will create a development fund of $3 billion, and other Arab producers may be pressed to "invest" in a development bank — where they probably will practice "neocolonialism" on their poorer brothers, who are now called the Fourth World. *Henry M. Pachter, "Imperialism in Reverse," Harper's, June 1974, p 68*

[1974, patterned on *Third World* (1965) the underde-
veloped countries of the world; coined by Robert McNamara, president of the World Bank, to distinguish such countries from the oil-rich nations of Asia, often grouped with the Third World] Compare FIRST WORLD, SECOND WORLD, THIRD WORLD. See also SOUTH.

four-wall, *v.t. U.S.* to rent a theater for the entire run of (a motion picture) and collect all the ticket receipts.

> "The picture ran into a lot of trouble," said Mr. Scott in his inimitably gentle growl, "because I originated a unique way of releasing it, with direct sales to exhibitors. I bypassed the distributors, and that got me into hot water. So now I'm four-walling the movie — leasing the theater for $240,000, paying for everything, including advertising, and taking whatever receipts I can get. It's been running for over three months, and the money is coming in at about $400 a week." *Guy Flatley, The New York Times, Sept. 23, 1977, p C6*

[1974, from the earlier (1954) adjective *four-wall*, referring to indoor theaters in contrast to drive-ins, and later (1967) applied to the kind of arrangement described above]

foxy, *adj. U.S. Slang.* very attractive especially to the opposite sex.

> If a woman is "sexy" she is over 30 and not to be trusted. The replacement is *foxy*, a "counter word" with plenty of connotation but no denotation. *William Safire, "Vogue Words Are Trific, Right?" The New York Times Magazine, March 21, 1976, p 111*

[1971, apparently derived from Black English *fox*, meaning an attractive young girl, popularized by the boxer Muhammad Ali in the 1960's]

frac·tal ('fræk təl), *n.* any of a class of highly irregular and fragmented shapes or surfaces that are not represented in classical geometry. *Often used attributively.*

> Fractals arise in many parts of the scientific and mathematical world. Sets and curves with the discordant dimensional behavior of fractals were introduced at the end of the 19th century by Georg Cantor and Karl Weierstrass. Until now their use has been limited primarily to theoretical investigations in advanced mathematical analysis. Like the Koch curve, they were considered too bizarre for application to the real world. *Lynn Arthur Steen, "Fractals: A World of Nonintegral Dimensions," Science News, Aug. 20, 1977, p 123*
>
> FRACTALS shows that it is possible to remedy the absence of geometric representation in many of these shapes by using a family of shapes he calls fractals or fractal sets. Some fractal sets are curves, others are surfaces, still others are clouds of disconnected points, and yet others are so oddly shaped that there are no good terms for them in either the sciences or the arts. *Advertisement leaflet for FRACTALS, a book by Benoit B. Mandelbrot, 1979, p 2*

[1977, from Latin *frāctus* (past participle of *frangere* to break) + English *-al*]

frameshift, *adj. Molecular Biology.* present because of the deletion or insertion of one or two bases in the DNA chain, so that the sequence of bases is read in incorrect groups of three during translation.

> These mutagens are called frameshift mutagens because the reading frame of the messenger RNA (mRNA) is shifted

by the addition or deletion of a base, and this effect distinguishes them from the usual mutagens that cause base pair substitutions. *Bruce N. Ames, et al., "Epoxides of Carcinogenic Polycyclic Hydrocarbons Are Frameshift Mutagens," Science, April 7, 1972, p 47*

Two of the other Salmonella strains have "frameshift" mutations in "hot spots" or clusters with a different base composition, thus making them sensitive to different classes of mutagens. *"Monitor: Mutating Bacteria Spot Carcinogenic Chemicals," New Scientist, Oct. 18, 1973, p 167*

[1971] Compare MISSENSE.

rancicize or **francisize**, *v.t. Canadian.* to cause to adopt or change to the French language.

Whether Quebec separates or not, there is a feeling among Anglos that things will never be the same for them as the province moves to "francicize" business and restrict the right to English-language education for newcomers. *Maclean's, April 4, 1977, p 18*

[1977, from Canadian French *franciser* (literally) to make French]

rancization or **Francization**, *n. Canadian.* the process of adopting or changing to the French language. *Often used attributively.*

Now, business firms that wish to be eligible for government premiums, subsidies, concessions, contracts, etc. must hold "francization" certificates. Individuals who wish to join professional corporations—a prerequisite to many types of employment—must demonstrate their proficiency in French. *G. Richard Tucker, "French Becomes Official Language of Quebec," The Linguistic Reporter, Dec. 1975, p 3*

Companies with 50 or more employees would have to obtain certificates of "Francization" by 1983. Certificates would be issued when the companies met stated norms, such as a "satisfactory" knowledge of French by management and the use of French in advertising. *David M. L. Farr, "Canada," The 1978 World Book Year Book, p 236*

[1974, from Canadian French *francisation*, from *franciser* to FRANCICIZE]

▶ In the sense of "the act of making French in nationality, customs, manners, etc.," *Francization* was borrowed from French *francisation* in the late 1800's (OED 1888), and revived during 1959-1962 to designate President DeGaulle's plan for Algeria's complete integration with France. The Canadian use of the term surfaced in July, 1974 with the passage of Quebec's Official Language Act, which declared French the single official language in the province. In August, 1977 Quebec enacted the Charter of the French Language (also known as Bill 101), which made use of French mandatory in legislation, justice, administration, labor, and education and decreed that consumers must be informed in the French language about products and services offered for sale in Quebec.

ranco, *n., pl.* **-cos**, *adj. Canadian.* —*n.* a Canadian of French descent; French-speaking Canadian.

Liberal Pierre de Bane . . . thinks that discussion will speed a settlement—but while agreeing with him that everybody should have their say, I doubt that the question can ever be settled to everyone's satisfaction, or that true affection can be induced as between Francos and Anglos in Canada. *The Province (Vancouver), June 9, 1973, p 4*

—*adj.* of or relating to French Canadians.

Heady with the new sense of Franco preeminence after more than a century of Anglo power, the radicals feel the time has come to be decisive. It may well be, experts say, that Levesque has chosen caution. *The Manchester Guardian Weekly (The Washington Post section), Nov. 12, 1978, p 16*

[1973, perhaps abstracted from *Francophone* French-speaking Canadian, by influence of ANGLO]

Fran·quis·ta (fræn'kis tə), *n.* a follower of the policies of Francisco Franco (1892-1975), dictator of Spain from 1936 to 1975, especially one of the ultraconservative members of the BUNKER. *Often used attributively.*

Waiting for the ceremonies to begin, the crowd began to chant. "You notice it! You can feel it! Franco is here!" Then the Spanish national anthem boomed over the loudspeakers, and the Franquistas snapped to attention and put their palms forward in the straight-arm Fascist salute. *Time, Dec. 4, 1978, p 58*

[1972, from Spanish, from *Franco* + *-ista* -ist]

fratricide, *n.* the destruction of nuclear missiles launched in a second wave by the explosion of the warheads of the missiles fired in the initial attack.

The violent movement of the air near the explosion, the large amounts of debris that rise rapidly into the upper atmosphere after the explosion, and the persistently high level of radioactivity emanating from the expanding fireball combine to create another effect, known as interference, screening, or fratricide (the latter term coined by the Pentagon). *Kosta Tsipis, "Physics and Calculus of Countercity and Counterforce Nuclear Attacks," Science, Feb. 7, 1975, p 395*

An additional factor in a massive attack involving many warheads arriving at about the same time in the same area is "fratricide" among the incoming missiles. In a concentrated attack the atmospheric disturbances created by the first warheads to arrive must necessarily destroy, disable or deflect many of the warheads that arrive later. *Sidney D. Drell and Frank von Hippel, "Limited Nuclear War," Scientific American, Nov. 1976, p 35*

[1974]

Freddie Mac, *U.S.* nickname for the Federal Home Loan Mortgage Corporation.

On a smaller scale, "Freddie Mac" operates to purchase existing loans from savings and loans, and 1974 was expected to establish a record high purchase total. *Stephen D. Messner, "Housing," The Americana Annual 1975, p 285*

[1974, patterned on earlier (1953) *Fannie Mae*, nickname for the Federal National Mortgage Association (from its abbreviation, *FNMA*)] Compare GINNIE MAE.

free agent, *U.S. and Canadian Sports.* a player who is not under contract to any professional team or club.

Under the Rozelle Rule . . . if a player becomes a free agent by playing out the option year of his contract and then signs with another team, the new team must compensate the old club with players or draft choices. *The New York Times, Oct. 19, 1976, p 47*

[1963] ▶ In sports this term was originally applied to nonprofessional players who attained fame for some skill or performance. The term gained wide currency in 1976, when a U.S. Court of Appeals ruled against the "reserve clause" which bound a professional baseball player to a particular team or to any team he was traded to. Soon football, basketball, and hockey made many players free agents. In turn the ROZELLE RULE (see the quotation above) was attacked because it effectively stopped teams from hiring free agents by failing to set a limit on the compensation a team would have to pay to the player's old team.

free agency: Earlier in the day, before the game, I had asked a couple of the Phillies veterans what they thought about free-agency and the enormous new sums of money that some players have begun to earn. *Roger Angell, "The Sporting Scene," The New Yorker, April 25, 1977, p 110*

freedom of information, freedom from governmental interference with the flow of information, especially unrestricted public access to government records and documents that do not violate an individual's privacy or endanger national security.

In the International Press Institute's annual review, published in December and entitled *Another Year of Lost Battles,* director Ernest Meyer stated that scarcely one-fifth of UN member countries enjoyed what could genuinely be called freedom of information. *Harford Thomas, "Publishing," Britannica Book of the Year 1973, p 567*

"Ninety per cent of the civil servants would like freedom of information. It's as they reach the top echelons and surround the ministers that they oppose it. There is an element of corruption and blatant incompetence." *New Scientist, Oct. 13, 1977, p 92*

[1967] *Abbreviation:* FOI

▶ The U.S. *Freedom of Information* Act (1967) was designed to prevent the executive branch from withholding information from Congress and the public. It was revised in 1974 to allow for judicial review of a complaint against the executive branch for withholding information. See EXECUTIVE PRIVILEGE.

free-free, *adj. Astrophysics.* unrestricted as a result of the movement of free electrons in highly ionized gas.

For the immediate neighbourhood of the Sun it is possible to use a combination of observations such as the difference in arrival times of pulsar signals at different frequencies or the relative intensities of the spectral lines of neutral and ionized calcium, combined with data on free-free absorption and emission. *"New Data on Interstellar Gas," Nature, Aug. 11, 1972, p 311*

[1965, from the phrase "free-free absorption" used in one of the Ossian poems by the Scottish poet James Macpherson, 1736-1796, to describe a dream of heaven]

free lunch, *U.S. and Canadian.* something that seems to be free but is not.

Many Republicans campaigned on the Kemp-Roth plan to cut federal income taxes by 33% over three years. . . . Even though voters want tax reductions, they were skeptical of a scheme that sounded so much like a free lunch. *"The Nation," Time, Nov. 20, 1978, p 18*

[1978, abstracted from the expression "there ain't no such thing as a free lunch," perhaps used origi-

nally in allusion to the practice common in the mid 1800's of giving saloon customers a free lunch with the purchase of drinks]

free school, a school in which pupils are free to choose and pursue their own subjects of interest without formal classroom instruction.

In hundreds of tiny private "free" schools and in public classrooms in nearly every state, the fixed rows of desks and the fixed weekly lessons have been abandoned. *"Education: Sober Chaos," Time, Jan. 3, 1972, p 44*

For the past six years free schools have almost been pet of the media. Too little of this coverage, however, has focused on the deep and often overwhelming problems that confront some of these schools: the terrible anguish about power and the paralyzing inhibition about the functions of the teacher. *Jonathan Kozol, "Free Schools: A Time for Candor," Saturday Review, March 4, 1972, p 54*

[1970] Compare ALTERNATIVE SCHOOL.

free schooler: From deschoolers and free schoolers, from the radical right and the radical left, the education system is under attack, and so are the teachers who work in it. *Stephen Jessel, The Times (London), Oct. 11, 1972, p 12*

freeze-fracture, *v.t., v.i.* to prepare a specimen for observation under an electron microscope by *freeze etching* (freezing rapidly and fracturing a specimen to show internal structure in three dimensions).

When a leaf is freeze-fractured it is easy to identify the epidermal layers, the spongy mesophyll with its air spaces and the vascular tissue. *Barbara Bole and Elizabeth Parsons, "A New Look at Plant Structure," New Scientist, Jan. 18, 1973, p 132*

Freeze-fracturing calls for freezing a sample of tissue at minus 150 degrees Celsius in liquid Freon and transferring the sample to a chamber that is then pumped down to high vacuum. The tissue is fractured by passing a microtome knife through it, and a platinum-carbon replica is made of the exposed surfaces. The replica can be examined in the electron microscope after the underlying tissue has been digested away. *L. Andrew Staehelin and Barbara E. Hull, "Junctions Between Living Cells," Scientific American, May 1978, p 141*

[1970]

Fre·li·mo or **FRELIMO** (frei'li: mou), *n.* a leftist guerrilla organization of Mozambique that fought against Portuguese control from 1964 to 1974. In 1975 it became established as the ruling political party of the newly independent country.

Frelimo's crucial support comes, however, from the Soviet Union and China. The Soviet Union supplies most Frelimo's weapons. Many Frelimo members have been trained in the Soviet Union or in China for guerrilla, terror and propaganda activities. *James Burnham, "The Protracted Conflict: Our Kind of War," National Review, Aug. 17, 1973, p 885*

[1967, from Portuguese, acronym for *Frente de Libertaçao de Moçambique,* Front of Liberation of Mozambique]

French fact, *Canadian.* the dominance of the French language and culture in Quebec, recognized especially after the emergence of the separatist movement in the 1960's; Quebec's French heritage and nationalism.

For many, the election crystallised the need to make

decision — to stay or leave; to accept the French fact and integrate, or pull up roots and start fresh elsewhere. *Angela Ferrante and Elaine Dewar, "Canada: Quebec's English: A Vanishing Minority," Maclean's, April 4, 1977, p 18*

[1974]

Frenglish, *n., adj.* English containing or spoken with French words and expressions.

It may be that one man's misfortune is another's good luck, and that "Frenglish" is none of a Frenchman's business. But at least it ought to be understood that language-borrowing isn't a one-way street. *Jacques Cellard, "Franglais or Frenglish?" The Manchester Guardian Weekly (Le Monde sec.), Jan. 29, 1972, p 14*

Wives especially, often arriving with little English, tend to feel lost at first in this seemingly unending conurbation with its bizarre customs and mentalities. Some never bother to learn more than the basic minimum of shoppers' Frenglish. But within a few months most come to terms with London and find their own circle of French friends. *John Ardagh, The Times (London), Feb. 11, 1976, p 11*

[1963, blend of *French* and *English*]

▶ Less common variants of this word are *Fringlish* and *Franglish*; *Franglais*, on the other hand, is French containing or spoken with English words and expressions.

freshperson, *n.* a freshman (used to eliminate supposed reference to sex in *freshman*).

Your poem "To His Coy Mistress" is under attack again, this time from a girl who wrote a paper on it for her college course in freshperson English. Here's the crux of her argument. *Peter Prescott, "To His Mistress, No Longer Coy," in a Letter to Andy [Andrew Marvell], Intelligence Digest, Feb. 1974, p 63*

[1972] See -PERSON.

▶ *Freshman* has applied to students of both sexes since the late 1800's, and *freshwoman* was used in the 19th century. *Freshperson* was contrived in the early 1970's but its use is much more limited than *chairperson* and *spokesperson*.

Friedmann universe, a model of the universe in which it does not expand indefinitely but reaches a state of maximum distention after which it begins to contract, both the expansion and contraction being of identical duration.

Numerous observations have shown that the universe appears to be pervaded by a background flux of electromagnetic waves that represent a blackbody at a temperature of 2.7 degrees K. Most cosmologists take this background as a relic of the original "big bang" that started the universe. On the whole this radiation is isotropic, the same in all directions, but some theories predict a minute anisotropy.... This leads to some cosmological conclusions: We live in a highly closed Friedmann universe. *"Physical Sciences: Blackbody and the Shape of the Universe," Science News, Aug. 18 and 25, 1973, p 108*

[1973, named for G. A. *Friedmann*, a 20th century German physicist]

Friends of the Earth, an organization of conservationists and environmentalists.

In less than two years the Friends of the Earth has precipitated action on issues ranging from wildlife protection and combating pollution from plastic packaging to exposing the risks to national parks and designated areas from oil

drilling and types of mining development new to Britain. *Pearce Wright, "Environment," The Times (London), June 29, 1972, p 4*

[1972] Compare GREENPEACE.

Friend virus, a virus that causes enlargement of the spleen in mice and replacement of normal spleen cells with cancerous ones.

A virus called the Friend virus is known to cause leukemia of the spleen in experimental animals. *"A Virus That Switches Off Cancer," Science News, Jan. 11, 1975, p 21*

[1967, named after Charlotte *Friend*, born 1921, an American microbiologist]

fringe theater, *British.* **1** a theater that stages low-cost and usually experimental plays.

Such performances are good value for thirty pence or so, but unfortunately the unreliable standards at fringe theatres reflect the pressure of productions staged under economic pressure. The Bush, Shepherd's Bush is the latest fringe theatre to make a desperate appeal for subsidy, and their current evening show, *Dracula*, provides a case for official support. *John Elsom, "Theatre: Bargains," The Listener, Feb. 15, 1973, p 223*

2 experimental drama such as that staged in fringe theatres.

The Great Ban, which opened in London's Soho district last week, stars York as a former actress who lapses into confused reveries, childhood recollections, and a brief impression of Marilyn Monroe. "An unintentional parody of all the worst excesses of fringe theater," blasted *Time Out* magazine. *"People," Time, Jan. 26, 1976, p 42*

[1970]

fringe time, the period of television broadcasting before or after prime time. Fringe time in the United States is usually considered as from 5 to 7 p.m. and 11 p.m. to 1 a.m.

Most TV stations refuse to sell time to politicians in the middle of their news programs, and that wipes out most of the valuable evening "fringe time." *Joseph Lelyveld, The New York Times, Jan. 13, 1976, p 17*

"We feel that original programming works best in fringe time," said Dick Ebersol, the head of NBC's late-night operations. *Frank Sean Swertlow, TV Guide, July 10, 1976, p A-1*

[1976] Compare PRIME TIME. See also FAMILY HOUR.

Frisbee golf, a game similar to golf but played with a Frisbee instead of a golf ball and clubs.

Frisbee golf rules are much the same as ordinary golf's, with each throw counting as one "stroke." A course has eighteen "holes," and each hole has a par. Fairways are laid out in any open area, sometimes using designated obstacles around or between which the Frisbee must be thrown. At the end of the fairway, there's some fixed object that the Frisbee has to hit or a basket or box that it has to land on. *Illustration legend, The New York Times Magazine, June 12, 1977, p 24*

[1977] Compare AIRBORNE SOCCER.

frog hair, *U.S. Slang.* money for use in political campaigns.

Disturbingly, many of the plaque owners were contractors or architects who stood to benefit from making political contributions — "frog hair," as such funds are known locally. *"The Credit-Card Governor," Time, Feb. 4, 1974, p 29*

[1972, paralleled on *hen's teeth*]

front, *n.* **up front,** *U.S. Informal.* **1** in advance.

The book then went to thirty other publishers. Change this, change that, they said. Mostly change the title. One offered $40,000 up front if all the proper changes were made. You had to be crazy to refuse. I was definitely crazy. *Abbie Hoffman, "Steal This Author," Harper's, May 1974, p 44*

2 in an open or straightforward manner.

He [John G. Heimann] noted that he fully favored programs to rebuild declining areas of cities and to revise eroding urban economies, but held that it would be better to finance such projects "up front" — that is, with Government appropriations or other means that permitted full and clear public knowledge of the total costs. *Joseph P. Fried, The New York Times, Nov. 13, 1976, p 21*

3 in the open or foreground.

. . . as good a team of working TV correspondents as then existed. But that was a while ago, and now Huntley and McGee are dead, Vanocur is at ABC as an executive, Newman is a media star in his own right, and Chancellor works up front, using his face muscles more than his leg muscles. *Michael J. Arlen, "The Air: 'The News'," The New Yorker, Oct. 31, 1977, p 124*

[1974] See UP-FRONT, *adj.*

front burner, on the (or **one's**) **front burner,** taking precedence or priority over others; of immediate and major concern.

In the U.S., most China analysts interpreted last week's pronunciamento as indicating that détente with Washington was still on Peking's front burner. *"China: The Unity Congress," Newsweek, Sept. 10, 1973, p 43*

On ABC's "Issues and Answers" Meany's admission of that fact was remarkable for the most influential man on the labor scene, who for obvious reasons normally keeps the jobs picture on the front burner. *The Manchester Guardian (The Washington Post section), June 4, 1978, p 15*

[1970] Compare BACK BURNER.

front-end, *adj.* *U.S.* provided or paid in advance to start a project.

Liddy, he [Magruder] said, drew a "substantial sum" in "front-end money" — $83,000 as it turned out — and went to work assembling his Mission Implausible operation. *"Inside Watergate," Newsweek, June 25, 1973, p 20*

How the grants are made remains to be worked out. In the past they have chiefly been up to 50 per cent of the cost of individual projects. The report advocates "front end" support which would involve large payments for R & D at the start of a programme that could reap commercial rewards later on. *Peter Marsh, "NEDO Chips in With Microelectronics Report," New Scientist, June 29, 1978, p 893*

[1970, perhaps abstracted from FRONT-END LOAD] See FRONT MONEY.

front-end load, sales commissions and other expenses that make up part of the early payments of an investor under a long-term contract for the purchase of mutual-funds shares.

The holders were paying for the privilege of having their money managed by portfolio wizards. Half of their first year's investment often went for the original sales commission, and late in 1966 the Securities and Exchange Commission indignantly declared these charges — the "front-end

load" — to be excessive. *John Brooks, "Annals of Finance The Go-Go Years," The New Yorker, July 3, 1973, p 38*

[1963, so called because the "load" (commissions and other charges) is paid at the beginning or "front end"]

front-end processor, a unit in a data-processing system which forwards data from terminals to the computer and back again.

The role of the communication-control unit varies with the system. It can act essentially as a computer and perform several functions, including routing commands and messages, checking errors and converting one data format to another. The unit is often called a front-end processor. *Hiroshi Inose, "Communication Networks," Scientific American, Sept. 1972, p 126*

[1972]

front four, *U.S. Football.* the four-man defensive line (two tackles and two ends) in a professional team.

So that is the jolly mood of the Cowboys one game into the season. . . . There is that excellent front four of Larry Cole, Jethro Pugh, Bob Lilly and George Andrie. *The New York Times, Sept. 27, 1970, Sports Sec., p 4*

[1966]

front-line, *adj.* of or having to do with a country that is close to or borders on a hostile nation or area of potential conflict.

Foreign Ministers of the so-called "front-line" states — Egypt, Syria, and Jordan — plus the Palestine Liberation Organization met in Riyad, Saudi Arabia, today with the ministers of the oil-producing Arab countries to discuss increased financial support for the countries that border Israel and carry the main economic burden of the Arab-Israeli dispute. *The New York Times, Jan. 10, 1977, p 9*

As more of the Rhodesian countryside falls to the rebels squabbling over territory could easily flare into fighting. Efforts by Nyerere and other front-line leaders to heal the breach have been to no avail. *"Tanzania: Nyerere's Appeal for Help," Time, Oct. 9, 1978, p 56*

One thing making such "front-line" states as Malaysia and Thailand more hostile to the boat people is the fear that the developed nations will cream off the most highly qualified and leave them with the rest. *The Economist, July 14 1979, p 13*

[1976]

front money, *U.S.* money paid, given, or shown in advance to initiate or support an undertaking; front-end money.

I've written six novels; if each had required $70,000 in front money, I'd still be making cement full-time. *D. Keith Mano, "Arts and Manners," National Review, Dec. 19, 1975, p 1480*

Competition among brokerage houses to recruit Wall Street's top salesmen has led to offers of front-money premiums and other incentives by would-be raiders. *Robert Metz, "Market Place," The New York Times, Oct. 12, 1977, p 56*

[1972]

Frostbelt, *n.* another name for SNOWBELT.

Like most conventional wisdoms, the arbitrary antithesis between "Sunbelt" and "Frostbelt" is a crutch that has crippled understanding of cities and their problems, and should be eschewed. In some of the frostiest of the "Frostbelt" cities—notably St. Paul, Minneapolis, Milwaukee, and Chicago—urban problems have been far less severe than in cities like St. Louis, Baltimore, and Oakland, where the snow falls less often or not at all. *T. D. Allman, "The Urban Crisis Leaves Town," Harper's, Dec. 1978, p 46*

[1978]

ru·gi·vore ('fru: dʒə vɔr), *n.* an animal, especially a primate, that feeds on fruits.

Those primate species that can utilize cellulose in leaves are referred to as folivores and are distinguished from frugivores, which cannot utilize cellulose. Of course, these basic categories do intergrade, since folivores may supplement their leaf diet with fruit. *J. F. Eisenberg, et al., "The Relation Between Ecology and Social Structure in Primates," Science, May 26, 1972, p 869*

[1972, from Latin *frūgis* fruit + English *-vore*, as in *carnivore*] Compare FOLIVORE.

Frye boot, a trademark for a heavy leather boot that reaches the calf and is adapted from traditional western boots.

The Frye boot is the obligatory accompaniment to the down jacket. . . . Frye boots—and they are everywhere around you—bag at the ankles so the wearer looks like a basset hound with old legs, wrinkled from the hard life it's known. Some of the Frye boots are decorated in Western designs; some are plain; all are heavy, thick-toed, good for stomping, or kicking a mugger. *Anne Roiphe, "Tweedledum and Tweedledee," The New York Times Magazine, Jan. 25, 1976, p 46*

[1976]

fry-up, *n. British Informal.* **1** a dish of fried food, usually leftovers quickly prepared in a frying pan.

With a deft flick Fred flung half a dozen bangers into his vintage frying pan, reached for the cracked cup containing the drippings from a month's fry-ups . . . *Ann Smith, The Sunday Times (London), April 11, 1971, p 11*

2 the making of such a dish or dishes.

You and Roy must come back for lunch. We'll have a good old fry-up. *Mavis Gallant, "In the Tunnel," The New Yorker, Sept. 18, 1971, p 37*

[1966]

FSO, abbreviation of *foreign service officer.*

"You were in Bonn?" "Three years." "Well, they probably thought that a change of scene . . ." "But I am an FSO." "You'll come to like it here," the chief of section said. *Ward Just, "Burns," The Atlantic, Aug. 1972, p 68*

[1965]

fuel air explosive, a cluster bomb that sprays vaporized fuel producing an explosion over a large area when ignited.

The bomb . . . is called a "fuel-air explosive." At a preset height, a film of kerosene-like inflammable liquid is squirted out to form a circle as much as 30 feet in diameter. *Lee Lescaze, The Manchester Guardian Weekly (The Washington Post section), Oct. 24, 1976, p 15*

[1973] *Abbreviation:* FAE

fuel cycle, the process which nuclear fuel undergoes in a reactor or in recycling for renewed use.

To a large degree the fear of terrorist theft has supplanted simple proliferation—an increase in the number of nuclear powers—as the Carter Administration's principal reason for opposing both the reprocessing of spent nuclear

fuels and the further development of the fast breeder reactor. The alternative being favored is the "once through," or "throwaway" fuel cycle, in which the depleted, highly radioactive fuel rods from nuclear power plants, containing about 1 percent of unspent uranium 235 and an equal amount of plutonium, would simply be stored indefinitely. *"Science and the Citizen: Breeders as Incinerators," Scientific American, May 1978, p 81*

[1976, short for *nuclear fuel cycle*]

fuelish, *adj. Especially U.S. and Canadian.* using excessive fuel.

A word to the fuelish:
Beginning Labor Day weekend, Canadians will again be bombarded by an advertising campaign urging energy conservation. The federal government will spend $820,000 in newspapers, magazines and on television encouraging homeowners to save fuel by reinsulating. *"Preview," Maclean's, Aug. 1976, p 13*

Curb your dog. Fight drug addiction. Watch out for deer. No littering or spitting. Don't be fuelish. Use your ashtray. *Russell Baker, The New York Times Magazine, April 24, 1977, p 14*

[1975, from *fuel* + *-ish*, coined as a pun on *foolish*]

fuelishly, *adv.:* The world's collective temper, already burning on a short fuse, was further aggravated by an international fuel shortage. Admonitions that people not be "fuelishly" wasteful did nothing to dampen the fires. *Paul C. Tullier, "Crises, Crusades, and Courage," The 1975 World Book Year Book, p 173*

full-court press, *U.S.* a vigorous, full-scale attack or offensive.

At the beginning of the year, and especially in his State of the Union address, he [President Carter] seemed to be pulling back from some of his most controversial proposals. But now he has gone to a full-court press. *James Reston, Washington, D.C., in a Letter to the Editor, The Times (London), April 6, 1978, p 5*

[1977, figurative sense of the basketball term (1951) for a defensive tactic in which strong pressure is applied on the offensive players all over the court in order to upset and disorganize them]

fulsome, *adj.* **1** very flattering or complimentary; profuse in praise.

I believe quite firmly that dictionary users have a real right to know what language attitudes are. If, in giving a formal talk, I say /núwkyələr/ and get blackballed for it, I have a perfect right to know what I did wrong. And I also have a right to know that when I use 'fulsome praise' to mean great and sincere praise, many will construe it as an insult. *Archibald A. Hill, Language, June 1970, p 248*

It is more or less commonly accepted . . . that "fulsome" (that is, "grossly excessive") means something like "extremely good or favorable" ("The chairman gave a fulsome eulogy of the speaker"). *Douglas Bush, "Polluting Our Language," American Scholar, Spring 1972, p 241*

2 full; rounded; complete.

The announcement that Prime Minister Begin is to come to Canada in the near future underlines my conviction that Sadat should be invited so that Canadians may have a fulsome view of the Middle East situation. *Heath MacQuarrie, Ottawa, in a Letter to the Editor, Maclean's, Oct. 2, 1978, p 17*

[1968, altered senses of the term meaning (since the 1300's) "offensive to normal tastes or sensibilities"]

fulsomely, *adv.:* We have been hearing so much, so fulsomely, about new-wave rock in the past year, that it was a distinct occasion to . . . listen to one of pop's greatest old-wave masters. *Robert Shelton, The Times (London), April 15, 1978, p 11*

▶ As the quotations under definition 1 show, this usage is viewed with disfavor in some quarters. Yet it has been gaining currency, probably because the first syllable is taken to mean "full" or "abundant" and therefore connoting approbation. The following quotation illustrates the usage in a neutral context:

In a serenade that made strong men quiver, fulsome colleagues rose to pay tribute to his decision to tolerate a compromise on the pending civil rights bill. *Tom Wicker, The New York Times, Feb. 27, 1968, p 42*

Historically the original meaning of *fulsome* was not pejorative, but rather the opposite. Derived from *full + -some*, the word meant "characterized by abundance, possessing or affording copious supply; abundant, plentiful, full" (OED *c*1250). Applied to the body, it meant "full and plump, fat, well-grown" (1340-70). Imperceptibly, however, these meanings shifted by extension to "overgrown" and then "coarse, gross, offensive to the senses," and finally, "offensive to good taste, especially from excess."

The new senses may represent a revival of the original approbative use of the word, as in the following quotation, in which *fulsome* means "very full":

Just heard someone on the radio say something like "Once you've known the rich, fulsome taste of organically grown fruits and vegetables and natural whole grains . . ." I'd never heard *fulsome*, which is usually used or misused in the term "fulsome praise," misused in quite that way before. But I like "the rich, fulsome taste." *Fulsome* is perhaps the most contra-onomatopoeic word in English. It sounds like *full* and *wholesome*, but in fact it means "disgusting, offensive." *Thomas H. Middleton, "Light Refractions: Fulsome's Folly," Saturday Review, July 21, 1979, p 10*

Fu Manchu mustache, a mustache that comes down vertically at the sides of the mouth; a thin, drooping mustache.

Roman is a boat bum, at 32, he wears shoulder length hair, Fu Manchu mustache and glasses thick enough to burn holes in the mainsail. *Peter Wood, The New York Times Magazine, Sept. 5, 1976, p 17*

He was a tall boy with a lot of curly hair and a Fu Manchu moustache. *Tom Wolfe, "The Intelligent Co-Ed's Guide to America," Harper's, July 1976, p 29*

[1964, named after *Fu Manchu,* a sinister Chinese doctor in the novels (1932-1948) of the English mystery writer Sax Rohmer] Compare ZAPATA MUSTACHE.

Functional Shifts. ▶ Dictionaries customarily identify each word by labeling part of speech to indicate the function, or functions, the word has in English syntax. However, as the language is used in each new generation or is applied to describe the changes in social attitudes or the developing needs of science and technology, words constantly shift in grammatical function: a word formerly used as a noun may be used as a verb, a noun begins to appear in the adjective position, and so on. In this dictionary, such shifts in function are noted chiefly in the etymologies and occasionally in usage notes. For example:

mainstream, *v.t.* . . . . [1974, verb use of the noun]
fail, *n.* . . . . [1968, noun use of the verb]
Gothic, *n.* . . . . [1972, noun use of the adjective . . .]
remote, *v.t.* . . . . [1970, verb use of the adjective]

Often identification of a shift in function depends on the context in which the word appears, though sometimes such a shift is marked by other observable changes that include inflectional endings (*-s* or noun uses such as *collectibles* and *singles*), or changes in stress (*rélet,* noun from *relét,* verb).

A common functional shift is from noun to verb. Technical language uses this device as a source of new expressions; for instance, ACCESS, BACKSTROKE, EXCESS, JETÉ, LESION, and POLYGRAPH are recorded as verbs in this book. Some general terms, such as RUBBISH and TOKE, were also converted from nouns to verbs.

Changes from verb to noun occur less frequently in our files, perhaps because nouns can easily be formed from verbs by derivation (see DERIVATIVES) through the addition of *-ation, -ment,* etc. However, verb phrases underlie numerous compound nouns; examples are BLOWBACK, FLAME-OUT, PASSALONG GIVEBACK, and BUY-OFF, and occasionally an adjective, such as BUYBACK. Conversely, noun phrases can become verbs, often initially used with a hyphen, as in SOFT-DOCK, *v.,* from *soft dock,* and BLUE-SHIFT *v.,* from BLUE SHIFT, but frequently dropping the hyphen to become solid COMPOUNDS with increasing use; for example DAYCARE, REDLINE, CARPOOL.

Noun use of adjectives is also common in words ending with *-ic,* such as ACRYLIC, TRANSURANIC, TRICYCLIC, and a number of nouns connected with medical descriptions: AUTISTIC, ASTIGMATIC, GERIATRIC, PREPSYCHOTIC. The appearance of such shifts can be explained by analogy with established noun use such as *alcoholic, fanatic, critic.*

Clear instances of shift from noun to adjective are more difficult to analyze because nouns share one of the adjective's characteristic uses, that of appearing readily in a position attributive to another noun, such as ADVOCACY in the term ADVOCACY JOURNALISM. Noun phrases and compounds include nouns in this use, as *throw* in THROW WEIGHT and *tube* in TUBE SOCK, and many noun entries in this book include examples of attributive uses.

Sometimes functional shifts are difficult to determine because new words appear almost simultaneously in several parts of speech, such as UPLINK, *n.* and *v.,* DEACCESSION, *v.* and *n.,* UPMARKET, *adj.* and *adv.*

fun·di ('fun di:), *n.* (in eastern and southern Africa) a skilled person; craftsman; expert.

I get sick after the sack—ulcers and headaches, and the

young medical fundi tells me it's my alcohol consumption — nothing serious provided I keep away from the brown bottles and plastic mugs. Fair enough! *The Rhodesia Herald, April 20, 1973, p 10*

The stress on cooperative production and on village involvement — through the survey team, training of local *fundis*, village meetings, etc. — provides a basis by which the village can control both the production and use of these technologies. . . . In practical terms, we may find that this group of *fundis* will contribute considerably more towards their community, for example by building a school and a village dispensary. *Joseph Hanlon, "Not Just Another Windmill," New Scientist, Sept. 14, 1978, p 758*

[1972, from Swahili, from Bantu *fund-* instruct, teach]

fund-raiser, *n. U.S.* a formal dinner or other social gathering to raise funds; a fund-raising function or event.

White House aide Jerry Jones says Ford's trip to Georgia, a week before Reagan was to announce, was Ford's "last speech to a Republican fundraiser for a long time and maybe forever." *"For the Record," National Review, Dec. 5, 1975, p 1326*

He [Woodie Guthrie] was perhaps an even bigger hit with the upper-middle-class liberals and leftists at fund-raisers than he was among the poor. *Pauline Kael, The New Yorker, Dec. 13, 1976, p 149*

[1970, apparently extended from earlier meaning (1960) "a person who raises funds"]

funk, *v.i. U.S. Slang.* to swing pleasurably (to agreeable music).

There were organic peanut-butter-and-honey sandwiches to eat, free liquor and carrot juice to drink, live rock from a group called the Stoneground to funk to and a spacious denim pillow in the seatless rear cabin to play games on. *"Life and Leisure: Flying High," Newsweek, Nov. 26, 1973, p 116*

[1973, back formation from *funky* fine, excellent (originally, a black jazz term meaning earthy, unpretentious, rooted in the blues)]

fu·o·ro (fyu:'or ou), *adj.* of or having to do with any of a group of very young, distant, variable stars (T Tauri stars) that exhibit eruptive activity which changes their brightness, spectrum, and apparent shape.

Although two of the fuoro stars have remained close to peak brightness for years, V 1057 appears to be sliding back to its previous condition. It has declined by a magnitude and a half in five years. So perhaps the fuoro phenomenon is not permanent, and after n number of years, the star goes back to the T Tauri class again. *Dietrick E. Thomsen, "A Funny Thing Happened on the Way to the Main Sequence," Science News, Jan. 10, 1976, p 27*

[1976, coined by Viktor Ambartsumian, an Armenian astronomer, from *FU Ori*nis, a nebula in which the first star of this type was observed]

Furbish lousewort, a rare, endangered species of lousewort (genus *Pedicularis*) discovered in Maine in 1880 and thought to be extinct until rediscovered in 1976.

The Furbish lousewort, despite its unprepossessing name, is not without a certain modest charm when it first emerges in the springtime along the steeply sloping banks of the St. John River. Its leaves are delicate and fernlike. Its stem is slender and, in due season, it diffidently puts forth two or three pale yellow blossoms. *Philip Shabecoff, The New York Times Magazine, June 4, 1978, p 39*

[1976, named after Kate *Furbish*, its discoverer] See SNAIL DARTER.

fu·ror col·li·gen·di ('fyur ɔr,kɑl ə'dʒen dai), *Latin.* a rage for collecting.

Both brothers [Albert and Henry Berg] were collectors; when they were·boys — they were the sons of a tailor — both worked as pages in the Cooper Union Library, where early browsing led to the *furor colligendi.* *"The Talk of the Town," The New Yorker, March 25, 1972, p 30*

[1971] See COLLECTIBLES.

fusion, *n.* a blend of jazz and rock or other popular musical styles. *Often used attributively.*

Fusion enjoys a crucial advantage over mainstream and avant-garde jazz: it "crosses over" a wide range of radio formats, a key element to selling any music today. Top Forty, Album Oriented Radio (AOR) and progressive FM radio regularly include fusion artists like Stanley Clarke, Weather Report and Chick Corea on their playlists. *Michael Segell, "The Children of 'Bitches' Brew'," Rolling Stone, Jan. 11, 1979, p 43*

[1976] Compare CROSSOVER[1].

futuristics, *n.* the art or practice of making forecasts about future developments, especially in science and technology, and future trends, as in art, fashion, etc., and their effect upon society.

Some writers, such as Bertrand de Jouvenel, have objected to the term 'futurology', because an 'ology' is a science which deals with things that exist, and the future *per definitionem* never exists, so let us call it 'futuristics'. *Dennis Gabor, Innovations, 1970, p 102*

An equally sinister projection, made by Dr. James Dator, a popular futurist at the University of Hawaii, which prides itself on its "futuristics" department, was that the fiftieth state could become a center for "retraining" or "retooling" lower-middle-class American workers in preparation for the future shock of the leisure age. *Francine du Plessix Gray, "Profiles: The Sugar-Coated Fortress — II," The New Yorker, March 11, 1972*

[1970] Compare DELPHOLOGY.

fuzzbuster, *n. U.S. Slang.* an electronic device for detecting radar.

High Times: What's been the greatest technical advance in the marijuana smuggling business?
Eby: The fuzzbuster. Modify that box just a little bit and you can tell whenever radar is coming at you. *A. Craig Copetas, "Robert Eby," High Times, Jan. 1979, p 53*

[1977, from *fuzz* slang term for the police (1920's) + *buster* one that busts; so called because it destroys the effectiveness of police radar]

fuzzbuzz, *n. U.S. Slang.* fuss or inconvenience; bustle; commotion.

Descending from ship or train or plane, with a minimum of immigration fuzzbuzz, the F.F. [Foreign Friend] sees the world's most intensively cultivated fields, wheat and rice and sorghum and countless vegetables, pressing to the edge of every road, rail and airport runway. *Michael Demarest, "China Says: 'Ni Hao!' " Time, Oct. 23, 1978, p 62*

fuzz tone

[1960, probably from *fuzz* a blur + *buzz* humming sound, formed to suggest confusion and noise]

fuzz tone, a fuzzy quality given to the sound of an electric guitar by distorting certain amplified sound waves.

Either vibrato or tremolo can be added to tones electronically, and a variety of novelty effects, such as "fuzz tone," can be produced. *Earle L. Kent, "Musical Instruments," McGraw-Hill Yearbook of Science and Technology 1971, p 276*

[1968]

fuzzy set, a mathematical set whose elements converge or overlap with those of other sets.

In many fields of science, problems having an element of uncertainty and imprecision are conventionally treated according to the concepts and methods of probability theory. However, there are also situations in which the imprecision stems not from randomness but from the presence of a class or classes (that is, fuzzy sets) that do not possess sharply defined boundaries. *Thomas L. Saaty, "Operation Research: Some Contributions to Mathematics," Science Dec. 8, 1972, p 1069*

[1972; see Lofti Zadeh's *Fuzzy Sets*, 1965]

G

G, a symbol used in the United States to designate motion pictures recommended for general audiences.

The Motion Picture Association of America's Production Code and Rating Administration . . . has been classifying movies (G, PG, R or X) for the stated purpose of providing the public with information that would forestall the impulse toward local censorship. *Vincent Canby, "The Court's Impact on Movies," The New York Times, July 3, 1973, Sec. 2, p 1*

[1968] ► Symbols for a voluntary system of rating films were introduced in the United States in November, 1968 by the Motion Picture Association of America. Originally the categories were *G* (General audience), *M* (Mature audience), *R* (Restricted, under 16 not admitted without adult), *X* (under 16 not admitted). The new code was debated and criticized. One of the categories was renamed *GP* and then *PG* (Parental Guidance) before the new U.S. code began to enjoy widespread acceptance.

While the rating system adopted in the U.S. is new and controlled by the film industry, the British have been rating films since 1914, but not until 1970 was the newly elaborate system applied by the British government's Board of Film Censors. It parallels in general the one of the U.S. film industry: *A* (Adult discretion), *AA* (Accompanied by Adult), *U* (Universal exhibition), *X* (restricted to adults).

In Canada, each province has its own film censorship board. For example, Ontario has two ratings but no symbols: *Restricted* (to those over 18) and *Adult* (entertainment), a category often accompanied by a warning about content.

In Australia there are four censorship classifications: *G* (General exhibition), *NRC* (Not Recommended for Children), *M* (Mature, for audiences over 15), *R* (Restricted exhibition, under 18 not admitted).

gag order, *U.S.* a court order prohibiting members of the news media from reporting or publicly commenting on an issue that is before a court of law.

When the Supreme Court last year virtually banned direct "gag orders" on the press, reporters thought they had won a decisive victory. But the victory has since been diluted by the emerging possibility that indirect curbs may be legal, a trend for which the Supreme Court last week provided support. *Virginia Adams and Tom Ferrell, "Making Moot the First Amendment," The New York Times, Jan. 15, 1978, Sec. 4, p 7*

[1976, perhaps from a combination of *gag rule* limiting debate in a legislature and *restraining order*] Compare PRIOR RESTRAINT.

gal operon, a group of genes which control the metabolism of galactose sugar in bacteria, important in genetic research.

In the middle of the duplex there was an unpaired region where the picked-up segment of bacterial DNA (including the *gal* operon) was not complementary to the viral DNA. *Allan M. Campbell, "How Viruses Insert Their DNA Into the DNA of the Host Cell," Scientific American, Dec. 1976, p 111*

[1972, *gal*, short for *galactose*]

galvanic skin response, a measure of the resistance of the skin to the flow of electricity between two electrodes attached to a person's hand, used to indicate the degree of stress or anxiety of the subject.

Prior to meditation, volunteer meditators and control subjects took the Minnesota Multiphasic Personality Inventory (MMPI) and were measured for spontaneous galvanic skin response (GSR). GSR is a measure of the degree of stability of the autonomic nervous system which is correlated to such things as resistance to stress and reduced physical impulsivity. *"Behavioral Sciences: Meditating in Prison," Science News, Sept. 8, 1973, p 152*

[1970]

game-breaker, *n.* *U.S. Football.* a play or player that determines the outcome of a game.

With the new 3-4 defense choking off the long run and seamless zone defenses in the secondary denying all but the perfectly thrown pass, the big play is often the game-breaker in the N.F.L. [National Football League] this season. Often that play comes from the little men, especially on kickoff and punt returns. *"Sport: Runts in the Big League," Time, Dec. 5, 1977, p 75*

[1969]

game park, a large tract of land, especially in Africa, set aside as a game preserve.

Because the game parks offer so much that is unique, they are regarded as Kenya's number one tourist attraction; and this is as it should be, for nothing can compare with the experience of viewing game in such surroundings. *The Times (London), Aug. 26, 1978, p 11*

[1970] Compare SAFARI PARK.

gamma-ray astronomy, the study and detection of sources of celestial gamma radiation, including the study of GAMMA-RAY BURSTS.

Gamma-ray astronomy finally achieved a measure of sophistication with the launch of the American SAS-2 satellite in 1972 and the European COS-B satellite in 1975. In addition to the detection of a flux of gamma rays whose intensity varies with the 33-millisecond period of the pulsars in the Crab Nebula, a dozen other sources were revealed in data analyzed as of mid-1977. *Kenneth Brecher, "Astronomy," Britannica Book of the Year 1978, p 207*

[1966]

gamma-ray burst, a sudden, short, powerful emission of gamma rays detected by orbiting astronomical satellites about five times a year.

Gamma-ray bursts are stirring the kind of excitement among astronomers and astrophysicists that the discovery of pulsars, quasars and X-ray stars did in the 1960's.

Gamma-ray bursts are short in duration, sometimes less than one second, and staggering in their power. *Patrick Young, "A New Cosmic Puzzle: Gamma-Ray Bursts," Encyclopedia Science Supplement (Grolier) 1974, p 24*

[1974] *Abbreviation:* GRB. Compare X-RAY BURST.

gamma-ray laser, another name for GRASER.

Packing the wallop of a miniature A-bomb and able to penetrate a wall several feet thick, the gamma-ray laser ... could create a revolution in scientific research and weapon development. *John H. Douglas, Science News, Jan. 5, 1974, p 8*

[1974]

Gang of Four, a group of high officials of the Chinese Communist party that opposed westernizing influences in Chinese culture and modernization of industry. Its members were arrested and purged in the power struggle following the death of Mao Tse-tung (Mao Zedong) in 1976.

Although this tour was planned before Mao's death, his official heirs are capitalizing on it to add their denunciation of the infamous "Gang of Four"—the coterie of disgraced former top bureaucrats, among them Mao's widow Chiang Ch'ing, who once determined what China's 850 million people could see on stage and screen. *Marci McDonald, "The Great Leap—and Pirouette—Forward," Maclean's, May 2, 1977, p 70*

We heard [in China] denunciations of the Gang of Four for past abuses from almost everyone. Their removal from power is said to be the most significant political event since the 1949 revolution. The Gang of Four and Lin Piao are clearly the current domestic villains, and they are blamed for the excesses of the Cultural Revolution and the suppression of modern development. It has been said that radical movements thrive when some devil has been identified for condemnation. The Gang of Four certainly fills that role admirably. *E. E. David Jr., "China: Objectives, Contradictions, and Social Currents," Science, Feb. 9, 1979, p 514*

[1976, so called in reference to Mao's wife, Chiang Ching, and three of her allies, who led the radical faction in the Shanghai Communist Party organization] See CONFUCIAN, ANTI-CONFUCIAN, CAPITALIST ROADER.

ganz·feld ('gants‚felt), *adj.* of or having to do with a method of testing for extrasensory perception in which outside stimuli, especially those received by sight and hearing, are neutralized to prevent interference with internally produced imagery.

Sitting alone with Ping-Pong ball halves over my eyes, a red light shining in my face and earphones piping the sounds of the sea into my head, I must have looked as foolish as I felt. But I had asked for it. This was the ganzfeld setup in the parapsychology lab at Maimonides. My task was to think out loud for 30 minutes while someone on the outside listened but did not answer. *Robert J. Trotter, "Excursion into ESP?" Science News, Nov. 10, 1973, p 300*

[1973, from German, from *ganz* whole, all + *Feld* field]

garage sale, a sale of old or used household belongings, held in a garage or other part of a house.

Garage sales, especially those in old neighborhoods, are a sometime source of interesting old things, although the truly worthwhile old stuff may not be out for sale simply because the householder thinks of it as junk. *Joseph Gribbins, "A Connoisseur's Guide to Junk," American Home, March 1976, p 82*

[1967] Compare TAG SALE, YARD SALE.

garbageology, *n.* the study of a culture or society by recording the contents of its refuse.

The unarguable theory behind this garbageology is that if we can learn about ancient peoples by studying their garbage, we can learn even more about present society the same way: "It's all there in the trash," the professor says. *National Review, Feb. 6, 1976, p 70*

[1976, from *garbage* + *-ology* scientific study] See ETHNOARCHEOLOGY.

GARP, *n.* acronym for *Global Atmospheric Research Program.*

One of the tasks of GARP is to collect data describing the complete atmosphere, *i.e.*, from the surface to about 30 km (19 mi). Since the inception of GARP there has been significant progress in the development of satellites equipped with radiometric instruments that can measure surface temperatures as well as the distributions of temperature and humidity with altitude. *Louis J. Battan, "Atmospheric Sciences," 1978 Britannica Yearbook of Science and the Future (1977), p 283*

[1974]

gar·ry·ow·en (‚ger i:'ou ən), *n. Rugby.* a high, hanging kick used to advance the ball down the field.

213

The provincial XV includes five men on national duty at Lansdowne Road on Saturday. One of these is the stand-off, Ward, and it may safely be assumed that all Munster rugby men are praying not only that he will be on target as a goal kicker but also as a hoister of garryowens, under which his forwards will advance like the hounds of hell. *Peter West, The Times (London), Oct. 31, 1978, p 8*

[1965, from *Garryowen,* the name of an Irish rugby club noted for its use of such kicks] Compare CHIP-KICK.

gas-guzzling, *adj.* Especially U.S. and Canadian. consuming excessive quantities of fuel.

Chevys sold in 1985 will be compacts or subcompacts. Engines will be smaller and more fuel-efficient, using fuel injection and turbocharging (which force feeds air into the engine and improves combustion) to maintain at least some of the peppiness of a gas-guzzling V8. *Time, Oct. 9, 1978, p 93*

The smart folks in the sportfishing industry decided a while back that the days of heavy tackle, expensive boats, and gas-guzzling outboards might be headed for trouble, so they bet on fly-fishing. *"Topics: Doing Without," The New York Times, June 6, 1979, p A26*

[1968]

gas guzzler: Ever since North Americans faced the fact that fuel reserves are finite, some drivers of the big cars with huge V-8 engines have felt guilty. While they reveled in powerful six-seaters, environmentalists kept telling them their gas-guzzlers were sinful. *Murray McGregor, "Energy: Pop Goes the Diesel," Maclean's, Nov. 28, 1977, p 69*

gas·o·hol ('gæs ə‚hɔ:l), *n.* **1** a blend of gasoline and ethyl (grain) alcohol, used as fuel in internal-combustion engines.

In half a dozen major cities, Brazilians now fill the tanks of their car with "gasohol," a mixture of 80 percent gasoline and 20 percent ethyl Alcohol. *The Manchester Guardian Weekly (The Washington Post section), Sept. 10, 1978, p 15*

Supporters of gasohol say that its use will conserve scarce petroleum supplies and also reduce surplus farm crops, which can be used to produce alcohol. *"Congressman Urges Government to Issue Rule on Lead in Gasohol," The New York Times, Jan. 14, 1979, p 40*

2 Gasohol, a trademark for such a product.

Nebraskans just completed two million miles of on-road testing of Gasohol—a trademarked blend of 10 percent ethyl (or grain) alcohol and 90 percent unleaded gasoline. *"Gasohol Takes to the Road," Science News, Oct. 29, 1977, p 280*

[1974, from *gas*oline + alc*ohol*] Compare DIESOHOL.

► The gasoline-alcohol mixture was first developed in the U.S. in the 1930's and sold in the Midwest under the trade name Agrol (from *agr*icultural alcohol). The term gasohol became current after the energy crisis of 1973-74 led to a search for alternate sources of fuel.

GASP, *n.* U.S. acronym adopted by various antismoking and antipollution groups.

Kessiloff is an advocate of GASP (Group Against Smoker's Pollution) who feels that cabdrivers have a right to clean air in their taxis. A Winnipeg ordinance prohibits drivers from smoking while carrying passengers but no such law extends to cab patrons. *Rosalie Woloski, "Lips That Touch Nicotine Can Call Another Cab," Maclean's, March 22, 1976, p 24*

[1969] ► This acronym has been used as the name for *Group Against Smoke and Pollution, Gal. Against Smoke and Pollution, Greater Washington Alliance to Stop Pollution,* etc.

gas-ripened, *adj.* ripened by treatment with ethylene gas.

The regulation stated that the vine-ripened tomatoes had to be larger than gas-ripened tomatoes produced in the U.S. *"The USDA Meets the Consumer Interest," Consumer Reports, Jan. 1976, p 5*

[1976]

gas tail, the part of a comet's tail that consists of ionized molecules blown away from the coma by the solar wind.

A color photograph of Comet Bennett showed the dust tail to be yellowish. . . . The gas tail, on the other hand, was blue, because of characteristic emissions of the ionized molecules present. *Robert D. Chapman, "Comets: Especially Kohoutek," Encyclopedia Science Supplement (Grolier) 1974, p 12*

[1974] Compare DUST TAIL. See also ANTITAIL.

gas·tri·no·ma (‚gæs trə'nou mə), *n.* a disease characterized by multiple ulcers in the stomach, caused by excess secretion of gastrin, resulting from a pancreatic tumor.

While some specialists remain skeptical of the value of cimetidine in the treatment of other ulcer diseases, they are virtually unanimous in acclaiming it for gastrinoma. *Gilbert Cant, "Worrying About Ulcers," The New York Times Magazine, Nov. 6, 1977, p 76*

[1977, from *gastrin* + *-oma* diseased condition] Compare ZOLLINGER-ELLISON SYNDROME.

gate, *n.* one of the locations in the nervous system, especially along the spinal cord, at which pain signals are controlled according to the gate-control theory.

Twirling the acupuncture needles, these researchers hold, creates a flood of sensations—but none that contain pain—racing to the gates. These sensations, in effect overwhelm the capacity of these "gates" so that the pain sensations of a surgical procedure are not transmitted to the areas of the brain where pain is registered and felt by the patient. *Harry Schwartz, "Acupuncture: The Needle Pain-Killer Comes to America," The New York Times, June 4, 1972, Sec. 4, p 7*

[1968]

-gate, a combining form added to nouns and meaning any scandal resembling Watergate; a scandal involving charges of corruption and usually of cover-up. The following are examples of its use:

Cattlegate: B. Dale Ball, director of the state Agriculture Department, was accused by several state legislators of masterminding a "Cattlegate" coverup to minimize the problem. . . . In the face of public pressure, however, he made a dramatic turnabout and endorsed a law which he had previously opposed, restricting the sale of PBB-contaminated products. *Charles W. Theisen, "Michigan," The Americana Annual 1978, p 330*

Hollywoodgate: Judy Garland's ex-husband Sid Luft accused David Begelman, president of Columbia Pictures and a central figure in the unfolding "Hollywoodgate" drama, of embezzling up to $100,000 from the late singer while managing her career. *Richard Gooding, New York Post, Jan. 30, 1978, p 1*

Koreagate: The continually expanding scandal over the Park regime's influence peddling on Capitol Hill has already been called a "Koreagate." *Jonathan Steele, The Manchester Guardian Weekly, Dec. 5, 1976, p 6*

Lancegate [Bert *Lance*, former director of Office of Management and Budget]: Although Lancegate has encouraged the British press to expose the financial shenanigans of Tory Reginald Maudling, the question is asked: Why are the Americans doing this to themselves? *William Safire, The New York Times, Sept. 29, 1977, p 35*

Muldergate, *n.:* The South African government seems to have given little thought to former information minister Connie Mulder, who was forced to drop from the government, parliament and party positions because of the "Muldergate" scandal. *The Weekly Review (Nairobi, Kenya), March 30, 1979, p 19*

Nannygate: Canada's "Nannygate" furor—touched off by Transport Minister Otto Lang's attempt to arrange a free armed forces flight for his family's Scottish nanny . . . *Julianne Labreche, Maclean's, Jan. 24, 1977, p 46*

Oilgate: Had the government proclaimed a stern law and then winked at its offenders? Who knew about the misdeeds? How much did they know? The affair that Britons were dubbing "Oilgate" threatened to reach into the highest places. *Time, Oct. 2, 1978, p 43*

Quakergate: Quakergate is the new scandal brewing, and two Pennsylvania congressmen are accused. *People Weekly, Feb. 13, 1978, p 32*

[1973, abstracted from WATERGATE]

► Most words formed with *-gate* last only for the newsworthiness of the event: *Dallasgate, Floodgate, laborgate, Muldergate,* or as a nonce word to relieve some writer's style: *headachegate* or *sewergate.* However, the combining form persists in spite of the short life of most of the creations that make use of it. A discussion of *-gate* words by I. Willis Russell and Mary Gray Porter appears in "Among the New Words," a regular column in the quarterly journal of the American Dialect Society (*American Speech*, Fall 1978).

gate-control theory or **gate theory,** a theory that assumes the existence of specific locations in the body at which sensation of pain can be blocked off from awareness.

An increase in the sensory input at the site of needling [in acupuncture] and application of electricity might send impulses up the spinal cord to the brain and jam the circuits—in line with [Pat] Wall's pain gate-control theory. "*Acupuncture Goes American*," *Science News, Aug. 5, 1972, p 84*

One theory of pain that has been widely cited as a possible explanation of acupuncture is the so-called gate theory, developed by Wall and Ronald Melzack. This theory rejects the long-held idea that sensations of pain are transmitted directly from the receptors to the brain via nerve structures. *Emanuel M. Papper, "Acupuncture: Medicine or Magic?" 1974 Britannica Yearbook of Science and the Future (1973), p 60*

[1968] See ACUPUNCTURE.

gauge theory, *Physics.* any theory that attempts to establish relationships between fundamental physical forces such as electromagnetism, the weak force, the strong force, etc.

Nearly 11 years ago Abdus Salam and Steven Weinberg independently proposed a simple "gauge theory" which would unify two of the fundamental forces of nature: the weak interaction, which is responsible for the "beta decay" of atomic nuclei and allows the Sun to burn, and the electromagnetic interaction which creates light and chemical forces. To everyone's delight the . . . theory fitted beautifully with two great discoveries of the 1970s: neutral currents (discovered, incidentally, in Gargamelle) and the charmed quark. "*Monitor: New Threat to Unified Field Theory*," *New Scientist, April 20, 1978, p 151*

[1977] See HIGGS MESON.

Gault, *adj. U.S.* of, relating to, or providing legal protection and rights to minors.

The Gault decision established, nationwide, children's right to counsel, though only in the adjudication stage. The Court, however, has yet to address itself to the question of the rights of so-called status offenders, or PINS. *Lis Harris, "A Reporter At Large: Persons in Need of Supervision," The New Yorker, Aug. 14, 1978, p 56*

[1973, from the Supreme Court ruling (1967) that Gerald *Gault* was denied due process under the Fourteenth Amendment when committed to reform school without being informed of his rights] Compare MIRANDA.

Gay Lib, 1 a militant movement of homosexuals protesting discrimination in business, etc.

Why, ultimately, would I not subscribe to Gay Lib—or to Women's Lib, or Black Power, or Welsh Nationalism? It is because, though it may be the fact I am 'gay' or a woman or black or Welsh, I don't want to make it the business of my life. *P. N. Furbank, "Books: A Man and His Words," Review of "The Survival of English" by Ian Robinson, The Listener, Aug. 16, 1973, p 220*

2 a member or supporter of this movement.

Being a politician, Mr Jenkins may calculate that the Gay Libs can muster more votes than the Christian community can. *David Lang, London, in a Letter to the Editor, The Times (London), Sept. 3, 1976, p 13*

[1972, shortened from *Gay Liberation* (1970), on the pattern of *Women's Lib*]

gene bank, a place in which specific genetic materials are stored alive for study and research.

The idea behind creation of such "gene banks," of course, isn't really anything new. Plant breeders have been collecting, sorting, and storing plant materials gathered from all over the world for years, especially for use in plant-breeding experiments. *Robert Cooke, Improving on Nature, 1977, p 117*

[1972]

general adaptation syndrome, physical and mental changes by which the body responds to prolonged stress. See the quotation for the details.

Just as Cannon investigated how the body responds when confronted with an emergency demand, Selye began to study how it responds when faced with stressors for long periods of time. He concluded that the body responds to continued stress in three stages, which together he called the general adaptation syndrome: the alarm reaction, in which the person or animal becomes aware of the stressor; the stage of resistance, in which the body adapts to the stressor; and the stage of exhaustion, in which the body loses its ability to adapt. If the stress continues beyond this point, homeostasis cannot be maintained and illness will result. *Judith E. Randal, "Stress: The Ticking Bomb," The World Book Science Annual 1977 (1976), p 31*

[1972, coined by Hans Selye, Canadian physician born in Austria in 1907, an authority on stress]

Ge·ne·ra·li·tat (ˌʒe ne rɑ: liˈtɑ: t), *n.* the autonomous government of Catalonia reestablished in 1977.

The Generalitat's executive council has been installed in the old Gothic palace which was its headquarters before and during the Civil War. *The Manchester Guardian Weekly (Le Monde section), March 19, 1978, p 11*

[1976, from Catalan, from *(Diputació del) General (de Catalunya)* Deputation of the General of Catalonia, the body's original name + *-itat* -ity]

genesis rock, a rock or rock formation thought to be contemporary with the formation of the planet, moon, or other celestial body where it is found.

In addition these Apollo 15 astronauts returned a piece of anorthosite, a plagioclase-rich rock formed at depth. It had been hoped that the sample would prove to be a "Genesis rock" as old as the moon itself—about 4.6 billion years—but this hope was not realized: the rock was dated as 4.15 billion years old. *William Lee Stokes, "Geology," The Americana Annual 1972, p 303*

Important clues to the origin of the solar system lie in "genesis rocks." These are rocks that have retained their character from nearly 4.6 billion years ago. *Clark R. Chapman, "The Nature of Asteroids," Scientific American, Jan. 1975, p 24*

[1972]

gene splicing, another name for RECOMBINANT DNA RESEARCH.

Gene splicing, the much-heralded technique generally known as recombinant DNA research, became more of a reality during the year. Gene splicing involves newly developed techniques by which scientists can incorporate genetic material from one organism into the DNA of another. *Nicholas Wade, "Science and Research," The 1978 World Book Year Book, p 473*

[1977] See SPLICE.

gene therapy, elimination of genetic defects by genetic engineering.

Other strategies of gene therapy . . . would be to implant normal cells (cells with the right genes and chromosomes) in developing embryos, or to synthesize viruses to carry the needed enzymes. *Joseph Fletcher, The Ethics of Genetic Control, 1974, p 55*

The success obtained by Berg and colleagues Richard Mulligan and Bruce Howard is the first glimmer of a different and still distant vision, that of "gene therapy"—replacing defective genes with their normal counterparts. *Science News, Oct. 28, 1978, p 292*

[1972]

genetic counseling, the counseling of prospective parents on possible inheritable defects, based chiefly on examination of the parental chromosomes or of the fetal cells in the amniotic fluid of a pregnant woman.

People who know or suspect the possibility of an inherited disorder in their family often want to know if they are likely to have a child with the disorder. Genetic coun-

seling is available to these people and their physicians. *Lynn Lamoreux, "Genetic Engineering," Encyclopedia Science Supplement (Grolier) 1977/1978 (1977), p 61*

[1974] Compare GENETIC SCREENING.

genetic counselor: As a dividend, the test also ascertains the sex of the child. "But do you want to know?" my friends asked. Of course. I was dying to know. "We'll be glad not to tell you," said Lynn Godmilow, my genetic counselor at Mount Sinai Hospital. *Nora Ephron, "Having a Baby After 35," The New York Times Magazine, Nov. 26, 1978, p 28*

genetic marker, a gene or genetic characteristic that can be identified and followed from generation to generation.

In 1973 it was discovered that the great majority of patients suffering from ankylosing spondylitis have a characteristic "genetic marker," HA W-27. This marker could be used to identify persons at risk of developing ankylosing spondylitis. *Suzanne Loebl, "Arthritis," Encyclopedia Science Supplement (Grolier) 1975, p 271*

[1967]

genetic screening, study of the genetic composition of an individual to find and correct inherited defects or to detect defects that may be passed on to offspring.

The best known and most widely used type of genetic screening is the testing in early infancy for the condition known as PKU (phenylketonuria), a disorder that may doom its victims to incurable mental retardation. The ill effects are preventable by adherence to a strict diet, if the dieting begins early enough in infancy. *Harold M. Schmeck, Jr., "Research Council Backs Genetic Screening As an Aid to Health," The New York Times, June 24, 1975, p 55*

In July, a committee of the National Academy of Sciences reported the results of their 2 1/2-year study of genetic screening. The committee decided that it was too soon to recommend mass screening programs for communities. However, it strongly endorsed the genetic screening of individuals under the proper circumstances—for example, when the medical history of a parent suggests the possibility of genetic abnormalities in a child. *Earl A. Evans, Jr., "Biology," The 1976 World Book Year Book, p 218*

[1972] Compare GENETIC COUNSELING.

gene transplantation, another name for RECOMBINANT DNA RESEARCH.

In a letter to two major scientific publications in July 1974, a group of leading biologists proposed a six-month ban on most research in this area so that scientists could have an opportunity to better evaluate the hazards of gene transplantation. *Eugene R. Katz, "Genetics," The Americana Annual 1975, p 265*

[1974]

genital herpes, a viral disease in which vesicles occur in the genitals.

These two viral forms are responsible for the common cold sore, herpes keratitis (a severe eye infection) and genital herpes, a venereal disease more common than syphilis. *"Seaweed Versus Viruses," Science News, June 5 and 12, 1976, p 361*

[1976]

genitality, *n.* the focus of attention on genital organs.

At one point we find [Norman] Mailer cheering Germaine Greer for saying in her book, *The Female Eunuch* . . . that clitoral stimulation is "the index of the desexualization of the whole body, the substitution of genitality for sexuality." *V. S. Pritchett, The Atlantic, July 1971, p 42*

[1968, from extension of meaning "normal sexual response in the genital organs" (1950's)]

gentleperson, *n. U.S. (often used humorously or ironically)* a replacement of *gentleman.*

The ideological egalitarianism of these gentlepersons is uninhibited by thought, by analytical rigor, or by moral refinement. One gets the creepy feeling that, really, the lot of them make no distinction between the way of life of a free or relatively free society, and the way of life of a totalitarian society. Congress will have to take second place in my evening prayers. *National Review, June 20, 1975, p 685*

[1975] See -PERSON.

► The capitalized, plural form *Gentlepersons* is occasionally used as a neutral salutation in letters.

gen·tri·fy ('dʒen trə,fai), *v.t.* **1** to convert (a poor or working-class property or area) to one that is more expensive or exclusive, especially in order to raise property value.

It was useless to buy up sub-standard housing, when council's put most of their improvement budgets into gentrifying their own older estates. *Rosemary Righter, The Sunday Times (London), March 30, 1975, p 53*

He and others in the community are complaining that the new people, almost all of them white, are prosperous, civic-minded and far too eager to buy and renovate rundown houses. These newcomers are "gentrifying" working-class Islington and should be resisted, not welcomed, Mr. Pitt, a 31-year-old community worker, says. *Robert D. Hershey Jr., The New York Times, Sept. 22, 1977, p A2*

2 *Figurative use.*

Labour's class of '71 was a younger and more radical group than the previous Labour administration. It had recovered from the Sporle corruption case in the late 1960s and was—in its own words—a gentrified council, dominated by professional people from Putney rather than people from the working-class areas. *Christopher Warman, "Uneasy Neighbors," The Times (London), Dec. 17, 1976, p 30*

[1973]

gentrification, *n.:* "Gentrification" goes hand-in-hand with inefficient use of the housing stock because "gentrified" properties tend to be underoccupied. Local, working-class people cannot afford the high rents, let alone buy the properties, so their children are forced to move away. *The Times (London), Aug. 15, 1977, p 3*

From Boerum Hill in Brooklyn to Capitol Hill in Washington the fastest growing social problem was not the departure of the white middle class; it was the displacement of the poor and nonwhite, as affluent, taxpaying professionals bid up the prices on brownstone houses and cooperative apartments in what once were dismissed as unsightly slums. Urban specialists now refer to this process as inner-city "gentrification." *T. D. Allman, Harper's, Dec. 1978, p 42*

Transferred use.

Such pretentions are compounded by the usual inverted snobbery of the middle classes who have "gone slumming" to save a bob or two and then, to their amazement, enjoyed it. To that extent Skytrain is to cheap travel what early Islington was to the property market. It's "gentrification" of the air. *The Manchester Guardian Weekly, Jan. 29, 1978, p 19*

ge·o·co·ro·na (,dʒi: ou kə'rou nə), *n.* a region of ionized hydrogen surrounding the earth at a distance of forty to eighty thousand miles from its surface.

The geocorona, which is produced by the solar wind—a varying flow of protons and electrons from the sun—streams away from the earth on the side opposite the sun, and the moon will be at right angles to that stream, so Dr. Page expects a spectacular shot of the earth looking like a comet with a bright front and a tail thousands of miles long. *Henry S. F. Cooper, Jr., "Letter From the Space Center," The New Yorker, April 8, 1972, p 108*

[1960, from *geo-* earth + *corona* a ring or halo]

geomagnetic storm, see the quotation for the meaning.

The term geomagnetic storm is used for worldwide fluctuations in the Earth's field with a scale of about 100 over a period of several hours, caused by the impact of a solar plasma front on the magnetosphere. A number of Russian scientists have claimed that there is a real association between geomagnetic storms and the incidence of various human diseases. *B. J. Lipa, et al., "Letters to Nature: Search for Correlation Between Geomagnetic Disturbances and Mortality," Nature, Jan. 29, 1976, p 302*

[1972]

geometrodynamics, *n.* the use of multiple connected geometrical structures to study electric, magnetic, and gravitational phenomena as parts of a single process.

"There is nothing in the world except empty curved space. Matter, charge, electromagnetism and other fields are only manifestations of the curvature of space." John Wheeler, prophet of geometrodynamics wrote these words in 1957 and remains as passionately committed to this philosophy as he was then. *New Scientist, Sept. 26, 1974, p 828*

Even modern approaches such as geometrodynamics get a mention. *P. C. W. Davies, Review of "Space, Time and Spacetime" by Lawrence Sklar, Nature, Feb. 6, 1975, p 485*

[1972, from *geometric* + *connecting -o- + dynamics*]

geophysical warfare, the modification of environmental conditions, such as weather and cosmic radiation, as a weapon of war.

Perhaps the most exotic form of geophysical warfare concerns tampering with the electrical behaviour of the ionosphere, that ionised region of the atmosphere which extends from 50 km or so up to hundreds of kilometres above the surface of the Earth. Techniques for disturbing radio communication by "punching holes" in the ionosphere with nuclear explosions have long been discussed. *Nicholas Valéry, "The Shape of War to Come?" New Scientist, June 17, 1976, p 629*

[1972]

ge·o·pres·sured ('dʒi: ou'preʃ ərd), *adj.* under great pressure from geologic forces.

The most speculative, but perhaps also the largest, potential source of natural gas is the geopressured zone of the Gulf Coast. This zone . . . consists of large aquifers at depths of 2500 to 8000 meters. These aquifers are characterized by high temperatures (above 150°C) and pressures that are as much as twice those of conventional water at comparable depths. At such temperatures and pressures . . . nearly all organic matter is eventually converted to methane. *Thomas H. Maugh II, Science, Feb. 13, 1976, p 550*

geriatric

[1968, from *geo-* earth, of the earth + *pressured*]

geriatric, *n.* a geriatric patient; one suffering from a disease of old age.

Writing to the local newspaper last week, a £14-a-week nurse suggested a solution to the miner's dispute: ban all hospital treatment for miners, and send geriatrics and mental defectives back to their pit villages. *Ruth Hall, New Statesman, Jan. 25, 1974, p 105*

[1974, noun use of the adjective (1920's)]

ge·ron·to·pho·bi·a (dʒəˌrɑn təˈfou bi: ə), *n.* fear, dislike, or hatred of old age or old people.

A few years ago the great intellectual enemy of the movement was called gerontophobia—fear of aging, loathing of the aged . . . The target has shifted from gerontophobia to ageism. . . . Gerontophobia could be inflicted only upon the old. Ageism, on the other hand, is a social prejudice against people of *any* age. Just as whites might be victims of black racism, and men may sometimes be the objects of female chauvinism, so young people can be (in early America actually were) targets of ageism too. *David Hackett Fischer, "Books Considered," Review of "The New Old" and "Aging and The Elderly," The New Republic, Dec. 2, 1978, p 35*

[1978, from Greek *gérōn, -ontos* old man + English *phobia*] See AGEIST, GRAY POWER.

get, *v.* **get off on,** *U.S. Slang.* to get a thrill from; be pleased by; enjoy greatly.

"A lot of people get off on getting into a loft," says Mrs. Walz, whose guest lists are sprinkled with Upper East Side names. "Some uptown people have never seen a loft before, so it's fun for them to stand in the street and yell and release themselves." *Georgia Dullea, "The High Lives of Loft People," The New York Times, Sept. 15, 1977, The Home Sec., p 25*

[1973] ► An earlier meaning of this phrase is "to get high on," perhaps from *to get off* "to feel the effects of a drug," and *to get on* "to smoke marijuana."

ghet·to·ism (ˈget ouˌiz əm), *n.* the formation or existence of a ghetto and the attitudes a ghetto generates.

I resent ghettoism as much from my own point of view as from that of its victims. I do not like living in a city where whole acres of territory are out of bounds to me. I want to visit Harlem; I object to being told that, if I value my own life and those of my wife and son, I'd better get out of the West Side and join the show biz people and literary agents and publishers nearer the Park. If I'm to live in New York, I want to belong to it. More than that, I want it to belong to me. *Anthony Burgess, The New York Times Magazine, Oct. 29, 1972, p 38*

[1972]

ghost, *U.S. —n.* an absentee who is counted as present at school or at work.

"High schools were being allocated funds according to the total register, although many pupils attended class sporadically. So the high school division created the category of long-term absentee, defined as any youngster absent from school for 20 consecutive school days. This was the first official acknowledgment of the existence of this part of the school population. These are your ghosts." *Susanna Doyle, The New York Times, Nov. 14, 1976, Sec. 12, p 7*

—v.i. (of an absentee) to be counted as present.

The waterfront investigation began in response to reports of widespread "ghosting" by many longshoremen, who were listed on payrolls by their foremen even though they were not present. *The New York Times, April 19, 1976, p 14*

[1976]

giant otter, a rare, endangered species of otter (*Pteronura brasiliensis*), up to seven feet in length, found in South America.

In September last year the International Fur Trade Federation announced a voluntary ban on trading in skins of the tiger, snow leopard, clouded leopard, La Plata otter and giant otter. *Pearce Wright, "Earth's Friends Want to Ban Wildlife Skins," The Times (London), Jan. 26, 1972, p 16*

[1971]

gi or **gie** (gi:), *n.* the costume worn for judo or karate (often used in combination, as *judo-gi, karate-gi*).

All karate students start out as white belts wearing a uniform called a "gie." *The (Eastchester, N.Y.) Observer, July 20, 1972, p 4*

[1963, from Japanese *ki* clothing]

GIGO (ˈgaiˌgou *or* ˈgi:ˌgou), *n.* acronym for *garbage in, garbage out* (in reference to unreliable data fed into a computer that produces worthless output).

Most of us are familiar with GIGO—garbage in, garbage out—and we try in our systems to eliminate the vast printouts from the computer. *Ed Williams, New Scientist and Science Journal, March 11, 1971, p 575*

Fred Reif, a Berkeley physicist turned educator, is only a little kinder than Twain: New technology and curriculum changes, he says, can be beneficial, but "it's a matter of GIGO—Garbage In, Garbage Out. You put garbage into a computer, you get garbage out." Simply investing money into new ideas isn't enough. *John H. Douglus, "Science Education: The New Humanity?" Science News, March 24, 1973, p 186*

[1966]

Ginnie Mae, *U.S.* **1** nickname for the Government National Mortgage Association.

"Ginnie Mae" has been more active than ever before, particularly in the area of "pass-through" securities where "Ginnie" guarantees securities issued by lenders that represent loans in which the net principal and interest on the mortgage loan are passed through to investors each month. *Stephen D. Messner, "Housing," The Americana Annual 1975, p 285*

2 a stock certificate issued by this agency.

Ginnie Maes—which normally come in minimum amounts of $25,000—provide both high interest yields and also return part of your investment to you each month. Any brokerage firm can provide you with complete details. *William A. Doyle, "Investor's Guide: Ditch Losing Fund," New York Post, Dec. 1, 1978, p 65*

[1975, from pronunciation of the abbreviation *GNMA,* patterned on earlier (1953) *Fannie Mae,* nickname for the Federal National Mortgage Association (from its abbreviation, *FNMA*)] Compare FREDDIE MAC.

Gis·card·i·an (ʒisˈkɑr di: ən), *n.* a follower or supporter of Valéry Giscard d'Estaing, President of France since 1974 and its Minister of Finance in the 1960's and early 1970's.

218

Weeks of backroom negotiations between Giscardians and Gaullists failed to produce a compromise on a candidate. *"France: A Duel Over City Hall," Time, Jan. 31, 1977, p 31*

—*adj.* of or relating to Valéry Giscard d'Estaing, his followers, or his policies.

The Giscardian regime's grand design could have been to bring about those "necessary changes in French society" the President alluded to when he presented his property reform plan. But the achievements fall far short of the lofty goals which were announced. *Thomas Ferenczi, The Manchester Guardian Weekly (Le Monde section), Oct. 26, 1975, p 13*

[1967, from French *Giscardien*]

Giscardism, *n.:* Gaullism still has a popular base which Giscardism has never achieved. *Charles Hargrove, The Times (London), Dec. 1, 1976, p 7*

Giscardist, *n., adj.:* The Socialist leader, François Mitterrand . . . has charged the Government with failure to prevent the drought-related problems. The Communist Party complained that the Giscardist majority in Parliament refused to debate the issue. *James F. Clarity, The New York Times, July 8, 1976, p 3*

giveback, *n. U.S.* the surrendering of fringe benefits or other advantages gained previously by a labor union, usually in return for an increase in wages or other concessions by management.

New York City and its Transit Authority are both demanding givebacks to compensate for pay increases sought by their unions. *The New York Times, March 26, 1978, p 1*

Murdoch got most of the rest of the staff cut he was looking for by laying off eighteen people at the bottom of the seniority roll. That left an imposing list of givebacks still on Murdoch's "must" list. *A. H. Raskin, "A Reporter At Large: The Negotiation," The New Yorker, Jan. 22, 1979, p 61*

[1978, from the verb phrase *give back*]

glass arm, an injured or sore arm resulting from tendons weakened or damaged by throwing or pitching balls.

Countless more suffered chronic maladies ranging from the annoying, like athlete's foot and jock itch, to the exotic and painful, like glass arm (loss of throwing ability from damaged tendons, common in baseball players), hollow foot (a strained instep found in ballet dancers) and web split (splitting of skin between the fingers). *"Medicine: How Sports Hurt," Newsweek, April 2, 1973, p 65*

[1966, patterned after *glass jaw* (of a boxer)] Compare SURFER'S KNOB, TENNIS TOE. See also SPORTS MEDICINE.

glass cord, cord made of fiberglass.

Another material that may make possible cheaper radials is glass cord. Glass cord can save tiremakers as much as $1 per tire, and some companies have already started to make glass-belted radials. *Robert W. Henkel, "Tires," Encyclopedia Science Supplement (Grolier) 1972, p 397*

[1968]

glasshouse effect, another name for *greenhouse effect.*

According to Dr Sawyer the direct effect of carbon dioxide on mankind is negligible, with atmospheric content now being 319 parts per million to be compared with about 290 parts per million at the end of the nineteenth century. The

indirect effect—the trapping of heat within the atmosphere, the so-called glasshouse effect—is however not so easily evaluated. *"Environment: A Mixed Bag," Nature, May 5, 1972, p 5*

[1972]

glass tissue, *British.* a fabric made of fiberglass.

Glass tissue, of which the initial annual production will be about 60 square metres, can be used as a base for roofing materials, wall covering, and other building purposes. *Margaret Walters, The Times (London), April 2, 1976, p 20*

[1976]

Gleit·zeit ('glait, tsait), *n.* German word for FLEX-TIME.

"Flextime," the term which the jargon-ridden world of management has inevitably given the concept, has its origins in West Germany. *Gleitzeit,* or gliding time, has already been applied there on a substantial scale. *"Flexibility and Work Time," The Times (London), April 19, 1972, p 23*

[1971, contraction of German *gleitende Arbeitszeit* gliding worktime]

gliding shift, *Especially British.* a work shift that functions on flextime.

In 1970, Lufthansa German Airlines tried out the system in one of its offices. It then extended it to many other units and now is considering putting its technical workshops on a comparable program, with "gliding shifts." *U.S. News and World Report, June 19, 1972, p 102*

[1972]

gliding time, *Especially British.* another name for FLEXTIME.

In West Germany some 3500 firms have adopted "gliding time." In one form of the plan, company doors are open from 7 am to 7 pm and factory or office workers can come in any time they like provided they are around for "core time" from 10 am to 3 pm. *Ian Low, "Taking the Drag Out of the Job," New Scientist, Jan. 4, 1973, p 27*

[1972, translation of German *Gleitzeit*] Compare SLIDING TIME.

glitch, *Astronomy.* —*n.* a sudden change in rotation of a celestial body, especially a pulsar.

From the Earth one sees, first, a long slow decrease in the pulsar frequency as radiation saps the spin energy of the pulsar; strains build up in the crust, causing the glitch, and instantaneously the frequency increases . . . Based on those ideas a mathematical model of the glitch has been developed. *The Times (London), Jan. 13, 1976, p 14*

—*v.i.* to undergo a glitch.

Several times, however, the Crab and Vela pulsars were observed to begin suddenly to pulse faster, or "glitch." This was attributed to "starquakes," in which the star suddenly readjusted its shape for its slower rotation period. *Kenneth Brecher, "Astronomy," Britannica Book of the Year 1977, p 152*

[1970, extended from earlier meaning "a sudden mishap or malfunction" (1962)] Compare SPIN-DOWN, SPIN-UP.

glitter rock, a form of rock music in which performers wear glittering makeup and costumes.

Going solo, he [Lou Reed] anticipated and helped launch both the underground and the glitter rock extravagances of the early 70s. *Time, April 24, 1978, p 79*

"Glitter" rock appeared to be fading fast, although the antics of such as David Bowie and Alice Cooper continued to sell to live and television audiences. *Noel Coppage, "Popular Records," The Americana Annual 1975, p 478*

[1973] Also called DECA-ROCK. Compare PUNK ROCK.

glitter rocker: Outfitted in an orange and white soccer uniform—and mink warm-up coat—Glitter Rocker **Elton John** came to the Los Angeles Coliseum last week to greet his newest employee. *Time, March 15, 1976, p 46*

glitz, *n. U.S. and Canadian.* glitzy condition or appearance; dazzle.

Helping Creley and Negin recreate the glitz and glitter of Paris gone-by are Richard Adams as Chevalier, Taborah Johnson as Josephine, Liliane Stilwell as Piaf and Barbara Law as Mistinguett. *Meriké Weiler, "Elegance Is Elegance Even 50 Years Later," Maclean's, Nov. 27, 1978, p 4*

[1978, back formation from GLITZY]

glitz·y ('glit si:), *adj. U.S. and Canadian.* glittering; dazzling; showy; flashy.

This son of Glasgow . . . dreamed of crowning Toronto's new boom-town status with a genuinely glitzy film festival. *John Fox, Maclean's, Oct. 3, 1977, p 70*

Individuals like Rachel and Geri Wagner are bright, educated. . . . They can be seen in Bloomingdale's, Marshall Field, Neiman-Marcus; in glitzy restaurants, health clubs, tennis courts, theaters and bookstores. *William Brashler, "The Black Middle Class: Making It," The New York Times Magazine, Dec. 3, 1978, p 35*

[1968, probably from German *glitz(ern)* to glitter + English *-y*]

GLM, abbreviation of GRADUATED LENGTH METHOD.

In GLM, beginners start without poles and are first taught how to walk up the hill herringbone style. This is accomplished by Chaplinesque manoeuvres of the feet. *Martin Myers, "The Trials of a Middle-Aged Skier," Maclean's, Jan. 1974, p 25*

[1972]

glosser, *n.* any shiny or glossy cosmetic, especially one for the lips.

Miss Japan curled her eyelashes with a pair of tiny tongs. Miss Lebanon creamed off her shoulder with a cotton wool ball and Miss Bahamas smacked her lips over a raspberry flavoured glosser. *Tina Brown, The Sunday Times (London), Nov. 16, 1975, p 43*

[1974, from *gloss, v.* to make glossy + *-er*]

glu·can ('glu: kən), *n.* a large carbohydrate isolated from the cell wall of bakers' yeast and other fungi, shown experimentally to be effective in the treatment of microbial diseases.

These polysaccharides are glucans which are commonly referred to in the literature as dextran, they form a major component of the bacterial plaque matrix, and may be responsible for adhesion of the bacterial plaque to tooth enamel. *S. J. Challacombe, et al., Nature, July 28, 1972, p 219*

[1967, from *glucose* + *-an* suffix indicating an anhydride of a carbohydrate]

glu·co·re·cep·tor (‚glu: kou ri'sep tər), *n.* a cell in the brain, sensitive to the presence of glucose.

Experiments in my laboratory had demonstrated that the satiety centers contain cells that are particularly sensitive to glucose and hormones, such as insulin, to which the rest of the brain does not respond. We suggested that the rate at which these cells, called glucoreceptors, take up glucose from the blood determines whether the satiety centers are active and the feeding centers quiet or, conversely, whether the satiety centers are quiet and the feeding centers active. *Jean Mayer, "A Matter of Fat," The World Book Science Annual 1973 (1972), p 121*

[1972, from *glucose* + *receptor*]

glu·on ('glu:‚αn), *n.* an elementary particle thought to be the carrier of the strong force which binds quarks together.

The particle—called a gluon—was identified through research in Hamburg, West Germany, . . . by bombarding protons in high-energy atom smashers. *"New Particle: Missing Link to Einstein Theory?" Daily News (New York), Aug. 29, 1979, p 24*

If a fundamental theory of matter called quantum chromodynamics, or QCD, is correct, the gluon must exist, and if the scientists had failed to find it in their new experiment, much of the theoretical work in physics in the past decade would have been in serious doubt. *Malcolm W. Browne, "Detection of the Elusive 'Gluon' Exciting Scientists," The New York Times, Sept. 2, 1979, p 1*

[1972, from *glue* + *-on* elementary particle] See COLOR FORCE.

gly·co·syl·ate ('glαi kə sə‚leit), *v.t. Biochemistry.* to add a carbohydrate chain to (a protein) to form a glycoprotein.

One of the general facts that seems to have emerged is that proteins with carbohydrate chains attached to their outer end always span the membrane. The histocompatibility antigens have such chains (or in technical terms, are glycosylated). *"Proteins in Membranes, Floating or Sunk," New Scientist, Oct. 20, 1977, p 152*

[1971, back formation from *glycosylation*]

gly·co·syl·a·tion (‚glαi kə sə'lei ʃən), *n. Biochemistry.* the addition of a carbohydrate chain to a protein to form a glycoprotein.

In vitro synthesis of interferon should permit one to approach the question of the role of carbohydrate substitutions in interferon activity. Interferon has long been known to be a glycoprotein but whether the glycosylation is essential for activity remains unclear. *David Metz, "News and Views: Interferon Translated," Nature, Feb. 5, 1976, p 363*

[1963, from *glycosyl* carbohydrate radical derived from a glycose (simple sugar) + *-ation*]

gob pile, *U.S.* a large accumulation of refuse from a mine, especially slime and silt from washing coal.

Sixty miles to the east, near the village of Nokomis, a second gob pile will soon be coming down, ending the runoff of sulfuric acid water into a tributary of the Kaskaskia River. *Seth S. King, The New York Times, Nov. 26, 1976, p B-14*

[1972]

godfather, *n. Slang.* **1** the head of a Mafia family or other group involved in organized crime.

Just to run down the names of the nearly dozen capos—all subordinate to the family boss, or godfather, as he is also called—heading the different regimes within the family . . . illustrates what this investigator means when he says the Colombo combine is deep into "everything." *Fred. J. Cook, "A Family Business: Hijacking, Bookmaking, Policy, Dice*

Games, Loan-Sharking and Special Contracts," The New York Times Magazine, June 4, 1972, Sec. 6, p 91

We meet a Puerto Rican Godfather who radiates pride of family and neighborhood connections and has incorporated tape cassettes into his numbers operation to avoid incriminating policy slips. *Newsweek, June 17, 1974, p 98*

2 *Transferred sense.*

Through direct-mail bombardment, the right alerts its friends to a particular cause and adds to its converts. In this letter-box war for American minds, the top general is Viguerie, who is considered by friend and foe alike the "godfather" of the New Right. *"Right On for the New Right," Time, Oct. 3, 1977, p 24*

Some critics say the I.R.A. has become a children's army.... The youngsters, they say, are manipulated by a little band of experienced "godfathers" who make the plans but never risk their own lives. *The New York Times, Feb. 13, 1978, p A12*

[1972, from *The Godfather*, title of a popular motion picture (1972), based on a novel (1969) by Mario Puzo] Compare DON.

God's Eye, a small cross made of twigs, branches, etc., around which colored yarn or thread is wound in geometric patterns, popular in Mexico and the southwestern United States as a decoration or as a symbol of good fortune.

An ancient and comparatively little known craft that is presently undergoing a revival in this country is the making of *ojos de dios* (God's Eye) hangings and talismans. *Diane Thomas, "Take Two Crossed Sticks, Some Yarn, and ..." The New York Times, July 11, 1976, Sec. 2, p 29*

[1966, translation of Mexican Spanish *ojo de dios*, literally, eye of god; so called because it originally represented the eye of a deity (and was used in worship) among some Indians]

God slot, *British Slang.* a religious program on radio or television.

Just as we have to be given God-slots at chosen times, so, it seems, we must have our [comedy programs] carefully allocated. Let us pray. Let us laugh. *The Times (London), July 25, 1977, p 9*

[1972]

God squad or **God committee,** *U.S. Slang.* a group of advisors to a hospital staff on ethical procedure in cases of terminal illness, severe birth defects, elective surgery, etc.

The whole concept of an ethics committee to determine the fate of any patient is one that is being discussed with increasing frequency in medical and legal circles not just in the United States but also throughout the world. Such committees go by different names and sometimes are irreverently called "God Squads" and "God Committees." *Lawrence K. Altman, "Quinlan Case Stirs Debate on Ethics," The New York Times, June 27, 1976, Sec. 1, p 1*

[1976]

gold, *adj. U.S.* of or designating a phonograph record that has sold a million copies or an album with sales of a million dollars.

His records sell extremely well — since 1964 he has had three gold albums . . . and three gold singles. *William Whitworth, The New Yorker, March 1, 1969, p 38*

His [Flip Wilson's] net income is well upward of

$1,000,000 a year. This comes mainly from earnings from his show and royalties from his four comedy LPs (one of them a gold disk). *"Television: When You're Hot, You're Hot," Time, Jan. 31, 1972, p 60*

[1969, so called from the award, a gold phonograph record, given to the performers] Compare PLATINUM.

► In Canada *gold* is applied to records that have sold between 50,000 and 100,000 copies:

Her last six singles all shot to number one on the national country music charts, and the first album she recorded for RCA, after years of being ignored by the company, went "gold" (it sold more than 50,000 copies in Canada). *Ron Base, "Sex in the Heartland," Maclean's, Sept. 5, 1977, p 31*

golden handshake, *British.* **1** a large sum of money given as severance pay.

O'Farrell, with 3 1/2 years of a five years' contract to go, was assured of a golden handshake of about £40,000, while the other two, not under contract, were "compensated." *Alan Dunn, The Manchester Guardian Weekly, Jan. 6, 1973, p 28*

2 the payment of such a sum of money.

You make the proposal that the golden handshake is the solution to the job stagnation problem in British universities. *Josie A. Beeley, Glasgow, "Golden Handshake," in a Letter to the Editor, Nature, Feb. 13, 1975, p 496*

[1963]

golden oldie or **golden oldy,** something old or long-established that is very popular or is being revived to become popular.

Their latest album (*Grateful Dead*, Warner Bros K66009, stereo, £3.99), which is made up of live excerpts from such shows, contains . . . such golden oldies as 'Johnny B. Goode' and 'Not Fade Away'. *Tim Souster, The Listener, Jan. 27, 1972, p 123*

But football, truly a Golden Oldie, remains as it is — a sport in which not all the participants can be picked up simultaneously by a single camera. *"Football: Old Faces, New Faces," The New Yorker, Nov. 27, 1978, p 126*

[1966]

golden palm, a motion-picture award presented annually at the Cannes Film Festival in France.

The golden palm for the best short film went to Marcell Jankovics, a Hungarian director, for *Kuzdok* ("The Fight"). *The Times (London), May 28, 1977, p 3*

[1967, translation of French *palme d'or*]

Golden Triangle, 1 an area of southeastern Asia growing a large portion of the world's raw opium. It consists of the Yunnan province in China, northeastern Burma, northern Thailand, and northern Laos.

Both the opium and the morphine base almost certainly originated in the so-called "golden triangle" where the opium poppy grows in abundance. *Bangkok Post, April 22, 1973, p 1*

. . . Thai coöperation in stemming traffic in narcotics in the so-called Golden Triangle — the area where Burma, Laos, and Thailand come together. *Robert Shaplen, "Letter from Thailand," The New Yorker, July 14, 1975, p 79*

2 geographic area characterized by high yield or productivity.

In the area of greatest population concentration, the

birth rate was found to be more than double that of the outlying regions. The result of this trend could be to entrench the so-called Golden Triangle, the industrial area that extends from the Midlands of England to the Gulf of Genoa. *Paul Cheeseright, "Can Europe Clean Itself Up?" Nature, Jan. 1 and 8, 1976, p 2*

[1972] See BROWN SUGAR.

goldie, *n. U.S.* a gold record or album.

In the three years since he emerged from the ashes of the legendary Jeff Beck group to record "The Rod Stewart Album," the wiry singer who almost became a soccer pro has had two gold solo albums and another goldie with his group, Faces. *"Music: Soccer Rocker," Newsweek, Sept. 11, 1972, p 75*

[1969, from GOLD + -*ie* (diminutive suffix)]

gon·zo ('gɑn zou), *adj. U.S. Slang.* crazy or wild; extremely eccentric; bizarre.

Gonzo Journalism supplements the techniques of the novelist with the techniques of the lunatic. *Richard Todd, "Left, Right, Gonzo!" Review of "New Journalism" by Tom Wolfe, The Atlantic, July 1973, p 100*

Politics, in any case, has nothing to do with this gonzo record, which transcends mundane concerns and speaks, as rock henceforth *must* speak, to universal themes alone. *David Brudnoy, "Rock: Faith Triumphant," National Review, June 21, 1974, p 707*

Rock's gonzo guitarist Ted Nugent ... began grandstanding, chomping on Nancy's booted leg and, when she didn't kick, tussling with her on a sofa. Finally, he drew a blood-curdling yelp when he whipped out a knife and laughingly sliced her blouse up the front. *People Weekly, Oct. 2, 1978, p 95*

[1972, from Italian *gonzo* simpleton, blockhead, perhaps shortened from *Borgonzone* Burgundian]

▶ The phrase *gonzo journalism* first appeared in the book *Fear and Loathing in Las Vegas* (1972) by Hunter S. Thompson, a correspondent for the magazine *Rolling Stone*, in reference to his reporting. With the popularity of the book, and the continuing influence of NEW JOURNALISM, the phrase caught on and *gonzo* was apparently abstracted from the phrase. Its popularity was further increased by the name of an eccentric character in the *Muppets*, a group of puppets appearing in a popular television series.

good buddy, *U.S. Informal.* 1 form of address used especially by CB radio operators.

"Hey, there, eastbounders. You've got a Smokey in the grass at the 93-mile marker. . . . he's takin' pictures."

"Aaay, we definitely thank you for that info, good buddy. We'll back 'em down a hair." *Michael Harwood, "America With Its Ears On," The New York Times Magazine, April 25, 1976, p 64*

2 a CB radio operator.

Perhaps the biggest problem is overcrowding, which can turn "good buddies" into nasty rivals. CBers are supposed to limit calls to five minutes, and those who do not are called "ratchet jaws." *Robert K. Johnson, "Citizens Band Together," The 1977 World Book Year Book, p 267*

[1976]

good news, *U.S. and Canadian.* a pleasant person or a desirable or satisfying condition.

A two-year-old says *bastek* for *basket* until she reaches a state of readiness to make the change. When that happens ... her memory bank rings up *basket* for all time. The child experiences a flash of delight: getting it right is good news. *June Callwood, Maclean's, Jan. 1973, p 32*

Bradley is good news on many levels. Ten years' service as a city councilman have made him a professional specialist in urban problems. *Shana Alexander, "And Now, The Good News," Newsweek, July 23, 1973, p 27*

[1972, patterned on earlier (1970) *bad news* an undesirable or troublesome person or condition]

▶ In the early 1970's *good news, bad news* jokes became a fad in the United States. According to *Time* magazine (June 5, 1972, p 75), "The gags probably originated a few years ago as spoofs of the in-flight announcements made by airline pilots. For example: 'This is your captain speaking. I have some good news and some bad news. The goods news is that we're ahead of schedule. The bad news is that our navigational equipment has failed and we have no idea where we are.' "

Others have dated jokes back to high school and college use in the 1950's, to parlor games of the 1940's, and even to comic vaudeville routines of World War I vintage. The following are three examples of nonjocular contexts:

From the Mayor on down there is good news ... in the fact that the concept of Federal revenue sharing without the inevitable tangle of governmental strings is now law. Now for the bad news. *William E. Farrell, "Revenue Sharing: Good News and Bad for the Budget Man," The New York Times, Oct. 22, 1972, Sec. 4, p 6*

The market has already discounted all of the bad news and ... when the good news arrives in the form of a Mideast peace treaty or record corporate-earnings reports, the market shrugs or retreats. *Jack Egan, "Good News, Bad News: Stalemate on Wall Street," New York Magazine, April 9, 1979, p 10*

Mayor Koch unveils his $13 billion budget for fiscal 1980 today as he tries to balance the good fiscal news with the bad. *Charles Koshetz, "Budget: First the Good News . . . ," New York Post, April 26, 1979, p 5*

See EUPHOBIA.

Good News Bible, a modern-English translation of the Bible, published by the American Bible Society in 1976.

The accuracy of the latest and much-heralded translation of Holy Scripture, the Good News Bible, the millionth copy of which has just been presented to the Queen, has been challenged by Dr Eric Kemp, Bishop of Chichester. He says he finds it incredulous that those famous words of St Paul about "flesh" and "lower nature" have, in his episcopal view, been altogether mistranslated. *Badon Hickman, The Manchester Guardian Weekly, Feb. 6, 1977, p 4*

[1976, *Good News*, from *gospel*, in Old English *gōdspell* or *gōdspel*, *gōd* good + *spel* news, story, tidings]

good ole boy, 1 *U.S.* a Southerner who is typically easy-going, unpretentious and gregarious.

The core of the good ole boy's world is with his buddies, the comfortable, hyperhearty, all-male camaraderie, joshing and drinking and regaling one another with tales of assorted, exaggerated prowess. *Bonnie Angelo, "Manners: Those Good Ole Boys," Time, Sept. 27, 1976, p 47*

This is the world of the Good Ole Boy, the country hick from down in the hollow, his innocent, God-fearing eyes scanning the world of corruption laid out before him at every crossroad grocery store, supermarket, and shopping center. *Johnny Greene, "The Dixie Smile," Harper's, Sept. 1976, p 18*

2 *Transferred use.*

If I could take a transsexual and make her seem like everybody's best friend—just a good ole boy—then I succeeded. *John Irving, in an Interview with Maclean's, Maclean's, June 11, 1979, p 6*

[1976, *ole* alteration of old (as in *Grand Ole Opry*) to represent Southern pronunciation]

goose, *v.t. Slang.* **goose up,** to push or prod; raise; lift.

The book needs goosing up. *Ray Gosling, Review of "Elvis" by Jerry Hopkins, The Times (London), July 10, 1972, p 7*

But what's the use of goosing up wages if the cities' workers live in dreary, faceless prisons. *Allan Fotheringham, Maclean's, June 28, 1976, p 52*

[1972, figurative use of earlier (1880's) slang sense of "to poke in the buttocks so as to startle"]

gork, *n. Slang.* a person who has lost the function of his brain as a result of senility, stroke, disease, etc.

Like many other physicians, I have cared for hopelessly brain-dead people (referred to by the less genteel as "vegetables" or "gorks") who, due to the tragedy of our technological times, have been maintained by machines and nutritious solutions. *Mary E. Costanza, Boston, in a Letter to the Editor, Harper's, Nov. 1974, p 127*

[1972, of unknown origin]

gorp, *n. U.S.* a mixture of dried fruit and nuts, seeds, etc., used for snacks.

We carried water, lunch, iron, and gorp. Gorp is a secret strengthening mixture favored by climbers and other desperate types, consisting of peanuts, raisins, dried apricots (optional), and bittersweet chocolate bits. *John Skow, "Second Man on a String," The Atlantic, June 1974, p 49*

[1972, probably related to earlier U.S. slang verb *gorp* to eat greedily, of unknown origin]

gos·syp·lure (ˈgɑs əpˌlur), *n.* the sex attractant of the pink bollworm, a larva which feeds on cotton bolls.

Gossyplure proves the old adage that nothing exceeds like excess. When it is sprayed on a cotton field, it so saturates the air with female pink bollworm moth pheromone that the male moths sometimes go on indiscriminate sex orgies. They try to mate with sticks, stones, vegetation or anything else in the vicinity. However they react, they are seldom able to find the available females; they soon become so accustomed to the scent that they no longer respond to it. The result: a sharp drop in the population of caterpillar young. *"Environment: It Makes Scents: Using Sex Against Bugs," Time, May 22, 1978, p 95*

[1976, from New Latin (*Pectiniphora*) *gossyp*iella the pink bollworm + English *lure*] Compare DISPARLURE, MUSCALURE.

Gothic or **gothic,** *n.* a novel, motion picture, or play characterized by a lurid or gruesome atmosphere; a work in the Gothic style.

The books are there to prove it on every paperback bookrack in North America. Not only those that he [Dan

Ross] refers to simply as "Gothics," as in "The Gothic that I'm doing now has a Jack-the-Ripper theme," but nurse romances, detective stories and westerns. *Alden Nowlan, "Paperback Hero," Maclean's, Sept. 1974, p 60*

This little gothic in a high-school setting has a script by Lawrence D. Cohen taken from Stephen King's unassuming potboiler about a miserable, repressed high-school senior . . . who has never been accepted by other kids. *Pauline Kael, "The Current Cinema," The New Yorker, Nov. 22, 1976, p 177*

[1972, noun use of the adjective; see GOTHICKRY]

gothickry, *n. British.* a Gothic theme, mood, or style.

But it is an earlier genre of gothickry that predominates, a world (or other world) in which the hero can write about the "miasma of hatred which, even to this day, seems to rise through the soil of his grave." *Review of "Father Figure" by Beverley Nichols, The Times (London) Literary Supplement, March 10, 1972, p 272*

[1971, from *Gothick*, *gothick*, deliberate archaic spelling of *Gothic*, *adj.* + -*ry*, noun suffix]

GPM, abbreviation of GRADUATED PAYMENT MORTGAGE.

GPM's, insured by the Federal Housing Administration (FHA), enabled many more families to buy their first homes. Under this plan, introduced in 1976, payments increase gradually for a specific number of years and then level off. *"Housing," The 1979 Compton Yearbook, p 166*

[1978]

grade creep, *U.S.* the automatic promotion of people in the civil service by regularly raising the level of their jobs in the job classification system (GS-1, GS-2, etc.).

Agriculture Secretary John A. Knebel, conceding that the Ford Administration failed to prevent a "grade creep" in jobs in his department over the past eight years, has appealed to agency officials to tighten safeguards against over-grading Government posts. *The New York Times, Jan. 9, 1977, p 36*

[1976]

graduated length method, a method of ski instruction in which beginners start on short, maneuverable skis and advance through progressively longer skis as their ability improves.

The Graduated Length Method makes it possible to develop skills in a week that take several seasons on long skis. I later discovered that GLM is a source of great annoyance to skiers who have had to learn the long, hard way. *Martin Myers, "The Trials of a Middle-Aged Skier," Maclean's, Jan. 1974, p 25*

[1972]

graduated payment mortgage, *U.S.* a mortgage on which monthly payments are low in the early years after purchase of a house, rising gradually thereafter.

Graduated payment mortgages (GPMs) are new, too, and were also created for the young house hunter. Here payments rise as the homeowner gets older, on the theory that his or her income will be rising as well. Graduated payment mortgages come in government-insured, privately-insured, and uninsured programs. *Ruth Rejnis, Her Home, 1980, p 25*

[1976] Compare VARIABLE RATE MORTGAGE.

223

graft-versus-host, *adj.* of or denoting a condition in which transplanted cells of a donor attack the cells of the recipient's body, instead of the more common reaction in which the recipient's body rejects the transplanted cells.

In bone marrow and thymus transplants, one runs the added risk of the transplanted tissue rejecting the patient to whom it is given. Thus, donor marrow cells produce lymphocytes that recognize the patient's tissue as being foreign to themselves. The result, known as graft-versus-host (GVH) disease, is usually deadly unless the reaction is very mild. *Barbara J. Culliton, Science, April 13, 1973, p 170*

The injected lymphocytes reacted immunologically against . . . that part of the hybrid rats' cells that they recognized as foreign, and some of these lymphocytes produced anti-DA antibodies. This is part of what is known appropriately as a graft-versus-host reaction. *Jacques M. Chiller, "Immunology," The World Book Science Annual 1977 (1976), p 293*

[1963]

grandfather, *U.S.* —*adj.* relating to or based upon rights or privileges possessed prior to the passage of a new law or regulation.

Some lawyers opposed to the Concorde insisted that it would be perfectly legal to lay down noise rules that would bar the Concorde and, under a "grandfather" exemption, still allow other planes now using the airport and exceeding those new noise limits to keep operating at Kennedy. *Richard Witkin, "The Port Authority and the Concorde," The New York Times, Oct. 10, 1977, p 12*

—*v.t.* to exempt (a person or company) from the restrictions of a new law or regulation.

Cablecasting . . . systems in the top 100 markets operating on March 31, 1972, are "grandfathered"—not required to conform to new regulations—until March 31, 1977. *Mary Alice Meyer Phillips, "Cable Communications—A Springboard to Tomorrow," Britannica Book of the Year 1973, p 656*

As a subdivision that had been filed before the new laws went into effect, Chambers Point was exempt from their requirements—what real-estate people call "grandfathered." *The New Yorker, Oct. 30, 1978, p 152*

[1965 for adj., from *grandfather clause,* referring to a clause in the constitution of some Southern states restricting voting rights to those whose fathers or grandfathers voted before the Civil War; 1968 for verb, verb use of the adjective]

granny annexe, *British.* a part of a house set aside as an apartment for an old relative.

A ground floor "granny annexe,"—with no stairs and easy access to the garden—is a sensible way of helping elderly relatives who want to retain their independence, yet need to know that someone is close at hand. *Bill Eykyn, "Shoparound," The Times (London), Sept. 9, 1978, p 10*

[1978]

gra·no·la (grə'nou lə), *n.* a mixture of dry oats, brown sugar, nuts, raisins, etc., used especially as a health food.

One nice thing about a working-class commune: bacon and eggs and potatoes for breakfast—no granola. *Barbara Garson, Harper's, June 1972, p 72*

Other health foods—crunchy granola, for example—and all the up-to-the-minute superheroes have also been re-

created with paint and glitter; $7, in sizes ranging up to 12. *"On and Off the Avenue," The New Yorker, Nov. 26, 1973, p 107*

[1970, originally a trademark, ultimately from Italian *grano* grain, wheat, corn + -*ola* a diminutive suffix]

graph·i·ca·cy ('græf ə kə si:), *n.* skill in the graphic arts.

It seems that the individual who excels in literacy, numeracy and graphicacy (all needed in good measure by the first-class geographer) is indeed rare. *W. G. V. Balchin, "Replacing the Three Rs with the Four Aces," The Times (London), April 19, 1977, p 12*

[1972, from *graphic* + -*acy* (noun suffix), patterned on *literacy*] Compare ORACY.

graph·i·cate ('græf ə kit), *adj.* skilled in the graphic arts; able to draw, map, engrave, etc.

The new BA studies start this coming October and are much more broadly construed aiming to nurture numerate, literate and graphicate geographers experienced in the applications of their subject to real problems. *Juliet Williams, Geographical Magazine, July 1972, p 673*

[1972, from *graphic* + -*ate* (adj. suffix), patterned on *literate*]

graphite fiber, a fibrous material made of graphite, similar to fiberglass.

Thornel is a remarkable graphite fiber, produced by Union Carbide, which when used to reinforce high performance plastics, creates a material that can have five times the strength and stiffness, for equal weight of metals. *Advertisement by Union Carbide, Scientific American, Jan. 1977, p 69*

[1970]

graph theory, *Mathematics.* the study of sets of points joined by lines.

Network analysts rely heavily on graph theory, a branch of mathematics that was founded with Leonhard Euler's formulation and solution of the first graph-theory problem in 1736. *Howard Frank and Ivan T. Frisch, Scientific American, July 1970, p 94*

While the solution to this problem is of no practical use to cartographers, the century-long endeavor to solve it generated a whole new branch of mathematics called graph theory that has been of crucial importance to the development of such fields as operations research and computer science. *Lynn A. Steen, "Mathematics," 1978 Britannica Yearbook of Science and the Future (1977), p 353*

[1964]

gra·ser ('grei zər), *n.* a device similar in function to a laser, which uses gamma rays to produce a beam of great energy and penetrating power.

Grasers . . . are hypothetical devices which would generate coherent radiation in the range of 0.05-5A (0.0005-0.5 nm) by inducing radiative transitions between isomeric nuclear states. They are not to be confused with so-called nuclear lasers, in which the radiation generated is of optical frequency although the laser is pumped by nuclear radiation. *George C. Baldwin, "Laser," McGraw-Hill Yearbook of Science and Technology 1976, p 228*

[1974, acronym for *ga*mma-*r*ay *a*mplification by *s*timulated *e*mission of *r*adiation; patterned on *laser*] Also called GAMMA-RAY LASER.

grasshopper, *n. U.S. Slang.* a marijuana smoker.

I could not see how they were more justified in drinking than I was in blowing the gage. I was a grasshopper, and it was natural that I felt myself unjustly imprisoned. *Eldridge Cleaver, quoted by Norman E. Zinberg and John A. Robertson, Drugs and the Public, 1972, p 206*

[1968]

grass mask, a breathing mask attached to a marijuana pipe to conserve the smoke.

Contemporary pipes are also made of metal, glass and acrylic plastic. The grass mask is a pipe fitted with a plastic nose shield to ensure that you lose nothing you want to inhale; the water pipe filters the smoke through water, wine or whatever flavored cooling agent you like. *Anthony Astrachan, "Pot Luck," The New York Times Magazine, March 21, 1976, p 21*

[1976]

Grasstex, *n.* a trademark for a type of tennis court surface. See the quotation for details.

The new courts, known as Grasstex, are composition courts with grit-free surfaces. It was felt that this surface, with its top layer of natural fibres reinforced by emulsified asphalt, provided a cushioning effect that, in Cumberland's view, made Grasstex preferable to its sister product, Laykold. *Rex Bellamy, "Tennis: Cumberland Open Five New Courts," The Times (London), Sept. 24, 1976, p 11*

[1976, from *grass* + *tex*ture] Compare ASTROTURF, HAR-TRU.

gravitational radiation, radiation of *gravitational waves* (energy-carrying waves of gravitational force).

Our own galaxy is a spiral type with most of the matter in a plane. Gravitational radiation may be emitted by objects in orbits lying in this plane. *Popular Science, May 1972, p 192*

Gravitational radiation is supposed to be detected by vibrations that it causes as it passes through large aluminum cylinders. *Science News, Aug. 18 and 25, 1973, p 108*

[1970]

grav·i·ti·no (ˌgræv əˈti: nou), *n.* a hypothetical elementary particle with a spin of 3/2, postulated in the theory of SUPERGRAVITY.

Others are worried by the growing complexity of the theories and the proliferation of the supposedly "basic" building blocks of matter. There is talk of hundreds of them: quarks of different "colors" and "flavors," gluons that bind them inseparably, leptons, bosons and, in one formulation that includes gravity, "gravitinos." *The New York Times, Aug. 6, 1979, p A9*

[1977, from *gravit*on the unit particle of gravitational force + *-ino,* as in *neutrino*]

gray, *n.* an international unit for measuring absorbed doses of ionizing radiation, equal to 1 joule per kilogram. It is intended to replace the older name *rad.*

Among the SI's [Système International] derived units with special names are those for . . . radioactivity (the becquerel, or spontaneous nuclear transitions per second) and absorbed dose of radiation (the gray, or joules per kilogram). *"Science and the Citizen," Scientific American, March 1976, p 60A*

[1975, named after Louis Harold *Gray,* a British radiobiologist]

graymail, *n. U.S.* a threat of possible public exposure of government secrets during prosecution in a trial.

The graymail problem extends beyond espionage — to bribing foreign officials, lying to Congress about intelligence activities abroad, and investigating and harassing innocent dissidents. . . . Secret proceedings would not eliminate graymail. But the procedure would let all parties know where they stand and reduce the number of cases that cannot be prosecuted. *"Minimizing the Blackmail in Graymail," The New York Times, July 25, 1979, p A22*

[1979, originally a term used in the Central Intelligence Agency as a euphemism for *blackmail*]

Gray Panther, a member of an organization promoting the interests of the elderly in America.

Gray Panthers have been on the prowl nationwide for over six years. As they prey on the various existing forms of ageism, they deftly uncover issues of trenchant public interest: health care, housing, income security, utilities, crime. *Carol Mackenzie, "Gray Panthers on the Prowl," in The New Old: Struggling for Decent Aging, 1978, p 310*

Associations are being spawned in great profusion by the age movement today. They range from cultural and political and economic organizations of high sophistication to basement centers where "senior citizens" in rocking chairs listen to Lawrence Welk and make macaroni jewelry. The Grey Panthers rage against those places as "geriatric playpens." Others rail against the Grey Panthers too. *David Hackett Fischer, Review of "The New Old" and "Aging and the Elderly," The New Republic, Dec. 2, 1978, p 34*

[1974, from *gray*-haired or hair + *panther*; patterned on *Black Panther* (1965)] Compare GREEN PANTHER.

gray power, *U.S.* the power of the elderly to assert their rights.

Consider the Gray Power reflected in the congressional bill banning mandatory retirement at sixty-five. *"On and Off the Avenue," The New Yorker, Dec. 12, 1977, p 122*

Age is yet another denominator. The group awareness of senior citizens — "Gray Power" — is a considerable phenomenon in Florida, Arizona, and California. At the other end of the age chart, more and more legal rights are being defined for children. *Kevin Phillips, "The Balkanization of America," Harper's, May 1978, p 41*

[1977, from *gray*-haired or hair + *power*; patterned on *black power* (1966)] See AGEIST, GERONTOPHOBIA.

graywater, *n.* waste water which can be recycled, as from a sink or washing machine, and does not drain from toilets and other sources of heavy contamination.

His pamphlet on graywater (recycled water from sink and shower) had been adopted by the local water utility as the western drought tightened. *Kenneth S. Brower, "The Urban Farm," The Atlantic, Jan. 1978, p 61*

[1978]

GRB, abbreviation of GAMMA-RAY BURST.

We compared notes and gained confidence that these quite unexpected GRBs were real. They occur at an unpredictable time, in unpredictable parts of the sky and last no more than a few seconds. During 4 1/2 years of nearly constant alert, we found 41 GRBs that had activated two or more distant satellites. *Ian B. Strong, "The Case of the*

green ban

Baffling Bursts," The World Book Science Annual 1976 (1975), p 201
[1975]

green ban, (in Australia) the refusal of trade union members to work on environmentally and socially objectionable projects.

> As leader of the 40,000-member Australian Builders' Laborers Federation, he [Jack Mundey] was the bloke who invented the green ban—labor's veto over projects that threaten the environment. Shop steward, spare that tree. *Allan Fotheringham, Maclean's, June 28, 1976; p 52*

[1974]

green belt, a strip of land adjacent to desert which has been irrigated and planted in order to stop desertification.

> One of the most tangible products of the UN conference will probably be six "transnational" or cooperative intergovernmental experimental projects, involving 29 countries, that have been developed to halt desertification and to demonstrate how countries can work together to solve common problems. These projects include establishment of "green belts" in the northern and southern fringes of the Sahara, to extend from the Atlantic Ocean to the Red Sea, to limit grazing and allow regeneration of some of the region's lost farming land. *Science News, Oct. 29, 1977, p 285*

[1977] ▶ The earlier (1930's) meaning of this term is an area of parkland set aside around a city or town to restrict further urban growth or development.

green currency, any of the artificial units of account, such as the green pound, created in 1969 to protect the European Economic Community's common farm prices from the fluctuations of the currencies of its member nations.

> The present debate about German farming, whether held in France, Italy or Britain, centres on money. It is claimed that the green currency system is used by the West German Government to keep up the incomes of part-time smallholders. *Hugh Clayton, "Critics of German Farming Ignore History," The Times (London), Nov. 13, 1978, p 1*

[1977]

greenfield, *adj. British.* of, relating to, or built in a rural or undeveloped area.

> In this study we have considered plants of the kind which may be decided upon for "greenfield" construction in the UK some years ahead. *Frederick Cartwright, New Scientist, May 4, 1972, p 253*

> It is becoming apparent that greenfield sites close to urban areas are in short supply and it is probable that future development will be concentrated on the refurbishment of existing premises. *The Times (London), June 12, 1978, p 12*

[1963]

greenlining, *n. U.S.* any of various methods used to combat the practice of REDLINING.

> Now a spirited fight against redlining is mounting across the U.S. by the residents of declining neighborhoods. Their tactic: to make investments in the inner city financially attractive to lenders once again, a process that community groups call "greenlining." *"Greenlining of America," Time, May 27, 1974, p 72*

> One pressure tactic, called "greenlining" by a Chicago community group, the Citizens Action Program, which has employed it, is to threaten to withdraw residents' savings deposits en masse from institutions that decline to make mortgage and home improvement loans in the depositors' neighborhoods. *William E. Farrell, " 'Redlining' Gains U.S. Legal Status," The New York Times, Jan. 26, 1976, p 46*

[1974, patterned on *redlining*]

green lung, *British.* a park or other area of planting in a city.

> The English with their gift for enjoying their country have managed to preserve fragments of the ancient past. The parks, "the green lungs," once the hunting preserves of the early monarchs, which give London such refreshment today, are a prime example. *Edward Weeks, The Atlantic, May 1970, p 131*

[1962, 1969, in reference to production of oxygen in plants]

green monkey disease, another name for MARBURG DISEASE.

> The mystery fever from which scores of people are reported to have died in the southern Sudan and across the border in Zaire is caused by the Marburg virus—the "green monkey disease"—the World Health Organization said today. *The Times (London), Oct. 15, 1976, p 9*

[1967]

Green Panther, *U.S. (used disparagingly)* a militant or vocal protector of the natural environment.

> There is another problem. To minority groups, sensitivity about the landscape goes hand in hand with indifference to human needs. In the ghetto, environmentalists are known as "Green Panthers." *Mary Ellen Leary, "California," The Atlantic, Nov. 1973, p 26*

[1973, from *green*, color associated with environmentalists + *panther*; patterned on *Black Panther* (1965)] Compare GRAY PANTHER. See EAGLE FREAK.

Greenpeace, *n.* a militant environmentalist movement involved especially in protecting animals from whalers, trappers, and other hunters.

> The shambling New Brunswick Liberal . . . is about to be subjected to the piranha-like peckings of Greenpeace, the scruffy band of ecofreaks who take on nations—and usually win. *Alan Fotheringham, Maclean's, Feb. 21, 1977, p 64*

> The seal hunt is indeed a sickening and unnecessary event. . . . Greenpeace seeks a ban on the commercial hunting of harp and hood seals. We believe that only the aboriginal hunt can be justified, provided that this limited hunting can be proven to be within safe environmental boundaries. *Allan Thornton, "The Canadian Seal Hunt: A Reply," New Scientist, April 13, 1978, p 83*

[1977] Compare FRIENDS OF THE EARTH.

green pound, the unit of account by which farm prices are expressed in sterling within the European Economic Community.

> He [Agriculture Minister Peter Walker] persuaded his European colleagues, moreover, to accept a devaluation of 5 per cent in the "green pound," the national unit of exchange for farm produce. *The Manchester Guardian Weekly, July 1, 1979, p 3*

[1974] See GREEN CURRENCY.

green time, the length of time during which traffic is able to move uninterruptedly through a series of traffic lights showing a green light.

The basic idea is to make more efficient use of the precious "green time" that keeps traffic moving on the roadways. Ideally, the computer program coordinates traffic signals so that platoons of vehicles can run smoothly from one green light to another, with a minimum number of stops for red lights or congestion. *Popular Science, Jan. 1971, p 53*

[1968]

greenway, *n. Especially U.S.* a strip of parkland, usually connecting larger parks, designed for pedestrians and bicyclists. *Often used attributively.*

"Our next proposal, by the way, is for an eight-block Ruppert Greenway, running from Central Park, through the Green here, to Carl Schurz Park, on the East River." *William Hodgson, The New Yorker, June 24, 1972, p 28*

Governor McCall and others favor a program of public acquisition of "greenway" land along both banks, but the program has lagged. *James E. Bylin, "Rescue of a River," Encyclopedia Science Supplement (Grolier) 1973, p 215*

[1966]

grief therapy, supportive therapy for the bereaved; psychological help for those who have sustained the death of a spouse, a child, etc.

So successful was this first attempt that five grief therapy groups are now operating. Each is composed of both men and women in similar stages of grief and need. As the need for a highly-trained counselor ebbs, a counselor of less expertise is gradually worked into the group. *Virginia Fraser and Susan Thornton, "An Inventory of Innovative Programs," in The New Old: Struggling for Decent Aging, 1978, p 429*

[1973] Compare DEATH THERAPY.

gri·ot (gri:'ou *or* 'gri: at), *n.* a traditional poet, musician, and storyteller of western Africa.

Ouologuem writes as a *griot*—"a troubadour, member of a hereditary caste whose function it is to celebrate the great events of history and to uphold the God-given traditions." *John Updike, "Books," The New Yorker, Nov. 13, 1971, p 187*

By working backward through slave records, talking to linguists and finally interviewing African *griots*, native oral historians, he [Alex Haley] succeeded in tracing his slave ancestor, Kunta Kinte, back to a particular village, Juffure, in an interior section of Gambia. *Newsweek, Aug. 5, 1974, p 74*

[1959, 1966, from French, probably of African origin (compare Wolof *gewel* oral historian)]

gross, *U.S. Slang.* —*adj.* applied to anything objectionable.

True enough, "gross" has always meant something coarse and vulgar. But as used by the teens, it runs the gamut of awfulness from homework to something the cat contributed to the ecology. *Frank Bunker Gilbreth, Jr., Saturday Review, July 29, 1972, p 71*

—*v.t.* Usually, **gross out.** to affect with disgust, horror, shock, etc.

Instead of subtle plot twists, they [horror films] offer dangling limbs, effusing guts and gruesome decapitations—and audiences are lining up in droves to be "grossed out." *Michael Musto, "Yecch!" New York Post, June 7, 1979, p 35*

[1968 for verb; 1972 for adj., extended from the original meaning (OED 1532) "extremely coarse in behavior or morals"]

gross domestic product, the gross national product of a country minus the net payments on foreign investments.

One of the most important agents of change was the tourist, whose spending generated an increase in local consumption, in imports, and in the gross domestic product. *Philip Sherlock, "The Commonwealth Caribbean: The West Indies," The Annual Register of World Events in 1969 (1970), p 112*

In terms of one key indicator, per capita gross domestic product, the developed economies registered an increase of 43 percent in the course of the decade, compared with only 27 percent for the underdeveloped economies. *"Science and the Citizen," Scientific American, Sept. 1972, p 64*

[1964, patterned on *gross national product* (1940's) the total monetary value of all goods and services produced in a country during a year]

gross-out, *U.S. Slang.* —*n.* someone or something disgusting, boring, or otherwise objectionable.

Well, it's just toooo much (late '40s). A real drag ('50s), a bad trip ('60s), and, naturally, a gross-out ('70s). As the new decade approaches, so does a new lingo of youth. *Lynn Ludlow, "Youth Lingo: Facing Up to a Change," San Francisco Examiner & Chronicle, April 1, 1979, Sec. A, p 12*

—*adj.* variant of GROSS.

Disgusting; wild or orgiastic, as in "That was a real gross-out party." *Benjamin G. Kohl, "A Note on GROSS OUT," American Speech, Spring-Summer 1973, p 157*

[1973, from GROSS OUT, v.]

ground pollution, environmental pollution caused by the seepage of toxic chemical wastes buried in the ground, especially in dumpsites and landfills.

Ground pollution's greatest threat is to the national drinking supply. More than 100 million Americans depend upon ground water as the major source of life's most vital fluid. *Michael H. Brown, "Love Canal, U.S.A.," The New York Times Magazine, Jan. 21, 1979, p 41*

[1979]

groundprox, *n.* a navigational device in an aircraft which alerts a pilot to change the craft's attitude to avoid crashing into the ground.

Groundprox (*New Scientist,* vol. 68, p 280) is a system for warning a pilot that he is flying into the ground. At the heart of the Plessey system is the Plessey MIPROC, which processes inputs such as the altimeter reading and emits an electronically synthesised command—"pull up" or "climb"—if the plane is in danger. *"Groundprox on the Way," New Scientist, March 4, 1976, p 508*

[1975, short for *ground prox*imity warning system]

ground truth, information about the earth obtained by direct examination of features on the ground in order to verify information gathered by satellite or other airborne means.

The atmosphere may prove to be so dense that it will throw the instruments off; indeed, scientists involved in these experiments, some of whom are skeptical about the accuracy of data from an orbiting spacecraft, will be scattered around the world to get what they call "ground truth." *Henry S. F. Cooper, Jr., "A Reporter at Large: Skylab," The New Yorker, May 5, 1973, p 128*

[1971]

grouper, *n. U.S.* one of a group of young people who have pooled their resources to rent a vacation cottage.

The three young women decided to become "groupers" and take part shares in "Snug Cozy," which means that for $375 each they will be allowed to spend every other summer weekend there, with a group of 13 other hopefully amiable "groupers," no more than 8 of whom will be allowed per weekend. *Judy Klemesrud, " 'Groupers' Plan for Sun and Sociability," The New York Times, March 26, 1976, p 41*

[1966]

group grope, *U.S. Slang.* **1** petting or similar sexual play by a group of people.

Nevertheless she'd gone along with group-grope, gang-bang . . . and other perversions for her plump pal's sake, deferring her preferences to his. *John Barth, Harper's, Oct. 1972, p 82*

2 a form of encounter-group therapy which stresses close physical, and especially tactile, contact between members of a group.

It's a group grope at Esalen . . . an orgy of touching, palpating, feeling, stroking. *Martin Gardner, The New York Review of Books, Jan. 26, 1978, p 22*

[1969]

groupie[1], *n. Informal.* **1** a follower or admirer of a celebrity; fan.

Steve Doyle . . . is a groupie. No, not the kind of groupie that chases after rock singers. Steve's serious. He *works* for his idol, and his idol happens to be a presidential primary contender. *Lynn Sherr, "Here Come the Political Groupies!" Saturday Review, June 10, 1972, p 22*

Groupies have been around a long time — camp followers of the rich or famous, this heavyweight champion or that president. John F. Kennedy took several groupies into the White House with him. *Garry Wills, New York Post, Oct. 13, 1978, p 59*

2 a devotee or enthusiast; aficionado.

Court groupies and Hearst case buffs arrived from all over the country; some had taken leaves from their jobs to see as much of the six- to eight-week trial as possible. *"The Law: Piloting Patty's Defense," Time, Feb. 16, 1976, p 46*

. . . a radical-chic restaurant where Toronto artists, entrepreneurs and culture groupies hang out. *Meriké Weiler, "Frontlines: A Poet of Light and Space and Time," Maclean's, Dec. 11, 1978, p 6*

[1971, extended from the original meaning (1967) of a teen-age fan who follows after rock-group musicians] Compare JUNKIE.

groupie[2], *n. Especially U.S. Informal.* a consortium or group of associated companies designated by the term *Group.*

Last year's groupies included the Medallion Group, the American Recreation Group, the Wellington Fund reorganized as Vanguard Group of Investment Companies and Clinton Oil, to the Energy Reserves Group. *"Business Roundup: Group Inc.?" The New York Times, May 23, 1976, Sec. 3, p 17*

[1971, from *group* + *-ie*, probably influenced by GROUPIE[1]]

Group of 77, a group of United Nations diplomats representing the underdeveloped countries of the world.

The 114 third-world nations, represented by the so-called "Group of 77," would have the "common heritage of mankind" husbanded by an international body generally referred to as the Authority. *William Wertenbaker, "Mining the Wealth of the Ocean Deep," The New York Times Magazine, July 17, 1977, p 32*

The Group of 77 (the term used to describe developing countries in the North/South negotiations) formulated a tough draft of the code. *Paul Harrison, New Scientist, Nov. 2, 1978, p 354*

[1967, so called because originally it represented 77 nonaligned nations at the United Nations Conference on Trade and Development]

grunge (grənʤ), *n. U.S. Slang.* something that is bad, inferior, ugly, or boring.

Your average American rock-and-roll fan can stand the Dolls' brand of high-strung urban grunge only if it comes from somewhere besides New York — preferably England. *Ellen Willis, "Rock, Etc.," The New Yorker, Nov. 19, 1973, p 234*

[1965, corresponding to the adjective *grungy* (1965)]

GSR, abbreviation of GALVANIC SKIN RESPONSE.

GSR is a measure of the degree of stability of the autonomic nervous sytem which is correlated to such things as resistance to stress and reduced physical impulsivity. *"Behavioral Sciences: Meditating in Prison," Science News, Sept. 8, 1973, p 152*

The GSR showed that he was under no unusual stress. His heart rate remained essentially the same. *Elmer and Alyce Green, "The Ins and Outs of Mind-Body Energy," The World Book Science Annual 1974 (1973), p 144*

[1970]

GUIDO or **Gui·do** ('gɑi dou), *n. U.S. Aerospace.* an engineer in charge of a space flight; the chief navigation officer in a mission-control center.

The men in the [front row] never feel more like pilots than during a rocket burn. As soon as the GUIDO got the trajectory information from the FIDO, he punched the numbers into a white keyboard in front of him, preparatory to loading (or, as GUIDOs say, "uplinking") the data into the computer aboard the spacecraft. *Henry S. F. Cooper, Jr., "Annals of Exploration: An Accident in Space—I," The New Yorker, Nov. 11, 1972, p 107*

[1969, probably from *Guid*ance *O*fficer] Compare RETRO.

gu·lag or **Gu·lag** ('gu:,lɑ:g), *n.* **1** a shortened name for GULAG ARCHIPELAGO.

Perhaps the most profound influence of all . . . was the moral impact in the West of Alexander Solzhenitsyn whose revelations of the character and scale of the Gulag made it electorally imperative as well as morally necessary for the Western Communist parties to come to full terms with Stalinism. *Peter Jenkins, The Manchester Guardian Weekly, Nov. 20, 1977, p 5*

Dissent was punished long before there was a gulag. It was in recognition of this simple but basic fact that the Founders took such pains to disperse power and safeguard individual freedoms. *The New York Times, June 13, 1978, p A18*

2 a forced labor camp, especially for political prisoners.

To tell these workers that they are foreigners, living in black *gulags,* and can express their political voice only in distant homelands is sheer fantasy. *Henry Grunwald, "Arguing with South Africa," Time, June 27, 1977, p 37*

The erosion of God's presentness from daily life and from the legitimacy of political power generated the need to institute a surrogate damnation on earth (a Hell aboveground), this surrogate being the Nazi, the Soviet, the Chilean, and the Cambodian Gulags. *George Steiner, The New Yorker, Sept. 4, 1978, p 98*

[1974, from Russian *GULag*, acronym for *G*lavnoye *U*pravleniye *Lag*erei Chief Administration of (Corrective Labor) Camps; popularized in *The Gulag Archipelago*] See ZEK.

Gulag Archipelago, the network of prisons and forced labor camps in the Soviet Union established by Stalin for criminals and political prisoners.

All the *aggressive* elements, all the influential elements in society — this was especially the case in Britain — admired what they called the 'unprecedented progressive experiment taking place in the USSR', while we were being strangled by the cancerous tentacles of the Gulag Archipelago, while millions of hard-working peasants were being sent to die in Siberia in midwinter. *Alexander Solzhenitsyn, "On the Brink of a Cataclysm," The Listener, March 25, 1976, p 358*

... a horror that can be thought of only in the images conjured up by the words "Auschwitz" or "Gulag Archipelago." *Henry Kamm, "The Agony of Cambodia," The New York Times Magazine, Nov. 19, 1978, p 42*

[1974, from *The Gulag Archipelago*, a series of books by Aleksandr Solzhenitsyn, Russian author, born 1918] Also shortened to ARCHIPELAGO.

gundown, *n.* the act of shooting or killing with a gun.

This aborted son of a godfather seems a compendium of every gangster classic since "Little Caeser" — complete with the obligatory gundowns in barbershop and restaurant, initiation blood ritual, tribal meetings and formalized Sicilian mating dances. *P. D. Zimmerman, "Blood for Sale," Film Review of "The Valachi Papers," Newsweek, Nov. 27, 1972, p 100*

[1969, from the verb phrase *gun down*]

gunge (gəndʒ), *n. British Slang.* a soft, sticky mass; goo; gunk.

Carl Sagan and B. N. Khare have obtained a rough match between the interstellar infrared bands and those they have obtained from solid residues produced by discharge or ultraviolet irradiation of various gaseous mixtures of chemically abundant compounds.... They call this solid material tholin (after the Greek word for muddy), but it seems likely that chemists will continue to call this rather familiar material "gunge." *New Scientist, Jan. 11, 1979, p 93*

[1969, probably alteration of *gunk* (1940's), originally *Gunk*, a U.S. tradmark for a liquid soap]

Gush E·mu·nim ('gu:ʃ e mu:'ni:m), a militant, religious, and ultranationalistic movement in Israel.

Government officials spoke of a plan to establish 20 more Jewish settlements in the West Bank over the next four years, but when members of *Gush Emunim*, the fanatical religious organization, tried to found two illegal settlements on the hills above Jerusalem last week, soldiers quickly evicted them. *"Cooling It in Egypt and Israel," Time, Jan. 8, 1979, p 34*

[1976, from Hebrew, literally, bloc of the faithful]

Guts Frisbee, Also, **Guts.** a game in which competing teams throw and try to catch a Frisbee (lightweight plastic disk).

The name of the game is Guts Frisbee, and to a growing number of serious competitors it is the greatest sport around. Two five-member teams stand on boundaries set 15 yards apart and take turns hurling a Pro Model Frisbee so hard, or on so tricky a trajectory, that no opponent can make a clean one-handed grab. *"Modern Living: Flipped Disks," Time, July 17, 1972, p 52*

There are well-developed games like Guts, where teams of five, 15 yards apart, engage in an all-out, 100 m.p.h., flying disk war. *Stancil E. D. Johnson, "Frisbee Imperiled," The New York Times Magazine, July 18, 1976, p 47*

[1972] Compare AIRBORNE SOCCER.

gy·rase ('dʒaɪˌreɪs), *n.* an enzyme which changes double-helix DNA into superhelical DNA.

Gyrase uses energy from ATP molecules to "super coil" the DNA double helix in the direction opposite the twist of the helix. The stored mechanical energy from such super coiling makes a local region of the helix easier to open.... Gyrase so far has been best studied as an aid to replication of DNA, but recently scientists have begun investigating its potential role in RNA production. DNA strands must separate to serve as templates for messenger RNA involved in protein production. *Science News, June 10, 1978, p 372*

[1977, from *gyrate* + *-ase* enzyme]

gyr·o ('yir ou; *Anglicized* 'dʒaɪ rou), *n.* a type of Greek sandwich. See the quotation.

Soyer circled the area, took his time, and settled for a Greek *gyro* — mounds of thinly sliced, garlicky pressed beef and lamb on pita bread. *Helen Drees Ruttencutter, "Profiles: String Quartet," The New Yorker, Oct. 23, 1978, p 101*

[1972, from Modern Greek, from Greek *gŷros* turn, rotation; so called from the meat being roasted on a spit]

gyrodynamics, *n.* the study of the dynamics of rotational motion.

Although he has spent most of his life in an academic environment, starting at Edinburgh University where he was awarded a PhD for his study of gyroscopes, [Leonard] Maunder's work has kept him in close touch with industry. He has also carried out research on engineering dynamics and gyrodynamics and the stress analysis of structures. *The Times (London), July 23, 1976, p 19*

[1976, from *gyro-* circle, spiral + *dynamics*]

H

ha·ba·tsu (hə'bɑːt suː), *n. sing.* or *pl.* (in Japan) a faction or clique, especially in a political party.

The *Habatsu*. These local baronies within the larger grouping of the party, can thus serve as a useful safety valve for surplus energies. Each faction boss has in turn his own ... relationship with the party leader and it is this that holds the whole together. *Michael Hornsby, The Times (London), June 26, 1972, p 12*

[1971, from Japanese]

hab·er·dash ('hæb ər ˌdæʃ), *v.t. U.S.* to make or style (clothing).

When nothing's too good for you, associate with a shirtdress that's haberdashed with details worthy of the most exacting taste. *Advertisement by Saks Fifth Avenue, The New Yorker, Dec. 16, 1972, p 59*

[1972, back formation from *haberdashery*]

ha·dal ('hei dəl), *adj.* of or relating to the very deep part of the ocean, ranging from depths of 6500 to 11,000 meters.

Later the reader is taken from the intertidal with its diverse wealth of life progressively lower over the floor of the continental shelf and slope eventually to the profound depths of the ultra-abyssal or hadal zone. *C. M. Yonge, Review of "Life in the Sea" by Gunnar Thorson, Nature, May 19, 1972, p 180*

[1964, from *Hades* the nether world + *-al*]

Hag·e·man factor ('hæg ə mən *or* 'heig mən), a substance in blood plasma necessary for rapid coagulation of blood.

In addition to promoting clotting, activated Hageman factor can initiate the function of other enzymes in the blood plasma which ultimately increase vascular permeability, contract isolated smooth muscles, induce pain and dilatation of the blood vessels (thus increasing blood flow to the area), and even cause the white blood cells to stick to injured areas of blood vessels and subsequently traverse this barrier into surrounding tissues. *Virginia H. Donaldson, "Blood," McGraw-Hill Yearbook of Science and Technology 1971, p 133*

[1963, named after a patient in whom a deficiency of this substance was first noticed]

hair implant, a graft or grafting of strands of artificial hair (usually made of an acrylic fiber) stitched into a bald area of the scalp or attached to small metal barbs forced into the scalp under pressure.

Hair implants have been advertised by a number of clinics across the country. ... Unlike the transplantation of actual hair from one part of the scalp to another, synthetic implants trigger the body's natural defense mechanisms, usually causing the rejection of the artificial hairs. *Matt Clark and Dan Shapiro, "Medicine: Bald Men Beware," Newsweek, Feb. 19, 1979, p 54*

[1974] Compare HAIR TRANSPLANT.

hairologist, *n. U.S.* a specialist in the care and treatment of hair.

Fancier shops now boast resident "hairologists" whose only mission is to prescribe the proper natural treatment and conditioning for feeble follicles. *"Modern Living: Summer Shortcut," Time, July 16, 1973, p 59*

[1973, from *hair* + *-ologist*, as in *cosmetologist* (1920's) a specialist in cosmetics]

hair transplant, a graft or grafting of one's own hair by removing follicles and inserting them in a bald area of the scalp.

He's a no-sell advertisement for hair transplants; his haven't taken, and he combs the few remaining blond strands from left to right over the crown of his head. *Jack Batten, "Dr. Jekyll and Mr. Hull," Maclean's, March 1973, p 29*

[1973] Compare HAIR IMPLANT.

Hal·a·phone ('hæl əˌfoun), *n.* a large electronic device used during the performance of an orchestra to produce special effects by picking up the sounds of individual instruments and blending and modifying them in various ways.

In the first performance of the piece by the Lincoln Center Chamber Music Society, the Halaphone not only transmuted the instrumental sounds electronically, but sped those sounds around the concert hall via loudspeakers pinned to the walls. Boulez remained onstage cuing the technicians. *"Music: Crack in the Wall," Time, Jan. 22, 1973, p 44*

[1973, from Peter *Hal*ler, name of its inventor + connecting *-a-* + *-phone* sound]

Haldane principle, the principle that government research agencies be completely insulated from government departments that benefit from the research.

The National Research Council has evolved into the embodiment of the so-called Haldane principle that government research and development should be the responsibility not of mission-oriented departments but of an independent agency. *"Science in Canada: Call for End to the Haldane Principle in Canada," Nature, Aug. 11, 1972, p 305*

[1966, named after J. B. S. *Haldane*, 1892-1964, British geneticist who headed the committee which enunciated this principle]

half-board, *n. British.* the provision of a bed, breakfast, and one other meal each day (as by a hotel or boarding house). *Often used attributively.*

We were grateful we had only half-board so that we could justify eating outside the hotel at least once a day. *Diana Patt, "Half Board Is a Gourmet's Licence," The Times (London), April 1, 1977, p IV*

[1975, patterned on *full board* (1910) the provision of a bed and all meals]

half-life, *n.* a period of flowering or prosperity preceding decay or decline.

Alas, in the mercurial cosmetics business, almost all products have short half-lives, and Charlie sales have started to decline. But before they did, Bergerac and Revlon were ready with both an explanation and a new product. *"Cosmetics: Kiss and Sell," Time, Dec. 11, 1978, p 90*

[1963, figurative of "the time it takes half of a particular substance to break down or decay"]

hal·o·bac·ter·i·a (ˌhæl ou bæk'tir i: ə), *n.pl.; sing.* **-i·um** (-i: əm). rod-shaped bacteria of a group that thrives in areas with very high salt concentrations.

Halobacteria are salt-loving cells that inhabit stagnant puddles and salt flats at the edge of tropical seas. . . . They turn water orange and red herrings red and turn sunlight into chemical energy on their "purple membranes." These bacteria are, all in all, very strange organisms. *"Purple Salt-Lover Captures the Sun," Science News, March 6, 1976, p 149*

[1976, from *halo-* salt (from Greek *háls, halós*) + *bacteria*]

hal·o·car·bon (ˌhæl ou'kar bən), *n.* a compound of carbon and one or more halogens (fluorine, chlorine, etc.).

Concern over the tenuous, but vital, ozone layer which surrounds the Earth has centered around the possible effects of exhaust gases from supersonic transport and the space shuttle, and latterly those which may result from the halocarbons used in packaged aerosol canisters. *"Analysing the Stratosphere at Sub-mm Wavelengths," New Scientist, May 29, 1975, p 492*

[1964, from *halogen* + *carbon*] Compare CHLOROFLUOROCARBON.

hal·o·meth·ane (ˌhæl ou'meθ ein), *n.* a compound of methane and one or more halogens (chlorine, fluorine, etc.).

Halomethanes . . . used as refrigerants or as propellants for aerosol spray cans, are another hazard to the earth's ozone shield. *Eugenia Keller, "Chemistry," The Americana Annual 1975, p 175*

Among other nasty organic and man-made intruders, every sample contained chemicals called halomethanes, which some scientists believe can cause cancer in humans. *Maclean's, March 20, 1978, p 16*

[1975, from *halogen* + *methane*] Compare CHLOROFLUOROMETHANE.

hal·o·per·i·dol (ˌhæl ou'per ə dɔ:l), *n.* a tranquilizing drug used in the treatment of acute and chronic psychosis. *Formula:* $C_{21}H_{23}ClFNO_2$

Doctors know that two groups of drugs, which include chlorpromazine and haloperidol, are remarkably effective

in relieving the thought disorders, hallucinations and extreme withdrawal of schizophrenia, a chronic psychosis that affects one person out of every 100. *"Exploring the Frontiers of the Mind," Time, Jan. 14, 1974, p 57*

[1967, from *halogen* + piperidine + *-ol*]

hammer, *n. U.S. Slang.* an accelerator.

"Yeah, good buddy, you got a county mounty there at marker three-oh. He's eastbound and he's got the hammer down." *Marshall Schuon, "Using Citizens Band on Vacation," Family Circle, Aug. 1976, p 20*

drop the hammer, to accelerate.

And "modulating," (talking) while "dropping the hammer" (accelerating) is more dangerous to the driver than to his speech. *Stefan Kanfer, Time, Jan. 2, 1978, p 36*

[1975]

ha·na·mi·chi (ha: na:'mi: tʃi:), *n.* a raised runway leading to the stage in the Japanese Kabuki theater.

Hanamichi is the ramp extending from stage to rear of theatre which allows the actor to show off at close quarters . . . hanamichi will be on view at Sadler's Wells from August 15 when a Japanese Kabuki season opens. *The Times (London), Aug. 3, 1977, p 14*

[1971, from Japanese, from *hana* flower + *michi* way] Compare HASHIGAKARI.

hand, *v.* **hand up,** *U.S.* to deliver (an indictment) to a higher judicial authority.

Both men pleaded not guilty to the charges, which were handed up by a special grand jury. *Tom Goldstein, The New York Times, May 14, 1976, p 1*

[1973] ▶ The verb phrase *hand down* means "to announce (a legal decision or opinion)." A judge hands down a decision, whereas a grand jury hands up an indictment.

handle, *n. U.S.* Usually, **have** or **get a handle on,** to have a means of directing or guiding; control.

It follows that if we could only get a better handle on the arms-building phenomenon, we could do something about it; turn it around. *The Manchester Guardian Weekly (The Washington Post section), May 29, 1977, p 15*

Carter's State of the Union speech failed to convince foreign moneymen that the Administration has a handle on the economy's problems. *Time, Jan. 30, 1978, p 20*

[1972]

hands-on, *adj.* designed for or encouraging personal participation or involvement.

Skyline is a "magnet" school, attracting students from all over the city to its special offerings; it also is a new concept in "career education" (not to be confused with "vocational education") that combines fast-paced academic work with hands-on training for real jobs. *Peter A. Janssen, Saturday Review, Nov. 11, 1972. p 37*

"Hands on" instruction includes how to measure blood pressure, how to use stethoscopes, how to use otoscopes (for mothers to determine whether their youngsters' eardrums are red and inflamed or normal looking), and, optionally, how—in lab sessions—to test stool samples for blood. *Robert C. Yeager, "The Self-Care Surge," Encyclopedia Science Supplement (Grolier) 1979 (1978), p 259*

[1971, patterned on *hands-off*]

hand·tec·tor ('hændˌtek tər), *n.* a hand-held electronic metal detector, used especially in airports to screen for the presence of weapons.

Held close to a person's body the handtector detects any inordinate amount of metal . . . hidden beneath the clothing. *Robert R. Rodwell, "Technology in the Streets of Ulster," New Scientist, April 6, 1972, p 17*

[1972, from *hand* de*tector*]

hang, *v. U.S. and Canadian Slang.* **1 hang loose,** to stay calm; relax; take it easy.

In the meantime, my survival plan is to hang loose, trust my own perceptions, and wear out my Rod Stewart and Joy of Cooking records. *Ellen Willis, "Rock, etc.," The New Yorker, Feb. 26, 1972, p 81*

"In Marin Countyese, people talk of being laid back, mellow, hanging loose and getting their thing together." *Herbert Mitgang, "Behind the Best Sellers: Cyra McFadden," The New York Times Book Review, Oct. 16, 1977, p 54*

2 hang tough, to remain firm in resolve; persevere.

Washington has adhered to a policy of "no concessions" to the terrorists. It will not accede to demands put forward as a condition for the hostages' release, it will not negotiate such terms, and it will not put pressure on other Governments to yield. In the interests of deterring future terrorism, America hangs tough. *Judith Miller, "Bargain With Terrorists?" The New York Times Magazine, July 18, 1976, p 7*

Chrétien decided to hang tough rather than give in to opposition demands for sweeping cuts in personal income taxes. *Ian Urquhart, "Lord Let There Be Light!" Maclean's, Nov. 27, 1978, p 22*

[1968, related to older slang expressions of like form and meaning, such as *hang in there, hang on*]

hang-glide, *v.i.* to ride a hang glider.

More often she [Lily Tomlin] plunges at random into her seemingly inexhaustible repertory of impersonations: a crazy woman of the streets, a quadriplegic whose goal is to hang-glide off Big Sur. *Brendan Gill, "The Theatre," The New Yorker, April 4, 1977, p 81*

[1974, back formation from *hang glider* or *hang gliding*]

hang glider, 1 a device somewhat like a kite. The rider controls the gliding and soaring while holding onto a bar suspended from the kite. It is usually launched by running off a hill or cliff.

My first hang glider had a sail consisting of .004-inch polyethylene. The machine weighed 40 pounds empty. It served me well for many ground-skimming flights until the sail began stretching, which degraded the glide ratio. *Michael A. Markowski, quoted by C. L. Stong, "The Amateur Scientist," Scientific American, Dec. 1974, p 139*

Also called ROGALLO.

2 the rider of such a device.

"It is the most beautiful, the quietest, the cleanest sport," says one hang glider. "It is as close to the elements as you can get," says another. "It is the ultimate natural high." *Jurate Kazickas, "Hang Gliding—The Craziest Sport," Sunday News (New York), Sept. 16, 1973, p 28*

Also called ROGALLIST, SKY SURFER.

[1972]

hang gliding: It's called hang gliding, sky surfing or self-soaring—one of man's fantasies since the mythical days of Daedalus and Icarus. But in the past three years, self-propelled flying has become a reality—and one of the fastest-growing sports in the country. *"Life and Leisure: Go Fly a Kite," Newsweek, Sept. 17, 1973, p 82*

hangout, *n. U.S.* disclosure, exposure, or openness.

As Alan, Peter Firth is equally astonishing; he and Roberta Maxwell as the stable girl play the most blazingly effective nude scene in our age of Total Hangout. *Newsweek, Nov. 4, 1974, p 60*

For Congress to agree to less than full cooperation from Korea would be to acquiesce in a kind of cover-up, in what not so long ago was dubbed a modified limited hangout. *The New York Times, Jan. 8, 1978, Sec. 4, p 18*

[1974, from the phrase *let it all hang out*]

► This term was in part popularized by use in the White House tapes transcribed during the Watergate affair.

hangtime, *n. U.S. Football.* the amount of time a punt stays in the air. The longer the hangtime, the greater the opportunity for the defensive team to tackle the receiver.

A whistle sent the Mariners into a punting drill and a football soared into the sky above the treetops of this affluent North Shore community. It wasn't a particularly long kick, but Rush liked the hangtime. *Steve Cady, "Coaching Is an Incurable Disease," The New York Times, Aug. 26, 1976, p 41*

[1971]

hap·pen·stan·tial (ˌhæp ənˈstæn ʃəl), *adj. U.S.* accidental; happening by chance.

We are not "others," say women, we are human beings like you in whom there exists merely a happenstantial sex difference. *Elizabeth Janeway, "The Weak Are the Second Sex," The Atlantic, Dec. 1973, p 96*

[1958, 1966, patterned on *circumstantial* (adjective form of *circumstance*); from *happenstance* (blend of *happen* and *circumstance*)]

happy hour, a time in the early evening when alcoholic drinks are served, especially at a club bar or cocktail lounge, sometimes at reduced prices.

So, this being the content of your happy hour, you decide to break your iron-clad rule, that rule of rules, and have eleven drinks instead of the modest nine. *Donald Barthelme, The New Yorker, July 17, 1971, p 26*

A recruit needs neither height (five-feet two-inches will do) nor education (grade 8) to begin making $536 a month and having the privilege of buying beer for 40 cents a bottle during Happy Hour. *Roy MacGregor, Maclean's, Nov. 6, 1978, p 23*

[1967]

happy talk, a form of news broadcasting in which reports are tailored to an informal style with emphasis on light subjects.

What Happy Talk means in fact is that the consumer-listener-viewer gets an inverted perspective of the world in which he lives. Even for domestic news, he is fed reaction rather than analysis. *Brenda Maddox, "Media: Happy Talk," The Listener, Aug. 30, 1973, p 295*

I think broadcast journalism has done much to expand news definitions . . . something which I think is long overdue. Yes, there have been excesses . . . the happy talk, the newscasters in clown suits. *Columbia Journalism Review, March/April 1976, p 83*

[1973]

hardball, *n. U.S. and Canadian Slang.* Usually, **play**

hardball, (to use) tough, aggressive methods and tactics. *Often used attributively.*

The inducements ranged from the withholding of campaign appearances by the First Family to the granting of photographs with the President, jobs in Federal agencies and seats on Federal commissions. It was hardball of the rawest kind, an insider's game that one would not previously have associated with the softspoken Washington outsider. *Martin Tolchin, "New Pro in the White House," The New York Times Magazine, Dec. 17, 1978, p 34*

The sense of discouragement left by the breakdown of the private meetings caused the publishers to issue an ultimatum to Moffett: if he did not break off the formal negotiation by two o'clock the next afternoon, Friday, September 15th, they would walk out on their own. . . . At a meeting with the publisher's negotiators, Moffett said, "Evidently, you guys have decided that you are going to play hardball." *The New Yorker, Jan. 29, 1979, p 62*

[1973, figurative use referring to "serious" or "professional" baseball (as opposed to *softball*); a usage popularized by Patrick J. Buchanan, a White House speechwriter during the administration of President Nixon]

hard bubble, an aberrant magnetic bubble that causes disruption of the memory in a computer, usually formed spontaneously in the operation of a circuit.

The hard bubbles are more stable than the previously known "normal" bubbles and have different dynamic properties. Instead of moving only parallel to the drive field, the hard bubbles have a velocity component perpendicular to the field and would in general move at some angle to it. *"Physical Sciences: Hard Magnetic Bubbles," Science News, Oct. 21, 1972, p 264*

[1972] Also called QUANTIZED BUBBLE.

hard copy, printed copy in a computer or data-processing system.

Some keyboards used for perforating tape are converted typewriters and therefore generate hard copy; others are designed solely for tape perforation and therefore operate "blind," that is, without preparing any record of keystrokes other than the punched paper tape. Hard copy seems to be advantageous for relatively untrained or part-time operators but less advantageous for the professional. *P. L. Andersson, "Composition (Type)," McGraw-Hill Yearbook of Science and Technology 1970, p 159*

[1964]

hard-core, *adj.* **1** completely uninhibited, graphic, or explicit in presenting or describing sexual acts.

The exploration of unacknowledged desires is the process that is the most compelling structural requirement in hard-core pornography. *Horace Freeland Judson, "Skin Deep," Harper's, Feb. 1975, p 47*

That breakthrough film which uses hard-core sex as a dramatic expression of meaningful human relationships has yet to be made. *Frank Rich, "Riding the New Wave of Porno," New York Post, Nov. 29, 1975, p 14*

2 hard to cure of addiction; resisting treatment.

Mostly, the users, even the heroin users, weren't strung-out hard-core junkies. I'd say many of them came from middle-class families. *John Brooks, "Annals of Finance: The Go-Go Years," The New Yorker, July 3, 1973, p 61*

—*n.* Also, **hard core.** hard-core pornography.

California is busy withdrawing the liquor licences of strip-joints and bars putting on sex-shows. Hard-core may fetch the customers, but hard liquor brings in the profits: and hundreds of such saloon-keepers have suddenly developed a passionate concern for the Constitution in general and the First Amendment in particular. *Alistair Cook, "Porn Laws," The Listener, July 27, 1973, p 120*

He had seen it during World War II, when he served as a Navy lieutenant. In Casablanca, as watch officer for his ship, he had seen his men bring back locally produced pornography. He knew the difference between that hardest of hard core and much of what came to the Court. He called it his "Casablanca Test." *Bob Woodward and Scott Armstrong, The Brethren, 1979, p 194*

[1963 for adj. def. 1, 1972 for def. 2, from meaning "firm or unyielding"; 1973 for noun] Compare SOFT-CORE.

hard dock, a joining of orbiting spacecraft by mechanical coupling.

Finally, they depressurized the command module, went to an open-cockpit condition to carry out a dramatic series of maneuvers—and achieved a hard dock. *"The Skylab Rescue Mission," Newsweek, June 4, 1973, p 60*

[1971]

hard-dock, *v.i.:* Their frustrations were far from over. At least five attempts to redock with the space station after the futile repair work failed. The crew finally hard-docked late the first night by hot wiring the retract mechanism of the docking probe with a cable. This involved donning their spacesuits again, depressurizing the spacecraft and removing the forward hatch to work on the probe and drogue. *"First Week in Space for the Crew of Skylab," Science News, June 2, 1973, p 353*

hard porn, hard-core pornography.

Ain't Misbehavin' (Focus) is an extraordinary compilation film which relies heavily on naughty footage from private (sic) collections from 1907 to the Forties. Not hard porn, it nevertheless contains some surprisingly rude bits from the earliest days that have earned it, some 70 years later, an X certificate. *Gavin Millar, "Cinema: Revelations," Review of "Ain't Misbehavin'," The Listener, March 6, 1975, p 314*

[1975] Compare SOFT PORN.

hard-wired, *adj.* **1** (of a computer circuit or component) wired directly to a computer.

The decoding of the instruction can be done in several ways. One method employs a "hard-wired" decoder, in which an array of gates selects a unique combination of active output lines for each possible combination of bits in the operation code. *William C. Holton, "The Large-Scale Integration of Microelectronic Circuits," Scientific American, Sept. 1977, p 89*

The coordinates, speed, course and other data of other nearby vessels can also be entered, either via the keyboard or directly from another source via a hard-wired link. *"Technology: Computerised Navigator Is a Ship's Saviour," New Scientist, Nov. 2, 1978, p 360*

2 *Figurative use.*

It appears to me that there are a long list of such human traits and that a large percentage of them are shared with primates. For example the facial expressions of human beings really appear to be hard-wired and in many instances comparable to those found in the chimpanzee. *The New York Times, Feb. 26, 1978, Sec. 4, p 18*

[1971]

hard-wiring, *n.:* It is pre-eminently a clandestine device, hidden away, and so the first constraint the bug-maker meets is size. The next is the means of passing on the signal — radio transmission, carrier wave system, or directly by cable. In the trade, the use of an ordinary cable is known as "hard wiring." *New Scientist, Nov. 23, 1978, p 600*

Ha·re Krish·na ('haː re kriʃ nə), a member of the International Society for Krishna Consciousness, a sect devoted to the Hindu god Krishna; a follower or adherent of KRISHNA CONSCIOUSNESS.

The tangible outcome of the arranged marriage among the Hare Krishnas can be seen in certain temples in the Western U.S. In Los Angeles, seventy married devotees are raising fifty infants under five years old; in Dallas, about two hundred Hare Krishna offspring aged five to fourteen from all over the world attend a special Sanskrit school. *Faye Levine, "Wraparound: Where Marriages Are Arranged," Harper's, May 1974, p 9*

[1972, from the title of a love chant or mantra (1968) used by the sect, from Hindi, literally, Lord Krishna]

har·tree ('haːˌtriː), *n.* a unit of energy in nuclear physics, approximately equal to 27.21 electron volts.

Orbital energy is given below each diagram in hartrees, and charge density is plotted in electrons per cubic bohr. *Illustration legend, "Chemistry by Computer," Scientific American, April 1970, p 58*

[1970, named for Douglas R. *Hartree*, born 1897, English theoretical physicist]

Har-Tru ('haːˌtruː), *n. U.S.* a trademark for an artificial surface for tennis courts, made from crushed greenstone.

Many American tennis enthusiasts, I am sure, have wondered if we were not too hasty in ripping up the grass courts used for the championships at Forest Hills and replacing them with Har-Tru. *Herbert Warren Wind, The New Yorker, Oct. 9, 1978, p 148*

[1976, from *Hard* + *True*, a reference to the physical quality of such courts] Compare ASTROTURF, GRASSTEX.

harvest index, the percent of total plant weight represented by the harvested product.

With many crops, particularly cereals, the trend is to increase the harvest index, that is, weight of harvested product/total plant weight of the crop, and this is of special significance for multicropping in that an over-abundance of vegetative parts tends to delay maturity. *"Multiple Cropping: Research in India," Nature, Sept. 1, 1972, p 9*

[1970]

ha·shi·ga·ka·ri (ˌhaː ʃiː gaːˈkaː riː), *n.* a bridgelike passageway over which performers enter or leave the stage in the Japanese No theater.

By now one is used to the formalised stage, the raised rosewood platform, the pine-tree background, the hashigakari (or bridgeway) leading to a curtained doorway. *Michael Billington, "The Arts: Oh, Noh," The Manchester Guardian Weekly, June 16, 1973, p 22*

[1967, from Japanese, from *hashi* bridge + *-gakari* between two] Compare HANAMICHI.

hash marks, *U.S. and Canadian.* the broken in-bounds lines or markers on a football field.

The hash marks are used to position the ball on the playing field after it has been downed either out of bounds or too close to the boundaries to permit reasonable play. Moving the hash marks closer to the center of the field has given offensive players — particularly wide receivers and running backs — more room to maneuver, while the defenses have more ground to cover. Also, field-goal kickers now enjoy a better angle. *"Sport: Joe Namath and the Jet-Propelled Offense," Time, Oct. 16, 1972, p 47*

[1967, so called from their supposed resemblance to *hash marks* or military service stripes]

hash oil or **hashish oil,** tetrahydrocannabinol (THC), the active ingredient of marijuana and hashish.

Hash oil is hard to detect; it can be mixed with coffee or wine, and because it has no distinctive odor, it is often dabbed onto ordinary cigarettes and smoked in public with impunity. *"Life and Leisure: 'The One'," Newsweek, Sept. 11, 1972, p 63*

Mr Salman said today that about 4,000 kilograms of the drug and 34 kilograms of hashish oil had been confiscated by the police in recent months and added that "the authorities have stepped up efforts to crack down on the hashish trade." *The Times (London), Sept. 7, 1977, p 6*

[1972, so called because of its resemblance to motor oil]

hat, *n. Especially U.S. Slang.* any bribe or illicit bonus, such as that offered as graft for protection against prosecution, or the extra money collected by the recipient himself rather than through a bagman.

The discussion about enlarging the staff turned on the question of whether the plainclothesmen should hire a civilian to make the monthly pickups from the gamblers. This finally was rejected because the policemen involved did not want to lose the $200 monthly bonus or "hat" for the dangerous job of making the pickups themselves. *David Burnham, "Corrupt Police: The Next Board Meeting May Be in Jail," The New York Times, May 7, 1972, Sec. 4, p 11*

The black market price — what Greeks refer to as "the hat" — are the difference between what the government says the local butcher can charge for a piece of veal, and what the shopper actually has to pay for it. Some Athenians say that the hat is driving their household expenses up by 15% a year. *"Greece: An Unlikely Boom," Time, Feb. 19, 1973, p 82*

[1971, from the expression "buy yourself a hat" used in offering an initial bribe]

haut (ou), *adj.* having a high tone or style; high-class.

We who suffered the pangs of stretching out now hang loose, line up at the cinema, down an egg cream at the haut café, and, after hours, in copious time, enjoy a mellow joint with friends. *Richard Goldstein, "Performing Arts: Also Sprach Grand Funk Railroad," Harper's, Oct. 1971, p 32*

In fact, I was green with envy under my gray cheeks. Here was a man of the *hautest* of *haut-mondes*. A fabulous winter vacationer on the slopes of Mount Sybaris. *Russell Baker, "Radical Chic," The New York Times Magazine, Dec. 26, 1976, p 4*

[1970, abstracted from such phrases as *haut monde* and *haut ton*, ultimately from French *haut* high; compare obsolete *haut* high, haughty (OED 1430)]

ha·vu·rah (xaːˈvuː raː), *n., pl.* **ha·vu·rot** (xaː vuː ˈrout), any of various informal Jewish fellowship groups formed, especially in colleges and universities in the United States, as an alternative to traditional, synagogue-centered activities and practices. *Often used attributively.*

Each such group—there are now hundreds all over the U.S.—is a close-knit community that meets for prayer sessions, meals, classes and discussions on Judaism. While *havurah* members do not necessarily live together or pool their finances, they share an intense commitment to making religion part of everyday living. *"Religion: Kosher Earth Catalog," Time, Jan. 10, 1977, p 57*

[1972, from Hebrew *hăbhurāh* fellowship]

ha·ya·shi (hɑ:'yɑ: ʃi:), *n.* a Japanese orchestra.

The hayashi music of spare flutes and sparse drums was first-rate, and I suspect the two flute players are among the finest in Japan. *Geoffrey T. Hellman, The New Yorker, Nov. 4, 1972, p 86*

[1971, from Japanese]

Hay·flick limit ('hei flik), a natural limit to the lifetime of cells in a culture.

If the fibroblasts come from old tissue their potential for dividing in culture is much reduced: the average number of divisions declines by 0.20 for each year of the donor's life in human tissue. Leonard Hayflick of Stanford University, the man whose name has been given to this limited division potential (the Hayflick limit), believes the laboratory observations do have some relevance to the normal ageing phenomenon. *Roger Lewin, New Scientist, Nov. 29, 1973, p 615*

[1971, named after Leonard *Hayflick,* born 1928, an American microbiologist who discovered it]

Haz·chem ('hæz₁kem), *n. British.* a system of labeling containers of potentially dangerous chemicals by a special code to facilitate their safe handling or disposal in an accident.

The immediate appeal of Hazchem is due to its simplicity and directness—it tells the fireman exactly what he wants to know. However, hopes that it would gain acceptance widespread enough to forgo legislation have been dashed. "The absence of specific and obligatory rules for all operators and hauliers is seriously weakening" the development of Hazchem, Bill Aston (Deputy Chief Constable of Cleveland Constabulary) told a conference. *Lawrence McGinty, New Scientist, May 5, 1977, p 262*

[1976, from *haz*ardous + *chem*ical]

HCS, abbreviation of *human chorionic somatomammotrophin,* a hormone that originates in the outermost membrane of the amniotic sac enclosing the fetus (chorion) and promotes growth, mammary development, and milk secretion.

Later, the developing placenta produces a polypeptide hormone called human chorionic somatomammotrophin, or HCS. By and by the placenta produces this hormone in enormous quantities—about a gramme a day. This alone suggests the hormone is functional. But till now there has been no convincing explanation of its function. *"Monitor: Do Hormones Stop a Mother Rejecting Her Foetus?" New Scientist, July 5, 1973, p 4*

[1971]

HDL, abbreviation of *high density lipoprotein,* a lipoprotein containing more protein than lipids, thought to carry excess cholesterol out of body tissues to the liver for excretion.

Any cholesterol program should be directed, at least in part, toward raising the supply of these "good" cholesterol-disposing HDLs in the bloodstream, as opposed to the "bad" cholesterol-depositing LDLs. *Time, Nov. 21, 1977, p 119*

[1974] Compare LDL and VLDL.

head end, a location in a cable television system where a central antenna receives, amplifies, filters, and sometimes changes the frequency of a signal before it is passed into the cable leading to local subscribers. *Often used attributively.*

Whatever the source, the signals go into the "head end," which is the master control station and nerve center of a cable system. . . . If the signals are exceptionally weak, they are usually boosted by a preamplifier so that the head-end equipment can process them satisfactorily. *William T. Knox, "Cable Television," Scientific American, Oct. 1971, p 22*

[1969]

head restraint, a support for the head attached to the back of an automobile seat to prevent injury to the neck by a sudden jolt in a crash.

The devices may have been made in Detroit, but they were mandated in Washington, and they join a formidable list of items forced on Detroit in the past few years: head restraints, shoulder belts, engine blow-by devices, side marker lights, locking steering columns, fire-resistant fabrics, impact-resistant fuel tanks. *"The 1973 Cars: Year of the Bumper," Newsweek, Sept. 18, 1972, p 76*

[1972]

head trip, *Slang.* **1** an informal psychological or exploratory excursion into the mind.

"Folie En Tête" is her own title for this book, and exactly right. A head-trip, lasting 180,000 words. *William Cooper, The Sunday Times (London), July 18, 1971, p 26*

"[Robert] Crumb is creating a whole new way of thinking, a whole new head trip," says Gary Arlington. "People really relate to his stuff. It's like opening up your mind and seeing it in a mirror." *Thomas Maremaa, The New York Times Magazine, Oct. 1, 1972, p 68*

2 to engage in a head trip.

Dr John Lilly did much of his celebrated dolphin research with US military money. When, however, he shifted from studying the dolphin mind to exploring the inner recesses of his own—head tripping to Americans—military interest in the man ought properly to have ceased. *"Ariadne," New Scientist, July 19, 1973, p 176*

[1971]

head-up display, a secondary visual display of data relayed from instrument readings, projected on a windshield enabling a driver or pilot to keep his eyes on the course or path ahead.

Twelve Yorkshire police cars are currently testing head-up displays—projections of the car's speed onto the windscreen. *"Technology Review: Yorkshire Police Testing Space-Age Dashboard," New Scientist, Nov. 22, 1973, p 546*

The other development, the head-up display, also enhances automatic-landing safety by helping the human pilot, having been brought down to the runway by electronics, to make the transition from instruments to the outside world by optically putting all essential instrument data in the windscreen. *The Times (London), Sept. 4, 1978, p VII*

[1964]

health maintenance organization, an organization that provides subscribers with comprehensive health care for a fixed fee.

Health maintenance organizations can be a third option for the Medicare recipient. An HMO is a one-stop shopping center that offers a broad range of health services—including hospitalization, preventive care, diagnosis, and nursing—for a fixed monthly or yearly premium. We believe that the kind of care a good HMO provides can be ideal for older people. *Consumer Reports, Jan. 1976, p 27*

Five years ago, President Nixon coined the term Health Maintenance Organization to describe prepaid health groups—those organized medical services that allow a family to pay one set fee for almost all medical care. *Nancy Hicks, The New York Times, May 17, 1976, p 16*

[1971] *Abbreviation:* HMO

HEAO, abbreviation of *high-energy astronomy observatory,* any of a series of unmanned earth satellites that gather data on X-ray stars, gamma-ray bursts, and other astronomical phenomena, the first of which was launched in August, 1977.

HEAO-1, at 7,000 pounds (3,175 kg) the heaviest unmanned earth orbiting satellite ever launched, carried a new generation of experiments that dwarfed earlier rocket and satellite experiments. *Pitt G. Thome, "Space Exploration," The Americana Annual 1978, p 443*

[1971]

heat island, an industrial area or populated region in which the heat radiated is measurably greater than in the surrounding area.

The first report of the Royal Commission on Environmental Pollution mentions that temperatures are usually higher in urban areas than in nearby rural areas and that the warmth of the city helps to reduce space heating costs. These urban 'heat islands', as they have been termed, affect the distribution of atmospheric pollution, and geographers have pioneered their study. *The Geographical, Aug. 1972, p 787*

[1964]

heat-seeking missile, a guided missile with an infrared device to home in on objects that radiate heat, such as aircraft engines and factory facilities.

In Guinea over the last eight weeks "Estrela" heat-seeking missiles have been used with some effect against the Portuguese air force. *James McManus, The Manchester Guardian Weekly, June 9, 1973, p 7*

[1966]

heavy-metal, *adj. Especially U.S.* of or relating to a type of rock music with a heavy beat and sometimes harsh amplified instrumental effects.

The next kings of that musical thunder known as heavy-metal rock might very well be an English rock quartet called Queen. *Henry Edwards, The New York Times, Jan. 18, 1976, Sec. 2, p 17*

This is heavy-metal music with easy-listening inflections, rock fierce enough for the FM stations, flighty enough to fit right into Top 40 AM radio. *Time, Sept. 25, 1978, p 76*

[1974, partly from the association with rock groups that popularized it: *Led Zeppelin* and *Iron Butterfly;* partly from the amplified "metallic" guitar effects in the music]

heavy rail, of or belonging to a system of trains running as part of a conventional railroad system.

Transit specialists generally consider heavy rail transit, such as the subways, surface and elevated trains of the New York City system, to be the best and most efficient way to move large numbers of people through heavily traveled corridors. *Ernest Holsendolph, The New York Times, Sept. 13, 1977, p 22*

[1976] Compare LIGHT RAIL.

heavy rock, another name for PROGRESSIVE ROCK.

Heavy rock remained a vital force. One of the most broadly accepted groups was Aerosmith, whose lead singer, Steve Tyler, was compared with Mick Jagger of the Rolling Stones. *Leonard Feather, "Popular Music," The 1977 World Book Year Book, p 417*

[1973; *heavy,* slang word meaning "serious"]

hegemony or **hegemonism,** *n.* a Chinese Communist term for an expansionist foreign policy, applied especially to the Soviet Union.

The talks had been suspended for almost three years, in large part due to Soviet pressure on Japan to avoid signing a treaty with an "anti-Soviet" clause opposing "hegemony"—which is China's jargon for the Soviet threat. *Robert Whymant, "Japan and China Vow Peace," The Manchester Guardian Weekly, Aug. 20, 1978, p 6*

This became a central theme of Chinese pronouncements. The conflict in Vietnam could be seen as "resistance to hegemony." In 1972 Mao decreed: "Dig deep, store rice, never seek hegemony." He was surely referring to a presumed military threat from the United States, even as he was referring to the Soviets. *Daniel Patrick Moynihan, "Say 'Hegemony' and Duck!" Daily News (New York), Feb. 4, 1979, p 42*

He [Vice-Premier Teng Hsiao-ping] then flew to Thailand, Malaysia and Singapore, signing scientific exchange agreements and preaching endlessly against Soviet "hegemonism." *"Visionary of a New China," Time, Jan. 1, 1979, p 13*

[1970, special use of *hegemony* "leadership or dominance of a state" as translation of Chinese (Pinyin) *pa-ch'uan-chu-i,* literally, doctrine of domination; 1965 *hegemonism,* patterned on *imperialism*]

► This use began to appear in American and Chinese joint communiqués after the establishment of trade and other relations between the two countries in 1971 (see CODE WORD and PING-PONG DIPLOMACY).

heightism, *n.* an attitude of contempt for or discrimination against short people.

Worst of all, we usually end up marrying a short man, thereby having to share the life of one of those less successful victims of heightism. *Lia Schipper, Time, Oct. 25, 1971, p BI-1*

[1971, patterned on *ageism, sexism, racism*]

hei jen ('hei 'rən; *Anglicized* 'hei 'dʒen), (in China) young people who run away from rural factories and communes to live and work illegally in the cities.

According to reports reaching Hong Kong, as many as 1,000,000 rusticated youths have gone AWOL, creating a serious urban crime problem. Once back in the cities, the deserters become *hei jen* (black persons) who have no registered abode. *Time, July 27, 1970, p 22*

[1966, from Chinese, literally, black people]

hei·mish or **hai·mish** ('hei miʃ), *adj. Especially U.S. Slang.* cozy; friendly; informal.

The restaurant attracts this crowd not only because of its *heimish* cuisine but because of its five-man team of countermen, a couple of whom mainly provide countertalk entertainment and a couple of whom mainly provide food. *"The Talk of the Town: Counterman," The New Yorker, May 15, 1978, p 28*

[N.Y. Mayor] Koch served as a street speaker then, and again four years later, developing a style that is more *haimish*—homey—than sophisticated or rousing. *Time, Oct. 3, 1977, p 23*

[1966, from Yiddish, literally, homelike]

Heim·lich maneuver ('haim lik), a first-aid procedure to dislodge food or some object from a person's windpipe. The rescuer embraces the choking victim from behind, beneath the rib cage, and presses a closed fist under the breastbone with a quick upward thrust.

Frank Field's report on the Heimlich maneuver to help someone who is choking on food resulted in 300 similar letters citing life-saving instances. You see, on News Center 4 Frank does a lot more than just give weather reports. *Advertisement by News Center 4 WNBC-TV, The New York Times, Nov. 19, 1976, p C-26*

[1975, named after Henry J. *Heimlich*, an American surgeon who devised the procedure] See CAFÉ CORONARY.

Heimlich's sign, a proposed hand signal to indicate that one is choking on food.

"Heimlich's sign" is a universal signal that the victim can use and that a rescuer can recognize to indicate that this accident has occurred. The victim grasps his neck between thumb and index finger of one hand to signal "I'm choking!" *Henry J. Heimlich, "When Someone Chokes on Food," Encyclopedia Science Supplement (Grolier) 1976, p 229*

[1976] See HEIMLICH MANEUVER.

Heinz bodies, aggregates of hemoglobin visible in red blood cells in certain conditions.

The unstable haemoglobins are a group of well-defined haemoglobin variants associated clinically with haemolytic anaemia of varying severity. The nature of the amino-acid substitutions reduces the stability of the haemoglobin molecule, and this results in precipitation within the red cell and formation of characteristic inclusions called Heinz bodies. *Christine C. Winterbourn and R. W. Carrell, Christchurch, New Zealand, "Letters to Nature," Nature, Nov. 17, 1972, p 180*

[1970, named after Robert *Heinz*, 1865-1924, German physician who first described them]

helihop, *v.i.* to go short distances from place to place by helicopter.

At 3:35 p.m., the shuffling exercise routine in Mountjoy Prison was noisily disturbed when a helicopter suddenly settled in the yard, scattering prisoners in all directions. One Mountjoy warder thought it was a surprise visit from Defense Minister Patrick Donegan, who is fond of helihopping round the country. *"Ireland: The Canny Copter Caper," Time, Nov. 12, 1973, p 74*

[1966, from *heli-* helicopter + *hop*]

heliskiing, *n.* skiing on high mountains reached by helicopter.

For the dedicated disciples of winter who follow the snow from continent to continent, heli-skiing is the ultimate experience and the top of the mountain is the last frontier. *Graham Fraser, Maclean's, Jan. 9, 1978, p 52*

[1976, from *helicopter skiing*]

helium shakes or **helium tremors,** another name for HIGH-PRESSURE NERVOUS SYNDROME.

The high-pressure neurologic syndrome is indeed called "helium shakes" in diver's vernacular, but in truth has nothing to do with helium. The high pressure neurologic syndrome has been clearly shown to result from increased hydrostatic pressure. Indeed, helium tends to offset it, but inadequately. *Peter M. Winter, Seattle, Wash., "Divers and Gases," in a Letter to the Editor, Science News, May 29, 1976, p 339*

[1970]

hemiretina, *n.* half of the retina of the eye.

The Polaroid filters are arranged so that each eye receives a different image. Using a technique developed by Bela Julesz of the Bell Telephone Laboratories, the author presented one random-dot pattern to the right hemiretina of the right eye and a slightly different random-dot pattern to the right hemiretina of the left eye. In other trials the pattern was presented to the left hemiretinas. *Doreen Kimura, "The Asymmetry of the Human Brain," Scientific American, March 1973, p 75*

[1970 from *hemi-* half + *retina*]

He-Ne laser ('hi:'ni:), a laser that is activated by exciting a mixture of helium and neon gases.

The visible output of these He-Ne lasers is a coherent beam of monochromatic light at a frequency of 6328 angstroms. *Morton Grosser, "A Little Light on The Subject," The Atlantic, June 1971, p 93*

The experiment raises anew the serious question of how to define the metre. The error of the NBS [National Bureau of Standards] result arises mainly from comparing the miserable standard of length, based on incoherent krypton radiation, with the He-Ne laser. *"Monitor: Lasers Time Light With Unprecedented Accuracy," New Scientist, Nov. 16, 1972, p 376*

[1971, *He-Ne* from *He*, symbol for helium + *Ne*, symbol for neon]

hepatocarcinogen, *n.* a substance that causes cancer of the liver.

It is interesting that in the two most sophisticated parts of the world, Europe and North America, liver tumours are the least common, and so far no known experimental hepatocarcinogen has been unequivocably implicated in human liver cancer. *Lionel Mawdesley-Thomas, "Toxicological Tangle," New Scientist, Aug. 30, 1973, p 494*

[1972, from *hepato-* liver + *carcinogen*]

hepatocyte, *n.* a cell of the liver.

Specific fluorescence was also found in the cytoplasm of spindle-shaped cells growing out from the original liver tissue and it was considered that these fibroblast-like cells phagocytosed the antigen produced by the hepatocytes. *"Growing Hepatitis B Virus," Nature, Jan. 25, 1974, p 177*

[1972, from *hepato-* liver + *-cyte* cell]

herb, *n. U.S. Slang.* marijuana.

"My parents didn't make enough money. I used to burglarize places that had the stuff I wanted. I didn't like people feeling sorry for me." "Selling herb is the easiest life

237

there is . . . until you get busted." *"To Be Young, Black and Out of Work," The New York Times Magazine, Oct. 23, 1977, p 40*

[1977, perhaps patterned on *weed* and *grass* earlier (1930's) slang terms for marijuana]

Her·big-Ha·ro object ('hər big 'hɑ: rou), any of a number of small bright nebulas believed to be associated with the early stages of stellar formation.

Herbig-Haro objects are another of the many curious classes of objects in the sky. Small, nebular and reddish, they have spectra consisting of emission lines of various elements with a very weak continuous spectrum in the background. Efforts to explain what they are have not adequately fit the data, but some astronomers have suggested that Herbig-Haro objects may be very early phases of stellar evolution. *"37 New Herbig-Haro Objects," Science News, Oct. 28, 1978, p 296*

[1972, named after George *Herbig*, an American astronomer, and Guillermo *Haro*, a Mexican astronomer, who first discovered such objects] See YSO.

her·ma·type ('hər mə,taip), *n.* a coral that forms reefs.

It should be noted that there are two kinds of stony corals: those that build true reefs and those that do not. The reef-building corals—called hermatypes from the Greek *hermatos*, "mound"—contain within the inner tissue layer a symbiotic alga that speeds the calcification process. *Peter W. Glynn, "The Coral Reef Community," 1977 Britannica Yearbook of Science and the Future (1976), p 205*

[1976, back formation from *hermatypic* reef-building, from Greek *hérma* reef + English *-typic* of the type] Compare AHERMATYPE.

heroin baby, the infant of a woman addicted to heroin, usually born prematurely and with a craving for the drug.

At Kings County Hospital in Brooklyn, one in every 50 births is reported as a heroin baby. No one knows how many others are not diagnosed or reported. In 1971, the births of more than 550 heroin babies were recorded by the Department of Health in New York City. *Sophy Burnham, "The Heroin Babies: Going Cold Turkey at Birth," The New York Times Magazine, Jan. 9, 1972, p 18*

[1972] Compare BOARDER BABY.

he/she, he or she (used as a pronoun of common gender when the antecedent may be either male or female).

The author rejects volunteer work as merely a way "to fill in the time" and claims that he/she needs "real work." For the person truly willing to give of himself or herself, especially the teacher, the only difference between volunteer work and "real work" is in the pay check, *not* in the work. *Georgia Dunbar, New York, "How Old Is Old? The Readers Reply," The New York Times, Sept. 5, 1977, p 17*

Parents are wise not to make flat statements telling the teen what he/she should or should not do and letting it go at that. *Jacqueline Simenauer, "Guiding Your Child," New York Post, March 9, 1979, p 24*

[1976, patterned on combinations such as *and/or*] Compare HIM/HER, HIS/HER, S/HE. See also -PERSON.

Recent concern over sexism in language causes many writers to avoid using *he* as a genderless antecedent (e.g. "If a person wishes to succeed, *he* must work hard"). The most common replacement is "he or she."

The formula *he/she* developed from "he or she," and since its introduction in the early 1970's it continues to gain in popularity over other proposed substitutes (e.g. *co, hesh, tey*). Its use is restricted mainly to print, though orthographically it is often considered unappealing, but *he/she* has a clear advantage for those who are loath to recast their sentences, because it is both short and acceptable to both sexes. By contrast, a shorter version, *s/he*, is not widely accepted even though it is favored by some feminists.

Attempts to DEGENDER the third person singular pronoun are probably best known by the substitute *thon* (for *that one*), proposed in 1858 by Charles C. Converse. *Thon* was entered in the original edition (1913) of Funk & Wagnalls New Standard Dictionary and in Webster's New International Dictionary, Second Edition (1934). In addition, Funk & Wagnalls listed *he'er* for "he and she," *him'er* for "him or her," and *his'er* for "his or her." None of these coinages survived, despite occasional attempts at reviving them.

According to some writers, the search for a genderless pronoun to replace *he* where "he or she" is meant is unnecessary and wasteful, since we already have such a pronoun. The word is the plural form *they*. In the following passages, two authors, separated by a span of 20 years, argue for its acceptance:

The English language most needs . . . one word to mean "he or she." Nobody is likely to go as long as an hour without encountering this need. We have the plural "they" to apply to the genders indiscriminately; why must we be deprived of an equivalent singular word? "Everybody," says the average person defiantly, "should speak as they please." "Wrong!" thunder the grammarians. "The antecedent 'everybody' being singular, you must say '. . . as he or she pleases.'" So again . . . we have a Hobson's choice. *Albert H. Morehead, "English at a Loss for Words," The New York Times Magazine, Sept. 11, 1955, p 27*

In the stubborn case of the masculine generic pronoun, the candidate that seems most likely to succeed is a word already in wide use, they. Despite grammarians' efforts to restrict it to plural antecedents, *they* is already commonly used both in speech and writing as an alternative to the awkward "he or she." What critics of this usage seem not to know, or decline to acknowledge, is that *they* and its inflected forms have been used for centuries by reputable writers from Shakespeare ("Everyone to rest themselves") to Shaw ("It's enough to drive anyone out of their senses") to Scott Fitzgerald ("Nobody likes a mind quicker than their own"). *Casey Miller and Kate Swift, Words and Women, 1976, p 135*

hes·i·fla·tion (,hez ə'flei ʃən), *n. Economics.* a condition of halting, spasmodic growth accompanied by high inflation.

During 1977 the world economy suffered through sporadic periods of four different types of economic conditions: stagflation (slowing "real" growth and accelerating inflation), hesiflation (a stuttering economic growth pattern combined with strong inflationary pressures), disinflation (a selective slowing down but not elimination of inflation), and deflation (sharp price declines in certain economic sectors). *Robert H. Trigg, "Stock Exchanges," Britannica Book of the Year 1978, p 644*

[1978, from *hesit*ation + *inflation*] Compare BOTTLENECK INFLATION, SLUMPFLATION.

het·er·o·fil ('het ər ə fil), *adj. British.* (of a synthetic fiber or fabric, especially nylon) composed of more than one type of filament to reduce static electricity, improve resistance, etc.

A British fibre producer announced plans to make textiles by the spun-bonded process, using heterofil fibres of his own invention. *Peter Lennox-Kerr, "Industrial Review: Textiles and Fibres," Britannica Book of the Year 1974, p 377*

[1968, from *hetero-* other, different + *fil*ament]

heteronuclear RNA, a form of ribonucleic acid (RNA) found in the nucleus of mammalian cells.

In recent years, it has become apparent that in mammalian cells the appearance of messenger RNA is preceded by the synthesis of a "giant" species of RNA, called heteronuclear RNA (or HnRNA), which is confined to the nucleus. The role of HnRNA is still nuclear; it may be concerned with events taking place strictly within the nucleus, or it may be the precursor of messenger RNA (or it may be both). *Eugene Goldwasser, "The Making of a Red Blood Cell," New Scientist, June 8, 1972, p 560*

[1971]

hexadecimal, *adj.* using the decimal number 16 or its equivalent as a base, especially in computer arithmetic systems.

The hexadecimal numeral system uses the base 16, as contrasted with the base 10 of the decimal system and base 2 of the binary system. *R. Clay Sprowl, "Computers," Encyclopedia Science Supplement (Grolier) 1971, p 143*

[1968, from *hexa-* six + *decimal*]

hex·os·a·min·i·dase (₁hek sə sə'min ə₁deis), *n.* either one of a pair of enzymes, a deficiency of which causes various degenerative diseases of the central nervous system.

The Baltimore program owes its origin to several recent scientific discoveries in the field of molecular biology. One was the identification of the enzyme hexosaminidase-A, the lack of which causes Tay-Sachs disease. *"Medicine: Genetics for the Community," Time, Sept. 13, 1971, p 40*

[1969, from *hexosamine* an amine derivative of a hexose + *-id* related to + *-ase* enzyme]

Higgs meson, a hypothetical meson (highly unstable subnuclear particle) with large mass and zero spin, whose existence is predicted by the gauge theory.

Higgs mesons, an exotic class of new particles as massive as atomic nuclei, will be the physics of the next decade. . . . The role of the Higgs mesons has been played down—except at a highly abstract level. For although in theory they orchestrate the symmetry break-up Higgs mesons are not easily seen. They are likely to be very heavy (7 to 100 GeV) and will interact only weakly with ordinary matter. *Robert Walgate, "Weinberg Plugs Higgs Mesons," New Scientist, Feb. 17, 1977, p 381*

[1974, named after the British physicist Peter Higgs, who first proposed it]

high-level, *adj.* intensely radioactive.

The AEC has 80 million gallons of liquid waste at their defence establishments in Hanford, Washington; Idaho Falls, Idaho; and Savannah River, Georgia. The waste is temporarily in ground-level tanks but the AEC hopes to store the high-level waste in geological formations, other than salt, which are located directly beneath the establishments. *Gerald Wick, "A Salty Graveyard for Nuclear Waste," New Scientist, March 16, 1972, p 589*

[1971] Compare LOW-LEVEL.

high-level language, a computer programming language which employs terms and grammar often found in the vocabulary of the user.

A variety of computer languages enable the computer and the user to "communicate" with each other. The most popular high-level language for home-computer use is BASIC (an acronym for Beginners All-purpose Symbolic Instruction Code). Although not the most powerful language, its English instructions are relatively simple to master. *Arthur P. Salsberg, "Computers and Electronics," 1978 Collier's Encyclopedia Year Book (1977), p 205*

[1970]

high-pressure nervous syndrome, a condition of nausea, dizziness, and tremors often experienced by deep-sea divers, thought to be caused by the effects of respiration of a helium-oxygen mixture under high pressure.

Commercial divers can now descend to 1,000 feet by breathing a helium-oxygen mixture, but using this mixture also exposes them to the high-pressure nervous syndrome, characterized by mental deficits and trembling hands. Adding nitrogen to this breathing mixture can reduce the dangers of the syndrome. *"Biomedicine: Progress in Underwater Medicine," Science News, Nov. 6, 1976, p 296*

[1973] Also called HELIUM SHAKES.

high-rise, *adj.* raised up; elevated.

High-rise shoes run the gamut of style, color and height. *"Modern Living: The Elevated Look," Time, Aug. 21, 1972, p 46*

"High-rise" handlebars, which force a small child to steer with elbows at chinlevel, and the long, narrow "banana" seats, which invite additional passengers, are major contributors to instability—and may cause additional accidents. *The Reader's Digest, Aug. 1974, p 38*

[1965, extended from the sense of "tall" (apartment house)]

high-tech ('hai'tek), *n.* a style of design or interior decoration that uses objects and articles normally found in factories, warehouses, restaurant kitchens, etc., or that imitates the stark functionalism of such equipment.

High-tech, in case you haven't heard, is the tag line for a home furnishings trend that's catching on fast. It's an interior design style that uses utilitarian industrial equipment and materials, out of context, as home furnishings. *Madeline Rogers, "The Nuts and Bolts of High-Tech," Daily News (New York), Feb. 11, 1979, p 8*

Attributive use.

A cultural and administration center in construction now by Vasconi and Pencreac's is a far more sophisticated building, but its version of the current "high-tech" vogue of mechanical effects, with its brightly colored metal panels, has little to do with anything else around it. *Ada Louise*

high-technology

Huxtable, "Cold Comfort: The New French Towns," The New York Times Magazine, Nov. 19, 1978, p 168

[1978, coined by Joan Kron and Suzanne Slesin, American interior decorators, from high-style technology]

high-technology, *adj.* of or relating to advanced, highly specialized, and sophisticated technology.

High-technology goods such as computers, aircraft and electronics comprise the most vital part of the U.S. export mix. *"A Crushing New Money Crisis," Newsweek, Feb. 19, 1973, p 61*

A five-year study by the Commerce Department of six "mature" corporations (such as General Motors and Bethlehem Steel), five "innovative" companies (including Polaroid and IBM) and five "young high-technology" firms (among them, Marion Labs and Digital Equipment) turned up some telling figures. *"The Innovation Recession," Time, Oct. 2, 1978, p 63*

—*n.* Usually, **high technology.** advanced, highly specialized, and sophisticated technology, involving extensive research and development.

Professor Jewkes went on to argue that the only thing that is "high" about high technology is the level of risk involved. High technology is technology that private companies will not finance because they cannot see a reasonable return on their investment. *"Technology: High Risk Research," Nature, Nov. 10, 1972, p 66*

[1967] Compare LOW-TECHNOLOGY.

Hilbert space, *Mathematics.* a space with an infinite number of dimensions generalized from ordinary or Euclidean space.

A special kind of Banach space called Hilbert space had the property that numerous splittings of a desirable kind existed. *Irving Kaplansky, "Mathematics," Britannica Book of the Year 1972, p 447*

[1964, named for David *Hilbert*, 1862-1943, a German mathematician]

him/her, *Especially U.S.* him or her (used as the objective case of HE/SHE to indicate common gender).

I could not help children if I did not believe that every child is as positive as his/her unique life situation allows him/her to be. *Annette Covino, Great Neck, L.I., N.Y., "The 'All of You'," in a Letter to the Editor, The New York Times, Oct. 17, 1977, p 28*

[1977]

hip-shooting, *adj. U.S.* haphazard, reckless, or impulsive.

"Structuralism" is an umbrella-word if ever there was one, and Dr. Martin makes it cover a number of dim definitions. Under the umbrella he delivers a great many hip-shooting generalizations about American culture, America today, the incompatibility between American and Christian directions, etc. *Walter Arnold, Review of "Three Popes and the Cardinal" by Malachi Martin, Saturday Review, April 8, 1972, p 61*

[1968, from the phrase *shoot from the hip* (figurative use) act or speak recklessly or impulsively]

his/her, *Especially U.S.* his or her (used as the possessive form of HE/SHE to indicate common gender).

... the author's suggestions regarding what needs to be researched about est, for example, effects on the trainee's sense of responsibility, his/her freedom from resentment,

240

"righteousness" and domination, and his/her flexibility in points of view. *Morris B. Parloff, "Books: How Werner Got It," Psychology Today, Nov. 1978, p 147*

[1977]

Hispanic, *n. U.S.* a Spanish-speaking person of Latin-American origin or descent, living in the United States.

The 68-person unit includes twelve blacks, twelve Hispanics, and two women; all of them . . . can be called instantly when a hostage action develops. *"The Hostage Squad," Newsweek, June 25, 1974, p 90*

[1972, noun use of the adjective]

Hispano, *adj., n.* another name for HISPANIC.

About 15 per cent of Denver's students are black and another 20 per cent are Hispano (the local term for those with Latin-American roots). Most of the blacks live in central or northwestern Denver. The Hispanos are also concentrated in a few areas. *Christopher Jencks, "Busing—The Supreme Court Goes North," The New York Times Magazine, Nov. 19, 1972, p 41*

[1972, short for *Hispano-American* (1900), originally applied to the descendants of Spaniards living in the southwestern U.S.; later (1960's) extended to include Mexican-Americans of the same area]

his·ti·di·ne·mi·a (ˌhis tə di'ni: mi: ə), *n.* a hereditary disorder associated with a high level of the amino acid histidine in the blood and characterized by lowered growth rate and increased susceptibility to infection.

In humans, physicians disagree as to the effect of the biochemical abnormality. At first it appeared to be associated with mental retardation and speech defects, but now many human geneticists believe histidinemia produces no demonstrable effect on the nervous system. *Science News, Feb. 5, 1977, p 86*

[1967, from *histidine* (coined as German *Histidin* in 1896, from Greek *histíon* tissue, web) + *-emia* blood condition (from Greek *haima* blood)]

his·to·com·pat·i·bil·i·ty antigen (ˌhis tou kəm,pæt-ə'bil ə ti:), any of various proteins in the blood that stimulate rejection of foreign tissue, used as markers to determine genetic compatibility between different tissues for a successful graft or transplant.

At the root of the rejection problem in transplantation surgery are the histocompatibility antigens, the cellular markers which label the grafted tissue as foreign and lead to its attack by the host's immunological defence mechanism. *"Fishing for the Molecules of Rejection," New Scientist and Science Journal, June 24, 1971, p 733*

[1969, from *histo-* tissue (from Greek *histós* web) + *compatibility*] Compare HLA. See also H-Y ANTIGEN.

His·to·sol ('his tə,sɔ:l), *n.* (in U.S. soil taxonomy) any of a group of wet soils consisting mainly of organic matter such as forest litter and plant residues.

Most of the soils formerly called Intrazonal are included in the orders of Vertisols, Inceptisols, and Histosols. *Guy D. Smith, "Zonality of Soil," McGraw-Hill Encyclopedia of Science and Technology, 1971, vol. 12, p 489*

[1971, from *histo-* tissue (from Greek *histós* web) + *-sol* (from Latin *solum* soil)] Compare ALFISOL, ARI-

DISOL, ENTISOL, MOLLISOL, OXISOL, SPODOSOL, ULTISOL.

hit[1], *n. Underworld Slang.* a planned murder, especially one carried out by a mobster.

Indeed, mob sources have been saying that Nunziata's death was a "hit," ordered by the Gambinos because they feared the detective might talk about the heroin thefts. *"Crime: Missing Evidence," Time, Jan. 1, 1973, p 92*

"I've done some hits — you know, a contract. It was right after I got out of prison, and I needed some bread." *James Willwerth, "Portrait of a Mugger," Harper's, Nov. 1974, p 92*

[1963, from the slang verb meaning to kill (1950's)]

hit[2], *n.* a successful comparison or matching of two items of data in a computer.

The computer responds with a postings count (a tally of the number of items in the data-base "hits" which match the search statement) and a list of these is held in a temporary store and assigned a number by which it can be identified for printing or for incorporation in a subsequent search statement. *David Magrill, "Information at the Touch of a Button," New Scientist, Jan. 12, 1978, p 77*

[1970, extended from the sense of "a successful stroke" (OED 1815)]

hit list, *Slang.* **1** a list of persons to be killed.

At the end of June, the Red Brigades issued a "hit list" of thirty prominent anti-Communist journalists and editors. *Michael A. Ledeen, "The Fourth Estate: Cultural Terrorism," Harper's, Sept. 1977, p 99*

ZANU, one of two Rhodesian nationalist guerrilla organisations, meanwhile issued a "hit list" of supporters of the interim Government, describing them as "priority military targets." *The Manchester Guardian Weekly, Nov. 26, 1978, p 7*

2 a list of persons or projects to be removed or eliminated.

A particular sore point was Carter's original "hit list" of 32 water projects. The President compromised and restored 14 of the originally doomed projects. *"Gunfight at the Capitol Hill Corral," Time, June 6, 1977, p 11*

One top mandarin is convinced that the Tories are keeping a "hit list" of Liberal civil servants who would be dumped. *Robert Lewis, "Winning by Default," Maclean's, Feb. 21, 1977, p 29*

[1976; see HIT[1]] Compare ENEMIES LIST.

hit man, 1 *Underworld Slang.* a man paid to murder; a hired killer.

A mobster hit man named Joseph Rodriguez was spilling detail after gory detail about the 1972 slaying of Mafia Boss Emmanuel ("Nello") Cammarate. *"Holiday for Homicide," Time, May 31, 1976, p 46*

In his confession to the FBI, Townley has named six Cubans he recruited as hitmen against Letelier. Three of them have been arrested in the past two months. Two more are on the run from the FBI. *Michael Cockerell, "Chile's Watergate," The Listener, June 22, 1978, p 791*

2 *Transferred sense.*

Every [ice hockey] team employs swashbuckling "hit men" and "enforcers." Chicago Black Hawk defenseman Keith Magnuson has taken boxing lessons from a former world bantamweight champion. *Bill Surface, The Reader's Digest, March 1976, p 34*

[1970; see HIT[1]]

hit squad or **hit team, 1** a group of hit men.

Dellacroce dispatched hit teams of his own toward Danbury. . . . Belatedly, Morris Kuznesof, chief federal probation officer in Manhattan, wrote Danbury Warden Raymond Nelson that he had received information "from a highly reliable source that an attempt to murder Mr. Galante will be made at your institution." *Time, Nov. 13, 1978, p 37*

2 a group or unit of terrorists.

They [the German Baader-Meinhof gang] are a self-appointed hit squad for a revolution none of them have yet been able to articulate. Whatever the jargon of their ransom notes, they . . . horrify most older people on the left here, who blame them, reasonably, for the backlash the entire left endures after each gloating act of third-generation violence. *Jane Kramer, "A Reporter in Europe: Hamburg," The New Yorker, March 20, 1978, p 44*

[1976; see HIT[1]]

hit woman, *Underworld Slang.* a woman paid to murder.

Blanche Wright, accused 'hit' woman. *Picture legend in the Reporter Dispatch (White Plains, N.Y.), Feb. 14, 1980, p A14*

[1980]

hive-off, *n. British.* the formation of a new or subsidiary company by distribution of stocks. The equivalent U.S. term is *spin-off.*

To involve governments in the collaboration between companies or changes in industrial structure (mergers, take-overs, "hive-offs," etc.), adding the complexities of diplomacy and international financing to the normal burdens of running the affairs of large companies. *Ieuan Maddock, "Can Science-Based Companies Survive?" New Scientist, Sept. 6, 1973, p 566*

[1965, from the verb phrase *hive off* to separate or remove from a larger unit]

HLA or **HL-A,** abbreviation of *human leucocyte antigen* or *histocompatibility locus antigen,* histocompatibility antigens in white blood cells of humans.

Compatibility between donor and recipient, generally highest among relatives, is gauged according to similarities in two individuals' immune systems as measured in the H-LA . . . system. *Betty Corday, Science News, March 21, 1970, p 297*

The individuality of tissue from different human beings is asserted primarily by the protein products of genes at four loci on the short arm of chromosome No. 6; the major histocompatibility complex, designated *HLA.* Genes *A, B* and *C* code for antigens inserted in the cell membrane, and gene *D* is apparently involved in the manufacture of antibodies. *Scientific American, Jan. 1978, p 64*

[1967]

HMO, abbreviation of HEALTH MAINTENANCE ORGANIZATION.

The best (and biggest) of the HMOs take care of their members with 65 percent less hospitalization than the national average (even excluding the chronically ill): HMO subscribers and their families don't go into the hospital as often and don't stay there as long when they do. Yet, by and large, they are satisfied: HMOs have grown steadily and now service over six million people, a number equal to the entire population of Sweden. *Robert Claiborne, "The Great Health Care Rip-Off," Saturday Review, Jan. 7, 1978, p 11*

[1973]

HnRNA, abbreviation of HETERONUCLEAR RNA.

Investigators of this critical process have identified markers for following the parts of the HnRNA that are degraded, as well as markers for following the parts converted to m-RNA. This work has helped clarify the role of the strange polyadenylic acid (poly-A) sequences, 200 units long, that are added at the end of the HnRNA molecules before m-RNA is produced. *Stephen N. Kreitzman, "Biochemistry," The Americana Annual 1975, p 126*

[1971]

ho (hɔ:), *n. U.S. Slang.* a prostitute.

Much of the Milners' evidence runs counter to prevalent beliefs, like the one that pimps are sinister Svengalis who entice innocents into prostitution by stringing them out on heroin or other hard drugs. "The truth is," say the Milners, "that only a few of the hos are masochists or junkies." *Arthur Cooper, Review of "Black Players: The Secret World of Black Pimps" by Christina and Richard Milner, Newsweek, Jan. 15, 1973, p 70*

[1971, alteration (influenced by Black English pronunciation) of *whore*]

hoc tap ('hɑk 'tɑp), the Vietnamese term for RE-EDUCATION.

But "rehabilitation" does not involve only those who served under the former regime. Everyone is subjected to "hoc tap," a kind of retraining course (without surveillance or travel away from home) that comprises talks and discussions on revolutionary policies and on Vietnam's recent history. *Hugues Tertrais, "Reconstruction in Vietnam: Back to the Land," The Manchester Guardian Weekly (Le Monde section), Feb. 8, 1976, p 13*

[1976, from Vietnamese]

hog, *n. U.S. Slang.* **1** a motorcycle, especially a large one.

A hog, of course, is a motorcycle, and the Angels have long been first among riders of the open road. *"Hell's Angels 4, Breed 1," Time, March 22, 1971, p 10*

2 a large automobile.

His name was Teddy Johnson but they called him 'Eldorado' because that was the kind of hog he drove. He was involved in numbers and other hustles and used the Post Office job for a front. *James Alan McPherson, "The Story of a Scar," The Atlantic, Dec. 1973, p 80*

[1967, probably so called from its *hogging* the road]

hoi·sin sauce ('hɔi'sin), a thick dark-red sauce made with soy beans, garlic, and various spices, used in Chinese cooking.

Most large towns will have one Chinese grocery store (those restaurants have to get their stuff somewhere) and you can find hoisin sauce, oyster sauce, dried mushrooms, and suddenly you can cook just about any dish you've ever eaten in your local Chinese restaurant, and a good many others besides. *Ray Smith, "Finding Yourself," Maclean's, Sept. 1973, p 54*

[1965, from Chinese (Canton)]

hold, *n.* **on hold,** *U.S.* **1** on a telephone connection held open automatically until someone is available to take the call.

Phone calls sometimes come in from Florida, Nova Scotia, and Missouri; the callers may be put on hold for an hour or more. They do not seem to mind. *James Stevenson, The New Yorker, Aug. 14, 1978, p 39*

2 *Figurative use.* in a suspended state; put off; delayed.

"A massive reorganization of our elevator operation, based on a two-year engineering study, has been 'on hold' for over a year pending the results of the Department of Investigation-Housing Authority probe," Mr. Christian said. *Edward Ranzal, The New York Times, Aug. 25, 1976, p 33*

[1975]

hold-harmless, *adj. U.S.* relating to or designating a part of a government aid program that spares the recipient group or locality from further harm or deterioration, usually by providing aid equal to or above that of a specified year.

Pending disputes involve a so-called "hold-harmless" provision, under which the Federal Government is to absorb program costs above the amount paid by state and local governments during 1972 in the former welfare grants for the aged, blind and disabled poor. *"New York is One of 31 States Disputing U.S. on Aid to Poor," The New York Times, April 11, 1976, p 38*

[1976, from the legal phrase *hold harmless* to make free from loss or liability, originally (OED 1418) *save harmless*]

holding pattern, a condition in which no progress is made; a static or stationary situation.

Analysts noted that prices in recent sessions have been in a "holding pattern" pending fresh news developments. *Alexander R. Hammer, "Stocks Edge Up in Amex Trading," The New York Times, March 23, 1976, p 48*

While most nonprofit arts organizations manage to stay in business, recent studies for the National Endowment for the Arts (NEA) suggest that the spiral of labor and other costs has forced them into a "holding pattern." *Peter P. Jacobi, "The Money Crunch in the Arts," The 1978 World Book Year Book, p 132*

[1970, figurative sense of the term meaning a circular pattern flown by aircraft waiting to be cleared for landing]

-hol·ic (-'hɔːl ik), a variant of -AHOLIC, as in:

carboholic [from *carbohydrate* + -*holic*]: To remedy the problem, I have devised a special diet for carboholics (detailed in my book. Dr. Solomon's Easy No-Risk Diet), which balances the proportion of carbohydrates, protein and fats. *Neil Solomon, "The Carboholics," New York Post, Dec. 29, 1976, p 30*

chocoholic [from *chocolate* + -*holic*]: Mrs. Marcus, a self-professed chocoholic, has left no mint patty unturned in her search for the ultimate chocolate experience. *Frank J. Prial, "Secrets of a Chocoholic," The New York Times, May 16, 1979, p C1*

colaholic [from *cola* + -*holic*]: The "colaholics" reported a strong craving for their favorite drink and complained that without it, they could not perform as well when studying and taking exams. *Mark Bricklin, Prevention, July 1974, p 87*

computerholic: There are clearly more "computerholics" in Britain than many in the business ever imagined. *Nicholas Valéry, New Scientist, May 19, 1977, p 405*

crediholic [from *credit* + -*holic*]: Only a handful are true "crediholics"—people who get some kind of excitement about always being in debt and in a bind about paying bills. Most simply yield to the temptation to overspend. *"Merchants of Debt," Time, Feb. 28, 1977, p 39*

mariholic [from *marijuana*+*-holic*]: So — just like the speed freaks, alcoholics, mariholics and junkies — people using liquid diets against a virus or diarrhea, others undergoing diuretic therapy, and those who just prefer drinking to eating, *all* are raising their own B vitamin requirements. *Rich Wentzler, The Vitamin Book, 1978, p 28*

petroholic: It is, of course, the craving for crude that keeps the game going. Petroholic economies everywhere remain excessively hooked on Demon Oil. *Time, May 7, 1979, p 70*

[1972]

hollow foot, a foot with an abnormally high longitudinal arch.

Countless more suffered chronic maladies ranging from the annoying, like athlete's foot and jock itch, to the exotic and painful, like glass arm (loss of throwing ability from damaged tendons, common in baseball players), hollow foot (a strained instep found in ballet dancers) and web split (splitting of skin between the fingers). *"Medicine: How Sports Hurt," Newsweek, April 2, 1973, p 65*

[1973] Compare SURFER'S KNOB, TENNIS TOE. See also SPORTS MEDICINE.

hol·on ('hal an), *n. Philosophy.* any whole which is a part of a larger whole; a distinct entity.

By remembering the dynamic status of these "holons" — at one moment the nodes from which other branches spring, at another the boughs that lead to the main trunk — the scientist will overcome the atomistic fallacy: the erroneous image of complex units as mere composites of small, divisible parts. *George Steiner, "Books," The New Yorker, March 6, 1971, p 107*

Things of all kinds are made of holons — things like hearts and livers, where people are concerned — which have a natural tendency towards autonomy but also a tendency towards integration. But people are also holons, and they are in part impelled by the 'integrative tendency', which accounts for ESP, clairvoyance, psychokinesis and the other phenomena by which Arthur Koestler is fascinated. *John Maddox, "Books: Holons," Review of "The Roots of Coincidence" by Arthur Koestler, The Listener, Feb. 10, 1972, p 187*

[1970, coined by the Hungarian-born British author Arthur Koestler, born 1905, from Greek *hólos, hólon* whole]

home-beat, *n. British.* a policeman's beat in or near the area in which he lives.

PC Prendergast's home-beat is at the more commercial end of Notting Hill, with boarding houses and small and large hotels. *Peter Evans, " 'Local' Policemen Help to Ease Notting Hill's Tensions," The Times (London), July 31, 1972, p 3*

[1971]

home computer, a microcomputer for home use, usually consisting of a cassette tape recorder that transfers data from cassette programs to the microprocessor and a video screen that displays the desired information.

A new generation of home computers is beginning to emerge. With these, you take them home, plug them in, and begin using them. Costs vary widely and there is a lot of market maneuvering. *William J. Hawkins, "New Home Computers," Encyclopedia Science Supplement (Grolier) 1979 (1978), p 113*

Since 1975, when home computers made their debut, some 200,000 have been sold, despite a serious dearth of programs. *Madeline Rogers, "You" section, Daily News (New York), Feb. 4, 1979, p 3*

[1977] Compare PERSONAL COMPUTER.

homeland, *n.* any of various regions of southern Africa set aside by the Republic of South Africa as separate tribal Bantu states.

The second of South Africa's nine tribal homelands to be granted "independence," Bophutha Tswana (literally meaning "that which binds the Tswana") is not recognized by any country in the world except South Africa and another homeland, Transkei, which became independent last year. *"South Africa: The Birth of Bophutha Tswana," Time, Dec. 19, 1977, p 40*

[1963, extended from the original sense (OED 1670) "one's native land"] Compare TOWNSHIP.

▶ The usual name for such regions or states during the 1950's and 1960's was *Bantustan* (from *Bantu* + *-stan*, as in *Baluchistan, Pakistan, Afghanistan*). During the 1970's *homeland* replaced Bantustan, which seemed to convey a racial tone.

home-port, *v.t.* to establish a port for (part of a naval fleet) in a location near its theater of operations.

Junta leaders, who have given up their American limousines in favor of Mercedes-Benzes, have blocked the U.S. Navy's plans to home-port a Sixth Fleet aircraft carrier in Greece. *Time, April 19, 1974, p 41*

Both vessels will be home-ported at Lahaina and according to Drew, will operate in waters south of Hawaii with their catches slated for export and the local market. *Robert McCabe, "Maui Experiment Is First Step to Great Fishing," Honolulu Star-Bulletin, Feb. 5, 1973, p C-20*

[1972, from the noun phrase *home port*]

home-porting, *n.:* The rationale of what is called "home-porting" here [in Athens] is that this affords the Sixth Fleet essential facilities, strengthening its position as a key force on NATO's flank and also as a guardian of U.S. commitments to Israel. But Athenian comfort and culture for the wives and kiddies are not required for that. *C. L. Sulzberger, "A Navy Home Away From Home," The New York Times, Oct. 15, 1972, Sec. 4, p 15*

homesteading, *n. U.S.* short for URBAN HOMESTEADING.

The "homesteading" scheme, whereby citizens could gain title to dilapidated houses by repairing them and living in them for a minimum period, was gaining in popularity. *Hiroshi Daifuku, "Historic Preservation," Britannica Book of the Year 1975, p 363*

[1975]

homophobia, *n.* fear, dislike, or hatred of homosexuals.

The task force reached an agreement that secular society should forbid job discrimination against homosexuals and repeal laws that regulate the private sexual behavior of consenting adults. It urges the church to work against "homophobia," the fear and loathing of homosexuals. *Time, Jan. 30, 1978, p 85*

[1969, from *homo*sexual + *phobia*]

homophobic, *adj.:* Herbert Gold is a heterosexual. Although it is possible for straights to write positive articles about gays, Gold's treatment leaves something to be desired. While obviously not rabidly homophobic, his con-

243

sciousness, sensitivity and awareness are not what they could be. *Colette Holt, New Haven, in a Letter to the Editor, The New York Times Magazine, Dec. 4, 1977, p 34*

ho·mo·pol·y·nu·cle·o·tide (ˌhou məˌpal iːˈnuː kliː-əˌtaid), *n.* a substance composed of nucleotides of the same kind.

At Merck, Sharpe and Dohme a process for the preparation of homopolynucleotides has been scaled up to commercial level using immobilized polynucleotide phosphorylase covalently coupled to cellulose. *Howard H. Weetall, "Enzyme," McGraw-Hill Yearbook of Science and Technology 1974, p 176*

[1968, from *homo-* same + *polynucleotide*]

ho·mo·pol·y·pep·tide (ˌhou məˌpal iːˈpep taid), *n.* a substance composed of peptides of the same kind.

Homopolypeptides provide good model systems for various aspects of proteins. Recent advances in high polymer and solid state physics have enabled the vibrational aspects of the simpler homopolypeptides to be treated as normal—but complicated—polymers. *Leonard Finegold and Jesse L. Cude, Nature, July 7, 1972, p 38*

[1966, from *homo-* same + *polypeptide*]

honor box, *U.S.* a type of newspaper vending machine. See the quotation.

The blue-and-white newspaper-vending machines that have been multiplying on city streets as newsstands approach extinction . . . are called "honor boxes," because they open when the price of a paper is deposited, the customer being trusted to take just one. *A. H. Raskin, "A Reporter At Large: The Negotiation," The New Yorker, Jan. 22, 1979, p 56*

[1978]

hooker, *n. Slang.* **1** a hidden difficulty; catch.

With neither a colonizing past to overcome, nor an imperialistic present to dissemble, with tireless diplomats and an abundant store of selfless common sense, Canada can be trusted by nearly everyone. But—and this is the hooker—Canadian statesmen will only be effective if they speak softly while they carry their slim dispatch cases from capital to capital, from crisis to crisis. *Charles Taylor, "Quiet Hypocrisy," Maclean's, Oct. 1974, p 57*

2 an intriguing or catchy opening, as of a show or a story.

Her [Barbara Walters'] values are conventional, whether they pertain to the structure of a television program ("It should have a hooker, a teaser and a conclusion"), social intercourse . . . or society in general. *James Conaway, The New York Times Magazine, Sept. 10, 1972, p 46*

[1967 for def. 1; 1968 for def. 2]

hoot owl, *U.S.* the midnight shift in a mine, factory, or the like. *Often used attributively.*

The newer men, the trainees, can be shuttled around at will. On the hoot owl they usually end up as laborers. *Laurence Leamer, "Eccles No. 6: Working the Seam in a West Virginia Coal Mine," Harper's, Dec. 1971, p 102*

[1968, in allusion to the owl's nocturnal habits]

horizontal divestiture, the disposal of a company's holdings in operations or businesses producing products similar to its own.

Mr. Carter favors horizontal divestiture—prohibiting energy companies from owning competing forms of fuel—and

the issue seems sure to be discussed early in the year. *Steven Rattner, "Missing for Years: An Energy Policy That Encourages Self-Reliance," The New York Times, Jan. 9, 1977, Sec. 3, p 35*

[1975] Compare VERTICAL DIVESTITURE.

horizontal proliferation, increase in the number of nations that possess nuclear weapons.

"Horizontal proliferation" or sideways spread . . . is the danger that seventh, eighth, and *n*th countries will acquire the means to make bombs. *"Comment," The Manchester Guardian Weekly, Jan. 29, 1978, p 10*

It is clearly recognized by both sides that vertical proliferation and horizontal proliferation need to be attacked as mutually inseparable problems. *Vipin Chandra, Norton, Mass., in a Letter to the Editor, The New York Times, Jan. 15, 1978, Sec. 4, p 20*

[1976] Compare VERTICAL PROLIFERATION.

horsenapping, *n.* the theft of a horse, especially a racehorse.

The horsenapping at Claiborne happened in late June. Somebody cut a wire fence and made off with Fanfreluche, a mare that had been Canada's horse of the year in 1970 and had produced a colt that won the same distinction twice. *Red Smith, "Focus on Sports," The 1978 World Book Year Book, p 56*

Attributive use.

This lady has unwisely taken her eye off her $3,700 thoroughbred gelding "Prince," evidently unaware that horsenapping gangsters could get up to $5,000 for him on the Belgium-Luxembourg underground meat market. *Picture legend, High Times, Jan. 1979, p 105*

[1978, from *horse* + kid*napping*]

hospice, *n.* an institution for the care of the terminally ill.

From Britain has come the idea of the "hospice," an inpatient facility specially designed for the dying: cheerful, homelike, full of plants and families (including young children). There are about thirty such places in Britain now, but the idea has been slower to take root in the United States. The hospice in New Haven, for instance, has been in operation with a home-care program for more than two years. *Tabitha M. Powledge, "Death as an Acceptable Subject," in The New Old: Struggling for Decent Aging, edited by Ronald Gross, Beatrice Gross, and Sylvia Seidman, 1978, p 159*

[1976, extended from the older meaning (1890's) of a home for the destitute or the sick] Compare PALLIATIVE CARE UNIT. See also DEATH.

hospitality suite, a room or set of rooms in which guests of a company or organization are received and served refreshments.

NBC, with great aplomb, secured for itself two aged but air-conditioned railroad parlor cars, parked them on a spur across from the convention hall and went into business with the most elegant hospitality suite in town. *"Convention Report," TV Guide, Aug. 28, 1976, p A2*

[1965]

host, *n.* a computer used simultaneously by various operators at different terminals; multiple-access computer.

An example is the situation where a central computer—a "host" in the current jargon—wishes to communicate with a variety of different types of terminal. At present this entails not only having a separate access port for each terminal active at a given moment, but also providing special support software for each terminal type. *Timothy Johnson, "Electronic Post for Switching Data," New Scientist, May 13, 1976, p 52*

[1970, specialized sense of the term meaning one who provides lodging for guests (OED 1303)]

hot-dog, *v.i.* (of a skier, skateboarder, etc.) to perform acrobatics or stunts.

"And when I ski, I hotdog. I wouldn't recommend it for everyone, but racing no longer gives me the expression I need; I had to progress from there. Hotdogging lets me be free; I enjoy self-realization in sport." *Suzy Chaffee, quoted in Town and Country, Jan. 1975, p 57*

[1972, originally (1960's) applied to surfers]

hot-dogger, *n.:* For advanced practitioners, a whole new style of baroque skiing has developed. Known as "freestyle," "exhibition" or "hot-dog" skiing, the form emphasizes acrobatic stunts rather than downhill speed. Hotdoggers build up repertoires of twists, turns, spins and somersaults. *"Skiing: The New Lure of a Supersport," Time, Dec. 25, 1972, p 60*

hotliner, *n. Canadian.* the host of a radio or television program which broadcasts conversations with people who telephone the studio.

Al, our muckraking, scabpicking, intrepid, Icelandic but otherwise clean-living reporter, was interviewed on the spot by A. C. Grudge, the well known hotliner. *The Province (Vancouver), April 28, 1973, p 53*

The unlikely events lurched to a start last November when Vancouver radio hot-liner Ed Murphy offered to send his listeners a list of Murphy-collected government boondoggles and examples of waste. *Maclean's, Oct. 23, 1978, p 66*

[1973, from *hot line* (1966) a radio or television call-in program + *-er*]

hot rock, an underground heat reservoir without the water needed to bring its geothermal energy to the surface.

The US Department of Energy (DOE) expects to make LASI the lead agency for the country's "hot rock" geothermal programme. While the US has so far exploited only conventional hydrogeothermal resources where there is underground water available to bring the energy to the surface, the DOE estimates that there is something like a hundred times as much energy in hot dry rocks. *New Scientist, March 23, 1978, p 784*

[1975]

hot spot, any of various regions of the earth where molten material in the earth's mantle is carried upwards, heating the crust above.

The oceanic "hot spots" which may be the source of mid-Pacific volcanic islands may be several hundred km wide and may well up from mantle depths. *"Monitor: The Problem of Atmospheric Evolution," New Scientist, Nov. 29, 1973, p 607*

Scattered around the globe are more than 100 small regions of isolated volcanic activity known to geologists as hot spots. Unlike most of the world's volcanoes, they are not always found at the boundaries of the great drifting plates that make up the earth's surface; on the contrary, many of them lie deep in the interior of a plate. Most of the hot spots move only slowly, and in some cases the move-

ment of the plates past them has left trails of extinct volcanoes. The hot spots and their volcanic trails are milestones that mark the passage of the plates. *Kevin C. Burke and J. Tuzo Wilson, "Hot Spots on the Earth's Surface," Scientific American, Aug. 1976, p 46*

[1971] See PLUME.

hot tray, a tray with an electric heating element built in underneath its surface to keep food hot.

The magazine had gotten a surprisingly negative response to an ad for hot trays that ran in the sample issue (The slogan was: "Women: stand up for your right to sit down at dinner time"). *Mary Breasted, Saturday Review, July 15, 1972, p 10*

[1970]

hot tub, a large tub or vat that is electrically heated or filled with hot water, used for bathing, often in a group, as a form of relaxation or physical therapy.

He could clearly hear the burbling sounds of water in the fiber-glass and redwood hot tub that had been installed in the backyard. *Time, June 18, 1979, p 62*

How does the young modern executive unwind after work? By dipping into a swimming pool? No, the pool is yesterday's status symbol. The hot tub is the wave of the future, according to spa manufacturers and dealers across the country. *Mark Lundahl, "Hot Tubs Are Receiving Warm Welcome," Today (New York), Sept. 20, 1979, p B2*

[1973] Also called SPA.

hot tubbing: Santa Barbara has become the center of a new fad called "hot tubbing" — outdoor communal soaking at temperatures of 104 to 120 degrees. *"Life and Leisure: Rub-a-Dub-Dub," Newsweek, Aug. 20, 1973, p 50*

hot-wire, *v.t. Slang.* to start the engine of (an automobile, airplane, etc.) by short-circuiting the ignition switch.

Her David-and-Jonathan 16-year-olds hustle pool-players for money, hot-wire cars, get shot at, flunk chemistry exams. *Jean MacGibbon, "Adolescent's-eye-view of Life," The Sunday Times (London), Dec. 5, 1971, p 43*

Well, on *Columbo*, the millionaire would plot the perfect murder. He would attend a business convention in another city, secretly fly back by hot-wiring an associate's private plane, drown the girl. *"Show Business and Television: A Cop (and a Raincoat) for All Seasons," Time, Nov. 26, 1973, p 118*

[1966]

houseperson, *n.* a person who manages a household.

That evening, on TV, she [Margaret Thatcher] looked a winner: her *sang froid*, hairdo, and clarity of diction perfect, but her well-known persona of a chilly suburban houseperson infused with a new warmth, real or assumed. *"London Diary," New Statesman, Feb. 7, 1975, p 172*

One may empathize with the plight of the Mesa Verde houseperson by getting down on hands and knees to try the back-straining job of grinding a few dried red, blue and yellow corn kernels in a stone mortar. *R. V. Denenberg, The New York Times, Feb. 22, 1976, Sec. 10, p 7*

[1975, used to replace *housewife* or *househusband*] See -PERSON.

house-sit, *v.i. Especially U.S.* to live in and take care of a house while the regular occupants are away.

If you want to house-sit in a remote vacation home for a year or so, pick the area where you want to go, contact local real estate agents who may know of these homes, and write letters of inquiry to resort directors. *Robert Coram, "To the House-Sitter, a Contented Owner Means a Free Vacation," The New York Times, Dec. 10, 1978, p 14*

[1977, back formation from *house-sitter* (1973), patterned on *baby-sitter*]

house-sitter, *n.: Housesitters, NY Suburbs, Summer.* Suburban home with nice garden and cat looking for reliable "au pair" caretakers during owner's absence from July through mid-September. *Classified Ads: Rentals, The New York Review of Books, March 4, 1976, p 39*

hou·tie ('hou ti:), *n.* a derogatory term used in Zimbabwe (Rhodesia) to refer to a black African.

Then, with perhaps an unfortunate turn of phrase, he added: "The catchword of the battalion is 'We just want to slay houties.'" Afterwards Colonel Rich explained to foreign correspondents that the term "houtie" meant Africans. It is in fact an Afrikaans word meaning "wooden head" and has tended to replace "kaffir" and "munt" as a derogatory term for blacks. *Michael Knipe, "Rhodesian Lads March Out to War," The Times (London), May 15, 1976, p 4*

[1976, shortened from Afrikaans *houtkop*, literally, wooden head] Compare AF. See also TERR.

hoverbed, *n.* a device for supporting a person with burnt or ulcerated skin on a cushion of air.

The block will provide all in-patient services needed to complete the accident and emergency centre next door. It will have a regional burns unit, including two revolutionary "hoverbeds" for badly burned patients. *Belfast Telegraph, Feb. 2, 1973, p 3*

[1967, from *hover-* (as in *hovercraft*, 1959) + *bed*]

hovertrailer, *n.* an air cushion vehicle for carrying heavy loads over a marsh, bog, mudflats, plowland, and the like.

Two hovertrailers linked side by side have been used to transport a 27-ton tracked piledriver over marshy ground along the line of an electricity transmission line in Holland. *"Hovertrailers Rescue Bellyflops," New Scientist, June 21, 1973, p 756*

[1967, from *hover-* (as in *hovercraft*, 1959) + *trailer*]

HTGR, abbreviation of *high temperature gas-cooled reactor* (a nuclear power reactor using uranium and thorium as fuel, graphite as moderator, and helium as coolant).

With a total absence of combustion products the HTGR is certainly the most environmentally attractive source of energy available today. *Douglas J. Holloway, Encinitas, Calif., in a Letter to the Editor, Science News, Nov. 17, 1973, p 307*

[1968] Compare HTR.

HTR, abbreviation of *high temperature reactor* (a nuclear reactor in which the temperature is high enough to generate mechanical power).

Both in Germany and the United States, there is great interest in the HTR system as the medium term for generation. *John Davies, "Parliament, August 8, 1972: Major Nuclear Reactor Programme," The Times (London), Aug. 9, 1972, p 6*

[1967]

huay·co ('wai kou), *n.* a large landslide common in Peru.

Although a mud- and earthslide (called *huayco*) covered Yungay and a nearby village beneath tons of debris and took thousands of lives, the principal cause of the high death toll was strong earth vibration that led to the collapse of innumerable poorly designed structures. *Leonard M. Murphy, "Seismology," Britannica Book of the Year 1971, p 661*

[1970, from American Spanish, from Quechua]

Hugo, *n.* an annual award for the year's best work in science fiction.

The yearly awards for excellence in science fiction are called Hugos. . . . With greater justice, they might be called Herberts, in recognition of Herbert George Wells. *Jack Williamson, "H. G. Wells: The Man Who Discovered Tomorrow," Saturday Review, Jan. 1, 1972, p 14*

[1967, named for *Hugo* Gernsback, 1884-1967, American editor, publisher and inventor, who founded the first science-fiction magazine, *Amazing Stories*, in 1926]

humanistic psychology, a branch of psychology dealing with the emotions, needs, and potential development of the normal individual.

Although [Abraham H.] Maslow later became president of the American Psychological Association, he saw his own humanistic psychology as a "third-force" alternative to strict Freudianism and its off-shoots, which ruled the psychoanalytic profession, and to the behavioristic psychology that had become dominant in most university psychology departments. *Calvin Tomkins, The New Yorker, Jan. 5, 1976, p 42*

[1971]

humanistic psychologist: No one could have mistaken the Squaw Valley meeting of the humanistic psychologists for an academic conference. *Leo Litwak, The New York Times Magazine, Dec. 17, 1972, p 19*

human rights. ▶ This 200-year-old phrase rose to new prominence in 1976 as the expression of a major political policy of the American government. As a theme of his inaugural address and in addressing the United Nations in 1977, President Jimmy Carter emphasized that body's responsibility to promote human rights throughout the world:

All the signatories of the UN Charter have pledged themselves to observe and to respect basic human rights. Thus, no member of the United Nations can claim that mistreatment of its citizens is solely its own business.

By campaigning for human rights the President temporarily made the issue a part of American foreign policy.

The Administration's vigorous espousal of human rights was implemented in its open verbal support of dissidents struggling for basic freedoms and in the action of selectively curtailing aid to countries whose governments violated rights and freedoms of its citizens. These efforts had little impact on the governments they were meant to influence. Instead with the LINKAGE of the human-rights issue to negotiations with the Soviet Union (see BASKET, SALT II), the two countries' policy of DÉTENTE appeared to be endangered. Yet American insistence on raising the issue of human rights gave prestige and impetus to the work of such groups as AMNESTY INTERNA-

TIONAL and probably encouraged the formation of dissident movements such as CHARTER 77.

The term *human rights* has been in the English language since the French Revolution, perhaps first used by Thomas Paine, in his *Rights of Man* (1791), where he translated the French *droits de l'homme* as "human rights." Considered self-evident in meaning, it was not defined in dictionaries until the late 1970's.

The phrase "human rights" can seldom if ever have been so ragingly fashionable as it is today. The anniversary of the Crucifixion is perhaps a good moment to stop and ask ourselves what human rights are and where they come from. The most authoritative text on the subject is presumably the Universal Declaration of Human Rights, to which the great majority of member-states of the United Nations have formally subscribed, even though only a small minority of them come anywhere near applying it in practice. *"Human Rights and Wrongs," The Times (London), April 9, 1977, p 13*

In Belgrade, the diplomats of the European nations were talking about "human rights"—a concept so different in the Communist states that it clearly could not be reconciled with the theories of individual rights in the West. *The New York Times, March 5, 1978, Sec. 4, p 19*

human sciences, the formalized studies or sciences that deal with the activities of human beings, such as anthropology, language, literature, psychology, religion, and sociology.

The magisterium's role is to express "what is true," [Yves] Congar emphasized, while today's theologian is expected to chart new modes of defining those truths. "The theologian must be in constant contact with human sciences, with latest developments in all kinds of thought ..." *"Taming the Theologians," Time, Nov. 13, 1972, p NY13*

Acquisition of language by humans is among the most recalcitrant problems in human sciences. *"Monitor: What About the Third R?" New Scientist, Nov. 22, 1973, p 526*

[1971]

hu·mint or **HUMINT** ('hyu: mint), *n.* the gathering of secret intelligence by the use of spies (as opposed to electronic surveillance, etc.)

Among the more practiced perpetrators of mayhem on the English language are members of the US intelligence community. Already they have flattened the phrase communications intelligence (the fruits of electronic surveillance or code breaking) into "comint" and reshaped human intelligence (information from spies) into "humint." *Time, July 25, 1977, p 30*

[1977, acronym for *human intelligence*] Compare ELINT, SIGINT.

hu·mon·gous (hyu:'maŋ gəs), *adj. U.S. Slang.* extremely large or great; colossal; tremendous.

Her normal speaking voice has a light Southern accent. She uses expressions like "the whole megillah" (meaning the whole long story) and "humongous" (meaning huger than huge and more tremendous than tremendous). *"The Talk of the Town," The New Yorker, Aug. 16, 1976, p 26*

The surge of slang is, in a word, humongous. Go for it! *Lynn Ludlow, "Youth Lingo: Facing Up to a Change," San Francisco Sunday Examiner & Chronicle, April 1, 1979, p 12*

[1976, apparently a fanciful coinage from *huge* and *monstrous*]

180-degree or **hundred-and-eighty-degree,** *adj.* complete; hundred-percent.

Still, as one diplomat in Paris noted, "The Chinese now are open and forthcoming; the slogans, polemics and jargon have disappeared from their conversation. It's a 180-degree change from the old days." *"China's Marco Polo Act in Europe," Newsweek, Jan. 22, 1973, p 31*

Taft, as you'll recall, was a stick-in-the-mud on most economic and social issues, but ... midway in his senatorial career he did a hundred-and-eighty-degree turnabout on this issue, and became a forceful advocate of federal aid to education. *"The Talk of the Town," The New Yorker, Feb. 3, 1975, p 21*

[1972, figurative use of the measurement of a straight angle, one equal to a complete turnabout or the opposite side of a circle or arc]
► As an adverb in the sense of "completely" the form *180 degrees* is also sometimes used, as in the following quotation:

I mean, those glancing insights, those adolescent knight-errantries, aren't they old news? Haven't our tastes altered 180 degrees? *Stefan Kanfer, "Holden [Caulfield] Today: Still in the Rye," Time, Feb. 7, 1972, p 50*

hunter-killer satellite, an artificial satellite designed to search out and destroy enemy satellites.

Last year's resumption of Soviet tests of a hunter-killer satellite in earth orbit has moved the United States to draw up its own plans to wage war in space. *Thomas O'Toole, "U.S. Ready for War in Space," The Manchester Guardian Weekly (The Washington Post section), Jan. 23, 1977, p 16*

There are a couple of hundred (overtrained) blue-eyed boys in Los Alamos, New Mexico, working on hunter-killer satellites and directed energy weapons like satellite-launched high-energy lasers. *Michael Thomas, Rolling Stone, Jan. 11, 1979, p 78*

[1976, extended from the older (1951) meaning of *hunter-killer* designed for finding and destroying enemy submarines] Also called KILLER SATELLITE, SATELLITE KILLER. See ASAT.

hush kit, *British.* a combination of sound-absorbent linings and modified jet pipe nozzles fitted to jet engines to reduce noise.

Engine manufacturers have been working for the past four years to develop hush kits and claim to have had a large degree of technical success. Fitted to new BAC 1-11 airliners, the Rolls kits have reduced the 90-decibel noise "footprint" produced on the ground by the two Spey engines from 25 to 12 1/2 square miles. *Arthur Reed, "Cost Rules Out the Silencing of Older Aircraft," The Times (London), March 19, 1976, p 5*

[1973]

hustle or **Hustle,** *n.* a lively dance for couples done to disco music, characterized by intricate footwork, dips, and spins.

Each week an extra kick or a fancy turn sets off a new variation and a new challenge. There is the advanced hustle, which resembles a jitterbug, the beginner's hustle, which is the dance reduced to its simplest steps, and the Latin hustle, which has the most complicated footwork and spins. There is also a Bronx hustle, Queens hustle, Brooklyn hustle and others that do not have names. *Dena Kleiman, "The 'Hustle' Restores Old Touch to Dancing," The New York Times, July 12, 1975, p 27*

—*v.i.* to dance a hustle.

Again, as in times long past, "Would you like to dance?" means "Can you dance?" There's no more ad libbing, no way to fake it. Either you Hustle—or you sit. If the question can be answered affirmatively, there is then the moment while you figure out which Hustle your partner is dancing. *"The Hustle—And How to Do It," Sunday News (New York), Jan. 11, 1976, p 41*

[1975]

H-Y antigen ('eitʃ 'waɪ), a protein that determines the action of the male chromosome (Y chromosome) in mammals, found on the surface of cells in males.

Mary Lyon, at Harwell, and her colleagues in America, showed that only the Y chromosome carried the genetic blueprint for production of a surface protein, the so-called HY antigen, which acted as the stimulus for developing testes. By filling out understanding of the process of sex determination (already understood in the female) this discovery showed how, in future, disastrous upsets in the process might be avoided. *John Newell, "Science, Medicine and Technology," The Annual Register of World Events in 1975 (1976), p 360*

The Y chromosome sex determinant gene was identified in all seven of them [hermaphrodites]. Specifically, the protein that is encoded by this gene, the so-called H-Y antigen, was present in cells from all the subjects. *"The Genetic Basis of Hermaphroditism," Science News, Oct. 16, 1976, p 246*

[1976, from *histocompatibility + Y* chromosome + *antigen;* so called because it was originally thought to be a HISTOCOMPATIBILITY ANTIGEN, since it caused skin grafts in genetically identical mice to be rejected when male skin was grafted on females]

hy·brid·o·ma (ˌhaɪ brə'dou mə), *n.* a hybrid cell formed by CELL FUSION.

Tissue typing . . . is the labour to which immunologists foresaw the end when they made the first antibody-secreting hybridoma: a hybrid between an ordinary mouse antibody-secreting cell, which has only a limited lifespan, and an immortal tumour cell from a mouse myeloma. *"Hybrid Cells Are a Good Source of Antibody," New Scientist, July 27, 1978, p 271*

Hybridoma technology is . . . nearly ready for application in research, diagnosis and possibly treatment. This is the result of fusing two different kinds of cells—lymphocytes fused to myeloma cells provide information for producing just that one pure antibody. *Lewis Thomas, New York Post, Dec. 24, 1979, p 13*

[1978, from *hybrid + -oma* mass, tumor, as in *myeloma* a malignant tumor of the bone marrow]

hy·bri·my·cin (ˌhaɪ brə'maɪ sən), *n.* any of various antibiotic drugs made by combining the components of other antibiotics.

These two deoxystreptamine analogs, streptamine and 2-epistreptamine, are in fact parts of two other antibiotics, streptomycin and spectinomycin, respectively. Hence the new antibiotics were given the name hybrimycins, since they can be considered hybrid antibiotics, with the streptamine or 2-epistreptamine ring coming from streptomycin or spectinomycin, respectively, and the remaining rings coming from the neomycins. *W. Thomas Shier, "Bacterial Genetics," McGraw-Hill Yearbook of Science and Technology 1971, p 121*

[1969, from *hybrid + -mycin,* suffix in the names of antibiotics derived from soil bacteria (from Greek *mýkēs* fungus)]

hy·can·thone (haɪ'kæn₁θoun), *n.* a chemical substance that causes mutations in bacterial and mammalian cells, used as a drug in the treatment of schistosomiasis. *Formula:* $C_{20}H_{24}N_2O_2S$

Sterling-Winthrop Research Institute has produced hycanthone, a one-shot treatment for schistosomiasis, a worm disease almost as widespread and devastating as malaria, and has reported 80 percent cure rates. *Frank P. Mathews, "Medicine," 1971 Collier's Encyclopedia Year Book, p 336*

[1970, from *hydroxymethyl thioxanthenone,* part of the chemical constituents]

hy·del (haɪ'del), *adj.* (in India) hydroelectric.

The Rana Pratap hydel station has again started generating power. Its first unit started functioning last night after the reported sabotage by the striking engineers on Monday. *The Hindustan Times Weekly, April 29, 1973, p 6*

[1973, contraction of *hydro*electric]

hy·dril·la (haɪ'drɪl ə), *n.* a soft aquatic weed that was introduced from Asia into Florida in the 1960's as an aquarium plant and that has since spread throughout the southeastern United States.

This year, the almost indestructible hydrilla has blanketed the 1,600-acre lake [Trafford], choking fish and destroying navigation. *Newsweek, Jan. 13, 1975, p 74*

Hydrilla . . . appears to have the potential of becoming the most serious submersed weed problem in the United States. It is a major problem in the Panama Canal Zone and in several other countries. *David L. Sutton, "Aquatic Weeds," McGraw-Hill Yearbook of Science and Technology 1978, p 96*

[1970, from New Latin *Hydrilla (verticillata),* the species name, probably diminutive of Latin *hȳdra* hydra]

hydrofracturing, *n.* a method of opening a passageway for oil by pumping water under high pressure down an oil well that has gone dry to crack the rock and allow more oil to seep into the well, used also to pump water to and from hot rock reservoirs for use as a power source. *Also used attributively.*

The challenge is to sink wells and shatter this rock so that water from the surface can penetrate it and become heated. The hot water or steam would then be piped up and used to drive a power plant. Holes must be drilled into such rock and some process, such as underground nuclear explosions or "hydrofracturing," must be used to shatter the rock so that water can penetrate it. *Walter Sullivan, "Earth's Heat: Furnace Below the Crust," The New York Times, Nov. 5, 1972, Sec. 4, p 8*

Passing into verb:

At the deepest level attempted, 5,320 meters, the tests reached the 1,000-bar safety threshold of the well pipe without hydrofracturing the local gabbro zone. *"Earth Sciences: Dry Oil Well Becomes Scientific Success," Science News, April 24, 1976, p 267*

[1970, from *hydro-* water + *fracturing* cracking]

hydrolab, *n.* a vessel designed for research under water for an extended period.

Meanwhile, after years of having the hydrolab underwater laboratory-residence used primarily for testing man's survival in a strange environment, scientists have begun to use the facility for extensive research at 50-foot depths near the Bahamas. From March 13 to 20, ichthyologist C. Lavett Smith of the American Museum of Natural History, and two companions, lived in the 16- by 8-foot habitat to study the microcosm around a coral reef. *"Diving for Knowledge of the Ocean's Life," Science News, April 7, 1973, p 221*

[1969, from *hydro-* water + *lab*]

hydrophilic, *n.* a contact lens made of a plastic material that absorbs water to become soft and flexible; soft lens.

It is estimated that within a couple of years between 30 and 40 per cent of the contact lens market will be taken by the hydrophilics. *Priscilla Hodgson, The Sunday Times (London), Oct. 24, 1971, p 10*

[1971, noun use of the adjective meaning "readily absorbing water"]

hy·lol·o·gy (hai'lal ə dʒi:), *n.* the study of the properties of materials used in science and technology; materials science.

The problem in arriving at these priorities, of course, is the very diversity of what constitutes "materials research." As a separate discipline, the field has existed for only about two decades, and only now has the Academy suggested that the term "hylology" (the study of matter) be applied to this amorphous realm. *"Materials Research: A Call for New Directions to Avert Future Crises," Science News, Jan. 26, 1974, p 53*

[1974, from Greek *hýlē* substance, matter + English *-ology* study of]

hy·per ('hai pər), *adj. U.S. and Canadian Slang.* overly excited or stimulated; emotionally charged.

The quiz kids are about as sensitive as meat grinders. They scratch and claw for every point, lips smacking and eyes glittering. . . . One boy was so hyper he fell off the set minutes before the game was to begin; he climbed back up and did the show with a broken wrist. *Heather Robertson, "Television," Maclean's, Feb. 1973, p 85*

One of Culver's characteristics, noted by his friends, is objectivity about himself. As he talks now about the staff, this comes out, "I know I can be hyper and intimidating and aggressive, and I have to be careful not to expect too much of them." *The New Yorker, Sept. 11, 1978, p 65*

[1971, adjective use of the combining form *hyper-*, meaning excessive or perhaps from *hyper*active]

hyperalimentation, *n.* intravenous feeding that provides the necessary foods and nutritive substances to patients who cannot ingest them through the alimentary canal.

Thousands of people across the country who cannot digest or absorb their food are benefiting, though less conveniently, from . . . intravenous hyperalimentation. By using this technique, which involves pumping nutrients directly into the bloodstream, doctors are able to keep alive patients with shortened guts, inflamed bowels, and immunological defects that prevent proper digestion of food. It is also used for burn victims and people receiving drug or radiation treatment following cancer surgery. *Time, Oct. 9, 1978, p 104*

[1970, from *hyper-* extreme, excessive + *alimentation*]

hypercomplex, *adj.* **1** of or designating the most structurally complex cells of the visual cortex.

A typical complex cortical cell responds only to a slit, a bar or an edge. Cortical cells also have stringent requirements for the width and orientation of the stimulus. Hypercomplex cortical cells require that the stimulus also have a specific length. *Barbara Gordon, "The Superior Colliculus of the Brain," Scientific American, Dec. 1972, p 78*

2 of or designating any algebraic number or system involving quaternions.

Buff studied hypercomplex analysis, which deals with a calculus for functions of quaternions, variables in complex mathematics analogous to numbers. *Science News, March 7, 1970, p 244*

[1969 for def. 1; 1970 for def. 2; both from *hyper-* extremely, excessively + *complex*]

hy·per·lip·id·e·mi·a (ˌhai pərˌlip ə'di: mi: ə), *n.* an abnormally large amount of fatty or oily substances (lipids) in the blood.

It is currently recommended that children with one of the known genetic forms of hyperlipidemia (elevated blood levels of certain fats) be placed on an appropriate diet. *William E. Segar, "Medicine: Pediatrics," The Americana Annual 1973, p 452*

A national register of people suffering from hyperlipidaemia, a rare form of heart disease, is being compiled in Oxford. . . . Hyperlipidaemia is a severe biochemical abnormality characterized by a greatly increased level of fats in the blood — not cholesterol but triglycerids. *The Times (London), Oct. 24, 1978, p 2*

[1969, from *hyper-* excessive + *lipid* + *-emia* blood]

hy·per·lip·o·pro·tein·e·mi·a (ˌhai pərˌlip ə prou ti:ni: mi: ə), *n.* an abnormally large amount of lipids and proteins combined (lipoproteins) in the blood.

Dr M. C. Stone (Leigh Infirmary, Lancashire) discussed the role of diet in the management of hyperlipoproteinaemias. He and his collaborators have developed a simple method for studying the serum lipoprotein pattern by a combination of membrane filtration and nephelometry. *"Nutrition: Diet and Heart Disease," Nature, July 28, 1972, p 194*

[1969, from *hyper-* excessive + *lipoprotein* + *-emia* blood]

hyperrealism, *n.* a style of painting and sculpture characterized by extremely lifelike representation of persons and objects.

Hyperrealism, as predicted, is popping up in the galleries, represented here by Michael Leonard, who has actually been practising it for some time. His style is immaculate, his subjects intimate, the tone as green and shady as a day in the park. *Caroline Tisdall, "Real Life Artists?" The Manchester Guardian Weekly, Aug. 26, 1972, p 21*

[1970, from *hyper-* extreme + *realism*] Compare PHOTOREALISM.

hyperrealist, *adj., n.:* Robert Bechtle/Alan Kessler—Hyperrealist paintings of California back yards by a painter who has a deadly eye for the banal. / What look like well-worn tools offered up at a lawn sale—handsaws, files, hatchets, crossbars—are really hand-carved-and-painted wooden sculptures. *The New Yorker, Jan. 2, 1978, p 7*

The proof of a really good exhibition is whether it makes you see things differently afterwards, and the exhibition of American Hyper-realists and European Realists at the National Centre of Contemporary Art (CNAC) in Paris did just that. *Richard Roud, "The Object of the Exercise," The Manchester Guardian Weekly, May 11, 1974, p 21*

hypnodrama, *n.* the acting out of a situation under hypnosis; psychodrama performed by a hypnotized person or persons.

We were to be hypnotized, and were then to participate in a hypnodrama. We encircled the fieldstone fireplace in the center of the large dining hall as Ira Greenberg of the Camarillo, Calif., State Hospital led the session. He described hypnosis as a "control of our controls." It was a technique, he said, that enabled us to concentrate deeply and regress to forgotten states; once these states were recalled, hypnodrama could be used to act them out, enabling us finally to gratify the unsatisfied nurture needs of infancy. *Leo Litwak, " 'Rolfing,' 'Aikido,' Hypnodramas, Psychokinesis, and Other Things Beyond the Here and Now," The New York Times Magazine, Dec. 17, 1972, p 22*

[1966, from *hypnosis* + *drama*]

I

i·ai·do (i:'ɑi dou), *n.* a Japanese form of fencing using a single-edged sword slightly curved toward the point.

In martial arts activities closely related to kendo, the 17th All-Japan Iaido (Quick-Sword-Draw) Championships were held on October 31 in Fukushima Prefecture. *Andrew M. Adams, "Kendo," Britannica Book of the Year 1977, p 201*

[1976, from Japanese, from *iai* drawing a sword + *-dō* way]

i·at·ro·gen·e·sis (ɑi‚æt rou'dʒen ə sis), *n.* the inducing of a disease, disorder, symptom, etc., by a physician through treatment, diagnosis, or other medical activity.

I include in clinical iatrogenesis the inevitable unwanted side effects of most powerful treatments or interventions which are foreseen and accepted by the doctor; those which are *not* foreseen, either because of his negligence, or because of his ignorance, or because of lack of scientific evidence on such treatments — this is a second category. Third, I include there all that damage that results from wrong judgment systems breakdown; lack of communication between patient and doctor; mix-up of information in the treatment establishment. *Ivan Illich, Maclean's, Dec. 13, 1976, p 4*

[1976, from Greek *iātrós* physician + English *genesis* origin]

IBA, abbreviation for *Independent Broadcasting Authority* (of Great Britain).

In the meantime he pursued his case against the ITV [Independent Television] documentary on Andy Warhol before the Appeal Court. Counsel for the Independent Broadcasting Authority said the IBA's board had now seen the film and fully concurred with its executive's decision that it be broadcast. *William Hardcastle, "Britain's Week," The Listener, Feb. 1, 1973, p 137*

[1971, replacing earlier (1954) *ITA*, abbreviation of Independent Television Authority]

i·bu·pro·fen (‚ɑi byu:'prou fen), *n.* a drug which reduces the inflammation of arthritis and rheumatism without the gastrointestinal upset associated with aspirin. *Formula:* $C_{13}H_{18}O_2$

In 1974 Boots won the Queen's award for export achievement. One of its drugs, ibuprofen, contributed significantly to that success. *The Times (London), Feb. 2, 1977, p 20*

[1970, from *isobu*tylphenyl*pro*pionic acid + *-fen* (probably alteration of *phen*yl)]

ice station, a scientific research station in the Arctic, serving especially to monitor ice movement, weather, sea, and other environmental conditions.

Charles Knight . . . has had several periods of residence and work on drifting ice stations in the Arctic; he notes that one of them, ARLIS I (Arctic Research Laboratory Ice Station I) "was the first attempt at an austere station, and it did succeed in being austere." *Scientific American, Jan. 1973, p 11*

[1968]

ICU, abbreviation of *intensive care unit*, a medical unit equipped with lifesaving and monitoring devices for the care of critically ill patients.

Nearly every patient in the ICU is attached to a respirator, with a tube running from his nose to a white accordion-pleated cylinder, encased in glass, that expands and then flattens with a rhythmic sighing sound. *Joyce Maynard, The New York Times Magazine, May 23, 1976, p 80*

[1972] Compare CCU.

i·den·ti·kit (ɑi'den ti‚kit), *n. British.* a device used in police work to reconstruct faces from memory by using line-drawn variations of facial features to make a composite picture that approximates the description supplied by witnesses. *Often used attributively.*

Parts of the picture — for instance, of a face — can be lifted with a light pen and deposited on another face across the screen. This makes the construction of identikit-style pictures easier than before. The computer can even be programmed to divide the picture in two and replace the left with the right half and then the right with the left. *"Micromagic With TV Picture Store," New Scientist, Sept. 29, 1977, p 798*

Figurative use.

Twenty-five years as a policeman had taught him that no character was without its complications, its inconsistencies. Only the young or the very arrogant imagined that there was an identikit to the human mind. *P. D. James, Shroud for a Nightingale, 1971, p 154*

[1962, from *identi*ty + *kit*; originally from the trademark spelled *Identi-Kit*] Compare PHOTO-FIT.

Idioms. ► An idiom is a phrase or expression with meaning that is occasionally literal, but often is metaphorical or allusive, and not at all transparent. Idioms generally add force and color to the language, especially to informal speech and writing; however, they are susceptible to becoming clichés, such as the current POINT IN TIME.

Of the various aspects of language construction, idioms show perhaps the greatest variety and are also the hardest to classify. Some are simple verb phrases with literal meanings: ADOPT OUT is one such idiom that replaces the traditional phrase "give up for adoption." HAND UP is less literal but a useful term in law. GET OFF ON and SIGN OFF ON are similar in form but different in application: the first belongs to the slang of drug users, the second to the jargon of bureaucrats. The widespread expression COULD CARE LESS is an alteration of the old phrase "couldn't care less." The use of GOOD NEWS, BAD NEWS is a reference to a type of joke, yet it has become a commonplace phrase in journalistic writing. The colloquial GIVE A FOR INSTANCE combines two older constructions, the verbal "give an instance" with the adverbial "for instance."

Among current idioms are such figurative expressions from sports as RUN WITH THE BALL, TOUCH BASE WITH, and PLAY CATCH-UP. From the theatrical world come GET ONE'S ACT TOGETHER, DO A NUMBER ON, and TAKE, FIVE, the last of which probably derives ultimately from military use by way of the theater. Politics has provided LIGHT AT THE END OF THE TUNNEL, ON THE RESERVATION, and TWIST IN THE WIND.

Often the metaphor or implied comparison is clear even where the source or origin of the phrase is uncertain. The following examples illustrate:

EGG ON ONE'S FACE, embarrassed and humiliated.
GO BARE, carry no insurance.
GO DOWN THE TUBE, be lost or finished.
OFF THE WALL, unconventional, offbeat.
ON THE FRONT BURNER, of immediate concern.
ON THE MONEY, on target.
TAKE A BATH, sustain a loss or reversal.

Some of the idioms recorded in this dictionary are not strictly new but are entered because they have been revived or become especially current in recent years. For example, the idiom MARCH TO A DIFFERENT DRUMMER, meaning to be different or unconventional, is a paraphrase of a famous epigram in Thoreau's *Walden* (1854). Other old idioms are *the* TROUBLES and *playing the* DOZENS.

Idioms are listed in the dictionary in boldface under their key verbs, nouns, and adjectives, as **could care less** under **care, take a bath** under **bath,** and **go bare** under **bare.**

Ig, abbreviation of *immunoglobulin,* used especially in combination with a letter to designate any of various types, as in the subentries that follow:

IgA, a protein antibody acting against bacteria.

Our skin acts as a formidable barrier against infection, but our other coverings are not so impervious: the mucous membranes that line our lips, the soft covering of our eyes, the inside of our nose and cheeks, the linings of our mouth, throat and stomach. To keep organisms from entering through these moist, open surfaces, our body in its evolutionary wisdom coats them with IgA antibodies, which will attack any microbe, stopping it from getting into the bloodstream or down into the deeper layers of our bodies. *Ronald J. Glasser, "The Body Is the Hero," The Reader's Digest, Oct. 1976, p 263*

A protective immunological substance called secretory IgA is abundant in mother's milk. Studies have found that secretory IgA appears to prevent viruses from locking themselves to the membranes of living cells, the first step in infection. *Sunday News (New York), Sept. 23, 1979, p 42*

IgD: In man, there are two minor or less abundant classes, IgD and IgE, which have delta and epsilon heavy chains, respectively. Although the function of IgD is unknown, IgE antibodies are responsible for reaginic hypersensitivity reactions. *Frank W. Putnam, McGraw-Hill Yearbook of Science and Technology 1975, p 238*

IgE, a protein antibody acting against allergic substances.

Further experiments indicated that this substance, called reagin, is produced in allergic people in response to such allergens as molecules from pollens and foods. It is similar to the way immunoglobulins, or antibodies, are produced. . . . Then, in 1967, immunologists Kimishige and Teruko Ishizaka, a husband-and-wife team at the National Jewish Hospital and Research Center in Denver, proved that reagin was a new type of immunoglobulin, now called immunoglobulin E, or IgE. *Robert N. Hamburger, "Attack on Allergy," The World Book Science Annual 1977 (1976), p 154*

IgG, a protein antibody causing agglutination of bacterial cells.

Some antibodies called IgG and IgM, may pass from the blood into the mouth in the minute amounts of fluid that normally seep out of the crevices where the gingivae meet the teeth. These crevicular antibodies adhere to bacteria and enhance the action of certain white blood cells, which engulf and destroy *S. mutans. Simon W. Rosenberg, "A Vaccine Against Tooth Decay," The Americana Annual 1978, p 174*

IgM, a protein antibody acting against gram-negative bacteria.

However, IgM, the phylogenetically and ontogenetically earliest immune globulin, can be produced in large amounts despite the most severe malnutrition. If the diet of mice is qualitatively adequate and only moderately restricted, stimulation of the cell-mediated immune system and increased resistance against viral diseases and neoplasia result. *Werner Dutz, "Biological Stress," McGraw-Hill Yearbook of Science and Technology 1978, p 21*

[1965]

im·age·a·ble ('im i dʒə bəl), *adj. Psychology.* (of a word, phrase, etc.) able to evoke a mental image.

This attribute [imagery-concreteness] is highly correlated with performance in many memory tasks, such that imageable, concrete words are remembered better than nonimageable, abstract words. *John Richardson, "Imagery and Memory," New Scientist, Oct. 5, 1972, p 32*

[1967, from *image, v.,* to represent, portray + *-able*]

imageability, *n.:* Most work in imagery and memory has concerned attributes of verbal items. The two chief properties which have been investigated are imageability (usually abbreviated to "I") and concreteness (C). *John Richardson, "Imagery and Memory," New Scientist, Oct. 5, 1972, p 32*

immersion, *n.attrib.* of or having to do with an intensive course of oral instruction in a second language, especially in a bilingual area.

immersion course: He [Robert Lorne Stanfield] also has a wry, self-deprecating sense of humor that can make him the funniest man at a small party. Discussing his public speaking style, he once told me: 'I've been taking immersion courses in French, you know. Some of my friends say what I really need is an immersion course in English.' *"Tory Leader Robert Stanfield: 'I Am What I Am,'" Time, Nov. 13, 1972, p 35*

immersion school: In Winnipeg, a total of 1,123 students were enrolled in immersion courses this fall, and Ecole Sacre-Coeur, the city's largest immersion school, recorded a jump in enrollment from 334 to 560 students between 1974 and 1975. *"Canada: A Terminal Failure to Communicate?" Maclean's, Nov. 1, 1976, p 21*

[1972]

immune complex, *Medicine.* an aggregate formed by an antigen and its antibody. Immune complexes may cause agglutination, precipitation, and other immunological reactions.

Anti-DNA antibodies are the hallmark of this disease, and such antibodies are demonstrable in virtually all cases. Circulating immune complexes of DNA—anti-DNA undoubtedly cause some of the lesions of acute nephritis and vasculitis. *Gene H. Stollerman, "Medicine: Rheumatic Diseases," 1975 Britannica Yearbook of Science and the Future (1974), p 280*

[1973]

immune complex disease: In the light of the evidence that the kidney disease was caused by an antigen-antibody complex, it was called "immune complex" disease. *Abner Louis Notkins and Hilary Koprowski, "How the Immune Response to a Virus Can Cause Disease," Scientific American, Jan. 1973, p 26*

immune surveillance, another name for IMMUNOLOGICAL SURVEILLANCE.

Cellular immunity evolved specifically to hunt down and destroy cancer cells that are constantly emerging in all of us. This concept of "immune surveillance" was taken up and championed by Sir Macfarlane Burnet and is now accepted, in some form, by most immunologists. *New Scientist, Sept. 26, 1974, p 807*

[1973]

immunity bath, *U.S. Law.* a grant of immunity allowing a witness to confess to any crime without risking future prosecution.

The traditional reluctance of Congress, the courts, and the executive branch to wield such a potent weapon [immunity] carelessly grew out of several factors—among them the fear that corrupt prosecutors would give "immunity baths" to those guilty of serious crimes. *Richard Harris, "Annals of Law," The New Yorker, April 12, 1976, p 99*

[1969] Compare USE IMMUNITY.

immunoadsorbent or **immunoadsorbant,** *n.* a chemical substance that adsorbs antigens or antibodies.

EBV-infected cells are homogenized and the immunoad-

sorbent is immersed in the mixture. The antigens cling to the antibodies and when the immunoadsorbent is removed, the antigens come with it. The antigens are then freed from the immunoadsorbent and concentrated. *Science News, July 14, 1973, p 32*

Gluteraldehyde fixation of the cells . . . has been widely used in immunology to make fixed preparations of antigens (immunoadsorbants) which allow the adsorption and isolation of antibody and cells bearing antibodylike receptors. *C. J. Sanderson, "Vaccination," McGraw-Hill Yearbook of Science and Technology 1976, p 400*

[1973, from *immuno-* immunological + *adsorbent* or *adsorbant*]

immunodeficiency, *n.* inability of the immune system to produce antibodies in sufficient number or strength to fight infection.

The granulocytes and macrophages in our bloodstream are only part of our immune system. Indeed, if they were all we had, we would not survive long. Those children born with immunodeficiency have all the granulocytes they need, yet they die within months from infections. *The Reader's Digest, Condensed from the Book "The Body Is the Hero" by Ronald J. Glasser, Oct. 1976, p 262*

[1971, from *immuno-* immunological + *deficiency*]

immunodeficient, *adj.:* One experimental approach to treating immunodeficient individuals, who are likely to die of overwhelming infection if their immune systems cannot be restored, is transplantation of bone marrow or thymus tissue. *Barbara J. Culliton, "Restoring Immunity: Marrow and Thymus Transplants May Do It," Science, April 13, 1973, p 169*

immunological surveillance, a monitoring process by which the body's immune system detects foreign cells.

Immunological surveillance, first proposed by Macfarlane Burnett, is now widely accepted in principle, even though it begins to look in need of some modification. The theory says that T cells roam the body looking for foreign cells, including incipient cancers, which are summarily destroyed. *"When Friends Are Disguised as Enemies Are Disguised as Friends," New Scientist, Sept. 13, 1973, p 606*

[1973] Also called IMMUNE SURVEILLANCE, IMMUNOSURVEILLANCE.

immunoprecipitation, *n.* the process of separating a substance in an insoluble form by combining specific antibodies and antigens.

As a rule immunoprecipitation procedures are necessary to visualise the small amount of virus-specific polypeptides. The specificity of the immunoprecipitation was checked as follows. Immunoprecipitation of control injections . . . by addition of anti-AMV [Avian Myeloblastosis Virus] serum, gives rise predominantly to two polypeptides with molecular weights of 190,000 and 50,000, respectively. *Martin Salden, et al., Nijmegen, The Netherlands, "Letters to Nature," Nature, Feb. 26, 1976, p 698*

[1972]

immunoregulation, *n.* the process by which the immune system of the body is regulated.

Understanding T-cell suppression is potentially important to understanding immunoregulation. For example, it is possible that allergic individuals have congenital or acquired deficiencies in this suppressive activity that permit uncontrolled production of allergy-causing antibody. It may be that desensitization works in the treatment of some allergies by boosting the number of suppressor cells. *Jacques M. Chiller, "Immunology," The World Book Science Annual 1975 (1974), p 306*

[1974]

immunosorbent, *n.* another name for IMMUNOAD-SORBENT.

The role of animal rotaviruses in human disease and the exchange of rotaviruses is not known. . . . This report describes the use of an enzyme-linked immunosorbent assay to distinguish members of the rotavirus group. *Robert H. Yolken, et al., "Enzyme-Linked Immunosorbent Assay for Identification of Rotaviruses from Different Animal Species," Science, July 21, 1978, p 259*

[1974]

immunosuppress, *v.t., v.i.* to suppress the immune response of (an organism) against a foreign substance.

Further studies are under way to confirm that the technique selectively immunosuppresses at the cellular and subcellular levels. *"A Possible Answer to Transplant Rejections," Science News, May 6, 1972, p 295*

There is evidence that those individuals in whom the capacity to respond to an immunological challenge is decreased, *i.e.,* those who are immunosuppressed, have a high incidence of cancer. *Nathaniel I. Berlin, "Cancer Research," 1976 Britannica Yearbook of Science and the Future (1975), p 364*

[1967, back formation from *immunosuppression* (1965)]

immunosurveillance, *n.* another name for IM-MUNOLOGICAL SURVEILLANCE.

This new work has now established that it *is* the antibodies in myasthenics which are behind the diseases' symptoms. For some reason the immuno-surveillance of these patients has broken down, and they are interpreting their own acetylcholine receptors as "foreign," and coating them with antibody. There is no hint just yet as to the reason why this should be happening. *"Antibodies Coat Muscle Receptors in Myasthenia," New Scientist, Sept. 14, 1978, p 769*

[1974]

IMP or **imp¹,** abbreviation of *International Match Point,* a unit of scoring used in European contract bridge tournaments.

The Italians staged an incredible rally. They won by 26 IMP's, 215-189, with the entire margin swinging on the 92nd deal. *Richard L. Frey, "Contract Bridge," 1976 Collier's Encyclopedia Year Book (1975), p 209*

With eight boards to be played Scotland were trailing by 24 imps, but in a great rally they scored 28-4 imps to make the match an exact tie. *"Wales Ahead in Camrose Cup Bridge," The Times (London), Jan. 20, 1976, p 14*

[1963]

Imp or **imp²,** *n.* acronym for *indeterminate mass particle,* a hypothetical nuclear particle with no well-defined rest mass.

One of the first things to come up is an explanation of why all searches for free quarks have failed to find them. Imps have the property that their size increases rapidly with age. This means that very soon after quarks are produced they get too large to interact effectively with electrons and ionize atoms. *"Catch an Imp and Find a Quark," Science News, Jan. 14, 1978, p 23*

[1977]

impact aid, *U.S.* Federal financial assistance to a school district where children of government employees attend school.

"Impact aid," as it is called, goes to four hundred and fifteen of the four hundred and thirty-five congressional districts. This year, the Administration proposed to reduce funds for children whose parents are federal employees but do not live in federal installations, on the theory that these people do pay property taxes. *Elizabeth Drew, "Phase: Engagement With the Special-Interest State," The New Yorker, Feb. 27, 1978, p 64*

[1970]

impact statement, a review of the possible consequences of a proposed idea or project, especially one affecting the environment.

In the first draft of an impact statement on the transportation of radioactive materials near and through large, densely populated areas, the agency counted in 1975 in New York City approximately 280,000 radioactive shipments including twelve shipments of the Brookhaven spent elements or thirteen per cent of the national total. *Fred C. Shapiro, "Radiation Route," The New Yorker, Nov. 13, 1978, p 146*

[1973]

imperial presidency, the Presidency of the United States viewed as exceeding in power and authority the executive role provided by the Constitution.

One area in which the imperial presidency is as regal as ever is the matter of international airline routes: by law the President can bestow on any airline of his choice the right to fly between any American city and any foreign one and he need not bother to state a reason. *"Playing Politics With Airlines," Time, Jan. 16, 1978, p 46*

[1973, from *The Imperial Presidency* (1973), by Arthur M. Schlesinger, Jr., born 1917, American historian]

imperial president: The "imperial" Presidents in global affairs — from Roosevelt to Nixon — did not so much usurp their great powers as find them conferred because public fears and ambitions were then so widely shared. *"The Consensus That Died at Tet," The New York Times, Feb 19, 1978, Sec. 4, p 16*

implied consent, *U.S. Law.* consent to forfeit certain rights or to assume certain responsibilities when one applies for some privilege, such as a driver's license.

The governor also paid tribute to the "implied consent" law which allows testing of drivers suspected of drunkenness. *The Tuscaloosa News (Alabama), June 19, 1974, p 6*

[1969] ► This term should not be confused with IN-FORMED CONSENT.

implosion, *n. Psychology.* a method of treating a phobia by dramatically confronting the patient with the situation or object feared.

A more drastic technique, similar to throwing a baby into a pool to teach it how to swim, is known as "implosion" — a patient might be driven to a large empty field and left there for hours to cope with his fears. The theory is that terror drains away once it is faced directly. *Time, Nov. 7, 1977, p 58*

[1969, specialized sense of the word meaning "a bursting inward"] Compare FLOODING. See also AGORAPHOBIA.

253

impoverished, *adj.* containing fewer stimuli than those provided in a standard laboratory environment.

The team found that rats placed in "enriched" environments — cages holding toys, mazes and other rats — developed, among other things, thicker cerebral cortices than those isolated in bare, or "impoverished," cages. *"Birth Pill Hormones Found to Affect Rat Brains," The New York Times, May 22, 1976, p 11*

[1972]

impulse purchase or **impulse buy,** something purchased impulsively, especially without consideration of cost, quality, or utility.

Write out a list and stick to it. Impulse purchases will be thrust at you; most of them you don't *really* need. *Walter Stewart, "The Games Supermarkets Play," Maclean's, Aug. 1974, p 16*

Our games are cheap enough to be impulse buys. *Gwen Nuttall, The Times (London), Sept. 26, 1971, p 61*

[1971; cf. earlier (1955) *impulse buying*]

In·cep·ti·sol (in'sep tə,sɔ:l), *n.* (in U.S. soil taxonomy) any of a group of widely distributed soils of recent origin, characterized by a slight development of soil horizons.

The remaining broad groups of soils, the Alfisols, Entisols, Spodosols, and many Inceptisols, fall between the two extremes, both in nutrient losses during formation and in fertility levels. Mountainous regions, with their great variety of soils, also belong to this intermediate group. Collectively these occupy about 35% of the land surface. *Roy W. Simonson, "Soil," McGraw-Hill Yearbook of Science and Technology 1972, p 374*

[1971, from *inception* + *-sol* (from Latin *solum* soil)] Compare ARIDISOL, HISTOSOL, MOLLISOL, OXISOL, ULTISOL, VERTISOL.

income maintenance, *U.S.* money paid by a government to provide the poor with a regular income.

They have shown, for example, that it is possible to provide the poor with a secure income without killing their motivation to work, suggesting that a "negative income tax" or "income maintenance" system could be a viable policy. *Amitai Etzioni, "Social Science vs. Government: Standoff at Policy Gap," Psychology Today, Nov. 1978, p 24*

[1972]

incomes policy, any government policy to check inflation resulting from wage and cost increases.

Galbraith urged the cause of a militant incomes policy in the form of direct wage-price controls — a message that President Nixon put into effect in August 1971, to the great advantage of the country and the President's re-election prospects. *Paul A. Samuelson, "The Morning After," Newsweek, Nov. 13, 1972, p 88*

What is needed, therefore, is some kind of government participation in the wage bargaining process — an incomes policy, in short — which will directly secure a reduction in the size of pay claims. This is not a piece of straightforward economics, like controlling the money supply, but more in the nature of continuous or repeated exercises in internal diplomacy. *Peter Oppenheimer, "Books: Opinions About Inflation," Review of "An Incomes Policy for Britain," edited by Frank Blackaby, The Listener, March 8, 1973, p 313*

[1963] ► The term was originally used by British economists and referred chiefly to a policy of the

Labour government during the 1960's. It began to be used in the United States about 1970, especially in the sense of a policy that would use any means to curb inflation short of full wage and price controls.

incommutation, *n. U.S.* another name for REVERSE COMMUTING.

In regard to Westchester, the report explained the growth of incommutation as a result of the movement of major companies and industries into the suburbs, combined with the decision of employes to remain in the central cities. *Tom Pica, "They Commute in Reverse," The Herald Statesman (Yonkers, N.Y.), Jan. 22, 1974, p (not recorded)*

[1974, from *in* + *commutation*]

IND, abbreviation of *investigational new drug,* (the status of) a drug approved by a regulatory agency for experimentation and research.

The Committee for Freedom of Choice in Cancer Therapy . . . point to the plot of the U.S. Food and Drug Authority granting Andrew McNaughton an IND — permission to test a new drug on humans — then 10 days later taking it away when he didn't come up with the required information on the drug's safety. *Marci McDonald, "Cashing in on Cancer," Maclean's, Jan. 1976, p 26*

[1970]

in·dé·pen·dan·tiste (æ dei pã dã ti:st), *n.* a supporter or advocate of political independence for the Province of Quebec.

[Camille] Laurin explains that he became an *indépendantiste* partly through his experience with Canadian medical groups and associations, in which, over the years, he felt less and less as though he belonged. "I wasn't part of the club," he says. *Graham Fraser, "All the Premier's Men," Maclean's, Jan. 10, 1977, p 29*

[1968, from Canadian French, from French *indépendant* independent + *-iste* -ist] Compare PÉQUISTE.

in·de·pen·den·tis·ta (,in de,pen den'ti:s ta:), *n.* a supporter or advocate of political independence for Puerto Rico.

Statehooders and *independentistas* agree on only one thing — that commonwealth status is colonial status, and degrading. By and large statehooders are conservatives, the commonwealth leaders are left-centrists, and the *independentistas* are leftists. *John Bartlow Martin, "A Commonwealth's Choice," Harper's, Dec. 1977, p 18*

[1967, from Spanish, irregularly formed from *independencia* independence + *-ista* -ist] Compare FALN.

indexation, *n.* variant of INDEXING (def. 1).

Basically, indexation simply means attaching escalator clauses based on some relevant yardstick of inflation to various long-term contracts. Wages and rents, for example, would be raised periodically to keep step with the cost of living. Interest payments on bonds and bank deposits would be adjusted upward or downward in line with the inflation rate (chart). And the tax system would be readjusted so that corporate and individual income gains that merely reflect inflation are not taxed away, resulting in a loss of real income. *"Economists Differ Sharply Over Whether Escalator Clauses Help Fight Inflation," Business Week, May 25, 1974, p 147*

[1963, from *index* + *-ation*]

indexed, *adj. Economics.* adjusted to changes in a

cost-of-living index (or a similar indicator of changes in the value of money).

It is the indexed National Savings Bond recommended by the Page Committee. For ordinary savers — and a few still survive — it would be a rock of assurance in the flood of inflation. *The Manchester Guardian Weekly, July 26, 1974, p 15*

Brazil has now developed into what could be termed an "indexed economy," where practically every area of the economy has some sort of adjustment mechanism for inflation. *The New York Times, April 7, 1974, p F14*

[1972]

index fund, *U.S. Finance.* an investment fund made up of stocks selected for their relative values to match the performance of the market over a period of time.

Index funds, though popular, are few. Their clients include other institutions, some of which buy shares because their managements believe that they must put at least some of the money they control into the index to avoid accusations of investing imprudently. *Robert Metz, "Market Place," The New York Times, Jan. 14, 1977, p D2*

[1976, so called from its being based on Standard & Poor's index of 500 stocks]

indexing, *n. Economics.* **1** adjustment of income, prices, interest rates, etc., to a cost-of-living index or similar indicator of change in the value of money.

A band of conservative economists . . . are vigorously touting "indexing," a system that in theory preserves the buying power of money by tying all paper values to a price indicator. *Time, May 13, 1974, p 110*

The new handy pain reliever we're being offered instead of a miracle cure, is called "indexing" — a way to adjust nearly everybody to the realities of rising prices; a system that hitches incomes, various other payments and taxes to changes in the cost-of-living. *Ray Magladry, "Indexing: Income Geared to Inflation Is No Cure," Maclean's, Nov. 1974, p 118*

2 a correlating of the prices of basic commodities to the prices paid by underdeveloped countries for industrial imports.

Mr. Kissinger is opposed to the concept of "indexing," a system of linking the price of oil and other raw materials to the cost of industrial goods that poor nations must import. *"Kissinger to Urge Resources Bank for Third World," The New York Times, May 3, 1976, p 3*

[1972]

index-link, *v.t. Especially British, Economics.* to adjust according to a cost-of-living index or similar indicator.

Of all the factors which have contributed to the drop in consumption the most important has been tax increases. . . . A commitment by the Government to index-link cigarette tax would be a major reform. A move to make the tax progressively steeper would be an even better deterrent. *The Manchester Guardian Weekly, June 12, 1977, p 10*

[1970]

index-linked, *adj.:* There are more than one would think, in the private sector, who also have index-linked pensions. *The Listener, Jan. 15, 1976, p 41*

index-linking, *n.:* "Index-linking is not the panacea some people make it out to be — indeed it can create a false sense of security," says another company. *The Sunday Times (London), June 1, 1975, p 49*

in·do·meth·a·cin (ˌin dəˈmeθ ə sən), *n.* an analgesic drug used in the treatment of arthritic disorders to reduce inflammation and fever. *Formula:* $C_{19}H_{16}ClNO_4$

This manoeuvre might well eliminate the gastrointestinal side-effects of drugs such as indomethacin used to treat rheumatoid diseases. *Graham Chedd, New Scientist and Science Journal, June 24, 1971, p 745*

[1963, from the chemical constituents *indo*le + *methy*l + *acetic* acid + *-in* (chemical suffix)]

industrio-, a combining form meaning "industrial" or "industrial and _____."

industrio-economic: We may expect to see before very long something resembling an industrio-economic "inner cabinet" consisting of the Chancellor of the Exchequer, the President of the Board of Trade, the Minister of Labour, the Minister of Technology and the Prime Minister. *Peter Jenkins, The Manchester Guardian Weekly, Sept. 7, 1967, p 4*

industrio-nuclear: Having heard that football was a vital metaphor for understanding industrio-nuclear America, we drove to Washington to discover what could be learned about the country. *Russell Baker, The New York Times Magazine, Oct. 3, 1976, p 6*

industrio-scientific: Basically, the qualifying concept is "plant used in manufacture" (with special dispensations for ship-repairing, mining, quarrying, construction and industrio-scientific research, and for computers, ships and hovercraft). *Peter Wilsher, The Sunday Times (London), Dec. 4, 1966, p 54*

[1966]

inertia-reel belt, a seat belt with a take-up reel which adjusts automatically the length of the belt to fit people of different sizes.

Early belts were often poorly designed, being difficult both to adjust and to release. Furthermore, static belts can hold the driver in so effectively that he is unable to reach essential controls. Finally, they tend to drag on the floor and get dirty. Most of those points have been met by the inertia-reel or automatic belt, which has become increasingly popular in the past two years or so. *Peter Waymark, "Motoring: New Seat Belts Overcome Design Defects," The Times (London), July 15, 1976, p 31*

[1964] Compare PASSIVE RESTRAINT.

infill, *adj.* designed to fill in a vacant space or area.

On aircraft noise, however, the report is considerably "softer." It proposes that new and infill housing should be allowed in areas that government policy would not allow. *"London Kept Quiet by Financial Stringency," New Scientist, Feb. 12, 1976, p 338*

[1964]

infinity microphone, transmitter, or **bug,** an extremely sensitive and far-ranging listening device concealed in a telephone.

And the CIA is believed to be making extensive use of the "infinity microphone" — a device billed as the world's most effective bug. Hitched to the victim's telephone, it can transmit either phone conversations or voices in the room; it uses telephone current for power, and can't be found with a radio detector. It can be switched on from anywhere in the world, merely by ringing the victim's number, apologizing for a misdial, waiting for the victim to hang up and then sounding a signal note. It will keep transmitting until the listener hangs up. *Newsweek, July 30, 1973, p 17*

Then there is the telephone, which can be used both to listen into phone conversations and to bug a whole room. There is a particularly pleasing device on offer known as an "infinity transmitter," or more commonly as Monitel. *Peter Hillmore, "Whisper Not Between These Walls," The Manchester Guardian Weekly, Sept. 4, 1977, p 5*

The "infinity" bug . . . can be used from any corner of the world's telephone system. In the United States, although not in Europe, this type of device is activated by the sending of a special tone while calling the desired phone. The phone never rings, and instead the caller is able to eavesdrop through the infinity bug's microphone. *Duncan Campbell, "Personal Surveillance Devices," New Scientist, Nov. 23, 1978, p 601*

[1973]

in·fi·tah (,in fi tɑːx), *n.* the policy of opening Egypt's economy to foreign capitalist investment, associated with the administration of President Anwar Al-Sadat.

Inflation has now shot up to 25 per cent and *infitah* has aggravated some of the long-standing problems plaguing Cairo, where it takes a miracle to make a public service function. *The Manchester Guardian Weekly (Le Monde section), June 11, 1978, p 13*

[1976, from Arabic *infitāh*, literally, an opening, from *fataḥa* to open]

inflation-proof, *v.t.* to protect (investments, savings, etc.) from inflation, especially by indexing.

So far as the Civil Service is concerned, the cost of inflation-proofing the pensions of 260,000 retired civil servants was 1.5 per cent of the wages bill for the Civil Service, at a time when, on the basis of outside pay movements, the salaries of serving civil servants were being increased by 32 per cent. *John Dryden, "Civil Servants—Their Numbers, Their Salaries and Their Privileges," The Listener, Jan. 15, 1976, p 41*

[1973, verb use of earlier (1967) adjective]

influenza A, B, and **C,** three types of influenza viruses having different degrees of virulence.

Part of the problem of distinctions among the strains of influenza viruses may have been resolved in 1972 when the World Health Organization adopted new nomenclature for influenza viruses. The gist of the semantic change was that different strains of the viruses—such as A_1, A_2, and so forth—should henceforth all be classified simply as influenza A. *Thomas H. Maugh II, Science, April 9, 1976, p 131*

Influenza C is an insignificant cause of human illness. Influenza B is a perennial problem but does not change dramatically and rarely causes widespread epidemics or severe illness. Influenza A is another story. . . . The A flu virus has been the cause of all the deadly pandemics of influenza for which a cause has been established—that is, all the global outbreaks since the flu virus was discovered in 1933. *Jane E. Brody, The New York Times, July 23, 1976, p A22*

Both kinds of variation are observed in influenza *A* viruses, but only antigenic drift has been detected in influenza *B* viruses. Influenza *C* virus is rarely isolated. *Martin M. Kaplan and Robert G. Webster, "The Epidemiology of Influenza," Scientific American, Dec. 1977, p 91*

[1972]

in·flump ('in,fləmp), *n.* another name for SLUMPFLATION.

Albert Sommers, economist for the business-oriented Conference Board and the man who coined the term "in-

flump" to describe the current mess, argues that renewed stimulus would become politically inevitable—and since it would be mistimed, the effect would inevitably be more inflation. *Larry Martz, et al., "The Economy: Can They Fix It?" Newsweek, Feb. 24, 1975, p 65*

[1975, blend of *inflation* and *slump*]

in-form, *adj. British.* in good form; well conditioned and coached for competition.

One in-form player Revie did not pick was Birmingham's Trevor Francis. "He is definitely a player for the future. I was tempted to put him in this time, but I have been happy with the players up front," Revie said. *The Times (London), Nov. 3, 1976, p 10*

[1964]

informational picketing, *U.S.* picketing by workers to publicize demands or grievances.

Under an executive order, unionized Government workers are prohibited from picketing. But union lawyers said the picketing ban should exempt so-called "informational picketing," such as is conducted in Kentucky and New York. *The New York Times, Oct. 3, 1976, p 45*

[1976]

information art, art concerned with the communication or representation of information.

. . . to arrive at found objects, ready-mades, conceptual art, information art, anti-form heaps, earth art it is necessary only to discard Picasso's compositional objectives in "Man with a Hat" and to elaborate upon his pasted-in news items and aging paper (processed art). *Harold Rosenberg, "The Art World," The New Yorker, March 11, 1972, p 118*

Harold Rosenberg moans on . . . about the serial follies of Pop Art, Sharp-focus Realism, Conceptualist Art, Information Art, Earth Art. *Geoffrey Grigson, Review of "Art on the Edge: Creators and Situations" by Harold Rosenberg, The Listener, Feb. 5, 1976, p 156*

[1972 Compare PERFORMANCE ART, POST-OBJECT ART, STORY ART]

information pollution, a profusion of information, especially unnecessary or redundant information produced by researchers, journalists, broadcasters, etc.

One of the subjects which he hinted strongly that he would like the panel . . . to consider is "information pollution." If there is too much information, he said, there is a danger that people will ignore all of it and return to idiosyncratic politics, based on gut reaction. *Martin Sherwood, "Will Dahrendorf Reorganise British Science?" New Scientist, June 12, 1975, p 594*

[1973]

information system, any method of processing information, especially by a data-processing system.

Information science and technology is concerned with devising means for providing more efficient access to documents and improving the dissemination of information. To accomplish these tasks it is necessary to gather together large quantities of raw information and to process them into a form that is more easily transferable and usable. When these processing procedures are integrated into an efficiently functioning unit, the result is called an information system. *Harold Borko, "Information Science and Technology," 1973 Britannica Yearbook of Science and the Future (1972), p 258*

[1971]

informed consent, consent to surgery or medical experiment conditional upon the patient's or subject's understanding of what is involved.

A California law giving mental patients the right to refuse convulsive therapy and psychosurgery . . . requires informed consent by the patient or, with court permission, a guardian. "Informed consent" is defined to mean that the patient must be told the reason for treatment, the probability of side effects, and that there exists a division of opinion as to the efficacy of the treatment. *"ECT Cut in California," New Scientist, Sept. 1, 1977, p 535*

Some skeptics doubt that enough embryo transplants have been done on primates and other mammals to justify trials on man and also wonder if the patients know enough about the risks to give "informed consent." *Time, July 31, 1978, p 69*

[1974]

in·fra·di·an (in'frei di: ən), *adj.* of or relating to biological rhythms or cycles that recur less than once per day.

Neurobiologic rhythms are organized according to the complexity of the space in which they operate and the frequency at which they recur. Figure 1a defines rhythms in three frequency ranges: less than one per day (infradian), about one per day (circadian) and more than one per day (ultradian). *J. Allan Hobson, "Body Rhythms," McGraw-Hill Yearbook of Science and Technology 1977, p 147*

[1977, from *infra-* below + Latin *diēs* day + *-an*]

infrared astronomy, a branch of astronomy dealing with the nature and sources of infrared radiation in space.

Infrared astronomy is beginning to study such things as intensity variations and polarizations in infrared sources, to chart their positions more accurately and to obtain better resolution of their spectra. *"New Infrared Astronomy Results Include First from Orbit," Science News, Sept. 7, 1974, p 150*

[1965]

in·fra·son·ics (ˌin frə'san iks), *n.* sound waves below the frequency of those audible to the human ear, especially as produced during severe storms.

At the other end of the sound spectrum are frequencies below those which can be heard. This is the world of infrasonics. The noise here ranges from about 20 cycles per second down to one cycle per second. *Mary Plumbly, "Noise," The Sunday Times Magazine (London), Jan. 26, 1975, p 20*

[1969, from *infrasonic, adj.* (1920's)]

ink-jet, *adj.* of or designating a high-speed printing or typing process in which jets of ink are broken up into magnetized droplets and deflected under computer control to form letters and numbers on paper.

Ink-jet printing. A wide variety of methods exist involving continuous flow and stop/start jets of ink aimed at plain paper. The Mead Dijit system uses 512 continuous jets of ink which are acoustically broken up into tiny equal sized drops in precise follow-my-leader columns. *"New Trends in Plateless Printing," New Scientist, June 10, 1976, p 575*

Two of the three models in this family . . . use IBM's unique ink-jet printer, which offers faster speeds than automatic typewriters, combined with high-quality and a variety of "type" styles. *Kenneth Owen, The Times (London), Jan. 27, 1977, p 23*

[1973]

inoperative, *adj.* deprived of force or effect; nullified; invalidated.

Whenever necessity required him to swear loyal reconciliation and fealty to the King of France, his mortal enemy, he promptly engaged in treacherous intrigues with the King of England, leaving his knightly oaths to become, in the White House word, inoperative. *Barbara W. Tuchman, "History as Mirror," The Atlantic, Sept. 1973, p 44*

Suddenly the "official spokesman" of a great national leader is telling us things which, a day or so later, turn out to be "inoperative." *James Brady, New York Post, Feb. 3, 1979, p 9*

[1973] ▶ The usage was popularized by President Nixon's press secretary, Ronald Ziegler, who referred to contradictory statements as being "inoperative." The word has existed in English in the sense "not working or operating" at least since 1631 (OED).

inside skinny, *U.S. Slang.* secret or confidential information.

It was clear to everyone that he had inside information, "inside skinny," as Nora called it. *Ward Just, "Nora," The Atlantic, May 1973, p 45*

On balance, the book is well worth reading (with appropriate grains of salt), but to get the real inside skinny we shall have to wait until you-know-who's memoirs tell us what the butler really saw. *J. L. Johnson, Review of "Cold Dawn: The Story of SALT" by John Newhouse, National Review, Sept. 14, 1973, p 1007*

[1972, probably from the idea of getting *inside the skin* of a subject]

in·son·i·fy (in'sa: nəˌfai), *v.t.* to charge (an object) with high-frequency sound waves, especially to form an acoustical hologram (that becomes a three-dimensional picture when reconstructed with laser light).

A variety of interesting scanning schemes is possible by choosing various combinations of scanning motion involving four basic elements. These elements are (1) the source of sound used to insonify the object, (2) the object, (3) the receiver, and (4) the pointlike light source. *Byron B. Brenden, "Holography," McGraw-Hill Yearbook of Science and Technology 1973, p 218*

[1965, from *in-* into + Latin *soni-* (combining form of *sonus* sound) + English *-fy* to make] Compare SONICATE.

In·sta·mat·ic (ˌin stə'mæt ik), *n.* a trademark for a lightweight, fixed-focus camera with a nonadjustable lens, made by the Eastman-Kodak company.

"Hey, there's Sonny Bono," said Carol Troy. "Where's my Instamatic?" *"The Talk of the Town," The New Yorker, Nov. 29, 1976, p 33*

"It would be difficult to catch from so frail a craft," I laughingly said. "Catch? Dew, there's a simpleton you are. Instamatics we use, not harpoons. We make pictures." *"Compass Travel Guide," Punch, Jan. 21, 1977, p 107*

[1964, from *insta*nt + auto*matic*]

instance, *n.* **give a for instance,** *U.S. Informal.* to give an example or illustration.

"Give me a for-instance, Rabbi," Dr. Muntz suggested. "All right. Since we're talking about wills, I'll give you an example from the laws of inheritance." *Harry Kemelman, Wednesday the Rabbi Got Wet, 1976, p 205*

"I'll give you a for instance," a man named Irving Goltz told us while he chewed on a fried chicken wing. "My real name was Irving. For a while there, they called me Sidney, and then, all of a sudden, they were calling me Sussy. Don't ask me why." *"The Talk of the Town," The New Yorker, June 26, 1978, p 26*

[1971, probably translation of Yiddish *gebn a tsum bayshpil*]

instant book, a book, such as an anthology or a reprint of a government report, that requires little editing or rewriting to prepare for printing.

Yale University Press has simply reprinted this surprisingly readable document (*The Double-Cross System in the War of 1939 to 1945*) on the coded doings of Garbo, Tricycle and the rest, and bargain-priced the instant book at $6.95. *Melvin Maddocks, "Books," Time, March 13, 1972, p 83*

[1968]

instant camera, a camera which takes individual photographs and develops each picture soon after it is taken.

The resultant small size of the negative means that it must be enlarged for printing and viewing. This both adds a process which is missing from the instant cameras, such as the Polaroid, and can introduce defects that are absent on the original negative. *"Technology: New Lens May be Bee's Knees for Compact Cameras," New Scientist, Dec. 23-30, 1976, p 720*

[1964] See INSTANT PHOTOGRAPHY.

instant lottery, *U.S.* a lottery in which the player can immediately determine from the markings on the ticket whether he has won a prize, without having to wait for a drawing.

The game will be a variation of the state's most recent instant lottery in which players rubbed off a wax covering to reveal a set of numbers. In the new lottery, each ticket will cost $1 and will contain 16 numbers. There are six ways to win, depending on which numbers are shown to be circled when the wax is rubbed off. *The New York Times, Aug. 31, 1977, p 33*

[1976]

in·stant·on ('in stæn,tan), *n.* a hypothetical quantum unit for the interaction occurring between states of the lowest energy.

It now seems likely that the key to understanding QCD [quantum chromodynamics] relies on a detailed knowledge of the vacuum state — that is, a state of zero energy. Previously believed empty, it appears to contain "pseudoparticles" otherwise called instantons, which can affect the interactions between the quarks. *James Dodd, "Instantons and the Real World," New Scientist, March 30, 1978, p 858*

Instantons are mathematical, but they have a physical effect: In their presence the gluons feel forces. So nothing can affect something. *Science News, April 15, 1978, p 228*

[1978, from *instant* + *-on* elementary unit or particle] Compare AXION.

instant photography, a photographic process that develops each picture soon after it is taken.

The manufacturing of film and cameras for instant photography, with the photographic darkroom incorporated into the film itself, has been dominated by the Polaroid Corporation. *Victor McElheny, "Kodak to Unveil Instant Camera," The New York Times, April 13, 1976, p 47*

[1976]

instant replay, *U.S. and Canadian.* a videotape replay of an event, especially a play in sports, which can be shown as soon as the event is completed.

TV instant replay multiplies analysis and assigns error in the press boxes, after a goal has been scored, sports writers and sportcasters rush to the TV screen for the instant replay, usually shown in slow motion. When a goalie looks bad on a goal now, he looks bad over and over again. Instant replay might pick up the forward who missed his check, or the defenseman out of position: what it never fails to pick up is an awkward miss or a faked-out drop to the ice. *Jack Ludwig, Maclean's, Feb. 1973, p 80*

[1973] The corresponding British term is ACTION REPLAY.

in·su·lin·o·ma (,in sə lə'nou mə), *n.* a benign tumor of the islets of the pancreas (islets of Langerhans) that secretes insulin.

The best-known example of this is the insulinoma of the pancreas, which causes the plasma to contain an unusually high amount of insulin much of which can be in the form of "pro" insulin. *Stephen B. Baylin, "Tumor," McGraw-Hill Yearbook of Science and Technology 1977, p 415*

[1962, from *insulin* + *-oma* tumor (from Greek *-ōma* noun suffix)]

In·tal ('in,tæl), *n.* a trademark for CROMOLYN SODIUM.

It took Fisons, a British company, seven years to get its Intal, an anti-bronchial medication, approved by American authorities, even after registration was granted in Britain. *Clyde H. Farnsworth, "Drugs in Europe: Collision of Interests," The New York Times, March 21, 1976, Sec. 3, p 6*

[1969, from *int*erference with *al*lergy]

in·te·grase ('in tə,greis), *n.* a viral enzyme that promotes the insertion of the virus's DNA into the genetic material of a bacterial cell.

The enzyme product of a specific viral gene (dubbed integrase) is required for the insertion of viral DNA; mutant viruses lacking this enzyme are unable to enter the lysogenic state. *Allan M. Campbell, "How Viruses Insert Their DNA Into the DNA of the Host Cell," Scientific American, Dec. 1976, p 109*

[1974, from *integr*ation + *-ase* suffix meaning enzyme] Compare EXCISIONASE.

integrated injection logic, a type of integrated circuit used in microprocessors and semiconductor memories.

The circuit is an example of the semiconductor technology called integrated-injection logic, or I²L. A distinguishing feature of I²L circuits is that some regions of the chip function as elements of more than one transistor. *Picture legend, James D. Meindl, "Microelectronic Circuit Elements," Scientific American, Sept. 1977, p 70*

[1976]

integrated optics, the use of highly compact units of optical fibers to control and guide the flow of light in optical instruments and devices activated by or using light, such as in communication systems.

The need for transmission, repeating, and receiving terminals for the fiber links has given rise to yet a new field, "integrated optics." In this area the effort is aimed at duplicating for light the feat that integrated electronics has already achieved for electricity, the ability to manipulate the flow of light in miniature, monolithic optical circuits. *Amnon Yariv, "Fiber Optics: Communications System of the Future?" 1975 Britannica Yearbook of Science and the Future (1974), p 47*

[1974]

intelligent, *adj.* (of a machine) able to solve problems, make fine distinctions, and perform other logical operations.

A new electronic camera from Japan represents a step towards the concept of the "intelligent" camera—one which can decide for itself how to produce the best possible photograph from any given set of circumstances. *"How Soon Before Cameras 'Think' for Themselves?" New Scientist, May 18, 1978, p 452*

The eye of the gadget "memorizes" the underside of the object it is guarding, and of course the alarm "hits" if that object is removed. In addition, it is so "intelligent" that it knows immediately if a piece of paper or even a sliver of the same material it is guarding is slid under the object in an attempt to remove it without detection. *William H. Honan, "The Perils of Guarding King Tut's Treasures," The New York Times Magazine, Dec. 17, 1978, p 108*

[1974] Compare SMART. See also ARTIFICIAL INTELLIGENCE.

intensivism, *n.* the breeding and raising of animals herded together in a small area.

Wherever intensivism has taken control, severe problems of disease and environmental damage have arisen. *The Times (London), Nov. 15, 1972, p 24*

[1968, from *intensive (husbandry)* + *-ism*]

interconnect, *adj.* *U.S.* of or having to do with the interconnection of private telephone facilities with the general telephone network.

Virtually overnight, an "interconnect" industry sprang up offering Bell customers the chance to buy a variety of new terminal equipment—and interconnect it to A.T.&T.'s lines. *Milton R. Benjamin and William H. Read, The New York Times Magazine, Nov. 28, 1976, p 114*

[1973, adjective use of the verb]

intermediate technology, a form of technology that combines small scale, simplicity, and self-sufficiency with present-day tools and methods.

Providing practical edge to the theory, a number of intermediate or "appropriate" technology groups, inspired by Schumacher's philosophy, now exist in several Western nations, including Germany, Switzerland, Canada, and the United States. The U.S. group, Intermediate Technology (IT) of Menlo Park, California, explains its goals: "We take our name from the original concept with which Schumacher's name is associated around the world. *"Intermediate Technology Sends Down Roots," East West Journal, Sept. 1977, p 30*

What the poor need most of all is simple things—building materials, clothing, household goods, agricultural implements—and a better return for their agricultural products. ... All these are ideal fields for intermediate technology. *E. F. Schumacher, Small Is Beautiful, 1973, p 186*

[1973] Compare ALTERNATIVE TECHNOLOGY, APPROPRIATE TECHNOLOGY.

internalization, *n.* *U.S.* a method of transacting sales of stock securities within brokerage offices instead of transmitting trading orders to the floor of an exchange.

For the public . . . internalization could lead to drastic changes in the way that securities are bought and sold. Although there is no question that it would result in more sites where Big Board stocks are traded, in addition to the exchange itself, there is a raging controversy among those with and without axes to grind as to whether it would lead to better prices and greater access to the marketplace by the individual investor. *Leonard Sloane, "Internalization, a Different Way to Trade Stock," The New York Times, Jan. 17, 1977, p 37*

[1977] Compare EXTERNALIZATION.

interoperability, *n.* **1** the ability to operate together or jointly; cooperation.

Defenders of the existing regime—although many concede there is scope for greater "inter-operability" between the home and foreign services—contend that . . . the Foreign Office has developed a sharp commercial edge while remaining a political instrument which is still the envy of others, including the Americans and the French. If it were to be integrated with the home departments what would happen to its superb communications? *Peter Jenkins, "Abolition of Foreign Office?" The Manchester Guardian Weekly, May 1, 1977, p 4*

2 coordination of communication systems, equipment, etc., used by member countries in an alliance.

While nationalistic pride will probably continue to prevent full standardization, there have been gains in what NATO jargon terms interoperability. Two years ago, for example, few of the airbases in NATO countries could service any but their own warplanes. By next year, most bases will be able to accommodate all NATO aircraft. *Time, Dec. 11, 1978, p 43*

[1965, from *inter-* one with the other, between + *operability* condition of being operable]

interpandemic, *adj.* occurring between pandemic outbreaks of a disease.

Our present vaccine policy . . . recommends the preferential immunization of the estimated 45 million Americans unusually susceptible to influenza complications (pneumonia and death) even in interpandemic years. *Edwin D. Kilbourne, The New York Times, Feb. 13, 1976, p 33*

[1970, from *inter-* between + *pandemic*]

interpulse, *n.* a secondary or intermediate pulse occurring in a pulsar.

There may be two pulses in the pulsar, a main pulse strong in radio but weak in X-ray and an interpulse strong in X-ray but weak in radio. *"Astronomy: X-ray Pulses from Vela Pulsar," Science News, Jan. 27, 1973, p 58*

[1969, from *inter-* between + *pulse*]

interstate, *n.* *U.S.* a highway extending between States; an interstate highway.

Since the restaurant adjoined a motel, most of the breakfast crowd were regular denizens of the Interstate: traveling salesmen; irritable young matrons in hair curlers with inert infants in tow; members of some obscure rock combo, all surly and haired-over. *William Hedgepeth, Saturday Review, Sept. 2, 1972, p 13*

The wildcat blockades, which began early in the week on interstates in the East and quickly spread to other parts of the country, led to angry confrontations with police. *Newsweek, Dec. 17, 1973, p 74*

[1965, noun use of the adjective (1844)]

intervention, *n. U.S. Education.* instruction or tutoring of children by their parents.

I, for one, am tired of the past decade's scramble to discover some magic period during which interventions will have particularly great payoffs. Some experts emphasize the nine months *in utero;* Pines and White, the period between 8 and 18 months; others, the entire preschool period; and yet others emphasize adolescence. *Edward Zigler, New Haven, "Filling the Preschool Gap," in a Letter to the Editor, The New York Times Magazine, Jan. 18, 1976, p 42*

[1976]

intractable, *adj. Mathematics.* a problem for which a polynomial algorithm cannot be given.

The inclusion of guessing in the definition of these problems suggests strongly to many mathematicians that *P* and *NP* are not the same set and hence that efficient algorithms can never be found for the intractable problems in the class *NP. Harry R. Lewis and Christos H. Papadimitriou, "The Efficiency of Algorithms," Scientific American, Jan. 1978, p 105*

[1977] Compare NP-COMPLETE.

In·tro·pin ('in trə pin), *n.* the trademark for a drug that stimulates the action of the heart.

Intropin (dopamine hydrochloride), a compound that increases the heart's ability to contract and may restore blood pressure when it is dangerously low during shock, such as after a heart attack or open-heart surgery. Although chemically related to adrenalin and other stimulant drugs, Intropin exhibits differences in activity, expecially in increased blood flow to the kidneys and less abnormal heart rhythm. *Arthur H. Hayes, Jr., "Drugs: New Drugs," The World Book Science Annual 1977 (1976), p 268*

[1976]

in·van·dra·re ('in₁van dra: rə). *n.sing.* or *pl. Swedish.* a worker who has immigrated to Sweden to take advantage of the labor shortage and high wages.

Most *invandrare* in Sweden work in clean, progressive factories, and they work by law, for Swedish wages. Predrag takes home eighteen hundred kronor a month after taxes — about four hundred and ten dollars — which is more than five times what he used to make in Yugoslavia. *Jane Kramer, "Profiles: The Invandrare," The New Yorker, March 22, 1976, p 48*

[1976] ► This is the Swedish equivalent of the German term *Gastarbeiter* (literally) guest worker.

investigative reporting or **investigative journalism,** news gathering by investigation, as of crime or corruption when official investigation is lagging.

Two prominent Japanese journalists, at a luncheon meeting with their foreign colleagues here the other day, talked for two hours in Japanese about the problem and used "investigative reporting" in English throughout. *"Tokyo Press Slow to Dig Into Graft," The New York Times, April 11, 1976, p 4*

[1972]

in vitro fertilization, another name for EXTERNAL FERTILIZATION.

In-vitro fertilization, the method by which Louise Brown was conceived ... was developed in England by Dr. Patrick Steptoe and physiologist Robert Edwards to help women who cannot conceive because their Fallopian tubes are blocked. *Susan Jacoby, "Should Parents Play God?," The Reader's Digest, June 1979, p 110*

[1974]

in·works ('in'wərks), *adj. British.* carried on or taking place within a factory or works.

He added: "In hindsight, it might have been sensible to announce it, but there was no major hazard involved. It was a purely internal, local, inworks business." *Pearce Wright, "Two Men Are Contaminated Trying to Trace Source of Windscale Radioactive Leak," The Times (London), Dec. 11, 1976, p 2*

[1976]

I/O, abbreviation of *input-output* (operations or parts of a computer).

The disparity in the speed of electromechanical I/O and electronic components resulted in ineffective use of the more expensive resources (processor and memory), since these were often idle pending completion of the slower I/O operations. *Joel S. Birnbaum, "The Future Computer," McGraw-Hill Yearbook of Science and Technology 1977, p 42*

[1971]

iodine-xenon dating, a method of determining the age of a geological specimen by calculating the time it has taken radioactive xenon to decay into the iodine present in the specimen.

Iodine-xenon dating has established that iron sulphide in the Orgueil carbonaceous meteorite is one of the oldest known meteoritic mineral phases, and probably dates from the condensation stage of the early Solar System. *John F. Kerridge, Los Angeles, Cal., "Letters to Nature: Formation of Iron Sulphide in Solar Nebula," Nature, Jan. 22, 1976, p 189*

[1967] Compare AMINO-ACID DATING, RUBIDIUM-STRONTIUM DATING, THERMOLUMINESCENT DATING. See also AGE-DATE.

i·o·do·chlor·hy·drox·y·quin (₁ai ə dou₁klɔr hai-'drɑk sə kwin), *n.* a drug used to treat amebic dysentery and infections caused by certain protozoans and bacteria. *Formula:* C_9H_5ClINO

Another potentially harmful drug that the vacationer may encounter in many countries is an anti-diarrheal preparation called Entero-Vioform (iodochlorhydroxyquin). When taken for long periods, says the Medical Letter, this remedy can sometimes produce eye and nerve damage. *"And Don't Drink the Water," Newsweek, June 11, 1973, p 116*

[1972, from *iodo-* iodine + *chlor-* chlorine + *hydroxyl* + *quin*oline]

i·on·o·phore (ai'ən ə₁fɔr), *n.* any of various substances capable of transporting ions across lipid barriers in a cell.

The class of compounds known as ionophores has attracted increasing attention during the past decade because of the remarkable cation selectivities shown by these substances. Their ability to carry ions across lipid barriers caused the term "ionophores" to be suggested in 1967 for all compounds having this property. These compounds are generally cyclic, although several are known in which cyclization occurs only upon complexation with a cation. Those studied initially were of natural origin, namely, valinomycin, nonactin, and monensin. *Reed M. Izatt and James J. Christensen, "Ionophore," McGraw-Hill Yearbook of Science and Technology 1974, p 245*

[1967, from *ion* + connecting *-o-* + *-phore* combining form meaning thing that carries (from Greek *phóros* carrying)]

o·pon (i:'pɑn), *n.* a full-point score in judo, equivalent to a knockout in boxing.

Last night the first judo gold medal was won by the strong and skillful heavyweight from the Soviet Union, Sergei Novikov. He threw his opponent, Gunther Neureuther, forcibly on to his back to score an *ippon* to which there is no reply, ending a scheduled 10-minute bout in 79 seconds. *Jim Railton, The Times (London), July 28, 1976, p 11*

[1967, from Japanese, literally, point]

I.R.A. or **IRA**, *U.S.* abbreviation of *individual retirement account.*

I.R.A.'s were established by the Employee Retirement Income Security Act of 1974 to allow individuals not covered by an employer pension plan to set up a plan of his or her own. With an I.R.A., a person can put 15 percent of his earnings each year up to a maximum of $1,500 in a special account and build up an untaxed nest egg until normal retirement age. *Leonard Sloane, "Personal Finance: Retirement Accounts," The New York Times, March 18, 1976, p 61*

[1974] Compare KEOGH PLAN.

iren·ol·o·gy (ˌai rə'nɑl ə dʒi:), *n.* the study of peace, especially as part of international relations.

Peace-making is at last becoming a subject of serious study, engaging some of our most talented scholars. Variously called "Peace Studies," or "Irenology," this is rapidly developing as an independent field. *Joseph J. Fahey, "Irenology, the Study of Peace," in a pamphlet published by The Christophers, New York, Feb. 1974*

Irenology has received new impetus with an infusion of fresh ideas about human conflict from the fields of psychology, anthropology, sociology, economics, politics and history. *"Peace and Conflict Studies (Irenology)," Murdoch University (Australia) Handbook and Calendar 1975, p 66*

[1974, from *irenic*, ultimately from Greek *eirênê* peace, + English *-ology*; compare *polemology* (1968) the study of war]

Ir gene, a gene that determines immunological response to various antigens, such as viruses.

The discovery of the existence of Ir genes was only the first of several surprises. The next came when attempts were made to map them—that is, pinpoint the location of the genes among the chromosomes. It turned out that not only were they nowhere near the genes controlling antibody structure, but that they appeared to be tucked away right in the middle of the genes determining graft rejection, those coding for the so-called histocompatibility antigens. *Graham Chedd, "Genetics, Immunity and Disease," New Scientist, May 25, 1972, p 431*

The interaction between T cells and B cells that leads to antibody production . . . requires that both types of cell have identical IR genes. *Jacques M. Chiller, "Immunology," The World Book Science Annual 1975 (1974), p 306*

[1972; Ir abbreviation of *immune response*]

ir·ghiz·ite ('ir gəˌzait), *n. Geology.* a tektite rich in silica, discovered in Kazakhstan, U.S.S.R.

The irghizites are small black objects averaging about half a gram in weight. (Most tektites weigh a few grams.) They are warty, twisted objects. . . . Their chemical composition according to Kurt Fredrikson of the Smithsonian Institution, is remarkably uniform from specimen to specimen; it is unlike that of any local rocks and is very similar to that of the tektites found in Java. *John A. O'Keefe, "The Tektite Problem," Scientific American, Aug. 1978, p 116*

[1977, from *Irghiz*, a town near which it was discovered in a shallow crater + *-ite* rock, mineral]

ir·i·dol·o·gy (ˌir ə'dɑl ə dʒi:), *n.* a method of inspecting the iris of the eye which is supposed to aid in medical diagnosis.

Iridology can identify an organ that has degenerated enough to become cancerous. The basis for iridology is the neuro-optic reflex, an intimate marriage of the estimated half million nerve filaments of the iris with the cervical ganglia of the sympathetic nervous system. *Jessica Maxwell, "What Your Eyes Tell You About Your Health," Esquire, Jan. 1978, p 56*

Hoax or not, iridology has been practised and studied in Europe since the first iridology chart was developed in the early 1800s. There are now an estimated 10,000 European practitioners, though North America has only about 1,000, most of them in the United States. *Maclean's, Feb. 6, 1978, p 58*

[1971, from *irid-* of the iris (from Greek *îris, íridos* iris) + *-ology* study of] Compare SANPAKU.

iridologist, *n.:* The eye has been called the window to the soul. Less poetically, iridologists call it the map to the body's trouble spots. *Terry Poulton, "Health: Your Eyes May Be Trying to Tell You Something," Maclean's, Feb. 6, 1978, p 56*

Iris, *n.* acronym for *infrared intruder system*, an alarm system which is set off when a beam of infrared light is interrupted.

Iris (infrared intruder system) is . . . effective over distances of up to 200 metres between its two component parts, a beam transmitter and sensor. The infrared beam is very narrow—a 40 mm cylindrical "pipe" links the two components, which work off a 12 volt dc supply. *"Technology Review: Vietnam-style Sensors in Ulster—and at Home," New Scientist, Aug. 24, 1972, p 386*

[1972, influenced by the proper name *Iris*]

iron, *n. Slang.* **pump iron**, to lift weights; be a weight lifter.

When Lisa Lyon, 26, met muscleman-actor Arnold Schwarzenegger two years ago . . . she began to pump iron, and—voila—today the 5-3 cutie can heft 265 lbs. like straw. *New York Post, Oct. 19, 1979, p 7*

[1976, popularized by the motion picture "Pumping Iron" (1977)]

iron-pumper, *n. Slang.* a weight lifter.

The generation now turning 40 is the one that never trusted anyone over 30. Its members . . . are among the most fanatical cyclists, joggers, iron-pumpers, lap-swimmers, rope-jumpers and cross-country skiers. *"Ready, Set . . . Sweat!" Time, June 6, 1977, p 83*

[1977, from *pump iron* (see IRON)]

ISBN, abbreviation of *International Standard Book Number*, a number assigned to new books, especially to facilitate ordering.

The International Standard Book Number (ISBN) for numbering of books by publishers was widely adopted. At the meeting of the International Standards Organization Technical Committee 46, Documentation, at Scheveningen, Neth., in September further progress was made with the introduction of the International Standard Serials Number for the identification of periodical publications, and of the International Standard Record Number for records, tapes, and cassettes. *Anthony Thompson, "Libraries," Britannica Book of the Year 1973, p 413*

[1972]

ISD, abbreviation of *international subscriber dialing,* a system of direct dialing of telephones between participating countries.

Users of Britain's 15 million telephones with international subscriber dialling are now able to dial Moscow direct. ISD has also started to Bombay. *The Times (London), Nov. 16, 1976, p 4*

[1972]

island of stability, a group of superheavy chemical elements with highly stable nuclei.

For a number of years efforts have been under way at the University of California, Berkeley, and at Dubna in the Soviet Union to create elements in the so-called "island of stability" centered on 114 by smashing heavy atoms together. Likewise, various researchers have reported evidence that such elements exist—or that they have left behind their decay products. *Walter Sullivan, "Superheavy Element Is Believed Found," The New York Times, June 18, 1976, p B6*

[1970] Compare SEA OF INSTABILITY.

isobutyl nitrite, a colorless liquid chemical prepared from isobutyl alcohol, inhaled by drug users for its stimulant effects. *Formula:* $C_4H_9NO_2$

A kind of poor man's cocaine, isobutyl nitrite is known to users as a "popper" because its effects are similar to those of its restricted chemical cousin, amyl nitrite. Poppers have become the newest cheap kick for increasing numbers of people; manufacturers estimate that 5 million Americans regularly inhale the chemical, both on the dance floor and later in bed. Some people use it as a quick upper during the day. *Time, July 17, 1978, p 16*

[1978] Also, BUTYL NITRITE.

i·so·glu·cose (ˌaɪ səˈgluːˌkoʊs), *n.* a sugar substitute extracted from starchy crops such as maize and wheat flour.

Taxation of competing products should not be used as a means of disposing of food surpluses by compelling consumers to eat the dearer product. This principle is breached by the present proposal by the European Commission to tax isoglucose—a cheap sugar substitute made from cereals—to make it less competitive with sugar. *The Times (London), Feb. 16, 1978, p 12*

[1977, from *iso-* alike (from Greek *ísos* equal) + *glucose*]

I·so·prin·o·sine (ˌaɪ souˈprɪn ə siːn), *n.* a trademark for an experimental drug used to fight viral infection by stimulating the B cells and T cells of the immune system. *Formula:* $C_{52}H_{78}N_{10}O_{17}$

Thirty-nine volunteers were randomly chosen to receive either Isoprinosine or a placebo tablet. They were then challenged with a cold virus. Of the 19 volunteers receiving Isoprinosine, 5 became ill, whereas 14 out of 20 in the placebo group did. *Joan Arehart-Treichel, "Where Are Those Antiviral Drugs?" Science News, March 20, 1976, p 187*

[1971]

I²L, abbreviation of INTEGRATED-INJECTION LOGIC.

I²L is already faster than all the MOSFET technologies. On the other hand, the compact architecture of integrated-injection logic makes it a natural candidate for large-scale

integration. *James D. Meindl, "Microelectronic Circuit Elements," Scientific American, Sept. 1977, p 81*

[1976]

Ivorian, *adj.* of or relating to the Ivory Coast (a republic in western Africa, independent since 1960)

The black Ivorian élite, who can be seen enjoying a "elevenses" of caviar and champagne, support the President's free enterprise system. *Richard West, "Africa," The Sunday Times Magazine (London), Oct. 10, 1971, p 43*

—*n.* a native or inhabitant of the Ivory Coast.

It is hardly surprising that Mr Houphouet-Boigny has sounded the call for "Ivorisation." He has his Finance Minister, Konan Bedie, and Minister of the Plan Mohamed Teikoura Diawara, working actively to increase the role of Ivorians in national life. *Andre Fontaine, The Manchester Guardian Weekly (Le Monde section), March 24, 1973, p 15*

[1966, from French *Ivoirien,* from Côte d'*Ivoire* Ivory Coast + *-ien* -ian]

-ization, noun suffix now often used in the sense of "the transferring of establishments, institutions, or positions of authority or power (to a specified ethnic or national group)." The suffix is added to proper name adjectives and nouns usually ending in *-an*

Ivorianization: One explanation is that Mr. Yacé has been pressing behind the scenes for more vigorous application of a program of "Ivorianization," in which foreigners in high corporate and governmental positions are replaced by Ivorians. *John Darnton, The New York Times, July 14, 1976, p 2*

Libyanisation: In the first of two articles from Tripoli, David Hirst reports on how Libyanisation is going awry. *David Hirst, The Manchester Guardian Weekly, March 6, 1971, p 4*

Malaysianization: But some misunderstandings still prevail over the policy of Malaysianization. *Dick Wilson, The Times (London), Nov. 27, 1970, p IV*

Moroccanization: King Hassan . . . continued his direct control of political life and sought to extend the 'Moroccanization' of agriculture, industry and commerce. *Peter Kilner, "Morocco," The Annual Register of World Events in 1973 (1974), p 234*

Zairianization: Marred by corruption, mismanagement and political favoritism, the "Zairianization" of small- and medium-sized foreign firms had seriously disrupted some sectors of the economy. *Edouard Bustin, "Zaire," The Americana Annual 1977, p 557*

[1958] ▶ The new meaning of this suffix developed from the practice of replacing foreign managers with native citizens, especially non-Europeans, as part of the process of decolonization and the emergence of independent African and Asian nations during the 1960's and 1970's.

Originally *-ization,* when added to proper names (*Americanization, Germanization, Japanization, Mexicanization,* etc.) meant "the act or process of making or becoming (American, German, Japanese, etc.) in form or character." Use of the suffix in the sense of a transfer of authority to native citizens became prominent between the World Wars when the British adopted a policy of *Indianization,* increasing the number of native Indians elected to the legislature of India. Usage began to spread during the 1950's with the coining of *Egyptianization* (a synonym for "nationalization of foreign holdings") and *Nigerianization*. During the early 1970's *Vietnamization* became an important political term for transferring conduct of the Vietnam war to the Vietnamese and withdrawing American forces from Vietnam. *Cambodianization* and *Laosization* carried similar senses.

Current usage applies to developing countries of Africa, Asia, and Latin America. Compare -IZE. See also BUMIPUTRAIZATION.

ize, suffix now often used to form transitive verbs in the sense of "to transfer (establishments, institutions, or authority) to members of a specified ethnic or national group." Such verbs often derive by back formation from nouns in -IZATION.

Algerianize: "By 1980, the El Hadjar metal works will be 100 per cent Algerianized." There are 5,000 workers at El Hadjar now; within eight years there will be 15,000. *Edward R. F. Sheehan, The New York Times Magazine, April 23, 1972, p 22*

Ivorianize: The decision-making posts in the Civil Service are now totally Ivorianized and private firms have had to report and say what their plans are in this direction between now and 1980. *Alan Rake, The Times (London), March 25, 1977, p II*

Jordanize: Moves were also made to "Jordanize" the armed forces after the hijacking of a Jordanian airliner on November 6, 1974, by members of a group calling itself the "free officers." *Roy E. Thoman, "Jordan," 1976 Collier's Encyclopedia Year Book (1975), p 311*

[1958]

J

, n. *U.S. Slang.* a marijuana cigarette.

If they have never heard the terms in Vietnam, the POW's will quickly learn about "bummers" ("unpleasant experiences, especially with drugs"), "joints" ("marijuana cigarettes, jays, j's, reefers") and "munchies" ("to be hungry, usually after ingesting marijuana"). *"Newspeak for POW's," Newsweek, Feb. 12, 1973, p 68*

[1973, from abbreviation of *joint*, slang for marijuana cigarette] Also spelled JAY.

, n. variant of J PARTICLE.

The discovery two years ago of the heavy particles called psi or J continued to reverberate through all of particle physics, extending this year to the discovery and later to the photographing of particles that openly show the property called charm. *Kendrick Frazier, Science News, Dec. 18-25, 1976, p 387*

[1974]

Ja·cuz·zi (dʒəˈku: zi:), n. **1** a trademark for a device which swirls water in a bath.

West Coast home furnishing shows this fall feature . . . Waterford wood stoves from Ireland, as often and as prominently as Jacuzzis and hot tubs last year. *Thomas Hopkins, "Helping Us Live Better Alternately," Maclean's, Nov. 27, 1978, p 14*

2 a bath equipped with such a device.

I don't blame them for saying they'll move the team to Jidda if the city here won't build them a new upper deck and an executive Jacuzzi. *Calvin Trillin and Edward Koren, "The Inquiring Demographer," The New Yorker, Dec. 11, 1978, p 37*

[1966]

Ja·kob-Creutz·feldt disease (ˈyɑ: kəpˈkrɔits felt; *Anglicized* ˈdʒei kəbˈkrɔits felt), variant of CREUTZ-FELDT-JAKOB DISEASE.

It was diagnosed as Jakob-Creutzfeldt disease, and there are few recorded cases of it. Something about a galloping degeneration of the nerve cells. The prognosis for him: up to six months. Cause? Nobody knows. *William F. Buckley, Jr., "Death of a Christian," Condensed from "Execution Eve," The Reader's Digest, Sept. 1976, p 31*

[1973]

ja·mais vu (ˌʒɑ: me ˈvu:; *French* ʒɑ me ˈvʏ), *Psychology.* the illusion that one has never experienced the situation one is in, although it is in fact a familiar situation.

The experience of having been somewhere before—déjà vu—is said to be a purely physical experience which affects the frontal lobe of the brain which provides the impression that one has dreamt the identical situation previously. The same explanation is applied to the opposite feeling—jamais vu—when one momentarily fails to recognize a familiar situation. *Chauncy Stark, The Auckland Star (New Zealand), (Weekender section), March 31, 1973, p 3*

[1968, from French, literally, never seen, patterned on déjà vu (1903)]

Ja·na·ta (dʒəˈnɑ: tə), n. a coalition political party in India that defeated the long-ruling Congress Party and gained control of the government from 1977 to 1979. *Often used attributively.*

Indira Gandhi's return to the parliamentary stage in India last week, after nearly two years' absence, set off twitches of anxiety in the governing Janata coalition. *Barbara Slavin and Rosanne Klass, "Mrs. Gandhi Back In Center Stage," The New York Times, Nov. 12, 1978, Sec. 4, p 2*

For a while last year it seemed that the Janata wave had, in a handful of weeks, achieved the vital breakthrough. Congress, the party of Nehru, had governed too long, split too frequently: it was tired and discredited. *"Mrs. Gandhi,*

Unwelcome But Inevitable," The Manchester Guardian Weekly, Nov. 19, 1978, p 1

[1972, from Hindi, literally, People's group]

jar·go·naut ('dʒɑr gəˌnɔːt), *n. Humorous.* a person who uses jargon excessively.

So *Clinical* is inexorably coming to mean something like its opposite; and the doctors will have to invent a new word for their purpose. There is poetic justice of a sort if this happens. Members of the medical profession have often been unscrupulous and piratical Jargonauts with other men's jargon themselves. *Philip Howard, The Times (London), April 1, 1976, p 16*

[1963, blend of *jargon* and *argonaut*, probably influenced by *argot*]

Jaws of Life, a hydraulic device shaped like a pair of scissors in which the jaws are used to force apart or lift things, especially in rescue work.

Dale Greene doesn't remember the crash, the way his car wrapped around the tree trunk. . . . All he knows is that he is alive, and he gives credit to a machine called "the Jaws of Life," which freed him from the wreckage in around five minutes. *George Vecsey, "Rescue 'Jaws' Are Lifesavers, Not Killers," The New York Times, Sept. 6, 1976, p 17*

[1976, probably patterned on *kiss of life* (1963), British name for mouth-to-mouth resuscitation]

jay, *n. U.S. Slang.* a marijuana cigarette.

Several enterprising youths mingled with the crowds selling buttons saying "Have a Nice Jay" for $1 (jay is another word for marijuana cigarette) and bags of what they said were "legal smoking herbs" for $4. *"Hundreds March for Marijuana," The New York Times, May 16, 1976, p 28*

[1973, from pronunciation of *j*, abbreviation of *joint*] Also spelled J.

jazz loft, *U.S.* an upper floor in a building used as a club or concert hall where jazz, especially experimental jazz, is played.

Studio We, run by DuBois and Sultan, is one of the earliest jazz lofts. It is located in the squalor of a slum at 193 Eldridge Street, not far west of the famous Katz's delicatessen. *Stanley Crouch, "Jazz Lofts: A Walk Through the Wild Sounds," The New York Times Magazine, April 17, 1977, p 40*

[1976] Compare LOFT JAZZ.

jeaned (dʒiːnd), *adj.* wearing jeans.

They're 22, . . . jeaned and meticulously casual; perfectly young. *Bill Cameron and Elaine Dewar, Maclean's, Sept. 1973, p 36*

There was a festive atmosphere in the square as jeaned supporters settled down with their blankets to pass the night there and to see how their party would do. *Patricia Clough, The Times (London), June 22, 1976, p 7*

[1968] Compare DENIMED.

jeanswear, *n.* jeans of various styles for chiefly casual wear.

Jeans departments are readying themselves for a flood of related jeanswear which designers are beginning to produce. *Jacqueline McCord, "Blue-Jean Country," The New York Times Magazine, April 29, 1979, p 116*

[1979]

Jen·sen·ism ('dʒen səˌniz əm), *n.* the theory that in-

telligence, as measured by IQ tests, is largely determined by heredity.

Indeed, the term "Jensenism"—used, rightly or wrongly, to represent a belief that blacks are intellectually inferior t whites—has found its way into the educational lexicon. *Jerold K. Footlick, "Jensen for the Defense," Newsweek March 19, 1973, p 63*

I think part of the reason I paid as much attention to [the hereditability of intelligence] as I did when I wrote th *Harvard Review* article was that I felt that it had been to tally neglected in American psychology, and especially i American educational psychology. Part of 'Jensenism could probably be seen as a reaction against extreme and to me, unreasonable environmentalism. *Arthur Jensen quoted in "Jensenism—A Discussion," The Listener, Jan. 4 1973, p 14*

[1970, from Arthur R. *Jensen,* an American educa tional psychologist, born 1923, who suggested the theory + *-ism*] Also spelled **jensenism.**

Jensenist, *n., adj.:* Critics of the Jensenist line say that hi conclusions are illogical and based on inadequate evidence *Oliver Gillie, Science Journal, Sept. 1970, p 9*

Jensenite, *n., adj.:* More chilling is the call by some jer senites for the exercise of "eugenic foresight" or that of th physicist William Shockley for voluntary sterilization pr grams for people with lower than normal IQs. *Norman Daniels, "The Smart White Man's Burden," Harper's, Oc. 1973, p 25*

He firmly believes in the Jensenite figure of 80 per cer as the proportion of an individual's IQ that is inherited i advanced countries, and indeed thinks that the figure fo real intelligence (whatever that is) is still greater. *Graham Chedd, New Scientist and Science Journal, Sept. 30, 197 p 722*

jetabout, *n.* a person who travels by jet aircraft.

Kuala Lumpur, as well as other cities, is taking on th look of Bangkok or Singapore: luxury hotels; . . . loads o "jetabouts," mostly Australians crammed into Boeings fo two days here, two there, with a glimpse of the country be tween hotel rooms. *Jacques Decornoy, The Mancheste Guardian Weekly (Le Monde section), July 13, 1974, p 13*

[1974, patterned on *gadabout, layabout,* etc.]

je·té (ʒə'tei), *v.i. Ballet.* to leap from one foot to th other.

Since the show's emphasis is on the ability of dancers t act, as well as to glissade, jeté and pirouette, the show ha also become an actor's workshop. *Barbara Gelb, "Produc ing—and Reproducing—'A Chorus Line'," The New Yor Times Magazine, May 2, 1976, p 19*

[1968, verb use of the noun, ultimately from French

jetfoil, *n. Especially British.* a jet-powered hydrofoil

In September P&O is making a brave financial commit ment to the Thames and, three times a day, its jetfoil wi 'fly' down the river from the heart of London to Belgiu and back for less than it costs to go by plane. *Jenny Ba raclough, "Unloved Flows the Thames," The Listener, Ma 10, 1979, p 638*

[1974, from *jet* + hydro*foil*]

Jew for Jesus, a member of a missionary grou evangelizing among Jews and maintaining they ar Jews who accept Jesus as a Jew and as the Messiah

Some of the recent returnees, however, are hardly wha

Israeli legislators had in mind: zealous young Jews for Jesus whose purpose in coming to the Promised Land is to engage in aggressive Christian evangelism. *"Religion: Unwelcome Immigrants," Time, March 26, 1973, p 111*

[1972] Also called JEWISH CHRISTIAN.

ewish Christian, 1 a person claiming to be both a Jew and a Christian, especially a JEW FOR JESUS.

Though Jewish Christians come from all ages and backgrounds, they are predominantly young spiritual refugees from secularized Jewish homes, liberal synagogues, the drug culture or radical politics. *Time, June 12, 1972, p 67*

2 of or pertaining to Jewish Christians; claiming to be both Jewish and Christian.

The aggressiveness of some groups toward the conversion of Jews and the appearance of "Jewish Christian" sects aroused some apprehension among Jewish leaders. *Alfred P. Klausler, "Religion," Britannica Book of the Year 1973, p 584*

[1972]

iggly or **jiggle,** *adj. U.S. Slang.* sexually suggestive; titillating.

NBC had catapulted itself out of last place in the Nielsen ratings with "jiggly" shows and promotional ads. *" 'Stomachs Are Turning' Over Jiggly TV," New York Post, Oct. 24, 1979, p 15*

[1978]

INS (dʒinz), *n. U.S.* acronym for *Juvenile(s) In Need of Supervision.*

These children, who are variously labelled Persons in Need of Supervision (PINS), Children in Need of Supervision (CINS), Juveniles in Need of Supervision (JINS), or Wayward Minors, depending on the state they live in, will be guilty of nothing more serious than being a burden or a nuisance. *Lis Harris, "A Reporter at Large: Persons in Need of Supervision," The New Yorker, Aug. 14, 1978, p 55*

[1972] See MINS.

ob bank, a computerized job-placement service run by a government department.

The computer is an ideal tool for compiling and cleaning lists, so both DoE [Department of Employment] and DL [Department of Labour] developed computer job banks which produce periodic print-out lists of available jobs. *"Computers Get to Work on Unemployment," New Scientist, Aug. 31, 1972, p 437*

[1971] Also called JOB CENTRE.

ob centre, *British.* a variant of JOB BANK.

The cost of each job centre placing, based on the job centre's running costs, including premises, salaries and other expenses, is £22. How many private employment agencies do the job so cheaply? Job centres place 30 per cent to 40 per cent more people in jobs than the older-type offices they replace. *J. S. Cassels, The Times (London), Nov. 25, 1976, p 17*

[1971]

ogging pants, ankle-length pants similar to sweat pants, worn especially in cold weather for jogging.

Hunting, fishing, and hiking clothes were extremely popular. Among these items were . . . jogging pants tied at the ankle, and billowing sweat shirts. *Kathy Larkin, "Fashion," 1977 Collier's Encyclopedia Year Book (1976), p 260*

[1974]

jogging shoe, a soft sneaker or sneakerlike shoe with a cushioned sole, for jogging.

The piece begins as Gordon and Setterfield circle the space slowly in a jog-walk. They wear satin gym pants, white shirts, jogging shoes. An atmosphere of trial, of self-tempering, begins to gather. *Arlene Croce, "Dancing," The New Yorker, May 15, 1978, p 126*

[1978]

joint, *n. Racing Slang.* a small battery-operated device for applying an electric shock, used illegally to stimulate a racing horse.

For years, dishonest jockeys have experimented with tiny hand-carried shock-makers that can be applied to the horse's neck in the homestretch. But the "joint" is usually an unreliable accomplice, because many horses become angry and contrary when the men on their backs give them electric shocks. *Pete Axthelm, "Sports: How Not to Fix a Race," Newsweek, July 9, 1973, p 59*

[1972]

joint custody, a legal agreement between divorced or separated parents to share the custody of their children.

Six-year-old Tommy Mastin, the central figure in a controversial child-rearing arrangement known as joint custody, leads something of a double life in Gainesville, Fla. On Mondays, Wednesdays and Sundays, Tommy lives with his father at Oak Forest, a luxury apartment complex on the city's south side. *Georgia Dullea, "Joint Custody: Is Sharing the Child a Dangerous Idea?" The New York Times, May 24, 1976, p 24*

[1976]

joint float, a controlled float of the currencies of several countries, established to prevent large fluctuation in any one of the currencies, especially the controlled float established in 1972 by France, West Germany, Belgium, the Netherlands, Luxembourg, Norway, Sweden, and Denmark.

Mounting speculation about impending adjustments to currency parities within the European joint float . . . caused new uncertainty and much confusion in European financial centres. *Melvyn Westlake, The Times (London), Jan. 31, 1976, p 15*

[1973] Compare SNAKE.

Jonah word, any word which a chronic stutterer has difficulty uttering in ordinary conversation.

A person trained in the Van Riper method may attack a Jonah word like "mother" by prolonging the first syllable into a long mooing sound. The result may not be exactly like normal speech, but it is better than trying to talk through sealed lips. For some reason, prolonging the vowel sound often gets the stutterer through the block and into the next word. *Gerald Jonas, "A Reporter at Large: The Disorder of Many Theories," The New Yorker, Nov. 15, 1976, p 146*

[1976, from *Jonah,* the name of the Biblical character, in allusion to one who brings bad luck, a jinx]

Jones or **jones,** *n. U.S. Slang.* **1** Often, **the Jones.** drug addiction.

A gang member named Sly, 22, a tall black who lost a college basketball scholarship because of his habit, put it this way: "I was arrested three times for robbery and larceny. Drugs were ruining my life. But then the Brothers got hold of me and wouldn't let me out of their sight. You get a guy on the Jones and that's what you have to do." *Time, April 3, 1972, p 18*

2 a narcotic, especially heroin.

"Jones" is slang both for heroin and its craving (as in "his jones came on him so bad"). The top ghetto jones-man, as pragmatic as a dumdum bullet, hunts his upstart challengers with stunning, careless cruelty. *S. K. Oberbeck, Review of "The Jones Men" by Vern E. Smith, Newsweek, Oct. 14, 1974, p 120*

[1970, apparently from the common proper name *Jones*, but the connection is obscure]

Jo·vi·ol·o·gist (ˌdʒou viːˈɑl ə dʒist), *n.* astronomer who specializes in the study of the planet Jupiter.

It's been scarcely four months since Pioneer 10 gave earthlings their first good look at Jupiter, and the Joviologists are still finding new causes for excitement every time they reexamine their data. *"Jupiter Revisited: The Rosetta Stone," Science News, April 13, 1974, p 236*

[1974, from Latin *Jovis* genitive of *Jupiter* + English *-ologist* student of]

J particle, another name for PSI PARTICLE.

The most striking feature of the J particle is its very long lifetime. The J particle lives from a hundred to a thousand times longer than all known mesons of heavy mass. Whenever objects in nature are found much more stable than expected, there is reason to be curious. There must be some hidden cause, some yet unknown effects of new principles that change the anticipated course of events. *Samuel C. C. Ting, "J Particles," McGraw-Hill Yearbook of Science and Technology 1976, p 226*

[1975, named by Samuel C. C. Ting of the Massachusetts Institute of Technology, who led in its discovery at the Brookhaven National Laboratory in Long Island, New York, partly from the initial letter of *jump* and partly because the letter *J* resembles the Chinese character for *Ting*]

J-psi particle, another name for PSI PARTICLE.

What the two scientists had to tell each other was precisely the 'same thing: using different techniques, both had discovered a new subatomic particle — now known as the J/psi particle — a finding that turned the field of elementary particle physics on its collective ear. *R. James Turner, "Science: Small, Smaller, Smallest," Maclean's, Jan. 10, 1977, p 48*

[1977]

jugate, *n. U.S.* a button showing two heads, especially one which pairs the pictures of a Presidential candidate and his running mate.

Pollack's own collectibles run heavily toward buttons. He owns more than 50,000. He keeps them in file drawers in his bedroom. If he could find the button of his dreams, it would be the Cox-Roosevelt 1920 campaign button.

"I guess everybody thinks about owning a Cox-Roosevelt jugate," he said. "It goes for $2500 on up. I've seen one; I've touched it." *Lewis Grossberger, New York Post, Sept. 13, 1975, p 9*

[1974, noun use of the adjective (OED 1887) meaning joined or overlapping, as two busts on a coin]

juke, *U.S.* —*v.t.* to pretend to make a movement or play in American football to mislead (an opponent); fake.

"My game is to juke the tough guys," he [O. J. Simpson] says. "I put the okey-doke on them, just bounce around an look for daylight. No one is going to get me to put my hea in Dick Butkus' lap." *"Sport: Year of the Okey-Doke, Time, Dec. 24, 1973, p 57*

—*n.* an act of juking in American football; a fake.

Pruitt puts on "a lot of jukes and lateral movement" s that he does not get hit head on. *"Sport: Runts in the B League," Time, Dec. 5, 1977, p 76*

[1973, originally (1958) verb intransitive, probabl from earlier verb (OEDS 1937) *juke* to dance, ulti mately of West African origin]

jump jockey, *British.* a rider in a steeplechase.

Graham Thorner, that most determined of jump jockey rode his heart out three times over fences in stamina sa ping conditions at Worcester yesterday for a double o When Lad and Breakwater and a neck second on Toy Fla *The Times (London), Jan. 25, 1977, p 12*

[1970]

junk bond, *U.S.* a high-risk, noncorporate bon that is bought at less than face value.

What they will also get is a piece of a fund that specia izes in deep-discount bonds — sometimes known as "jun bonds" — that have enabled FIFI over the last several year to run up one of the most enviable performance records i the industry. Junk bonds, because they carry a muc higher risk quotient than corporate bonds, typically offer much higher return. *Richard Phalon, "Personal Inves ing," The New York Times, Jan. 29, 1977, p 28*

[1976]

junk food, quickly prepared or ready-made foo often containing a large proportion of food substi tutes, and usually rich in carbohydrates, such as im itation potato chips or cheap commercial baker products.

One thing most camps try to do is cut down on junk foo children are accustomed to. *Richard Flaste, "How to Pic a Camp," The New York Times Magazine, March 20, 197 p 91*

"There is a huge junk food industry providing empty ca ories . . . the trouble is that these junk foods will not fill th nutritional gap, though big profits could be made." *Hug Clayton, "Margarine Health Claim Challenged," Th Times (London), Feb. 25, 1977, p 5*

[1973]

junk gun, another name for SATURDAY NIGHT SPE CIAL.

The 1968 Federal Gun Control Act banned the import many of these so-called "junk guns." But under pressu from various gun lobbyists, the landing of gun parts was n stopped. This led naturally to the profitable gun-assembl business. *R. Z. Sheppard, Time, Nov. 26, 1973, p 131*

[1973]

junkie, *n. Informal.* one who is addicted to som (specified) thing; enthusiast; devotee.

For all I know, people may exist who like to see the names in print. John Lennon and Yoko Ono were said to b print junkies. *Germaine Greer, The Listener, Nov. 15, 197 p 671*

The campaign of antisepsis began soon after h [Solzhenitsyn] was expelled from the Soviet Union in 197 ("He suffered *too* much—he's crazy." "He's a Christia zealot with a Christ complex." "He's an agrarian reactio ary." "He's an egotist and a publicity junkie.") *Tom Wolfe,* *"The Intelligent Co-Ed's Guide to America," Harper's, July 1976, p 34*

Barbara Mikulski, a Democratic member of Congress from Baltimore . . . told me why she was here: "I'm a new-idea junkie. In 1968 and 1972, the Party wasn't in touch with what was going on out there with the people." *Elizabeth Drew, "A Reporter at Large: Constituencies," The New Yorker, Jan. 15, 1979, p 60*

[1972, transferred and figurative use of the slang word for a drug addict (1920's)] Compare GROUPIE[1] (def. 2).

u·so ('yu:ˌsou), *n.* any of a group of young leftist members of the Social Democratic Party of West Germany.

One problem is that one can't talk about the Social Democrats at the moment without discussing their left-wingers, especially the powerful young socialist movement known as Jusos for short. The Jusos, roughly speaking, are moderate Marxists educated during the student upheavals four or five years ago: their aim is gradually to phase out capitalism by reforms rather than revolution. *Neal Ascherson, The Listener, Jan. 31, 1974, p 139*

His [Chancellor Schmidt's] first order of business was to lay down the law to the young Marxists, known as Jusos, whose demands for nationalization, more welfare programs and more state controls were angering the conservative workers who were the party's backbone. *Clyde H. Farnsworth, The New York Times Magazine, May 2, 1976, p 82*

[1971, from German, short for *Jungsozialisten,* literally, young socialists]

u·va·bi·one (ˌdʒu: vəˈbɑi oun), *n.* a terpene of the balsam fir which is a naturally occurring hormone similar to the juvenile hormone that prevents insects from reaching sexual maturity.

William Bowers and his colleagues at the Insect Physiology Laboratory, Agricultural Research Service (ARS), Beltsville, Maryland, isolated and determined the structure of this "paper factor," now called juvabione. Juvabione, which is found in the wood of the balsam fir, only affects members of one family of "bugs." *Jean L. Marx, "Insect Control (II): Hormones and Viruses," Science, Aug. 31, 1973, p 834*

[1968, from *juv*enile (hormone) + *Abi*es (balsamea), New Latin name of the balsam fir + horm*one*]

juvenile-onset diabetes or **juvenile diabetes,** the form of diabetes that develops early in life (usually before the age of 20) and is much more severe, although less widespread, than MATURITY-ONSET DIABETES.

Juvenile-onset diabetes is treated with injections of insulin derived from the pancreases of cows and pigs. The patient's diet must also be controlled so that the minimum amount of insulin is required and so that concentrations of sugar in the blood do not fluctuate too widely. *Thomas H. Maugh II, "The Two Faces of Diabetes," The World Book Science Annual 1978 (1977), p 54*

[1976]

juvenile-onset diabetic or **juvenile diabetic:** There are an estimated 10 million diabetics in this country; one million juvenile diabetics, most of whom suffer from absolute insulin deficiency. *Elizabeth Stone, "A Mme. Curie from the Bronx," The New York Times Magazine, April 9, 1978, p 98*

ju·ve·nil·i·za·tion (ˌdʒu: və nə ləˈzei ʃən), *n.* an arrest in the development or maturation of an insect, especially by action of juvenile hormones.

72% of the treated *Pyrrhocoris* larvae formed adultoids which showed effects ranging from a marked juvenilization of the wings to the formation of supernumerary sixth instar larvae. By contrast, untreated larvae in similar conditions consistently formed normal adults. *Lynn M. Riddiford and James W. Truman, Cambridge, Mass., "Letters to Nature," Nature, June 23, 1972, p 458*

[1972]

ju·ve·noc·ra·cy (ˌdʒu: vəˈnak rə si:), *n.* rule or government by young people.

A young McGovernite woman, 24-years-old, demanded to be made vice chairman of the Platform Committee to represent youth, "an oppressed minority." The Committee rushed to oblige. Then, on television, she spoke about "child molesting," and, according to the *Village Voice,* gave "the most rotten, bigoted speech of the whole Convention." The perils of juvenocracy. *Lewis S. Feuer, "Democrats Versus Democracy," National Review, Oct. 27, 1972, p 1180*

[1972, from *juven*ile + connecting *-o-* + *-cracy,* as in *aristocracy*]

K

K or **k,** *n.* a unit of computer memory capacity equal to 1000 (or 1024 in the binary system) characters, bytes, or words.

Does the idea of a 10 million K RAM stretch credulity too far? It shouldn't because this device is already here. Dutch electrotechnical giant Philips recently demonstrated a random access memory (RAM) that can hold up to 10^{10} bits of information, that can be written on by a user and on which any bit, or character, can be located within a quarter of a second. *John Stansell, "Optical Storage Is Light Years Ahead," New Scientist, Nov. 23, 1978, p 611*

[1966, from *k*, symbol for *kilo-*, prefix for 1000] See KILOBYTE.

ka·be·le (kɑː'bei lei), *n.* variant of KEBELE.

In addition, there are mass organizations with great power, such as the peasants' associations, the trade unions and the kabeles, or urban dwellers' associations. Originally created by the Dergue and the ideologues, they now have millions of members and their own imperatives. Their tribunals sit on criminal and civil cases. Kabele leaders collect rents and can evict tenants. *Michael T. Kaufman, "A Reign of War in the Land of Sheba," The New York Times Magazine, Jan. 8, 1978, p 26*

[1977]

ka·bou·ter (kə'bɑu tər), *n.* any of a group of Dutch political activists promoting pacifism and anarchism.

The Dutch protesters passed on all they had learnt about . . . pollution to an Antwerp offshoot of the *kabouters* (literally dwarfs or pixies), Holland's newest antisociety movement. But protest was in vain. *John Lambert, The Times (London), May 31, 1972, p III*

[1970, from Dutch]

ka·in·ic acid (kei'in ik), a chemical substance derived from a species of red alga, used especially to kill intestinal worms. *Formula:* $C_{10}H_{15}NO_4$

Kainic acid, a potent substance that is now the standard treatment for intestinal parasites, comes from a red seaweed, *Digenia simplex*, eaten by the Japanese from time immemorial for the same purpose. *Anil Angarwal, "Eye of Newt and Toe of Frog," New Scientist, Nov. 2, 1978, p 367*

[1962, probably from Greek *kainós* new + English *-ic* (adj. suffix)]

Kam·pu·che·a ('kɑːm puː'tʃiː ə), *n.* the official name of Cambodia since 1975.

A vitriolic attack on Canada's record in Indochina and its treatment of the underprivileged at home has been made by the government of Cambodia, now known as Democratic Kampuchea. Canada's hands are said to be "stained with the blood of the people of Kampuchea" . . . say the Cambodians. *David Allen, "Cambodia: The Best Offense . . ." Maclean's, Sept. 25, 1978, p 25*

[1976, from Khmer (language of Cambodia)] See KHMER ROUGE.

Kampuchean, *adj., n.:* Speaking two days after Vietnam and the Soviet Union signed a friendship and cooperation treaty in Moscow, Mr Wang said at a banquet last nigh "The Chinese Government and people resolutely suppo the Kampuchean people's just struggle in defence of the independence." *The Times (London), Nov. 7, 1978, p 9*

Peking's technicians have been providing expertise i telecommunications and irrigation, while 49 North Korean attempted (unsuccessfully, as it turned out) to teach th Kampucheans to fly MiG aircraft. *Time, Jan. 22, 1979, p 33*

ka·rak·te·ris·ti·ka (ˌkɑː rɑːk te'riːs tiː kə), *n.* a character reference by one's employer or superior which a Soviet citizen applying for an exit visa i required to submit with his application.

To Svechinsky's surprise, the Moscow OVIR announce that, yes, it too would accept applications (in duplicate, ac companied by six photos, permission from parents, and *karakteristika*, or character reference, from the place o work). *Anatole Shub, "From Russia with Chutzpah," Harper's, May 1972, p 77*

[1972, from Russian *kharakteristika* character ization] Also spelled KHARAKTERISTIKA.

ka·ree·ba or **ka·re·ba** (kə'riː bə), *n.* a short-sleeved shirt worn with matching trousers by Jamaican men.

The guests sauntered from booth to booth viewing . . . the latest kareebas. *Week-End Star (Kingstown, Jamaica) Sept. 28, 1973, p 6*

He [Michael Manley] was wearing a blue *Kareba* suit, the open-necked, loose-fitting African garb he popularized i Jamaica in line with third-world fashion. *Stephen Davis The New York Times Magazine, July 25, 1976, p 32*

[1972, probably of African origin]

karma, *n.* an aura or quality (good or bad) felt to be emanating from a person, place, or thing.

Disney World alone attracts 1,000,000 visitors a month t its 27,000 acres of fun and games—and school is not eve out yet. "It's great karma, man," noted one long-haire California youth as he emerged from the Mickey Mous Review. *Time, May 15, 1972, p 77*

Laid back though they are, Los Angelenos can be a touchy as anyone else when the karma feels wrong. *Davi Cobb, "Exit Laughing," Maclean's, Dec. 27, 1976, p 28*

[1970, extended sense of the Hindu and Buddhist term (OED 1828, from Sanskrit) meaning the acts and thoughts that determine a person's fate; hence. fate or destiny]

Karman cannula or **Karman catheter,** a device for performing an abortion by vacuum aspiration. See the quotation for details.

The Karman cannula is a narrow, blunt, flexible plasti tube, closed at the end and notched. Attached to any vacuum-creating apparatus it effects suction abortion i about two minutes. Since the cannula is blunt and soft, the risk of uterine perforation is virtually nil. *Stephanie Mills "The Cannula Abortion," Harper's, April 1974, p 107*

[1972, named after Harvey *Karman*, an American designer of surgical instruments, who invented it]

CIA or **K.C.I.A.**, abbreviation of *Korean Central Intelligence Agency.*

For all of its zeal, the KCIA is regarded in Washington as a ham-handed offspring of the U.S. CIA — which has helped finance the KCIA in the past. The KCIA does not bother to gather intelligence from South Korea's closest enemy, North Korea. *"Investigations: Koreagate on Capitol Hill?" Time, Nov. 29, 1976, p 14*

[1976]

e·be·le (kə'bei lei), *n.* any of the self-governing neighborhood associations formed in the towns and cities of Ethiopia by the military government which deposed Emperor Haile Selassie in 1974.

To manage the confiscated urban property and to act as agents of administration, the government established a series of kebeles. The kebele is thus the basic urban unit of the Ethiopian revolution — what the soviet was to the Russian Revolution and the commune was to the Chinese revolution. *Joseph Kraft, The New Yorker, July 31, 1978, p 40*

[1976, from Amharic] Also spelled KABELE.

eller plan or **Keller method,** a method of college instruction in which the subject matter of a course is divided into study units students are allowed to master at their own pace.

The Keller Plan as applied to science instruction in college was the subject of a comprehensive survey during the year. Evaluation of the results of a large number of experimental and questionnaire-type investigations revealed a surprisingly consistent advantage of PSI over the orthodox lecture-discussion procedure. *Melvin H. Marx, "Behavioral Sciences: Psychology," 1975 Britannica Yearbook of Science and the Future (1974), p 195*

[1973, named after Fred S. *Keller*, an American psychologist who proposed it in 1968] Also called PSI.

e·ogh plan ('ki: ou), *U.S.* any of various plans by which self-employed individuals set aside part of their yearly income as a tax-deferred annuity or retirement fund.

Keogh plans permit self-employed people . . . to deduct each year as much as 15 percent of what they earn (up to a maximum of $7,500 annually), tuck the money into an insurance annuity, mutual fund or savings bank, and pay no taxes on the interest or dividends credited to the account until they retire. *Richard Phalon, "Personal Finance: Self-Pension Woes," The New York Times, Dec. 27, 1976, p C-14*

[1976, named after Eugene J. *Keogh*, born 1907, a Congressman from Brooklyn, N.Y., who sponsored a legislative bill for such a plan] Compare I.R.A.

e·pone ('ki:ˌpoun), *n.* a trademark for a highly toxic chlorinated hydrocarbon formerly widely used as a pesticide. *Formula:* $C_{10}Cl_{10}O$

Kepone . . . is shown to cause brain and liver damage, sterility and possibly cancer in exposed workers. Allied Chemical Corporation, the manufacturer, was fined $13 million for dumping Kepone-laden wastes into Virginia's James River, destroying the fishing industry downstream. *Jane E. Brody, "Chemicals: Health Is the New Priority," The New York Times, Jan. 9, 1977, Sec. 3, p 39*

Industrial waste from the plant, laced with the pesticide kepone, flowed through the city's sewer system. *The New Yorker, Jan. 3, 1977, p 65*

[1972] Also spelled **kepone.** Generic name, CHLORDECONE.

Kev·lar ('kevˌlar), *n.* a trademark for a strong, lightweight, synthetic fiber developed to substitute for steel in automobile tires, cables, and many other products.

Lined with Kevlar, a synthetic fiber that is lighter than nylon and five times as strong as steel, these contemporary garments are virtually bulletproof and knife-resistant. Already worn by police in seven U.S. cities, the "soft body armor" also has considerable appeal within the bullet-prone private sector as well. *"Fashion Plating," Newsweek, Feb. 24, 1975, p 56*

[1973]

keypad, *n. British.* a small panel or console with a set of buttons for operating an electronic calculator or other machine.

Telephones equipped with a 12-button keypad can be used for data communication or retrieval — for example, in a shop to check a customer's credit balance or in a factory to record job progress or staff attendance. *Kenneth Owen, "Telecommunications: Technology of Tomorrow Is Here Today," The Times (London), June 8, 1976, p 10*

[1967, patterned on *keyboard*]

keyphone, *n. British.* a push-button telephone.

Looking exactly like a conventional instrument, except for its 10-button keypad in place of the rotary dial, the Keyphone is being sold to the public as "the phone with the modern touch." *Nicholas Valéry, "Debut for the Telephone on a Chip," New Scientist, April 11, 1974, p 65*

[1967, from *keyboard* + *phone*]

khan·ga or **kan·ga** ('ka:ŋ gə), *n.* a colorful cotton fabric or garment of East Africa, with traditional patterns printed on the borders.

One-of-a-kind khangas from Kenya are used as body wraps and head wraps, or the ends may be tied to form a carryall. Made of hand-printed cotton, they've been prewashed until they're as soft as oversize hankies. *Picture legend, "Fashion: From Africa," The New York Times Magazine, April 11, 1976, p 100*

[1963, from Swahili] Also called KITENGE.

kha·rak·te·ris·ti·ka (ˌxa: ra:k te'ri:s ti: kə), *n.* variant of KARAKTERISTIKA.

According to one Soviet scientist who has traveled abroad, the crucial document is a kharakteristika, or character reference, from one's institute. *Christopher S. Wren, The New York Times, June 16, 1976, p 16*

[1972]

Khmer Rouge (kə'mer 'ru:ʒ), the Communist guerrilla force (and from 1975 to January 1979 the Communist government) of Cambodia (Kampuchea).

In "The Politics of Food," an apologia for the evacuation of Phnom Penh, the Indochina Resource Center criticizes the use of the term "Khmer Rouge" as pejorative and/or illiterate. But it is used by Sihanouk and it will be employed in this article in the same sense as he employs it — as a shorthand for that section of the FUNK [National United Front of Kampuchea] which took control of Cambodia after April 17, 1975. *William Shawcross, "Cambodia Under Its New Rulers," The New York Review of Books, March 4, 1976, p 24*

In order to counterbalance a neutrality hitherto tilted

towards the Khmer Rouge, Thailand sent the 50,000 refugees into a sector held by the Vietnamese and their allies in Phnom Penh. *Roland-Pierre Paringaux, The Manchester Guardian Weekly (Le Monde section), July 1, 1979, p 11*

[1970, from French, literally, Red Khmer] See KAMPUCHEA.

khoum (ku:m), *n.* a monetary unit in Mauritania introduced in 1973, equal to 1/20 of a ougiya.

At the end of June, on the same day as a total eclipse of the sun brought hundreds of visitors to Mauritania, the new currency was launched. The denominations were the ougiya (worth 5 CFA francs) and the khoum (worth one CFA franc). *Kaye Whiteman, "French-Speaking West and Central Africa," The Annual Register of World Events 1973 (1974), p 274*

[1973, from Arabic]

kickboxing, *n.* a form of boxing, especially popular in Oriental countries, in which kicking with bare feet is permitted.

From karate, Mr. Rothman and his friends have graduated to the more dangerous kickboxing, an Americanized karate. Wearing boxing gloves and sneakers, the kickboxers fight full force and Mr. Rothman admits "you can get hurt." He described it as the "ultimate" in fighting and self-defense. *The Observer (Eastchester, N.Y.), July 20, 1972, p 4*

[1971]

kickboxer, *n.:* In the featherweight contest Cambridge's Griffin understandably came out somewhat perplexed against Oxford's former Thai kickboxer, Weeraworawit. *The Times (London), March 4, 1978, p 17*

kickturn, *n.* the lifting of the front of a skateboard and moving it left or right by pressing down and pivoting on the back wheels.

Children preferred boards with "kicktail" curves, helpful in performing such stunts as kick-turns. *The Times (London), Dec. 1, 1977, p 2*

[1965]

ki·dol·o·gy (ki'dɑl ə dʒi:), *n. British, Informal.* a subject of humor or ridicule; something comic or laughable.

It is hard to see their [French wines] making much headway here in Britain where the indiscriminate use of the word *Château* is a popular piece of kidology. *The Times (London), Nov. 22, 1976, p 17*

[1964, from *kid* to joke with, fool, tease + *-ology* study of]

kidvid, *n. U.S.* children's television programs. *Often used attributively.*

Yet, beyond those business-as-usual cartoons, a greening has been transforming the kid-vid wasteland, and the catalyst is yesteryear's bore—educational (now public) television. *Christopher S. Wren, Saturday Review, Sept. 16, 1972, p 54*

It's a new world for Anne, an innocent abroad now in that special region of televisionland known as kidvid, an industry within an industry where, says one broadcaster, "We don't think of them as little people, but as little customers." *Joan Barthel, "Boston Mothers Against Kidvid," The New York Times Magazine, Jan. 5, 1975, p 15*

[1971, from *kid* child + *video*]

killer bee, 1 an African honeybee (*Apis mellifera adansonii*), usually black with yellow abdominal bands, noted for its extreme aggressiveness when disturbed.

Such behavior has earned the insect names like the "killer bee" or the "Mau Mau bee." The bee is also a hard worker and an excellent producer of honey, especially tropical and semi-tropical environments. It was for these reasons that Brazilian authorities decided, in 1956, to import the African bee. *George Alexander, "About The Killer Bees," Encyclopedia Science Supplement (Grolier) 1976, p 93*

2 any of various hybrids of this African bee and native Brazilian bees that have been spreading from Brazil since the late 1950's, attacking in swarms anything that disturbs their hives.

The northward and southward expansion of the bee's range from the original point of release [has] . . . led predictions that the "killer bees" might eventually spread reign of terror throughout the U.S. *Scientific American, Jan. 1976, p 63*

[1976]

killer satellite, another name for HUNTER-KILLER SATELLITE.

Killer satellites are small spacecraft. They carry explosive charge which destroys itself and any nearby satellite on detonation. *The Times (London), Dec. 16, 1977, 16*

[1972]

killer weed, another name for ANGEL DUST.

Angel dust . . . is called killer weed because it causes numbness in the arms and legs and because it makes some users feel "dead." *Marcia Kramer, "Angel Dust, the New Killer in Town," Daily News (New York), Feb. 23, 1978, p .*

[1978]

kill shot, a shot in racquet games that is very difficult or practically impossible to return.

Third, the squash ball is smaller and not as lively as the racquetball. Combined with the smaller court and telltale, this leads to longer rallies and puts the emphasis skillful placement of shots rather than power. Very few points are ended by an irretrievable "kill" shot—a bread-and-butter play in racquetball or tennis. *Bill Bruns, Mon. Dec. 1977, p 93*

[1976]

ki·lo·byte ('kil ə,bait), *n.* a unit of computer information equal to one thousand bytes.

The data are recorded on the magnetic tape inside the cartridge in a diagonal fashion. Each stripe contains 4 K (kilobytes) of data. A total of 67 diagonal stripes represent one cylinder on disk. *James L. Pyle, "Computer Memory," McGraw-Hill Yearbook of Science and Technology 1979, p 148*

[1973, from *kilo-* 1000 + *byte* unit of computer information usually equal to 8 bits] Compare MEGABYTE

ki·lo·met·rage (kə'lɑm ə tridʒ), *n.* the number of kilometers covered or traveled.

He [the lorry driver] is paid according to milage (or rather kilometrage). *Edmund Stevens, "Making a Killing on Russia's Open Roads," The Times (London), June 23, 1976, p*

The difference between a united and divided Jerusalem is nothing in terms of kilometrage, but everything in terms of having a unified capital. *Terence Smith, The New York Times, April 9, 1976, p 2*

[1976, from French *kilométrage*]

ki·na ('ki: nə), *n.* the monetary unit of Papua New Guinea (an independent country since 1975).

In line with a decision made in the spring of 1974, Papua New Guinea adopted a new currency as of April 19, 1975. The kina, which is divided into 100 toeas, will circulate with the Australian dollar, to which it is equivalent, until the end of the year. *Thaddeus F. Tuleja, "Papua New Guinea," 1976 Collier's Encyclopedia Year Book (1975), p 398*

[1975, from the native name]

ki·nin·o·gen (kai'nin ə dʒən), *n. Biochemistry.* an inactive precursor in the blood of any of various kinins (polypeptides forming in tissues in response to injury).

A recent report described the immunoglobulin E (IgE) mediated release of a new mediator . . . which is an arginine esterase and generates kinin from kininogen. *Harold H. Newball, "Allergic Reaction," McGraw-Hill Yearbook of Science and Technology 1977, p 126*

[1968, from *kinin* (1954, abstracted from *bradykinin*, 1949) + connecting *-o-* + *-gen* thing that produces (from Greek *-genês* born)]

Kir·li·an ('kir li: ən), *adj.* of or relating to Kirlian photography.

Those who are interested in the details of how to make Kirlian motion pictures may feel free to write to me. *Gary K. Poock, Science News, Dec. 1, 1973, p 339*

Among the factors that obviously influence a person's Kirlian signature, explains physicist William Tiller of Stanford University, are chemical changes on the skin surface brought about by such unmysterious substances as sweat and body oils, the topology of a person's fingerprints, the electrical energy in the outer cells of the skin and physical buckling of the film when the electric spark passes through it. *Newsweek, March 4, 1974, p 55*

[1972, abstracted from KIRLIAN PHOTOGRAPHY]

Kirlian photograph, an image obtained on film by Kirlian photography.

The body's aura, he continued, is more intense inside a pyramid. He took from his desk two Kirlian photographs of a living butterfly. The one made outside the pyramid showed only a faint white aura. The one made inside showed a bright blue aura that extended several inches beyond the butterfly's wings. *Martin Gardner, "Mathematical Games," Scientific American, June 1974, p 118*

[1972] Also called ELECTROPHOTOGRAPH.

Kirlian photography, a process that records on photographic film the field radiation of electricity supposed to surround living things. By passing an electric charge through an object a bright glow is detected emanating from the object.

Work in Russia recently has photographed, by Kirlian photography, the energy emissions from the acupuncture points. *Sydney Rose-Neil, New Scientist, Aug. 10, 1972, p 309*

Kirlian photography . . . produces startling photographs of pulsating, multicolored lights streaming from the human body and from plants. *Lisa J. Shawver, "Science Focuses on a 'Light of Life'," Science News, Sept. 29, 1973, p 202*

Many psychics and their followers believe that paranormal powers may be dependent on mysterious auras or "energy flows," phenomena that they say can be recorded by Kirlian photography. *Time, March 4, 1974, p 70*

[1972, named after Semyon D. and Valentina K. Kirlian, Russian researchers who invented the process] Also called RADIATION-FIELD PHOTOGRAPHY. See BIOPLASMA.

ki·ten·ge (ki'teŋ gi:), *n.* another name for KHANGA.

Women and girls were so committed to minis that when those dresses were banned they immediately saw an alternative in the kitenge . . . and began tying them around their legs. *Mohamed Sengooba, Voice of Uganda, March 14, 1973, p 6*

[1964, from Swahili]

kneecapping, *n.* the act of shooting or drilling through the kneecaps of a person as a punishment.

. . . I.R.A. "hit men" punish detractors and defectors, by subjecting them to "kneecapping." "It used to be done with guns," Clutterbuck will tell a class matter-of-factly, "but lately they've been running an electric drill through the knee in such a way that even after medical treatment there's a peculiar, easily identifiable walk." *E. J. Kahn, Jr., "Profiles: Richard Lewis Clutterbuck," The New Yorker, June 12, 1978, p 60*

The Red Brigades . . . last week took responsibility for the "knee-capping" of three more Italian industrial figures. *"At Last, Italy Gets a President," The New York Times, July 9, 1978, Sec. 4, p 2*

Passing into verb.

Terrorists 'Kneecap' 10 At School In Italy. *Headline in New York Post, Dec. 12, 1979, p 43*

[1975]

kneeling bus, *U.S.* a bus with a pneumatic suspension system that will lower its body to the level of a curb so that passengers do not have to negotiate a step.

Pledging that his own administration would be "sensitive to the special needs of the aging," Mr. Koch promised, among other things, . . . the deployment of "kneeling" buses "on routes where they will serve the greatest number of people who need them." *Charles Kaiser, The New York Times, Aug. 29, 1977, p 21*

[1977]

knees-up, *n. British.* a lively party or celebration.

I'm sure the Ferryboat at Whitchurch won't mind my saying that they're good for a knees-up any night of the week. *John Hall, The Manchester Guardian Weekly, (Le Monde section), May 30, 1970, p 14*

The street party . . . wasn't exactly a Cockney "knees-up," but everyone was having a ball. *Carol Kennedy, "The U.K.: Doing It up Royally," Maclean's, June 27, 1977, p 40*

[1963, from a popular song beginning "Knees up, Mother Brown!" and a dance associated with it]

known quantity, *Figurative.* a well-known or familiar person or thing.

411 dailies with 30 million circulation back Ford. They tend to emphasize that he is a known quantity. *"The Nation: Who's for Whom," Time, Nov. 8, 1976, p 13*

Have people become so accustomed to the series idea from television viewing that they go to another Dirty Harry movie because it's a known quantity? *Pauline Kael, "The Current Cinema: Dirty Harry," The New Yorker, Jan. 24, 1977, p 86*

[1976, patterned on *unknown quantity*, an algebraic term]

ko·ban ('kou₁ba:n), *n.* a police substation in Japan.

Foot patrols are characteristic of police work in Tokyo, and every few city blocks has a *koban*, or police booth, manned by one to a dozen men who patrol the neighborhood constantly. Each *koban* policeman is responsible for about 150 households, and is required to visit each of these households at least twice a year. *Gilbert Geis, "Crime," The Americana Annual 1975, p 197*

[1967, from Japanese *kōban*]

Ko·hou·tek (kə'hou tek), *n.* a comet discovered on March 7, 1973 beyond the orbit of Mars by Lubos Kohoutek, a Czech astronomer working at the Hamburg Observatory.

What set Kohoutek apart from other comets is that its passage was subjected to more scientific observation than ever before. The attention resulted because Kohoutek was discovered while still distant from the Sun, allowing ample time to organize observations by a variety of techniques. The comet was observed in many wavelengths of the electromagnetic spectrum, from the far-ultraviolet through the radio frequencies, and by observatories throughout the world. *William C. Schneider, "Skylab," McGraw-Hill Yearbook of Science and Technology 1975, p 51*

[1973] See OORT'S CLOUD.

ko·mi·teh (kou'mi: tei), *n.* any of the revolutionary committees with wide police powers formed in Iran after the deposition of the Shah in 1979.

Ayatollah Mahdavi Khani, supreme commander of the komitehs, announced they would be phased out and their militiamen incorporated into the now-moribund national police force. Prime Minister Mehdi Bazargan again attacked the komitehs, calling for an end to their "rule of revenge." *"Islamic Komitehs Back Off, For Now," The New York Times, April 29, 1979, p 2E*

[1979, from Persian, probably from English *committee*]

Kon·do effect ('kan₁dou), *Metallurgy.* an increase in the resistance of dilute alloys of magnetic materials in a nonmagnetic environment as the temperature is lowered.

Disappearing superconductivity has been observed once before in certain alloys which exhibit the "Kondo effect" (a minimum in electrical resistance at low temperatures). The new compound ErRh4B4 shows no sign of a Kondo effect. *"Case of the Vanishing Superconductivity," New Scientist, June 30, 1977, p 778*

[1969, named after J. *Kondo*, a physicist who predicted it in 1964]

Ko·re·a·gate (kɔ:'ri: ə₁geit), *n.* See the quotation for the meaning.

The scandal, which is sometimes called "Koreagate" here, gained public attention last fall through American newspaper reports that Park Tong Sun, a Korean businessman in Washington, had made payments in cash to American legislators to obtain favorable consideration of American military and economic support of South Korea. *Andrew H. Malcolm, The New York Times, Jan. 9, 1977, Sec. 1, p 12*

[1976, from *Korea* + -GATE]

ko·za ('kou zə), *n.* a staff unit in Japanese universities for teaching and research, consisting of a professor,

272

an associate professor, several assistants, and technical personnel.

Each *koza* is funded separately and functions almost independently, with each worker making a virtual lifetime commitment to this particular group. *Science News, Aug. 19, 1978, p 125*

[1972, from Japanese, literally, academic chair, professorship]

Krishna, *n.* Short for HARE KRISHNA.

Forrest Nichols, a security guard at O'Hare in charge of regulating solicitors, said that each Krishna averaged $125 to $150 a day in solicitations and that the airport got about five complaints a week about them. *Wayne King, The New York Times, Dec. 22, 1976, p 31*

[1976]

Krishna Consciousness, a form of Hinduism devoted to the god Krishna, founded in the United States in 1966 by Swami Prabhupada (A. C. Bhaktivedanta), an Indian guru born in 1896 in Calcutta.

Some meditation practices are avowedly religious and integral to the beliefs of the group itself such as with Hinduism, Buddhism, the Vedanta Society, Sivananda Yoga, Krishna Consciousness, and the Self-Realization Fellowship. *Russell Chandler, New York Post, Feb. 26, 1977, p 23*

[1973] See HARE KRISHNA.

Kru·ger·rand ('kru: gər₁rænd), *n.* a one-ounce gold coin of South Africa, with the obverse showing a bust of President Paul Kruger, first struck in 1967.

Gold is the country's major export and the advertising campaign behind the Krugerrand is designed to help South Africa sell more of the precious metal. The coin is being promoted not for its numismatic value—as a collector's item—but as a convenient way to own gold. *Richard Phalon, "Personal Finances: Krugerrands Drawing U.S. Investors' Interest," The New York Times, Oct. 9, 1976, p 28*

[1969, from Afrikaans, from Paul *Kruger* (1825-1904) + *rand* South African monetary unit]

Ku·gel·blitz or **ku·gel·blitz** ('ku: gəl₁blits), *n.* a very rare type of lightning that appears in the form of blazing spheres which move slowly and disappear without an accompanying sound. Its common name is the English equivalent *ball lightning.*

Writing in Nature (vol 245, p 95) R. C. Jennison of the University of Kent at Canterbury, proposes that the mysterious spheres of Kugelblitz (the more dramatic-sounding Teutonic name) may be some sort of stable standing waves of electromagnetism; the balls, usually about 20 cm in diameter, are "a phase-locked loop of electromagnetic radiation in the intense field associated with lightning activity. *New Scientist, Sept. 27, 1973, p 792*

[1968, from German *Kugelblitz*, literally, ball lightning]

ku·mi·te (ku'mi: ti:), *n.* a sparring event or exhibition in karate, similar to sparring in boxing except that attacks are stopped just short of contact with the target.

Japanese also won the men's team kumite final as well as the individual and team titles in the *kata* (prescribed forms), for both men and women. *Andrew M. Adams, "Combat Sports," Britannica Book of the Year 1978, p 255*

[1965, from Japanese, literally, set hand]

kun·da·li·ni (₁kun də'li: ni:), *n.* (in Hindu yogic tradition) the mystic life force or spiritual energy which lies dormant at the base of the spine until it is awakened by the practice of yoga.

The mystics want "a lofty class of men," of scientists with elevated kundalinis who will keep watch over the race. *William Irwin Thompson, Review of "The Yogi and the Physicist" by Gopi Krishna, Harper's, Nov. 1972, p 125*

Kundalini, often referred to as the "serpent power" because it is symbolized by a coiled snake, can be concentrated and channeled through the spine into the brain — a process . . . not yet identified by modern science. The systematized process for accomplishing this upward flowing of energy is known as kundalini yoga. *John White, Kundalini, Evolution and Enlightenment, 1979, p 21*

[1971, from Sanskrit *kuṇḍalinī*, literally, coiled up]

kung fu (ˌkən ˈfuː), a Chinese method of fighting without weapons in which the hands and feet are used to strike blows at vulnerable parts of the body.

Unlike the hard, powerful style of karate, kung fu involves softer, fluid movements, all of which have philosophical meanings. "Kung fu is a way of life," says Ronald Dong, an instructor in the White Crane Kung Fu School in San Francisco. *"Life and Leisure: The Kung Fu Craze," Newsweek, May 7, 1973, p 76*

A Chinese Buddhist monk, expert in the deadly art of kung fu, who uses his skill only in self-defense . . . *Heather Robertson, "Kung Fu and the Cult of the Gentle Hero," Maclean's, Jan. 1974, p 78*

[1966, from Chinese (Canton) *kung fu*, literally, boxing art] See WU SHU.

ku·ro·ma·ku (ˈkuː rəˈmɑː kuː), *n. sing.* or *pl.* a Japanese of great power and influence, especially one who acts behind the scenes.

The system also involves the behind-the-scenes machinations of the *kuromaku*, or "black curtain" wirepullers — influential power brokers whose connections with violent rightwing nationalist groups and gangsters enable them to use coercion and intimidation to accomplish what money and influence alone cannot. *Jerome Alan Cohen, "Japan's Watergate: Made in U.S.A.," The New York Times Magazine, Nov. 21, 1976, p 105*

A few days later he introduced Kotchian to another of Japan's top power brokers, Ryoichi Sasakawa. Like Kodama, Sasakawa was a *kuromaku*; in fact, now that Kodama is in trouble as a result of the Lockheed scandal, and is sick besides, Sasakawa is regarded as the last of Japan's great old-time fixers. *Robert Shaplen, "Annals of Crime: The Lockheed Incident — I," The New Yorker, Jan. 23, 1978, p 69*

[1974, from Japanese, literally, black curtain, a term taken from the Kabuki theater and extended to mean "wirepuller, manipulator"]

Kwan·za (ˈkwɑːn zə), *n.* an Afro-American cultural festival celebrated during the seven days preceding New Year's Day.

Although Africans themselves don't celebrate Kwanza, it has been growing in popularity in black communities here since the early 60s, when it was developed by Los Angeles black leader Maulana Ron Karenga, founder of the organization US. *Stephen Gayle, "Harlem Has Celebration of Its Own," New York Post, Dec. 31, 1973, p 7*

[1971, from Swahili *kwanza* beginning; so called probably in reference to a festival of first fruits]

Kwok's disease, Chinese restaurant syndrome, a sensation of flushing, dizziness, and headache, produced by eating food seasoned with monosodium glutamate.

Several years ago, Chinese restaurants became a centre of scientific attention as a result of what was later called "Kwok's disease" — numbness in the back, followed by general weakness, and palpitations — a syndrome caused by too lavish addition of the flavouring agent monosodium glutamate to the chop suey. *"B. Cereus for a Change," New Scientist, March 28, 1974, p 796*

[1972, named after Robert *Kwok*, an American physician, who first described it]

L

laboratory disease, a disease induced, especially in laboratory animals, for experimental purposes.

This graft-v.-host syndrome is a "laboratory disease" procurable at will by a variety of methods, most simply by inoculating newborn mice or rats with a few million lymphocytes from adult donors of another strain. *Alan E. Beer and R. E. Billingham, "The Embryo as a Transplant," Scientific American, April 1974, p 43*

[1974]

lac·to·fer·rin (ˌlæk təˈfer in), *n.* an iron-binding protein found especially in mammalian milk, important in providing resistance to certain infections.

Lactoferrin . . . deprives certain bacteria, most often staphylocoecus and *E. coli*, of the iron they need to survive. *Robin Marantz Henig, "The Case for Mother's Milk," The New York Times Magazine, July 8, 1979, p 42*

[1973, from *lacto-* milk + Latin *ferrum* iron + English *-in* (chemical suffix)]

lacto-ovo-vegetarian, *n.* another name for OVO-LAC-TARIAN.

Technically, I'm a lacto-ovo-vegetarian, which means that I eat milk products and eggs as well as vegetables. A stricter vegetarian is called a vegan. *"The Talk of the Town," The New Yorker, March 17, 1975, p 32*

[1952, 1975, from *lacto-* milk + *ovo-* egg + *vegetarian*]

lad·der·tron (ˈlæd ərˌtrɑn), *n.* an electrostatic generator (for accelerating charged particles) consisting of a ladderlike series of metal rungs separated by plastic insulating material to form a current-carrying belt.

The laddertron . . . has a much greater current carrying capacity than either the conventional belt or the pelletron and has the advantage of greater mechanical rigidity. *"Nuclear Structure Facility: Ten Years On," Nature, May 26, 1972, p 192*

[1972, from *ladder* + *-tron* (accelerating) device, as in *cyclotron, bevatron*]

La·e·trile (ˈlei əˌtril), *n.* the trademark for an anticancer drug obtained by hydrolyzing amygdalin (a compound derived from almonds, apricot pits, and other seeds) and oxidizing the resulting glycoside. It is supposed to release cyanide into the body to kill cancer cells. *Formula:* $C_{14}H_{15}NO_7$ Often spelled **laetrile.**

We drive up a dusty sidestreet to a makeshift former warehouse which houses the Cytopharmaca factory, where primitive equipment and a handful of lethargic Mexicans in lab coats grind the small brown apricot kernels imported from U.S. canning factories into a fine white, cyanide-rich powder that emerges, several steps later, as the yellow tablets and pale serum known as Laetrile. *Marci McDonald, "Cashing In On Cancer," Maclean's, Jan. 1976, p 23*

Laetrile . . . is found in the kernels of many fruits, notably apricots, peaches, plums and bitter almonds. It is also found in cassava, lima beans and numerous other plants in a slightly different chemical form. The notion of using Laetrile as a cancer drug got its first major impetus in the United States in 1920 when Ernst T. Krebs Sr., a California physician, tried apricot pits as a cancer treatment. Laetrile received another big shove in 1952 when Ernst T. Krebs Jr., a biochemist, developed a purified form of Laetrile for injection. *Joan Arehart-Treichel, Science News, Aug. 6, 1977, p 92*

There is no scientific evidence that Laetrile helps cancer patients, and there is some thin evidence that it may do harm, especially when taken orally. Doctors at the Massachusetts General Hospital, for example, recently testified that a child named Chad Green showed signs of cyanide poisoning as a result of oral Laetrile treatments given him by his parents. *Eliot Marshall, "Laetrile's Day in Court," Science, Feb. 9, 1979, p 528*

Under the patent name, Laetrile, it is touted, at a high price, as a cure for cancer. The medical and political controversy surrounding this unorthodox treatment is concentrated mainly in the United States, but the treatment has its adherents all over the world. *John Ziman, The Listener, June 22, 1978, p 800*

[1949, 1968, from *l-mandelonitrile*, the chemical name of the compound, from *levorotatory* + German *Mandel* almond + connecting *-o-* + English *nitrile*]
Also called VITAMIN B₁₇.

laetrilist, *n.*: These data were leaked by someone within SKI [Sloan-Kettering Institute] and found their way, via Dr John Richardson, the Californian physician whose arrest led to the formation of the Committee for Choice in Cancer Therapy, to a Los Angeles newspaper. Although successive mouse experiments—both by Sugiura and others—proved negative, SKI was accused of concealing information by the laetrilists. *Jon Trux, "Few Data to Support Laetrile," New Scientist, June 30, 1977, p 768*

If, say, the Laetrilists, the pancreas fails in its mission, these cells scatter throughout the body . . . and this, they say, is the basis of cancer. *The New York Times Magazine, Nov. 27, 1977, p 48*

▶ Although patented by a British firm in 1958 and banned by the U.S. Food and Drug Administration from importation and interstate shipment and sale since 1963, Laetrile's sudden popularity in the 1970's stirred controversy over whether a patient's right to select his own treatment should override the government's efforts to protect its citizens from treatment whose claims of medical effectiveness, either as a cure or a preventive, remain unproved. The U.S. Surgeon General has also warned that the drug's high concentration of cyanide may be lethal. Nevertheless, 13 states have legalized Laetrile owing to public pressure.

Laf·fer curve ('læf ər), *Economics.* a curve showing a correlation between tax rates and economic activity. See the quotation for details.

The "Laffer curve" . . . is a simple parabola, drawn to demonstrate that if the tax rate were 100 per cent, revenues would be zero. If the tax rate were zero, revenues would be zero. As tax rate rises, so does revenue—up to a point where tax evasion builds up, people prefer leisure and unemployment to work, and the growth of output slows down. *Frances Caincross, "The British Taxation System Is an Ass," The Manchester Guardian Weekly, July 30, 1978, p 4*

[1978, named after Arthur *Laffer*, an American economist, who devised it]

La·grang·i·an point (lə'grein dʒi: ən), *Astronomy.* a location between heavenly bodies where centrifugal force neutralizes gravitational force so that an object in that location remains stationary.

Back in 1772 the astronomer Joseph Louis Lagrange showed that in those places any object remained stationary with respect to the moon. As the moon moved about the earth, any object in either of those places would also move about the earth in such a way as to keep perfect step with the moon. The connecting gravities of earth and the moon would keep it where it was. . . . The two places ideally are merely points in space and are called "Lagrangian points." *Isaac Asimov, "Colonizing the Heavens," Saturday Review, June 28, 1975, p 12*

[1962, named after Joseph Louis *Lagrange*, 1736-1813, the French mathematician and astronomer who postulated the existence of such points] Also called LIBRATION POINT. See SPACE COLONY.

laid-back or **laidback**, *adj. Slang.* calm, cool, and relaxed; nonchalant.

Yates' tenacity in a fight might come as a surprise to those whose judgment is based on his apparent laidback manner. *"Midwest," Chicago Sun Times, Oct. 3, 1976 (page not known)*

Of all the clichés about west coast living . . . the most offensive is that life out here is "laid back," as if even the most aspiring members of the artistic community are sitting around waiting for someone to peel them a grape while the real hustlers are back east getting things done. *Judith Timson, "Theatre: The Playwrights of the Western World," Maclean's, Jan. 9, 1978, p 62*

Sharks, the ad tells us, are "built for destruction," but then so is the barnacle in a laid-back sort of way. *Colin Tudge, "Sharks in Books," Review of "Dangerous Sea Creatures," New Scientist, Nov. 2, 1978, p 377*

[1969, perhaps originally in allusion to the posture of riders on motorcycles fitted with a long seat and a backrest] See LAY.

Laing·i·an ('læŋ i: ən), *adj.* of or having to do with the theory that mental illnesses are understandable as natural and often therapeutic responses to stress in family and other social situations.

She [Doris Lessing] began in that novel to explore the theme of non-verbal consciousness: the now-familiar Laingian argument that language is the first and strongest of the prison-houses with which our civilisation enslaves the free self. *Ronald Bryden, "Books: Laingian Soarings," Review of "The Summer Before the Dark," The Listener, May 10, 1973, p 623*

The subject of this documentary film is the condition of the mentally ill in Italy. . . . The approach is somewhat Laingian, for we realise when Bellocchio interviews the mothers that if anyone ought to be behind bars, it should be them, and not their mixed-up offspring. *Richard Roud, "Socialist Benefit," The Manchester Guardian Weekly, July 26, 1975, p 21*

—*n.* an adherent or follower of Laing's theories and therapeutic methods.

In addition, although I find Dr. Redler's reluctance to bare "innermost feelings" both admirable and utterly unique among Laing's followers, I remain in my "arrogance" (suspicion would have been a better word, but Laingians are wretchedly imprecise in their use of the language) more than a little dubious. *Richard Schickel, Harper's, July 1971, p 10*

[1967 for adj.; 1971 for noun, from R. D. *Laing*, born 1927, Scottish psychiatrist, who formulated the theory] See ANTIPSYCHIATRY.

lambda, *n.* a virus which infects the bacterium Escherichia coli, important for its ability to incorporate the E. coli genes into its own system and transfer them to the cells of other organisms. *Often used attributively.*

In particular, lambda has played a crucial role in our understanding of how genes are controlled at the molecular level, and of the events that lead up to copying out of these genes (in the form of messenger RNA) in the process of transcription. *"Where Enzymes Drift, Queueing for Genes," New Scientist, June 29, 1972, p 727*

Merrill used a special virus—the Lambda virus, a favorite tool for biologists who want to tamper with the genes—to infect the cells. The genetic information needed to correct a deficiency in galactose metabolism had been inserted into the virus's DNA by having it first infect the bacterium E. coli to pick up the missing genetic instructions. *Robert Cooke, Improving on Nature, 1977, p 76*

[1965, from the Greek letter λ, perhaps because of a resemblance in shape] See LAMBDOLOGY.

Lamb dip, a narrowing or decrease in resonance manifested in the output signal of a gas laser.

If a quartz cell containing methane is inserted into the laser, however, a resonance (the Lamb dip) much narrower (50 to 100 khz) than the broad spectral range can be achieved. *William D. Metz, "Physics with Lasers: High Resolution Coming of Age," Science, Feb. 18, 1972, p 740*

[1968, named after Willis E. *Lamb*, Jr., born 1913, an American nuclear physicist who postulated this form of resonance in 1962]

lamb·dol·o·gy (læm'dɑl ə dʒi:), *n.* the study of the virus lambda.

"Lambdology" has long remained an esoteric science. The book attempts to make it accessible to all biologists. This is a very welcome effort, since the results and concepts emanating from the study of phage lambda will undoubtedly find applications in a variety of other fields; they already inspire the thoughts of those who study genetic recombination, DNA replication, cell differentiation, morphogenesis, and the transformation of animal cells by oncogenic viruses. *Maxime Schwartz, "Phage Studies," Review of "The Bacteriophage Lambda" by A. D. Hershey, Science, Feb. 11, 1972, p 617*

[1972, from LAMBDA + -*ology* study of]

lambdologist, *n.*: Lambdologists, whose discoveries have laid bare in extraordinary and fascinating detail the complicated biology of bacteriophage lambda, may seem particularly prone to lapse into a shorthand language which rapidly becomes almost totally incomprehensible to the outsider. *"Lambda Phage: How Gene N Works," Nature, Jan. 14, 1972, p 82*

land art, another name for EARTH ART.

Akin to both Contemporary Primitivism and Conceptualism was Land Art, or Earthworks. Michael Heizer, Robert Smithson, Walter De Maria, and Richard Serra all created large outdoor sculptures using the materials of the environment as their structural components. These sculptural forms could be either ephemeral or permanent in nature. *Robert J. Loescher, "Art and Art Exhibitions," Britannica Book of the Year 1977, p 144*

[1970]

Land·sat ('lænd,sæt), *n.* a United States artificial satellite designed to gather data about the earth's natural resources; an EARTH RESOURCES SATELLITE.

The Landsat satellites circle the earth in near-polar, sunsynchronous orbits 14 times per day at altitudes of about 910 kilometers. *Philip W. Guild, "Discovery of Natural Resources," Science, Feb. 20, 1976, p 709*

Landsats . . . make fast, accurate and cheap surveys of forests and crops. Landsat images were used last year to create a geologic map of Minnesota covering 84,000 square miles at a cost of 65 cents a square mile, as compared with $118 a square mile for maps produced by people on foot. Landsats have located deposits of copper, chromium and manganese as well as new sites for tuna and shrimp fishing. *The New York Times, Feb. 5, 1978, Sec. 4, p 18*

[1975, from *Land satellite*] Compare DOMSAT, MARISAT.

► Formerly (1968) called *ERTS* (acronym for *Earth Resources Technology Satellite*), this type of satellite was renamed *Landsat* in 1975.

language planning, the formulation and implementing of a program to standardize a language, as by choosing between alternative forms, dropping archaisms, etc., or to control language development, as by recommending new usage and meanings, or to promote use of a language or dialect, as by selecting among dialects for different purposes (such as in religion, education, law courts, etc.) or selecting a standard dialect.

Language planning . . . has its own built-in dialectic between goals such as modernization, unification, and tradition; every decision involves a compromise. *"Deciding What to Speak," Review of "Can Language Be Planned?" edited by Joan Rubin and Bjorn H. Jernudd, The Times Literary Supplement, July 7, 1972, p 773*

There is an unwritten and unspoken assumption that with the advent of cultural pluralism, many of the abuses against minorities would vanish. Many who advocate a move toward cultural pluralism have this view in mind. Unfortunately, studies of language planning in other countries clearly demonstrate that the issue is not merely one of a

policy of language change, but also a conscious shift in the power structure. *Robert N. St. Clair, "The Politics of Language," Word, April 1978, p 50*

[1968; see *Introduction to a Theory of Language Planning* (1968), by V. Tauli]

language universal, any linguistic feature that is found in all natural languages.

The child is limited by his innate linguistic endowment, the inborn sense of abilities which are reflected in language universals and which are common to all children speaking all languages in all cultures. *Neil Smith, "Puggles and Lellow Lollies," The Listener, Dec. 2, 1971, p 760*

At the beginning of Chapter 3, L presents the well-known Chomskyan doctrine on the innateness of language universals. No one doubts (18) 'that children are biologically disposed to acquire a language'—at least I have encountered no doubters. What does seem doubtful is that 'the structural properties that all languages have in common' are so peculiar and unpredictable that only a theory of special creation will account for them. If they are NOT peculiar, then it becomes a nearly hopeless task to decide which of them have survived by genetic evolution (wired in), which by cultural evolution (acquired), and which will inevitably be invented anew every time a child learns its first language. *Fred W. Householder, Review of "The Study of Syntax: The Generative-Transformational Approach to American English" by D. Terence Langendoen, Language, June 1971, p 456*

[1966; see *Language Universals with Special Reference to Feature Hierarchies* (1966), by J. H. Greenberg] Also called LINGUISTIC UNIVERSAL.

La Pla·ta otter (lə 'plɑː tə), an endangered species of American otter, found in Argentina.

In September last year the International Fur Trade Federation announced a voluntary ban on trading in skins of the tiger, snow leopard, clouded leopard, La Plata otter and giant otter. *Pearce Wright, "Earth's Friends Want to Ban Wildlife Skins," The Times (London), Jan. 26, 1972, p 16*

[1970, from *Rio de la Plata* in eastern Argentina]

laser bomb, 1 a bomb with nonnuclear explosives, released by an aircraft and guided to its target by laser beams.

Those laser bombs, according to the protesters, have since caused havoc to the dike systems of North Vietnam, thus endangering the lives of thousands of peasants when the moonsoon season brings flooding. *"Feedback: Scientists' Vietnam Protest," New Scientist, Sept. 28, 1972, p 590*

2 a hydrogen bomb detonated by a laser beam.

A "laser bomb" would be an H-bomb in which the intense heat of a laser beam—perhaps the most powerful and concentrated form of light in the universe—would be used to trigger the hydrogen explosives, instead of the A-bomb trigger now required. *Sunday Post-Herald (Hongkong), June 24, 1973, p 7*

[1970; earlier (1967) *laser-guided bomb*]

laser cane, a walking stick that emits infrared laser light which is reflected by surrounding objects and received as tones in a light-sensitive device to help blind people detect obstacles.

Laser canes provide an optical echo at three vertical angles, warning the blind user of objects overhead and at his feet, as well as straight ahead. The laser cane communicates its information by both tones and touch. *Picture* legend, "New 'Eyes' for the Blind," *The World Book Science Annual 1976 (1975), p 73*

[1975]

aser fusion, nuclear fusion induced by high-energy pulses of radiation from a laser.

The laser fusion concept, on the other hand, eliminates the whole problem of magnetic containment. A pellet of frozen hydrogen is dropped into a relatively simple round vessel made of metal alloys. This vessel, as first designed, is filled with molten lithium to absorb heat. Midway in its descent the pellet is hit by a short, powerful pulse of laser light through a porthole in the sphere. The burst of energy instantly sets off a small thermonuclear reaction. *Lawrence Lessing, "Laser Fusion: Tomorrow's Energy?" Encyclopedia Science Supplement (Grolier) 1975, p 337*

Forum participants listened attentively to the announcement by [Nikolai] Basov that he and colleagues at the P. N. Lebedev Physical Institute in Moscow reached a confinement time and plasma density necessary to demonstrate breakeven laser fusion—something the United States is not yet able to claim. *Janet Raloff, Science News, Nov. 26, 1977, p 361*

[1972] See LAWSON CRITERION.

aser memory, a computer memory that retrieves information by a scanning laser beam.

The first laser memories were of the block-oriented variety; thus they were quite slow (requiring many milliseconds) in locating a block but then could read a block of 150,000 bits extremely quickly, about three bits every microsecond. Future designs are expected to reduce the initial delay substantially. *John R. Rice, "Information Sciences," 1976 Britannica Yearbook of Science and the Future (1975), p 321*

[1975]

aser ranging, a method for determining precise distances by measuring the time it takes a pulse of laser light to return from an object.

Lageos [Laser Geodynamic Satellite] has as its *raison d'être* the experimental assessment of the possibilities of laser ranging in studies of movements of the Earth's crust and its poles. It may also serve for measuring solid Earth tides and, as a necessary adjunct of accurate plate movement determinations, the more precise fixing of reference points on the world's land-masses. *"Plate Tectonics With a Two-Foot 'Golfball' Satellite," New Scientist, June 3, 1976, p 525*

[1968]

laser ranger: The "laser ranger," a very precise surveying instrument, is another application. It is really laser radar and is sometimes called lidar. This device sends out a light pulse that reflects off a distant object. The time it takes the beam, traveling at the speed of light, to make the round trip, provides a precise measurement of the distance. *James L. Tuck, "Lasers Today: Still Not in Full Focus," The World Book Science Annual 1974 (1973), p 204*

ast hurrah, *U.S. and Canadian.* a final act or effort at the end of a career.

It isn't enough to dismiss Richard Daley's victory as the truly last hurrah: that phrase has been applied to him every four years, and each time he has been born again out of the phoenix flame of his presumably dead self. *Max Lerner, "The New-Old Politics," New York Post, Feb. 28, 1975, p 37*

No player anywhere, you thought at those moments, can lift a hockey crowd the way Bobby Hull can. But what were these moments? Were they symbols of . . . a move ever

upward in the calibre of play? Or symbols simply of Hull's last hurrahs? *Jack Batten, "Dr. Jekyll and Mr. Hull," Maclean's, March 1973, p 56*

[1972, originally applied to the final campaign of a veteran politician, from *The Last Hurrah,* the title of a novel (1956) about an Irish-American political boss (believed to be modeled on Mayor James M. Curley of Boston), by Edwin O'Connor, 1918-1968]

Las Vegas line, *U.S.* the betting odds set by bookmakers on a number of football games.

What began to agitate lottery officials here about their odds was a statement by Joseph L. Zambanini, a Wilmington tile contractor who says that he is an amateur oddsmaker and has access to "the Las Vegas line," the gambling underworld's football point spread. *Ben A. Franklin, "Delaware Will Pay Off on Lottery That Was Canceled and Reinstated," The New York Times, Dec. 15, 1976, p A18*

[1976, from *Las Vegas,* Nevada, where the odds used by most bookmakers originate] Compare LINE.

Las Vegas Night, *U.S.* a legal gambling event conducted by a nonprofit organization to raise money.

Under the regulations set up by the [New York State] Legislature last year, religious and charitable organizations can hold Las Vegas Nights once a month to raise money for themselves. Games are limited to blackjack, roulette, craps and other competition where players are pitted against the house. Prizes are limited to $1,000 a game a night, with top prizes of $100 for each player. *The New York Times, Jan. 30, 1977, p 35*

"Might I point out, Sergeant Drago, that we had a Hawaiian Luau just last year, whereas it's been three years since we've had a Las Vegas Nite?" *Cartoon legend, The New Yorker, Nov. 6, 1978, p 200*

[1973, from *Las Vegas,* Nevada, famous for its gambling casinos]

laugher, *n. U.S. and Canadian Slang.* a game so absurdly one-sided as to be laughably easy to win.

The game was a laugher, 8-0 Jets. The level of play was often closer to senior amateur than to NHL [National Hockey League] professional. *Jack Batten, Maclean's, March 1973, p 56*

[1971] ► Originally (1963) restricted to baseball games.

launder, *v.t.* **1** to give (money obtained illegally) the appearance of being lawfully gained, usually by channeling it through a respectable enterprise.

It was Lansky who developed the worldwide network of couriers, middlemen, bankers, and frontmen that allows the underworld to take profits from illegal enterprises, to send them halfway around the world and then have the money come back laundered clean to be invested in legitimate businesses. *Nicholas Gage, The Atlantic, July 1970, p 65*

A Queens grocer who used his store to "launder" more than $80,000 in stolen welfare and pension checks was convicted yesterday in Brooklyn Federal Court for possession of stolen mail and conspiracy to cash the checks. *New York Post, Jan. 14, 1976, p 7*

2 to make (any illegal commodity, etc.) seem lawfully obtained; give (something) the appearance of being acceptable.

Some authorities suspect that much of the food Havana is now importing from other countries actually is U.S.-

grown and has been "laundered" by international traders before being shipped to Cuba. *Parade, Sept. 26, 1976, p 9*

The grand jury report . . . describes a situation in which inconsistent title laws among the various states allow unscrupulous dealers to "launder" the mileage of cars. *"Odometer Fraud Called Widespread," The New York Times, May 3, 1976, p 35*

3 to remove any blemish from; clear of faults; whitewash; sanitize.

But now, after a year in Nowheresville, Bourne has been laundered—and born again. *"People," edited by Jane O'Hara, Maclean's, May 7, 1979, p 39*

[1970, from the idea of "cleansing" "dirty" money] See MONEY-WASHING.

► **Launder,** def. 1 became current during the 1972-74 investigations into the Watergate scandal, in connection with funds contributed to the Nixon campaign that were deposited in a Mexican bank and then used to finance various illegal campaign activities. See also the note under *laundry*.

laundry, *n.* a place, usually in a foreign country, where money from an illegal source is laundered.

For no flourishing power block will tamely submit to a sudden and arbitrary exclusion from influence. It will resort to the Mexican laundries and to other roundabout routes, preferably within the law but, well, if it can't be done legally . . . *Ferdinand Mount, "The Limits of Hypocrisy: A British View of Watergate," National Review, Jan. 18, 1974, p 77*

Law-enforcement authorities . . . began to suspect what Louis Chesler was up to. His Canadian and Bahamian companies provided a convenient "laundry" for illegitimate mob money looking for a way to reach legitimate usage within the United States. *Lucian K. Truscott, "Hollywood's Wall Street Connection," The New York Times Magazine, Feb. 26, 1978, p 22*

[1974] ► *Laundermat* was used in this sense in 1969:

On a more complex level, Wall Street crime involves the use of secret foreign bank accounts and other financial gimmicks to defraud the U.S. Government and to provide a convenient "laundermat" for organized crime in "bleaching" illegal profits from narcotics and gambling. Thus cleansed the money can be reinvested in legitimate businesses. *"Crime: Brothers to Dillinger," Newsweek, Dec. 15, 1969, p 90*

lav·a·lier or **lav·a·liere** (ˌlæv ə'lir), *n.* a very small microphone hung around the neck or clipped to the clothing of the user. *Also used attributively.*

Another kind of microphone, the *lavalier*, . . . may be in camera view, or hidden in the clothing. *Sig Mickelson and Herbert Zettl, "Television: Microphones," The 1974 World Book Year Book, p 570*

Individual interviews were carried out with all members of the group, yielding the individual data we needed on each individual. A series of group sessions was held in which the speech of each member (picked up from a lavaliere microphone) was recorded on a separate track. *William Labov, Sociolinguistic Patterns, 1972, p 210*

[1960, extended sense of the term (1950's) for a pendant hung from a chain worn around the neck, ultimately from the name of the Duchess of *La Vallière*, mistress of Louis XIV]

Law·son criterion ('lɔ: sən), *Physics.* **1** the requirement that for a nuclear fusion reaction to yield a gain in energy the product of the confinement time of plasma (highly ionized gas), measured in seconds, and the density of the plasma, measured in ions per cubic centimeter, must exceed a certain number, usually 10^{14}.

Under the Lawson criterion, a very high density can be made to compensate for a very short confinement time. *Dietrick E. Thomsen, Science News, Oct. 17, 1970, p 323*

The fundamental criterion for a successful fusion reactor is that it should confine the hot fuel long enough so that a sufficiently large fraction will react and thereby release appreciably more energy than was invested in fuel heating. This is known as Lawson's criterion. *Harold P. Furth, "Nuclear Fusion: Power Source of the Future," 1973 Britannica Yearbook of Science and the Future (1972), p 112*

2 Also called **Lawson number.** a number which indicates the gain in energy obtained in a fusion reaction.

B. Grant Logan and his Berkeley colleagues compute that a multiple-mirror consisting of 40 cells will contain a plasma with 4×10^{16} particles per cu.cm for about 11.9 milliseconds. This configuration is about five times the Lawson criterion. *"Is Fusion's Missing Link a Chain of Magnetic Mirrors?" New Scientist, Jan. 27, 1972, p 191*

The Lawson number, expressed in seconds per cubic centimeter, specifies the break-even condition on the assumptions that no more than a third of the energy released must be fed back to sustain the reaction. *John L. Emmett, et al, "Fusion Power by Laser Implosion," Scientific American, June 1974, p 24*

[1969, named after the British physicist J. D. *Lawson*, who formulated it in the 1960's]

lay, *v.i.* **lay back,** *Slang.* to relax; take it easy.

A society that has no heroes will soon grow enfeebled. . . . Its individual members will also be enfeebled. They will "hang loose" and "lay back" and, so mellowed out, the last thing of which they wish to hear is heroism. *Henry Fairlie, "Too Rich for Heroes," Harper's, Nov. 1978, p 33*

After a three-year hiatus from composing, Valdy has decreed "there'll be no more laying back." *Marsha Boulton, "The New Valdy Puts His Shoes On," Maclean's, Jan. 22, 1979, p 4*

[1978, from LAID-BACK]

layered look, a fashion in clothes in which garments of various types and lengths are worn one over the other; the fashion of LAYERING.

The best season classics for women are pre-washed jeans topped by a printed T-shirt, a front-tied work shirt, wrapped head, espadrilles, wooden bangle bracelets and a pouchy canvas shoulder bag. This layered look offers the added option of taupe-tinted aviator sunglasses and a perfect tan. *Jacqueline McCord, "Dressing Up for the Hamptons," The Herald Statesman (Yonkers, N.Y.), Aug. 21, 1975, p 13*

High-fashion designers are making casual clothes for men. Here, the "layered look": an outdoorsy shirt worn with a vest and . . . covered with a rough jacket. *Picture legend, 1978 Collier's Encyclopedia Year Book (1977), p. 250*

[1972]

layering, *n.* the wearing of garments of various types and lengths one over the other.

What makes the layering plausible is that clothes are increasingly unstructured and pliable so they don't stand away from the body. Not a new development, of course, but one that is taking over. *Bernadine Morris, "Grace Note to the Fashions of the '70's," The New York Times, Sept. 16, 1975, p 36*

Layering, the art of piling garment upon garment, also aided a rich look. Layering savvy consisted of double blouses, multiple sweaters of varying lengths, pants under tunic dresses, jumpers over dresses, double coats (a paper-thin rain shell over a warm wool, knit, or fur version), hoods under hats, and shawls over everything. *Kathryn Zahony Livingston, "Fashion," The 1976 World Book Year Book, p 309*

[1971, coined in 1950 by Bonnie Cashin, born 1915, an American fashion designer]

layperson, *n.* a person who does not belong to the clergy or to a profession or, sometimes, to any specified group; a layman or laywoman.

Cary, the NCC's (National Council of Churches) first black president, succeeds the council's first woman president, Cynthia Wedel, an Episcopal layperson. *James H. Stentzel, "Religion," 1974 Collier's Encyclopedia Year Book (1973), p 457*

Hospital ethics or review committees . . . have been looked to by some laypersons as possible arbitrators of the decisions to begin or discontinue extreme efforts to maintain life. *Leonard C. Lewin, "Bioethical Questions," Harper's, Aug. 1978, p 29*

In a field where the layperson is typically either ignorant or misinformed, "The Tenant Survival Book" will be a serviceable handbook for the curious and the convinced alike. *Allen R. Bentley, Review of "The Tenant Survival Book" by Emily Jane Goodman, The New York Times Book Review, Nov. 19, 1972, p 48*

[1972; see -PERSON]

LCD, abbreviation of *liquid crystal diode* or *display,* a device in which a transparent liquid turns opaque when an electric current is passed through it, used to obtain dark numbers on a light field in digital watches, calculators, etc.

The second advice I would give, despite arguments to the contrary from many experts, is that you should buy LCD models. The letters stand for Liquid Crystal Display and that means that you have a continuous display of hours and minutes or, where relevant, date, month and seconds. *The Times (London), May 14, 1977, p 23*

[1973] Compare LED.

LD, abbreviation of LEARNING-DISABLED.

The LD youngsters, although of average or better than average intellectual level, had either failed a grade or were near failure and were about two years behind controls in oral reading achievement. *Science News, Dec. 10, 1977, p 389*

[1977]

LDL, abbreviation of *low-density lipoprotein,* a lipoprotein containing more lipids than protein, thought to carry cholesterol from the liver to various tissues.

Cholesterol destined for delivery to the body tissues circulates in a package termed LDL, or low-density lipoprotein (high levels of which are correlated with heart disease). *"Wounded Arteries Collect Cholesterol," New Scientist, March 16, 1978, p 730*

[1976]

leafleteer, *n.* a person who hands out leaflets.

When I left the plant there were leafleteers at the gate distributing *Workers' Power. Barbara Garson, "Luddites in Lordstown," Harper's, June 1972, p 69*

Two leafleteers were hauled before the court for handing out a document which on the face of it could be held to be contemptuous, and the judge only released them when it became apparent that they had sought police permission before beginning to hand out the leaflet. *Colin Amery, New Statesman, Oct. 17, 1975, p 466*

[1970, from *leaflet, v.i.,* to distribute leaflets (1962) + -eer one connected with]

▶ *Leafleteer* in the sense of "a writer of leaflets" developed in the late 1800's.

leakproof, *adj. U.S.* protected or secure against the disclosure of secret or confidential information.

The President . . . continues to urge that the six leaky congressional committees dealing with intelligence be consolidated into one leakproof joint committee. *"Intelligence: New Policemen to Battle Abuses," Time, March 1, 1976, p 11*

[1976, figurative extension of *leakproof* (OEDS 1926); influenced by *leak* disclosure of secret information]

leaky, *adj.* not secure against disclosure of secret or confidential information.

IBM's Operating System for Multiprogramming with a Variable number of Tasks (OS/MVT) does not prevent unauthorised reading of files when used on certain computers. The system is used widely, but is commonly known to be leaky and is being replaced increasingly by other IBM operating systems which provide better security. *Joseph Hanlon, "Comment: Leaky Systems," New Scientist, June 16, 1977, p 626*

[1976, figurative extension of *leaky* (OED 1606); influenced by *leak* disclosure of secret information]

leap second, a second of time as measured by an atomic clock, that is added or omitted each year by international agreement to compensate for changes in the earth's rotation.

The leap second grows out of science's pressing need for extremely accurate clocks. *"And Now, the Leap Second," Time, Dec. 27, 1971, p 37*

In the new regime, the adjustment will be made by inserting a whole second called a leap second when this becomes necessary. *Alan Hunter, The Times (London), Jan. 4, 1972, p 11*

[1971, patterned on *leap year*] See UNIVERSAL COORDINATED TIME.

learning disability, a condition associated with the nervous system which interferes with mastery of a skill such as reading and calculation with numbers.

With widespread confusion and uncertainty surrounding both the causes and effects of various types of learning disabilities, it is not surprising that a wide variety of terms has been applied to the condition. A recent Government report found 38 different names in common use, including minimal brain damage or dysfunction, psychoneurological inefficiency, cerebral dysfunction, neurological handicap, perceptual handicaps, communication disorder and association deficit pathology. A number of more specific terms are also in common use: dyslexia (inability to read), dysgraphia (inability to write), dyscalculia (inability to manipulate numbers) and developmental aphasia (inability to receive or express spoken words). *C. P. Gilmore, "The Strange Malady Called Learning Disability," The New York Times Magazine, March 2, 1975, p 15*

[1960, patterned on *reading disability* (1930's)]

learning-disabled, *adj.* having a learning disability.

Only the special-education teachers know which children have been designated as moderately retarded, emotionally impaired or learning disabled. *Psychology Today, April 1975, p 36*

Within the "learning disabled" group there were five distinct clusters of disorders. . . . It is particularly interesting that many of the "learning-disabled" children's neurometric abnormalities were very similar to those of the senile patients, and it may be that the two groups share common sorts of cognitive malfunctions. *Jeremy Cherfas, "Neurometrics Gets More Out of Brainwaves," New Scientist, Nov. 10, 1977, p 360*

[1974] *Abbreviation:* LD

Le·boy·er (lə bɔː'yei; *Anglicized* lə'bɔi ər), *adj.* of or relating to a method of childbirth that is as painless as possible for the newborn by avoiding the use of forceps, using a quiet, dimly lit room for delivery, and placing the infant in a warm bath upon birth.

One couple wanted their baby to have a Leboyer bath, but the baby didn't even want to leave his mother's arms for that long. *Nadine Brozan, "New Childbirth Center: Baby Born in Morning Was Home by Evening," The New York Times, March 27, 1976, p 30*

If additional follow-up studies continue to show beneficial effects for children born the Leboyer way, it seems likely that nonviolent delivery may become an accepted way of birth. *Robert J. Trotter, "Leboyer's Babies," Science News, Jan. 22, 1977, p 59*

[1976, named for Frederick *Leboyer*, a French obstetrician who presented his ideas in *Birth Without Violence* (1975)] See ALTERNATIVE BIRTHING.

LED, abbreviation of LIGHT-EMITTING DIODE.

LED's are most often used in small sizes, which mates them well to small portable devices such as pocket calculators. Most LED's emit red light, although yellow and green are becoming available and blue is being worked on. *Alan Sobel, "Electronic Numbers," Scientific American, June 1973, p 72*

[1970] Compare LCD.

left-brain, *n.* the left hemisphere of the brain. *Often used attributively.*

The brain's two large cerebral hemispheres . . . are now commonly known as left-brain and right-brain. The reason is that, once the corpus callosum has been cut, the two sides of the brain appear to possess such independent capacities and mental properties that each merits a separate name. *Roger W. Sperry, "Left-Brain, Right-Brain," Encyclopedia Science Supplement (Grolier) 1976, p 50*

They conclude that while alcohol can affect left-brain functions, such as speech and language, such disruptions did not show up using the amount of alcohol employed in their study. *Science News, April 30, 1977, p 281*

[1976, perhaps abstracted from *left-brained* (OEDS 1890)]

leg·he·mo·glo·bin ('leg,hi: mə'glou bən), *n.* the oxygen-carrying pigment in legumes, essential for symbiosis with nitrogen-fixing bacteria.

There is now evidence that the enigmatic leghemoglobin in *Azotobacter* of root nodules, which is not essential for nitrogenase activity, serves to provide oxygen to the system at a very low concentration. *John R. Postgate, "Nitrogen Fixation," McGraw-Hill Yearbook of Science and Technology 1974, p 308*

[1968, from *legume* + *hemoglobin* the oxygen-carrying substance in the blood]

legionnaires' disease or **legionnaire's disease,** a serious and sometimes fatal form of pneumonia characterized by high fever, chills, abdominal pain, and lung congestion. It is caused by a previously unclassified species of small, rod-shaped, gram-negative bacteria.

From such studies it appears that Legionnaires' disease is caused by a common bacterium present in soil or water. In four instances the organism was discovered in air cooling or air-conditioning equipment. The organism may be trapped in these devices, sprayed as an aerosol to the surroundings, and then inhaled by a susceptible individual. *Charles Marwick, "Legionnaires' Disease Marches Into Place," New Scientist, Nov. 30, 1978, p 670*

Legionnaire's disease . . . struck 12 residents of Nottingham and 19 residents of other British cities as well between July 1973 and April 1978, according to the June 16 MORBIDITY AND MORTALITY WEEKLY REPORT, published by the Center for Disease Control. British scientists have not yet tracked down the origins of the infections. Six patients developed symptoms during or within seven days of returning from a holiday in Spain, but each had stayed at a different resort. *Science News, July 1, 1978, p 9*

[1976, so called because the disease was first identified in an outbreak at an American Legion convention in Philadelphia in July 1976]

leg warmers, knitted coverings for the legs extending from the ankles to the upper thighs.

Practicality is never far from real-life fashion, so last chilly winter found all the trendy girls . . . well preserved against chilblain on the nether half. Leg-warmers, accessory of every freezing dance rehearsal room, emerged as a stylish cover-up for girls who had never heard of an entrechat. *Prudence Glynn, "Shopping," The Times (London), March 30, 1976, p 10*

[1976]

Lei·den·frost phenomenon ('lai dən,frɔ:st), *Physics.* **1** a phenomenon in which a hot surface repels a liquid by generating a thin layer of insulating vapor.

You may use many common household liquids in place of water in investigating the Leidenfrost phenomenon, but first you should eliminate any that are flammable or likely to explode near an open fire or on a hot surface. *Jearl Walker, "The Amateur Scientist," Scientific American, Aug. 1977, p 129*

2 an analogous hypothetical phenomenon applied to the relationship of matter to antimatter in the boundaries where particles and antiparticles meet.

If matter and antimatter are separated, there must be boundary regions, and in these regions annihilations should occur. The annihilations should produce gamma rays that would go a long distance from their source. Neither of these effects are observed. Some astronomers invoke the so-called Leidenfrost phenomenon: A few annihilations at the border maintain a pressure that keeps large amounts of matter and antimatter apart. *Dietrick E. Thomsen, "Does the Universe Need Antimatter?" Science News, March 31, 1973, p 212*

[1967, translation of German *Leidenfrostsche Phä̈nomen,* named after Johann G. *Leidenfrost,* 1715-1794, a German physician who discovered the insulating phenomenon]

leisure suit, a suit for informal wear, consisting of an open-collar, shirtlike jacket and matching trousers.

They posed for photographs, Mr. Badillo sober in a navy-blue suit, Mr. Hirschfeld resplendent in an open-collared leisure suit. *Charles Kaiser, The New York Times, Aug. 29, 1977, p 21*

[1972] See SHIRT-JACKET.

leopard-skin cease-fire, a cease-fire in which each side remains in control of the areas it occupies.

Elsewhere in the country, the Communists have been maneuvering to put themselves in as advantageous a position as possible when the projected leopard-skin cease-fire occurs. *Robert Shaplen, "Letter From Vietnam," The New Yorker, Jan. 13, 1973, p 78*

[1972, so called from the spotty or irregular arrangement of the areas occupied, suggesting a leopard's skin] See LEOPARD SPOT.

leopard spot, any of a number of separate areas held by a military force, especially at the time of a cease-fire.

The exact number of these isolated strongpoints or clandestinely administered villages will only be known when the communist leadership emerges after the ceasefire. The Americans insist that the leopard spots are relatively few, but anticipate many claims and much flag competition in the Mekong Delta. *Louis Heren, The Times (London), Nov. 23, 1972, p 8*

The war itself, in which more than 35,000 have been killed, has exacerbated the divisions between the nation's Christian and Moslem communities and the Palestinians, who, in Lebanon as refugees, became embroiled in its civil fighting. The war also has left the nation in a state of "leopard spot," de facto partition, with different factions in control of noncontiguous areas. *The New York Times, Nov. 14, 1976, Sec. 4, p 1*

[1969; see LEOPARD-SKIN CEASE-FIRE]

lesion, *v.t.* to cause a lesion in.

Jouvet also has a critical experiment he wants to perform. If dreams are the replay of the genetic code, they should not be affected by the environment. Earlier, he recalled that he had lesioned in cats the "brake" that prevents them from moving while they dream. *David Cohen, "The Purpose of Dreaming," New Scientist, March 15, 1973, p 604*

[1972, verb use of the noun]

less developed, economically underdeveloped, especially in technology and industry.

Less-Developed Nations experienced even more severe inflation than the industrial countries. *Warren W. Shearer, "Economics," The 1977 World Book Year Book, p 307*

There are hundreds of millions of poor people in the less developed countries, and very few trained experts. *Harford Thomas, "The Third World Looks to Its Own," Britannica Book of the Year 1978, p 338*

[1963] ► See the note under DEVELOPING.

lethal yellowing, a disease of palm trees first dis-covered in Jamaica and becoming widespread in the United States, caused by a viruslike microorganism.

The primary cause of the epidemic called "lethal yellowing" seems to be a virulent mycoplasma – a microorganism without cell walls. The organism is so low in the order of things that it cannot be classified as either plant or animal. *Jean Craighead George, "The Battle to Save Florida's Palms," Encyclopedia Science Supplement (Grolier) 1977/1978 (1977), p 196*

[1973]

leu·en·keph·a·lin (ˌlu: en'kef ə lin), *n.* a chemical that overcomes or reduces pain, produced normally in the brain and consisting of a peptide chain having the amino acid leucine at its end.

In the first of the three *Nature* papers (vol 261, p 423) a large research group from Sandoz Ltd in Basle report the analgesic effects of met- and leu-enkephalin when injected directly into mouse brains. Met-enkephalin is more potent than the leu- variety, but both bind less strongly to brain receptors than does morphine. *"Monitor: More Answers on the Brain's Own Opiate," New Scientist, June 10, 1976, p 578*

[1976, from *leu*cine + ENKEPHALIN]

le·vam·i·sole (lə'væm əˌsoul), *n.* a drug originally used as a deworming agent, found to stimulate cellular immunity and used experimentally in the treatment of cancer and other diseases. *Formula:* $C_{11}H_{12}N_2S$

The beneficial effect of Levamisole is due to its action in improving the body's natural defences against infection. Levamisole was introduced several years ago in the treatment of parasitic infections, and it was only later that it was found to stimulate the natural immune system which gives protection against bacterial and viral infections. *"Science Report: Virology: Winter Cold Cures," The Times (London), Feb. 20, 1976, p 8*

Many researchers believe that one of the body's two immune mechanisms, . . . cell-mediated immunity, apparently retards cancerous growth. By a yet-undefined mechanism, levamisole increases cellular immunity when it is below normal. *Arthur H. Hayes, Jr., "Drugs," The World Book Science Annual 1977 (1976), p 264*

[1976, from *levo*rotatory + *amide* + alteration of *azole*]

lex·i·gram ('lek səˌgræm), *n.* any figure or symbol used to represent a word.

So far the scientists have created 125. To avoid ambiguity, explains [Ernst] von Glaserfeld, each lexigram has only one meaning, unlike English in which most words have more than one definition. *Robert J. Trotter, "I Talk to the Animals," Science News, June 2, 1973, p 360*

On each of the variously colored keys is a different geometric form; the forms are the words – or "lexigrams," as the scientists call them – of Yerkish. *"Lessons for Lana," Time, March 4, 1974, p 74*

[1973, from Greek *léxis* word + English *-gram* something written; compare earlier (OED 1836) *lexigraphy* a system of writing in which each character represents a word]

lez, *n.; pl.* **-zes.** *U.S. Slang (often used disparagingly).* a lesbian.

In an editorial expressing approval of the Supreme Court's refusal to consider the case of a man who was de-

281

nied a job by a state government because of his homosexuality, the *News* broadened its views on the subject only to the extent of offering its readers a larger selection of sobriquets: "Fairies, nances, swishes, fags, lezzes—call 'em what you please." *Calvin Trillin, "U.S. Journal: Manhattan," The New Yorker, July 15, 1972, p 64*

[1972, alteration (influenced by the pronunciation) of earlier (1956) *les*, short for *lesbian*]

LGM, abbreviation of *little green man* (a whimsical reference to intelligent extraterrestrial life).

Looking for LGM's: Intelligent aliens may be neither little, green, nor men, but if any are there, NASA wants to look for them. *Dietrick E. Thomsen, Science News, Nov. 20, 1976, p 332*

[1968, originally applied to pulsars by their discoverer, the English astronomer Antony Hewish (born 1924); so called from the popularized characterizations of extraterrestrial beings found in early science fiction and fantasy writings] See SETI.

LH-RH, abbreviation of *luteinizing hormone-releasing hormone*, a hormone secreted by the hypothalamus (now also produced synthetically) that causes the pituitary gland to release luteinizing hormone, which in females stimulates ovulation and estrogen production and in males stimulates release of testosterone.

LH-RH plays a key role in the onset of puberty, is the mediator responsible for the release of the ovulatory quota of LH [luteinizing hormone], and is necessary for normal implantation and maintenance of pregnancy. *Andrew V. Schally, "Endocrine Mechanisms," McGraw-Hill Yearbook of Science and Technology 1978, p 164*

Production of that luteinizing-hormone-releasing hormone, or LHRH, stops when oestrogen reaches a certain level in the circulation. That feedback inhibition is part of the system of hormonal checks and balances which regulate the reproductive process, and which lead to problems such as amenorrhoea when they go wrong. *The Times (London), May 5, 1978, p 16*

[1971]

lib, *n. Informal.* freedom from discrimination.

Susan Struck won a near three-year "maternity lib" battle. The Air Force, reversing its stand on automatic dismissal for giving birth, has reinstated her to active duty. *"The Nation: Women's Lib: Confrontations Galore," The New York Times, Dec. 3, 1972, p 2*

The authors reject any suggestion that the study is a call for children's suffrage or other simplistic notions associated with kids' lib, but at the same time they talk about the "dimensions of the struggle ahead. We believe very strongly that what is at stake in our discrimination against children and youth is not only the rights of the young but the human rights of our society." *Warren Gerard, "Kids Without Rights," Maclean's, Nov. 20, 1978, p 41*

[1971, short for *liberation*, as in *Women's Lib*, *Men's Lib*, etc.] Compare ANIMAL LIB, GAY LIB.

libber, *n. Informal.* **1** a member or follower of Women's Lib; a Women's Liberationist.

The doctor sees through Kate and sees Sheila's worth. Achievement has made her more lovable. It's a pop conversion of women's liberation into: The libbers get the princes. *Pauline Kael, "The Current Cinema," Review of "Sheila Levine," The New Yorker, Feb. 3, 1975, p 86*

2 a member or follower of any liberation group.

'Gosh, I never expected the happy ending', exclaims the narrator at the end of yet another of Ms Kavan's bleak forays among ghastly freakers-out and assorted libbers: nor did the reader. *Valentine Cunningham, "Glum," New Statesman, March 28, 1975, p 424*

Neither left-wing nor right-wing himself, Wolfe will continue to irritate zealous left wingers just so long as American society continues to be dominated by the left-libbers. *Barbara Amiel, "A Society's Monitor," Maclean's, Nov. 6, 1978, p 6*

[1971, abstracted from *Women's Libber*]

libbie, *n. U.S. Informal.* a member or follower of Women's Lib; LIBBER.

Decter's major charge against the libbies is that, basically, they seek not equal responsibility with men but flight from responsibility, that, faced with those choices before them regarding their individual modes of existence, women, having made their choices, are now unwilling to bear the consequences. *Pat Kennedy, Review of "The New Chastity and Other Arguments Against Women's Liberation" by Midge Decter, National Review, Dec. 22, 1972, p 1416*

[1971, from *lib* + *-ie*, diminutive suffix]

liberated, *adj.* freed from or rejecting traditional sexual and social roles, especially the passive or secondary role traditionally assigned to women in society.

From her [Linda Wolfe's] feminist point of view, she contends that liberated women now enjoy the sexual freedom that men have always enjoyed, and that they are, therefore, behaving as shabbily as men have always behaved sexually. *Judson Hand, "Books: A Feminist View of Women's Role in the Sexual Revolution," Sunday News (New York), June 29, 1975, p 18*

Though a successful working woman, and "liberated" in many respects, she will marry no man who is on a social or intellectual level lower than her own. *Sam Blum, "The Re-Mating Game," The New York Times Magazine, Aug. 29, 1976, p 18*

[1970, from past participle of *liberate*, *v.*, influenced by Women's *Liberation*, *liberationist*, etc.] See SEX ROLE, MARRIAGE.

liberationist, *n.* a member or follower of any liberation group, especially of Women's Liberation.

While certain liberationists might applaud the idea of freeing women from the nine-month pregnancy period, they might be appalled at the exploitation of another woman. *Willard Gaylin, The New York Times Magazine, March 5, 1972, p 48*

Emma Lou Thornbrough's *T. Thomas Fortune: Militant Journalist* recovers the life and times of a black liberationist who lived from 1855 to 1928 and became one of the country's leading journalists. *Daniel R. Barnes, "Literature: American Literature," The Americana Annual 1973, p 416*

—*adj.* advocating or supporting liberation, especially Women's Liberation.

In June a group of young women . . . launch a monthly news magazine to be called *Spare Rib*. As its clever, acid title suggests, its tone will be liberationist. *Prudence Glynn, The Times (London), April 24, 1972, p 7*

[1970, abstracted from *Women's Liberationist*]

► The 19th-century use of this term (OEDS 1869)

was restricted to the members of the "Liberation Society" of England which advocated disestablishment. The current form is an independent derivation.

liberation theology, a Christian theological movement which views God as acting through historical processes to free mankind from social and political oppression.

Some advocates of "liberation theology" have indeed embraced violence, joining guerrilla movements. But more have expressed their convictions peacefully. In Honduras, priests helped to found the National Peasant Union, a force for land reform; in Ecuador, priests organized Indian cooperatives; in Brazil, Chile and El Salvador they have spoken out forcefully against violations of civil rights by the ruling regimes. *"A Voice Against 'Liberation Theology',"* The New York Times, Jan. 30, 1979, p A18

[1974] Also called THEOLOGY OF LIBERATION.

liberation theologist: A group of liberation theologists ... worked round the clock preparing documents on the desperate state of Latin America's masses. *Alan Riding, "Latin Church in Siege," The New York Times Magazine, May 6, 1979, p 44*

libration point, another name for LAGRANGIAN POINT.

All libration points, however, are not alike . . . Points L-1, L-2, and L-3 are fairly unstable. The other two points — L-4 and L-5 — seem to be fairly stable. Space scientists are now very interested in those "stable" points. *Michael Cusack, " 'Hanging In' at L-5," Encyclopedia Science Supplement (Grolier) 1975, p 358*

[1973, so called because an object at a Lagrangian point is likely to *librate* or sway at times under the influence of the competing gravities of the bodies between which it is located]

lifeboat ethic or **lifeboat ethics,** a set of values which in a crisis assigns priorities according to urgency or expediency rather than on the basis of humanitarian or other moral principles.

Dr. [Garrett] Hardin, an ecologist at the University of California, Santa Barbara, is well known as an advocate of triage or "the lifeboat ethic," in world food matters. He has argued that as global food shortages become more intense, the United States should not grant food aid but instead should permit famines to reduce the number of people in developing countries. *"Food Experts Fear Long-Term Shortage," The New York Times, Dec. 5, 1976, p 67*

Is there a basis for hope that the circular dilemma of runaway population growth, poverty, and hunger can be solved? The neo-Malthusians despair that the gap between population and food can ever be overcome and fear that governments may be forced to practice triage and lifeboat ethics. The cornucopians emphasize that the earth's resources are far from exhausted and that there are facts which justify optimism. *David M. Burns, "The Food in Our Future," The Manchester Guardian Weekly (The Washington Post section), Nov. 26, 1978, p 18*

[1974, by analogy with an overcrowded lifeboat from which a number of passengers must be cast for the rest to survive] Compare TRIAGE.

life care, a type of housing in which apartments and medical services are purchased for life. *Often used attributively.*

As you have probably guessed, life care does not come cheap. Costs of the apartments range from $20,000 for an efficiency unit to $50,000 and more for a two-bedroom unit for two apartment occupants. After paying the initial buying fee, a resident pays a monthly service charge, like rent or a condominium maintenance fee, which varies but generally starts at from $400 to $500. *Ruth Rejnis, Her Home, 1980, p 117*

[1963]

life president, Also, as a title, **Life President.** the president of a republic, especially in Africa, who is elected to or assumes the presidency for life.

President Banda is not only life-president of the country, but life-president of the ruling Malawi Congress Party as well. He is also his own Minister of Agriculture, Foreign Affairs, Public Works and Justice. *The Times (London), July 4, 1978, p 16*

[1972] Also called PRESIDENT-FOR-LIFE.

life-support, *adj.* **1** containing or providing the necessary equipment, material, or treatment to keep a person alive, especially in adverse circumstances.

Also to be deferred was the development of improved space suits, life-support backpacks, and astronaut maneuvering units for use with the shuttle. *Mitchell R. Sharpe, "Space Exploration," Britannica Book of the Year 1976, p 627*

The fetus reaches viability (the capability of surviving, given the appropriate life-support facilities) . . . ordinarily at about 24 weeks. *Christopher Tietze and Sarah Lewit, "Legal Abortion," Scientific American, Jan. 1977, p 22*

2 of or involving the capacity to support life, especially wild life.

The final category was life support value, including a marsh's ability to absorb carbon dioxide, produce oxygen, support waterfowl and other animals and protect cities and beaches from the damaging effects of storms. *Bayard Webster, "Study Upgrades Value of Tidal Marshes." The New York Times, Jan. 8, 1976, p 24*

— *n.* Also, **life support.** the equipment, material, or treatment necessary to keep a person alive.

Basic life support is an emergency first-aid procedure that includes . . . the proper application of cardiopulmonary resuscitation (CPR). Advanced life support also includes the use of electrical and mechanical equipment, intravenous fluids, and drugs as needed for complete emergency care. *Irwin J. Polk, "Medicine," The Americana Annual 1975, p 372*

New legislation was urgently required, some doctors urged, to make it easier to decide when life-support should be discontinued. *John Newell, "Science, Medicine and Technology," The Annual Register of World Events in 1975 (1976), p 358*

[1970, abstracted from earlier (1962) *life-support system*]

liftback, *n.* an automobile with a slanted back that opens upward.

The Celica models comprise a 1600 two-door coupé and a range of two-litre liftbacks with tailgate and folding rear seat. *The Times (London), Jan. 12, 1978, p 70*

American Motors, whose mainstay nowadays is its Jeeps, has also struck a blow of sorts for slipperiness by replacing its boxy Gremlin with a sleeker-looking liftback called the Spirit. *Time, Oct. 9, 1978, p 93*

[1978, patterned on earlier (1970) *hatchback*]

283

light

light, *n.* **(see the) light at the end of the tunnel,** (to glimpse) the prospect of success during a long and perilous venture.

The Secretary of State has repeatedly said that he will not help companies where there is no light at the end of the tunnel. . . . Even now there are serious doubts whether the group is capable of eking a profit four years hence. *Victor Keegan, The Manchester Guardian Weekly, March 11, 1972, p 10*

A proposal for a federal Ireland . . . could be the light at the end of the tunnel—in contrast to further well-meaning British suggestions, which only add fuel to the fire. *James Fitzpatrick, "A Way Out of Ireland's Dilemma?" National Review, Aug. 30, 1974, p 979*

[1967] ► The expression was popularized during the Vietnam War by U.S. government spokesmen predicting the imminent victory of South Vietnam and an end to the American involvement in the war. Opponents of the war frequently ridiculed the expression, and some of them attributed the light to an onrushing train coming from the other direction. See the note under PROTECTIVE REACTION.

light-emitting diode, a semiconductor that emits light whenever a suitable electric current is applied across it, used widely to produce the glowing digits in electronic calculators, digital watches, etc.

The most popular type of display on present hand-held calculators is the light emitting diode (LED). This gives small, red digits which can switch rapidly. *Nicholas Valéry, "Shopping Around for a Calculator," New Scientist, May 31, 1973, p 549*

[1970]

light-minute, *n.* the equivalent of a minute in a light-year (the distance light travels in a year).

Suppose that the Sun is suddenly switched off. We on Earth, about eight light-minutes away, will see a dark spot appear in the centre of the Sun some eight minutes after switch off. *Dr. Andrew Fabian and Dr. James Pringle, "Cosmic Gamma-ray Bursts," New Scientist, Feb. 6, 1975, p 313*

[1975] Compare LIGHT-SECOND.

light pipe, a fine glass fiber or transparent plastic rod that conducts light.

Light pipes . . . have, until now, absorbed and lost too much light. While high losses are acceptable for many applications—over short lengths in scientific instruments, for example—low loss fibres are essential for long distances. *"Technology Review: Fibre Optic Loses Less Light," New Scientist, Sept. 21, 1972, p 488*

The Vivitar VI keeps the negative cool by carrying the light from lamp to negative by means of a Lucite "light pipe" illumination system. *Harvey Fondiller, "Report From the 1976 Photokina," The New York Times, Oct. 3, 1976, p 34*

[1965]

light pollution, the excessive glare of street lights, advertising signs, and the like, in a city and its environs.

Looking for possible new sites Walker prepared maps of California and Arizona on which he drew exclusionary circles around regions where urban light pollution was too strong for good observatory siting. *Dietrick E. Thomsen, "Light Pollution," Science News, Dec. 15, 1973, p 382*

[1971, patterned on earlier *air pollution, thermal pollution, etc.*] Compare SOUND POLLUTION.

light rail, of or belonging to a railroad system built with light rails and using lightweight rolling stock, such as streetcars.

Brookline passengers board a "light rail" vehicle, one of 175 modern trolley cars for the Massachusetts Bay Transportation Authority system. *Picture legend, "Transit," The 1978 World Book Year Book, p 509*

[1976, shortening of *light railway* (OCS 1910)] Compare HEAVY RAIL.

light-sculpture, *n.* a sculptured work made of transparent material and electric wiring that causes it to light up.

The show looks great. A blue neon light-sculpture, designed by artists Val Strazoveck and Cork Marchesky, dominates the stage. *Gratten Gray, "Music: For Charlebois, Quebec Is Not Enough," Maclean's, Sept. 1974, p 82*

[1968] Compare SOUND SCULPTURE.

light-second, *n.* the equivalent of a second in a light-year (the distance light travels in a year).

The sun is 500 light-seconds away, the nearest star 100 million light-seconds distant, the "edge" of the universe 400 million billion (4×10^{17}) light-seconds away, and ever receding. *Jesse L. Greenstein, "Astronomy for the '70s," 1974 Britannica Yearbook of Science and the Future (1973), p 409*

[1973, patterned on earlier *light-month, light-week, light-day*] Compare LIGHT-MINUTE.

Li·kud (li:'ku:d), *n.* a right-wing coalition party in Israel that was formed in 1973 and became the ruling party in May 1977.

To the surprise of Washington, if not to that of his countrymen, Begin became Premier after his Likud coalition won a narrow victory in last May's national election, thereby ending 29 years of Labor-led coalition governments. *Time, Jan. 2, 1978, p 13*

[1973, from Hebrew, literally, alliance, union]

li·lan·ge·ni (,li: la:ŋ'gei ni:), *n.; pl.* **e·ma·lan·ge·ni** (,ei ma: la:ŋ'gei ni:), the monetary unit of Swaziland, introduced in 1974.

As Swaziland is part of the Rand Monetary Area, visitors do not even have to change money. South African rand and the local currency, the lilangeni (plural emalangeni) which is pegged to the rand, are used interchangeably. *Denis Taylor, "Swaziland," The Times (London), Sept. 6, 1978, p I*

[1976, from siSwati (a Bantu language) *li-*, singular prefix + *-langeni*, the root of the word for money]

limiting nutrient, a chemical which retards eutrophication.

Some researchers have claimed that internal sources of carbon may sometimes be the limiting nutrient in lake eutrophication and that phosphates and nitrogen may be less important than earlier thought. *"Environment: Atmospheric CO_2 and Eutrophication," Science News, Oct. 7, 1972, p 238*

[1971]

Li·mou·sin (li: mu:'zã; *Anglicized* ,lim ə'zi:n), *n.* any of a breed of hardy beef cattle from France.

Further, the new breed had to be evaluated competitively against native breeds. It was under these regulations that

Limousin cattle were subsequently imported from France and Simmental cattle from Germany and Switzerland. *David Allen, "Breeding Bulls for Higher Steaks," New Scientist, Feb. 15, 1973, p 357*

[1970, named for a region in central France]

line, *n.* Usually, **the line.** *U.S. and Canadian.* the betting odds set by bookmakers for a number of nonracing sports contests, especially in football.

Who decides what the point spread will be? Theoretically, the bookmaker decides and the bettor bargains him out of it. Realistically, both get it from an expert. For years, the "line" — which is what the point spread for a number of games is called — came from a group of experts in Minneapolis. *William Barry Furlong, "Of 'Lines,' 'Point Spreads' and 'Middles'," The New York Times Magazine, Jan. 2, 1977, p 15*

The line, published in many daily newspapers, establishes for bookmakers and bettors across the continent the team favored to win each game and by how many points. *Hal Quinn, "Millions Betting Millions Against the Spread," Maclean's, Jan. 22, 1979, p 35*

[1964] Compare LAS VEGAS LINE.

liner pool, a swimming pool made with a heavy vinyl lining inside an excavated hole.

He finally decided, rightly, that for the do-it-yourself enthusiast the "liner" pool is the best bet . . . Not surprisingly, these liner pools evidently take up about 80 per cent of the American home pools market. *Tom Hey, "Change: Taking the Plunge in a Do-It-Yourself Pool," The Times (London), April 15, 1972, p 8*

[1971]

linguistic universal, another name for LANGUAGE UNIVERSAL.

In relation to the total number of spoken languages, our studies remain statistically almost insignificant. 'It is still premature to expect,' says one linguist, 'that we can make any except the most elementary observations concerning linguistic universals and expect them to be permanently valid. Our knowledge of two-thirds or more of the world's languages is still too scanty (or in many instances non-existent).' *George Steiner, On Difficulty, 1974, p 152*

[1971]

linkage, *n.* the principle or policy of bargaining, especially in international relations, in which seemingly diverse issues are related in an attempt to force an agreement on each issue, at least one of which by itself would be less likely to be resolved.

He [Henry Kissinger] also reaffirmed his commitment to the concept of "linkage" which he defined as an understanding of the interrelationship of foreign policy issues, and called President Carter's decision to cancel the B-1 bomber "a unilateral unreciprocated concession" that violated the linkage principle. *Carey Winfrey, "Kissinger Appraises U.S. Foreign Policy," The New York Times, Sept. 20, 1977, p 6*

"Linkage" is back, kind of, under the patronage of Zbigniew Brzezinski, seconded last week by his chief, Jimmy Carter. We refer to the doctrine that holds, in its most common variant, that if the Russians act badly in third countries, the United States will withhold its cooperation in some other policy area in which the Russians have special interest. *"Back to Linkage," The Manchester Guardian Weekly (The Washington Post section), March 12, 1978, p 16*

The issue of linkage — that is, relating Israeli withdrawal from the Sinai Peninsula to political changes for the occupied West Bank and Gaza Strip — remains a major stumbling block. *Time, Dec. 11, 1978, p 52*

[1973] See DÉTENTE, HUMAN RIGHTS.

▶ The term was popularized by Henry Kissinger as assistant to the President for national security affairs (1969-75). Its first use in a political context was by James N. Rosenau in *Linkage Politics* (1969).

lip·o·some ('lip ə͵soum), *n.* a microscopic membranous capsule made by the action of ultrasonic vibrations on a suspension of fats in water. Liposomes are used especially to enclose a drug or other substance to be released in a specific part of the body.

During the year, liposomes were successfully tested as an experimental form of cancer treatment, used to carry drugs selectively to the site of a tumour. They were also used for the first time to treat diseases caused by lack of essential enzymes. The liposomes were employed to carry the missing enzymes to the liver, where they were required. Liposomes were also used to make vaccines much more potent. It was discovered, at the clinical research centre at Northwick Park Hospital, in Harrow, that vaccines made into liposomes stimulated the immune system much more effectively. *John Newell, "The Sciences," The Annual Register of World Events in 1974 (1975), p 397*

[1972, from *lipo-* fat (from Greek *lípos*) + *-some* body; an earlier (1940's) meaning of this term is a droplet of fat in the cytoplasm of a cell]

liposomal, *adj.:* The researchers are now tagging the liposomes with antibodies that should help direct the liposomal-packaged enzymes to the appropriate target cells. Weissmann remains optimistic that liposomal-enzyme packets will eventually benefit persons with various defective or deficient enzymes. *Science News, July 22, 1978, p 60*

lip·o·trop·in (͵lip ə'trou pin), *n.* a hormone of the pituitary gland that promotes the breakdown of fat in the body and that is a chemical precursor of the natural opiates of the brain called endorphins.

The C-terminal region of lipotropin, named C fragment, has been found as an intact polypeptide in the pituitary gland and the C fragment is also released from lipotropin by mild digestion with trypsin *in vitro*. *A. F. Bradbury, et al., "Letters to Nature: C Fragment of Lipotropin Has a High Affinity for Brain Opiate Receptors," Nature, April 29, 1976, p 793*

In schizophrenics an enzyme defect might lead to an imbalance in the endorphins produced from the original large pituitary chemical (known as beta lipotropin). Different enzyme deficiencies might lead to the variety of symptoms seen in different kinds of schizophrenia. *Nature-Times News Service, "Neuropharmacology: Schizophrenia," The Times (London), Nov. 4, 1976, p 14*

[1964, from *lipotropic* preventing the accumulation of fat (from Greek *lípos* fat + *tropé* a turning) + *-in* (chemical suffix)]

lipspeaker, *n.* a person who is skilled in using lip movements to communicate with the deaf.

"Lip Speakers" are used. These are people who are easy to lip-read and they repeat what is being said without "voice." It is not strictly simultaneous translation because the lipspeakers try to use the main speaker's actual words, and run two or three words behind. *F. Holloway, Essex, in a*

lip-synch

Letter to the Editor, New Scientist, Oct. 12, 1978, p 125

[1977, patterned on *lip reader*]

lip-synch ('lip₁siŋk), *v.i.*, *v.t.* to move the lips in synchronization with recorded sound, words, voices, etc., often silently.

"Please bear with me tonight, Licia. The old persona's on the fritz, and I'm just lip-synching." *Lee Lorenz, Cartoon legend, The New Yorker, Oct. 21, 1972, p 31*

Unlike a true NHL [National Hockey League] player, Dryden didn't . . . mark off an entire season by lip-synching his way through *The Godfather. Jack Ludwig, "Ken Dryden, Hockey's Lonely Forerunner," Maclean's, Feb. 1973, p 27*

[1970, verb use of noun phrase *lip synch*, *lip sync* (1961), short for *lip synchronization*]

liquid chromatography, chromatography renamed to distinguish it from *paper chromatography*, *gas chromatography*, and other methods.

Another technique, this one for separation of complicated mixtures, became prominent this year. The technique is liquid chromatography, and although the principles involved have been well known for a long time, there was an explosion of interest this year because of the newly discovered power of the method for separating nucleotides, the sugar-base compounds that are the building blocks of DNA and RNA. *Edwin S. Weaver, "Chemistry," 1973 Collier's Encyclopedia Year Book (1972), p 219*

[1972]

liquid membrane, a thin film of oil encapsulating a water globule or water surrounding a globule of oil, stabilized by an agent that reduces surface tension. Liquid membranes are able to isolate a substance from its surroundings or to separate it from other substances.

The team tested both aspirin and phenobarbital and found that liquid membrane solutions will remove 95 percent of each drug within five minutes from acidic solutions (such as those found in the stomach). *"Liquid Membranes Trap Assorted Poisons," Science News, April 17, 1976, p 246*

This flexibility suggested obvious uses for liquid membranes as timed-release agents in long-term drug administration. *Charles M. Cegielski, "Applied Chemistry," 1978 Britannica Yearbook of Science and the Future (1977), p 278*

[1976]

liquid protein, a preparation of concentrated protein, once widely used as a food substitute to reduce weight but later considered unsafe as a diet.

Liquid protein consists, essentially, of protein processed from the gelatin in cowhide or from some other source of connective tissue. It supposedly provides patients with just enough low-calorie nutrition to help them survive the rigors of near-starvation diets. *"Liquid Protein: A Deadly Diet," Science News, July 29, 1978, p 70*

Unlike the popularized diets often labeled "liquid protein" and available over the counter, the Optifast program can only be prescribed by physicians trained by Dr. Vertes at the Mt. Sinai Hospital. *Nancy Beach, "How to Diet and Keep Fit Safely," The New York Times Magazine (Fashions of the Times), Nov. 12, 1978, p 70*

[1967]

lit crit ('lit 'krit), *Especially British, Informal.* **1** literary criticism.

Alas, the title is a publisher's trick, concealing a fairly orthodox work of literary criticism: criticism, it is true, dressed up a little and fitted into a thesis, but lit crit nonetheless. *Margaret Drabble, Review of "Towards Androgyny," by Carolyn Heilbrun, The Listener, Sept. 27, 1973, p 416*

2 a literary critic.

Unfairly, the novel that is an "easy read"—accomplished, well-paced, absorbing, rather than knotted up in sensitivity—seems to be at a disadvantage with lit crits. *Review of "Down the Rabbit Hole" by Anthony Paul, The Times Literary Supplement, Aug. 25, 1972, p 985*

[1968, from *lit. crit.* (1963), abbreviation of *literary criticism*]

Li·tek ('lai tek), *n.* the trademark for a fluorescent light bulb designed to last up to ten years and consume 70 percent less energy than ordinary bulbs.

Unlike a conventional light bulb, the Litek bulb has a magnetic coil that is energised by electronic circuitry in its base. The coil produces a magnetic field that excites mercury gas in the bulb. The gas emits ultraviolet light, which produces visible light as it strikes a phosphor layer on the inside surface of the bulb. *"Energy File: Light Relief," New Scientist, March 18, 1976, p 626*

[1976, probably irregular acronym for *Light Technology Corp.*, the company established by its inventor, Donald D. Hollister, an American physicist, to develop the device]

lithium, *n.* a salt of the element lithium, used as a psychotherapeutic drug.

Dr Michael Pare of St Bartholomew's Hospital spoke of the use of lithium to hold back the recurrence of attacks of depression. 'Lithium is a very simple substance', he said. 'It's very similar to sodium and potassium: in other words, lithium salts are very similar to common salt. . . . If a person's depressed, lithium will not cure it, but when the person has been cured of his depression with anti-depressant drugs or ECT, lithium can be used to prevent a recurrence. It's a mood-stabiliser.' *"Depression—Symptoms and Cures," The Listener, Oct. 18, 1973, p 515*

[1970, short for *lithium carbonate* (1967)]

live-in, *adj.* living with another, especially as a mate, without being married.

[He] was sitting on the floor of his cabin, passing a joint on a bobby-pin roach holder to his live-in girlfriend, one of those wandering women of the 60's, pretty and insubstantial, who light their untenanted souls by plugging into whatever scene they stumble onto. *Ted Morgan, "The Good Life," The New York Times Magazine, July 4, 1976, p 20*

—*n.* a live-in person.

Now she devotes her time to writing, pottery, Ben, her live-in (American for permanent boy friend . . .), friends, cats and plants. *Linda Blandford, The Manchester Guardian Weekly, March 6, 1977, p 19*

[1969, from *live-in*, originally in the sense of "live-in maid" or "live-in help"] Compare COHABITEE, ROOMMATE. See also MARRIAGE.

live·ware ('laiv₁wer), *n.* the personnel involved in computer work, such as operators, programmers, and systems analysts.

Computing people, programs and machines—in the jargon, liveware, software and hardware—will be busy interacting next week at the British Computer Society's Datafair '73 conference and exhibition at Nottingham University. *The Times (London), April 6, 1973, p 32*

[1966, patterned on *hardware, software*] Compare MIDDLEWARE.

living will, a document expressing a person's wish to be allowed to die in case of an incurable illness or injury rather than be kept alive by artificial means.

It also would have provided for litigation to enforce a so-called living will, stipulating that life sustaining treatment be abandoned should the signer "by reason of brain damage or degeneration" become "permanently incapable of giving directions." *William A. McGeveran Jr., "A Right to Die?" 1977 Collier's Encyclopedia Year Book (1976), p 336*

[1972] See DEATH.

lockdown, *n. U.S.* a condition or period in which the inmates of a prison are kept in their cells all day under maximum security.

The shooting occurred nine days after the officials lifted a month-long "lockdown," prompted by gang-related racial battles in July in which three prisoners were killed. *"Around the Nation: White Inmate Is Killed by San Quentin Guard," The New York Times, Aug. 29, 1977, p 18*

[1974, from the verb phrase *lock down*]

lockwasher, *n.* or **lock washer,** *Cell Biology.* a helical form occurring in the structure of protein as a result of some dislocation.

There is no evidence that short helical portions of protein, that is those structures known as "lockwashers," occur freely under any conditions in cells of the tobacco plant. *W. F. Harris, "Dislocations in Tobacco Mosaic Virus," Nature, Dec. 1, 1972, p 296*

Making the solution abruptly more acidic (down to pH 5) converts the disks directly into short helical "lock washers" of just over two turns, in length; the lock washers then stack in imperfect register and eventually anneal to yield helixes of indefinite length that are structurally very similar to the virus particle except that they are devoid of viral RNA. *P. J. G. Butler and A. Klug, "The Assembly of a Virus," Scientific American, Nov. 1978, p 64*

[1971]

locomotive, *adj.* having the capacity to stimulate or accelerate economic growth.

What can be done? The OECD [Organization for Economic Cooperation and Development] recommends prompt efforts by West Germany and Japan, two "locomotive" economies, to speed up growth. Since Japan is already trying to stimulate its economy, the obvious target of the OECD appeal is West Germany, which has consistently rejected expansionist economic policies. *Time, Jan. 9, 1978, p 45*

[1977, transferred sense of adjective "having the power of locomotion . . ." (OED 1657)]

loft jazz, *U.S.* an innovative form of jazz, often performed in an informal setting, such as a loft.

There are other signs that New York's loft jazz, one of the few authentic underground musical activities left in the city, is about to go overground on a national scale. Alan Douglas . . . recorded the entire spring festival at Studio Rivbea and plans to issue a series of loft jazz anthology records. *Robert Palmer, "Loft Jazz Goes on a Three-Day Toot," The New York Times, June 4, 1976, p C17*

The music produced in the lofts ranged from transcendental to abysmal, but the counterfestival, along with the appearance of a series of Rivbea-recorded albums, *Wildflowers,* on a national label, drew wide attention to the loft-jazz scene. *Ed Ward, "Popular, Rock, Soul, Jazz, and Country Music," 1978 Collier's Encyclopedia Year Book (1977), p 383*

[1976] Compare JAZZ LOFT.

Lom·o·til (ˈlɑm ə,til *or* ˈlou mə,til), *n.* a trademark for a drug that temporarily paralyzes the peristaltic contractions of the alimentary canal, used especially to treat traveler's diarrhea. *Formula:* $C_{30}H_{32}N_2O_2 \cdot HCl$

Lomotil is an "anti-diarrhoeal" creeping into common usage in the rich world. Salesmen on missions abroad take it in their emergency medication packs, lest they succumb to "Delhi belly." *Mike Muller, New Scientist, March 31, 1977, p 786*

[1969]

long-term memory, the part of the memory which consists of a permanent store of information.

Long-term memory has no obvious limits on the amount which we can store in it, but now there is the difficulty of retrieving the material. It seems likely that whereas forgetting in short-term memory is caused by the interfering effects of distracting events and involves permanent loss of the items, forgetting in long-term memory arises largely because the material is inaccessible — the information is still stored in the system but we can't get it out. *Fergus Craik, "When Memory Fades . . ." New Scientist, Feb. 24, 1972, p 428*

[1970]

look-ahead, *n.* the ability of a computer to perceive or calculate in advance different possibilities, steps, etc.; foresight.

In a few board games, computer programs play better than the best humans; these are games in which the intellectual mechanisms we know how to program, such as look-ahead and evaluation, are adequate for successful play. *John McCarthy, "Mechanical Servants for Mankind," 1973 Britannica Yearbook of Science and the Future (1972), p 102*

Look-ahead . . . is defined in Hayes and Levy's excellent book on the first world computer chess championship, Stockholm, 1974 as "the search for a solution to a problem by examining the branches of a tree of possibilities." *The Times (London), April 15, 1978, p 9*

— *adj.* characterized by or involving this ability.

When this scheme was actually implemented in the late 1950's with an IBM 704 computer, a look-ahead search of two full moves took eight minutes. *Albert L. Zobrist and Frederic R. Carlson, Jr., "An Advice-Taking Chess Computer," Scientific American, June 1973, p 93*

[1972] See INTELLIGENT.

look-down radar, another name for DOWN-LOOKING radar.

Any armed U.S. penetration of Soviet airspace will be at low altitude. Low-flying aircraft can only be tracked by a look-down radar since the ground masks land-based radars. Neither the MiG-25 nor any other Soviet aircraft has a look-down radar that works over land. *Science News, March 5, 1977, p 147*

[1972]

loon, *v.i. British Slang.* to spend time foolishly; frolic or clown.

All except one have been banned from riding at one time or another, and most of them boast of flouting the ban. . . . 'Looning about on our bikes' means riding far beyond the speed limit, chasing along the pavement, riding straight over roundabouts; it also means buzzing oncoming motorists and playing chicken with trucks. *William Cran, "Looning About on Our Bikes," The Listener, July 12, 1973, p 37*

The hippy penchant for play survives in the way sisters enjoy . . . "looning" together, that is, dancing and clowning around for fun. *Angela Carter, "The Language of Sisterhood," in The State of the Language, edited by L. Michaels and C. Ricks, 1980, p 233*

[1968, probably back formation from *loony* foolish, crazy (1872)]

loon pants, Also **loon trousers** or **loons,** *n. pl. British.* tight-fitting pants that flare from the knees down, designed for informal wear.

Dress manufacturers who are in despair at the number of young customers in loon pants and T-shirts might now consider hiring not a designer but another Johann Strauss to restore a desire for expensive extravagant dress. *Prudence Glynn, The Times (London), Dec. 5, 1972, p 15*

[1971, from LOON or panta*loon*]

lo·pho·phor·ate (ˌlou fəˈfɔr it), *n.* an invertebrate animal having a fan of ciliated tentacles (lophophores) about its mouth, especially an extinct species (*Odontogriphus omalus*) discovered in 1976 and believed to have been the source of the toothlike, conical fossils called conodonts.

The discovery of a new Cambrian lophophorate . . . with conodont-like teeth from the Burgess Shale of British Columbia was described as highly significant. It represented still another type of possible "conodont animal" found in the fossil record in the past few years and suggested that some conodonts were lophophorates. *Robert E. Boyer, "Geological Sciences," 1978 Britannica Yearbook of Science and the Future (1977), p 288*

[1977, from *lophophore* (from Greek *lóphos* crest, comb + *-phóros* bearing) + *-ate* (noun suffix)]

lordotic, *adj.* of or relating to the characteristic arching posture of certain female mammals during mating.

In contrast, even when given high doses of estrogens, the capacity for showing normal female behavior—such as the "lordotic" response, typical in female rats and guinea pigs, in which the back is deeply arched and the genitals raised and presented to the male—was dramatically diminished. It was as if, during the period of prenatal life, some inner behavioral dial had been set at "male." *Maggie Scarf, "He and She: The Sex Hormones and Behavior," The New York Times Magazine, May 7, 1972, p 103*

[1971, derivative of *lordosis* arching posture (1941). The original meaning of *lordotic* (1856) was pertaining to or affected with an anterior curvature of the spine.]

Lords·town syndrome (ˈlɔrdzˌtaun), *U.S.* a condition of restlessness and discontent among workers resulting from the sameness of automated assembly-line work.

Union leaders . . . contended that what passed for job dis-

satisfaction—the so-called Lordstown syndrome—was no new, could be resolved by increasing job security and pa through traditional collective bargaining procedures, an was at most limited to special work situations and specia circumstances. *Harvey L. Friedman, "Dissatisfactio Among Workers Causes Concern: 'Lordstown Syndrome', The Americana Annual 1974, p 331*

[1973, named after the fully automated assembly plant of General Motors in *Lordstown*, Ohio, where workers first went on strike over the job dissatisfaction issue]

Lou Gehrig's disease, a disease of the central nervous system accompanied by degeneration of the muscles.

In Boca Raton, Fla., physician Murray Sanders of the Sanders Research Institute is experimenting with a combination of venoms from the cobra and African snake, the krait, to treat victims of a central nervous system disease called amyotrophic lateral sclerosis, also known as Lou Gehrig's disease because it killed the great baseball player *Constance Holden, "Venom for Science," The World Book Science Annual 1977 (1976), p 351*

[1965, named after Henry *Lou*is *Gehrig*, 1903-1941]

love-bombing, *n. U.S.* the outpouring of contrived affection by members of a cult towards a potential convert.

Love-bombing, a term coined to describe the typical pattern of early encounters with cults, overwhelms the visitor with a barrage of apparent fellowship, concern and affection, purveyed by solicitous and ever-smiling devotees. As part of the softening-up process various noble-sounding plans are trotted out: setting up a utopian community where the dream of true brotherhood and harmony will be realized. *Melvin S. Finstein, New Brunswick, N.J., in a Letter to the Editor, The New York Times, Nov. 28, 1978, p A22*

[1975]

love bug, a small black fly of the southeastern United States, related to the March fly. The love bug flies only during daylight, feeds on dead vegetation, and appears at springtime in very large numbers, often covering windshields and clogging radiators of automobiles.

An exotic new driving hazard faces motorists in the American resort of Miami this summer—the love bug. The love bug population, report scientists, is on the increase and is spreading down the Florida peninsula at the rate of 20 miles every year. The love bug is a flying insect rather like an elongated housefly. *Celia Haddon, "Love Bug Invasion," The Sunday Times (London), July 13, 1975, p 8*

[1966, so called because they are often seen in pairs]

Lower Forty-eight or **Lower 48,** *U.S.* the forty-eight states of the continental United Sates excluding Alaska.

People arrive steadily. And people go. They go from Anchorage and Fairbanks—let alone the more exacting wild. Some, of course, are interested only in a year or two's work, then to return with saved high wages to the Lower-Forty-eight. *John McPhee, "A Reporter at Large: Coming Into the Country—I," The New Yorker, June 20, 1977, p 49*

[1976] ► The name is used chiefly in Alaska to refer to the rest of the continental United States. Others, such as weather forecasters, use it occasionally.

low-level, *adj.* not intensely radioactive.

Solidified high-level wastes are generated by commercial reprocessing plants that remove waste fission products from fuel that has been used in nuclear power stations; low-level wastes are contaminants in solid materials, principally in the transuranium elements (such as plutonium) generated at AEC installations. *James D. Lyman, "Nuclear Energy," 1971 Collier's Encyclopedia Year Book (1970), p 385*

[1970] Compare HIGH-LEVEL.

lowriding, *n.* *U.S.* a style of cruising in an automobile practiced especially in California and New Mexico. See the quotation for details.

Farther east, on Whittier Boulevard, young Hispanics express themselves with a unique form of Saturday night fever known as "low riding"—cruising in ornately decorated autos equipped with hydraulic pumps that lower the chassis to within inches of the roadway so as to produce showers of sparks as the car bounces along the street. *Time, Oct. 16, 1978, p 52*

[1978]

lowrider, *n.:* The custom is called lowriding. The car a lowrider drives—almost always a sedan produced by the General Motors Corporation—is also called a lowrider. *Calvin Trillin, "Low and Slow, Mean and Clean," The New Yorker, July 10, 1978, p 70*

"The police will never be able to drive the low-riders away," said Luis Martinez, a 22-year-old East Los Angeles auto mechanic on his way home from a movie. "Cruising is a way of life here. The boulevard was closed New Year's Eve but it didn't help because the low-riders just went to another place." *The New York Times, Sept. 4, 1979, p A6*

low-technology, *adj.* of or relating to old, unsophisticated technology limited to the production of basic commodities.

Because the U.S. no longer commands such a high share of the world's high-technology market, it no longer can offset its large imports of low-technology items such as shoes and clothing. *Time, Oct. 2, 1978, p 59*

[1973]

L-PAM ('el'pæm), *n.* a nitrogen mustard used as an anticancer drug. *Formula:* $C_{13}H_{18}Cl_2N_2O_2$

Fisher and his colleagues at the 34 centers have found a 36 percent reduction in death two years after giving patients the drug L-PAM as an adjunct to a radical mastectomy. *Science News, Feb. 5, 1977, p 91*

[1974, from *l*-phenylalanine mustard]

LRF, abbreviation of *luteinizing (hormone) releasing factor,* a hormone secreted by the hypothalamus that causes the release of luteinizing hormone (which stimulates cells in the ovary and the testes).

The results of the experiments may prove to be even more important if further experimentation shows LRF can affect copulation in humans. LRF may be helpful in the treatment of impotence in males where no organic defect can be found. It may also become useful as a cure for frigidity and infertility in women. *"A Third Hormone That Can Induce Mating," Science News, July 14, 1973, p 21*

[1970] Also called LH-RH. Compare TRF.

lucid dream, a dream which involves some conscious control by the dreamer.

There is a little-known kind of dream in which you feel much as you do now—awake, conscious, rational. It's called the lucid dream. During an ordinary dream your mind suddenly "wakes up" or becomes lucid and logical, yet you are still in the dream world. The lucid dream is an altered state of consciousness (ASC), a drastic change in the pattern of your mind's functioning. *Charles T. Tart, "New Classifications," Harper's, Dec. 1974, p 111*

[1974]

lude (lu:d), *n.* a slang name for QUAALUDE.

Because "ludes," as the students call them, are so abused as a "fun" drug, pharmacists are constantly on the watch for phoney prescriptions. *William Lowther, "All the President's Boys," Maclean's, Aug. 21, 1978, p 22*

The calming effects of Ludes spill over from pure recreational use into a drug that helps you cope with life. The user who begins by taking Ludes for fun finds himself using them to take the edge off all pressure situations. *Henry Post, "The Quaalude Life Style," Cue (New York), Oct. 28, 1979, p 27*

[1978, short for *Quaalude*] Compare QUAD².

Lu·ing ('lu: iŋ), *n.* a breed of beef cattle produced by interbreeding the offspring of Shorthorn bulls and purebred Highland cows.

Welsh Black cattle have spread far beyond the borders of the principality to produce beef on all but the highest hills, while the newest on the scene is the Luing. *"Agriculture," The Times (London), Aug. 14, 1972, p 14*

[1970, named for the island of *Luing* off the west coast of Scotland, where the breed was produced]

luminosity, *n.* *Nuclear Physics.* the number and density of accelerated particles in a beam.

The higher-energy, higher-luminosity storage rings would also be very useful for the study of the weak interaction. The weak interaction tends to get overwhelmed by strong-interaction effects at low energies. At higher energies it should come into its own. *Dietrick E. Thomsen, "Storage Rings," Science News, May 19, 1973, p 329*

[1973]

lu·mi·some ('lu: mə‚soum), *n.* a light-emitting particle in the cells of animals that emit light; a unit particle of bioluminescence.

"Lumisomes" contain all the various molecules which have previously been identified as part of the bioluminescent system. So the list of sub-cellular organelles increases, and lumisomes take their place with lysosomes, peroxisomes and the rest. *"A Global View of Cells Gets the Green Light," New Scientist, July 12, 1973, p 66*

[1973, from Latin *lūmen, -inis* light + English *-some* body]

lump·ec·to·my (‚ləm'pek tə mi:), *n.* the surgical removal of a tumor in the breast.

In the "simple" mastectomy, the breast is removed but the lymph nodes are not touched, and in the "partial" mastectomy or "lumpectomy," only the tumor and a surrounding section of normal breast tissue are excised. *Newsweek, Oct. 7, 1974, p 34*

The treatment involves limited excision of the tumor (lumpectomy), irradiation (both external and internal), and most recently, chemotherapy (drug therapy) when cells have spread beyond the immediate breast area. *Maureen R. Michelson, "There Are Alternatives to Mastectomy," Ms., Jan. 1979, p 29*

lumpenprole

[1972, from *lump* + *-ectomy* surgical removal (from Greek *ektomē* a cutting out)] Also called TYLECTOMY.

lum·pen·prole or **lum·pen·prol** ('ləm pən‚proul), *n.* one of the lumpenproletariat; an unintellectual, unenlightened worker.

Once we were one-dimensional, then (in an appendix) we were revolutionary students, a little later flower-people, hippies, counter-culture cadres (a blend presumably of Marx's Bohemia and lumpenproles?). *Gwyn A. Williams, Review of "Counter Revolution and Revolt" by Herbert Marcuse, The Manchester Guardian Weekly, Feb. 17, 1973, p 26*

The Autograph Hound, by John Lahr (Knopf). An interesting, if somewhat shallow, first novel . . . that takes us through one frenetic week in the life of Benny Walsh: lumpenprol, loser, busboy, autograph collector. *"Books: Briefly Noted," The New Yorker, March 17, 1973, p 129*

[1971, short for *lumpenproletarian* (1930's), influenced by *prole* (1930's) a proletarian]

lunar mass, the mass of the moon (7.35×10^{25} g.), used as an astronomical unit of mass.

As measured from radio signals received at Earth, the motion of the spacecraft provided a new estimate of the mass of Jupiter—heavier than previously thought by 1 lunar mass. Also, it showed the lunar masses of the Galilean satellites as being: Io, 1.22; Europa, 0.67; Ganymede, 2.02; and Callisto, 1.44. *Eric Burgess, "Space Probe," McGraw-Hill Yearbook of Science and Technology, 1975, p 383*

[1974]

lunchtime abortion, *Informal.* an abortion performed by vacuum aspiration.

May we remind our correspondent that legal abortion is not nearly as safe as she would like to think? . . . Even the Karman catheter (lunchtime abortion) carries at least a 13 per cent complication rate. *Debby Sanders and Amanda Binns, Warwickshire, in a Letter to the Editor, New Statesman, May 16, 1975, p 661*

[1972, so called because of the short time it usually takes to complete it]

luteinizing hormone-releasing factor, the full name of LRF.

Still another hormone, luteinizing hormone-releasing factor (LH-RH or LRF), is secreted by the hypothalamic region of the brain. LH-RH serves as a master switch over luteinizing hormone, the sex hormones and ovulation. *Joan Arehart-Treichel, "Birth Control in the Brave New World," Science News, Feb. 10, 1973, p 93*

[1970]

lux·on ('luk‚san), *n.* any elementary particle with zero mass that moves at the speed of light.

Other particles with proper mass of zero, such as neutrinos and gravitons, also travel at the speed of light. Bilaniuk suggested that all such zero mass particles be termed "luxons" from a Latin word for "light." *Isaac Asimov, "The Ultimate Speed Limit," Saturday Review, July 8, 1972, p 54*

[1971, from Latin *lūx* light + *-on* elementary particle] Compare TARDYON.

Lyme arthritis (laim), a painful form of arthritis accompanied by fever and large red skin patches believed to be caused by a virus transmitted by insects or ticks.

Alerted by the Connecticut data, doctors in Massachusetts, Rhode Island and New York have since discovered instances of Lyme arthritis in their own areas. These cases suggest that the disease may have been misdiagnosed or overlooked in the past and may actually be widespread. *"Medicine: Diagnosing Lyme's Malady," Time, June 13, 1977, p 56*

[1976, named after *Lyme*, a town in southern Connecticut where the disease was first observed in 1975]

lym·pho·kine ('lim fə‚kain), *n.* any of various chemical agents secreted by T cells which have been activated by suitable antigens. Lymphokines are involved in cell-mediated immunity and other processes affecting cells.

The activation of T cells also results in the production and release of soluble mediators of cellular immunity called lymphokines, an array of substances with beneficial or adverse effects on the operation of both branches of the immune mechanism. *M. Michael Sigel, "Immunology: Humoral and Cellular Immunity," 1974 Britannica Yearbook of Science and the Future (1973), p 280*

The T-lymphocytes receive the antigen in an appropriate form through the intermediary of the macrophages. Some of them kill the foreign microbe cells directly. Others secrete various lymphokines, substances that take part in the defense through various mechanisms. *Lucien Israel, Conquering Cancer, 1978, p 20*

[1971, from *lympho*cyte lymph cell + Greek *kīnein* to move]

lym·pho·tox·in (‚lim fə'tak sən), *n.* a lymphokine having a toxic effect on cells derived from a tumor.

One of these mediators is known to attract inflammatory (white) cells and another can keep the inflammatory cells at the site of the infection. A third mediator, lymphotoxin, can destroy uninfected as well as infected cells, and a fourth is the now well-known substance interferon, which can inhibit the replication of viruses. *Abner Louis Notkins and Hilary Koprowski, "How the Immune Response to a Virus Can Cause Disease," Scientific American, Jan. 1973, p 25*

[1972, from *lympho*cyte lymph cell + *toxin*]

M

M₁, M₂, M₃. See these entries in their alphabetical places (**M-one, M-two, M-three**).

ma and pa, variant of MOM AND POP.

Says Roger Kennedy, terminal manager for a grocery wholesaler: "We've been reluctant to hire women because the job involves unloading heavy cases at Ma and Pa grocers." *Time, April 26, 1976, p 100*

Ali's Alley, 77 Greene St., between Spring and Broome Sts. . . . Sort of a ma-and-pa jazz loft, owned and managed by drummer Kashied Ali. *"Goings on About Town," The New Yorker, Jan. 15, 1979, p 6*

[1963]

MAC (mæk), *n.* acronym for the *Municipal Assistance Corporation,* created in 1975 to alleviate New York City's fiscal crisis.

The most that MAC could do was to buy time, but the time was promptly squandered when [Mayor] Beame and his associates incited the unions with threats of wholesale firings and provoked MAC officials with their refusal to produce facts and figures. *M. J. Rossant, Harper's, Jan. 1976, p 70*

[1975] Also called BIG MAC.

machine intelligence, another term for ARTIFICIAL INTELLIGENCE.

IBM describes the assembler as a programmable, adaptable machine tool, not a robot. Though it is similar to work carried out by machine-intelligence researchers at Edinburgh University, its designers insist they are not in the artificial intelligence business. *Kenneth Owen, The Times (London), March 26, 1976, p 19*

[1966]

macroengineering, *n.* engineering dealing with extremely large and complex projects. *Also used attributively.*

For the first time a one-day discussion was held on "macroengineering" projects — the construction of things so big size alone makes them different from all other things. Past examples include the pyramids and the Panama Canal (successful) and Charlemagne's Rhine-Danube canal (a flop). *Virginia Adams and Tom Ferrell, The New York Times, Feb. 19, 1978, Sec. 4, p 7*

[1964, from *macro-* large + *engineering*]

MAD (mæd), *n.* acronym for MUTUAL ASSURED DESTRUCTION (a concept of nuclear deterrence based on the ability of each side in a conflict to cause intolerable damage to the other in retaliation for a nuclear attack).

Since about the middle of the last decade, the strategic deterrent has been designed according to the concept of Mutual Assured Destruction — MAD for short. The theory has been that if both the United States and the Soviet Union had enough nuclear weaponry to destroy one other power, even after suffering a first strike, neither would hit first. *Joseph Kraft, "Who's Running the Country?" The Atlantic, April 1974, p 65*

In the acronymically MAD era of mutually assured destruction, atomic warfare is clearly absurd. *Geoff Watts, "Age of the Guerrilla," New Scientist, Sept. 14, 1978, p 785*

[1973, coined by Donald G. Brennan, born 1926, an American military strategist and mathematician]

Mafiology, *n.* the study of the Mafia crime syndicate.

These key events in current Mafiology are skilfully described from young Bonanno's viewpoint. *John Pearson, Review of "Honour Thy Father" by Gay Talese, The Times (London), March 16, 1972, p 11*

[1971, from *Mafia* + *-ology* study of]

mag·con ('mæg₁kɑn), *n.* a concentration of magnetic material on the surface of a moon or planet.

Magnetic concentrations ("magcons") in the lunar surface could, if of sufficient extent and field strength, interact locally with the solar wind when the magcons are on the daytime lunar side. *P. Dyal, et al., "Measurements of Lunar Magnetic Field Interaction with the Solar Wind," Nature, April 21, 1972, p 381*

This magnetisation would be random and confined to an exceedingly thin shell. But if that is accepted it becomes exceedingly difficult to explain . . . the 'magcons' inferred from disturbances recorded by the Explorer 35 satellite. *S. K. Runcorn, "An Ancient Lunar Magnetic Dipole Field," Nature, Feb. 27, 1975, p 702*

[1972, from *magnetic concentration,* patterned on (1968) *mascon* (from *mass concentration*)]

magic bullet, a drug or other medicinal agent that is able to destroy specific disease-causing bacteria, viruses, cancer cells, or the like without harming the host.

Every investigator in the field has at one time or another dreamed of discovering this "magic bullet," and as yet no one has succeeded. *Christian de Duve, "Chemotherapy II: In Search of a "Magic Bullet," Harper's, June 1976, p 55*

We realized that there is a great diversity of taste and smell disorders, with a great variety of causes, and we are forced to conclude that zinc is no magic bullet. That is to say, it is a drug like other drugs. Magic bullets are rarer than people like to think. There are, for example, insulin-resistant diabetics. And the famous antibiotics are far from being comprehensively effective. *Berton Roueché, "Annals of Medicine," The New Yorker, Sept. 12, 1977, p 116*

Another important factor in the development of an effective cancer therapy is that it should act like a "magic bullet," killing cancer cells while doing a minimum of damage to normal ones. *"Science and the Citizen," Scientific American, May 1978, p 92*

[1967, originally used in reference to the pioneering efforts of the German biochemist Paul Ehrlich (1854-1915) to discover a chemical that would kill bacteria without harming human beings, which led to his discovery of the antisyphilitic drug arsphenamine (also known as Salvarsan or 606)]

magic mushroom, 1 a mushroom of western North America containing psilocybin, an alkaloid which produces hallucinatory effects when eaten.

The autumn rains and fertile pastures propagate thousands of little mushrooms of the psilocybe species, commonly known as magic mushrooms. Renowned for their ability to produce a vividly colored "high" when a few are ingested, the mushrooms annually attract hundreds of "psilocybarites" . . . to the river valleys of the Pacific Northwest. *Mark Budgen, Maclean's, Oct. 16, 1978, p 16*

2 *Transferred Use.* any hallucinogenic mushroom.

In the ancient Near East, there was another "magic mushroom" cult, which probably influenced the religious concepts of the Greeks, Jews, and early Christians, and which still lingers in Siberia. *Norman E. Zinberg and John A. Robertson, Drugs and the Public, 1972, p 68*

[1966]

magic spot, a compound of guanosine and four or five phosphate groups, whose appearance in cells is believed to inhibit the synthesis of ribosomal RNA.

A further twist to the story of ribosomal RNA synthesis was . . . an unusual substance, guanosine tetraphosphate (ppGpp), otherwise christened "magic spot." This has the interesting property that its amount in bacterial cells is inversely correlated with the rate of ribosomal RNA synthesis; the more magic spot a cell contains, the less ribosomal RNA it makes. *Andrew Travers, "Factors That Help to Read the Genes," New Scientist, Feb. 10, 1972, p 326*

[1970, so called from the unexpected spots this compound causes to appear on chromatograms used to analyze the nucleotide component of bacterial cells]

mag-lev or **mag.lev** ('mæg‚lev), *n.* a high-speed railway train riding on superconducting magnets over a magnetic field that is around the rails that guide the train. *Often used attributively.*

But the most interesting possibility is to try to use magnetic levitation to lift trains. The German mag-lev system uses attractive magnets pulling up towards a steel plate. A railway rail is T-shaped, which means there are two surfaces that magnets could pull up against on each rail. *"Technology Review: . . . and Mag-lev for German Trains," New Scientist, Sept. 20, 1973, p 685*

[1968, from *magnetic levitation*]

magnetic bubble, a tiny, circular magnetic domain that can be moved at extremely high speed through an integrated circuit on a wafer of crystalline material. Each bubble represents a unit of binary information, so that its movement from one circuit to another can form a single calculation in a computer.

Magnetic bubbles are small cylindrical domains within a piece of magnetized matter in which the magnetization is opposite to that of the bulk of the material. The domains can be made to move by application of a driving field.

"Physical Sciences: Hard Magnetic Bubbles," Science News, Oct. 21, 1972, p 264

A magnetic bubble, which holds one bit of information may be one micron in diameter, or smaller. A disk one inch in diameter can hold 10 million bubbles, equivalent to a sizable book. *Stacy V. Jones, "Memory Bubble Invented for I.B.M. Typewriters," The New York Times, April 17, 1976, p 27*

[1970] Also called BUBBLE and BUBBLE DOMAIN. See also BUBBLE MEMORY and HARD BUBBLE.

magnetic domain, a zone of uniform magnetization in a thin film of ferromagnetic material.

A magnetic domain is that portion of a substance in which the electron orbits of all the atoms are lined up in the same direction. A magnetic domain is in effect a small magnet within the substance. A substance will act as a large magnet when all or most of its magnetic domains (little magnets) line up in the same direction. *Michael Cusack, "Magnetic Bubbles," Encyclopedia Science Supplment (Grolier) 1972, p 390*

[1970]

magnetodisk, *n.* a cylindrical region of strong magnetic lines on the boundary of a magnetosphere (area dominated by a planet's magnetic field).

According to one model of this magnetodisk or "current sheet," it resembles the wide, floppy brim of a fedora hat, with one side cocked up and the other cocked down. Close to Jupiter, the sheet lies in the plane of the magnetic equator. *Henry T. Simmons, "Visit to a Large Planet: The Pioneer Missions to Jupiter," 1976 Britannica Yearbook of Science and the Future (1975), p 31*

[1974, from *magneto-* magnetic + *disk*]

magnetosheath, *n.* a thin region surrounding the magnetosphere of a planet that acts like an elastic medium transmitting the kinetic pressure of the solar wind onto the planet's magnetic field.

IMP [Interplanetary Monitoring Platform] also confirmed another theory that the electric field outside of the earth's bow shock is zero, but as the plasma [highly ionized gas] moves across the bow shock, the particles become accelerated inside the magnetosheath. *"Space Sciences: Tracking the Sun's Magnetic Field Lines," Science News, April 1, 1972, p 219*

Yet far stranger discoveries remain. Some half a million miles later—twice the distance from the earth to the moon, a surprisingly small distance on Jupiter's vast scale—the spacecraft left the tumultuous magnetosheath and entered the magnetosphere proper, the main body of the planet's magnetic field. *"A Pioneer View of Jupiter," Science News, Dec. 8, 1973, p 356*

[1968]

magnetotactic, *adj.* exhibiting magnetotaxis.

Richard Blakemore of the Woods Hole Oceanographic Institution reported finding bacteria that respond to magnetic forces by swimming toward the earth's north magnetic pole. Blakemore called these organisms "magnetotactic." *Joan Schuman, "Biology," Encyclopedia Science Supplement (Grolier) 1976, p 67*

[1976]

magnetotail, *n.* the elongated part of the earth's magnetosphere that extends away from the sun in a form resembling the tail of a comet.

The continuum seems to consist of two components, one which fills the whole magnetosphere and magnetotail and which is permanently trapped between the plasmasphere and magnetosheath, and another component which can penetrate the magnetosheath to propagate freely into the solar wind. *Dyfrig Jones, "Source of Terrestrial Non-Thermal Radiation," Nature, April 22, 1976, p 686*

[1973, from *magneto*sphere + *tail*] See SUBSTORM.

magnetotaxis, *n.* movement of an organism in response to a magnetic field.

Iron-rich beads probably play a role in magnetotaxis in bacteria. The bacteria crowd to one edge of a waterdrop under the influence of the earth's magnetic field, then migrate in opposite direction when a magnet is placed there. *Picture legend, "Microbiology," The World Book Science Annual 1977 (1976), p 309*

[1963, from *magneto-* magnetic + *taxis* movement (in a particular direction) in reaction to an external stimulus]

magnet school, *U.S.* a school with superior facilities or curricula, designed to attract enrollment by pupils, especially of different races.

The concept of magnet schools with the educational excellence to draw enough white students to accomplish voluntary integration has shown such promise that it is being viewed as a way to help Boston out of its school busing brouhaha. *The Wall Street Journal, May 19, 1975, p 1*

[1972]

mag wheel, *U.S.* a shiny metal rim or wheel of a sports car. Mag wheels have no hubcaps.

It is Del Rio Customs, a garage that equips cars with elaborate racing stripes and mag wheels. *"The Muscle and Soul of the A's Dynasty," Time, June 3, 1974, p 65*

[1972, *mag* short for *magnesium*, the metal used to give it a silvery appearance]

mail bomb, an explosive device hidden in a letter or parcel so that it may explode when opened by the recipient.

Last October, Taiwan's governor, Shieh Tung-min, had his left hand amputated after he was injured by a bomb mailed inside a dictionary, and two other officials had close escapes from other mail bombs. *Robert Shaplen, "Letter from Taiwan," The New Yorker, June 13, 1977, p 86*

[1972, perhaps replacing the earlier (1948) *letter bomb*] Compare PARCEL BOMB.

mailgram, *n. U.S.* a letter transmitted electronically between post offices for regular mail delivery.

Mailgrams, a combination of letter-telegram, which are cheaper than telegrams and faster than a letter, now exceed U.S. telegram volume. On Sept. 6, 1974, mailgrams were first transmitted by satellite. *David R. Bloodsworth, "Postal Service," The Americana Annual 1975, p 466*

[1970, from *Mailgram*, trademark of the service developed jointly by the U.S. Postal Service and the Western Union Telegraph Co.]

mainstream, *v.t., v.i. U.S.* to place (handicapped or exceptional children) in regular classes with normal students whenever possible; integrate into the academic mainstream.

The Philadelphia School District is committed to mainstreaming, or enrolling mildly-handicapped students in reg-

ular classes. . . . They are also mainstreaming the gifted. Since the mathematics curriculum is non-graded, the student can easily move from a special class to a regular class. *Report from Association of American Publishers, Inc., New York, March 2, 1976, p 4*

Of the children who cannot be mainstreamed, the group that seems to disturb school officials most is the emotionally handicapped. *David Milofsky, "Schooling the Kids No One Wants," The New York Times Magazine, Jan. 2, 1977, p 28*

[1974, verb use of the noun]

mainstreaming, *n.*: In the U.S. advocates of "mainstreaming" became more insistent that handicapped students could get effective education in regular classrooms. They would have handicapped students receive much of their instruction with peers, but they did point up the need for special training for regular classroom teachers, special education personnel to assist classroom teachers, and special materials. Advocates of mainstreaming recognized the necessity of having some separate special education facilities and programs. *Tudor David and Joel L. Burdin, "Education," Britannica Book of the Year 1976, p 306*

mainstream smoke, the smoke that passes through the length of a cigarette or cigar.

First, a distinction must be drawn between two types of cigarette smoke. The gases which a smoker draws into his mouth are called mainstream smoke, while the smoke which drifts off the tip of a cigarette is called sidestream. *Jon Tinker, "Should Public Smoking Be Banned?" New Scientist, Aug. 9, 1973, p 313*

[1973] See PASSIVE SMOKING.

maintenance drug, a narcotic given legally to an addict in doses large enough to maintain the drug's effect and prevent withdrawal symptoms.

At present, [Herbert Jay] Sturz concedes the advantages of oral methadone over heroin as a maintenance drug. Both are addictive, but oral methadone lasts 24 to 36 hours while heroin, which must be injected, lasts only for six hours, requiring repeated injections. *James M. Markham, The New York Times Magazine, July 2, 1972, p 7*

[1972] See METHADONE MAINTENANCE.

major, *n.* Usually, **majors,** *pl.* a large oil-producing company.

Together these eighteen or twenty "majors" control an astonishing 94 per cent of America's crude-oil reserves, 70 per cent of its crude-oil production, 86 per cent of its gasoline sales. Even the phrase "oil company" has become a misnomer, for the majors are much more than that. *Newsweek, March 4, 1974, p 12*

[1963] Compare SEVEN SISTERS.

mal·a·dapt (,mæl ə'dæpt), *v.t.* to adapt poorly or improperly.

Speaking of criminals, some governments have engaged in some evil practices, using the tools of your trade, science. Suppose neurology makes great strides in the future in terms of things it's possible to do with the mind, and some government maladapts your discoveries. *"Interview With Dr. Wilder Penfield," Maclean's, April 19, 1976, p 4*

[1976, back formation from *maladapted* (1956) or *maladaptation* (1877)]

mal·a·dept (,mæl ə'dept), *adj.* not adept or skilled; inexpert.

Within the Conservative and Labour parties, the most

likely candidates for these seats are Westminster MPs ready to retire from the back benches, candidates who have unsuccessfully fought a British election, and those too youthful or maladept to have been nominated. *Richard Rose, "The European Parliament," The Times (London), Feb. 11, 1976, p 14*

[1976, from *mal-* badly, poorly + *adept*]

male bonding, fellowship or camaraderie among males.

Buried within . . . the Gilgamesh epic is an adolescent-male myth of the wonderful world without women which still surfaces in male writings. It is the earliest extant tale of male bonding and the diabolic influence of women. *Elizabeth Fisher, Woman's Creation, 1979, p 323*

In Milburn, an aging group of Ivy League types who've known each other since they were pups is holding its regular Chowder Society meeting. Their purpose: a highly ritualistic evening of male bonding, as the feminists call it, moderate drinking of excellent liquor and the telling of, you've guessed it, ghost stories. *Judson Hand, Daily News (New York), April 1, 1979, p 18*

[1972]

male chauvinist pig, a derogatory or humorous term for a man who regards himself or all men as superior to women.

Now somebody . . . hit on the idea of having him proclaim himself the world's ranking male chauvinist pig. Grinning from ear to ear, he put out the most outrageous possible statements about the pathetic inferiority of women, except in the boudoir and the nursery. He actually succeeded in baiting into fury the brave but totally humourless vanguard of Women's Lib. *Alistair Cooke, "The Hustler," The Listener, Sept. 27, 1973, p 398*

Like it or not, put off as you might be by Tullio's impersonation of the Italian male chauvinist pig, years before the phrase, you have to say that it withstands inspection as a monumental reminder, something placed indelibly on the record. *Archer Winsten, "Visconti's 'Innocent' a Classic," New York Post, Jan. 12, 1979, p 39*

[1972, from *male chauvinist* (1970) and *pig*, a derogatory slang term for an obnoxious person] *Abbreviation:* MCP. Compare FEMALE CHAUVINIST PIG.

male chauvinist piggery: In its single-minded, five-year assault on male chauvinist piggery, the women's liberation movement has spawned hundreds of practical guides to help sisters infiltrate everything from karate to carpentry. *Elizabeth Peer, "Dirty Words," Newsweek, Feb. 4, 1974, p 78*

mal·o·lac·tic (ˌmæl ou'læk tik), *adj.* of or relating to the conversion of malic acid to lactic acid and carbon dioxide in wine by the bacterium *B. gracile.*

A Nicolas buyer told me that some cooperatives and private growers in the Midi had to be taught how to vinify correctly: "Some of them didn't know that wine undergoes two fermentations—one alcoholic, the other malolactic." *Pierre-Marie Doutrelant, "Too Much Body, Too Little Bouquet," The Manchester Guardian Weekly (Le Monde section), Sept. 8, 1973, p 13*

[1967, from *malic* + connecting *-o-* + *lactic*]

man, *n.* ► Concern during the 1970's with eliminating sexism in the English language focused especially on the word *man*. In an attempt to DEGENDER the language extensive use of the occupational suffix *-man*, as in *fireman, policeman,* etc., was criti-

cized as implicitly favoring the male sex. Likewise critics contend the use of *man* in the generic sense (*working man, early man, man as toolmaker*) obscures the role of women in society, since this sense is confused with another common meaning of *man,* "an adult male." Some efforts to restrict the use of *man* have met with a degree of success.

The National Conference of Catholic Bishops will vote next month on a . . . second proposal [that] would authorise the priests to "substitute an inclusive word or phrase" in the church's prayers wherever "the generic term 'man' or its equivalent is found." Instead of "man," the committee suggests, priests can say "men and women," "the human family," or "the human race." Instead of "all men," they could use "all persons," or "all people." And instead of "brothers" or "sons," they could use "brothers and sisters" and "sons and daughters." *Washington Correspondent, The Guardian, Oct. 25, 1979, p 5*

In Old English, *man* had two of the primary senses, meaning "human being" (as opposed to animals) and "adult male" (as opposed to women). This ambiguity caused little trouble since Old English also had several words distinctive of sex, such as *wer* (or *waépman*) for "adult male" and *wíf* (or *wífman*) for "adult female." But changes in usage caused *wíf* and *wífman* to become *wife* and *woman,* while *wer* and *waépman* became obsolete and disappeared from the language by the end of the Middle English period.

These developments left Modern English with the word *man* alone bearing the burden of meaning for both "human being" and "adult male." While this twofold sense of *man* existed originally in other Germanic languages, the generic sense of "human being" was subsequently taken over by a derivative, as in German and Dutch *Mensch,* Swedish *människa,* Danish *menneske,* etc. English, however, did not develop such a derivative and *man* retained the built-in ambiguity that lies at the root of its present difficulties:

When a language refers to the human species as "man," . . . what does that say about which sex is considered the primary one? "Whether we are aware of it or not," says Madeline Hamermesh, an English instructor at Normandale Community College, "every time we say *man* and do not include women, we are subconsciously shutting out women." . . . Not only is *man* exclusive, notes Hamermesh it is confusing. If a newspaper headline, for example, says "Man's last hope . . . ," does it refer to a dying man or to the fate of humanity? *Suzanne Perry, "It's No 'Ms.-take',", The Minneapolis Star, March 12, 1979, p 1B*

Accordingly in a study conducted at Drake University in 1972, reported in *Words and Women: New Language in New Times* (1976), by Casey Miller and Kate Swift, when *man* was used in the generic sense, students (both male and female) asked to select pictures to illustrate "Social Man," "Industrial Man," and "Political Man," selected pictures that evoked images of males only.

This point of view has led to serious efforts in many large publishing houses to establish guidelines for avoiding sexist language. These guidelines succeeded in popularizing such nongender terms as camera operator, firefighter, law-enforcement or police officer, and mail carrier in place of camera-man, fireman, policeman, and mailman. Even less male-oriented terms such as chessman and man-made are replaced by "chess piece" and "of human origin," and frequently the -man ending in titles is replaced by -person, as in chairperson, Congressper-son, spokesperson (see -PERSON). At the same time many words with feminine endings are avoided in favor of neutral substitutes, such as flight attendant and homemaker in place of stewardess and house-wife.

However, it seems doubtful that certain time-honored feminine and masculine designations, such as the distinguishing pairs master/mistress, hero/heroine, duke/duchess will soon, if ever, disappear. Nevertheless, there have been proposals to replace the salutation Ladies and Gentlemen with "Gentle-people" or "Gentlepersons," but these expressions have gained little acceptance so far. An increasing use of woman to replace man in women-oriented contexts is also evident (see WOMAN).

Exaggerated demands to alter or abolish all words with the syllable "man" in them (e.g. manager, man-date), regardless of the etymological meaning are generally disclaimed by members of the women's rights movement.

See also the note under HE/SHE.

Manchurian candidate, a person who has been brainwashed by some organization or foreign power to the extent of obeying their orders automatically.

Embarrassing pop-psychology aside, the Schlafly-Ward thesis seems to be that Kissinger is a sort of Manchurian Candidate, planted in government by . . . members of the Council on Foreign Relations. He totally subscribes, say the authors, to the CFR one-world, better-Red-than-dead philosophy. John R. Coyne, Jr., "Overkilling Kissinger," National Review, June 6, 1975, p 624

[1972, from The Manchurian Candidate, title of a novel about a brainwashed assassin (1959) by Richard Condon, born 1915, American novelist, and of a motion picture (1962) based on the novel]

Manhattanize, v.t. to build up (a city) with high-rise office and apartment buildings and other large-scale projects.

The net result of this has been to "Manhattanize" Paris (Maine-Montparnasse and the Defense areas are among the less glorious examples of this trend). Andre Fermigier, "Haussmann's Paris Threatened." The Manchester Guard-ian Weekly (Le Monde section), Aug. 31, 1974, p 11

[1972, from Manhattan, borough of New York City noted for its skyscrapers + -ize]

Manhattanization, n.: The expansion of the financial-dis-trict high rises is part of a process now known in San Fran-cisco as Manhattanization. . . . The business leaders of the Bay Area have for some years been transforming San Fran-cisco into a center of financial institutions and corporate headquarters which they see as Wall Street West. Calvin Trillin, "U.S. Journal: San Francisco," Newsweek, Dec. 19, 1977, p 116

man-month, n. one month of an individual's work

taken as a unit of time in business and industry.

In-depth studies will involve . . . "up to 60 man-months of professional effort over a period of 18 months." Preliminary studies will involve "up to 18 man-months of professional effort over 12 months." New Scientist, May 24, 1973, p 473

[1971, patterned on earlier man-hour, man-week, etc.]

man-portable, adj. capable of being carried or moved by a man (as distinguished from several men or a vehicle).

"The tactical world," he said, "will be dominated by sys-tems that are cheap and widely distributed: man-portable antitank and antiaircraft weapons, unmanned remotely piloted vehicles . . ." Phil Stanford, "The Automated Bat-tlefield," The New York Times Magazine, Feb. 23, 1975, p 36

Deferred — a helicopter borne antitank missile and the Milan man-portable missile. David Fairhall, "Defence Cuts Challenged," The Manchester Guardian Weekly, March 27, 1977, p 5

[1973]

man-rad, n. a dose of one rad (100 ergs per gram) per individual, used as a unit of absorbed radiation.

The annual cost in the United Kingdom of health physics services in the hospitals together with the costs of struc-tural shielding amounted to some £580,000 per year. This resulted in a consequential saving of 140,000 man-rads, that is about £4 per man-rad saved. "Code of Practice for Radi-ation Protection," Nature, Jan. 4, 1974, p 6

[1972] Compare MAN-REM.

man-rem, n. a dose of one rem (1 roentgen of high-voltage X-rays) per individual, used as a unit of ab-sorbed radiation.

"The total future cost of one man-rem in terms of health costs paid in present dollars, is between $12 and $120." "Environmental Mutagenic Hazards," Science, Feb. 14, 1975, p 509

[1973] Compare MAN-RAD.

mantle plume, a large upwelling of molten material from the earth's mantle.

Mantle plumes are . . . hypothesized by some scientists to account for, among other things, the creation of volcanic island chains in the Pacific. "Earth Sciences: Plates, Plumes and Yellowstone," Science News, Aug. 17, 1974, p 105

[1972] Also called PLUME. See HOT SPOT.

mao-tai ('mau'tai), n. Also, **mao tai.** a potent Chinese liquor distilled from millet.

Hitting the U.S. market, Mao-tai, China's 112-proof vodka-like drink with which Richard Nixon and Chou En-lai plighted their troth . . . "For the Record," National Review, Jan. 5, 1973, p 6

Speeches of welcome accompanied by toasts in the fiery colourless mao-tai begin early and may go on sporadically to the soup (the last course). Michael Gill, The Listener, Oct. 4, 1973, p 443

[1970, from Chinese mao tai (Maotai, town in China where it is made)]

► This term was popularized in the West after President Nixon's visit to China. It should not be confused with mai tai (1963), a Hawaiian drink made with rum.

295

Marburg disease

Mar·burg disease ('mɑr,bərg), a contagious, often fatal virus disease characterized by high fever and hemorrhaging, transmitted to man by West African green monkeys of the species *Cercopithecus aethiops*.

Three laboratories . . . have now confirmed that specimens from the Sudan/Zaire fever contain a virus similar to that of Marburg disease. Several hundred people have already died in the current outbreak, and as a result control measures have been tightened up at ports and airports throughout the world. *"This Week: New Outbreak of Marburg Disease," New Scientist, Oct. 28, 1976, p 199*

[1969, named after *Marburg*, West Germany, where several laboratory technicians died from the disease in 1967 after handling green monkeys] Also called GREEN MONKEY DISEASE.

Marburg virus, 1 the large virus causing MARBURG DISEASE.

The World Health Organization said today that studies with electron microscopes of specimens received from Zaire and the Sudan revealed a virus that appeared to be similar in form to the Marburg virus. *"W.H.O. Identifies Cause of New African Fever," The New York Times, Oct. 15, 1976, p A5*

2 another name for MARBURG DISEASE.

If we did not study viruses in the laboratory, we would be helpless against outbreaks of new diseases, such as the Marburg virus or Lassa fever of recent years. *Joshua Lederberg, 1974 Britannica Yearbook of Science and the Future (1973), p 301*

[1971] Compare EBOLA VIRUS.

Mar·i·sat ('mær ə,sæt), *n.* a satellite for maritime communications of the U.S. Navy, commercial shipping, and offshore industries.

The first launch of a communications payload during the reporting period was that of *Marisat 3*, on Oct. 14, 1976. This geostationary maritime communications satellite was stationed above the Indian Ocean. *Marisat 1* and *2* cover the Atlantic and Pacific oceans, and thus *Marisat 3* completes the Marisat system's global coverage of shipping lanes. *John F. Clark, "Space Flight," McGraw-Hill Yearbook of Science and Technology 1978, p 342*

[1976, from *Mari*time *sat*ellite] Compare LANDSAT.

Mar·ka·ri·an galaxy (mɑr'kɑ: ri: ən), any of a class of galaxies characterized by unusual shapes and a strong emission in the ultraviolet part of the spectrum.

The Markarian galaxies, under their broad umbrella of excess ultraviolet, contain many different types: Seyferts, Zwicky objects, Haro blue galaxies, many giant galaxies, many dwarf galaxies, distant galaxies and close galaxies; even quasars might be numbered among them. One of them, Markarian 132, is the brightest object in the universe with an absolute magnitude of about minus 27. *Dietrick E. Thomsen, Science News, Aug. 18-25, 1973, p 117*

[1969, named after B. E. *Markarian*, an Armenian astronomer who discovered the first such galaxies in 1968]

markup, *n. U.S.* the process of putting a legislative bill into final form. *Often used attributively.*

Almost all congressional committees do their most important work – deciding the final details of legislation – in secret; these are called "mark-up" sessions. *Elizabeth Drew, "Washington," The Atlantic, Sept. 1972, p 17*

The Judiciary Subcommittee is now beginning its markup of the bill, and the best estimate is that the measure will reach the House floor for consideration in April. *Townsend Hoopes, in a Letter from Association of American Publishers, Inc., Feb. 20, 1976, p 2*

[1967, from the *marking up* of a bill with various proposals, compromises, etc., by members of the committee in charge]

MARMAP ('mɑr,mæp), *n.* acronym for *Marine Resources Monitoring Assessment and Prediction*, a survey of the kinds and amounts of living marine resources available to the United States.

The U.S. National Marine Fisheries Service is, for example, conducting a research program (MARMAP) designed to reveal the distribution of larvae and breeding areas over the continental shelf of North America. *John B. Pearce, "Marine Biology," The Americana Annual 1974, p 367*

[1971]

marriage, *n.* ▶ New liberalizing patterns of social conduct have affected the institution as well as the traditional definition of marriage. The classic legal definition of marriage as "the condition of one man and one woman united in law for life" (*Black's Law Dictionary*) has been altered by such innovations as CONTRACT MARRIAGE, OPEN MARRIAGE, and SERIAL MARRIAGE. Even the standard dictionary definition, "the condition of being a husband and wife" (which avoids direct reference to "man and woman") has been called into question by the existence of homosexual marriages:

The move toward legally sanctioned marriages between persons of the same sex is considered by homosexual rights groups to be an important part of their national drive to overcome what they regard as discriminatory laws. *Grace Lichtenstein, The New York Times, April 27, 1975, p 49*

Marriage as an institution has been challenged particularly by the trend, common especially among young adults, to avoid it entirely and live together with no formal obligation to each other. Such sexual partners or mates have been given various names to replace "husband and wife," for example COHABITEE, ROOMMATE, LIVE-IN.

In turn, many LIBERATED couples substitute either PERSON or *spouse* in formal applications. *Spouse* is sometimes preferred even where the reference is specifically to a married woman:

Spouse abuse, better known as wife beating, was one of many women's issues permeating legislative sessions. *Ralph Wayne Derickson, "State Government," The 1978 World Book Year Book, p 486*

Spouse is also the preferred term for the new legal definition of ALIMONY, which makes either or both husband and wife liable without distinction. In cases of PALIMONY, however, where there is no formal husband-and-wife relationship, *cohabitee* or some other substitute is preferable.

marriage encounter, a method of renewing and enhancing marital relationships in which a small group of married couples meet, usually on a weekend, and engage in frank discussions and exploration of feelings between husbands and wives.

Dialoguing is what Marriage Encounter is all about. It is a technique you will not learn ... except during an encounter weekend, a form of communication that cannot be taught properly by one couple or through the printed word. It is also a very sensitive undertaking. *Kitty Hanson, "A Weekend of Shared Feelings," Daily News (New York), July 31, 1979, p 29*

The *marriage encounter*, a movement Catholic in origin but nondenominational in outlook and participation. . . . There is nothing typically Catholic about either the marriage encounter or the charismatic renewal, or indeed about much that is new in the Catholic Church. *Henry R. Stern, "The Changing Language of American Catholicism," American Speech, Summer 1979, p 88*

[1975] *Abbreviation:* ME.

Marsquake, *n.* a major seismic disturbance on the planet Mars.

Even though the Viking 1 lander successfully touched down, it suffered a few malfunctions. Its seismometer refused to uncage upon command and remained out of order permanently. Thus, no data on Marsquakes could be recovered. *Mitchell R. Sharpe, "Space Probes," 1977 Britannica Yearbook of Science and the Future (1976), p 396*

[1974]

martial artist, a practitioner of the martial arts, such as karate and kung fu.

Martial artists who dispatch their enemies by puncturing their jugulars bare-fingered are on a level of combat which is either too high or too low for this scenario. *The Listener, Sept. 5, 1974, p 310*

[1970, from *martial arts* (1930's) the Oriental arts of self-defense] See WU SHU.

MARV, *n.* acronym for *Maneuverable Reentry Vehicle,* a rocket-launched offensive missile with several nuclear warheads that can be maneuvered to change course or vary speed to avoid interception by defensive missiles during reentry into the earth's atmosphere.

Also included under this heading are $248 million for advanced research on MARV's, a "follow on" generation of highly accurate maneuverable reentry vehicles. *"Science and the Citizen," Scientific American, March 1974, p 44*

—*v.i.* to equip with a MARV warhead.

They invented MIRV's (multiple independently targetable re-entry vehicles) and are now busy MARVing (MARV's are maneuverable re-entry vehicles) the MIRV's, so that they can be maneuvered right onto their targets. *William Epstein, "Scientists and Arms," The New York Times, Feb. 18, 1976, p 37*

[1972, patterned on earlier (1967) *MIRV,* acronym for *Multiple Independently-targeted Reentry Vehicle*]

mass driver, a device for propelling or launching materials from the moon or other body in space to a space colony under construction.

Getting off the earth itself may always be difficult and rather expensive. But, once you are in space, some old but still untried ideas for propulsion become feasible. We have heard about the mass driver, for instance, which hurls

rocks and might be used for fetching asteroids. *"The Santa Claus Machine and the Seeding of the Universe," The Listener, July 6, 1978, p 13*

[1975]

materials-intensive, *adj.* requiring great use of or expenditure on materials.

The relatively less materials-intensive switching technology is substituting for transmission technology, a trend that has been given enormous impetus by the integrated circuit which is doing for switching what it is doing for calculators. *A. G. Chynoweth, "Electronic Materials: Functional Substitutions," Science, Feb. 20, 1976, p 731*

[1972, patterned on earlier *capital-intensive* (1959), *labor-intensive* (1957)]

maturity-onset diabetes, the form of diabetes that is more widespread, occurs later in life, and is usually less severe than JUVENILE-ONSET DIABETES.

Maturity-onset diabetes (because it usually shows up after the age of 40) definitely "appears to have a strong hereditary tendency," the editorial continues. "It has been calculated that 60% of the children of two maturity-onset diabetics will themselves develop mild diabetes by the age of 60. *"Science and the Citizen: Diabetes: More than One Disease?" Scientific American, Feb. 1976, p 56*

[1976]

maturity-onset diabetic: All maturity-onset diabetics are found concordant as opposed to only 50% of juvenile-onset diabetics. This suggests that in maturity-onset diabetes inheritance is the primary factor, while in some juvenile-onset diabetics environmental factors are consequential. *Shih-Wen Huang, "Diabetes," McGraw-Hill Yearbook of Science and Technology 1978, p 139*

Maun·der minimum ('mɔːn dər), a period of irregular solar activity between about 1645 and 1715, characterized especially by the virtual absence of sunspots.

During a 70-year period in the late 17th and 18th centuries, sunspots and other signs of activity all but vanished from the sun. Historical evidence for this period, called the "Maunder minimum," coincided with a very clear picture of the minimum shown as a radiocarbon anomaly in tree rings formed at the time. *"The Sun Since the Bronze Age," Science News, March 5, 1977, p 152*

Auroral displays occur during periods of high solar activity but, during the Maunder minimum, far fewer aurorae were recorded than in either of the 70-year periods preceding or following. *Keith Hindley, "The Long Years of the Quiet Sun," New Scientist, Aug. 25, 1977, p 467*

[1976, named after E. Walter *Maunder,* a 19th-century British solar astronomer who first described it in 1890; so called because of the minimal solar activity recorded]

maxi, *n.* something very large.

The worst outbreak so far this year occurred on April 3 and 4, when a fusillade of 100 tornadoes, more than half of them maxis, struck in a 14-state area over a 12-hour period. More than 300 people died. *"Earth Science: Year of the Killer Tornado," Science News, Sept. 7, 1974, p 152*

[1967, abstracted from *maxi-*, meaning very large, as in *maxi-budget, maxi-order*]

MBD, abbreviation of MINIMAL BRAIN DYSFUNCTION.

The hyperkinetic child is being recognized as a true behavioral aberration or diagnostic entity. Also called MBD, for "minimal brain dysfunction," this handicap causes children to be extremely overactive, distractible, of short attention span, impulsive, aggressive, and fluctuant in mood. Great trials to their parents and teachers, these children can apparently be calmed down by antidepressive drugs. *Frank P. Mathews, "Medicine," 1973 Collier's Encyclopedia Year Book (1972), p 377*

[1971]

MBFR, abbreviation of *mutual and balanced force reduction,* designating the proposal that the armed forces in both western Europe under NATO and eastern Europe under the Warsaw Pact be simultaneously and proportionately reduced.

One prime aim of NATO diplomacy now ought to be to rescue the talks on MBFR from a state of relaxed and (apparently) amiable deadlock and to introduce a needed note of stridency. *"Despatches from the Front," The Manchester Guardian Weekly, Nov. 6, 1977, p 10*

[1971]

MCP, abbreviation of MALE CHAUVINIST PIG.

A senator who voted against her [Anne Armstrong] might once have been thought unchivalrous, but in the liberated air of today, he would be branded by every woman in his state as an MCP — male chauvinist pig. *Alistair Cooke, "A Lady from Washington," The Listener, Jan. 15, 1976, p 38*

Some MCPs still regarded woman as a sex object ... sexist and racist attitudes had to be rubbished once and for all. *Tom Tickell, The Guardian (London), Dec. 28, 1979, p 10*

[1972]

MDA, abbreviation of *methylene dioxyamphetamine,* a hallucinogenic drug derived from amphetamine.

MDA ... has a high abuse potential, is without currently accepted medical use in treatment in the United States and lacks accepted safety for use under medical supervision. *"Behavioral Sciences: Another Bad Trip," Science News, Aug. 18-25, 1973, p 110*

[1972] Compare DPT, PMA, PCP.

MDC, abbreviation of *more developed country.*

Of particular relevance is the development of insight and assessment of policy alternatives that could lead to narrowing of the gap between the less developed (LDC) and more developed (MDC) countries. *Lemuel Wingard, "Enzyme Engineering: A Global Approach," New Scientist, Nov. 21, 1974, p 565*

[1973, patterned on *LDC* (1967) for *less developed country*]

ME, abbreviation of MARRIAGE ENCOUNTER.

ME was born in Spain in the 1950s, the brainchild of Gabriel Calvo, a young priest working with couples in Barcelona. It was discovered in 1968 by an American Jesuit, Chuck Gallagher, who saw in it the antidote for the "overemphasis on personal fulfilment in today's life," as he explains. *André McNicoll, Maclean's, May 2, 1979, p 6*

[1979]

meal pack, *U.S.* a frozen meal prepackaged in a tray to be heated before serving.

Meal packs constitute 30 percent of all lunches served in New York City public schools. *Edward C. Burks, The New York Times, Sept. 29, 1977, p 39*

[1976]

Meanings. ▶ A source of new vocabulary is the development of new meanings in existing words, usually either through figurative and transferred uses (such as "a FIRESTORM of criticism") or in technical coinages such as the specialized meanings of CHARM in nuclear physics and WORD in molecular biology.

A figurative sense can provide a vivid comparison. ADRENALIN, a hormone used to stimulate the heart, when used figuratively is extended to mean "something that stirs to action; a stimulant or stimulus." Figurative use of LAUNDER extends its meaning to the "cleansing" of money from illegal or disreputable sources. CLONE, until recently confined to the scientific meaning of two or more individuals duplicated or propagated asexually from a single ancestor, now has two distinct figurative senses in popular usage: (1) a carbon copy or replica and (2) an automaton or robot. Some phrases that have taken on figurative meanings are FIRST COUSIN, HOLDING PATTERN, and TUNNEL VISION.

Transferred senses involve changes in the area or scope of a word's use, as when ALTRUISM describes self-sacrificing behavior among animals. A meaning may be narrowed down by specialization or broadened by generalizing. For example, in the field of nuclear physics we find such common words as FLAVOR, TRUTH, and BEAUTY in highly specialized transferred senses. In molecular biology, the concept of a genetic alphabet has stimulated transfer of the meanings of WORD, SYNONYM, SENTENCE, and PALINDROME to specific applications associated with the genetic code. Slang and argot also put common words to specialized uses: CB (citizens band) radio operators have attached new meanings to words like APPLE, EARS, BREAK, and HAMMER. Computer engineers have given a specialized meaning to EMULATE and its derivatives. Economists have added a narrow meaning of FLOAT, chemists the meaning of ANALOGUE, and drug users the meaning of SMOKE.

On the other hand, a restricted meaning can be widened or generalized. For example, EXECUTIVE (as in *an executive suite*) was gradually extended to describe anything sophisticated and expensive such as *executive housing.* The word METAPHOR has been broadened to apply to anything that represents or symbolizes something else (as in "The croquet game is the author's metaphor for the absurdity of the human condition"). VACUUM CLEANER can mean "any suction-producing device," and BEAUTIFUL has been generalized in informal usage to mean fashionable or elegant.

Other changes in meaning come about because of social factors. Certain words develop derogatory meanings as a result of changes in customs, values, and even specific events that affect the attitudes of people. A word like WAREHOUSE, when applied to the type of large, impersonal institution to which the mentally ill or the poor are relegated, acquires a derogatory meaning.

Conversely, words formerly considered as derog

atory or negative are sometimes rehabilitated and given approbative meanings. The use of BLACK as a racial epithet, formerly avoided as impolite or even derogatory, was upgraded by the civil rights movement through the use of such slogans as "black is beautiful" and "black power."

Some words evolve new meanings that completely reverse their established ones. FULSOME, used for centuries in the sense of "grossly excessive," is now frequently used to mean "very flattering or complimentary" (though originally the word had the favorable meaning of "abundant, plentiful"). Changes in meaning stimulated by social factors also include euphemism, or the use of mild or indirect expressions to avoid harsh or offensive ones, as when a prisoner or convict is called a CLIENT (see EUPHEMISMS).

Some new meanings come about by a morphological process, such as shortening or derivation (see CLIPPED FORMS, DERIVATIVES). Thus ANCHOR, from *anchorman*, is only distantly related to a ship; an ALPINIST takes part in an ALPINE skiing competition but is not the same *Alpinist* who climbs high mountains; and a SEMINARIAN participates in a *seminar* not necessarily as a *seminarian* from a theological seminary. Ultimately some of these new meanings for old words will become an enduring part of English, though the USAGE is not fully acceptable or comfortable in the vocabulary at the present time.

me decade, a name applied to the 1970's to characterize the seemingly obsessive preoccupation individuals had with their personal happiness or self-gratification during that decade.

Broadly, the premise of the "me decade" . . . is that great numbers of people are disdaining society to pursue existence as narcissistic massage buffs, om-sayers, encounter groupies and peacocks. *Time, Dec. 25, 1978, p 84*

The conservative 1970s were called the "Me Decade," especially by people clinging to the myth that the 1960s were years of selflessness. Odd, isn't it, that the slogan of the "selfless" '60s was "Do your own thing." *George F. Will, "The Illusion of Progress," Newsweek, Nov. 19, 1979, p 59*

[1977, coined by the American journalist Tom Wolfe, born 1931] Compare ME GENERATION.

media event, 1 an event deliberately staged or promoted for extensive coverage by the communications media; a pseudo-event.

The reason that some phenomenon or other is declared to exist as a trend is that powerful interests have invested in that existence. (The "media event," which is no event at all until the network camera crews tramp in to make it so, is one example of the attempt to shape the world to subjective corporate fiat.) *Kennedy Fraser, "Reflections: The Fashionable Mind," The New Yorker, March 13, 1978, p 93*

2 a minor event made to seem important by excessive or exaggerated publicity.

The vogue phrase for coverage that overwhelms an occasion and by magnification distorts it is "media event." *Thomas Griffith, "Newswatch," Time, March 8, 1976, p 62*

3 a special or outstanding event, especially in broadcasting or communications.

Among the top "media events" of 1977 were David Frost's historic televised interviews with former President Richard Nixon, presented in four 90-minute segments at weekly intervals. *Henry S. Sloan, "Biography: David Frost," The Americana Annual 1978, p 119*

[1976]

me·di·a·gen·ic (ˌmiː diː əˈdʒən ik), *adj. Especially U.S.* suitable for or appealing to the broadcasting or communications media.

[Gerald] Ford hopes to find someone youngish and mediagenic, politically moderate enough to balance his own brand of Midwest conservatism. *"Who'll Be the Ex-Veep's Veep?" Newsweek, Aug. 19, 1974, p 32*

[1972, from *media* + -*genic*, as in *photogenic, telegenic, radiogenic*]

mediaman, *n.* another name for MEDIAPERSON.

Not everyone has been bored. I have found people to be more polite and philosophical than is usual at election time, as if they wanted to identify themselves with the impartial experts and media-men, rather than the partisans: there has been a tendency to look down on politicians, who actually hold *beliefs* and make *decisions. The Listener, Feb. 28, 1974, p 260*

[1974]

me·di·a·mor·pho·sis (ˌmiː diː əˈmɔr fə sis), *n.* the transformation or distortion of facts by the media.

Thus, where the Vice President is concerned after this reinauguration, the question is not what [he] is really like. Mediamorphosis notwithstanding, a great many people seem to know, and from all electoral accounts, he seems to be doing just fine. *Victor Gold, Newsweek, Jan. 29, 1973, p 9*

[1971, from *media* + meta*morphosis*]

mediaperson, *n.* a reporter or correspondent of one of the media.

The Braves' attendance so far strongly suggests that if Hank should waft the record-breaker during a home game the deed will be witnessed by more mediapersons than Atlantans. *Roger Angel, "The Sporting Scene," Newsweek, July 16, 1973, p 52*

[1973; see -PERSON]

media-shy, *adj.* fearful of the media; nervous about being interviewed or reported on by journalists.

A man who was involved with the Monkees from their conception to demise, but who is media-shy and insists on remaining anonymous, tells me he has seen it happen to every person he's known who becomes the object of mass worship. *Sara Davidson, The Atlantic, Oct. 1973, p 64*

[1973, patterned on *camera-shy* (1920's)]

Medibank, *n.* the national health insurance program of Australia.

More than two million Australians have begun a 24-hour strike in protest against proposed changes to Medibank, the national health scheme introduced by the former Labour Government. *"General Strike Brings Australia to a Halt," The Times (London), July 12, 1976, p 1*

[1975, from *medical* + *bank*]

Medicaid mill, *U.S.* a private clinic where several doctors offer medical services under the Medicaid program, engaging in excessive or illegal billing for services that are unnecessary or never performed.

299

mediocritize

The investigation of Medicaid mills is unusually difficult because, unlike nursing homes and day-car centers, they usually do not exist as corporate entities. Rather, groups of doctors share an office, with each billing Medicaid separately under his own name. *Linda Greenhouse, "Curbs Imposed on Medicaid Mills in Carey Plan to Save $50 Million," The New York Times, Oct. 6, 1976, p 1*

[1975, patterned on *diploma mill, propaganda mill,* etc.] See PING-PONG, FAMILY GANGING.

me·di·oc·ri·tize (ˌmiː diːˈɑk rə taɪz), *v.t.* to make mediocre; reduce to the ordinary or banal.

Leticia Kent, a journalist and a critic, describes Barbara [Walters] as "chameleonlike. At first she was anti-student and antifeminist. She was even against women wearing slacks.... 'Today' is one of the most mind-controlling programs, and the banal patter on the show is appalling. She exercises a mock-critical role. Everything is mediocritized, I don't know if it's her, or the medium." *James Conaway, The New York Times Magazine, Sept. 10, 1972, p 50*

[1972, back formation from *mediocritization* (1968), from *mediocrity* + *-ization*]

mediocritization, *n.:* I subscribe more to my own theory of our general mediocritization (or would if the word itself were less unwieldy). People who are led to feel that it is basically desirable to let mass-produced precooked frozen foods nourish their families are perhaps the general run, or will be in a few years. *M. F. K. Fisher, Esquire, Aug. 1970, p 124*

MEDLARS (ˈmɛdˌlɑrz), *n. U.S.* a computerized system for obtaining bibliographical data compiled from medical literature.

The National Library of Medicine, in Bethesda, Maryland, has an information-retrieval service (MEDLARS) designed to index the medical literature in twenty-three hundred periodicals. *Lewis Mumford, The New Yorker, Oct. 24, 1970, p 63*

[1964, from *Medical Literature Analysis and Retrieval System*] Compare MEDLINE.

MEDLINE (ˈmɛdˌlaɪn), *n. U.S.* a direct-line computerized system for obtaining bibliographical data compiled from medical literature, introduced in 1972.

Previously, hospitals, medical schools, medical libraries, and related research institutes had access to medical literature through an automated system called MEDLARS.... In using MEDLARS, a physician or researcher would generally write or telephone a request for a search on a given topic to the National Library of Medicine in Washington. A week or longer would lapse before he would receive the results. Now, through MEDLINE, each user installation would have its own computer terminal connected to a centralized data processing system and would be able to search a large body of the more frequently used medical literature and receive listings of relevant citations in minutes. *Harold Borko, "Information Science and Technology," 1973 Britannica Yearbook of Science and the Future (1972), p 259*

[1972, from *MEDLARS* + *line* telephone or communications line]

meg·a·byte (ˈmɛg əˌbaɪt), *n.* unit of computer information approximately equal to one million bytes.

Edinburgh University, according to *Computing* magazine, has requested permission from the Universities Computer Board to install 1,600 megabytes of Telex disc memory. *The Times (London), Nov. 12, 1976, p 16*

[1973, from *mega-* one million + *byte* unit of computer information usually equal to 8 bits] Compare KILOBYTE.

megadose, *n.* a very large dose of a drug, medicine, vitamin, etc.

Studies with college students in Canada have shown that megadoses of vitamin C can protect against the common cold. *Robert J. Trotter, Science News, July 28, 1973, p 60*

—*v.t.* to provide with a megadose.

In the scramble for a cure in the past half-century, patients have been lobotomized, tranquilized, psychoanalyzed, starved, chilled, shocked with electricity and mega-dosed with vitamins. *Terry Poulton, "Health: Schizophrenia," Maclean's, Dec. 26, 1977, p 42*

[1972, from *mega-* very large + *dose*]

megatanker, *n.* a very large tanker, especially one exceeding 200,000 tons.

Japan, which has concentrated on the construction of these megatankers, in 1972 launched 13 million tons of merchant ships representing nearly 50 percent of the total world tonnage and nearly double the total output of Sweden, West Germany, Great Britain, Spain, and France. *Paul M. Danforth, "Transportation," 1974 Collier's Encyclopedia Year Book (1973), p 540*

[1970] Compare SUPERSHIP.

me generation, the adult generation of the ME DECADE.

It may have taken them a little longer, but right now, 1978, middle-class blacks have been seized by the "Me Generation." They are looking at themselves, their bodies, their minds, their golf swings, wardrobes and investment portfolios. *William Brashler, "The Black Middle Class: Making It," The New York Times Magazine, Dec. 3, 1978, p 140*

The quest for identity also accounted for the self-improvement programs associated with the human-potential movement—a farrago that included such quick-fix therapies as "primal scream" and "rolfing." Much of it, observers complained, typified the "me" generation's insistence on magical solutions and gratification. *Larry Martz et al., "The Limits of Power," Newsweek, Nov. 19, 1979, p 96*

[1977, coined by the American journalist Tom Wolfe, born 1931; term influenced by *Now Generation* (of the 1960's)]

meltdown, *n.* the melting of the fuel core of a nuclear reactor.

What concerns these nuclear engineers—and many of their fellow protesters—is not any possibility that a conventional nuclear plant will blow up in a mushroom cloud and wipe out a city. All but a few ignorant hysterics recognize that that is impossible. What they do fear, however, is a "meltdown," which can occur if a reactor loses the water used to control the temperature of its uranium core. *"Environment: The Struggle over Nuclear Power," Time, March 8, 1976, p 69*

Even if there were to be a meltdown, the release of radioactivity would be retarded by the very strong reactor vessel, which typically has walls six to 12 inches thick. Finally, once this reactor vessel melts through, the radioactive material would still be inside the containment building, which is equipped with many devices to precipitate the volatile radioactive elements (mainly iodine, cesium and strontium) and prevent them from escaping to the outside. *H. A. Bethe, "The Necessity of Fission Power," Scientific American, Jan. 1976, p 25*

[1965, from the verb phrase *melt down*] Compare BLOWDOWN, EXCURSION. See also CHINA SYNDROME.

᥉em·con ('mem,kɑn), *n. Especially U.S., Informal.* a memorandum of a conversation.

The U.S. negotiators prepare memorandums known as "memcons" on any "unofficial" point — or hint — of substance a Russian offers, and the Soviet side presumably does the same. *Time, Aug. 14, 1978, p 11*

[1973, from *memo* + *conversation*]

᥉é·nage à qua·tre (mei,nɑːʒ a 'ka trə), a household of four people whose relationship involves sexual intimacy between all or several of the members.

Trevor, in hospital with broken limbs (having slipped on a frog!), is visited by a liberated Irene with Shirley and Eric, all ready for a *ménage à quatre*. *John Elsom, "Theatre: Marriage Beds," The Listener, Jan. 29, 1976, p 121*

"One simply does not marry men who are Siamese twins!" was the premise of Judith Rossner's novel, *Attachments*. But Nadine and Diane do — and what begins as prurient interest in "academic" sexual positions becomes a rather conventional *ménage à quatre* rife with frustrations and complaints about who's washing all the dishes. *Frederick S. Plotkin, "Literature," Britannica Book of the Year 1978, p 515*

[1963, from French, literally, household of four, patterned on *ménage à trois*]

᥉en·go·vi·rus ('meŋ gou,vai rəs), *n.* a virus that causes inflammation of the brain and heart muscle (encephalomyocarditis). It belongs to the picornavirus group.

There are shifts in allegiance to various hypotheses as new findings occur; for example, early studies with vaccinia [and] mengovirus . . . all indicated that interferon acts at a translation level. *"News and Views: How Does Interferon Act?" Nature, Aug. 18, 1972, p 369*

Researchers at the Max Planck Institute for Cell Biology in West Germany report that the cytoplasm of the unicellular giant alga Acetabularia can produce specific proteins directed by RNA from the animal Mengo virus. *Science News, Jan. 6, 1979, p 8*

[1970, from *Mengo*, apparently the name of its discoverer + *virus*]

᥉enstrual extraction, a method of terminating possible pregnancy by evacuating the uterus.

In several gynecological offices and clinics the technically legal process of "menstrual extraction" is now being employed as a means of terminating suspected pregnancy at its earliest stage. The procedure involves slipping a soft, thin flexible plastic tube into the uterus, exerting suction with a syringe, and drawing out most of the uterine lining, with any fertilized egg that happens to be present. For a woman whose period has been delayed no more than two weeks it is a simple and safe treatment, requiring no anesthesia. *Frank P. Mathews, "Medicine," 1974 Collier's Encyclopedia Year Book (1973), p 348*

[1972] Compare SALINE, VACUUM ASPIRATION. See also KARMAN CANNULA.

MEOW (mi:'au), *n.* a derisive acronym for *moral equivalent of war*. See the quotation.

One of Jimmy Carter's more memorable phrases was his description of his energy bill as "the moral equivalent of war." But the Administration has stumbled so badly in trying to get the program through Congress that the campaign has come to be known by the biting acronym MEOW. *"Energy: Some Action at Last on Meow," Time, May 1, 1978, p 65*

[1978]

MEP, abbreviation of *Member of the European Parliament*.

It has already been laid down in Strasbourg that MEPs "shall vote on an individual and personal basis" and "they shall not be bound by anyone's instructions and shall not receive a binding mandate." Moreover, "it is not desirable that chairmen or members of committees should enter into direct contact, as MEPs, with governmental or other national authority." The Community interest is meant to override the national interest. *The Times (London), Aug. 8, 1977, p 15*

[1976] See EUROPEAN PARLIAMENT.

merc (mərk), *n. Informal.* a mercenary.

The articles pull few punches. This month, for example, we can lie in our baths and delight ourselves with "Rhodesia is Ready!" "Operation Diablo: US mercs and financiers oust a red regime." *Simon Winchester, "The Death Dealers," The Manchester Guardian Weekly, June 20, 1976, p 6*

A squad of Dutch and West German mercenaries invaded the platform and took possession — on behalf of the foreign minister himself. In a daring predawn raid six days later, Bates and four other armed men retook Sealand and ousted the mercs. *"Europe: New Nation Established on Sea Platform," High Times, Jan. 1979, p 108*

[1967, by shortening]

mer·ce·nar·ism ('mər sə nə,riz əm), *n.* the act or practice of being a mercenary soldier.

Derek Roebuck, professor of law at Tasmania University, another member of the commission, said it was not improper for the court to establish a crime of mercenarism as international and national law. *The Times (London), July 1, 1976, p 7*

[1976]

Mer·ten·si·an mimicry (mər'ten ziː ən), *Zoology.* close resemblance of a noxious animal to one that is less noxious.

Three major forms of mimicry have been observed, or at least are thought to exist, in nature — Batesian mimicry, in which a defenseless organism bears a close resemblance to a noxious one; Mullerian mimicry, in which noxious species tend to resemble each other, and Mertensian mimicry, in which a mimic is more strongly protected than its model. Which of these forms of mimicry is involved in the case of nonvenemous and moderately venemous snakes resembling the red, yellow and black ringed pattern of the deadly coral snake? *"Coral Snake Mimics," Science News, Feb. 26, 1977, p 139*

[1977, named after R. *Mertens*, a herpetologist who first described this type of protective mimicry]

mesc, *n. Especially U.S., Slang.* mescaline.

[Relevant Teen-ager 1971] is off everything at the moment — pot, hash, speed, acid, STP, mesc, psyl, coke, scag — because "It's all a bummer, man; I got my head to-

mesocyclone

gether. "*Sherman B. Chickering, "Staying Hip: 1971,* 18. *Dropout from Senior Year of High School*," *Harper's*, Sept. 1971, p 63

[1970, by shortening]

mesocyclone, *n.* a cyclone of up to ten miles in diameter that develops in the vicinity of a large thunderstorm.

The Norman instrument, operated by the National Severe Storms Laboratory and the National Weather Service, sweeps oncoming storms with a radar beam and monitors echoes of the beam returned by water droplets and ice crystals. The echoes are translated into a display which can indicate to meteorologists the characteristic signatures of mesocyclones, from which tornadoes are born, and the tornadoes themselves. "*Radar Detection of Tornadoes*," *New Scientist, April 6, 1978, p 7*

[1975, from *meso-* midway, intermediate + *cyclone*]

message unit, *U.S.* a unit used by a telephone company to charge for calls that are timed, such as long-distance calls.

But then Joe Smith got tough: "Come off it, bo'. You wanna meet Mr. Howard Hughes or not? Time is money and you have just cost me 10 message units, though life is cheap here in Mexico." *Richard R. Lingeman, The New York Times Book Review, Feb. 27, 1972, p 55*

[1963]

metalloenzyme, *n.* an enzyme containing metal ions that are essential for its activity.

Enzymes in which transition metals are tightly incorporated are called metalloenzymes, since the metal is usually embedded deep inside the structure of the protein. If the metal atom is removed, the protein usually loses its capacity to function as an enzyme. *Earl Frieden, "The Chemical Elements of Life," Scientific American, July 1972, p 57*

[1971, from *metall*ic + connecting *-o-* + *enzyme*]

metaphor, *n.* something concrete thought of as resembling and hence representing an idea, quality, or condition; a symbol.

His metaphor for the insincerity of the governmental approach is the moratorium on whale hunting taken at the Stockholm conference. "Canada was boastfully associated with the United States and France who are both blowing off bombs in the water where the whales live. There's the inconsistency, the cynicism, the PR gesture." *Phyllis Webb, Maclean's, June 1973, p 76*

One of Mr. Nixon's tax dodges provides a metaphor for his relation to the places where he spends his time. *Hendrik Hertzberg, "Wraparound," Harper's, July 1974, p 4*

Having heard that football was a vital metaphor for understanding industrio-nuclear America, we drove to Washington to discover what could be learned about the country. *Russell Baker, The New York Times Magazine, Oct. 3, 1976, p 6*

[1971, extended sense of the term meaning an implied comparison in language, e.g. "the sea of life," "Life's but a walking shadow," etc.]

met·en·keph·a·lin (ˌmet enˈkef ə lin), *n.* a painkilling chemical produced in the brain and consisting of a peptide chain having the amino acid methionine at its end.

Met-enkephalin is more potent than the leu- variety, but both bind less strongly to brain receptors than does morphine. "*Monitor: More Answers on the Brain's Own Opiate*," *New Scientist, June 10, 1976, p 578*

[1976, from *methionine* + *enkephalin*] Compare LEU-ENKEPHALIN.

methadone maintenance, the use of methadone as a maintenance drug in treating heroin or morphine addiction.

Addicts attempting to withdraw from heroin, morphine, or the like . . . go to treatment centers for methadone maintenance. The largest program is in New York City and is headed by Dr. Vincent Dole and Dr. Marie Nyswander, who began the push for methadone maintenance and have done most of the original clinical research. *Norman E. Zinberg and John A. Robertson, Drugs and the Public, 1972, p 112*

[1972]

meth·an·o·gen (məˈθæn əˌdʒən), *n.* any of a group of methane-producing microorganisms genetically distinct from bacteria and plant and animal cells.

The most striking thing about the methanogens is that they survive only in warm environments entirely free of oxygen—on the sea floor, in sewage, in the stomachs of cattle or in the hot springs of Yellowstone National Park. They thrive by converting carbon dioxide and hydrogen into methane, the principal component of natural gas. *Peter Gwynne, "The Oldest Life," Newsweek, Nov. 14, 1977, p 53*

[1977, coined by Ralph S. Wolfe, an American microbiologist, from *methane* + connecting *-o-* + *-gen*, suffix meaning something that produces] Also called (as a group) ARCHAEBACTERIA.

methanogenic, *adj.*: They were all conspicuously remote from the other bacteria. This cuts right across any classification on the basis of form; but then it is quite reasonable to suppose that form in bacteria is not the important evolutionary pointer that it is in higher, many-celled animals. Is there any other indication in the methanogenic biochemistry that these organisms are distinct from other bacteria? "*Protein-Making Machinery Was a Clue to Ancient Organisms*," *New Scientist, Dec. 1, 1977, p 565*

meth·a·qua·lone (ˌmeθ əˈkwei loun), *n.* a nonbarbiturate drug that reduces anxiety and induces sleep, widely used as a narcotic. *Formula:* $C_{16}H_{14}N_2O$

Because methaqualone was believed to be non-addictive when it first went on the U.S. market in 1965, it was not placed under the special Federal restrictions that govern substances whose harmful potential has been proved, including morphine, barbiturates, LSD and amphetamines. "*Medicine: Warning on 'Sopers',*" *Newsweek, Feb. 12, 1973, p 65*

Methaqualone, a powerful central nervous system depressant . . . is a grossly abused pill. It has a reputation among "swingers" as an aphrodisiac; it is supposed to make the sensations of sex more intense and longer lasting. "They have the same effect as martinis, except there's no hangover," says one who knows. Also, like martinis, they make you drowsy. *William Lowther, Maclean's, Aug. 21, 1978, p 22*

[1968, from *methyl* + connecting *-a-* + *quinazolinone*, chemical components of the drug] Trademark, QUAALUDE. See SOPOR.

metro or **Metro,** *U.S. and Canadian.* —*adj.* of, relating to, or extending over a region including a large city and its suburbs.

The Valley of the Sun—Metro Phoenix—includes the

302

satellite cities of Scottsdale, Paradise Valley, Tempe, Mesa (founded by Mormons), Glendale, and the retirement communities of Youngstown and Del Webb's Sun City. *Town And Country, Jan. 1976, p 99*

Even to the extent that it represents a "spreading out" of existing metro areas, the more recent pattern of sprawl is producing an organization of urban life which may be as different in kind as it is in degree. *Charles L. Leven, "The Cities: A Continuous Crisis," The Americana Annual 1978, p 49*

—*n.* a municipal government extending over a metropolitan area.

Metro handles public transit, police, welfare, ambulance services, and housing for the elderly. Local governments take care of many services, from firefighting to parking lots. *Anthony Astrachan, "A City That Works," Harper's, Dec. 1974, p 15*

[1962, short for *metropolitan (area)*]

met·ro·ni·da·zole (ˌmet rəˈnai dəˌzoul), *n.* a drug used to treat trichomoniasis (a disease infecting the vagina and causing abortion and sterility in cattle), used experimentally in cancer chemotherapy. *Formula:* $C_6H_9N_3O_3$

A kind of shock wave ran through the community of chemotherapists not long ago when Sutherland of Great Britain showed that metronidazole, which I have already mentioned in connection with radiotherapy, not only sensitized cells to radiation but, independently of radiation, could also kill cells in phase G—a result that is yet to be confirmed but the possible significance of which can be readily imagined. *Lucien Israel, Conquering Cancer, 1978, p 106*

[1963, from *metro-* (from Greek *mētrā* uterus, cervix) + *ni*troimid*azole*, chemical constituent of the drug]

Mex·i·cal·i revenge (ˌmek səˈkæl iː), *Slang.* traveler's diarrhea acquired in Mexico.

He brought his own food, water, and liquor to Acapulco to avoid the embarrassment of his 1970 trip when nearly all of his guests developed classic cases of "Mexicali revenge" after being fed local produce. *Leo Janos, "The Last Days of the President," The Atlantic, July 1973, p 38*

[1973, from *Mexicali*, city in northwestern Mexico] Also called AZTEC TWO-STEP, MONTEZUMA'S REVENGE.

► See the note under DELHI BELLY.

Mexican brown, a type of dark-colored heroin produced in Mexico.

William Smitherman, the U.S. attorney in Arizona, says his state has become perhaps the most important conduit for heroin entering the country. So-called "Mexican brown" cascades across the Nogales frontier, often in light aircraft that skim the desert to avoid radar surveillance. *Robert Miller, Maclean's, Nov. 15, 1976, p 34*

Since becoming boss, Galante . . . has begun re-establishing the family's Southeast Asian connection, broken by federal narcotics agents six years ago. One sign of his success is the white Asian heroin that has begun reaching New York to compete with the more common Mexican brown. *Time, May 16, 1977, p 36*

[1975] Compare BROWN SUGAR.

MIA or **M.I.A.** (ˌem aiˈei), *n. Especially U.S.* a member of the armed forces reported as missing in action.

This month the Young Lawyers Section of the American Bar Association started a service to aid the 1,600 families of P.O.W.s and M.I.A.s across the country. *"Aid for War Wives," Time, Nov. 1, 1971, p 46*

"We shall under no circumstances abandon our POWs or MIAs (missing in action) wherever they are," he [President Nixon] said. *The Times (London), Oct. 17, 1972, p 6*

[1968, from the abbreviation of *missing in action*]

Mi·chae·lis constant (maiˈkei lis), *Biochemistry.* a measure of the affinity of an enzyme for the substance it acts upon, equal to the concentration at which the reaction occurs at 50% of the maximal rate. *Symbol:* km

In the oyster adductor muscle, as in other organisms, malic enzyme is fully reversible; however, the Michaelis constants for pyruvate and carbon dioxide are so high that in vivo the oyster enzyme probably functions only in the direction of pyruvate production. *P. W. Hochachka and T. Mustafa, Science, Dec. 8, 1972, p 1057*

[1970, named after Leonor *Michaelis*, 1875-1949, an American chemist]

micro, *n.* short for MICROCOMPUTER.

The real importance of micros, he notes, rests upon the fact that both processor and memory circuits have become units of mass production. Some peripheral machines are also moving in the same direction. Although the impact of the new micros will be so much wider than the area of the traditional data-processing department, Mr d'Agapeyeff says, the opportunity for data-processing management remains. *The Times (London), Sept. 12, 1977, p 7*

[1972]

microcomputer, *n.* a very small, low-cost electronic computer containing one or more microprocessors.

The trend toward smaller and smaller computers continued in 1974 with the rapid development of the microcomputer. The heart of the microcomputer is a tiny chip of silicon packed with thousands of transistors. This chip, called a microprocessor, functions in the same way as the central processing unit in a standard computer. Thus small-scale memory systems and other units can be linked with the chip to produce a complete microcomputing device. *Steven Moll, "Computers and Mathematics," Encyclopedia Science Supplement (Grolier) 1975, p 90*

[1972, from *micro-* very small + *computer*] See HOME COMPUTER, PERSONAL COMPUTER.

microcontinent, *n.* a slab of continental rock thought to have been isolated and separated from a larger parent continent during the process of continental drift.

Rockall Bank is supposed to be one such isolated fault block—a microcontinent left behind in the splitting apart of Greenland and northern Europe. Its east and west boundaries represent the torn edges of the splitting; its southwestern one, a transform fault dislocating the ocean floor in a shearing movement. *"Monitor: Glomar Challenger Drills Into the Atlantic Margin," New Scientist, June 24, 1976, p 701*

[1965, from *micro-* very small + *continent*]

microfilament, *n.* an extremely fine and very long fiber in the cytoplasm of cells, associated with protoplasmic movement and cytoplasmic division.

Cytological and biochemical studies have demonstrated that microfilaments are virtually identical to actin, one of

303

the major contractile proteins found in all skeletal, cardiac, and smooth muscle cells. The cytological evidence centers on the observation that microfilaments in a wide variety of animal and plant cells interact with a portion of the other major muscle protein, myosin. *R. Goldman, "Cell Biology," McGraw-Hill Yearbook of Science and Technology 1977, p 155*

[1970]

microfilamentous, *adj.:* The actin and myosin of the microfilamentous system interacted with each other while floating just under the membrane. *Bryn Jones, "How Cells Move and Associate," New Scientist, June 5, 1975, p 553*

mi·cro·me·tas·ta·sis (ˌmɑi krou məˈtæs tə sis), *n.; pl.* **-ta·ses** (-tə siːz). the spread of small, residual cancerous growths from one organ to another.

Studies of breast tissue removed during surgery have revealed that even when there was only one small identifiable lump in the breast, there were, in a majority of cases, micrometastases elsewhere in the breast, the lymph nodes of the armpit and the nodes beneath the *pectoralis major,* or major chest muscle. *"Breast Cancer: Fear and Facts," Time, Nov. 4, 1974, p 109*

[1974, from *micro-* very small + *metastasis* spread of cancerous cells (from Greek *metástasis* removal)]

mi·crop·o·lis (mɑiˈkrɑp ə lis), *n.* a miniature or compact city; a small area containing many of the facilities of a city.

Colony Square, a hundred-and-one-million-dollar project that is described by its builders as a "micropolis," will have two office towers, a hotel, a shopping center, luxury apartments, town houses, condominiums, and a two-thousand-car underground garage, all on eleven acres of land about a mile from the center of the city. *Fred Powledge, "Profiles: A New Politics in Atlanta," The New Yorker, Dec. 31, 1973, p 33*

[1972, from *micro-* very small + Greek *pólis* city; patterned on *metropolis*]

microprism, *n.* any of the minute prisms in the focusing screen of a camera that produce a blur when the subject is not in proper focus.

The viewfinder of the Contax RTS has some unique features. In addition to the interchangeable viewing screen with a central micro-prism, an illuminated scale across the top of the finder area indicates the maximum aperture of the lens in use and the actual aperture setting. *Arthur Rothstein, The New York Times, Sept. 26, 1976, p 36*

[1965]

microprocessor, *n.* a small silicon chip containing the circuitry for a central processing unit of a computer.

A single microprocessor, the size of a half a stick of gum, can contain 3,000 transistors along with other components that are the equivalent of a room-size computer of 10 years ago. A decade ago a computer of this capability cost several hundred thousand dollars. Today, using the mass-produced microprocessor, one can be had for $200. *Boyce Rensberger, The New York Times, May 4, 1976, p 23*

Microprocessors, the small-scale computing units on silicon chips that serve as the processing units of microcomputers, are being used to control fuel and emissions and gasoline mileage on some 1977 and 1978 automobiles. And cars may soon come equipped with microprocessor-controlled safety devices. *Jane Samz, "Computers and Mathematics,"*

Encyclopedia Science Supplement (Grolier) 1979 (1978) p 98

[1970] See MICROCOMPUTER.

micropublication, *n.* a book, periodical, or the like published in greatly reduced form, especially on microfilm or microfiche.

Most micropublications have been produced not for their qualities of space saving and archival permanence, but because they can provide cheap good quality reproductions for a very small market. ... Micropublications can be economically viable even if as few as five copies are sold, and are able, therefore, to provide on the most specialised subjects information that would otherwise be inaccessible. *F H. Gregory, London, "Micropublishing," in a Letter to the Editor, New Scientist, April 27, 1972, p 230*

[1971]

micropublish, *v.i., v.t.* to publish in greatly reduced form, especially on microfilm or microfiche.

An important development in micropublishing, the production of newspapers on microfilm is announced today. From January 1 The Washington Post will be micropublished by Newspaper Archive Developments Ltd., a subsidiary of Times Newspapers Ltd. *The Times (London), Oct. 12, 1978, p 21*

[1970]

microquake, *n.* a very weak seismic vibration of a magnitude of 2.5 or less on the Richter scale.

A second type of 'quake in the stellar crust is brought about by angular strains ... perpendicular to the stellar axis of rotation. When these strains are too large, you get a microquake in which a small portion of the equatorial bulge suddenly effectively rotates in such a way as to relieve some angular strain energy. *David Pines, "Starquakes," New Scientist, May 30, 1974, p 546*

McNally and her six co-workers would also help design the experiment, based on their work with monitoring swarms of "microquakes" in Southern California. *"Oaxaca Quake Was 'Trapped' After All," Science News, Dec. 16, 1978, p 422*

[1973] Compare SILENT QUAKE.

microsample, *n.* a minute or microscopic sample of a substance.

Protons are also being used in many laboratories to analyze microsamples, such as air- and water-pollution filtrates. *David J. Nagel, "Ion Excitation of X-Rays," McGraw-Hill Yearbook of Science and Technology 1974, p 435*

[1973]

microstudy, *n.* a study of a very small, specific, or minor part of a subject or field.

One of the important conclusions emerging from the discussion was the view that anthropology needs to expand its horizons beyond microstudies to deal with the national and international considerations that can impinge upon even the most apparently isolated village. *Raymond Lee Owens, "Behavioral Sciences: Anthropology," 1975 Britannica Yearbook of Science and the Future (1974), p 192*

[1972]

microteaching, *n.* a method of training teachers. See the quotation for details.

After sixteen years both as a student at Stanford University and a teacher in the university's Graduate School of Education, Allen claimed much of the credit for "microteaching," an intensive teacher-preparation program involving skill development through the use of videotape, differentiated staffing, and flexible scheduling in secondary schools, among other achievements. *Henry S. Resnik, "Are There Better Ways to Teach Teachers?" Saturday Review, March 4, 1972, p 48*

[1971; so called from the analysis of very small segments of practice teaching employed in this method]

microtexture, *n.* the small structural characteristics or composition of a rock, stone, etc.

The basic facts about designing road surfaces giving good wet grip have been known for a decade or more. The first such fact is that if a surface is to provide good wetted friction at any speed, it must have a coarse microtexture and adequate fine-scale roughness at the 0.01-0.10 mm size level. *Anthony Curtis, "The Tarmac Connection," New Scientist, Jan. 13, 1977, p 67*

[1965]

microtextural, *adj.*: The aim of the conference was an assessment of the role of . . . microtextural and microtectonic information in the interpretation of geological processes. *K. R. McClay, "Microtextures and Rock Deformation," Nature, April 8, 1976, p 483*

microtransmitter, *n.* a very small electronic transmitting device, used in surveillance, tracking, and the like.

Other devices spray the thief with incapacitating chemicals or phosphorescent dyes or even tag the poor devil with a microtransmitter so that he can be pursued, if need be, to the four corners of the earth. *William H. Honan, "The Perils of Guarding King Tut's Treasures," The New York Times Magazine, Dec. 17, 1978, p 108*

[1973]

microwave sickness, an illness described in Russian medical literature as caused by low-intensity microwave radiation that affects the circulatory, cardiovascular, and central nervous systems.

The Soviets recognize a distinct "microwave sickness" among radar workers and others exposed to microwaves on their jobs. This "sickness" is characterized, they say, by headaches, irritability, anxiety, disturbed sleep, fatigue, forgetfulness, decreased efficiency, and inability to concentrate. *Marion Steinmann, "Microwaves: Waves of the Future?" Encyclopedia Science Supplement (Grolier) 1977/1978 (1977), p 193*

[1976]

middle distillate, a petroleum product that is volatilized at medium temperatures in oil refineries.

The allocation program for the so-called "middle distillates" – including heating oil and diesel fuel – gives priority to all fuel-producing firms, farmers, mail transportation, cargo freight and vital community services such as hospitals and mass transit. *"The Trials of Allocation," Newsweek, Dec. 10, 1973, p 92*

[1952, 1973]

middle manager, a person occupying an intermediate position in management, such as an executive who is responsible for day-to-day operations but not for overall policymaking.

The workers are currently finalising a structure which will create a governing council, which appoints a general manager. The existing middle-managers and foremen are expected to retain their present jobs. All the unskilled men and women will continue to have full interchangeability between jobs. *John Fryer, The Sunday Times (London), Jan. 12, 1975, p 50*

John S. Dyson, The New York State Commissioner of Commerce, proposed yesterday that all middle managers in the state government be stripped of their Civil Service status to make them more effective, innovative and responsive to the needs of the public. *Michael Sterne, The New York Times, Nov. 24, 1976, p 56*

[1966, from earlier (1954) *middle management*]

middle-of-the-road, *adj.* of or relating to the type of popular and standard music that appeals to a broad audience.

No matter what critics and prophets looked for, sales of records showed that the public was reacting against the amateurism that characterized much rock music, preferring the greater craft and professionalism of such middle-of-the-road singers as the Carpenters. *William Livingstone, "Records and Recordings," 1975 Collier's Encyclopedia Year Book (1974), p 448*

[1973, so called because such music avoids extremes of fashion or innovation, employing familiar, established themes and styles]

mid·dl·es·cence (₁mid ə'les əns), *n.* the period or condition of life between about 40 and 65; the middle age of a person's life.

The Spouse Gap [by] Robert Lee and Marjorie Casebier. Middlescence – the new crisis years of marriage – is the subject of this unique book. The authors examine problems that face middle-aged married couples and offer some exciting possibilities for bridging "the spouse gap" and recreating a full life together. *Advertisement, The Atlantic, Nov. 1971, p 142*

A humorist has called our condition "middlescence." . . . But we will stick with the original putdown: middleaged. *Michael Kernan, "Middle Age Is Still Right, So There!" New York Post, Feb. 10, 1979, p 15*

[1965, from *middle (age)* + *-escence*, as in *adolescence* and *senescence*]

middlescent, *adj.*: Most of us, however, in middlescent years – say about 30 to 65 years old – just want to get and stay in shape, manage our stressful lifestyle, live a little longer. *Herme Shore, "What's Healthier? To Jog or Not?" The Jewish Week-American Examiner, Aug. 26, 1979, p 28*

middleware, *n.* computer software designed for tasks that are intermediate between control programs and application programs. Middleware includes any program needed for the chosen tasks of a particular installation.

According to Mr. Barney Gibbens of Computer Analysts and Programmers, middleware is a collection of techniques . . . based on a design approach in which the controls – for example, the checking and recovery of large files – are divorced from the application programs. Each can then move independently of the other. *The Times (London), April 6, 1973, p 32*

[1970, from *middle* + *ware*, as in *software, hardware,* LIVEWARE]

mid·i- ('mid i:-), combining form meaning of medium or intermediate size; mid-sized. It is added to nouns, as in the following examples:

midibus, *n.:* The National Bus Company's experimental rural "midibus" has been running around the Fenland villages for a month and most people seem to think it a good idea. *Michael Baily, "Roving Rural Bus Helps Commuters and Villagers," The Times (London), June 23, 1976, p 3*

midicarrier, *n.:* The whole concept of switching from Nimitz class carriers, which cost $2,000 million each, to midi-carriers costing half that much, will have to be re-evaluated. *Richard Whittle, The Manchester Guardian Weekly (The Washington Post section), June 19, 1977, p 17*

midicomputer, *n.:* Midicomputer for laboratory automation. Charles Sederholm of IBM Corp., Palo Alto, Calif., has pioneered the effort for the laboratory automation concept. *Max Tochner, "Computer-Assisted Analytical Chemistry," McGraw-Hill Yearbook of Science and Technology 1971, p 62*

[1970, generalized from the earlier (1967) meaning "reaching to the mid-calf" (of garments)]

midlife crisis, a crisis or turning point experienced on becoming middle-aged, caused especially by the realization that one's youth is over.

The Center for Applied Behavioral Sciences in Topeka, Kan., gives seminars in which executives are taught how to solve personal problems, how to relax and how to cope with "midlife crisis." *Kathy Slobogin, "Stress," The New York Times Magazine, Nov. 20, 1977, p 50*

Mid-life crisis; should you take a lover or redo your house? *F. Solod, Vogue, Sept. 1978, p 506*

[1972] See MIDDLESCENCE.

mi·grain·eur (mi: grə'nœr), *n.* a person who siffers from migraine headaches.

Migraineurs also speak of small white skunks with erect tails, the rippling pattern of windblown water, mice and rats, Turkish carpets and Brobdingnagian or Lilliputian vision. Migraineur Lewis Carroll is thought to have conceived his scenes for "Alice's Adventures in Wonderland" during his auras. *Alan Anderson Jr., "Managing Headache," The New York Times Magazine, May 8, 1977, p 52*

[1971, from French *migraine* migraine + *-eur* agent suffix]

mi·gro·naut ('mai grə,nɔ:t), *n.* a person who is forced to travel as a migrant for lack of a country that will admit him; displaced person.

Called "shuttlecocks" or "migronauts" in the press, these Asians have traveled from airport to airport throughout the world until the British, faced with Amin's decree, have finally relented and agreed to take in every British citizen. *Stanley Meisler, "Uganda," The Atlantic, Dec. 1972, p 34*

[1970, from *migrate* + connecting *-o-* + *-naut* traveler (as in *astronaut*)] Compare BOAT PEOPLE.

Mi·lan·ko·vich (mə'læŋ kə'vitʃ), *adj.* of or relating to the theory that slow cyclic changes in direction and tilt of the earth's axis and eccentricity of its orbit are linked to major climactic changes.

On the face of things, the Milankovitch process seems to explain very satisfactorily the climatic fluctuations of the past two million years, the so-called Quaternary Ice Age. But sceptics have doubted whether quite small changes in insolation could account for such major features as the advance of an ice sheet. *Nature-Times News Service "Science Report: Geology: Milankovitch and Ice Sheets," The Times (London), May 7, 1976, p 19*

[1975, named for Milutin *Milankovich*, a Yugosla geologist who published this theory in 1941]

Milankovitcher, *n.:* Looking outside the Earth itself, th solid basis of present work is seen both in the latest deve opments of the "Milankovitchers," and in the recurrir (but now at last established) idea of a link between solar a tivity and climate. *John Gribbin, "Climate and the Glob Economy," New Scientist, Aug. 28, 1975, p 470*

mimic board, a board or screen for displaying i diagrammatic form, often with lights, a complex sy tem, now especially one controlled by a compute such as a public utility distribution system.

Static mimic boards have been a fixture in dispatch ar control centers for many years, and they are gradual being replaced by new boards with varying amounts of d namic capability and compatibility with the control cor puter. The types range from the simplest addition of ligh at selected locations to displays in which all variable visu elements can be changed dynamically by computer or oth remote command. *Sol Sherr, "Control Systems," McGra Hill Yearbook of Science and Technology 1975, p 147*

[1975]

min·don ('mɑin,dɑn), *n.* a hypothetical particle matter that carries mental or telepathic messages

Columbia University's Gerald Feinberg . . . thinks th psychic transmissions may one day be linked to as yet u discovered elementary particles, so-called mindons or ps chons. *"Science: Reaching Beyond the Rational," Tim April 23, 1973, p 86*

[1972, coined by the Hungarian-born British write Arthur Koestler, born 1905, from *mind* + *-on* el mentary particle or unit]

mini-black-hole, *n.* *Astronomy.* a hypothetic black hole of extremely small size with a mass a low as 1/100,000 of a gram.

Most papers on black holes (those warped regions space from which light cannot escape) deal with entities stellar or galactic mass. Stephen Hawking injected son variety with his idea that mini-black-holes in the ma range 10^{-5} to 10^{-15} g might also exist. These have the a tonishing property that quantum fluctuations cause them evaporate . . . *"Monitor: Stars May Be Making Black Hol Right Now," New Scientist, June 2, 1977, p 527*

[1973]

minibudget, *n.* a supplemental budget introduce to adjust the economy of a country, especially du ing fiscal emergencies.

Chrétien and his officials . . . produced one budget ar two minibudgets in the year, to turn the economy aroun Concedes a battered Chrétien: "The job is tougher than expected." *Ian Urquhart, "From Bad to Worst Maclean's, Sept. 25, 1978, p 15*

[1966]

minicalculator, *n.* a pocket-size electronic calcula tor, consisting of a numerical keyboard and a ligh ing panel on which the digital readout appears.

A typical minicalculator will add, subtract, multiply, divide, giving an eight-digit answer with a floating decim point. *Ronald A. Schneiderman, "Electronics," The Amer cana Annual 1973, p 265*

[1972] Also called POCKET CALCULATOR.

minicourse, *n.* a brief course of study.

The idea of a short January term, sandwiched between the regular semesters, has become institutionalized in recent years, and students on hundreds of campuses will be staying around next month for so-called minicourses. *Gene I. Maeroff, "Semester Break Yields to the Minicourse," The New York Times, Dec. 15, 1976, p D21*

[1972]

minifestival, *n. Especially U.S.* a small-scale festival; a festival in miniature.

Churches will serve as sites for afternoon concerts and social suppers, and local groups will also be involved in "minifestivals," a group of outdoor activities taking place in various parks and gardens that will feature South Carolina storytellers, gospel and blues singers, puppets, mimes, crafts and instant theater. *Grace Glueck, "Spoleto U.S.A.," The New York Times Magazine, May 22, 1977, p 37*

[1976]

minimal brain dysfunction, a disorder of undetermined mechanism exhibited in the behavior and/or learning capacities of some children, but generally overcome to a degree with maturity. It is often characterized by poor muscular coordination, brief span of attention, difficulty in perception and verbalization, hyperactivity, eye imbalance, etc.

Some scientists use the term minimal brain dysfunction to describe a collection of behavioral symptoms that are presumed to represent a disturbance of brain activities. *Robert L. Isaacson, "Psychology," The World Book Science Annual 1974 (1973), p 348*

What is the cause of hyperactivity? ... It is possible that these children sustained some brain damage during pregnancy or birth; however, the data in support of this are not compelling and certainly do not justify the alternative description of the condition as "minimal brain dysfunction." *New Scientist, Nov. 2, 1978, p 351*

[1962] *Abbreviation:* MBD. Compare LEARNING DISABILITY.

minimill, *n.* a small-scale steel mill utilizing locally collected scrap metal.

The increasing . . . construction of minimills near large cities with ample scrap supplies will further open markets for steel scrap. *S. L. Blum, "Tapping Resources in Municipal Solid Waste," Science, Feb. 20, 1976, p 672*

[1972]

miniminded, *adj.* mindless; stupid.

In recent months, producers have become shrewdly sensitive to the public's insatiable appetite for escapist epics, for jumbo-budgeted, miniminded movies that rock no boats and make no statements bulkier than "Beware of the Shark!" *Guy Flatley, The New York Times Magazine, Feb. 8, 1976, p 34*

[1965]

min·i·mine ('min i,mi:n), *n.* a poisonous substance obtained from the venom of bees.

At the California Institute of Technology, an injection of minimine—a toxic polypeptide isolated from the bee venom—into fruit fly larvae was found to result in one-quarter-size adults that were normal in every way except that their individual cells were miniature. *John G. Lepp, "Zoology," 1973 Britannica Yearbook of Science and the Future (1972), p 338*

[1971, from *minim* very small (amount or size) + *-ine* (chemical suffix)]

minimum purchase, *U.S.* a minimum amount that can be purchased at one time, especially a minimum amount of gasoline that must be sold to each purchaser in order to prevent drivers from topping off their gas tanks.

Several states including New Jersey are intensifying efforts to make sure that gasoline stations comply with "minimum purchase" rules. Motorists with four- and six-cylinder cars are restricted to buying no less than $4 worth of gasoline; motorists with eight cylinder autos must buy at least $8 worth. *Ward Morehouse III, The Christian Science Monitor, Nov. 20, 1979, p 10*

[1979] See ODD-EVEN.

minimum tillage, another name for NO-TILLAGE.

No plowing. For millennia, farmers have turned over the land with plows before tilling it, cultivating it and putting in seed. Now, machines are available that combine several operations in a process called minimum tillage. One machine, on which Garst and a partner hold the patent, cuts a V-shaped furrow in unplowed land and simultaneously drops in seed. Says Garst: "In a sense, we have gone back to the pointed stick." *Time, Nov. 6, 1978, p 101*

[1977]

mininuke, *n. Especially U.S. Slang.* a small nuclear weapon designed for use in combat.

A better way to describe the present device would be to consider it as only one type of a new generation of what have been called "mininukes." By being able to control the amount of radiation, fallout and blast from these tiny H-bombs, the Pentagon can now deploy nuclear weapons capable of performing a whole new range of tactical functions. *Science News, July 23, 1977, p 61*

[1975, from *mini-* small, little + *nuke* nuclear weapon] Compare ENHANCED RADIATION WEAPON. See also WARFIGHTING.

miniplanet, *n.* a small or minor planet.

The solar system yielded yet another of its secrets in November when Charles Kowal of the Hale Observatories, Pasadena, Calif., announced discovery of a "miniplanet" circling the Sun between the orbits of Saturn and Uranus. *Kenneth Brecher, "Astronomy," Britannica Book of the Year 1978, p 205*

[1977] See OBJECT KOWAL.

mini-series, *n.* a short series of dramatizations, performances, or the like.

There has been friction behind the scenes over a low-budget mini-series called *Royal Suite*, whose installments are linked, like those of Neil Simon's *Plaza Suite*, by the fact that they all take place in the same hotel room. *Martin Knelman, Maclean's, Sept. 20, 1976, p 62*

Twenty-eight concerts are scheduled between now and next June; you can buy subscriptions to the entire program or one of seven mini-series. *Carol Lawson, The New York Times, Sept. 23, 1977, p C22*

[1973]

minitank, *n.* a highly mobile lightweight tank.

Pentagon researchers have designed a vehicle with rapid acceleration so it could scoot for cover before an antitank missile could hit it. The 20-ton minitank would carry an armor-piercing 75mm gun for destroying heavy tanks while racing around the battlefield. *George C. Wilson, "Army Leaders Keep Faith in the Tank," The Manchester Guardian Weekly (The Washington Post section), Nov. 27, 1977, p 16*

[1973]

minor tranquilizer, any of a group of mild tranquilizers used to treat anxiety or tension, that are usually ineffective in serious neurotic or psychotic disorders.

In a country where 100 million people are regular consumers of alcohol (of them, 10 million are alcoholics), where doctors write an estimated 100 million prescriptions each year for the so-called "minor tranquilizers," such as Valium and Librium, the age-old practice of mixing alcohol and drugs has reached unprecedented and staggering proportions. *William Stockton, "Dual Addiction," The New York Times Magazine, Aug. 6, 1978, p 10*

[1969]

MINS (minz), *n. U.S.* acronym for *Minor(s) In Need of Supervision.*

Legislatures rewrote juvenile codes to include *Gault* rights, but deep-seated public apathy and the resistance of the "child savers" had not extended reform beyond label changing. To deny Gault-type hearings to children not accused of specific crimes, new categories were devised with amusing acronyms: PINS, CINS, or MINS (persons, children, or minors in need of supervision). *Lisa Aversa Richette, "Do We Need a Bill of Rights for Children?" Britannica Book of the Year 1973, p 409*

[1972] See also JINS.

MIPS (mips), *n.* acronym for *million instructions per second.*

The Army's plans for a network of 288 processing elements, each with a processor—for input, arithmetical operations and output—were hit by lack of money after only 11 were built. Nevertheless, those 11 can handle a total throughput of 100 MIPS. Simulation of the full array suggested it could handle 800 MIPS. *"US Looks for Bigger Warlike Computers," New Scientist, April 21, 1977, p 140*

[1974]

miracle fruit, the fruit of a West African tree (*Synsepalum dulcificum*) of the sapodilla family, containing a substance that makes sour food taste sweet.

Miracle fruit comes from a wild shrub, in tropical West Africa, whose red berries have long been used by natives to make their sour palm wine and acid maize bread more palatable. Its secret is a taste-modifying protein. *"Sweet Tooth Technology Without Tears," New Scientist, Jan. 1, 1970, p 21*

Other plant materials suggested as sources of anthocyanins for food colors are Concord grape juice, cranberries, red cabbage, miracle fruit, Roselle (a tropical shrub of the Hibiscus family), blackberries, elderberries, and others. *F. J. Francis, "Food," McGraw-Hill Yearbook of Science and Technology 1978, p 176*

[1964] Compare SERENDIPITY BERRY. See also MIRACULIN.

mi·rac·u·lin (mə'ræk yə lin), *n.* a protein derived from MIRACLE FRUIT.

Miraculin is a glycoprotein from the miracle berry which modifies the taste of food so that even sour foods taste sweet. Miraculin was marketed at one time by the Miralin Corporation as a sweetener in dietetic foods. *G. Norris*

Bollenback, "Food," McGraw-Hill Yearbook of Science and Technology 1976, p 181

[1973, from *miraculo*us + *-in* (chemical suffix), named after the MIRACLE FRUIT] Compare MONELLIN, THAUMATIN.

Mi·ran·da (mə'ræn də), *adj. U.S.* of, relating to, or upholding the legal rights of a person suspected of a crime to remain silent and to be represented by a lawyer, especially during questioning by police.

Miranda card: Police used a "Miranda card" to read a Mexican immigrant his rights before arresting him in connection with the barroom slaying of Ernesto Miranda—the man whose name was given to a landmark Supreme Court decision on defendants' rights. *"A Miranda Suspect Gets Rights," New York Post, Feb. 2, 1976, p 15*

Miranda rights: On TV, when cops like . . . Starsky and Hutch club someone on the head, they explain that there was no other way. The law doesn't apply to them, and reading a prisoner his Miranda rights is just a joke, since they know their prisoners are guilty. *Pauline Kael, The New Yorker, Nov. 8, 1976, p 140*

Miranda rule: The report acknowledges that factors in the poor conviction record may include . . . such restrictions on police power as the still controversial Miranda rule, which requires the arresting officer to inform the suspect of his rights to counsel and to remain silent. *Time, Sept. 26, 1977, p 60*

Miranda warning: The United States Supreme Court . . . has once again limited the application of the so-called Miranda warnings, further narrowing the conditions under which a suspect must be advised of his legal rights. *"The Nation: The Narrowing of Miranda," The New York Times, Jan. 30, 1977, Sec. 4, p 2*

[1967, from the Supreme Court ruling (*Miranda* vs. Arizona, 1966) in the case of Ernesto *Miranda*, a Mexican immigrant convicted of a crime in 1963 in Phoenix, Arizona] Compare GAULT.

mi·rex or **Mi·rex** ('mɑi,reks), *n.* a highly toxic and persistent chlorinated hydrocarbon compound, used widely as an insecticide, especially to control fire ants.

The tools used by man to control his environment often contain unknown dangers. DDT, for example, was once heralded as the ultimate pesticide, then was deemed an insidious killer. Now the U.S. Government finds itself in court defending a new pesticide called Mirex, which conservationists claim has toxic side effects. *Time, Nov. 2, 1970, p 40*

Mirex may again be used against the fire ant in the southern states despite the program's recent cutback. *David R. Zimmerman, Natural History, Jan. 1976, p 16*

[1962, origin uncertain]

► Despite its frequent appearance in print with an initial capital, *mirex* is not registered as a proprietary name or trademark.

misevolution, *n.* abnormal evolution of a cell, viral particle, etc.

According to Dr. Temin, human cancer is probably brought about by a "misevolution of a normal cellular information transference process"—a mistake that can be caused in several ways, viruses perhaps being one of the ways. *"The 1975 Nobel Prize in Physiology or Medicine," Encyclopedia Science Supplement (Grolier) 1976, p 91*

[1972, from *mis-* bad, wrong + *evolution*]

misfuel, *v.i., v.t.* to supply (a motor vehicle) with the wrong type of fuel, especially leaded gas in a vehicle designed for unleaded gas.

As long as gas — and especially unleaded gas — remains in short supply, many motorists will undoubtedly keep right on misfueling their cars whatever the consequences. *David Pauly, et al., "Gas-Pump Games," Newsweek, July 16, 1979, p 78*

[1979] See ENERGY CRISIS.

missense, *adj. Molecular Biology.* involving or resulting from the insertion of the wrong amino acid in a protein molecule.

The additional material consists of amino acids added on to the N-terminal, or start of the molecule. Although this could be an artefact of the cell-free system, investigation shows that there are no major "mis-sense" errors . . . , no termination or initiation errors, and essentially no breakdown of the product during the incubation. *New Scientist, Aug. 8, 1974, p 309*

[1965, from *mis-* wrong + *sense*, as in *nonsense* (1961) that does not specify a particular amino acid] Compare FRAMESHIFT.

missionary position, the face-to-face position in sexual intercourse with the male on top of the female.

In the South and Midwest . . . said one lawyer, "the law proscribes even married people from using anything but the missionary position" in their sexual relations. *Anthony Mancini, "The Sex Laws," New York Post, June 21, 1975, p 23*

[1969, apparently so called because of the belief that it was not practiced in primitive societies until its introduction by missionaries]

mission control, a command center that controls space flights from the ground.

Instead of launching the cosmonaut team, Soviet mission control had to raise the orbit of Salyut 2 by engine thrust on 4 April. *"Clever Manoeuvring Salvages Soviet Space Station," New Scientist, April 19, 1973, p 157*

[1964]

mission controller: By the following day, mission controllers had devised a kind of Rube Goldberg extension of the damaged fender, using four plastic terrain maps and two clamps. This seemed to work well enough. *"Apollo 17 Strikes Paydirt," Newsweek, Dec. 25, 1972, p 46*

mission specialist, a scientist responsible for coordinating scientific experiments aboard a spacecraft or during space exploration.

"Mission specialists," . . . with a variety of scientific and engineering backgrounds, may become involved with spacewalks, payload handling and maintenance, and actual experimental operations. All six of the selected women are in the mission-specialist category. *Science News, Jan. 21, 1978, p 36*

[1977] Compare PAYLOAD SPECIALIST. See also PI.

Mit·be·stim·mung ('mit bə‚ʃtim uŋ), *n.* (in West Germany and some other European countries) the right of workers to participate in corporate management; codetermination.

West German unions are normally famous for their self-restraint, and one source of moderation has been *Mitbe-*

stimmung: that means the election of workers onto boards of management as opposed to boards of directors. *Neal Ascherson, The Listener, Jan. 31, 1974, p 139*

[1970, from German, from *mit* with, together with (co-) + *Bestimmung* decision, determination] Also called WORKER PARTICIPATION.

mi·tose (mai'tous), *v.i.* to undergo cell division.

The small DNA tumour viruses — polyoma virus and simian virus 40 — share the property of inducing nondividing cells which they infect to initiate a round of DNA synthesis; if the cells are non-permissive and survive, they subsequently mitose. *"SV40 Induces Nuclear Acidic Protein Synthesis," Nature, June 16, 1972, p 371*

[1972, back formation from *mitosis*]

MLR, abbreviation of *minimum lending rate,* the official interest rate of the Bank of England, which corresponds to the U.S. Federal Reserve discount rate.

There was considerable political pressure on the Government, not least from its supporters, to intervene either by making funds available at a low rate of interest, as was done by the previous government, or by lowering MLR. *The Manchester Guardian Weekly, July 15, 1979, p 3*

[1973]

MMT, abbreviation of *Multiple Mirror Telescope.*

The MMT is the first of a new class of large telescopes: it has a number of small mirrors, rather than a single large one, collecting the light from stellar objects. The six 72-inch mirrors have the light gathering power of a single 176-inch mirror, making MMT the world's third largest telescope. *"MMT's Mirrors Reflect on the Stars," New Scientist, June 8, 1978, p 647*

[1973]

mne·mon ('ni:‚mɑn), *n.* a minimal unit of information stored in the brain or nervous system; a theoretical unit of memory encoded in a nerve-cell pathway.

If a mnemon in an octopus brain is thought of as a single word on a signpost — a simple "Stop" or "Go" — then the mnemons in a human brain must be equivalent to whole sentences, paragraphs, even books, containing elaborate "programs" for guiding our future thoughts, feelings, and actions. *"The Talk of the Town," The New Yorker, Aug. 16, 1976, p 23*

[1965, from Greek *mnēmē* memory + English *-on* elementary unit]

modulate, *v.i. U.S. Slang.* to talk over a CB radio.

The person who installs a CB set and adopts a "handle" (nickname) and starts "modulating" on the air, is creating a character and reaching out to others while still maintaining anonymity. *"Modern Living: The Bodacious New World of C.B.," Time, May 10, 1976, p 79*

[1976]

mole, *n.* **1** a machine that bores holes through soil and rock, used especially to make tunnels.

On land, tunnel work may be a cut-and-cover operation, a drill-blast-muck sequence, or a boring operation with a mechanical machine called a mole. . . . The tunnel borer, or mole, has 36 cutters, weighs 200 tons, and is designed to cut through sandstone and siltstone at the rate of 20 feet (6 meters) per hour. A laser beam guides the machine through the rock formation. *William H. Quirk, "Tunnels," The Americana Annual 1972, p 689*

2 a secret intelligence agent who builds a legitimate cover over a period of years by not engaging in spying activities until he is tapped for an important mission.

A 'mole' is, I think, a genuine KGB term for somebody who burrows into the fabric of a bourgeois society and undermines it from within—somebody of the Philby sort who is recruited at a very tender age. . . . They're people about whom, at a certain time, you guess the pattern of their ideological development, if you're a talent spotter working for the Russian Secret Service, and you winkle them into a corner, and say: 'We appreciate your feelings about this, but just keep very quiet—sooner or later we will need you and when we do we will tell you.' *John le Carré, The Listener, Jan. 22, 1976, p 90*

A leak is detected in Castle's department. Counter-intelligence suspects a "mole"—the word used to designate a traitor in one's secret midst, a burrower from within who is working under the mandate of a foreign espionage organization. *George Steiner, "Books: God's Spies," The New Yorker, May 8, 1978, p 151*

Also called SLEEPER.

[1965 for def. 1; 1976 for def. 2; both transferred senses of *mole* burrowing mammal]

Mol·li·sol ('mɑl ə,sɔ:l), *n.* (in U.S. soil taxonomy) any of a group of soils with well-defined horizons, formed under vegetation and usually yielding rich cereal crops.

Mollisols. These soils of cool-temperate grasslands have been formed in weakly weathered regoliths on young land surfaces. Major areas are in the north-central United States and adjacent Canada, the Ukraine and Siberia, and the pampas of Argentina. *Roy W. Simonson, "Soil," McGraw-Hill Yearbook of Science and Technology 1972, p 372*

[1971, from Latin *mollis* soft + *-sol* (from Latin *solum* soil)] Compare ALFISOL, ARIDISOL, ENTISOL, HISTOSOL, INCEPTISOL, OXISOL, SPODOSOL, ULTISOL, VERTISOL.

mom and pop, *U.S.* **1** of or relating to a small, family-run retail business.

Shortages of natural gas have forced industries and utilities in some areas to switch to oil. . . . Something had to give. What gave were the "mom and pop" independent filling stations. Almost entirely dependent on surplus gasoline of "brand name" distributors, the independents suddenly found themselves cut off from supplies as the major petroleum companies moved to protect their own dealers. *John H. Douglas, Science News, May 26, 1973, p 342*

"It's a Mom and Pop deli. That's Pop." *Cartoon legend by B. Tobey, The New Yorker, Nov. 29, 1976, p 45*

2 *Transferred use.*

What started out as a "Mom and Pop" television shop, with two reporters and six line producers, has grown into a factory, employing more than 70 people, including 21 producers and 16 film editors. *Harry Stein, "How '60 Minutes' Makes News," The New York Times Magazine, May 6, 1979, p 29*

[1962 for def. 1; 1972 for def. 2; so called because many such businesses are operated by a husband and wife] Also called MA AND PA.

Monday clubber, *British.* a right-wing Tory.

The 11 contenders for John Boyd-Carpenter's safe seat include a strong contingent of Monday Clubbers, headed by

Dr Rhodes Boyson, headmaster of Highbury Grove Comprehensive School. *The Times (London), Feb. 4, 1972, p 12*

[1970, from *Monday Club* (1962), a British right-wing Conservative social and political organization] Compare TRIBUNITE.

M₁ or **M-1** ('em'wən), *n. Economics.* money supply consisting of currency and demand deposits.

The Fed reported that the basic money supply, known as M-1 and referring to currency in circulation plus checking account balances, had climbed from $304.3 billion in the statement week ended Sept. 8 to $308.8 billion in the week ended Sept. 15. *Terry Robards, The New York Times, Sept. 24, 1976, p D1*

[1974; *M*, abbreviation of *money*] Compare M_2, M_3.

▶ M_1 represents the generally accepted idea of money. According to economists who favor this basic definition, there is a well-established relationship between the growth of M_1 and the overall course of the economy. Other economists dispute this and propose the broader concepts of M_2 and M_3 which incorporate money that can be readily converted into M_1. Some go further and include large certificates of deposit (M_2' or M_2 prime), and savings bonds and credit union shares (M_4), and so on. Only M_1, M_2 and M_3, however, are generally in use among economists.

mon·el·lin ('mɑn ə lin *or* mou'nel in), *n.* a protein derived from an African berry, having a taste about 30,000 times sweeter than sugar.

Many other sweeteners, both naturally occurring and synthetic, are in various states of research and development. These include monellin (from the serendipity berry) and thaumatin, both protein sweeteners. *G. Norris Bollenback, "Food," McGraw-Hill Yearbook of Science and Technology 1976, p 182*

[1972, from *Monell* Chemical Senses Center at the University of Pennsylvania (where the protein was isolated) + *-in* (chemical suffix)] Compare MIRACULIN.

mo·nen·sin (mou'nen sən), *n.* a fermentation product of a species of streptomyces, widely used as an additive to beef cattle feed. Monensin is also noted for its ability to carry ions across lipid barriers.

Feedlot cattle will normally eat only enough to satisfy their energy needs, Muller says, so monensin does not increase their average daily weight gain. But since they get more energy per unit of feed, it does decrease their consumption by a little more than 10 percent, or by about 1 kilogram of feed for every kilogram of weight gained. *Thomas H. Maugh II, "The Fatted Calf: More Weight Gain with Less Feed," Science, Feb. 6, 1976, p 453*

Monensin is less soluble in acid and base than in octanol so it remains within the membrane. It picks sodium ions from the basic solution, carries them across the membrane and releases them into the acid solution. *"Chemistry: Man Made Membrane, Almost Alive," Science News, Nov. 30, 1974, p 348*

[1974, from *(Streptomyces cinna)monensis*, the name of the organism from which it derives + *-in* (chemical suffix)] See IONOPHORE.

money, *n.* **on the money,** *U.S. and Canadian Slang.* on target; precisely to the point.

Richard Nixon may never make things perfectly clear, but Peter Klappert's article "Let Them Eat Wonderbread" on political double talk from a poet's vantage point was right on the money. *Joseph Bauer, Toledo, Ohio, in a Letter to the Editor, Saturday Review, Nov. 4, 1972, p 28*

[1971, patterned on similar older phrases such as *on the button, on the nose*]

money-washing, *n.* the act or practice of channeling illegally obtained funds to make them seem legitimate; laundering of money. *Often used attributively.*

The undercover activities reportedly ranged from disrupting the Democratic primaries to secret fundraising, questionable "money-washing" operations and the preparation of dossiers on various prominent Democrats. "*Watergate: Plenty to Probe,*" *Newsweek, Feb. 12, 1973, p 26*

[1972] See LAUNDER.

monobuoy, *n.* a large floating structure anchored several miles offshore to serve as a mooring place for megatankers or other large vessels that cannot be accommodated at a conventional port.

The journey from Thistle's tanker loading buoy, 130 miles north-east of the Shetlands, to the Humber monobuoy took the tanker two days, and discharge of the cargo about 24 hours. *The Times (London), April 17, 1978, p 19*

[1972] See SUPERPORT.

monoclonal antibody, a specific antibody produced in the laboratory by fusing cells that are genetically distinct and cloning the resulting hybrids so that each hybrid cell produces the same antibody.

Biologists are trying to obtain a monoclonal antibody that will bind interferon, a natural substance that fights viral infections. . . . Other active areas of research already underway include development of monoclonal antibodies that enhance organ transplants, that diagnose and monitor leukemia and that detect subtle changes in the nervous system. *Julie Ann Miller, "The Cloning of an Antibody," Science News, Dec. 23 and 30, 1978, p 447*

The technique for making monoclonal antibodies was developed only five years ago. . . . A whole new industry is developing to exploit the potential of these highly precise antibodies. Their first use is likely to be in medical diagnosis such as the important task of identifying hepatitis infections in a person or blood sample. *Harold M. Schmeck, Jr., "Advances in Gene-Splicing Hint Scientific-Industrial Revolution," The New York Times, Jan. 27, 1980, p 31*

[1972] See CELL FUSION, RECOMBINANT DNA RESEARCH.

monster, *n. Especially U.S. Slang.* a singer or musician of very broad public appeal; a musical superstar.

Behind the headlines the Average White Band is an exciting group with the potential to be what the music business calls "monsters," musically and commercially. *Maureen Orth, "Music: Scottish Soul," Newsweek, March 24, 1975, p 81*

[1974]

Mon·te·zu·ma's revenge (ˌmɑn təˈzu: məz), *Slang.* traveler's diarrhea acquired in Mexico or from eating Mexican food.

"I do hope this doesn't last too long. I had a Mexican meal last night and I've got Montezuma's revenge," said

one of the dozen or so photographers shuffling about in the cold and wet. *The Times (London), Jan. 6, 1977, p 17*

[1962, named after *Montezuma* II, 1480?-1520, an Aztec ruler of Mexico during the Spanish conquest] Also called AZTEC TWO-STEP, MEXICALI REVENGE.

▶ See the note under DELHI BELLY.

Mon·to·ne·ro (ˌmɑn touˈnɛr ou; *Anglicized* ˌmɑn təˈnɪr ou), *n.* a member of a left-wing Peronist organization in Argentina, engaged in urban guerrilla activities.

In recent months, the Montoneros, a political and guerrilla organization of Marxists and leftist followers of the late President Juan Domingo Perón, have repeatedly denounced the activities of the Argentine military intelligence in Mexico and other countries where there are Argentine exiles. *The New York Times, Jan. 29, 1978, p 13*

[1970, from Spanish, literally, bushwhacker, guerrilla]

mood ring, a ring with a stone that supposedly changes color as the wearer's mood changes. It consists of quartz incorporating liquid crystals which have the property of changing colors with small changes in temperature.

I was so pleased to see . . . the Mood Ring — a finger ornament which changes colour with the wearer's emotions. *Donald Gould, "Emotional Jewellery," New Scientist, Oct. 30, 1975, p 298*

Keyano [a toy bear, mascot of the Commonwealth Games] is coming on like mood rings and pet rocks. "People who never thought of buying souvenirs during the Games suddenly want them for Christmas gifts," reports Dorothy Fairweather. *"A Little Logo Goes a Long Way," Maclean's, Nov. 6, 1978, p 16*

[1975]

moonchild, *n.* a person born under the sign of Cancer, June 21-July 21.

She was a Cancerian, a Moon child with no light of her own but the reflected blaze of the Sun. *Katinka Loeser, "The Houses of Heaven," The New Yorker, April 3, 1971, p 40*

Into his life and villa moves the external present in the form of Jill, a rich moonchild on the run from a mother in Connecticut and a pusher in New York. *Michael Ratcliffe, Review of "Rabbit Redux" by John Updike, The Times (London), April 6, 1972, p 7*

[1969, because of the influence of the moon on the house of Cancer; used instead of *Cancer* because of association with the disease]

Moonie, *n.* a follower of the Reverend Sun Myung Moon and member of his Unification Church; an adherent of Moonism.

The Greens have a personal motive for their campaign. Last year, two of their children left home to cast their lot in with "the Moonies" — 7000 hardcore converts who live in guarded "training centres" across the US. *Charles Foley, San Francisco, "Parents Battle 'Messiah',"" The Fiji Times, Jan. 10, 1976, p 12*

The Federal Government, however, has some ways of coping with the cults. At the moment an interagency task force . . . is being organized to investigate the financial transactions of the Moonies. *Time, Dec. 11, 1978, p 38*

[1975, from Sun Myung *Moon*, born 1920, Korean industrialist and religious leader + *-ie*]

mooning, *n. U.S. Slang.* the act or practice of displaying one's buttocks.

And one boy rhapsodizes about his success at "mooning," a boyish trick of sticking one's bare behind out the window at passing girls. All these things are essentially ugly and debasing. Yet *Grease* treats them unevasively and with good comic effect. *Henry Hewes, "Kid Stuff Retrospective," Saturday Review, July 15, 1972, p 64*

[1972, from *moon* or *moons,* old slang noun (1700's) meaning buttocks] Compare STREAKING.

Moonism, *n.* the beliefs, teachings, and practices of the Reverend Sun Myung Moon and his Unification Church, combining elements of fundamentalist Christianity and Buddhist philosophy.

Six days later I was to get a new insight into Moonism — this time by observing an intense process of withdrawal which has become known in the language of religious cultism as "deprogramming." *John Cotter, "Moonism: There Isn't an Easy Way Out," Daily News (New York), Dec. 3, 1975, p 54*

[1975, from Sun Myung *Moon* (see MOONIE) + *-ism*]

moon pool, a shaft in the center of a deep-sea mining ship, through which equipment is lowered and raised.

There was also a giant "moon pool" in the ship's bottom, with doors that could swing open to take aboard bulky "mining machinery" from below. *Newsweek, March 31, 1975, p 31*

Later this year, Deepsea Miner II will arrive there. Its crew will lower a dredge through the moonpool by attaching some 450 sections of pipe, one by one, until the dredge hits the ocean floor. *William Wertenbaker, "Mining the Wealth of the Ocean Deep," The New York Times Magazine, July 17, 1977, p 30*

[1971]

MOR, *U.S.* abbreviation of MIDDLE-OF-THE-ROAD (used especially in radio programming).

"Now a copyright like 'I Write the Songs' is *worth* something; a Sinatra will work it into his act, for instance. Or — and this is certainly something you didn't see a few years ago — a song will break MOR [middle of the road, easy listening] and then cross over to top-40." *Clive Davis, The New York Times Magazine, April 24, 1977, p 86*

[1973]

mor·phac·tin (mɔr'fæk tən), *n.* any one of a group of chemical compounds, derived from fluorene and carboxylic acid, which affect plant growth when applied at various stages and in varying strengths.

Morphactin . . . need merely be applied to the leaves of young cucumber plants that are beginning to flower. The chemical causes the flowers' ovaries to develop into fruit without first being pollinated, as is normal. *William C. Steere, "Botany," The World Book Science Annual 1972 (1971), p 282*

[1966, from *morphogenesis* + *active* + *-in* (chemical suffix)]

MOSFET ('mas,fet), *n.* acronym for *metallic oxide semiconductor field effect transistor,* a type of transistor widely used in microprocessors, computer memories, and other electronic circuits.

In a typical MOSFET two islands of n-type silicon are created in a substrate of p-type material. Connections are made directly to the islands, one of which is called the source and the other the drain. On the surface of the silicon over the channel between the source and the drain a thin layer of silicon dioxide (SiO_2) is formed, and on top of the oxide a layer of metal is deposited, forming a third electrode called the gate. *James D. Meindl, "Microelectronic Circuit Elements," Scientific American, Sept. 1977, p 74*

[1967]

Möss·bau·er spectroscopy ('mœs,bau ər), spectroscopic study using the Mössbauer effect for analysis and measurement.

With very few exceptions the application of Mössbauer spectroscopy to biology has involved measurement and interpretation of the resonant gamma-ray absorption of ^{57}Fe, the stable isotope which makes up 2% of the iron in nature. *George Lang, "Mössbauer Effect," McGraw-Hill Yearbook of Science and Technology 1977, p 305*

[1962, named after Rudolf *Mössbauer,* born 1929, a German physicist who discovered the *Mössbauer effect,* enabling changes in gamma radiation to be measured with great precision]

mo·to ('mou tou), *n.* one of the heats that make up a cross-country motorcycle race.

A Grand Prix motocross race actually consists of two heats, or "motos," each lasting for about 45 grueling minutes. *Pete Axthelm, Newsweek, July 9, 1973, p 58*

[1973, back formation from *moto-cross* (1950's)]

motor home, a motor vehicle with a long body designed and furnished to serve as living quarters for recreational travel or for camping.

Steve Ford . . . is touring scenic backwaters of the Far West with his boyhood friend Kevin Kennedy in a 27-ft. motor home. *Time, Oct. 11, 1976, p 24*

[1966] ► Not to be confused with a *mobile home* (1950's), which is a trailer designed to be used as a permanent, year-round home and which ranges from 29 to 70 feet in length and 8 to 14 feet in width.

Mo·town ('mou,taun), *n.* a style of rhythm and blues with a strong beat, which originated in Detroit, Michigan. *Often used attributively.*

Think of Michael Walden: he plays funky, Detroit low-down, Motown. But he plays better than most of the famous names, and he's only 22. *Lucien Malson, "Jean-Luc Ponty: Transatlantic Jazzman," The Manchester Guardian Weekly (Le Monde section), March 8, 1975, p 14*

Would *you* want to hear French hits from the past 30 years done with a Motown beat? *Curt Davis, "Motown With French Feelings," New York Post, April 20, 1979, p 45*

[1970, from the trademark of a record company based in Detroit, a blend of *Motor Town,* nickname for Detroit]

movement, *n.* Usually, **the Movement,** the Women's Liberation movement.

My editor in New York, Lisa Drew, began writing "Ms." on her letters to me. The feminist Kate Millett had just written a grumpy Doubleday book, *Sexual Politics,* and the office was full of The Movement. *June Callwood, Maclean's, Jan. 1973, p 32*

[1970] Also called WOMEN'S MOVEMENT. Compare SISTERHOOD.

MRCA, abbreviation of *multi-role combat aircraft,* a swing-wing type of combat aircraft jointly developed by Great Britain, Italy, and West Germany.

The third partner in the MRCA project is Italy, and each of the three countries will have its own assembly line for this advanced fighter-bomber with its variable-geometry wing and top speed well over twice that of sound. *Arthur Reed, The Times (London), June 22, 1977, Special Report: West Germany, p V*

[1970]

Mr. Clean, *Informal.* a person of impeccable morals or reputation, especially a politician or other public figure regarded as incorruptible.

The board . . . handed the top job to Jerry MacAfee, a tough, outspoken Texan who was dubbed "Mr. Clean" by the Toronto *Star* during his term as president of Gulf Oil Canada Ltd. *Ian Urquhart, Maclean's, Feb. 9, 1976, p 47*

The Lockheed payoffs are clearly an example of what the Japanese poetically refer to as *kuroi kiri* (black mist), or corruption. Ironically, Premier Miki could profit from the public anger; he has earned a reputation as his party's Mr. Clean. *Time, Feb. 23, 1976, p 36*

There were serious fears that Mr Callaghan might have damaged his reputation as "Mr Clean" by confirming his son-in-law's appointment. *The Manchester Guardian Weekly, May 22, 1977, p 1*

[1971, from the trademark of a liquid cleanser]

MSY, abbreviation of *maximum sustainable yield,* the largest amount of a natural resource that can be taken every year without impairing the ability of the resource to renew itself.

From a strictly biological point of view, the optimal harvest strategy is to remove no more and no less than the MSY each year. . . . In the case of the whales, by adding economic to biological considerations, one finds that the optimal harvest strategy may be to harvest at a rate either above or below the MSY. *Kenneth E. F. Watt, "Environment," 1978 Britannica Yearbook of Science and the Future (1977), p 310*

[1972]

M₃ or **M-3** ('em'θri:), *n. Economics.* the overall money supply of a country, including M_2 and deposits in savings and loan associations and the like and certificates of deposit.

According to figures for October, M_3 (a money supply measurement which includes cash as well as current and deposit bank accounts) was rising at an annual rate of 14 and a half per cent—compared to the target range of 9 to 13. *"Dearer Money—Bad Move at a Bad Time," The Manchester Guardian Weekly, Dec. 4, 1977, p 1*

[1974; *M,* abbreviation of *money*] ▶ See the note under M_1.

M₂ or **M-2** ('em'tu:), *n. Economics.* the money supply of a country, including M_1 and commercial-bank time deposits except certificates of deposit.

In five out of seven months for M_1, and four out of seven months for M_2, the actual rate of growth has fallen short of the desired rate, and in the past two months, drastically short. *Milton Friedman, "What Is the Federal Reserve Doing?" Newsweek, March 10, 1975, p 63*

M2, the broader category of money supply, climbed $1,700m in the latest week, averaging $711,900m against a revised $710,200m a week earlier. *"Money Supply Growth*

in US Still on Target," The Times (London), Aug. 21, 1976, p 15

[1974; *M,* abbreviation of *money*] ▶ See the note under M_1.

Mud Man or **mudman,** *n.* one of a native people of Papua New Guinea who daub themselves with mud and wear grotesque clay masks to frighten their enemies.

In this anthropologist's dream world, many people—like the Mud Men of Goroka—still live in something akin to the Stone Age. *"Birth (Reluctant) of a Nation," Newsweek, Nov. 19, 1973, p 69*

[1971]

mug·gee (ˌməˈgiː), *n.* a person who is attacked or robbed violently; the victim of a mugger.

It is no use saying a mugger is a symptom of social problems. For someone in a dark street who is about to become a muggee, the 'symptom' is the problem. *"Ideas: In Hot Blood," Newsweek, Sept. 16, 1974, p 53*

Old Sam is full of ideas: in a press release . . . he suggests that, when attacked, the muggee should "try not to make any ethnic slurs . . . soft whistling or humming are okay while you are being stripped of your valuables." *Walter Stewart, Maclean's, March 22, 1976, p 14*

[1972, from *mug,* v. + *-ee*]

multiflex, *adj.* of or relating to a complex offensive system of formations in American football in which the backs and ends may assume a number of different positions to confuse the opposing team.

Because it takes a great deal of experience, poise and ability to run Harvard's multiflex offense, the loss of Davenport is even more crippling. *Deane McGowen, The New York Times, Sept. 23, 1977, p D14*

[1977, from *multi-* many + *flexible*]

mul·ti·me·ric (ˌməl tiːˈmer ik), *adj. Chemistry.* (of a group of molecules) held together by weak bonds.

There are two possible ways in which such multimeric DNA molecules might be generated—by recombination or by some failure to terminate replication—and evidence for one or other mechanism has been obtained by workers investigating the replication of various phages and viruses. *"Origin of Multimeric ø X174 DNA," Nature, May 26, 1972, p 196*

[1968, from *multimer* group of molecules held together by weak bonds (coined in 1959 from *multi-* many + *-mer* part, as in *polymer*) + *-ic*]

multinational, *adj.* having branches, subsidiaries, plants, and the like in many countries.

The multinational company has been a key factor in increasing skills, creating jobs and promoting economic growth in the developing world, and in trebling the international flow of investment capital in the past ten years. *Alastair Buchan, "The Emerging Agenda: Multinationalism," The Listener, Nov. 22, 1973, p 696*

—*n.* a multinational company.

The author is concerned that numerous multinationals will prove so powerful politically as well as economically that they will often find themselves in open conflict with many of the countries across whose borders they operate. *H. Lee Silberman, Review of "The Multinationals" by Christopher Tugendhat, Saturday Review, March 11, 1972, p 66*

multinationalism

Some multinationals have been described as "sovereign states." The metaphor is more than apt, and one consequence of its currency is that the federal intelligence community no longer automatically equates the national interest with the multinationals' investments. *Jim Hougan, "A Surfeit of Spies," Harper's, Dec. 1974, p 52*

[1968 for adj.; 1971 for noun; earliest adj. meaning (OEDS 1926), "consisting of many races or nationalities"] Also called TRANSNATIONAL.

multinationalism, *n.:* As chairman and chief executive officer of the Singer Co., Kircher, 57, runs a worldwide enterprise that could serve as a model of U.S.-based corporate multinationalism — and to get a close-up view of the global company's role in the world, NEWSWEEK reporters have been studying Singer's operations. *"Global Companies: Too Big to Handle?" Newsweek, Nov. 20, 1972, p 98*

multinationality, *n.:* In engine production in particular, opportunities for moving towards multinationality and market expansion are real and attainable: it is substantially this path that the whole European Motor industry is taking. *Umberto Agnelli, The Times (London), Feb. 23, 1972, p VI*

multiphoton, *adj.* involving a number of photons.

As ionisation cannot take place with the absorption of a single photon, most laser physicists believe that multiphoton processes are in operation. *"Monitor: Photon Scattering Lights Up Ionised Plasmas," New Scientist, Jan. 20, 1972, p 130*

Important progress in a promising new technique to separate isotopes, known as multiphoton isotope separation, is reviewed in *Science* by Dr Arthur Robinson, of the research laboratories at Los Alamos. *"Science Report: Nuclear Power: Isotope Separation," The Times (London), Oct. 12, 1976, p 17*

[1970]

multiple aim point system, a system for reducing the vulnerability of stationary missile silos to nuclear attack by shuttling missiles within underground tunnels in a series of empty silos.

One solution to the theoretical problem has been the proposed "multiple aim point" system (MAP) for deploying ICBMs — a shell game in which the US Minuteman force would be deployed in only a small proportion (say 10 percent) of greatly increased numbers of missile sites. This cure could be worse than the imagined disease. It would invite a nuclear strike against all possible sites, including the empty ones, risking American casualties. *Edward Kennedy, "SALT II Will Enhance Western Security," The Manchester Guardian Weekly, Oct. 29, 1978, p 7*

[1978] See MX.

multiprobe, *n.* a spacecraft carrying several other craft designed to be released as planetary probes.

Ground controllers with the Pioneer Venus project at NASA's Ames Research Center in Palo Alto, Calif., sent a radio message to . . . a complex craft known as the multiprobe. Weighing nearly a ton, the multiprobe resembled a tall hatbox, about 2.5 meters across and 2.9 meters high, with four large, conical mushrooms growing on its lid. "Resembled" — past tense — because the mushrooms are no longer there. The radio signal was the first step in setting them free, to become individual, instrument-laden probes. *Science News, Nov. 25, 1978, p 356*

[1978]

multi-track, *v.t.* to record, especially on tape, on several sound tracks.

On *Heart Food* she is helped a lot by engineering, which has enabled her to multi-track her vocal lines. *Stephen Holden, "Records: Heart Food, Judee Sill," Rolling Stone, May 24, 1973, p 56*

[1972, verb use of earlier (1950's) adjective, as in *multi-track recording*]

munch·ies ('mən tʃi:z), *n.pl. U.S. Slang.* a desire for food, especially after smoking marijuana (often in the phrase *to have the munchies*).

If they have never heard the terms in Vietnam, the POW's will quickly learn about "bummers" ("unpleasant experiences, especially with drugs"), "joints" ("marijuana cigarettes, jays, j's, reefers") and "munchies" ("to be hungry, usually after ingesting marijuana"). *"Newspeak for POW's," Newsweek, Feb. 12, 1973, p 68*

[1971, from earlier slang *munchie* (OEDS 1917) something to munch on, a snack]

mu·ni ('myu: ni:), *n. U.S. Informal.* a municipal bond or other security issued by a city.

Paragon . . . mounted an expensive advertising campaign aimed at peddling "munis" to the masses and last year sold $750 million worth of securities. *"Business and Finance: Problems at Paragon," Newsweek, Aug. 13, 1973, p 82*

[1973, short for *municipal*]

Mup·pet ('məp it), *n.* any of a group of puppets manipulated by the hands of one or more persons representing animal characters and people, which became popular in 1970 on the American television show for children *Sesame Street*.

In its simplest form a Muppet is a sleeve, one end of which is so stitched as to allow a human hand to operate as the thing's mouth; above that are sewn two glass eyes. How these lengths of felt are then transmuted into live, endearing individuated and, above all, hilariously funny characters I dare not begin to analyse. It cannot depend wholly on the skill of the hidden forearms responsible for the manipulation; maybe it is a magic inherent in the felt. *Alan Coren, "The Muppet Show," The Times (London), Oct. 25, 1976, p 10*

Henson, who plays Kermit . . . says that "muppet" was simply a word that sounded good to him. The sound combination of puppet and marionette is merely an explanation that happens to sound logical. Logic peeling aside, a Muppet is (most of the time but not always) a largish arm puppet, whose body contains the arm and whose head surrounds the hand of its operator. *Time, Dec. 25, 1978, p 71*

[1976, alteration of *puppet*; coined by Jim Henson, who created this group of puppets]

mus·ca·lure ('məs kə,lur), *n.* the sex attractant of the female housefly, first isolated and identified in 1971.

Initial field tests of muscalure, a newly identified sex attractant for houseflies, showed that the attractant more than tripled the response of flies to several traps and baits. *Marcella M. Memolo, "Agriculture," 1974 Britannica Yearbook of Science and the Future (1973), p 159*

[1973, from Latin *musca* fly + English *lure*] Compare DISPARLURE, GOSSYPLURE.

muscle car, *Chiefly U.S.* a medium-sized automobile with a large engine and heavy-duty suspension system, designed for high power and speed.

. . . a thunderous avalanche of Barracudas, G.T.O.s, Javelins, Challengers, Hondas, Harleys, Cougars, Vettes, pickups, Furys, Darts, choppers, and various aging muscle cars as the players and spectators come dragging out of the parking lot. *James Stevenson, The New Yorker, Aug. 30, 1976, p 28*

[1968] Compare PONY CAR.

muscle pill, an informal name for ANABOLIC STEROID.

A group of West German sports doctors is challenging the Olympic ban on anabolic steroids, contending the "muscle pills" are harmless to physically mature athletes if dosages are carefully controlled. *The New York Times, Oct. 27, 1976, p 48*

[1976]

mu·se·que (mu:'sei kei), *n.* a slum area in Angola.

Luanda has two faces. One is of a town of fine old colonial buildings and modern blocks of flats, built by the Portuguese for their own use. The other is of the museques, the sprawling shanty towns that encircle the city and which are rarely seen by whites except from the window of a passing car. *Nicholas Ashford, "Back-Street Idealism in Angola," The Times (London), Feb. 6, 1976, p 14*

[1972, from Portuguese]

mutual assured destruction, the full form of MAD.

Referring to reports and warnings issued by the more vigorous critics of SALT, Culver says, "One of their major pegs is that the Soviets do not share our strategic-nuclear-doctrine concepts of deterrence and mutual assured destruction . . ." *Elizabeth Drew, "A Reporter at Large: Senator—I," The New Yorker, Sept. 11, 1978, p 51*

[1973]

MX, *n.* an experimental intercontinental ballistic missile with multiple warheads, designed to be moved within underground tunnels.

Most ominous is the plan to develop the huge mobile ICBM, the MX, that would be equipped with as many as ten nuclear warheads. This deadly counterforce weapon would threaten Soviet ICBM forces and invite a similar response. *George B. Kistiakowsky, "False Alarm: The Story Behind Salt II," The New York Review of Books, March 22, 1979, p 38*

[1976, from the abbreviation of *missile, experimental*] See MULTIPLE AIM POINT SYSTEM.

N

Na·der·ite ('nei də,rait), *n.* an advocate of consumerism, especially one who follows methods used and advocated by Ralph Nader.

Lowell F. Jones, a businessman in Minnesota who ran afoul of the consumerists a couple of years back, has a horrifying tale to tell. The Naderites play plenty rough . . . *Priscilla L. Buckley, National Review, May 10, 1974, p 507*

—*adj.* of or relating to the form of consumer protection practiced and advocated by Ralph Nader and his group.

Although British consumerists like to feel they can tub-thump with the best of them, it's noticeable that our brand of consumerism is generally very much more respectable than the American Naderite sort. *Alisdair Fairley, The Listener, July 12, 1973, p 67*

Of dispute there is plenty, with strong contributions and interjections from such inexorable critics as . . . James Turner, Naderite author of The Chemical Feast, and founder and co-director of Consumer Action for Improved Food and Drugs. *New Scientist, Aug. 8, 1974, p 345*

[1972, from Ralph *Nader*, born 1934, American lawyer and consumer advocate + -*ite*]

nail bomb, a homemade explosive consisting of nails tied around sticks of dynamite.

A nail bomb looks very much like half a brick and often the only means of distinguishing between a stone-thrower and a nail-bomber is that a light enough stone may be thrown with a flexed elbow whereas a nail bomb is usually thrown with a straight arm as in a bowling action. *The Times (London), April 20, 1972, p 5*

[1970]

nail bomber: The lives of the soldiers were at risk from attendant snipers and nail bombers. *Michael Lake, The Manchester Guardian Weekly, April 29, 1972, p 6*

naked call, *U.S.* an option to buy a stock or other security not actually owned by the seller.

So far this month there have been more than enough buyers to snap up the shares. Some were speculators who had sold "naked calls"—that is, speculators had sold to other investors options to buy at pre-fixed prices that the sellers of the options did not own. As the deadline approached two weeks ago for the options to be exercised, the option sellers had to rush into the market. *"Stock Market: In the Grip of a 'Buying Panic'," Time, Feb. 2, 1976, p 52*

[1976]

nal·ox·one (næl'ɑk soun), *n.* a chemical substance that acts as an antagonist to narcotics by blocking the nerve receptor sites that absorb the narcotics. *Formula:* $C_{19}H_{21}NO_4$

An antagonist, such as naloxone, is chemically similar to a specific drug—in this case, morphine. When given to an addict, it blocks the euphoria usually produced by heroin, or the analgesic effect of morphine. *"How Heroin Hits the Brain," Newsweek, March 19, 1973, p 55*

The experimenters found they could reverse the effects of the beta-endorphin, which has some of the characteristics of morphine, by injecting naloxone, a chemical used as an antidote for morphine overdose. *"Ideas and Trends: Hints on the Chemical Nature of Schizophrenia," The New York Times, Nov. 7, 1976, Sec. 4, p 7*

[1969, from *N-allylnoroxymorphone*, the chemical name] Compare NALTREXONE.

nal·trex·one (næl'trek soun), *n.* a nontoxic chemical substance used experimentally as an antagonist of narcotics. *Formula:* $C_{20}H_{23}NO_4$

Multiple emulsions (oil in water in oil) containing the narcotic antagonist Naltrexone are being developed as "timed-release" drug systems for addicts. Naltrexone blocks the opiate "high," but must be injected too frequently for successful use in out-patient treatment centers. *Science News, April 17, 1976, p 246*

[1973, from the chemical components *N-allyl* + *-trex-* (as in *methotrexate*) + *-one* (chemical suffix)] Compare NALOXONE. See also CLONIDINE.

nan·no·fos·sil ('næn ou₁fas əl), *n.* a small or microscopic fossil.

Up to 60 percent of the rock consists of nanno-fossils, relics of the smallest kinds of plankton, according to a report by Robert E. Garrison of the University's geology department. *Science News, Oct. 7, 1967, p 348*

By the time the first Pliocene white ooze was deposited the Mediterranean must have been filled to the brim. Then the present system of exchange with the Atlantic would have been in operation. The white ooze is a typical oceanic sediment, made up almost entirely of the skeletons of microfossils and nannofossils. *Kenneth J. Hsü, "When the Mediterranean Dried Up," Scientific American, Dec. 1972, p 33*

[1967, from *nanno-* very small (variant of *nano-* small) + *fossil*]

nan·o·amp ('næn ou₁æmp), *n.* one billionth (10^{-9}) of an ampere.

Rats with induced currents of between 5 and 15 nanoamps in amputated limbs quite definitely achieve a striking degree of organised recovery and partial regeneration compared with controls. *New Scientist, Jan. 20, 1972, p 127*

[1972, short for earlier (1962) *nanoampere*]

nan·o·at·om ('næn ou₁æt əm), *n.* one billionth (10^{-9}) of an atom of any element.

The initial rate of respiration was 216 nanoatoms of oxygen per minute. The addition of 0.1 m*M* glucose induced an increased rate of oxidation (270 nanoatoms per minute) which lasted approximately 50 seconds. *D. H. Koobs, Science, Oct. 13, 1972, p 127*

[1972, from *nano-* one billionth + *atom*]

narrative art, another name for STORY ART.

Jean Le Gac—Photographs and printed commentary (the genre has been labelled "narrative art") by a French practitioner who works in the touching belief that the time and effort required of the viewer to digest his lengthy captions and relate them to the pictures is well spent. *"Goings On About Town: Galleries—SoHo," The New Yorker, Feb. 2, 1976, p 11*

[1975]

narrowcasting, *n. U.S.* transmission of television programs by cable; CABLECASTING.

Arnie Rosenthal's "The Big Giveaway," New York cable television's first game show, began live narrowcasting on public-leased Channel J from a Manhattan Cable TV studio on East Twenty-third Street to eighty thousand apartments and houses and eight thousand hotel rooms and a couple hundred bars on the southern half of Manhattan Island. *"The Talk of the Town," The New Yorker, March 15, 1976, p 26*

[1972, from *narrow* + *-casting*, as in *broadcasting* because of the limited range of cable transmission]

▶ This term has been in existence for over thirty years, although not in the sense recorded here. In the Fall 1978 issue of *American Speech* ("Among the New Words," p. 217), I. Willis Russell and Mary Gray Porter traced the word back to 1948 as "a term used by its opponents to describe subscription radio." According to Russell and Porter, this meaning disappeared because subscription radio and TV were not widely accepted at that time. Another sense of this word, recorded since 1958 but rarely used, is "radio or TV programming aimed at a restricted or specialized audience." The following quotation illustrates this use:

Don Durgin, NBC-TV president, lately has plumped for "broadcasting rather than narrowcasting," implying that too much prime-time programming has had older-age "skew" and too little has appealed to *all* ages. *TV Guide July 18, 1970, p 20*

NASDAQ ('næz₁dæk), *n. U.S.* acronym for *National Association of Securities Dealers Automated Quotations*, a computerized information system providing price quotations on securities traded over the counter.

At least 30,000 publicly traded over-the-counter issues remain outside the NASDAQ system, an association spokesman estimated. For these securities, the primary source of data is the National Quotation Bureau, which compiles quotations from about 750 securities dealers. *Frederick Andrews, The New York Times, Dec. 29, 1976, p 37*

[1968]

national lakeshore, *U.S.* a recreational area adjoining a lakeshore, preserved and administered by the Federal government.

The nation's first National Lakeshore, Indiana Dunes on the shores of Lake Michigan, was established on September 8. *Andrew L. Newman, "Conservation," The 1973 World Book Year Book, p 282*

[1972] ▶ Like the national parks and monuments, the national lakeshores, of which there were four by 1975, are maintained by the U.S. National Park Service of the Department of the Interior.

Native American, *U.S.* an American Indian.

The Indians . . . have suffered a great deal from the white man, though of course they suffered a great deal from fellow Native Americans before whitey arrived. And not all the statistics are exactly genocidal in their implications. *William F. Buckley Jr., National Review, April 27, 1973, p 487*

There were disappointed minorities—black, Spanish-speakers, Native Americans—who had felt that the partisanship the privileged, young upper middle class had shown during the civil rights movement in the 1950s and 1960s had been insincere, self-indulgent and fleeting. *Margaret Mead, Culture and Commitment, 1978, p 110*

[1973] ▶ This name was popularized in the early 1970's by civil-rights activists to emphasize that the Indians were the earliest native inhabitants of America and to call attention to the discriminatory practices they were subjected to over the centuries. The new name probably derives from the designation *Native American Church* (known since the early 1950's), referring to a religious denomination of American Indians which combines traditional Indian beliefs and rituals with aspects of Christianity.

Ironically, the name *Native American* was used in the 1840's to refer to a member of the Know-Nothing political party (the Native American Party) whose aim was to keep control of the U.S. government in the hands of native-born citizens. This use disappeared (along with the party) by the turn of the century.

In the southwestern United States, *Native American* (DA 1811) has been used to refer to Spanish-speaking residents of European ancestry. See the related entries AIM, APPLE (def. 1), UNCLE TOMAHAWK.

nautical archaeology, the branch of archaeology that deals with the recovery and study of historic or ancient objects (as those found in shipwrecks) from beneath the sea.

The first move in making nautical archaeology in Britain a true academic discipline and establishing an appropriate university qualification is the inauguration of an Institute of Maritime Archaeology at the University of St. Andrews. *New Scientist, June 28, 1973, p 825*

[1972]

needle therapy, another name for ACUPUNCTURE.

In the intervening days, I found acupuncture to be almost a part of the dove-gray Paris air. Every day I met someone who was either going or had gone for needle therapy. *Eileen Simpson, "Acupuncture (à la Française)," Saturday Review, Feb. 19, 1972, p 47*

[1972]

neg·a·bi·na·ry ('neg ə,bai nə ri:), *adj., n.* (expressing) a negative binary number.

The answer to the question about negabinary palindromes is that the smallest composite number that is palindromic in negabinary is 21. Its plus form is 10101, its minus form is 111111. *Martin Gardner, "Mathematical Games," Scientific American, May 1973, p 105*

[1973, from *nega*tive + *binary*]

negative euthanasia, another name for PASSIVE EUTHANASIA.

Negative euthanasia refers to withdrawal of treatment from a patient who as a result is likely to die somewhat earlier than he otherwise would. . . . Many of those who favor negative euthanasia also recognize that appropriate care of the terminally ill may include "positive" procedures, such as giving morphine, (which, among other effects, may advance the moment of death). *Robert S. Morison, "Dying," Scientific American, Sept. 1973, p 60*

[1972]

negative interest, *Finance.* money deducted from or paid on interest.

Treasury bills are now 7.5% to 8.5% on an annual basis, CDs slightly higher. But inflation is at 12% to 13%. So you have a negative interest rate that swells the demand for credit. *David T. Kleinman in an Interview "As I See It," Forbes, Aug. 15, 1974, p 27*

Switzerland, traditional safe citadel for flight capital from all over the world, two weeks ago in effect slammed shut its bank vaults to foreigners. Among other things, it ordered

banks to charge foreigners 40% a year "negative interest" for the privilege of keeping deposits in Swiss francs. *Time, March 20, 1978, p 61*

[1973]

negative option, the choice one has of keeping and paying for or accepting the obligations of an unsolicited product received in the mail or of returning it to the sender. The practice is also called *inertia selling* in Great Britain.

Unsolicited credit cards may be new to Great Britain, but they are notorious — and illegal — in the US. The chaos that followed the launches of the US versions of Access several years ago brought such a public outcry that two years ago today a law took effect banning unsolicited cards. Even the negative option or inertia selling technique used by Lloyds Bank, where the consumer has 10 days to refuse the card, is banned in the U.S. *New Scientist, Oct. 26, 1972, p 206*

[1972]

neoantigen, *n.* an immunity-stimulating protein formed in a cell infected by a slow virus.

Immune complexes of antibody and circulating neoantigens are deposited and lead to inflammation, as in lupus nephritis. Antibody may also combine with neoantigens on tissue cells . . . so that inflammation results in various tissues. *Paul E. Phillips, "Immunopathology," McGraw-Hill Yearbook of Science and Technology 1975, p 240*

[1971, from *neo-* new + *antigen*]

neoconservatism, *n. U.S.* a moderate form of conservatism that favors many liberal reforms while opposing big government and that often sides with business interests on political and economic issues.

What is not often realized, however, is how much of the currently fashionable "neoconservatism" is made possible by the rapid exertions of government in the recent past to meet the real problems of this society. *David S. Broder, "A New Skepticism About Uncle Sam," The Manchester Guardian Weekly (The Washington Post section), Feb. 5, 1978, p 15*

A cluster of mandarins, including the Harvard triumvirate of Nathan Glazer, Daniel Bell and James Q. Wilson, and New York's tart-tongued Sen. Daniel Patrick Moynihan modulated their New Deal progressivism into a cautious new social critique, dubbed "neo-conservatism" by socialist Michael Harrington. *"The Limits of Power," Newsweek, Nov. 19, 1979, p 95*

[1976]

neoconservative, *U.S. —adj.* of or characterized by neoconservatism.

To be sure, there are signs of change in the intellectual community. A few neoconservative intellectuals like Irving Kristol, Edward Banfield, and Pat Moynihan are leaning in the New Majority direction. *Kevin Phillips, "Conservative Chic: The Evolving Style of the New Republican Majority," Harper's, June 1973, p 70*

—n. an adherent or advocate of neoconservatism.

The neoconservatives' claim that big government tends to become unpopular and eventually illegitimate deserves more attention than liberals or radicals have given it. Unfortunately, it also deserves more attention than neoconservatives have given it. *Christopher Jencks, Review of "The Neoconservatives" by Peter Steinfels, The New York Times Book Review, July 1, 1979, p 17*

[1973]

ne·o·mort ('ni: ou'mɔrt), *n.* a body whose brain is dead but with some other organs kept functioning by a respirator and other artificial means.

Whatever is possible with the old embalmed cadaver is extended to an incredible degree with the neomort . . .

Uneasy medical students could practice routine physical examinations . . . everything except neurological examinations, since the neomort by definition has no functioning central nervous system. *Willard Gaylin, "Harvesting the Dead," Harper's, Sept. 1974, p 26*

"Should neomorts arise . . ." Toward the programme's end I gathered that . . . even with most advanced techniques, the management of these semicadavers is exceptionally difficult beyond 24 hours: they need, so it appears, much the same amount of nursing as anyone with a totally incapacitating stroke — and that is quite a lot. *David Wade, The Times (London), June 19, 1976, p 10*

[1974, coined by Willard Gaylin, an American psychiatrist, from *neo-* new + Latin *mortuus* dead]

neo-Pentecostal, *adj.* of or relating to a movement in Protestant and Catholic churches of the United States which emphasizes Pentecostal beliefs and practices such as faith healing, speaking in tongues, and the exorcism of demons.

She had a session with a pioneer in the Neo-Pentecostal movement that was just then beginning to introduce healing and other "gifts of the Holy Spirit" into mainstream churches. *Time, April 26, 1976, p 42*

—*n.* a member of a neo-Pentecostal church or sect; a CHARISMATIC.

The most radical innovation among neo-Pentecostals is the creation of charismatic "households" in which married couples, singles, clergy and nuns come together for shared prayer and mutual support. *Newsweek, June 25, 1973, p 85A*

[1971] See DISCIPLING, EXORCISM.

neo-Pentecostalism, *n.:* Roman Catholic "neo-Pentecostalism," a movement that stressed prayers and speaking in tongues, attracted thousands. *Martin E. Marty, "Ecumenism In the '70s," The 1973 World Book Year Book, p 177*

neo-Pentecostalist, *n.:* Like other Neo-Pentecostalists, Stapleton believes in miraculous physical healings, but has played down her own involvement in them. *Time, April 26, 1976, p 42*

Ne·o·ri·can (ˌni: ou'ri: kən), *U.S.* —*n.* a New Yorker of Puerto Rican origin or descent.

Manny Santel is doubtless the luckiest man in Mosquitos. A skilled worker and union leader at the Aguirre mill, he won a $17,000 lottery. . . . But he is an exception, a relatively sophisticated returnee from New York (those who come back are called *Neoricans*, a term touched with envy and resentment). *Time, Feb. 16, 1976, p 15*

—*adj.* of or being a New Yorker of Puerto Rican origin or descent.

His ragged Spanish also has caused problems, although it is now improving. Terry and her Neorican friends at school are severely rebuked by classmates if they are overheard speaking in English. *William Stockton, "Going Home: The Puerto Ricans' New Migration," The New York Times Magazine, Nov. 12, 1978, p 90*

[1972, influenced by *neo-* new, from NUYORICAN]

neovascularization, *n.* the growth or spread of new capillaries in the body, especially in a tumor.

Neovascularization also seems to be important in some diseases other than cancer. For example, one would like to know why capillaries invade the vitreous humor of the eye in diabetes and overrun the cornea in trachoma, leading in both cases to blindness. *Judah Folkman, "The Vascularization of Tumors," Scientific American, May 1976, p 73*

[1976]

nerd (nərd), *n. U.S. and Canadian Slang.* a foolish or ineffectual person; jerk.

As the novel begins, the hero, another loser named Walter Starbuck, is serving time for a contemptible minor role he played in the Watergate scandal. . . . He's 67 years old and a nerd, but he still has lots of energy. *Judson Hand, "Books," Review of "Jailbird," by Kurt Vonnegut, Jr., Sunday News (New York), Aug. 26, 1979, Leisure section, p 7*

[1965, originally hot-rod and surfing slang, probably an alteration of earlier slang (1940's) *nert* stupid or crazy person, itself an alteration of *nut*] Also spelled NURD.

nerdy, *adj.:* With her [Gilda Radner] came her stable of TV characters, from the crudely candid Roseanne Rosannadana to the nerdy Lisa Loopner — all of whom did just fine. *"Gilda Live," Newsweek, Aug. 13, 1979, p 3*

nerve growth factor, a protein that stimulates the growth of sympathetic and sensory nerve cells.

Nerve growth factor is a protein found in special abundance in mouse salivary glands and in certain snake venoms. It has a unique biological activity as a potent and specific stimulant of the growth of postganglionic sympathetic neurons and sensory neurons. These effects are seen most prominently in the sympathetic or sensory ganglia of young animals when the neurons are not fully developed. *L. Iversen, "Neurochemical Manipulation," Science, Jan. 12, 1973, p 171*

[1966] *Abbreviation:* NGF

net economic welfare, *U.S. Economics.* a measure of a country's economy, consisting of the gross national product corrected to account for certain nonmaterial factors, such as the cost of industrial pollution and the value of expanded leisure.

The new indicator, which M.I.T.'s Samuelson calls "net economic welfare," or N.E.W., is based on a pioneering study by Yale Professors William Nordhaus and James Tobin. Basically, N.E.W. tries to measure some of the more slippery realities not included in G.N.P. *"Economy and Business: Theory: A Gauge of Well-Being," Time, April 9, 1973, p 98*

[1973]

networking, *n.* a computer system in which several computers and data banks are linked together. *Also used attributively.*

Time-sharing and networking are "multi-access" systems. Several individuals or companies have access to and can use a single computer system. In all such systems, each user has the impression that the entire computer is at his disposal. Actually, the machine may be serving many users at once. *Tom Alexander, "The Computer Rip-Off," Encyclopedia Science Supplement (Grolier) 1975, p 98*

[1973]

networked, *adj.:* Mainframes, as large computers are called, will be needed only for work requiring special facilities — large programs, graphics display and so on — so it would be sensible to build networked systems enabling expensive machines to serve a large number of users. Networking also means that particular jobs can be run on special machines rather than many machines handling all types of jobs which is inefficient. *"Armchair Science," New Scientist, Sept. 7, 1978, p 669*

neuroethology, *n.* the branch of ethology dealing with the nervous system; study of the neural basis of animal behavior.

Jörg-Peter Ewert ("The Neural Basis of Visually Guided Behavior") is professor of zoology and head of the department of neuroethology at the newly founded Gesamthochschule Kassel (Integrated University of Kassel) in West Germany. *"The Authors," Scientific American, March 1974, p 16*

[1972]

neurogenetics, *n.* the branch of genetics dealing with the nervous system; study of the genetic development, features, etc., of the nervous system of animals.

Current neurogenetics is based primarily on research with animals such as mice, *Drosophila, Paramecium, Daphnia,* and nematodes, in which it is difficult or impossible to study the physiology of particular neurons. *David Bentley, Science, Feb. 28, 1975, p 760*

[1972]

neurogeneticist, *n.:* The team, coordinated by . . . neurogeneticist Dr. Eva Andermann, is trying to stop the death toll from Tay-Sachs — six families have now lost sons and daughters to the disease — by identifying couples who both carry the Tay-Sachs gene mutation and thus run a 25% chance of having a Tay-Sachs child. *Glen Allen, "Medicine," Maclean's, April 19, 1976, p 57*

neurolinguistics, *n.* the study of the relationship between the human nervous system and language.

The field of neurolinguistics is concerned with elucidating the relationships between language and the central nervous system; it draws upon the research, analytical tools, and hypotheses of linguistics, psychology, neurology, and neuroscience. Since the 19th century the principal source of data has been the patient with brain damage; hence, for ethical as well as practical reasons, the accumulation of knowledge in this field has been slow and difficult. *Harry A. Whitaker, "Neurolinguistics," McGraw-Hill Yearbook of Science and Technology 1976, p 287*

[1961, coined by the American linguist Edith C. Trager, born 1924]

neuroregulator, *n.* any of a group of chemical substances that function specifically in communication between nerve cells, including substances that transmit impulses between nerve cells (neurotransmitters) and those that amplify or dampen neuronal activity.

A seemingly diverse group of substances, neuroregulators have in common a role in communication processes among neurons. In that respect, they differ from substances such as glucose and oxygen, which are involved primarily in the metabolic maintenance of the cell. They also differ from second messengers, such as cyclic AMP and cyclic guanosine monophosphate (GMP), which help to translate neurotransmitter or neuromodulator signals into metabolic events. It only recently has become clear that many neuroregulators in the brain do not satisfy the criteria for neurotransmitters. *Jack D. Barchas, et al., "Behavioral*

Neurochemistry: Neuroregulators and Behavioral States," Science, May 26, 1978, p 965

[1978]

neuroscientist, *n.* a specialist in any of the sciences dealing with the nervous system.

American neuroscientists at the meeting hailed his [Levon A. Matinian's] findings as a monumental achievement which might make it possible to treat victims of spinal cord injury, brain injury, stroke, and multiple sclerosis successfully. Until recently, neuroscientists thought that repairing damaged nerves in the brain and spinal cord was impossible. *Joan Arehart-Treichel, "Medicine," 1977 Collier's Encyclopedia Year Book (1976), p 353*

[1965, from *neuroscience* (1963) + *-ist*]

neu·ter·cane ('nu: tər,kein *or* 'nyu: tər,kein), *n.* a storm with high winds, which originates to the north of the normal Atlantic hurricane area.

A neutercane comes into being when pretropical storm conditions and an invading cold air mass coincide. Winds are driven both by the heat of condensing water vapor and the push of the cold air mass. *Boyce Rensberger, "Science/ Medicine: A Storm for Some Seasons," The New York Times, Sept. 10, 1972, Sec. 4, p 13*

[1972, from *neuter* + hurric*ane*]

neutral current, a weak interaction between nuclear particles in which no charge is exchanged. *Often used attributively.*

Towards the end of 1973, physicists had taken a big step towards unifying the laws of the universe into a single, cohesive system, with their discovery of so-called 'neutral currents'. These had unified the mathematics describing radioactivity and electro-magnetism. *John Newell, "The Sciences," The Annual Register of World Events in 1975 (1976), p 395*

A neutral-current process is one in which two particles interact without exchanging a unit of electric charge. If a neutrino strikes a proton and bounces off, and the neutrino remains a neutrino and the proton remains a proton, that's a neutral-current interaction. . . . A search for neutral-current processes was undertaken, and they were discovered in 1973. *Science News, July 8, 1978, p 20*

[1974] Compare SEMISTRONG FORCE. See also B PARTICLE, GAUGE THEORY, HIGGS MESON, WEINBERG-SALAM THEORY.

neutron bomb, another name for ENHANCED RADIATION WEAPON.

The Pentagon proposal to introduce a new generation of tactical nuclear weapons into Europe is truly alarming. Included are the so-called "neutron bombs," a term used to describe new 8-inch nuclear artillery shells and new warheads for Lance surface-to-surface missiles. These weapons, under development since 1972, are designed to produce a prompt burst of neutrons and gamma-rays capable of delivering sufficiently large radiation doses at ranges of several hundred metres to incapacitate exposed persons in a matter of minutes and kill almost all of them in a day or two. *Frank Barnaby, "New-Generation Weapons," New Scientist, July 14, 1977, p 68*

[1961] ► Although references to this weapon appeared in print sporadically during the 1960's, they became frequent and widespread after President Carter's announcement in 1977 that he supported military requests for its development.

319

neutron poison, an element that readily absorbs large numbers of neutrons. The rods used in a nuclear reactor to control a chain reaction are made of these elements.

The operation of the reactor might also have been modified by a decrease in the quantity of neutron poisons present. . . . In this way neutron poisons may have been "burned out" of the ore soon after the reactor began operating. If the initial amounts of elements such as lithium and boron were large enough, this effect could have been a major factor controlling the reactor. *George A. Cowan, "A Natural Fission Reactor," Scientific American, July 1976, p 40*

[1963]

NEW, *U.S.* abbreviation of NET ECONOMIC WELFARE.

NEW is the corrected version of GNP—corrected (1) to subtract from the conventional calculation those *non-material disamenities that have been accruing as costs to our economy* whether or not they have been recognized and charged against the industries and activities that cause them and corrected (2) to add in items irrationally excluded from GNP (such as housewives' services in the home, value of expanded leisure and so forth). *Paul A. Samuelson, "From GNP to NEW," Newsweek, April 9, 1973, p 102*

[1973]

New Alchemist, a member of a group advocating methods of agriculture that utilize renewable resources, avoid the use of pesticides, and protect the environment from the destructive aspects of modern technology.

The New Alchemists built a greenhouse that is heated by solar energy, grows most of the community's food supply, and recycles its own wastes. It has a system of transparent screens and shutters that lets in the heat and traps it. They grow fruits and vegetables, and have devised a miniature river, powered by a windmill pump, that runs through the greenhouse and is stocked with fish. The algae in the circular river act as solar absorbers, helping to heat the system, as well as providing food for the fish. *Ted Morgan, "Looking for: Epoch B," The New York Times Magazine, Feb. 29, 1976, p 65*

[1975, from *New Alchemy* Institute, organized in 1972 by John Todd, an American oceanographer and biologist, to study and explore alternative methods of agriculture] See ALTERNATIVE TECHNOLOGY, APPROPRIATE TECHNOLOGY, ARK.

new archaeology, an approach to archaeology that makes extensive use of technological and statistical apparatus and seeks to establish scientific procedures to explain and test theories about the past.

The innovative methodological developments of the so-called new archaeology became part of standard operating procedure, and schisms between proponents of alternative approaches were less pronounced. *David A. Fredrickson, "Archaeology," Britannica Book of the Year 1976, p 129*

[1972]

new archaeologist: Humphrey Case, Deputy Keeper of the Department of Antiquities at the Ashmolean Museum in Oxford, would be the first to call himself one of the new archaeologists, but like many of his colleagues he has certain reservations about it. *Magnus Magnusson, "The New Archaeology," The Listener, Jan. 20, 1972, p 70*

New Journalism, journalism characterized by personal involvement of the reporter, deeply probing interviews, psychological speculation, and use of dramatized chronology, detailed description, etc.

According to Tom Wolfe, the New Journalism has taken on the sacred trust abandoned by the novel, social realism. There is something to this idea, but the reader quails when Wolfe energetically compares the decade of such figures as Rex Reed, Dick Schaap, Jimmy Breslin, Gay Talese, and Tom Wolfe to the age of Balzac and Dickens. *Richard Todd, Review of "New Journalism," by Tom Wolfe, The Atlantic, July 1973, p 99*

[1972] ► See the note under GONZO.

New Journalist: I worry about the health of Dr. Hunter Thompson. . . . He is the most creatively crazy and vulnerable of the New Journalists, seemingly, and scattered throughout his dispatches are alarming reports on his health. *Kurt Vonnegut, Jr., Review of "Fear and Loathing: On the Campaign Trail '72," by Hunter S. Thompson, Harper's, July 1973, p 92*

news hole, *U.S.* the space devoted to news and features in a newspaper or magazine; nonadvertising space.

Newspapers have much more room, and it is easier for them to expand the news hole. *"The Media: Stories Behind the Story," Newsweek, May 27, 1974, p 87*

[1962]

New Smoking Material, British trademark for a tobacco substitute with a cellulose base, used in cigarettes.

In the Hammersmith tests, 200 men smoked cigarettes containing 30 per cent New Smoking Material (a cellulose synthetic) and ordinary cigarettes for 20 months, without knowing which they were smoking. *New Scientist, June 17, 1976, p 619*

[1973] *Abbreviation:* NSM. Compare CYTREL.

newsperson, *n.* a person who reports the news; a reporter, correspondent, or newscaster.

Some of "Today's" critics charge that it is unseemly for a newsperson to do commercials. *Elizabeth Peer, Newsweek, May 6, 1974, p 58*

We are used to chairpersons, of either sex, camerapersons, newspersons (they usually work for "a media"), and congresspersons. *The Times (London), Nov. 24, 1977, p 1*

[1972; see -PERSON]

new wave, a more restrained and sophisticated form of punk rock developed in the late 1970's.

Unlike the Stranglers and other bands who wish to dissociate themselves from the punks by calling themselves "new wave," the Clash still play the driving, relentless songs that forced the invention of the pogo-dance. *The Times (London), Dec. 14, 1979, p 11*

Punk soon turned to new wave, which especially in the United States meant a more deliberately clever, even arty approach to rock minimalism. *John Rockwell, The New York Times, Aug. 13, 1979, p C-16*

[1977]

Nex·tel ('nek stel), *n.* the trademark for a synthetic substance that resembles blood, used in plays, motion pictures, etc.

Besides looking realistic when applied, Nextel coagulates and cakes as it dries, just like real blood. But here the similarity ends: Nextel dries to a soft powder that can be simply brushed off costumes, thus reducing cleaning costs. *Roger Field, "The Technology of TV Violence," Saturday Review, June 10, 1972, p 51*

[1972]

NGF, abbreviation of NERVE GROWTH FACTOR.

When a minute amount of NGF is added to an isolated sympathetic ganglion in a laboratory tissue culture, projections sprout in large numbers from the cell cluster, forming a halo of nerve fibers around it in six to 10 hours. *"Science and the Citizen," Scientific American, Dec. 1976, p 52*

[1966]

ngul·trum (əŋˈgul trəm), *n.* the monetary unit of Bhutan, introduced in 1974.

Bhutan's first currency notes were released in Thimphu in April. Called ngultrums, they were at par with the Indian rupee, which would remain legal tender. *Govindan Unny, "Bhutan," Britannica Book of the Year 1975, p 109*

[1974, from Bhutanese (a Tibetan language)]

nickel-and-dime, *v.t.* or **nickel and dime,** *U.S. Informal.* **1a** to pay close attention to minor expenditures.

Joe DePrimo, 25, returned from Vietnam with a Bronze Star and worked his way through New York's Richmond College with the help of G.I. benefits and part-time jobs. Two and a half months after earning his B.A. in psychology, he is still looking for work. "I nickeled-and-dimed it all through college," says DePrimo, the first in his family to get a degree. *"The Permanent War Prisoners," Newsweek, March 5, 1973, p 24*

b to get or achieve by paying close attention to minor expenditures.

But this is not the first time Mr. Carter has tried to wriggle out of a tough political problem by compromising with special economic interests. And what passed for good tactics last fall has become bad strategy. The economy is rapidly being nickeled and dimed into double digit inflation. *The New York Times, Feb. 2, 1978, Sec. 4, p 18*

2 to treat cheaply or stingily, especially by paying too close attention to minor expenditures.

J. Paul Getty once kept a pay phone at his English mansion, but he wasn't the sort to nickel and dime his women — except possibly his wives. *Time, June 28, 1976, p 38*

[1963]

ni·date (ˈnaɪˌdeɪt), *v.i. Embryology.* to become implanted in the uterus.

In 1971, Shettles was the first investigator to actually implant an artificial or laboratory conceptus in a woman's womb, doing it at the implantable or "blastocyst" stage of sixty-five or more cell divisions (about five days' growth). . . . The egg transfer was done only to see if it would nidate, which it did; it was not done to bring it to birth. *Joseph Fletcher, The Ethics of Genetic Control, 1974, p 66*

[1962, back formation from *nidation* (1892), from Latin *nidus* nest + English *-ation*]

Nielsen rating, *U.S.* the percentage of households tuned in to a specified radio or television program, based upon an automatic sampling of households by the A. C. Nielsen marketing research organization.

It was the Nielsen ratings, that arcane métier that dictates the longevity of all the programs we see on the home screen. *Goodman Ace, "The Hello and Goodby Season," Saturday Review, Jan. 8, 1972, p 4*

Nielsen ratings were based on mechanisms — "audimeters" — inserted in a sampling of television sets, keeping a record of stations tuned. Their use in radio had dated from 1935, but they became especially prestigious in television. *Erik Barnouw, Tube of Plenty, 1975, p 133*

This was the decade in which culture was quantified as never before in our mass society, where numbers tell the story from political polls to Nielsen ratings to box-office grosses. *"Culture Goes Pop," Newsweek, Nov. 19, 1979, p 112*

[1963]

nif gene, a gene involved in nitrogen fixation.

One of the earliest goals of such work — as should be obvious with the emphasis on soybeans — is to try to make the nif gene settle into a type of plant where it's not normally found. *Robert Cooke, Improving on Nature, 1977, p 135*

Even if *nif* genes could be incorporated into the cells of a plant such as corn, that would probably not be enough to create a self-fertilizing crop. One problem that would remain to be solved, for example, is the protection of the nitrogenase from oxygen. *Winston J. Brill, "Biological Nitrogen Fixation," Scientific American, March 1977, p 81*

[1974; *nif*, from *ni*trogen-*f*ixing]

Nine, *n.* **the Nine,** the nine nations of the European Economic Community since 1973.

The Nine are due to agree then on a new round of farm price increases, which would go hand in hand with Britain's second alignment to Community price levels under the timetable set out in the Treaty of Accession. *Richard Norton-Taylor, The Manchester Guardian Weekly, March 9, 1974, p 7*

Said one French diplomat: "Kissinger is attempting to bring the Nine into an Atlantic system whereby they will be able to take only decisions that are approved in Washington." *Henry's Seven Deadly Sins," Time, April 1, 1974, p 26*

The Soviet Union has given the EEC until Friday to submit a list of vessels to be licensed for fishing within the Soviet sector of the Barents Sea. The Russians have also told the nine that their fishermen must keep within a total catch limit of 1,800 tonnes . . . *Michael Hornsby, The Times (London), Sept. 28, 1977, p 1*

[1973] ▶ The European Economic Community, popularly known as the Common Market, or between 1957 and 1973, *the Six*, comprised Belgium, France, Italy, Luxembourg, The Netherlands, and West Germany. On January 1, 1973, Denmark, Ireland, and Great Britain joined the group, known thereafter as *the Nine*. Then, in May 1979 Greece was accepted as the tenth member, effective as of January 1, 1981, and the Common Market *Nine* will probably be known as *the Ten*.

NLP, *U.S.* abbreviation of *neighborhood loan program*, a state-sponsored plan that provides low mortgage and down-payment requirements, designed especially for redlined sections of a city.

The neighborhoods eligible for the NLP are chosen in consultation with municipal officials. They have to be basically stable and primarily residential, areas where decay and blight have not reached too advanced a stage and where financing has been difficult. *Ruth Rejnis, Her Home, 1980, p 24*

[1979]

no-cut contract, *U.S. and Canadian.* a contract in professional sports guaranteeing that the signer will not be eliminated from a team's roster.

Joe Thomas reportedly is demanding a five-year, no-cut contract at more than $350,000 a year with the Baltimore Colts. Thomas, who has been credited with rebuilding the franchise, is the pro football club's general manager. *Steve Cady, The New York Times, Jan. 5, 1977, p A18*

[1976]

no-fault, *n.* or **no fault,** *Especially U.S. — adj.* **1** of or denoting a form of divorce which is granted without either party having to prove the other guilty of causing the dissolution of the marriage.

Already accepted by 25 of the United States, the no-fault concept eliminates the adversary role; the courts accept an acknowledgment of irretrievable marriage breakdown by both spouses as sufficient grounds for divorce. *Paul Nowack, "Till Divorce Do Us Part," Maclean's, April 19, 1976, p 30*

2 of or involving any method of reaching a settlement or awarding damages without having to resort to legal action.

A related "no fault" plan was recently endorsed by the American Medical Association. "When a patient is aggrieved, he should be paid appropriate compensation, and he should not have to take his chances in court to get it," [Gerald J.] Lustic says. *"Science and the Citizen: Doctor's Dilemma," Scientific American, March 1975, p 49*

— n. any system in which the fault, guilt, or responsibility of a party is eliminated as the basis for compensation or settlement.

There remains, for instance, the right to sue in court for damages sustained in an auto accident. And as long as this right remains, there's no pure no fault. *Gregg Kakesako, "No-Fault Behind Closed Doors Again," Honolulu Star-Bulletin, April 2, 1973, p A-10*

Under no-fault, an injured driver is reimbursed for medical expenses and lost wages by his own insurance company, regardless of who caused the accident. *"The Senate Buys No-Fault," Time, May 13, 1974, p 108*

[1972, extended from the earlier (1967) sense of a form of automobile accident insurance]

no-frills, *adj.* stripped to or providing the bare essentials; without extras or embellishments.

In 1974 the CAB flatly rejected a proposal by London-based Laker Airways to fly regular "no-frills" flights between New York and London for $125 each way. *Peter H. Schuck, "Why Regulation Fails," Harper's, Sept. 1975, p 28*

In suburban areas around the country, builders are turning out no-frills houses that sell for prices ranging in most areas from about $20,000 to $36,000. *"Modern Living: Now, the No-Frills House," Time, Feb. 23, 1976, p 62*

[1963, from the phrase *(with) no frills*] Also, **no-frill.**

no-growth, *adj.* designed to prevent, decrease, or restrict growth (as of an area, a population, or an economy).

California's legal system is already clogged with lawsuits provoked by local zoning restrictions or "no growth" rulings. *Mary Ellen Leary, "California," The Atlantic, Nov. 1973, p 31*

Mr Roy Shaw, secretary-general of the Arts Council, commented: "It is still a no-growth budget, which means we shall have to disappoint clients who were hoping to de-

velop in new directions." *The Times (London), April 3, 1976, p 3*

[1972]

no-hair theorem, *Astronomy.* the axiom that black holes of the same mass, charge, and spin are indistinguishable regardless of what they are made from.

Apart from these three properties [mass, angular momentum and electric charge] the black hole preserves no other details of the object that collapsed. This conclusion, known as the theorem "A black hole has no hair," was proved by the combined work of Carter, Werner Israel of the University of Alberta, David C. Robinson of King's College, London, and me. The no-hair theorem implies that a large amount of information is lost in a gravitational collapse. *S. W. Hawking, "The Quantum Mechanics of Black Holes," Scientific American, Jan. 1977, p 36*

[1976]

No·Ho ('nou,hou), *n.* an area of New York City, in lower Manhattan, noted as a growing center of avant-garde art, music, film, and fashion.

The Newport-New York Jazz Festival may be losing some of its stars to mass culture and failing to tap the loyal audience that listens to the avant-garde in the lofts of SoHo and NoHo, but one suspects that it will continue to survive and prosper. *Robert Palmer, "It's That Jazz Time Again," The New York Times Magazine, June 12, 1977, p 87*

[1976, from its being situated *N*orth of *Ho*uston Street]

nonachiever, *n. U.S.* **1** a student who fails to achieve passing grades.

The most recent serious disturbance at our high school was set off not by blacks, but by a gang of white "nonachievers" from relatively low-income families, who started a fight with long-haired middle-class white seniors. *Walter Goodman, The New York Times Magazine, April 9, 1972, p 104*

2 any person, especially a youngster, who lacks accomplishment.

With scoreboard lights flashing and father shouting, a boy has much more than his self-evaluation at stake. The rewards after the game are sweet for the achiever, but bitter for the nonachiever. There is no overt punishment, just the punishment of being left out. *Warren T. Farrell, "Growing Up Male in America," The 1974 World Book Year Book, p 101*

[1972, patterned on *underachiever* (1959), *overachiever* (1960)]

non·ac·tin (nə'næk tin), *n.* an antibiotic derived from a species of streptomyces, noted for its ability to carry ions across lipid barriers. *Formula:* $C_{40}H_{64}O_{12}$

The class of compounds known as ionophores has attracted increasing attention during the past decade because of the remarkable cation selectivities shown by these substances. . . . These compounds are generally cyclic, although several are known in which cyclization occurs only upon complexation with a cation. Those studied initially were of natural origin, namely, valinomycin, nonactin, and monensin. *Reed M. Izatt and James J. Christensen, "Ionophore," McGraw-Hill Yearbook of Science and Technology 1974, p 245*

[1968, probably from *non-* not + *active* + *-in* (chemical suffix), because of its unusual inertness to chemical compounds]

nonaerosol, *adj.* not using a propellant, especially a fluorocarbon, under pressure.

The Bristol-Myers Company has introduced an antiperspirant deodorant pump spray . . . It is the first nonaerosol deodorant spray to be marketed in South Africa. *The New York Times, Sept. 23, 1977, p D9*

[1977] See AEROSOL.

noncampus, *adj.* not having a campus; providing instruction from other than a specific location or headquarters.

A somewhat similar development, begun in the 1971-72 academic year, was the Vermont Regional Community College, a non-campus, community-based instructional system that covered much of the state. *Tudor David and Kenneth G. Gehret, "Education," Britannica Book of the Year 1973, p 265*

[1972]

Nonce Words. ► A type of new word that seldom finds its way into a dictionary is the nonce word. It is coined specifically for the occasion; it fills a momentary need and is recorded in a single occurrence or in a particular piece of writing. Nonce words are arbitrary COINAGES that soon disappear, even if they appear in important books by famous writers. A number of entries in the OED are labeled *nonce word*; for example, *nowhereness* (1838. Sterling) and, notably, *Mammonolatry*, "the worship of Mammon," coined by Coleridge in 1820.

Nonce words are mainly used in literary or general writing, though a few are introduced into scientific or technical works. In the latter, new words are usually coined to name new inventions, discoveries, concepts, techniques, etc., with the serious intention of having them become standard names or terms. They die out, however, because what they name is not generally accepted. In literary essays or popular articles the writer chooses particular words to create a distinctive style, to produce a fresh, interesting effect, or to make a point in an original or memorable way; hence it is in this kind of writing that nonce words are most frequently found.

An example of the effective use of nonce words is a satiric essay by Charles Fazer ("Postscript On the Millenium," *New York Times*, Sept. 10, 1979, p A27), in which the author discusses a condition he calls *Sixtomania*, a morbid preoccupation with the years 1960 to 1969 which can take the forms of *Sixtophilia* or *Sixtophobia*. *Desixtification*, the only treatment for this disease, permits recovered patients to attain the condition of *Sixtostasis*, a balanced, detached attitude toward the 60's. These nonce words, derived from the word *sixty* used as a combining form, helped the author make his point much more trenchantly than if he had used only standard words.

Like most new words, nonce words are formed with existing elements in the language, its standard words, combining forms, and affixes. Because nonce words are often playful or fanciful coinages, many are puns, or humorous PATTERNED FORMS (like PALIMONY based on *alimony*). For example:

herstory [pun on *history*, as if *his-* were the masculine pronoun]:

Although psychobabble cannot be blamed for the ludicrous semantics of "herstory" for history, those feminists seduced by its bland pseudopsychology have made it too obvious a target for mockery. *Christopher Reed, "Psychobabble Enigma," The Manchester Guardian Weekly, Jan. 22, 1978, p 19*

petishism [pun on *fetishism*]:

Of more serious concern to naturalists is the genetic degeneration of many pet species. In the frantic race to keep up with petishism, fast-buck breeding mills are churning out more and more diseased, spavined and moronic beasts. *"The Great American Animal Farm," Time, Dec. 23, 1974, p 64*

smotherlove [pun on *mother love*]:

Whatever the starting point, Lovecraft is a marvellous subject for a biographer. A life-long victim of smotherlove, he developed a remarkable range of neuroses and illnesses. *The Times (London), March 25, 1976, p 13*

Other typical nonce words are blends, back formations, compounds, and derivatives, such as:

yumptious [blend of *yummy* and *scrumptious*]:

Kiddies' Special. Yumptious eats for the young and the young in heart. *Time, Oct. 2, 1978, p 100*

Deheroize [from *de-* opposite of + *heroize*] is a good example of the best kind of nonce word: it is self-defining and the meaning and function of each component are clearly understood.

His pre-World War II associations with the America First Committee, and with those of Nazi-tainted views, deheroized him only momentarily. *Alden Whitman, The New York Times Magazine, May 8, 1977, p 15*

A new word or phrase that gains currency usually suggests or stimulates the formation of nonce words. For example, the popularity of *workaholic* spawned many nonce words with the ending -AHOLIC, and similarly -GATE was used to produce many nonce words to describe episodes similar to the WATERGATE affair. During the 1960's *theater of the absurd* inspired the formation of other similar constructions, such as *Theater of the Streets, theater of despair, Theater of the Mind*. And in the mid-1970's the frequent use of EXECUTIVE PRIVILEGE stimulated the coinage of such nonce phrases as *journalistic privilege, judicial privilege, scholar's privilege*, and *theatrical privilege*.

Nonce words lend variety and flavor to language even if they do not become part of its permanent stock of words.

nonconsumptive, *adj.* not consuming, destroying, or exploiting natural objects or resources.

He [Edward Hoagland] is a "nonconsumptive" user of the forest, a man with exceptional powers of observation, reflection and appreciation. He neither hunts nor fishes but takes long solitary hikes and prefers conversing with old farmers, trappers and woodsmen. *R. Z. Sheppard, Time, April 2, 1973, p 88*

[1970]

noncontact, *adj.* of or involving a game or contest in which no physical contact occurs or is required between the players or competitors.

In Michigan, New Jersey, New York, and Indiana, girls won the right to play on noncontact boys' teams. *Bill Braddock, "Sports," The Americana Annual 1974, p 535*

[1972]

noncooperativity, *n.* the lack or absence of COOPERATIVITY.

The three different enzymes shown exhibit respectively noncooperativity (*top row*), positive cooperativity (*middle row*) and negative cooperativity (*bottom row*). *Daniel E. Koshland, Jr., Scientific American, Oct. 1973, p 63*

[1973]

noncountry, *n.* a country that lacks the characteristics of most countries, such as a homogeneous population, natural borders, and a history as a nation.

The reason Cyprus is unable to handle its own affairs is not that it is a nonaligned country but a noncountry. Its Greek-speaking and Turkish-speaking population don't think of themselves as Cypriots the way French-speaking Swiss and German-speaking Swiss consider themselves Swiss. *C. L. Sulzberger, "The Role of a Noncountry," The New York Times, Aug. 27, 1972, p 15*

[1970, patterned after *non-book, nonplay* (1960's)]

nonearthly, *adj.* originating or existing outside the earth.

Man has long regarded the stars, sun, moon and planets as the homes of gods and demons. In countless myths, man is helped and civilized by them. In some tales, the extraterrestrial (nonearthly) beings are fully human, at least physically. These themes have survived in present-day science fiction and fantastic stories, including many flying-saucer reports. *Richard S. Young, "Astronomy: Life on Other Worlds," Encyclopedia Science Supplement (Grolier) 1972, p 9*

[1970] ► This term is preferred in an outer-space context to *unearthly,* which is suggestive of the supernatural or unnatural.

nonmarket, *adj.* not included in the labor market.

Economists . . . have traditionally chosen not to measure a housewife's productivity because it falls in the so-called nonmarket sector, along with such activities as charity work and unpaid political canvassing. *Keith Love, "How Do You Put a Price Tag on a Housewife's Work?" The New York Times, Jan. 13, 1976, p 39*

[1976]

nonorgasmic, *adj.* unable to have orgasm.

Higher levels of glucose and insulin, as well as lower levels of nitrogen, phosphorus, cholesterol, and calcium, were found in the blood of "nonorgasmic women." *Byron T. Scott, "General Medicine," 1977 Britannica Yearbook of Science and the Future (1976), p 364*

—*n.* a nonorgasmic person.

Deprived of a stable father-figure, the non-orgasmic in this study seemed to be unable to face the blurring of personal boundaries which goes with full physiological orgasm. *Alex Comfort, Review of "The Female Orgasm" by Seymour Fisher, The Listener, April 26, 1973, p 549*

[1973] Compare ANORGASTIC.

nonpermissive, *adj. Biology.* not permitting replication (of genetic material, viruses, etc.).

Temperature-sensitive mutants of bacteria had been ob-

tained that are defective in initiating DNA replication at a high or nonpermissive temperature, where the mutation is phenotypically expressed. *James C. Copeland, "Life Sciences: Molecular Biology," Britannica Book of the Year 1973, p 420*

[1972] Compare PERMISSIVE.

nonprint, *adj.* that does not include printed matter, such as books, magazines, and newspapers, but is recorded on tapes, films, and the like.

In its celebration of reading, this annual event (the 16th), sponsored by the American Library Association and the National Book Committee, again failed to recognize the presence of nonprint media in libraries. *Dan Bergen, "Libraries," The Americana Annual 1974, p 346*

In general, nonprint materials reflect the worst kind of tokenism. An example we viewed of this was a film on women narrated by a man with the only woman speaker in the film being one who spoke *against* the equal rights amendment. *"Women: A Recommended List of Print and Non-Print Materials . . . ," Mediacenter (New York), May 1975, p 6*

[1968]

nonstandard analysis, *Mathematics.* a method of studying the properties of infinitely large and infinitely small numbers, and of systems that incorporate such numbers.

Nonstandard analysis, a revolutionary new approach to classical calculus, is deeply rooted in mathematical logic, the study of the reasoning processes of mathematics itself. *Lynn A. Steen, "Mathematics," 1977 Britannica Yearbook of Science and the Future (1976), p 355*

[1971, invented in 1960 by the German-born American logician Abraham Robinson, 1918-1974]

nontarget, *adj.* not being the object under attack, study, experimentation, etc.

They pointed out that while such substances would be of potential use against a broad spectrum of pests, they might, by the same token, affect nontarget species. *Peter W. Miles, "Life Sciences: Zoology," Britannica Book of the Year, 1974, p 424*

[1971]

non-thing, *n.* **1** something nonexistent; nothing.

She [Germaine Greer] cannot blame female weakness because she has convinced all of us that this is a non-thing. *Frank Cauchi, London, Ont., "Letters," Time, Aug. 14, 1972, p 8*

2 something insignificant; meaningless thing; trifle.

. . . a large and deadening apparatus which explains among other non-things that William Dean Howells spelt 'millionaire' with two n's, or that in *Tom Sawyer* on a specified number of occasions 'ssst!' is printed as 'sssst!' *D. J. Enright, The Listener, Nov. 29, 1973, p 751*

[1972]

non·tu·plet (nɑn'təp lit), *n.* one of nine offspring born at one birth.

Geraldine Brodrick gave birth last week to nontuplets (nine babies) in Australia, the first such recorded birth. *Jane E. Brody, "Multiple Births: How to Have a Baby or Nine," The New York Times, June 20, 1971, p 7*

[1971, from Latin *nōnus* ninth + English *-tuplet* as in *quintuplet, sextuplet,* etc.]

noodge (nudʒ), *n.* variant of NUDZH.

. . . Rabbi Ben Kaddish, the holiest of all ninth-century rabbis and perhaps the greatest *noodge* of the medieval era. *Woody Allen, The New Yorker, June 20, 1970, p 31*

[1968]

nor·ad·ren·er·gic (ˌnɔr ə drəˈnər dʒik), *adj.* producing or activated by the adrenal hormone noradrenaline (norepinephrine).

Injections of amphetamines such as Dexedrine or amphetaminelike drugs such as Ritalin stimulate the noradrenergic systems and usually make a normal person more active and enhance his pleasurable experiences. *Robert L. Isaacson, "Psychology," The World Book Science Annual 1974 (1973), p 350*

[1963, from *noradren*aline + Greek *érgon* work + English *-ic*] Compare CATECHOLAMINERGIC, DOPAMINERGIC, SEROTONERGIC.

Nordic, *adj.* of or relating to ski competition involving cross-country racing and ski jumping.

A series of errors and mishaps added interest to the Olympic men's 4 × 10 kilometres cross-country relay race . . . in which Finland took their second Nordic gold medal of the games. *The Times (London), Feb. 12, 1976, p 10*

Nordic disciplines gained more active following outside their traditional north European strongholds, especially in Switzerland and the U.S. *Howard Bass, "Winter Sports," Britannica Book of the Year 1977, p 732*

[1963, so called from such competition having originated in the Nordic or Scandinavian countries] Compare ALPINE.

North, *n.* the industrialized, technically and economically advanced countries of the world.

During a four-day Conference on International Economic Cooperation held in Paris last week by 16 industrialized nations and 19 "poor" ones (which included some *nouveau riche* oil-producing countries), the North made what it considered a generous offer, especially given its painfully slow economic recovery. The South grudgingly accepted the package, but termed it quite inadequate and refused to give anything in exchange. *"Conflict Between North and South," Time, June 13, 1977, p 30*

[1976, so called because most of the industrialized countries lie in the northern latitudes] Compare SOUTH. See also FIRST WORLD.

▶ *North* and *South* are economic designations into which the countries of the world can be roughly divided (see the note under DEVELOPING). The *North/South* distinction first appeared in the expression *North-South dialogue*, referring to a protracted debate concerning the obligations and expectations of each group of countries in a redistribution of the world's wealth. In this scheme the North is expected to provide increased economic and technological aid to the South as recompense for past colonial exploitation.

Norwalk agent, a cube-shaped viral particle identified in 1972 as the causative agent of intestinal flu.

They decided to examine stool specimens from hepatitis A patients using immune electron microscopy. Kapikian had previously used this method for detecting, in a stool filtrate, the Norwalk agent, which is similar to the hepatitis A virus. The Norwalk agent was found to be associated with a form of acute infectious nonbacterial gastroenteritis — intestinal flu — in humans. *"Visualization of Infectious Hepatitis Virus," Science News, Dec. 8, 1973, p 359*

[1972, named after *Norwalk*, Ohio, where it was first isolated]

noseguard, *n.* the defensive player in American football directly opposite the offensive center; a middle guard.

The Princeton coach also expressed pleasure with the play of his defensive line, especially Pete Funke, the noseguard, and two tackles, Matt McGrath and Joe Luncie, both sophomores. *Deane McGowen, The New York Times, Sept. 28, 1977, p 32*

[1976, probably so called from his central position on the defensive line]

nose wheelie, *U.S.* the raising of a skateboard's back wheels off the ground by putting one's weight on the front.

So many children perform "nose wheelies" and "tail wheelies" (tipping back or front) that some skateboards are now being manufactured with snubbed noses and flipped-up tails. *Judi R. Kesselman, "Skateboard Accidents," Encyclopedia Science Supplement (Grolier) 1977, p 260*

[1976]

nosh·er·y (ˈnaʃ ər iː), *n. Slang.* a restaurant.

Richard Newport's Space-1999-with-touches-of-Conran restaurant is more than an expense account, sturgeon-egg noshery. *The Times (London), July 14, 1977, p 14*

Pronto, a trendy East Side Italian restaurant, is offering a Sunday brunch for the first time, and similar affairs at other nosheries are S.R.O. *Time, Oct. 2, 1978, p 88*

[1963, from *nosh* to nibble, snack, eat + *-ery*, as in *eatery, bakery*]

no-show, *n.* **1** a person who fails to show up, as for an appointment.

The Levitt audit said there was no requirement to determine when . . . the "no-shows" had become ineligible, and hence no chance to recover any fraudulent payments. The "no-shows," the report said, might involve deaths, moving away from the city or changes in income. *Peter Kihss, "Levitt Cites Medicaid Payments to Ineligibles in New York City," The New York Times, June 2, 1976, p 23*

2 an act or instance of not showing up; nonappearance.

In many instances, say prosecutors around the country, the loss of one key witness means no case. Though statistics of witness no-shows are spotty and hard to come by, a recent study in high-crime Brooklyn, N.Y., by the Vera Institute of Justice found that as many as half the witnesses required to come to court for trial just did not show up. *Time, Sept. 11, 1978, p 41*

[1966, transferred senses of the term (1940's) meaning "a person who reserves a seat on an airplane, etc., and neither cancels nor claims it"]

no·taph·i·ly (nouˈtæf ə liː), *n.* the collecting of banknotes as a hobby.

Notaphily is the name of the hobby, and, as Mr. Narbeth points out in "Collect British Banknotes," it has one great advantage over other hobbies — "You are actually saving money and getting real pleasure from it . . ." *Oliver Pritchett, The Manchester Guardian Weekly, Dec. 12, 1970, p 17*

[1970, from Latin *nota* note (for banknote) + English

325

not-for-profit

-*phily* love of (from New Latin -*philia*, from Greek *philía* love)]

notaphilic, *adj.*: Biafran £1 notes were printed, but it appears the war with the Nigerian Government ended before they were used. However, the notes found their way on to the notaphilic market. *Patrick O'Leary, The Times (London), Jan. 27, 1976, p 17*

notaphilist, *n.*: Another kind of note which is highly prized was produced by the Chinese of the Ming dynasty — the Ming vases, you might say, of the notaphilists. *Donald Wintersgill, The Manchester Guardian Weekly, June 12, 1971, p 17*

not-for-profit, *adj. U.S.* not formed to make profit; nonprofit.

Ever since the United States Customs Service moved out of the building, several years ago, the New York Landmarks Conservancy (a not-for-profit organization that preserves and reuses buildings of architectural and or historical significance) and the Custom House Institute . . . have been putting on a variety of shows. *"The Talk of the Town," The New Yorker, Sept. 11, 1978, p 29*

[1966] ► During the 1970's this term became almost as common in the United States as *nonprofit.*

no-tillage or **no-till,** *n.* a method of farming in which a seedbed is prepared without tillage by spraying a covering of mulch with herbicide and applying fertilizer. *Often used attributively.*

Differences in response of crops to tillage do exist on different soils, and tillage system selection should be tailored to specific soil characteristics. No-tillage is the most desirable system under some conditions, while moldboard plowing may be the most desirable system under others. *Glover B. Triplett, Jr., "Soil and Crop Practices in Agriculture," McGraw-Hill Yearbook of Science and Technology 1978, p 79*

We experimented with no-till corn and soybeans last year. No-till worked especially well on land that had a good mulch. *"Thomas Williams Helps Spread New Farming Ideas," The Progressive Farmer, June 1974, p 29*

[1971] Also called MINIMUM TILLAGE, ZERO TILLAGE.

NOW or **N.O.W.** (nau), *n.* acronym for *National Organization for Women.*

Women's Liberation formally began with the founding in 1966 of the National Organization for Women, which remains the largest and most influential movement group, the original umbrella under which other groups pressed their individual programs. Its membership has doubled to 18,000 in the past year; around 255 chapters now exist in 48 states. N.O.W. has led assaults in Congress and the courts on issues ranging from child care to abortion reform. *"Women's Liberation Revisited," Time, March 20, 1972, p 29*

[1968, influenced by *now* immediate]

NOW account, *U.S.* a savings account which may be used by the depositor to write checks against, much as if it were a checking account, and which usually bears interest.

The NOW accounts were clearly popular, and were a particular boon to pensioners who were recently authorized to have their Social Security checks deposited directly in a savings bank. *Iver Peterson, The New York Times, May 12, 1976, p 31*

[1973, from *NOW*, abbreviation of *negotiated order of withdrawal,* the checklike instrument used in such accounts]

no-win, *adj.* **1** not likely to be won; not leading to victory.

For a long time, these officials looked the other way. Why? Well, they said, they were afraid that active efforts to find out which children were in the extortion ring and to punish them would expose them to charges of "police tactics." The principal's main concern was that it was a "no-win" situation. *Amitai Etzioni, "Do As I Say, Not As I Do," The New York Times Magazine, Sept. 26, 1976, p 65*

2 not played or engaged in to win; noncompetitive.

An offshoot of a 1973 New Games Tournament, staged by *Whole Earth Catalog* Creator Stewart Brand, the foundation is now a growing national enterprise. Its goal is nothing less than to change the way Americans play, mainly by replacing competitive games with cooperative "no win" pastimes. *Time, Sept. 11, 1978, p 54*

[1962, from *no, adj. + win, v.*]

NO$_x$ (naks), *n.* acronym for *nitrogen oxide* or *nitrogen oxides.*

[Robert] Fri also announced a one-year delay of implementation of the 1976 standards for emissions of nitrogen oxides (NO$_x$). EPA will recommend a modified NO$_x$ standard to Congress this fall, and Fri says some sort of special electronic feedback catalyst system will be required to meet that new standard. *"How U.S. Cities Can Meet Air Standards," Science News, Aug. 4, 1973, p 71*

[1972]

NP-complete, *Mathematics.* of or belonging to a class of problems that are impractical to solve because no polynomial algorithm can be given.

Several typical examples can be used to illustrate the wide variety of problems currently known to be NP-complete. One example is known as the Traveling Salesman's Problem. In this problem a salesman is given a list of cities and a road map telling him the shortest route between each pair of cities. The salesman would like to begin at his home city, visit all the other cities, and return to his home city, traveling the least total distance in the process. The problem of finding this shortest route has recently been shown to be an NP-complete problem. *Ronald L. Graham and Michael R. Garey, "The Limits to Computation," 1978 Britannica Yearbook of Science and the Future (1977), p 184*

Since *NP*-complete problems capture the difficulty of all other problems in *NP*, it is widely thought today that all *NP*-complete problems are computationally intractable. A proof that a problem is *NP*-complete is usually considered a strong argument for abandoning further efforts to devise an efficient algorithm for its solution. *Harry R. Lewis and Christos H. Papadimitriou, "The Efficiency of Algorithms," Scientific American, Jan. 1978, p 107*

[1976, from *nondeterministic* polynomial + *complete*]

NRC, abbreviation of *Nuclear Regulatory Commission,* a U.S. government agency established in 1975 to regulate the operation of nonmilitary nuclear facilities, especially nuclear power plants.

At a press conference at which the NRC was sharply criticized for complacency and being too close to the nuclear industry, Rep. James Weaver, D-Ore., also raised the possibility of blocking licenses for new plants until the dangers of nuclear facilities are brought into focus. *Norm Brewer, "Regulatory Commission Probe Likely," Today (New York), April 3, 1979, p A2*

[1976]

NREM sleep ('en,rem), another name for SYNCHRO-NIZED SLEEP.

These two phases are already present in the infant from birth on. Compared with the adult there are a number of differences: in the nature of some of the brain wave criteria; in the fact that infants invariably begin sleep with an REM phase whereas adults start with NREM sleep; and so on. *Rudolf Schaffer, "Behavioural Synchrony in Infancy," New Scientist, April 4, 1974, p 16*

[1965; *NREM*, acronym for *nonrapid eye movement*]

NSM, abbreviation of NEW SMOKING MATERIAL.

The controversial NSM advertisements were approved by the authority and the Department of Health before they appeared . . . Unlike those for cigarettes, these advertisements can make health claims and do not have to carry a health warning. Critics argue that they could mislead smokers. *The Times (London), July 6, 1977, p 19*

[1973]

nu body, another name for NUCLEOSOME.

About half of the DNA in chromatin was found to be associated with nu bodies and the remainder with the threads connecting them; recent data, however, suggests that more, perhaps over 70%, of the chromosome DNA is associated with nu bodies. *Robert Haselkorn, "Molecular Biology," 1977 Britannica Yearbook of Science and the Future (1976), p 344*

[1976; *nu*, said to be derived from the Greek letter *nu* but probably short for *nucleus*]

nu·cle·o·cap·sid (,nu: kli: ou'kæp sid), *n.* the nucleic acid of a virus together with the shell enclosing it.

The RNA of the influenza virus is found in five to seven discrete pieces, each in its own nucleocapsid, and its total mass is about 4 million daltons. Each of the pieces . . . is an intact gene that controls at least one characteristic of the virus. *Thomas H. Maugh II, "Influenza: The Last of the Great Plagues," Science, June 8, 1973, p 1044*

[1972, from *nucleo-* nucleic acid + CAPSID outer shell of a virus]

nucleochronology, *n.* the chronology or sequence of time in which chemical elements are formed from the nuclei of hydrogen, especially in the evolution of stars and planets.

These nucleochronologies, coupled with the observed abundances of heavy elements in the stars and theories of star formation, have been used by various investigators in proposing detailed theories of the entire history of the galaxy. Further work on the correlation of nucleochronology with other astronomical information should yield important results in the near future. *David N. Schramm, "The Age of the Elements," Scientific American, Jan. 1974, p 77*

[1972, from *nucleo-* nucleus + *chronology*]

nucleochronometer, *n.* a chemical element or isotope that serves as a standard for measuring or determining nucleochronology.

We have estimated the relative *p*-process production of ^{146}Sm and propose a measurement which would enable it to become a nucleochronometer. *Joan Audouze and David N. Schramm, "^{146}Sm: A Chronometer for p-Process Nucleo-*synthesis," Nature, June 23, 1972, p 447*

[1972, from *nucleochrono*logy + *-meter* measuring device]

nucleocosmochronology, *n.* the chronology or time sequence of the formation of the universe or any part of it, such as the solar system, determined especially by nucleochronology.

The history of these countless nuclear events is written in the chemical elements out of which the earth and the rest of the universe are made. By properly interpreting this history we can assign a date to the formation of those elements. From this date we can infer the age of the universe itself. The scientific discipline that is concerned with these techniques is called nucleocosmochronology. *David N. Schramm, "The Age of the Elements," Scientific American, Jan. 1974, p 69*

[1972, from *nucleo-* + *cosmo-* universe + *chronology*]

nu·cle·o·ni·um (,nu: kli:'ou ni: əm), *n.* an elementary particle consisting of a nucleus and an antinucleus in a bound state, formed when matter and antimatter come into contact.

To understand the process by which nucleonium is formed in a matter-antimatter encounter, one may consider a specific, hypothetical example of a collision between a neutral atom X and a singly ionized antiatom $\bar{Y}$, which is lacking one positron. *David L. Morgan, Jr., "Antimatter," McGraw-Hill Yearbook of Science and Technology, 1974, p 102*

[1974, from *nucleon* nuclear particle + *-ium* (suffix for chemical elements)]

nu·cle·o·some ('nu: kli: ə,soum), *n.* the basic structural unit of chromatin, the constituent of chromosomes, consisting of a roughly spherical body made up of 200 base pairs of DNA and eight basic protein molecules called histones.

Chromatin is the DNA and protein package that makes up the chromosomes of higher organisms, and it is generally believed to consist of a series of gobs of DNA-plus-protein, arranged like pearls on a string. The gobs are known as nucleosomes, and the holy grail of chromatin research has been the nucleosome crystal. Once he has a crystal, the molecular biologist can use the most powerful tool in his possession—X-ray crystallography—to solve its structure. *"Pearls, Platysomes and Gene Packaging," New Scientist, Sept. 22, 1977, p 727*

Each nucleosome contains two molecules each of the four histone types H2A, H2B, H3, and H4. Closely associated with the histones to form the nucleosome "core" are 140 base pairs of the DNA; the remaining DNA is less closely associated with histone and forms a bridge or linker between adjacent cores. *Bruce A. J. Ponder, "Nucleosome," McGraw-Hill Yearbook of Science and Technology 1978, p 278*

[1976, from *nucleo-* + *-some* body] Also called NU BODY.

nucleosomal, *adj.:* They suggest that H1 is bound to a short (30 base pair) terminal stretch of nucleosomal DNA which can be removed by nuclease treatment . . . without significantly disturbing the basic nucleosome structure. *Tom Barrett, "Role for Histone H1 in Chromatin Condensation?" Nature, April 15, 1976, p 577*

nude mouse, any one of a laboratory-bred strain of mice that have no thymus glands and therefore lack the immune defenses provided by T cells.

There is also the case of the "nude mouse." The nude mouse is . . . very prone to disease. But it is not more prone than any other mouse to cancer. So it seems that T cells cannot be playing a very large part in the natural defence of the body against cancer. However, that does not mean that it is entirely defenceless. More recent research has shown clearly that there are tumour-killing cells, both in the blood of cancer patients and in that of normal people. But they are not (or apparently are not) T lymphocytes. Nude mice, for instance, have them. What they are remains, for the time being, a mystery. *"An Efficient New Killer Makes Its Entrance on the Immunological Scene," New Scientist, Feb. 2, 1978, p 291*

[1974, so called from its being hairless]

nudzh or **nudge** (nudʒ), *n. U.S. Slang.* a nuisance; bore; pest.

"He's not a writer, he's a nudge. On the phone twice a day asking how's it going!" *William Cole, The New York Times Book Review, Dec. 7, 1972, p 56*

Discharged from prison, Lou Jean Poplin — sometime beautician, full-time *nudzh* — must first spring her husband . . . from the minimum-security prison. *Time, April 15, 1974, p 92*

[1968, from Yiddish *nudyen* to bore, pester, from Russian *nudnyi* tedious, boring; related to *nudnik* a bore, pest (1920's)] Also spelled NOODGE.

► The spelling *nudge* was influenced by the English word *nudge* push, poke (pronounced nədʒ).

number, *n.* **do a number on,** *Chiefly U.S. and Canadian Slang.* **1** to hurt or harm, especially by deception or trickery.

I was on my own among male relatives, male bosses, male lovers who were all, at one time or another doing numbers on me. *Myrna Kostash, "Courting Sappho," Maclean's, Nov. 1974, p 19*

The wife was shaken. "If I'm doing a number on the kid, I want to know about it," Mrs. Bryan said. *Janet Malcolm, "A Reporter At Large: The One-Way Mirror," The New Yorker, May 15, 1978, p 40*

2 to make fun of in a sly or mocking way; subject to derision or ridicule.

Fearless Johnny Carson stepped out before the camera last night on his "Tonight" show and did a number on his new boss, NBC president Fred Silverman . . . with this line: "Freddy Silverman has just canceled his mother." *"Headliners: Johnny Zaps Freddy," New York Post, Dec. 1, 1978, p 10*

In fact, there is a real social disadvantage for those of us who are limited to one standard language, and others sometimes do a number on us because of it. Black Americans who successfully navigate in the white offices of standard English, for instance, still employ the mother tongue, sometimes to remind the white folks around them that black is beautiful or proud or indomitable. *William Greider, "Don't Pay the Purists No Mind, Honey," The Manchester Guardian Weekly (The Washington Post sec.), Jan. 6, 1980, p 17*

3 to flirt with, especially in a subtle or devious manner.

I coolly flicked the ashes of my Lucky Strike — into my half-finished brandy and soda. I don't think she noticed — her big baby blues were too busy doing a number on my bloodshot brown ones. *Francis M. Dattilo, Jr., "Farewell My Coupe," Spectator, Winter 1979, p 15*

4 do a number, to do a (specified) act, performance, or routine.

"I did a bag-lady number on one of the platforms here in the bus station last year, and I almost got arrested. They thought I was the real thing." *Joan Avril, "The Talk of the Town," The New Yorker, Oct. 17, 1977, p 40*

[1974, patterned on *do a job on* with apparent extension from the phrase *do one's number* to perform one's act or routine in a show, etc.]

number cruncher, *Informal.* a computer designed to perform complicated and lengthy numerical calculations.

Figures of 40-50 MIPS have been claimed for . . . the Texas Instruments Advanced Scientific Computer (ASC) in contrast to a conventional giant number-cruncher like the CDC 7600 at 10 MIPS. *Dennis Parkinson, "Computers by the Thousand," New Scientist, June 17, 1976, p 626*

Aiming to develop their own "number crunchers," as the fast new U.S. machines are called, Moscow is designing a large computer, specified the BESM-10. Supposedly, it will be capable of 15 million operations per second. *Time, Aug. 1, 1977, p 45*

[1966, so called for its ability to break down large computational tasks]

number crunching, *Informal:* A new HP 1000 F-Series computer system — the Model 45 — provides number-crunching power previously obtainable only with much larger and more expensive systems. This is made possible by a fast new central processing unit and a new real-time executive operating system. *Advertisement for Hewlett-Packard, Scientific American, Sept. 1978, p 104*

numbered account, a bank account identified only by a number and not by the holder's name.

Most [Swiss] banks try to dissuade depositors from opening a numbered account on the grounds that Swiss banking secrecy covers all accounts. The vetting of credentials is much stricter, the deposit higher (as much as $50,000 for some banks) and one pays for the service. In return, the identity of a holder of a numbered account is known only to two or three high bank officials. *Rod Chapman, "The Gnomes Keep Smiling," The Manchester Guardian Weekly, June 9, 1973, p 27*

Along with a more or less stable currency, Panama now has, under Torrijos, banking laws of alluring flexibility: numbered accounts like Switzerland's, no local taxes on offshore earnings, no restrictions on taking money out of the country. *E. J. Kahn, Jr., "Letter from Panama," The New Yorker, Aug. 16, 1976, p 72*

[1965]

numerical taxonomy, the classification of plant and animal species based on a quantitative analysis by means of computers.

In the second edition of their work on numerical taxonomy, Peter Sneath and Robert Sokal stated: "Numerical taxonomy is a revolutionary approach to biological classification. . . . Instead of qualitatively appraising the resemblance of organisms on the basis of certain favored characters, a taxonomist using this new methodology will attempt to amass as many distinguishing characters as possible, giving equal weight to each." *John G. Lepp, "Zoology," 1975 Britannica Yearbook of Science and the Future (1974), p 338*

[1974]

nu·me·ro u·no ('nu: mə,rou 'u: nou), *U.S. and Canadian.* the first, best, or most important of a kind; number one.

All the Bicentennial rhetoric and campaign jingoism can't cover up the fact that we're not Numero Uno. *Victor Grant Backus, "America, Good and Bad," Time, June 21, 1976, p E6*

Now along comes the 22-year-old Miss Evert, numero uno, a two-time defending champion, with a winning streak on clay that spans four years and 112 matches. *Neil Amdur, The New York Times, Sept. 10, 1977, p 19*

Margaret Laurence's *The Stone Angel* was adjudged numero uno, a popular choice. *Mordecai Richler, Maclean's, March 20, 1978, p 67*

[1963, from Spanish *número uno* or Italian *numero uno*]

ıurd (nərd), *n. U.S. and Canadian Slang.* variant of NERD.

When Collins condescends to the help of a greenhorn (John Lazarus)—a nurd in heavy, black-rimmed glasses and an early-morning bouffant—he does it because it amuses him, temporarily. The kid's a klutz, but he's also a link with the outside world. *Lawrence O'Toole, "Films," Review of "Skip Tracer," Maclean's, Dec. 18, 1978, p 49*

[1965]

nurdy, *adj.:* The nurdier clients want foil. They don't want golden-brown Brillo pads. "They want potatoes cooked in an oven in foil," Otto says. "If the potatoes are in foil, that's gourmet." *John McPhee, The New Yorker, Feb. 19, 1979, p 92*

Nu·yo·ri·can or **New·yo·ri·can** (ˌnuː yɔr'riː kən), *adj., n. U.S.* variant of NEORICAN.

A book of poems by more than a dozen of these Nuyorican writers, "Nuyorican Poetry, an Anthology of Puerto Rican Words and Feelings," has just been published by William Morrow & Company, in English and Spanish or both—a "Nuyorican dialect" that the writers see as just being born. *David Vidal, " 'Nuyoricans' Express Pain and Joy in Poetry," The New York Times, May 14, 1976, p D17*

Puerto Ricans on the island have a name for these reverse migrants: Neoricans (sometimes spelled Newyoricans). As Neoricans, the family of Manuel Ortiz-Peña is typical, a microcosm of the returning islanders. *William Stockton, "Going Home," The New York Times Magazine, Nov. 12, 1978, p 20*

[1972, from Spanish *Nueva York* or English *New York* + Puerto *Rican*]

O

ıAPEC (ou'ei pek), *n.* acronym for *Organization of Arab Petroleum Exporting Countries,* a subgroup of OPEC.

By way of explanation, OAPEC spokesmen argued that a sizable increase was warranted because "persistent erosion" of the dollar and inflation in the developed countries had cut the real price of a liquid barrel of oil almost by half since 1973. *Time, Oct. 9, 1978, p 94*

[1969]

ıAU, abbreviation of *Organization of African Unity,* an association of 49 African countries, formed by 30 of them in 1963.

Nigeria and Tanzania carry special weight within the OAU, the first because it is black Africa's most populous and militarily most powerful state, the second because it is the spokesman of the front-line states (in the Rhodesian conflict). *Jean-Claude Pomonti, The Manchester Guardian Weekly (Le Monde section), July 9, 1978, p 11*

[1963]

ıbduct, *v.t. Geology.* to push (one crustal plate of the earth) on top of another.

In Newfoundland, however, they recognize examples of their first category of ultramafic rocks—sheet-like masses analogous to ophiolite complexes of oceanic lithosphere obducted later than the Permian. *"Continental Drift: Pre-Permian Probing," Nature, Dec. 15, 1972, p 383*

Many recent reports on the nature of ophiolites from various parts of the world have clearly pointed up the problem of comparing oceanic lithosphere with preserved slabs of supposed older oceanic crust obducted onto the margins of continents. *Robert G. Coleman, "Structural Geology," Mc-Graw-Hill Yearbook of Science and Technology 1974, p 393*

[1972, from Latin *obductus,* past participle of *obdūcere* to cover over, from *ob-* over + *dūcere* to lead; formed on the analogy of *subduct*] Compare SUBDUCT.

▶ *Obduct* in the general sense of "to cover over" is recorded in the OED as obsolete since 1646. Compare SUFFOSION.

Object Ko·wal ('kou əl), a planet about 100 miles (160 kilometers) in diameter, discovered between Saturn and Uranus in 1977.

The new planet's . . . motion is locked in resonance with the movement of Saturn. The time for five revolutions of Saturn in its orbit is almost exactly equal to that for three revolutions of object Kowal. There are also possible resonances with Jupiter and Uranus, a situation which would make the orbit of the new planet particularly stable. *Keith Hindley, "Chiron—The Celestial Centaur," New Scientist, Feb. 2, 1978, p 300*

[1977, named after Charles *Kowal,* the astronomer who discovered it at the Hale Observatories in Pasadena, California] See MINIPLANET.

obsidian dating, a method of determining the age of a geological or archaeological specimen containing volcanic glass (obsidian) by measuring the amount of water absorbed.

In contrast one can agree that the wealth of detail in the section on obsidian dating is fully justified because this is a technique which by virtue of its low cost and relative simplicity should be within the technical competence of a small archaeological unit to set up and operate, and the chapter provides enough practical detail to make this possible. *Harold Barker, Nature, Aug. 11, 1972, p 360*

[1968]

occupational medicine, a branch of medicine dealing with the treatment and prevention of disorders related to one's occupation or work.

Murray has admiration for some of the French legislation which insists that the employer of 3000 people must have a full-time doctor trained in occupational medicine. *Ian Low, "The Unions' Doctor," New Scientist, June 14, 1973, p 697*

[1970]

ocean engineering, a branch of engineering dealing with the design and development of equipment for use in the ocean, such as underwater sensing devices.

Dr Ken Ridler of NRDC was . . . roaming up and down the country trying to whip up enthusiasm for ocean engineering, and broadcasting the fact that this was one area where the corporation would be pleased to invest its money. *Tony Loftas, "Sealbeaver—Failure by Default?" New Scientist, July 13, 1972, p 75*

[1965]

ocean-floor spreading, another name for SEA-FLOOR SPREADING.

Ocean-floor spreading processes, Talbot contends, swept the "scum" together, piling it up in a skimming action to form "micro-continents." *"Monitor: Untangling the Saga of Continental Evolution," New Scientist, April 6, 1972, p 6*

[1972]

oceanization, *n.* the gradual conversion of crustal material characteristic of continents to the type of material found beneath the oceans.

The Soviet tectonician Belousov has gone so far as to invoke extensive 'oceanisation' of continental crust to account for the ocean basins; he has in consequence totally rejected plate tectonics and explains first order structures exclusively by vertical motions. *A. Hallam, "Basin Tectonics," Nature, Feb. 6, 1975, p 396*

[1970, from *ocean* + *-ization*]

ocean-thermal, *adj.* relating to or making use of the temperature differences between the (warm) surface water and (cold) deep water of the ocean.

William E. Heronemus, a University of Massachusetts professor who has done extensive research in both windpower and ocean-thermal technology, believes that if we wanted to, we could have the first commercial-sized ocean-thermal-differences power plant in place and making electricity in the Gulf Stream off Florida within six to eight years. *Michael Harwood, The New York Times Magazine, March 16, 1975, p 46*

[1974]

och·ra·tox·in (‚ouk rə'tɑk sən), *n.* any of various highly poisonous substances secreted by some strains of a mold found in grain. Grain feed containing ochratoxin may find its way into eggs and meat.

Some of the history of ochratoxin A demonstrates the point. First encountered in South Africa in the early 1960s, this toxin is produced by the mould *Aspergillus ochraceus* isolated from grain. *R. Drennon Watson, New Scientist, April 22, 1976, p 170*

[1972, from (*Aspergillus*) *ochra*ceus, the species of mold + *toxin*]

Ock·er ('ɑ kər), *n. Australian.* a type of working class Australian man who often reacts to social pressures in a bigoted and self-righteous manner.

A legacy of colonial brutality and puritanical inhibition still sends the Ocker in search of sporadic release through "rorts" of formidable rowdiness and binds him to a veritable cult of intolerance and ethnocentricity. *Shirley Hazard, "Letter from Australia," The New Yorker, Jan. , 1977, p 58*

[1973, from the name of a character played in a television series by the Australian actor Ron Frazer. *Ocker* is a common Australian variant of the name *Oscar*] Compare ALF GARNETT, ARCHIE BUNKER.

Ockerism, *n.:* The new Australian boorishness is known as Ockerism, from a slob-like character called Ocker in television series—the embodiment of oafish, blinkered self-satisfaction. *The Listener, Sept. 12, 1974, p 334*

odd-even, *adj. U.S.* of or having to do with a system of odd and even numbering, especially in relation to a method of restricting the sale of gasoline in a period of shortage, the sales being contingent upon a matching of odd and even numbered days on the calendar with odd and even license plate numbers.

Panicky motorists bluffed and bribed to beat the odd-even system, and station operators took most of the heat. *Tom Morgenthau et al., "The Energy Plague," Newsweek, July 2, 1979, p 24*

Maryland would reimpose odd-even rationing if the state projected that gasoline supplies would fall substantially below expected demand. Odd-even plans have proved to be a comparatively simple method of cutting long lines at gas stations when supplies become tight. *Ward Morehouse II, "US Driving Fast Toward 'Odd-Even' Gas Again," The Christian Science Monitor, Nov. 20, 1979, p 10*

[1979] See MINIMUM PURCHASE, TOP OFF.

off-air, *adj., adv.* **1** directly from a radio or television broadcast with a sound or videotape recorder.

Indeed all domestic machines have in common the provision of sockets which enable them to record programs "off air" with the minimum of fuss and so breach copyright with the maximum of ease. *New Scientist, April 6, 1978, p 9*

The "post-fade" facility now being incorporated in two new tape recorders from Philips Electrical will be welcomed by enthusiasts who wish to tape broadcast music. But as such it has already brought protests from the British Phonographic Industry, a trade association which continually strives to discourage off-air taping. *"Technology: New Fade in Tape Recording," New Scientist, Dec. 23-30, 1976, p 719*

2 broadcasting by cable instead of over the airways.

Essentially, these rules require that systems in the top 100 markets must have at least 20 broadcast channels . . . for each off-air channel and nonvoice return communication capacity. *Mary Alice Mayer Phillips, "Cable Communications—A Springboard to Tomorrow," Britannica Book of the Year 1973, p 656*

[1972] Compare ON-AIR.

off-book fund, a secret fund used for improper or illegal disbursements of money.

The company disclosed it had funneled $65,000 to $90,000 in corporate funds through an "off-book" fund between 1968 and 1973. The money was used for domestic political contributions. *Michael C. Jensen, "3 Directors Out at R. J. Reynolds," The New York Times, May 29, 1976, p 1*

BP says that the four off-book funds in four counties have been closed. Funds in those accounts totalled £126,000, of which about £56,000 was paid to minor government officials, custom officials, "in order to get them to perform duties which they were not otherwise obligated to perform." *Roger Vielvoye, "£56,000 secret payments by BP," The Times (London), June 4, 1977, p 1*

[1976, so called from its being *off the books*, i.e., not on any official bookkeeping record]

off-road, *adj.* made or used for traveling off public roads and highways, such as dune buggies, snowmobiles, and heavy trucks are.

The American deserts are among the last wild areas remaining in the United States. These beautiful, fragile environments are now being laid waste by the mindless operation of off-road vehicles. *Mark A. Wilson, Wooster, Ohio, "Forum: Off-Road," Time, Jan. 12, 1976, p 7*

The complaints, which came from about five British manufacturers, concerned the prices of 30-tonne and 15-tonne Russian trucks of the type for off-road operations such as earthmoving and quarrying. *Edward Townsend, "Price Increase on 'Dumped' Trucks," The Times (London), Feb. 10, 1977, p 19*

[1973]

off-roader, *n.:* To the rest of us, an abundance of specialized life forms provides opportunity for study and quiet reflection—re-creation of mind and body that often conflicts with the tumultuous pursuits of off-roaders. *Stanley L. Cummings, "Forum: Off-Road," Time, Jan. 12, 1976, p 7*

offshore fund, an investment company operating from abroad, usually as an investment trust or mutual fund.

The SEC [Securities and Exchange Commission] proposed that previously unregulated hedge funds (private funds) as well as offshore funds (outside the United States) be subjected to controls. *William G. Dewald, "Stocks and Bonds," The 1972 World Book Year Book, p 522*

[1970]

off-the-wall, *U.S. Slang.* —*adj.* unconventional; unusual.

[Denis] Brian knows how to startle the over-interviewed with off-the-wall questions that get surprising answers: Ever see a ghost? What makes you cry? *D. Crinklaw, National Review, Jan. 4, 1974, p 47*

Goin' South has a consistent personality that reflects the off-the-wall sensibility of its hero. Nicholson's straight-faced use of unappetizing extras makes us see the whole film through Moon's somewhat stoned eyes. *Time, Oct. 9, 1978, p 100*

—*adv.* Also, **off the wall.** unconventionally.

"I just thought it was off-the-wall funny," says Lear. "When I told my wife Frances about the idea, she said, 'Norman, this time you've gone too far—even for you.' But it worked. It was funny." *Time, April 5, 1976, p 74*

[1974, probably from handball or squash court usage, meaning "not expected, startling"]

o·fu·ro (ou'fu: rou), *n.* a large tub or vat filled with hot water, used in Japan for bathing.

The concept of the hot tub, essentially a wooden tub filled with hot water (102 degrees Fahrenheit to 105 degrees Fahrenheit as a rule), is hardly new—the Japanese have been bathing communally in their ofuros for centuries. *Ruth Robinson, "The Hot Tub Goes Northeast," The New York Times, Oct. 13, 1977, p 48*

The Japanese custom of the communal bath, *ofuro,* with one large tub of hot water shared by all members of a family, presented a perfect opportunity for the early application of solar energy on a commercial scale. *John H. Douglas, "A Project Called Sunshine," Science News, April 22, 1978, p 263*

[1964, from Japanese]

-o·hol·ic (-ə'hɔ:l ik), a variant of -AHOLIC, as in:

bloodoholic, *n.:* [Yury] Mamleev writes about such Soviet *bizarreries* as a psychopathic vampire, a kind of bloodoholic, who is trying to stay on the wagon, or at least on the Moscow bloodmobile (he manages to refrain from killing people when he gets a job in a bloodbank). *Carl R. Proffer, "Writing in the Shadow of the Monolith," The New York Review of Books, Feb. 19, 1976, p 12*

Cokeoholic, *n.:* Does it help your election choice to know that Trudeau's office contains a regular box of chocolates to appease his sweet tooth? And that Clark is a Coke-oholic, who relishes junk food? *Alan Fotheringham, Maclean's, May 1, 1978, p 88*

[1973]

oilberg, *n.* a large mass of oil floating in the sea.

No scientists are willing to forecast the effects of the oil now spreading seaward from the *Argo Merchant.* Most believe that if the globs of oil, called oilbergs because most of their mass is below the surface, continue to move east, the damage will be held to a minimum. *"Environment: Oil Is Pouring on Troubled Waters," Time, Jan. 10, 1977, p 45*

[1977, from *oil* + ice*berg*]

oil diplomacy, diplomacy involving relations between oil-importing and oil-exporting countries.

A prime goal of U.S. oil diplomacy over the past two years has been to break up the Organization of Petroleum Exporting Countries. *"Oil: Living with OPEC," Time, Jan. 19, 1976, p 54*

[1975]

oiling, *n.* an act or instance or being covered with oil from an oil spill.

Volunteers helping to save bird victims of oil-tanker disasters take note: "the degree of oiling has little impact on the bird's chances of survival and should not be used as a criterion for euthanasia." *"Oiled Seabirds Get in the Swim," New Scientist, April 27, 1978, p 213*

[1973]

oil minister, a government official in charge of or representing the interests of an oil-producing country.

At the June meeting of OPEC in Quito, Ecuador, the Shah's oil minister, Jamshid Amuzegar, blocked a move by Saudi Arabia to lower the price of oil by $2 on the posted price of $11.65 per barrel. *"Reports and Comment: Iran," The Atlantic, Sept. 1974, p 20*

[1974]

oil spill, the accidental escape of oil into a body of water, often resulting in the destruction of water plants and birds and the pollution of shoreline.

oil weapon

If we can't stop all the oil spills, can we at least clean up the messes they cause? That takes technology and trained people, and cleaning up oil spills is a new and primitive art. Equipment and techniques do exist — floating booms and chemicals to corral the oil, pumps and skimmers to pick it up, straw and "sorbents" to mop it, chemicals to disperse it, materials to sink it, microorganisms to eat it. *Michael Harwood, "The Rising Tide of Oil Spills," The New York Times Magazine, April 9, 1978, p 33*

Specifically, we have been warned: — that the pollution of the seas by oil spills and chemical runoff may be annihilating the phytoplankton that renews much of the oxygen in the atmosphere . . . *Theodore Roszak, Person/Planet, 1978, p 35*

[1971] See CYCLONET, SKIMMER.

oil weapon, the threat of withholding oil or raising its price, used as a means of pressuring or controlling countries that depend upon oil imports for their energy needs.

The new President . . . was a keen opponent of President Nixon of the United States and an advocate of the so-called 'oil weapon'. It came as no surprise, therefore, when on 16 April he announced the nationalization with compensation of the 22 oil companies operating within Venezuela, to be completed in 24 to 36 months. *Peter Calvert, "Venezuela," The Annual Register of World Events in 1974 (1975), p 105*

[1974] See PETRO-.

O·ka·za·ki fragment, piece, or **segment** (‚ouka'za: ki:), a fragmentary form of bacterial DNA, occurring during replication and later linked with other fragments to form the long double-helical strand of the typical DNA molecule.

Some enzyme other than the usual RNA polymerase may be . . . involved in starting off the Okazaki fragments of bacterial DNA. *"Molecular Biology: How DNA Is Replicated," Nature, Nov. 3, 1972, p 14*

[1968, named after Refii *Okazaki*, a Japanese geneticist who first identified the fragments]

O·klo phenomenon ('ou‚klou), the occurrence of a series of natural nuclear chain reactions during the accretion of a rich deposit of uranium over a billion years ago in what is now a uranium mine in southeastern Gabon.

It is not generally appreciated that a natural example of geological containment of high-level wastes for many millions of years exists at the site of a uranium mine in Gabon. The "Oklo phenomenon" as this has come to be termed, is an occurrence of natural chain fission reactions which took place in a uranium deposit in Precambrian times, and which were moderated by groundwaters. Many of the resultant actinides and fission-products are still fixed in the host rocks in the reactor zones despite 1800 million years of subsequent exposure to geological processes. *Neil Chapman, et al., "Nuclear Waste Disposal: The Geological Aspects," New Scientist, April 27, 1978, p 226*

[1976, named after *Oklo*, the uranium mine where the phenomenon was discovered in 1972]

O·kun's law ('ou kənz), a formula in economics by which an increase in unemployment is correlated with a decline in the gross national product.

Okun's Law . . . starts from the basic premise that it takes about 4 per cent real growth in the gross national product just to keep unemployment from rising — and much

more than that to bring it down. . . . On average, it takes that much of a rise in activity to keep the jobless rate from rising as new workers enter the labor force and as productivity improves.

Okun's Law, that is, asserts that growth in production must exceed some minimum value in order to keep unemployment from rising as labor productivity increases and the need for labor declines, relative to output. *Barry Commoner, The New Yorker, Feb. 16, 1976, p 90*

[1970, named after Arthur M. *Okun*, 1928-1980, an American economist who devised the formula]

Olympiad, *n.* a variant of OLYMPICS.

After Varna, Fischer did play from time to time in international chess — notably at the Havana Olympiad in 1966. *George Steiner, "The Sporting Scene," The New Yorker, Oct. 28, 1972, p 76*

Preeminent in women's bridge was the British pair, Mrs. Rixi Markus and Mrs. Fritzi Gordon. They were runaway victors in the women's Pairs Olympiad. *Harold Franklin, "Contract Bridge," Britannica Book of the Year 1975, p 193*

[1961]

Olympics, *n.* a series of contests patterned on the Olympic Games by including a variety of events, having an international representation, etc.

Keith Brown of Baltimore took individual honors at the National Junior Olympics that ended today by becoming the first athlete in the 10-year history of the event to win three gold medals. *The New York Times, Aug. 24, 1976, p 26*

It may be inspiring to watch tiny Nadia Comaneci arch into a flawless parallel-bar handstand . . . but for sheer spine-tingling, heartrending drama and a basic tug deep in the stomach, nothing can compare with the World Culinary Olympics. *Marci McDonald, Maclean's, Dec. 13, 1976, p 31*

[1976]

OMA ('ou mə), *n. U.S.* acronym for *orderly marketing agreement,* a negotiated agreement between governments to restrict imports of a specific product when they jeopardize the employment, production, and sales of the importing country's industry.

The Administration has negotiated an OMA limiting imports of Japanese color-TV sets to 41% of their 1976 level (a restriction that obviously has not stopped Zenith from concluding that it will benefit by becoming a foreign manufacturer). Another OMA limits imports of shoes from Korea and Taiwan to 25% and 20% respectively. *"Economy and Business," Time, Oct. 17, 1977, p 53*

[1977]

O·mah ('ou ma:), *n.* another name for SASQUATCH.

At the same time, a more modest effort is under way to track down the Western Hemisphere's own Abominable Snowman — a large, shaggy, ape-like creature variously called Sasquatch or Bigfoot or Omah that is said to roam the mountains and forests of the Pacific Northwest. *"The Abominable Sasquatch," The New Yorker, Oct. 9, 1972, p 40*

[1972, of uncertain origin; perhaps related to *Omaha*]

OMB, abbreviation of *Office of Management and Budget,* a U.S. government agency established in 1970 to replace the Bureau of the Budget.

Those whose pet projects have been cut out of Federal budgets allege that the OMB is the real power in the Government, a kind of bureaucratic Cardinal Mazarin. *Science News, May 22, 1971, p 349*

[1970]

omnisex or **omnisexual,** *adj.* of or involving individuals or activities of all sexual types.

Chief attraction was the New York Dolls, a gaudy "omnisex" rock group. *"Newsmakers," Newsweek, Nov. 12, 1973, p 69*

The Dice Man is a blackly comic amusement park of a book, replete with vertiginous roller coaster rides of the spirit, feverish omnisexual trips through the tunnel of love. *Time, Nov. 1, 1971, p 60*

[1971, from *omni-* all + *sex(ual)*].

omnisexuality, *n.:* Nothing much for anyone, actually, in this film about the omnisexuality of a footman hero (Michael York) who sidles up to an Austrian countess (Angela Lansbury) and also to her son and to everyone else in sight. *"Goings On About Town," The New Yorker, Jan. 15, 1972, p 16*

on-air, *adj.* broadcast or broadcasting over the airways, instead of transmission by cable.

A WNET spokesman noted that both the total amount raised by the station and the size of the average donation exceeded the levels of all previous on-air campaigns for funds. *Les Brown, The New York Times, March 23, 1976, p 62*

Cable-TV's greatest objection to the bill is that it establishes the principle that cable owes fees for all the on-air television programs it carries. *John M. Gunn, "Television and Radio," The Americana Annual 1975, p 546*

[1973] Also, OVER-THE-AIR. Compare OFF-AIR.

on·co·gen·e·sis (ˌaŋ kə'dʒen ə sis), *n.* the process of producing tumors.

But these, as well as congenital chromosome anomalies, which likewise carry a risk of leukemia or solid tumors, are on the whole rare, and, although their study may illuminate mechanisms of oncogenesis, their impact on the sum total of human malignancy is quite small. *N. B. Atkin, "Cancer Research," Science, Jan. 6, 1978, p 60*

[1967, from *onco-* tumor (from Greek *ónkos* bulk, mass) + *genesis*]

on·cor·na·vi·rus (aŋˌkɔr nə'vai rəs), *n.* any of a group of tumor-producing viruses that contain RNA.

We now report that six oncornaviruses, including the human "candidate" virus RD-114, can be distinguished from each other. Even immunologically similar viruses from the same species can be identified as to type. This technique permits rapid identification of new virus isolates by comparison with known strains. *Daniel J. Haapala and Peter J. Fischinger, Science, June 1, 1973, p 972*

[1972, from *onco-* tumor + *RNA* + *virus*] Compare CORONAVIRUS, PAPOVAVIRUS, RETROVIRUS.

one-on-one or **one-to-one,** *adj., adv.* U.S. and Canadian. with one competitor, candidate, etc., directly confronting another; on a person-to-person basis.

A former pro player himself, Shue believes in solid defense, heads-up rebounding—and run, run, run. But his Bullets were strictly one-on-one operators who drew raves for their artistry—only to lose the big games. *Newsweek, March 5, 1973, p 51*

The President responds, "Politics is a one-on-one relationship, because if you don't feel some warmth and friendship with people, then you ought not to be in politics." *Elizabeth Drew, The New Yorker, Jan. 17, 1977, p 73*

They acknowledge that she now has a sizable, varied political base but suspect that it is unexpandable and that, one-on-one after a contentious primary, she will lose. *Maurice Carroll, The New York Times Magazine, June 26, 1977, p 38*

Ellis Rabb was alarmingly persuasive as the older actor. Once again Mamet had demonstrated his particular talent for one-to-one conversations. *Henry Popkin, "Theater," The Americana Annual 1978, p 493*

[1967 for *one-on-one*, originally a sports term (especially basketball and football); 1965 for *one-to-one*, extended from the sense (used in mathematics, statistics, etc.) of "matching exactly one element with another," as in *one-to-one correspondence*]

onlend, *v.t., v.i. British.* to lend (borrowed funds) to others.

The aim of the "corset," reintroduced as part of the June economic package, is to restrict the capacity of the banks to bid in funds which they then on-lend, creating new bank deposits and increasing the money supply. *John Whitmore, The Times (London), Aug. 18, 1978, p 15*

[1972]

Oort's Cloud (urts *or* ɔrts), a great swarm of comets traveling in elliptical orbits around the solar system at distances of up to 13 trillion miles from the sun.

Comets exist by the billions in . . . Oort's Cloud, coalesced from the swirling dust and gases in the original solar nebula, from which the sun, earth and other planets and moons were formed. *"Special Report: Kohoutek: Comet of the Century," Time, Dec. 17, 1973, p 91*

[1965, named after the Dutch astronomer Jan H. Oort, born 1900, who first proposed its existence]

op-con or **ops-con,** *n. U.S.* operations control.

"Burns, we want control of this operation. If there *is* an operation. We've got men on the ground, we've got very good op-con. American interests are involved, and don't forget that. This is what the Deputy Director wants, and that is what we will have." *Ward Just, "Burns," The Atlantic, Aug. 1972, p 71*

He led me up a narrow flight of stairs to a gallery overlooking a control room at Goddard, very much like the Mission Control Room in Houston, which is called Operations Control, or OpsCon, and from which engineers sitting at four rows of consoles were supervising the communications and tracking network. *Henry S. F. Cooper, Jr., "Letter From the Space Center," The New Yorker, April 17, 1971, p 129*

[1971, by shortening]

OPEC ('ou pek), *n.* acronym for *Organization of Petroleum Exporting Countries,* formed in 1960.

The economists, with their trained inability to understand the real world, had an even simpler solution. Paper money (dollars, marks, etcetera) would flow to OPEC, whose members would have to spend it, lend it, or bury it in the sand. If they spent it, we would get the oil, and pay for it with our exports, a workable exchange even if at unfair prices. *Miles Ignotus, "Seizing Arab Oil," Harper's, March 1975, p 45*

[1960] Compare OAPEC.

▶ The abbreviation appeared occasionally (mostly with periods, as *O.P.E.C.*) during the 1960's. With the advent of the energy crisis of the early 1970's the organization and its abbreviated name gained world-wide prominence. See ENERGY CRISIS.

open contract, *Underworld Slang.* a murder assignment open to any mobster.

According to some reports, there had been an "open contract" on Joe for months—that is, virtually ever since the Colombo shooting. . . . Some detectives insist, however, that they never heard of any such thing as an "open contract" until the phrase began to appear in the press; mob bosses, they insist, don't leave such matters to chance. *Fred J. Cook, The New York Times Magazine, June 4, 1972, p 96*

[1972] See CONTRACT.

open-date, *n.* a date stamped on packaged food to show when the food was packaged or when it is no longer fresh. *Often used attributively.*

New labeling regulations came into force in Britain, and comprehensive proposals were made for a system of open-date marking of prepacked foods. *H. B. Hawley, "Food," Britannica Book of the Year 1973, p 306*

—*v.t.* to put an open-date on (packaged food).

I congratulate those manufacturers who have been willing to open-date their products. *Stewart M. Lee, Beaver Falls, Pa., in a Letter to the Editor, The New York Times, Sept. 1, 1977, p 30*

[1971] Compare PULL-DATE.

open-dating, *n.:* Mr. Leonard Reeves-Smith, chief executive officer of the National Grocers' Federation, said: "We have always maintained that agitation for open-dating did not represent the view of the majority of consumers. The average housewife has few complaints about freshness." *The Times (London), March 16, 1973, p 14*

open education, a system of instruction, especially at the elementary-school level, emphasizing individualized activities and free discussions, as an alternative to traditional methods of instruction.

[John] Bremer, 45, is, after all, a noted advocate of "open education," the creator of Philadelphia's innovative Parkway School (the "school without walls," where students use the community as their place of learning). *Clive Cocking, Maclean's, March 1974, p 77*

[1973] See ALTERNATIVE SCHOOL.

open marriage, a form of marriage in which the spouses agree to remain socially and sexually as independent as if they were single.

Others are trying to meld the two modes through "open marriage" covenants that permit each party to form a variety of relationships—by no means just physical—with members of the opposite sex. *Newsweek, July 16, 1973, p 58*

Advocates of "open marriage" have argued that the partners in a monogamous relationship need the freedom to develop as individuals outside the bonds of the relationship while retaining primary emotional ties with the wife or husband. But some people are unable to tolerate change, growth, or even privacy in a partner, and thus the strain can grow too great to permit the relationship to continue. *Estelle Fuchs, The Second Season, 1977, p 221*

[1973, coined by George and Nena O'Neill, U.S. anthropologists and authors of the book *Open Marriage* (1973)] Compare CONTRACT MARRIAGE, SERIAL MARRIAGE. See also MARRIAGE.

open-space, *adj.* of or characterized by the use of movable partitions and furniture as space dividers instead of rigid partitions and walls.

Although traditional concepts of architectural design still

appealed to some, a contemporary concept, the open-spac plan, gained increasing popularity in the early 1970's. . . contemporary designers of homes, offices, or schools, mad striking design statements that exploited to the full sur light, trees, and view and efficiently accommodated th needs of the building's occupants. *Jeanne G. Weeks, "Inte rior Design," The Americana Annual 1972, p 351*

A return to basics, if it is projected as a cure, is bound t prove as disappointing as open-space architecture. *Willia Raspberry, The Manchester Guardian Weekly (The Wash ington Post section), Dec. 18, 1977, p 12*

[1972]

open university, a college or university without reg ular classroom instruction.

Under the auspices of the State University, New Yor opened its first "open university." It teaches its student largely by remote control—mailed assignments, televisior tape recordings, and independent study. These are au mented by periodic guidance, discussion, and testing se sions with faculty members at specially designated learnin centers. *Fred M. Hechinger, "Education," The 1972 Worl Book Year Book, p 331*

[1971, probably influenced by the *Open Universit* (1967), a British educational institution that teache adult students by a series of television programs]

opera window, a small ventless window on eithe side of the back seat of an automobile, usuall behind a rear side window.

Imperial Le Baron by Chrysler makes its 1975 appea ance with only minor styling changes, the most conspicu ous of which is a new narrow opera window for rear sea passengers. *Picture legend, "Cars for 1975: Compact an Subcompact," Ebony, Jan. 1975, p 74*

[1972, patterned on *opera light* either of two outsid lights by the passenger doors of an automobile]

o·pi·oid ('ou pi:ˌɔid), *n.* a synthetic drug that resem bles morphine, heroin, etc., in its effects. *Often use attributively.*

The I. G. Farbenindustrie laboratory at Höchst am Mai created methadone in the search for a morphine substitut late in the Second World War, when Germany was cut o from opium supplies. Yet it is a narcotic—an "opioid"—f in action it is fundamentally similar to morphine or heroi and it is fully as addictive. *Horace Freeland Judson, "A R porter at Large: The British and Heroin," The New Yorke Oct. 1, 1973, p 97*

[1972, from *opium* + *-oid*, suffix meaning "(on like"]

▶ An *opiate* (OED 1603) is a preparation or natura derivative of opium (e.g. morphine, codeine). A *opioid* is a synthetic substitute for an opiate that di fers from it chemically but resembles the action c effect of an opiate.

Op·ta·con ('ap təˌkan), *n.* a trademark for an elec tronic device that enables a blind person to read o dinary printed matter by touch. The device consist of a small camera connected to light detectors an vibrating tactile pins that convert printed charac ters of a text into a vibrating pattern of the shape c the characters which can be felt by the blind pe son's fingertip.

The Optacon is primarily a reading aid: a letter beneat the camera excites a corresponding pattern of vibration the tactile array, which the user can feel with the index finger. Nearly 2,000 blind people use the Optacon, and after a year or two of experience they can read 40 to 60 words per minute. *New Scientist, May 19, 1977, p 394*

[1972, from *optical*-to-*tactile* *converter*] Compare CORTICAL BRAILLE, TEXT-TO-SPEECH.

op·to·a·cous·tic (͵ɑp tou ə'ku:s tik), *adj.* of or having to do with the modulation of light energy by means of sound waves.

Some of the recent studies in the field of measuring atmospheric contaminants have been concerned with the use of the optoacoustic method in determining the level of concentration of trace gases in the lower atmosphere. *K. B. McAfee, Jr., "Atmospheric Contaminants Measurement," McGraw-Hill Yearbook of Science and Technology 1977, p 140*

[1973, from *opto-* of vision or light, optical + *acoustic* of sound] See ACOUSTOOPTICS.

or·a·cy ('ɔr ə si:), *n.* the ability to express oneself orally and to understand the speech of others.

Why is there such great interest in dyslexia and no interest in dis-functional oracy? In all but the deaf, effective oracy precedes any effective literacy: in learning literacy a functional ability to communicate in the mother tongue is thus a condition of being communicated with thereafter in literacy from the printed page. *Sir James Pitman, The Times (London), Dec. 6, 1973, p 9*

[1965, from *oral* + *-acy* (noun suffix), patterned on *literacy* (1883), *numeracy* (1959)] Compare GRAPHICACY.

oral history, 1 the tape-recording of interviews with persons who witnessed or participated in historical events.

The creative aspects of recent British research — concern for the visual (buildings, landscapes, the urban environment, crafts) and interest in oral history — depend on universally available cameras and tape recorders, yet they are strongly based in indigenous historical tradition. *Asa Briggs, "The Boom in Social History," The Manchester Guardian Weekly, June 9, 1973, p 25*

Since 1970 . . . oral history has evolved into a full-blown movement, feeding the mills of scholarship and gossip alike with thousands of miles of taped reminiscences, justifications (both candid and self-serving), secrets and trivia. *Kenneth L. Woodward, "The Pen vs the Tape Recorder," Newsweek, Aug. 5, 1974, p 74*

2 a historical account based on tape recordings or typescripts of such interviews.

A $100,000 grant from the Ford Foundation is supporting an oral history of the civil-rights movement during Dr. [Martin Luther] King's lifetime. *Henry P. Leifermann, The New York Times Magazine, Nov. 26, 1972, p 68*

Evidence from the oral history of Masai age sets clearly demonstrates that a halophytic vegetation covered the basin during the past century. *"Climate and Ecological Change in East Africa," Nature, Jan. 12, 1973, p 88*

3 any account based on verbal recollections or information, as distinguished from written records.

She never spoke of him with anything but affection. . . . Yet at one time, according to the oral history of the town, she and Jake had decided on divorce. *John Fischer, Harper's, Feb. 1973, p 25*

oral historian: The historian must be prepared to see and define the problems and to remind and even spur as well as to check and supplement the forgetful subject. In short, a tape recorder does not of itself make an "oral historian." *Seymour S. Cohen, Science, March 7, 1975, p 827*

[1972] ▶ Although the term *oral history* was used occasionally in the 1960's by historians, chiefly in connection with the John F. Kennedy Library, it became very current about 1972, as the method attained popularity both among social historians and writers on contemporary affairs.

orange paper, a document published by a British or Commonwealth ministry in which a program of reform or modification of existing policy is proposed.

The first step toward that goal followed in the same year with publication of a government "orange paper" that proposed, as a key element of reform, the provision of "an acceptable basic annual income for all Canadians" — in effect, a guaranteed annual income aimed especially at the "working poor." *Ian Urquhart, Maclean's, June 14, 1976, p 23*

[1976, patterned on earlier (1967) *green paper* a government document in which a proposal is put forward for national discussion]

org, *n. Informal.* organization.

Inside the Toronto org, I saw one ceremony that might be construed as worship. It was an hour-long "Sunday service" opening with a recitation of the Scientology creed, which is reminiscent of the United States Declaration of Independence. *John Saunders, "The Weird World of Scientology," Maclean's, June 1974, p 77*

[1962, by shortening]

organic metal, *Chemistry.* a polymer with high electrical conductivity.

"Organic metals" are tantalizing chemists and physicists both with the challenge of understanding unusual properties and the potential for novel technological applications. Most solids composed of an array of molecules are good insulators, instead of conductors, because electrons associated with one molecule cannot jump to another. But the new materials are surprisingly good conductors, and their conductivity is strictly temperature dependent. Although they conduct electricity, these solids retain organic characteristics (such as solubility in organic solvents) that may offer a number of new industrial possibilities. *Science News, Sept. 10, 1977, p 171*

[1977]

or·ga·no·hal·o·gen (ɔr͵gæn ou'hæl ə dʒən), *adj.* of, relating to, or denoting any of a group of highly toxic organic compounds containing one or more halogens.

Three categories of waste disposal were included in the proposed regulations. The first was for agents totally banned. These were the organohalogen compounds, such as the organochlorine pesticides and polychlorinated biphenyls. *Pearce Wright, "Europe to Act on Pollution of N Atlantic," The Times (London), Feb. 16, 1972, p 7*

The Convention prohibits the dumping at sea of certain dangerous substances, including . . . organohalogen compounds and highly radioactive materials. *Colin Norman, "Cancer Controversy Recommences," Nature, Jan. 1 and Jan. 8, 1976, p 5*

[1972, from *organo-* organic + *halogen*]

Oriental

Oriental, *n.* short for ORIENTAL JEW.

The Orientals hold down the majority of the service and production jobs in Israel. Some twenty-five to fifty per cent of the Europeans (depending on date of arrival) are in professional and managerial posts, as against only ten to fifteen per cent of the Orientals. *Joseph Kraft, "Letter from Israel," The New Yorker, April 7, 1973, p 74*

[1972]

Oriental Jew, an Israeli Jew of Middle Eastern or North African origin or descent (as distinguished from Israelis of European origin or descent).

Today the Israeli Arabs enjoy a standard of living that is not only considerably above that of the average Egyptian or Syrian but also higher than that of Israel's Oriental Jews. *Time, April 12, 1976, p 38*

Thousands of blue-collar workers and so-called Oriental Jews—from North Africa, Yemen and Iraq, the bottom of the economic and educational scale—were tired of Labor. *Marvin Kalb, "The New Face of Israel," The New York Times Magazine, July 17, 1977, p 33*

[1972]

Oriental Shorthair, any of a breed of green-eyed cats with a long body of uniform color, developed in Europe by crossing Siamese with other oriental cats.

Newly recognized by the Cat Fanciers Association, the Oriental Shorthair cat is one of this country's newest breeds, combining the stylized body type of the Siamese with the richest colors of other shorthair felines. *Nancy Rubin, The New York Times, Jan. 28, 1979, Sec. 12, p 7*

[1979]

-oriented, a combining form added to nouns to form adjectives, meaning "geared to, directed toward," now increasingly used, as in:

action-oriented, *adj.:* Magic Mountain: No Disneyland imitator, this park is an action-oriented playground featuring thrills and excitement. *Edwin A. Roberts, Jr., The National Observer, June 9, 1973, p 16*

change-oriented, *adj.:* "Then again, these hillmen are implacably tradition-bound, or 'not change-oriented,' to use the expression of an unusually disheartened visiting sociologist." *Claire Sterling, "Nepal," The Atlantic, Oct. 1976, p 283*

cops-and-robbers-oriented, *adj.:* . . . a welcome relief from the strident, cops-and-robbers-oriented dramas of commercial television. *Michael J. Arlen, The New Yorker, March 24, 1975, p 79*

golf-oriented, *adj.:* "It was," says the Rangers' golf-oriented center, Peter Stemkowski, "like getting a two on a par-five hole." *Stan Fischler, Boys' Life, Dec. 1972, p 10*

identity-oriented, *adj.:* The American Indian is a classic example. He was identity-oriented, occasionally warlike and hostile, but seldom motivated by aggression or fear. The American frontiersmen were survival-oriented, and all but eliminated the Indian in the acquisition of power and land. *William Glasser, Saturday Review, Feb. 19, 1972, p 27*

land-oriented, *adj.:* It's estimated that Southern city dwellers spent $1.4 billion on land-oriented recreation last year. *C. G. Scruggs, "5 Big Changes Ahead in Southern Agriculture," Progressive Farmer, Jan. 1973, p 20*

outdoor-oriented, *adj.:* As pleasant and hospitable as their surroundings, they take obvious pride in their outdoor-oriented life-style. *John Reddy, The Reader's Digest, Dec. 1971, p 148*

sports-oriented, *adj.:* Ironwood, Palm Desert. Exclusive sports-oriented community on 900 acres. *Town and Country, June 1974, p 43*

[1961, from the past participle of *orient, v.,* "to adjust, correct, or put into the right relationship" (OED 1850)]

or·tho·char·mo·ni·um (ˌɔr θou tʃɑr'mou ni: əm), *n.* a name for the PSI PARTICLE according to the charm theory.

They designate the charmed-quark-charmed-antiquark bound state as "charmonium" and say that what has been found is specifically orthocharmonium. *Dietrick E. Thomsen, Science News, Jan. 25, 1975, p 60*

[1975, from *ortho-* straight + CHARMONIUM] See QUARK.

or·tho·don·ture (ˌɔr θə'dɑn tʃər), *n.* the straightening or adjusting of irregular teeth; orthodontia.

More and more adults are wearing braces on their teeth, and smiling, because orthodonture today can be done with braces that are removable for special occasions. *The New York Times Magazine, Nov. 26, 1978, p 130*

[1969, from *orthodontics* the branch of dentistry dealing with the straightening of teeth + *-ure* (noun suffix), as in *denture;* perhaps influenced by a corruption in the pronunciation of *orthodontia*]

orthophoto or **orthophotograph,** *n.* a composite photograph of terrain, made by joining narrow strips of other photographs so that the finished picture is fully correct in scale, position, etc.

The orthophoto produced in this manner, although similar in appearance to an aerial photograph, is in fact quite different. Whereas an aerial photograph of rolling or mountainous terrain will have inherent scale and angular distortions, the orthophoto is true to scale; shapes, angles, and distances are correct. *George G. Alexandridis, "Highway Engineering," McGraw-Hill Yearbook of Science and Technology 1972, p 245*

Despite developments in air survey techniques, leading to the introduction of orthophotographs . . . conventional cartographic resources are now unable to keep pace with the accelerating rate of information collection. *E. P. J. Williams, The Times (London), May 21, 1976, p 15*

[1964, from *ortho-* straight + *photo(graph)*]

orthovoltage, *n.* X-ray radiation therapy using voltages of 200,000 to 500,000 volts. *Often used attributively.*

It is unlikely that further sophistication of either radiation dosage or localization will result in an increased rate of cure (witness the rather disappointing gains in progressing from orthovoltage to the accelerator [the use of proton beams in radiotherapy]). *Louis G. Jacobs, Science, June 9, 1972, p 1071*

[1970, from *ortho-* straight, normal + *voltage*]

OSHA ('ou ʃə), *n. U.S.* acronym for *Occupational Safety and Health Administration,* created by Congress in 1971.

OSHA was empowered to set national standards to replace a welter of conflicting health and safety guidelines, send inspectors to factories, stores and offices to check on compliance, levy stiff fines on violators and even order unsafe businesses to close down. *"OSHA Under Attack," Time, July 8, 1974, p 48*

[1972]

os·so·bu·co (ˌas ou'bu: kou), *n.* an Italian dish of braised veal shanks, made with olive oil, white wine, anchovies, etc.

There are five pastas costing $3.75 and $4.00, and three entrées at $6.25, including osso buco. *Nika Hazleton, "Delectations," National Review, July 18, 1975, p 780*

[1971, from Italian, (literally) bone marrow] Also spelled **osso bucco.**

os·to·my ('as tə mi:), *n.* any operation in which a part of the intestine or urinary tract is removed and an artificial opening (stoma) is made for the passage of waste products; a colostomy, ileostomy, ureterostomy, etc.

An ostomy may become necessary because part of the intestine or urinary system is affected with cancer or an inflammatory disease. . . . Although the ostomy operation involves major surgery, it is a relatively safe procedure. *Neil Solomon, New York Post, Dec. 1, 1979, p 25*

[1976, abstracted from *colostomy, ileostomy,* etc.]

OTC or **O.T.C.,** abbreviation of *one-stop inclusive tour charter,* an airline tour package that combines low-cost air fares with discount arrangements at a single destination.

To their credit, travel agents have devised ingenious plans to make the tourist's dollar work more efficiently. This year's prime example: the one-stop-inclusive tour charter, or OTC. Approved last fall by the Civil Aeronautics Board, OTC plans allow travelers to choose among dozens of destinations at prices that include air fare, hotel room, ground transportation, taxis and tips. *"Economy and Business: Travel: Back to Wings and Wheels Again," Time, Aug. 23, 1976, p 53*

[1976] Compare ABC, APEX, SUPER SAVER.

OTH, abbreviation of OVER-THE-HORIZON.

Unlike conventional radar, over-the-horizon, or OTH, radar is not restricted in its range by the curvature of the earth. By reflection from the ionosphere OTH radar can penetrate to great distances, making possible the detection of missiles soon after they are launched. *Ted Greenwood, "Reconnaissance and Arms Control," Scientific American, Feb. 1973, p 22*

[1967]

ou·gi·ya or **ou·gui·ya** (wa:'gi: yə), *n.* the monetary unit of Mauritania introduced in 1973.

In a second slap at France, the republic of Mauritania replaced the French franc with a new currency unit called the *ougiya*. *"Africa: Unbinding the Ties," Newsweek, Aug. 27, 1973, p 36*

[1973, from Arabic] See KHOUM.

outlaw country, another name for PROGRESSIVE COUNTRY.

B. W. Stevenson, also on the bill, is a country-music performer who spills over into rock; probably he could fit into the currently popular "outlaw country" genre. He filters his country sounds through present day rock-and-roll. *Ian Dove, "Ace, British Group, at the Bottom Line," The New York Times, Feb. 15, 1976, p 65*

[1976]

out-of-body, *adj.* characterized by or involving dissociation from one's own body; having to do with parapsychological phenomena in which a person sees himself and his surroundings from an external position in space.

Noyes speculates that out-of-body experiences may be projections the brain makes to negate death, to pretend we are only witnessing it as a spectator. *William Lowther, "Medicine: Some People Who Have Died—and Lived to Tell the Tale," Maclean's, June 14, 1976, p 50*

[1971, alteration of earlier (1958) *out-of-the-body*]

outrageous, *adj. U.S., Slang.* used admiringly, especially by teenagers, of something shocking, daring, etc.

But that is not at all what's wanted by the fans of Kiss (at least according to the kids I talked to). What they want is outrageousness. *("Outrageous,"* spoken with heavy emphasis on the "rage" and overweening approval in the voice, is today's slang for defiant or flamboyant behavior, going against the rules: 50's-style rebellion with a twist. Think of James Dean in drag.) *Colette Dowling, "An Outrage Called Kiss," The New York Times Magazine, June 19, 1977, p 66*

R. Couri Hay, celebrity columnist for the *National Enquirer* and star and producer of his own celebrity-interview show on Channel C, local cable-TV station: "The invitation was first-class. All the important media people were there. The narrated slide show of Elvis was outrageous. I just couldn't believe the dialogue." *"The Talk of the Town: Recollections," The New Yorker, Nov. 27, 1978, p 34*

[1977]

outreach, *n. U.S.* any deliberate and systematic effort to provide health care, jobs, and other social services to needy groups or communities. *Often used attributively.*

A joint committee study . . . showed that 1890 colleges had significant capabilities in areas involving nutrition, environmental quality, psychology, consumer education, rural development, community health, and outreach to the rural poor. *Peter H. Schuck, "Discrimination as Public Policy," Saturday Review, June 23, 1972, p 48*

His was also the first black gospel group to play at Nashville's Grand Ole Opry. His Soledad concert was arranged at the request of an independent ex-con outreach group called The Way Inn. As for his own motivations in singing the Lord's praises to such a group of desperate men, Crouch explains: "I'll hook them any way I can." *Time, Jan. 9, 1978, p 14*

[1968, extended sense of the term meaning "act of reaching out" (OED 1870)]

Oval Office or **Oval Room,** *Especially U.S.* the office of the Presidency of the United States.

And if Congress should decide that a President is no longer to be held broadly accountable for the conduct of his most personal appointees, it would obviously encourage future Presidents to wink at every sort of skulduggery so long as nothing could be traced to a specific directive from the Oval Office. *Arthur M. Schlesinger, Jr., Harper's, May 1974, p 15*

Neither corruption of language nor corruption extending from the Oval Room can much longer mask the perilous need for the new energy resources so long suppressed. *William Rodgers, "The Exxon-Nixxon Axis," The Nation, Jan. 5, 1974, p 16*

[*Oval Office* 1969; *Oval Room* 1974; transferred from the literal sense of the private office of the President, a large oval room in the White House]

▶ In the current sense this term became popular in the context of the Watergate affair. In its literal sense it appeared in the 1930's, when the office was built.

Oval Officer, an appointee to the staff of the President of the United States.

John J. Wilson, attorney for former Oval Officers Haldeman and Ehrlichman, said that, realistically, he expected them both to be indicted. *National Review, March 15, 1974, p 290*

[1974]

overdose, *v.i.* **1** to become sick or die from an overdose of a narcotic.

He overdosed in Miles's bathroom and cut himself in a fall. *Newsweek, March 26, 1973, p 22*

Dr Gisela Oppenheim, consultant psychiatrist at the drug dependence unit at Charing Cross Hospital, said she wrote to Dr Vignoles asking him not to prescribe for one of her patients. "This boy's life is in danger as he is overdosing," she wrote. *The Times (London), March 14, 1973, p 3*

2 *Figurative use.*

Though Wenders overdoses on mood, he creates the right apprehensiveness for a Highsmith story. But he's trying to do eighteen other things, too; he "enriches" the plot with incidental speculative themes. *Pauline Kael, "The Current Cinema," The New Yorker, Oct. 17, 1977, p 176*

By day's end, the children will be pale and testy, overdosed on anticipation and excitement. *Linda Bird Francke, The New York Times, Dec. 24, 1978, Sec. 4, p 11*

[1972, verb use of the noun, probably influenced by the earlier (OED 1758) transitive verb meaning "to give too large a dose to"]

overdub, *n.* the addition of recorded vocal or instrumental parts to a recording; the blending of several or multiple layers of sound in one record.

In 1971 Mike Oldfield began work on a composition entitled 'Tubular Bells' and now, after 2,300 overdubs, 'Tubular Bells' is available on record as the first release from Virgin Records of Notting Hill Gate. *John Peel, "Pop Music: 'Tubular Bells'," The Listener, June 7, 1973, p 775*

[1973, noun use of earlier (1965) verb]

overground, *adv., adj.* **1** in the open; public or publicly.

But in Hainan, and later in Japanese-occupied Burma, the socialism of the embryo officer corps was mingled with what can only be called Japanese fascism.

The new force saw little serious combat. But it became of pivotal importance in both the overground and underground politics of Burma under the Japanese and it saw itself very much in the Japanese mould. *Martin Woollacott (from Bangkok), "Burma's Iron-Bound Road to Xenophobia," The Manchester Guardian Weekly, May 11, 1974, p 6*

2 belonging to or recognized as acceptable to, established society or culture.

Next, I got a part in what you might call an "overground" movie—huge budget and lots of stars. *F. P. Tullius, The New Yorker, Sept. 9, 1967, p 40*

When the American activist Abbie Hoffman published his "handbook of survival and warfare," . . . the book clearly bore a price and, beneath the spoof imprint "Pirate Editions," that of an "overground" publisher, Grove Press. *"Commentary," The Times Literary Supplement, Jan. 21, 1972, p 66*

[1967]

overmike, *v.t.* *U.S.* to amplify too much with a microphone.

Because the show, like all Broadway shows, is damnably overmiked, it is hard to tell what the quality of her voice may be. *Brendan Gill, "The Theatre," The New Yorker, May 2, 1977, p 90*

[1972, from *over-* too much + *mike, v.* (1957) to transmit on or use a microphone]

override, *n.* *U.S.* the act of overriding or nullifying.

A few days before the scheduled Assembly vote, Tony Daugherty, [Governor Jerry] Brown's legislative liaison chief, told me, "In all candor, we have not worked it the way we would a normal override." With the backing of strong Democratic majorities . . . Brown had never been overridden; in fact there had been only two successful overrides of a governor's veto in all the years since Earl Warren. *David S. Broder, The Atlantic, Jan. 1978, p 36*

[1974, noun use of the verb]

overspend, *n. British.* **1** the act of overspending; excessive spending.

. . . in the words of the report, that "the larger the proposed technological step, the larger the probability of overspend." *"A Lame Duck," The Manchester Guardian Weekly, Aug. 11, 1973, p 15*

2 an amount overspent; overexpenditure.

An overspend of £100,000 is a probability, therefore. *Robin Marlar, The Sunday Times (London), May 30, 1971, p 22*

[1971, noun use of the verb]

overstayer, *n. British and Australian.* a visitor to a country who remains longer than permitted by the terms of the entry visa.

"I do not think an unconditional amnesty is right, but I think the Home Office could adopt a much more liberal attitude to overstayers, particularly to people from Cyprus or Rhodesia." *Lord Avebury, The Times (London), Sept. 17, 1976, p 4*

Auckland Police Association chairman P. Ngata says the methods used to track down overstayers were "quite abhorrent." . . . He had a departmental memo which said that police were to round up illegal immigrants and overstayers of all races. *National Business Review (Auckland, N.Z.), Nov. 10, 1976, p 5*

[1976]

over-the-air, *adj.* variant of ON-AIR.

Although studies have been prepared proposing or assuming the end of over-the-air broadcasting in favour of cable, such efforts seem hardly more than academic exercises. *Mary Alice Mayer Phillips, "Cable Communications—A Springboard to Tomorrow," Britannica Book of the Year 1973, p 657*

[1972]

over-the-horizon, *adj.* of or denoting a type of radar that uses reflections from the ionosphere to detect objects beyond the horizon.

The department is spending $50,000 to explore over-the-horizon radar as a spotting tool. Used now to give distant early warning against missiles, submarines and warships, a single radar installation of this type located at, say, Denver could cover the entire 1,500-mile border from the Gulf of Mexico to the Pacific. *"The Periscope: Dew-Line For Drugs," Newsweek, Sept. 17, 1973, p 19*

[1967] *Abbreviation:* OTH

over-tonnaged, *adj.* having too great a tonnage; oversized for its kind.

Russian expansion has not been in the bulk trades — which are free and open to all and in which she is under-tonnaged — but in the liner trades, which are largely closed and in which she is already over-tonnaged. *Michael Baily, The Times (London), June 13, 1977, p 19*

[1968]

over-tonnaging, *n.:* The report stated that this would produce over-tonnaging which in turn would reduce the efficiency of vessel utilization and result in increased shipping costs. *The Times (London), Jan. 12, 1976, p 17*

overwash, *v.t.* to wash over; cover with water.

A typical barrier island is overwashed by a storm that drops sand on vegetated areas. *Dietrick E. Thomsen, "As the Seashore Shifts," Science News, June 17, 1972, p 397*

— *n.* a being overwashed; inundation.

Beach houses, motels, restaurants and the US Navy base at Cape Hatteras . . . are shielded from normal storms, salt spray and overwash by the artificial dunes. *"Coastal Protection Lost in the Wash," New Scientist, Jan. 4, 1973, p 25*

[1972]

overwithhold, *v.t.* *U.S.* to withhold too large an amount of (personal tax) from a taxpayer.

Some developments, such as the federal refund of over-withheld income taxes in 1972, were expected to stimulate the economy further in the first half, particularly if, as some estimates have it, more than $5 billion is handed back to consumers who were overwithheld. *Jackson Phillips, "Economy of the U.S.," The Americana Annual 1973, p 243*

[1972]

OVIR (ou'vir), *n.* the Soviet government bureau that issues exit visas for foreign travel.

I could enumerate for you a few of the innumerable bureaucratic atrocities of OVIR, not that anyone knows them all. But I could give you a list of the names of all those criminals, down to the women clerks. *Cynthia Ozick, The New Yorker, May 9, 1977, p 38*

[1972, from Russian, acronym for (the Russian equivalent to) *Office of Visas and Registrations*]

o·vo·lac·tar·i·an (ˌou vouˌlæk'ter i: ən), *n.* a vegetarian whose diet includes dairy products and eggs.

"Ovo-lactarians" supplement their plant food with eggs and milk; "granivores" eat only seeds and grains; "fruitarians" consume only fruits; "vegans" refrain from utilizing any animal product whatever. *Stefan Kanfer, Review of "The Vegetable Passion" by Janet Barkas, Time, March 10, 1975, p K5*

[1975, from *ovo-* egg + Latin *lactārius* of milk + English *-an*] Also called LACTO-OVO-VEGETARIAN.

own-label, *adj.* *British.* bearing a retail store's label as brand name instead of the manufacturer's label.

Denis Defforey, director-general of Carrefour hypermarket group, has stirred up rival distributors and many manufacturers by introducing 50 own-label items costing up to a third less than equivalent branded goods. *The Times (London), June 15, 1976, p 21*

[1972, variant of *own-brand* (1970)]

Ox·i·sol ('ɑk səˌsɔ:l), *n.* (in U.S. soil taxonomy) any of a group of highly weathered and leached soils of tropical regions.

Oxisols may require millions of years to form from unweathered material. *Paul F. Smith, "Soil," McGraw-Hill Yearbook of Science and Technology 1976, p 367*

[1972, from *oxide* + *-sol* (from Latin *solum* soil)] Compare ALFISOL, ARIDISOL, HISTOSOL, etc.

oxygen walker, a small portable oxygen tank for persons suffering from emphysema or other lung diseases, and heart disease.

My father used a newly developed Union Carbide "oxygen walker" for over a year prior to his death from emphysema in 1970. The "walker" was filled from a liquid oxygen tank and its use enabled him to retain mental alertness and a certain degree of physical mobility in spite of the emphysema and the tranquilizing medications that he was receiving. *Molly Gordon, Bainbridge Island, Wash., in a Letter to the Editor, Science News, Nov. 6, 1976, p 291*

[1976]

o·ze·ki (ou'zei ki:), *n.* a champion sumo wrestler ranking immediately below the grand champion.

Me, I'm a belt man. It is a thing of joy to witness my favorite, a trim but powerful ozeki, or champion, named Takanohana, come out of the . . . initial charge, with his legs crouched and his head up and his arms slashing away at his opponent. *Richard Halloran, "Notes of a Sumo Wrestling Fan," The New York Times, Jan. 6, 1974, Sec. 10, p 11*

[1966, from Japanese *ōzeki*] Compare YOKOZUNA.

ozone shield, the layer of ozone about 20 to 40 miles above the earth's surface that shields the earth from excessive ultraviolet radiation.

Man's assaults on the ozone shield, in the form of SST flights, aerosol sprays and other chemicals, are continuous and could permanently deplete the layer. *"Science: Ozone Alert," Time, Feb. 23, 1976, p 46*

Atmospheric chemists have predicted that man-made chemicals will thin the earth's ozone shield, and the sun's harsh rays will then increase skin cancer prevalence and alter global climate. Now by jet, laboratory experiments and computer, the chemists are challenging and substantiating that gloomy prediction. *Science News, Sept. 23, 1978, p 212*

[1976] ► Earlier terms for this part of the atmosphere were the still current *ozone layer* (1951) and *ozonosphere* (1952).

ozone sickness, a condition caused by inhalation of ozone seeping into jet aircraft at altitudes over 40,000 feet. It is characterized by itchy eyes, headaches, chest pains, and drowsiness.

Because ozone sickness is such a recent peril to air safety, many vexing questions remain unanswered. Why does the sickness hit frequently during the early months of the year? Why does it occur more often over the Pacific Ocean? What's the best remedy? Pan Am has already installed charcoal filters in its six 747SP jets, and the company reports the problem solved. *Julianne Labreche and William Lowther, Maclean's, April 17, 1978, p 30*

[1978]

P

P-A-C, abbreviation of *Parent, Adult, Child,* used in transactional analysis to designate the three ego-states within every individual.

The analysis of transactions in terms of P-A-C is what the theory of T.A. is all about. There is no doubt in the minds of its advocates that T.A. works better than other methods. As Dr. Harris once wrote: "If only one hour were available to help someone, the method of choice would be a concise teaching of the meaning of P-A-C and the phenomenon of the transaction." *Kenneth Lamott, The New York Times Magazine, Nov. 19, 1972, p 43*

[1972]

pacemaker, *n.* an electronic device for relieving certain symptoms of neurological disorders by sending signals to electrodes implanted under the scalp.

In the last year, three dozen [epileptic] patients have had the pacemaker implanted. . . . Even if the pacemaker's results turn out to be short lasting, experts believe that the fact that it works at all could lead to a new understanding of how the brain controls movement and perhaps to simpler nonsurgical methods of treating abnormal movement disorders. *Jane E. Brody, "Brain 'Pacemaker' Is Helping Some With Handicaps," The New York Times, Sept. 22, 1973, p 15*

[1973, transferred from the earlier (1955) sense of an artificial pacemaker for the heart, a device implanted near the heart to control its beat] Compare ESB, STIMOCEIVER.

pach·y·ceph·a·lo·saur (ˌpæk ə səˈfæl əˌsɔr), *n.* a plant-eating dinosaur of the Cretaceous period, characterized by a thickened, dome-shaped skull covered with knobs and spines.

Pachycephalosaurs probably used their reinforced skulls as battering rams during competitive courtship display—rather like living goats and sheep. *Richard A. Thulborn, "Dinosaur," McGraw-Hill Yearbook of Science and Technology 1973, p 163*

[1973, from New Latin *Pachycephalosaurus,* the genus name, from *pachy-* thick (from Greek *pachýs*) + *cephalo-* head (from Greek *kephalê*) + *saurus* lizard (from Greek *saûros*)]

pachycephalosaurian, *adj.:* Galton . . . has suggested that the greatly thickened skull roof of the pachycephalosaurian dinosaurs was correlated with the use of the head in pushing and ramming during intraspecific combat, like that seen today in mountain sheep. *Barry Cox, "Fossilised Fury," Nature, April 29, 1976, p 748*

packet, *n.* a segment of data or information processed as a unit in a computerized communications system.

A customer's message was treated as one or more packets, about 1,000 or so bits in length, with its destination address and other relevant information included among the bits. The packet could route itself through a special communications network, which generally utilized minicomputers at the junction or branch points. *Ernest R. Kretzmer, "Communications," 1975 Britannica Yearbook of Science and the Future (1974), p 216*

—*v.t.* to segment data or information into units for processing in a computerized communications system.

Most terminals do not have the capability to "packet" their data, so a "terminal processor" at the local exchange is interposed to accept the characters sent by the terminal, packet them, and convert them if necessary into a standard format. *Timothy Johnson, "Electronic Post for Switching Data," New Scientist, May 13, 1976, p 352*

[1973 for noun; 1976 for verb]

packet-switched, *adj.* using a packet-switching communications system.

New data transmission services—in particular packet switched links now being introduced, in which blocks of data from different users are interleaved along main communication links—raise new problems of data security. *Duncan Campbell, "Whose Eyes on Secret Data?" New Scientist, March 2, 1978, p 593*

[1976]

packet-switching, *n.* the transmission of data or information in segments over a computer network, each unit of transmission restricted to a maximum size and bearing a specific address. *Often used attributively.*

The technique . . . is known as "store and forward" or packet-switching. Messages are temporarily stored as they arrive at a centre; only when the message has been completely and accurately received is it forwarded to the next centre; and so on in succession through the various centres en route. *Kenneth Owen, "Telecommunications: Seat Reservations—by Computer," The Times (London), May 17, 1972, p III*

[1971]

paddy, *n. U.S. Slang.* a derogatory name for a white man, especially among speakers in American black and Spanish-speaking communities.

There were a few years, beginning in the late sixties, when almost any Mexican *barrio* in Southern California was dangerous territory for Anglo police. For those years . . . gang members were transformed into Brown Berets, street toughs began thinking of themselves as Chicano militants, juvenile offenders learned to refer to the rest of the world as "the Anglo-dominant society" instead of "paddies." *Calvin Trillin, "U.S. Journal: Riverside, Calif.," The New Yorker, Feb. 5, 1979, p 101*

[1966, probably from *Paddy*, nickname for an Irishman (OED 1780), also slang term for a policeman (as in *paddy wagon*), from the diminutive form of the Irish name *Padraig* or *Patrick*] Compare BLUE-EYED DEVIL.

page, *v.t.* **1** to contact someone by sending a radio signal to a small receiver he is carrying that has a warning sound activated by the radio signal.

An executive moving from country to country will be accessible to paging in any of the company's establishments by carrying a pager in his pocket, as he would a pen. *The Times (London), April 27, 1973, p 15*

A thief was caught in Sydney, Australia, when police "paged" him in the pocket paging device he had stolen. *Reader's Digest, Jan. 1980, p 82*

2 to contact and regulate (an electrical appliance) by means of an electronic remote-control device operated by a keyboard.

The digital signal pages only those wall modules set to the number you keyed. If you page a light, for example, you can also page it to turn on, off, or you can even dim it. . . . You can page an appliance such as your coffee maker or toaster to turn on or off. *Advertisement in Science News, May 5, 1979, p 304*

[1973, specialized use of the verb meaning to find or contact someone by means of a page boy (OEDS 1904) or a public-address system (1920's)]

pager, *n.* a small electronic device used to page someone.

A Boston narcotics peddler used top-line $300 models to keep track of his 13 pushers — until he went to jail and the pushers made off with the pagers. The users most thoroughly hooked on pocket page calls may be . . . well, hookers. The gadgets are standard equipment for Las Vegas professionals. *Time, May 5, 1977, p 67*

[1973]

page-turner, *n.* a very interesting book, especially a fast-moving novel that is an adventure story, science–fiction or detective story.

As they say in the story departments out at The Burbank Studios, this one is a real page turner. *Walter Wager, quoted in The New Yorker, Oct. 30, 1978, p 155*

If it is possible to ignore the moral issues that West himself raises and then drops, *Proteus* can be clear sailing. Connoisseurs of page-turners will feel right at home in a world where a woman can still be described as a "leggy redhead," where grins are "crooked," where a Jewish character says "oy vay" and a Scotsman says "aye." *Time, Jan. 22, 1979, p K6*

[1972]

pair, *v.t. U.S.* to combine the white and black pupils of (schools that are close to each other).

The administration of Pres. Jimmy Carter seemed to be leaning toward busing and pairing (or clustering) schools to mix students from predominantly white or black schools. Under the pairing plan, an elementary school is formed from two or more different schools so that students will attend a racially mixed class even though they may reside in segregated neighbourhoods. *Tudor David and Joel L. Burdin, "Education," Britannica Book of the Year 1978, p 343*

[1964]

paired-associate learning, *Education, Psychology.* a form of learning in which words, numerals, pictures, etc., learned in pairs become associated so that one of the pair can serve as a stimulus to recall the other.

Paired-associate (PA) learning apparently differs from serial learning mainly in benefiting to a larger degree from past verbal experience. PA learning can be more influenced by verbal mediational processes than serial learning. *Arthur R. Jensen, Genetics and Education, 1972, p 264*

[1963]

pa·laz·zos (pə'lɑ:t souz), *n.pl.* or **palazzo pants,** women's loose, wide-legged trousers.

Unlike jeans, which tend to reveal everything, palazzos conceal everything, even fat hips, skinny thighs and thick calves. *"Modern Living: Baggy Britches," Time, Sept. 11, 1972, p 49*

She [M. McPartland] is wearing an ensemble that has clearly been thought out to the last fold: a close-fitting cranberry turtleneck, a gold belt, brocaded cranberry-and-gold palazzo pants, and a gold pocketbook. *Whitney Balliet, The New Yorker, Jan. 20, 1973, p 56*

[1972, from earlier (1965) *palazzo pajamas,* ultimately from Italian *palazzo* palace, large mansion]

paleoenvironment, *n.* the oceanic or terrestrial environment in the time before the ages of human history.

As it enters its second decade, the Deep Sea Drilling Project is shifting its objectives. The *Challenger*'s most recent voyage, Leg 63, completed the transition . . . from hard rock geophysics and tectonics to paleoenvironment — studies of changes in ocean ecology with time as reflected in the sediments. *Science News, Jan. 6, 1979, p 6*

[1971, from *paleo-* ancient, prehistoric, of geological times + *environment*]

paleohabitat, *n.* the habitat of an animal that lived in the time before the ages of human history.

Further, systems of biostratigraphy based on different organisms have been conceived in isolation, not integrated, and these systems can individually apply no further than the principal paleohabitat (represented by facies — rock sequences reflecting major Earth environments) of the studied organism. *Erle G. Kauffman, "Biostratigraphy," McGraw-Hill Yearbook of Science and Technology 1974, p 118*

[1972, from *paleo-* + *habitat*]

paleolatitude, *n.* the location of a landmass with respect to the equator at the time it was formed.

The geologically young island of Hawaii — which is still coming out of the sea floor — has no paleolatitude. More exactly, its present and paleolatitudes are the same, since it has not had time to move on the earth's surface. *Igor Lobanov-Rostovsky, "Seamounts: Keys to the Earth," Encyclopedia Science Supplement (Grolier) 1973, p 186*

[1972, from *paleo-* + *latitude*]

paleoprimatology, *n.* the study of prehistoric primates.

Palaeoprimatology is a subject the very existence of which depends on the fact that teeth, unlike other parts of the body, are immutable, being "fossils" from the start; and it is hardly surprising that most of our knowledge of evolutionary lineages has been formulated under the "tyranny of the teeth." *John Napier, Review of "The Functional and Evolutionary Biology of Primates,"* edited by Russell H. Tuttle, *New Scientist, Sept. 13, 1973, p 642*

[1972, from *paleo-* + *primatology* study of primates]

pal·i·mo·ny ('pæl ə‚mou ni:), *n. U.S. Slang.* alimony or its equivalent demanded by a person for having lived with someone without being married.

The latest case of "palimony" involves a Los Angeles court demand . . . by Kayatana Harrison for $4 million of the fortune amassed by comic Flip Wilson, who, she says, was a longtime, live-in boyfriend. *Lynn Langway, "Newsmakers," Newsweek, Feb. 19, 1979, p 59*

The Lee Marvin palimony case . . . shows that—married or not—people who live together cannot avoid a shared responsibility. *Daily News (New York), April 20, 1979, p 35*

[1979, blend of *pal* and *alimony*] See ALIMONY, COHABITEE, MARRIAGE.

palindrome, *n. Molecular Biology.* a segment of double-stranded DNA (the genetic material in cells) having identical sequences of nucleotides on both strands.

A 24-nucleotide stretch reads identically (with one flaw) in opposite directions beginning at its center. The researchers suggest that this segment could bind a protein important for messenger RNA function. Mirror-image sequences, called palindromes, of a different type are known in bacteria, but such an arrangement of nucleotides has not been described in globin or other mammalian genes. *Science News, May 7, 1977, p 295*

[1975, transferred sense of the term (*c*1629) meaning a word, number, etc., that reads the same backward and forward] Compare SENTENCE, SYNONYM, WORD.

palindromic, *adj.:* Restriction enzymes . . . recognize a single palindromic nucleotide sequence on the DNA helix and make staggered cuts in both chains of the helix whenever this sequence appears. *"Science and the Citizen: To Clone a Gene," Scientific American, Jan. 1977, p 48*

palliative care unit, *Especially Canadian.* a hospital facility for the care of the terminally ill.

Charette is one of the stars in a film just released by the National Film Board of Canada called *The Last Days of Living.* His co-stars are a dozen patients, at the Royal Victoria Hospital (RVH) who are dying of cancer, their families, and the staff of the palliative care unit at the RVH. *Bonnie Price, "No Fear of Dying: A Film About the Gift of Death," The Saturday Gazette (Montreal), Feb. 2, 1980, p 45*

[1975] *Abbreviation:* PCU. Compare HOSPICE.

pan·cu·ro·ni·um (‚pæn kyu'rou ni: əm), *n.* or **pancuronium bromide,** a synthetic drug similar to curare, used as a muscle relaxant. *Formula:* $C_{35}H_{60}Br_2N_2O_4$

Pancuronium . . . acts on muscle fibers as it does on motor nerve terminals. *Annibal Galindo, Science, Nov. 17, 1972, p 754*

An investigation indicated that at least 18 of the victims —including nine of those who died—had been given Pavulon, or pancuronium bromide, a synthetic variant of curare, the lethal plant toxin used by South American Indians to tip poison darts. Anaesthesiologists sometimes administer Pavulon to surgical patients to relax their muscles. *Time, March 22, 1976, p 47*

[1970, probably from *pan-* all, general + *curare* + *-o* + *-ium,* chemical suffixes]

paperback, *v.t. Chiefly British.* to publish as paperback.

They suspect they may have a best-seller on their hand but they think it's too bulky to paperback. *Philip Oake The Sunday Times (London), Feb. 16, 1975, p 56*

[1971, verb use of the noun]

pa·po·va·vi·rus (pə'pou və‚vai rəs), *n.* any of a grou of viruses containing DNA which are associate with or known to cause various types of tumors an growths in mammals.

The virus . . . found in 8 out of 18 kidney-transplant p tients, belongs to a group known as the papovaviruses, th human version of which has only recently come to ligh *"Bringing Human Viruses Out of Hiding," New Scientis Feb. 8, 1973, p 285*

The human papovavirus belongs to the same group viruses as the monkey virus SV40, which is known to caus tumours on rodents. *The Times (London), Feb. 6, 1973, p 14*

[1964, from *papilloma-polyoma-vacuolation* + *virus*] Compare ONCORNAVIRUS.

Pap·u·a New Guinean ('pæp yu: ə), a native or in habitant of Papua New Guinea, an independen country (since Sept. 16, 1975) consisting of the east ern half of New Guinea and a chain of island including the Bismarck Archipelago, Bougainvill and Buka in the Solomon Islands, and the Trobrian Islands; Papuan.

In 1976, in an attempt to establish a sense of nation identity, Papua New Guineans were encouraged by th prime minister to wear national dress to work every Frida *A. R. G. Griffiths, "Papua New Guinea," Britannica Boo of the Year 1977, p 550*

[1972]

par·a·char·mo·ni·um (‚pær ə tʃar'mou ni: əm), *n.* hypothetical form of the PSI PARTICLE according t the charm theory.

Paracharmonium (a version with slightly different quan tum numbers, but still charmed) should also exist at slightly different mass, and they think it ought to be looke for. *Dietrick E. Thomsen, Science News, Jan. 25, 1975, p 60*

[1975, from *para-* beside, supplementary + *char monium*] Compare ORTHOCHARMONIUM.

par·a·le·gal ('pær ə‚li: gəl), *adj.* of, relating to, or as sociated with the law in an auxiliary capacity.

It was epitomized in a letter from a young paralega worker, Adam Bennion, to Charles R. Nesson, a Harvar Law School professor who was one of the defense attor neys. *Sanford J. Ungar, "Pentagon Papers," The Atlantic Aug. 1973, p 12*

Women in Scarsdale feel a great pressure to be involve in something. "They're all getting Ph.D.s or have a job i psychiatric or paralegal work . . ." one resident told me *Alex Shoumatoff, "Profiles: Westchester," The New Yorker Nov. 13, 1978, p 129*

—*n.* a paralegal aide.

Operating with local foundation financing out of a refur bished downtown factory building, the clinic's three attor neys and three paralegals can devote personal attention t individual problems that overburdened legal-aid attorneys and probation officers do not have time for. *"The Law: Ne*

Clinics for Kids in Trouble," Time, April 18, 1977, p 46

[1968, from *para-* near, subordinate + *legal*]

arallel computer, a computer having several processors that enable it to handle a large number of computations for a problem at the same time instead of serially.

The computer is the ILLIAC IV, and it is the first truly parallel computer—that is, a computer capable of working on a problem in parallel, simultaneous operations. The ILLIAC IV can do 64 identical operations in parallel. *Alan J. Perlis, "Computers and Mathematics," Encyclopedia Science Supplement (Grolier), 1972, p 122*

[1970] See PARALLELISM.

arallelism, *n.* or **parallel computation,** the simultaneous handling of a large number of computations for a problem by a computer.

The advantages to be gained by parallel computation are still largely unknown. In some important applications parallelism can increase the computation speed almost indefinitely. It is important to note that in some situations there is no substitute for speed. That is, one hour of computation at 100 MIPS cannot be replaced by 100 hours at 1 MIPS. Examples of this include weather prediction (it does no good to take 48 hours to compute a 24-hour weather forecast). *John R. Rice, "Computers," 1975 Britannica Yearbook of Science and the Future (1974), p 219*

[1974]

arallel slalom, a slalom skiing race in which two competitors race at the same time over courses roughly equivalent in length and difficulty.

The Nations' World Series, a new event, was notable in that it provided that amateur circuit with its first taste of head-to-head "parallel slalom" skiing, with two skiers racing down parallel courses against each other, rather than against the clock. *Roger Allaway, "Sports: Skiing," 1975 Collier's Encyclopedia Year Book (1974), p 504*

[1974] Also called DUAL SLALOM.

Par·a·lym·pics (ˌpær əˈlim piks), *n.* an international sports competition patterned on the Olympics, in which the participants are paraplegics or others confined to wheelchairs.

These four, and 380 other handicapped athletes from 31 states, are competing in the 20th national Wheelchair Games . . . The top finishers in the various classes—determined by the severity of the handicap—will represent the United States in the upcoming "Paralympics" in Toronto, Aug. 3 through 11, against teams from 51 other countries. *Tony Kornheiser, The New York Times, June 12, 1976, p 15*

[1965, from *paraplegic* + O*lympics*] See OLYMPICS.

pa·ram·e·ter·ize (pəˈræm ə təˌraiz), *v.t.* to represent (physical effects or phenomena) by the use of parameters, as in fitting the scale of the data to the scale of the phenomena under study.

By parameterizing the effects of small-scale motions in the solar atmosphere in terms of an eddy viscosity, it was shown that giant convection cells . . . give rise to a differential rotation which agrees in all qualitative aspects with that observed on the sun. *F. H. Busse and C. R. Carrigan, "Laboratory Simulation of Thermal Convection in Rotating Planets and Stars," Science, Jan. 9, 1976, p 83*

[1973, back formation from *parameterization* (1964), from *parameter* + *-ization*]

parameterization, *n.:* Parameterization is necessary because cloud processes occur on a much smaller scale than that separating the grid points (about 10 km or more) in the model hurricanes. Most current parameterizations of cloud effects assume that the clouds heat the adjacent air by direct turbulent transfer of their own excess warmth. *Joanne and Robert H. Simpson, "Hurricane," McGraw-Hill Yearbook of Science and Technology 1974, p 229*

paramilitarist or **paramilitary,** *n.* a member of a paramilitary force.

It was feared that the failure of the warring Catholic and Protestant factions [in Northern Ireland] to reach any kind of agreement on power-sharing would inspire paramilitarists on both sides to try to fill the political vacuum. *James Lewis, Manchester Guardian Weekly, March 7, 1976, p 1*

Senator Wilson was firmly opposed to violence and, unlike most Ulster politicians, did not carry a gun; his body had thirty knife wounds. Responsibility for this deed was claimed by a group of Protestant "paramilitaries" calling themselves the Ulster Freedom Fighters. *Anthony Bailey, "A Reporter at Large," The New Yorker, May 8, 1978, p 61*

[1973, from *paramilitary, adj.*]

► These terms have been applied chiefly to the paramilitary units in Northern Ireland.

paraphysics, *n.* the study of physical phenomena attributed to psychic forces; the physical aspects of parapsychology.

Professor Werner Schiebeler of Ravensburg Polytechnic has lectured on "An Introduction to Parapsychology and Paraphysics," in addition to his normal lectures, since 1970. *"Feedback: Can Paraphysicist Dematerialise Objections?" New Scientist, March 6, 1975, p 566*

[1973, from earlier (1950's) *paraphysical* relating to such phenomena as telekinesis, levitation, etc., from *para-* beside + *physical*]

► In recent years *paraphysics* has been suggested by some students of extrasensory phenomena as a replacement of *parapsychology*, on the grounds that these phenomena cannot be adequately accounted for by psychology and their proper area of study might be physics.

par·a·sail·ing (ˈpær əˌsei liŋ), *n.* the act or sport of soaring in a parachute while being towed by a motorboat, car, or other fast vehicle.

The ultimate panoramic view is probably best gained by parasailing, where the intrepid traveller is attached to a parachute and pulled along behind a motorboat to rise in the air like a kite over the water. *The Times (London), Feb. 18, 1978, p 13*

[1969, from *para*chute + *sailing*]

parascience, *n.* any field of study considered outside the traditional realm of science because its principles, hypotheses, or data cannot be rigorously tested in accordance with the scientific method.

Theory constitutes the reigning body of scientific principles or hypotheses, and in science, as opposed to what may be called "parascience," practice should by definition be explicable by, and based on, theory. *Lord Zuckerman, "Theory and Practice In and Out of Science," The Times Literary Supplement, Nov. 17, 1972, p 1393*

The boom in "parascience" is causing concern to some scientists in the United States. Last week the Committee for the Scientific Investigation of Claims of the Paranormal

held a press conference in New York to deplore the growing flood of uncritical media coverage of such subjects as
astrology, parapsychology, spoon bending, and other
topics. *"Parascience Under Attack," New Scientist, Aug. 18,
1977, p 395*

[1965, from *para-* beyond + *science*]

para-transit, *n.* a system of transportation, often
without fixed schedules or routes, that uses automobiles, vans, and buses to carry passengers and
usually supplements an urban transit system.

Para-transit was the rather sinister name given to another range of cheap solutions aimed at bridging the gap between private cars and conventional public transport. Para-
transit covered a multitude of services, including shared
taxis, jitney buses, dial-a-ride, and car pools. *Richard Case-
ment, "Urban Mass Transit," Britannica Book of the Year
1976, p 673*

[1975]

parcel bomb, an explosive device in the form of a
parcel or package; MAIL BOMB.

Last month in Malatya, a provincial center about 300
miles southeast of Ankara, a parcel bomb killed the town
mayor, Hamid Fendoglu, a Kurd. *Nicholas Gage, "The Violence of Extremism Grips Turkish Politics," The New York
Times, May 7, 1978, Sec. 4, p 6*

[1971]

parenting, *n.* **1** the process of caring for and raising
a child.

Our study of adopted children, *Growing Up Adopted*,
published recently, indicated that . . . "it is the single-
minded, unconditional desire, together with the emotional
maturity to provide a loving, caring home, which is the hallmark of good parenting." *Mia Kellmer Pringle, "Readers'
Letters," The Times (London), Oct. 30, 1972, p 8*

"When we ask whether sex determines parenting, we
can say that neither males or females are innately programmed to parenthood nor do they inherit distinct styles
of parenting . . . Parenting is mostly learned from identification with models." *Mary Read Newland, Review of "Parenting" by Sidney Cornelia Callahan, The New Republic, Jan.
5 and 12, 1974, p 31*

2 the act or process of producing offspring; reproduction; procreation.

The eight modes or methods of parenting can be listed
very simply. (1) The coital-gestational way. (2) Artificial insemination of a wife with her husband's sperm, without any
assistance or input from a third party. (3) Artificial insemination of a woman with a donor's sperm. (4) Egg
transfer from a wife, inseminated by her husband and then
transferred to another woman's womb for substitute gestation . . . *Joseph Fletcher, The Ethics of Genetic Control,
1974, p 40*

[1963]

park-and-ride or **park-ride,** *adj. U.S.* designed to
enable suburban commuters to park their cars at
railroad stations, bus terminals, etc., and complete
their trip into the city by public transportation.

From park-and-ride facilities to bus—rapid transit
transfer terminals, Chicago's commuters are increasingly
able to step from one mode of transportation to another
quickly and conveniently. *"Transportation: Chicago: Inter-
modal Systems," Science News, Sept. 15, 1973, p 170*

Metro . . . took over and revived the countywide transportation network, creating a park-ride system to bring in

344

suburbanites. *"The Nation: Those Movers Who Shak
Seattle," Time, Dec. 12, 1977, p 36*

[1972]

parole, *n.* the discretionary authority, granted to the
Attorney General by the U.S. Immigration and Na
tionality Act, to admit refugees into the country or
an emergency basis.

The bills differ . . . substantially in how they allo
policymaking power. Mr. Eilberg would end the discre
tionary "parole" authority extensively used by attorney
general and replace it with congressionally written guide
lines. Mr. Kennedy would retain parole and give the execu
tive branch flexible new authority to cope with unexpectec
refugee flows. The executive departments have been slow
to coordinate their positions. Uncertainty over the future
flow from Indochina is a particular complication. *"U.S. Pol
icy on Refugees," The Manchester Guardian Weekly (The
Washington Post section), April 9, 1978, p 16*

Attributive use.

In 1973 . . . Attorney General John Mitchell granted Sovi
ets "parole" immigration status—reserved for persons
being given refuge from persecution in their homeland.
*Faubion Bowers, The New York Times Magazine, Sept. 26,
1976, p 27*

—*v.t.* to admit into the country under parole.

A section of that act [Immigration and Nationality Act]
states that the Attorney General "may in his discretion
parole into the United States temporarily . . . any alien applying for admission," and this section was invoked by the
Ford Administration shortly before the fall of Vietnam to
allow up to a hundred and fifty thousand refugees from
Vietnam and Cambodia to enter the country. *Robert Shaplen, "A Reporter at Large: Survivors," The New Yorker,
Sept. 5, 1977, p 35*

[1967, transferred sense of the term (a1616) meaning the discretionary release of a prisoner]

▶ Although *parole* in this unrecorded sense has existed since the passage of the 1952 Immigration and
Nationality Act, the term appeared infrequently in
print and only when a new influx of refugees raised
questions about their admission and status. The
wave of refugees from southeastern Asia (see BOAT
PEOPLE) during the 1970's brought the word into
currency.

parrot's perch, a device or method of torture.

Describing one regular torture, the parrot's perch, the
document says victims are suspended from a horizontal
pole, with their knees doubled over the bar and their hands
tied to their ankles behind their backs. *Leonard Greenwood,
The Manchester Guardian Weekly, Feb. 1, 1976, p 6*

[1972, translation of Portuguese *pau de arara* (literally) perch of ara (a kind of macaw)]

Parsons table, a square or rectangular table of
simple design, with the legs extending from the four
corners of the underside of the tabletop.

The eclectic approach, combining traditional French and
English styles with such contemporary designs as the Parsons table, steel-and-glass or steel-and-leather pieces, the
wall system, and sectional upholstered pieces became
fairly widespread. *Helen W. Harris, "Interior Design," 1972
Collier's Encyclopedia Year Book (1971), p 286*

[1967, probably named after its designer]

partial, *v.t.* Usually, **partial out.** to remove the influence of (one or more relevant variables) in a statistical correlation.

Initial ability could affect the amount learned by the students. Therefore, in preference to a simple correlation between the objective and subjective measures of teaching effectiveness, a partial correlation between the two measures was obtained. This statistic "partials out" the effect due to initial ability, or, in effect, describes the relation between amount learned from the instructor and student rating of the instructor, with initial ability held constant. *Miriam Rodin and Burton Rodin, "Student Evaluations of Teachers," Science, Sept. 29, 1972, p 1165*

[1972, verb use of adjective, probably abstracted from *partial correlation*]

particle beam, 1 a stream of charged nuclear particles produced in a particle accelerator.

Particle beams . . . are the source for much of what is known about the structure of the atom and its constituent particles. To create such a beam, negatively charged electrons, positively charged protons or the charged nuclei of atoms may be swung past successive rows of magnets in devices called accelerators, speeding up each time a magnet is passed and acquiring more energy. *Malcolm W. Browne, The New York Times, Dec. 4, 1978, p D11*

2 a stream of charged nuclear particles directed through the atmosphere by a beam weapon.

Particle beams fired from the ground or space at close to the speed of light—186,000 miles a second—have been suggested as a means of stopping enemy nuclear missiles before they reach the U.S. *"Scientists Push $1B 'Death Ray' Research," New York Post, Jan. 22, 1979, p 12*

Also called CHARGED PARTICLE BEAM.
[1978]

particle-beam weapon, a beam weapon that fires particle beams.

The idea of a particle-beam weapon is to produce a copious burst of energetic particles, be they electrons, protons, ions (or, as the Soviets now seem to be suggesting, neutral [?] particles), send them X kilometers through the atmosphere and zap! there goes your capital city ("biological target") or, more likely, zap! there goes your incoming cruise missile. *Science News, Aug. 19, 1978, p 117*

[1978]

Par·ti Qué·be·cois (par'ti: kei be'kwɑ:), a political party in Quebec advocating political independence and separation from the rest of Canada. Formed in 1968, it gained control of the provincial government of Quebec in 1976.

The victory of the Parti Québécois in the November 15 election implied on the part of the voters a willingness to put . . . the question of independence to a referendum. If it does not pass, and if the PQ is elected once more, the question will be put again. *John Harney, Maclean's, Dec. 13, 1976, p 12*

Surely—this book was published three years after the Parti Quebecois came to power, remember—there will be in the final chapters a revaluation, a reconsideration of the dogmas of a decade ago. *William Johnson, The Globe and Mail (Toronto), Jan. 7, 1980, p 10*

[1968, from French] See PÉQUISTE.

▶ As the above quotations show, English periodicals in Canada vary greatly in their use of accent marks on French loanwords. Some Anglo-Canadian writers regard the use of accent marks in loanwords as an affectation, while others render them scrupulously. In the first quotation, the second accent mark is an error resulting from hypercorrection.

par·vo·vi·rus (ˌpɑr vou'vai rəs), *n.* a virus containing DNA and found chiefly in rodents and apes.

The bacteriophage øX174 . . . has many features of resemblance to the parvoviruses of vertebrates. *Frank Fenner, "Various Groups of Viruses," Science, July 28, 1972, p 343*

[1971, from Latin *parvus* little + English *virus*]

passalong, *n.* U.S. an increase in the costs of a producer or someone who provides a service, that is passed along in the form of increased prices, rent, etc.

This meant that production costs could no longer be offset to the same degree, and, in industry after industry, the consequent cost increase was passed along to the consumer in the form of higher prices. As this "pass-along" accelerated, prices began rising at an inflationary rate. *Seymour Melman, "Beating 'Swords' Into Subways," The New York Times Magazine, Nov. 19, 1978, p 48*

[1977, from the verb phrase *pass along*]

pass-fail, *n.* the system in which a student either passes or fails a course instead of receiving a grade in numbers or letters, such as A, B, C, etc.

As with many other colleges of late, Hobart and William Smith also offer such options as . . . pass-fail instead of grades, study off-campus or abroad or at another school, and independent study in a major field. *Donald Johnston, The New York Times, June 25, 1972, Sec. 4, p 9*

—*v.t.* to pass or fail (a student) instead of giving a grade in letters or numbers.

I would much have preferred to pass-fail my students. They could have relaxed more and learned more if we'd all concentrated on education instead of grades. *James G. Driscoll, "Grade Beef, Not Students," The National Observer, July 1, 1972, p 10*

[1972, noun and verb use of earlier (1963) adjective *pass-fail*]

passive belt, an automobile safety belt that automatically holds an occupant in a seat, especially by laying across a shoulder upon the closing of a door.

In model year 1982, all standard-size cars will get an automatic protective system; in 1983, midsize cars [will] get a passive belt or air bag. *Charles E. Dole, "Midyear Auto Update," The Christian Science Monitor, May 8, 1979, p B7*

[1977]

passive euthanasia, the causing or hastening of the death of an incurably ill or injured person by withholding life-sustaining treatment.

In the United States, most right-to-die measures introduced in 15 states from 1969 through 1974 would have permitted only the withholding or termination of treatment (so-called passive euthanasia) or, occasionally, the administration of pain-killing drugs in dosages that risk death. *William A. McGeveran, Jr., "A Right to Die?" 1977 Collier's Encyclopedia Year Book (1976), p 336*

[1975] Also called NEGATIVE EUTHANASIA. Compare ACTIVE EUTHANASIA.

passive restraint, a safety device in an automobile that automatically protects a passenger from serious injury in an accident.

Passive restraints are devices designed to protect occupants in collisions, without the need for occupants to take any active step, such as buckling belts. The air-bag, which automatically inflates in a crash, or passive belts, which are attached to the front door and automatically fold across front-seat occupants when the door closes, have been tested and can meet the Government's requirement. *The Times (London), July 4, 1977, p 20*

[1970]

passive smoking, the inhalation by nonsmokers of smoke from other people's cigarettes, cigars, and pipes.

Although the amount was small relative to that measured in smokers, the doctors said, "the fact that some nicotine is present in the urine of almost all nonsmokers suggests that episodes of passive smoking are common in urban life." *Lawrence K. Altman, "Nicotine Absorbed from Air by Nonsmokers in Urban Life," International Herald Tribune, Feb. 4, 1975, p 3*

Passive smoking can injure the health of nonsmoking wives, children, infants and unborn babies, as well as people with chronic heart and lung diseases and allergies to tobacco smoke. *Jane E. Brody, "Nonsmokers Try to Clear the Air," The New York Times, Nov. 22, 1978, p C1*

In a study at the Long Beach Veterans Administration Hospital, Aronow tested the effects of passive smoking (breathing smoke-contaminated air) on ten men with severe coronary-artery disease. *Time, July 17, 1978, p 73*

[1975] See MAINSTREAM SMOKE, SECONDHAND SMOKE, SIDESTREAM SMOKE, SMOKE POLLUTION.

passive smoker: Throughout the country, "passive smokers" are beginning to speak out. Growing numbers of nonsmokers are trying to rid their environment of a pervasive pollutant that is a general nuisance to most and a genuine health hazard to some. *Jane E. Brody, The New York Times, Nov. 22, 1978, p C1*

pat-down search, *U.S.* a search, especially for concealed weapons, conducted by running the hands over a person's outer clothing; a frisking.

Everyone trying to enter the courtroom is scanned by electronic devices; there is a pat-down search by guards who also rummage through purses and briefcases; photographs are taken of each new visitor. *"The Law: The Longest Trial," Time, July 19, 1976, p 43*

[1974] Compare SKIN SEARCH, TOSS.

patient-day, *n.* a unit for calculating the cost of running a hospital, clinic, etc., based on the expense of providing care and facilities to one patient for one day.

More specifically, planners must decide such things as the average hospital cost per patient-day, the number of patient-days per capita and ultimately the share of national income that is devoted to health care. *Martin S. Feldstein, "The Medical Economy," Scientific American, Sept. 1973, p 159*

[1967, patterned on *man-day* (OEDS 1925)]

patrial, *n.* a native or natural-born citizen of a country, and in Great Britain, one who has such status by adoption or naturalization or whose parent or grandparent had such status.

Commonwealth citizens with a grandparent born here would not need a work permit or be subject to supervision. But they would not share the privilege of "patrials" or immunity from deportation and they would have to apply initially for entry. *David McKie, "UK Closes Door on Mass Immigration," The Manchester Guardian Weekly, Feb. 3, 1973, p 11*

[1971, noun use of the adjective meaning "of one's native country" (OED 1629)]

pa·tri·ate ('pei tri:,eit), *v.t. Canadian.* to transfer the authority to amend (Canada's constitution, embodied in the British North America Act of 1867) from the British government to Canada's federal government.

For most Canadians, . . . the failure to agree on a simple thing like patriating the constitution must seem puzzling. But it is not patriation that has proven so contentious. Rather, it is the division of powers between Ottawa and the provinces. Provinces that want more power for themselves, notably Quebec and, latterly, Alberta, fear that if they agree to patriation they will lose their biggest bargaining chip. *Ian Urquhart, "Lament for a Nation: The Colony that Can't Grow Up," Maclean's, Nov. 13, 1978, p 26*

[1976, from Latin *patria* native country + *-ate*, (verb suffix), influenced by *repatriate*]

patriation, *n.:* "The maintenance of the legitimate and historical powers of the provinces may be at stake if patriation is carried forward unilaterally," Premier Peter Lougheed of Alberta declared this week. *Robert Trumbull, The New York Times, April 10, 1976, p 2*

patrimonial sea or **patrimonial waters,** the waters within which a coastal state may exercise sovereignty over natural resources.

In principle, Australia is ready to accept new laws which would provide a territorial sea of 12 miles, a patrimonial sea of 200 miles, and retain existing rights to explore the continental shelf even if it extends beyond 200 miles. *Paul Webster, The Manchester Guardian Weekly, June 30, 1973, p 6*

[1972] Compare EXCLUSIVE ECONOMIC ZONE.

Patriotic Front, a black nationalist organization formed in Zimbabwe-Rhodesia in 1976 as an alliance of ZANU and ZAPU to represent a united front against the white Rhodesian government.

The Patriotic Front has the full backing of the black African states most closely involved in the Rhodesian conflict and claims to be the political voice of the guerrillas fighting against white minority rule. *The New York Times, Jan. 16, 1977, p 7*

[1976]

Patterned Forms. ▶ Many new words are patterned or modeled on older words. The form and meaning of the new word shows the direct influence of its forerunner. A patterned form may be a simple word, an acronym, a blend, a compound, a derivative, an idiom, or even a foreign term; it is distinctive because it might never have been coined had a previous form or pattern of forms not existed to serve as the blueprint for its creation. However, the form or forms given in these etymologies are not necessarily to be interpreted as the one word which served as the pattern.

Patterned forms included in this dictionary are indicated in the etymology by the phrase "patterned on" as shown in the following examples.

The dates in parentheses give a rough indication of the length of time a pattern has been established in the language.

businesspeak. . . . [1971, blend of *business* and *speak*, patterned on *Newspeak* and *doublespeak*, the artificial languages in George Orwell's novel *1984*]

oracy. . . . [1965, from *oral* + *-acy* (noun suffix), patterned on *literacy* (1883), *numeracy* (1959)]

pink-collar. . . . [1977, patterned on *white-collar* (1928), *blue-collar* (1950), and *gray-collar* (1968) . . .]

pit lizard. . . . [1972, patterned on *lounge lizard* (1920's)]

A new word or expression may eventually become a pattern itself for newer forms, inspiring the coinage of similar words or expressions. Thus *sexism*, which was patterned on *racism*, became in turn the pattern for *ageism*, HEIGHTISM, SPECIESISM, and other words in *-ism* where the suffix often suggests prejudice or discrimination. Similarly, *black power* became the pattern for GRAY POWER and the name *Black Panther* became the model for GRAY PANTHER and GREEN PANTHER. The revival of interest in *acupuncture* not only spawned such forms as STAPLEPUNCTURE and QUACKUPUNCTURE but also inspired the revival of ACUPRESSURE. And the hybrid economic condition *stagflation* begot the more recent hybrids SLUMPFLATION and HESIFLATION.

Older and well-established terms, however, are the usual models for new words created by pattern. The forms RIDERSHIP and VIEWERSHIP are natural descendants of the pattern represented by *readership* (1920's) and *listenership* (1940's). There would probably be no word spelled WHYDUNIT without the preceding *whodunit* (1930). The DEBIT CARD of today is surely indebted to the *credit card* of the 1950's. The competitive COOK-OFF owes as much to *bake-off* (1952) as SAILOFF owes to the earlier FLY-OFF. But probably the oldest models are *adolescence* (OED *c*1430) and *senescence* (OED 1695), on which the coinage MIDDLESCENCE was patterned. Another very old pattern word is *double-entendre* (OED 1673), the apparent model for SINGLE-ENTENDRE.

Patterned forms are often deliberately coined as contrastive terms. A BRAIN GAIN is the reverse of a *brain drain*; to DECRUIT contrasts with to *recruit*; and BASSE COUTURE is the opposite of *haute couture*. A SOUND-ALIKE, however, may also be a *look-alike* (1940's), and a LIPSPEAKER is usually an excellent *lip reader* (*c*1900).

Analogy, the tendency to imitate or follow what is accepted and generally used in the language, also provides a stimulus for patterned formations. Analogy is active on all levels of language (pronunciation, inflection, spelling, etc.), forcing varying degrees of uniformity and standardization. The new patterned forms of language reinforce existing lexical patterns and stimulate the formation of ones as they are needed.

patz·er ('pats ər), *n. Especially U.S. Slang.* an amateur or unskilled chess player.

Peter Andrews, a well-known freelance writer, describes himself as a patzer, or wood-pusher, at chess. *Saturday Review, Aug. 19, 1972, p 13*

Not that there weren't a sufficient number of patzers hulking over boards stenciled on park benches or, like me, amateurishly tinkering with plastic pieces and folding cardboard boards as an occasional pastime . . . *Mel Watkins, Review of "Chess and the Dance of Death" by Alexander Cockburn, The New York Times Book Review, March 16, 1975, p 10*

[1968, probably from German *Patzer* bungler, from *patzen* to bungle]

Pave Paws, acronym for *Precision Acquisition of Vehicle Entry, Phased Array Warning System,* a radar system that detects ballistic missiles launched at sea at a range of over 3,000 miles.

Pave Paws has no moving parts. Its thin 2° beam is electronically focused and steered at high search rates by 10,000 antenna elements fixed to two faces of the radar building. Quick to note that the military operates facilities today which are 20 times more powerful than Pave Paws, Lt. Col. Paul T. McEachern who presented the case for the Air Force, repeatedly assured residents that "the power densities will be well below the values at which any health impact will occur." *Lee Torrey, "Pave Paws Stalks US Microwave Standard," New Scientist, Feb. 2, 1978, p 30*

[1976]

Pav·u·lon ('pæv yə,lɑn), *n.* a trademark for PANCURONIUM.

To suppress the shivers, the infant was dosed with Pavulon, a derivative of curare, a poison used by South American Indians to paralyze game. *David Harris, "The Short Happy Life of a Child of 'The Land'," The New York Times Magazine, June 11, 1978, p 32*

[1970]

Pay Board or **pay board,** a government board in charge of establishing general standards for wage increases.

U.S. Pay Board announced guidelines on the granting of fringe benefits to workers. *Britannica Book of the Year 1973, p 43*

Phase Two of the Government's anti-inflation programme officially began, and the new Pay Board formally came into being to hear unions' complaints that the present freeze was dealing unfairly with their members. *William Hardcastle, The Listener, April 5, 1973, p 437*

[1972] Compare PRICE COMMISSION.

pay cable, *U.S.* a system for transmitting a fixed number of special television programs by coaxial cable for a monthly charge.

For the first time in its long, flickering career, pay television—now known as "pay cable"—is making a highly visible challenge to the networks' oligarchic hegemony over video entertainment. *Harry F. Waters, "Entertainment: 'Pay Cable'," Newsweek, March 31, 1975, p 73*

Pay cable, offering regular cable subscribers movie-and-sports packages at a special figure, grew at a comfortable rate during the year, despite persistent charges of interference by on-air broadcasting interests. *John M. Gunn, "Television and Radio," The Americana Annual 1976, p 537*

[1974]

payload specialist, a specialist on scientific experiments aboard a spacecraft.

Two British and six American scientists are on the short list from which two candidates will be chosen for a new breed of astronaut, called payload specialists, to carry out 13 experiments on the second flight of Spacelab 2 in 1981. *The Times (London), April 29, 1978, p 5*

[1977] Compare MISSION SPECIALIST. See also PI.

PBB, abbreviation of POLYBROMINATED BIPHENYL.

PBBs, which are no longer manufactured for use in this country, had been used as a flame retardant. In 1974 that chemical was accidently mixed with animal feed in Michigan and contaminated livestock and food. Recent studies have identified adverse health effects on some farm residents. *Science News, Nov. 5, 1977, p 297*

[1976]

PBS, abbreviation of *Public Broadcasting Service* (the network of noncommercial television stations in the United States).

In what it called an "experiment," PBS abandoned floor reporting and trained its cameras only on speakers at the rostrum. This technique, the network said, would give viewers a delegate's-eye view of the proceedings. *Joseph Morgenstern, Newsweek, Sept. 4, 1972, p 89*

[1971] Compare PTV.

P.C., *U.S.* abbreviation of *Professional Corporation.*

A doctor whose medical practice has been incorporated for tax purposes must use the initials "P.C.," for professional corporation, after his name. *"What the Initials Mean," The New York Times, Jan. 30, 1976, p 10*

Mr. Goodfriend, whose law firm has helped half a dozen other law firms make the switch from partnership to PC in the last nine months, said that most PCs are small firms with one or two lawyers. *"Partners Go to PCs: Less Tax, More Pension," The National Law Journal, June 4, 1979, p 10*

[1976]

PCB, abbreviation of *polychlorinated biphenyl,* any one of a group of highly toxic and persistent chemical substances used in industry especially as electrical insulators and in plastics manufacture. Since 1976 the manufacture of PCBs has been discontinued in the United States.

In Ontario alone, more than 220 tons of deadly polychlorinated biphenyls or PCBs are currently being stored as liquid waste under varying conditions at sites throughout the province — many of them in urban areas — because there is no incinerator anywhere in Canada capable of destroying them. *Judy Dobbie, "Environment: It's Enough to Make You Sick — or Dead," Maclean's, Oct. 2, 1978, p 50*

[1966]

PCM, abbreviation of PROTEIN-CALORIE MALNUTRITION.

The biochemical lesions in PCM are still incompletely understood but are of obvious importance. The syndrome has been called the greatest killer of infants and young children and the major cause of retarded child growth and development in today's world. *Joan L. Caddell, "Nutrition," McGraw-Hill Yearbook of Science and Technology 1971, p 298*

[1971]

PCP, a trademark for the depressant drug phencyclidine, used illegally in powder form as the narcotic popularly called ANGEL DUST.

The San Francisco office of the United States Department of Justice's Bureau of Narcotics and Dangerous Drugs was feverishly trying to locate what is believed to be the largest manufacturing plant of PCP in California. Phencyclidine hydrochloride is a hallucinogen, an animal tranquilizer which provides an acid-like high and, doctors say, gradually damages the brain. *Joe Eszterhas, Rolling Stone, May 24, 1973, p 30*

[1970, from the abbreviation of *p*henyl*c*yclohexyl*p*iperidine, also (by contraction) the drug's generic name *phencyclidine*] Compare DPT, MDA, PMA.

PDL, *British.* abbreviation of POVERTY DATUM LINE.

The PDL is, in fact, so low a standard that most social researchers use the concept of the Minimum Effective Level to express the minimum income needed for an African family to lead a decent life. *Adam Raphael, The Manchester Guardian Weekly, March 17, 1973, p 4*

[1973]

Peace People, a movement of Catholics and Protestants organized to promote peace in Northern Ireland.

There were the Peace People, for instance, who over the past two years and despite their failings, have at least proved to Protestants, that Catholics truly want an end to violence and to Catholics that the Protestants desire likewise. *The Times (London), Aug. 24, 1978, p 12*

[1976]

peace studies, a course or program of studies dealing with the subject of peace among nations and the means of achieving it.

Some £75,000 was raised during 1972 toward the establishment of a chair of peace studies at the University of Bradford, Yorkshire. *Edwin Bronner and Clifford Haigh, "Religion: Protestants," Britannica Book of the Year 1973, p 591*

[1972] Compare IRENOLOGY.

peak experience, a profoundly affecting spiritual or mystical experience.

In place of the behaviorists' mechanistic concept of human nature as a network of conditional responses, [Abraham] Maslow posited a human nature that is partly species-wide and partly unique. Most of us, according to Maslow, are capable, moreover, of what he termed "peak experiences" — breakthrough moments of deep emotional understanding or intensity, the most dramatic examples of which are the spiritual revelations of saints and mystics. *Calvin Tomkins, "Profile: Michael Murphy," The New Yorker, Jan. 5, 1976, p 42*

[1974]

peak shaving, the pumping out of liquefied natural gas from storage tanks during periods of peak demand.

Cryogenic storage of natural gas is a rapidly growing technique; at 76 locations in the U.S. "peak shaving" operations involving liquefied natural gas are in use or under construction. There is no technical reason why a similar peak shaving technique cannot be employed with liquid hydrogen. *Derek P. Gregory, "The Hydrogen Economy," Scientific American, Jan. 1973, p 16*

[1960, so called because the natural gas is "shaved off" during periods of great demand]

PEC, abbreviation of PHOTOELECTROCHEMICAL CELL.

In effect, a PEC cell splits H_2O just as may be done in electrolysis by electrical current from a battery or other energy source. But in this case, the energy comes from sunlight. *Harry B. Gray, "Chemistry," The World Book Science Annual 1977 (1976), p 261*

[1976]

-pe·di·a or **-pae·di·a** (-'pi: di: ə), a combining form used in names of sections of an encyclopedia. See the quotations for examples of words using this combining form.

The first volume, propaedia, will be introductory. . . . Next comes micropaedia, a 10-volume ready-reference dictionary of 10,300 pages, lavishly illustrated in colour. Finally, there is macropaedia, 19 volumes of substantive essays ranging the world of learning. *The Times (London), Jan. 12, 1974, p 12*

The Alphapedia was conceived as a finding device for the Colorpedia. *Hugh Kenner, Review of The Random House Encyclopedia, Harper's, Dec. 1977, p 105*

[1974, abstracted from *(en)cyclopedia* or *(en)cyclopaedia*]

pe·do·chem·i·cal (ˌpi: dou'kem ə kəl), *adj.* of or having to do with the chemical composition of, or changes in, soil.

The sources of trace metals in soils include those derived from geochemical and pedochemical weathering of rocks which make up the parent materials of soils. *Albert L. Page, "Soil Chemistry," McGraw-Hill Yearbook of Science and Technology 1974, p 381*

[1974, from Greek *pédon* soil + English *chemical*]

pelican crossing or **pelican,** *n. British.* a crosswalk with traffic lights that can be activated by a pedestrian.

One particular concern is the pelican crossing: old people tend to distrust them, fearing that the lights will change before they can reach the other side of the road, and will deliberately choose other (and more dangerous) places to cross. *Peter Waymark, "Motoring," The Times (London), Feb. 19, 1976, p 27*

The GLC [Greater London Council] survey . . . studied 40 pelicans which had been converted from zebras; 31 pelicans where there had been no previous controlled crossing, and 32 pelicans with vehicle-actuated equipment. *"Technology: How Safe Are Pelican Crossings?" New Scientist, June 24, 1976, p 702*

[1968, formed irregularly from *pedestrian light controlled,* and patterned on *zebra crossing* (1952) a crosswalk painted with black and white stripes]

pel·le·tron ('pel ə,tran), *n.* an electrostatic generator of metal beads or pellets separated by insulating material to form a current-carrying belt for accelerating charged particles.

Charge flows off smoothly after contact, so there is no spark abrasion. In most Pelletrons the returning pellets are charged opposite to the ingoing ones to give current doubling. *Raymond G. Herb, "Particle Accelerator," McGraw-Hill Yearbook of Science and Technology 1976, p 316*

[1972, blend of *pellet* and *-tron*] Compare LADDERTRON.

penholder, *n.* or **penholder grip,** a way of gripping a table tennis paddle in which the handle is held like a pen, with the blade pointing down.

The penholder, preferred by the East, is gripped with the thumb and forefinger and employs only one side of the bat. It saves you rubber and provides enormous mechanical advantage. Almost every Oriental champion uses it with shattering effect. *Stefan Kanfer, "The Demonic Game of Plock-Plack," The New York Times Magazine, April 2, 1972, p 52*

[1971]

pen register, an electronic device connected to a subscriber's telephone line at an exchange that prints the numbers called and the date, time, and duration of telephone calls.

Because a pen register automatically keeps a record of whom someone calls, when, and how often, and because the phone company, some businesses, law enforcement, and the intelligence community use them, pen registers are becoming the focus of a new kind of debate over a citizen's right to privacy as guaranteed by the Fourth Amendment. *Deborah Shapley, "Pen Registers: The 'Appropriate Technology' Approach to Bugging," Science, Feb. 17, 1977, p 749*

[1966, patterned on earlier *pen recorder*]

pen·ta·dec·a·pep·tide (ˌpen tə,dek ə'pep taid), *n.* a proteinlike molecule consisting of 15 amino acids.

In the report, published in July, 1972, the investigators describe how they isolated an active substance they named "scotophobin" . . . In view of their uncertainty as to the precise structure, they synthesized three pentadecapeptides. They reported that one had biological and chemical properties identical to those of the naturally occurring material. *Earl A. Evans, Jr., "Biology: Scotophobin," The 1974 World Book Year Book, p 226*

[1972, from *pentadeca-* fifteen (from Late Greek *pentadeka-*) + *peptide*]

pen·ton ('pen,tan), *n.* a group of five interdependent units in the outer protein shell of a virion (virus particle).

After a further 3 days . . . during which time there is a loss of pentons from the virion and a consequent greater susceptibility to disruption, DNA was extracted from purified virions. *J. K. McDougall and A. R. Dunn, "Letters to Nature: In Situ Hybridization of Adenovirus RNA and DNA," Nature, April 14, 1972, p 347*

[1971, from *pent-* five + *-on* elementary unit]

people journalism, a form of journalism, chiefly pictorial, devoted to the activities of celebrities.

"People journalism" . . . had its origins in Time magazine, in a department called "People," which was eventually allowed to swing as a single between its own covers on supermarket counters. Even we, at the Times company, have spawned an "Us." In "people journalism," the media become as important as the personages they cover. *"Topics," The New York Times, Dec. 6, 1979, p A30*

[1979]

pep·stat·in (pep'stæt in), *n.* a chemical compound that inhibits the action of certain enzymes, which break down proteins. Pepstatin has been isolated from various species of streptomyces.

Pepstatin could become a valuable tool for investigating the role of renin in various forms of experimental hypertension. *F. Gross, et al., "Inhibition of the Renin-Angiotensinogen Reaction by Pepstatin," Science, Feb. 11, 1972, p 656*

péquiste

[1972, from *pep*sin + -*stat* inhibiting substance + -*in* (chemical suffix)]

pé·quiste or **Pé·quiste** (pei'ki:st), *n.* a member of the PARTI QUÉBECOIS.

The Péquistes are off and running. A referendum is promised (its timing is uncertain but the general expectation is that it will come in about two years) and ministers speak confidently of their future as an independent nation. *Ivan Barnes, "The Canadians: Separatists Pose Greatest Challenge," The Times (London), June 3, 1977, p 1*

—*adj.* of or relating to the Parti Québecois.

Let's suppose that the péquiste government succeeds in its first 18 months in office in delivering the goods in the rather modest pledges it made during the campaign. *Claude Ryan, Maclean's, Dec. 27, 1976, p 8*

[1973, from Canadian French *péquiste*, from (the French pronunciation of) *P.Q.*, abbreviation of Parti Québecois + -*iste* -ist] Compare INDÉPENDANTISTE.

pe·ren·ni·ty (pə'ren ə ti:), *n.* continuance for a long time; permanence; perpetuity.

M Chirac told party officers yesterday that his objectives were to insure the perennity of Gaullism and to win the next general election. *The Times (London), Dec. 20, 1976, p 4*

[1972, from French *pérennité*, from Latin *perennitās*, from *perennis* perennial]

▶ This is a reborrowing or revival of a 17th-century word. The OED records it as obsolete, citing three instances of its use in 1597, 1641, and 1713. The related word *perenniality* (derived from *perennial*) has been in use since the mid-1800's though not nearly as frequently as the synonyms *permanence* and *perpetuity*.

per·flu·o·ro·chem·i·cal (pər,flu: ər ə'kem ə kəl), *n.* any of a group of chemical compounds in which hydrogen has been replaced by fluorine. Emulsions of such chemicals have been used in experiments as short-term substitutes for blood.

The perfluorochemicals, like blood itself, can carry oxygen and carbon dioxide, since both of these gases are very soluble in these compounds. *Edwin S. Weaver, "Biochemistry," 1974 Collier's Encyclopedia Year Book (1973), p 172*

—*adj.* of or relating to such chemicals.

Research toward breathable liquids has progressed from pressurized saline to the use of perfluorochemical liquids. *Janet H. Weinberg, Science News, Sept. 28, 1974, p 202*

[1973, from *per*- of the highest valence + *fluoro*- fluorine + *chemical*] See ARTIFICIAL BLOOD.

performance art, a form of theatrical performance or presentation which combines dancing and acting with music, photography, films, and other art forms.

Related to the "happenings" of the '60s was the Performance Art of the '70s, theatrical in presentation or form and sculptural in concept. The artist or performers present an internalized commentary between their bodies and the environment. This kinetic imagery, however, is both personal and general, for it is self-referential in content but usually ritualistic in form. Performance Art was centered in the U.S., England, and West Germany. *Robert J. Loescher, "Art and Art Exhibitions," Britannica Book of the Year 1977, p 144*

Performance art. Distinctions between painting, sculp-

350

ture, theater, and choreography were merged and blurred. Diaghilev's teams of composer, dancer, and painter, were reconstituted often in one person. *Henry Geldzahler, "Art: Abandonment of the Heroic," New York Post, Dec. 29, 1979, p 15*

[1973] Compare INFORMATION ART.

performance artist: One of the most controlled and sophisticated performance artists is David Gordon, who also happens to like words, although he classifies himself as a dancer, not a writer. (I don't know of many writers who have been attracted to the form; those who have been have generally seen it as no occasion to lay their verbal gifts aside.) *Arlene Croce, "Dancing," The New Yorker, May 15, 1978, p 126*

performance contract, *U.S.* a contract by a private educational business firm to improve the educational performance of public-school students to a specified level for an agreed-on fee.

Roger R. Sullivan, president of Behavioral Research Laboratories, which has performance contracts operating in seven cities but was not one of the companies used in the test, said: "We feel that a performance contract, done properly, can be a great asset to American education." *U.S. News and World Report, Feb. 14, 1972, p 52*

[1971]

performance contracting: More than 30 cities have experimented with "performance contracting," and one poll showed that two-thirds of the nation's school board members were interested in trying it. *Time, Feb. 14, 1972, p 42*

performance contractor: The program was further marred by a number of complaints that employees of the performance contractor were using corporal punishment to control and discipline students. *Albert Shanker, "Where We Stand," The New York Times, Jan. 2, 1972, Sec. 4, p 7*

performance theater, a form of theater in which productions are developed cooperatively by the actors.

Some of the brightest moments in U.S. theater in 1970 were to be found on the avant-garde front, in particular, with what was sometimes referred to as "performance theater." In this new kind of work . . . actors . . . either improvised without a written text, or freely adapted an old (dramatic or nondramatic) text, or had a text written to suit their needs by a playwright who worked with them as a member of the company. *Julius Novick, "Theater," The 1971 Compton Yearbook, p 458*

[1970]

per·i·na·tol·o·gy (,per ə nei'tal ə dʒi:), *n.* the medical study of the period around childbirth, especially the period including five months preceding birth and the first month after.

[The] chief of the Maternal and Child Health Center's division of perinatology described to the press and a large number of hospital personnel today the problems that were posed in caring for and then separating the twins. *Roy R. Silver, "6-Month-Old Siamese Are Separated," The New York Times, Sept. 29, 1977, p 39*

[1976, from *perinatal* (1950's) of or relating to the period around childbirth (from *peri*- around + *natal*) + -*ology* study of]

perinatologist, *n.:* At the same time that perinatologists have been concerning themselves with what goes on in the life of the fetus during its nine months of development, the birth process itself has become safer for the newborn, most dramatically through the use of fetal-heart monitors. *Rita Kramer, "Revolution in the Delivery Room," The New York Times Magazine, July 11, 1976, p 21*

permissive, *adj. Biology.* permitting replication (of genetic material, viruses, etc.).

In non-permissive primary mouse embryo cells some 24 h after infection with SV40 [a virus] the extent and pattern of transcription are almost identical to that in permissive cells late in infection. *"Hidden Subtleties," Nature, Oct. 13, 1972, p 368*

[1972] Compare NONPERMISSIVE.

person, *n.* ► 1. *Redefinition of "person" to exclude unborn child.* During the 1970's the 800-year-old word *person* was redefined and put to new uses owing largely to the influence of the WOMEN'S MOVEMENT. One far-reaching refinement of the meaning of *person* occurred in January, 1973, when the U.S. Supreme Court ruled (in *Roe v. Wade*) that "the word person, as used in the 14th Amendment, does not include the unborn." As this meant that a fetus is not entitled to constitutional protection until it becomes "viable" (defined as at approximately seven months), the ruling invalidated the antiabortion laws of many states, in effect legalizing abortion in the United States. See the note under ABORTION. See also TEST-TUBE BABY.

2, *Use of "persons" to replace "people." Person* in the plural has for some time been invading the domain of *people;* it is the universal plural in notices, for example: "Capacity 13 persons." This plural now produces sentences such as "How many persons attended the lecture?" and "Their best friends are usually persons involved in the arts."

3. *Use of "person" as a genderless designation.* More generally, person is increasingly used as a replacement for both *man* and *woman.* For example, a classified advertisement may seek a "person Friday" instead of a "girl Friday." To a lesser extent, *person* replaces *boy* and *girl,* especially for teenagers; for younger boys and girls *child* remains acceptable, though it tends to be displaced by *person* in institutional surroundings, such as schools and hospitals. See the entries PERSONKIND and PERSON-YEAR.

The most obvious new use of *person* is to replace *-man* or *-woman* in scores of established compounds. See -PERSON below.

The following quotations illustrate the use of *person* to eliminate reference to gender, even whimsically:

Chairman briefly became chairperson, but many now settle simply for chair, as in "she was the chair of the committee." . . . The Naval Academy wisely insists that its women will be called midshipmen. Person is still acceptable when used independently to designate either a man or a woman. When White House Press Secretary Ron Nessen mentions future Government appointees, he is very careful these days to speak of person instead of man. *Time, Jan. 5, 1976, p 13*

Then Anne Wexler . . . talks about the child-care centers set up during the campaign, how they had been "manned on a full-time basis." "You mean *personned* on a full-time

basis," quips a male AP reporter in a surprising burst of feminism. *Lynn Sherr, Saturday Review, Aug. 5, 1972, p 6*

► See MAN, WOMAN.

person-, a combining form sometimes used in place of *man* and *woman* in compounds to avoid reference to the individual's gender. The following are examples, some that show the strain to which legitimate efforts can lead:

personhole, *n.:* When the city council of Woonsocket, R.I., three weeks ago approved some job descriptions that eliminated supposedly sexist language, a utility man became a utility person, whose duties included "building personholes." Ever since, Woonsocket has been the butt of jokes from as far away as California. *Time, Oct. 2, 1978, p 37*

person-ness, *n.:* Thomas Savage's *Daddy's Girl* (Ballantine, 95c) is one of those small, beautifully written novels often overlooked in the hardcover crush. It's a "lost lady" story about cheeky, bright Marty Linehan, whose father deserted her mother, and who muddles through too many marriages and lovers, and far too much liquor, seeking some assurance of her own person-ness. *Review of "Daddy's Girl" by Thomas Savage, Saturday Review, April 29, 1972, p 74*

person-trip, *n.:* The number of "person-trips" (one person taking one trip) exceeded 660 million, an improvement of 16 percent, and the total number of miles traveled amounted to more than 541 billion, a gain of 14 percent. *John Brannon Albright, "Notes: Out of Town It's July Fourth, Too," The New York Times, June 27, 1976, Sec. 10, p 25*

[1970] See also entries below for compounds in *person-* having specialized meaning or greater-than-average frequency.

-person, a combining form used in place of *man* and *woman* in compounds to avoid reference to the individual's gender. Often, however, compounds in *-person* are applied specifically to women, as when a prime minister who is a woman is referred to as a *statesperson,* and such usage defeats the purpose of the replacement.

The plural of compounds ending in *-person* may be *-persons* or *-people;* see for example ADPERSON. Some of the commonly used compounds are main entries in this book, e.g. ANCHORPERSON, LAYPERSON, SPOKESPERSON. Some compounds in *-person* (e.g. *henchperson*) are fabricated facetiously or for comic effect. The following are recent examples of the use of this combining form.

businessperson, *n.:* If there is a budding business-person in your vicinity, check the local Farmers Home Administration office listed under the U.S. Department of Agriculture in the telephone book. *"Setting Up In Business," Woman's Day, March 1974, p 24*

councilperson, *n.:* No caption-writer in his normal senses would solemnly employ such ludicrous words as "councilpersons" and "chairpersons" and "salespersons." *Anthony Lejeune, "America Through British Eyes," National Review, Feb. 6, 1976, p 92*

fisherperson, *n.:* Check your impulse to indulge in salty vernacular, especially when among veteran fisherpersons. *Paul W. Wales, "Fish and How to Capture Them," The New Yorker, Sept. 6, 1976, p 24*

► The U.S. Department of Labor uses *fisher* instead

of *fisherperson* or *fisherman*. *Fisherperson* is as tautologous as *fisherman;* in both terms the *-er* performs the same function as *man* or *person*. See also the note under HE/SHE.

henchperson, *n.:* This week Chairperson Mitchell and her henchpersons looked at the way education brainwashes girls into accepting a submissive domestic role. *Phillip Whitehead, The Listener, March 1, 1973, p 286*

houseperson, *n.:* The Pastry Bureau is supposed to (and probably does) busy itself in teaching the British houseperson to take more interest in better pastry. *Harold Wilshaw, The Manchester Guardian Weekly, Oct. 19, 1975, p 21*

marksperson, *n.:* The Army has decided that all women soldiers donning their new uniform after June 30 must become qualified "markspersons" with the M16 rifle. *The Tuscaloosa News (Alabama), March 26, 1975, p 8*

policeperson, *n.:* If, for whatever reason, it has been determined necessary to be of a certain height to be a policeperson, then it seems to follow that only those men and women above that height should be considered. *Barbara Deinhardt, New Haven, Conn., in a Letter to the Editor, Newsweek, Nov. 13, 1972, p 15*

repairperson, *n.:* Need a Fix? . . . Making home repairpersons from finger smashers. *Headline in The National Observer, May 25, 1974, p 6*

second baseperson: The parents of a sometimes second baseperson say they will seek a federal injunction to allow their 8-year-old daughter to play without the protection of a boy's plastic athletic protector cup. *"Boys Will Be Boys, But . . . ?" The Tuscaloosa News (Alabama), June 14, 1975, p 7*

sideperson, *n.:* The saturnalia ended with Alice's [Cooper] four gasping sidepersons receiving oxygen from the kindly police. *Maureen Orth, "Music: Mr. America," Newsweek, May 28, 1973, p 65*

spaceperson, *n.:* Applications are invited from suitably qualified candidates for the post of the first British spaceperson. *Alan Hamilton, The Times (London), June 3, 1977, p 1*

workperson, *n.:* The actual manufacture and distribution of the fixtures themselves is . . . rather a matter for the engineers than for workpersons. *Teresa May Alcott, "Why All Women Must Now Arise," Esquire, Dec. 1972, p 226*

yachtsperson, *n.:* If you are a yachtsperson and have never visited Edgartown, go. *M. Phillip Copp, Town and Country, Aug. 1974, p 37*

[1972, generalized chiefly from *chairperson* (1971), though influenced by earlier *salesperson* (OEDS 1928) and perhaps *tradesperson* (OED 1886)]

personal computer, a microcomputer that fits in a small area, such as a desk top, and can be programmed and operated by one person.

We started a little personal-computer manufacturing company in a garage in Los Altos in 1976, Now we're the largest personal-computer company in the world. We make what we think of as the Rolls-Royce of personal computers. It's a *domesticated* computer. People expect blinking lights, but what they find is that it looks like a portable typewriter, which, connected to a suitable readout screen, is able to display in color. There's a feedback it gives to people who use it, and the enthusiasm of the users is tremendous. *"The Talk of the Town," The New Yorker, Nov. 14, 1977, p 41*

We visualized the personal computer of the 1980s as a notebook-sized package whose front side was a flat-screen reflective display, like a liquid-crystal watch face . . . The machine would be completely self-contained. However, it

also could be connected to hi-fi sets to create music, to other personal computers for group projects . . . *Alan C. Kay, "Programming Your Own Computer," The World Book Science Annual 1979 (1978), p 185*

[1977] Compare HOME COMPUTER.

personal flotation device, *U.S. and Canadian.* any device designed to keep a person afloat.

Personal flotation devices, (as the Coast Guard calls life jackets, life vests and other kinds of life preservers), must be bought in the proper size—and not necessarily "the bigger the better." *Bill McKeown, Popular Mechanics, June 1973, p 30*

[1972] *Abbreviation:* PFD

personal rescue enclosure, *U.S.* another name for BEACHBALL.

Hard-pressed for elbow room in the shuttle's crew-carrying orbiter section, engineers at the National Aeronautics and Space Administration's Johnson Space Center in Houston have developed the beachball, called the "personal rescue enclosure," as a compact escape system to replace bulky spacesuits in case the orbiter becomes disabled or a crew member is injured. *"Beachballs to the Space-Shuttle Rescue," Science News, May 22, 1976, p 327*

[1976]

personkind, *n.* the human race; humanity (used in place of *mankind* to eliminate the reference to *man*).

Readers and writers of both sexes must resist onefully any meaningless neologisms. To do less is to encourage another manifestation of prejudice—against reason, meaning and eventually personkind itself. *Stefan Kanfer, "Sispeak: A Msguided Attempt to Change History," Time, Oct. 23, 1972, p 79*

There really are people who think it is very funny to refer to "personkind" . . . and one clown even wrote a letter to the *Daily Another Newspaper* beginning "Person," instead of "Sir." *Bernard Levin, The Times (London), Jan. 13, 1976, p 14*

[1972] See PERSON.

▶ *Humankind* is an alternate term that has been in the language since about 1645.

person-year, *n.* a unit of work equivalent to the work done by one person in one year, usually calculated without absence, or a unit of life lived in one year, used to calculate medical or population statistics (used in place of *man-year* to eliminate the reference to *man*).

The results of a massive study—"based on a total of 29,217 person-years of experience"—into the effect of a cholesterol-lowering diet on deaths from coronary heart disease have just been published in Lancet. *"Diet Halves Heart-Disease Deaths," New Scientist, Oct. 26, 1972, p 190*

Expressed another way, in a population of constant size the birth rate is the number of births per person-year lived and the average duration of life is the number of person-years lived per birth. *Ansley J. Coale, "The History of the Human Population," Scientific American, Sept. 1974, p 44*

[1972] See PERSON.

pet·a- ('pet ə-), a prefix meaning one quadrillion of any standard unit in the international meter-kilogram-second system of measurements.

In deriving units the SI [Système International] emphasizes that they should be formed from the base and supplementary units in a coherent manner. One result of this principle is a series of 16 prefixes that should be applied to the basic units to indicate large or small quantities. For large quantities they are deka (10^1), hecto (10^2), kilo (10^3), mega (10^6), giga (10^9), tera (10^{12}), peta (10^{15}) and exa (10^{18}). *"Science and the Citizen," Scientific American, March 1976, p 60A*

[1976, probably from the Greek root *peta-* spread out]

petro-. Originally *petro-* was used as the combining form of Greek *pétra* meaning "rock" or *pétros* meaning "stone," as in *petrography*. Later, *petro-* became a combining form for "petroleum" (= rock oil) and was used chiefly to form technical or scientific terms such as *petrochemical* and *petrolization*.

A new meaning arose during the mid-1970's as a worldwide ENERGY CRISIS developed. When the states belonging to OPEC substantially increased the price of petroleum, they greatly increased their wealth and influence, particularly in the formation of Western nations' Middle Eastern policy. At that time *petro-* began to acquire the meaning "based on or having to do with the wealth and power of the oil-exporting countries, especially those of OPEC." The following are some examples.

petrobillions, *n.pl.*: Top Arab leaders have now decided not to put their petrobillions into U.S. Treasury bonds . . . *Arnaud De Borchgrave, Newsweek, Oct. 7, 1974, p 52*

petrocrat, *n.* [*petro-* + bureau*crat*]: A new order is the ultimate goal of the petrocrats. Their aim is to lead many of the Third World nations in an economic revolution that is already bringing a radical redistribution of the world's wealth and political power. *"Man of the Year: Faisal," Time, Jan. 6, 1975, p 12*

petrocurrency, *n.*: Part of sterling's strength may be its position as the "petro-currency" and opinion is growing that the continued high rates and a strong currency will make Britain a haven for the even greater OPEC cash surpluses which will accumulate following the latest oil price rise. *William Darling, "UK 'Heading for Slump'," The Manchester Guardian Weekly, July 15, 1979, p 3*

petrofunds, *n.pl.*: As 1974 drew to an end there was increasing recognition that "recycling" petrofunds meant merely the piling of debt on top of debt. *Miroslav A. Kriz, "International Exchange and Payments," Britannica Book of the Year 1975, p 294*

Petro-Islam, *n.*: The United States will again be underscoring the importance it attaches to Saudi Arabia's role as a power broker in the Middle East, the driving force that one Egyptian writer calls "Petro-Islam." *Bernard Gwertzman, "Saudi Arabia, Mideast Power Broker," The New York Times, Oct. 23, 1977, Sec. 4, p 2*

petromoney, *n.*: The boom in Arab property purchases in London has attracted its fair share of Saudi money. Hotels and apartment buildings have fallen to the tidal wave of petro-money. *Peter Hobday, The Times (London), Special Report: Saudi Arabia, Sept. 24, 1976, p II*

petropolitics, *n.*: The energy crisis . . . may have been artificially imposed, but its implications stretch far beyond petropolitics. *Time, Dec. 3, 1973, p 44*

petro-sterling, *n.*: Moreover, while most of world oil trade goes on in dollars, a significant amount also takes place in British pounds. So we have petro-sterling as well as petrodollars. *Richard N. Cooper, Saturday Review, Jan. 25, 1975, p 11*

See also PETRODOLLARS and PETROPOWER.

petrodollars, *n.pl.* surplus dollars accumulated by oil-exporting countries, especially when used for loans and investments in oil-importing countries.

Iran, seeking investment outlets for its petrodollars, said it had tentatively agreed to infuse $300 million into the ailing carrier, enough to ease Pan Am's current financial strain. *David Pauly and James Bishop Jr., "Airlines: Pan Iran Airways," Newsweek, March 3, 1975, p 60*

petrodollar, *singular noun and attributive use.*

There are many other kinds of help we could give the Arabs . . . but all they seem to want from us is arms. Since 1973, we have sold them more than $12 billion worth. Not that we mind. It is an effective way to recycle the petrodollar. *Tom Gervasi, "Eagles, Doves, and Hawks," Harper's, May 1978, p 21*

. . . the unpredictable financial consequences of the massive petrodollar surpluses being acquired by the oil states. *John Palmer, The Manchester Guardian Weekly, Nov. 16, 1974, p 3*

[1973] See RECYCLE, def. 3.

petropower, *n.* **1** the financial or political power of oil-rich countries.

It was a devastatingly ironic example of petropower. The Libyan Arab Foreign Bank will lend Fiat $104 million and spend an additional $311 million to buy newly issued Fiat stock and bonds. *Time, Dec. 13, 1976, p 65*

2 a country having power based primarily on possession of abundant supplies of petroleum.

Iran has thus blossomed into a formidable petropower—a regional political force that must be reckoned with and even, perhaps, one of the world's potentially great nations. *Karsten Prager, "Iran," Britannica Book of the Year 1975, p 37*

[1975]

PFD, *U.S. and Canadian.* abbreviation of PERSONAL FLOTATION DEVICE.

This new PFD is not intended to supplant the outstanding worth of the MoT [Ministry of Transport]-approved jacket. The aim is to increase the chances of survival in the water; it won't guarantee it. . . . The big "must" of course is that the PFD's must be designed to float a person in a safe position, and pass a stiff leak test. *Consumer Contact (Ottawa, Canada), June 1972, p 1*

Coast Guard approved PFD's may include life rings, buoyant cushions, buoyant vests, or buoyant jackets. . . . You are legally required to carry at least one PFD for every person in the boat. *"Boating: Life Savers," Field and Stream, April 1973, p 83*

[1972]

PG, a symbol used in the United States to designate motion pictures not restricted to any age group but requiring parental discretion and guidance. The approximate British equivalent is *A*.

The picture meticulously avoids nudity, and gets its reward: a PG rating from the M.P.A.A. *Pauline Kael, "The Current Cinema," The New Yorker, Dec. 23, 1972, p 55*

In *Whatever Happened to Randolph Scott*, the Statler Brothers examine the plight of the movie-oriented family man who must plow through G, PG, R and, especially X ratings. *Time, May 6, 1974, p 53*

[1968, abbreviation of *P*arental *G*uidance]

▶ See the note under G.

PGM, abbreviation of *precision-guided munition.*

Phalangist

The development of PGMs was greatly stimulated by the very effective use made of laser-guided bombs in Vietnam ... A PGM may be an air-to-air, air-to-surface, surface-to-air, or surface-to-surface weapon and may be fired from an artillery piece, aircraft, ship, or vehicle, or be launched by an individual soldier. *Frank Barnaby, "Precision Warfare," New Scientist, May 8, 1975, p 305*

[1975]

Pha·lan·gist (fə'læn dʒist), *n.* a member of the Phalange, a conservative Christian paramilitary organization and political party in Lebanon.

Hundreds of Moslem and leftist gunmen, backed by armored vehicles yesterday drove right-wing Phalangists from the towering, battered Holiday Inn, gaining an important military and psychological victory. *James M. Markham, "Beirut Leftists Seize Holiday Inn in Heavy Assault," The New York Times, March 22, 1976, p 1*

Attributive use.

The appalling civil war, between the alliance of Lebanese Muslims and Palestinian radicals on one side and the Phalangist forces representing the hitherto economically dominant Christian element in Lebanese society on the other, had begun in April 1975. *A. C. Turner, "Middle East," The Americana Annual 1977, p 333*

[1958, 1970, from French *Phalangiste*, from *Phalange*, the party name, originally the French name of the Spanish fascist *Falange* party founded in 1933, ultimately from Latin *phalanx, -angis*, from Greek *phálanx, -angos* rank of soldiers]

phal·lo·crat ('fæl ə,kræt), *n.* one who believes in the superiority or rule of the male sex; a male chauvinist.

Granted, not every art historian has been as nobly certain of the natural order as that unruffled Italian phallocrat; yet the fact remains that until quite recently, the work of women artists did not have a history. *"Art: Rediscovered—Women Painters," Time, Jan. 10, 1977, p 60*

"Women's cooking is made by little changes, not great inventions," Mr. Gault said. "Although I don't know, I've met women . . . of course, they may have been men."

"He's not a democrat, he's a phallocrat," one of the men said laughing. *Flora Lewis, "For French Chefs, Fraternité et Egalité," The New York Times, Sept. 28, 1977, p 46*

[1977, from French *phallocrate*, from Greek *phallós* penis, phallus + *krátos* rule]

phallocratic, *adj.:* A young heart trapped in an aging body, the private energy crisis of nature, is a suitable case for fictional treatment. But the phallocratic and medical detail meant to be portentous becomes absurd. *Philip Howard, "Fiction," Review of "The Way Out" by Romain Gary, The Times (London), June 30, 1977, p 14*

phar·ma·co·ki·net·ics (,far mə kou ki'net iks), *n.* **1** the reaction of the body to particular drugs; the way a drug is absorbed, distributed, metabolized, etc., in the body.

The magnitude of the antitumour effect depends on a complex interaction between cell kinetics and pharmacokinetics. *Kurt Heilmann, New Scientist, Sept. 27, 1973, p 748*

Compare BIOAVAILABILITY.

2 the study of the absorption, distribution, metabolism, etc., of drugs.

From pharmacokinetics . . . has come the concept of

minimal alveolar concentration (MAC), which is defined as the concentration of an anesthetic that must be present in the lungs before anesthesia can be achieved. *Stanley A. Feldman, Britannica Book of the Year 1969, p 491*

[1966, from *pharmaco-* drug (from Greek *phármakon*) + *kinetics*]

phen·cyc·li·dine (fen'sik lə,di:n), *n.* a depressant drug used to immobilize animals, and illegally as a narcotic popularly known as ANGEL DUST. *Formula:* $C_{17}H_{25}N$

And if you want to see a Siberian tiger, *Panthera tigris altaica*, "immobilized with phencyclidine and promazine . . ." turn to the photographs. *Arthur Bourne, New Scientist, May 14, 1970, p 345*

By any name, phencyclidine (PCP) is the most dangerous drug to hit the streets since LSD became widely available a decade ago. Its use is growing rapidly; a National Institute on Drug Abuse (NIDA) study found that nearly a third of the young patients reporting to drug-treatment centers have tried PCP and one-fifth used it regularly. *"Behavior: PCP: 'A Terror of a Drug'," Time, Dec. 19, 1977, p 53*

[1964, short for *phenylcyclo*hexyl piper*idine*] *Abbreviation:* PCP

phen·met·ra·zine (fen'met rə,zi:n), *n.* a drug related to amphetamine that mimics the action of the sympathetic nervous system, used as an appetite depressant. *Formula:* $C_{11}H_{15}NO$

Pressure is now coming from several other European countries, including Denmark, Finland, Iceland, Norway, Sweden and Yugoslavia, to reclassify amphetamines (and also the related compounds methylphenidate, phenmetrazine and pipradol) as dangerous drugs. *Oliver Gillie, Science Journal, Feb. 1970, p 7*

[1965, from *phenyl* + *methyl* + *tetra-* four + *azine*]

Philadelphia chromosome, an abnormally small, chromosome found in the blood-forming cells of many patients with chronic myelocytic leukemia.

In each chapter appropriate and informative tables and figures are included: the lack of a picture of a metaphase with the Ph[1]-chromosome (Philadelphia chromosome) is regrettable since the chromosomal anomaly is the only consistent and characteristic one established to date for any mammalian malignancy. *Avery A. Sandberg, "Tumor Cytogenetics," Review of "The Role of Chromosomes in Cancer Biology" by Leo C. Koller, Science, April 27, 1973, p 401*

[1963, so called because it was discovered by Peter C. Nowell of the University of Pennsylvania School of Medicine in *Philadelphia*]

phone phreak ('foun ,fri:k), Also spelled **phone freak.** a person who uses electronic equipment illegally to make free telephone calls.

Placing the signals related to a call on separate circuits . . . will also increase greatly the difficulty that so-called "phone phreaks" have in placing long-distance calls without paying toll charges by using devices that imitate the phone system's internal tone signals. *Victor K. McElheny, The New York Times, Jan. 18, 1976, p 7*

[1972, *phreak*, alteration of *freak* by influence of *phone*] Also shortened to PHREAK. See BLUE BOX.

phone phreakdom: The pharaoh of phone phreakdom, a loose-knit organization of tech heads who try to rip off the phone company with sophisticated home-concocted electronic devices, got busted in nearby Stroudsburg last year

354

by Ma Bell's security squad for operating a computer "capable of theft of telecommunications service." *High Times, Jan. 1979, p 40*

phone phreaking: A new offensive against "phone phreaking" may have claimed its first victim last month. An alleged phone phreak had dialled a motoring organisation. . . . But, in mid-call, his line was abruptly crossed by the Post Office's special phone phreak detectives. *"Battle With Phone Phreaks Hots Up," New Scientist, April 3, 1975, p 29*

phor·bol ('fɔr‚bɔːl), *n.* any of a class of chemicals derived from various tumor-producing compounds in croton oil, used in biochemical research.

The phorbols prevented the differentiation of stem cells. The power of different phorbols to prevent the differentiation of mouse red blood cells turned out to correspond to their power to promote skin tumours caused by chemical carcinogens. *The Times (London), Aug. 22, 1977, p 14*

[1976, from Greek *phorbé* pasture, food, fodder + English *-ol* an alcohol]

photic driver, a weapon combining strobe lights and ultrasound, for use in riot control.

The Army has stopped short of introducing the strobe lights of the projected "photic driver" with their ability to induce epileptic fits, but its use could still be guaranteed to produce another anti-Army and communally divisive outcry. *Robert Rodwell, New Scientist, Sept. 20, 1973, p 668*

One of the most controversial is the photic driver, a new form of crowd dispersal weapon designed to help armies and police forces to counter riot situations. The machine resembling the strobe lighting effects used in discotheques, combines flashing lights and ultrasonic sound waves to produce an overpowering feeling of sickness. *The Times (London), Oct. 3, 1973, p 2*

[1973, *photic* of or using light, from Greek *phōs, phōtós* light]

photobiologist, *n.* a specialist in photobiology (the branch of biology dealing with the relation of light to living things).

Solar energy research is nothing if not multidisciplinary, and architects and engineers rub shoulders with plant breeders and photobiologists. *Eleanor Lawrence, "Solar Energy in Britain," Nature, Jan. 3, 1975, p 2*

[1970, from *photobiology* (1958)]

photocall, *n. British.* a session in which publicity pictures are taken of celebrities or government officials. The U.S. equivalent is PHOTO OPPORTUNITY.

Mr Callaghan had a particularly busy time. Yesterday he put his nose into the fresh air only once for a photocall for which only a third of the assembled leaders turned up. *Ronald Faux, The Times (London), June 13, 1977, p 5*

[1967, from *photo* photograph + *call* invitation or request to appear (as in *curtain call*)]

photodegrade, *v.t., v.i.* to decompose by the action of light, especially sunlight.

Kenneth W. L. Moilanen and Donald G. Crosby of the University of California at Davis have demonstrated two routes by which DDT may have photodegraded into PCBs, using wavelengths which occur in sunlight. *"Monitor: PCB Pollution May Stem from DDT Breakdown," New Scientist, May 24, 1973, p 462*

[1973, back formation from *photodegradation* (1950's)]

photodegradable, *adj.:* One pound of active ingredient is 900 times as effective as a pound of pesticide and must be applied only half as often, the developers claim. The fibers, made of an acetal resin, are photodegradable and the EPA found the system had no ill effects on wildlife, soil and water. *Science News, June 3, 1978, p 360*

photodissociate, *v.t.* to dissociate chemically by the absorption of light.

A meteorite impact, Veverka suggests, could crack the fragile crust, producing a huge fountain of dilute ammonia that is quickly photodissociated by ultraviolet light into hydrogen and nitrogen. *Jonathan Eberhart, Science News, Jan. 1, 1977, p 12*

[1970, back formation from *photodissociation* (1940's)]

photoelectrochemical cell, an electrochemical cell that produces current when exposed to light, used experimentally to convert solar power to chemical energy.

As might be suspected, the central element of the photoelectrochemical cell is the photoelectrode. Virtually any electrode material will give photoeffects, and it has been known for over 100 years that irradiation of an electrode can result in the nonspontaneous flow of electric current in the external circuit. *Mark S. Wrighton, "Conversion of Sunlight to Chemical Fuel," McGraw-Hill Yearbook of Science and Technology 1978, p 14*

[1973] *Abbreviation:* PEC.

photoelectrode, *n.* an electrode that is stimulated to action by light.

Another idea that the team came up with was to etch the photoelectrode to improve light pick-up. Whereas previously they had at best achieved power conversion efficiencies of around 1.2 per cent, after etching efficiencies improved to around 9 per cent. *"Monitor: New Charge for Re-Chargeable Solar Battery," New Scientist, June 10, 1976, p 579*

[1973]

photoenvironment, *n.* an environment marked by the presence of light.

The layer [of plankton], which had migrated downward at dawn, rose again by 50m. at eclipse totality, some three hours after sunrise, lagging slightly because the rate of swimming was too slow to permit the animals to maintain themselves exactly in the optimal photoenvironment. *Ernest Maylor, "Marine Biology," Britannica Book of the Year 1976, p 469*

[1976]

photo essay, an article or book presenting a subject chiefly through photographs.

What is the future of the self-published photo essay? It may not replace the coffee-table spectacular, the scholarly monograph, or the book pegged to current events, but the new photography book is finding a growing audience of its own. *Gene Thornton, "Personal Encounters," Saturday Review, Dec. 2, 1972, p 67*

"The Other Hampton," a photo-essay on the black community of Bridgehampton, Long Island, has been published by Grossman. *The New Yorker, Feb. 11, 1974, p 128*

[1971]

photo essayist: When *Life* magazine ceased publication on December 29, some observers said the era of the black-and-white photo essay in print was over. What had in fact

Photo-Fit

happened, however, was that the photo essayist had moved on to other media—even as reader interest was moving—while *Life* (and *Look*, which had died a year earlier) stuck stubbornly to their old patterns. *Rus Arnold, "Photography," The 1973 World Book Year Book, p 462*

Pho·to·Fit ('fou tou‚fit), *n. British.* the trademark for a system of reconstructing faces from memory by using photographic alternatives of five basic facial features (forehead, eyes, nose, mouth, and chin) to make a composite photograph that approximates the description supplied by witnesses.

A new system to help the police in identification cases has been developed by a British company in cooperation with the Home Office. It is called the Photo-Fit and is a development of the Identikit system but uses photographs instead of line drawings. *Norman Fowler, The Times (London), April 23, 1970, p 5*

photofit, *Attributive use.*

The police had distributed photofit likenesses of the three men who murdered Signor Occorsio in his car as he was leaving his home to go to the law courts. *Peter Nichols, The Times (London), July 12, 1976, p 4*

[1970]

pho·to·graph·i·ca (‚fou tou'græf ə kə), *n.pl.* items of interest or of value to devotees of photography, such as antique cameras and related equipment once owned by famous photographers.

At many of the world's leading auction houses the traditional emphasis on the fine arts and expensive jewelry has had to make room, in recent years, for a new phenomenon: the burgeoning sales of photographica, the images and equipment identified with the first years of photography. *George Gilbert, "Rediscovering Photographica," 1978 Collier's Encyclopedia Year Book (1977), p 46*

[1972, from *photograph* + *-ica* by analogy with such words as *erotica* and *esoterica* or from plural of (assumed) New Latin *photographicum*]

pho·to·i·som·er·ize (‚fou tou ai'sɑm ə‚raiz), *v.t.* to change the isomeric form of (a substance) by the action of light.

Exposure to light photoisomerizes the retinal [visual pigment of retina] and initiates a series of changes in the configuration of opsin as its deep red color is replaced by light yellow. *Jeremy Baptist, "Molecular Biology: Biophysics," 1973 Britannica Yearbook of Science and the Future (1972), p 301*

[1972, back formation from *photoisomerization* (1962)]

photonovel, *n.* a novel in the form of photographs, usually with dialogue inserted in the style of comic-strip balloons.

Make way for the latest rage: Photonovels are here. Equipped with the plots of soap operas, models as characters, the color of the finest slick magazines, and comic book . . . formats, two new monthly magazines, "Darling" and "Kiss" are bound to be hits. These photonovels are the American counterparts of magazines that have been raging successes in Europe for decades. *Andrea Diehl, "Photonovels: Soapy and Clean," Daily News (New York), July 11, 1978, p 40*

Mr. Stewart, as head of Fotonovel Publications, presides over a staff of 15, turning out two 168-page photonovels a month. *Ray Walters, "Paperback Talk," The New York Times Book Review, July 22, 1979, p 27*

[1978, from Spanish *fotonovela*, from *foto* photo + *novela* novel]

photo opportunity, *U.S. and Canadian.* a session in which publicity pictures are taken of celebrities or government officials. The British equivalent is PHOTOCALL.

A husky, bearded veteran of Vietnam War coverage who now watches the White House for CBS, ruminated glumly on the morning's events: "This is the sort of thing that eats up our time. Photo opportunities, briefings, releases, more photo opportunities. Most of it doesn't mean a damn thing. But the White House grinds it out and we eat it up." *J. Anthony Lukas, "The White House Press 'Club'," The New York Times Magazine, May 15, 1977, p 22*

[1976]

photopile, *n.* a device for storing a supply of light energy from the sun to be used as fuel.

Photopiles were developed for use in space exploration, where cost is of comparatively little importance, but they are still much too expensive to be widely used on earth. *Pierre Langereux, "Power From the Sun," Nature, April 8, 1976, p 477*

[1976, from *photo-* light + *pile* battery, as in *galvanic pile*]

photorealism, *n.* a style of painting and sculpture having the realism of a photograph.

Photorealism's sudden emergence in the Whitney's "New Realism" show of 1970 caught most critics unprepared: Those who had cut their eyeteeth on various kinds of abstraction . . . were at a loss when confronted with these huge, photographically meticulous canvases that looked like oversized picture postcards. *Ruth Berenson, National Review, May 11, 1973, p 530*

[1971] Compare HYPERREALISM.

photorealist, *n., adj.:* To the photorealists of the turn of the sixties, nudity, reproduced to the last pore and hair curl, ranks with automobiles and storefronts as preferred data of painting and sculpture. *Harold Rosenberg, The New Yorker, Nov. 4, 1972, p 121*

Photorealist sculpture is there, too, though Ludwig's choice does not run to the extravagant voyeurism of John de Andrea's copulating couple, or Duane Hanson's disturbing Bowery Bums. *Caroline Tisdall, The Manchester Guardian Weekly, April 21, 1973, p 24*

phreak (fri:k), *n.* short for PHONE PHREAK.

So far, British phreaks have tended to avoid the sophisticated electronic devices used by many US phreaks. *Joseph Hanlon, "Fiddling the Telephone," New Scientist, April 5, 1973, p 23*

[1973] ▶ *Phreak* is also an easy variant of *freak* for any whimsical purpose. For example, *name phreak* is Herb Caen's term for a person who contributes a note on an oddity in a personal name to his column in the San Francisco *Chronicle*.

phy·to·a·lex·in (‚fai tou ə'lek sən), *n.* any substance produced by a plant to counteract infection.

One basis of resistance to fungal attack is the accumulation at the site of infection of compounds toxic to the potential pathogen. The production of these "phytoalexins" by the host is triggered by chemical "elicitors" of pathogenic origin. *Peter L. Webster, "Botany," Britannica Book of the Year 1977, p 466*

[1963, from *phyto-* plant + *alexin* (1892) substance in blood serum that can destroy bacteria]

PI or **P.I.**, *U.S.* abbreviation of *principal investigator*, a scientist or scholar in charge of a particular experiment or study.

One source quotes a high official in the NASA Pioneer office: "If Pioneer survives, it'll be the first time in this mission that I've been right and all the PI's (principal scientific investigators—the experimenters) have been wrong." *Science News, Nov. 24, 1973, p 325*

[1969]

pi·ca·dil·lo (pik ə'dil ou; *Spanish* pi: kɑ:'di: you), *n.* a Spanish and Latin American dish of ground meat mixed with tomatoes, garlic, onion, olives, and capers.

Who would have ever guessed, for instance, that the old Mexican street near downtown Los Angeles that looks as if it was restored by the MGM set department . . . would have one place that served delicious hand-patted soft tacos packed with picadillo. . . ? *Calvin Trillin, "Any Decent Barbecues in This Town?" The Atlantic, April 1974, p 68*

[1965, from Spanish, literally, ground meat, hash]

pickpocket, *v.t.* to rob by picking pockets.

Another customer breaks in to scold Lewis, saying, "This is the biggest ripoff place in Brooklyn. Two of my friends were pickpocketed here last week and I had to give them carfare home." *John McPhee, "A Reporter at Large," The New Yorker, July 3, 1978, p 60*

[1963, verb use of the noun (1591) meaning a thief who picks pockets; the verbal noun *pickpocketing* was originally used by Dickens in *Oliver Twist* (1838) and is still in use]

PIDE or **Pi·de** ('pi:ˌdə), *n.* the former secret intelligence organization of Portugal.

Angry workers and intellectuals gathered this afternoon in front of the Santa Clara military court, where one of the most prominent officials of the political police—known colloquially as PIDE—is on trial. *Marvine Howe, The New York Times, Jan. 7, 1977, pA3*

[1964, from Portuguese, acronym for *Policía Internacional e de Defêsa do Estado* International and State Defense police] Compare BOSS, DINA, SAVAK.

piggyback, *v.t., v.i. U.S. and Canadian.* to add or join up to something else as an extra load (in various transferred and figurative uses).

The Senate is engaged in its old game of trying to piggyback a tax-cut rider onto important legislation—this time a bill raising the debt ceiling. *Business Week, June 22, 1974, p 108*

A Mackenzie Valley pipeline transporting this U.S. gas provides us as Canadians with access to our frontier gas which can "piggyback" on the U.S. gas. *Donald Mackay, Maclean's, May 30, 1977, p 22*

Senator Bayh remarked, "If we are going to amend the Constitution of the United States, each amendment ought to stand on its own legs, and not piggyback on another amendment." *Martin Tolchin, The New York Times, Sept. 16, 1977, p A14*

[1968, extended from the verb sense "to carry loaded truck trailers on railroad flatcars" (1953)]

pimp, *v.t., v.i. U.S. Slang.* to profit from or live off another, as a pimp does.

"I think it unfortunate that black personalities, or leaders (those who actually command people), allow themselves to be used, pimped, in this way." *Earl Anthony, The New Republic, April 4, 1970, p 29*

"That child been pimpin' off his mother since he was three years old." *Time, Jan. 11, 1971, p 43*

[1970, verb use of the noun; cf. *pimp, v.i.* (OED 1636) to work as a pimp; pander]

pi·ña co·la·da ('pi:n yə kou'lɑ: də), an alcoholic drink made with pineapple juice, coconut (syrup, milk, or meat), and rum.

Norma inspected his work. "These are wild," she said. "There's only one thing to do: get some piña coladas and stay up all night. I'm game." *John Updike, The New Yorker, Aug. 21, 1978, p 32*

[1967, from Spanish, literally, strained pineapple]

pin·e·al·ec·to·my (ˌpin i: ə'lek tə mi:), *n.* surgical removal of the pineal gland.

Pinealectomy is known to affect the locomotor activity pattern of the house sparrow. *K. Homma, et al., Science, Oct. 27, 1972, p 224*

[1970, from *pineal* (gland) + *-ectomy* surgical removal (from Greek *ektomé* a cutting out)]

pinealectomize, *v.t.*: A group of starlings were pinealectomised, and injected daily, at the same time each day, with melatonin. The results were clear-cut. Over 95 per cent of the birds showed a clear entrainment of their activity rhythms to the injections, settling down to sleep very soon afterwards. Melatonin levels normally rise in the evening, so it looks like the pineal has a cast-iron case. *"On the Track of the Time Switch," New Scientist, Dec. 21-28, 1978, p 932*

ping-pong, *v.t., v.i. U.S.* to refer (a patient) needlessly to various specialists, especially in a clinic.

The Senate investigators, all of whom had been pronounced in excellent health by Congressional doctors at the beginning of the inquiry, . . . were "ping-ponged" to neurologists, gynecologists, internists, psychiatrists, podiatrists, dentists, ophthalmologists, pediatricians. *The New York Times, Sept. 5, 1976, Sec. 4, p 1*

The sending of a patient to eight or ten doctors for needless, Medicaid-reimbursed tests and treatments is known to the trade as "ping-ponging." *"On and Off the Avenue," The New Yorker, Dec. 13, 1976, p 121*

[1975, extended from the figurative verb sense "to bounce or toss back and forth" (1952), from *Ping-Pong*, trademark for table tennis equipment] See FAMILY GANGING.

ping-pong diplomacy, the establishment of trade and other relations between the United States and the People's Republic of China, begun when an American table tennis team went to China in 1971.

The extraordinary transformations of the past two years, commencing almost ludicrously with "ping-pong diplomacy," but going on to . . . the de facto exchange of diplomatic recognition between Washington and Peking, did not result from some wishful brain-wave of Nixon or Kissinger. *"Peking-Washington Rationale," National Review, March 30, 1973, p 352*

[1971]

pink-collar, *adj. U.S.* of or relating to occupations in which women predominate.

Congress continually condescends to legislate the lives of pink- and blue-collar workers, although less than 2 percent of the legislators have stooped to such jobs for more than three months at a stretch. *Darcy Veach, Madison, Wis., in a Letter to the Editor, Harper's, July 1977, p 4*

Working women are still disproportionately herded into so-called pink-collar jobs—teaching, clerical and retail sales work. The median salary for American women last year was only 60% that of American men. *Time, Nov. 28, 1977, p 14*

The "silent 80%" is what they're often called—the women who do the low-paid, dead-end, unglamorous pink- and blue-collar jobs. *Beverly Stephen, "Working Class Heroines," Sunday News (New York), Dec. 9, 1979, p 3*

[1977, patterned on *white-collar* (1928), *blue-collar* (1950), and *gray-collar* (1968), the color pink being traditionally associated with the female sex]

PINS (pinz), *n.pl. and sing. U.S.* acronym for *Person(s) In Need of Supervision*, a legal term for a child or adolescent with behavioral problems.

The Family Court Act defines PINS as any youngster under 16 "who is a habitual truant or who is incorrigible, ungovernable or habitually disobedient and beyond the lawful control of parent or other lawful authority." *Richard Severo, The New York Times, Dec. 14, 1976, p 42*

There are, for many reasons, still far more girls than boys who are PINS, and girls are usually confined in institutions for far longer periods than boys. *Lis Harris, "A Reporter at Large," The New Yorker, Aug. 14, 1978, p 58*

[1968] Compare JINS and MINS. See also STATUS OFFENDER.

Pin·yin ('pin'yin), *n.* a system for transliterating Chinese into Roman characters.

The new system, known as Pinyin, for the Chinese word meaning "transcription," has been adopted in the United Nations and by the United States Board on Geographic Names, which determines the spelling of place names for Government use. . . . In switching to the Pinyin style, The Times will retain a handful of well-known conventional names, such as Peking and Canton, because they are deeply rooted in English usage. For some names the various spelling systems coincide, as in Shanghai. *"Times Due to Revise Its Chinese Spelling," The New York Times, Feb. 4, 1979, p 10*

[1974] ▶ The Pinyin system was introduced in China in 1958 as a teaching aid, but it was not utilized to communicate with foreigners until recently. The most widespread Romanized system is the Wade system, devised in the mid-1800's by Sir Thomas Wade, a British diplomat and Chinese scholar and revised by H. A. Giles for his *Chinese-English Dictionary* (1892).

In the Pinyin system, the late Chairman Mao Tse-tung's name is rendered Mao Zedong, and the late Premier Chou En-lai's name is spelled Zhou Enlai. Some examples of place names are:

Conventional spelling	Pinyin
Canton	Guangzhou
Fukien	Fujian
Kiangsu	Jiangsu
Nanking	Nanjing
Peking	Beijing
Szechwan	Sichuan
Tientsin	Tianjin

Following is a partial table of the Pinyin alphabet showing the pronunciation of characters with their approximate English equivalents. The corresponding characters in the Wade system are given in parentheses for reference. (Source: *Beijing Review*, Jan. 5, 1979)

a (a), pronounced as in English *far*
b (p), as in *be*
c (ts), as in *its*
ch (ch), as in *church*, strongly aspirated
d (t), as in *do*
e (e), as in *her*
ei (ei), as in *way*
g (k), as in *go*
h (h), as in *her*, strongly aspirated
i (i), as in *eat*, or as in *sir* (in syllables beginning with c, ch, r, s, sh, z, and zh)
j (ch), as in *jeep*
k (k), as in *kind*, strongly aspirated
o (o), as in *law*
p (p), as in *par*, strongly aspirated
q (ch), as in *cheek*
r (j), as in *run* (but not rolled), or as the z in *azure*
s (s, ss, sz), as in *sister*
t (t), as in *top*, strongly aspirated
u (u), as in *too* (also as in French *tu* or German *München*)
x (hs), as in *she*
y, as in *yet* (used in syllables beginning with *i* or *u* when not preceded by consonants)
z (ts, tz), as in *zero*

pi·on·i·um (pai'ou ni: əm), *n.* a short-lived quasiatom consisting of a pion (pi-meson) and a muon (mu-meson), unstable nuclear particles.

Pionium is produced in the decay of the K meson to a muon, a pion, and a neutrino. In about one in ten million decays the muon and pion remain bound together by their electrostatic attraction. The resulting neutral pionium atom moves undetected away from the line of the K beam. *"Monitor: Exotic Atom Has Pion and Muon in Thrall," New Scientist, June 10, 1976, p 578*

[1976, from *pion* + *-ium* (suffix for chemical elements)]

pion therapy, a method of destroying cancer tumors by concentrating an intense beam of pions on the cancerous tissue and causing a miniature atomic explosion that damages the atoms and molecules of the target cells.

"It will take years to say whether pion therapy is superior to other treatments," says Malcolm Bagshaw, a radiation oncologist from Stanford University, who is visiting Los Alamos. "We are looking for local control where cancer has started. We probably can't do much about a cancer that has spread through the body." Local control is important, because a large proportion of cancer patients die from continued growth of the primary tumor, and chemotherapy and immunotherapy are weak in their ability for local control. Nevertheless, pion therapy will have to show significant improvements over alternates, to be worth the expense and effort. *Science News, Dec. 9, 1978, p 414*

[1970]

pi·qua·da (pi'ka: də), *n.* a small electric needle used as an instrument of torture.

Technology also has a place. One instrument widely used in some Latin American torture centres is an electrical refinement of the straight pin called the piquada, which is inserted under the victim's fingernails. *"Building a Better Thumbscrew," New Scientist, July 19, 1973, p 141*

[1972, alteration of Spanish *picada*, puncture]

pit, *n.* **the pits,** *U.S. Slang.* the worst; the most undesirable or unpleasant place, condition, circumstance, etc.

"Get me back into the novel or marry me," Emma told Kugelmass. "Meanwhile, I want to get a job or go to class, because watching TV all day is the pits." *Woody Allen, The New Yorker, May 2, 1977, p 38*

They take a special delight in bad-mouthing the old hometown and state. First of all, this state was good enough for them for about 55 years. Suddenly, it's the pits! *"Hooray for Missouri," Dear Abby Column, New York Post, Oct. 10, 1978, p 91*

[1976, probably from plural of *pit* a deep place; abyss; hell] Compare ARMPIT.

pit lizard, *U.S. Slang.* a female fan or follower of automobile racing drivers.

Some of the women stand out because you see them there every day — and most likely would see them next Sunday at the race in Richmond, Virginia, or the following race in Bristol, Tennessee. "Pit lizards," camp followers, or dedicated racing fans, whatever you choose to call them, they are part of the scene and their presence is pleasing to racing men. *William McIlwain, "Speed, Sex, and Heroes," The Atlantic, June 1973, p 77*

[1972, patterned on *lounge lizard* (1920's)]

pit road, the road off an automobile racing course where the pits are located to service the competing cars.

The race stewards had declared that no replacement cars would be allowed to start the race and neither would any driver who had failed to complete the first lap, which meant that all those who finished the lap in the pit road would also be excluded. *John Blunsden, The Times (London), July 19, 1976, p 8*

[1976]

PL, abbreviation of PRODUCT LIABILITY.

Many PL problems relate directly to product quality control and reliability. *Kenneth E. Case, "Quality Control," McGraw-Hill Yearbook of Science and Technology 1974, p 361*

[1974]

plan·i·fi·ca·tion (ˌplæn ə fə'kei ʃən), *n. Especially U.S. and Canadian.* the act or process of planifying; systematic planning.

He also expects the increase in business concentration to erode the functioning of markets, necessitating ever more "planification of capitalism" . . . *Tibor Scitovsky, Harper's, June 1976, p 102*

As for his government of technocrats and bureaucrats, nearly all of us, French and English, businessmen and workingmen, have been frustrated to the screaming point by their *planifications*, financial chaos and the obvious fact that most of their programs create more problems than they solve. *Hugh MacLennan, Maclean's, Nov. 1, 1976, p 14*

[1967, from French, from *planifier* PLANIFY]

plan·i·fy ('plæn əˌfai), *v.t. Especially U.S. and Canadian.* to plan systematically; subject to thorough planning.

"We have established in recent years the most planified market that ever existed," said Louis Camu, chairman of the Banque de Bruxelles. "Every day the price for eggs, for example, is fixed by a computer in Brussels and then transmitted to the people who buy, sell and transport them." *Time, April 23, 1973, p 79*

[1973, from French *planifier*]

plank·to·troph·ic (ˌplæŋk tou'traf ik), *adj.* feeding on plankton.

The . . . theory demands that planktotrophic larvae are primitive, and evidence of direct development in supposedly primitive members of many phyla is dismissed without proper discussion. *R. B. Clark, "Whence Metazoa?" Nature, Dec. 1, 1972, p 285*

[1972, from *plankton* + *-trophic* (from Greek *trophé* nourishment)]

plant·i·mal ('plæn tə məl), *n.* a living cell formed by fusing the protoplast of an animal cell with that of a plant cell.

James Hartmann, quoted in a recent Miami Herald article, speculates on a stronger potential application for "plantimal" cells: A living, meat-type substance might eventually be grown, he says, that builds animal protein by converting the sun's energy directly to chemical energy, much as a plant does. *"Animal? Vegetable? No. Plantimal," Science News, July 31, 1976, p 70*

Already, in some instances, cells as different, as distantly related as a mouse and man, as tobacco plant and man, have been induced to fuse and form new cells which were neither man nor mouse, neither plant nor animal. Indeed, those plant-animal hybrids are already being called "plantimals." Such strange new hybrid cells haven't yet been grown up successfully into strange new creatures. *Robert Cooke, Improving on Nature, 1977, p 130*

[1976, from *plant* + an*imal*]

plasma panel, a panel displaying information from an electronic computer or the like, consisting of an array of gas-filled cells which can be selectively ignited to display any letter, number, diagram, etc.

[Jurg] Nievergelt programmed Race Track for the University of Illinois's Plato IV computer-assisted instruction system, which uses a new type of graphic display called a plasma panel. Two or three people can play against one another or one person can play alone. *Martin Gardner, "Mathematical Games," Scientific American, Jan. 1973, p 108*

Optical display devices that have become popular for computers and pocket calculators within the last year utilize light-emitting diodes (LED), liquid crystals, plasma panels, or fiber optics. All have considerably faster response times than . . . cathode-ray-tube (CRT) terminals. *Murray Sargent III and William Swindell, "Optical Computer," McGraw-Hill Yearbook of Science and Technology 1974, p 322*

[1972]

plas·mon ('plæzˌmɑn), *n. Physics.* a quantum of longitudinal excitation of an electron gas.

Graphite is known to have a sharp plasmon at about 7eV [electron volts]. *J. E. Houston, "Electron Spectroscopy," McGraw-Hill Yearbook of Science and Technology 1976, p 174*

plasticated

[1966, from *plasma* (highly ionized gas) + *-on* elementary particle or unit]

plasticated, *adj.* plastic, synthetic, or artificial (chiefly figurative use).

Marco Ferreri's *The Last Woman* [a film] is set in an immediately recognizable context—a modern industrial wasteland of high-rise apartment blocks and plasticated entertainments. *Richard Combs, The Times (London), Oct. 15, 1976, p 13*

[1972, from past participle of *plasticate, v.* (1960) to knead rubber by means of a plasticator or (1962) to make plastic by adding a plasticizer]

plastic bullet, a bullet made of polyvinyl chloride plastic and discharged from a specially designed gun, used in riot control.

The grim news from Belfast focused attention for the first time on the plastic bullet, the sleeper among the new generation of British anti-riot weapons. Basically it is rather shorter than a rubber bullet and made of PVC. A cylinder 1 1/2 inches in diameter and rather over four inches long, it looks like a thick white lump of candle. *Jonathan Rosenhead, "A New Look at Less 'Less Lethal' Weapons," New Scientist, Dec. 16, 1976, p 672*

[1976] Compare RUBBER BULLET.

plastic credit, the use of credit cards in place of cash or checks.

We were told then and now that the advantage of plastic credit is that it reduces paperwork, consolidates all bills down into one (to be paid by a single check at the end of the month), and moves us rapidly, inexorably toward the "checkless society." *Douglas Davis, Newsweek, June 30, 1975, p 11*

[1971] Compare PLASTIC MONEY. See also DEBIT CARD.

plastic money, credit cards.

One advantage of using "plastic money"—bank credit cards in place of cash—was the interest-free ride if monthly bills were paid on time. But now the free ride is rapidly disappearing, and users of Master Charge cards and Bank-Americards should take notice. *Terry Robards, The New York Times, Sept. 11, 1976, p 27*

Plastic money is taking on a new form that seems sure to make it even more widespread on the British banking scene. *"Plastic Money May Soon Cash-In," New Scientist, Feb. 17, 1977, p 398*

[1974]

plate·glass ('pleit,glæs), *adj.* of, relating to, or designating the newer British universities founded especially since the 1950's.

The collective academic phenomenon now known as the Plateglass universities coincides with a break in the great graduate bull market of the 1950s and 1960s. *Christopher Driver, The Manchester Guardian Weekly, May 22, 1971, p 13*

The new universities, particularly the new foundations, which are familiarly called "the plateglass universities" because of their architecture, were expected to be innovative institutions, breaking away from conventional models of organization, course structure, and degrees. *John Walsh, "Higher Education in Britain," Science, June 1, 1973, p 938*

[1968, so called because of the *plate glass* often used in the building of these universities, in contrast to the *redbrick* universities built in the 1800's]

360

plate-tectonic, *adj.* of or relating to the theory of plate tectonics, according to which the land masses of the earth consist of slowly moving crustal blocks called plates.

During Permian and Triassic time, between about 200 and 250 million years ago, the quiet of the western coast of South America gradually gave way to rumblings brought on by the incipient breakup of the supercontinent Pangaea and the onset of the plate-tectonic cycle that is still under way. *David E. James, "The Evolution of the Andes," Scientific American, Aug. 1973, p 65*

[1969]

platinum, *adj.* of or designating a record album that has sold a million copies.

The Austin sound—redneck rock or progressive country—began crossing over from country to pop charts and racking up sales once scarcely dreamed of in the country field. In the past two years, three such albums have gone platinum, in trade parlance (i.e., sold 1 million copies). *Time, Sept. 18, 1978, p 81*

[1971, so called from the award, a platinum album, given to the performers] Compare GOLD.

PLATO or **Pla·to** ('plei,tou), *n.* a computer-based individualized system of instruction.

Plato operates through visual display terminals that connect directly to the large-scale computer and interact through lesson materials in the computer's memory. Users see their instructional materials in the form of text, numbers, animated drawings, and other graphics.

The student interacts with the computer-stored lesson materials in somewhat the same manner as with a teacher. *William D. Smith, "Control Data Computer To Be Used In Education," The New York Times, April 15, 1976, p 57*

[1963, acronym for *Programmed Logic for Automatic Teaching Operations*]

plea-bargain, *Especially U.S.* —*n.* Often, **plea bargain.** an agreement between a prosecutor and a defendant or his attorney to allow the defendant to plead guilty or give testimony against others in return for a reduced charge or some other concession by the prosecution.

The vast majority of criminal sentences in the United States—between 80 percent and 90 percent in some jurisdictions—are the result of "plea bargains" in which the defendant "waives" his constitutional right to trial in exchange for a "good deal." *Alan Dershowitz, "Doing Time," Harper's, Jan. 1974, p 8*

Encouraging plea-bargains as a means of expediting the criminal process is a mere palliative, and ultimately self-defeating. *Irving R. Kaufman, "The Injustices of Plea-Bargaining," The New York Times, Dec. 13, 1976, p 35*

Twenty-two of them said that they had pleaded guilty because of a plea-bargain—an offer made through counsel to the effect that if they pleaded guilty, they would receive lesser sentences than if they fought their cases and were convicted. *The Times (London), Sept. 24, 1977, p 13*

—*v.i.* to make a plea-bargain.

Miller plea-bargained with Jaworski to get Kleindienst off with a misdemeanor charge. *Time, Sept. 9, 1974, p 14*

The effect of the 1972 decision was to change North Carolina's discretionary into a mandatory death penalty law. There can still be discretion, opponents of the penalty claim, even where the penalty is mandatory under the law. The prosecution can plea-bargain and bring a lesser charge, and the governor can exercise executive clemency.

"The Court Faces Death," National Review, May 9, 1975, p 494

[1968 for noun; 1973 for verb; back formations from plea-bargaining (1963)] Compare DEAD UP.

plea-bargaining, n.: Some eighty per cent of the convictions obtained in New York State are the result of plea-bargaining — pleading guilty to a lesser offense than the original charge in the hope of obtaining leniency. Susan Sheehan. "Annals of Crime: A Prison and a Prisoner," The New Yorker, Oct. 24, 1977, p 66

plei·o·typ·ic (ˌplai əˈtip ik), adj. characteristic of cellular multiplication or growth.

Important parameters determining rate of growth include membrane transport, protein and RNA synthesis, and protein degradation. These characteristics fluctuate in a coordinated way with fluctuations in growth rate; together they are known as the pleiotypic programme. "What Does the Cell Switch Switch On?" New Scientist, July 12, 1973, p 64

[1972, from pleio- more, multiple (from Greek pleiōn) + typic]

PLO, abbreviation of Palestine Liberation Organization, a military and political organization representing the Palestinian Arabs, dedicated to the reunification of pre-1948 Palestine as a secular Arab state.

It is not malicious or propagandist to offer the view that Israel is not at present helping to expand the peace process begun at Camp David. Neither, for that matter, is the PLO, whose charter explicitly calls for the destruction of the State of Israel and whose occasional utterances do little to dilute that unacceptable commitment. Editorial, The Manchester Guardian Weekly, July 8, 1979, p 10

[1965] Compare AL FATAH.

► The PLO was founded in 1964 at a conference of Arab leaders in Cairo. In 1974 it was recognized by most Arab governments and by the United Nations as the legitimate representative of the Palestinians.

PLR, British. abbreviation of PUBLIC LENDING RIGHT.

I would be opposed to PLR if it infringed on public libraries, but librarians are not expected to work for nothing. Dan Jacobson, "Taking Sides on PLR," New Statesman, Dec. 19, 1975, p 796

[1969]

plug, n. **pull the plug, 1** to remove life-support equipment, such as a respirator, from a person who is permanently comatose, irreversibly brain-damaged, or terminally ill.

He also foresees — perhaps thinking wishfully — that "Community Ethics Boards" will be empowered to "pull the plug" in cases where meaningful life has ended. Walter Sullivan, The New York Times, Jan. 25, 1976, Sec. 3, p 56

The Euthanasia Society claims 50 to 60 per cent of medical men pull the plug when life chances are nil and the prognosis is negative. "Dear Meg," New York Post, May 14, 1979, p 24

2 Figurative use.

Cowles, pointing out that Harper's is, in effect, being kept afloat by the parent Minneapolis Star and Tribune Co., even hinted he might pull the plug in preference to "indefinitely" subsidizing the magazine. Time, March 22, 1971, p 48

[1966] See DEATH, EUTHANASIA.

plug compatible, capable of being connected in auxiliary or peripheral functions to various computers.

The 1970 IBM took in more than $1.1 billion in revenues from peripheral products that were plug compatible with its mainframe units. All other manufacturers of plug compatible equipment combined took in a little more than $100 million on products designed for IBM computers. William Rodgers, Harper's, May 1974, p 82

[1974]

plumber, n. U.S. a person whose job is to investigate and stop leaks of government secrets.

Ford is not averse to that important, although unofficial, branch of government called cronyism. Cronies, if they are well placed and well chosen, can tell even a President what he needs to know, and perform a few tasks without the aid of "plumbers." Saul Friedman, Harper's, Aug. 1974, p 22

[1972] ► The term became current during the Watergate affair. The White House plumbers were assigned in 1971 to investigate security leaks, but soon thereafter turned to various illegal activities which included the Watergate burglary.

plum book, U.S. Informal. an official government publication that lists the available government positions which the President may fill by appointment.

While the number of positions in the plum book is about 5,000, the turnover would be only about half that number since many apolitical persons would be retained. Yet if Mr. Carter makes good his campaign promise to restructure the bureaucracy it could be that many of these positions will be abolished next year and patronage seekers will have to look elsewhere for jobs. Richard D. Lyons, "Job Seekers Buy Up Federal 'Plum Book,' " The New York Times, Nov. 21, 1976, Sec. 1, p 28

There are about 350,000 federal civilian employees in and around Washington, but when Mr. Carter arrived in town he could make only 2,200 appointments from what is known as the "Plum Book." This document, which is in fact yellow and entitled Policy and Supporting Positions, presents the Administration with the list of available patronage. Tom Bethell, "Witnesses of the New Order," Harper's, June 1977, p 34

[1965, from plum a choice position or appointment (OED 1891)]

plume, n. short for MANTLE PLUME. Often used attributively.

The mechanism that generates hot spots must be sought in the mantle. They may be surface manifestations of "plumes": rising, columnar currents of hot but solid material. The plumes might well up from below the asthenosphere, at a phase-change boundary a few hundred miles inside the mantle. Kevin C. Burke and J. Tuzo Wilson, "Hot Spots on the Earth's Surface," Scientific American, Aug. 1976, p 49

[1972]

PMA, n. abbreviation of paramethoxyamphetamine, a potent hallucinogenic drug derived from amphetamine.

Other than the hallucinogens presently controlled by the Act though, only two others have found their way to the illicit market in any quantity. These drugs, called PMA and MDA, are derivatives of amphetamine. "Home Office Plans Blanket Drugs Ban," New Scientist, Dec. 9, 1976, p 572

[1967] Compare DPT, PCP.

poblacion

po·bla·ci·on (ˌpou blɑ: si:'oun), *n.; pl.* **-o·nes** (-'ou-nes). a shanty-town or slum in Chile.

During the three turbulent years of Salvador Allende's administration, the poor of the poblaciones never wavered in their support of his government. *"Slaughterhouse in Santiago," Newsweek, Oct. 8, 1973, p 54*

[1971, from Spanish *población* village, settlement]

po·bla·dor (ˌpou blɑ:'dɔr), *n.; pl.* **-do·res** (-'dɔ: res). an inhabitant of a poblacion in Chile.

Yes, tracts such as this one do continue to be circulated in Chile. This particular one covers everything — infant mortality, malnutrition, school dropouts, prostitution by young children, and evictions of the *pobladores. Charles Vanhecke, The Manchester Guardian Weekly (Le Monde section), Aug. 8, 1976, p 12*

[1976, from Spanish, villager, settler] Compare ROTO.

pocket calculator, another name for MINICALCULATOR.

I also have my own pocket calculator, which goes up to a million dollars and you could leave the housekeeping to me, leaving yourself free to fly around to Washington, Paris, etc. *M. B. K. Thibgrift, Punch, March 26, 1975, p 518*

The promise lies in the continuing advance in military technology based on microelectronics, symbolized by the ubiquitous pocket calculator. *Philip Morrison and Paul F. Walker, Scientific American, Oct. 1978, p 55*

[1973]

point in time, *U.S. and Canadian.* a particular time. Used especially in the phrases:

at that point in time, then.

Saying "at that point in time," when you mean "then," requires a lot of time and wears down the audience. *Russell Baker, The New York Times, Aug. 11, 1974, p (not known)*

at this point in time, now.

"At this point in time, dinner is served." *Cartoon legend, The New Yorker, June 23, 1973, p 41*

[1973] ► This phrase became a cliché during the Watergate hearings (1973-74), although evidence of its earlier use in scholarly and literary sources has been cited (see *American Speech,* Spring-Summer 1973, pp 159-60). For example:

Daringly, in section 5 [of "The Bear"], he takes us back to a point in time three years before Isaac's act of renunciation. *Cleanth Brooks, William Faulkner: The Yoknapatawpha Country, 1963, p 269*

point man, *U.S. and Canadian.* a representative in dealings with others, especially with others who are considered opponents.

As the head of the 10-member "interest section" in Havana, Mr. Lane will be serving as a direct channel of communications with the Cubans and as the point man for American policy. *Joseph B. Treaster, "Scholarly U.S. Diplomat," The New York Times, Sept. 2, 1977, p A3*

[1972, figurative use of the hockey term for a defenseman assigned to an offensive position (the "point") within the attacking zone, especially during a power play; also, in U.S. military usage, the soldier in front of a patrol]

point-of-sale, *adj.* of, relating to, or placed in the location where sales are made or recorded in a store, etc.

A kit with a slew of point-of-sale material had to be prepared and sent to agents by Aug. 23, and an ad to recruit new agents had to be made and placed. *Philip H. Dougherty, "Advertising: Next Move for New York Lottery," The New York Times, Sept. 21, 1976, p 60*

Electronic cash registers linked to computers — point-of-sale systems, in the jargon — are continuing their move into the main department stores. A £2m commitment to 500 point-of-sale terminals for 12 regional stores was announced yesterday by Lewis's, one of the department store companies. *The Times (London), Aug. 3, 1977, p 17*

[1972] *Abbreviation:* POS

pointy-head, *n. U.S. Informal (often derogatory).* an intellectual; egghead; highbrow.

He shouted some and lied some, but he told those people they were being screwed by pointy-heads in Washington and New York — and they clapped hands. *Richard Reeves, The New York Times Magazine, March 12, 1972, p 106*

[1972, back formation from POINTY-HEADED]

pointy-headed, *adj. U.S. Informal (often derogatory).* intellectual; eggheaded; highbrow.

Groups widely believed to have been at the center of the shifting conspiracy against the common weal have at various times included . . . the pointy-headed bureaucrats, the Establishment, the system, the straights, the New Left nihilists, the Mafia, the oil companies, the media, and the CIA. *Hendrik Hertzberg and David C. K. McClelland, "Paranoia," Harper's, June 1974, p 52*

Before Frank Mankiewicz arrived on the scene, the few people talking about NPR [National Public Radio] at all were saying the wrong things: "Pointy headed" . . . "elitist" . . . "inaccessible" . . . were some of the comments. *Christopher Swan, The Christian Science Monitor, Nov. 20, 1979, p 816*

[1968, coined by George C. Wallace, born 1919, former governor of Alabama]

Po·la·vi·sion ('pou lə, viʒ ən), *n.* a trademark for motion picture equipment that develops its film in the cartridge automatically after the film is exposed, introduced by the Polaroid Corporation in 1977. See the quotation for details.

The system, christened Polavision, uses three minutes of special Super 8 film sealed in a non-standard cassette which fits only a Polaroid camera. After exposure the cassette is loaded into a Polavision player. A small sachet containing just 12 drops of developer is automatically ruptured and the film is rewound and processed. Ninety seconds later it is ready for projection by the player onto a back projection screen the size of a small TV set. *"Technology: Instant Movies Coming Europe's Way," New Scientist, April 13, 1978, p 88*

[1977, from *Pola*roid + *vision*]

po·le·mol·o·gist (ˌpou lə'mɑl ə dʒist), *n.* an expert in polemology (the study of war).

Polemologists say two things helped Israel's victory, at the material level, over the Arab armies: they were the Startron [an aid for improving night vision] and the American-made 155 cannon. *Maurice Denuziere, The Manchester Guardian Weekly (Le Monde section), Jan. 9, 1977, p 11*

[1977, from *polemology* (1968) + *-ist*]

police lock, a metal bar that sets against a door and extends diagonally out to the floor.

The first thing I saw was the apartment door. It was closed and the police lock was on. Its bar was in place, braced between the door and the floor. There was no way the woman could have entered the apartment. *Laura Furman, "Last Winter," The New Yorker, March 1, 1976, p 34*

[1972, perhaps because these locks are recommended by police for their effectiveness]

po·li·cier (ˌpou li'syei), *n.* a detective story; whodunit.

The film climaxes, as all *policiers* apparently must, with a car chase, but it is nowhere near as interesting as the successful off-casting of nice Hal Holbrook as a heavy. *Richard Schickel, "Cinema," Review of "Magnum Force," Time, Feb. 11, 1974, p 64*

[1969, short for French *roman policier*, literally, police novel]

Po·li·sa·ri·o (ˌpou li'sɑr i: ou), *n.* **1** Also, **Polisario Front.** a guerrilla organization fighting for independence of the former Spanish Sahara (Western Sahara) ceded by Spain to Mauritania and Morocco in 1976. *Often used attributively.*

France is supporting Mauritania and Morocco against the Polisario in what is in practice a latter-day colonial war between Arabs. *"Out of Step in the Sahara," The Manchester Guardian Weekly, Jan. 1, 1978, p 1*

Algeria and the Polisario Front, a Saharan nationalist movement, want independence for the area's nomad population. They have armed guerrillas who say they will fight to the death for the area, now occupied by more than 20,000 Moroccan troops. *"Unrest Persists in West Sahara," The New York Times, May 16, 1976, Sec. 1, p 15*

2 a member of this organization.

The Moroccan army launched a search-and-destroy campaign against the Polisarios. Apparently in response, Algerian units crossed into the Sahara. *"North Africa: Armor at the Oasis," Time, Feb. 9, 1976, p 42*

[1975, from Spanish (*Frente*) *Polisario*, acronym for (*Frente*) *P*opular para la *Li*beración de *Sa*guia el Hamra y *Rio* de Oro (Popular Front for the Liberation of Saguia el Hamra and Rio de Oro, the two zones of Western Sahara]

Pollutant Standards Index, *U.S.* a standard index for measuring the amount of air pollution.

The Pollutant Standards Index will gauge air quality on a scale from 0 to 500. Intervals will be geared to the measured levels of five major pollutants: carbon monoxide, oxidants, particulates, sulfur dioxide and nitrogen dioxide. "Good" air will fall in the 0-to-50 range, "moderate" air from 50 to 100, "unhealthful" from 100 to 200, "very unhealthful" from 200 to 300, and "hazardous" above 300. *"Uniform U.S. Index to Measure Air Pollution Rate," The New York Times, Aug. 24, 1976, p 31*

[1976] Compare AMBIENT AIR STANDARD.

pollution tax, a proposed tax on companies or their products that create environmental pollution.

Mr. Miller said that if special financing was needed to help meet the new noise rules, he preferred a so-called "pollution tax" in the form of a tax imposed on planes in inverse proportion to the amount of noise suppression achieved. Revenues would be allocated for further noise-reduction efforts. *Richard Witkin, "Airlines Seek Aid in Quieting Planes," The New York Times, Dec. 2, 1976, p 51*

[1972]

pol·y ('pɑl i:), *n.* **1** *British, Informal.* a polytechnical school.

Those people who feel that polys should be "upgraded to university status" are implicitly and unfairly judging them as second-rate institutions. *Martin Sherwood, New Scientist and Science Journal, May 27, 1971, p 514*

Is the growth in student members to be stopped in universities and slowed down in polys, in spite of bigger age groups, higher proportions reaching A-levels, and more demand for women's places? *"Cash Threat to Universities," The Manchester Guardian Weekly, Nov. 2, 1974, p 10*

2 polyester fiber.

Brushed Nylon Gown with matching trim, back placket and elasticized sleeve cuffs. Comfortable 100% brushed nylon with poly trim. *Carroll Reed, Winter Holiday 1979-1980 Catalog, Item B, p 20*

[1970 for def. 1, short for *polytechnic, n.* (OED 1883); 1974 for def. 2, short for *polyester* (1951)]

poly A, a substance found in ribonucleic acid, made up of a long sequence of nucleotides containing adenine.

Sau-Wah Kwan and George Brawerman of Tufts University have recently uncovered evidence that poly A is able to bind certain proteins to messenger RNA. *Stephen N. Kreitzman, "Biology: Biochemistry," Encyclopedia Science Supplement (Grolier) 1973, p 84*

[1970, from *poly-* many + *A*, abbreviation of *adenine*] Also called POLYADENYLIC ACID.

pol·y·ad·e·nyl·ic acid (ˌpɑl i:ˌæd ə'nil ik), another name for POLY A.

Poliovirus virion RNA contains a single covalently bound sequence of polyadenylic acid which is approximately 49 nucleotides long. *Science, May 5, 1972, p 526*

[1970]

pol·y·bro·mi·nat·ed biphenyl (ˌpɑl i:'brou mə nei tid), any of a group of highly toxic and persistent chemicals related to the polychlorinated biphenyls, used as a fire retardant and additive in plastics, and regarded as a dangerous contaminant.

600 pounds of a closely related chemical, polybrominated biphenyl, were shipped to a Michigan cattle feed plant in 1973. The contaminated feed nearly wiped out the state's dairy industry. *Bill Dampier, "Environment," Maclean's, Feb. 9, 1976, p 55*

The chemical, polybrominated biphenyls, or PBB's, is a close relative of PCB's, an industrial pollutant that has become widespread through the environment and has been shown in heavily exposed people in Japan and upstate New York to cause liver and thyroid abnormalities, nerve damage, skin lesions, pregnancy problems and, in laboratory animals, cancer and growth retardation. *Jane E. Brody, "Farmers Exposed to a Pollutant Face Medical Study in Michigan," The New York Times, Aug. 12, 1976, p 20*

[1976] *Abbreviation:* PBB

polydrug, *adj.* of or relating to the use of many kinds of narcotics.

What most concerns the military are "polydrug abusers," servicemen taking a mixture of drugs that become addictive. Abuse seems to be greater in units outside the United States, and the drugs vary. In Korea, the problem is barbiturates. In Germany, it is heroin, methaqualone and amphetamines. In the United States, it is LSD, cocaine, heroine, and PCP, or phencyclidine, commonly known as "angel dust." *Bernard Weinraub, "A Fog and a Furor Over GI Drug Use," The New York Times, July 30, 1978, Sec. 4, p 4*

[1972]

polygraph, *v.t.* to give a lie-detector test to.

"Polygraph them all. I don't know anything about polygraphs and I don't know how accurate they are," the President said, "but I know they'll scare the hell out of people." *Time, July 29, 1974, p 20*

[1971, verb use of *polygraph* lie detector (1940's)]

pol·y·logue ('pɑl i:,lɔ:g), *n.* **1** a conversation involving a number of characters in a play, etc.

Radio writers are sometimes advised to eschew monologue in favour of the less artificial polylogue; Mr Curram's excellence in soliloquy suggests one reason for this recommendation: the majority of actors cannot carry it off as he can. *David Wade, The Times (London), March 18, 1972, p 8*

2 a discussion involving a number of participants.

It is much too soon to speculate what will come of the parleys that began in December 1975. They would be useful even if the "polylogue" among the more than two dozen countries, deemed to be representative of developed and developing countries, merely begins to reveal the priorities among the numerous aims of the participants. *Hans H. Landsberg, Science, Feb. 20, 1976, p 640*

[1971, from *poly-* many + dia*logue*]

Pom·e·ran·chuk theorem (,pɑm ə'ræn tʃək), *Physics.* a theorem which states that in a high energy region a particle and its antiparticle should have approximately the same total cross section when interacting with a target.

The Pomeranchuk theorem is based on the symmetry of matter and antimatter. It says that although the proton-antiproton cross section can at low energies be a little larger than the proton-proton cross section, at high energies the two cross sections should tend to the same value. *Science News, March 17, 1973, p 165*

[1970, named after Isaak Y. *Pomeranchuk*, a Soviet theoretical physicist, who postulated it]

pom·e·ron ('pɑm ə,rɑn), *n. Physics.* a theoretical "pole" formed in a high energy region where total cross sections of interacting particles have become constants. *Also used attributively.*

For "elastic" two-body scattering, where only momentum and angular momentum are exchanged (the particles remain themselves), the appropriate "Regge pole" is called the "Pomeron" after the Russian physicist Pomeranchuk. The Pomeron differs markedly from all other Regge families. If the Pomeron were simple, then the total cross sections (or interaction rates) for hadron-hadron scattering would remain constant (or decrease) as the energy is increased. *Christopher Micharel, New Scientist, March 27, 1975, p 797*

[1974, from *Pomer*anchuk theorem + *-on* elementary unit or particle]

Pom·pe's disease ('pɑm pəz), a metabolic disorder that prevents the normal storage of glycogen in the body.

In Pompe's disease glycogen builds up in the liver, heart and muscle and the average age at death is five to six months. *Gregory Gregoriadis, New Scientist, Dec. 27, 1973, p 890*

[1970, named after J. C. *Pompe*, a Dutch physician of the 1900's]

Pong, *n.* Often popularly spelled **pong.** a trademark for any of various video games simulating such sports as hockey and tennis.

Clutching a handful of quarters, the college student settled in at a video console. Twiddling a set of dials, he sliced an electronic table-tennis "ball" back and forth across the screen. As the game wore on, he muttered intently: "I'm a prisoner of pong." *"King Pong," Newsweek, Dec. 17, 1973, p 91*

My dream is to be an airline stewardess, but I'm not old enough. In the meantime, I operate a pneumatic tie-wrap gun and make harnesses for electronic pong games. *Quoted from "Working" by Bill Owens in The New York Times Magazine, Sept. 4, 1977, p 9*

[1973]

pony car, *U.S.* a medium-sized automobile.

NASCAR [National Association for Stock Car Auto Racing] is very seriously considering switching from full-size models to so-called "pony" cars, the Dodge Aspens, Chevrolet Novas, Ford Granadas and such, beginning with the 1978 season. *The New York Times, Oct. 28, 1976, p 55*

[1976, originally (1968) applied specifically to certain small, sporty cars modeled after the Ford Motor Company's Mustang, suggesting the name *pony*] Compare MUSCLE CAR.

pooper-scooper, *n. Especially U.S.* a scooplike device for picking up the droppings of a dog, horse, etc.

Though most New Yorkers' initial reaction was that the law is probably unenforceable, retailers reported brisk sales of sanitary devices ranging from 15¢ disposable cardboard shovels to $11, long-handled pooper scoopers equipped with a flashlight for nocturnal emitters. *Time, Aug. 14, 1978, p 73*

[1972, *pooper,* from *poop,* U.S. slang (chiefly a children's) term for feces + *-er,* suffix added to rhyme with *scooper* device used to scoop up]

popper, *n. Slang.* **1** an ampule of amyl nitrite, inhaled by drug users for its stimulant effect.

Later Roman tells me that just before the crucial take he gave her a popper—i.e. crushed an amyl nitrite capsule under her nose. *Kenneth Tynan, "The Magnetic Pole," The Sunday Times (London), Nov. 7, 1971, p 43*

2 another name for ISOBUTYL NITRITE.

As a result of aggressive marketing, poppers quickly spread to avant-garde heterosexuals. Marketed under such trade names as Bullet, Crypt and Locker Room, isobutyl nitrite is sold openly in some record stores, boutiques and pornographic bookstores. Poppers sell for $4 to $6 for about half an ounce, enough for up to 15 sniffs. *Time, July 17, 1978, p 16*

[1969, so called from the popping sound made when it is broken open]

pop-rock, *n.* popular music in the style of rock with a strong beat, repetitive phrasing, electronic instruments, etc. *Often used attributively.*

The millionaire pop-rock star Mick Jagger, leader of the Rolling Stones . . . *Albin Krebs, "Notes on People," The New York Times, Nov. 9, 1976, p 28*

[1966, from *pop* (short for *popular*) + *rock*]

pop-rocker, *n.*: Vancouver's pop-rocker *Nick Gilder* has the look of a Vienna Boys Choir refugee and the sweet high sound of a castrato, so no wonder he's trying to change his image. *Jane O'Hara, "People," Maclean's, Nov. 13, 1978, p 45*

population biology, a branch of biology dealing with the distribution of animal and plant populations.

For example, we are told that salinity is the principal factor underlying marine distributions today, and ecological-evolutionary aspects of population biology, which have proved so fruitful in application to zoogeography, are scarcely mentioned. *James W. Valentine, Nature, April 7, 1972, p 298*

[1972]

population genetics, a branch of genetics dealing with the frequency and distribution of genes, mutants, genotypes, etc., among animal and plant populations.

The study of population genetics has in general become a powerful tool for unraveling human history and prehistory and particularly for solving problems of the origin and dispersal of plants and animals. Each individual study, however, brings out limitations in both the organism being investigated and the approach made to the study. To obtain greater precision in the interpretation of complex events it is therefore desirable to study a number of species. *Neil B. Todd, "Cats and Commerce," Scientific American, Nov. 1977, p 100*

[1972] Also called QUANTITATIVE GENETICS.

population geneticist: The book, in fact, represents a useful contribution in an area of enquiry shared by population geneticists, taxonomists and natural historians. *K. R. Lewis, Review of "Plant Speciation" by Verne Grant, Nature, May 5, 1972, p 55*

pop wine, *U.S.* a sweet, fruit-flavored wine.

The alcoholic tide has been pushed higher by the fast-selling, inexpensive pop wines, which disguise their alcoholic content with sweet fruit flavors. *"Alcoholism: New Victims, New Treatment," Time, April 22, 1974, p 76*

[1971, probably from *pop*, as in *soda pop* carbonated soft drink] Also called SODA-POP WINE.

porn- or **porno-,** variant combining forms meaning "pornographic" or "pornography," freely attached to many words, sometimes to form puns such as *pornfield* and *pornucopia.* The following are some examples of use:

pornbook, *n.*: the author is content to employ his demonic imagination on an almost routine device for writing a pornbook: the step-by-step story of filming the most elaborate stag flick in history. *Time, Aug. 24, 1970, p 64*

pornfield, *n.*: Browsers are not noticeably furtive. A young actor cheerfully leafs his way through the pornfield, whistling Mozart. *Norman Shrapnel, "The Abuses of Literacy—5: The Porn Market," The Times Literary Supplement, Feb. 11, 1972, p 159*

porno-chic, *n.*: Undoubtedly one of the major trends of the year was not towards the art film, but towards porno-chic. *Clive Barnes, The Times (London), Jan. 10, 1976, p 5*

pornoflick, *n.*: An occupational hazard of film criticking is coming to hate movies, to sit grim-faced through laff-riots, yawn during thrillers, peek at a newspaper by the light of a 10-watt aisle bulb during pornoflicks . . . *David Brudnoy, National Review, Nov. 9, 1973, p 1251*

pornoland, *n.*: Another nice quiet restaurant, this one in a contradictory location, is the Ceylon India Inn at 148 West 49th, deep in the heart of pornoland. *John Canaday, The New York Times, April 9, 1976, p 33*

porno-violent, *adj.*: "A Clockwork Orange" might be the work of a strict and exacting German professor who set out to make a porno-violent sci-fi comedy. *Pauline Kael, The New Yorker, Jan. 1, 1972, p 50*

pornshop, *n.*: Their researches have caused them to travel hundreds of yards, from one Soho pornshop to another and one saloon bar to several more. *Bernard Levin, The Times (London), Feb. 8, 1972, p 12*

[1963, abstracted from *porn* and *porno, adj., n.* (1962)]

portability, *n. U.S.* the condition permitting a worker to transfer pension contributions and entitlements to another pension fund when he changes his place of employment.

But one feature of the proposed Senate legislation rankles business. Both bills provide for "portability"—which allows employees to change jobs and carry accumulated pension benefits with them without having to start from scratch at the new job. *"Pensions: The Reformation Begins," Newsweek, Sept. 24, 1973, p 98*

[1972, derived from *portable, adj.* applied to a pension plan (1963)]

POS, abbreviation of POINT-OF-SALE.

Point-of-sale (POS) equipment emerged with unexpected strength as a giant in the retail industry. POS systems were basically real-time, data-collection computer terminal systems. They replaced traditional electromechanical cash registers and checkout devices. *Ruth M. Davis, "Computers," Britannica Book of the Year 1977, p 208*

[1972]

position, *v.t. U.S.* to market (a product or service) by appealing to a particular segment of the market in order to emphasize uniqueness and difference from the competition.

Sports Illustrated positioned itself as a third newsweekly instead of just another sports magazine, and its circulation rose. *Ted Morgan, "New! Improved! Advertising!" The New York Times Magazine, Jan. 25, 1976, p 56*

How much slick advertising can a college undertake before compromising the tone of the specific institution and higher education in general? Admissions directors now attend professional workshops in marketing, and they seek Madison Avenue advice on "positioning" their product among rivals. *Richard W. Moll, "The College Admissions Game," Harper's, March 1978, p 27*

[1973]

positive euthanasia, another name for ACTIVE EUTHANASIA.

The situational ethicist, who derives much of his philosophical base from classical utilitarian, or consequential, ethics, sees relatively little difference between negative and positive euthanasia, that is, between allowing to die and causing to die. *Robert S. Morison, "Dying," Scientific American, Sept. 1973, p 60*

[1972]

postcode, *v.t. British.* to provide with the postcode (group of letters and numbers identifying a postal area in Great Britain).

On the letters side, 13 offices were equipped with code-

365

sorting machinery, although not all were fully operational. Almost every address in the U.K. was expected to be post-coded by early 1973. *"Postal Services," Britannica Book of the Year 1973, p 558*

[1972, verb use of the noun (1968)]

posted price, a price for crude petroleum used as a reference for calculating the taxes and royalties paid by oil companies to the oil-producing countries.

Posted prices are not the prices at which the companies sell the oil but are a yardstick against which the revenues and royalties which make up the producer countries' revenue are calculated. *Egyptian Mail, June 2, 1973, p 4*

The central concept was "the posted price," a figure that in principle—though not in fact—represented the price at which crude-oil extracting divisions of the companies sold oil to their refining divisions. *Joseph Kraft, "Letter from Opec," The New Yorker, Jan. 20, 1975, p 64*

[1963] ► This term gained currency during the ENERGY CRISIS of the mid-1970's caused by the great rise in the price of oil.

post-fade, *n.* a mechanism for turning on and off the erasing head of a tape recorder to erase unwanted passages from a recording.

Post-fade on an open reel machine is an answer to the prayer of anyone taping music off-air and seeking to eliminate dull tracks and much of the excruciating disc-jockey chat. *"New Fade in Tape Recording," New Scientist, Dec. 23/30, 1976, p 719*

[1976]

post-modern, *adj.* **1** of or relating to POST-MODERN-ISM; characterized by a departure from or rejection of twentieth-century modernism in the arts.

"Post-modern" . . . denotes a period in which the radical aberrations of modern thought and modern art have at last been shaken off. . . . If some outstanding modernist artists can be admired as masters, the post-modern critic argues, they are illuminated craftsmen, like artists of other times, and owe nothing to vanguardist dogmas. *Harold Rosenberg, "Inquest Into Modernism," The New Yorker, Feb. 20, 1978, p 99*

In his latest book, *The Language of Post-Modern Architecture* (1977), Jencks [the English architecture critic Charles Jencks] complains that "any building with funny kinks in it, or sensuous imagery" has come to be labeled Post-Modern, and suggests that the term should be restricted to hybrid, "impure" buildings that are designed around historical memory, local context, metaphor, spatial ambiguity and an intense concern with architectural linguistics. *Robert Hughes, "Architecture," Time, Jan. 8, 1979, p 52*

2 following or going beyond the modern in ideas, values, technical advances, etc.

Europeans since the Second World War mostly have been content to accept America at the evaluation we ourselves are inclined to set—as the "postmodern" society, model for the world, or social laboratory for mankind . . . *William Pfaff, "Reflections: The French Exception," The New Yorker, Jan. 24, 1977, p 69*

[1976 for def. 1, probably back formation from *post-modernism;* 1969 for def. 2, from *post-* coming or developing after + *modern*]

post-modernism, *n.* a movement or style in art, architecture, literature, etc., characterized by a departure from or rejection of twentieth-century mod-

ernism (including modern and abstract art, avant-garde writing, functional architecture, etc.) and represented typically by works incorporating a variety of classical or historical styles and techniques.

My ambition has been to write splendidly engaging stories without turning my back on the history of what happened in our medium and in our culture since the decline of realism at the turn of the century. Some critics have called this postmodernism, and that seems to me a useful term to describe it, so long as it's not a mindless atavism or regression which denies that the first half of the century has happened. *John Barth, The New York Times Book Review, Sept. 24, 1972, p 36*

Post-modernism has no use for vanguards. In fact, the essential connotation of "post-modern" may be "a period without vanguards." *Harold Rosenberg, "Inquest Into Modernism," The New Yorker, Feb. 20, 1978, p 100*

The term "post-modernism" became a rubber stamp to explain everything from Christo's "Running Fence," which meandered with epic grace across 24 miles of California, to the performance art of Chris Burden, who went so far as to have himself shot to break down the boundaries between art and life. In architecture, post-modernism meant the reaction against the long-running supremacy of the International Style, which froze architectural form into ice cubes of space, by a growing number of architects including an apostate International stylist, Philip Johnson. *"Culture Goes Pop," Newsweek, Nov. 19, 1979, p 118*

[1971, from *post-* coming or developing after + *modernism,* patterned on *post-impressionism* (*c*1910) etc.]

post-modernist, *adj., n.:* The controversy over modern art was never merely between the artists and their public but also between different groups of artists: even as the avant-garde seemed to have triumphed, to have taken over the academics and become an orthodoxy, a generation of artists has arisen which considers itself "post-modernist," and which includes some who are willing to renew the dispute. *Rackstraw Downes, The New York Times Book Review, Dec. 31, 1972, p 6*

In this war of words, [Reyner] Banham accused [Charles] Jencks and the post-modernists of not being able to reject modernism totally. *Ada Louise Huxtable, " 'Towering' Achievements of '78," The New York Times, Dec. 31 1978, p 21*

post-object art, a form of art that attempts to eliminate or minimize the art object itself by stressing the theories, ideas, or personality of the artist.

Although there were at least two large exhibitions of post-object art—the "ungainly genres" as they are called—interest in such production may have waned as its sensationalism has given way to difficult searches for quality. The Walker Art Center offered "Projected Images," an exhibition by six artists who use film and video to create light environments. *Joshua B. Kind, "Visual Arts," The 1975 World Book Year Book, p 529*

[1971] Also called ANTI-OBJECT ART.

post-synch, *v.t., v.i.* to synchronize sound with motion-picture action after a scene or film has been photographed.

Tati always dubs and post-synchs his sound tracks after shooting—every word of the script, and also every buzz and every clicking high heel on overpolished tiles, which are noises that he often raises above words, following the reality of people's attention and throwing film conventio out of the window. *Penelope Gilliatt, "Profiles," The New Yorker, Jan. 27, 1973, p 46*

[1967, short for *post-synchronize* (1950's)]

pots de vin (pou də 'væ̃), *French.* bribery; (literally) pots of wine.

On a less monumental scale, these managers assert, *dash, baksheesh, pots de vin, la mordida*—in a word, bribery—is an accepted practice, necessary in many countries to get any business done. *"Scandals: The Big Payoff," Time, Feb. 23, 1976, p 30*

[1976]

pov·er·ti·cian (ˌpɑv ər'tiʃ ən), *n. U.S. (derogatory use)* a person in the administration of a government antipoverty program, especially one who profits privately from such a program.

Despite some successes, Lyndon Johnson's War on Poverty is too well remembered as one in which benefits often trickled up to the so-called poverticians—the programmers, social workers and suppliers to the needy. *Time, Aug. 29, 1977, p 18*

The Koch administration's distaste for what the Mayor has called "poverty pimps" and what Deputy Mayor Herman Badillo describes as "poverticians" has been a hallmark of its opening days in office. *The New York Times, Jan. 24, 1978, p 24*

[1977, from *poverty* + *-ician*, as in *politician*]

poverty datum line, *British.* another name for POVERTY LEVEL.

Seven companies were paying some employees below the poverty datum line (PDL) which is defined as the lowest possible amount on which a family can live under humanly decent conditions in the short run. *The Times (London), Dec. 15, 1977, p 1*

[1973]

poverty level, a minimum level of income set as the standard of adequate subsistence, below which a person or family is classified as living in poverty.

It is said that 24.3 million Americans—more than 10 percent of the population—were classified as poor in 1974, up from 23 million in 1973. . . . The poverty level is defined as an annual income of $5,038 for a nonfarm family of four. *"Rich-And-Poor Gap Was Widened in '74," The New York Times, Feb. 2, 1976, p 13*

Widespread complacency in West Germany about unemployment may have been shaken by the disclosure that at least a million people are living below the poverty level because they or their breadwinners are out of work. *Patricia Clough, The Times (London), Feb. 2, 1978, p 5*

[1966] ► The variant *poverty line*, which appeared about the same time as *poverty level*, continues to be used.

poverty trap, *British.* a condition in which people receiving government benefits cannot increase their income without losing some of those benefits.

The poverty trap (he said) is a scandal; it is becoming virtually impossible for the family below the national wage to improve its position. *The Times (London), Jan. 30, 1976, p 6*

[1972]

power game, *Especially British.* any scheme or maneuver to increase one's power over others.

Presentation of a journalists' union card can tighten up slack service in a restaurant in no time at all. While I was there, one other sort of power game was taking place: the elections for a new head of the painters' union. Grants, bursaries and priceless travel awards are in the gift of the person who holds this post and it necessarily carries a fair degree of pull. *Stephen Bayley, "The Almost Free," The Listener, June 8, 1978, p 724*

[1970]

power-sharing, *n.* a proposed coalition between the Protestant and Catholic factions in the government of Northern Ireland.

Privately, Government officials as well as Catholics and Protestants in Northern Ireland held out scant hope that the Government's plan for resumption of a convention of Catholics and Protestants could achieve a breakthrough on the issue of power-sharing. *Bernard Weinraub, The New York Times, Jan. 13, 1976, p 1*

[1970] Compare DEVOLUTION.

power tower, a power station which generates electricity with solar energy. The tower, which is surrounded by mirrors, is equipped with a device that absorbs their reflections and converts the solar energy to heat, which produces steam used to drive turbine generators.

Despite a solar research budget that has soared from less than $1 million to $290 million, the cost of making electricity from photovoltaic cells or from a power tower on which a field of mirrors is focused remains out of sight. *Edward Cowan, "And Still U.S. Energy Alternatives Are Weak," The New York Times, Dec. 5, 1976, Sec. 3, p 7*

[1972]

PQ, abbreviation of PARTI QUÉBECOIS.

The PQ, whose platform calls for Quebec to break away from the Canadian confederation but to establish a customs union with Canada after independence, took over the government of the province by winning 70 of the 110 seats in the provincial legislature. *John Dafoe, "Quebec," 1978 Collier's Encyclopedia Year Book (1977), p 466*

[1970]

P.R. or **p.r.,** *v.t. U.S. Informal.* to influence, persuade, or manipulate by means of public relations.

[Joe] McGinniss expressed doubts that any conceivable advertising campaign could resell the President. "It's a lost cause," the writer said. "They seem to have finally p.r.'d themselves into a corner that they can't p.r. themselves out of. *"Public Opinion: The Reselling Of the President?" Time, July 9, 1973, p 20*

[1966, from the abbreviation of *public relations*]

prac·to·lol ('præk təˌlɔːl), *n.* a beta-blocking drug used to control irregular heart rhythms. *Formula:* $C_{14}H_{22}N_2O_3$

At a conference prompted by concern about adverse reactions to practolol, a useful drug which produces adverse reactions in a small number of patients, Sir Eric said: "Modern medicines have become so powerful that there must be some doubt about the ability of one person to comprehend fully every new production." *John Roper, The Times (London), April 1, 1977, p 4*

[1972, from *propoxyacetanilide* (chemical constituent of the drug) + *-olol,* as in *propranolol*] Compare PROPRANOLOL.

pra·sa·dam (prə'sɑː dəm), *n.* (in Hinduism) food, usually fruit, offered first to God or to a saintly person who thereby confers a blessing and purification upon the person eating it.

There's a big feast of "prasadam" — the Hindu-style veggies which they claim bestow spiritual rewards in the very tasting. *Judith Wax, "Sharing a Son With Hare Krishna," The New York Times Magazine, May 1, 1977, p 40*

[1972, from Sanskrit]

prayer breakfast, *U.S.* a Christian prayer meeting combined with a breakfast.

The prayer-breakfast movement, evangelical in origin, has been taken up enthusiastically by mainline Protestant churches and by Mormons and Christian Scientists. It is nondenominational in emphasis, like the great revivals and crusades. *Gary Wills, " 'Born Again' Politics," The New York Times Magazine, Aug. 1, 1976, p 9*

Nowadays, no politician in the vicinity of Atlanta at the appropriate time would dream of skipping the Governor's Annual Prayer Breakfast. *E. J. Kahn, Jr., "Profiles," The New Yorker, Feb. 6, 1978, p 46*

[1976]

preaddict, *n.* *U.S.* a person who has tried or experimented with a narcotic and is therefore considered a potential addict.

But under American conditions — with heroin, so to speak, widely available except to investigators — research into occasional users would be difficult and its meaning debatable, for many American specialists automatically consign all such users to the ranks of what they call pre-addicts. *Horace Freeland Judson, "A Reporter at Large: The British and Heroin," The New Yorker, Oct. 1, 1973, p 81*

[1967]

preatmospheric, *adj.* coming or occurring before the formation of the atmosphere.

The shallow craters could be the result of preatmospheric bombardment of the planet [Venus]. *Everly Driscoll, "Our Cratered Sister Planet," Science News, Aug. 4, 1973, p 72*

[1972]

precarcinogen, *n.* a chemical precursor of a cancer-producing substance.

The concept that the chemical to which the animal is exposed is often not the molecular species which induces the tumour has given rise to a new group of terms: precarcinogen, for the parent compound; proximate carcinogen for more carcinogenically active decomposition products; and ultimate carcinogen for the product which reacts with some critical cellular component and thus induces cancer. *Peter Magee, "Nitrosamines: Ubiquitous Carcinogens?" New Scientist, Aug. 23, 1973, p 433*

[1973]

prefade, *v.t.* to cause (a new fabric or garment) to look faded.

With the rise of George McGovern, the Democrats have donned the love-beads, prefaded denims and purple sunglasses of affluent liberalism. *Kevin Phillips, The New York Times Magazine, Aug. 6, 1972, p 9*

[1972]

pregalactic, *adj.* existing before the formation of a galaxy or galaxies.

If the technique of comparing brightness and color distribution works throughout as well as hoped, it may provide a thread on which to hang details of a theory of galactic evolution from the gassy chaos of the pregalactic universe through ellipticals and spirals to disks. *Dietrick E. Thomsen, "Astration and Galactic Evolution," Science News, Nov. 6, 1976, p 300*

[1976]

pre-metro, *n.* an underground passageway for streetcars.

Interest continued in light rail systems, ranging from the "pre-metros" of such cities as Bonn and Brussels to revived streetcar (tram) systems and very light systems, such as those at airports. *David Bayliss, "Urban Mass Transit," Britannica Book of the Year 1978, p 680*

[1968, from *pre-* before + *metro* underground railway, subway]

preprocessor, *n.* a computer program for performing preliminary operations on data before further processing.

PM3 is a translator that allows programs to be written in a shorthand, thus saving programming time. Known as a Cobol pre-processor, PM3 takes shorthand statements and converts them to proper Cobol statements that will be accepted by the computer. *"Choosing Computer Technology for Government Aid," New Scientist, Nov. 30, 1972, p 510*

[1972]

preprogrammed, *adj.* programmed in advance; preset; predetermined.

How does one reconcile the known malleability of behavior with a preprogrammed and rigidly "wired" nervous system? *Eric R. Kandel, Scientific American, July 1970, p 58*

Many behavioral scientists and neuroscientists now believe that much of the brain's activity is preprogramed and that some unknown portion of it is genetically determined. *Science News, Nov. 25, 1978, p 362*

[1968]

preprohormone, *n.* a large molecule that is the precursor of a prohormone.

Preprohormones seem to exist only at stages before the final protein gets off the production line. And Günter Blobel and his associates believe that its function is as a production directive. *"Extra Ends Tell Protein Where to Go," New Scientist, Aug. 4, 1977, p 291*

[1977, from *pre-* before + PROHORMONE]

preproinsulin, *n.* the preprohormone of proinsulin.

The researchers concluded that insulin is made on the ribosome as part of the much larger preproinsulin. Evidence suggests that the extra amino acid sequence is needed to guide the newly synthesized hormone from the ribosomal surface . . . to the Golgi apparatus in which the hormone is stored as proinsulin. *Earl A. Evans, Jr., "Biochemistry," The 1978 World Book Year Book, p. 221*

[1976, from *pre-* before + PROINSULIN]

prepsychotic, *n.* a person with a predisposition to psychosis.

LSD has inspired a number of horror statistics, and it is certainly true that there is danger of long-term damage or difficult reentry into society for prepsychotics and teenagers who use the drug casually and without proper supervision. *Norman E. Zinberg and John A. Robertson, Drugs and the Public, 1972, p 49*

[1972, noun use of the adjective (1950's)]

presenter, *n. British.* a newscaster who introduces or coordinates a television or radio broadcast. The approximate U.S. equivalent is ANCHOR.

American television presenter Barbara Walters hit the headlines when she agreed to switch networks—from NBC to ABC—on the strength of a $5 millions contract. *Richard Roud, The Manchester Guardian Weekly, Jan. 9, 1977, p 19*
[1966, from *present* to introduce (the various parts of a broadcast) + *-er*]

pres·er·va·tor ('prez ər,vei tər), *n. U.S.* a person responsible for the preservation of a park, scenic or historic site, etc.

A Columbia University professor of architectural history will be named the first Preservator of Central Park, according to Edwin L. Weisl Jr., the Parks, Recreation and Cultural Affairs Administrator, *The New York Times, Sept. 29, 1974, p 25*
[1974]

president-for-life, *n.* variant of LIFE PRESIDENT.

As the young [Jean-Claude] Duvalier settled into his role of president-for-life, the battle for the real power in Haiti came to the fore. *Karl M. Schmitt, "Haiti," The Americana Annual 1973, p 331*
[1972]

presidential, *adj.* of or characteristic of a president; considered to have qualities, such as decisiveness and dignity, appropriate of a president.

The President fared better with Cathy Marceau, 23, a Los Angeles computer programmer. "Ford was very presidential," she said. "Carter seemed hesitant. Too many 'wells' and 'uhs'." *Time, Oct. 4, 1976, p 21*
[1963]

presidentiality, *n.:* Local political satirists and cartoonists . . . were preoccupied with variations on jokes about teeth, stumbling, grits, and calculated Presidentiality. *Andy Logan, "Around City Hall," The New Yorker, Sept. 27, 1976, p 60*

press kit, memorandums, sample newspaper articles, or other information handed out in a package to reporters and writers, especially at a press conference.

Mr Sean O Bradaigh, the Provisionals' publicity officer, who dispenses elaborate press kits in neat plastic folders to legions of journalists from Europe and America, says that Yugoslavia comes nearest to their ideal. *John Clare, "The IRA's Separate Roads to Unity," The Times (London), Feb. 16, 1972, p 14*
[1963]

Pres·tel (pres'tel *or* 'pres tel), *n.* a service of the British postal system that connects subscribers to a computer by telephone and displays information from it on a television screen.

Prestel . . . is now looking increasingly less like a straightforward system that provides information by linking TV sets to a computer, and more like a fully-fledged computerised data network. Prestel's change in emphasis will undoubtedly hasten, at a rate not foreseeable a year ago, the acceptance of the "personal" computer in the home or in the office. *"Prestel Impressions," New Scientist, Nov. 9, 1978, p 418*

[1978, probably blend of *presto* quick + *tele*phone and *tele*vision] Compare DATEL. See also TELETEXT, VIEWDATA.

preteen-ager or **preteenager,** *n.* a person approaching adolescence; a boy or girl approximately between 10 and 12 years of age; a preadolescent.

In her first tournament, as a preteen-ager in Southern California, she [Billie Jean King] was ordered out of a group picture because she was wearing shorts instead of a tennis dress. *Time, March 20, 1972, p 103*

Crime among teenagers—and even preteenagers—has skyrocketed in recent years. *Robert Famighetti, "Juvenile Crime," 1976 Collier's Encyclopedia Year Book (1975), p 212*
[1965] ▶ A more informal synonym, *preteen*, has been in use since about 1959.

pre·vi·a·ble (pri:'vai ə bəl), *adj.* before being able to live, especially outside of the uterus.

The legal distinction between killing a pre-viable fetus (now condoned by the court) and a viable one (here the court encouraged the states to limit abortion) is in conflict with church or secular teachings. *Marc Lappé, "Abortion and Fetal Research: A Reconsideration," Britannica Book of the Year 1976, p 382*
[1972]

Price Commission or *(especially British)* **Prices Commission,** a government commission established to regulate price increases.

Meanwhile, the Price Commission permitted only a few food processors to increase prices, and it urged the food industry to hold its requests for increases to a minimum. *Alma Lach, "Food," The 1973 World Book Year Book, p 341*

'We believe it is necessary,' the Prime Minister informed one of his questioners, 'to have this as a feature'—he was referring to the Pay Board and Prices Commission—'certainly for the next three years . . . to show the world that we are going to continue to deal with inflation . . .' *Andrew Boyle, "Britain's Week," The Listener, Jan. 25, 1973, p 105*
[1972] Compare PAY BOARD.

primal, *n.* the release of repressed childhood emotions, as by emitting primal screams or through other techniques of PRIMAL THERAPY.

One of the major aims of the therapy is to help a person fully relive an early personality-shaping experience. When this occurs, he is said to have a primal. After a primal the patient often realizes truths about himself and gains new insights which will help him achieve significant personality changes. *Thomas Verny, "Medicine: Primal Therapy: Finding Peace Through Pain," Maclean's, Feb. 1974, p 8*
[1972, probably shortened from *primal scream*]

primal scream or **primal screaming,** a scream or fit of screaming uttered by a patient in PRIMAL THERAPY.

Some of the more volatile schools of analysis (Fritz Perls' gestalt therapy, Alexander Lowen's bioenergetic approach, Janov's primal scream) teach the desirability of giving vent to one's feelings through verbal or physical acts of aggression. *Robert J. Trotter, "Let It All Out: Yes or No?" Science News, Oct. 14, 1972, p 254*

The quest for identity also accounted for the self-improvement programs associated with the human-poten-

primal therapy

tial movement—a farrago that included such quick-fix therapies as "primal scream" and "rolfing." *Newsweek, Nov. 19, 1979, p 96*

. . . the impulse that's lately sent so many people into transcendental meditation and primal screaming and astrology and est and all the other byways of the human-potential movement. *Nancy McGrath, "Learning With the Heart," The New York Times Magazine, Sept. 25, 1977, p 102*

[1972]

primal therapy or **primal scream therapy,** a method of psychotherapy developed by the American psychologist Arthur Janov. See the first quotation for details.

They are all patients in the pre-intensive stage of primal therapy, a new form of intensive psychotherapy which attempts to rid people of their neuroses by having them relive those early experiences that stunted the healthy development of their personalities. *Thomas Verny, "Medicine: Primal Therapy: Finding Peace Through Pain," Maclean's, Feb. 1974, p 8*

She is an educated, upper-middle-class New York woman of 34 who . . . paid seven psychiatrists and six psychologists more than $75,000 for treatment ranging from Freudian analysis to primal-scream therapy. *Julie Baumgold, "Agoraphobia: Life Ruled by Panic," The New York Times Magazine, Dec. 4, 1977, p 46*

[1972] Also called SCREAM THERAPY.

primal therapist: Primal therapists believe that patients can only free themselves of these neuroses by reaching back into their childhood and fully reliving the original traumatic experiences. *Thomas Verny, "Medicine: Primal Therapy: Finding Peace Through Pain," Maclean's, Feb. 1974, p 8*

primary care, medical care basic to diagnosis and treatment of an illness or condition of the body, usually the first step in seeking specialized treatment.

The AMA, in turn, called for half of the new M.D.s to go into "primary care" specialties—general practice, internal medicine, pediatrics, and obstetrics-gynecology. *Byron T. Scott, "General Medicine," 1975 Britannica Yearbook of Science and the Future (1974), p 272*

Primary-care physicians include general practitioners, internists and pediatricians, most of whom do not perform surgery and were not hard hit by new insurance rates on the first of the year. *"2-Day Coast Strike Urged on Primary-Care Doctors," The New York Times, Jan. 21, 1976, p 30*

[1974]

primary health worker, a formal or official name for a BAREFOOT DOCTOR.

Primary health workers might be described as "first aiders," trained to recognize common symptoms that require simple treatment. *Harford Thomas, "The Third World Looks to Its Own," Britannica Book of the Year 1978, p 339*

[1978]

primary production, the first link in an ecological food chain, usually consisting of green plants but in some systems of analyzing the food chain it includes bacteria.

The lower forms of life have now taken over the abundant food supply once consumed by the whales. There are not a lot of different species there, but what is there is

370

abundant. "The abundance of life at the level of primary production of vegetation is enormous," he [Jacques Cousteau] says. *"With Cousteau in the Antarctic (by Satellite)," Science News, Feb. 17, 1973, p 103*

[1970]

primary producer: Several species of bacteria use reduced inorganic compounds, such as ammonia, nitrite, and hydrogen sulfide, as energy sources and fix carbon dioxide. These may also be considered primary producers. *William J. Wiebe, "Microbial Ecology," McGraw-Hill Yearbook of Science and Technology 1978, p 144*

prime time, the period of television broadcasting that attracts the largest number of viewers. Prime time in the United States is usually considered as from 7 to 11 p.m.

The number of minutes that can be used for commercial messages on television is limited in industry practice to six per hour during "prime time"—which is the four hours of evening programming when most of the potential television audience has its sets on—and up to twelve per hour at other times. *Edward Jay Epstein, "Onward and Upward With the Arts," The New Yorker, March 3, 1973, p 60*

[1961] Compare FRINGE TIME. See also FAMILY HOUR, NIELSEN RATING.

Princeton Plan, *U.S.* a plan to give college students a recess (usually of two weeks) in an election year so that they may work for the election of candidates of their choice.

An idea widely heralded on college campuses emerged in 1970 from the student uprisings that followed the American invasion of Cambodia. Instead of seeking change through violent rebellion, why should not students work within the electoral system for reform? This was the basis for the so-called Princeton Plan. . . . The plan was copied at many schools. *Fred M. Hechinger, The New York Times, Feb. 6, 1972, Sec. 4, p 9*

[1970] ► During the 1960's the term *Princeton Plan* was the name of a plan to achieve racial balance in public schools by pairing a school of predominantly white students with one of black students so that all students in certain grades attend the same school. Both *Princeton Plans* originated at Princeton University.

print journalism, *Especially U.S.* the gathering of news or the writing for newspapers and magazines as distinguished from newsgathering and reporting for television and radio.

Federal statute and administrative rulings impose restrictions on broadcasting that do not exist for print journalism. *"Who Decides Fairness?" Time, Feb. 4, 1974, p 59*

"Media" suggests that there is no difference in purpose and function between print journalism and television journalism; that within print journalism there is no difference in function and purpose between *Time* and the New York *Times. Henry Fairlie, The Atlantic, Jan. 1975, p 29*

[1972] Compare BROADCAST JOURNALISM, ELECTRONIC JOURNALISM.

print journalist: Earlier this week, we of the Broadcasting Press Guild held a lunch to hand out scrolls to the winners of our 1974 television awards. I should explain that the Guild is composed of print journalists who write about broadcasting. *The Listener, April 10, 1975, p 466*

print press or **printed press,** *Especially U.S.* the

editors and journalists of newspapers and magazines, or newspapers and magazines themselves, as distinguished from radio and television.

Although the print press was in there plugging, the week clearly belonged to television. *Newsweek, Feb. 26, 1973, p 55*

Nixon, who by then had developed equivocal feelings, to say the least, about the printed press, could still manage a kind word on behalf of the electronic media. *Thomas Whiteside, The New Yorker, March 17, 1975, p 41*

[1973]

pri·or·i·tize (prai'ɔr ə,taiz), *v.t.* **1** to arrange in order of importance; establish priorities for.

I do have a special interest, based on what I hope is a creative self-perception. It is to upgrade my potential. When I prioritize my goal/objectives, that comes first. *Edwin Newman, "My College Essay . . ." The New York Times Magazine, Jan. 16, 1977, p 29*

2 to give preference or priority to.

New York's financial problems don't come from "bloated" social services. This crisis was caused by a system that prioritizes money for the Pentagon and the banks' debt service before our needs. *Catarino Garza, "Why I Am Running for Mayor," The New York Times, Oct. 8, 1977, p 23*

The thousand-odd delegates to the . . . conference sat dutifully in the Winter Gardens from 9 am until midnight adding composite resolutions, referring back amendments, and "prioritizing" motions as only they know how. *Ian Bradley, Blackpool, in a Letter to the Editor, The Times (London), April 8, 1978, p 3*

—*v.i.* to establish priorities.

Next, you need to sift the essentials from the nonessentials. You need to establish priorities—or, as Mrs. Habeeb says, the second step is to Prioritize. In other words, just who are you and what are you? Are you a Perfectionist, a Compulsive Doer, a Lick-and-a-Promise Type, or an Out-and-Out Slob? *"The Talk of the Town," The New Yorker, Oct. 16, 1978, p 35*

[1972] ▶ In the first quotation above, *prioritize* is used in a context intended to parody the jargon of social scientists. Though this and other words in *-ize* (e.g. *finalize*, widely used since the 1940's but established in Australian English since the 1920's) have had difficulty finding initial acceptance among conservative users of the language, derivatives using *-ize* and borrowings ending in *-ize* have long been a part of English. Some examples: *sympathize* (1591), *Christianize* (1593), *philosophize* (1594), *idolize* (1598), *satirize* (1610), *monopolize* (1611), *realize* (1611), *legalize* (a1716), *eulogize* (a1810), *radicalize* (1823). See also STRATEGIZE.

prior restraint, *U.S.* a court order prohibiting publication of material or disclosure of proceedings deemed by the court to interfere with due process, threaten national security, and the like.

Judges concerned that their trials remain valid began to issue gag orders and prior restraints on the press. They have done so 45 times since the Sheppard case, and 12 times in the past year. *Fred W. Friendly, "A Crime and Its Aftershock," The New York Times Magazine, March 21, 1976, p 18*

Nobody seemed to have noticed that the government has very little power to impose even its benign intentions, that it lost the Pentagon Papers case and every other case in which it attempted to impose prior restraint. *Lewis H. Lapham, "The Art of Innocence," Harper's, April 1976, p 12*

If prior restraint (prevention of publication) has a chilling effect on free speech, then obligatory disclosure of notes (enforcement of publication) has a chilling effect on free thought. *"The Talk of the Town," The New Yorker, Aug. 14, 1978, p 23*

[1972, so called from its being imposed before the actual appearance of the material in print]

proabortion, *adj.* favoring or permitting induced abortions, especially abortion-on-demand.

"I got into the abortion issue when I started teaching criminal law in 1963," Professor [Robert] Bryn said recently. "I decided to study it because at first everything I came across seemed to be proabortion. So, I found some other people who were also disturbed . . . and we sort of formed our own group, Metropolitan Right to Life." *Fred C. Shapiro, The New York Times Magazine, Aug. 20, 1972, p 34*

[1972, from *pro-* favoring + *abortion*] Compare ANTIABORTION. See also ABORTION.

proabortionism, *n.:* My impression is that it is the upper middle class . . . who are the social "headquarters" of proabortionism, as of liberal attitudes in general, in this country. *M. J. Sobran, Jr., "Abortion: The Class Religion," National Review, Jan. 23, 1976, p 28*

proabortionist, *n.:* The anti-abortionists came across as narrow and vengeful, their arguments a primitive reaction against what threatened their sexual hang-ups. . . . The proabortionists came across as equally fanatical upholders of women's right to abortion. *Peter Black, The Listener, April 26, 1973, p 537*

Compare ABORTIONIST, ANTIABORTIONIST.

problematics, *n.pl.* a complex of problems and uncertain conditions.

Mr. Schrag is, admirably, for pluralism, and he suggests at the end that the way out of our present predicament is to *institutionalize* (his word) pluralism in all possible ways. The assertion itself and some of the examples he then offers (decentralizing schools, police forces, health services) show that he has devoted little thought to the inherent problematics of institutionalization. *Robert Alter, Review of "The Decline of The WASP" by Peter Schrag, The New York Times Book Review, March 5, 1972, p 40*

[1970, from *problematic, adj.* (OED 1609)]

prob·le·ma·tique (prɔb lə ma'ti:k), *n.* the complex of interrelated problems, especially of pollution, urban decay, shortage of resources, inflation, etc., affecting technologically advanced and industrial countries.

MIT nuclear engineering professor David J. Rose proposes one partial solution: the establishment of new, interdisciplinary institutions dedicated to *problematique*, the current European term for such issues as energy, environmental quality, transportation and public health. *John H. Douglas, Science News, Aug. 10, 1974, p 92*

Peter Roberts . . . says that the Meadows' team model that provided the basis for *The Limits to Growth* and the earlier model developed by Professor Jay Forrester "suffered from such substantial shortcomings that they cannot be considered useful tools for enhancing understanding of the 'problematique'." *"Model Behaviour by the British Government," New Scientist, Oct. 6, 1977, p 7*

[1972, from French, from the adjective *problema-*

371

tique problematic; originally a usage of the CLUB OF ROME]

problem bank, *U.S.* a bank listed by a government regulatory agency as having financial problems.

Combining bank supervision in one agency was an idea that developed from the well-publicized "problem bank" situation. Many institutions had gotten into difficulty during the recession from bad loans, particularly those involving real estate. *Robert D. Hershey, Jr., "Banking," The Americana Annual 1977, p 114*

[1976]

product liability, *U.S.* a manufacturer's responsibility for any damage, loss, or injury caused by his product.

"The whole area of product liability is getting expensive and litigious, "says Dr. Alan R. Hinman, director of the Center for Disease Control's immunization division, "and the companies are self-insuring—for several million dollars' worth, even, of claims . . ." *Dodi Schultz, "Who Is Liable When Something Goes Wrong?" The New York Times Magazine, May 7, 1978, p 154*

[1974] *Abbreviation:* PL

prog (proug), *n. British, Informal.* program.

A new series of BBC-2 commences at 8 pm: . . . In tonight's prog, Anthony Smith has a look at the world's newest national park, created two years ago on the eastern border of Bavaria in West Germany. *"The Week Ahead," New Scientist, June 15, 1972, p 644*

[1972, by shortening of *programme*]

pro·grade ('prou,greid), *adj.* moving in the same direction of rotation as the celestial body being orbited.

All known prograde satellites (those going the same way as the majority of rotary motions in the solar system), except Phobos, . . . are gradually increasing their distance from their planets. Retrograde satellites have the opposite condition. They come closer and ultimately crash into the planet. Thus retrograde satellites gradually disappear. *Science News, March 24, 1973, p 180*

[1968, from *pro-* forward + retro*grade*] See CORO-TATE, RESONANCE.

progressive country, *U.S.* a form of country music that stresses social themes in the lyrics and innovative techniques in instrumentation.

The "progressive country" artists include such Nashville rebels as Waylon Jennings, Willie Nelson, songwriter Billy Joe Shaver, Tompall Glaser, and Bobby Bare. These artists share a dislike for the more facile sentimentality of mainstream country music, as well as for its tried-and-true chord changes, instrumental setups, and formulaic production. *Ed Ward, "Music," 1975 Collier's Encyclopedia Year Book (1974), p 364*

[1974] Also called OUTLAW COUNTRY.

progressive lens, a bifocal or multifocal lens with no outwardly visible lines and with a gradual change of focus that provides clear vision at all distances.

American Optical Corp., the largest American maker of lenses, recently introduced *Ultravue*, a progressive lens made of plastic. *"How to Buy Eyeglasses," Consumer Reports, Nov. 1977, p 649*

[1976]

progressive rock, a technically elaborate and often experimental form of rock music.

Two progressive-rock bands—one led by former Door [Doors, a rock group] Ray Manzarek and another, a German specimen called Passport—share the stage . . . *"Goings On About Town," The New Yorker, March 24, 1975, p 6*

[1968] Also called HEAVY ROCK. Compare ART ROCK.

progressive rocker: Concerts grew ever bigger and more depersonalized. . . . It was, in the words of Robert Fripp, one of the most interesting of the British progressive rockers turned reductionist, a time for "dinosaurs." *The New York Times, Aug. 13, 1979, p C16*

progressive soul, *U.S.* a form of soul music incorporating elements of jazz and disco music.

Rufus, the progressive soul band that features Chaka Khan as vocalist, faced high expectations at the Felt Forum on Saturday night. *Robert Palmer, The New York Times, April 12, 1976, p 37*

[1974]

prohormone, *n.* a chemical substance that is the inactive precursor of a hormone.

The natural [parathyroid] hormone is initially produced as a prohormone, which is a linear chain of 106 amino acids. The prohormone is rapidly converted into its storage, or glandular, form, which is a chain of only 84 amino acids. *Earl A. Evans, "Biochemistry," The World Book Science Annual 1974 (1973), p 263*

[1973, from *pro-* anterior, before + *hormone*] Compare PREPROHORMONE.

proinsulin, *n.* the prohormone of insulin.

It turned out that proinsulin (the inactive precursor of insulin) had a fairly low affinity for the receptor. *"Membrane Receptors Grab Insulin," New Scientist and Science Journal, Sept. 23, 1971, p 669*

Proinsulin consists of a single polypeptide chain containing the A and B chains and the C peptide, all linked covalently. *William A. Frazier, et al., "Nerve Growth Factor and Insulin," Science, May 5, 1972, p 482*

[1968, from *pro-* anterior, before + *insulin*]

pro-life, *adj.* opposed to legalized abortion, especially in advocating or supporting antiabortion laws; RIGHT-TO-LIFE.

Catholics do constitute the backbone of the pro-life movement, and the action performed in defense of the sanctity of life . . . reflect a new militancy whose object will eventually be to correct other of recent years' mistaken developments besides the legalization of abortion. *Gary Potter, Washington, D.C., in a Letter to the Editor, The New York Times, Jan. 29, 1978, Sec. 4, p 16*

[1972, from *pro-* in favor of + *life*] See ABORTION.

pro-lifer, *n.:* Besides the big corporations and the unions, virtually every interest group has a representative in Washington, from the Grey Panthers, the senior citizens' campaign, to the "pro-lifers," who oppose abortion. *Jonathan Steele, "America in Crisis," The Manchester Guardian Weekly, Sept. 3, 1978, p 5*

▶ Like *right-to-life*, the term *pro-life* is used and promoted chiefly by antiabortionists, since it implies that those who favor unrestricted abortions are against "life."

promo, *U.S. Informal.* — *n.* an advertisement, promotional announcement, or other presentation.

The misadventures of Roger and his gifted cat are not as "marvelously funny" as the promos for the book explain on the jacket. *Marvin Kitman, The New York Times Book Review, April 16, 1972, p 8*

— *adj.* used for promoting some person or thing; promotional.

The boss controls the newspaper and assorted promo material, which is likely to feature pictures of himself peering knowingly into a mine face or welding machine. *Wilfred Sheed, "What Ever Happened to the Labor Movement?" The Atlantic, July 1973, p 62*

[1962 for noun, short for *promotion* publicity and advertising; 1970 for adjective]

pro·nase ('prou,neis), *n.* an enzyme that breaks down proteins into simple compounds, derived from a species of soil bacteria and used in biomedical research.

Previously, Beatrice Mintz and Carl Illmensee of the Cancer Institute in Philadelphia had used a particular enzyme called pronase to remove the zona pellucida (protective covering) surrounding embryos. After the coverings were removed, the embryonic cells were sticky, and two embryos could be pushed together to form a single embryo. *Science News, Oct. 22, 1977, p 263*

[1965, probably from *protein*ase enzyme that breaks down proteins to peptides]

pronatalism, *n.* support or advocacy of childbearing and, generally, an expanding rate of birth.

"Pronatalism" as editors Ellen Peck (author of "The Baby Trap") and Judith Senderowitz (a vice president of Zero Population Growth) explain is "any attitude or policy that is 'pro birth,' that encourages reproduction, that exalts the role of parenthood." *Letty Cottin Pogrebin, Review of "Pronatalism: The Myth of Mom and Apple Pie," The New York Times Book Review, Feb. 23, 1975, p 36*

[1972, from earlier (1950's) *pronatalist, adj.,* from *pro*- favoring + *natal*ity birth rate + *-ist*]

pro·neth·al·ol (prou'neθ ə,lɔ:l), *n.* a beta-blocking drug that controls irregular heartbeat. *Formula:* C₁₅H₁₉NO

. . . the selective blockade of epinephrine by the beta adrenergic blocking agent pronethalol. *Earl W. Sutherland, "Studies on the Mechanism of Hormone Action," Science, Aug. 4, 1972, p 404*

[1964, from *prop*yl + am*ine* + *methyl* + naphth*alene* + menthan*ol*]

Proper Names. ► This book is in general concerned with common vocabulary and not with names of persons and places. However, important proper names can come to be used as ordinary nouns (as in World War II *Munich* meant "appeasement" and *Quisling* became a synonym for "traitor"). Probably the most famous proper name to have emerged during the 1970's is WATERGATE, originally the name of a building complex in Washington, D.C., which took on several meanings, produced various derivatives and even a combining form (-GATE), and thus quickly became part of the contemporary language.

The entries in this book include various types of proper names and words formed from proper names that can be classified as follows:

1. Common nouns (and sometimes verbs) from names of persons or places, such as BARGELLO (noun and verb), ROGALLO, SIEMENS.

2. Fictitious characters used as stereotypes or personifications: ARCHIE BUNKER, MR. CLEAN, OCKER, STRANGELOVE.

3. Names used in figurative and transferred senses: BERLIN WALL, CHECKPOINT CHARLIE, ANDROMEDA STRAIN, CATCH-22.

4. Names formed from common nouns or from other names: ANIK, BACKFIRE, HARE KRISHNA.

5. Nicknames and other special names of places, people, or things: BEEB, BERMUDA TRIANGLE, BIG APPLE, SOHO.

6. Names of organizations, associations, political parties, etc.: JANATA, KHMER ROUGE, RED ARMY, RED BRIGADES.

7. Names of peoples and languages: BENINESE, TASADAY, AMERICAN SIGN LANGUAGE, DARI, YERKISH.

8. Abbreviations and acronyms representing names of organizations, associations, agencies, programs, etc.: AIM, CETA, OAU, OSHA.

9. Derivatives: nouns, verbs, adjectives, etc., derived from names of persons and places: FERMIOLOGY, FINLANDIZE, MOONIE, NADERITE.

10. Phrases (usually technical terms) naming things after a person or place (eponyms): FOSBURY FLOP, HEIMLICH MANEUVER, LORDSTOWN SYNDROME, MARBURG DISEASE, MAUNDER MINIMUM, OKLO PHENOMENON.

propfan, *n.* an eight-bladed propeller driven by a jet engine for subsonic aircraft.

On flights of up to 1,500 miles, the prop fan would be 40% more fuel economical, since a propeller is more efficient than jet thrust during climb-outs and letdowns. *Time, Aug. 14, 1978, p 65*

Attributive use.

Lockheed, under contract from NASA, also delved into fuel-economic aircraft with . . . a four-engined, 200-passenger transport employing "propfan" engines — essentially advanced turboprop engines with smaller-diameter, eight-bladed propellers. *Warren C. Wetmore, "Transportation," The Americana Annual 1977, p 512*

[1977, from *propeller* + *fan*]

Proposition 13, *U.S. and Canadian.* a law or measure for reducing authority to impose taxes, especially on property, etc. (used in reference to the measure passed by voters in California in June, 1978 to reduce property taxes by more than 50 percent). *Often used attributively.*

Appreciative of what the city [New York] had endured during the last three years of retrenchment, . . . Felix Rohatyn, chairman of the Municipal Assistance Corporation said recently — "We have gone through our own Proposition 13." *Andy Logan, "Around City Hall," The New Yorker, Sept. 4, 1978, p 85*

The post office is caught in a vise between the union and treasury board, Ottawa's watchdog over spending. Buoyed by the Proposition 13 mood in the country, treasury board is cracking down on civil service wages as part of its program of restraint. *Ian Urquhart, Maclean's, Oct. 2, 1978, p 23*

Sen. William Proxmire of Wisconsin . . . points out that to give American cities today what Europe got under the Marshall Plan would be to inflict mass cutbacks in urban spending that not even the lunatic fringe of the Proposition 13 crowd would espouse. *T. D. Allman, "The Urban Crisis Leaves Town," Harper's, Dec. 1978, p 48*

History records . . . a catchy little ditty called "Proposition 13" as a box office smash with the only audience that counts, the voters. *Brad Knickerbocker, The Christian Science Monitor, April 18, 1979, p 1*

[1978, from the name of the California initiative, also known as the Jarvis-Gann initiative or amendment, after its authors and main sponsors, Howard Jarvis and Paul Gann] See TAX REVOLT.

pro·pran·o·lol (prou'præn ə₁lɔːl), *n.* a beta-blocking drug that controls irregular heartbeat, high blood pressure, and angina pectoris. *Formula:* $C_{16}H_{21}NO_2$

Propranolol was found by chance to be effective in relieving mental symptoms in patients given the drug for physical disease. Propranolol is not a tranquilizer (it slows and steadies the heartbeat) but it can relieve some of the symptoms of anxiety such as palpitations and a racing pulse. *The Times (London), Dec. 28, 1974, p 12*

[1966, from iso*pro*pylamino-*propanol* (chemical constituents of the drug) + -*ol* (chemical suffix)] Compare PRACTOLOL.

proprietary, *n. U.S.* a business secretly owned by the Central Intelligence Agency.

Most of the agency's existing proprietaries, the report said, are shell corporations with paper assets that are used to provide agents with working cover or to hide the agency's operations. But the report found that the operating proprietaries had been used heavily in the past to extend the C.I.A.'s presence abroad, to provide support for paramilitary operations, to disseminate propaganda and to manage the agency's private investments. *John M. Crewdson, "C.I.A. Secretly Owned Insurance Complex and Invested Profits in Stock Market," The New York Times, April 27, 1976, p 25*

[1975]

pros·ta·cy·clin (₁pras tə'sai klin), *n.* a hormonelike substance that inhibits the aggregation of blood platelets and dilates blood vessels, produced naturally by enzymes in arterial cells.

Chemists have succeeded in synthesising a natural substance which it is hoped may lead to the prevention of heart attacks and strokes in people with atherosclerosis. The compound, prostacyclin, synthesized in America by the group headed by Dr U. F. Axen, of the Upjohn Company, is thought to protect human beings from the formation of blood clots inside healthy blood vessels. *"Science Report," The Times (London), April 2, 1977, p 16*

[1976, from *prosta*glandin (any of the class of hormonelike substances to which prostacyclin belongs) + *cycle* + -*in* (chemical suffix)] Compare THROMBOXANE. See also ENDOPEROXIDE.

protected village, an enclosed and guarded camp or settlement in Rhodesia and, now, in Zimbabwe to which black villagers are relocated by the government in areas of black nationalist guerrilla activity.

There are now 50 protected villages in Rhodesia, and nearly 100,000 tribesmen live in them. Most have been built in the past two years. New ones are being built as funds become available. *Michael T. Kaufman, "From an Embattled Land," The New York Times, July 11, 1976, p 35*

There were reports . . . of black voters being forced into voting especially in the so-called 'protected villages' in the warzone. Despite Smith's claims to the contrary there were strong indications that the guerrillas did succeed in preventing some of the population from going to the polls. *The Weekly Review (Nairobi), April 27, 1979, p 25*

[1975] See PATRIOTIC FRONT.

protective reaction, *U.S.* **1** a bombing raid on an enemy target conducted in self-defense or retaliation. *Often used attributively.*

A secret Air Force investigation concluded that the Commander of the Seventh Air Force, Gen. John D. Lavelle, had ordered at least 28 unauthorized raids into North Vietnam and later reported them as "protective reaction"—a defensive action. *Seymour M. Hersh, The New York Times, June 18, 1972, Sec. 4, p 1*

An aggressive attack by an armada of airplanes, which most speakers of English call simply an *air raid,* was instead spoken of as a momentary defensive strategy, a *routine limited duration protective reaction. Peter Farb, Word Play, 1974, p 136*

2 *Transferred use.*

The same is true of people who believe themselves persecuted and harassed by "enemies" who are out to "get" them—and who, as a sort of "protective-reaction strike," persecute and harass these same "enemies." *Hendrik Hertzberg and David C. K. McClelland, "Paranoia," Harper's, June 1974, p 52*

[1970] ▶ During the early 1970's the phrase *protective reaction strike* was appropriated by protesters against the Vietnam War as a mocking euphemism. This use of the term is exemplified in the following quotation:

And, of course, Vietnam was the great source of that kind of thing. 'Bombing, bombing, why do you always say bombing?' one of the military spokesmen was quoted as saying. 'These are protective reaction strikes.' *Edwin Newman, quoted by Tony Cash, The Listener, Jan. 15, 1976, p 45*

See EUPHEMISMS. See also **light at the end of the tunnel** under LIGHT.

protein-calorie malnutrition, a form of malnutrition common in economically depressed areas, and characterized by deficiencies in protein and overall caloric intake that lead to depletion of magnesium and potassium in the body.

The spectrum of protein-calorie malnutrition (PCM as it is known to workers in the field) varies from a diet that is relatively high in calories and deficient in protein (manifested in the syndrome known as kwashiorkor) to one that is low in both calories and protein (manifested in marasmus). *Jean Mayer, "The Dimensions of Human Hunger," Scientific American, Sept. 1976, p 40*

[1971]

protein clock, a hypothetical biological mechanism regulating the rate of evolutionary changes in the protein of a species.

By plotting the genetic differences between the flies against time, measured by the known evolution of the islands, Carson was able to predict the points at which each species evolved and the speed of the protein clock. This speed, he suggests, is a rate of 1 percent genetic difference per 20,000 years. *"Hawaiian Flies: Setting the Protein Clock," Science News, Feb. 21, 1976, p 118*

[1976, patterned on *biological clock*]

protoporcelain, *n.* early pottery that resembles porcelain, especially ancient reddish pottery of China made white with kaolin and given a thick glaze.

Finely textured, hard-glazed "protoporcelains" of the Shang gave way to more hastily created pottery, designed for utilitarian purposes. *John H. Douglas, "A New Vision of Classical China," Science News, Dec. 21 and 28, 1974, p 395*

[1973]

protostellar, *adj.* of or relating to the protostars (star-forming gaseous matter); giving rise to stars.

Computer simulations of spherical, protostellar clouds of stellar masses, collapsing under self-gravity, have been developed by Richard Larson and by C. C. Hayashi and his collaborators. *Stephen E. Strom, "The Formation of Stars," 1977 Britannica Yearbook of Science and the Future (1976), p 76*

[1971]

proved reserves or **proven reserves,** the amount of oil or natural gas that can be removed profitably from available sources.

In considering resources of oil and gas one encounters a category that has no exact counterpart in world coal statistics: the concept of "proved reserves." The term refers to discovered and well-delineated reserves that can be extracted by available techniques at current costs and sold at current prices. *Sam H. Schurr, "Energy," Scientific American, Sept. 1963, p 116*

The Israelis have also found major natural gas fields in the northern Sinai. Proven reserves amount to over 35 billion cubic feet. *Jim Lederman, "Middle East," New York Post, Dec. 29, 1978, p 5*

[1960]

prox·e·mics or (*British*) **prox·ae·mics** (prak'si:- miks), *n.* (*pl.* in form, *sing.* in use). the relative degrees of physical proximity tolerated by members of an animal species, cultural group, etc.

Meanwhile the essential biology studies whole animals and plants. And in animals we have in recent years learned how important is social behaviour and proxaemics in the fullness of life and our understanding of it. *Frank Fraser Darling, Review of "Production, Pollution, Protection" by W. B. Yapp, New Scientist, June 1, 1972, p 520*

[1972, from *proxemic* (1967) of or involving physical proximity]

proximity talks, diplomatic discussions in which disputing parties occupy separate but proximate locations while a mediator moves back and forth between them.

Carter began conducting what is known in diplomacy as "proximity talks." Because Sadat and Begin were in lodges less than 100 yds. apart, Carter was able to move easily from a bilateral conversation with one to a chat with the other. *Time, Sept. 25, 1978, p 12*

[1973] Compare SHUTTLE DIPLOMACY.

PRT, abbreviation of *personal rapid transit* (an au-

tomated system of small passenger cars that stop at individual destinations by pushing a button).

For the passenger, a PRT would seem like a cross between an automatic lift and a monorail. Units will run out-side on elevated beams, but they will have no driver and when they stop—often inside building lobbies—the doors will open and close automatically. *Joseph Hanlon, "Personal Rapid Transit Comes to the U.S.," New Scientist, May 25, 1972, p 429*

[1972]

pseudorandom, *adj.* produced in sequences that imitate statistical randomness of sampling or distribution; not truly random.

Instead of using a short pulse to provide a broad-band rf [radio frequency] source, pseudorandum noise can be used to modulate the monochromatic rf and thus excite nuclei with a range of resonance frequencies. If this is done, the output noise is no longer random since it contains signals from the nuclear resonances. *Edwin D. Becker and T. C. Farrar, "Fourier Transform Spectroscopy," Science, Oct. 27, 1972, p 367*

[1961]

pseudorandomly, *adv.*: Each alarm is interrogated pseudo-randomly every 2-3 seconds and a small PDP8 computer identifies the change of state on a visual display unit. *"Alarming Growth," New Scientist, June 3, 1976, p 529*

pseudovirion, *n.* a virion (infectious viral particle) that contains nucleic acid from the host cell.

In another experimental approach, virus-like particles which contain pieces of cellular DNA (pseudovirions) instead of viral DNA are being used as the vector for DNA-mediated genetic modification. *Theodore Friedmann and Richard Roblin, "Gene Therapy for Human Genetic Disease," Science, March 3, 1972, p 952*

[1970]

psi (saɪ), *n.* short for PSI PARTICLE.

The first candidates were the particles discovered in 1974 at the Brookhaven National Laboratory and at SLAC [Stanford Linear Accelerator Center], which were named *J* or psi. It was immediately proposed that the psi consists of a charmed quark and a charmed antiquark, a combination called charmonium. *Scientific American, April 1976, p 55*

[1974]

PSI, abbreviation of *Personalized System of Instruction,* another name for the KELLER PLAN.

The most attractive feature of PSI for students was self-pacing; the students take a short examination on a unit of instruction whenever they feel they are ready and are allowed to repeat the examination without penalty or prejudice if they do not pass. *Melvin H. Marx, "Behavioral Sciences: Psychology," 1975 Britannica Yearbook of Science and the Future (1974), p 195*

[1973]

psi·khush·ka ('psi: xu:ʃ kə), *n. pl.* **-ki** (-ki:). Russian slang term for a PSYCHOPRISON.

The dissidents who have spent time in these *psikhushki* —the word they have coined for these madhouses—estimate that several thousand political offenders are currently undergoing "treatment" in their wards. *Ludmilla Thorne, "Inside Russia's Psychiatric Jails," The New York Times, June 12, 1977, p 27*

psion

[1976, from the Russian combining form *psikh-*, *psikho-* psych-, psycho-]

psi·on ('sai,ɑn), *n*. another name for the PSI PARTICLE.

Various particles, known as "psions," have been discovered in the last year and a half that are thought to possess charm as a hidden property. *"Subatomic Particle Manifesting 'Charm' Reported on Coast," The New York Times, June 9, 1976, p 17*

[1976, from *psi (particle)* + *-on* elementary particle]

psionic, *adj.*: By now, something like nine members and cousins of the psionic family have been catalogued, and there may be more to come. *"Charm at Last: How Sweet It Is," Science News, June 5 and 12, 1976, p 356*

psi particle, any of a group of subatomic particles of large mass and long lifetime. Psi particles are classed as hadrons composed of a charmed quark and a charmed antiquark.

The main significance of the discovery of the psi particle was that it provided compelling evidence for the existence of a fourth kind of quark, which had earlier been named the "charmed" quark. *Martin L. Perl and William T. Kirk, "Heavy Leptons," Scientific American, March 1978, p 50*

[1974, so called by its discoverers (at the Stanford Linear Accelerator in Palo Alto, Calif.) from the resemblance of the paths made by daughter particles to the Greek letter *psi* (Ψ)] Also called J PARTICLE and PSION. See QUARK.

PSRO or **P.S.R.O.,** abbreviation of *professional standards review organization*, a regional medical review board.

The PSRO's would be empowered to review patients' records and track down instances of unnecessary treatment and overlong hospital stays. *Newsweek, Dec. 17, 1973, p 94*

P.S.R.O.'s . . . were established in the hope of providing health care economically through the evaluation of the quality of care being provided in hospitals. *The New York Times, Jan. 14, 1978, p 20*

[1973]

psychic healer, a person who cures the sick by means of psychic power or energy transmitted through touch, meditation, prayer, etc.

Psychic healers have achieved many cures that cannot be denied — or even explained in conventional scientific terms. *Newsweek, April 29, 1974, p 67*

Only after he has done his persuasive best do I admit to Dr. Kirklin that I have hedged my bets. A psychic healer in New York, mobilized by a friend, will be devoting the next day to transmitting restorative waves down the Eastern seaboard specifically in my direction. *Douglass Cater, "How to Have Open-Heart Surgery (and Almost Love It)," The New York Times Magazine, May 14, 1978, p 60*

[1974]

psychic healing: Psychic healing may or may not involve religious faith. Often it requires no faith at all. Some believe that anyone can heal. Others believe that only certain people can heal. *Charles W. Bell, Sunday News (New York), Aug. 12, 1979, p 55*

psychic numbing, a denial of reality induced as a protection against overwhelming and unacceptable stimuli.

How did so many doctors manage to preside over killings while viewing themselves as idealists? . . . [Robert Jay] Lifton concludes that they invoked two standard psychological forms of self-delusion: the first is "psychic numbing"; at Auschwitz, for example, doctors talked compulsively about technical matters to avoid confronting the reality of all the horrors around them. *"Doctors of the Death Camps," Time, June 25, 1979, p 68*

[1970]

psychic surgeon, a psychic healer who claims to be able to remove diseased tissues from the body.

Still farther from the pale of reason are claims of the so-called "psychic surgeons" of the Philippines and Brazil. These spiritual healers not only "cure" tennis elbow and the like, but supposedly "operate" on the critically and terminally ill without benefit of scalpel or anesthesia, removing "cancerous tissue" and other "tumours" from the credulous sufferers for substantial fees. *Lawrence K. Lustig, "Science and Superstition: An Age of Unreason," Britannica Book of the Year 1976, p 271*

[1976]

psychic surgery: One programme was about psychic surgery, practised mainly in the Philippines. Surgeons grope into a patient's stomach and produce blood and entrails, leaving no scar. Sometimes patients say they feel better, although in some cases the blood and entrails have been shown to belong to chickens. *The Times (London), Dec. 19, 1977, p 12*

psychobabble, *n*. psychological jargon, especially the jargon of psychotherapy groups.

It dawned on Rosen that her words were nothing more than "psychobabble" hippie argot laced with psychiatric terms to give the impression of weight and meaning. *Kaspars Dzeguze, "How to Talk Stupid and Influence People," Maclean's, April 17, 1978, p 74*

According to the practitioners of currently fashionable psycho-babble, we live in the best of times because more and more people are "being upfront" about their feelings and "doing their own thing." *William Colgan, The New York Times, July 18, 1979, p A23*

Another key verb in psychobabble is *hang*, meaning to act, behave, comport oneself. The injunction to "hang loose" is familiar and expressive, conveying a quintessentially Californian state of relaxed readiness for new experience . . . "So if you want me to hang in there any longer, you're gonna have to bring your energies to reconstituting this marriage entirely." *David Lodge, "Where It's At: California Language," in The State of the Language, ed. L. Michaels and C. Ricks, 1980, p 509*

[1977, coined by the American author Richard D. Rosen in his book *Psychobabble: Fast Talk and Quick Cure in the Era of Feeling* (1977), from *psychological* + *babble*]

psychobabbler, *n*.: Meanwhile I stand on the roof of my Mill Valley house, watching the flood of psychobabble rising, ever rising, and wishing I knew how to turn the situation around. It won't be easy. The psychobabblers not only outnumber the rest of us, but, what is worse, they have The Force on their side. *Cyra McFadden, "Semantic Spinach, or, Mellowing Out in Sunny California," The New York Times Magazine, Nov. 20, 1977, p 124*

psychobiography, *n*. the story of a person's life from the point of view of psychoanalysis; a psychoanalytical biography.

376

There are various objections to psychobiography. First, few biographers have any formal training in psychoanalysis. Secondly, which school of psycho-analytic theory is to be followed: Freud, Jung or another? *Bevis Hillier, Review of "Aubrey and the Dying Lady" by Malcolm Easton, The Times (London), Oct. 5, 1972, p 11*

It is the paradox of psychobiography that it resolutely ignores the feasts of available information to pounce, with the trumpets at full blast, on a mere crumb. *Edwin M. Yoder Jr., Review of "Dimensions of a New Identity," by Erik H. Erikson, National Review, Aug. 16, 1974, p 936*

And, as often occurs in psychobiography, unless evidence is abundant and conclusive, alternative interpretations, often equally plausible, can be argued. *Nathan G. Hale, Jr., Review of "Freud and His Followers" by Paul Roazen, The New York Times Book Review, Jan. 12, 1975, p 26*

[1967, from *psycho*analysis + *biography*]

psychobiographer, *n.*: Melville kept his secrets to himself, though he left behind the sort of clue that makes as cheery a sight for the psychobiographer as the first fire of fall. *Richard Todd, The Atlantic, Dec. 1975, p 114*

psychobiographical, *adj.*: Its [the book's] aims are simpler and less ambitious; it makes no large historiographical, mythological or psychobiographical assumptions, offering instead an inquiry into the transformations of Greek and Roman concepts of heroic virtue. *Frank Kermode, Review of "Hero and Saint" by Reuben A. Brower, The New York Times Book Review, Dec. 10, 1972, p 36*

psychoenergetic, *adj.* of or involving the use of psychic energy, as in psychokinesis (mentally influencing the movement of objects) and radiesthesia (being sensitive to energy radiations).

To move forward and reliably identify psychoenergetic effects via high-voltage photography, we must carefully monitor those physiological parameters that can directly influence the streamer process and which can be altered by mental or emotional changes in the living organism. *William A. Tiller, "Are Psychoenergetic Pictures Possible?" New Scientist, April 25, 1974, p 163*

[1972]

psychoenergetics, *n.*: While the experimental conditions were not perfect, the events at Birkbeck do represent a major step forward in the new field of experimental psychoenergetics. *Jack Sarfatt, "Off the Beat: Geller Performs for Physicists," Science News, July 20, 1974, p 46*

psychogeriatrics, *n.* the study and treatment of psychological disorders affecting the elderly.

The eastern opium dens of the past will be replaced by state controlled hallucinogenic centres which will provide a supervised escape from the technological horrors of the 21st century. In the expanding field of psychogeriatrics these drugs will become the mainstay in the management of such patients. *Peter Schiller, "Psychiatry's Future," New Scientist, June 15, 1972, p 637*

[1972]

psychohistory, *n.* **1** historical study and writing that uses the methods of psychology and especially of psychoanalysis.

THE PRESIDENTIAL CHARACTER: *Predicting Performance in the White House.* By James David Barber. A fascinating experiment in psychohistory in which psychological factors are brought to bear on evaluating the performances of the presidents of this century, and a frame-work is suggested for predicting the character of future administrations. *"SR Reviews Books," Saturday Review, Dec. 2, 1972, p 88*

There are repeated attempts in the mode of psychohistory (acknowledgments are made to Erik Erikson) to link the acts of the man to the experience of the child. *Benjamin DeMott, "Life and Letters: Capital of Russia," The Atlantic, Feb. 1974, p 87*

2 an historical account or analysis using these methods.

Yes, he would attempt what no one else had even thought of daring to venture—a multi-angular psychohistory of the man whose very name suggested deep affinity with Capricorn's own verbal compulsions. *Joseph Epstein and Gerald Graff, "Gabby," The New Yorker, Oct. 1, 1973, p 34*

[1969]

psychohistorian, *n.*: When the same techniques are applied to history by psychohistorians, it is always the "psycho-" that wins over the "-history." Psychohistory is just another example of the "growing habit of psychologizing," says Jacques Barzun in *Clio and the Doctors. Earl Shorris, "Market Democracy," Harper's, Nov. 1978, p 98*

psychological pricing, the pricing of a product to enhance its value or increase its sales appeal.

Psychological pricing is the old gimmick of taking a price to the nearest figure of nine; if normal markup methods will produce a price of, say, 25 cents for a can of peaches, the store will boost it to 29 cents and the customer will think he is getting a bargain cut down from 30 cents. *Walter Stewart, "The Games Supermarkets Play," Maclean's, Aug. 1974, p 63*

[1972]

psy·chon ('saiˌkɑn), *n.* a theoretical particle of matter bearing a psychic message.

He writes with precise lyricism about other observed or putative sub-atomic entities: quarks, mindons, psychons, the ghostly neutrinos which have no physical properties and fall in billions through space and matter. . . . *A. S. Byatt, "Books," Review of "The Roots of Coincidence" by Arthur Koestler, The Times (London), Feb. 10, 1972, p 12*

[1972, coined by the Hungarian-born British writer Arthur Koestler (born 1905), from *psych-* + *-on* elementary particle or unit] Compare MINDON.

psychoprison, *n.* a psychiatric hospital for the criminally insane in the Soviet Union.

During the past decade, it has become increasingly routine for the Soviet regime to put dissidents onto the judicial conveyor belt that dispatches them to corrective labor camps and to psychoprisons, roughly in a ratio of ten to one. *Harvey Fireside, Soviet Psychoprisons, 1979, p 64*

[1979] Also called PSIKHUSHKA. See AMINAZIN, SLUGGISH SCHIZOPHRENIA, SULFAZIN.

psychosynthesis, *n.* a method of psychotherapy combining psychoanalysis with various exercises and meditation techniques adopted from oriental philosophy and religion by Roberto Assagioli, an Italian psychiatrist.

Psychosynthesis—This multidimensional growth therapy developed in Italy now is attracting increasing attention in the U.S. It uses various forms of group and individual therapy, including meditation. written self-analysis, guided daydreams (fantasies) and music. *New York Post, Feb. 26, 1977, p 23*

These have included growth groups, encounter groups, T-groups, sensory-awareness training, Arica training, the Gurdjieff method, psychosynthesis, Zen, etc. *Morris B. Parloff, "How Werner Got It," Psychology Today, Nov. 1978, p 136*

[1973] ► Formerly (1950's) this term designated a form of psychotherapy that opposed psychoanalysis, especially by discouraging such processes as abreaction and catharsis and stressing instead the development of a strong, reality-centered ego.

psy·toc·ra·cy (sai'tak rə si:), *n.* an autocratic government in which the behavior of people is regulated by psychological means.

According to the authors of *Requiem for Democracy?* [Lewis M. Andrews and Marvin Karlins], behavior-control technology has placed us on the threshold of regulating our own psychosexual evolution. This evolution can go toward *participatory democracy*, with its emphasis on human individuality and initiative, or toward what they call *psytocracy*, with manipulative emphasis on human conformity and passivity. *Psychology Today, April 1971, p 24*

[1971, from *psychological* + au*tocracy*]

PTV, abbreviation of *public television* (noncommercial TV).

After 20 years of rather dry, highbrow fare, PTV came up with some creative, audience-attracting productions that are helping to alter its old image. *Kathryn Rose, "Television and Radio Broadcasting: Public Television," 1972 Collier's Encyclopedia Year Book (1971), p 542*

[1971] Compare PBS.

public, *adj.* **go public,** to come before the public with confidential information; present private information in public.

A foretaste of what [John] Dean had already told committee staffers in a secret rehearsal leaked into print last week, and his accusations promised to be explosive indeed when he went public. *Newsweek, July 2, 1973, p 13*

Quickly there came more figures and helpful explanations from Mobil, Shell, Gulf, Standard of Indiana and Exxon. The decision to go public with company data, even on a small scale, represents a new era. *"The Oil Information Shortage," The New Republic, Jan. 26, 1974, p 7*

The dispute went public at the weekend, when one of the National Weather Service forecasters, in giving his bulletin, remarked: "... We attempt to give an honest and scientific appraisal of weather situations and are not intent on scooping anybody on a news story." *The Times (London), Feb. 15, 1978, p 5*

[1968, transferred sense of the financial term (1950's) meaning "to make a public offering of stock to raise capital"]

public access, *Especially U.S.* television broadcasting on channels set aside by law for the exclusive use of community groups and other segments of the public. *Often used attributively.*

Some half-dozen cities have experimented sporadically with public access, and New York City's two cable operators ... are now beaming 150 hours of do-it-yourself TV each week over their public-access channels. *Newsweek, April 9, 1973, p 83*

[1972] Compare ACCESS².

public-interest law, *U.S.* a branch of law dealing

with class action suits and other legal means of protecting the general interests and welfare of the public.

Meites chose public-interest law, he says, because he "couldn't bother with the conventional lawyer's willingness to take either side." *Time, May 24, 1971, p 44*

In the United States ... there has developed over the last five years a new department of jurisprudence: public-interest law, in which the courts are used as an integral part of the campaign for clean air, unpolluted rivers, quieter cities, and unbulldozed landscapes. *Jon Tinker, "Is English Law Too Stuffy for Pollution?", New Scientist, Sept. 28, 1972, p 547*

[1970]

public-interest lawyer: Three public-interest lawyers in San Francisco, acting on their own, filed a class-action lawsuit against "Henry Kissinger *et al.*" on behalf of parents in Vietnam to reunite them with these non-orphans as quickly as possible. *Tracy Johnston, The New York Times Magazine, May 9, 1976, p 14*

public key, a cryptographic key used without risk of decoding by others because the letter values assigned to a second key are needed for decoding. *Often used attributively.*

The authorised recipient of these messages has publicised his "public key," the numbers R and S. But only he knows the prime factors of R. With this knowledge, the encrypted message can be quickly rendered into plain text by a similar function C^T (modulo R). But calculation of the vital decrypting factor, T, is only possible if you know the prime factors of R. And only the person who published the key will thus be able to understand such messages. *Duncan Campbell, "The Revolution in Cryptography," New Scientist, March 2, 1978, p 594*

[1978]

Public Lending Right, *British.* a royalty paid to authors based on the number of times their books are borrowed from public libraries.

The comparatively new notion known as Public Lending Right has already placed authors on a collision course with librarians, who regard the proposed law as an intrusion and a nuisance, and with some government officials, who look upon professional writing as a pleasant risk instead of as a property right. *Herbert Mitgang, "Britain Weighs Library Royalty," The New York Times, Oct. 14, 1976, p 34*

[1969] *Abbreviation:* PLR

pu·ka ('pu: kə), *n.* a small, perforated white shell common on Hawaiian beaches, used for stringing on a wire to form a necklace or bracelet. *Often used attributively.*

Necklaces of puka shells, liquid silver, coral birds, turquoise cylinders and African trading beads are giving diamonds a run for their money these days. *Tobi Frankel, "Baubles, Bangles and Beads," The New York Times Magazine, Jan. 4, 1976, p 38*

In a show of solidarity, Vancouver's blue-jean literati, led by aging poetry guru and University of British Columbia Professor Warren Tallman, dusted off their puka beads and held a series of parties last month. *Thomas Hopkins, "Tempest in the West: Art vs. Boondoggles," Maclean's, Oct. 23, 1978, p 66*

[1974, from Hawaiian, literally, hole, perhaps short for *pukaihu* hole in a pearl shell]

pu·la ('pu: lə), *n.; pl.* **-la** or **-las.** the monetary unit of Botswana, equal to 100 thebe.

The pula was introduced in 1976 replacing the South African rand which had been used as Botswana currency since independence. The pula is valued at par with the rand. *George T. Kurian, "Botswana," Encyclopedia of the Third World, 1978, p 176*

[1976, from the Setswana word for rain]

pull-date, *n.* a date, stamped on packaged food, after which the food is no longer fresh and may not be sold in its regular shelf space at full price.

The council strongly urged that labeling for processed foods include serving size, a list of ingredients, nutritional information, and the pull-date. *Robert A. Skitol, "Consumer Affairs," 1973 Collier's Encyclopedia Year Book (1972), p 248*

[1972] Compare OPEN-DATE.

pull tab, a metal tab that is pulled to open a can or container.

They guzzle all day and all night; they garland themselves with the pull tabs from beer cans. *Pauline Kael, "The Current Cinema," The New Yorker, March 4, 1972, p 89*

A quick-release pull tab is provided so that when the container has served its useful purpose the protective film can be stripped away and the main body of the container dissolved in water. *Adrian Hope, "Patent News: Plastic Container That Can Be Dissolved in Water," The Times (London), Feb. 18, 1976, p 24*

[1963]

punctuational, *adj.* characterized by periods of little or no change punctuated by episodes of rapid change.

Punctuated equilibrium provides a model for the "small" level of speciation and its consequences. But a preference for punctuational over gradual tempos may be asserted at more encompassing levels of the history of life itself. This history is not, as many people assume, a tale of slow progress, leading to greater complexity of form and greater diversity of kinds and numbers. It is, in important respects, a series of plateaus punctuated by rare and seminal events that shift systems from one level to another. *Stephen Jay Gould, "Evolution: Explosion, Not Ascent," The New York Times, Jan. 22, 1978, Sec. 4, p 6*

[1978]

punctuationalism, *n.:* The alternative theory is called... "punctuationalism." According to this, the diversity of life has come about as a result of sporadic adaptations by small, well-defined groups confronted by a new environment, interspersed with long periods of little or no change. *"Missing, Believed Nonexistent," The Manchester Guardian Weekly, Nov. 26, 1978, p 1*

punctuationalist, *n.* A convinced punctuationalist, he contrasts bivalves and mammals to support (unconvincingly, I believe) the hypothesis that rate of evolution is determined by rate of speciation. *Robert E. Ricklefs, Review of "Patterns of Evolution as Illustrated by the Fossil Record," edited by A. Hallam, Science, Jan. 6, 1978, p 58*

punk, *n.* **1** short for PUNK ROCK or PUNK ROCKER.

Lou Reed has stayed with punk, ... nailing his colours firmly to the mast of traditional rock and roll. *Clive Bennett, The Times (London), April 27, 1977, p 14*

The critics heap abuse and the punks gather up each salvo like evil-smelling flowers. The game is to shock. To

goad. To enrage. To *move.* There is no ideology. Only a vague desire for power and potency. The implements are guitar, bass and drums, amplified to an ear-bleeding volume. The music is corporate (no solos), two and three chord pedantry; endings are ragged and the words are generally unintelligible. *Tom Hopkins, "Dada's Boys," Maclean's, June 13, 1977, p 42*

No matter, he survived punk, and Talking Heads are going to survive us all. Now I know why they didn't like it when I used to compare them to the Beatles, even before they had a disk to their name. *Michael Newman, "The Diadem of Pop Culture," High Times, Jan. 1979, p 123*

2 a style of clothing worn and popularized by performers of punk rock.

Classic punk is on sale at Boy, a unisex shop offering Gary Gilmore memorial T-shirts, multi-zippered jackets and shirts whose cuffs are attached to the shoulders by chains. *Sandra Salmans, "Where to Go in London," The New York Times, Sept. 26, 1977, p 38*

3 a person who follows punk fashions in clothing, makeup, etc.

"The Punks are also rebelling against a very repressive atmosphere. Kids have even been arrested for wearing T-shirts some people consider offensive," adds Pamela, showing off a Punk sporting naked cowboys, another the Queen's head with an obscene connotation. *Ruth Preston, "Punk Fashion: It's Fun and It's Bad," New York Post, June 9, 1977, p 42*

—*adj.* of or characteristic of punk rock, punk rockers, and the style of ragged clothes and garish makeup and decorations worn and popularized by punk-rock groups.

The British punk bands are a community linked by anger and frustration. They are, within the music world, a rebuke to the bourgeois excesses. *Time, July 11, 1977, p 47*

Kent ... wears yellow jeans and a t-shirt whose shoved-up sleeves are held in place with pink safety-pins. He's got a punk crew-cut, but not Paris punk. Kent is provincial punk, lead singer with a group from the Lyon suburbs called the Starshooters. *Pierre Georges and Dominique Pouchon, "Amour Toujours," The Manchester Guardian Weekly (Le Monde section), Jan. 29, 1978, p 13*

[1972]

punk rock, a form of rock music resembling early rock 'n' roll, played and sung in an aggressive, rowdy style by performers usually made up in ragged clothes.

Punk rock has been stealing up on us for some time now, with the original tales of torn clothes cobbled together with safety pins being superseded by more bizarre ones concerning punk fans transpiercing their cheeks, Afghan zealot style, with those same safety pins. *Michael Church, "Catching up with Punk: The London Weekend Show," The Times (London), Nov. 29, 1976, p 11*

Actually, "punk rock," as it is called, has brought about some useful changes in popular music, as many respected rock critics have pointed out, and its roots can be traced back to the very origins of rock itself and perhaps even a little bit farther. *Garrison Keillor, The New Yorker, May 30, 1977, p 38*

[1972, from *punk* young hoodlum] Compare GLITTER ROCK, NEW WAVE.

punk rocker: In between cutting up their bodies with broken glass and switchblades, spitting up on stage, and thinking up new names to "shock," Punk rockers sing and play — execrably. *Maclean's, June 13, 1977, p 1*

purchasing-power bond, a bond in which the amount of annual interest and final repayment are not stated as a fixed sum but adjusted to an index.

The issuance of purchasing-power bonds on a large scale is a prerequisite for any extensive issuance of price-escalated life insurance, in order to provide the appropriate assets to match such liabilities. *Milton Friedman, "More On Living With Inflation," Newsweek, Oct. 29, 1973, p 96*

[1973]

Pur·ex or **pur·ex** ('pyuˈr eks), *adj.* of or designating a system for reprocessing nuclear fuel by which both pure uranium and pure plutonium are produced.

Similar efforts would be needed in any demonstration of the existing Purex recycling process on breeder fuel. That process is used in several countries, including the United States, for both weapons and power programs. *The New York Times, Feb. 28, 1978, p 49*

[1971, from *plutonium* reduction by solvent *ex*traction, probably influenced by *pure*] Compare CIVEX.

purple membrane, a membrane under the cell wall of halobacteria, capable of changing sunlight into chemical energy in a process resembling photosynthesis.

When light shines on the gloriously purple membrane the pigment molecules change shape slightly and shoot out a proton. This proton pumping sets up a mini-electrical potential which can be harnessed to generate important biochemicals (particularly ATP) for the bacterium, and to transport nutrients from the outside to the inside. *"This Week: Electricity and Fresh Water from Bacteria?" New Scientist, March 11, 1976, p 547*

[1976]

push-in crime or **push-in job,** *U.S. Slang.* a mugging at the door of a person's home.

The Senior Citizens Robbery Unit is assigned all cases involving indoor robberies of Bronx victims over the age of 60. Many of these crimes are the so-called "push-in" jobs that occur when a robber or group of robbers waits in a hallway for a victim to come home, and then pushes him or her into the apartment. *Judy Klemesrud, The New York Times, Nov. 13, 1976, p 11*

[1976] Compare CRIB CRIME.

pyramid selling, *Especially British.* a method of extending the number of franchises held by a chain of stores in which a company pays its franchise holders to recruit new franchise holders, instead of restricting them to the sale of the company's products.

The new orders, issued under powers of the Fair Trading Act . . . "will crack down on objectional features of pyramid selling." Significantly the new regulations will put an end to the payment of substantial sums to join a pyramid-selling organisation. *Alex Brummer, "Collapse of Pyramids?" The Manchester Guardian Weekly, Nov. 3, 1973, p 11*

[1971]

py·re·throid (paiˈri: θrɔid *or* paiˈreθ rɔid), *n.* any of a group of fast-acting insecticides similar to the natural pyrethrins but made synthetically.

A potent new pesticide one hundred times as effective as DDT began extensive trials. Known only by the code name NRDC 143, it was a new synthetic pyrethroid, a chemical similar to the pesticides extracted from the pyrethrum flower but much more powerful and longer-lasting. *John Newell, The Annual Register of World Events in 1973 (1974), p 404*

[1971, from *pyrethr*in + *-oid* (one) like] See RESMETHRIN.

Q

QCD, abbreviation of QUANTUM CHROMODYNAMICS.

In the QCD theory quarks interact by exchanging a gluon, a quantum of the electromagnetic force. Naively applied, this picture is insufficient. To improve on the simple model theorists suggested that quarks have a side-to-side motion within the proton, for example a transverse momentum of their own. *"New Quark Theory Already Under Threat," New Scientist, Nov. 9, 1978, p 435*

[1977]

Quaa·lude ('kwei,lu:d), *n.* a trademark for a sedative and hypnotic drug having addictive properties. Generic name, METHAQUALONE.

There's a new entry: Quaalude, the brand name of a white pill that acts as a depressant. Vassar used twenty thousand of them in three weeks, and they tell of one Brooklyn college that uses five thousand a day. *"The Week," National Review, Dec. 8, 1972, p 1332*

It is four months since Dr. Bourne, one of President Carter's key advisers, wrote his disastrous prescription for Quaalude—time, that is, for a less hysterical view of official Washington's drug scene. *Michael Halberstam, Psychology Today, Nov. 1978, p 129*

[1972] Also called LUDE, QUAD², and SOPOR.

quack·u·punc·ture ('kwæk yə,pəŋk tʃər), *n.* the misleading or fraudulent use of acupuncture by dishonest practitioners.

FDA is concerned that acupuncture does not fall into the category of "quackupuncture." *FDA Consumer, May 1973, p 23*

Acupuncture anesthesia does indeed work. . . . Unfortunately, acupuncture has become an American fad instead of the subject of serious experimental research. Acupuncture in America has become transformed into "quackupuncture." *Samuel Rosen, "On 'Quackupuncture'," The New York Times, May 28, 1974, p 39*

[1973, blend of *quack* and *acupuncture*]

quad¹, *adj., n.* short for QUADRAPHONIC or QUADRAPHONY.

Domestic quad listening needs two additional loudspeakers over stereo, and two more amplifiers, plus the black box which allocates some of the sound to the rear left/right and others to the front left/right. *The Listener, Oct. 23, 1975, (page not known)*

Quad is a new medium in which the musical experience is heightened. *"Music: The Mod Quad," Newsweek, Feb. 5, 1973, p 65*

[1970]

quad², *n.* a slang name for QUAALUDE.

On the street and on campus, methaqualone is known by various corruptions of its trade names: "quads" (from

Qaalude, made by William H. Rorer, Inc.). . . . It was so popular among the young people who camped out at last year's political conventions that Miami Beach's Flamingo Park was dubbed "Quaalude Alley." *"Medicine: The Deadly Downer," Time, March 5, 1973, p 73*

[1973, by shortening and alteration of *Quaalude*] Compare LUDE.

quad³, *n. U.S.* a unit of energy equal to a quadrillion British thermal units. One quad is equivalent to 24 million metric tons of petroleum.

Without any new initiatives the need for imported oil will rise steadily from about 12 quads at present to more than 60 in the year 2000. *H. A. Bethe, "The Necessity of Fission Power," Scientific American, Jan. 1976, p 21*

Although it is by far the most abundant indigenous energy source, coal ranks only third in consumption. Last year, it provided Americans with an estimated 14.1 quads of energy, or the equivalent of roughly seven million barrels of oil a day. That satisfied barely 18 percent of total energy needs. In 1973, coal provided 13.3 quads. *The New York Times, July 16, 1979, p A12*

[1974, short for *quadrillion*]

quadraphonic, *adj.* of, having to do with, or using quadraphony.

Quadraphonic music has stereo buffs drooling these days and last week was something of a milestone for the new technique: the first American recording session of symphonic music in the round. The work: Bela Bartok's tumultuous "Concerto for Orchestra," tailor-made for the four-speaker quad play-back system. *"Music: Sound in The Round," Newsweek, Jan. 1, 1973, p 40*

[1972, alteration of earlier (1970) *quadriphonic*] Also called FOUR-CHANNEL, QUADRASONIC.

quadraphonically, *adv.:* The sound track, reproduced quadraphonically, makes the floor hum and the seats vibrate, and the songs come out in bounteous cascades. *Jay Cocks, "Cinema," Review of "Ladies and Gentlemen, The Rolling Stones," Time, May 6, 1974, p 90*

quadraphonics, *n.* variant of QUADRAPHONY.

The system requires, for the best reproduction, one channel fewer than the number of speakers. So a commercial model with three channels and four speakers (quadraphonics requires four channels) looks the most likely development. *The Times (London), Dec. 23, 1974, p 12*

[1972, alteration of earlier *quadriphonics*]

quadraphony, *n.* any system of high-fidelity sound reproduction involving signals transmitted through four different channels.

The big question for me was whether, in the process of attempting to wrap the listener of the future in quadra-

381

phony, music-making would slip out by the back door. *Edward Greenfield, "Classical," The Manchester Guardian Weekly, April 28, 1973, p 23*

[1972, from *quadraphonic*, alteration of earlier *quadriphonic*] Compare AMBISONICS, SURROUND-SOUND.

quadrasonic, *adj.* another term for QUADRAPHONIC.

One of the most popular Sibelius symphonies, recorded once again, this time in what is called compatible quadrasonic sound; i.e., the sides can be played on a standard stereo machine as well as on four-channel equipment. *Winthrop Sargeant, "Concert Records," The New Yorker, April 28, 1973, p 142*

[1972, alteration of earlier (1970) *quadrisonic*]

quadrasonics, *n.* another name for QUADRAPHONY.

Two competing approaches to quadrasonics emerged: the "purist" approach, in which four separate sound tracks were recorded from four microphones and then played back separately to four speakers, and the "matrix" approach, in which two specially encoded channels were fed into a decoder where they were electronically adjusted and then split up and fed to the four speakers. *Stephen Scrupski, "Electronics," The 1972 Compton Yearbook, p 230*

[1971, alteration of earlier *quadrisonics*]

quadrominium or **quadraminium,** *n.* another name for FOURPLEX.

In Chicago, Dayton and some West Coast areas, four-dwelling condominiums—or "quadrominiums"—have become the fastest selling form of housing. *"Quadrominium Hunting Near Chicago," Time, March 29, 1971, p 51*

The same economies are present in various other forms of new housing, such as quadraminiums and townhouses. *Business Week, July 13, 1974, p 58*

[1971, from *quadro-* or *quadra-* four + con-do*minium*]

Qua·li·täts·wein (ˌkwa: liːˈteitsˌvain), *n.* any German wine officially guaranteed as originating from grapes grown in several specified regions.

Qualitätswein, the next rung on the ladder, is really just a better grade of table wine, but it must come from a specified region, must be made from certain grape varieties and must have enough sugar in the must—the name given to the crushed grapes just before fermentation—to produce 7.5 percent of natural alcohol during the fermentation process. *Frank J. Prial, "Cultivating Weinsmanship," The New York Times Magazine, Dec. 10, 1978, p 178*

[1972, from German, literally, quality wine]

► The corresponding official designation for French wines is *appellation contrôlée.*

quan·go (ˈkwaŋ gou), *n. British.* a government body or organization with independent powers.

Quangos cover a large field. The National Enterprise Board (chairman £31,850, deputy £26,000, seven members £1,000 a year each) is a quango. So is the Water Services Staff Commission (one unpaid chairman, four members receiving £125 a year). They descend from the familiar (the Post Office) to the arcane (Committee for Terotechnology), take in the enormous (90 area health authorities), and . . . include the local (King's Lynn Conservancy Board) and the specialist (Ship's Wireless Working Party). *Caroline Moorehead, "Trying to Track Down the Elusive 'Quangos'," The Times (London), Oct. 5, 1976, p 4*

I notice the Right-wing Tories who attack quangos never

mention the House of Lords, the biggest quango of them all. *W. E. Baugh, Manchester, in a Letter to the Editor, The Manchester Guardian Weekly, July 15, 1979, p 2*

The machinery of the Dartmoor National Park Authority is an object lesson in Britain's complex bureaucracy. It operates autonomously under its national park officer, Ian Mercer. But Mr Mercer is responsible both to this committee, which is part of Devon County Council, and to the Countryside Commission, a "quango" financed from central government. *Robert Waterhouse, "Dartmoor: Infinite Variety," The Manchester Guardian Weekly, Jan. 20, 1980, p 20*

[1975, acronym for *quasi-autonomous national governmental organization*] See ACAS.

quantitative genetics, another name for POPULATION GENETICS.

The study of the genetic basis of individual differences in intelligence in humans has evolved in the traditions and methods of that branch of genetics called quantitative genetics or population genetics, the foundations of which were laid down by British geneticists and statisticians such as Galton, Pearson, Fisher, Haldane, and Mather and, in the United States, by J. L. Lush and Sewall Wright. *Arthur R. Jensen, Genetics and Education, 1972, p 104*

[1972]

quantized bubble, another name for HARD BUBBLE.

A stumbling block was, however, identified by workers at Bell Telephone Laboratories . . . who reported the existence of a new form of magnetic bubble, namely the "hard" or "quantized" bubble. *"Solid State: Hard and Soft Bubbles," Nature, Nov. 24, 1972, p 184*

[1972]

quantum, *adj.* of sudden, spectacular significance or effect; representing a major breakthrough.

A major lesson of the energy crisis is that we must retreat from some of our quantum technological advances. *Mark Goodman, "Final Tribute," New Times, March 22, 1974, p 68*

Xerox . . . refers to the dry, electrostatic copying process (a quantum improvement over earlier wet photographic methods) finally developed in 1938 in a one-room laboratory behind a beauty parlor in Astoria, Queens, by a penurious patent attorney named Chester F. Carlson. *Time, March 1, 1976, p 69*

[1971, abstracted from the earlier *quantum jump* (1955) and *quantum leap* (1970) a sudden, spectacular advance]

quantum chromodynamics, the theory that quarks possess a quantum property called color, of which there are three that combine in each quark to produce the force that binds quarks together.

For fifty years physicists have searched for a theory of strong interactions, yet it is only in the last year or so that a possible solution has emerged. This is the theory of quantum chromodynamics, which has now made the surprising prediction that a remarkable new kind of elementary particle should exist. Such a claim allows the theory to be put to experimental test. *The Times (London), Feb. 16, 1978, p 14*

If a fundamental theory of matter called quantum chromodynamics, or QCD, is correct, the gluon must exist, and if the scientists had failed to find it in their new experiment, much of the theoretical work in physics in the past decade would have been in serious doubt. *Malcolm W. Browne,*

"Detection of The Elusive 'Gluon' Exciting Scientists," The New York Times, Sept. 2, 1979, p 1

All this is pulled together in a theory called quantum chromodynamics (QCD) analogous to the thoroughly-proved quantum electrodynamics which describes the interaction of particles through electromagnetic forces. *Robert C. Cowan, "Particle Physics: Poised for a Breakthrough," Technology Review, Dec./Jan. 1980, p 11*

[1977] Also called CHROMODYNAMICS. See QUARK.

quark, *n.* ► In 1961 the American physicist Murray Gell-Mann proposed that all subatomic particles are composed of combinations of three fundamental particles which he called *quarks* (after a word in Joyce's *Finnegan's Wake*). The three types of particles (FLAVORS) were what are now called the DOWN QUARK, the UP QUARK, and the STRANGE QUARK. However, the discovery of new classes of particles suggested the possibility of a fourth quark. Such a quark would exhibit a property which was called CHARM, and the search for particles containing CHARMED quarks led to the discovery of the PSI (or J) PARTICLE in 1974. Such a particle was also called CHARMONIUM.

Then in 1977 the discovery of the UPSILON gave support to the existence of yet a fifth quark, the BOTTOM QUARK, having the property of BEAUTY. This spurred the search for a symmetrical companion to the bottom quark called TOP QUARK whose property was given the name TRUTH. The top quark would bring the number of quarks to six. However, as many as eighteen types of quark are possible according to the theory of QUANTUM CHROMODYNAMICS, which holds that each quark possesses a quantum state or property called COLOR. It is the COLOR FORCE which binds quarks together, and the carrier of this force is a particle called GLUON, which moves at the speed of light and becomes stronger as the distance between quarks increases.

A variation in the combination of the basic three-quark model was advanced in 1977 when physicists proposed a particle built from two quarks and two antiquarks, which they called BARYONIUM.

The quark theory has not been accepted by all physicists. The BOOTSTRAP and REGGE theories, for example, conceive of matter in terms of abstract mathematical models rather than in terms of fundamental physical building blocks such as quarks. Although evidence of the existence of subparticles continues to accumulate as particle accelerators reach higher and higher energy levels, no free quarks have been seen so far, though physical evidence for the gluon continues to mount promisingly.

qua·si·at·om ('kwei zɑi'æt əm), *n.* a short-lived nuclear particle resembling an atom.

Quasi-atoms are systems in which particles not normally found in atoms become bound together in a way analogous to the proton and electron in a hydrogen atom and exhibit an atom-like hierarchy of discrete energy levels. Examples are positronium (electron and positron) and muonium (electron and muon). Quasi-atoms are generally unstable structures either because they are subject to matter-antimatter annihilation (positronium) or because one or more of their constituents is radioactively unstable (muonium). *Science News, June 5 and 12, 1976, p 356*

[1975, from *quasi-* part, near + *atom*] See PIONIUM.

quasifission, *n.* a type of nuclear fission in which the target and projectile nuclei do not fuse before splitting but retain their original forms.

When nuclear physicists began to strike heavy nuclei against each other in heavy-ion accelerators, they expected that projectile and target would fuse into a new compound nucleus, and the compound nucleus would then fission according to its own internal dynamics, producing two new fragments. What the physicists found instead was mostly what is called quasifission: Target and projectile form a momentarily bound system, but it seems to remember what the original nuclei were. When it splits, its fragments tend to reproduce the projectile and target. *"Physical Sciences: Quasifission and Energy," Science News, Jan. 17, 1976, p 41*

[1974, from *quasi-* part, near + *fission*]

quasimolecule, *n.* a structure formed by a combination of quasiatoms.

Basically, electron ejection from an atom or a quasimolecule is due to the time-varying electric field acting on the electron as the collision partners pass each other. If the collision partners have comparable atomic numbers, it must usually be assumed that the electrons in both adjust their orbits so as to form quasimolecular states from which an electron will be removed. *W. E. Meyerhof, "Atomic Physics," McGraw-Hill Yearbook of Science and Technology 1975, p 115*

[1972, from *quasi-* part, near + *molecule*]

quasimolecular, *adj.:* The large class of "quasimolecular" transitions offers some hope to those who seek an energy storage system. These are transitions in which the upper level is a bound complex of atoms, molecules, or mixtures of the two, while the lower level is a transitory state existing only very briefly while the components of the complex fly apart. *Malcolm McGeogh, "Lasers for Fusion," New Scientist, July 24, 1975, p 207*

Qube (kyu:b), *n.* the trademark for a two-way cable television system that allows subscribers to participate in some programs.

From the demonstrations I saw, Qube seem very coy about flashing up the actual size of the sample behind all its impressive percentages, and the total imponderable is, of course, over whose finger is on the button. *Peter Fiddick, "Towards an Electronic Democracy?" The Listener, May 10, 1979, p 650*

[1977]

quick and dirty, *U.S. Slang.* easily and cheaply made or done; of inferior quality.

President Carter announced an indefinite deferral of the reprocessing of commercial spent fuel, and Congress passed the Nuclear Antiproliferation Act, but a study by Oak Ridge National Laboratory concluded that any country with access to spent fuel could build a "quick and dirty" reprocessing plant to produce bomb-grade plutonium. *"Science and Society," Science News, Dec. 24, 1977, p 438*

[1977, probably extended sense of *quick-and-dirty* (1968) slang term for a cheap eating place, itself an alteration of *quick and filthy* (1940's)]

quick fix, *Informal.* a hasty, superficial remedy or solution to a problem.

At first, Schreiber called Dreyfus' proposal a gimmicky, vote-getting "quick fix." Replied Dreyfus: "It is a quick fix, I agree. But what do they want—a slow fix?" *Time, Oct. 16, 1978, p 43*

Then, Gerald Rafshoon, the smooth Atlanta ad man who helped get Mr. Carter elected, was on his way to Washington, bringing along a bag of media gimmicks and public-relations quick fixes that he is still employing today, as the President approaches another campaign. *B. Drummond Ayres Jr., "The Importance of Being Rosalynn," The New York Times, June 3, 1979, p 39*

Attributive use.

The quest for identity also accounted for the self-improvement program associated with the human-potential movement—a farrago that included such quick-fix therapies as "primal scream" and "rolfing." *Newsweek, Nov. 19, 1979, p 96*

[1966; influenced by *fix* slang term for a shot of a narcotic. See FIX.]

quiet room, a locked, cell-like room used in some psychiatric hospitals to seclude intractable patients.

The researchers found that persons diagnosed as schizophrenic and manic-depressive were placed in the quiet room more often than were those with personality disorders and depressive neuroses. Schizophrenics were the most frequently secluded group. *"Behavior: 'Quiet Room' Can Be Disturbing," Science News, June 4, 1976, p 360*

At the South Florida State Hospital, a 72-year-old woman lies.... Dehydrated and suffering from a compound fracture of the hip, she had been left unattended in the "quiet room." *"Mental Patients: A 'Forgotten Minority' in U.S.," U.S. News & World Report, Nov. 19, 1979, p 49*

[1976]

quin·a·crine mustard ('kwin ə krin), a bright-yellow fluorescent compound that stains chromosomes selectively, used especially to determine the sex of fetuses during pregnancy.

T. Caspersson and his colleagues at the Karolinska Institute, Stockholm, ... showed that when hamster and bean chromosomes were stained with a compound called quinacrine mustard, and viewed with long wavelength ultraviolet light, the chromosomes fluoresced differentially along their length. *Peter Pearson, New Scientist and Science Journal, March 18, 1971, p 606*

The male Y chromosome could be made to fluoresce brightly in human cells when stained with quinacrine mustard. *H. E. Kubitschek, "Life Science: Molecular Biology," Britannica Book of the Year 1974, p 419*

[1970] ► As an antimalarial drug, quinacrine in hydrochloride form has been known since the 1930's.

quin·es·trol (kwi'nes trɑl), *n.* a long-acting, synthetic estrogenic hormone. *Formula:* $C_{25}H_{32}O_2$

In cases of primary sterility in women in which the drug clomiphene was unsuccessful, the addition of quinestrol (an estrogen) to the treatment regime produced a much higher yield of successful pregnancies. *Frank P. Mathews, "Medicine: Gynecology," 1972 Collier's Encyclopedia Year Book (1971), p 345*

[1970, from *quinic* acid + *estrogen* + *-ol* (chemical suffix)]

quor·ate ('kwɔr it), *adj. British.* containing or consisting of a quorum.

Even if the union general meeting was quorate, the council has a right to reject same by a two-thirds majority. *A. S. Gani, President, Union of Students, University of Sheffield, in a Letter to the Editor, The Times (London), Feb. 23, 1972, p 13*

The chairman noticed that more than a dozen of the 18 members of the Committee had drifted from the room and he was forced to suspend the proceedings as unquorate. *New Scientist, Sept. 4, 1975, p 541*

[1972, from *quorum* + *-ate* (adj. suffix)]

quota system, *U.S.* a system in which a number or percentage of blacks, women, etc. must be admitted or hired in order to achieve equality or redress past discrimination in education and employment.

The President ordered all government agencies to expunge any trace of a strict quota system from federal programs. *Robert L. Canfield, "Ethnic Groups," The Americana Annual 1973, p 283*

A quota system is the other side of the coin of the federal government's intervention requiring racial and economic integration. *Oscar Newman, Community of Interest, 1980, p 25*

[1963] See AFFIRMATIVE ACTION.

► Before its application to civil rights, this term was used chiefly in reference to the system of quotas limiting the number of immigrants into a country.

qwer·ty or **QWERTY** ('kwər₁ti:), *n.* an informal name for the standard typewriter keyboard.

Typewriters have become so refined mechanically that they almost operate themselves; the keyboard designed in 1872, however, remains basically the same. Today you and I and about fifty million other people in the English-speaking world still use qwerty. *Charles Lekberg, "The Tyranny of Qwerty," Saturday Review (Science), Sept. 30, 1972, p 37*

The Dvorak keyboard differs from the QWERTY in several ways. The most important difference being the placement of the vowels, a, e, i, o, u, on the home row, off the left hand. *"At the Keyboard," Word Processing World, May-June 1975, p 46*

[1972, from *q, w, e, r, t, y,* the first six keys in the upper row of letters of a standard typewriter's keyboard]

R

R, a symbol used in the United States to designate motion pictures to which persons under 16 or 17 are not admitted unless accompanied by an adult. The approximate British equivalent symbol is *AA*.

"Goin' Down the Road," which is perhaps the most uncorrupt movie in town, and a movie that will probably suffer at the box office because of its gentleness, has been rated R (or restricted) by the Motion Picture Association of America. *Pauline Kael, The New Yorker, Oct. 31, 1970, p 131*

What was once R is now GP, and what was X only a year ago is now R. *Time, April 5, 1971, p 40*

[1968, from *R*estricted] ► See the note under G.

racemization, *n.* a method of determining the age of a fossil specimen by measuring the amount of right- or left-handed rotation of polarized light passed through crystals of amino acid contained in the specimen.

The newly dated remains include a skull found in a sea cliff near Del Mar, Calif., dated at 48,000 years old, and a 44,000-year-old skull fragment found near La Jolla, Calif. The new dating technique, called *racemization*, measures amino acids in human bones. In crystalline form, these acids rotate light waves passed through the crystals. In living bone tissue, they always rotate the light to the left. After an organism dies, the amino acids gradually change their geometry so the light is rotated to the right. . . . The dating method is considered a major breakthrough in fossil dating because the carbon-14 method is reliable only to about 40,000 years into the past. *Fred Plog, "Anthropology," The 1975 World Book Year Book, p 196*

[1971, extended sense of *racemizing* (changing from an optically active compound to one without polarized rotation that is optically inactive)] See AGE-DATE.

race walking, the sport of walking competitively for speed.

Nihill knows that race walking, which really is his second sporting love, for he wanted to be a boxer, has cost him a better career. *John Rodda, The Manchester Guardian Weekly, Aug. 26, 1972, p 24*

[1961]

ra·con·tage (ra kɔ̃:'taʒ), *n.* a storytelling; anecdotage.

The foreign correspondent shares honours with the diplomat when it comes to racontage. Anyone with a taste for humour . . . will relish this pot-pourri of oriental anecdotes, exposures, scandals and adventures from the doyen of Far East reporters. *Review of "Foreign Devil" by Richard Hughes, The Times Literary Supplement, Oct. 20, 1972, p 1244*

[1971, from French, from *raconter* to relate; cf. *raconteur* (1829) one skilled in telling stories or anecdotes]

racquetball, *n. U.S. and Canadian.* a game similar to handball, in which two or four players strike a ball with short-handled, stringed racquets.

Racquetball is played on a regulation handball court (20 by 40 feet) with the ceiling in play and a 20-foot-high front wall as your basic target. You swing what resembles a sawed-off tennis racquet at a lively, hollow rubber ball. *Bill Bruns, "Swinging Through Winter," Money, Dec. 1977, p 91*

[1974]

radar trap, a section of road in which the speed of vehicles is monitored by police using radar.

For the first time patrol cars will be able to measure accurately the average speed of cars without having to follow them at a constant distance or use radar traps. *"Technology Review: 'Ello, 'Ello, 'Ello . . . A New Speed Trap," New Scientist, Aug. 23, 1973, p 446*

[1963, probably short for *radar speed trap* (1958) and patterned on *speed trap*]

radiation-field photography, another name for KIRLIAN PHOTOGRAPHY.

Psychologists, psychiatrists, biologists and physicists, as well as investigators of psychic phenomena, are looking into Kirlian photography (also known as radiation-field photography) as a new way of observing energy fields associated with living organisms. *Lisa J. Shawver, "Science Focuses on a 'Light of Life'," Science News, Sept. 29, 1973, p 202*

It deals with Kirlian photography, here somewhat more properly called radiation field photography. *Lester del Rey, "The Reference Library," Analog, July 1976, p 163*

[1973]

ra·di·es·the·sia (ˌrei di: es'θi: ʒə), *n.* the psychic power to detect energy radiating from hidden objects, involved in such phenomena as the ability to identify colors with the hands or to locate water with a divining rod.

He [Anthony Roberts] . . . takes heart in the revival of interest in the old arts such as water-divining, radiesthesia (picking up energy from the landscape) and geomancy (the ability to find sites where energy abounds). *Jonathan Sale, Review of "Atlantean Traditions in Ancient Britain" by Anthony Roberts, The Times (London), June 19, 1976, p 14*

[1959, from *radi*ation + *esthesia*, feeling, sensitivity, or from French *radiesthésie*] See EYELESS SIGHT, RADIONICS, PSYCHOENERGETICS.

radio astrometry, the branch of radio astronomy

dealing with the magnitudes and positions of radio sources.

In addition to this ability to map radio sources with fine resolution, the instrument is expected to prove valuable in radio astrometry, that is, the study of the precise positions of radio sources on the celestial sphere. *Simon Mitton, "Newest Probe of the Radio Universe," New Scientist, Oct. 19, 1972, p 139*

[1972]

radio echo sounding, a method of determining the depth of a body of water, an ice mass, etc., by measuring the echoes of very high frequency radio waves transmitted through it from the surface or the air.

Contributions to the International Antarctic Glaciological Project . . . included 40 hours of aerial radio-echo sounding of the Lambert Glacier. *John Arnfield Heap, "Antarctica," Britannica Book of the Year 1975, p 74*

[1972]

radiolabel, *v. t.* to label or tag (a substance) by adding a radioactive isotope to the substance and tracing it through one or more chemical reactions.

Variations in the composition of the antisera would make each antiserum a unique target for radiolabelling with consequent variations in results. *K. I. Welsh, et al., Nature, March 6, 1975, p 67*

—*n.* a radioactive isotope used to radiolabel a substance.

The use of a radiolabel makes the technique expensive, Purcell concedes, but the expense is justified by the increased sensitivity. *Thomas H. Maugh II, Science, June 16, 1972, p 1226*

[1970 for verb; 1972 for noun]

ra·di·on·ics (ˌrei diːˈɑn iks), *n.* the use of electronic devices to detect and study the radiation of energy in radiesthesia.

Nevertheless, some Western scientists have begun investigating radiesthesia and radionics (using instruments to detect the energy involved). . . . Specifically, they are experimenting with devices capable of detecting or measuring various "psychoenergetic fields," which the Soviets have reported finding associated with the human body and with plants. *Samuel Moffat, "The Psychic Boom," 1973 Britannica Yearbook of Science and the Future (1972), p 81*

This book is of considerable interest in presenting in a stimulating way the background to . . . alternative forms of therapy, such as osteopathy, chiropractic, postural therapy, acupuncture, psychic healing, radionics, homeopathy, naturopathy and yoga. *Malcolm Jayson, Review of "The Book of the Back" by Brian Inglis, New Scientist, Sept. 14, 1978, p 782*

[1972, from *radiation* + electro*nics*]

▶ During the 1950's the term *radionics* developed to designate the technology dealing with electronic devices in radios, high-fidelity systems, television sets, etc.

ra·di·o·phon·ics (ˌrei diː ouˈfɑn iks), *n. British.* sounds produced over the radio, especially sounds made by tape recorders, stereophonic systems, and other electronic devices.

By way of nine programmes all worth listening to . . . we came to *PM Reports*, introduced by a frenzied and mean-

ingless jangle of radiophonics. *"Radio: Francis Dillon Listens in Hospital," The Listener, Nov. 8, 1973, p 648*

[1972, from earlier *radiophonic* of or relating to sound broadcast]

radio pulsar, a pulsar that emits radio pulses, as distinguished from optical or X-ray pulses.

Russell A. Hulse and Joseph H. Taylor of the University of Massachusetts found the first radio pulsar in a binary system in July, 1974. Their discovery establishes that a neutron star can form as one of a relatively low-mass binary pair without disrupting the system. *Riccardo Giacconi, "High-Energy Astronomy," The World Book Science Annual 1976 (1975), p 240*

[1972]

rainmaker, *n. U.S. Slang.* a business executive, especially a partner in a law firm, who has high political connections and promises to use them to bring in business.

Rainmakers can come up dry: ex-Attorney General Ramsey Clark did so much free *pro bono* work that he lost money for his former New York firm. *Time, April 10, 1978, p 65*

But the firm's reputation as a political one comes primarily from Mr. Shea's activities. In legal parlance, a "rainmaker" is a business-getter, and in the Shea Gould firm, Mr. Shea rattles the sky and produces thunderstorms. *Tom Goldstein, "William Shea Law Firm Makes Business of Power," The New York Times, Dec. 6, 1978, p B1*

[1968, in allusion to the American Indian *rainmaker* (OED 1775), who promised to produce rain by supernatural means]

rainmaking, *n.:* This trial, like most trials, has created jargon all of its own. Witnesses speak, for instance not of dates on the calendar as May or June, say, but as "time frames," which was a holdover from the Senate Watergate hearings. "Rainmaking" is another. It has come to mean at the trial the promise a lawyer makes to his client to keep him happy, a promise a lawyer has no intention of keeping. *Martin Arnold, "Sears Testimony Studied by Jury," The New York Times, April 28, 1974, p 51*

rallycross, *n.* an automobile competition in which drivers in small groups race to achieve the fastest time around a short course.

With the reduction in rally events the other branches of the sport have blossomed—sprints, hillclimbs, rallycross, . . . and drag racing. *The Times (London), July 13, 1973, p VII*

[1968, from *rally* + *cross* (as in *moto-cross* an automobile race)] Compare AUTOCROSS.

rallyman, *n.* a person who participates in an automobile rally, especially one who races cars in a rally.

But down in the forests something stirs. It is the sound of innumerable club rallymen taking part in overnight events. More drivers than ever apparently want to go rallying—but on a more reasonable scale. *Judith Jackson, "Motoring: Is the Monte Rally Going Bust?" The Sunday Times (London), Feb. 2, 1975, p 13*

[1967]

RAM, *n.* acronym for *random-access memory,* a computer memory in which access to data can be chosen at random.

Appropriately programmed RAM's—up to 16 kbit [kilobits] per circuit—can store any program in the machine in a "standby" mode. Coupled with this "plug-in" programming, a user-programmable file containing two metal nitride-oxide semiconductor RAM's—each with 1 kbit per circuit—can retain information indefinitely without power. *"Technology," New Scientist, June 24, 1976, p 704*

[1975] Compare ROM.

ran·chi·to (rɑːnˈtʃiː tou), *n. American Spanish.* **1** a small ranch.

Many descendants of the *pobladores* still live in villages that seem dominated by cracked adobe or on tiny *ranchitos* with a garden patch and a few head of cattle. *Calvin Trillin, "U.S. Journal: Costilla County, Colorado," The New Yorker, April 26, 1976, p 122*

2 a small hut.

The "ranchitos" of tin and bricks wind round the valley and spill out down the impressive 22-kilometre motorway to the sea. *David Pallister, "Cadillacs and Squalor: Letter from Caracas," The Manchester Guardian Weekly, Oct. 31, 1976, p 8*

[1976]

ran·dom·ic·i·ty (ˌræn dəˈmis ə tiː), *n.* random quality or condition; randomness.

Environmental randomicity of various kinds may have important implications in triggering evolutionary sequences that would be impossible or unlikely in non-stochastic environments. *Scott A. Boorman, Review of "Geographical Ecology" by Robert H. MacArthur, Science, Oct. 27, 1972, p 392*

Most of these phenomena are characterized by a great deal of randomicity associated with the chaotic nature of turbulence. *Peter J. Westervelt, "Sound," McGraw-Hill Yearbook of Science and Technology 1977, p 390*

[1972, from *random* + *-icity*, as in *elasticity, electricity*, and other words formed from adjectives in *-ic*]

RANN, *n. U.S.* acronym for *Research Applied to National Needs*, a program of the National Science Foundation, created to explore ways of solving social, environmental, and health problems.

Faced with a host of federal agencies sponsoring research on fossil fuels and nuclear sources, RANN should concentrate on unconventional sources, such as solar energy. *Deborah Shapley, "NSF: Engineers' Policy Group Urges More Software for RANN," Science, Dec. 22, 1972, p 1272*

[1971]

rapid water, *U.S.* a nontoxic polymer slurry that is mixed with water in fire-fighting pumping apparatus to decrease friction and accelerate the rate of flow. It is manufactured under the trademark *Ucar*.

Engine 60, on East 143d Street, is one of the busiest fire companies in the city, and has been without rapid water since last May. When queried yesterday, a spokesman for the Fire Department acknowledged that supplies of the additive were low and that many other companies in the city equipped to use rapid water were out of it. *Glenn Fowler, "New York City Firemen Short of a Chemical for 'Rapid Water,'" The New York Times, Aug. 21, 1976, p 22*

[1976]

rap parlor, *U.S.* a euphemism for a place of prostitution.

"In 1970 we didn't have a dial-a-anything that advertised, no porno movie houses, no rap parlors and only four adult bookstores all of which were within one block of each other," he [James M. O'Meara] said. "Now there are adult movie houses all over the city, about 15 rap parlors, for which there's no control whatsoever, and porno bookstores everywhere." *The New York Times, Feb. 7, 1978, p 6*

[1975, from *rap* as in *rap session*, because such establishments disguise their illegal activities by claiming to conduct rap sessions] Compare BODY SHOP, def. 1.

Ras·ta (ˈræs tə), *n.* short for *Rastafarian*, a member of a cult in the West Indies advocating a militant black nationalism and worshiping the former ruler of Ethiopia, Haile Selassie.

What the Rastas really believe . . . is a little hard to grasp, partly because it takes days just to understand the patois and mainly because they spend most of their waking time on the verge of vanishing into delicious, weed-induced delirium. *Kevin Doyle, "Foul Wind for Jamaica," Maclean's, Dec. 13, 1976, p 52*

The overwhelming majority of reggae's exponents are devout Rastas. *Timothy White, "Bob Marley: All You Need is Love," Rolling Stone, Jan. 11, 1979, p 97*

[1963, ultimately from *Ras Tafari*, the title and surname of Emperor Haile Selassie] See DOWNPRESS, DREADLOCKS.

Rastafarianism, *n.* the practices and beliefs of the Rastafarians.

A significant minority of young West Indian males in England are rejecting the values of white, English society and expressing pride through Rastafarianism in being black, according to a report published today by the Social Science Research Council research unit on ethnic relations. *Peter Evans, The Times (London), Nov. 23, 1978, p 30*

[1977, from *Rastafarian* (see RASTA) + *-ism*]

► According to Tracy Nicholas, *Rastafari, A Way of Life* (1979), Rastafarians refer to their practices and beliefs as *Rastafari*.

ratchet effect, intermittent advance, increase, growth, etc.

During the last decade and a half the SNP [Scottish National Party] has advanced by a ratchet effect. If they are stuck for a moment at their latest peak that does not mean they will stay stuck for ever. *The Manchester Guardian Weekly, May 22, 1977, p 4*

Because they want to be reelected, Congressmen are generally on the lookout for ways in which to increase government programs. This is because enlarged federal programs enlarge the number of constituents that a Congressman can "service," thus adding to the number of voters who will be suitably grateful on election day. The result is a powerful ratchet effect, with federal programs and expenditures getting larger, but almost never smaller. *Tom Bethell, "The Wealth of Washington," Harper's, June 1978, p 57*

[1970]

ratchet jaw, *U.S. Slang.* a person who talks too much or too long over citizens band radio; chatterbox.

Perhaps the biggest problem is overcrowding, which can turn "good buddies" into nasty rivals. CBers are supposed to limit calls to five minutes, and those who do not are called "ratchet jaws." But even without the ratchet jaws, some CBers on crowded highways or in urban and suburban areas never get a chance to talk. *Robert K. Johnson, "Citizens Band Together," The 1977 World Book Year Book, p 267*

[1976, from the comparison of the moving jaw to the jerky motion and clattering noise of a ratchet mechanism]

raunch (rɔːntʃ), *n.* **1** untidiness; sloppiness; shabbiness.

Calvin Coolidge High is an actual Manhattan school building, its rust and raunch unretouched for the camera. *Time, Aug. 18, 1967, p 63*

2 crudeness, vulgarity, or tastelessness.

Bette Midler is . . . no Streisand, her material is blue and her songs are old. Yet she's been camped out at one of Broadway's biggest theatres for several months now, making raunch respectable in a sellout revue called Clams on the Half Shell. *Bart Mills, "Bette Midler," The Manchester Guardian Weekly, Aug. 2, 1975, p 20*

There are bars that are all elegance, and bars that are all raunch, and bars that breathe both elegance and raunch and therefore are considered chic. *John Corry, "Bars: Elegance and Down-Home Chic," The New York Times, July 9, 1976, p C19*

[1964, back formation from *raunchy* (1955)]

ra·za·kar (rɑː zɑːˈkɑr), *n.* a member of an auxiliary military force in Pakistan, especially in the former East Pakistan (now Bangladesh).

The Pakistan Army is clearing up the border belt to make room for para-military forces — razakars — who are being stationed along the vulnerable sectors on their side of the control line in Jammu and Kashmir. *"Razakar 'Huts' Dot Kashmir Border," The Hindustan Times Weekly, June 10, 1973, p 1*

[1971, from Urdu]

razor job, *British Informal.* a ruthless attack; hatchet job.

This key passage occurs early in . . . the section which is the book's real beginning. It sets the tone for a spectacular razor-job on American pedagogy: PhD-mills, symbolmongering, the lot. *Review of "The Performing Self" by Richard Poirier, The Times Literary Supplement, Feb. 4, 1972, p 127*

[1971]

reaction shot, a motion-picture or television camera shot of a performer's face to show an emotional reaction or response.

His [Michael Jackson's] lack of experience as a screen actor works partly to his advantage; his ingenuousness is touching, though there are too many reaction shots of him being self-consciously dear, and you want to yell "Cut!" to the editor. *Pauline Kael, "The Current Cinema," The New Yorker, Oct. 30, 1978, p 141*

[1974]

reactor zone, an area showing the remains or evidence of the OKLO PHENOMENON.

Nature, not man, had constructed the world's first nuclear-fission reactor. Eventually six reactor zones were identified in the Oklo pit, four of them in strata that had not yet been mined. *George A. Cowan, "A Natural Fission Reactor," Scientific American, July 1976, p 36*

[1976]

reading wand, *British.* an electronic device that reads and records the coded information on the labels of retail goods.

Much more information about the transaction can be entered and recorded, particularly on those ECR's [electronic cash registers] fitted with a so-called automatic reading wand. *Ron Brown, "Arrival of the Sales-Counter Computer," New Scientist, April 20, 1972, p 130*

[1972] See BAR CODE.

read-only memory, a computer memory in which the data cannot be altered by program instructions.

The decoding, timing and control circuitry . . . is principally governed by one or another of 320 instruction words (each consisting of 11 bits) delivered to the instruction register (and thence to the controller) from the read-only memory, so named because it contains a programmed set of operational instructions that cannot be changed after the manufacture of the calculator. Each instruction word, obtained from the read-only memory by nine-bit address words, establishes the operating rules that apply during one instruction cycle of 13 state times (39 clock cycles). *Eugene W. McWhorter, "The Small Electronic Calculator," Scientific American, March 1976, p 92*

[1968] *Acronym:* ROM

ready-faded, *adj.* made or designed to look faded; prefaded.

There's something rather precious about the washed-out look of, for instance, No. 50. I take it to represent fine art's answer to the ready-faded denim jean. *William Feaver, "Art: Diebenkorn," The Listener, Dec. 27, 1973, p 898*

[1973]

re·ag·gre·gate (riːˈæg rə‚geit *for verb;* riːˈæg rə git *for noun*), *v.i., v.t.* to form (cells or tissue) into a new mass or aggregate.

The idea that a piece of developing tissue from an embryo can be gently teased apart into its component cells, and that these will then reaggregate to form an apparently normal test-tube version of the tissue when gently shaken in solution, stems from Aaron Moscona of Chicago. *"A Brain Rewires Itself in a Test-Tube," New Scientist, Jan. 6, 1972, p 6*

— *n.* tissue that has reaggregated.

Spontaneous and evoked activities in the neuronal reaggregates were often synchronized, even between clusters that were 2 to 3 mm apart. *Stanley M. Crain and Murray B. Bornstein, Science, April 14, 1972, p 183*

[1966]

reaggregation, *n.:* As Gierer *et al.* show that even dissociated cells show some memory of their original position, it should be possible to find what kinds of biochemical treatment before reaggregation can disrupt this memory. *"Hydra as a Model Organism," Nature, Oct. 13, 1972, p 366*

reality therapy, a method of psychotherapy to help a person accept and adjust to reality.

This step-by-step handbook is designed not to judge therapies but to explain them. Among the guide's offerings are handy capsule descriptions of the kinds of treatment available (*e.g.,* "reality therapy": an approach emphasizing how to cope with a hostile environment). *"Behavior: Nader's Guide to Shrinks," Time, Jan. 5, 1976, p 64*

[1971]

recall, *n.* a request for the return of a product by its manufacturer for some necessary repair, especially to eliminate a possible hazard to the user.

When recalls are instituted, the auto companies estimate that only between 50 and 85 per cent of recalled vehicles are actually brought in for safety checks. *William Serrin, "Auto Recalls: If You Hear a Screech, Pull Over," The New York Times, April 23, 1972, Sec. 4, p 4*

[1972]

re·cep·to·rol·o·gy (ri,sep tə'ral ə dʒi:), *n.* See the quotation for the meaning.

One of the exciting advances in cell biology in the 1970s has of course been the birth of receptorology, the inelegant name given to the molecular study of receptor units. *Roger Lewin, New Scientist, Jan. 10, 1974, p 64*

[1972]

receptor site, an area or structure in a cell where the action of a drug or other substance takes effect.

The ways in which these proteins formed 'receptor sites', at which, and only at which, chemical messengers such as hormones could stimulate the cell to whatever action was required, was beginning to become an exact science. *John Newell, "Science, Medicine and Technology," The Annual Register of World Events in 1975 (1976), p 360*

[1972]

recertification, *n.* renewal of certification, especially by a certification board established in some field, such as nursing and aviation.

F. Bradley MacKimm, former publisher of Medical World News and of MD Medical Newsmagazine, two of the more popular magazines for physicians, is . . . this time taking advantage of a recent development in the medical profession, recertification. From his office . . . he'll begin publishing Family Practice Recertification in April and delivering it to more than 70,000 family physicians. *Philip H. Dougherty, The New York Times, Jan. 26, 1979, p D11*

[1973]

re·com·bi·nant (ri:'kam bə nənt), *n.* a gene or genetic substance made from recombinant DNA.

The widespread use of *E. coli* bacteria in this new genetic research increases its dangers. . . . Thus every laboratory working with *E. coli* recombinants is staffed by potential carriers who could spread a dangerous recombinant to the rest of the world. *Liebe F. Cavalieri, "New Strains of Life—or Death," The New York Times Magazine, Aug. 22, 1976, p 59*

Meanwhile, many scientists are eager to proceed with recombinant research, because DNA recombinants offer a promising lead in the search for possible links between viruses and cancer. *Edwin S. Weaver, "Biochemistry," 1977 Collier's Encyclopedia Year Book (1976), p 164*

—*adj.* of or having to do with recombinant DNA or recombinant DNA research.

By the way: The tragic results from recombinant gene experimentation can be hypothesized also from chance mutation, and that without interference of man. No safety rules possible can prevent that from happening. *Bernard Foster, Bronx, N.Y., in a Letter to the Editor, Science News, April 9, 1977, p 227*

[1976, so called because it is produced by *recombining* fragments of DNA molecules obtained from different organisms] Compare ARTIFICIAL GENE.

recombinant DNA, a form of DNA produced in the laboratory by recombining fragments of DNA molecules obtained from different organisms. The recombined molecules are introduced into a host cell and become a part of its permanent genetic complement.

Research in recombinant DNA may create viral and bacterial mutants that, should they ever escape from the laboratory, could rapidly kill off whole species of plants and animals, including the human species, and so create ecological chaos. *Theodore Roszak, Person/Planet, 1978, p 35*

Human insulin has been produced at last by genetically engineered bacteria in a California laboratory—an achievement that catapults recombinant DNA technology into the major leagues of the drug industry. *Science News, Sept. 16, 1978, p 195*

[1976]

recombinant DNA research, the methods and procedures by which DNA fragments from different organisms are recombined in the laboratory to produce new or altered genes which are then inserted into host cells to assume specific genetic functions.

The work is called recombinant DNA research because it involves breaking apart chains of deoxyribonucleic acid (DNA), the chemical that carries genetic data, and recombining them in various ways. *Daniel L. Hartl, "Genes: Handle With Care," The World Book Science Annual 1978 (1977), p 28*

I am not opposed to recombinant DNA research as such. I have said, and I still believe, there are some wonderful results to be derived from genetic engineering—and some that may literally be essential for the survival of our civilisation. But I see also a darker potential for biological and social chaos and I would hope to maximise the former and minimise the latter. *Robert Sinsheimer, "An Evolutionary Perspective for Genetic Engineering," New Scientist, Jan. 20, 1977, p 150*

[1976] Also called GENE-SPLICING and GENE TRANSPLANTATION. Compare CELL FUSION.

► Recombinant DNA research is generally regarded as the first major step in the development of genetic engineering, the process of altering, adding, or removing genes to produce new living forms and characters. Genes transplanted into bacteria by means of this technique can cause the bacteria to produce cheaply an endless supply of important and scarce hormones and other body chemicals. But many feared that the technique could unintentionally give rise to harmful or dangerous forms of life (see ANDROMEDA STRAIN), since the source of the genetic material implanted in the bacteria may be from any animal, plant, microbe, or virus.

The technique has many variations. The most widely used method consists of joining DNA molecules of any organism to bacterial molecules called plasmids which carry genes but reproduce independently of the chromosomes. In order to SPLICE or ANNEAL the donor DNA to the plasmid DNA, a RESTRICTION ENZYME is used to cleave the two molecules at RESTRICTION SITES in such a way that both have STICKY ENDS. When the plasmid is reintroduced into bacteria, the new genes it carries begin to function as part of the bacteria's natural genetic makeup.

recombinational repair

Besides plasmids, viruses can also be combined with a higher organism's DNA to serve as carriers of genes. This form of GENE SPLICING has caused concern because some viruses can infect human cells and transmit disease, and a group of prominent scientists issued a call in 1974 for a worldwide voluntary moratorium on recombinant DNA experiments that were potentially BIOHAZARDOUS.

Nevertheless, by 1979, fears of the potential hazards of recombinant DNA research had diminished considerably, supported largely by the finding that the strains of bacteria used in the research did not survive outside the laboratory. At the same time the promised benefits of recombinant DNA research began to appear.

In December 1977 a group of researchers at the University of California succeeded in synthesizing and inserting into bacteria a gene that codes for the hormone SOMATOSTATIN, causing the gene to EXPRESS itself — to produce the hormone. In July of the following year another group performed similar experimental production of insulin in rats and the EXPRESSION of the gene. These successes did much to calm doubts about the value of recombinant DNA research. See also MONOCLONAL ANTIBODY, TEST-TUBE BABY.

recombinational repair, self-repair of a strand of the DNA molecule.

The third mechanism is under the control of the genes involved in genetic recombination and is called recombinational, or Rec, repair. It appears to repair single-strand breaks in the sugar-phosphate backbone that are induced primarily by such ionizing radiation as X rays, and by certain chemicals. *1973 Britannica Yearbook of Science and the Future (1972), p 303*

[1971] Compare DARK REPAIR, EXCISION REPAIR.

reconciliation room, another name for ROOM OF RECONCILIATION.

Another Catholic editor, *Commonweal's* John Deedy, believes the church is already "well down the road" toward elimination of individual confession. Whether those low-lit "reconciliation rooms" will prove him wrong remains to be seen. *"Religion: Out of the Box," Time, March 15, 1976, p 44*

[1976]

recreational vehicle, a vehicle for leisure or recreational activities, such as a camper or trailer.

The desert becomes dotted with oases of recreational vehicles clustered into base camps for target shooters, hunters, bird watchers, wild-flower enthusiasts, backpackers, bicyclists, fossil collectors, gem prospectors and even, improbably, fishermen. *"Life and Leisure: Up the Sandbox," Newsweek, April 30, 1973, p 73*

In glinting procession, often oblivious of the 55-m.p.h. limit, gas guzzlers and recreational vehicles are already rolling down the interstates. San Francisco is dense with tourists. Millions are expected in Florida before summer's end. *Lance Morrow, "A Comfortable Season," Time, July 4, 1977, p 31*

[1966] *Abbreviation:* RV. Also called RECVEE.

re·cu·sal (ri'kyu: zəl), *n.* a declaring unfit; disqualification.

During the hearings, a South African application for the recusal of three judges — the President of the Court, Sir Muhammad Zafrullah Khan, Judge Luis Padilla Nervo of Mexico, and Judge Platon Morozov of Russia — was rejected as was an offer of an all-race plebiscite in Namibia to let the people themselves indicate whether they would prefer a South African or UN administration. *Noam Pines, "The Republic of South Africa," The Annual Register of World Events in 1971 (1972), p 224*

[1972, from *recuse* (1600's) to reject or disqualify as a judge + *-al*]

rec·vee or **rec-v** (ˌrek'vi:), *n. Informal.* acronym for RECREATIONAL VEHICLE.

In 1961, 83,500 "rec vees" were sold; last year the number was 740,000. There are now some 6.5 million rec-vee families in the U.S. *"Roughing it the Easy Way," Time, July 2, 1973, p 60*

You can learn a lot about people from the vehicles they drive. Silicon Valley folk appear to favour classy pick-ups and an incredible variety of so-called recreational vehicles, Rec-Vs or RVs. These range from modest vans (though embellished with exuberant paint-schemes, bulging portholes and, so help me, bay windows) to huge monsters, in appearance part furniture pantechnicon, part meat truck. *The Times (London), Nov. 22, 1978, p 18*

[1972, from *recreational* + *vee* or *v* (for *vehicle*)]

recycle, *v.t.* **1** to put to a new or different use.

Just about every hit or near-hit has been re-cycled and a fair number of them have been reactivated in single form and have reappeared in the charts. *John Peel, "Pop Music: Re-Cycling," The Listener, Oct. 4, 1973, p 463*

Most housewives bent on recycling their talents discover that what they must in fact recycle is their spirit — their initiative, perseverance, and aggressiveness. *Joan Hitzig, Harper's, Sept. 1974, p 93*

Recycled American series are becoming Arabian national pastimes. *I Dream of Jeannie* has even hit Saudi Arabia. *Esquire, Aug. 1975, p 78*

2 to renovate (an old building), especially for another function.

The sessions . . . will include visual presentations, discussions and on-site tours and will be augmented by an exhibit of recycled old buildings done by New England architects. *Preservation News, Sept. 1974, p 9*

Boston has recycled its majestic old market buildings and made them the exciting new hub of innercity life. *Time, Sept. 4, 1978, p 2*

3 to rechannel (surplus oil revenues) to oil-importing countries in the form of loans and investments.

So far, the recycling function has been fulfilled by commercial banks through the Eurodollar markets. The Arabs have been depositing dollars and (in smaller amounts) pounds sterling with banks in London and in New York. The banks, in turn, have been lending money to Britain, France, Peru, etc. *Forbes, Aug. 15, 1974, p 25*

Specifically, if the recycling of OPEC funds is to work at all, the Arabs must be brought into the Western financial tent — not kept out of it. *Julian M. Snyder, The New York Times, March 30, 1975, p 10*

[1972, transferred and figurative senses of the earlier meaning "to convert waste or discarded material to useful products"]

recycler, *n.:* In the realm of ideas, Hannah [Arendt] was a conservationist; she did not believe in throwing away what had once been thought. A use might be found for it; in her own way, she was an enthusiastic recycler. *Mary McCarthy, "Saying Good-By to Hannah," The New York Review of Books, Jan. 22, 1976, p 8*

red, *n. Slang.* a barbiturate capsule, especially Seconal (secobarbital).

Another is the case of a heroin addict who first "shot some reds" (that is, barbiturates) and then "fixed" with heroin following the barbiturates. *Edward M. Brecher, "So Why do Heroin Addicts Drop Dead?" The New York Times Magazine, Nov. 19, 1972, p 116*

[1966, so called from its color]

Red Army, 1 a terrorist group of Japan.

The Japanese Red Army. A fanatic, radical leftist movement whose cloudy ideology is part Mao, part Trotskyite permanent revolution, part Che Guevarism. Merged from a number of loosely knit radical groups, the Red Army has only about 40 active members but has been involved in terrorist exploits in Europe and the Middle East as well as Asia. The best known: the 1972 massacre at Lod Airport in which three Red Army terrorists, acting for the Palestinians, gunned down 26 people. *Time, Oct. 31, 1977, p 45*

2 Usually, **Red Army Faction.** a terrorist group of West Germany.

Clutterbuck goes on to say that although today's terrorists have comparable anti-authority aims, their motivations are by no means uniform. "Some, like the Palestinians and the members of the I.R.A., are nationalistic," he says. "Some, like the Red Army of Japan, the Red Brigades of Italy, and perhaps the Red Army faction of West Germany —the Baader-Meinhof Gang, in popular parlance—have broader and more widespread revolutionary goals. *E. J. Kahn, Jr., "Profiles: Richard Lewis Clutterbuck," The New Yorker, June 12, 1978, p 38*

[1972]

Red Brigades, an organization of Italian terrorists of the extreme left.

The Red Brigades . . . have also been blamed for a spate of attacks, including bank raids, assassinations and bombings. *Alvin Shuster, The New York Times, Dec. 16, 1976, p 3*

Between the kidnapping and the murder of Aldo Moro in Italy, a document was issued by the Red Brigades describing the doctrine and strategy of the Italian movement. It defined the ultimate objective of the Red Brigades as "to liberate man finally from bestial exploitation, from necessary labor, from misery, from fatigue, from social degradation." *William Pfaff, "Reflections: Terrorism," The New Yorker, Sept. 18, 1978, p 135*

Outside, in the headlines, the Red Brigades are blowing people's knees off. *Michael Thomas, Rolling Stone, Jan. 11, 1979, p 79*

[1972, translation of Italian *Brigate Rosse*]

red chicken, *Slang.* a crude form of heroin.

Most of those uncovered are turning out the crude No 3 heroin (known as . . . Red Chicken) for local consumption, but Government chemists see enough factories with the high quality No 4 heroin to suggest a sizable onward traffic, probably to America. *Patricia Penn, "The Narcotics Traffic in Hong Kong," The Listener, Nov. 11, 1971, p 644*

[1970]

Red Guard doctor, paramedic in China.

Analogous groups have also been trained in cities, such as "work doctors" in factories and "Red Guard doctors," who are housewives serving as physicians' assistants in neighborhood health clinics. *Charles M. Wylie, "Public Health," 1973 Collier's Encyclopedia Year Book (1972), p 477*

[1972, named after the *Red Guard* movement of young activists in the Maoist Cultural Revolution of the 1960's] Compare BAREFOOT DOCTOR.

redline, *v.t. U.S.* to subject (an old or blighted area of a city) to REDLINING; discriminate against by denying loans, mortgages, or insurance, especially to prospective property owners.

Banks, savings and loan associations, and other mortgage and brokerage houses in Detroit often "redlined" neighborhoods in the city, meaning blacks could not get mortgages in these areas. *William Serrin, Saturday Review, Aug. 26, 1972, p 14*

For the community that is redlined, that has conventional mortgage and loan money withdrawn, panic sets in. Through their economic discrimination, the lending institutions ensure a community's deterioration. *Student Lawyer, April 1975, p 36*

Once a collective decision is made by a group of banks to redline a community, that decision itself can become the critical factor in determining the community's future. *Oscar Newman, Community of Interest, 1980, p 88*

[1967, from *red line* supposedly drawn on a map to exclude certain areas]

redlining, *n. U.S.* the practice by certain banks, insurers, and other institutions of refusing to grant loans, mortgages, or insurance in old or blighted parts of a city because of the presumed risks involved.

Stopping banks and FHA firms from systematically denying applications for home-improvement loans in low-income neighborhoods, thus ensuring the further collapse of the neighborhood (the battle against this practice, called "redlining," has not yet been won). . . . *"Networks: Out to Win," Harper's, Dec. 1974, p 114*

Redlining involves a self-fulfilling prophecy, because an area shunned by lenders will, in fact, soon deteriorate for lack of the funds necessary for upkeep. *William E. Farrell, "Redlining, Whether Cause or Effect, Is No Help," The New York Times, Sept. 14, 1975, Sec. 4, p 2*

[1968; see REDLINE] Compare GREENLINING, SNOB ZONING, STEERING.

Red No. 40, an artificial coloring agent used in the United States in foods, drugs, and cosmetics as a substitute for the banned RED NO. 2.

The ruling may push up the price of many consumer products. Red No. 40 costs $8.50 per lb., *v.* $5.50 for No. 2, and manufacturers have to use 30% to 50% more of it to get the same color intensity as with Red No. 2. Even then, the colors do not come out quite the same, so chocolate pudding may look a bit greener. *"Regulation: Death of a Dye," Time, Feb. 2, 1976, p 53*

Early in 1977 the FDA indicated that Red No. 40 may also be banned because it causes cancer in mice. *Everett Edgar Sentman, "Too Many Watchdogs?" Britannica Book of the Year 1978, p 393*

[1976]

Red No. 2, an artificial coloring agent derived from naphthalene, formerly used in many foods, drugs, and cosmetics. It was banned in the United States in 1976 as a suspected carcinogen.

Red 2

Red No. 2 has many advantages as a coloring agent — persistence, stability, intensity, solubility, economy — and was often chosen over other red dyes such as Red No. 40. *"Red Dye No. 2 Dies a Slow Death," Science News, Jan. 24, 1976, p 55*

Red No. 2 gives the red colour to a wide range of foods, including jams, jellies, soft drinks, frankfurters, bottled red cabbage, salami, and blackcurrant drinks. *"This Week: Red for Danger There — But Not Here," New Scientist, March 25, 1976, p 659*

[1976] Also called RED 2. See DELANEY AMENDMENT.

Red 2, variant of RED NO. 2.

Red 2 has been the most widely used food color in this country, and it has always been touted as the "most thoroughly tested" of all the food colors. *Philip M. Boffey, "Color Additives: Botched Experiment Leads to Banning of Red Dye No. 2," Science, Feb. 6, 1976, p 450*

[1973]

reed relay, a device used as a switching unit in electronic telephone exchange systems.

One development has been a semielectronic exchange based on a device called a reed relay, in which two hairlike metal reeds are sealed in nitrogen in a glass ampoule. Because the reeds are so tiny, the time required to draw them together and to make the electrical contact is infinitesimal, and the telephone at the receiving end rings as soon as the caller has fed in the last digit. *Brenda Maddox, "The Global Telephone Network," Saturday Review, Oct. 28, 1972, p 41*

Reed-relay . . . switches are likely to be superseded at some time in the future by microelectronic digital switches. *The Times (London), Jan. 5, 1973, p 17*

[1971]

reeducate, *v.t.* to train or drill in a program of political indoctrination, especially in a communist country.

In Vietnam, Laos, and Cambodia . . . major efforts were made to revive the rural economy and to "reeducate" former opponents, but the Cambodians were clearly the most draconian in their approach. *David L. Williams, "Communist Movement," Britannica Book of the Year 1977, p 204*

[1971, extended from earlier meaning "to educate anew, especially in order to rehabilitate or reform"]

reeducation, *n.*: The P.R.G. [Provisional Revolutionary Government] has resorted to the time-honored Communist technique of "re-education" for its enemies, including some political prisoners arrested since August. Camps have been set up throughout the country for indoctrination sessions that usually last about three months. *"Vietnam: The Slow Road to Socialism," Time, Feb. 16, 1976, p 30*

"Re-education" is not a punishment in the ordinary penal sense. At best it is an administrative measure of unlimited duration imposed by the victor on the vanquished. *Roland-Pierre Paringaux, "Gulags in Name of Security," The Manchester Guardian Weekly (Le Monde section), Oct. 15, 1978, p 11*

Compare HOC TAP.

reel-to-reel, *adj.* consisting of or using an open supply reel and a take-up reel for winding and rewinding magnetic tape.

Tape cartridges have their appeal, too, particularly for the in-car user, but the software repertoire for them is lim-

ited. Then there is the open reel-to-reel tape system, for which pre-recorded tapes have dropped to a mere trickle from specialist suppliers, when available at all. *The Listener, Oct. 23, 1975, p ii*

[1961]

re·fuse·nik or **re·fus·nik** (ri'fyu:z nik), *n.* a Soviet citizen, especially a Jew, whose application for emigration is rejected.

I met Vladimir Sverdlin and Ilya Shostakovsky there who seemed to be close friends and who worked at organizing the "refuseniks" into some sort of cohesive body. *Michael Freedland, "What Freedom Means to 'Refuseniks' Who Finally Get Their Exit Permits," The Times (London), June 6, 1977, p 8*

Anatoly Scharansky, the celebrated 29-year-old refusnik was arrested last March at the Slepak apartment, where he had stayed for six months. *Mary McGrory, "A Soviet Jew's Message for the U.S.," New York Post, Dec. 6, 1977, p 45*

Orlov, who is a high energy physicist, was convicted of anti-Soviet agitation, a vague, catch-all charge often leveled at Soviet dissidents and refuseniks (persons who are refused a visa to Israel). *Science News, Sept. 2, 1978, p 165*

[1975, from *refuse* + *-nik* Russian suffix meaning one who is connected with something]

Reg·ge ('re dʒei), *adj.* of or having to do with a theory in particle physics that explains the behavior of strongly interacting subatomic particles in terms of mathematical poles and trajectories rather than as fundamental physical particles such as quarks.

Regge hypothesis: The members of each of these families are said to lie on a hypothetical curve called a Regge trajectory. . . . The idea that all hadrons lie on such trajectories, sometimes called the Regge hypothesis (even though Regge's original work did not involve hadrons), is now widely accepted. *John H. Schwarz, Scientific American, Feb. 1975, p 62*

Regge pole: The Regge pole is an abstract mathematical way of representing an entire class of physical situations. For example, all our Type 8 spikes can be described as originating from one Regge Pole, so that instead of needing an infinite number of mathematical terms to describe the behavior of Type 8 resonances, one can make do with the Regge pole alone. *Howard C. Bryant and Nelson Jarmie, Scientific American, July 1974, p 71*

Regge theory: The development of theoretical elementary particle physics has continued in two principal areas: current algebra and the quark model, and Regge theory. *San Fu Tuan, "Elementary Particle," McGraw-Hill Yearbook of Science and Technology 1970, p 179*

Regge trajectory: Another classification scheme, known as "Regge theory," groups particles with differing masses and "spins" (internal angular momenta) into families (called "Regge trajectories"). It is found that there is a correlation between the spin and mass of each resonance within a family such that the spin is proportional to the square of the mass. *Michael Green, "Some Elementary Particles May Be Strings," New Scientist, April 10, 1975, p 76*

[1962, named after Tullio *Regge*, an Italian theoretical physicist] Compare BOOTSTRAP. See also QUARK.

Reg·ge·ism ('re dʒei,iz əm), *n.* another name for REGGE THEORY.

There is now good evidence that Reggeism works in the following sense. The scattering region (where virtual particle exchanges give rise to exchange forces) and the resonance region (where the real particles exist after the fashion of molecular spectra) are described by a common entity called the trajectory function. *San Fu Tuan, "Elementary Particle," McGraw-Hill Yearbook of Science and Technology 1970, p 183*

[1970]

rehab, *n. U.S.* short for *rehabilitation.*

The vocational rehabilitation program — or "rehab" as it is often called — is jointly funded by the Alabama Department of Mental Health and the Vocational Rehabilitation Service of the state Department of Education. *Don Meissner, "At Bryce: One of Three Leave Through Rehab," The Tuscaloosa News (Alabama), Sept. 28, 1975, p D1*

A runaway from a therapy group stands with his nose pressed against a steel door and shrieks periodically. "He wants to go to rehab," a recreational aide explains. *Peter Koenig, "The Problem That Can't Be Tranquilized," The New York Times Magazine, May 21, 1978, p 46*

—*v.t.* to rehabilitate.

These were people who wanted to do good; who ... saw slums and dreamed of humane dwelling spaces (solid 1890s structures built practically with slave labor, now rehabbed to perfection, filled with greenery and occupied by urban planning consultants). *Tom Bethell, "The Wealth of Washington," Harper's, June 1978, p 43*

[1963 for noun; 1978 for verb; by shortening]

REIT (ri:t), *n. U.S.* acronym for *real estate investment trust,* a type of lending organization that invests in real estate holdings, such as developed property or construction projects.

Many banks, including Chase, organized their own REITs — a move that now seems to have been most unwise. As demand for commercial construction collapsed, many builders and property owners were forced into bankruptcy, and the REITs and the banks that they borrowed from were left holding the bag. *"Economy & Business: Banking: Digging Out of the Bad Debt Mess," Time, Jan. 26, 1976, p 50*

The Value Line Investment Survey calculated recently that a group of four REITs had run up an aggregate gain of 30% in the past three months. ... Such gains have been a long time in coming for many REITs. *Chet Currier, "REITs Regain Favor," Daily News (New York), June 4, 1979, p 36*

The trend is now back to syndicates, which were favored before REITs. REITs are still chancy for the first-time investor whose every dollar must count. *Ruth Rejnis, Her Home, 1980, p 163*

[1976]

rejection front, the Arab groups or countries that oppose any form of negotiation or settlement with Israel; rejectionists as a united front.

The Palestinian National Congress (parliament) has so far not been called upon to ratify the six-point agreement concluded by various Fedayeen organisations at the recent Tripoli conference. So this new platform, put together under pressure from the Rejection Front which deliberately rules out any compromise worked out with Israel, is still only a paper project and could be dropped at any time for a more conciliatory stance. *Eric Rouleau, "Moderates Turn On the Pressure," The Manchester Guardian Weekly (Le Monde section), Jan. 1, 1978, p 11*

[1976]

rejectionist, *n.* an Arab leader, group, or country that rejects any form of negotiation or accommodation with Israel.

The so-called rejectionists like Iraq and Libya, which oppose a permanent settlement with Israel, emerged largely discredited. *"Middle East: Offensive for Peace, Warning of War," Time, Dec. 6, 1976, p 32*

—*adj.* of or having to do with rejectionists; opposing any form of negotiation or accommodation with Israel.

There was no comment from the rejectionist states today about President Sadat's decision to return the latest draft Israeli-Egyptian peace treaty for further study. *The Times (London), Oct. 24, 1978, p 8*

[1975]

rejectionism, *n.:* West Bank residents have always tended toward the moderate end of the Palestinian political spectrum. Rejectionism, the political current that dismisses the idea of negotiating with Israel, exists, particularly among the young; it gains and loses strength as the situation changes but it is clearly a minority view. *The New York Times, Feb. 20, 1978, p 10*

relationship, *n.* a euphemism for a romantic attachment or affair.

A woman banker who came to the club only once told me she had a "relationship" but was looking for something better. "This fellow I'm seeing," she said, "would like to move in with me. He'd like all the conveniences of being married without the responsibilities. But I wouldn't live with him and I wouldn't marry him." *Sam Blum, "The Re-Mating Game," The New York Times Magazine, Aug. 29, 1976, p 18*

"I told you about Carl. He's the person with whom I'm having a relationship." *Cartoon legend, The New Yorker, Sept. 26, 1977, p 123*

[1967] See EUPHEMISMS.

relativities, *n.pl. British.* the relative differences in wages within and between groups of workers.

The Government had recognised that unfairness might have arisen. It was also to take a broad look at pay relativities, a word of which we were destined to hear much more. *Peter Cole, The Manchester Guardian Weekly, March 16, 1974, p 6*

[1973]

re·let (ˈriːˌlet), *n. British.* a dwelling unit that is let or leased anew.

Even allowing for the substantial numbers of relets from the existing stock, the magnitude of the loss of this source of housing in the new communities is evident. *Michael Harloe, The Times (London), Jan. 7, 1976, p 13*

[1972, noun use of the verb (OED 1812), pronounced (riːˈlet)]

remote, *v.t.* to extend to great distances.

At present, Beacon handles about 12 million passenger bookings a year. The system, which is based on Univac computer equipment, first came into operation in 1965. By 1967, the system had been "remoted" to principal cities throughout the United Kingdom and in 1968 to Paris, Amsterdam and Dublin. *"Technology Review: Beacon Flashes its Message as far as Rome," New Scientist, March 9, 1972, p 544*

[1970, verb use of the adjective]

remote sensor, a camera, radar unit, seismograph, or other instrument that gathers data, usually about features of the earth or other bodies in space, from an artificial satellite or space probe.

Instruments called remote sensors are well on the way to providing information vital to the solution of some of the worst problems of our environment—many of them being problems that technology itself has caused. *Peter Briggs, "Big Eye in the Sky," Encyclopedia Science Supplement (Grolier) 1972, p 392*

[1972, from earlier (1963) *remote sensing*]

ren·min·bi ('ren'min'bi:), *n.* the currency or legal tender of the People's Republic of China.

The outside world was still largely unfamiliar with the Chinese currency—the renminbi or people's currency. The basic unit of renminbi—which is abbreviated to RMB—is the yuan, represented by the symbol Y, and the subsidiary units are jiao (10 jiao = 1 yuan) and fen (10 fen = 1 jiao). *The Times (London), March 21, 1973, p III*

[1970, from Chinese (Pinyin) *rén-mín-bì*, literally, people's currency]

renormalization, *n. Physics.* the systematic replacement of infinities with experimentally observed values, used as a method of eliminating obstacles to theoretical formulations.

According to Einstein's famous energy-mass formula, the electron would then have an infinite mass, rendering it incapable of motion. To get around this problem, Feynman invented a rule called renormalization that enables the theorist to ignore these infinities. *Robert H. March, "The Quandary Over Quarks," The World Book Science Annual 1975 (1974), p 87*

Renormalization works in quantum electrodynamics and in the currently accepted field theories constructed to describe the strong interactions. For many years it seemed there was no convincing renormalizable theory of the weak interactions. *Daniel Z. Freedman and Peter van Nieuwenhuizen, "Supergravity and the Unification of the Laws of Physics," Scientific American, Feb. 1978, p 132*

[1969]

renormalize, *v.t. Physics.* to correct or adjust by the process of renormalization.

The second obstacle to a satisfactory theory is that many calculations involving the weak force quickly lead to infinite results. In electromagnetic theory similar divergences are handled by the process called renormalization. Until recently no one could see how to renormalize the divergences presented by the weak force. *"Science and the Citizen," Scientific American, Nov. 1972, p 50*

[1972, back formation from *renormalization*]

renormalizability, *n.:* All earlier attempts to implement such a programme, however, foundered on the rock of 'renormalisability'. That is to say, the higher order terms in the perturbation series were incalculable because of (unrenormalisable) infinities. *D. Bailin, Review of "Gauge Theories of Weak Interactions" by J. C. Taylor, Nature, April 22, 1976, p 736*

renormalizable, *adj.:* In the last few years, considerable progress has been made in unifying theories of electromagnetic and weak interactions of elementary particles and in constructing renormalizable models of weak interactions. *Benjamin W. Lee, "Force, Weak and Electromagnetic," McGraw-Hill Yearbook of Science and Technology 1974, p 194*

rent-a-crowd or **rentacrowd,** *n. Especially British, Slang.* a group of people paid or induced to form a crowd at a rally, demonstration, or the like.

In the end, the Ford campaign turned into a television ex-

travaganza, with the President shuttling from city to city to make pre-programmed appearances before rent-a-crowds, replete with "photo opportunities" but no "question opportunities" for the press. *Walter Stewart, Maclean's, Nov. 15, 1976, p 61*

I wish your paper would avoid the loaded term rent-a-crowd when reporting confrontations such as the recent one in Lewisham. The implication is absurd: journalese may be cheap, but to buy the services of 4,000 demonstrators would hardly be a cost-effective exercise in such a labour-intensive field. *Belinda Hollyer, North Carlton, Melbourne, in a Letter to the Editor, The Manchester Guardian Weekly, Sept. 18, 1977, p 2*

[1966, patterned on *rent-a-car* (1963) a car rental firm, and other terms formed with *rent-a-*, such as *rent-a-cop* (1963) a hired security guard] Compare BODY SHOP (def. 2), RENT-A-MOB.

rent-a-mob or **rentamob,** *n. British Slang.* a group of people paid or induced to act as a mob and especially to cause a riot.

Students are the prime targets of the anti-elitists because they can be so easily organised into Rentamobs by Labour's syndicalists and their allies (and future masters) even further to the Left. *Paul Johnson, "The Rise of the Know-Nothing Left," New Statesman, Sept. 26, 1975, p 356*

Trade unionists therefore all feel attacked and have rallied round to help our colleagues who have had 44 weeks of picketing. Charges of rent-a-mob are totally untrue and as a steward each morning, I can confirm all people I have spoken to are card carrying members of a trade union. *Chris Wright, in a Letter to the Editor, The Times (London), June 21, 1977, p 15*

[1970] Compare RENT-A-CROWD.

re·peg (ri:'peg), *v.t.* to give a fixed value to (a floating currency).

By the year's end, the Canadian dollar, which had been floating for over two and a half years, was regarded as very unlikely to be repegged before both the international situation and Canadian-U.S. relationships achieved a higher degree of stability. *Miroslav A. Kriz, "International Payments and Reserves," Britannica Book of the Year 1973, p 529*

[1972]

repetitive DNA, a form of DNA that contains multiple copies of a particular gene in each cell.

In all cases the repetitive DNA was located next to the single-copy DNA. The repetitive DNA was also shown to be in a sequence about 300 base pairs long, while the single-copy DNA adjacent to it was about 1,500 base pairs long. *Eugene R. Katz, "Genetics," The Americana Annual 1976, p 263*

[1975] See SPACER.

replacement level, the birth rate needed for a population to maintain itself.

The "total fertility rate"—a figure calibrated to the average completed family size at current fertility rates—was also up about 5 percent above the first third of last year. However, the current rate of 1.84 children per woman is still below the "replacement level" of 2.1 children for American society. *Science News, Aug. 13, 1977, p 101*

[1974]

rep·la·mine·form (ˌrep ləˈmiːnˌfɔrm), *n.* a process for duplicating organic skeletal structures in ceramic, metal, or polymer materials. *Usually used attributively.*

Biomaterials. Further development of synthetic membranes holds the promise of creating a totally implantable artificial kidney . . . and a new "replamineform process" can help replicate living structures in some suitable material. *Science News, Jan. 26, 1974, p 53*

[1972, probably from repl*i*cated + *amine* + *form*]

replant, *v.t.* to reattach surgically (a severed hand, finger, toe, etc.); implant anew.

From 1966 to 1971, the surgeons replanted 151 fingers. Eighty-five percent of the operations were successful. *"Chinese Medical Science: Replanting Severed Limbs and Fingers," Science News, June 16, 1973, p 388*

[1973]

replantation, *n.:* Replantation, members of the research group stress, must be based on a patient's general condition, on the nature of the trauma, and on the time limit for survival of the replanted limb. *"Chinese Medical Science: Replanting Severed Limbs and Fingers," Science News, June 16, 1973, p 388*

rep·li·car ('rep lə̩kar), *n.* a full-sized replica of a classic or antique automobile, usually sold in the form of a kit and containing an engine and other mechanical parts of modern design.

Most of the replicar companies are small, the result of individuals' efforts to meet a very present demand for the past. *Edmund K. Gravely, Jr., "Replicars: Appealing to Nostalgia," The New York Times, Jan. 28, 1979, Sec. 12, p 14*

[1979, blend of *replica* and *car*]

rep·li·con ('rep lə̩kan), *n.* any genetic element containing the structural gene to control its own replication.

This group . . . constitutes a replicon, of which there is just one in the E. coli chromosome and many on mammalian chromosomes. The bigger the chromosome the more replicons it has. *"Chromosomes Grow by Blowing Bigger and Bigger Bubbles," New Scientist, Sept. 13, 1973, p 607*

The replication of eukaryotic DNA has been extensively analyzed in the last few years, and significant problems that remain to be solved have been defined (for example, how are replicons turned on or off when the length of the S phase varies?). *Barbara A. Hamkalo, Review of "The Cell Nucleus" by Harris Busch, Science, March 21, 1975, p 1070*

[1972, from repl*ic*ation + *-on* elementary unit]

re·po ('ri:̩pou), *n. U.S. Finance.* an agreement in which a seller of securities, especially government bonds, agrees to buy them back after a specified period.

Mr. Hunt believes that repurchase agreements, or "repos," are the missing link. Repos make it possible for corporations to earn interest on funds with maturities of less than 30 days. *"A New Key to Leak in Money?" The New York Times, Feb. 5, 1979, p D5*

[1963, shortened from repo*ssess*, in allusion to the repurchase agreement]

reservation, *n.* **on the reservation,** *U.S. Informal.* remaining within a particular political party, faction, or group.

The appointment of Dean Burch . . . is another White House attempt to keep conservatives (as they say in White House lingo) "on the reservation." *Cato, "Letter from Washington," National Review, March 15, 1974, p 300*

[1971, patterned on earlier phrase (DA 1949) *off the reservation* going outside a political party, faction, etc., as by supporting another group's candidate; originally used in allusion to Indians who left their reservations]

res·me·thrin (rez'mi: θrin *or* rez'meθ rin), *n.* a quick-acting synthetic insecticide similar to the natural insecticide pyrethrin. *Formula:* $C_{22}H_{26}O_3$

We keep them [plastic sprayers] about a quarter full of "Sprayday," the spray based on resmethrin which has a wonderful knock-down effect on most insects. Resmethrin is about the least harmful spray you can use as an insecticide. *Roy Hay, "Gardening: Surviving the Drought," The Times (London), July 10, 1976, p 10*

[1971, probably from *res*in + blend of *meth*yl and pyr*ethrin*] Also called **BIORESMETHRIN.** See **PYRETHROID.**

resonance, *n. Astronomy.* a synchronous relationship between two motions of a celestial body (as the axial and orbital motions of the moon) or between the motions of two or more celestial bodies.

In the case of interplanetary resonances, the gravitational force between the two bodies has apparently brought the smaller one's motion into resonance with the motion of the larger.

The first resonance between an asteroid and a planet was reported last year by W. H. Ip and L. Danielsson, who found that the motion of Toro is controlled by a complicated resonance with the motions of the earth and Venus. *Dietrick E. Thomsen, "The Resonating Solar System," Science News, Feb. 17, 1973, p 105*

[1973] See **PROGRADE.**

resonate, *v.i. Astronomy.* to act in resonance; be in synchronous motion (with oneself or another celestial body).

Amor [an asteroid] resonates with the earth (three orbits to eight of the earth's) in such a way that, as seen from the earth, its orbit rotates until it has a close approach to the earth. *Dietrick E. Thomsen, "The Resonating Solar System," Science News, Feb. 17, 1973, p 105*

[1973] Compare **COROTATE.**

restorer gene, a gene of a plant, that prevents sterility, isolated for use as a fertility agent.

Called the restorer gene, it restores fertility to male-sterile plants and makes possible the breeding of hybrid sunflowers of consistent high quality with good yield. *Robert B. Rathbone, "Agriculture," 1973 Britannica Yearbook of Science and the Future (1972), p 162*

[1969]

restriction enzyme or **restriction en·do·nu·cle·ase** (̩en dou'nu: kli:̩eis), an enzyme that cleaves DNA strands (as of a bacterium or virus) at a specific site which matches the DNA fragment of another organism cut by the same enzyme, enabling segments of DNA from different sources to be joined in new genetic combinations.

The restriction enzyme EcoRI is an enzyme which conveniently chops DNA in such a way that the pieces have adhesive ends which can be used to stick the required gene, excised from the chromosome by the enzyme, into the replicating vehicle in which the same enzyme has hewn a suitable gap. The gap, however, must be in a part of the chromosome that the bacteriophage doesn't need in order to replicate, and that means that the particular sites on to which EcoRI likes to latch, must be on so-called non-essential parts of the genome. *"More Tools for Genetic Engineering," New Scientist, Dec. 12, 1974, p 799*

The discovery of restriction enzymes, enzymes that snip long chains of DNA into segments that can be separated and identified, not only helped open the field of recombinant DNA during the late 1970s, but in 1978 earned the three scientists who made the discovery a Nobel Prize in Medicine. *Science News, Dec. 23/30, 1978, p 451*

Today at least 80 enzymes, called restriction endonucleases, are known to cut DNA in different specific parts of the molecule. *Harold M. Schmeck, Jr., "The Tools That May Crack Life's Secrets," The New York Times, Nov. 12, 1978, Sec. 4, p E9*

[1970] Compare EXCISIONASE. See also RECOMBINANT DNA RESEARCH.

restriction site, the site at which a restriction enzyme cleaves DNA strands to be joined to the identically cut DNA of another organism.

The team synthesized an operator sequence of nucleic acid base pairs, then "glued on" two short DNA regions called restriction sites — the chemical equivalents to dotted lines where restriction enzymes can attack. They then snipped "holes" in small, circular chromosomes called plasmids and spliced in the operator region with restriction enzymes, one region per plasmid. *"Recombinant DNA: Impacts and Advances," Science News, June 19, 1976, p 389*

[1976] See RECOMBINANT DNA RESEARCH.

retarget, *v.t.* to direct to a new target.

The major outstanding question was whether Pioneer II, following along a year behind its predecessor, could safely be retargeted toward Saturn, a maneuver which would require a much closer pass to Jupiter — about 25,000 miles — for a gravity-assisted swingaround. *"A Pioneer View of Jupiter," Science News, Dec. 8, 1973, p 357*

One response that Bergerac has made is to retarget Revlon's lowest-priced line, Natural Wonder, once aimed specifically at teen-agers, to reach women aged 18 to 34 — not by changing the products, but by picturing slightly older females in the ads. *"Cosmetics: Kiss and Sell," Time, Dec. 11, 1978, p 88*

[1970]

ret·i·no·tec·tal (ˌret ə nouˈtek təl), *adj.* of or involving the network of nerve fibers connecting the retina with the dorsal part of the midbrain (tectum).

The mechanisms responsible for the formation of specific nerve connections have been analysed, most extensively in the retinotectal system of lower vertebrates: the axons of retinal ganglion cells connect selectively at local tectal sites to produce a map of the retina across the surface of the optic tectum. *Nature, Jan. 18, 1974, p 128*

[1972, from *retino-* retina + *tectal* of the tectum]

retirement community, *Especially U.S.* a residential community chiefly or exclusively for elderly people.

The well-to-do, who constitute less than 5 per cent of the over-65 population, often live in "retirement communities" which are actually old-age ghettoes in Florida or California. Old people don't like being segregated with other old people, but it's better than being isolated in a city apartment.

Jane Rosen, "American Way of Lingering Death," The Manchester Guardian Weekly, Feb. 22, 1975, p 16

Youngstown is, in many ways, the prototype of the modern, self-contained American retirement community that has begun to spring up throughout the Southwest and Florida. And the generational clash here could be a preview of things to come elsewhere as the average age of Americans increases, and more of the elderly flock together to live out their days. *Robert Lindsey, "Elderly in Arizona Town Fight to Keep Children Out," The New York Times, Jan. 29, 1976, p 35*

[1963]

re·tor·na·do (ˌre tɔrˈnɑː dou), *n.* **1** a Spaniard who has returned to Spain after working in another country.

There is no welfare system, though — which means that young men and women who have never had a job do not get any income from the government, and neither do the *retornados,* who are coming home from West Germany and France and Switzerland at the rate of forty or fifty thousand a year. *Jane Kramer, "A Reporter in Europe: Madrid," The New Yorker, March 21, 1977, p 108*

2 a Portuguese citizen who has returned to Portugal from one of its former colonies.

He is a retornado — he came back from "over there." A colonist? Come, he hadn't been 20 years in Angola when the dream came to an abrupt end outside the mob-besieged gates of Luanda's airport. *Dominique Pouchin, "Like Squaring the Circle," The Manchester Guardian Weekly (Le Monde section), May 7, 1978, p 13*

[1977, from Spanish and Portuguese, literally, returnee]

retro, *n.* a revival of the fashions, music, plays, etc., of an earlier time. *Often used attributively.*

The icy charms of the Group TSE's productions, beginning as far back as 1969's "Eva Peron," have been in the vanguard of the French vogue for "retro" (though the TSE is an Argentinian group, and a good deal of "retro" has been imported from the US). *Martin Even, "Nostalgia and Narcissus," The Manchester Guardian Weekly (Le Monde section), May 18, 1974, p 14*

We thought that if we closed our eyes, retro fashion would go away. No such luck. Everything from bustiers (read the Merry Widow bra of the 1950's) to chippie shoes has been copied and is now flooding the stores. If you loved the recent Paris fashions and think that the 40's and 50's were cute, then retro is your thing. *"Discoveries," The New York Times, Jan. 24, 1979, p C8*

[1974, from French *rétro,* *n.* and *adj.,* probably short for *rétrospectif* retrospective]

RETRO or **Retro,** *n. U.S.* an engineer specializing in the firing and action of the retrorockets of a spacecraft.

In the front row . . . sat three Flight Dynamics Engineers, the men responsible for the ship's trajectory: from right to left, the Guidance Officer, or GUIDO, who was the chief navigation officer; the Flight Dynamics Officer, or FIDO, who plotted the trajectory and made sure the spacecraft followed it; and the Retrofire Officer, or RETRO, who was in charge of the spacecraft's reëntry into the earth's atmosphere. *Henry S. F. Cooper, Jr., "Annals of Exploration: An Accident in Space—I," The New Yorker, Nov. 11, 1972, p 49*

[1969, short for *retrofire officer*]

retrofit, *v.t.* **1** to modify (older equipment) to include changes made in later production of the same model or type.

To help make up for the extra pollution generated by pre-1979 engines, the agency is proposing a program of retrofitting such engines with emission-control devices as these become technologically feasible. *"Aircraft Emissions Subject of New Guides," Science News, July 14, 1973, p 23*

2 to provide (an older vehicle, building, etc.) with equipment modified to include changes made in later models or other improvements.

Cars in Group III cities must be retrofitted with exhaust catalysts to remove pollutants and must impose some restrictions on downtown driving. *"How U.S. Cities Can Meet Air Standards," Science News, Aug. 4, 1973, p 71*

The federal government has . . . shaped legislation to provide grants to cities and states for "retrofitting" public buildings with solar energy systems. *Charles W. Moore and Robert J. Yudell, "Architecture," The Americana Annual 1977, p 95*

Conservation is often very expensive, especially when large plants must be converted to different fuels or "retrofitted" with more efficient equipment. *Time, April 25, 1977, p 31*

—*n.* the process of modifying equipment, etc., to include changes made in later models or other equipment.

We estimate that such technological improvements could cut present energy consumption by roughly one-third. These changes, however, require the production of new goods and services rather than a retrofit of existing systems. *Eric Hirst and Robert Herendeen, "A Diet Guide for Chronic Energy Consumers," Saturday Review, Oct. 28, 1972, p 66*

Ford is phasing in new locks and "there is a possibility of retrofit," meaning putting better locks on older cars, says Herbert Misch, a Ford vice president. *Jerry Flint, "Detroit's Blunders, on a Grand Scale," The New York Times, Jan. 11, 1976, Sec. 3, p 27*

[1969, verb use of earlier (1956) noun meaning a modification of an aircraft or part of an aircraft to incorporate changes made in later productions, ultimately from *retro*active re*fit*]

retrofittable, *adj.*: For instance, one proposed strategy is for retrofittable emission-control devices to enable older cars to meet 1975 or 1976 emission goals. *"Air Pollution: What Will the States Do?" Science News, June 10, 1972, p 372*

retrovirus, *n.* any of a group of tumor-producing viruses that use RNA instead of DNA to encode genetic information.

The RNA tumor viruses, which produce animal cancers, use RNA instead of DNA to encode their genetic information. They are often called "retroviruses" because they reverse a step in one central dogma of biology: DNA makes RNA makes protein. Viral RNA, once in a cell, must create double-stranded DNA molecules. Then the viral genes can slip into an animal chromosome. *"Viruses Prepare to Plug Into Chromosome," Science News, July 1, 1978, p 6*

[1977, from *retro*- backward + *virus*] Compare ONCORNAVIRUS. See also REVERTASE.

reuptake, *n.* the reabsorption of a chemical substance by a nerve cell after it has relayed an impulse.

Most of the norepinephrine active at the brain synapses

is "recycled," literally sucked back into the cell and conserved for future use, after relaying the nerve impulse. This sucking-back process, called "re-uptake," is the major means by which norepinephrine is "turned off." *Maggie Scarf, "From Joy to Depression," The New York Times Magazine, April 24, 1977, p 33*

[1976, from *re*- again + *uptake*]

reverse commuting, commutation from a city to the suburbs for work.

Mrs. Littlefield was among several private school officials who said they had begun to notice the phenomenon of "reverse commuting" by families who had become disillusioned with what they called the "barren" and expensive life of the suburbs. *"Private and Parochial Schools Begin Year on Note of Optimism," The New York Times, Sept. 15, 1976, p 88*

[1967] Also called INCOMMUTATION.

reverse commuter: But "reverse commuters," to whom the story refers, cannot afford the high housing cost of the inner-ring suburbs and therefore must live in the city while commuting to suburban jobs. *Robert J. Mangum, New York, in a Letter to the Editor, The New York Times, Sept. 4, 1970, p 26*

reverse discrimination, *U.S.* discrimination against individuals who are members of a dominant group by giving preferential treatment in education, employment, etc., to members of a minority group.

What has made these cases potentially explosive is the charge by those who fall outside the definition of minority groups, notably whites and Orientals, that the effect of these programs is "reverse discrimination." . . . Marco DeFunis had sued the University of Washington law school charging that it had practiced "reverse discrimination" against him by denying him admission in favor of less-qualified minority students. *"Justice: A Decision Not to Decide," Newsweek, May 6, 1974, p 50*

Only a nation of saints might reasonably anticipate that a long-sustained policy of reverse discrimination will have effects other than those associated with plain discrimination; that is, perpetuation of the antagonism and other barriers that separate black from white. *E. L. Pattullo, "Counterpoints," The Atlantic, Jan. 1978, p 77*

[1971] ► See the note under AFFIRMATIVE ACTION.

re·vert·ant (ri'vər tənt), *Genetics.* —*n.* an organism or strain that has reverted to an earlier type by mutation.

Examination of the chromosomes of such cells, according to Sachs, has shown that certain specific groups of chromosomes are always associated with malignancy and tend to be dropped in revertants, which conversely have more of another specific group of chromosomes, associated with nonmalignancy. *"Cancer Cells: Natural Selection or Gene Warfare?" New Scientist, June 28, 1973, p 799*

—*adj.* that has reverted to an earlier type by mutation.

The first step is the isolation of revertant strains having a normal phosphatase phenotype. Genetic mapping shows that the revertants can occur in either of two ways. *Alan Garen, Science, April 12, 1968, p 154*

[1966, from *revert*, v. + -*ant* (noun and adj. suffix)]

re·vert·ase (ri'vər,teis), *n.* an enzyme that causes the formation of DNA from a template of RNA, found in tumor-producing viruses containing RNA.

Recently, another important activity has been what

revolving door

Engelhardt calls their "Project Revertase"—revertase being the newly discovered enzyme . . . which can reproduce DNA using RNA as the template, thus reversing the central dogma of Crick about the unidirectional flow of genetic information from genes (DNA) to RNA to proteins. *Sarah White, "Soviet Biochemist," New Scientist, May 9, 1974, p 329*

[1974, from *reverse* transcript*ase*, the original name] See RETROVIRUS.

revolving door, a constantly recurring or repetitive round of activity; an automatic cycle or circular process.

The new airlift is designed to close or at least slow down the "revolving door" that allows apprehended aliens, after they have been taken back into Mexico at Tijuana, Juarez, Nuevo Laredo and other border cities, to repeat their attempts to reach the United States. *Everett R. Holles, "U.S. Airlifting Mexican Aliens Home," The New York Times, July 25, 1976, p 20*

The revolving door of the court system is expensive and fruitless. Prostitutes plead guilty; the judge slaps down a fine and lets them go. To pay the fine, they have to turn more tricks and soon wind up back in court. *Time, Oct. 2, 1978, p 48*

[1966, figurative sense of the term (1930's) for a door with sections that revolve on a central axis]

revolving-door, *adj.:* The courts dispense a revolving-door type of trial-less justice, where 95 percent of cases are disposed of by negotiated guilty pleas and where trials in the lower courts sometimes last five minutes. *Norman E. Zinberg and John A. Robertson, Drugs and the Public, 1972, p 216*

The woes of the wealthy Argonauts have become a national joke, thanks in part to the team's revolving-door policy with players, coaches and even owners. But how, oh how, do the Saskatchewan Roughriders manage to come up with a contender every year?" *Sports, Maclean's, Oct 4, 1976. p 65*

Reye's syndrome (reiz), a rare but often fatal children's disease which usually occurs after a common viral infection such as influenza and involves extensive brain, liver, and kidney damage.

First, repeated changing of blood is not the only known treatment for Reye's Syndrome. Along with the blood transfusions, the child undergoes dialysis, is given a powerful drug, L-dopa, to maintain nerve impulses, and holes are drilled into the patient's skull to relieve the pressure created by swelling of the brain. *Mary Donaldson, Fredericton, Canada, in a Letter to the Editor, Maclean's, June 28, 1976, p 9*

[1972, named after R. D. *Reye,* an Australian physician, who first identified the condition in 1963]

R factor, a genetic factor in some bacteria that codes for resistance to antibiotics and other antibacterial drugs, and that can be transmitted from one bacterium to another by conjugation.

Typhoid bacilli are among the bacteria that can acquire transferable resistance. This phenomenon occurs when bacteria that have survived exposure to an antibiotic by developing resistance to it pass on this resistance in the form of genetic material—the R factor—to other species or strains. *"Science Report," The Times (London), Aug. 4, 1972, p 14*

As in resistance to other drugs, trimethoprim-resistance is a characteristic inherited not through the main bacterial

chromosome, but through the existence of an autonomous, non-chromosomal carrier of genetic information known as an R-factor. R-factor-linked resistance is particularly disturbing because of the ease with which R-factors can be transferred from one bacterium to another. *New Scientist, July 18, 1974, p 118*

[1966, from Resistance *factor*]

rhom·bo·chasm ('rɑm bə,kæz əm), *n. Geology.* a rhomboid gap formed by tension between parallel and offsetting pairs of faults.

Figure 3*b,* approximately middle Triassic, shows two significant changes: a second rhombochasm begins to separate the arc segment from the Palaeozoic marginal basin fragment. *Richard A. Schweickert, "Early Mesozoic Rifting and Fragmentation of the Cordilleran Orogen in the Western USA," Nature, April 15, 1976, p 590*

[1972, from *rhombo-* shaped like a rhombus (from Greek *rhómbos* rhombus) + *chasm*]

rhyt·i·dec·to·my (,rit ə'dek tə mi:), *n.* cosmetic surgery that tightens the skin about the face and neck by removing fatty deposits, stretching loose muscle tissue, etc.; face-lift operation.

The face lift (rhytidectomy) corrects pendulous neck skin, wrinkled cheeks and jowls, and softens grooves from mouth to nose. Incisions are made along the frontal contour of the ear, under and behind the ear, and up the temple. *James Kelly, "Cosmetic Lib for Men," The New York Times Magazine, Sept. 25, 1977, p 124*

[1971, from Greek *rhytíd-, rhytís* wrinkle + *ektomē* excision] Compare BLEPHAROPLASTY.

► Although this term has been long used in medicine in the sense of "surgical removal of wrinkles," it has become in recent years generally synonymous with a face lift.

ri·ba·vi·rin (,rɑi bə'vɑi rin), *n.* a synthetic ribonucleoside that inhibits the replication of both DNA and RNA in viruses by interfering with the synthesis of nucleic acids. *Formula:* $C_8H_{12}N_4O_5$

At the present time only ara-A (Vira-A) and to a lesser extent ribavirin (Virazole) have shown promise in widespread clinical trials. Both drugs have antiviral activity at dose levels sufficiently below toxic levels to permit their systemic use. *J. C. Drach, Ann Arbor, Mich., "Antiviral Compound," in a Letter to the Editor, Science News, April 10, 1976, p 227*

[1975, probably from *ribonucleic acid* + *virus* + *-in* (chemical suffix)]

ridership, *n. U.S.* the number of passengers served by any transit system.

In many cities, bus ridership had been declining over the years until the energy crisis and Federal subsidies—which pay about three-fourths of the cost of a new bus—made buses more attractive than cars to many commuters. *Newsweek, Feb. 25, 1974, p 80*

Amtrak has not been failing; in fact, it has been extending its passenger train network, improving its equipment and schedules, and attracting increased ridership (up from 16.6 to 18.6 million annually). *Tom Wicker, "Energy Off the Rails," The New York Times, Sept. 2, 1977, p A21*

[1969, patterned on *readership* (1920's), *listenership* (1940's), VIEWERSHIP]

right-brain, *n.* the right hemisphere of the brain. *Often used attributively.*

Human beings are the only mammals whose left and right brains are specialized for quite different functions. . . . Because of the distinctly human differences in left-brain and right-brain, and the variations that genetic inheritance makes possible in brain physiology—and therefore in temperament and talents—each individual brain is truly unique. *Roger W. Sperry, "Left-Brain, Right-Brain," Encyclopedia Science Supplement (Grolier) 1976, p 50*

[1976] Compare LEFT-BRAIN.

righteous, *adj. Especially U.S. Slang.* genuine; true.

I admit to being totally subjective in my response to my work. But ultimately, I know. That's why I know my reaction to *Duddy Kravitz* is righteous. *Richard Dreyfuss, in an Interview with Cameron Crowe, Rolling Stone, Jan. 11, 1979, p. 88*

[1970, originally (1930's) jazz slang, especially of the quality of the music or the performance]

right-to-die, *adj.* permitting or advocating the withdrawal of extreme or artificial life-sustaining measures taken to prolong the life of an incurably ill or injured person.

A revolutionary "right-to-die" bill . . . will allow physicians to remove life support systems from patients who have authorized such action in advance. The act applies only in cases of irreversible injury or illness certified to be terminal by two physicians. *George S. Blair, "California," 1977 Collier's Encyclopedia Year Book (1976), p 177*

[1976] See DEATH, EUTHANASIA.

► The case of a young woman who lapsed into coma in April 1975 first brought this term and the issue to widespread public attention. Although she was not BRAIN DEAD, physicians believed that there was no reasonable expectation of recovery. The parents petitioned to remove the artificial respirator (pull the PLUG), arguing that the individual's right to die "with grace and dignity" took precedence over the state's interest and determination to forcibly preserve life by artificial life support.

The case gave impetus to the right-to-die movement permitting the use of a LIVING WILL in which a healthy person can direct that no life-support equipment shall be used if he becomes irreversibly comatose, terminally ill, etc.

right-to-life, *adj.* advocating or supporting laws that prohibit induced abortion, especially abortion-on-demand; PRO-LIFE.

Right-to-life propagandists take pains to refer to male and female fetuses as "unborn boy and girl babies" and during a 1972 referendum vote on a more liberal abortion law in a midwest state they had school children call voters on the telephone, saying in a piping youngster's treble, "This is the voice of a little unborn baby." *Joseph Fletcher, The Ethics of Genetic Control, 1974, p 109*

A vigorous "right to life" movement has successfully exerted pressure on some state legislatures to enact new restrictive laws and on many hospital administrators to prevent the delivery of abortion services in defiance of the decisions. *Christopher Tietze and Sarah Lewit, "Legal Abortion," Scientific American, Jan. 1977, p 22*

[1972] Compare ANTIABORTION. See also ABORTION.

► This term and its variant, *pro-life*, emphasize the "right of the unborn to life." To avoid the implied bias, some writers prefer *antiabortion* as an objec-

tive designation and *proabortion* as its antonym.

right-to-lifer, *n.* a person who advocates or supports antiabortion laws; ANTIABORTIONIST.

A woman is a responsible individual and should be permitted to decide for herself whether or not she wants an abortion. This seems rather obvious, but the "Right-to-Lifers" apparently belong to that stifling, archaic school of thought that holds that a woman is basically irresponsible and must be told what to do with her life. *Suzanne L. Clouthier, in a Letter to the Editor, Maclean's, Nov. 15, 1976, p 16b*

Buoyed by last week's victory, the right-to-lifers immediately began planning their congressional strategy for next year. They will press for a ban on all Medicaid abortions, without exception, and ask that these procedures be outlawed at military hospitals. They will also lobby against including abortions in any national health insurance program that Congress may consider in the future. *"Nation: New Limits on Abortion," Time, Dec. 19, 1977, p 12*

[1972]

ring·git ('riŋ git), *n.; pl.* **-git** or **-gits.** the monetary unit of Malaysia, also known as the Malaysian dollar.

The Malaysian High Court today also fined him 15,000 ringgit (£3,750) with the alternative of another six months' imprisonment, for abetment of a criminal breach of trust. *"Former Chief Minister of Selangor on Bail," The Times (London), Jan. 25, 1977, p 9*

[1967, from Malay]

riot shield, a shield used by members of a police or military force during a riot.

Later the Queen had a preview of some of what she will see during her jubilee visit to Northern Ireland next week. A review of the Royal Marines on Plymouth Ho included an officer and 30 men of 42 Commando, dressed for operations in Ulster and equipped with riot shields. *The Times (London), Aug. 6, 1977, p 2*

[1966]

ripple control, a method by which a utility company helps its customers save on the cost of electric power by automatically turning off water heaters during periods of peak consumer demand, when electricity is most expensive to produce.

So far, ripple control has worked: according to test results, the system has saved roughly $60 a year per heater in electricity costs, a saving that Green Mountain Power (G.M.P.) has returned to participants in the experiment in the form of monthly $5 rebates. *"Environment: Flattening the Peaks," Time, Sept. 6, 1976, p 33*

The ripple control scheme allows signals to be transmitted over the supply network so that the storage radiators can be switched on and off by the LEB [London Electricity Board] engineers to ensure that they only take power at the times when it is cheapest. *"Technology: Is Cheap Electricity Good For All Londoners?" New Scientist, June 30, 1977, p 784*

[1976]

ripple effect, a gradually spreading effect.

While adding to the nation's general economic woes, the ripple effects of the housing slump seem certain to add to the pressure on government policymakers to come up with help for home building. *John V. Conti, "Ripple Effect," The Wall Street Journal, Dec. 12, 1974, p 1*

It appears that when problems do occur, those of the wife were "least well tolerated" and produced a "ripple effect on all sexual relations" involving the couple. *Science News, July 29, 1978, p 70*

[1968] Compare ECHO EFFECT.

ripstop, *adj.* (of a lightweight fabric, especially a synthetic fabric) designed with a series of small ridged squares to contain tearing and prevent long rips.

Most popular of all [kites] are the dual control stunters, capable of exciting aerobatic performances, and thanks to ripstop nylon, comparatively indestructible. *Robin Young, The Times (London), Dec. 14, 1976, p 16*

[1970]

risk-benefit ratio, the relation between the risks taken and the possible benefits derived from any undertaking (such as the administration of a powerful drug in chemotherapy).

Whereas the majority of the investigators were what we called "strict" with regard to balancing risks against benefits, a significant minority were "permissive," that is, they were much more willing to accept an unsatisfactory risk-benefit ratio. *Bernard Barber, "The Ethics of Experimentation with Human Subjects," Scientific American, Feb. 1976, p 27*

Dr. Maurice B. Visscher . . . said in a review of the study in The New England Journal of Medicine that the results had found "no consensus among physicians about what risk-benefit ratios to the individual or to society will justify either therapeutic or pure-science studies." *Lawrence K. Altman, "Stricter Curbs Urged in Medical Research," The New York Times, Feb. 1, 1976, p 28*

[1975]

rite of reconciliation, (in the Roman Catholic Church) a new name for the sacrament of penance.

New procedures in the Sacrament of Penance give rise to the term *Sacrament* (or *Rite*) *of Reconciliation*. The clergymen questioned believe that the new name will eventually replace the old entirely . . . *Sacrament of Reconciliation* is milder in tone than either *Penance* or *Confession. Henry R. Stern, "The Changing Language of American Catholicism," American Speech, Summer 1979, p 84*

[1976] See ROOM OF RECONCILIATION.

roach clip or **roach holder,** *Slang.* any device used to hold the end of a marijuana cigarette when it is too small to hold in the fingers while smoking.

. . . lists of things: lanterns, mirrors, keys "with hollow ends," . . . candles, leather handbags, bejeweled roach clips. *Patrick Douglas, Harper's, April 1972, p 90*

An hour later, Petersen was sitting on the floor of his cabin, passing a joint on a bobby-pin roach holder to his live-in girlfriend. *Ted Morgan, "The Good Life," The New York Times Magazine, July 4, 1976, p 20*

[1967, from *roach* (c1938) slang term for the butt of a marijuana cigarette]

roadie, *n. Slang.* a person hired to assist singers or other performers on tour.

Queen's retinue includes technicians, roadies, sound and lighting engineers—needed to manage tons of equipment, including a dry-ice smoke generator and a bubble-blowing machine. Heavy rock, indeed. *"Music: Hail to Queen," Time, Feb. 9, 1976, p 71*

The Rolling Stones and their roadies load up one of Al's Convairs in L.A. during the group's seven-week tour this summer. *Picture legend, People Weekly, Oct. 9, 1978, p 82*

[1970, from *road* manager + *-ie*; probably patterned on *groupie* (1967) a fan or follower of singing groups]

roadman, *n.* a contestant in a race over public roads, especially a bicycle race.

The huge field of 146 riders seemed hell-bent on keeping the fast-finishing Burton well to the rear and with four laps to go and two roadmen 200 metres out in front, it seemed this has been achieved. *Michael Coleman, "Cycling: Winter in Ghent Gives Burton Extra Spring," The Times (London), May 25, 1976, p 9*

[1971, from *road* race + *man*]

road rash, *U.S. Slang.* a severe scrape or bruise suffered in a fall from a fast-moving skateboard.

"You get down low on the board to cut wind resistance, and you pray that the board slows enough so you can get off," said Fred Araujo. "If you get off prematurely, you get a road rash." *Frances Cerra, "Some Skateboarders in Rapture, Some in Traction," The New York Times, April 2, 1976, p 38*

[1976]

Roche lobe, a gaseous bulge formed in companion stars by each star's gravitational pull on the other.

The most widely held theory for the nova phenomenon is that the prenova is a close binary system consisting of a red dwarf, which is filling its Roche Lobe, spilling matter over towards a white dwarf companion . . . The nova outburst is believed to be due to the flow of material from the red star passing by way of an accretion disk to the white dwarf's atmosphere where it is compressed and heated by the gravitational field until it reaches the ignition temperature for hydrogen burning reactions. *P. J. Andrews, "Nova Cygni 1975," Nature, Jan. 22, 1976, p 172*

[1969, named after Edouard *Roche*, a French mathematician who in 1848 formulated the *Roche limit*, an area surrounding a planet within which any moon or satellite would be disrupted by the planet's gravitational force]

rock ballet, a ballet set to rock music.

Resident choreographer Gerald Arpino, with such works as "Kettentanz" and the solemn rock ballet "Trinity," has established himself as a major artist. *Hubert Saal, "A Diversity of Dance," Newsweek, Dec. 24, 1973, p 62*

[1972]

rocker, *n. Slang.* **1** a rock song or musical.

The lyrics to "Humpty Dumpty," a rocker about the futility of waiting for the king's men to put you together, are especially good. *Ellen Willis, "Musical Events," The New Yorker, Oct. 23, 1971, p 175*

2 a rock singer or musician.

Even in so broad a musical spectrum—part nostalgia, part status quo, part innovation—the jazz rockers are a stylish group apart. *"Improvising on the Beat," Time, July 8, 1974, p 37*

3 a fan of rock music, singers, etc.

Though no rock czar has yet successfully crossed over to direct films, United Artists figured he'd pull millions of rockers to see his movie. *Maureen Orth, "Movies: American Dreamer," Newsweek, Sept. 10, 1973, p 85*

[1964, from *rock*'n'roll + *-er*; probably influenced by earlier (1963) *Rocker*, a type of British teen-ager given to wearing leather jackets, riding in gangs on motorcycles, and dancing to *rock'n'roll* music]

rockfest, *n. U.S.* a rock music festival.

N.Y. Public Health Department says Watkins Glen rockfest's 600,000 attendance made it "largest public gathering ever recorded in the history of the U.S." *National Review, Aug. 31, 1973, p 922*

[1973, from *rock*'n'roll + *fest* festival (from German *Fest*)]

rock opera, a drama set to rock music.

There has been word of a black rock opera, the *first* black rock opera, and some days ago a lot of music-business people gathered in the Corinthian Room of the New York Sheraton Hotel to celebrate the news. *"The Talk of the Town: Two Gatherings," The New Yorker, Jan. 13, 1973, p 22*

This book's appearance is certainly timely, just before the opening in London of the rock opera *Evita* — and, it might be remembered, a couple of years after the fall of the second Peronista régime in March 1976. *John Brooks, Review of "Eva Peron" by John Barnes, The Listener, June 15, 1978, p 771*

[1971]

rock steady, an earlier form of reggae, a kind of rock music developed in the West Indies.

In the early and mid-60's, ska was followed by rock steady, a laid-back form of ska with less improvisation and more calypso. *Jon Bradshaw, "The Reggae Way to 'Salvation'," The New York Times Magazine, Aug. 14, 1977, p 28*

Mindful that ska, rock steady and reggae were once emulations of American R & B, soul and rock&roll, I can accept Marley's fascination with Seventies funk and rock idioms. *Timothy White, "Bob Marley: All You Need Is Love," Rolling Stone, Jan. 11, 1979, p 98*

[1967]

Ro·gal·list (rou'gæl ist), *n.* another name for HANG GLIDER (def. 2).

Rogallists have soared off Pikes Peak (14,110 feet). In California, flights have been made from Dantes View down into Death Valley, a 5800-foot drop. *Wolfgang Langewiesche, "The Flyingest Flying There Is," The Reader's Digest, Feb. 1974, p 90*

[1974, from *Rogallo* + *-ist*]

Ro·gal·lo (rou'gæl ou), *n.* another name for HANG GLIDER (def. 1).

A Rogallo is basically a triangular kite. It's launched with a running jump off a hill, and the pilot controls the flight with body english. *Paul Wahl, "Hang Gliders," Popular Science, May 1974, p 99*

[1973, short for *Rogallo* wing or kite, a kitelike device to slow down reentry of a space probe, invented about 1962 by Francis M. *Rogallo*, an American engineer working for NASA, from which hang gliders were developed]

role model, a person whose behavior in a particular role serves as a model or standard for another person to follow.

Indeed, the Air Force Academy tried to encourage this process of change artificially, by bringing in 15 female officers in January 1976, six months before the arrival of the first women cadets. The young officers went through an abbreviated version of basic training, then began acting as

"decoy" upperclassmen. In that way, the first real female cadets had role models of their own sex from the very beginning. *San Francisco Chronicle, Dec. 29, 1979, p 11*

It is suggested that black professionals are needed to provide "role models" for black children. *John Robertson, The New York Review of Books, Jan. 26, 1978, p 42*

We still need a clearer picture of a role model — one that does not include excessive nurturing, competition, submission, or seduction. *Susan Murray-Friend, Ann Arbor, Mich., in a Letter to the Editor, Ms., Jan. 4, 1979, p 4*

Here, his [Bettelheim's] explanation becomes an indictment of the immediate post-war generation, the parents of today's college boys and girls: in particular, he indicts the fathers for having abdicated their proper task of imparting values, and of presenting a role-model of adulthood which their sons could admire and accept. *G. M. Carstairs, "Youth: the New Constituency," The Listener, Sept. 14, 1972, p 330*

[1969]

role-play, *v.t.* to play the part of or represent (someone or something) in an improvised acting out of a real-life situation.

But the command to role-play a homosexual means venturing into an unknown area of experience. *T. E. Kalem, "Id-Olatry," Time, Nov. 1, 1971, p 60*

—*v.i.* to play a role or roles; enact what one conceives as an appropriate role in a particular situation.

The protean president can role-play, presenting himself as a *communal-tribal leader* on some matters, a *bureaucratic-entrepreneur* on other matters, and on still others a *problem-solver/manager. Warren G. Bennis, "Searching for the 'Perfect' University President," The Atlantic, April 1971, p 52*

Do children truly lack the capacity to role-play (to temporarily assume another person's perspective), which seems to be required for effective performance in any but the most routine and stereotyped communication situations? Or is it rather that children — even four-year-olds — have the ability to role-play but for one reason or another do not deploy the ability in certain experimental contexts? *Robert M. Krauss and Sam Glucksberg, "Social and Nonsocial Speech," Scientific American, Feb. 1977, p 104*

[1969, back formation from the earlier (1950's) psychosociological term *role-playing*]

Rolf·ing or **rolf·ing** ('rɑl fiŋ), *n.* a method of deep massage of the tissue around the muscles to make the body more supple and more efficiently oriented to the force of gravity.

Papa John has had a bad back for years, but last time he came to New York he had an hour of Rolfing, the deep-massage postural therapy, and he said the Rolfing had set him up. *"The Talk of the Town: Jamming With Papa John," The New Yorker, April 7, 1973, p 32*

The quest for identity also accounted for the self-improvement programs associated with the human-potential movement — a farrago that included such quick-fix therapies as "primal scream" and "rolfing." *Newsweek, Nov. 19, 1979, p 96*

[1972, from *Rolf* massage + *-ing;* named after Ida *Rolf,* 1897-1979, an American physiotherapist who developed this system]

rolfee, rolfer, *n.:* The rolfer claims that, following the rolfing program, energy flow is restored to areas of the body that have been enervated. Afterwards, the "rolfee" may breathe properly for the first time since childhood. In the course of these sessions, we are told, the rolfee is often liberated from the crippling psychic attitudes his body had preserved. *Leo Litwak, The New York Times Magazine, Dec. 17, 1972, p 30*

rollcage, *n.* a reinforcing structure of metal bars, and sometimes wire screen, built into a car or truck or over an open seat of a tractor to protect the driver.

It would be good to see the designer Robin Herd's special rollcage adopted by all constructors, and while they are at it, could they not agree to reverse the trend for ever wider tyres? *Julian Mounter, "Motoring," The Times (London), March 23, 1972, p 33*

[1972, from *roll*over or *roll*bar + *cage*]

roller, *n. U.S. Slang.* a policeman.

In the black community, the police, who are sometimes called "rollers," have not been particularly popular. There are still complaints, for instance, that in fights inside the schools the police are more likely to grab a black youth and send a white one on his way. *John Kifner, "The Men in the Middle," The New York Times Magazine, Sept. 12, 1976, p 112*

[1964]

roller disco, *Especially U.S.* **1** dancing to disco music while on roller skates.

Insport has a fairly light-hearted-looking pair of roller skates for indoor rinks or roller-disco. They have toe brakes, and track-shoe uppers in blue-and-yellow nylon; $75. *"On and Off the Avenue," The New Yorker, Dec. 4, 1978, p 203*

It's like stereo for the feet, and from the boardwalks of Venice, California, roller-skating has spread to New York, where roller-disco is raging, and now it's beginning to shake its well behaved booty in Canadian rinks too. *Marni Jackson, "Rollin': Stereo for the Feet," Maclean's, Jan. 8, 1979, p 38*

2 a ballroom with a roller-skating rink for disco dancing on roller skates.

Manhattan has several roller discos, such as the Metropolis on West 55th Street, but the true mecca is in Brooklyn, where the Empire Roller Disco has become the showcase for dancers. *Clyde Haberman, "The Roller Rage," The New York Times Magazine, July 8, 1979, p 30*

[1978]

rollerdrome, *n. U.S.* a roller-skating rink.

Many rollerdromes are equipped with game rooms, dance floors, and pro shops that sell skates and carrying cases on easy-payment "rollaway" plans. *"Eight-Wheel Drive," Time, April 8, 1974, p J13*

In New York, roller-disco moved uptown from its origins in Brooklyn rinks like the Empire Rollerdome, where skaters, mostly black, have taken disco to the third power: dancing on wheels at 20 mph. *Marni Jackson, "Rollin': Stereo for the Feet," Maclean's, Jan. 8, 1979, p 39*

[1974, from *roller* skate + *-drome* race course]

roller hockey, hockey played on roller skates.

Mr Edward Heath, the former Prime Minister, is reported to have nearly fallen off his seat with excitement while watching a game at the new roller hockey rink at Herne Bay, Kent, which he officially opened last month. He could not understand why roller hockey was not more popular in Britain today. *Diana Geddes, "A Sport Seeks Honour*

in Its Own Country," The Times (London), Oct. 20, 1976, p 12

[1976]

ROM, *n.* acronym for READ-ONLY MEMORY.

The Singer Company of New York City began selling a sewing machine that used an ROM to control stitch width, length, and density. *Marilyn J. Offenheiser, "Electronics," The 1976 World Book Year Book, p 298*

[1969] Compare RAM.

roommate, *n.* a euphemism for COHABITEE.

If you are planning to acquire a roommate or have one already, be warned that you are leaving yourself wide open to more legal entanglements than even a married couple faces. . . . First of all, you want to avoid getting socked with your roommate's debts. When you live with someone without being married, you assume absolutely no responsibility for his or her debts. *William Flanagan, "Unmarrieds and the Law," Esquire, Sept. 1979, p 12*

[1974, transferred sense of the term for a person who shares a room with another (OED 1838)]

room of reconciliation, (in the Roman Catholic Church) a room for confession in which the penitent and the priest can meet either face to face or separated by a screen.

Major changes are evident in all three forms [of the rite of penance] in the inclusion of Bible readings and prayers in which the penitent is expected to take part and the choice of speaking to a priest through a screen or openly in a special "room of reconciliation." *Kenneth A. Briggs, "Catholics Changing Concept and Practice of Confession," The New York Times, March 6, 1976, p 27*

The older *confessional,* or *confessional box,* is now joined by a *Room of Reconciliation. Henry R. Stern, "The Changing Language of American Catholicism," American Speech, Summer 1979, p 84*

[1976] Also called RECONCILIATION ROOM. See RITE OF RECONCILIATION.

ro·ta·vi·rus (ˌrou təˈvai rəs), *n.* any of a group of circular viruses with spoke-like projections that are related to the reoviruses and cause acute gastroenteritis in infants and newborn animals.

Rotaviruses . . . have a similar appearance by electron microscopy, making differentiation among them difficult. Rotaviruses derived from different host species were distinguished by postinfection serum blocking virus activity in an enzyme-linked immunosorbent assay. *Science, July 21, 1978, p 259*

[1976, from Latin *rota* wheel + English *virus*]

ro·to (ˈrou tou), *n.* a person of the poorest class in Spanish-speaking areas of Latin America, especially Chile; a slum dweller.

The visiting journalist, whatever his prejudices, inevitably falls among the middle class, and that class has no more contact with the life of the Chilean "roto" than the white burghers of Johannesburg have with the black inhabitants of the township of Soweto. *Richard Gott, The Manchester Guardian Weekly, Oct. 6, 1973, p 17*

[1970, from American Spanish, literally, broken or ragged (one)] Compare POBLADOR.

rotor, *n.* a turbulent mass of air that rotates horizontally about its axis, found especially in the area of some large mountain barriers.

Because mountain waves can be dangerous to aircraft, and because on occasion they generate intense "rotors" that can raise roofs from houses or topsoil from farms, it came to be recognized that atmospheric gravity waves were of direct significance to man. *C. O. Hines, "Gravity Waves in the Atmosphere," Nature, Sept. 8, 1972, p 74*

[1971, abstracted from earlier (1950's) *rotor cloud* a type of altocumulus cloud in which such an air mass is often found]

Ro·zelle rule (rou'zel), *U.S. Sports.* the provision in a contract between a free agent and a professional team which requires the team to give the free agent's former team either an agreed-upon compensation or a compensation set by the league commissioner.

The superstars will be the principal beneficiaries of Judge Larson's decision that the Rozelle rule violates the antitrust laws. . . . Even with the Rozelle rule, Joe Namath was able to negotiate a two-year contract for $900,000. *Theodore W. Kheel, The New York Times, Jan. 22, 1976, p 34*

Through the season of 1979-1980, a Rozelle Rule applies in basketball. That is, a team hiring a free agent must compensate his old team. *Red Smith, "Focus on Sports," The 1977 World Book Year Book, p 58*

[1974, named after Alvin Ray ("Pete") *Rozelle*, born 1927, commissioner of the National Football League since 1960, who established the rule] See FREE AGENT.

RPV, abbreviation of *remotely piloted vehicle*, a small, unmanned aircraft controlled by radio from the ground for use in target practice, bomb delivery, electronic reconnaissance, etc.

RPVs are, according to NASA, a safe and economic way of flight testing experimental aircraft. . . . Aviation Week (22 October) reports that the USAF has set up a new organisation to manage RPV programmes, and is considering the use of RPVs fitted with warheads as "kamikaze" planes. *New Scientist, Nov. 1, 1973, p 339*

One of these years, we'll be getting RPVs—remotely piloted vehicles (don't you like all the initials?). That will make being a pilot a cushy job: he sits at a TV console 200 miles away and gets the RPV to provide surveillance or relay radio messages or pinpoint targets for precision bombing. *Time, May 23, 1977, p 26*

[1970]

RSVP or **R.S.V.P.** (‚ɑr‚es‚vi:'pi:), *v.i.* to reply to an invitation.

I have not been very good about RSVPing; I'd need a full-time secretary bringing her own stationery and stamps. *Norbert Lynton, The Manchester Guardian Weekly, July 4, 1970, p 20*

Also, the party had been cleverly promoted, with each guest who had R.S.V.P.ed being sent a white beach towel and a green tank-top T-shirt that said "The Ritz" on them. *Judy Klemesrud, "A Rare Sight in August: Party for 600," The New York Times, Aug. 13, 1976, p B3*

[1970, verb use of the abbreviation (OED *a*1845) meaning "please respond" (French *répondez s'il vous plaît* reply, if you please)]

RTOL ('ɑr‚toul), *n.* acronym for *reduced take-off and landing* (referring to an aircraft that uses less than half the standard runway).

Interest continues, however, in RTOL (reduced TOL—indeed, the acronymology has become so bad that at the airport conference they referred to ordinary planes as CTOL—conventional TOL) which would take off in about 1200 m. *Joseph Hanlon, "Requiem for STOL," New Scientist, April 12, 1973, p 69*

[1972, patterned on *VTOL* vertical take-off and landing (1950's)]

rubber bullet, bullet made of hard rubber and discharged from a specially designed gun, used in riot control.

Police fired rubber bullets and smoke bombs and charged with batons to disperse a crowd of 10,000 on Sunday in one of the biggest anti-Government demonstrations seen here for many years. *"Batons Break up Barcelona Rally," The Manchester Guardian Weekly, Feb. 8, 1976, p 8*

[1972] Compare PLASTIC BULLET.

rubber-chicken, *adj. U.S. and Canadian.* of or having to do with the monotonous round of chicken dinners which a political figure, especially a candidate, is obliged to attend.

The listener is tempted to conclude that this therefore is merely another highly forgettable political speech, something redolent of the rubber-chicken circuit. *"Counterrevolution: The Inaugural," National Review, Feb. 16, 1973, p 192*

Departing from standard political fund-raising affairs, there wasn't a passed hat, a long-winded speaker or a rubber chicken dinner in sight last week when Consumer and Corporate Affairs Minister Warren Allmand tried to raise money for his riding association of Notre-Dame-de-Grâce. *"People," Maclean's, Dec. 25, 1978, p 31*

[1968; according to *Safire's Political Dictionary* (William Safire, 1978) "rubber-chicken circuit" was originally a vaudeville term referring to bookings in a number of theaters]

rubbish, *v.t.* **1** to treat with contempt; scorn; disparage.

History has dealt badly with the horse soldiers. Colonel Chivington is condemned because he won too big at Sand Creek; General Custer is rubbished because he lost too big at the Little Big Horn. *John Greenway, Review of "Crimsoned Prairie. The Wars Between the United States and the Plains Indians During the Winning of the West" by S. L. A. Marshall, National Review, May 11, 1973, p 536*

2 to wipe out; destroy.

With the half-a-dozen cries that could rubbish this Government and lay the United Kingdom politically waste in temporary suspension, the new year seems a fittingly brief, mellow moment . . . to praise Mr Harold Wilson. *"Comment: Harold Wilson," The Manchester Guardian Weekly, Jan. 4, 1976, p 6*

Sexist and racist attitudes had to be rubbished once and for all. *Tom Tickell, The Guardian (London), Dec. 28, 1979, p 10*

[1971, from Australian English (first recorded use, 1953, in G. A. Wilkes' *A Dictionary of Australian Colloquialisms*, 1978), figurative verb use of the noun]

ru·be·o·sis (‚ru: bi:'ou sis), *n. Medicine.* an abnormally reddish condition, especially of the iris.

The same procedure is used in the treatment of rubeosis, a common complication of diabetes in which the iris develops extra blood vessels. Thus enlarged, the iris cuts off circulation of aqueous humor. Previous techniques in treating rubeosis have not been satisfactory and Beckman reports his procedure is far safer to the eye. *"Medicine: Lasers for Glaucoma," Newsweek, Sept. 23, 1974, p 65*

[1974, from New Latin, from Latin *rubeus* red + *-osis* abnormal condition]

rubidium-strontium dating, a method of determining the age of a geological specimen by measuring the radioactive decay of rubidium to strontium in the specimen.

Rubidium-strontium dating has shown that the chondrites are the oldest objects scientists have sampled in the solar system. They are as old as the solar system itself, having crystallized 4.6×10^9 years ago. *Lawrence Grossman, "Condensation of the Solar System," McGraw-Hill Yearbook of Science and Technology 1974, p 36*

[1970] Also called STRONTIUM-RUBIDIUM DATING. Compare AMINO-ACID DATING, IODINE-XENON DATING, THERMOLUMINESCENT DATING. See also AGE-DATE.

ru·bre·dox·in (ˌruː brəˈdɑk sən), *n.* an electron-carrying protein found in anaerobic bacteria and associated with oxidation-reduction reactions in cells.

Also included in the iron-sulfur protein class are the rubredoxins, in which single iron atoms are attached to cysteine sulfurs. So far the rubredoxins have been found only in bacteria. The ferredoxin-type iron-sulfur clusters, on the other hand, are widespread in nature. *Richard Cammack, "Protein," McGraw-Hill Yearbook of Science and Technology 1977, p 353*

[1970, from Latin *rubr-, ruber* red + English re*dox* oxidation-reduction + *-in* (chemical suffix)] Compare FLAVODOXIN.

ruffling, *n.* cellular motion by means of thin folds that extend outward along the cells' forward edge, pulling the cell forward so that it flows over the fold as it extends new folds.

A hamster's kidney cell, magnified 16,200 times . . . travels by a process that is called "ruffling." *William J. Bell, "Zoology," The World Book Science Annual 1975 (1974), p 360*

[1973, from gerund of *ruffle, v.*]

rumble strip, a strip of highway pavement built with ridges which cause a vehicle to vibrate, alerting drivers to hazardous conditions ahead.

Driving aids, both on the road and in the vehicle, are being developed. On the road, they include ribbed "rumble strips" and painted striped markings which indicate to drivers that they should slow down when approaching hazards. *Kenneth Owen, "The Changing Pattern of Transport Research," The Times (London), June 18, 1976, p 19*

Most . . . have been heading west toward Birmingham when the accidents happened. Rumble strips and other warnings have been installed to remind drivers to slow down through the interchange. *Picture legend, "Another Truck Bites I-20- I-59 Dust," The Birmingham News (Alabama), Sept. 26, 1976, p 24-A*

[1966] Compare SLEEPING POLICEMEN.

rumdum, *U.S. Slang.* —*adj.* ordinary; average.

Ponicsan finds surprising depth and touching delicacy in the rumdum lives he weaves together—dime-store and din-

ner women, odd-job truckers and coal-mine cripples, a mom-smothered "reader" at the cigar factory who keeps the ladies amused, and even a foraging bunch of derelicts living communistically in the town dump. *Stephen K. Oberbeck, Review of "Andoshen, Pa." by Darryl Ponicsan, Newsweek, March 12, 1973, p 96*

—*n.* a person who is ordinary or average (as at a game or skill).

I have recently begun to play a game called racquet ball, and I find I would still rather look good than win, which is what I usually do: look good and lose. I beat the rum-dums but go down before quality players. *Joseph Epstein, "Obsessed With Sport," Harper's, July 1976, p 72*

[1973, probably extended sense of the slang term (1920's) for a drunkard; influenced by *humdrum*]

runaway star, a member of a binary star that flies off in a straight line at high velocity when the other member of the pair explodes as a supernova.

The exploding star has to lose a lot of mass in order to release the gravitational hold on the companion, and it is interesting that there are several runaway stars in the sky, whose high speeds have always been something of a mystery. Dr Sofia suggests that they are expelled by a slingshot effect when one member of a binary sheds mass catastrophically. *"Superheavy Envelopes Give Stars a Good Send-Off," New Scientist, March 30, 1972, p 680*

[1970]

run flat, *British.* an automobile tire that can be safely used after being punctured or deflated.

Whether the Michelin system will give such a good run-flat performance as the Dunlop Denevo remains to be seen. Dunlop, which puts the Denevo's lubricant inside containers instead of just squirting it inside the tyre, thinks not. The Denevo is good for at least 100 miles at 50 mph after puncturing. No figure is known for the Michelin run-flat, but it is said to be good enough for the car makers to dispense with the spare wheel. *The Times (London), Nov. 14, 1974, p 12*

[1972]

run-of-the-, a combining form, meaning ordinary, commonplace, as in the following quotations:

run-of-the-alley: The vulnerability of corporations to this kind of attack by revolutionaries or run-of-the-alley hoodlums even in the U.S. has been starkly dramatized recently by the abductions of Publishing Heiress Patricia Hearst in California and Newspaper Editor John ("Reg") Murphy in Atlanta. *Time, March 18, 1974, p 79*

run-of-the-house: Though he also treats run-of-the-house animals, like dogs and cats, Stone is best known for his work with wild species. *Newsweek, Oct. 22, 1973, p 122*

run-of-the-scale: Rossini and Puccini could get by, Lord Drogheda thinks, with run-of-the-scale performers, but for Verdi, Wagner, Strauss, and the bel canto operas of Donizetti and Bellini, nothing but the best. *Michael McNay, The Manchester Guardian Weekly, July 26, 1974, p 16*

run-of-the-universe: Tayler's book stands back from the whizz-bang of tomorrow's funny quasar. Instead the author shows, in general terms, what is known about the physics of run-of-the-universe galaxies. *Simon Mitton, review in New Scientist, Oct. 12, 1978, p xii*

[1965, abstracted from *run-of-the-mill*]

rush, *n.* **1** the intense sensation of pleasure produced immediately after taking a narcotic.

It is clear now that science can tell us nothing about why

a morphine addict says he gets a "rush" from his shot when he takes it in a deserted pad in the South End but, when given the same shot in the antiseptic ward of a modern general hospital, feels little or no pleasure. *Norman E. Zinberg and John A. Robertson, Drugs and the Public, 1972, p 99*

Some people use it [isobutyl nitrite] as a quick upper during the day. "I carry a bottle of it with me all the time," says Ron Braun, 28, a California carpenter. "If I'm bored and want a rush, I take a sniff. It's a short break during the day." *Time, July 17, 1978, p 16*

2 *Figurative use:*

It was amazing. Three layers of image. . . . Pictures can be laid down layer upon layer, the way sound is edited. I got a rush, standing there, contemplating the possibilities. *Eleanor Coppola, "Diary of a Director's Wife," The New York Times Magazine, Aug. 5, 1979, p 42*

[1969] Compare FLASH.

Russell rectifier, a hydraulic device for generating power from sea waves. See the quotation for details.

Russell rectifier. This device is a "wave rectifier." A large structure is divided into reservoirs, with valves designed so that waves drive seawater into a high level reservoir and empty a low level reservoir. This creates a "head" between the two reservoirs, and this can drive a water turbine. *Picture legend, "Waves a Million," New Scientist, May 6, 1976, p 310*

[1976, named after its inventor, Robert *Russell*, a British engineer] Compare SALTER DUCK. See also WAVE POWER.

Russian bear, a cocktail made with vodka, crème de cacao, and cream.

Americans spent an estimated $1.5-billion last year on this bland product [vodka], mostly to drink it mixed with fruit juices, as in Bloody Marys or screwdrivers, or even mixed with milk or cream, as in vodka milk punch or the Russian bear. *Roy Bongartz, " 'Little Water' With a Wallop," The New York Times Magazine, June 8, 1975, p 74*

[1975]

RV, abbreviation of RECREATIONAL VEHICLE.

As I drive back from a weekend in another valley—the incomparable Yosemite, in the Sierra Nevada mountains—the rear-view mirror seems to show a herd of stampeding RVs chasing me down the freeway. Latter-day covered wagons, but uglier. *The Times (London), Nov. 22, 1978, p 18*

[1976]

R-value, *n. U.S.* a measure of the resistance to heat flow provided by insulating material. A high R-value corresponds to a high level of insulation effectiveness.

The insulating value of any of the materials used in walls or ceiling is determined by its R-value. . . . Thickness is only an approximate indication of insulating value since 5 inches of one material may have just as much insulating value (just as high an R-value) as 6 inches of another. *Bernard Gladstone, "Homeowner's Guide to Insulation," The New York Times, Oct. 10, 1976, Sec. 2, p 46*

[1976, from *R*esistance] Compare U-VALUE.

S

sac·cade (sə'kɑ:d), *n.* the rapid jump made by the eye as it shifts from one fixed position to another.

What Ditchburn is mainly concerned with is not, however, a general physiology of vision, but how involuntary eye-movements, the so-called saccades and drift, affect visual performance. *Robert Weale, Review of "Eye-Movements and Visual Perception" by R. W. Ditchburn, New Scientist, Dec. 13, 1973, p 794*

First, a fast eye movement (called a saccade) carries the most sensitive part of the retina, the fovea, to the image of the target. *Emilio Bizzi, "The Coordination of Eye-Head Movement," Scientific American, Oct. 1974, p 100*

[1966, transferred from earlier applications in ménage, music, etc. (OED 1727-41, 1876) in the sense of a jerk or jerky movement, from French]

saccharin, *n.* ▶ This widely used artificial sweetener joined other important products (e.g., AEROSOL, RED NO. 2) that were declared potentially dangerous to human health.

In 1971 a report indicated that bladder cancer developed in rats after being on a diet containing 5 per cent saccharin for two years.

In 1977 a Canadian government study led Canada to ban saccharin in prepared foods and the U.S. Food and Drug Administration to invoke the DELANEY AMENDMENT banning saccharin in soft drinks and prepared foods. After public protest, Congress approved an 18-month delay on the ban.

Various new synthetic sweeteners, such as ASPARTAME, were introduced. In addition, potent sweeteners derived from exotic plants, such as MIRACULIN, MONELLIN, and THAUMATIN, were in various stages of research and development.

Recently published findings indicate saccharin was judged on inadequate testing.

It seems to strike most people as absurd, even outrageous, that saccharin has been indicted, convicted and condemned as a carcinogen. *Anthony West, "Of Rats and Men," The New York Times Magazine, May 15, 1977, p 88*

saccharinize, *v.t.* **1** to put saccharin in; sweeten with saccharin.

The Senate version requires all products that contain the artificial sweetener to be labelled with a warning that saccharin causes cancer in animals and "may increase your risk of contracting cancer." The House, by contrast, would require such a notice to be displayed only at the shop or other retail outlet where "saccharinised" products are actually bought. *"This Week: Sweet Success for Opponents of Saccharin Ban," New Scientist, Oct. 27, 1977, p 208*

2 *Figurative use.*

Thus Stone abases distinction in his very effort to honor it. Even his praiseworthy intention to bring great genius before large numbers of readers comes to seem suspect in the light of the corrupt and corrupting means he employs in censoring, simplifying, and saccharinizing it. *Steven Marcus, The Atlantic, April 1971, p 95*

[1971]

sack, *U.S. Football.* —*v.t.* to tackle (a quarterback) with the ball behind the line of scrimmage.

Namath played a half against the San Francisco 49ers, who have an outstanding pass rush — and he was sacked five times and intercepted once. *Leonard Koppett, The New York Times, Sept. 9, 1977, p B12*

—*n.* an act or instance of sacking.

The young defensive line he [Joe Thomas] drafted in 1973 and 1974 led the NFL in 1975 quarterback *sacks* (tackles behind the line of scrimmage) with 59. *Frank Litsky, "Football," The 1976 World Book Year Book, p 316*

[1972]

sado-maso, *adj.* of or relating to sado-masochism.

Dodeca, however, is fated to dramatize her author's sado-maso scene. *Martin Levin, Review of "Dodecahedron" by Tom Mallin, The New York Times Book Review, Dec. 31, 1972, p 18*

—*n.* a sado-masochist.

At present, the sado-masos are in the ascendant: their crowds are bigger, their uniforms shinier, more explicit. *Jonathan Raban, The Listener, Feb. 22, 1973, p 237*

[1970, short for *sado-masochist(ic)*]

safari, *n. attrib.* in or resembling a style of apparel originally worn by Europeans on African safaris:

safari boot: Footwear often consisted of sandals and "safari" boots and some of the men were shoeless. *"Ogaden Rebels Gaining Support Against Ethiopians," The New York Times, Aug. 29, 1977, p 3*

safari hat: White felt version of safari hat by Madcaps at $7 at Bergdorf's Bigi. Gray suede clutch bag by Morris Moskowitz is $55 at Bonwit's. *Thomasina Alexander, The New York Times Magazine, Sept. 17, 1972, p 53*

safari shirt: At Paraphernalia, the Basic Betsey at about £8 sold and sold and sold. Another seller was a bush shirt, "long before Yves Saint Laurent's safari shirt," explains Mrs. Young. *Ernestine Carter, The Sunday Times (London), Nov. 21, 1971, p 41*

safari suit: He [Yves Saint Laurent] endorsed fringes, nailhead studs, vinyl raincoats and chain belts, put women in pants with his three-piece trouser suits and his "smoking" tuxedo and popularized the safari suit, the long scarf and American-style sportswear. *Newsweek, Nov. 18, 1974, p 74*

[1967]

406

safari park, *Especially British.* another name for ANIMAL PARK.

"You are approaching lion country," a notice promises, warning you to close doors and windows against predators. The point is taken. Shopping around the safari parks certainly confirms one thought — that the low-income family on an outing these days can consider itself lucky if it gets back with its fleece. *Norman Shrapnel, "Kings of the Drive-In Jungle," The Manchester Guardian Weekly, Aug. 25, 1973, p 16*

I didn't like the idea of getting animals from the wild and putting them in restricted conditions. What we needed were much more extensive spaces. The emphasis in England now is on safari parks where the animals roam in large spaces. *Desmond Morris, quoted in Maclean's, Jan. 23, 1978, p 8*

[1972]

safe house, a house or other building used by intelligence agents or secret police as a place safe from surveillance.

Of the 107 prisoners interviewed by Amnesty, 71 said they had been tortured, often in "safe houses" where the methods of interrogation allegedly included prolonged beatings. *Brian Phelan, The Manchester Guardian Weekly, Sept. 26, 1976, p 8*

Agents developing informants had no access to special "safe houses" for meetings or special untapped phones or cars with licenses that couldn't be traced to the bureau, thus making meetings with prospective informants dangerous to everyone involved. *Nicholas Gage, "Has the Mafia Penetrated the F.B.I.?" The New York Times Magazine, Oct. 2, 1977, p 16*

[1971] See DEEP COVER.

safekeep, *v.t.* to keep safe; safeguard.

So, banking on Dictys to safekeep her, I'd set out for Samos on a tip from half-sister Athene, to learn about life from "art." *John Barth, Harper's, Oct. 1972, p 80*

[1972, back formation from *safekeeping, n.* (OED 1432)]

safety net, a guarantee of security or protection from financial or other losses; insurance.

The major London auction houses take great pains over attributions, checking with scholars and doing their own research. Nevertheless they work with a safety net in the form of their conditions of sale, which elaborately disclaim responsibility for the accuracy of attributions. *Geraldine Norman, The Times (London), Aug. 11, 1976, p 12*

Today's move follows . . . a $3.9 billion International Monetary Fund loan and agreement by Western bankers for a $3 billion "safety net" credit to stabilize Britain's official sterling reserves. *The New York Times, Jan. 25, 1977, p 45*

[1960, figurative extension in reference to the net to catch circus high-wire or trapeze artists or someone leaping from a building on fire]

safing, *adj. Astronautics.* designed to restore a condition of safety following a malfunction, such as a power failure.

Then came Launch Control again, reporting that the cut-off was initiated automatically by the terminal sequencer, and that "safing" procedures were now being carried out by the astronauts while Launch Control itself tried to identify the cause of the cut-off. *Graham Chedd, "Launch of the Last Apollo," New Scientist, Dec. 14, 1972, p 645*

[1972, probably short for *fail-safing,* participial form of *fail-safe, v.* (1949)]

Sa·hel (sə'heil *or* sə'hi:l), *n.* **1** Usually, **the Sahel.** a broad belt of semidesert on the southern edge of the Sahara, coextensive with Chad, Mali, Mauritania, Niger, Senegal, and Upper Volta. *Often used attributively.*

Today it should be possible to put increased scientific knowledge of the Sahel and modern techniques to use, not only to help the victims of drought but also to bring drought itself under control. Unfortunately, however, the Sahel is a very marginal region as far as international economics is concerned. *Jean Dresch, "Drought Over Africa," Encyclopedia Science Supplement (Grolier) 1974, p 157*

2 any part of the Sahel.

Finally, the existing parks are not an adequate sample of typical African ecosystems. They are heavily biased towards savannahs with their spectacular animals; sahel (arid savannah) and desert areas with their specialised plants and animals are seriously under-represented, as are tropical forests. *Jeremy Swift, "What Future for African National Parks?" New Scientist, July 27, 1972, p 193*

[1972, from Arabic *sāhel* shore, border]

Sahelian, *adj., n.:* The Sahelian countries are among the poorest in the world. A new expenditure of $1 million a year would be beyond the means of most. *Boyce Rensberger, "Plan for 'Green Belt' Near Sahara Revived," The New York Times, Sept. 7, 1977, p A12*

Even if climatologists were sure of this theory, and they aren't, it would simply add to rather than explain the Sahelians' troubles. Desertification was pinching their lives long before the rains failed here in 1968. The Sahelians have brought it upon themselves: and we — the rich, industrialized, superbly skilled, and technically superior we — have in effect been egging them on. *Claire Sterling, "The Making of the Sub-Saharan Wasteland," The Atlantic, May 1974, p 99*

Sah·ra·wi (saː'raː wiː), *n., pl.* **-wi** or **-wis.** an inhabitant of Western Sahara (the former Spanish Sahara) ceded by Spain to Mauritania and Morocco in 1976. *Often used attributively.*

The Sahrawi spend a quarter of their day attacking, a quarter switching position, a quarter repairing their vehicles, and a quarter drinking tea and sleeping. *Pierre-Marie Doutrelant, "Tireless Fighters for Sahrawi Freedom," The Manchester Guardian Weekly (Le Monde section), Aug. 29, 1976, p 12*

[1975, from Arabic, from *sahrā* desert, sahara] Compare POLISARIO.

sailoff, *n. U.S.* a race between two or more sailing vessels.

Dennis Connor of San Diego, a former Star Class world champion, bested an international field in a sailoff in capturing the Congressional Cup in the annual match-racing series off Long Beach, Calif., in March. *David M. Philips, "Sports: Yachting," 1974 Collier's Encyclopedia Year Book (1973), p 517*

[1970, from *sail off,* probably patterned on FLY-OFF, *bake-off,* etc.]

sal·bu·ta·mol (sæl'byu: tə mɔ:l), *n.* a beta-blocking drug used as a bronchodilator in the treatment of asthma and other allergies. *Formula:* $C_{13}H_{21}NO_3$

Clearly the order of potency of the catecholamines was

isoprenaline > adrenaline > noradrenaline. Salbutamol was about fourfold more potent than noradrenaline and dopamine was inactive at concentrations up to 100 μM. *S. R. Nahorski, Sheffield, England, Nature, Feb. 12, 1976, p 488*

[1972, from *sal* salt + *but*yric acid + *am*ine + *-ol* (chemical suffix)]

saline, *n.* the injection of a highly concentrated salt solution into the amniotic sac to induce an abortion; SALTING OUT.

St. Luke's Medical Center, with 137 beds available, does six D and Cs daily, 18 salines a week. *"Abortion in New York," Time, Sept. 7, 1970, p 48*

—*adj.* of or involving a saline.

The Court also held, 6 to 3, that it was unconstitutional for a state to bar the use, in abortions performed after the 12th week of pregnancy, of "saline amniocentesis," the most commonly used procedure. *Lesley Oelsner, The New York Times, July 2, 1976, p 1*

[1970, extended from the earlier sense of a salt solution used in physiology] Compare MENSTRUAL EXTRACTION, VACUUM ASPIRATION.

Sally Mae, *U.S.* nickname for the Student Loan Marketing Association.

The new law also continues government guarantees for private loans to students and provides for greatly expanding that program through creating a national Student Loan Marketing Association. "Sally Mae"—as the new association is called—is designed to increase the private funds available to students by buying loan paper from banks and other private lenders. *Eric Wentworth, "No Silver Spoon for Higher Education," Saturday Review, July 22, 1972, p 38*

[1972, from pronunciation of the abbreviation *SLMA,* patterned on *Fannie Mae* (1953), nickname for the Federal National Mortgage Association (from its abbreviation, *FNMA*)] Compare FREDDIE MAC, GINNIE MAE.

salsa, *n.* Caribbean dance music similar to the mambo but with elements of jazz and rock music.

At Barney Googles . . . you can hear both disco and highly spiced Latin music, called *salsa.* This blistering rhythm, Afro-Cuban in origin, is served up hottest at the Corso. *"Pop Performers," Time, July 19, 1976, p 21*

Meanwhile the music of the Spanish-speaking dance halls deepened with a new synthesis of black Cuban and black North American genres—*Salsa*—of which one monument can be arbitrarily selected, a composition called *Wampo,* played by the Larry Harlow orchestra. *Robert Farris Thompson, The Times (London), Jan. 16, 1977, p 1*

[1975, from American Spanish, literally, sauce]

salt-and-pepper, *adj. U.S.* involving or made up of a mixture of blacks and whites.

In the upper-income areas of the outer city, there is salt-and-pepper integration, a sprinkling of Negroes here and there, but it is insignificant. *Paul Delaney, The New York Times, June 1, 1971, p 28*

Detroit is a salt-and-pepper situation. A great mix of black and white. *George W. S. Trow, The New Yorker, Dec. 23, 1972, p 38*

[1971]

Salter duck, a mechanical device for generating power from sea waves, consisting of a line of vanes

linked to form a breakwater and shaped to rock in maximum response to waves.

It is called the "Salter duck"—perhaps because the device looks like a string of toy ducks bound side by side. As each individual "duck" rocks back and forth, the motion is transformed into electricity or hydraulic pressure. *"Energy: Britannia to Rule the Waves," Science News, May 29, 1976, p 344*

Sea Energy Associates at Lanchester Polytechnic have also been testing Salter duck systems and have gained information on wave conditions . . . and power output. *The Times (London), April 21, 1978, p 27*

[1976, named after the inventor, Stephen H. *Salter,* a British engineer] Compare RUSSELL RECTIFIER. See also WAVE POWER.

SALT I, Also **SALT 1. 1** the meetings for the first SALT agreement on nuclear weapons. *Often used attributively.*

Retired Adm. Elmo Zumwalt and others have complained that one-man diplomacy put Kissinger alone at the table with Soviet experts at critical moments in SALT I when the U.S. side needed its own technical specialists to judge the give and take. *Roger Morris, "Détente Is in the Eye of the Beholder," The New York Times Magazine, May 30, 1976, p 36*

2 the agreement resulting from these meetings.

Within the numerical limits of SALT 1, the Soviet Union has deployed much larger missiles than has the United States, achieving a throw-weight advantage of about three to one. *Ernest W. Lefever, "Disarmament and Arms Control," The Americana Annual 1976, p 210*

[1972, from *SALT* (1969), acronym for *Strategic Arms Limitation Talks*]

SALT II, Also **SALT 2. 1** the meetings for the second SALT agreement on nuclear weapons. *Often used attributively.*

SALT II is back on, says *Los Angeles Times* correspondent Robert Troth. The Soviets, says Troth, will agree to restrictions on their Backfire bomber and the United States will agree to restrictions on the range of its cruise missile. *National Review, Feb. 6, 1976, p 69*

2 the agreements resulting from these meetings.

SALT II will require congressional approval, and critics in Congress were quick to point out that the agreement will actually allow increases in the nuclear arsenals of both countries, thus hiking defense spending for some years to come. *Thomas M. DeFrank, "National Defense," The 1975 World Book Year Book, p 421*

[1972]

salting out, another name for SALINE.

The usual procedure for second-trimester abortions is saline injection, or "salting out." A heavy-gauge needle is inserted through the mother's abdomen and uterus and into the fluid-filled amniotic sac that surrounds the fetus. A half pint of amniotic fluid is withdrawn and replaced by an induction of highly concentrated salt solution. The solution usually terminates the life of the fetus within an hour. *Matt Clark with Mariana Gosnell, and William J. Cook, "A New Doctors' Dilemma," Newsweek, March 3, 1975, p 24*

[1970]

sambo, *n.* a form of judo wrestling that originated in the Soviet Union and is now featured in international competitions.

The first-ever world championship for Sambo wrestling wound up here tonight with the Russians making an almost unchallenged sweep of the gold medal tally, giving them an insurmountable lead for the overall honors at the World Wrestling Championships. *"Sambo Ends with USSR Gold Grab," The Tehran Journal, September 15, 1973, p 8*

The only thing that tarnishes Edinburgh's Maurice Allan's performance at Minsk last week in becoming the first Briton to win a world wrestling title since the 1908 Olympics is that the style in which he was successful, sambo, will not be contested at next year's Olympics. *John Goodbody, "Wrestling," The Sunday Times (London), Sept. 28, 1975, p 30*

[1964, from Russian, acronym for *samooborona bez oruzhiya* self-defense without weapons]

sa·mink ('sei,miŋk), *n.* a mutation mink fur resembling Russian sable.

With sable pelts bringing many times the price of mink, this had long been an aim of mink geneticists. Only about 1,500 "Samink" were raised in 1972, but an expansion program was launched on the basis of the pelt's initial reception. *Sandy Parker, "Furs," Britannica Book of the Year 1973, p 321*

[1972, from *sable* + *mink*]

sam·iz·dat (,sɑːm iz'dɑːt), *n.* **1** any underground press, especially in a Communist country.

Several people caught distributing underground publications have been arrested. Now for the first time the authorities are expected to put on trial an author for a work of fiction he has published. The book in question is Jiri Hrusa's novel "The Questionnaire," which was printed by the Prague Samizdat and is going to be published in Paris and Lucerne this autumn. *Marketta Kopinski, "Charterists Still Burrowing Away," The Manchester Guardian Weekly, Aug. 27, 1978, p 7*

New forms of *samizdat* also appeared in Poland, most significantly in the magazine *Zapis*, which specialized in good work turned down by the official magazines and publishing houses. *W. L. Webb, "Literature: Eastern Europe," Britannica Book of the Year 1978, p 526*

Attributive use.

To help coordinate nationwide *samizdat*, . . . Chojecki's printing establishment in a Warsaw apartment includes 20 typewriters, six crude presses and a skilled team of 30 people who help print, bind and distribute *samizdat* books. *"The World," Time, Dec. 12, 1977, p 55*

. . . the group has continued to work. It has produced a regular *samizdat* bulletin which chronicles cases of abuse. *New Scientist, May 25, 1978, p 493*

2 *Transferred use.*

There is much to be said for innovative publishing practices whereby the major mathematical assumptions and conclusions are published, with the full proofs supplied in manuscript form to the referees and available as *samizdat* to those who care to write to the author. *Judith May and Robert M. May, "The Ecology of the Ecological Literature," Nature, Feb. 12, 1976, p 446*

It may be that Gedin undervalues signs of resistance to these trends: the growth of cottage industry publishing by the radical Left, the women's movement and other far from insignificant interest groups. Is this our grander, capitalist form of soul-saving *samizdat* or is it—as he might put it—just a further sign that mainstream publishing is giving up the struggle to combine righteousness with readability? *W. L. Webb, "Going Out of Print," The Manchester Guardian Weekly, July 10, 1977, p 22*

[1977, extended from the earlier meaning (1967) referring to *samizdat* in the Soviet Union]

sam·iz·dat·chik (,sɑː miz'dɑːt tʃik), *n., pl.* **-chi·ki** (-tʃi ki:). a citizen of the Soviet Union who secretly publishes and distributes writings or literature banned by the government.

"To fill their reserves," the Saratov Kommunist reported, "the *samizdatchiki* seek ties with other cities. ˙. . . They arrive with copies of the originals, which have been given abroad. Immediately, blank sheets of paper go into the typewriters. They don't sleep nights . . . (copying) literary manuscripts . . . one copy for oneself, the rest for distribution." *Anatole Shub, The New York Times Magazine, Sept. 10, 1972, p 92*

[1972, from Russian, from *samizdat* the writings or literature of the Soviet underground press (from *sam* self + *izdat*, short for *izdatel'stvo* publishing) + -*chik*, agent suffix]

sand·burg ('zɑː;nt,burk; *Anglicized* 'sænd,bərg), *n.* a circular wall of wet sand, customarily built in Germany by seaside bathers to encircle themselves. It is often decorated with seashells, small sand sculptures, etc.

When the Germans take up position on the beach at the start of their holiday, they literally dig themselves in. They build what's known as a *sandburg*. The German word *burg* can mean castle, citadel, stronghold or fort. Certainly the German *sandburg* has little in common with the sandcastles you see on the beaches of Skegness or Teignmouth . . . It serves as a family's beach headquarters and, for the period of their stay, is just as inviolable as any permanent dwelling place. *Norman Crossland, "North Sea Sands," The Listener, Sept. 6, 1973, p 302*

[1970, from German *Sandburg* (literally) sand castle]

San·di·nis·ta (,sɑː;n di'niːs tɑː:) or **San·di·nist** ('sæn-də,niːst), *n.* a member of a leftist military and political organization in Nicaragua which overthrew the regime of President Anastasio Somoza Debayle and established a coalition government in 1979.

As any observer of Nicaraguan political life knows, there is at present no political force with any national standing except the Sandinistas. *Alma Guillermoprieto, "Somoza Clings On," The Manchester Guardian Weekly, July 8, 1979, p 5*

Attributive use.

Perhaps more than any guerrilla group in Latin America, Nicaragua's Sandinist National Liberation Front, or "El Frente," as the movement is known locally, has won the support or sympathy of broad sectors of the population, not just disenchanted youths, but non-Marxist intellectuals, conservative politicians, progressive priests and some wealthy businessmen. *Alan Riding, The New York Times, Jan. 29, 1978, p IV*

[1976, from Spanish *sandinista*, from Augusto César *Sandino*, a Nicaraguan general and rebel nationalist leader murdered in 1933 + -*ista -ist*]

S and M, abbreviation of sadism and masochism.

Says Zox, a Los Angeles photographer who has shot photos of women mutilating themselves: "S and M has been a trend in the arts for a while. It is just becoming a commercial trend." *Time, Feb. 7, 1977, p 58*

[1972]

sand wave, one of the moving ridges of sand on the surface of a desert or of the sea floor.

The sand waves and their movements are being studied by the Hydrographer of the Navy . . . and many other groups. A typical example is the Anglo-Dutch investigation of the Sandettie sandwave field which lies directly across one of the shipping routes into the North Sea from the English Channel. *James Lighthill, "Britain's Place in Ocean Science," New Scientist, Oct, 25, 1973, p 252*

[1972]

sanitation engineer, *U.S.* euphemism for a garbage and trash collector.

While the rubbish piled up last week—and newscasts reported that many of those "sanitation engineers" make more money than a lot of school teachers do—the bitterness against public servants who strike was unprecedented. *Harriet Van Horne, New York Post, July 9, 1975, p 36*

[1974] Compare SANMAN.

▶ Not to be confused with *sanitary engineer*, who plans and manages water-supply systems, air pollution standards, etc.

san·man ('sæn,mæn), *n. U.S. Informal.* a municipal garbage and trash collector.

The garbage collectors have one of the toughest jobs in the city: such a Sanman walks as much as fourteen miles a day behind a sanitation truck, and lifts as much as six tons of garbage a day, in all kinds of weather. Sanmen get more on-the-job injuries than either policemen or firemen. *"The Talk of the Town," The New Yorker, May 22, 1978, p 28*

[1977, short for *sanitationman*]

san·pa·ku (sɑ:m'pɑ: ku:; *Anglicized* sæn'pɑ: ku:), *adj.* characterized by an unhealthy condition that supposedly results from failure to follow a macrobiotic diet, which prescribes organically grown sugar, fruits, and vegetables in preference to meat, eggs, etc.

Ten minutes to lunch break, the publicist introduces a girl of about twenty who is very sanpaku—in fact, an inordinate amount of veinless white shows beneath the lampblack pupils—and almost intimidatingly beautiful. *Tom Burke, Esquire, Jan. 1972, p 118*

SICKNESS: If your vegetable is feeling *sanpaku* (droopiness, caused by a more than five-to-one yin-yang ratio), brew the little greenie a hot cup of Mu tea and settle down for a nice long chat. *F. P. Tullius, "Talking to Your Veggies," The New Yorker, Aug. 13, 1973, p 27*

[1965, from Japanese, literally, three-white, from the belief that the condition is manifested by three white areas around the iris of the eye instead of the normal two on either side of the iris]

Santa Marta gold, a strong variety of Colombian marijuana.

From them [dirt airstrips in Colombia] fly the night planes, their holds full of bales of Santa Marta Gold. The smokers say it is better than Mexican marijuana. U.S. authorities say it is three to ten times more potent than the Mexican. *Warren Gerard, Maclean's, April 2, 1979, p 26*

[1979, named after its place of origin, the Sierra Nevada de *Santa Marta* (in Guajira province, Colombia), and for its golden color] Compare COLOMBIAN GOLD.

san·te·ri·a (,sæn tei'ri: ɑ:), *n.* a religion or cult practiced in Cuba that combines African tribal and Roman Catholic rituals.

I believe that any discussion of contemporary Cuba is bound to be unsatisfactory if it does not deal with the long-range implications of institutionalized machismo (which Nicholson describes), the government's repressive response to Afro-Cuban religion (santeria) and to newer attempts of black Cubans to forge a separate identity. *Allen Young, Westwood, Mass., in a Letter to the Editor, Harper's, June 1973, p 100*

[1973, from Cuban Spanish *santería* (literally) activities of the *santeros;* see SANTERO]

san·te·ro (sæn'tei rou) or **san·te·ra** (sæn'tei rɑ:), *n.* a practitioner of the rituals of santeria.

Cuba now has . . . a leader who—in Professor Thomas's revealing and perceptive analogy—resembles a santero, a priest of the Afro-Cuban cults. *Colin McGlashan, The Manchester Guardian Weekly, Jan. 30, 1971, p 18*

Many of her fans will be surprised to learn that she is not a *santera*, a believer in the polytheistic saint-worshiping religion which provides a kind of cultural force to Cuban music. *Edmund Newton, "Singer Celia Cruz—Latins Call Her Queen," New York Post, Feb. 1, 1975, p 2*

[1971, from Cuban Spanish, from Spanish *santo* saint; so called from the cult's identification of Catholic saints with African deities]

Sas·quatch ('sæs,kwɑtʃ), *n.* a large, shaggy creature of legend that walks on two legs and lives in the mountains and forests of the Pacific Northwest.

Supposed sightings of Yeti and Sasquatch are disappointing evidence in favor of large manlike creatures living in the mountains of Asia and the Pacific Northwest or anywhere else. The eyewitness always turns out to be a victim of a hoax, commercially implicated, inept at keeping live specimens from getting away. *Dennis Chitty, Review of "Bigfoot" by John Napier, Science, Oct. 26, 1973, p 376*

This month's *Smithsonian* takes an engaging look at one man's determined search for the Sasquatch, an American cousin of the Abominable Snowman. *"Making Culture Pay," Time, Jan. 14, 1974, p 29*

[1972, apparently from a Salish Indian word meaning "wild men"; (1929 Canadian use attested in *A Dictionary of Canadianisms*)] Also called BIGFOOT and OMAH.

satellite, *v.t.* to transmit via communications satellite.

At 2 a.m. the telephone woke me. It was Peter Lynch, our contact in Tel Aviv (from where our film was being satellited). *The Listener, Dec. 19, 1974, p 826*

Somehow between ricocheting from Jerusalem to Damascus to Beirut to Zurich to Aswan, "satelliting" back his TV spots and getting his laundry attended to, Darius finds time to . . . unravel the dark, multilayered conspiracies of Israelis, Palestinians, the CIA and Vandenberg. *Lance Morrow, Review of "In the National Interest" by Marvin Kalb and Ted Koppel, Time, Dec. 19, 1977, p 99*

[1974, verb use of the noun]

satellite killer, another name for HUNTER-KILLER SATELLITE.

A "satellite killer," . . . could be ready in a year or so. The basic idea is for rockets to carry the killers into space where they will be launched to hunt their prey. Military sources have described the "killer" as a highly manoeuverable heat-sensing cylinder, about a foot long and eight inches in diameter, that will carry no explosives. Rather, it will ram the target satellite as both vehicles fly at thousands of miles an hour. *William Lowther, "It Came from Outer Space," Maclean's, Feb. 6, 1978, p 24*

[1977]

sat·sang ('sɑː't'sɑːŋ), *n.* a Hindu sermon or discourse.

Maharaj Ji decided to take his message of inner peace outside of India in 1970. He made his first appearance in the West in 1971 at a pop music festival in Glastonbury, Eng., arriving in a white Rolls Royce and taking the stage to deliver a *satsang* ("truthgiving") for five minutes before the microphone was shut off. *"Biography: Maharaj Ji," Britannica Book of the Year 1974, p 145*

—*v.i.* to deliver a satsang.

"The Perfect Master never comes or talks exactly as prophesied," a fat mahatma in a gray business suit is *satsanging* in front of the white satin throne. *Francine du Plessix Gray, The New York Review of Books, Dec. 13, 1973, p 38*

[1972, from Sanskrit]

Saturday night special, *U.S.* **1** a small handgun with a short barrel, usually made from imported parts.

The company is the only major producer of cheap pistols — "Saturday night specials" — in the city, and it continued assembling them in high volume even after Mayor Lindsay announced his determination to drive the concern out of the business or out of the city. *Will Lissner, The New York Times, March 13, 1973, p 35*

National statistics indicated that about half of all gun-related crimes involved "Saturday night specials," which . . . sell for less than $50 and are of .32 caliber or less. Although the Gun Control Act of 1958 banned importation of these weapons, its passage encouraged a thriving domestic production that now turns out about 200,000 "Saturday night specials" annually. *Gilbert Geis, "Crime," The Americana Annual 1976, p 199*

2 *Finance.* a public offer to buy shares of a company's stocks, made without warning to prevent the company from challenging the takeover bid.

After a recent federal district court ruling, the Saturday night special (the tactic in which a predator makes a lightning move to acquire a major line of stock before showing his hand) may never be the same again. *Becton Dickinson, "Business: Finance: New York," The Economist, July 14, 1979, p 97*

[1968 for def. 1, so called because of its frequent use in barroom and street fights on weekends; 1978 for def. 2, so called from such a bid by Colt Industries, a pistol manufacturer, to acquire a small firm, in the early 1970's]

SAVAK or **Sa·vak** (sæ'væk *or* sɑː'vɑːk), *n.* the former secret intelligence organization of Iran, abolished in 1979.

Like the KGB, Savak's primary role is domestic but it has also taken on a significant role abroad, monitoring the activities of the thousands of Iranian students in foreign colleges and universities. *William Branigan, "The Terror Called Savak," The Manchester Guardian Weekly (The Washington Post section), Sept. 12, 1976, p 17*

[1967, from the Iranian acronym for National Security and Intelligence Organization]

sax·i·tox·in (ˌsæk sə'tɑk sən), *n.* any of various nerve poisons obtained from shellfish that feed on toxin-forming dinoflagellates of the genus *Gonyaulax.*

Mussels, clams and other filter-feeding animals ingest the microorganisms, often concentrating the toxin in special organs. About half a milligram of the poison, called saxitoxin, is deadly to man. *Philip Morrison, "Books: Review of 'Neuropoisons: Their Pathophysiological Actions: Volume I: Poisons of Animal Origin'" by Lance L. Simpson, Scientific American, Jan. 1973, p 125*

[1966, from New Latin *Saxi(domus giganteus)* the Alaskan butter clam, from which the poison has been isolated + English *toxin*]

scaling, *n. Nuclear Physics.* a property or effect of the collision of high-energy electrons with protons, in which the electrons bounce off pointlike particles that are thought to be quarks, the constituents of protons.

Recent experiments at the Stanford Linear Accelerator Center (SLAC) involving the high-energy scattering of electrons from protons show the property known as scaling. Scaling is usually interpreted as direct evidence that the electric charge inside a proton at a given instant is localized at one point or a few points, that is, at the positions of the quarks. *John H. Schwarz, "Dual-Resonance Models of Elementary Particles," Scientific American, Feb. 1975, p 66*

[1970, from *scale*, probably in the sense of "to come off in scales, to peel"]

scanning electron micrograph, a photographic reproduction of an image formed by scanning electron microscopy.

These beautiful scanning electron micrographs impressively illustrate a new replication technique which enables the finer details of ice-crystal growth to be studied. *"Embryonic Snowflakes Are Caught in the Act of Growth," New Scientist, May 17, 1973, p 400*

[1972]

scanning electron microscopy, the use of a scanning electron microscope (in which a very fine beam of electrons scans an object and forms a three-dimensional image of it).

Scanning electron microscopy shows a tubule extending from a spore and attached to a host cell. *William Trager, "Some Aspects of Intracellular Parasitism," Science, Jan. 25, 1974, p 269*

The recent application of scanning electron microscopy to the field of immunology has sparked interest in the surface architecture of the immune cells called lymphocytes. *D. S. Linthicum, "Scanning Electron Microscope," McGraw-Hill Yearbook of Science and Technology 1976, p 270*

[1972]

Schedule 1, a U.S. government classification of drugs that are considered to have potential high abuse and no redeeming medical value, and whose possession and use is regulated by law.

Although marijuana is still classified, with heroin, as a Schedule 1 narcotic, it has become, for many, as American as blue jeans. *Jesse Kornbluth, "Poisonous Fallout from the War on Marijuana," The New York Times Magazine, Nov. 19, 1978, p 60*

[1973] Compare CONTROLLED SUBSTANCE.

schiz (skits or skiz), n. U.S. and Canadian Informal.
1 a schizophrenic.

Mother Rose is drinking vodka and muscatel in the laundry and conversing with the Virgin Mary; 300-pound Leland, an intermittently brilliant schiz, is going berserk in the basement. *Martin Levin, Review of "Season at Coole," by M. G. Stephens, The New York Times Book Review, July 16, 1972, p 30*

2 schizophrenia.

Schiz is all tied up with religion, art, psychology, politics, and countless other things. Studying these things from the angle of schiz and schiz from these fields is doubtlessly important, fascinating, and profound. *Mark Vonnegut, Boston, Mass., "Commentary: Why I Want to Bite R. D. Laing," Harper's, April 1974, p 92*

[1967, from *schizo*, shortening of *schizophrenia*]

schiz·zy or **schiz·y** ('skit si: or 'skiz i:), adj. U.S. Informal. schizophrenic.

This friend of mine—a bit of a schizzy dude, to be sure, but also a B.S. from Rensselaer Poly—has been telling me that if we go on muddying up the ecosphere, all the monarch butterflies will turn against us and eat up the entire world supply of sweet sorghum, rock salt, and anthracite coal, without which human life as we know it et cetera et cetera. *F. P. Tullius, "A Total Disaster," The New Yorker, Jan. 20, 1975, p 31*

[1974, from *schizo* or *schiz* + -*y* (adj. suffix)]

Schott·ky diode ('ʃɑt ki:), Electronics. a rectifier with a metal semiconductor.

Tiny Schottky diodes developed at General Electric are about the size of a match. In the foreground is the silicon wafer that when sectioned will form the heart of the device. *Picture legend, "Electrical," Britannica Book of the Year 1977, p 416*

"Schottky diodes" (using a metal semi-conductor junction) are simpler alternatives, and the most can be made of the structure's properties when it is applied to polycrystalline or amorphous thin-film cells. *John Wilson, "Amorphous Semiconductors in Action," New Scientist, Dec. 7, 1978, p 761*

[1968, named after Walter Hans *Schottky*, 1886-1976, Swiss-born German physicist, whose research led to its development]

science court, a proposed panel or board of scientists that would evaluate conflicting scientific claims in matters of public concern and present its findings to policymakers and the public.

The man behind the idea is Arthur Kantrowitz, chairman of the Avco Everett Research Laboratory near Boston, who sees the science court as a forum that would allow experts on both sides of technological issues to present their cases before a panel of scientist judges—men of renown in subjects similar to those under discussion, but without a stake in the issues at hand—in adversary proceedings that would be open to the general public. *Peter Gwynne, "Science Court to Judge Controversial Issues," New Scientist, Sept. 30, 1976, p 677*

The Science Court, by whatever name it might ultimately be known, offers a potential mechanism through which the status of knowledge or lack of knowledge on a controversial issue could be clarified in open forum as an input to the policymaking process. *John Noble Wilford, "28 Leaders Endorse Science Court Test," The New York Times, Jan. 2, 1977, p 28*

Perpich has proposed the creation of a "science court" that would have no legal status but would assess the line's potential dangers, if any, to the health of the farmers, their crops and their livestock. *Time, Feb. 6, 1978, p 34*

[1976]

scintiscanning, n. a method of detecting abnormalities in the body by recording with a scintillation counter the radiation of an injected radioactive isotope.

A new accelerator-produced radioactive nuclide, gallium-67, with a conveniently short half-life of 78 hours, is in many ways an ideal agent for localization of tumors by scintiscanning. *Frank P. Mathews, "Medicine," 1971 Collier's Encyclopedia Year Book, p 336*

[1970, from *scinti*llation counter + *scanning*]

scotophil or **scotophilic,** adj. having an affinity for or requiring darkness.

Actually the circadian rhythm was imagined to comprise two half cycles each of approximately twelve-hours duration, one of which was reckoned to be dark-requiring (scotophil), the other light-requiring (photophil). *Ronald Murton, "Behind the Face of the Biological Clock," New Scientist and Science Journal, July 29, 1971, p 254*

The measurement of the length of the day or the night was accomplished by an endogenous, or built-in, daily rhythm that consisted of two half-cycles, one photophic ("light-loving") and the other scotophilic ("dark-loving"). *D. S. Saunders, "The Biological Clock of Insects," Scientific American, Feb. 1976, p 115*

[1971, from *scoto*- darkness (from Greek *skótos*) + -*phil* or -*philic* attracted to, loving]

scrapnel, n. fragments of metal scattered by the explosion of a homemade bomb filled with scrap metal.

In other respects the new mines bear the usual hallmarks of the IRA's crude ordnance. . . . Like the electrically detonated mines before them, they are often ineptly placed so that their explosive power and scrap-metal "scrapnel" have not issued in the direction intended. *Robert R. Rodwell, "Technology in the Streets of Ulster," New Scientist, April 6, 1972, p 16*

[1972, blend of *scrap* and *shrapnel*]

scream therapy, another name for PRIMAL THERAPY.

One of the ways the psychiatrist has developed to release repressed emotion is scream therapy, described at length in his new book, "A Scream Away From Happiness." *Korea Times, March 4, 1973, p 4*

[1973, shortened from *primal scream therapy*]

scream therapist: That is what largely accounted for the initial appeal of the psychoanalysts, and for the subsequent appeal of transactional analysts, scream therapists, antipsychiatrists, and radical therapists of all sorts. None has any truly effective methods for treating mental illness, but each spares the patient the tortures that regular psychiatrists call "treatment." *Thomas Szasz, The Myth of Psychotherapy, 1979, p 45*

scrip, n. U.S. Informal. a prescription for a drug, especially a narcotic. Also used attributively.

[Leroy] Street and his fellow addicts had for some time been able to purchase heroin through venal "scrip" (prescription) doctors in Greenwich Village, who employed bouncers to keep order in their congested waiting rooms.

James M. Markham, "What's All This Talk of Heroin Main-tenance?" The New York Times Magazine, July 2, 1972, p 9

[1972, short for *prescription*]

scuzzy, *adj. U.S. Slang.* dirty; grimy.

Some early fumblings with girls, a lesson in how to get bluejeans properly scuzzy, and Ward's over-unsuccessful attempts to write a novel are especially memorable. *Review of "Cages" by Paul Covert, The New Yorker, Jan. 1, 1972, p 64*

[1972, origin uncertain; perhaps a blend of *scummy* and *fuzzy*]

Seabee, *n.* a large ship on which barges filled with cargo are loaded and transported.

Almost three football fields long, the seabee can carry up to 38 huge barges, which are lifted aboard by a 2,000-ton-capacity elevator built into the stern. When unloaded, the barges are towed into shore and can then be towed along inland waterways to their ultimate destination, thus mini-mizing cargo handling. *Paul M. Danforth, "Transportation: Sea Transport," 1972 Collier's Encyclopedia Year Book (1971), p 554*

BACAT is one of a number of systems for the sea trans-port of barges. It is distinguished from other services, like LASH (lighter aboard ship) and Seabee, because it uses narrower barges more useful in English canals. *"From Rotherham to Basel by Barge," New Scientist, Nov. 8, 1973, p 412*

[1971, perhaps influenced by *seabee* a member of the construction battalion of the U.S. Navy]

sea-floor spreading, *Geology.* the continuous for-mation of oceanic crust, caused by upwellings of magma from the earth's mantle at the mid-oceanic ridges when crustal plates are forced apart by the circulation of material within the earth.

As new material wells up through mighty splits such as the rift in the Mid-Atlantic Ridge, evidence suggests that it embarks on a gradual outward journey, in the process known as sea-floor spreading. *Jonathan Eberhart, "Ever Downward Beneath the Ocean Deep," Science News, Jan. 4, 1975, p 9*

So many apparently "cataclysmic" events – the giant rift that circles the earth and such high mountains as the Himalayas, for example – have been explained as results of the slow and steady operation of sea-floor spreading that continues today. *Stephen Jay Gould, "Catastrophes and Steady State Earth," Natural History, Feb. 1975, p 16*

Arabia and Africa have been drifting apart for the past four million years by a process known as seafloor spread-ing. Molten rock from the Earth's mantle wells up through a rift in the floor of the Red Sea and spreads out evenly on ei-ther side. That creation of oceanic crust is pushing Arabia and Africa apart at the rate of about 2cm a year and is responsible for the narrow trough in the centre of the Red Sea. *The Times (London), March 1, 1977, p 16*

[1968] Also called OCEAN-FLOOR SPREADING.

sea grant college, *U.S.* a college or university re-ceiving financial support from the government to conduct oceanographic research.

Massachusetts Institute for Technology has been named the "sea grant" college for Massachusetts. . . . A spokes-man said that the action followed seven years of M.I.T. ac-tivity in research, advisory services and education on ocean engineering, offshore oil, coastal management and new sea foods. *"M.I.T. Made a 'Sea Grant' College by Richardson*

for Oceanic Activity," The New York Times, Jan. 1, 1977, p 18

[1975, patterned on *land grant college* (1889)]

sea of instability, a group of superheavy chemical elements with highly unstable nuclei.

The element $Z = 105$ and $A = 262$ with the largest proton number is so unstable that it can only be produced in ex-tremely small amounts, and it disappears in a few minutes by radioactive decay. These known elements form a penin-sula in a plane of proton and neutron numbers, surrounded on three sides by a "sea of instability." *S. G. Thompson and C. F. Tsang, "Superheavy Elements," Science, Dec. 8, 1972, p 1047*

[1971] Compare ISLAND OF STABILITY.

Sea·sat ('si:,sæt), *n.* a United States artificial satellite designed to gather data about the ocean surface; an EARTH RESOURCES SATELLITE.

The experimental ocean-monitoring satellite known as Seasat was successfully launched on the evening of June 26, receiving its final kick into orbit from the modified Agena rocket that is also the body of the satellite itself. . . . Part of Seasat's contribution may be the ability to map the sea-surface winds every 24 hours at uniform, 1,400-km in-tervals. *Science News, July 1, 1978, p 4*

[1974, from *sea* sat*ellite*] Compare DOMSAT, LAND-SAT, MARISAT.

secondhand smoke, smoke inhaled unintentionally by nonsmokers.

Many individuals are sensitive to what they call "second-hand smoke." The prohibitionists set much stock by a 1972 pronouncement of a former Surgeon General, who reported that tobacco fumes "can contribute to the discomfort of many individuals" – who, presumably, also suffer from inhaling what passes for air in city streets. *Michael Demarest, "Time Essay: Smoking: Fighting Fire With Ire," Time, Jan. 12, 1976, p 36*

[1976] See PASSIVE SMOKING.

Second Lady or **second lady,** *U.S.* the wife or of-ficial hostess of a country's Vice-President or sec-ond-in-command.

Going to lunch with artists is sometimes risky, but we can report (for we were there, and mindful of the honor) that the Second Lady carried it off with élan. The seating arrangements were a triumph of tact. Mrs. Mondale sat at the midpoint of a long, narrow table . . . *"The Talk of the Town: Second Lady's Lunch," The New Yorker, May 30, 1977, p 30*

[1970, patterned on *First Lady* wife or official host-ess of the President (1940's)]

second language, 1 a language that is widely used or officially recognized in a country in addition to the national language.

English was declared the country's second language and teachers and teaching equipment were sent to make it so. *Tom Little, "Republic of Yemen," The Annual Register of World Events in 1971 (1972), p 211*

2 a non-native language used especially as the lan-guage of instruction in schools.

As more and more persons received specialized prepa-ration to teach English as a second language, the stronger grew a feeling of identification with a special discipline. *Harold B. Allen, "English as a Second Language," in Cur-rent Trends in Linguistics, Vol. 10, 1973, p 308*

Second World

[1963] ▶ In the sense of definition 2, the word *second* is not intended to be taken literally, since the language of school instruction referred to as a "second language" may be the third or even fourth language for many students. See ESL, TESOL.

Second World, 1 the industrialized countries of the world not including the United States and the Soviet Union. *Often used attributively.*

As far as "Second World" countries are concerned (in Chinese terminology, this refers to nations half-way between the Superpowers and the Third World), the Chinese no longer give priority to relations "between peoples," but are concentrating on links "between states." The most obvious example of that new policy is their rapprochement with the Japanese. *Philippe Pons, "Reshuffling Asia's Political Pack," The Manchester Guardian Weekly (Le Monde section), Nov. 19, 1978, p 12*

2 the socialist or Communist countries of the world.

The Smithsonian official called for involvement in global conservation efforts of the "second world — the socialist states, whose influence can be equal to our money, and whose active participation would go a long way to rationalize the apparent disparity in motivation between the 'have' and 'have not' nations." *Gladwin Hill, The New York Times, Dec. 1, 1976, p A-18*

[1974, patterned on *Third World* (1965) the underdeveloped countries of the world]

▶ The two meanings of the term correspond to two methods of classification. *Definition 1* resulted from the division of countries according to their economic power. Under this classification the most developed countries (especially the U.S. and the U.S.S.R.) constitute the FIRST WORLD and the least developed countries constitute the FOURTH WORLD. *Definition 2* corresponds to the original quasi-political scheme of Communist, non-Communist, and Third World countries. See the note under DEVELOPING.

security blanket, *U.S.* **1** a blanket, toy, or other familiar object carried around by a child for a feeling of security.

A worn, torn, one-eyed teddy bear about a foot long was my "security blanket." *Sylvia Porter, "Toys," Ladies' Home Journal, Dec. 1973, p 102*

Hutt clutches his mangy fur robe about him like a security blanket. *Melvin Maddocks, "The Theater," Review of "The Imaginary Invalid," Time, June 17, 1974, p 72*

2 *Figurative use.*

Tenure, the "security blanket" of the teaching profession, is in jeopardy at U.S. colleges. Reformers demand limits on the system's job guarantees. *"Are Lifetime Jobs for Professors in Jeopardy?" U.S. News and World Report, Dec. 11, 1972, p 55*

The hijacker, alternating between his seat and the galley in the rear of the aircraft, apparently was holding the rear rest room as his security blanket. *Neil Amdur, "The Pilot Said: 'There's An Armed Man Aboard'," Saturday Review, June 10, 1972, p 73*

Insecure investors are once again turning to gold as prices of stocks fall and rising inflation eats into yields on fixed-interest securities. But the golden security blanket comes in many patterns. *H. J. Maidenberg, "Commodities: Gold Depository Certificates," The New York Times, Oct. 17, 1977, (page not known)*

414

[1967, popularized by the American cartoonist Charles Schulz (born 1922) in the comic strip "Peanuts," in which a boy named Linus is depicted as inseparable from his blanket]

security guard, a guard privately hired, especially to protect a building or maintain order.

The image of the security guard projected in some bitingly funny television sketches by Mr Benny Hill as a baggy-trousered recidivist with cap askew and no idea of the whereabouts of the main gate, contains just enough truth to bolster public prejudice and misgivings. *The Times (London), July 7, 1978, p 6*

At Manual Arts High School in Los Angeles, an intruder robbed a female teacher. . . . "The school has a security guard," says the U.T.L.A.'s Roger Segure, "but he was on vacation and no one had replaced him." *Patricia O'Toole, "Casualties in the Classroom," The New York Times Magazine, Dec. 10, 1978, p 84*

[1960]

seed bank, a place for the storage and preservation of endangered plant species or varieties.

The United Nations Food and Agriculture Organization regards seed banks as vital to the prevention of worldwide famine. Because of the increasing use of high-yield hybrid grains, primitive food plants are rapidly disappearing. The numerous primitive strains developed special characteristics enabling them to fight off diseases or survive changes in local environments. Left with relatively few kinds of high-yield plants that are vulnerable to pests and disease, future generations face widespread famine unless the resistant primitive varieties are preserved for crossbreeding purposes. *Darlene R. Stille, "Assault on The Green Kingdom," The World Book Science Annual 1973 (1972), p 13*

[1972]

self-gravity or **self-gravitation,** *n.* the force of gravity which a body or system possesses or exerts upon itself or its constituent parts.

Computer simulations of spherical, protostellar clouds of stellar masses, collapsing under self-gravity, have been developed by Richard Larson and by C. C. Hayashi and his collaborators. *Stephen E. Strom, "The Formation of Stars," 1977 Britannica Yearbook of Science and the Future (1976), p 76*

Because eddies must occasionally collide with each other, turbulence within a [interstellar] cloud will provide an additional pressure capable of resisting self-gravitation and if the turbulence is intense enough, it may disrupt the cloud entirely. *Robert L. Dickman, "Bok Globules," Scientific American, June 1977, p 78*

[1968]

self-gravitating, *adj.:* The most significant difference arises from the fact that the angle between gravity and the vector Ω of angular velocity varies in self-gravitating bodies, while the two vectors must be parallel in the laboratory experiment. *F. H. Busse and C. R. Carrigan, "Laboratory Simulation of Thermal Convection in Rotating Planets and Stars," Science, Jan. 9, 1976, p 81*

self-reference, *n.* **1** *Logic.* a sentence or statement that is SELF-REFERENTIAL.

Many logicians have in recent years dismissed the Paradox of the Liar out of hand, on the ground that the paradox arises from allowing self-reference, that is, allowing sentences to refer to their own truth or falsity. . . . Tarski argues that no consistent language can contain the means for speaking of the meaning or the truth of its own expressions. When a language does allow self-reference, it is not surprising that it will lead to inconsistencies and paradoxes. *W. W. Bartley III, "Lewis Carroll's Lost Book on Logic," Scientific American, July 1972, p 45*

2 reference to oneself or itself.

"What they are really about," Professor Thompson writes of Kierkegaard's pseudonymous works, "is not ethics or aesthetics or theology or philosophy, but rather the imaginative act which founds all these disciplines," which means that "they are ultimately about themselves . . . a literature of self-reference." *R. J. Hollingdale, Review of "Kierkegaard" by Josiah Thompson, The Manchester Guardian Weekly, March 9, 1974, p 24*

[1972]

self-referential, *adj.* **1** *Logic.* (of a sentence or statement) asserting that it is itself true or false.

Natural languages are genuinely illogical, they say. . . . They claim that we are "*constantly* making self-referential statements"; their only reason for saying this seems to be that people sometimes say "what I am saying is true", yet it seems that we are not permitted "what I am saying is false." *Andrew Ortony, New Scientist, Oct. 8, 1970, p 83*

2 referring to oneself or itself.

No Name in the Street, a reconstruction of James Baldwin's activities and states of mind during the Sixties is less powerful, rhetorically, than *The Fire Next Time*, and, although self-referential, contains nothing to match the family remembrances in *Notes on a Native Son. Benjamin DeMott, "James Baldwin on the Sixties: Acts and Revelations," Saturday Review, May 27, 1972, p 65*

[1969]

self-referentially, *adv.*: In the apparently self-cancelling paradox of this kind of phrase Hegel isn't using language referentially or descriptively: he is using it 'self-referentially'. *Michael Moran, The Listener, Oct. 29, 1970, p 578*

semantic net, arrangement of data in the memory of a computer, designed to parallel the characteristics of human memory.

Past experience would be no longer "stacked," as it were, in mere formal sequence but interwoven in what are called "semantic nets." Such nets seem to account for the speed and accuracy with which verbal-visual associations between past and present intervene in our cognition of a new object or situation. *George Steiner, The New Yorker, Oct. 28, 1972, p 105*

A number of laboratories are exploring the use of relational structures — sometimes called "semantic nets" — for storing facts about storybook worlds extracted from English language input. *Donald Michie, "Computers and Chess," Encyclopedia Science Supplement (Grolier) 1973, p 139*

[1972]

semi-antique, *n.* **1** a rug or carpet approximately fifty years old, as distinguished from a genuine antique (at least 100 years old).

Although the real antiques were all woven or hand-knotted before 1873 (a date agreeable to United States Customs), there are also valuable semi-antiques (rugs made between 1870 and 1920) and a vast quantity of modern rugs, many of them using the same designs, the same dyes, and the same types of wool as their more distinguished ancestors. *"The Talk of the Town: Rising Market," The New Yorker, March 24, 1973, p 31*

2 any rug having an antique appearance.

Semi-antiques — a term used by dealers meaning the carpets are "old" or "used," from five years to 100 years old. *Ernest Dickinson, "Rug Importers Thrive," The New York Times, June 5, 1976, Sec. 8, p 8*

[1970]

semidwarf, *n.* a plant that is taller than a dwarf plant but still below the normal size of related species or varieties.

Nonlodging Rice was developed at the International Rice Institute. The varieties are semidwarfs with long stems, which hold the plant upright when the grain heads mature. Narrow leaves also aid photosynthesis by letting more sunlight penetrate. *Gunnar Myrdal, "The Transfer of Technology to Underdeveloped Countries," Scientific American, Sept. 1974, p 176*

[1974, noun use of earlier (1959) adjective]

semi-dwarfism, *n.*: Further development will depend on thorough understanding of the physiological and genetic bases of semi-dwarfism; the days when plant breeders simply cross the best with the best and hoped for the best are long since passed. *"What Is the Best Way to Make Wheat Short?" New Scientist, Feb. 8, 1973, p 286*

seminarian or **seminarist,** *n.* a participant in a seminar (course of study, conference, workshop, or the like).

Several of the first group of seminarians (as Esalen quaintly calls its paying guests) witnessed a nearly fatal attack on Dennis Murphy. *Calvin Tomkins, "Profiles: Michael Murphy," The New Yorker, Jan. 5, 1976, p 42*

Isaac Asimov, author of more than 100 books and one of the science-fiction seminarists, suggested that the long-distant eventual result of space exploration might be bonds with new outer-space life-forms very different from the human. *Tom Buckley, "Ship of . . . er . . . Philosophers," The New York Times, Dec. 17, 1972, p 2*

[1970, from *seminar* + *-ian* or *-ist*; compare *seminarian* or *seminarist* a seminary student]

semistrong force or **semistrong interaction,** *Physics.* a hypothetical force or interaction that is weaker than the strong force but more powerful than the electromagnetic force.

If the semistrong interaction could somehow be turned off, all the spin-1/2 baryons would have the same mass; they would degenerate into a single state. The semistrong force splits the degenerate state into particles of different mass, and the splitting is accompanied by the introduction of two new quantum numbers, isotopic spin and strangeness. *David B. Cline, Alfred K. Mann, and Carlo Rubbia, "The Search for New Families of Elementary Particles," Scientific American, Jan. 1976, p 46*

[1976] Compare NEUTRAL CURRENT.

senior citizenship, *U.S.* the condition of being an old or elderly person; old age.

Educators have begun to sense that this break in generational continuity . . . has deprived many old folks of a desired organic contact with the future and a feeling of usefulness that is often lacking in the status of "senior citizenship." *Fred M. Hechinger, "Education: Teaching: Grandpa Goes to Kindergarten," The New York Times, Oct. 29, 1972, Sec. 4, p 11*

A friend of mine in his 70s, a very lively fellow and extraordinarily cheerful, likes to while away his senior citizenship — what we used to call old age — by collecting droll statistics from government sources that confute the assumptions on which most Presidents and Congresses appear to run the government. *Alistair Cooke, "Focus on The Arts," The 1978 World Book Year Book, p 49*

[1972, from *senior citizen* (1955) + *-ship*] Compare THIRD AGE.

Sen·sur·round ('sen sə,raund), *n.* the trademark of a motion-picture sound effect consisting of low-frequency sound signals felt by the audience as vibrations and intended to make their experience of the film more realistic.

Universal is constructing several mechanical [King] Kongs ranging from 18 in. to 6 ft. tall. The movie will be in color and Sensurround, the vibration that made *Earthquake* so unpleasant. *"Show Business: Monkey Business," Time, Jan. 5, 1976, p 71*

We could logically have expected "Rollercoaster," the latest movie accompanied by seat-shaking Sensurround, to have plunged us into the boring depths of its predecessors, "Earthquake" and "Midway." *Christine Nieland, "Giving Them A Nice Ride for Their Money," The Commercial Appeal (Memphis), June 26, 1977, p 15*

[1974, blend of *sense* and *surround*]

sentence, *n.* any sequence of nucleotide triplets or codons that constitute a gene.

The sentences describing the amino-acid sequences of the different proteins of a cell are arranged end-to-end in the long DNA molecules of the nucleus. These sentences, the genes of an organism, when taken together give directions for making all of the proteins of the cell, including all of the enzymes that the cell is capable of making. Through the activity of these enzymes all of the other molecules of the cell (including even the DNA of the coding system) are made in turn. *Stephen L. Wolfe, "The Living Cell," 1976 Britannica Yearbook of Science and the Future (1975), p 62*

[1975] Compare WORD. See also EXPRESSION.

Septembrist, *n.* a member of the BLACK SEPTEMBER, a group of Palestinian Arab terrorists.

According to intelligence experts, the Septembrists maintain a few five- to ten-man cells throughout the Arab world and in Western Europe. *"Black September's Assassins," Newsweek, March 19, 1973, p 42*

[1972, patterned on *Septembrist* (in the French Revolution), *Octobrist* (in the Russian Revolution), etc.]

serendipity berry, the fruit of an African plant (*Dioscorephyllum cuminsii*), containing a substance that makes sour food taste sweet.

Mr. Ottinger said that the Library of Congress had conducted research on artificial sweeteners and had found eight in various stages of development, including monellin, an extract of the West African serendipity berry. *Richard D. Lyons, The New York Times, Oct. 5, 1977, p 16*

[1971, so called from the accidental discovery of its unusual property] Compare MIRACLE FRUIT.

serial-access memory, a computer memory in which the time it takes to retrieve data depends upon their location in storage.

One of the latest designs of a CCD [charge-coupled device] serial-access memory has storage for 65,536 bits on a chip measuring about 3.5 by five millimeters. The other principal form of microelectronic serial-access memory

exploits the mobility of magnetic bubbles. *David A. Hodges, "Microelectronic Memories," Scientific American, Sept. 1977, p 140*

[1977]

serial marriage, an arrangement of successive temporary marriages.

In talking about marriage, he felt quite confident that in the future there will be few people who will contract a life-long marriage. Instead the author had predicted people will gravitate towards serial marriage. In serial marriage partners remain married for 8-10 years, then without bitterness dissolve the marriage and start another. This way most could expect to be married four or five times in their life. *Royal Gazette (Bermuda), April 16, 1973, p 20*

One English practitioner proposed that we borrow from Latin the linguistic distinction between *pater*, the father of fact — a distinction that might be useful in today's "serial marriage" society as well as in the A.I.D. [artificial insemination by donor] situation. *Lillian Atallah, "Report from a Test-Tube Baby," The New York Times Magazine, April 16, 1976, p 52*

[1970] Compare CONTRACT MARRIAGE, OPEN MARRIAGE. See also MARRIAGE.

serial monogamy, the form of monogamy practiced in a SERIAL MARRIAGE.

"During the thirties and forties, we want someone who is charming, witty, intellectually stimulating and capable of keeping up with fresh demands and opportunities. In old age we seek a person who is sympathetic, understanding, and who also offers new insight into life." Kiviloo predicts that serial monogamy may become the most popular form of union in the next century. *Paul Nowack, "Till Divorce Do Us Part," Maclean's, April 19, 1976, p 30*

[1972]

se·ro·to·ner·gic (,sir ou tə'nər dʒik) or **se·ro·to·nin·er·gic** (,sir ou tə nə'nər dʒik), *adj.* producing or activated by serotonin, a substance that constricts blood vessels.

Fernstrom and Wurtman propose that the serotonergic nerve cells could function as "sensors" or transductors that convert information about peripheral metabolism into nerve signals. *Science and the Citizen: The Brain Feeds Itself," Scientific American, July 1973, p 51*

Here has been considerable controversy over whether opiate action is associated with some particular neurotransmitter. From the evidence various proponents have presented, one may conclude that the target of opiates is serotoninergic, or noradrenergic, or perhaps cholinergic. *"News and Views: Narcotic Action at the Molecular Level," Nature, Jan. 11, 1974, p 83*

[1972, from *serotonin* + Greek *érgon* + English *-ic*] Compare CATECHOLAMINERGIC, DOPAMINERGIC, NORADRENERGIC.

SES, abbreviation of *socioeconomic status*, a combination of social factors, such as education, and economic factors, such as income, used as a measure of rank in sociological studies.

The low SES child, like the average-intelligence child, is comfortable with his peers, thinks he is easy to like and perceives himself as popular. *Robert J. Trotter, "Self-Image," Science News, Aug. 21, 1971, p 131*

[1971]

ses·shin ('seʃ in), *n.* a long period of seclusion and meditation in Zen Buddhism, usually lasting from four to seven days.

The intensive period of Zen practice known as *sesshin* is "sustained self-effort," he [Philip Kapleau] explains in his book, *The Three Pillars of Zen*. *"Religion: Searching Again for the Sacred," Time, April 9, 1973, p 92*

With no deity to cling to, seven days of *sesshin* are a plunge into the inner self. *George Vecsey, "Buddhism in America," The New York Times Magazine, June 3, 1979, p 93*

[1972, from Japanese, from Chinese *ch'e hsin*] Compare ZAZEN.

SETI, abbreviation of *search for extraterrestrial intelligence,* a program to find ways of communicating with intelligent beings elsewhere in the universe.

Dubbed SETI, . . . the project is to be carried out over a period of six years by two teams of researchers. One team, at the Jet Propulsion Laboratory in Pasadena, Calif., will map the sky visible from that site using antennas at JPL's Goldstone tracking station in the Mojave Desert. The other team, at the NASA/Ames Research Center in northern California, will concentrate on our sun's cosmic neighbors, listening closely with large radiotelescopes to stars that lie within 100 light years of us. *Timothy Ferris, "Seeking an End to Cosmic Loneliness," The New York Times Magazine, Oct. 23, 1977, p 31*

[1976] Compare CETI. See also LGM, WATER HOLE.

Seven Sisters or **the Sisters,** a nickname for the world's seven largest oil companies.

The question asked of the international petroleum companies, the "Seven Sisters," can be asked of the grain companies as well: do they serve the interests of the United States or of themselves? *Dan Morgan, The Manchester Guardian Weekly (The Washington Post section), Jan. 25, 1976, p 17*

In the consuming countries, meanwhile, the Sisters faced painful marketing operations. *Time, Sept. 11, 1978, p 42*

[1963, transferred from the name of the Pleiades and probably influenced by the nickname for the seven Ivy League colleges originally for women] Compare MAJOR.

► In 1979, the seven largest oil firms were British Petroleum, Exxon, Gulf, Mobil, Royal Dutch Shell, Standard Oil of California, and Texaco.

sex-blind, *adj.* not discriminating between the sexes; unbiased as to a person's sex.

Spokesmen for several liberal groups, including the ACLU, declared yesterday that totally sex-blind job assignments are a violation of prisoners' rights. *Mike Hurewitz and Lindsy van Gelder, New York Post, March 30, 1977, p 3*

[1974, patterned on *color-blind*]

sex clinic, a clinic for the diagnosis and treatment of sexual problems.

The sex clinic is fast becoming as vital a part of the modern hospital as the emergency room and the intensive-care unit. . . . But even though low-income patients can get treatment, most people who come to sex clinics are white and upper-middle class. *"All About the New Sex Therapy," Newsweek, Nov. 27, 1972, p 65*

[1972] See SEX THERAPY.

sexo-, a combining form meaning "sex" or "sexual."

sexo-cultural, *adj.: Magic and Myth of the Movies* has enjoyed a large underground reputation, which was blown to the world a couple of years ago as a result of the role it is made to play in the sexo-cultural pilgrimage of Myron/Myra Breckinridge in Gore Vidal's novel, *"When Entertainment Is the Art," The Times Literary Supplement, Feb. 4, 1972, p 125*

sexographics, *n.pl.:* The Canadian hero, Adrian Dumas, tries to shake off his brutal iceman inheritance for a moral, ecological principle. . . . Although set in the 1980s, it has the staleness of the '60s. Bradley's sexographics are Neanderthal, and, while there's only one murder, there are several character assassinations. *Toba Korenblum, Maclean's, Jan. 22, 1979, p 44*

sexoscope, *n.:* The rival *Zeitung* fights back with such circulation builders as sex crossword puzzles, a dirty-poem page and lurid sexoscopes. *Time, Jan. 19, 1970, p 24*

sexotheological, *adj.:* Her delight, nostalgia, recollection, and state of total stimulation caused her to experience that process which in theological reference works . . . might be termed 'absolute self-fulfillment'; which, when embarrassingly reduced, is termed by clumsy erotologists and sexotheological dogmaticians an 'orgasm.' *Robert Sussman Stewart, "Group Portrait with Heinrich Boll," Saturday Review, Nov. 11, 1972, p 67*

[1966, formed on the model of *historico-, religio-,* and similar combining forms]

sex object, 1 someone used or serving exclusively to satisfy sexual needs.

Altogether, the Male Establishment never lets women forget that they are all but valueless to society except as sex objects (submissive vaginas and fruitful wombs) and as devoted domestic servants (at home or at work) of their superior menfolks. *Clare Boothe Luce, "Woman: A Technological Castaway," Britannica Book of the Year 1973, p 26*

She has an affair with a young man named Werner whom she uses as a sex object, but it is as unsatisfactory as it is brief. *Vincent Canby, The New York Times, April 24, 1979, p C-9*

2 an object of sexual interest, especially a sexually attractive woman.

Black actresses are beginning to be introduced as sex objects. Sheila Scott-Wilkinson is installed as resident girlfriend to the unpleasant Detective Chief Inspector Craven in *Special Branch* (Thames) and Cleo Sylvestre appeared in a supporting role in *Armchair 30* (Thames). *Phillip Whitehead, "Television: On Thinking White," The Listener, April 26, 1973, p 563*

The woman-as-sex-object, under wraps for the past few years mainly because of the influence of the women's movement, has returned this fall with a vengeance. You can see her on television, in the new . . . shows such as "Flying High" and "The American Girls," clones of "Charlie's Angels," where she wears a lot of make-up and bares a lot of skin and is, in general, a mental midget. *Judy Klemesrud, "The Return of the Sex Object," The New York Sunday Metro, Sept. 17, 1978, p 35*

[1972] ► *Sexual object* is an established term in psychoanalysis meaning any person or thing, such as a fetish, toward which sexual activity is directed, while *sex object* is an informal term of disparaging meaning in current usage, often reflecting biased male attitudes toward women. See also SEX ROLE.

417

sex role, activity or behavior regarded as suitable to one sex but not to the other.

Equal treatment would not necessarily mean the end of a housewife's legal right to support from her wage-earning husband, but such a benefit would also have to be available to the husband who stays home with the kids while his wife works. In other words, the amendment's backers want the law to operate according to what a person chooses to do and is able to do, rather than according to sex roles. *"The Law: Up from Coverture," Time, March 20, 1972, p 68*

Her Majesty's inspectors ask all secondary schools to review their curricula from top to bottom to ensure that subject choices are in future made on a basis of "a real equality of access" instead of traditional assumptions about sex roles. *John Ezard, "Children Moulded by 'Sexist' Schools into Traditional Roles," The Manchester Guardian Weekly, May 3, 1975, p 7*

[1968] ► This term of the social sciences that describes the social role of sex, such as childrearing versus hunting, has acquired a pejorative sense in current usage, implying that the roles assumed by the sexes are culturally conditioned and discriminatory towards women. See ROLE MODEL, SEX-TYPING.

sex shop, a shop selling pornographic books, erotic pictures, aphrodisiacs, and other paraphernalia related to sex.

The court . . . fully understood and had sympathy with the idea that the area had been degraded by an invasion of the sex industry. But the court was not concerned with sex shops: only with cinemas showing X certificate films. *The Times (London), Nov. 17, 1977, p 4*

[1972]

sex therapy, the treatment of sexual problems, such as impotence and frigidity, by techniques involving counseling, psychotherapy, and behavior modification.

Dr. Helen Singer Kaplan, director of sex therapy at New York Hospital, said that "pseudo sex researchers" and untrained therapists using experimental procedures were "taking advantage of people's vulnerability." *Jane E. Brody, "Experts Seek Ethical Guidelines for Sex Research and Therapy," The New York Times, Jan. 25, 1976, p 29*

Of the several major areas in which behavioral improvements were being promoted, none was so fast-growing or so controversial as sex therapy. Between 4,000 and 5,000 clinics and treatment centers were operating in the United States in 1977. The most crucial problem in the field was the high percentage of quackery. *Melvin H. Marx, "Psychology," 1978 Britannica Yearbook of Science and the Future (1977), p 392*

[1972] See SEX CLINIC.

sex therapist: "The scream therapist says, 'We are better than the transactional analyst,' who says, 'We are better than the group therapist,' who says, 'We are better than the sex therapist,' and so on." *Salvador Minuchin, quoted by Janet Malcolm, "A Reporter at Large: The One-Way Mirror," The New Yorker, May 15, 1978, p 78*

sex-typing, *n.* the assigning of sex roles; casting one into a role deemed appropriate to the person's sex.

Anyone who has had a girl-child and a boy-child knows that they are different. Even in families where there is no so-called 'sex-typing', a little girl will make a doll of anything, and a boy will put one on top of another as soon as he can hold an object in each hand. *Janet Hitchman, The Listener, Jan. 8, 1976, p 24*

[1972]

sex-typed, *adj.:* Although women 20 and over now account for one-third of the labour force, the vast majority are working in menial, sex-typed, or dead-end jobs. *Clare Boothe Luce, "Woman: A Technological Castaway," Britannica Book of the Year 1973, p 24*

sexual politics, any arrangement or social order in which members of one sex seek to dominate or exploit the other.

We have a choice between a *covert* sexual politics (what we've had for centuries) and an open examination of sexual politics (what feminism asks for). Keeping sexual politics under wraps requires, like all repression, tremendous energy. *Veronica Geng, "Onward and Upward," Harper's, Jan. 1977, p 6*

[1970, popularized by the American feminist leader Kate Millet, born 1934, in her book *Sexual Politics* (1970)]

sexy, *adj. Informal.* having popular appeal; attracting general interest.

Maddock, who retired as Chief Scientist at the Department of Industry last March, has applied much of his energy in recent years to publicising his belief that "the real red meat of the economy" is in humdrum engineering — electrical machinery, for example — rather than "sexy technology" such as tracked hovercraft. *"Pyke's Movements Uncertain," New Scientist, July 7, 1977, p 5*

British Admiral of the Fleet Sir Peter Hill-Norton dismisses the neutron bomb as "sexy for the media [but] a new dimension of warfare that we do not want to go into." *Time, April 17, 1978, p 10*

"The farmers are not a sexy protest group," added his press aide. "They just can't drum up the kind of sympathy here that, say, the blacks and the feminists can." *Anne Nelson, "A Long Row to Hoe," Harper's, May 1978, p 34*

[1965, extended from the meaning (1920's) "concerned with sex; sexually stimulating," probably by influence of *sex appeal* in the sense of "popular appeal; general attractiveness"]

sha·rav (ʃɑːˈrɑːv), *n.* a hot, dry easterly wind occurring in the Middle East in April and May.

One of the most dramatic results has been to provide a scientific basis for the tradition that ill winds such as the Föhn in Germany and the Sharav in the Near East can produce a malaise in humans. The malaise may occur because air ion imbalance affects the production of 5-HT in some individuals. *Albert Krueger, "Are Negative Ions Good for You?" New Scientist, June 14, 1973, p 670*

Jane goes off to visit an earlier love, Toby, now living in the uncomfortably warm climate of Israel, where the sharav is blowing and the Six-Day War is about to flare up. *The Listener, April 11, 1974, p 411*

[1972, probably from Arabic]

s/he, *pronoun. U.S.* she or he.

A child's sexual orientation is determined before s/he enters school. *Meryl Friedman and Marc Rubin, "Letters," American Educator, Winter 1978, p 65*

An older person is called "cranky" when s/he is expressing a legitimate distaste with life as so many young do. *Edith Stein, "What is Ageism?" in The New Old: Struggling for Decent Aging (ed. Ronald Gross, Beatrice Gross, and Sylvia Seidman), 1978, p 89*

A good deal of harmless fun has been poked at certain neologisms coined by the Women's Movement in its sexually egalitarian and sometimes even female supremacist zeal.... *S/he* to replace the offensively sectarian yet ubiquitous use of *he* as an impersonal pronoun? What? Have the girls no sense of proportion? *Angela Carter, "The Language of Sisterhood," in the State of the Language (ed. L. Michaels and C. Ricks), 1980, p 226*

[1978] Compare HE/SHE.

sheep-dip, *v.t. U.S. Slang.* to disguise (a military officer) as a civilian in order to use him as a spy in a civilian group.

American military officers engaged in C.I.A.-sponsored paramilitary operations are "sheep-dipped" for paramilitary duty—that is, they appear to resign from the military yet preserve their place for reactivation once their tour as civilians in paramilitary operations has ended. *The New York Times, April 27, 1976, p 23*

[1972, figurative verb use of the noun meaning a disinfecting mixture into which sheep are dipped]

shi·at·su or **shi·at·zu** (ʃiːˈaːt suː), *n.* a method of massaging or treating parts of the body by finger pressure to relieve pain, fatigue, etc. *Often used attributively.*

Due to a printer's error in the article on shiatsu finger-pressure massage, page 135 of the December issue of *Mademoiselle*, the amount of pressure to apply was grossly overstated. The suggested pressure is not 120 pounds, but 20 pounds. *"Erratum," The New Yorker, April 3, 1978, p 118*

Japanese shiatsu massage is available at several locations in addition to the Salon de Tokyo.... The undisputed *Sorbonne* of shiatsu is the Shiatsu Education Center of America, ... presided over by Wataru Ohashi, generally regarded as the foremost master of the art in America. Treatments as well as training are available here. *Nona Cleland, "There's the Rub," Sunday News (New York), June 3, 1979, p 43*

[1976, from Japanese *shiatsu*] Compare ACUPRESSURE.

shield, *adj. U.S.* intended to protect a journalist from having to disclose confidential sources of information, as a SHIELD LAW does.

Sen. Sam Erwin (D., N.C.) says he is all for so-called shield legislation to protect the rights of newsmen, but he says it's the toughest piece of legislation he's ever tried to write. *"For the Record," National Review, April 13, 1973, p 398*

Will there be a federal "shield" statute to protect the confidentiality of newsmen's sources? ... In the House generally, he said, "proshield forces are definitely stronger than antishield forces at this time." *"The Press: Subpoenas (Contd.)," Time, March 19, 1973, p 63*

[1972]

shield law, *U.S.* **1** a law which protects journalists from having to disclose confidential sources of information.

About twenty states have "shield laws"—some of them recently enacted or expanded—to protect reporters who claim confidentiality, and the trend has drawn support from conservatives as well as liberals. *"Nixon and the Media," Newsweek, Jan. 15, 1973, p 47*

Citing the First Amendment and a New Jersey "shield

law" giving a reporter the privilege of refusing to disclose confidential sources, Farber and the Times refused to turn over anything. The result: a head-on collision between the First and Sixth Amendments, between the constitutional claims of free press and fair trial. *"Piercing a Newsman's 'Shield'," Time, Aug. 7, 1978, p 74*

2 a law protecting a plaintiff's or witness's right to withhold private or confidential information.

There are now "shield laws" in 38 states to protect rape victims from inquiry during rape trials into their past sexual behavior. *Ralph Wayne Derickson, "State Government," The 1978 World Book Year Book, p 487*

[1972]

shin·kan·sen (ˈʃiːnˈkaːn sen), *n.sing.* or *pl.* a high-speed passenger train of Japan.

The Seikan tunnel, which was begun in 1972, will run between the main island on Honshu and the northern island of Hokkaido. The noted shinkansen, or bullet trains, and other trains, are to move throughout, bringing the northern frontier much more into the mainstream of Japanese life. *Richard Halloran, "Flood Threatens Japanese Tunnel," The New York Times, May 9, 1976, p 9*

[1973, from Japanese, literally, new railroad]

shirt-jacket, *n.* a lightweight, shirtlike jacket with an open collar and either long or short sleeves.

True, many leisure suits have shirt-jackets rather than the traditional jacket. It's possible, but more difficult, to dress up the shirt or Western style jacket, but then the man who buys one usually intends it only for casual wear. *Addis Durning, Daily News (New York), July 26, 1975, p 12*

[1973] Also, **shirt jacket.**

shirt-suit, *n.* another name for LEISURE SUIT.

From Gordon Deighton's spring collection at Trend in Simpsons, Piccadilly, W.1, this is a shirt-suit. *Antony King-Deacon, The Times (London), April 17, 1970, p 18*

Polyester doubleknit leisure shirt-suits $29.99. Your ticket to a comfortable, fashion-right summer! *Advertisement by Alexander's, Daily News (New York), July 2, 1975, p 31*

[1970]

shock front, the region in which the solar wind meets a planet's magnetic field, resulting in a BOW SHOCK.

None of the spacecraft crossed the shock front at a point directly between Venus and the sun, but a profile of the front can be constructed by plotting each crossing's distance from the sun and from the sun-Venus line. "The shock," Russell concludes, "is too close to the planet for all the solar wind flux to be deflected around the planet in the limited distance between the shock and the ionosphere." *Science News, March 19, 1977, p 185*

[1970, extended sense of the term (1950) meaning the outer region of an atmospheric disturbance caused by a rocket, an explosion, etc.]

shootout, *n. U.S. Soccer.* a tie-breaker introduced in 1977 by the North American Soccer League. Five players from both teams are given five seconds each to score one-on-one against the goalie; the team with the most goals receives one point to break the tie.

After a scoreless overtime, the two teams resorted to the shootout, the league's method to determine a winner when games end in a tie. Seninho converted the decisive kick in the shootout. It was the second time this season that Seninho had made the winning kick in a shootout against Washington. *Alex Yannis, The New York Times, Aug. 13, 1979, p C1*

[1977, figurative sense of the term meaning a gunfight, perhaps influenced by *shoot-off* a supplementary contest to decide a tie in a shooting match]

shopping bag lady, *U.S.* a vagrant, homeless, and often elderly woman who roams a city carrying her possessions in a shopping bag or bags.

On a nearby bench, apparently keeping an intermittent vigil on the vigil, were two shopping-bag ladies. They spent most of their time endeavoring to fix the mechanism of a rusty, skeletal umbrella someone must have discarded many rains ago. *Ron Rosenbaum, "The Subterranean World of the Bomb," Harper's, March 1978, p 104*

If you are not accosted by a drunk or degenerate, you might get lucky with a deranged shopping bag lady who will walk up to you, poke you in your upraised Daily News and shout something like, "Don't try to sweet-talk me, you freaking smuthound!" *William Reel, "All the Grief You Can Endure for 25 c.," Daily News (New York), Dec. 29, 1978, p 26*

[1976] Also shortened to BAG LADY.

short eyes, *U.S. Prison Slang.* a child molester.

For the cons the supreme sin is to be a "short eyes"—a sexual molester of children. On this one point everyone—black, white, Puerto Rican, Muslim fanatic and tough Irish Catholic—all come together, and the short eyes gets the book thrown at him, from ostracism to the indignity. of being dunked in the toilet to a final act of terrible "justice." *Jack Kroll, "In the Oven," Newsweek, April 8, 1974, p 81*

[1974]

short-life, *adj. British.* **1** lasting only a short time; short-lived.

More than 200 delegates were turned away from a London conference on disposable and short-life garments yesterday. *The Times (London), April 9, 1970, p 29*

2 having a short shelf life; perishable.

Short-life foods, with a recommended shelf life of three months or less, corresponding to a total life of up to as much as five months, "should be marked conspicuously with the *sell by* date in a prescribed form," such as *sell by* 02 SEP 72 or *sell by* 02 09 72. *Christopher Warman, "Standards Body Urges Date Stamps on Prepacked Food," The Times (London), July 6, 1972, p 2*

3 intended for transient occupancy; temporary.

The Greater London Council said in a letter pushed through her letterbox on Monday night, that it was taking possession of all the 26 short-life properties the charity was renting from it on April 1. One hundred people are housed in the 26 properties. *"GLC Takes Back Homes from Charity," The Times (London), April 1, 1976, p 7*

[1970]

short-term memory, the part of the memory which consists of information retained for only a short time.

This type of memory is referred to as short-term memory, because the number of events we can hold in this fashion is strictly limited, and forgetting is extremely rapid once our attention is diverted. *Fergus Craik, "When Memory Fades . . ." New Scientist, Feb. 24, 1972, p 428*

The necessary conclusion is that the initial storage of information, short-term memory, involves ongoing patterns of nerve impulses in circuits of nerve cells connected together by their fibers, while long-term memory is a lasting structural change in the pathway of cells. *Colin Blakemore, "The Unsolved Marvel of Memory," The New York Times Magazine, Feb. 6, 1977, p 46*

[1970]

shotgun, *n.* an offensive formation in American football in which the quarterback lines up several yards behind the center to receive a direct snap.

Staubach's talent is throwing from the shotgun—the old football stand-by that Coach Tom Landry had adapted for third-down passing plays. Staubach sets up 5 yds. behind scrimmage, back-pedals seven more after the snap and looks to hit any one of five receivers downfield. He says that the tactic allows him "to save a crucial couple tenths of a second"—time enough to read the defense, then choose one from a confusing mixture of possible passes in front of or behind opposing linebackers. *"Sport: Gunning for a Title," Time, Jan. 19, 1976, p 43*

[1963]

shoulder, *adj.* of or denoting an intermediate season of the year during which air travel is marginal, or the periods of time each day when heavy, rush-hour traffic begins to diminish.

Under the three-season concept, fares are at a peak in the June-August summer season, come down for the September-October and April-May "shoulder" periods, and normally are at their lowest in the relatively slack winter season. *Richard Witkin, "Ford Approves Rises in Certain Air Fares," The New York Times, Oct. 27, 1976, p 18*

Elliptical use.

Air fare from New York included in above prices: $312 winter, $352 shoulder, $402 peak. Day flight information from New York available on request. *Advertisement by TWA, National Geographic Magazine, Feb. 1979, p 4*

[1963]

shucking and jiving or **shuckin' and jivin',** *U.S. Slang.* a fooling or tricking of someone by creating a false impression or conveying false information; assuming a deceptive guise, posture, or facade.

"Sucking and jiving," "S-ing and J-ing" . . . are terms that refer to one form of language behavior practiced by the black when interacting with the Man (the white man, the Establishment, or *any* authority figure), and to another form of language behavior practiced by blacks when interacting with each other on the peer-group level. *Thomas Kochman, "Toward an Ethnography of Black American Speech Behavior," in Rappin' and Stylin' Out, 1972, p 246*

Harry Belafonte's shucking and jiving preacher in "Buck and the Preacher" was a particularly telling portrayal. When in trouble with the white folks, he grinned and preached, for that was his protective shield, but when he was with Buck he became a sly, crafty gunslinger. *John Dotson, "Movies: I Want Freedom to See the Good and the Bad," Newsweek, Oct. 23, 1972, p 82*

Shuckin' and jivin' is a verbal and physical technique some Blacks use to avoid difficulty, to accommodate some authority figure, and, in extreme cases, to save a life or to save oneself from being beaten physically or psychologically. *Herbert L. Foster, "Don't Be Put On! Learn About the Games Kids Play," Today's Education, Sept./Oct. 1975, p 52*

[1972, originally Southern Black English phrase, from verbs *shuck* and *jive*, both meaning to deceive, mislead (recorded since the 1920's] Compare the DOZENS, SIGNIFYING, SOUNDING, WOOFING.

shunt, *n.* *Slang.* an automobile crash or collision.

A crash – what is it like to crash at speed? During a shunt (racing slang for a crash) things appear to slow down. You watch the object that you are about to hit with a certainty that it is happening so abruptly that the wait before impact is unbearable. Already the mind is questioning what went wrong – error or mechanical failure? *Michael McHugh, "The Next Canadian Hero," Maclean's, Oct. 31, 1977, p 58*

The equipment is designed to reduce the high incidence of rear-end shunts on motorways and other roads carrying dense, fast traffic. *"Radar Eyes for German Drivers," New Scientist, Jan. 12, 1978, p 90*

[1965, probably noun use of *shunt*, *v.* to push or shove aside (OED 1706)]

shuttle, *n.* short for DIPLOMATIC SHUTTLE.

Thus [Ivor] Richard's shuttle has been dubbed by some officials and journalists in southern Africa a safari of salvation. *"Rhodesia: Richard's Safari of Salvation," Time, Jan. 17, 1977, p 30*

A week of furious diplomacy for the ever-smiling Mr Cyrus Vance left observers wondering whether his new-style shuttle (was it really very different from the kind practised by Dr Kissinger?) would obtain results. *"The Week," The Manchester Guardian Weekly, Aug. 21, 1977, p 5*

[1975]

shuttlecock, *n.* British name for MIGRONAUT.

"My impression is that the Government will view such cases sympathetically. Nor could they return families without papers as shuttlecocks to Uganda, even if they wished." *Peter Evans, "18 'Queue-Jumping' Asians a Threat to System of Entry," The Times (London), Sept. 6, 1972, p 2*

[1970]

shuttle diplomacy, diplomatic negotiations between hostile countries conducted by a mediator who travels between the belligerents.

The American Secretary of State hoped his latest exercise in shuttle diplomacy would lead to a formula for disentangling the warring armies and set the stage for an overall peace settlement in Geneva. *Newsweek, April 29, 1974, p 39*

With the rise of instant communication and shuttle diplomacy, foreign ministers and heads of state rely less and less on ambassadors as intermediaries. *Peter Pringle, "A New Kind of Envoy for the New Britain," The New York Times Magazine, July 2, 1978, p 10*

This can best be done by . . . sending U.S. Secretary of State Vance on yet another round of shuttle diplomacy between Jerusalem and Cairo. *New York Post, Feb. 1, 1979, p 22*

[1974, applied originally to U.S. Secretary of State Henry Kissinger's personalized diplomatic efforts in the Middle East] Compare PROXIMITY TALKS.

shuttle diplomat: Or consider Henry Kissinger. Understandably, Citizen K's style has changed perceptibly from that of the shuttle diplomat. To be sure, he jets by choice these days to Mexico rather than the Middle East. *Time, June 13, 1977, p 80*

Sicilian, *adj.* *U.S.* of or denoting a type of thick, bready, rectangular pizza. *Often used in the absolute form as a noun.*

In addition to plain whole pizzas at $4 each, onion-laden Sicilian squares at 60 cents and Neapolitan wedges for 55 cents, Famous Ray's offers the usual assortment of toppings. *Mimi Sheraton, "Goodbye to Classic Cookery and Hello Pizza," The New York Times, Aug. 17, 1976, p 44*

[1976]

sid·dhi ('sid i:), *n.* an occult or psychic power, such as the power to read minds or to become invisible, that is believed to arise especially through the practice of TRANSCENDENTAL MEDITATION.

As for the prisoners, some are no doubt looking forward to learning the advanced TM techniques called Siddhis. TM enthusiasts claim that by using Siddhis to refine control over mind and body, they can levitate and walk through walls. *Time, Nov. 13, 1978, p 84*

The International Meditation Society, founded and led by the Maharishi Mahesh Yogi, drew special attention in 1977 with its claim that advanced meditators might attain classical yogic powers (*siddhis*), such as levitation and invisibility. *H. Patrick Sullivan, "Hinduism," Britannica Book of the Year 1978, p 615*

[1972, from Sanskrit, literally, perfection, success]

sidefoot, *v.t.,* *v.i.* *Soccer.* to kick (the ball) with the side of the foot.

Wolverhampton dealt the knockout blow on the hour when Daley sidefooted an accurate pass from Kindon into the net. *Robert Armstrong, The Manchester Guardian Weekly, Nov. 23, 1975, p 28*

King thrashed a centre into the goal area. It ran to the centre-forward, who side-footed deliberately wide of Hansbury from six yards. *The Times (London), March 16, 1978, p 10*

[1963]

side-looking, *adj.* (of radar or sonar) transmitting signals at a slanting or acute angle to reflect a profile image.

Side-looking airborne radar, although costly, is valuable for mapping and other work in areas where constant cloud makes aerial photography almost impossible, such as in tropical rain forests. *Patricia Clough, The Times (London), April 8, 1976, p VI*

Surface ships would use electromagnetic devices and side-looking sonar, which gives a profile of objects on the bottom. *John W. Finney, The New York Times, Sept. 18, 1976, p 3*

The acute grazing angle of the microwave illumination of side-looking radar emphasizes the form of the land, and the large areas that can be surveyed under constant conditions favor the recognition of extensive features. *Homer Jensen, et. al., "Side-Looking Airborne Radar," Scientific American, Oct. 1977, p 93*

[1968] Compare DOWN-LOOKING.

sid·er·o·chrome ('sid ər ə,kroum), *n.* a chemical compound that transports iron across a cellular membrane into the cell, where the iron is metabolized.

In many cases the growth or activity of a microbial species depends upon the availability of iron. Microorganisms excrete siderochromes, which are trihydroxamates (or catechols) of low molecular weight that selectively chelate, or bind, iron. *Robert C. Eagon, "Microbiology,"*

1978 Britannica Yearbook of Science and the Future (1977), p 338

[1972, from *sidero-* iron (from Greek *sidēros*) + *chrome* chromium]

side-scan, *adj.* variant of SIDE-LOOKING.

Side-scan asdic (submarine detection device) with a slant range of one kilometre has been used most successfully for geological reconnaissance of the surface of the continental shelf and upper continental slope around western Europe. The technique is equivalent to the use of side-scan radar or oblique aerial photography for examination of the surface of the land. *A. H. Stride, Science Journal, Dec. 1970, p 56*

From a mooring on the loch, they [two zoologists] will lower a side-scan sonar instrument into the water and watch for any patterns of returned sound signals that suggest large moving objects below. *John Noble Wilford, "The Search Begins at Loch Ness," The New York Times, June 6, 1976, p 1*

[1970]

sidestream smoke, the smoke that drifts off the burning end of a cigarette or cigar.

According to the Lung Association sidestream and mainstream smoke emanating from the exhalations of cigarette smokers contain high concentrations of hazardous compounds, such as carbon monoxide, tar, nicotine and 3-4 benzpyrene, which is a suspected cancer-causing agent. *Mimi Sheraton, "Dining Out: Should Smokers Be Segregated?" The New York Times, Sept. 21, 1977, p C21*

[1973] Compare SECONDHAND SMOKE. See also PASSIVE SMOKING.

sie·mens ('si: mənz), *n.* the unit of conductance in the international meter-kilogram-second system of measurements.

Among the SI's [Système International] derived units with special names are those for . . . conductance (the siemens, or amperes per volt), magnetic flux (the weber, or volt-second), density of magnetic flux (the tesla, or webers per square meter), inductance (the henry, or webers per ampere), luminous flux (the lumen, or candela-steradian), illuminance (the lux, or lumens per square meter). *"Science and the Citizen," Scientific American, March 1976, p 60A*

[1971, named for Ernst Werner von *Siemens*, 1816-1892, German electrical inventor]

► In the 1800's Siemens' name was connected with many inventions, processes, and laws in the field of electrical research — among others, the *Siemens unit,* a measure of electrical resistance. His name has been revived to stand for a unit of conductance, a measurement of the characteristic opposite to that of resistance.

sig·int or **SIGINT** ('sig int), *n.* the gathering of secret intelligence by monitoring radio and other transmissions *(elint)* and intercepting the signals and messages transmitted *(comint).*

Generally speaking the larger part of the staff of all Sigint headquarters consists of scientists and engineers. Apart from actual cryptanalysis, there is a continuing need to improve intercept equipment. New forms of aerials capable of snatching the weakest signal out of the ether are constantly being devised. *John Marriott, "No Break in the Code War," New Scientist, March 2, 1972, p 467*

Questioned by Mr John Leonard, QC, for the Crown, he said Sigint was intelligence derived from the reception and analysis of foreign communications and other electronic emissions. . . . Sigint was the key component in the overall intelligence effort. *The Times (London), Oct. 14, 1978, p 2*

[1972, acronym for *signal intelligence*] Compare HUMINT.

sign, *v.* **sign off on,** *U.S. Slang.* to approve or allow (a plan, agreement, etc.) without actually signing or endorsing it.

The military bureaucracy, most notably the Joint Chiefs of Staff, would have to "sign off" on (Washington jargon for "approve") the American proposal. *John Newhouse, "Annals of Diplomacy: SALT," The New Yorker, May 19, 1973, p 90*

For example, people here don't really "agree" to a bill. They "sign off" on it — a subtle expression of much greater finality in a place where such things are prized — at which point they join their colleagues "on board" for the duration. *Steven R. Weisman, The New York Times, June 7, 1976, p 31*

[1971, originally used in the sense of "acknowledge as final," probably derived from *sign off* to announce the end of a broadcast, call an end to (anything)]

signifying or **signifyin',** *n. U.S. Slang.* a verbal game or contest in which the participants direct playful, teasing, or clever insults against each other.

Mary's indignation registers quite accurately the spirit in which some signifying is taken. This brings us to another feature of signifying: the message often carries some negative import for the addressee. *Claudia Mitchell-Kernan, "Signifying, Loud-talking and Marking," in Rappin' and Stylin' Out, edited by Thomas Kochman, 1972, p 320*

Although many of the retorts are stereotyped insults, some players achieve real proficiency. . . . Such skill in words is greatly admired in the black community, among both men and women, and "signifying" has taken on the wider meaning of "to top any preceding remark." *Peter Farb, Word Play, 1974, p 123*

[1970, from gerund of *signify*] Also called SOUNDING. Compare the DOZENS, SHUCKING AND JIVING, WOOFING.

silent quake or **silent earthquake,** a slippage or movement of a tectonic plate or plates, occurring without the ground-shaking or strong seismic waves that accompany observable earthquakes.

In some areas the descent of an oceanic plate generates little earthquake activity or produces "silent" quakes whose ground motions are so slow they are rarely observed. *Walter Sullivan, "Experts Discuss Mysteries of Shifting Ocean Floors," The New York Times, April 4, 1976, p 59*

He [Hiroo Kanamori] found that the Richter scale didn't rate many significant movements of the Pacific crustal plate, and he proposed "silent earthquakes" to account for the discrepancy in the slippage and the plate's movements. *"Revising the Richter Scale," Science News, Feb. 26, 1977, p 139*

[1976] Compare MICROQUAKE.

silo buster, *U.S. Military Slang.* a nuclear missile designed to destroy enemy silos to prevent a retaliatory attack.

If MX [an experimental missile] does go into full-scale development by virtue of that argument, the gap in America's second-strike submarine force will have helped tilt the American nuclear offense toward first strike. This is because the MX would be so accurate and powerful that it would fall into the first-strike category of "silo busters," especially in the eyes of the Soviets. *George C. Wilson, The Manchester Guardian Weekly (The Washington Post section), April 2, 1978, p 15*

[1977]

silo-busting, *adj.*: This [the MX] would give Washington the means to match Moscow in what defense analysts like to call "silo-busting" capability—the ability to launch pinpoint attacks against the opposing side's missile forces. *Richard Burt, "Search for an Invulnerable Missile," The New York Times Magazine, May 27, 1979, p 34*

sin bin, *Slang.* the penalty box in ice hockey.

There has been some discussion lately about the possibility of introducing a sin bin to football similar to ice hockey, with players being suspended from a game for five or ten minutes instead of being sent off altogether. *David Lacey, The Manchester Guardian Weekly, April 26, 1975, p 24*

[1971]

Sin·do·lor ('sin dǝ͵lɔr), *n.* an instrument which stops the pain of the dental drill with an electric current, eliminating the need for local anesthesia.

There is even a device for that most common of all miseries, dental pain. Developed three years ago by scientists at the University of Leningrad and called Sindolor, it is attached to a dentist's drill and sends a weak current through the patient's jaw. *Laurence Cherry, "Solving the Mysteries of Pain," The New York Times Magazine, Jan. 30, 1977, p 50*

[1973, apparently a trademark, probably from Spanish *sin* without + *dolor* pain]

sin·do·nol·o·gy (͵sin dǝ'nɑl ǝ dʒi:), *n.* the scientific study of the shroud of Turin, a cloth bearing the image of a life-size figure of a man thought to be Jesus Christ, kept in a chapel in Turin, Italy, since the 1500's.

Secondo Pia's photos, and better ones by Giuseppe Enrie, started the last phase in the long and vexed history of the shroud and opened up a new scientific discipline—sindonology. From the Greek *sindon*, via the Italian, *sindone*, which means shroud, sindonology is the study of the shroud—a lifelong romance with the paradox—and in particular two questions: what is the image composed of, and by what mysterious if not miraculous process was it formed? Sindonology is the physics of miracles. *Michael Thomas, "The Shroud of Turin," Rolling Stone, Jan. 11, 1979, p 79*

[1967, from (archaic or obsolete) *sindon* a shroud (from Latin, from Greek *sindôn*) + *-ology* study of]

sindonologist, *n.*: What most fascinates sindonologists ... is how the image got there. Historians have traced the shroud of Turin back to fourteenth-century France, a period in which many shrouds were venerated as the one from Jesus' tomb. *"Religion: The Shroud of Turin," Newsweek, Dec. 10, 1973, p 83*

single, *n.* Usually **singles,** *pl.* Especially U.S. and Canadian. an unmarried man or woman.

The sun was hot, and around the pool the singles were sizzling. The social director stepped briskly to a microphone and interrupted the *Love Story* theme blasting from the Muzak to announce that a fashion show was about to begin. *Mary Alice Kellogg, "Singles in the Suburbs, or, You Can Go Home Again," Saturday Review, June 24, 1972, p 16*

"Right now, I'm not looking for marriage, though friends often suggest I find a man. I've learned to cope very well, though I still feel like a spare wheel at parties. The problem with single parents is that they don't fit in with either the married couples or the singles. But since splitting up I've developed a deep sense of self-satisfaction. I've come to realize how much I really can do alone." *"Going It Alone: The Single Parent Starts A New Life," Maclean's, May 16, 1977, p 42*

Soviet singles also complain that it is difficult to meet prospective mates, especially after they leave university life and enter the working world. *"Soviet Singles Seldom Swing," Today (Westchester, N.Y.), Jan. 24, 1979, p B8*

[1969, noun use of the adjective]

single-blind, *adj.* of or based upon a test or experiment whose exact makeup is known to the researcher but not to the subject.

In a single-blind study, the physician knows whether he is giving a patient a drug or placebo but the patient does not know which he is receiving. *Barbara J. Culliton, "National Institutes of Health: The Politics of Taste and Smell," Science, Jan. 17, 1975, p 148*

The test we did on Rudy was single-blind: the patient didn't know the nature of the drug he was given but the doctor did. In a double-blind test, the true drug and the placebo are delivered to the clinician in containers labelled in a code known only to the investigator who prepared the medication. The doctor is as blind as the patient—he can't anticipate results. *Berton Roueché, "Annals of Medicine," The New Yorker, Sept. 12, 1977, p 115*

[1968, patterned on earlier (1950's) *double-blind*]

single-copy DNA, a form of DNA that incorporates only one gene of a particular kind in each cell.

Much effort went into understanding the relationship between two kinds of genes: those known to exist in general hundreds, or even thousands, of copies in the DNA of each cell (repetitive DNA) and those present only once (single-copy DNA). The relationship is critical, because models for gene regulation proposed that the single-copy DNA represents the active functional (structural) genes. The repetitive DNA represents the regulatory genes, whose role is to control the functional genes. *Eugene R. Katz, "Genetics," The Americana Annual 1976, p 262*

[1970]

sin·gle-en·ten·dre (͵siŋ gǝl ɑ:n'tɑ:n drǝ), *n.* a word, expression, or statement with an unmistakable and often indelicate meaning. *Also used attributively.*

And along New York City's Avenue of the Americas, where phalanxes of hard hats line the sidewalks at noon, passing office girls find themselves caught in a cross fire of single entendres. *"The Cities: Sidewalk Sexism," Newsweek, Sept. 3, 1973, p 90*

Jimmy Connors is the master of the single-entendre. He says what he wants, when he wants, to whom he wants. He is a Star. *Tony Kornheiser, "The Star You Love to Hate," The New York Times Magazine, April 10, 1977, p 20*

[1973, from *single* + French *entendre* to understand, mean; patterned on *double-entendre* (OED 1673)]

singlehood, the condition of being unmarried.

It is probable that singlehood with multiple sexual and love relationships, open marriage and traditional monogamy are already the major life-style choices. *Roger W. Libby, in a Letter to the Editors, Time, Dec. 9, 1974, p 86*

[1973]

singles bar, *Especially U.S. and Canadian.* a bar frequented by unmarried men and women.

When I visit the East Side singles bars, some of these upper-class snooty girls look down on you, you're just a lowly body builder. *Robert M. Strozier, The Atlantic, March 1974, p 44*

Here is a grown, experienced, loving woman—one you do not have to go to a party or a singles bar to meet, one you do not have to go to great lengths to get to know. *Ian A. Frazier, "Dating Your Mom," The New Yorker, July 3, 1978, p 25*

[1971]

single-sex, *adj. British.* intended for only one sex; not coeducational or unisex.

Ministers are also anxious that the proposals for single-sex training schemes should not look like reverse discrimination. The kind of plan they have in mind would be for engineering draughtsmen for example, where a firm could provide a scheme for women only to give them a chance of catching up. *Keith Harper, The Manchester Guardian Weekly, March 22, 1975, p 6*

[1975]

singularity, *n.* **1** *Astronomy.* a hypothetical point in space at which an object becomes compressed to infinite density and infinitesimal volume.

A singularity is a mathematical point at which an object such as a burnt-out star that has collapsed under its own gravity is . . . effectively crushed out of existence, although its gravity continues to exert an influence on the surrounding space. In practice, a singularity is surrounded by a region of space so distorted by gravity that nothing can escape; it is this region that constitutes the black hole. *Ian Ridpath, "Black Hole Explorer," New Scientist, May 4, 1978, p 307*

In what astronomers call catastrophic gravitational collapse, most of the matter contained in such a dying star begins falling in toward the stellar center. If the conditions are right, the matter crushes together with such enormous force that it literally compresses itself out of existence. The star becomes what mathematicians call a "singularity." Its matter is squeezed into an infinitesimally small volume, and it simultaneously becomes infinitely dense and has an infinitely high gravitational force. At the point of singularity, time and space no longer exist. *Time, Sept. 4, 1978, p 53*

We do not know whether black holes, as such, exist, and whether within them singularities provide links to other realms of space and time. *Walter Sullivan, Black Holes, 1979, p 267*

See EVENT HORIZON, WHITE HOLE, WORMHOLE. **2** *Mathematics.* a point at which the continuity of a surface, function, etc., is broken.

The functions studied in ordinary calculus are quite capable of offering complete descriptions of such things as planes, spheres, and less regular surfaces. But functions offer very awkward and inadequate descriptions of the more complex surfaces common among soap films. Such surfaces have what mathematicians call "singularities"—that is, edges and vortices caused by the surface branching or intersecting with itself. *Lynn Arthur Steen, "Solving the Great Bubble Mystery," Encyclopedia Science Supplement (Grolier) 1976, p 127*

[1971]

singulary, *adj. Linguistics.* being or consisting of a single factor; not being one of a pair.

It might at first seem enough to say that any segment which is glottalized or nasal is marked in that respect, one that is not is unmarked. Glottalization and nasality could then be regarded as singulary, not binary features, either present or absent in a particular case. *Wallace L. Chafe, Univ. of California, Berkeley, Language, March 1970, p 116*

[1970, patterned on *binary*] Compare UNARY.

Sinophobia, *n.* distrust or fear of China or something having to do with China.

A stunning glimpse of Moscow's Sinophobia was provided; on learning of plans for some "provocative" action or attack, the two sides—the United States and the Soviet Union—would take joint steps to prevent it, or, if it was too late for that, joint retaliatory action to punish the guilty party. *John Newhouse, "Annals of Diplomacy: SALT," The New Yorker, May 26, 1973, p 94*

[1973, from *Sino-* of China (from Late Latin *Sīnae* the Chinese) + *phobia*]

sin·se·mil·la (ˌsin səˈmil yə), *n.* a highly cultivated strain of seedless marijuana.

Last March they planted some high-class seed which had produced a splendid crop. It's called sinsemilla. "That's Spanish for without seed, see. The trick is to weed out all the male plants and leave just the females. They're the ones with the high THC content." *Charles Foley, "California: Up, Up and Away, Man!" Maclean's, Dec. 12, 1977, p 58*

Studies show that *sinsemillas* weed contains five times more tetrahydrocannabinol (pot's narcotic ingredient) than the common Mexican variety. *Time, June 12, 1978, p 22*

[1977, from Mexican Spanish, literally, without seed]

sin tax, *U.S. Informal.* a tax on tobacco, alcoholic liquor, gambling, etc.

Though federal taxes have been reduced since 1960, the cuts have been offset by severe increases in state and city income taxes, sales taxes, property taxes, Social Security taxes and "sin" taxes on liquor and cigarettes. *Time, March 13, 1972, p 66*

[1971, used originally (1963) in New Hampshire by opponents of state revenues which were obtained from activities regarded as of questionable value, if not sinful]

sissy bar, *U.S.* a curved metal support at the back of a motorcycle or bicycle seat.

Sissy bars will be lower this year. *Picture legend, Esquire, Feb. 1971, p 60*

Personals in this publication [*Easyriders*, a magazine for motorcyclists] have a forthright stormtrooper machismo about them. The woman's place is against the sissy bar. *John P. Sisk, "Strictly Personal," The Atlantic, June 1972, p 42*

[1970, so called disparagingly as suitable for sissies]

sister, *n.* a woman who supports or belongs to the Women's Liberation movement; a member of the SISTERHOOD.

Perhaps the most defiant of today's liberated young—the sort who are wed after seven months of pregnancy, then deliver at home with the husband superintending and a friend photographing—are making a profound statement about women, nature, and childbirth. I don't pretend to understand all of my "sisters." *Susan S. McDonald, "Commentary: Natural Childbirth (As If It Happened Any Other Way)," Harper's, June 1974, p 84*

At this initial meeting seven other "sisters" and I agreed we were there not to judge, but to listen, share and support. We could learn from each other, we felt, if we took time to sympathize. One thing we were going to "put together" in our group was a sense of camaraderie. *Jean Curtis, "When Sisterhood Turns Sour," The New York Times Magazine, May 30, 1976, p 15*

[1972]

sisterhood or **Sisterhood,** *n.* **1** Usually, **the sisterhood.** the group of women who support or belong to the Women's Liberation movement.

That book's ["The Liberated Woman and Other Americans"] stinging attack on the women's lib movement achieved for its author [Midge Decter] a place in the sisterhood's demonology right next to Hugh Hefner. *Arthur Cooper, "Fleeing from Men?" Review of "The New Chastity and Other Arguments Against Women's Liberation" by Midge Decter, Newsweek, Oct. 9, 1972, p 104*

For the first time in history, there is a real rallying of the Sisterhood that is being led by working women and their organisations. *Clare Boothe Luce, "Woman: A Technological Castaway," Britannica Book of the Year 1973, p 29*

2 the bond or community formed by such women.

Sisterhood across class lines is a myth. *"Ms. Blue Collar," Time, May 6, 1974, p 80*

Does this mean that only women left in the kitchen can make it into true sisterhood? Still locked into their "sexually oppressed" state, do they find sisterhood more attractive and easier to maintain? The rejection of sisterhood in favor of ambition doesn't sit well with many feminists. *Jean Curtis, "When Sisterhood Turns Sour," The New York Times Magazine, May 30, 1976, p 16*

[1972] Compare the MOVEMENT.

sit·ol·o·gy (sai'tal ə dʒi:), *n. Architecture.* the study of sites or locations for new buildings, especially ones that harmonize with natural surroundings.

They call on the resources of a new science called "sitology" in their proposal to call a halt to the massacre of nature and to start building without destroying our natural sites. *Jean-Pierre Quelin, "Sitology: The Rules of Landscape Harmony," The Manchester Guardian Weekly (Le Monde section), Jan. 18, 1975, p 14*

[1975]

situs picketing, *U.S.* another name for COMMON-SITE PICKETING.

After assuring Secretary of Labor Dunlop and the labor movement that he [Gerald Ford] would not veto a bill authorizing situs picketing, he reversed himself and led Dunlop to resign. *Sid Esterowitz, Brooklyn, N.Y., in a Letter to the Editor, The New York Times, Sept. 6, 1976, p 4*

[1963, from Latin *situs* location (used in law)]

ska (ska:), *n.* an earlier form of reggae, a kind of popular music developed in the West Indies.

The "Wailers" formed over ten years ago, in the days when 'Ska' was the popular music form in Jamaica. *Weekend Star (Kingston), June 29, 1973, p 15*

There was a speaker outside on the step blasting the current ska, which was a kind blend of syncopated Caribbean music, bebop and American soul, into the crowded streets.

Jon Bradshaw, "The Reggae Way to 'Salvation'," The New York Times Magazine, Aug. 14, 1977, p 28

[1964, origin unknown]

skag (skæg), *n. U.S. Slang.* heroin.

Lockhart Road, the central promenade, still throbs with pimps and barkers touting the talent behind the barroom doors, and heroin hustlers still push "skag" at 89 cents a fix in the alleys outside. *"Hong Kong: Good-by Suzie Wong," Newsweek, Feb. 19, 1973, p 44*

[1972, variant of *scag*]

skatepark, *n.* a smooth, paved area constructed for skateboarding, frequently featuring steeply slanted hills and sharply curved banks.

Frank Nasworthy . . . is breaking ground for a $60,000, 15 thousand-square-feet-of-concrete skatepark in Ft. Lauderdale which will feature a pro shop, a game room and "amenities for the parents." *Tony Hiss and Sheldon Bart, "Free as a Board," The New York Times Magazine, Sept. 12, 1976, p 85*

It would, of course, be far better if the boards were confined to sumptuous municipal skate parks. But for the rest, and while it lasts, what would the skateboarding millions be doing if their sport were banned? *"Comment: The Footpath Vigilantes," The Manchester Guardian Weekly, Jan. 15, 1978, p 10*

[1976, from *skate*board + *park*]

ski flying, the competitive sport of ski-jumping for distance.

The first world championship in ski flying, a technique differing from conventional ski jumping by emphasis on distance rather than style, was held on a giant 120-m. hill at Planica, Yugos., on March 24-26. *Howard Bass, "Skiing," Britannica Book of the Year 1973, p 612*

[1965]

ski flier: Ostensibly this is a documentary about Walter Steiner, the phenomenal record-breaking Swiss ski-flier. *David Robinson, The Times (London), Nov. 26, 1976, p 11*

skim, *U.S. Slang.* —*v.t., v.i.* to conceal part of (an income, such as the winnings of a gambling casino) to avoid paying taxes.

There was evidence of skimming . . . out of the casinos in order to dodge taxes. *Time, Dec. 21, 1970, p 63*

He . . . denied the Assemblyman's countercharge that Mr. Rosen had been "skimming" funds contributed by the residents for the strike. *The New York Times, March 1, 1976, p 27*

—*n.* an act or instance of skimming.

One of the men most responsible for exposing, or popularizing, the concept of a national criminal conspiracy called La Cosa Nostra, Pelequin has this to say about the Paradise Island transactions: "The atmosphere seems ripe for a Lansky skim." *Jim Hougan, Harper's, Dec. 1974, p 58*

[1966, from the idea of skimming (removing) the cream off the top of milk]

skimboard, *n.* a thin, often round, board about three feet in diameter, used for riding shallow water or receding waves on a beach.

Riding a skimboard, a youth glides over a comber-laved beach. Cold, treacherous currents make swimming risky. *Picture legend, "California's Land Apart—the Monterey Peninsula," National Geographic Magazine, Nov. 1972, p 688*

skimmer

[1972, from *skim* act of moving lightly (over water, ice, etc.) + *board*]

► Such boards have been known since the 1950's, but the term *skimboard* has rarely appeared in general periodicals since *surfboards* are far more popular.

skimmer, *n.* any of various devices for collecting oil from the surface of water in an oil spill.

A fleet of skimmers is steaming from Stavanger to suck up the oil and transfer it to waiting tankers. *Roger Vielvoye, The Times (London), April 25, 1977, p 1*

The French have developed skimmer gear that simply scoops up oily water and separates it into oil and water (it's said they had difficulty with this gear during the Amoco Cadiz spill). The French skimmer has one important advantage: It can be easily and quickly attached to most boats. *Michael Harwood, "The Rising Tide of Oil Spills," The New York Times Magazine, April 9, 1978, p 70*

[1972]

ski mountaineering, the sport of skiing on mountains or mountainous areas.

Ski mountaineering is gaining in popularity in the Albertan Rockies, and though the sport *seems* like cross-country skiing, it could be lethal to confuse the two. The backgrounds for most cross-country activity are groomed trails, open fields and even golf courses; the equivalent for ski mountaineering are glacier fields, narrow passes and avalanches. In ski mountaineering all the equipment is sturdier, particularly the skis. *Roy MacGregor, "Taking Winter in Stride," Maclean's, Oct. 1974, p 103*

[1972]

Skinnerism, *n.* the ideas and theories of the American behavioral psychologist B. F. Skinner, born 1904, especially his concept of controlling behavior through a system of rewards and reinforcements.

The second topic (behaviour control) might, for example, be an attack on Skinnerism and end with a code of practice for psychiatrists. Such a code would contain a patient's rights section and would . . . be presented in such a way that psychiatrists, anxious for a good public image, would adopt it. *"Feedback: Six Social Problems for Science," New Scientist, Dec. 13, 1973, p 789*

[1971] See BEHAVIOR MODIFICATION.

skin search, *Slang.* a search for illegal possessions by having a suspect undress.

So far, none of the three new guards in California's state prison system for men have been assigned to conduct "skin searches" of nude prisoners for contraband. *Time, March 26, 1973, p 64*

[1970] Compare PAT-DOWN SEARCH, TOSS.

skin-search, *v.t.*: Prisoners . . . had been skin-searched for weapons. *Peter Jenkins, The Manchester Guardian Weekly, Nov. 7, 1970, p 7*

skin vision, another name for EYELESS SIGHT.

Other types of bio-location being studied in the U.S.S.R. are dowsing and dermal-optical sensitivity, sometimes known as "skin vision." *Stanley Krippner and Richard Davidson, "Parapsychology in the U.S.S.R.," Saturday Review, March 18, 1972, p 57*

[1972]

ski touring, cross-country skiing, especially over large expanses of open country; hiking on skis as

opposed to cross-country racing or downhill skiing.

Ski touring represents a return to the way people skied before skiing got fancy. Scandinavians have been wild about cross-country for centuries. . . . *"Modern Living: Skiing—the Easy Way," Time, Jan. 17, 1972, p 68*

"Ski touring would be spoiled if too much emphasis is placed on the merchandising of fancy equipment, changing fashions, or organized area skiing, and on the promotion of the name resort." *Peter Wood, "The Unloneliness of the Long-Distance Skier," The New York Times Magazine, Dec. 18, 1977, p 19*

[1972] Compare X-C SKIING.

ski tourer: Somehow the noise seems more intrusive in the otherwise peaceful countryside, particularly to snowshoers, ski-tourers and others who enjoy the stillness of winter woods. *Berkeley Rice, The New York Times Magazine, Feb. 13, 1972, p 30*

sky·clad ('skai₁klæd), *adj.* (of witches) without clothes; unclothed.

The main ritual is conducted every month when the moon is full. If the ceremony is indoors, it is conducted "sky-clad"—in the nude. *"Religion: Witchcraft," Time, June 19, 1972, p 66*

Witches call their religion Wicca, from the Anglo-Saxon word meaning wisdom, which is the root of such words as witch, wizard and wicked. They practice a rite similar in form to Baptism in which infants are accepted into the faith. . . . Covens are encouraged, but not required, to worship outdoors, preferably "skyclad" or nude. *Sunday Post-Herald (Hongkong), July 22, 1973, p 22*

[1972, from *sky* + *clad* clothed, probably in the sense of "covered only by the sky," i.e. uncovered]

► The term was used occasionally in the early 1900's as an informal euphemism for "nude." Current interest in witchcraft and the occult (see EXORCISM) has revived it.

sky surfer, another name for HANG GLIDER (def. 2).

Most sky surfers first learn to fly on a Rogallo kite, which is often called simply a "wing." Many of them continue to fly the kite in preference to the hang gliders that were subsequently developed. The hang gliders have a higher level of performance than the kites, but they cost more and are more hazardous. *C. L. Strong, Scientific American, Dec. 1974, p 138*

[1973]

sky surfing, another name for HANG GLIDING.

Not all new words are serious or come from the striking events of the time. From sports, for instance, there is "sky surfing," in which participants tied to delta-wing kites glide down from cliffs. *"Books and the Arts: New Words Created for Changing Times," Bridgeport Sunday Post, April 14, 1974, p E4*

[1973]

Skytrain, *n.* the trademark for a system of low-cost, no-frills, air shuttle flights with scheduled but unreserved one-class service, introduced in Great Britain in 1977 by Laker Airways.

Britain's Freddy Laker has hired a Washington lawyer to protect Laker Airways' registered "Skytrain." Airlines, including Braniff, which applied for a no-reservation Dallas-London "Texas Skytrain" route, have already been warned politely but firmly to buzz off. *Time, Oct. 10, 1977, p 91*

"You know what I like most about Skytrain?" our friend

asked. "Once and for all, it scotches the notion that flying the Atlantic . . . has anything to do with glamour. . . . It's all one class on Skytrain." *"The Talk of the Town," The New Yorker, March 8, 1978, p 27*

[1972]

slam, *n. U.S. Slang.* Usually, **the slam.** short for SLAMMER.

This is the same Harvey Matusow who, at twenty-six, during the 1950s McCarthy inquests, played the role of ex-Communist finger man for the House Un-American Activities Committee and who ended up doing time in the federal slams for what amounted to perjury any way you slice it. *Carman Moore, Saturday Review, Nov. 4, 1972, p 65*

[1970]

slamdunk, *n. U.S.* a basketball shot made by jumping and slamming the ball forcefully down into the basket.

The only one-eyed candidate who would know how to put in a slamdunk on a New York playground has new financial life, a new strategy and a better record than he has been given credit for. *Tom Wicker, The New York Times, May 25, 1976, p 35*

[1976, from *slam* + *dunk, n., v.* (1955) jump and throw down into the basket] See STUFF.

slammer, *n. U.S. Slang.* Usually, **the slammer.** prison; jail.

No President has ever suffered the infamy and disgrace that this one did. It was even more ignominious than sitting in the slammer. *Leon Jaworski, quoted by Peter Goldman, "Was Justice Finally Done?" Newsweek, Jan. 13, 1975, p 19*

She sought to provoke Desai's Janata Party into rashly locking her up. . . . Then she could argue that her stay in the slammer had purged her of guilt for abuses during her term as India's one-woman ruler. *Time, Jan. 1, 1979, p 68*

[1967, from the *slamming* of the prison cell door (analogous to *lockup* meaning jail)]

SLBM, abbreviation of *submarine-launched ballistic missile.*

A freeze or limit on nuclear submarines would carry a lot of advantages from Washington's point of view but few from Moscow's. The sea is the most secure strategic environment, and the SLBM, as everyone agrees, is the one weapon likely to survive an uncertain future. *John Newhouse, "Annals of Diplomacy: SALT," The New Yorker, May 19, 1973, p 97*

Though the Soviets had more missile-firing submarines, U.S. subs were quieter, making them harder to detect, and many of the American SLBMs carried from ten to 14 warheads each. *"Arming to Disarm in the Age of Détente," Time, Feb. 11, 1974, p 18*

[1967] Compare SLCM.

SLCM, abbreviation of *submarine-launched cruise missile.*

The Navy contemplates placing both the strategic SLCM's and the tactical SLCM's aboard the present force of several hundred attack submarines, which now carry only tactical weapons and whose mission is to locate Soviet submarines and to guard American shipping. *Deborah Shapley, Science, Feb. 7, 1975, p 418*

[1970] Compare ALCM.

sleaze (sli:z), *n. Informal.* sleazy condition or quality; sleaziness; shoddiness.

The floodgates opened in 1966 when the Supreme Court, ruling on "Fanny Hill," declared that a work is pornographic only if it is "utterly without redeeming social value" — a definition that led directly to "Deep Throat" and the sleaze of today's Times Square. *"Pornography: A Turn of the Tide," Newsweek, July 2, 1973, p 18*

[1961, back formation from *sleazy* (OED *c*1645)]

sleazo, *adj. Slang.* sleazy.

Somehow she gets through to audiences where more polished performers fail. Her sleazo routines seem half-rehearsed. Her dirty jokes sound almost like last-gasp fill-ins for the cleaner lines she was supposed to deliver but forgot. *Bart Mills, "Bette Midler," The Manchester Guardian Weekly, Aug. 2, 1975, p 19*

[1972, from *sleaze* or *sleazy* + *-o*, as in *dumbo, socko, weirdo*, etc.]

sleep apnea, a temporary suspension of breathing that occurs during sleep. It may be caused by physical obstructions in the breathing tract, or by a neurological disorder.

One key question, of course, is — as with all crib-death theories — how many of the 7,500 to 10,000 deaths a year might be caused by this mechanism. Does sleep apnea cause a substantial fraction of the deaths? Or only a handful? *Marion Steinman, "Crib Death: Too Many Clues?" The New York Times Magazine, May 16, 1976, p 42*

Treatments are now available for narcolepsy and another recently discovered illness, sleep apnea. The apnea patient complains either of feeling sleepy all day, of his sleep not doing much good, or of difficulty in remaining asleep. All-night sleep recordings show that his breathing often stops for periods of 15 seconds or more during sleep. *Ernest L. Hartmann, "The Way We Sleep," The 1977 World Book Year Book, p 121*

[1976]

sleeper, *n.* another name for MOLE (def. 2).

The CIA call them 'sleepers', I think. They're people about whom, at a certain time, you guess the pattern of their ideological development, if you're a talent spotter working for the Russian Secret service, and you winkle them into a corner, and say: 'We appreciate your feelings about this, but just keep very quiet — sooner or later we will need you and when we do we will tell you.' *John le Carré, The Listener, Jan. 22, 1976, p 90*

[1955, 1976, so called from his being inactive for a time, as one who sleeps or hibernates]

sleeping policemen, *British.* a series of ridges built across the surface of a road to deter motorists from speeding.

The problem of designing barriers which allow cyclists to pass but deter motorists is typical. "Sleeping policemen" type humps are allowed — but only for a year at a time. A footpath can be extended to form a ramp across the mouth of a road, but the legal procedures for building this are quite different to those for erecting a barrier or railings. *New Scientist, Nov. 2, 1978, p 349*

[1973] Compare RUMBLE STRIP, SPEED BUMP.

sleight-of-mouth, *n. Informal.* skillful use of words to deceive; verbal legerdemain.

The ambitious [William H.] Sullivan has sometimes been accused of "sleight-of-mouth" tricks — of changing his views to suit the policy of the moment. *Time, Feb. 19, 1973, p 21*

There are, perhaps, three-quarters of a million people in camps and prisons across the sub-continent who would win freedom from an agreement. They are not, frankly, to be sacrificed any longer to political sleight of mouth. *"The Prisoners Must Be Freed," The Manchester Guardian Weekly, April 21, 1973, p 1*

[1973, patterned on *sleight-of-hand*]

slide, *n.* another name for BOTTLENECK.

It is called "slide" or "bottleneck," a style of guitar playing in which something like a piece of broken glass is used to fret the strings to produce a strong, lowdown sound. A few decades ago it was the sound of a whole genus of American music that might be called backroads blues. *"The Wizard of Slide," Time, Oct. 21, 1974, p 99*

[1972]

sliding time, *U.S.* another name for FLEXTIME.

In West Germany, some 3,500 firms have adopted "sliding time." In one form of the plan, company doors are open from 7 a.m. until 7 p.m., and factory or office workers can come in any time they like, provided that they are around for "core time," from 10 a.m. to 3 p.m., and they put in a 40-hour week. *Donald M. Morrison, "Is the Work Ethic Going Out of Style?" Time, Oct. 30, 1972, p 97*

[1972, translation of German GLEITZEIT] Compare GLIDING TIME.

slim·nas·tics (ˌslim'næs tiks), *n.pl.* exercises to help a person lose weight.

Mrs. Mason sets a no-nonsense athletic schedule. At Stanley, "every single girl, every single day, has one hour of tennis, one hour in the pool, one hour of slimnastics." *Chris Chase, Saturday Review, Aug. 19, 1972, p 74*

"Straight exercise is dull," said one woman in green leotard and tights at the Yonkers Y. "I've taken slimnastics and interpretive dancing, but this seemed exciting and fun." *Ursula Mahoney, "Belly Dancing," The New York Times, Nov. 24, 1974, p 39*

[1967, blend of *slim* and *gymnastics*]

slingshot, *n.* a space-flight using the gravitational pull of a celestial body to accelerate sharply, usually in order to change course.

The next flight now scheduled is for 1973, a "slingshot" that will pass close to Venus on its way to Mercury. *Raymond N. Watts Jr., "The Exploration of Venus," Encyclopedia Science Supplement (Grolier) 1971, p 350*

Meanwhile, the long trip from Jupiter to Saturn has been productive in its own right. The "slingshot" trajectory between the worlds has carried Pioneer 11 about 16° above the plane of the ecliptic, making it the first spacecraft ever to provide earthlings with a look "down" on the solar system. Date of the Saturn encounter: Sept. 1, 1979. *"Pioneer 11: Looking Good for Saturn," Science News, June 18, 1976, p 391*

[1971] Compare SWINGAROUND.

slow infection, an infection that is often fatal, caused by a virus that is present in the body, usually for a long time (slow virus) before it becomes active.

The Fore, a primitive tribe in New Guinea, were the main victims of kuru, the first known slow infection of man. *Picture legend, "Agents of Slow Death," The World Book Science Annual 1976 (1975), p 57*

[1972, patterned on *slow virus*] See CREUTZFELDT-JAKOB DISEASE, SSPE.

sluggish schizophrenia, a presumed mental illness often ascribed in the Soviet Union to political dissidents.

"Even if one should accept the diagnosis of sluggish schizophrenia in these and similar cases," Chodoff said, "one must wonder why a disease without delusions, hallucinations or agitated behavior should require injections of chlorpromazine (an antischizophrenic drug) for its treatment." *Science News, Sept. 10, 1977, p 165*

The Institute of Psychiatry of the Soviet Academy of Medical Sciences has isolated a curious, but convenient, new form of mental illness, which only affects people in the Soviet Union. There are no clinical symptoms for 'sluggish schizophrenia', as it is known, but one of its symptoms is described as a paranoid delusion about reforming society. *John Simpson, "The Disease of Conscience," The Listener, July 20, 1978, p 70*

[1977, translation of Russian *stertye shizofreniya*] See PSIKHUSHKA PSYCHOPRISON.

slump·fla·tion (sləmp'flei ʃən), *n. Economics.* a condition of unemployment and business decline accompanied by increasing inflation.

The downturn was aptly described by such words as "inflationary recession," "stagflation," or even "slumpflation"—words coined to recognize not just that inflation coexisted with recession, stagnation, or slump, but that inflation brought about such conditions. *Miroslav A. Kriz, "Economy, World," Britannica Book of the Year 1975, p 251*

The $16 billion in rebates and tax credits might be too weak to jolt the economy out of its alarming slumpflation. *"The Nation: Ford's Risky Plan Against Slumpflation," Time, Jan. 27, 1975, p 13*

[1975, from *slump* + *inflation*] Also called INFLUMP. Compare HESIFLATION.

S-M or **s-m,** abbreviation of: **1** sado-masochism.

The taboo currently under the heaviest assault is sado-masochism—sexual pleasure derived from dominating and inflicting pain on a partner or from being hurt. Porn-film makers long avoided "S-M," as it is known in the trade, because they were convinced that it would drive away customers. *"The Porno Plague," Time, April 5, 1976, p 61*

2 sado-masochist.

"The Story of O" is even more self-defeating: It's a soft-core film that reduces the S-M sex of Pauline Reage's novel to a series of anguished facial close-ups. *Frank Rich, "Riding the New Wave of Porno," New York Post, Nov. 29, 1975, p 40*

[1974] Compare S AND M.

smackhead, *n. U.S. Slang.* a user or addict of heroin.

It includes an imbecilic meeting of narcotic agents ... and a macabre, incredibly funny conversation with a Georgia cop, who is warned of a smackhead migration to his state because they like warm weather. *Crawford Woods, Review of "Fear and Loathing In Las Vegas: A Savage Journey to the Heart of the American Dream" by Hunter S. Thompson, The New York Times Book Review, July 23, 1972, p 17*

[1972, from *smack* heroin + *head* drug addict]

smart, *adj. U.S. Military Slang.* guided to a target by sophisticated sensor devices.

Such projectiles—the Army has named them "smart rounds," after the "smart bombs" used in the air war against North Vietnam—would carry a sensor device (infrared or electromagnetic) which could "lock on" to a target by "reading" its "signature," and correct the trajectory of a shell so that it lands on target. *Michael T. Klare, "The Army of the 1970s," the Nation, Jan. 26, 1974, p 108*

Thousands of so-called "smart" weapons, guided bombs and antitank missiles, have been added to U.S. stockpiles overseas. *Michael Getler, "Crack German Forces Key to NATO Strength," The Manchester Guardian Weekly (The Washington Post section), March 13, 1977, p 15*

The last columns of the article and the final tables showed our current proposals for a U.S. military budget of the 1980's; this included a sharp reduction in spending, based much more on our appraisal of current weapons and troop deployments than on the "smart" weapons of the future. *Philip Morrison and Paul E. Walker, "Letters," Scientific American, Jan. 1979, p 10*

[1972] Compare INTELLIGENT.

smarts, *n.pl.* Sometimes also **smart.** *U.S. and Canadian Slang.* good sense; intelligence; brains.

"But the river has been good to me. There's enough here to keep you going. You start in docking, and if you've got enough smarts you try to climb." *Berton Roueché, "A Reporter at Large: The River World," The New Yorker, Feb. 26, 1972*

Some failed simply because they just didn't have the smarts it takes to get into a U.S. medical school and stay in. *Michael Seiler, The Tuscaloosa News (Alabama), May 19, 1974, p 4D*

Mrs. Maynard said that Mr. Miller, a former West Virginia miner whom she has never met, lacks "backbone" and "doesn't have enough smart to run a union as big as the United Mine Workers." *The New York Times, Oct. 9, 1977, p 26*

She also had the smarts, as did Shaver, to get a U.S. agency behind her. *Lawrence O'Toole, "The Girls of Autumn," Maclean's, Nov. 13, 1978, p 54*

[1968, noun use of the adjective] Compare STREET-SMARTS.

smashball, *n.* a racquet game in which two or more players hit a ball back and forth with smashing force.

Smashball, a new racquet type game popular in Israel and Greece, comes to Central Park. . . . The game resembles tennis without the bounce, court or net — or ping pong without the table. *Picture legend, "New Racquet," New York Post, April 28, 1975 (page not known)*

[1975]

smog, *v.t.* to envelop in smog.

When we hear that Tokyo citizens are confined to their homes, that Los Angeles residents are smogged in, then we get worried. *Rollene W. Saal, Saturday Review, Oct. 31, 1970, p 32*

Furthermore, conventional geodesy depends on clear lines of sight, and in the Los Angeles basin these are often smogged out. *Science News, Aug. 24, 31, 1974, p 136*

[1970, verb use of the noun]

smoke, *Slang.* —*n.* marijuana (sometimes also applied to hashish).

"So one night I'm high on smoke, and I walk into this bar. I see a dude named Cuba. He is from the island, you dig it, and he is into numbers and he does some things in drugs." *James Willwerth, "Portrait of a Mugger," Harper's, Nov. 1974, p 92*

Twenty tons of smoke in 40-pound plastic-wrapped bales was nailed aboard the shrimper *Tomahawk* near a canal-

side home in *Tybee Island, Florida,* by county and DEA fuzz. *"High Crimes: Bust Biggest 'Mother' of All — 112 Tons at Sea," High Times, Jan. 1979, p 32*

blow smoke, to smoke marijuana (or hashish).

Everybody blew smoke there. You could buy hash. A guy who hung out there sold little balls of hash for a dime — ten dollars. I bought from him, and then we busted him. *John Brooks, The New Yorker, July 3, 1973, p 60*

—*v.i., v.t.* to smoke marijuana (or hashish).

"If you smoke, you are your own dealer: It's the same with acid. Smoking is so natural it's unnatural to talk about it. The biggest danger is not the dope but the fact you're breaking the law." *Tom Mangold, "Midweek Programmes (BBC 1) on Drug-Taking and the Drug Trade," The Listener, Sept. 6, 1973, p 306*

[1973]

smoke detector, a device sensitive to smoke, used to warn people of a fire by making a loud sound when smoke enters its vents. It is usually encased in plastic and attached to a wall or ceiling.

Smoke detectors work either through photoelectric cells or an ionization device, but fire officials generally agree that there is minimal difference in effectiveness between the two. *"Modern Living: Hot Item: A Life-Saving Squawk," Time, Jan. 10, 1977, p 36*

The Savoy has won permission to keep its fire doors open — with magnetic catches that release automatically when a smoke detector flashes the alarm. *Israel Shenker, The New York Times Magazine, Dec. 24, 1978, p 21*

[1977]

smoke pollution, tobacco smoke regarded as a pollutant.

To determine how much nicotine nonsmokers absorb from smoke pollution, the investigators did two series of experiments on 39 urban nonsmokers. *Lawrence K. Altman, International Herald-Tribune, Feb. 4, 1975, p 3*

[1975]

Smokey or **smokey,** *n.* Also, **Smokey Bear.** *U.S. Slang.* a policeman or a state trooper, especially one who patrols a highway.

C.B.-ers with their colorful pseudonyms and jargon may warn of Smokey's presence — but in hundreds of instances they have helped the police catch drunken and hit and run drivers and have sped ambulances to accident scenes. *Ernest Dickinson "Business Tunes In on Citizens Band," The New York Times, March 7, 1976, Sec. 3, p 5*

Once limited to truckers and their Smokey Bear antagonists on highway patrols, Citizens Band radio has grown to the point where about 20 million American "good buddies" have CB rigs in their cars or homes. *Time, Jan. 23, 1978, p 66*

[1975, so called from the resemblance of some state troopers' wide-brimmed hats to the forest-ranger hat worn by *Smokey (the) bear,* an animal character warning against forest fires in signs of the U.S. Forest Service]

smoking gun or **smoking pistol,** a piece of definitive, indisputable evidence, especially of a crime.

It was not clear, however, whether these new allegations were what had persuaded Ribicoff and Percy to call for Lance's resignation. In fact, there may well be no "smoking gun" — no incontrovertible, black-and-white evidence of wrongdoing by Lance. *Time, Nov. 19, 1977, p 8*

A spokesman for the Center for Disease Control refused to comment last night on the finding of the bacteria in Macy's water tower. But Dr. Marr said: "We haven't got a smoking pistol. Unfortunately, everyone is zeroing in on this as a cause, but the case isn't that strong." *The New York Times, Jan. 12, 1979, p D14*

[1974, in allusion to the crime-fiction stereotype of a person found at the scene of a crime holding a recently fired, still smoking gun in his hand]

▶ This usage arose during the Watergate affair, when evidence among the White House tapes and papers was sought to show conclusively that the President was involved in the Watergate cover-up.

SMSA, abbreviation of *Standard Metropolitan Statistical Area* (official designation of a metropolitan area in the United States).

An SMSA consists of a city of 50,000 or more and the county in which it is located, plus adjoining counties that meet certain criteria of metropolitan character and are closely integrated with the central city, as through commuting, for example. (In New England, the basic units are towns rather than counties.) *Conrad Taeuber, "Population Trends of the 1960's: Notes," Science, May 19, 1972, p 777*

Changes in the definition of "standard metropolitan statistical area" (SMSA), by which U.S. urban areas are outlined, were ordered on April 27 by the Office of Management and Budget. The changes added to, subtracted from, or merged various densely populated areas. As a result, 26 new areas were designated as SMSA's, 12 existing SMSA's were merged into 6 new ones, and several other SMSA's were expanded. *James M. Banovetz, "City: Pollution Control," The 1974 World Book Year Book, p 259*

[1966]

snail darter, a species of small perch that feeds on snails, discovered in the Tennessee River in 1973 and unknown elsewhere.

The 3-in-long snail darter is exerting an influence far out of proportion to its size. In June the U.S. Supreme Court stopped construction of the $116 million Tellico Dam because it would wipe out the diminutive fish, thereby violating the 1973 Endangered Species Act. Now the snail darter is endangering the very law that protected it. *Time, Oct. 16, 1978, p 84*

Now that it is a *fait accompli*, and all appeals are lost, I and my family would like to mourn the passing of the snail darter into oblivion, and to express our outrage at legislation that knowingly doomed a species of life on this planet. *Nancy Scott, Irvington, N.Y., in a Letter to the Editor, The New York Times, Dec. 25, 1979, p 22*

[1976] See FURBISH LOUSEWORT.

snake, *n.* Usually, **the snake.** a system of jointly floated currencies whose exchange rates are allowed to fluctuate within narrow limits against each other but within a wider margin against other currencies, established in 1972 by France, West Germany, Belgium, the Netherlands, Luxembourg, Norway, Sweden, and Denmark.

The country [Sweden] also pulled out of the European monetary "snake," the collection of currencies tied to the West German mark, because Stockholm wanted to devalue the krona much more than snake rules allow. Because their economies are closely tied to Sweden's, Denmark and Norway felt obliged to devalue their own currencies by 5%, but neither followed Sweden out of the snake. *Time, Sept. 12, 1977, p 49*

Much as the French would join with Britain in preferring a system which required prompt and effective intervention when the warning bells on the snake ring, the exact details are of secondary importance. The latest intention is that the snake (which is an arrangement by which all the member currencies are linked to each other) should be equipped with a warning system capable of identifying which currencies are responsible for undue fluctuations within the system. *Peter Jenkins, "Britain Rejects Both the Snake and the Apple," The Manchester Guardian Weekly, Oct. 29, 1978, p 10*

Attributive use.

Under his proposals countries whose currencies are already in the EEC "snake" system will have to follow common monetary budgetary and wider economic policies. For the time being the non-snake currencies will have to make progress as best they can until conditions are right for them to join the snakes. *John Palmer, "Forget Dog Licences, What About Crises?" The Manchester Guardian Weekly, Jan. 18, 1976, p 8*

[1973, shortened from *snake in the tunnel*, a name for this system derived from the graphic representation of the narrow fluctuations allowed between the jointly floated currencies that supposedly resembled a wriggling *snake*, as compared to the wider band of fluctuations permitted against other currencies of the world that supposedly resembled a *tunnel*] Compare JOINT FLOAT.

SNG, abbreviation of *synthetic* (or *substitute*) *natural gas.*

Shortage of natural gas in the US now makes it necessary for that country to rely on SNG in future as a valuable energy source. *Eric Braithwaite, "Molybdenum, the Pervasive Element," New Scientist, Sept. 20, 1973, p 680*

SNG consists essentially of methane, CH_4. Like natural gas, it has a heating value of about 1,000 British thermal units (B.T.U.) per cubic foot. *Frederick C. Price, "Chemical Technology," The World Book Science Annual 1974 (1973), p 272*

[1972]

snob zoning, U.S. the use of zoning requirements (such as "one acre per house") to keep poor or less affluent people from purchasing property, especially in the suburbs.

Also, court actions were initiated in some suburban communities to prevent the use of "snob zoning" to exclude "low-income families. *Allan F. Thornton, "Housing," The Americana Annual 1973, p 337*

[1956, 1973] Compare REDLINING.

snort, *n. Slang.* **1** an act of inhaling a narcotic through the nostrils.

"Everyone assumed it was coke." In fact, it was "China White" heroin. Those who sniffed became ill. . . . Cher, who didn't take a snort, is credited with saving Bassist Alan Gorrie's life by walking him around all night, preventing him from lapsing into a coma. *"People," Time, March 3, 1975, p 49*

2 the narcotic inhaled.

At night, the whores and pimps and pushers take over. . . . Want a fix? A snort (cocaine)? A smoke? *Tom Mangold, "Midweek Programmes (BBC 1) on Drug-Taking and the Drug Trade," The Listener, Sept. 6, 1973, p 304*

[1973] Compare TOOT.

Snowbelt, *n.* the northern region of the continental United States extending east to west.

Snowbelt representatives contended time after time that their region was being shortchanged. They said that the formulas were originally drawn when the Sunbelt was poor and the Snowbelt was rich. They argued that the situation had been reversed, and they promised to lobby tirelessly on Capitol Hill to revise the formulas. *B. Drummond Ayres Jr., "Regional Divisions Intensified by Dispute Over Aid to Sunbelt," The New York Times, Sept. 28, 1977, p 75*

[1977, patterned on *Sunbelt*] Also called FROSTBELT.

snuff film or **snuff movie,** a pornographic motion picture that culminates in the actual murder of one of the actors.

Even the sexual uses of women are getting more sinister. In addition to rape, pornography and prostitution, we now have "snuff films," presented as a real, you-are-there slaughter of a woman hired to "act" in the movie – and this is presented as titillating. *Letty Cottin Pogrebin, "Sexism Rampant," The New York Times, March 19, 1976, p 33*

FBI agents are now zeroing in on two specific "snuff" films they believe may portray the grisly death of pretty Philadelphia English teacher Susan Reinert. . . . The names of these two movies are "After Satan" and "The Satan Cult." The supposed snuff films may show people involved in her killing and perhaps the killing itself, officials believe. *Michael Shain, New York Post, Sept. 17, 1979, p 15*

[1975, from "*snuff* out" to extinguish, kill]

snurf·ing ('snər fiŋ), *n.* the act or sport of riding on a special board over snow. See the quotation for details.

Snow surfing (or "snurfing") through deep powder is all the rage in Utah, where two snurfers have invented the "Winterstick," a 5-foot-long, 14-inch-wide foam-cored plastic board with three small "skegs," or fins, on the underside like a surfboard. To prevent the board from running amok when the rider falls off, a safety rope is attached to the back. The snurfer hooks his feet under a strap on top, stands sideways on the board, grasps the safety line and banks off down the hill, blanketed in a powdery cloud of snow. *"Life Style: Skiing Without Skis," Newsweek, Feb. 3, 1975, p 69*

[1970, blend of *snow* and *surfing*]

soap, *n.* U.S. short for *soap opera.*

Strangely, none of the catastrophes on soaps – and nearly every soap event is a catastrophe – are set up with much sentiment. *Renata Adler, "The Air," The New Yorker, Feb. 12, 1972, p 79*

A lot of things are happening to soaps these days. In what is one of the worst ever prime-time TV seasons, the soaps are prospering by offering sex and sorrow in the afternoon. Each year they become more "relevant" and, sometimes, realistic. *"Television: Sex and Suffering in the Afternoon," Time, Jan. 12, 1976, p 46*

[1971, replacing earlier (1950's) slang *soaper*] Compare SUDSER.

soa·per ('sou pər), *n.* U.S. Slang. variant of SOPOR.

Many students here have been frantically doing soapers for more than a year, knowing little about the dangers and caring only that the pills are a great way to get loose. I appreciate TIME's report of the frightening results of methaqualone abuse. *Lisa Sidner, Oxford, Ohio, in a Letter to the Editor, Time, March 26, 1973, p K2*

[1972]

social contract, an agreement between labor unions and government in which the unions limit their demands for wage increases in exchange for economic and social policies favorable to workers.

The government announced an agreement with business and labor leaders in October to limit wage increases and to ban both strikes and layoffs for 180 days. Implementation of this "social contract," which did not include agricultural associations, was uncertain. *Ronald M. Schneider, "Argentina," 1976 Collier's Encyclopedia Year Book (1975), p 132*

The relative labor peace has been achieved only because the [British] Labor government's "social contract" with the all-powerful unions is still holding. The unions continue to accept, albeit grudgingly, the government's ceiling of a maximum 6-pound pay increase. *Felix Kessler, "The Pound's Slump May Be Misleading," The Wall Street Journal, Nov. 12, 1976, p 12*

[1974] ► The term was introduced in Great Britain in 1974 by Prime Minister Harold Wilson, apparently echoing the 18th-century phrase for the agreement forming the basis of human society according to Rousseau's *Contrat Social* (1762).

sociobiology, *n.* the study of the biological basis of social behavior, especially as such behavior is transmitted genetically.

These models ascribe social behavior to a kind of genetic imperative – that is, behavior of individuals evolves so as to maximize their genetic contribution to the next generation. This far-reaching notion is the basis of an emerging field of inquiry known as sociobiology, which seems to be having an impact on the design of field studies of animal behavior and is also attracting the attention of social scientists as well as stirring up controversy among them. *Gina Bari Kolata, "Sociobiology (1): Models of Social Behavior," Science, Jan. 10, 1975, p 50*

Sociobiology purports to offer explanations of animal behavior, including human, in terms of survival strategies exploited by individuals within species. As things worked out at the Dahlem meeting, the term "naturalistic approach" in the conference task was effectively replaced by "sociobiology": the question, therefore, became, are moral norms simply part of a clever stratagem for getting us to behave in a way dictated by our genes? *Roger Lewin, "Biological Limits to Morality," New Scientist, Dec. 15, 1977, p 694*

[1975, popularized by the book *Sociobiology: The New Synthesis* (1975) by the American zoologist Edward O. Wilson]

sociobiological, *adj.:* Sociobiological theories of altruism have been applied to primate behavior by Richard Alexander of the University of Michigan in Ann Arbor and by others. *Gina Bari Kolata, "Sociobiology (1): Models of Social Behavior," Science, Jan. 10, 1975, p 50*

sociobiologist, *n.:* Some sociobiologists go so far as to suggest that there may be human genes for such behavior as conformism, homosexuality and spite. Carried to an extreme, sociobiology holds that all forms of life exist solely to serve the purposes of DNA, the coded master molecule that determines the nature of all organisms and is the stuff of genes. *Time, Aug. 1, 1977, p 54*

► In the 1950's and 1960's the term *sociobiology* was used in the general sense of the study of society according to the concepts and methods of biology. In the current sense of the term, the apparent assumption that social behavior among all animals,

431

including human beings, can be genetically transmitted and be subject to biological evolution, has stirred controversy.

socioecology, *n.* social grouping or organization as related to or influenced by the environment.

The comparative study of the ecology and behaviour of pachyderms is not only interesting, but also instructive, because it can contribute to a broader understanding of mammalian socioecology in the same way that studies of other groups such as primates and antelopes have done. *Andrew Laurie and Robert Oliver, "Pachyderms in Peril," New Scientist, Sept. 15, 1977, p 658*

[1975, from *socio-* social, of society + *ecology*]

soda-pop wine, variant name of POP WINE.

The cultural forces that produced this band of celebrants have lately included a merchandising milestone—the development of what are sometimes called "soda-pop wines." *Calvin Trillin, "U.S. Journal: Breaux Bridge, Louisiana," The New Yorker, May 20, 1972, p 102*

[1972]

soft-core, *adj.* simulating or suggesting sexual acts; not graphic or explicit in presenting erotic activity.

It is soft-core pornography which represents the true degradation of sex. And also its maximum exploitation; since the teasing and the taunting is interminable, and because it never delivers the goods, the customers can be strung out for years, going to film after film, hoping *this* time to see a *little* more than the last time. *John Hofsess, "Misadventures in the Skin Trade," Maclean's, July 1974, p 58*

—*n.* Also **soft core.** soft-core pornography.

Attempts to retract into soft-core, like *Deep Throat II*, in which the explicit scenes are all off-camera, have failed. *"Lust's Labor Lost," Time, May 13, 1974, p 99*

. . . Dennis Hopper (Adult) Publications churn out soft-core for hard men. *Julian Barnes, Review of "The First of All Pleasures" by Deanna Maclaren, New Statesman, July 4, 1975, p 30*

[1966 for adjective; 1973 for noun; patterned on *hard-core*] Compare HARD-CORE.

soft-dock, *v.i.* to join orbiting spacecraft without a mechanical coupling, as by nylon line, etc.

The astronauts soft-docked with the station, took a dinner break and planned their method of attack. *Science News, June 2, 1973, p 352*

[1973] Compare HARD-DOCK.

soft energy, energy derived from SOFT TECHNOLOGY.

Naturally enough, the book concentrates on soft energy technologies. There are sections on: tools, invention, solar, wind, transport, steam, biofuels, building, and integrated systems. Biofuels, for example, covers, among other things, methane makers and wood stoves. *Michael Kenwood, Review of "Soft-Tech," edited by J. Baldwin and Stewart Brand, New Scientist, Oct. 12, 1978, p xviii*

[1977]

soft landing, *U.S. Economics.* a slowing down of the rate of economic growth without causing a recession or high unemployment.

According to White House economists, it now looks as if the third-quarter real-growth rate of the gross national product will be almost exactly the 4 per cent a year that the

Administration has been looking for. "That is right on the button for an at least temporary soft landing," said one. *"Prices: A Temporary Respite," Newsweek, Oct. 15, 1973, p 86*

Public Service Jobs—Going slow on those easily given commitments for federal funds to provide public service jobs at the local level as insurance for a "soft landing" against the recessionary consequences of the money squeeze would be prudent politically as well as fiscally. *Eliot Janeway, The Tuscaloosa News (Alabama), Sept. 15, 1974, p 38*

[1973, transferred from the earlier aerospace term (1959) meaning a slow landing of a spacecraft to avoid damage]

soft path, the method or approach of SOFT TECHNOLOGY.

By following the soft path, a smooth transition would be made from the era of oil and gas to an era of renewable energy sources—sun, wind, tides, streams, and liquid fuels derived from vegetation. *J. Dicken Kirschten, "A New Alternative in the Energy Crisis," Britannica Book of the Year 1978, p 143*

[1977]

soft porn, soft-core pornography.

The mystery deepens when it comes to the soft porn which sweeps in rivers of flesh along the edges of the pavements on a fine day. Newspaper kiosks are thatched in *Playboys* and *Penthouses*. Where there is something more than usually explicit on show—though the publisher's wrapper covers the middle of the action—men collect. *Robert Dundas, "Hard Politics, Soft Porn," New Statesman, March 21, 1975, p 361*

[1974] Compare HARD PORN.

soft technology, a form of technology that relies on solar power, wind power, and the like, instead of on large, costly machinery; APPROPRIATE TECHNOLOGY.

The term "soft technology" was coined amid the British counter-culture in 1970. Technology which is soft is gentle on its surroundings, responds to it, incorporates it, feeds it. A nuclear power-generating station doesn't qualify. A wooden windmill with cloth sails grinding local grain does. *"Wraparound," Harper's, April 1974, p 6*

Another example would be underground architecture. I may be biased in being particularly interested in the innovative end of things. But it seems to be energy-saving, it seems to be material-saving, and these are things that supposedly make soft technology good. *Stewart Brand, quoted by Wade Greene in "The Selling of Soft Tech," Psychology Today, Nov. 1978, p 73*

[1973]

So·Ho ('sou‚hou), *n.* an area of New York City, in lower Manhattan, noted as a center of avant-garde art, music, film, and fashion.

A tour of SoHo, the bustling neighborhood in downtown Manhattan, is a must for visitors who want a firsthand look at New York's famous art community. Much livelier than the Establishment art scene to be found along upper Madison Avenue, SoHo has live-in artists, low-rise buildings and ground floor or walk-up galleries. *Grace Glueck, "Art People," The New York Times, July 9, 1976, p C22*

[1973, from its being situated *So*uth of *Ho*uston Street; name probably influenced by the *Soho* district in London] Compare NOHO.

ɔl (sɑl), *n.* a Martian day, consisting of 24 hours, 37 minutes, and 22 seconds.

The squat little lander seemed to get through its first sol (as the Martian day . . . is called) without any problems. The temperature at night sinks to about −127°F but warms up to a more comfortable −5°F when the sun comes up. *Michael Binyon, The Times (London), July 22, 1976, p 1*

On sol 8 — the eighth sol, or day, after the first of the Viking landers had touched down on Chryse Planitia, a great basin in the northern hemisphere of Mars — the craft's sampler arm extended straight out and then dropped to the ground. *Henry S. F. Cooper, Jr., "A Reporter at Large: The Search for Life on Mars," The New Yorker, Feb. 5, 1979, p 41*

[1976, probably from Latin *sōl* the sun, since a Martian day represents one rotation of the planet with respect to the sun]

ɔlar, *n.* short for SOLAR POWER.

A few days ago, Senator Charles H. Percy, Republican of Illinois, recanted his support for the breeder and recommended the transfer of funds to "conservation, solar and coal." *Edward Cowan, "And Still U.S. Energy Alternatives Are Weak," The New York Times, Dec. 5, 1976, Sec. 3, p 7*

[1976]

ɔlar collector, any of various devices that catch and store radiation of the sun for use in heating, producing electric power, etc.

The solar collectors placed on the south side of the house at an angle of 48° cover an area of 20 sq.m. Each collector contains 18 evacuated glass tubes about 1 m long and 7 cm in diameter, equipped with integrated heat reflectors. *Günter Sandscheper, New Scientist, Aug. 14, 1975, p 382*

A solar collector is plastic paneling installed in a building's roof to catch the sun's rays. The heat builds up inside much the way it does inside a parked car with closed windows on a summer day. The heat is usually transmitted to a water tank or to radiators by hot water. *Edward Cowan, "Solar Heat Competitive With Electric, Agency Finds," The New York Times, Dec. 30, 1976, p 14*

[1966] Also shortened to COLLECTOR. See FLAT-PLATE COLLECTOR.

ɔlar farm, a large area with solar collectors for storing heat and converting it to electric power.

One technique . . . involves spreading a "solar farm," consisting of piping containing a mixture of chemicals, over 25 sq.mi. of desert. Heated by the sun, the mix would be used to make steam, which would power turbines. *"Environment: Solar Energy," Time, May 7, 1973, p 49*

[1972]

ɔlar pond, any of various devices consisting of long, flat containers filled with water to absorb radiation of the sun and convert it into heat.

"Still another example is the solar ponds of Israel, which . . . consist of large containers about a meter deep with black bottoms. The bottom half of the pond is filled with salt water, the top half with fresh. The black bottom absorbs solar radiation and heats the adjacent salty water. *Seelye Martin, "The Amateur Scientist," Scientific American, June 1971, p 127*

A solar pond acts as a collector. However, it differs from other collectors in that the pond can also store heat energy. *David Crabbe and Richard McBride, The World Energy Book, 1978, p 164*

[1961, from the resemblance of such a device to a *pond*]

solar power, energy derived from radiation of the sun and converted to heat energy or electric energy.

The term solar power today encompasses a great deal more than most people think. Actually, it may be appropriately applied to . . . such seemingly disparate activities as generating electricity with windmills, burning wood and producing methane gas from cow manure. *Michael Harwood, The New York Times Magazine, March 16, 1975, p 42*

If all new houses built for the next 30 years could be fitted with solar heating panels . . . and if an equal number of existing houses were converted, domestic solar power could then substitute for about 4 per cent of Britain's energy needs. *Kenneth Owen, The Times (London), March 26, 1976, p VI*

[1974]

sol·i·ton ('sɑl ə,tɑn), *n. Physics.* a quantum unit for a solitary wave of energy caused by a single disturbance.

Solitons themselves appear when exact solutions of the classical field equations are quantised. They actually represent new "particle states," and carry a quantum number called soliton number. Solitons have actually been around in solid state physics for some years, in the guise of nondispersive waves. There is a simple way of showing the dispersion of a wave, demonstrated by throwing a stone into a pond: the ripples, of course, get flatter and wider as they spread outwards, but in the analogy a soliton ripple would always remain the same height and width: it would progress over the surface maintaining its initial form. *Stephen Wilson, "How Do Quarks Get Confined in Fields?" New Scientist, Feb. 16, 1978, p 435*

[1975, from *solit*ary + *-on* elementary unit or particle]

so·ma·to·me·din (,sou mə tə'mi: din), *n.* a hormone secreted by the liver which promotes the action of the growth hormone somatotropin.

Growth hormone does not act directly on growing cartilage. It causes the liver to secrete another hormone: somatomedin. The somatomedin molecule is much smaller than the growth hormone molecule, but its structure is not yet known. *J. M. Tanner, "Growing Up," Scientific American, Sept. 1973, p 42*

Extremely high doses of growth hormone, which is in short supply, and a recently discovered substance called somatomedin, which is needed by growth hormone to perform its many growth activities, may be used someday to increase the height of constitutionally short children. *Angela Haines, "Controlling Height," The New York Times Magazine, April 4, 1976, p 75*

[1973, from *somato*tropin + Late Latin *mediāri* to intervene, mediate + English *-in* (chemical suffix); because it modifies the action of somatotropin]

so·ma·to·stat·in (,sou mə tə'stæt in), *n.* a hormone produced primarily in the hypothalamus that inhibits the release of various other hormones, especially those regulating growth of the body and glucagon and insulin production.

Before somatostatin, diabetes was viewed as a disease in which one hormone, insulin, was important: diabetes was described as a disease characterized by a shortage of insulin. Now it is known that two hormones are involved in diabetes. The second hormone is glucagon, produced by the pituitary—and the production of glucagon is regulated by the brain hormone, somatostatin. *Edward Edelson, "Discovery of Brain Hormones a Giant Step for Doctors," Sunday News (New York), June 22, 1975, p 74*

Biologists in California have recently succeeded in making a synthetic gene for the human brain hormone somatostatin and inserting it into bacteria, where the hormone has been produced in milligram quantities. This is the first time an animal protein has been produced from a gene inserted into bacteria, and the achievement goes some way towards vindicating the claims of advocates of genetic engineering, who maintain that the techniques can be used for the cheap mass-production of medically important hormones and drugs. *The Times (London), Nov. 16, 1977, p 24*

[1973, from *somato*tropin the growth hormone affected by this + *-stat* combining form meaning regulating, controlling + *-in*, chemical suffix] See BRAIN HORMONE.

SOMPA ('sɑm pə), *n. U.S.* acronym for *System of Multicultural Pluralistic Assessment*, a system for testing intelligence of children by comparing the scores of children from similar social and cultural backgrounds to eliminate the bias in I.Q. tests ascribed to cultural differences.

The SOMPA technique would remove the "retarded" stigma from many children but leaves them in a position where they still need special educational attention but do not qualify for any funds. *Edward B. Fiske, "New Test Developed to Replace I.Q.," The New York Times, Feb. 18, 1976, p 28*

[1976]

son·i·cate ('sɑn ə,keit), *v.t.* to break up or disperse (any substance) by means of high-frequency sound waves.

Ten milliliters of the swollen gel pellet, containing 25 to 50 mg of DNA, were placed in a rosette flask cooled by an ice-brine bath and were sonicated with a Biosonik II sonicator. *Illustration legend, "Reports: Chromatin Fragments Resembling V Bodies," Science, Jan. 17, 1975, p 174*

—*n.* a particle of a substance that has been sonicated.

After specified periods of culture, cells were collected by centrifugation . . . and disrupted by sonication in 1 ml of buffer appropriate for each enzyme assay. Enzyme activities of the lymphocyte sonicates were determined by radioisotopic assay methods as previously described. *David Calle, et al, Nature, Jan. 17, 1975, p 214*

[1972 for verb; 1968 for noun; both apparently back formation from *sonication* (1964), probably from ultra*sonic* + *-ation*] Compare INSONIFY.

sonicator, *n.*: The cells were brought to a volume of 0.35 to 0.5 ml and then sonicated for 3 minutes in an Insonator model 1000 sonicator (Savant Instruments). *Science, March 9, 1973, p 1001*

sonic guide or **Sonicguide**, *n.* an ultrasonic transmitting and receiving device mounted on eyeglasses, similar to radar, and enabling a blind person to sense objects ahead of him.

[The] statement that electronic aids such as the sonic guide have not been popular with blind adults and that only 5 per cent can use them is misleading. The sonic guide was extensively evaluated during 1971-72 when professional mobility specialists in New Zealand, Australia, the US, and England trained over 100 blind people to use them. Some 78 per cent declared that the benefits they derived from th "glasses" made the considerable trouble and personal e pense of being trained away from home worthwhile. *Lesl Kay and Edward Strelow, New Scientist, June 23, 197 p 709*

[1977]

Son·nen·feldt doctrine ('sɑn ən,felt), the polic that the United States should not encourage polit cal uprising in the Communist satellite countries c Eastern Europe because it might lead to Soviet ir tervention and to the danger of an incident escala ing into world war.

The Sonnenfeldt doctrine suggests that the real intere of the Eastern European countries lies in building link with the Soviet Union based on a more genuine partnersh to a situation in which the Russians would no longer want t dominate by sheer exercise of military power. *Hella Pic "East is East, and West is West . . . ," The Manchest Guardian Weekly, April 11, 1976, p 9*

Did they take seriously the so-called Sonnenfeldt do trine about encouraging secure Soviet dominion in its ov sphere as a guarantee of world peace, and nearly pan when Carter seemed to annul it? Do they feel s endangered by hidden pressures? *Flora Lewis, "Europe (Almost) Upbeat View of America," The New York Tim Magazine, Aug. 7, 1977, p 38*

[1976, named after Helmut *Sonnenfeldt*, born 192(American official who proposed it]

so·por or **so·per** ('sou pər), *n. U.S. Slang.* a sedativ and hypnotic sold as a white tablet; QUAALUDE.

Methaqualone—known on the street as sopor or qua lude—is a nonbarbiturate hypnotic downer. It is prescribe to induce sleep and is legal when sold by prescription. Th drug was thought to be non-habit forming but Judi M LaForme, director of the University of Wisconsin Madiso Drug Information Center, says, "Now it looks as though may be addictive." In excess or in combination with alcoh the drug causes loss of motor coordination, and may caus the user to black out. *Science News, March 10, 1973, p 1£*

Methaqualone has become the sixth best-selling sedativ in the U.S. on the legal market; in addition, a huge supp of the drug has been diverted to campus and stre pushers, who have found an apparently insatiable mark for the "sopers" (catchall slang for the several brands methaqualone) at 25 to 50 cents a pill. *"Medicine: Warnin on 'Sopers'," Newsweek, Feb. 12, 1973, p 65*

[1972, from *Sopor*, a trademark for this drug] Als spelled SOAPER.

sortie lab, sortie can, or **sortie module,** variar names for SPACELAB.

The nations also agreed to develop a space laborato sometimes called the sortie lab, which will be placed in earth orbit in the cargo bay of the space shuttle, now bei built by NASA. *Science News, Aug. 11, 1973, p 87*

NASA has offered Europe the "sortie can"—a pre surised laboratory module that is to swing out from th cargo bay of the orbiting shuttle. *Nicholas Valéry, New Sc entist, July 6, 1972, p 3*

The main part of what remains is the so-called sort module—a 12-man passenger compartment which fits in the cargo bay of the orbiter. *Kenneth Owen, "Space Tec nology," The Times (London), July 7, 1972, p 17*

[1972] ► The origin and usage of *sortie* as the firs element in these compounds is discussed in the fo lowing quotation:

The Americans . . . call it the sortie-can or sortie-lab because it will go for excursions into space and return to Earth after a week or so. When the proposal came last year that Europe should tackle this integral package of the overall shuttle programme it was referred to as the sortie-lab. Objections arose at once. In French, it was pointed out, *sortie* means to leave with no suggestion of return. The name for the Europeans was duly changed to the over-used and colourless "spacelab." But this in turn prompted mutterings notably from the non-French majority of ESRO [European Space Research Organization] staff who were heard to say that an "ascenseur" in French did not change its name when it changed direction. *"More Language Problems in Space," New Scientist, June 14, 1973, p 702*

sots, *n.* a form of dissident Soviet art that satirizes the style of socialist realism.

Others, done in a sort of pop-art style the artists called "sots," made fun of socialist realism, the officially imposed genre of heroic optimism that dominates everything from propaganda posters to landscapes. One was a portrait of a stern-faced worker with his finger at his lips and the admonition "Don't babble." Another, in Moscow at the time of the New York show, depicted a pure white factory releasing billows of clear blue air to cleanse the filthy atmosphere. *David K. Shipler, The New York Times, Oct. 31, 1977, p 2*

[1976, from Russian, short for *sotsialist* socialist (realism)]

sound, *v.t. U.S. Slang.* Usually, **sound on.** to engage (someone) in sounding.

Somebody can "sound on" somebody else by referring to a ritualized attribute of that person. *William Labov, "Rules for Ritual Insults," in Rappin' and Stylin' Out, edited by Thomas Kochman, 1972, p 274*

The game begins when one youth "sounds" another to see if he will play. That is done either by "signifying" . . . or by "the dozens." *Peter Farb, Word Play, 1974, p 122*

[1972]

sound-alike, *n.* some person or thing that sounds just like another.

And to Monsieur D—and Auguste D—and the other sound-alikes, we should add the name of D—Hoffman who is as personally implicated in this critical narrative as Poe was in his stories and verses. *R. W. B. Lewis, Review of "Poe Poe Poe Poe Poe Poe Poe" by Daniel Hoffman, The American Scholar, Autumn 1972, p 683*

[1970, patterned on *look-alike, n.* (1940's)]

sounding, *n. U.S. Slang.* another name for SIGNIFYING.

This interchange, quoted from a study by William Labov, is an example of "sounding," a type of verbal contest common among lower-class black American adolescent boys. Sounding involves the exchange of usually obscene insults and invective which might well, in other circumstances, lead to violence: in sounding, however, one fights with words rather than with fists. *Donald Brenneis, New Scientist, May 4, 1978, p 280*

[1972] Compare the DOZENS, SHUCKING AND JIVING, WOOFING.

sound pollution, excessive noise of motor vehicles, jet planes, machinery, etc., considered harmful to the environment.

Sound pollution has been gaining increased attention and new regulations limit the amount of noise to which workers and the general public can be subjected. But concern so far has been concentrated on the nuisance value of noise one actually hears. *"Environmental Sciences: What You Don't Hear Can Hurt You," Science News, Dec. 8, 1973, p 361*

[1970] Also called AUDIO POLLUTION. Compare LIGHT POLLUTION.

sound sculpture, a sculptured work made of metal rods or other material that can emit pleasant sounds.

The most recent artist to put the mall to work is Liz Phillips, a young woman who specializes in "sound sculpture." Miss Phillips calls the sound sculpture in the mall "City Flow," and its special trick—it is, by the way, genuinely tricky—is the ability to translate the human traffic in the mall into electronic sounds that the passers-through hear. *"The Talk of the Town: Output," The New Yorker, April 18, 1977, p 31*

[1970] Compare LIGHT-SCULPTURE.

South, *n.* the less industrialized, technically, and economically advanced countries of the world.

Today, any regional struggle over who is to become managing director of the I.M.F. [International Monetary Fund] is far less likely to be one between the United States and Western Europe as between the "North" and the "South"—that is, the developed, industrial countries and the so-called developing countries, some oil-rich and others oil-poor; some well on the way to industrialization, and others desperately poor, with per capita incomes of $200 a year or less. *Leonard Silk, The New York Times, Sept. 22, 1977, p 43*

The turbulent years of the 1970s have witnessed an uneasy confrontation between the North and the South, and a largely unresolved debate on a whole series of specific economic problems. The truth of the matter is that the fortunes of the developed and developing countries are more and more intertwined in our increasingly interdependent world. *Robert S. McNamara, "Will We Face Up to the New Balance of Wealth?" Newsweek, Nov. 19, 1979, p 144*

[1976, so called because most of the less industrialized countries lie in the southern latitudes] Compare NORTH. See also THIRD WORLD, DEVELOPING.

spa, *n. U.S.* another name for HOT TUB.

Unless bathers get out of the hot tub and replace the lost fluid, they will feel tired. Sometimes they faint. . . . Perhaps lulled by the too warm water and a bit of alcohol, they probably fell asleep minutes after settling into the spa. *"Hot Tubs Can Be Too Hot," Time, June 18, 1979, p 62*

Because of their small size, spas do not require as much energy or money to keep the water hot. In California, approximately $10 to $15 is required to heat a spa for an entire month. *Mark Lundahl, "Hot Tubs Are Receiving Warm Welcome," Today (New York), Sept. 20, 1979, p B-1*

[1979, extended sense of the term for a mineral spring used for cures (OED 1626) or a watering place having such a spring (1777)]

space, *n. Slang.* a person's position, attitude, or identity.

"Lucas is a good friend to me," she was telling us now, back on the track. "I was part of his space. For a while there, I really felt like the favorite . . ." *Elizabeth Macklin, "Circle of Friends," The New Yorker, May 7, 1979, p 45*

Finally, I would note the metaphorical use of the word *space* itself, meaning, well, where a person's at. "Kate wasn't really high on chest hair . . . but Leonard had a lot going for him otherwise, and Kate liked the space he was

space colony

in." David Lodge, "Where It's At: California Language," in The State of the Language (edited by Leonard Michaels and Christopher Ricks), 1980, p 511

[1978] See PSYCHOBABBLE.

space colony, a self-contained, self-supporting colony for human inhabitants to be established on a large artificial satellite in space, especially at any of various points where the gravitational fields of the earth and the moon balance each other.

The space colonies, the scientists pointed out, would provide an alternative to earth if the earth's resources ever reach the point of depletion. *"Future Vacation Spot: The L5 Libration Point," The New York Times, May 19, 1974, Sec. 4, p 6*

A growing number of lawyers and others have been urging that more attention be paid to the specialized legal problems that are likely to arise with increasing activity in space, such as in the possibly quasi-independent domains of future "space colonies." *"Space Law: Not If But How," Science News, Dec. 17, 1977, p 409*

The fundamental ideas about space colonies that make them different from other talk about space is that they would involve large numbers of people in an essentially inside-out manufactured planet, and extraterrestrial materials would be used to build these environments. *Stewart Brand, quoted by Wade Greene in "The Selling of Soft Tech," Psychology Today, Nov. 1978, p 78*

[1974] See LAGRANGIAN POINT, MASS DRIVER.

spaced, *adj. U.S. and Canadian Slang.* **1** stupefied or dazed by a narcotic.

Quite a few people came from the West Coast, mostly from Big Sur, bringing scores of children with them to New York.... For years they had been living in the hills with little more than their own minds to look at, taking lots of psychedelics in vast, empty spaces. They were spaced. *Winifred Rosen, Harper's, June 1973, p 32*

2 stupefied; dazed.

[J.] Fred [Muggs, the chimpanzee] looked really spaced. Roy and Buddy . . . said he hadn't slept a wink all night. *"The Talk of the Town," The New Yorker, March 31, 1975, p 26*

[1973, shortened from *spaced-out* (1965)] Compare SPACY.

spacefaring, *adj.* traveling in outer space; engaged in or having to do with space travel.

My own view when I first heard about pulsars was that they were perfect interstellar navigation beacons, the sort of markers that an interstellar spacefaring society would want to place throughout the galaxy for time-and-space fixes for their voyages. *Carl Sagan, "The Starfolk," Science News, Nov. 3, 1973, p 283*

—*n.* the act or practice of traveling in outer space; space travel.

The final moment of truth comes 18 months later when orbital tests begin. The shape of things to come in US spacefaring for the next generation depends on the outcome of these trials. *"Spaceship Enterprise Prepares to Glide to Earth," New Scientist, July 21, 1977, p 142*

In spacefaring we have found, for the taking, new realms for the human imagination. In the exploration and exploitation of space, these new realms . . . may not be infinite. *John Noble Wilford, "The Spinoff from Space," The New York Times Magazine, Jan. 29, 1978, p 29*

[1963, patterned on *seafaring*]

436

spacefarer, *n.:* Such an asteroid-ark might one day encounter spacefarers of another civilisation, members of an intellectual brotherhood between the stars that at this moment exists without our knowledge. *Ian Ridpath, New Scientist, June 27, 1974, p 772*

spacelab, *n.* a scientific laboratory in space, especially **Spacelab** (an orbiting space facility transported by space shuttle in a project of the European Space Research Organization).

Spacelab is carried to orbit by the shuttle orbiter. When it reaches the desired orbit, the shuttle's cargo bay doors are opened, Spacelab is checked out and prepared for its planned series of experiments. The module is connected to the orbiter so that it is an extension of the somewhat confined cabin, and forms a working area for the Spacelab crew. *David Shapland, "Space Science Prepares to Take Off," New Scientist, Feb. 28, 1974, p 551*

A Spacelab will be flown on one of the first missions after the shuttle completes its six orbital trials, and on board will be scientists from both Europe and the United States. *John Noble Wilford, "Shuttling Into Space," The New York Times Magazine, Aug. 7, 1977, p 56*

[1969, short for *space laboratory*, patterned on *Skylab* (1966)]

space-plane ('speis,plein), *n.* a spacecraft equipped with rocket engines but built and flown like an airplane for re-entry and landing.

In another year or so we should have the inauguration of a new kind of vehicle for space travel, the space shuttle.... Designed to take off like a rocket, fly in orbit like a spacecraft, and return to a runway landing like a glider, these huge spaceplanes are expected to make the near reaches of space more accessible than ever before. *John Noble Wilford, "The Spinoff from Space," The New York Times Magazine, Jan. 29, 1978, p 26*

[1961]

spacer, *n.* a segment of DNA that serves to separate genes of a specific type from one another.

Chemists from Moscow University have succeeded in synthesising a nucleotide complementary to a definite part of a small bacteriophage ("a virus" that infects bacteria), a part regarded as a spacer. The spacer is short, occupying a space between two of the three genes contained in the virus, and has a known sequence of nucleotides. *Sarah White, "Soviet Biochemist," New Scientist, May 9, 1974, p 329*

For the production of a small molecule of RNA that resides in ribosomes ... there are no less than 20,000 identical genes separated from each other by an inert DNA "spacer." *"Genetic Engineers Are Assembling Gene Factory," New Scientist, April 1, 1976, p 4*

[1972] See REPETITIVE DNA.

Spaceship Earth or **spaceship earth,** the planet Earth and its inhabitants, conceived of as a spacecraft with its passengers who depend on its limited resources to survive.

What may happen between now and then is that the world will stop thinking in terms of superpowers and more in terms of Spaceship Earth. Perhaps the massive problem of cleaning up our seas and oceans will make the superpowers realize that the global political power game is being overtaken by events. *Giovanni Agnelli, "One Europe —Three Views," Newsweek, Jan. 1, 1973, p 23*

Without the weak force, the sun and other stars would have shut down long ago and "spaceship earth," if it existed at all, would be a cold and dreary place made up of pure hydrogen. *Sheldon L. Glashow, "The Hunting of the Quark," The New York Times Magazine, July 18, 1976, p 36*

We also demonstrate our respect for "spaceship earth," the concept of accepting that there are limitations on the world's resources and that their use is a matter of common international concern. The more enlightened oil exporters, by the way, endorse "spaceship earth" themselves. *Stephen S. Rosenfeld, "Energy and Power," The Manchester Guardian Weekly (The Washington Post section), May 8, 1977, p 17*

[1970, coined by R. Buckminster Fuller, born 1895, American designer and author, in his book (1969) *Operating Manual for Spaceship Earth*]

space warp, an imaginary rupture or discontinuity in interstellar space that facilitates travel between the stars and galaxies.

A writer who wants to use the entire galaxy as a backdrop for a story cannot simply ignore the theoretical speed limit [of light]; this would be an unforgivable *gaffe*. But hardly anyone will object if the writer makes use of a "space warp" . . . or "hyperspace"—shorthand expressions that refer to cosmic anomalies where the laws of Einsteinian physics do not apply. *Gerald Jonas, "Onward and Upward With the Arts: Science Fiction," The New Yorker, July 29, 1972, p 43*

Other people have suggested that there is a "hole in the sky" in the Triangle region, a place that one can enter but cannot leave. It may be some kind of fourth dimensional "space warp" that will some day return all the lost travelers and ships and planes. *Steven Moll, "The Bermuda Triangle," Encyclopedia Science Supplement (Grolier) 1975, p 138*

[1960] Compare TIME WARP. See also WORMHOLE.

spacy or **spacey,** *adj. Slang.* **1** dazed; stupefied; dreamy.

A flautist was performing before a couple of hundred students . . . some giving merely spacy attention, some with acute professional eyes on a colleague. *Herbert Gold, "Walt Disney Presents: Adventures in Collegeland!" The Atlantic, Nov. 1972, p 55*

The myopically spacey Timothy Bottoms plays such characters as the gentlest and least harmful of the representative Americans in "The White Dawn"; he's frazzled, out of it, ineffective. *Pauline Kael, "The Current Cinema," The New Yorker, Nov. 8, 1976, p 139*

2 unconventional; eccentric.

Fiona Dean is 21 and comes from Basingstoke and she does strangely unalarming spacey clothes which actually look forward rather than sideways or back. *Prudence Glynn, "Fashion," The Times (London), July 4, 1972, p 15*

Her [Elizabeth Ray's] former boy friends generally describe her as nutty, spacy, neurotic or dim. *"Congress: Indecent Exposure on Capitol Hill," Time, June 7, 1976, p 12*

The solution to what Quebec *really* wants, it turns out, is a unique relationship with the rest of Canada to be known as "sovereignty-association." Even in a country where one of the major parties insists on calling itself both Progressive and Conservative, this spacey concept ranks high in the lexicon of political absurdities. *Peter C. Newman, "Editorial," Maclean's, Nov. 13, 1978, p 3*

[1971, from *space* + *-y* (adj. suffix); influenced by *spaced-out* (1965) stupefied by narcotics] Compare TRIPPY.

spaciness, *n.:* I remember the sleepless epiphanies of

1948—everywhere in America brainconsciousness was waking up, from Times Square to the banks of Willamette River to Berkeley's groves of Academe: little Samadhis and appreciations of intimate spaciness that might later be explain'd and followed as the Crazy Wisdom of Rinzai Zen. *Allan Ginsberg, "The Great Rememberer," Saturday Review, Dec. 2, 1972, p 63*

spa·ti·o·per·cep·tu·al (ˌspei ʃiː ə pərˈsep tʃu əl), *adj.* relating to or involving perception of the spatial properties (position, direction, size, form, distance) of objects.

Both the left and right hemispheres of the brain have been found to have their own specialized forms of intellect. The left, which controls the right side of the body, is highly verbal and mathematical, performing with analytic, symbolic, computerlike logic. The right, by contrast . . . performs with a synthetic, spatio-perceptual, and mechanical kind of information processing that cannot yet be simulated by computers. *Roger W. Sperry, "Left-Brain, Right-Brain," Encyclopedia Science Supplement (Grolier) 1976, p 53*

[1973, from *spatio-* spatial + *perceptual*] Compare VISUOSPATIAL.

spear carrier, 1 a person of secondary or minor importance; an underling.

His closest lieutenants, not to mention assorted spear carriers, have gone to jail or are about to stand trial for the same set of offenses of which Nixon is accused. *"Reflections on the Resignation: The Quality of Mercy," National Review, Aug. 30, 1974, p 956*

Many of Sheehy's findings were indeed reported earlier by academics; where she does cite experts they tend to be introduced as mere spear carriers in her own pageant. *"Behavior: The Gripes of Academe," Time, May 10, 1976, p 69*

2 the most active and important leader of a movement, party, or the like; a standardbearer.

No one went so far as to say that Agnew, the spearcarrier of the fall campaign, was as good as dumped with Connally coming on board, but the sly winks and smiles suggested it. *Richard J. Whalen, Harper's, Aug. 1971, p 30*

In Wisconsin on the same day Representative Morris Udall, the "liberal-progressive" spear carrier, will have to win to stay in the race. *Fred Emery, "US Presidential Elections 1976," The Times (London), March 18, 1976, p 10*

[1960 for def. 1, figurative use originally in allusion to stage extras or members of a chorus holding spears in the background; 1967 for def. 2, figurative use probably alluding to a military leader holding his spear up to rally forces]

spearing, *n.* **1** the illegal ramming of an opponent with the helmet in American football.

New rules for high school football in Pennsylvania call for automatic ejection for spearing, but coaches and players say referees either rarely see spearing or else fail to enforce the rule. *Time, Nov. 20, 1978, p 8*

2 the illegal jabbing of an opponent with a hockey stick.

Leafs were shorthanded through a spearing penalty to Kent Douglas. . . . Hull responded by taking a pass from Balfour and scoring on a quick slap-shot. *Globe and Mail (Toronto), Jan. 21, 1963, p 16*

[1963]

spe·cies·ism (ˈspiː ʃiːzˌiz əm), *n.* discrimination practiced by people against certain species of animals;

437

the misuse or exploitation of various animal species by human beings.

The antivivisectionists accuse the scientists of "speciesism," which means that the scientists are indifferent to the suffering of any species but humankind. Animals should have the same rights as humans to avoid suffering, the animal lovers say. The scientists reply that the real issue is human suffering and that the net effect of antivivisectionist success will be to slow efforts to help people live longer and healthier. *Edward Edelson, "Animals: Pro-Science and Conscience," Daily News (New York), May 27, 1979, p 59*

[1975, coined by Richard D. Ryder, an American psychologist and author, from *species + -ism*, patterned on *racism, sexism*] See ANIMAL LIBERATION.

speciesist, *adj., n.:* Paradoxically, the public tends to be "speciesist" in its reaction to animal experimentation: For many people, a test is permissible when it inflicts pain on a "lower" animal like a hamster, but not when the victim is a dog. *Patricia Curtis, "New Debate Over Experimenting With Animals, The New York Times Magazine, Dec. 31, 1978, p 21*

Sexists and racists have been superseded by speciesists. The humane side of the question is put in *Animal's rights: a symposium,* edited by David Paterson and Richard D. Ryder (Centaur Press, £6.50). *"Review of Books," New Scientist, May 10, 1979, p 465*

speckle interferometry, *Optics, Astronomy.* a method of recording and measuring extremely small displacements of an object by analyzing a series of images obtained when speckles of light reflected from the target object are photographed and combined into a single image.

Displacements can be measured by making a double exposure of an object on a single sheet of film. One exposure is made before the object moves and one is made after it moves. The technique, which is known as speckle interferometry, can also be used to map local deformations in stressed mechanical parts such as the components of telescope mountings, seismometers, optical benches and similar devices. *C. L. Stong, "The Amateur Scientist," Scientific American, Feb. 1972, p 106*

Another important use of binary stars is to calibrate the distance scale of the Universe. All distances in astronomy are based on knowledge of distances to stars in our Galaxy. The use of speckle interferometry now makes it possible to observe binary stars with separations nearly 10 times smaller than any previously observed. That corresponds to an increase in the volume of available space and number of stars by a factor of 1000. *Simon Worden, New Scientist, April 27, 1978, p 239*

[1972]

speckle interferogram: Astronomers can now use speckle interferograms of stellar objects to reconstruct a complete image of a star system, even when this is complex and unsymmetrical. *"Star Behind the Twinkle," New Scientist, Dec. 21-28, 1978, p 932*

spec·ti·no·my·cin (ˌspek ti nəˈmai sən), *n.* an antibiotic derived from a species of actinomycete, used especially against certain strains of gonorrhea that resist treatment by penicillin.

The only cure so far for the new strain is spectinomycin, a drug four times as costly as penicillin and hence not widely applicable in the Far East. But health officials are also concerned that a spectinomycin-resistant strain may develop if the drug is overused. *Julianne Labreche, "Medicine," Maclean's, Feb. 7, 1977, p 54*

The resistant organisms are dealt with very readily by the relatively new antibiotic spectinomycin. This drug is upwards of 30 times more expensive than penicillin, and it is not yet available in large bulk. Affluent countries may find it inconvenient and a little expensive to include spectinomycin in the anti-gonorrhoea weaponry, but it is feasible to do so. *Roger Lewin, "The Natural History of Gonorrhoea," New Scientist, April 28, 1977, p 204*

[1964, from (*Streptomyces*) *spect*abilis, the actinomycete (soil bacterium) from which the drug is derived + *actino*mycete + *-mycin* fungal substance (ultimately from Greek *mýkēs* fungus)]

spec·trin (ˈspek trin), *n.* a protein found in the membranes of red blood cells.

The two heaviest polypeptide components, with molecular weights of 255,000 and 220,000, are collectively known as spectrin. (Vincent T. Marchesi of the Yale University School of Medicine chose the name because he first isolated the components from "ghosts," the membranes of red blood cells that have been chemically deprived of their hemoglobin.) Spectrin accounts for about a third of all the protein in the red-cell membrane. *Roderick A. Capaldi, "A Dynamic Model of Cell Membranes," Scientific American, March 1974, p 27*

[1968, from *spectre* (from Latin *spectrum*) + *-in*]

spec·tro·he·li·om·e·ter (ˌspek trouˌhi: liːˈɑm ə tər), *n.* an instrument which measures the wavelengths of spectra from the sun.

The spectroheliometer showed that they [bright points, many as big as the earth] extended up from the chromosphere, where the temperature averages about ten thousand degrees, into the transition region between the chromosphere and the corona, where the temperature averages around seven hundred thousand degrees. *Henry S. F. Cooper, Jr., "A Reporter at Large: Life in a Space Station—II," The New Yorker, Sept. 6, 1976, p 40*

[1973, probably from *spectro*scope and *heliometer*]

speed bump, a low ridge of asphalt laid across a road to slow down vehicular traffic in a residential area or near a school.

Anyone who has driven on the Hackley Campus knows that our roads are narrow. Speed bumps have been put in at various places around the Campus to help limit speed. *News From Hackley (Tarrytown, N.Y.), Nov. 1977, p 3*

[1975]

sperm bank, a place for the storage of sperm to be used in artificial insemination.

Today, sperm banks have virtually revolutionized A.I.D. [Artificial Insemination by Donor] practice. Since semen can be kept frozen for years without loss of genetic quality, one of the clumsier aspects of A.I.D.—the synchronizing of donor-recipient appointments—has been eliminated. *Lillian Atallah, "Report from a Test-Tube Baby," The New York Times Magazine, April 18, 1976, p 17*

[1971, patterned on the older term *semen bank*] Compare EJACULATORIUM.

sperm banking: Biologist Mark Lappé of the Institute of Society, Ethics and Life Sciences in Hastings-on-Hudson, New York, is disturbed that commercial outfits are the first to introduce large-scale sperm banking. If it is worthwhile, he says, the government should be taking the lead. *Constance Holden, "Sperm Banks Multiply as Vasectomies Gain Popularity," Science, April 7, 1972, p 32*

spike, *v.t., v.i.* to slam the ball forcefully to the ground after a play in American football, especially after scoring a touchdown.

Says Assistant Coach Gary Bruch: "We're out there five days a week trying to teach high school kids to be good sports, working on the right ways to tackle and block. Then they go home and watch television, and what do they see? Pro players dancing in the end zone and spiking the ball to humiliate opponents, spearing, taking cheap shots." *Time, Nov. 20, 1978, p 8*

[1978, transferred sense of the volleyball term meaning to slam (the ball) into the opponents' court at a sharp, downward angle]

spin, *v.t., v.i.* **spin down** or **spin up,** *Astronomy.* (of a star, planet, etc.) to decrease or increase in rotation.

There's an unusual pulsar that spins extremely slowly. . . . This pulsar is spinning down so slowly that when the effects of its motion across the sky on its apparent (to us) spin rate are considered, it may actually be spinning up from the point of view of someone riding along with it. "*Physical Sciences: A Slow Pulsar and Cosmology," Science News, Oct. 30, 1976, p 280*

The gist of their thesis is that hydrodynamical coupling between the outer layers of the Sun and its core would pretty soon "spin down" the core to the same rate as the exterior—or the latter would alternatively be "spun up" to match the former. *New Scientist, June 29, 1967, p 751*

[1967; see SPIN-DOWN, SPIN-UP]

spin-down, *n.* **1** a decrease in the rotation of a star, planet, etc.

The D pulsars may not be so old as they appear; they may have started with small magnetic fields and thus suffered less spin-down from magnetic breaking. "*Classifying Pulsars," Science News, July 24, 1971, p 62*

Compare SPIN-UP. See also GLITCH.

2 angular momentum of an elementary particle in a direction opposite to that of spin-up.

In another "hybrid" technique, beta-ray spectroscopy has been combined with Mössbauer-effect spectroscopy to study the magnetic hyperfine field acting on an iron nucleus. With this technique, it is possible to calculate the difference between the spin-up and spin-down populations in each electron shell. *R. H. Herber, "Mössbauer Effect," McGraw-Hill Yearbook of Science and Technology 1973, p 287*

[1969 for def. 1; 1965 for def. 2]

spin-flip, *n.* a reversal in the direction of the spin of a nuclear particle or particles. *Often used attributively.*

Neutral hydrogen atoms emit 21-cm radiation by a somewhat unusual "spin-flip" process in which the spins of the hydrogen nucleus and its attendant electron switch from being parallel to antiparallel. *Tom Phillips and Michael Rowan-Robinson, "Molecules Among the Stars," New Scientist, Jan. 22, 1976, p 170*

[1971]

spin-flip laser, a laser in which the spin-flip of electrons is used to produce a highly monochromatic output.

In the spin-flip laser a spin resonance in a semiconductor—indium antimonide, for example—is used to achieve stimulated emission that can be tuned over a limited frequency range by changing an external magnetic field. *William D. Metz, "Physics With Lasers: High Resolution Coming of Age," Science, Feb. 18, 1972, p 740*

[1971]

spin-up, *n.* **1** an increase in the rotation of a star, planet, etc.

As these models accrete mass from outside they actually spin faster, explaining the otherwise very embarrassing observation that both Cen X-3 and Her X-1 are undergoing spin-up. "*Monitor: Are X-Ray Sources White Dwarf Stars?" New Scientist, Aug. 30, 1973, p 486*

Compare SPIN-DOWN. See also GLITCH.

2 angular momentum of an elementary particle in a direction opposite to that of spin-down.

The exchange field causes the 3d electrons to be split into two energy bands depending on spin: the spin-down band comes out with slightly higher upper and lower limits than the spin-up band. *New Scientist, Aug. 17, 1978, p 469*

[1969 for def. 1; 1965 for def. 2]

spi·ro·plas·ma (ˌspaɪ rəˈplæz mə), *n.* any of a group of microorganisms having a spiral shape and lacking a cell wall.

The organisms associated with corn stunt disease, and subsequently those associated with stubborn disease of citrus, have been shown to be unusual helical motile microorganisms now termed spiroplasmas. *Robert E. Davis, "Plant Disease," McGraw-Hill Yearbook of Science and Technology 1975, p 325*

A third possible spiroplasma has been found in natural populations of four closely related species of *Drosophila.* This agent, termed the sex ratio organism (SRO), is inherited maternally and associated with the absence of males in the progeny of infected females. *Joseph G. Tully, Bethesda, Md., "Letters to Nature," Nature, Jan. 15, 1976, p 118*

[1973, from New Latin, from *spiro-* coil (as in *spirochete*) + *plasma* protoplasm]

splanch (splæntʃ), *n. U.S.* a house that combines features of split-level and ranch type architecture.

He is supervising the construction of Carriage House of Roslyn. It is a suburban subdivision of 104 colonials, ranches and "splanches," a splanch being a cross between a split-level and a ranch house. All 104 houses were spoken for within weeks of the opening of the models last March. *The New York Times, Jan. 20, 1978, p A15*

[1961, from *spl*it-level + *r*anch]

splib (splib or, *occasionally*, spliv), *n. U.S. Slang.* a black person, especially a male.

Any other terms such as 'boy,' 'spook,' 'splib,' 'negro,' 'Uncle Tom,' 'nigra,' 'nigger,' or 'colored' carry connotations of prejudice and must be avoided. *Flora Lewis, The Atlantic, Jan. 1970, p 38*

"Boot" . . . is often used as a nickname by blacks, and as a term which, like "blood," "brother," or "splib," refers to blacks in general. *Thomas Kochman, "The Kinetic Element in Black Idiom," In Rappin' and Stylin' Out, 1972, p 169*

[1968, of unknown origin]

splice, *v.t. Molecular Biology.* **1** to join (a gene or DNA fragment of one organism) to that of another; recombine (strands of DNA molecules) from different organisms to form new genetic combinations.

The controversial research in question is a class of experiments that . . . include splicing the genes of a virus or bacteria to partially purified DNA from mammals or birds or from lower animals known to produce potent toxins or pathogens. *Science News, Jan. 29, 1977, p 70*

Under favorable conditions, the resulting fragment of foreign DNA may be incorporated, or "spliced," into the gap in the plasmid, closing the circle to create a hybrid molecule. Then, after the linkage is sealed by another enzyme, called DNA ligase, the modified plasmid is introduced into a host cell, such as *Escherichia coli*, a common bacterium, where it reproduces itself. *Edwin S. Weaver, "Biochemistry," 1978 Collier's Encyclopedia Year Book (1977), p 154*

2 to insert or transplant (a new or altered gene or DNA fragment obtained by the above means) into an organism such as a bacterium, to introduce a new character or trait into the host.

One valuable product has already resulted from the work: human insulin, manufactured by splicing fragments of DNA that manufacture the hormone in humans into an intestinal bacterium, causing it to start producing insulin on its own. *"The Key Breakthrough," Newsweek, June 4, 1979, p 64*

[1977] Compare ANNEAL. See also RECOMBINANT DNA RESEARCH.

split-brain, *adj.* of, relating to, or subjected to the surgical separation of the hemispheres of the brain.

No one who has watched a split-brain patient performing complex visual discrimination and recognition tasks processed wholly by the right hemisphere could possibly doubt the presence of consciousness in the sense in which the term is ordinarily used. *O. L. Zangwill, Review of "The Understanding of the Brain" by John C. Eccles, Nature, Jan. 11, 1974, p 121*

The so-called split-brain operations . . . involved severing a bit of brain tissue, known as the corpus callosum, that serves as the principal direct link between the left and the right cerebral hemispheres. After this radical surgery, the patients had fewer epileptic seizures. *"The Talk of the Town," The New Yorker, Nov. 8, 1976, p 36*

[1963] Compare LEFT-BRAIN, RIGHT-BRAIN.

split end, an offensive player in American football who is separated a few yards from either end of the line of scrimmage so that he can immediately run downfield to catch passes.

Rather, a Michigan split end, carried the ball on an end around three times, once for a touchdown, in a 21-6 overrunning of Northwestern last month. *"Football," The New Yorker, Oct. 16, 1971, p 166*

[1965]

Spod·o·sol ('spɑd ə,sɔ:l), *n.* (in U.S. soil taxonomy) any of a group of moist forest soils characterized by an ash-gray leached surface layer and an iron-rich layer beneath it.

The remaining broad groups of soils, the Alfisols, Entisols, Spodosols, and many Inceptisols, fall between the two extremes, both in nutrient losses during formation and in fertility levels. Mountainous regions, with their great variety of soils, also belong to this intermediate group. Collectively these occupy about 35% of the land surface. *Roy W. Simonson, "Soil," McGraw-Hill Yearbook of Science and Technology 1972, p 374*

[1967, from Greek *spodós* ashes + English *-sol* (from Latin *solum* soil)] Compare ARIDISOL, HISTOSOL, MOLLISOL, OXISOL, ULTISOL, VERTISOL.

spokesperson, *n.* a person who speaks for another or others; a spokesman or spokeswoman.

That leaves as the crucial qualities required of a new president the humane gifts — sensitivity, awareness, appreciation, flexibility — that make for an effective spokesperson for higher education but have no practical consequence for the day-to-day running of an institution. *Paul A. Lacey, "Casting About for a President," Science, March 28, 1975, p 1153*

The palace spokesperson immediately telephoned the man who should know about such things. He is Major General Peter Gillett, the secretary of the Central Chancery of the Order of Knighthood. He didn't immediately know. *Gareth Parry, The Manchester Guardian Weekly, Jan. 11, 1976, p 20*

[1972, from *spokes*man (OED *a*1540) or *spokes*woman (OED 1654) + -PERSON]

▶ For the plural, the form *spokespeople* also occurs, as in the following quotations:

As the Boston Tea Party of December 16, 1773 was re-enacted . . . spokespeople for the Indians showed up to announce that the re-enactment would be degrading to Indians. *"The Week," National Review, Jan. 18, 1974, p 69*

Opening my daily post has become marginally less predictable than in the past, including as it now does from time to time collages of swastikas and the bizarre maunderings of those (usually anonymous), who, if they are, as they would claim, spokespeople for the "white British race" would leave one in grave doubts for the collective sanity of that august body. *Steven Rose, "Minds Race," New Scientist, Dec. 7, 1978, p 791*

spork, *n. U.S.* a plastic spoon with blunt tines at the tip that can be used as a fork.

To eat the food, they frequently are crammed on benches at narrow tables as they try to cut meat, scoop up soup or wind up spaghetti with a spork. *Mimi Sheraton, "Lunches for Pupils Given Poor Marks," The New York Times, May 19, 1976, p 1*

[1976, blend of *spoon* and *fork*]

spo·ro·pol·len·in (,spɔr ə'pɑl ə nin), *n.* a durable substance that forms the outer wall of pollen grains.

There is no evidence of a vast and long lasting primitive soup, they say. . . . The only theory which at present fits the evidence is an extraterrestrial origin for life. They strongly argue for the value of analysis of sporopollenin, an insoluble organic material in the outer wall of pollen grains and related microspheres. Sporopollenin is superior as a biological marker and they use analysis to conclude in favour of the biogenic nature of constituents of meteorites. *New Scientist, Feb. 21, 1974, p 498*

[1968, from *sporo-* spore + *pollen* + -*in*]

sports medicine, a branch of medicine dealing with the treatment and prevention of injuries or illnesses that result from engaging in sports.

Dr. Sheehan, a cardiologist and internist in Red Bank, New Jersey, is medical editor for *Runner's World* magazine and a leading authority on sports medicine. *George Leonard, "Why Johnny Can't Run," The Atlantic, Aug. 1975, p 58*

Every coach who graduates from the Leipzig Institute . . . has been through a five-semester sports medicine course that begins with chemistry and physics, goes on to biomechanics and ends with an introduction to practical sports medicine. *Craig R. Whitney, "Sports Medicine Shares in*

East German Success," The New York Times, Dec. 22, 1976, p 24

[1972] See GLASS ARM, HOLLOW FOOT, SURFER'S KNOB, TENNIS TOE.

spray-paint, *v.t.* to paint with a spray can or spray gun.

Greyhound will no longer charter buses for Osmond travel since fans spray-paint love notes on the buses. *Newsweek, Sept. 3, 1973, p 89*

A profusion of abandoned Greek villages remain to be populated, each house with its special number spray-painted on the front ready to receive Turkish Cypriots from the south. *Tony Rocca, The Sunday Times (London), April 20, 1975, p 9*

[1966]

spread, *n. U.S. and Canadian.* the number of points by which a stronger team may be expected to defeat a weaker team, used in betting, especially on football games.

How does a bookie make money? He charges about 10% for handling the bets, a fee called "vigorish." And he manipulates the spread. Let us say Minnesota Vikings are favored by eight points over Green Bay Packers. If too much money is bet on Minnesota, the spread is increased to nine points, or 10 points, whatever it takes to achieve a balance. *Martin O'Malley, Maclean's, Oct. 3, 1977, p 61*

[1967, shortened from the earlier (1953) *point spread*] Compare LINE.

spring roll, *Especially British.* a Chinese egg roll.

The large Chinese business population has brought to Bangkok innumerable Chinese restaurants catering for all tastes, from a spring roll at 20 baht to food more tempered to assumptions about tourists' palates. *"Thai for Two," The Times (London), Feb. 14, 1976, p 10*

[1967]

spy satellite, an artificial satellite equipped with cameras and electronic sensing devices for ground surveillance.

Costs would be high if western Europe tried to compete with the super powers, who launch spy satellites at the rate of about 30 a week during a crisis, but a far smaller number could conceivably provide all the information needed. *Ron Brown, "Comment: A European Spy in the Sky?" New Scientist, Nov. 1, 1973, p 315*

The Air Force . . . funds the overhead-reconnaissance program—mostly spy satellites—for the entire U.S. intelligence community. *"Trying to Expose the CIA," Time, April 22, 1974, p 22*

[1960] See EYE-IN-THE-SKY.

s quark, short for STRANGE QUARK.

In the quark model these particles are distinguished by the presence of an s quark or an s̄ antiquark, which respectively carry strangeness quantum numbers of −1 and +1; the other quarks have zero strangeness. *Roy F. Schwitters, "Fundamental Particles with Charm," Scientific American, Oct. 1977, p 58*

[1976]

squid, *n.* a very sensitive device for measuring weak magnetic fields, typically consisting of a thin film of superconducting niobium placed around a small quartz rod. Exposure to a magnetic field sets up a circulating current in the device.

Squids are proving useful in a number of studies where sensitivity to minute magnetic fields can yield information. Medicine, psychology, geophysics and metrology are especially active right now and physicists representative of those working in these fields were invited to discuss squids at the recent meeting of the American Physical Society in Chicago. *Science News, April 9, 1977, p 234*

[1976, acronym for *superconducting quantum interference device*]

Sri Lan·kan ('sri:'la:ŋ kən), **1** a native or inhabitant of the Republic of Sri Lanka, the official name of Ceylon since 1972.

"A Sri Lankan works only every other day," complained Prime Minister Ranasinghe Premadasa recently, noting that between the abundance of Buddhist holidays and liberal trade-union work regulations, Sri Lankans work an average of only 178 days per year. *High Times, Jan. 1979, p 111*

2 of or having to do with Sri Lanka.

China . . . agreed to export 200,000 tons of rice in exchange for 67,000 tons of Sri Lankan rubber. *Norman D. Palmer, "Sri Lanka (Ceylon)," The Americana Annual 1977, p 481*

[1974, from Pali *Sri*, an honorary prefix, and *Lanka* island, from Singhalese *laka* + English *-an*]

SRO, abbreviation of *sex-ratio organism*, a microorganism, believed to be a spiroplasma, that infects female fruit flies and causes the death of their male offspring.

Most attempts to understand why only the males die have dealt with manipulations of the chromosomes of flies carrying and transmitting the SRO. Hemolymph containing SROs was injected into females of a number of special stocks of *D. melanogaster. David L. Williamson, "Sex determination," McGraw-Hill Yearbook of Science and Technology 1975, p 361*

[1975]

S.R.O. hotel, *U.S.* a welfare hotel for single occupants.

Peter Koenig made it appear that S.R.O. hotels are almost the only facilities available to chronic mental patients. There are others. One such facility is the adult foster home, which offers services and supervision for dependent adults who cannot manage alone but do not require skilled care. *Ethel Sheffer, New York, in a Letter to the Editor, The New York Times Magazine, July 2, 1978, p 39*

[1967, *S.R.O.* abbreviation of *single-room occupancy*]

SSBN, a naval designation for a nuclear-powered submarine capable of launching ballistic missiles.

The Navy provided the strategic deterrent of four SSBNs, each with 16 Polaris A-3 missiles with MRV, under independent British control. *Robin J. Ranger, "Defense: United Kingdom," Britannica Book of the Year 1976, p 238*

[1972, from SS (symbol for *submarine*), *B*allistic, *N*uclear] See SLBM.

S sleep, *n.* short for SYNCHRONIZED SLEEP.

Each sleeper spends about three-fourths of each cycle in S sleep (the S standing for synchronized delta waves, with from one to four peaks per second, that mark the deepest stages of this form) and the rest of the cycle in "paradoxical" D sleep. *Philip Morrison, "Books," Review of "The*

441

Functions of Sleep" by Ernest L. Hartmann, Scientific American, May 1974, p 133

[1974] Compare D SLEEP.

SSPE, abbreviation of *subacute sclerosing panencephalitis,* a chronic brain disease chiefly affecting children, thought to be caused by the measles virus or by an unknown variety of slow virus (a virus with a long period of latency).

SSPE causes stiffness, jerkiness, mental deterioration and death in young people. *"Biomedical Sciences: Polio Vaccine and Slow Virus Diseases," Science News, Nov. 3, 1973, p 286*

In contrast to kuru and CJD [Creutzfeldt-Jakob disease], SSPE raises some different problems. Measles is a common virus which most of us encounter in childhood. SSPE is a rare disease and yet the same virus seems to be involved. Here is a fascinating example of a virus undergoing two quite different types of interaction in the same host. *Richard Kimberlin, "Viral Origins for Chronic Brain Disease," New Scientist, Nov. 18, 1976, p 382*

[1968] See SLOW INFECTION.

Sta·bex ('stei͵beks), *n.* a system by which the European Economic Community compensates for any drop in the export earnings of developing countries in Africa, the Caribbean, and the Pacific.

On Stabex—the export stabilising mechanism, Ouko said the ACP had proposed that an additional 60 commodities be brought under the scheme. *The Weekly Review (Nairobi), July 27, 1979, p 21*

[1976, from *stabilize* + *exports*]

sta·ple·punc·ture ('stei pəl͵pəŋk t∫ər), *n.* a form of acupuncture in which small metal pieces are inserted into parts of the outer ear to enable a person to twist them at will when having pain, discomfort, etc.

The other fat fad to incur the displeasure of the A.M.A. is "staplepuncture," which is based on the theory—so far unconfirmed—that there are "obesity nerve endings" in the ear. Doctors who practice the art place surgical staples in their patients' ears and instruct them to wiggle the metal clips with their fingers whenever they feel like cheating on the 400-calorie-per-day diet that accompanies the treatment. *"Fat Faddists, Beware," Time, Dec. 16, 1974, p 106*

[1974] Compare ELECTROACUPUNCTURE.

stargaze, *v.i.* to watch famous actors or other celebrities as a fan does.

He [Christopher Porterfield] and his roommate, Dick Cavett, frequently got backstage at the Shubert Theater to stargaze at close range. "In those days," says Porterfield, "I regarded performers with a mixture of fascination and awe. Since then I've become more fascinated and less awed." *Ralph P. Davidson, Time, Sept. 25, 1972, p 1*

[1970, extended from the original meanings (1600's): (1) to study the stars; (2) to daydream]

stargazer, *n.:* Stargazers could expect to see Jeanne Moreau, Jack Nicholson, Jane Fonda, Richard Burton and Marlon Brando, slated to close the festival with "Last Tango in Paris," directed by Italy's brilliant Bernardo Bertolucci. *Charles Michener, "At the New York Movie Orgy," Newsweek, Oct. 9, 1972, p 91*

stargazing, *n.:* Nureyev and Bruhn danced the male lead roles. Although critical reception was generally poor, *Raymonda* offered a fine opportunity for stargazing. *Nancy*

Goldner, "Dancing," The 1976 World Book Year Book, p 270

sta·ta·ry ('stei tə ri:), *adj.* (of army ants or a phase of their behavior) characterized by or coming to a standstill; stationary.

Schneirla was the first to demonstrate that army ants have a functional cycle composed of alternating nomadic and statary phases. During the nomadic phase colonies have a brood of larvae that usually develop into worker ants, and the colonies emigrate nightly for about two weeks. When the larvae spin cocoons, the colony enters the statary phase, in which it stays in one site for about three weeks and a new brood of eggs is laid. *Carl W. Rettenmeyer, "Social Insects," Review of "Army Ants: A Study in Social Organization" by T. C. Schneirla and Howard R. Topoff, Science, Jan. 28, 1972, p 402*

[1972, from Latin *statārius,* from *stāre* to stand]

▶ The OED records use of this term between 1581 and 1650 in the sense of "standing fast or firm; established; fixed." The revived or reborrowed term is so far restricted to the meaning shown above.

State of the State message, *U.S.* an annual speech by a governor to the state legislature, reviewing the state's development in the past year and outlining programs for the coming year.

Only 4 of the 39 governors who gave State of the State messages requested increases in sales or income taxes, the two major tax sources for the states. *Robert H. Weber, "State Government," The 1973 World Book Year Book, p 511*

[1967, patterned on the yearly U.S. Presidential *State of the Union message*]

State of the World message, *U.S.* a report on American foreign policy sent by the President to Congress.

In his State of the World Message, issued just prior to his China trip, the President suggested that Taipei and Peking negotiate their differences. *James Chace, "The Five-Power World of Richard Nixon," The New York Times Magazine, Feb. 20, 1972, p 47*

[1970, originally a report by President Nixon in February 1970, and afterward applied to similar reports]

statesperson, *n.* a statesman or stateswoman.

Much of the credit for last year's record goes to Indian statesperson Indira Gandhi, who wearied of democracy and is now dabbling in dictatorship. *"The Week," National Review, Jan. 23, 1976, p 17*

Ms Previn is not a political animal or, at least, not any more. She says she does not understand the very idea of someone being a politician. "I mean, to want to be a statesman, a statesperson, terrific. But a politician?" *"Rock-a-bye Baby," The Manchester Guardian Weekly, May 29, 1977, p 21*

[1976] ▶ The term is usually applied to a woman. See -PERSON.

static, *n. U.S. Informal.* noisy criticism; loud arguments.

This is the most difficult decision that I have ever had to make and I have no misconceptions as to the pain it is going to cause others and . . . the static I am going to receive. *James L. Buckley, Press Conference (March 19), National Review, April 12, 1974, p 417*

But the blond high jumper [Dwight Stones] fell short of setting yet another world mark. "I'm going to get a lot of static for this," he said after the meet. *Peter Bonventre and Vern E. Smith, "Sports: The High and Mighty," Newsweek, March 10, 1975, p 69*

[1967, probably extended from the earlier (1940's) slang sense "unpleasant interference in conversation, noisy chatter"]

status offender, *U.S.* a child or adolescent who, although not a delinquent, is placed under court jurisdiction because of habitual truancy, willful disobedience, and the like.

PINS are called status offenders because it is their state of being—their alleged "incorrigibility" or "unruliness," rather than any criminal offense—that brings them before the courts. Definitions of status offenders vary from state to state . . . *Lis Harris, "A Reporter at Large: Persons in Need of Supervision," The New Yorker, Aug. 14, 1978, p 56*

[1975]

status offense: The San Francisco law lost most of its muscle last year when California decriminalized all so-called status offenses—those acts, such as truancy, which would not be violations if committed by adults. *The New York Times, Jan. 6, 1978, p B6*

steady-state, *adj.* relatively stable; generally free from fluctuations.

X-ray still pictures of steady-state sounds, principally vowels, have been used for many years. *Timothy S. Smith, Language, March 1971, p 237*

A redistribution of wealth and a shorter working week would be sensible first steps in the replacement of growth economics by the steady state economics which is more realistic if the environment is to be considered. *Mark Burton, London, "Redundant Economics," in a Letter to the Editor, New Scientist, Feb. 3, 1972, p 292*

[1971, transferred sense of the term used in physics to describe a system that is essentially constant]

steamy, *n. U.S. Slang.* a pornographic motion picture.

The Rockne Theater aroused such ire when it began showing steamies that local matrons picketed in protest last summer. *"American Notes: What Price G?" Time, Jan. 24, 1972, p 8*

[1972, noun use of the adjective (in the sense of "sensual, erotic")]

steering, *n. U.S.* a practice in which real-estate agents steer or direct black clients to black or integrated communities without informing them of dwellings available for sale or rent in white communities.

Presidential candidate Jimmy Carter's stand on "ethnic purity" of urban neighborhoods, to "maintain the homogeneity of neighborhoods if they have been established that way," is clear support for residential "steering" which is now being tested in the courts. *Samuel M. Convissor, South Orange, N.J., "On Ethnic Purity," in a Letter to the Editor, The New York Times, April 13, 1976, p 32*

The Supreme Court ruled 7-2 Tuesday that a village and residents of a target area within it have the right to sue realtors for alleged "steering" of home buyers on the basis of race. *"High Court Rules on Racial 'Steering'," The Christian Science Monitor, April 18, 1979, p 2*

[1976] Compare REDLINING.

STEM (stem), *n.* acronym for *scanning transmission electron microscope,* an electron microscope that combines features of the scanning electron microscope (such as three-dimensional detail) with features of the transmission electron microscope (such as high-resolution power).

Albert Crewe and Michael Isaacson of the University of Chicago, while attempting to view biomolecular structures with a very-high-resolution STEM built in their own laboratory, instead obtained the first motion pictures of individual atoms. *Arthur L. Robinson, "Physical Chemistry," 1978 Britannica Yearbook of Science and the Future, p 277*

[1972]

Step·in·fetch·it ('step,ən'fetʃ,it), *n.* or **Stepin Fetchit,** *U.S. and Canadian.* a stereotype of a shuffling, fawning black servant; *by extension,* any servile black man. *Often used attributively.*

Mike Evans, who plays the young black neighbor Lionel, is obliged by his role to affect an occasional Stepinfetchit manner. It is the con act blacks sometimes employ to get what they want from whites. *Arnold Hano, "Can Archie Bunker Give Bigotry a Bad Name?" The New York Times Magazine, March 12, 1972, p 125*

The driver, from a small town outside Houston, though white, seemed to have taken a course at the Stepin Fetchit school of etiquette. No matter what I said, or asked, his answer was the same: "Yassuh." *Jack Ludwig, Maclean's, March 1974, p 70*

[1970, from *Stepin Fetchit,* stage name of a black American vaudeville actor who was typecast in the role of a shuffling, grinning, eye-rolling character in Hollywood films of the 1930's and 1940's, probably adopted from *Step-an'-fetch-it,* a nickname for any slow or lazy person]

sterile, *adj. U.S.* cleared for security purposes; screened to prevent access by enemy agents, etc.

The CIA had provided the plumbers with false identity papers, disguises, . . . two "safehouses" and a "sterile" telephone in Washington (permitting them to operate without being bugged or observed by rival spies from other government agencies). *Barry Farrell, Harper's, Oct. 1973, p 79*

The so-called sterile concourse—the long airport corridor that only ticketed, searched travelers may enter—means that a passenger must be searched each time he changes planes and concourses. *"Travel: What Price Security?" Newsweek, May 7, 1973, p 88*

[1973] See STERILIZE.

sterilize, *v.t. U.S.* to clear for security purposes, especially by omitting any potentially damaging material from a government document; render harmless.

Only a select few persons who have been specially cleared, and who live under special controls, will have access to this information, and before passing it on to other officials who must make use of it they will "sterilize" it so that it contains only what is needed for the legitimate purposes at hand, and no more. *Niles Copeland, "Dirty Tricks—Part II: There's a CIA in Your Future," National Review, Oct. 26, 1973, p 1170*

Sterilize—To remove identification marks from material to be used in clandestine operations. *"'Black-Bag Jobs' Among Spy Terms Defined in Report," The New York Times, April 27, 1976, p 26*

[1973]

ste·roi·do·gen·e·sis (stə,rɔi də'dʒen ə sis), *n*. the formation of steroids in the body.

The results suggest that previous evidence for direct involvement of vitamin A in steroidogenesis may have been due to the production of a secondary deficiency, a chronic scorbutic condition. *Kenneth A. Gruber, et al., "Reports: Vitamin A: Not Required for Adrenal Steroidogenesis in Rats," Science, Feb. 6, 1976, p 472*

[1972, from *steroid* + connecting *-o-* + *genesis*]

steroidogenic, *adj.*: These mucopolypeptide gonadotropins . . . stimulate the formation of the enzyme adenyl cyclase within the cell, which in turn converts ATP to cyclic AMP and activates steroidogenic enzymes. *A. E. Kellie, "Estrogen," McGraw-Hill Yearbook of Science and Technology 1973, p 185*

stew (stu:), *n. U.S. Informal.* an airplane steward or stewardess.

Before moving on to airline desk jobs, however, male stews are learning to appreciate the occupational hazards of the job-long flights: screaming babies, jet lag and lecherous passengers. *"Coffee, Tea or He," Newsweek, March 19, 1973, p 65*

[Al] Dellentash helps his stews aboard. Their outfits vary from shorts to long gowns, but pilot and co-pilot always wear uniforms. *Picture legend, People Weekly, Oct. 9, 1978, p 8*

[1973, by shortening]

stick, *v.t.* to hit or drive with a hockey stick.

After a scoreless first period, Dennis Hull, Yvan Cournoyer and Paul Henderson sticked home shots that wiped out a 1-0 Russian lead. *Bo Shembechler, "In Brief: . . . Embattled Canadians Outskate Russians," The Courier-Journal (Lexington, Ky.), Sept. 25, 1972, p B7*

[1972, verb use of the noun; past tense *sticked* parallels baseball use of *flied* ("hit a fly")]

Stickey or **Stickie,** *n.* a nickname for a member of the official Irish Republican Army. See the first quotation for details.

"Stickeys" (as they are disparagingly tagged by the Provisional wing because of the sticky backs of their Easter seals) maintain close ties with the minor-league Irish Communist party. *Gail Sheehy, "Stickeys and Provos," The New York Times Magazine, June 11, 1972, p 64*

Instead of "cops and robbers," Ardoyne children play "Martin Meehan and the soldiers."

"Martin was our leadership—who else could have got the clubs stopping selling drinks at half eleven? Who'll stop the boys fighting with the stickies?" *Victoria Brittain, The Times (London), Aug. 21, 1972, p 10*

[1972]

stick-slip, *Geology.* —*n.* the sudden, rapid displacement of rock along a fracture line, as distinguished from gradual, stable sliding. *Often used attributively.*

Theoretical and experimental work on the mechanisms of generation of earthquakes indicate that the presence of hot water along a rock fracture system tends to cause rock to move by creep and not by the process known as stickslip, which results in seismic shocks. *Robert W. Rex, "Power from the Earth," 1975 Britannica Yearbook of Science and the Future (1974), p 111*

—*v.i.* to undergo stick-slip.

The Moon is aseismic because its temperature-pressure

curve lies in the . . . field where rock fails by stable sliding rather than by stick-slipping. *L. Thomsen, Binghamton N.Y., "Letters to Nature: Implications of Lunar Aseismicity," Nature, Nov. 10, 1972, p 94*

[1971, so called from the intermittent slipping motion of the rock]

sticky ends, ends of single strands of DNA molecules that complement each other in the sequence of their nucleotides and can be linked up or reconnected in the presence of the enzyme ligase. Restriction enzymes are used to produce sticky ends.

Lambda DNA is a double helix throughout most of its length, but one end of each polynucleotide chain extends for 12 nucleotides beyond the double helix. These two single-strand chains are complementary to each other and are called "sticky ends." *Allan M. Campbell, "How Viruses Insert Their DNA into the DNA of the Host Cell," Scientific American, Dec. 1976, p 109*

The important point—discovered by Janet Mertz and Ronald Davis at Stanford University—is that these tiny DNA fragments are not snipped cleanly, smoothly, but that they have little single-strand tails left that are now referred to as "sticky ends."

Sticky ends, indeed, have turned out to be of utmost importance for genetic engineering research. Clever biochemists now use them as connectors for tying foreign bits of DNA to other pieces of DNA, to other genes. This would resemble the way railroad cars are assembled into a long line to make up a whole train. *Robert Cooke, Improving on Nature, 1977, p 50*

[1973] See RECOMBINANT DNA RESEARCH.

stim·o·ceiv·er ('stim ou,si: vər), *n.* a miniaturized radio device implanted in the scalp which through electrodes stimulates specific areas of the brain and transmits information from the brain to an outside receiver for study.

She was referred to Dr. Vernon Mark and his colleagues, who theorized that the trouble lay in epileptic disturbances of her amygdala, the "emotional thermostat of the brain." To prove their hypothesis, the neurosurgeons sought to induce a seizure artificially, using a stimoceiver, a remote-control device for sending and receiving electrical impulses. *"The Case of Julia: A Study in Switched-On Violence," 1973 Collier's Encyclopedia Year Book (1972), p 79*

[1967, from *stimu*late + connecting *-o-* + re*ceiver*] Compare ESB, PACEMAKER.

stish·ov·ite ('stiʃ ə,vait), *n.* an extremely dense form of quartz produced under very high pressure (as by the impact of a meteorite). *Formula:* SiO_2

The older craters have been identified thanks to the discovery that the explosive impacts in which they were formed left telltale transformations of the rock. These include tiny diamonds, greatly compressed forms of quartz (coesite and stishovite), shatter cones and minerals known as impactites. *Walter Sullivan, "Discovery of Soviet Crater Called a Sign That Earth Was Heavily Bombarded Even After Planet's Infancy," The New York Times, Oct. 24, 1976, p 26*

[1961, named after S. M. *Stishov*, a Russian geochemist who produced it in a laboratory in 1961 + *-ite*, mineral suffix]

stocker, *n. U.S.* a stock car, usually slightly modified, used in drag racing.

You simply can't believe the noise of these engines. Stockers, motorcycles, needle-nosed dragsters . . . tear the night apart for hours. *Alan Harrington, "Deus ex Machina," Harper's, Jan. 1976, p 20*

Members of the National Association for Stock Car Auto Racing . . . rolled up to the "diplomatic entrance" in their Day-Glo colored "stockers." *Time, Sept. 25, 1978, p 88*

[1972, from *stock* car + *-er*]

Stockholm syndrome, the desire of a hostage to please his captor, to cooperate with him, and to condone or justify his action.

Reports abounded that some of the Americans had expressed sympathy for their captors' cause. The explanation, as widely accepted as it was offered, was simple and quick in coming: The sympathy was a symptom of the "Stockholm syndrome." *Walter Reich, "Hostages and the 'Syndrome'," The New York Times, Jan. 15, 1980, p A19*

He had not succumbed psychologically. Rebhan had worried about the "Stockholm syndrome," the odd phenomenon whereby hostages begin to identify with their captors and even aid the very people who threaten their lives. *Gerald Moore, "Drama in Real Life: "Please Let Him Live to See the Baby!" The Reader's Digest, Jan. 1980, p 142*

[1978, named after an incident in which hostages were taken during a bank robbery in *Stockholm*, Sweden, in 1973, widely cited by social scientists to explain conversions among hostages]

stone, *adj. U.S. and Canadian.* complete; total; confirmed.

Big Ed [Muskie] was an adequate Senator—or at least he'd seemed like one . . . —but it was stone madness from the start to ever think about exposing him to the bloodthirsty thugs that Nixon and John Mitchell would sic on him. *Hunter S. Thompson, Fear and Loathing: On the Campaign Trail '72, 1972, p 159*

Admittedly the prospect of a new .400 hitter doesn't rank with the Second Coming—unless, of course, you're a stone baseball fan. *"Preview," Maclean's, July 11, 1977, p 13*

A rich Jewish boy from Boston and a stone intellectual (which is to say a nonintellectual with good credentials), Richard Alpert was prepared to give up everything—wealth, academia, Jewishness—to become the patriarch of mysticism's American-style *nouvelle vogue. Colette Dowling, "Confessions of an American Guru," The New York Times Magazine, Dec. 4, 1977, p 43*

[1968, adjective use of the adverb meaning completely, utterly (OED c1290), in such phrases as *stone broke* or *stone deaf*]

stonewall, *v.i.* to act in an obstructive or evasive manner.

He and his aides schemed to "stonewall," to make empty claims of "national security" and "executive privilege," to threaten the Speaker of the House, to maneuver prosecutors—all in order to keep the facts from coming out. *Anthony Lewis, The New York Times, May 20, 1974, p 31*

Brezhnev's *"nyet,"* however, put the Soviet Union on the defensive, and Moscow has since been working hard at trying to show it is not stonewalling on arms limitation. *Time, May 23, 1977, p 31*

—*v.t.* to resist, obstruct, or evade (an investigation, an opponent, etc.).

The President himself . . . served notice that he would stonewall any further demands for tapes in the Watergate scandal. *Newsweek, May 20, 1974, p 23*

Can Kennedy stonewall Chappaquiddick? *Headline, "The Insider," New Times, Aug. 8, 1974, p 8*

I had to do Ms. magazine and Clay Felker's been after me for years to do an interview. But I've stonewalled them. *"Katharine," Women's Wear Daily, Aug. 9, 1974, p 4*

There is never the remotest chance of a parliamentary investigation of the appallingly high number of nonwhite "suicides" that take place in police cells. . . . When beleaguered by criticism in the generally liberal English-language press in the country, the Afrikaners simply stonewall the issue. *Arturo Gonzalez, "A Nation of Murders," Maclean's, Nov. 14, 1977, p 54*

—*n.* Also, **stone wall.** an act or instance of stonewalling.

Ford repeated his view that the President's stone wall against the courts and Congress would produce an impeachment. *Saul Friedman, "In Praise of Honest Ignorance," Harper's, p 26*

Last fall . . . was a time when cries of "cover-up" and "stonewall" reverberated along the Tory benches in the Commons, and the government squirmed under almost daily revelations of shenanigans. *Maclean's, April 17, 1978, p 29*

[1974, a use made current during the Watergate hearings of 1973-74; extended from the term first used in Australian, and later British, political slang as a noun meaning Parliamentary obstruction (OED 1876) and as a verb, to use obstructive tactics in politics, especially by lengthy Parliamentary speeches; also a cricket term meaning to block balls persistently, to play solely on the defensive (OED 1889)]

story art, a form of art which presents a concept, description, or account by combining verbal and visual material.

An increasingly popular form this year was . . . story art—an offspring of conceptual art that sought to convey a lighter level of information than its parent. Captioned photographs, videotapes, and live performances documented intimate aspects of people's lives that frequently were amusing as well. *Nancy Harris, "Art: Year of Reassessment," 1976 Collier's Encyclopedia Year Book (1975), p 135*

[1975] Also called NARRATIVE ART.

straight-ahead, *adj. U.S.* not deviating from the norm; straightforward; standard.

I think a lot of artists who have gone in a fusion direction will realize that they don't have to do that exclusively, that they can play fusion music and make their money . . . and still play straight-ahead jazz, too. *Robert Palmer, "It's That Jazz Time Again," The New York Times Magazine, June 12, 1977, p 87*

[1976, from the adverbial phrase *straight ahead*]

Strangelove, *n.* a militarist who plans or urges large-scale nuclear warfare and destruction.

He displayed none of the usual fears about Strangeloves in disguise, no suppressed whiff of awe at the personified presence of the end of the world. *Ron Rosenbaum, "The Subterranean World of the Bomb," Harper's, March 1978, p 91*

That also was the period when everyone who believed that nuclear weapons should not be tossed into the sea except after the Soviet Union tossed theirs into the sea was labelled a Strangelove. *William F. Buckley, New York Post, April 12, 1979, (page not known)*

[1968, named for Dr. *Strangelove*, a mad military

445

nuclear-war strategist in a motion picture (1964) of the same name] Also called DR. STRANGELOVE.

Strangelovian or **Strangelovean,** *adj.:* Because it takes only about 100 warheads to kill 100 million people, both countries have long been able to rely on a Strangelovian strategic theory called "mutual assured destruction" (MAD) to deter a first strike by the other side. *"The Deadly Calculus of MIRVing," Newsweek, July 8, 1974, p 24*

Although the vocabulary is impenetrable, except to think-tank experts, and the concepts are often Strangelovean, the complex SALT negotiations may yet turn out to be the most important of the century. *Time, April 11, 1977, p 13*

strange quark, a type of quark (hypothetical nuclear particle) possessing a charge of $-1/3$ and a spin of $+1/2$.

When Murray Gell-Mann and George Zweig of the California Institute of Technology in Pasadena formulated the quark theory, a third quark was required. It was dubbed a strange quark because the particles that contained it acted in a strange way. The existence of the psi particle requires at least a fourth quark. *Robert H. March, "Physics: Elementary Particles," The World Book Science Annual 1977 (1976), p 324*

The neutron and proton may be made with up and down quarks only, but the other members of the octet require the strange quark. *Science News, Nov. 18, 1978, p 341*

[1974] Also called S QUARK. See QUARK.

strat·e·gize ('stræt ə,dʒaiz), *v.i.* to devise a strategy or strategies; lay out careful plans.

The [Alaskan] ground was white, the brooks and rivers frozen. The people slept for the most part in tents. They strategized about the federal bureaucracy—how to oppose it, how to melt out of its way. *John McPhee, "A Reporter at Large: Coming into the Country—II," The New Yorker, June 27, 1977, p 66*

Men in dark suits and homburg hats will be commissioning think tanks to strategise, and calculating kill ratios in case the unthinkable should come to pass with the Internal Revenue Service. *Peter Laurie, "The Shell Game," New Scientist, Sept. 21, 1978, p 873*

[1975, from *strategy* + *-ize;* see the note under PRIORITIZE]

stratified-charge engine, an internal-combustion engine in which the cylinder is divided into two chambers, with a fuel-rich mixture used for ignition in one chamber and a lean mixture for main combustion in the other.

The stratified charge engine was invented in the United States and developed by Honda of Japan. This is a lean-burning engine (that is, one using a high air to fuel ratio that permits oxidation of HC and CO), and Honda says it can meet all the U.S. statutory standards right now. *Constance Holden, Science, March 7, 1975, p 822*

Fuel economy and reduced exhaust emissions can both be obtained in so-called stratified-charge engines. *Kenneth Owen, The Times (London), Feb. 13, 1976, p 18*

[1972]

streak, *Slang.* —*v.i.* to dash in the nude through a public place, especially as a stunt or fad.

In the middle of the second Test between England and Australia at Lord's, this 24-year-old ship's cook took off all his clothes and 'streaked' across the pitch to win a £20 bet. Four months later, in Australia, three different men

were doing the same thing in one afternoon of a Test match against West Indies. *Doug Gardner, "Sport," The Annual Register of World Events in 1975 (1976), p 423*

There is something touchingly old-fashioned about the Athens campus; last spring, a few students were espied streaking. *E. J. Kahn, Jr., "Profiles," The New Yorker, Feb. 6, 1978, p 48*

—*v.t.* to streak through (a public area, event, etc.).

"And I was the first to streak a play. I got sort of a double notoriety." *"Streaking Coed Gets a Cold and the Freeze," New York Post, March 1, 1974, p 4*

They began drinking, and then they decided to streak the hotel lobby. So they did. They streaked the lobby. *Lowell Komie, Harper's, April 1979, p 63*

—*n.* an act or instance of streaking.

"There were solo streaks, but no private streaks. After all the variations that were tried, there was no new way to attract attention." *Dr. Joyce Brothers, quoted by Lee Dembart, "Streaking," The New York Times, May 19, 1974, p 35*

[1973, from the sense "to move very fast"]

streaker, *n.:* The [Academy Awards] festivities proceeded . . . as usual. No streakers, no scandals, no political filibusters. *Rex Reed, New York Post, April 11, 1979, p 54*

streaking, *n.:* I was anywhere from six to eight months ahead of . . . jogging, streaking, therapeutic screaming, running like an idiot, and your other ridick things. *Gordon Lish, Saturday Review, June 23, 1979, p 13*

street academy, *U.S.* a school formed in a poor section of a city to help high-school dropouts continue their education.

Taxpayers are rebelling at the escalating costs of running the schools; many large systems face bankruptcy. Splinter groups—free schools, alternative schools, private schools, street academies—are springing up everywhere. *Neil V. Sullivan, Saturday Review, Sept. 16, 1972, p 67*

[1968]

street-smarts, *n. U.S. Slang.* practical knowledge and understanding about the ways of city streets.

Such young women [who teach at a private school] . . . refuse to live in New York as though it were the Peter and Paul Fortress and they were enemies of the Czar. To be free, however, requires street-smarts, the cunning of the survivor. *John Leonard, "About New York: The Brearley Streetwise Crowd," The New York Times, Aug. 9, 1976, p 30*

They thought always about winning, and, one way or another, they almost always did win. Like the A's, these Yankees have street-smarts. They win. *Roger Angell, "The Sporting Scene," The New Yorker, Nov. 20, 1978, p 113*

[1972, from *street* + SMARTS]

street-smart, *adj.:* Norris also sought out local black leaders and followed their street-smart advice: Build a day care center for working mothers. Offer to put them on flexible hours, say, 8:30 a.m. to 2 p.m., or 1 to 5 p.m. Don't ask if the applicant has been arrested. Yes, many have been busted, but what difference does that make? *Time, April 3, 1978, p 61*

street value, the value of a narcotic on the illegal market.

Murphy called a news conference to announce that 57 pounds of heroin with an estimated street value of more than $10-million had been stolen. *David Burnham, New York: Police and Heroin: Incredible As It Seems . . . ," The New York Times, Dec. 24, 1972, Sec. 4, p 6*

[1972]

stress test or **stress testing,** a heart examination in which a cardiogram is taken during or immediately after performing strenuous exercise in order to test the heart's ability to function under stress.

An exercise electrocardiogram, or stress test, is a valuable tool in the diagnosis of heart disease. By recording heart activity during exercise, often on a treadmill, it is possible for a trained clinician to detect many coronary abnormalities well ahead of time. *Joe Graedon, The People's Pharmacy, 1976, p 272*

In any of 45 cardiac and pulmonary centers operated in 10 states . . . services include stress testing for potential heart-attack cases. *Jean Hall, "Stress Testing," The Herald Statesman (Yonkers, N.Y.), March 19, 1975, p 45*

[1973]

striker, *n. Soccer.* any forward, especially a center-forward.

Ten minutes into the second half Bob Paisley, the Liverpool manager, replaced McDermott with an extra striker, Johnson, but not until Dalglish began embarking on long lone runs at the middle of the Nottingham defence did Liverpool seem likely to score. *David Lacey, "Best Laid Plans Confounded," The Manchester Guardian Weekly, Sept. 24, 1978, p 23*

[1966]

string, *n.* or **string bikini,** a very brief bikini.

Winter vacation time is coming and the string bikini is still with us. . . . The string has come in for a lot of bad jokes but, actually, for a healthy, active woman, there is nothing immodest about it. *McCall's, Nov. 1974, p 10*

Its tourist brochures may feature come-on close-ups of itty-bitty string bikinis, but the government of Brazil takes a somewhat different view of female sexuality when the subject is treated seriously. *Marlise Simons, "A Brazilian Censor Tells All," Ms., Jan. 1979, p 98*

[1974, probably influenced by the *G string*]

stroke, *U.S. −v.t.* **1** to enhance (a person's) self-esteem, as by praise or flattery; boost the ego of.

"You go to a party up there, and instead of people making real conversation they stop the proceedings so somebody can sing opera or play the piano or do a tap dance. It's Show Biz, man—a bunch a' egomaniacal people using a captive audience to stroke themselves." *Larry L. King, The Atlantic, March 1975, p 44*

2 to persuade, cajole, or otherwise influence or manipulate.

Then he talks about the most desirable legislative outcome and the fallback positions. He tells his client, "It's looking pretty good. We'll stay on top of it." This is what is known as "stroking" the client. The Washington influencer —the lobbyist, the lawyer, the representative of one of the infinite number of trade associations—not only must keep informed but must also convince his clients that he is informed, is on top of things. Part of his job is to calm the clients' anxieties, and he spends a lot of time on the telephone doing this. *Elizabeth Drew, The New Yorker, Jan. 9, 1978, p 41*

−*n.* **1** something that enhances or reinforces self-esteem; approval or reward.

"The ability to give 'strokes' is a skill," says the public-relations specialist. (A "stroke" is a no-nonsense compliment, a bit of reinforcement. The women, instructed in its use, have been asking for, giving and getting "strokes" throughout the workshop.) *Gwyneth Cravens, "How Ma Bell*

is Training Women for Management," The New York Times Magazine, May 29, 1977, p 15*

2 power to persuade or cajole; ability to influence or manipulate.

Transcript P: What stroke have you got with Magruder . . . ? E: I think the stroke Bob has with him is in the confrontation to say, "Jeb, you know that just isn't so," and just stare him down on some of this stuff. *"White House Metaphors Made Perfectly Clear," New Times, May 31, 1974, p 29*

[1972, verb and noun definitions 1 were popularized by use in transactional analysis]

stroke house, *U.S. Slang.* a theater where pornographic films are shown.

He would fly to New York once a week, ostensibly to "work on a deal." Actually, he would camp in the 42nd Street stroke houses and come back with tales of what they were getting away with now. *Brutus, "Confessions of a Stockbroker," The Atlantic, July 1971, p 52*

[1970, from *stroke*, slang verb meaning to copulate]

strontium-rubidium dating, variant of RUBIDIUM-STRONTIUM DATING.

The ironstone sediments were dated . . . within analytical error with a date of 3.70 billion ± 140 million years for granitic gneisses (igneous rocks) in the Isua area determined by strontium-rubidium dating. *"Greenland Now Yields Oldest Sedimentary Rocks," Science News, Oct. 6, 1973, p 213*

[1973]

structural unemployment, unemployment resulting from changes in the structure of the economy, such as the introduction of automation, foreign economic influences, and population shifts.

The phenomenon that economists call structural unemployment is built into the economy, and is not diminished by rising levels of prosperity. Indeed, if you have a rising level of prosperity you get more of that kind of unemployment, because people can quit their unemployment benefits, and remain confident that they can get jobs again when their benefits run out. *S. I. Hayakawa, Harper's, Jan. 1978, p 40*

The problem of "structural unemployment" (the name sometimes given to the phenomenon of masses of people being put out of work by what amounts to a commendable increase in productivity) has only recently begun to be aired in public. *John Stansell, "Adjusting to Automation," New Scientist, May 4, 1978, p 274*

But there is a third form of joblessness, called "structural unemployment"—pockets of seemingly intractable joblessness that exist in varying degrees whether the economic cycle is in boom or bust. Because it is not directly related to the business cycle, many experts believe it susceptible to remedy even in a period of high inflation. *Philip Shabecoff, "Unemployment: The Structural Variety Is the Toughest," The New York Times, June 18, 1978, Sec. 4, p 4*

[1961]

stuff, *v.t. U.S.* to throw, drop, or slam a basketball down through the basket.

But size is not quintessential. Alabama's Kent Looney, a 5-ft. 9 in., 141-lb. guard, went over a 7-ft. opponent to stuff a rebound. *"Sport: The Year of the Superstuffers," Time, March 21, 1977, p 61*

[1967] See SLAMDUNK.

stun gun, a gun that shoots a dart connected by

wire, stunning the victim with an electric shock.

Promoted as a humane defensive weapon that will immobilize but normally not kill, the electric stun gun may be winning unwanted acceptance in the underworld as a sort of jailhouse insurance. *"Stun Guns Provide Latest 'Jailhouse Insurance',"* The Tuscaloosa News (Alabama), Oct. 26, 1975, p 10A

[1971] Compare TASER.

► The term has also been used for a kind of gun that fires a small bag of sand, bird shot, etc., designed for use in riot control.

stylostatistics, *n. Linguistics.* the use of statistical methods to analyze the style of a writer.

There are two essays in stylo-statistics, those by Jiří Krámský and Jaroslav Peprník. Both are based on extensive corpora, and both show that frequency of items or classes of items can be shown to correlate with time and type of writing. The first-mentioned essay takes up frequency of verb forms; the second confines itself to a narrow class, the verbs that introduce quotations. Both essays prove their points quite neatly. *Archibald A. Hill, Language, June 1971, p 452*

[1971]

subduct, *v.i., v.t. Geology.* to sink under the margin of a crustal plate; undergo or cause subduction.

When an oceanic plate collides with a continental one, the oceanic plate usually dives toward the mantle and is subducted. That is because the continental plates are thicker and more buoyant. *Kevin C. Burke and J. Tuzo Wilson, "Hot Spots on the Earth's Surface," Scientific American, Aug. 1976, p 53*

"The Juan de Fuca plate has been subducting," Riddihough says. "I see very little evidence that it has stopped now, so we have to assume that it still is." *Science News, Nov. 26, 1977, p 360*

[1970] Compare OBDUCT.

subduction, *n.:* When two plate margins converge, one plate undergoes subduction, which means that its leading edge buckles beneath the other plate and plunges diagonally downward into the earth's upper mantle to depths approaching 700 kilometers. The weight of the thick slab of descending lithosphere adds impetus to the motion of the entire plate, which, in effect, is making a long downhill slide from the elevated ridge crests to the mantle beneath the trenches. *Ursula B. Marvin, "Plate Tectonics," Britannica Book of the Year 1975, p 64*

An amount of crust equivalent to the amount added at a spreading ridge must return continuously to the mantle. This happens at subduction zones, where the oceanic lithosphere plunges into the asthenosphere, pulled down because the descending lithosphere is cooler and therefore slightly denser than the asthenosphere surrounding it. *Peter Molnar and Paul Tapponnier, "The Collision Between India and Eurasia," Scientific American, April 1977, p 32*

subemployed, *adj.* insufficiently or inadequately employed; underemployed, as of a part-time worker, or unemployed.

Those now subemployed could provide the additional services by working as policemen and firemen, teachers' aides, health workers, or in conservation, transit, recreation and antipollution jobs. *William Spring, et al., The New York Times Magazine, Nov. 5, 1972, p 56*

[1967]

subemployment, *n.:* In one study of low-income neighborhoods, the "sub-employment rate," including both unemployment and underemployment, was about 33 percent, or 8.8 times greater than the overall unemployment rate for all U.S. workers. *"Report of the National Advisory Commission on Civil Disorders," The 1969 World Book Year Book, p 547*

sublimit, *n.* a limit somewhat lower than a maximum limit.

Now the United States is reported to have agreed to allow modernization of the Soviet force of about 300 heavy missiles, and Moscow has accepted limits of 800 to 850 land-based missiles with multiple warheads. This would be a "sublimit" within an overall ceiling of 1,320 ballistic missiles bearing multiple warheads. *David K. Shipler, The New York Times, Oct. 22, 1977, p 3*

[1973]

sub·op·ti·mize (sə b'ɑp tə ̩maiz), *v.i.* to make optimal use of parts or subdivisions of a system, process, etc.

It is all very well to deduce these life valuations, but they are of no value if society does not act on them in some way. In the ... report the Sussex team says that "It is possible using the above scheme, however, to suboptimise across a set of projects and activities so that at least the adverse effects arising from these activities are more evenly distributed." *"Technology Review: Costing the Hazards of Technology," New Scientist, Dec. 14, 1972, p 638*

[1962, from *sub-* subordinate + *optimize* to make as effective as possible]

suboptimization, *n.:* A natural tendency is to try to cope with complexity by dividing the system into subsystems which will yield to independent solutions, and then combining the sub-solutions into a systems synthesis. Sub-optimization has a definite utility for certain situations but inherently it does not conform to the holistic idea that the total system is given meaning by the ways in which its components interact with each other when they are focussing on a given objective. *Ralph Parkman, The Cybernetic Society, 1972, p 198*

Another source of human frustration with large technological systems is what systems experts call suboptimization (failure to perceive the relation of optimum smaller systems to the larger whole). *Donald N. Frey, "Technology Control: A New Level of Choice," Britannica Book of the Year 1973, p 30*

subplate, *n. Geology.* a small crustal plate.

They [Robert B. Smith and Marc L. Sbar] propose in the August GEOLOGICAL SOCIETY OF AMERICA BULLETIN that the earth's crust in the intermountain West is divided into several subplates. Two of them, which they have named the Northern Rocky Mountain and Great Basin subplates, appear to be moving west with respect to the stable portion of the North American plate. *"Earth Sciences: Plates, Plumes and Yellowstone," Science News, Aug. 17, 1974, p 105*

[1970, from *sub-* secondary + (tectonic) *plate*]

subsonic, *n.* an aircraft that flies at speeds less than the speed of sound; a subsonic aircraft.

Flight International (November 27, 1975) published noise footprints for Concorde and the leading subsonics. *Jerome R. Ravetz, Leeds, England, in a Letter to the Editor, The Manchester Guardian Weekly, Jan. 18, 1976, p 2*

The subsonics will install new devices to reduce their noise to acceptable levels by 1985. *The New York Times, Sept. 28, 1977, p 36*

[1970, noun use of the adjective] Compare SUPER-SONIC.

substance P, a substance that acts somewhat like a peptide, found in the brain, spinal cord, and nerve cells, and thought to be associated with the production of the sensation of pain. *Formula:* $C_{63}H_{98}N_{18}O_{13}S$

It is known from classical neurology that pain signals are delivered to the spinal cord by small thin nerve fibres along which the signal travels fairly slowly. Some of those nerve fibres, Hökfelt and others discovered, release substance P. They may very well account for the substance P the Swedish team identified in the spinal cord. *"What Role Do Peptides Have in the Pain Gate?" New Scientist, Sept. 1, 1977, p 527*

Perhaps the strongest candidate among the neuropeptides for transmitter status is substance P, a chain of 11 amino acids. It is present in a number of specific neuronal pathways in the brain and also in primary sensory fibers of peripheral nerves. Some of these sensory neurons, whose cell bodies lie in sensory ganglia on each side of the spinal cord, contain substance P and release it from their axon terminals at synapses with spinal-cord neurons. Because substance P excites those spinal neurons that respond most readily to painful stimuli the substance has been suggested to be a sensory transmitter that is specifically associated with the transmission of pain-related information from peripheral pain receptors into the central nervous system. *Leslie L. Iversen, "The Chemistry of the Brain," Scientific American, Sept. 1979, p 148*

[1965, from *p*eptide]

substorm, *n.* a disturbance in the earth's magnetosphere (region dominated by the magnetic field) in which magnetic energy accumulated in the tail of the magnetosphere is suddenly released and dissipated, manifesting itself as an aurora or other magnetic phenomenon.

Substorms occur either in isolated form once every several hours (sometimes days) or in a rapid sequence consisting of several events per hour, often as the result of an interplanetary compression or expansion shock wave, triggered by a solar flare, impinging on the magnetosphere. This latter event represents a magnetic storm (historically, this is the reason why substorms have been called *sub*storms). *Juan C. Roederer, "The Earth's Magnetosphere," Science, Jan. 11, 1974, p 43*

[1966, from *sub-* subordinate, secondary + (magnetic) *storm*] See MAGNETOTAIL.

sub·ter·rene (ˌsəb təˈriːn), *n.* a drill heated to melt the rock through which it bores.

Scientists predicted that eventually the drills, called subterrenes, would be used for large-scale projects such as highway and railroad tunnels. *Frank A. Smith, "Transportation," 1973 Britannica Yearbook of Science and the Future (1972), p 336*

[1972, from Latin *subterrēnus* under the earth, subterranean; perhaps influenced by earlier *subterrene, adj.* (OED 1610), noun (OED 1854)]

sub·til·i·sin (səbˈtil ə sən), *n.* an enzyme that breaks down proteins, used especially in the study of protein synthesis.

These enzymes, and all but one of the others listed here, almost certainly have a common evolutionary origin. The exception is subtilisin, which has the same active site and catalytic function as trypsin but evolved independently. *Illustration legend, "A Family of Protein-Cutting Proteins," Scientific American, July 1974, p 86*

[1966, from New Latin (*Bacillus*) *subtilis*, a species of soil bacteria that was thought to produce it + English *-in* (chemical suffix)]

suburbanity, *n.* suburban quality or character.

At the same time that the suburbs have been taking on some of the less agreeable aspects of the cities they outlie, though, they have become startlingly less dependent on them—exchanging their suburbanity for self-sufficiency. *E. J. Kahn Jr., The New Yorker, Oct. 15, 1973, p 54*

California's opulent new Governor's mansion . . . does indeed capture California's quicksilver suburbanity. It has expansive verandas, teakwood floors, eight bathrooms and a caretaker assigned to collect golf balls sliced off the fairway of a nearby country club. *Time, July 18, 1977, p 22*

[1967]

suction method, another name for VACUUM ASPIRATION.

It is something of a surprise to hear that they [the Women's liberation movement] have now firmly launched a campaign for freely available abortions by the suction method—the so-called "lunch-time" abortion. This technique is about as difficult and traumatic as extracting a tooth and requires about the same amount of facilities and instrumentation. *"Feedback: Three Minute Abortions," New Scientist, May 11, 1972, p 336*

[1972]

sudser, *n. Especially U.S. Slang.* a soap opera.

Down to earth with *The Brothers*, the sudser with everything (BBC 1). *Clive James, "Television," The Listener, May 11, 1972, p 631*

His plays are worthlessly "moving"—lyricized sudsers with stand-up-comic numbers, and synthetic to the core. *Pauline Kael, "The Current Cinema," The New Yorker, Dec. 23, 1972, p 52*

[1968, from (soap) *suds* + *-er*, perhaps patterned on earlier slang *soaper* (1950's)] Compare SOAP.

suf·fo·sion (səˈfou ʒən), *n. Geology.* underground seepage of water into rock.

Headward extension will also be aided by sub-surface seepage or 'suffosion', helping to corrode the bedrock. It is evident that both suffosion processes and headcut migration will seek out weaknesses in the bed-rock such as joint-planes, zones of fault-line debris or seams of clay between harder sediments. *Clifford Embleton, "Vicissitudes of the Course-Changing River," The Geographical Magazine, June 1972, p 602*

[1966, from Latin *suffosio, -ōnis* a digging under, undermining, from *suffodere* to dig underneath]

▶ This is apparently a reborrowing of an obsolete term, recorded in the OED as used in the general sense of the Latin word between 1623 and 1648. Compare OBDUCT.

sug·gest·ol·o·gy (səg dʒesˈtɑl ə dʒi:), *n.* the study and use of suggestion, especially in teaching and psychotherapy.

Suggestology, the psychology of suggestion, has very wide application and it has achieved—according to Bulgarian scientists—striking results in the field of education, psychiatry, neurology and telepathy. It has nothing to do with hypnosis or sleep-teaching. *Gabriel Ronay, "Relax and Learn a Language with a Little Help from Bach," The Times (London), April 2, 1977, p 14*

[Dr. Georgi] Lozanov began to develop his ideas concerning Suggestology several decades ago while involved in research on the stimulation of memory through hypnotic therapy.... Lozanov's early experiments had to do with vocabulary learning in French and Greek, where students were shown to be able to acquire *passive* control over large numbers of words. *The Linguistic Reporter, Dec. 1979, p 7*

[1971, from *suggestion* + *-ology* study of]

suggestologic, *adj.:* His letter helpfully explains that, "apart from the specific suggestologic problems concerning the unconscious form of psychic interactions and the reserve capacities of the individual, . . . the symposium will also examine the problems of the place of suggestion in a number of spheres of psychological research." *New Scientist, Feb. 18, 1971, p 397*

sug·ges·to·pae·di·a (səg͵dʒes tə'pi: di: ə), *n.* the application of suggestology to learning; teaching through suggestion.

In an hour-long presentation to the Interagency Language Round Table in Washington DC, Dr. Georgi Lozanov, a Bulgarian psychiatrist, sketched the major tenets of his philosophy of learning, Suggestology, and described some of the practical applications of these tenets in his method of language instruction, Suggestopaedia. *The Linguistic Reporter, Dec. 1979, p 7*

[1977, from *suggesto*logy + Greek *paideiā* instruction]

suggestopaedics, *n.:* Since there are so many educational "wonder techniques" which eventually fizzle away, I asked Mr John E. Fobes, Unesco's deputy director-general to assess the Paris experiment with suggestopaedics. *Gabriel Ronay, "Relax and Learn a Language With a Little Help from Bach," The Times (London), April 2, 1977, p 14*

suicidogenic, *adj.* producing or conducive to suicide.

As a sociologist he [Emile Durkheim] had two interests, in identifying the 'suicidogenic currents' whose variation caused observed variations in suicide rates, and in tracing the pathology of his own society, whose suicide rate was far too high to be normal. *Alan Ryan, "Suicidogenic," Review of "Emile Durkheim: His Life and Work" by Steven Lukes, The Listener, March 22, 1973, p 383*

[1973, from *suicide* + connecting *-o-* + *-genic* producing]

su·i·se·ki (͵su: i:'sei ki:), *n.* the Japanese art of collecting and arranging stones.

"Suiseki is closely related to the natural forms of the universe. There are stones signifying calmness, pleasure, and happiness (as well as) a picturesque panorama." . . . As with all suiseki, the stones must be as found in nature, though they may be cleaned with a soft cloth or brush. However, they are never polished or sculpted. *Shirley Parenteau, "Stones That Speak With Symbolism," The New York Times, Aug. 8, 1976, p 24*

[1976, from Japanese, literally, flint]

sul·fa·zin or **sul·pha·zin** ('səl fə zin), *n.* a drug administered in Soviet psychiatric hospitals to treat mental illness and allegedly as a punishment. It consists of a one-percent solution of purified sulfur in

peach oil and it induces fever, weight loss, and exhaustion.

If a patient speaks out against such brutality, he is subjected to punishment by overdoses of drugs or injections of sulfazin that make it "painful for him even to stir . . ." *Harvey Fireside, Soviet Psychoprisons, 1979, p 82*

[1970, from Russian *sulfazin*] Compare AMINAZIN.

sul·fin·pyr·a·zone (͵səl fin'pir ə͵zoun), *n.* the generic name of ANTURANE.

The American research project was set up to test the theory that the risk of this further thrombosis might be reduced by treatment with a drug, sulfinpyrazone, which acts on the blood platelets, the small cells that start the process of thrombosis. *The Times (London), March 2, 1978, p 16*

[1960, from *sulfin*ic acid + *pyrazole* + *-one* (chemical suffix)]

Sullivan Principles, a set of principles under which American firms in South Africa pledge to follow nondiscriminatory employment practices.

I.B.M. has distributed the text of the Sullivan Principles to all its employees in South Africa. *E. J. Kahn, Jr., "Annals of International Trade," The New Yorker, May 14, 1979, p 144*

Out of a sense of social responsibility or business prudence, more than 100 American companies have adopted the Sullivan Principles. *George Vecsey, The New York Times Magazine, June 3, 1979, p 33*

[1977, named after their author, Leon H. *Sullivan,* born 1923, an American Baptist clergyman and member of the board of directors of General Motors]

summit, *v.i.* to engage or participate in a summit meeting.

Prime Minister Indira Gandhi is willing to summit with the chap (probably at the end of the month). *"International Notes: Political Etiquette," Time, June 5, 1972, p 40*

The presidential performance here continues to be played on a split screen, featuring . . . Nixon the President, summiting and clowning with the visiting Brezhnev, and Nixon, the suspect, seeking to elude the Watergate noose. *Don Greenberg, New Scientist, July 5, 1973, p 30*

[1972, verb use of noun meaning summit meeting]

su·mo·to·ri ('su: mou'tou ri:), *n., pl.* **-ris** or **-ri.** a practitioner of sumo, the Japanese form of wrestling.

Sumotori may look fat, says Jesse, "but anyone who [tries] socking a sumotori in the stomach will gladly go back to brick walls." *Stephen K. Oberbeck, "Push Comes to Shove," Review of "Takamiyama" by Jesse Kuhaulua and John Wheeler, Newsweek, Aug. 13, 1973, p 92*

The most disappointing *sumotori* of the year was Wajima, who for the first time in four years failed to win a single title. *Andrew M. Adams, "Combat Sports: Sumo," Britannica Book of the Year 1976, p 198*

[1973, from Japanese *sumōtori*] See YOKOZUNA.

Sunbelt, *n.* the southern region of the United States from Virginia to southern California. *Often used attributively.*

The most recent statistics for unemployment by area indeed show that joblessness is highest in the Northeast and lowest in the farm states, where there tend to be fewer major cities, and in the Sunbelt. However, in California and Florida, both part of the Sunbelt, unemployment has been higher than the national average. *Philip Shabecoff, "Jobs*

Move Faster Than the Jobless," The New York Times, Jan. 9, 1977, Sec. 3, p 43

There are still large numbers of whites-only country clubs and business clubs and residential areas. There are still no black chairmen of major industrial concerns or of big banks or black governors to be found throughout the Sunbelt states. *The Times (London), Sept. 29, 1977, p 1*

An even larger triple-width size, already seizing a good part of the mobile home market in California and other "sunbelt" regions, is beginning to make an appearance in other states. *Ruth Rejnis, Her Home, 1980, p 96*

[1972, coined by the American writer Kevin Phillips as *Sun Belt;* patterned on *corn belt, Bible belt,* etc.] Compare SNOWBELT.

sun block, a chemical substance, usually a cream, that protects the skin from sunburn. It provides more protection than a sunscreen.

There are various kinds of sun-tanning preparations which include differing combinations of these chemical sunscreens. These sun-tanning products are labeled in different ways according to the manufacturer. Products labeled as "sun blocks" usually screen out all, or almost all, damaging rays. *Alexandra Penney, "How to Stay Safe in the Sun," The New York Times Magazine, May 21, 1978, p 74*

[1977]

Sun Day, a day in May set aside by advocates of solar power to dramatize the need for expanded research and interest in the sun as an alternative energy source.

These observances on Wednesday, "Sun Day," are meant to spark a political movement that will "lead the United States into the solar era" just as Earth Day, eight years ago, dramatized the environmental movement. *"Wednesday Is Sun Day," The New York Times, April 30, 1978, Sec. 4, p 18*

Among other major spin-offs of Sun Day, Hayes described formation of two national organizations to promote a change in the political and social climate affecting solar energy development. The Solar Lobby, which should get underway within the next few months, will represent consumers on Capitol Hill. *Science News, May 13, 1978, p 310*

[1978]

sundown, *v.i.* to experience nighttime hallucinations because of strange surroundings.

During the day she was fine, if tired and dozing most of the time. But when darkness came she entered a shadowy world, a world seen only by her. In hospitals they call it "sundowning" and it is a common thing with old people when they are removed from a familiar environment and placed in the hospital. The darkness, the lack of familiar things around them, the strange sounds from the corridors cause a sort of sensory confusion which brings on hallucinations. *Sharon Curtin, "Aging in the Land of the Young," The Atlantic, July 1972, p 75*

[1972, verb use of the noun]

sunset law, *U.S.* a law requiring that government agencies, commissions, or programs be reviewed to assess their usefulness.

The recently enacted "sunset law" requires the House and Senate to take a look at every department between now and 1980 and abolish any which cannot justify their continued operation. *The Tuscaloosa News (Alabama), Sept. 26, 1976, p 8D*

A column on Colorado's "sunset law," which requires a yearly re-evaluation of spending programs, prompted legislators in eight other states to introduce similar measures. *Time, May 9, 1977, p 49*

Indiana's sunset law provides that agencies created by a governor's executive order terminate when that governor leaves office and that agencies created by legislative resolution end when the legislature adjourns. *Ralph Wayne Derickson, "State Government," The 1978 World Book Year Book, p 489*

[1976, from the figurative sense of *sunset* decline or close, because such laws terminate programs considered wasteful; influenced by SUNSHINE LAW]

sunshine law, *U.S.* a law which requires government bodies to conduct their regular sessions in public.

"Sunshine laws" are rapidly catching on in the states and cities and there are already cases where decision makers who have tried to settle things in private caucus have been hauled before the courts. *Peter Jenkins, "American Commentary," The Manchester Guardian Weekly, Aug. 1, 1976, p 8*

Congress in 1976 passed the nation's first federal "sunshine law," a measure that would open the proceedings of some 50 government boards and agencies to the press. *Donald M. Morrison, "Publishing," Britannica Book of the Year 1977, p 574*

[1972, so called originally because it was first enacted in Florida (the "Sunshine State"), later equated with the idea of "letting the sunshine in," or meeting in open session]

sunshine pill, *U.S. Slang.* a yellow or orange tablet containing the hallucinogenic drug LSD.

The police . . . could often be induced to tell of green-speckled sunshine pills, little blue-and-black mini-bennies, caps of fake mescaline that looked like brown sugar, and other underground pharmaceuticals that kept turning up in all the worst pockets. *Barry Farrell, "California Inquest," Harper's, May 1974, p 68*

[1970]

superbaryon, *n.* a hypothetical elementary particle whose existence has been postulated to account for the development of the universe after the Big Bang.

In addition to the standard model of the big bang there is a very speculative new hypothesis [which] assumes that massive "superbaryons" formed just after the big bang. The superbaryons were approximately the same size as ordinary baryons, but their mass was as much as 10^{38} times greater. *Jay M. Pasachoff and William A. Fowler, "Deuterium in the Universe," Scientific American, May 1974, p 117*

[1972]

superbolt, *n.* an unusually powerful bolt of lightning, releasing as much as 10 trillion watts of optical energy.

Winter storms over Japan, associated with a disproportionate share of the superbolts observed globally, have long been known for their anomalously intense lightning flashes. These are thought to occur between positively charged regions and the ground. This is in contrast to bolts derived from negatively charged regions, as in a typical summer storm, or from upper level cloud to cloud discharges. *Science News, July 2, 1977, p 15*

[1977]

super-bug, *n.* a bacterium that consumes large amounts of petroleum, produced by splicing genes from several strains of bacteria of the same species that digest petroleum.

The oil-eating bacterium contains genes from four different strains of *Pseudomonas* bacteria. That "super-bug" digests petroleum several times faster than any of the individual strains. A spokesman for General Electric says that the company will now reapply for the patent, but that the decision of the patent court may be appealed to the Supreme Court. *Science News, March 18, 1978, p 175*

[1975]

supercoil, *n.* another name for SUPERHELIX.

They suggest that a single DNA double helix is wound up into a supercoil with diameter 100 angstroms and pitch 110 angstroms, with histones holding the whole thing rigid by bonding between different parts of the supercoil. *"Monitor: Unravelling the Way Histones Hold Chromosomes Together," New Scientist, Nov. 16, 1972, p 378*

[1967]

supercoiled, *adj.*: The two strands of the DNA double helix are joined to form a duplex loop; these structures are "supercoiled," presumably so that the long DNA molecules can be fitted inside a cell. In the other kind only one of the DNA strands is joined; these molecules are not supercoiled. If a single break is made in one strand of a supercoiled molecule, the molecule loses its coils. *Royston C. Clowes, "The Molecule of Infectious Drug Resistance," Scientific American, April 1973, p 21*

su·per·crat ('su: pərˌkræt), *n. U.S.* an official of high rank; a powerful bureaucrat.

Under the unconventional—sometimes downright confusing—new chain of command, administrative control . . . will be largely limited to five supercrats, each bearing the title of "assistant to the President." *"The White House: Just Super," Newsweek, Jan. 15, 1973, p 15*

[1972, patterned on *bureaucrat*]

su·per·fec·ta (ˌsu: pər'fek tə), *n. U.S.* a form of betting in horse races in which the bettor must pick the exact order of the first four horses to finish in a race.

As for OTB [off-track betting] itself, the report recommends putting a five-percent tax on every wager (a $2 bet would cost $2.10) and channelling the play to gimmick betting—superfectas, exactas, and such. *Audax Minor, "The Race Track," The New Yorker, March 24, 1973, p 134*

[1971, blend of *super-* and *perfecta* (in which the first two finishers are picked)] Compare TRIFECTA.

superflare, *n. Astronomy.* a powerful stellar flare thought to be the source of gamma-ray bursts.

The superflare was part of an episode lasting more than two weeks, in which one or more "moderate-or-better" flares occurred almost every day. Ten such events were recorded on April 7 alone. If the more common, small flares are included, McIntosh says, the total during the two-week episode may have been as high as 200. *Science News, May 13, 1978, p 309*

[1973]

supergranular or **supergranulated,** *adj. Astronomy.* of, relating to, or forming supergranulations.

The result of the supergranular motions . . . is to spread the magnetic flux over very large areas of the solar surface,

even to the poles of the sun. *Robert Howard, "Recent Solar Research," Science, Sept. 29, 1972, p 1158*

Scientists see these supergranulated cells, as they are called, as the tops of convection currents bringing energy up from the center of the sun where it is generated by nuclear fusion. *William J. Cromie, "Research in Orbit," The World Book Science Annual 1975 (1974), p 140*

[1972]

supergranulation, *n. Astronomy.* any of a large number of gaseous cells of great density and heat that extend into the chromosphere from the deeper layers of the sun. *Often used attributively.*

The supergranulation "cells," unlike the small convective granulations visible on the Sun's surface, are of the order of 15 000 to 30 000 km across . . . with a central upflow of material which then flows outward with a velocity of about 500 m/s and then down back into the body of the Sun. *"Monitor: The Sun Spins Faster," New Scientist, Jan. 13, 1977, p 77*

[1972]

supergravity, *n. Physics.* the gravitational force that arises from a symmetry used to explain the relationship of different classes of fundamental particles.

The theory of supergravity suggests a new approach to unification. Supergravity is an extension of general relativity, and it makes the same predictions for the classical tests of Einstein's theory, such as the precession of planetary orbits . . . *Daniel Z. Freedman and Peter van Nieuwenhuizen, "Supergravity and the Unification of the Laws of Physics," Scientific American, Feb. 1978, p 129*

Since supergravity incorporates standard general relativity in a very fundamental and unique way, it was hoped that the additional constraints imposed by the added symmetry would cause the unmanageable infinities to cancel each other. This indeed happens to the lowest order corrections, though it fails to work from the third order on. *John H. Kay, Waltham, Mass., "Letters," Science News, May 12, 1979, p 307*

[1977] See GRAVITINO, SUPERSYMMETRY.

superhelix, *n.* a form of DNA consisting of a double helix coiled around itself.

Recent neutron diffraction studies indicate that the DNA is wound in a superhelix around the outside of this histone core. *Tom Barrett, "Role for Histone H1 in Chromatin Condensation?" Nature, April 15, 1976, p 577*

It is fairly clear that at the centre of this structure is a core of protein. Around the core is spun 1 3/4 turns of a helix of the double helix of DNA. The DNA is therefore said to be in a superhelix. That arrangement rather neatly explains most of the degradation products produced by the biochemists. *The Times (London), Sept. 3, 1977, p 14*

[1965] See GYRASE.

superhelical, *adj.*: Normal, double-helix DNA is spiral, like a loosely coiled spring. But DNA has also been isolated from cells in a superhelical form in which the helix is twisted around itself. Gellert and his co-workers found that the enzyme they discovered changed normal DNA into superhelical DNA. They named the enzyme gyrase. *Julian Davies, "Biochemistry," The World Book Science Annual 1978 (1977), p 251*

superhero, *n.* **1** a person greatly admired for extraordinary talents in some field; an extremely popular or accomplished athlete, performer, etc.

The [Grateful] Dead's relaxation is something which Eric

Clapton, former guitar superhero, is desperately trying to discover within his music. *Richard Williams, The Times (London), Sept. 12, 1970, p 19*

At first base, the superhero Henry Aaron of Atlanta struck up a conversation. *Wells Twombly, "Meet an Average Major Leaguer: Dirty Al," The New York Times Magazine, July 16, 1972, p 18*

2 an imaginary character endowed with superhuman powers for fighting crime, injustice, etc.

If your young friends have the current zeal for health foods and comic-strip superheroes your list might be taken care of in a single trip to Pinch Penny Pick-A-Pocket, where . . . health foods — crunchy granola, for example — and all the up-to-the-minute superheroes have also been re-created with paint and glitter. *"On and Off the Avenue," The New Yorker, Nov. 26, 1973, p 107*

[1965 for def. 1, from *super-* over, surpassing + *hero;* 1967 for def. 2, from *Superheroes*, title of a series of comic books about superhuman characters, a name influenced by *Superman*, comic-strip hero created in the 1930's]

superheroine, *n.*: Miss Comic Strip will be either male or female and selected for her originality of costume, ingenuity of stage presentation, and desirability as an imaginary superheroine. *The Times (London), Dec. 22, 1970, p 8*

A new series about teen-age superheroes, entitled "The Young Sentinels," will have among its principal characters a superheroine who is black. *Les Brown, The New York Times, Sept. 3, 1977, p 31*

superport, *n.* a very large port to accommodate megatankers and other large vessels, especially such a port built offshore.

. . . Promoting construction of more domestic oil refineries and superports for oceangoing tankers through legislation that would give Federal agencies authority to select sites for such facilities. *Peter J. Bernstein, "Handling a Fuel Crisis," Honolulu Star-Bulletin, Feb. 12, 1973, p A21*

[1969] Compare MONOBUOY.

super rat, a hardy rat resistant to most poison, capable of passing on the immunity to its offspring.

This company [Sorex] has developed an anti-coagulant which is particularly effective against super rats . . . , which are already prevalent in the United States and are now being reported in Europe and Asia. These animals are resistant to all previously available poisons. *"Queen's Awards for Technology," New Scientist, April 28, 1977, p 200*

[1976]

Super Saver, *U.S.* a type of low-cost, domestic air fare for passengers who purchase tickets 30 days in advance of travel and do not return before seven days.

On the other hand, the coast-to-coast Super Saver plan used by United, American and TWA has proved to be a profitable winner. Since April, on American alone, more than 450,000 passengers have taken advantage of the plan's discounts. *Time, Feb. 13, 1978, p 75*

[1978] Compare ABC, APEX, OTC.

supership, *n.* a very large ship, especially a megatanker.

However, new sources of competitive coal have opened up in Australia, Canada, and South Africa, and again the specter of superships rises to plague us. *Roger Ward,*

"Energy: Our Orphaned Superships," National Review, March 1, 1974, p 261

These superships . . . seem almost jerry-built. Overloaded and in dangerous waters, particularly off South Africa, they pose an ecological peril if they explode, crack up, or sink. *"Science Books of the Year: Supership by Noël Mostert," Encyclopedia Science Supplement (Grolier) 1975, p 281*

[1966]

super slurper, a material able to absorb large quantities of liquid at a rapid rate. It is a starch, such as corn flour, in the form of powder, flakes, or sheets copolymerized with acrylonitrile treated with a hot alkali.

The U.S. Department of Agriculture (USDA) increased the absorbability of its super slurper almost threefold. The newest modified version of this substance soaks up 5,000 times its weight of water. The material could be useful in such items as diapers or as a seed coating to promote germination. *Frederick C. Price, "Chemical Technology," The World Book Science Annual 1978 (1977), p 258*

[1976]

supersonic, *n.* an aircraft that can fly at speeds greater than the speed of sound; a supersonic aircraft.

The supersonics are coming — as surely as tomorrow. You will be flying one version or another by 1980 and be trying to remember what the great debate was all about. *Najeeb Halaby, Time, June 1, 1970, p 64*

The plane is no draw, and buyers aren't exactly falling over themselves to get to the factory. But they could make up their minds once the first results of employing the supersonic on a regular commercial run are known. *Jacques Isnard, "Commercial Gamble of Concorde," The Manchester Guardian Weekly (Le Monde section), Feb. 10, 1973, p 16*

[1964, noun use of the adjective] Compare SUB-SONIC.

superstardom, *n.* the status of a superstar.

The laws that apply to ordinary writers should be suspended for Norman Mailer. Apparently, in the eyes of one dazzled by his own celebrity, and in the eyes of his dazzled admirers, superstardom puts a man above the law, whether writer or President. *George P. Elliott, Review of "Marilyn" by Norman Mailer, Harper's, Oct. 1973, p 111*

Singer and songwriter Dolly Parton aimed for superstardom by shifting from country to popular music and making more road tours. *Picture legend, "Popular Music," The 1978 World Book Year Book, p 412*

[1968]

superstore, *n. Chiefly British.* a very large department store.

Some of Carrefour's giant out-of-town superstores in France seem almost like temples dedicated to the belief that the private car is the central spirit of the consumer religion. *Alisdair Fairley, "Information," The Listener, Dec. 30, 1971, p 919*

Superstores are not often built on High Streets. Rent and rates have grown so high that food would have to be sold at great speed to reach a turnover sufficient to cover costs. Moreover, superstores are designed for the car-borne shopper so that they need sites that will be bounded by their own customer car parks, not by double yellow lines. *The Times (London), May 5, 1978, p I*

[1965]

supersymmetry, *n. Physics.* the basis of a theory for unifying all the fundamental forces in nature by relating the symmetry of two broad classes of elementary particles, the fermions (such as protons and neutrons) and the bosons (such as photons and pions).

The symmetry operations of the hypothetical supersymmetry . . . assert that the fermions and bosons in a system of particles could be interchanged without substantially altering the system. Hence particles with integral spin and those with half-integral spin can be regarded as manifestations of a single underlying state of matter. *"Science and The Citizen," Scientific American, July 1977, p 59*

Studies of supersymmetry and exceptional groups have brought particle theory in contact with . . . new kinds of projective geometries. *Feza Gursey, "Symmetry Laws (Physics)," McGraw-Hill Yearbook of Science and Technology 1978, p 355*

[1977] See SUPERGRAVITY.

supracellular, *adj.* of or having to do with living organisms above the level of the cell.

Supracellular biologists, he maintained, have made a far greater contribution to the progress of cancer therapy than molecular biologists. *"Lord Zuckerman Defends His Position," Nature, Dec. 1, 1972, p 247*

[1972]

supragenic, *adj.* of or having to do with heredity above the level of the gene.

The true function of heterochromatic DNA remained unknown; however, according to Hatch and J. A. Mazrimus of the Lawrence Livermore Laboratory, it seemed to be important for supragenic functions of the chromosome, such as recombination and translocation. *H. E. Kubitschek, "Life Sciences: Molecular Biology," Britannica Book of the Year 1974, p 420*

[1972]

surfer's knob, a lump or nodule that develops under the skin especially on the knee and upper part of the foot of a surfer at points of contact with the surfboard.

Another result of his research, he [Dr. Christoph Wagner] maintains, is confirmation that the recurrent inflammations of the hand and arm suffered by musicians are the result of overtaxing their native skills — a musical variation on tennis elbow, football knee and surfer's knob. *Time, Dec. 25, 1972, p 49*

[1972] Compare HOLLOW FOOT, TENNIS TOE. See also SPORTS MEDICINE.

surgical strike, a swift military attack, especially a limited air attack.

This electronic super technology lends itself to a specific type of offensive called 'surgical strike'. In a surgical strike, you wipe out your target with great precision, avoiding any damage to nearby non-military installations. *The Listener, May 22, 1975, p 666*

Even the language of the bureaucracy — the diminutive "nukes" for instruments that kill and mutilate millions of human beings, the "surgical strike" for chasing and mowing down peasants from the air by spraying them with 8,000 bullets a minute — takes the mystery, awe, and pain out of violence. *Richard Barnet, "The Game of Nations," Harper's, Nov. 1971, p 55*

[1971]

sur·gi·cen·ter ('sər dʒə,sen tər), *n. U.S.* a surgical unit or facility for operations that do not require hospitalization.

A trend toward development of more outpatient or ambulatory care services by hospitals was also evident in 1972. A noteworthy development was the emergence of "surgicenters" where minor surgery can be performed on an outpatient basis. *Jerome F. Brazda, "Medicine: Hospitals," The Americana Annual 1973, p 450*

While the establishment has only recently begun to show a profit, it has spawned three satellite Surgicenters — in Sacramento and Palo Alto, Calif., and in Louisville — and inspired dozens of unaffiliated imitators in other cities. *Time, Oct. 10, 1977, p 96*

[1972, from *surgical center*]

surround-sound, *n. Especially British.* high-fidelity sound reproduction having the effect of surrounding the listener. *Often used attributively.*

All of the systems are capable of giving a generally pleasing and spacious surround sound, with the direct program in the front and the ambience developed by means of signals in the rear channels. *J. G. Woodward, "Four-Channel Stereophonic Sound," McGraw-Hill Yearbook of Science and Technology 1973, p 399*

The new surround-sound systems recognize that sound can come from literally any direction around the horizon, and they aim to convey this directional information in a smooth manner. *Kenneth Owen, "Music in the Round," The Times (London), June 24, 1977, p 19*

Inevitably, the next step of development — either from Nippon Columbia or others working more secretly in the field — must be the production of a disc which carries stereo or "surround-sound" in digital rather than analog fashion. *Adrian Hope, "Digital Sound Is on Its Way," New Scientist, Oct. 20, 1977, p 166*

[1972] Compare AMBISONICS.

survival guilt or **survivor guilt,** a feeling of guilt often experienced by survivors of a war, flood, etc., where others died.

Many residents also suffer from insomnia, crying spells, moodiness, and what has been called "survival guilt": unwarranted but painful self-reproach for having lived when others died. *"Behavior: After the Deluge," Time, Oct. 9, 1972, p 43*

Psychologists say it is common for returning veterans to suffer some form of "survivor guilt." *Michael Norman, "A Wound That Will Not Heal," The New York Times Magazine, Nov. 11, 1979, p 139*

[1971] See SURVIVOR SYNDROME.

survivor syndrome, symptoms, ranging from survival guilt to severe traumatic neurosis, often exhibited by survivors of a war, flood, etc., where others died.

Many Jews who escaped the Nazi horrors of World War II were scarred for life by "survivor syndrome" — chronic anxiety, flattened emotions, depression, guilt and recurring nightmares. Now, says Israeli Psychiatrist Samai Davidson, similar symptoms are turning up in the children and grandchildren of Holocaust survivors. *"Behavior: Legacy of Terror," Time, Feb. 21, 1977, p 48*

Psychologists call it the survivor syndrome. The survivor of some terrible ordeal, a concentration camp, for instance, or an earthquake, may pass several years in a state of apparently normal health, before entering a terrible depression and decline. It is as if the energy spent on readjustment gradually exhausts itself and the individual gives way to the trauma. *James Fenton, The Manchester Guardian Weekly, Nov. 5, 1978, p 7*

[1976]

suss, *v.t. British Slang.* Usually **suss out.** to figure out, as if by examination, study, or investigation.

Then there are those people who reckon they have got you all sussed out. "I know you really don't like too much help," they will yell, as you stand in the middle of Oxford Circus with traffic whipping all around you. *"Quiet, You Know," The Listener, Dec. 25, 1975 and Jan. 1, 1976, p 853*

The tacky-chic room of Tanya McCallin's set . . . suggested that once again Miss McCallin had sussed out the characters of a play and placed them in the surroundings they deserved. *Ned Chaillet, "Abigail's Party/Hampstead," The Times (London), April 22, 1977, p 11*

[1975, originally (1920's) a shortening and alteration of *suspect*]

suture, *n. Geology.* the line between crustal plates of the earth.

The Mid-Atlantic Ridge represents the suture, or master fracture, that separates several of the 20 giant plates that form the earth's outer shell. *Thomas X. Grasso, "Geology," The 1975 World Book Year Book, p 342*

The Vardar Zone is thought to include a line of "sutures" formed where two continental blocks converged, sweeping up an intervening ocean floor. *Walter Sullivan, "Earth's Plates Converging in Quake Area," The New York Times, May 8, 1976, p 8*

[1972]

SVD, abbreviation of SWINE VESICULAR DISEASE.

SVD is confined to pigs — and pigs in Britain do not, as do many cattle, sheep, and deer, wander at large over vast areas of countryside. *Colin Tudge, New Scientist, March 8, 1973, p 556*

[1972]

SV40, abbreviation of *Simian Virus 40,* a virus that causes cancer in monkeys, widely used in genetic and medical research.

The possible use of polyoma and SV40 as vectors has caused some concern, particularly because SV40 can infect human cells and evidence of SV40 infections has been found in some cases of neurological and malignant diseases in humans. But scientists have not yet . . . demonstrated that SV40 can cause human disease. *Daniel L. Hartl, "Genes: Handle With Care," The World Book Science Annual 1978 (1977), p 34*

SV40 carries its genetic blueprint on a single circular piece of DNA, the viral chromosome. So far five genes have been identified. The genetic instructions are encoded in the sequence of the chemical subunits (nucleotides) strung together to make the DNA molecule. It is the complete sequence of those nucleotides that has been determined by Professor Walter Fiers and his colleagues at Ghent, and, independently, by Dr S. M. Weissman and colleagues at Yale. *The Times (London), May 12, 1978, p 18*

[1963]

swap meet, *U.S.* a market or bazaar where cheap or used articles, especially of handcraft, are bartered or sold.

The latest way that Californians have discovered to use up their golden hours is by going to what is called a "Swap Meet." (To be sure, there are swap meets in New Jersey, on Long Island, even in Georgia. Nobody, however, is interested in how people use up their lives in New Jersey, Long Island or Georgia). *John Leonard, "Handcraft Swapping at Drive-Ins: A Bit of California Dreaming," The New York Times, Jan. 17, 1976, p 30*

[1976]

SWAPO or **Swa·po** ('swɑ: pou), *n.* acronym for *South-West Africa People's Organization,* a black independence movement in Namibia.

A settlement in Namibia is relevant only if it ends the guerrilla war in the north; but because SWAPO has been excluded from decision-making on the future of the territory, the guerrilla war is only beginning. Possibly, the warlike noises that the South African Minister of Defence, Mr. P. W. Botha, and his generals have been making, are meant to exaggerate South Africa's military aggressiveness, as a deterrent to Swapo's intentions; but if the predicted SWAPO offensive materialises, the war talk will become a reality. *Stanley Uys, "Black Prospects in South Africa," The Manchester Guardian Weekly, Jan. 2, 1977, p 9*

[1967]

swart ge·vaar ('swɑrt xə'fɑr), the alleged threat to the white population by the black majority in South Africa.

Any movement away from the old . . . *swart gevaar* style of politics is to be welcomed. *The Cape Times, April 14, 1973, p 9*

While heavily armed police stood guard around the smoldering ruins of Soweto — a satellite township for nearly 1 million blacks on the outskirts of Johannesburg — sporadic rioting broke out in neighboring ghettos and in black suburbs near Pretoria. In both cities, whites rushed to buy arms and ammunition for protection against the so-called *swart gevaar* . . . although at no time were any white communities threatened. *"South Africa: After Soweto, Anger and Unease," Time, July 5, 1976, p 40*

[1966, from Afrikaans, literally, black peril; compare *yellow peril* (OED 1900)]

SWAT or **S.W.A.T.** (swɑt), *n. Especially U.S.* a paramilitary police unit trained in the use of special weapons. *Often used attributively.*

The flak-jacketed Special Weapons and Tactics teams had conducted themselves as in an exercise at Quantico or Benning, pouring 1,200 rounds into the target without bringing death or injury to anyone outside. Only twenty-three SWAT-schooled officers had actually engaged in the shooting. *Barry Farrel, "A Let-Burn Situation," Harper's, Sept. 1974, p 32*

SWAT cops dress in black paramilitary uniforms with soft guerrilla-style jungle hats. *David Blundy, "The SWAT Squads," The Sunday Times (London), Aug. 31, 1975, p 9*

Policemen were all over the sidewalk. Many of them were wearing blue baseball caps, like the S.W.A.T. teams on TV. *"The Talk of the Town," The New Yorker, Aug. 7, 1978, p 18*

[1968, from the acronym for Special *W*eapons *a*nd *T*actics (squad or team) or Special *W*eapons *A*ttack *T*eam]

sweat equity, *U.S.* a share or interest in a building earned by a tenant for contributing his services to the building's maintenance or renovation.

A group of poor, racially mixed tenants took over a nearby city-owned tenement, stripped the shabby interiors and are building modern apartments to replace the narrow, cold-water flats. . . . In return for their "sweat equity," the builder-residents will make payments as low as $80 per month and ultimately own the building as a cooperative. *"People's Cathedral," Time, July 16, 1973, p 43*

Today, after getting the loan and investing hundreds of thousands of hours of their own labor, called sweat equity, in the six-story building, the young people have shown what urban homesteaders can do in neighborhoods so decayed some people are ready to write them off as hopeless. *Michael Sterne, "A Loan and Some 'Sweat Equity' Restore a Battered Tenement," The New York Times, Oct. 7, 1977, p 1*

[1968] See URBAN HOMESTEADING.

sweet spot, the spot on the face of a racquet, bat, club, stick, etc., where a ball or puck is most effectively hit.

Many players swear by their new racquets. New Jersey Insurance Executive James Slote has bought five different racquets during the past two years and finally settled on the outsized Prince, which promises a sweet spot 3 1/2 times that of normal racquets. *"Sport: Those Super Racquets," Time, Dec. 27, 1976, p 50*

Almost every player noticed a definite improvement in his game. 77% hit the sweetspot more often with it. *Advertisement by Dunlop, The New Yorker, May 14, 1979, p 125*

[1974, originally used in reference to golf clubs]

swimming pool, a tank of water for cooling and temporarily storing low-level radioactive wastes from a nuclear power plant.

Next to each nuclear reactor core there is a "swimming pool" where burned up fuel elements are stored. . . . The water cools the hot fuel and shields workers from its lethal radioactivity until it dies down in intensity. *David F. Salisbury, "Is the Nuclear Power Dream Fading?" Encyclopedia Science Supplement (Grolier) 1979 (1978), p 185*

[1978, from its resemblance to a pool]

swine flu, a virulent form of influenza caused by a virus originally isolated in swine and believed to be related to the virus which caused a pandemic in 1918-1919.

The very possibility that the swine flu virus had once again become infectious to humans was enough to trigger a series of trip-hammer decisions. *Edward Edelson, "Medicine Rallies to Fight the Flu," Sunday News (New York), April 18, 1976, p 58*

The death of an American army private in New Jersey prompted Canadian health authorities to undertake the largest mass inoculation program in the country's history. The soldier had died of viral pneumonia caused by an aggressive strain of influenza known as swine flu. *Michael Enright, "No Ounce of Prevention," Maclean's, Nov. 1, 1976, p 23*

[1976]

swine vesicular disease, a virus disease of swine in which blisters develop on the tongue and hooves as they do in foot-and-mouth disease. It originally appeared in Italy in 1966 and first broke out in Great Britain in 1973.

Swine vesicular disease, which has already prompted the slaughter of about 30,000 pigs, and cost £1/2 million in compensation alone . . . is probably not spread to any great

extent via the air; transmission is by contact with an infected animal or through infected feed. *Colin Tudge, New Scientist, March 8, 1973, p 556*

[1972]

swingaround, n. a spacecraft trajectory in which a planet's gravitational field is used to alter the direction of travel.

Physicist Harry Ruppe . . . envisions a wide range of solar missions using various techniques to get there such as planetary swing-arounds, auxiliary rockets and the space shuttle. *Jonathan Eberhart, "Run for the Sun," Science News, Aug. 3, 1974, p 75*

[1974] Compare SLINGSHOT.

swin·gle ('swiŋ gəl), n. Chiefly U.S. and Canadian Slang. a fashionably lively and sexually active single person.

At the same time, the sheer number of singles, meshed with the media's seductive imagery (singles who swing are jauntily dubbed "swingles"), is gradually revising society's view of its unwed members. *"Life and Leisure: Games Singles Play," Newsweek, July 16, 1973, p 53*

Let's look at the single girl's sex life from a practical point of view. All those how-tos, all that advice to swingles are still based on the old you-be-the-master-I'll-be-the-slave idea. *Betty Jane Wylie, "The Joy of Fidelity," Maclean's, Sept. 1974, p 40*

[1967, blend of *swinging* and *single*]

switch trading, international trading in commodities paid for by services, benefits, rare commodities, etc., instead of by currency.

The other principal method of barter involves a bilateral agreement, with a clearing mechanism, which is known as switch trading. *Melvyn Westlake, The Times (London), Jan. 26, 1972, p 19*

What Intertel does is . . . sanitize public images; shred red tape, monitor relevant government legislation, and lobby; advise on geopolitical "switch-trading opportunities." *Jim Hougan, Harper's, Dec. 1974, p 54*

[1972]

syl·i ('sil i: *or* 'si: li:), n. the monetary unit of Guinea, which replaced the franc in 1972.

Finance. Monetary unit: syli, with an official rate (Sept. 22, 1975) of 20.46 sylis to U.S. $1 (free nominal rate of 42.40 sylis = £1 sterling). Budget (1972-73 est.) balanced at 4.5 billion sylis. *"Guinea," Britannica Book of the Year 1976, p 373*

[1973, from the Susu (West African language) word for elephant, the symbol of the Guinea Democratic Party]

syn-, a combining form meaning "synthetic," added to nouns.

synjet, *n.:* In the long term, the choice must be between jet fuel derived from synthetic crude (synjet) or a wholly new type of fuel. *Bill Sweetman, New Scientist, June 7, 1979, p 818*

synoil, *n.:* The future looks bright indeed — provided that coal can be economically turned into synthetic oil and natural gas. So far several plants have been . . . designed to turn 2,700 tons of high-sulfur Illinois coal into 22 million cu.ft. of "syngas" and 3,000 bbl. of "synoil" each day. *Time, March 1, 1976, p 47*

synroc, *n.* [*syn-* + *rock*]: The Australian National University has carried out tests that show that buried synroc will be more stable when it comes in contact with underground water than the products of either vitrification or the super-calcine method of disposing of nuclear wastes. *"Nuclear Waste Disposal," New Scientist, Nov. 30, 1978, p 669*

Synthane, *n.* [*syn-* + *methane*]: Economical ways to make a high-heat gas from coal to rival natural gas is a goal of several projects. One such project, sponsored by the U.S. Bureau of Mines, uses a nickel-based catalyst. Even a pilot demonstration of this "Synthane" process is at least three or four years away, however, and no competing process seems nearer. *Ed Nelson, "Energy," The World Book Science Annual 1973 (1972), p 307*

synzyme, *n.:* It therefore comes as a considerable surprise to discover that a synthetic enzyme (or synzyme), put together in a chemical laboratory according to really rather simple reasoning and certainly very arbitrary design, actually outperforms the real thing. *"Monitor: A Fake Enzyme That Improves on Nature," New Scientist, Sept. 21, 1972, p 472*

[1972, abstracted from *synthetic*] See also the main entries SYNCRUDE, SYNFUEL, and SYNGAS.

syn·ap·ti·ne·mal complex or **syn·ap·to·ne·mal complex** (si͵næp tə'ni: məl), a threadlike protein structure present between chromosomes especially during the synaptic stage of meiosis.

Electron microscopy has revealed the presence of a tripartite structure (the synaptinemal complex) associated with meiotic chromosomes. Apparently restricted to germ cells, the complex is thought by some to represent the point-to-point pairing of homologs preparing for or undergoing exchange. *Rhoda F. Grell, "Cell Division," McGraw-Hill Yearbook of Science and Technology 1972, p 134*

The dominant theme was the study by electron microscopy of the synaptonemal complex (SC), an organelle of remarkable uniform dimensions and appearance in a wide range of eukaryotes. *"The Meiotic Process," Nature, Jan. 15, 1976, p 82*

[1969, from *synaptic* + connecting *-i-* or *-o-* + *-nemal* (from Greek *nêma* thread + English *-al*)]

syn·ap·to·some (si'næp tə͵soum), *n.* a structure containing parts of nerve endings thought to represent the synapse.

The most remarkable feature of synaptosomes is that the attachment of the surface membranes of the two nerve cells (the synaptic junction) remains intact even though each of these membranes has been torn from its cell during the homogenisation. It is possible to isolate from synaptosomes the two synaptic membranes still joined by the intact synaptic junction, and it is this preparation which is used as a starting point for studies of the chemical structure of the junction itself. *Andrew Matus, "Molecular Architecture of Nerve Connections," New Scientist, Jan. 8, 1976, p 57*

[1971, from *synaptic* + connecting *-o-* + *-some* body]

synaptosomal, *adj.:* For each analysis, the cerebral cortices of one control and one experimental mouse were homogenized gently in isotonic sucrose and crude synaptosomal fractions were prepared. *Science, Jan. 18, 1974, p 220*

synchronized sleep, the form of sleep in which little or no dreaming occurs.

Synchronized sleep . . . is characterized by slow brain waves, regular pulse and breathing, and the absence of rapid eye movements. *Ernest L. Hartmann, "The Way We Sleep," The 1977 World Book Year Book, p 112*

[1975] Also called NREM SLEEP and S SLEEP. Compare DESYNCHRONIZED SLEEP.

syn·crude ('sin͵kru:d), *n.* synthetic crude oil produced especially from low-grade (high-sulfur) coal.

Looking at the alternative power sources for private transport, the survey reckons that the most likely ones are a synthetic liquid fuel (such as methanol or syncrude) derived from coal, or electricity stored in batteries. *Peter Waymark, The Times (London), Dec. 9, 1976, p 27*

[1974, from SYN- + *crude*]

syn·fu·el ('sin͵fyu: əl), *n.* any synthetic fuel, such as SYNCRUDE or SYNGAS.

They note, in particular, that on an energy-equivalent basis a lot more CO_2 is released from production and combustion of synfuels than from the direct burning of coal. *Luther J. Carter, "A Warning on Synfuels, CO_2, and the Weather," Science, July 27, 1979, p 376*

[1975, from SYN- + *fuel*]

syn·gas ('sin͵gæs), *n.* synthetic gas produced especially from low-grade coal.

Becoming a feedstock for "syngas" would open a major new potential for coal, especially the now stymied high-sulfur varieties. *"Economy and Business: King Coal's Return: Wealth and Worry," Time, March 1, 1976, p 47*

[1975, from SYN- + *gas*] Compare BIOGAS.

synonym, *n.* a nucleotide triplet or codon in the genetic code that may be substituted for another to produce the same amino acid.

There are more than 60 translator RNA molecules, each corresponding to an RNA code word for one of the 20 amino acids. Because there are synonyms in the code, as many as six different translator RNA molecules may link to the same amino acid. *Stephen L. Wolfe, "The Living Cell," 1976 Britannica Yearbook of Science and the Future (1975), p 66*

[1975] Compare WORD. See also CODE WORD (def. 2), EXPRESSION, PALINDROME, SENTENCE.

syn·te·ny ('sin tə ni:), *n.* location of several genes on the same chromosomal strand.

Genes that are on the same chromosome will therefore usually be expressed together. . . . Assaying a number of clones for various human enzymes therefore provides information on the synteny of genes. *Dietrich Schneider, "The Sex-Attractant Receptor of Moths," Scientific American, July 1974, p 39*

[1973, from *syn-* together + Latin *tenia* band]

syntenic, *adj.:* The demonstration that two or more genes are syntenic . . . and the assignment of genes or groups of syntenic genes to particular chromosomes can be accomplished in three basic ways. The first and best-established method involves following the segregation of genetic markers in informative families. *R. P. Creagan and F. H. Ruddle, "Somatic Hybridization," McGraw-Hill Yearbook of Science and Technology 1975, p 375*

synthetic-aperture radar, a radar system that combines microwave signals reflected from the ground along the path of an aircraft or satellite to form an image of high resolution.

One of those sensors, however, does a job that is huge even on Seasat's scale: Called a synthetic-aperture radar (SAR), it carries a 2.1-by-10.7-meter antenna that works as the equivalent of a conventional radar antenna 14.8 *kilome-*

ters long. Such a monster would span more than 160 football fields—nearly 36 New York World Trade Centers—laid end to end. *Science News, Aug. 5, 1978, p 89*

[1976]

systems dynamics, the use of mathematical models to simulate the forces that produce a problem, trend, or development within a system or systems.

In demonstrating the usefulness of a "systems dynamics" approach to specific problems considered at a disaggregative level—as is done effectively in the papers on "DDT Movement in the Global Environment"; on "Mer-

cury Contamination," and on "The Eutrophication of Lakes"—this objective may have been achieved. *Michael Lloyd, Review of "Towards Global Equilibrium," edited by Dennis L. and Donella H. Meadows, New Scientist, March 22, 1973, p 680*

[1972]

systems dynamicist: Securing a higher rate of industrial investment can, for instance, provide short-term gains for the economic well-being of many people. But the long-term result might be, say the systems dynamicists, an aggravation of the original problem. *Richard H. Gilluly, "Limits to Growth," Science News, March 25, 1972, p 202*

T

TA, abbreviation of TRANSACTIONAL ANALYSIS.

For the vast majority who use it, "TA"—as it is known—is neither panacea nor curse, but is one therapeutic comment among many that has both practical advantages and distinct limitations. *Kenneth A. Briggs, "Growing Number in Clergy Using 'I'm O.K., You're O.K.' Counseling Concept," The New York Times, Feb. 29, 1976, p 37*

TA, or transactional analysis . . . is a system of psychotherapy which encourages practitioners to give "strokes" or emotional rewards, like a kind word or a nice smile, to get desired responses. *The Times (London), April 13, 1977, p 12*

[1972]

tab·bou·leh (tə'bu: lə), *n.* a Middle Eastern salad made with chopped garden vegetables and cracked wheat.

Malca's *tabbouleh* is surprising: its major ingredients are parsley, tomatoes, and scallions with just a sprinkling of cracked wheat—rather than the other way around—and it is mixed with lemon juice and olive oil. *"On and Off the Avenue: The Christmas Table," The New Yorker, Dec. 20, 1976, p 91*

[1965, from Arabic (in Lebanon and Syria) *tabbūla*]

tach·y·on·ic (ˌtæk i:'ɑn ik), *adj.* of or having to do with tachyons (hypothetical elementary particles that travel faster than the speed of light).

A tachyonic electron would radiate all its energy . . . in about 10^{-19} seconds. *"News and Views: Tachyons and Gravitons," Nature, Jan. 7, 1972, p 11*

Large sums of money have already gone down the drain, the authors believe, in efforts to detect tachyons by methods that imply tachyonic communication. *Martin Gardner, "Mathematical Games," Scientific American, May 1974, p 121*

[1971, from *tachyon* (1967)]

TACV, abbreviation of *tracked air cushion vehicle*, a high-speed train that rides on a cushion of air over a concrete track.

The British developed their Hovertrain, the French their Aerotrain and the U.S. Federal Railroad Administration its TACV. *Henry H. Kolm and Richard D. Thornton, "Electromagnetic Flight," Scientific American, Oct. 1973, p 18*

[1969]

tadpole galaxy, any of a group of radio galaxies (sources of intense radio signals) having an elongated structure whose shape suggests a tadpole.

Tadpole galaxies appear to be an interesting variation on normal radio sources, one in which the familiar double structure is distorted by motion through the surrounding gas. *"The Magnetic Skeleton of a Cosmic Tadpole," New Scientist, Jan. 16, 1975, p 118*

[1973]

tae·kwon·do ('tai₁kwan'dou), *n.* a method of self-defense developed in Korea, using powerful kicks and punches to disable an opponent.

Developed in Korea, tae kwon do is generally, except by Koreans, considered a style of karate. Like Japanese and Okinawan styles, it has origins traceable to China. *"The East at a Glance," Esquire, Aug. 1973, p 73*

Ford lunched with the troops and watched a taekwondo, the traditional Korean martial art, championship match between two divisions. *"President Ford's Far Eastern Road Show," Time, Dec. 2, 1974, p 17*

[1966, from Korean]

ta·ga·ri (tə'gɑ: ri:), *n.* a popular Greek shoulder bag, usually made of brightly patterned, coarse wool.

European stores still offer many bargains for the perspicacious visitor. In Italy, Fendi handbags and Nazareno Gabrielli shoes cost 25% less than they do in the U.S. Greece's hand-woven shoulder bags, called *tagari*, are priced at only $7. *Time, June 19, 1978, p 79*

[1967, from Modern Greek *tagári* peasant bag]

tag sale, a sale of old or used household belongings in which items for sale carry price tags.

. . . a tag sale where the prices are within anyone's reach

458

but the merchandise is mostly too shabby or useless to bother with. *John W. Schulz, Forbes, Aug. 15, 1974, p 103*

[1974] Compare GARAGE SALE, YARD SALE.

tailback, *n. British.* a long line of automobiles and trucks caused by an obstruction on the road.

On the northbound carriageway of the M1, there was a 12-mile tailback, while westbound drivers had long delays on the M4, aggravated by an accident between Slough and Maidenhead. *The Times (London), Aug. 26, 1978, p 1*

[1977]

tailgating, *n. U.S.* a social gathering, especially of football fans outside a stadium, at which refreshments or a meal are served from the tailgate of a station wagon, the rear of a van, etc.

Tailgating started years ago at Ivy League games, where alumni would serve genteel picnics from the backs of their station wagons. Cold chicken and Chablis was a typical menu. . . . The super bowl of tailgating occurs when the Green Bay Packers visit the Minnesota Vikings. *"Modern Living: The Other Super Bowl," Time, Oct. 15, 1973, p 87*

[1973]

ta·ka or **tak·ka** (ˈtɑː kə), *n.; pl.* **-ka** or **-kas.** the monetary unit of Bangladesh, introduced in 1972.

Mr. [S. A.] Karim is Political Secretary for the Ministry of Foreign Affairs in the new government. Like all Bengalis, he can draw a salary of no more than 2,000 takas, or about $275 a month. *William S. Ellis, "Bangladesh: Hope Nourishes a New Nation," National Geographic Magazine, Sept. 1972, p 302*

"People without Government housing have to find 1,000 takka a month (£33 at the market exchange rate) for rent while their pay has been cut to 1,500 takka, and everything they consume has gone up between 100 and 300 per cent." *Walter Schwarz, The Manchester Guardian Weekly, Oct. 27, 1973, p 6*

[1972, from Bengali]

talking head, a person shown talking on a television or motion-picture screen.

Television often achieves its best effects by moving in close. 'Talking heads' can be superb television. I remember vividly, after more than a decade, A. J. P. Taylor's scintillating lectures on British prime ministers, delivered standing in a studio and looking straight into a camera from behind his floppy bow tie. *Norman Moss, The Listener, Jan. 22, 1976, p 70*

"The Memory of Justice" is, in Ophuls's deprecatory phrase, "another talking-head movie," an assembly of many recent interviews interspliced with stock footage. *Michael Wood, The New York Times Magazine, Oct. 17, 1976, p 37*

Len Maguire . . . is no glamorous figure—he probably wouldn't even get an audition as a television "talking head." *Ernest Leogrande, "Movies," Daily News (New York), May 30, 1979, p 27*

[1973, originally used (in television industry parlance) chiefly in the plural as a derogatory reference to an interview, documentary, etc., that lacks visual excitement or interest]

talking shop or **talk shop,** *British.* a group or organization considered too weak or ineffectual to do anything more than engage in argument and discussion.

It was H. Wilson himself who said "royal commissions take minutes but last years." They are an all too familiar device—used too much by this present Government—for pushing awkward questions under the carpet. They can become meaningless talking shops. *"Balm to the Doctors' Fury," The Manchester Guardian Weekly, Oct. 26, 1975, p 6*

Sir Michael is opposed to any such council. In the first interview he has given to the press since taking office, he said: "I have said that if it does not have any power it is merely another talk shop, and if it does have power, it undermines the governors." But he recognizes the demand for some body that would issue an occasional sharp rebuke to the BBC. *The Times (London), July 24, 1973, p 4*

[1960, applied originally to Parliament; probably influenced by verb phrase *talk(ing) shop* (1850's)]

talk jockey, *U.S.* the host of a radio program which solicits telephone calls as part of the broadcast.

One of the most imitated and controversial new formats was the sex-oriented talk show in which female listeners discuss intimate details of their love lives by telephone with male "Talk Jockeys" (T.J.'s). *June Bundy Csida, "Radio," The 1973 World Book Year Book, p 479*

[1972, patterned on *disk jockey* (1940's)] Compare DISCO JOCKEY.

tall ship, a square-rigged sailing vessel, used chiefly as a training ship for naval cadets.

The Tall Ships—the great sailing ships from around the world—captured the national imagination, and they seemed to do so simply because they did, not because we were told that they should. *Elizabeth Drew, "A Reporter in Washington, D.C.," The New Yorker, Sept. 20, 1976, p 110*

Operation Sail, aided by the American Sail Training Association, brought 16 tall ships, old windjammers, and 77 smaller craft (60 of them manned by 3,000 cadet trainees) across the Atlantic Ocean. *Bill Braddock, "Sailing," The Americana Annual 1977, p 474*

[1976] ► The spectacular procession of sailing ships during the U.S. Bicentennial celebrations in 1976 made this a popular term and substantially widened its usage beyond John Masefield's "Sea-Fever" (1902):

I must go down to the seas again, to
   the lonely sea and the sky,
And all I ask is a tall ship and
   a star to steer her by . . .

But the phrase precedes Masefield by three centuries (OED 1582).

ta·ma·ru·go (ˌtɑ mɑːˈru gou), *n.* a tree (*Prosapis tamarugo*) of Chile, related to the mesquite.

The tamarugo . . . grows in a part of Chile's desolate Atacama Desert where no rain falls in most years. Salt deposits, which are death to most plants, are so thick and widespread there that, except for the tamarugo groves, the area looks like a desolate moonscape. Chilean scientists have found that tamarugo leaves and pods are rich in protein, and large herds of sheep now graze on them. . . . The tamarugo may also be useful in developing livestock industries in other salt desert regions. *Noel D. Vietmeyer, "Prospecting for Green Gold," The World Book Science Annual 1977 (1976), p 72*

[1976, from Spanish, probably from Pampa del *Tamarugal*, name of plateau in the Atacama desert of northern Chile]

tan·noy (ˈtæn ɔi), *British.* —*n.* a public-address system.

A little tannoy fanfare sound, and out come six competitors, never more than six to a race, led by kennel lads. *Ray Gosling, "A Night at the Dogs," The Listener, March 1, 1973, p 262*

A tannoy, droning out the while, is heard intoning "The major of Hackney." *The Times (London), July 28, 1973, p 12*

—*v.i.* to broadcast over such a system.

The Portuguese Socialist leader arrives behind a convoy of tannoying cars and almost bounces into the crowd. *Robert Fisk, The Times (London), April 24, 1976, p 4*

[1969 for noun, from *Tannoy* (1960) the trademark of such a system; 1966 for verb]

tape-delay, *n.* **1** a delay between recording on a tape recorder and the programming of the recording on a broadcast to eliminate possible unwanted material.

Most television people have treated the common public with great mistrust, filtering them through auditions, then through moderators, and then, as a final safeguard, through a tape-delay for blips, before allowing them to appear on the air. *Jonathan Price, "Video Pioneers: From Banality to Beauty: TV As a New Form of Visual Art," Harper's, June 1972, p 92*

"When the show gets started, I'll phone the callers back and keep four of them on hold for Lou Adler to choose from. So far, sixty per cent of the calls have been about snow removal, but we're going to use only two on the air, so that there will be a broad range of subjects discussed. We're also on a fifteen-second tape delay to prevent abusive language." *"The Talk of the Town," The New Yorker, Feb. 6, 1978, p 27*

2 the tape recording of a segment of live music to play it back in order to create a fuller sound or the effect of an echo by combining the taped segment with the continued live performance.

The hallmarks of this style are well-known: asymmetrical riffs, cool-jazz harmonies, interlocking polymetric loops, striding tunes in octaves on fuzz bass and organ, tape-delay and wah-wah filtering effects. *Tim Souster, "Pop Music: Soft Machine," The Listener, July 26, 1973, p 127*

[1966]

ta·phon·o·my (tə'fan ə mi:), *n.* **1** the processes and conditions which plant and animal matter are subject to as they become fossilized.

A survey by Michael R. Voorhies of the University of Georgia on the taphonomy (sequence and arrangement of fossil deposition) and population dynamics of an early Pliocene . . . *W. E. Swinton, The Americana Annual 1970, p 528*

2 the study of the processes and conditions of becoming fossilized.

In the years since it was founded the project has brought together workers from many countries who represent many different disciplines: geology, geophysics, paleontology, anatomy, archaeology, ecology and taphonomy. *Alan Walker and Richard E. F. Leakey, "The Hominids of East Turkana," Scientific American, Aug. 1978, p 54*

[1969, from Greek *táphos* tomb + -*nomy* suffix meaning system or field of knowledge]

taph·o·nom·ic (ˌtæf ə'nam ik), *adj.:* We made a taphonomic analysis to determine if they were aquatic or land animals. *Robert T. Bakker, "A New Image for Dinosaurs," The World Book Science Annual 1977 (1976), p 55*

taphonomist, *n.:* The Russian scientists have brought together a team of geologists, geophysicists, palaeontologists and a group of taphonomists: the last belong to a speciality created in Russia for studying the way animals and plants are preserved in their burial sites. *The Times (London), March 2, 1974, p 19*

TAPS (tæps), *n.* acronym for *Trans-Alaska Pipeline System.*

The start-up of the pipeline—known as TAPS—marks the virtual completion of a project which has cost eight of the world's biggest oil companies some $15 billions. In about four weeks' time that first oil will reach the pipeline's shipping terminal at Valdez on the southern Alaskan coast. *Charles Cook, The Manchester Guardian Weekly, June 26, 1977, p 6*

[1970]

ta·ra·ma·sa·la·ta or **ta·ra·mo·sa·la·ta** (ˌtar ə mə sə'la: tə), *n.* a Greek appetizer consisting of a light creamy paste of fish roe mixed with bread crumbs or boiled potato, grated onion, dill, etc.

The Justin de Blank shop will have the same food as in Elizabeth Street—home-cured bacon from Wiltshire, quiches, kipper pate, taramasalata and so on. *"Counterpoint," The Times (London), March 10, 1972, p 9*

Taramosalata: red fish-roe spread, usually made with carp. *"Middle Eastern Muddle," Cue Magazine, Jan. 22 thru Feb. 4, 1977, p 11*

[1965, from Modern Greek *taramosaláta*, from *taramâs* fish roe + *saláta* salad]

tardive dys·ki·ne·sia (ˌdis kə'ni: ʒə), a neuromuscular disorder marked by involuntary twitching of facial and other muscles, occurring as a complication of prolonged therapy with antipsychotic drugs.

A main side-effect of their long-term use is that the patient may develop tardive dyskinesia, a nervous disorder resulting in constant spasms and twitches of the facial muscles and uncontrollable movements of the tongue, lips and jaws. As well as being extremely unpleasant, it may interfere severely with speaking and eating. *The Times (London), Oct. 25, 1978, p 21*

Scientists suspect that the cause of tardive dyskinesia is a lack of acetylcholine, which is depleted by years of using antipsychotic drugs. *Bill Gottlieb, "Brain Food," Prevention, Sept. 1979, p 182*

[1976, *dyskinesia* from *dys-* bad, abnormal + -*kinesia* combining form meaning motion, movement, from Greek *kínēsis*] *Abbreviation:* TD

tar·dy·on (ˈtar di:ˌan), *n.* elementary particle that moves at a velocity less than the speed of light.

It is perfectly possible to convert a particle from one class to another. For example, an electron and a positron, both of which are tardyons, can combine to form gamma rays. . . . There would seem, then, to be no theoretical objection to the conversion of tardyons to tachyons and back again, if the proper procedure could be found. *Isaac Asimov, "The Ultimate Speed Limit," Saturday Review, July 8, 1972, p 56*

If they [tachyons] exist, they would have the property of moving faster than light. By contrast, all the more mundane matter that we know about that moves at less than the speed of light would be lumped under the general heading of "tardyons," or "slowly moving ones." *James S. Trefil, "Traveling Faster Than Light," Encyclopedia Science Supplement (Grolier) 1979 (1978), p 309*

[1970, coined by Olexa-Myron Bilaniuk, an American physicist, patterned on *tachyon*] Compare LUXON.

Tartan Turf, the trademark of an artificial surface resembling grass, used especially for playing fields.

I stand behind the batting cage, watching in awe as Bobby Tolan, Joe Morgan, Pete Rose, Johnny Bench, and Tony Perez lace a rookie pitcher's fat deliveries far out into the unnaturally green reaches of the artificial Tartan Turf. *J. Anthony Lukas, "Way to Go, Jonathan Seagull!" Saturday Review, Nov. 11, 1972, p 7*

[1966] Compare ASTROTURF.

Ta·sa·day (ˌtɑː sɑːˈdɑi), *n.; pl.* **-day** or **-days.** a member of a cave-dwelling forest people of Stone-Age culture, discovered in 1971. *Often used attributively.*

The Tasaday are a . . . people recently discovered in the rain forests of the Philippines who may have had no contact with the outside world for centuries. Until this decade they were food gatherers; in other words they may exemplify the human state at a time when it had only just moved from the animal level. *William Golding, The Manchester Guardian Weekly, Oct. 4, 1975, p 21*

[1971, named by their Filipino discoverers after a range of nearby mountains] Compare ACHÉ, YANOMAMA.

Ta·ser ('tei zər), *n.* the trademark of a small gunlike device for firing electrified darts which temporarily immobilize a person.

Unlike a real gun, the Taser is not supposed to cause permanent damage. *Steven Aaronson, "Technology," Encyclopedia Science Supplement (Grolier) 1976, p 345*

The Montgomery County incident is not the first in which the Taser was used to commit a crime. Last September a Taser was used to hold up a gas station attendant in Miami. *"Robbery Victims Cowed by Taser," New York Post, Jan. 14, 1976, p 24*

—*v.t.* to immobilize with a Taser.

A powerful transformer within the Taser generates 50,000 volts when a trigger is pressed. This jolt, sent through the wires into the darts, which have been shot into the skin or clothing of the victim, cause him to become "Tasered." *Fred Ferretti, "Zap!" The New York Times Magazine, Jan. 4, 1976, p 13*

[1971 (patented in 1974), from *Tele-Active Shock Electronic Repulsion*; form influenced by *laser*]

tau, *n.* a weakly interacting elementary particle with a mass about three and a half thousand times that of the electron.

The tau joins the lepton group of particles, which interact only through the forces of the weak nuclear interaction responsible for the radioactive decay of nuclei and electromagnetism. The electron is the best known member of the family. *James Dodd, New Scientist, Dec. 21/28, 1978, p 935*

The number of massive leptons that exist limits the possible number of quark flavors. At the moment three massive leptons are known: the electron, the muon and the tau. If that is all the massive leptons there are, then quark flavors are limited to six. But there could be more massive leptons. They are limited by the number of possible neutrinos. (Neutrinos are leptons with zero mass.) *Science News, Jan. 20, 1979, p 43*

[1978, from the Greek name of the first letter of Greek *tríton* third, adopted to indicate that the particle is the third charged lepton after the electron and the muon]

tax disc, *British.* a small, round sticker, affixed usually to the windshield of a motor vehicle, indicating road tax for that vehicle has been paid.

The Government yesterday acted against protests in Cornwall over road tax laws imposed by Westminster. More than 100 motorists have said they will not renew their tax discs. Instead, they want the ancient Cornish Stannary Parliament, which was revived in 1974 after a 222-year break, to issue discs of its own. *The Times (London), Aug. 1, 1978, p 4*

[1972]

taxmobile, *n. U.S.* a bus or other motor vehicle serving as a traveling tax-service facility.

"Taxmobiles" staffed with agents now trundle through back-country roads in Tennessee and into shopping centers in California bringing tax assistance to all who want it. *"Taxes: The War On Refund Mills," Time, March 12, 1973, p 92*

[1973, from *tax* + auto*mobile*, patterned on *art-mobile, bloodmobile, bookmobile*]

tax revolt, *U.S.* a vote or lobbying effort to reduce property taxes that are considered to be excessive.

That angry noise was the sound of a middle class tax revolt erupting, and its tremors are shaking public officials from Sacramento to Washington. *"Sound and Fury Over Taxes," Time, June 19, 1978, p 13*

The tax revolt of the middle 1970's coincided with the emergence of single-issue lobbying as a potent technique of legislative and electoral politics. . . . This suggests that the tax revolt that burst into full bloom in 1978 may continue to gain breadth and momentum. *Edward Cowan, "Taxpayers' Revolt," 1979 Collier's Encyclopedia Year Book (1978), p 579*

[1978] ▶ The term became current with the passage in June 1978 of PROPOSITION 13, an amendment to the California state constitution which cut back the state's property taxes 57 per cent. The success of this popular initiative encouraged taxpayers throughout the country to put on the state ballots similar measures designed to reduce increasing government taxation.

Tay-Sachs ('tei,sæks), *n.* a fatal hereditary disease of children characterized by degeneration of the cells of the central nervous system. It is caused by a deficiency of the enzyme hexoaminidase.

A team of Montreal medical specialists has discovered Tay-Sachs in proportions never known before in the last place they might have looked—among non-Jewish French Canadians in the heartland of eastern Quebec. *Glen Allen, "Medicine," Maclean's, April 19, 1976, p 57*

—*adj.* of or relating to this disease.

Tay-Sachs carriers—people who have the Tay-Sachs gene—are 10 times more prevalent among the Jewish population who have their ancestral origins in central and eastern Europe. *William Stockton, "Death in the Family," The New York Times Magazine, Sept. 12, 1979, p 29*

[1976, shortened from *Tay-Sachs disease* (1951), named after Warren *Tay*, 1843-1927, an English ophthalmologist, and Bernard *Sachs*, 1858-1944, an American neurologist]

TCDD, abbreviation of *tetrachlorodibenzo-p-dioxin*, a very poisonous and persistent impurity present in herbicides, also known as dioxin.

TCDD . . . is recognised as one of the most powerful foetus damaging (teratogenic) chemicals known, and has been shown experimentally to be at least a million times more potent than thalidomide. *Anthony Tucker, The Manchester Guardian Weekly, Aug. 15, 1976, p 9*

TCDD is one of the most toxic substances known to man, and . . . Dow Chemical is the world's largest producer of the herbicide 2,4,5-T, which is contaminated with TCDD yet is used in spray operations affecting millions of acres of this country's forestlands, rangelands, pasturelands, and utility and railroad rights of way each year. *"The Talk of the Town," The New Yorker, Dec. 18, 1978, p 27*

[1971]

T cell, or **T-cell,** *n.* a lymph cell that defends the body against disease and foreign matter.

T cells are responsible, among other things, for the rejection of transplants, resistance to fungal infections and killing cells infected with viruses. *The Times (London), Jan. 25, 1978, p 11*

Back in the "Dark Ages" of immunological research — say five years ago — only two major kinds of white blood cells appeared to serve as immunological defenders of the body. These were B cells and T cells. T cells, however, have since been found to consist of at least three different subpopulations — killer T cells (credited with killing tumors and other "enemies"), helper T cells (henchmen to the killer T cells) and suppressor T cells (moderates that keep killer Ts from going overboard in slaying the enemy). *Science News, Nov. 18, 1978, p 342*

[1970, from *thymus-derived cell*] Also called T LYMPHOCYTE. Compare B CELL. See also LYMPHOKINE.

tchotch·ke ('tʃɔtʃ kə), *n. U.S. Slang.* a showy trifle or toy; trinket; gewgaw; bric-a-brac.

A New York, N.Y. Boutique, to the left of the entrance, [is] stocked with a careful selection of New York's best tchotchkes. These include thirteen-inch-long matchbooks . . . , bronze Empire State Buildings with thermometers in them . . . , candles that look like bottles of Pepsi; and, naturally, candles that look like apples. *"The Talk of the Town," The New Yorker, Aug. 1, 1977, p 14*

[1968, from Yiddish *tshotshke*] Also spelled TSATSKE.

TD, abbreviation of TARDIVE DYSKINESIA.

TD is fairly common among chronic mental patients who have taken antipsychotic drugs for a substantial period of time. Scientists also believe that inadequate acetylcholine production may be linked to other ailments such as mania and memory loss. *Science News, Feb. 11, 1978, p 85*

[1976]

T-dress, *n.* a T-shirt long enough to be worn as a dress.

Jackets, at $10, and T-dresses, at $21, are summer items and are where you can find them. *Lawrence Van Gelder, "Mapping Out an Underground Style," The New York Times, Sept. 18, 1976, p 11*

[1967, from *T-shirt + dress*]

teachware, *n.* audio-visual material used in teaching.

Audio-visual equipment exhibitors comprised the largest group of represented countries. Half the companies showing AV equipment came from outside Germany, mainly from the US and France. These two countries each provided another word for the audio-visual vocabulary; "teachware" from the Americans and the "videogramme" from the French. *Garry Pownall, "AV View," New Scientist, May 11, 1972, p 346*

[1972, from *teach, v. + -ware*, as in *software*]

team-teach, *v.i. U.S. and Canadian.* to practice or engage in team teaching.

Two answers to this problem . . . are to teach science ethics to college students by presenting them realistic case studies and to bring industrial scientists into the universities to team-teach. *"Corporate Scientists: Ethics of Dissension," Science News, Feb. 28, 1976, p 135*

[1976, back formation from TEAM TEACHING]

team teaching, a method of classroom instruction in which two or more teachers skilled in separate subjects are jointly responsible for teaching a group of students.

Team teaching, in which a master teacher and several specially selected and prepared assistants approached a single classroom as a team, . . . *Fred M. Hechinger, "Education: Reforms: Program That Flunked," The New York Times, Dec. 10, 1972, Sec. 4, p 5*

[1961]

Technical Terms. ► Many technical terms are common words to which the specialist assigns a highly restricted meaning, often one that is totally unfamiliar to the nonspecialist. Most dictionaries enter a considerable portion of the specialized vocabularies of the arts and sciences, and the technical terms included in this dictionary are those which have appeared with increasing frequency in recent years in general or popular periodicals. Their appearance in these sources indicates an expansion of general interest in technological achievement.

Many of these terms were used in their specialized fields a long time before they began to appear in general circulation. For example, the term EXECUTIVE PRIVILEGE was first used in some legal cases in the early 1950's, but it was not until the 1970's that it attained widespread currency. The term LACTO-OVO-VEGETARIAN goes back at least to 1952, but a revival of interest in vegetarianism popularized it in 1975.

A number of new scientific terms, such as MAGNETOTAXIS, NUCLEOSOME, PHYTOTOXIN, STEROIDOGENESIS, have been formed in the classical pattern, derivative of Latin and Greek stems and are typical of the terms long familiar in the international scientific world. But there are other creations of individualistic and often whimsical terms such as QUARK and CHARM in nuclear physics, GENE-SPLICING and STICKY ENDS in molecular biology, WHITE HOLE and WORMHOLE in astronomy, and FUZZY SET in mathematics that do not follow the established patterns. Some of these inspire the formation of whole groups of similar words. Thus, *charm* became the model for FLAVOR, COLOR, TRUTH, and BEAUTY. The analogy of the genetic code with the alphabet led to the use of such common words as SENTENCE, WORD, and SYNONYM to designate various sequences of nucleotides.

A consequence of advancing technology with its increasing specialization of meaning is that a dictionary definition is often no longer fully understood by the person who does not have some previous knowledge of the principles and basic vocabulary of the field (for example, the six entries RECOMBINANT, RECOMBINANT DNA, RECOMBINANT DNA RESEARCH, RECOMBINATIONAL REPAIR, RESTRICTION ENZYME, and RESTRICTION SITE). The quotations, etymologies, cross-references, and explanatory notes which accompany the bare defintions should help the nonspecialized reader understand the terms, but some basic knowledge (the meaning of "gene," "molecule," and "enzyme") is assumed as a general education comes to encompass more exposure to technical fields.

Among the physical sciences, some of the most productive contributors of new technical terms in recent years have been:

biochemistry (CYTOCHALASIN, ETHIDIUM, EN-KEPHALIN, ENDORPHIN),
physics (AXION, INSTANTON, TARDYON),
astronomy (WHITE HOLE, SINGULARITY, BLUE SHIFT, BOW SHOCK),
geology (ARMALCOLITE, CLAST, OBDUCT, PLUME).

As study progressed there were other prolific contributors of new technical terminology:

psychology (ETHOGRAM, FLOODING, HYPNO-DRAMA),
economics (FLOAT, M₁, OKUN'S LAW),
education (ACCOUNTABILITY, COMPREHENSIVIZA-TION, MAINSTREAM).

Technological fields as diverse as military defense, environment, and energy have produced an abundance of terms: DIAL-UP, GRASER, BEAM WEAPON, TRI-CAP, HEAT ISLAND, CO-GENERATION, and TERTIARY RECOVERY.

A study of the technical terms included in this book will show contributions from over seventy specialized areas. Some examples from various other fields include:

aerospace (BIOSHIELD, SLINGSHOT, TIMELINE),
art (COLOR-FIELD, DE-ACCESSION, PHOTO-REALISM).
architecture (ECOTECTURE, POST-MODERNISM),
broadcasting (CRAWL, MEDIAGENIC),
communications (COMPANDING, TELETEXT),
cookery (GYRO, PICADILLO),
dancing (HUSTLE, SALSA),
fashion and design (BEANBAG, HIGH-TECH, LAYER-ING, RETRO),
finance (DEGEAR, FAIL),
history (CLIOMETRICS, PSYCHOBIOGRAPHY),
journalism (FACTOID, NEWS HOLE),
literature (LIT CRIT, PHOTONOVEL),
music (HEAVY-METAL, FUSION),
narcotics (BONG, THAI STICK),
photography (FALSE COLOR, REACTION SHOT),

politics (CONVERGENCE, MARKUP),
printing (INK-JET, VIDIFONT),
recording (CLAP TRACK, DOLBY),
sports (BEATOUT, EVENTING),
transportation (FLY-DRIVE, WET LEASING).

technicism or **technism,** *n.* excessive emphasis on practical results, technical methods, and procedures; that which relies too much on mechanical tools, etc.

Mylai exposed us as victims of the increasing impersonal technicism of the style of warfare evolved in Vietnam; it was "just another job to be done" with "American know-how." *Francine du Plessix Gray, Saturday Review, Nov. 18, 1972, p 77*

In our highly developed technological society we have adopted, usually without knowing it, the implicit ideology called "technism," which places central value on what can be measured with numbers, assigns numbers to what cannot be measured, and redefines everything else as self-expression or entertainment. *Kenneth Keniston, The New York Times, Feb. 19, 1976, p 35*

[1971]

technicist, *adj.:* A technicist society indifferent to location and continuity will undermine itself by wrecking the structures of meaning on which any society must rest. *The Times (London), March 16, 1974, p 16*

technify, *v.t., v.i.* to provide with or adopt technical materials, methods, etc.; make or become technically efficient.

It relies on money and technology in unparalleled quantities. This method is designed to be effective against other industrial and technified countries, whose organisation can be so disrupted that they simply can no longer function. *Eric Hobsbawm, The Listener, May 18, 1972, p 640*

They internalized their intelligence activities with headlong speed. They technified senselessly — charts, graphs, bugs, concealed cameras, dart guns, phone taps, the most expensive monitoring equipment ever to appear on any agent's expense voucher, where a single inside source and a few intelligent questions would have been enough. *Andrew St. George, "The Cold War Comes Home," Harper's, Nov. 1973, p 82*

[1972]

technology transfer, the transfer of new or advanced technological information, especially from the developed to the less developed countries of the world.

Technology transfer is sometimes used to describe information dissemination, but this is only a part of the technology transfer process. *Footnote, Arthur A. Ezra, "Technology Utilization: Incentives and Solar Energy," Science, Feb. 28, 1975, p 713*

Regarding technology transfer, the . . . paper calls on the developed nations to "ensure full and free access to those technologies that are essential to [Third World] development, including advanced technologies." New technology should be supplied to the developing world on favourlable terms, which were not spelt out. *"Group of 77 Calls the Shots," New Scientist, June 7, 1979, p 825*

[1973]

technosphere, *n.* human technology; the technological activities of mankind.

It is encouraging to see so much evidence of concrete results relevant to the urgent environmental tasks of assist-

463

ing the biosphere to hold out against the brutal impact of the technosphere. *Max Nicholson, Review of "Ecology and Reclamation of Devastated Land," edited by Russell J. Hutnik and Grant Davis, New Scientist, Dec. 13, 1973, p 792* [1972]

tectonomagnetism, *n.* anomalies in the earth's magnetic field caused by stresses in the earth's crust.

Tectonomagnetism . . . is attracting increasing interest as a method of monitoring local changes in Earth stress. *P. M. Davis and F. D. Stacey, Brisbane, Australia, "Letters to Nature: Geomagnetic Anomalies Caused by a Man-made Lake," Nature, Dec. 8, 1972, p 348*

[1972, from *tectonic* (of the earth's crust) + connecting *-o-* + *magnetism*]

tectonomagnetic, *adj.:* Theory has it that stress in the earth's crust causes local anomalies in the magnetic field . . . If it could be quantified, the so-called tectonomagnetic effect could provide a means of monitoring stress on faults and eventually forecasting earthquakes. *"Earth Sciences: The Magnetism of Stress," Science News, Dec. 23, 1972, p 408*

teeny, *n. Informal.* a teen-ager.

Prince Andrew, the 16-year-old son of Queen Elizabeth, has proved the favorite among royal visitors with many Canadians. "He's the biggest thing for teenies since Bjorn Borg," said one person. *The New York Times, July 29, 1976, p 26*

[1971, from *teen-ager* + *-y* diminutive suffix]

TEFL ('tef əl), *n.* acronym for *teaching English as a foreign language.*

There is a growing awareness of the similarities of the various types of English teaching, as well as a recognition of the need for communication among teachers. Well-designed TESL or TEFL curricula, regardless of the type of program, share certain objectives and principles which emphasize the need for integration of the student into the target language community through carefully designed linguistic and cultural instruction. *Newsletter of the American Dialect Society, Nov. 1974, p 45*

[1963] Compare ESL, TESOL, TOEFL.

teh ch'i ('te 'tʃi:), **1** a vibration detected by an acupuncturist when an acupuncture point is reached.

The traditional Chinese doctors could tell whether a person was a likely candidate for acupuncture through a phenomenon called Teh Ch'i. Teh Ch'i is a vibration in the acupuncture needle that the doctor feels as he pushes through the surface layers of skin and begins twirling. *The Rhodesia Herald, April 6, 1973, p 27*

2 the sensation experienced by the patient when an acupuncture point is reached.

First, the correct point must be chosen in order to affect the required zone of the body; second, the needles at the correct point must elicit a special sensation called t'eh chi which has four qualities: heaviness, swelling and numbness, and soreness. *Pat Wall, New Scientist, Oct. 3, 1974, p 34*

[1973, from Chinese]

teleconference, *n.* a conference of a group of people linked by long distance telephone.

Other specialized European satellite services envisaged

include public data networks, private computer networks, remote printing, "teleconference" facilities and, in the longer term, videophone and electronic mail services. *Kenneth Owen, "Plugging the Sea Platforms Into the Telephone Network," The Times (London), Jan. 16, 1976, p 19*

[1974, from *tele-* long-distance + *conference*]

teleconsultation, *n.* a medical consultation made by means of long-distance telemetric equipment, closed-circuit television, etc.

Besides live seminars originating at the National Medical Audiovisual Center in Atlanta, there will be computer-assisted instruction (the satellites also handle computer data), "tele-consultation," allowing the VA doctors to consult with specialists at teaching institutions, and even full patient-case presentations and diagnosis. *Jonathan Eberhart, "A People Satellite," Science News, April 6, 1974, p 227*

[1971]

telecopier, *n.* a machine for transmitting and reproducing graphic material (such as written copy and drawings) over telephone lines.

The back of the plane looks more like a business office than like a campaign plane: a desk with two electric typewriters; . . . and a telecopier (which takes down copy that comes over a telephone). *Elizabeth Drew, "A Reporter in Washington, D.C.," The New Yorker, Jan. 10, 1977, p 46*

[1970]

telemedicine, *n.* the practice of medicine by means of telemetric, telephone, and television apparatus.

As well as these universally significant impacts, the video telephone will also play a part in . . . medicine ("decades hence, medical historians might write that telemedicine was only an easier way to deliver poorer quality health care"). *Michael Kenward, "Assessing the Impact of the Video Telephone," New Scientist, Sept. 20, 1973, p 694*

[1970]

tel·e·o·nom·ic (ˌtel i: əˈnɑm ik), *adj.* governed or determined by an overall purpose.

In the end you come to the conclusion that teleonomic behaviour is a necessary defining characteristic of living beings. *Sir Peter Medawar in Conversation with Jacques Monod, "The Ethic of Knowledge," The Listener, Aug. 3, 1972, p 137*

C. S. Pittendrigh in *Behaviour and Evolution,* suggested that the word teleological should be reserved for cases where the idea of the end (goal) precedes the use of the means, and the world teleonomic for cases where the ends result from means that lack design (intent)—as when adaptive traits are produced by random mutations and natural selection. *William H. Gilbert, "Correspondence: Teleological vs Teleonomic," Nature, March 20, 1975, p 176*

[1971, derivative of *teleonomy* (1970), from *teleo-* end, purpose + *-nomy* system of rules]

telephone bank, rows of telephones operated especially by volunteers to solicit votes, charitable contributions, etc.

The mobilization of labor . . . included . . . telephone banks in 638 localities, using 8,058 telephones, manned by 24,611 union men and women and their families. *John A. Davenport, National Review, Aug. 2, 1974, p 866*

One such recruit . . . worked telephone banks turning people out for ward conventions, the first step in the delegate selection process. *Time, June 28, 1976, p 12*

[1972]

teletext, *n.* a communications system in which printed information transmitted by television is displayed on a screen by a special encoder attached to the set.

While the general benefits of teletext are becoming familiar, its potential for deaf viewers has been largely overlooked. Together with the Post Office's proposed telephone-linked View-data service, teletext could help to revolutionize communications for the deaf and the hard of hearing. *Kenneth Owen, "Electronics Put the Blind and Deaf in Closer Touch With the Printed Word," The Times (London), Jan. 7, 1977, p 17*

Viewdata and teletext, which allow a viewer to display a "page" of information from a choice of several hundred, will convert television sets into home terminals. *Raymond L. Boggs, in a Letter to the Editor, The New York Times Magazine, Sept. 23, 1979, p 110*

[1975, from *tele*vision + *text*]

temp, *n.* a temporary employee, especially a typist or secretary.

He asked: "What are your ambitions? What sort of secretary do you want to be?" "The top!" she said with a surprising burst of energy. "Well, not really, I want to earn enough to drive about in my own car. Maybe I'd like to be a temp later on." She probably couldn't have said anything more disastrous. The company would not be keen to train someone who was going to take off to become a temp. *Polly Toynbee, The Manchester Guardian Weekly (Le Monde section), July 2, 1978, p 19*

—*v.i.* to work as a temporary employee.

Most of the students had given as their explanation for deciding to temp: "To gain office experience before taking up a permanent job." *The Times (London), Oct. 2, 1978, p III*

[1965 for noun; 1973 for verb; shortened from *temporary*]

tem·peh ('tem pei), *n.* a food of Indonesia, made by fermenting soaked, hulled soybeans with rhizopus fungus and frying them in deep fat.

A student researching in physics at the Australian National University believes that tempeh, a soya bean-based food used in Indonesia for 2000 years, could help to fill empty stomachs in underdeveloped areas. *"Shorter News: . . . And Feeding Them," The Geographical, March 1972, p 428*

The use of fabricated soya protein illustrates the peculiar attractiveness of meat to Western tastes; in the East soya beans are converted domestically by a fermentation process into a kind of cheesecake called *tempeh*, thus contributing equal nutritional value while suiting a different taste. *Magnus Pyke, "Food," 1973 Collier's Encyclopedia Year Book (1972), p 294*

[1966, from Indonesian *tempé*]

10-4 or **ten-four,** *interj. U.S. Slang.* a term meaning "message received," "affirmative," "OK," used especially by citizens band radio operators.

"Aaay, we definitely thank you for that info, good buddy. We'll back 'em down a hair. You a westbound?"

"Aaay, 10-4 on that. You got the Jack of Diamonds on this end, and we definitely westbound. How's it look over your shoulder, good buddy?" *Michael Harwood, "America With Its Ears On," The New York Times Magazine, April 25, 1976, p 64*

"Ten four old buddy, see you on the flip" they yell as their trucks pass in a roar of spray and fumes. And they rejoice in communicating at last after decades of stern silence, glaring from behind the television pictures of their windscreens. *Simon Winchester, "Where American Grit Lives On," The Manchester Guardian Weekly, May 30, 1976, p 1*

[1963] ► The term was used earlier by police and other radio operators in the *ten code* to minimize air time: "leaving the air" (*10-7*), "repeat message" (*10-9*), and "trouble, emergency" (*10-34*). See the note under CB.

tennis toe, severe bruising of the toenails of tennis players, caused by abrupt stops which rupture small blood vessels in the toes.

Known for the severe throbbing pain it causes, tennis toe can be recognized by a swelling of the toe with a purple discoloration below the nail. According to the Podiatry Society of the State of New York, it can be prevented by wearing thick socks and well-fitted sneakers so that the foot doesn't slide inside the shoe. *Roscoe Tanner, "Tennis Pro Warns of Tennis Toe," New York Magazine, June 4, 1979, p 9*

[1973, patterned on *tennis elbow*] Compare HOLLOW FOOT, SURFER'S KNOB. See also SPORTS MEDICINE.

tensor light or **tensor lamp,** a high-intensity lamp with a hinged metal shaft that can be extended to various positions.

Thad and I had really nice offices with tensor lights all over the place. *James Dickey, Deliverance, 1970, p 17*

The hall has . . . fifteen dart boards along the walls, and tables and chairs in the middle. Each board has its own tensor lamp and a line taped eight feet in front of it. *Steven Warner, The Atlantic, Aug. 1973, p 75*

[1970, from *Tensor*, trademark (1962), from New Latin *tensor* thing that stretches, from Latin *tendere* to stretch]

tent trailer, a lightweight trailer that serves as a base for a canvas tent that unfolds for camping.

BOAC's latest holiday idea is worth mentioning here. Simply, the Landcruise holiday provides you with a motorcaravan or a car with a caravan or tent trailer and leaves you free to wander at will. *John Carter, "Summer Holidays: Advance Booking Will Bring Transatlantic Boom," The Times (London), Dec. 28, 1972, p 11*

[1965]

teph·ro·chro·nol·o·gy (,tef rou krə'nal ə dʒi:), *n.* a chronology of volcanic eruptions, based on the examination and dating of ash deposits.

The remaining four chapters deal with thermoluminescent dating of ceramics, archaeomagnetic dating of pottery kilns and tephrochronology. *M. S. Tite, Review of "Scientific Methods in Medieval Archaeology," edited by Rainer Berger, Nature, Feb. 11, 1972, p 344*

[1968, from Greek *téphra* ashes + connecting *-o-* + English *chronology*]

—**tephrochronological,** *adj.:* Apart from those for which the historical record is good, the only way to discover if the volcano has a long history of violent activity is to conduct a thorough "tephrochronological" study of the area. *Basil Booth, "Predicting Eruptions," New Scientist, Sept. 9, 1976, p 527*

ter, *n.* variant of TERR.

We have to drive very slowly on dirt roads so that we can

watch out for land mines, which the ters [short for terrorists—the Rhodesians' term for the guerrillas] love planting. In fact, you aim the vehicle over existing tire tracks, and any disturbed soil has to be investigated. *Diana Sanford, "Living in Fear," National Review, March 30, 1979, p 416*

[1976]

ter·a·hertz ('ter ə,hərts), *n. Physics.* one trillion cycles per second; 10^{12} hertz.

Four scientists at the National Bureau of Standards' Boulder, Colo., laboratories found the absolute frequency of an emission from a helium-neon laser to be 88.376245 terahertz. *Science News, Feb. 5, 1972, p 85*

[1970, from *tera-* one trillion + *hertz*]

ter·a·volt ('ter ə,voult), *n. Physics.* one trillion electron volts.

For Fermilab, Congress will be asked to support a development program looking toward the creation of a proton beam of about 1,000 GeV, or one teravolt (TeV), in the present accelerator tunnel by adding a new doughnut-shaped vacuum tube fitted with superconducting magnets. *"Science and the Citizen: Teravolt Territory," Scientific American, Feb. 1975, p 40*

[1975, short for *tera-electron-volt*]

ter·a·watt ('ter ə,wat), *n. Physics.* one trillion watts.

The Laboratory for Laser Energetics of the University of Rochester, recently dedicated its latest and largest piece of equipment, which will hit a target with six laser beams delivering a total of 3 or 4 terawatts of power. *Science News, Nov. 4, 1978, p 309*

[1969]

Ter·com ('ter,kam), *n.* a computerized guidance system in a cruise missile that controls its flight path.

Tercom is one of the terminal-guidance techniques currently being developed in conjunction with the U.S. cruise-missile program. The system relies on a set of digital maps stored in the memory of the missile's on-board computer. *Kosta Tsipis, "Cruise Missiles," Scientific American, Feb. 1977, p 28*

[1976, acronym for *terrain contour matching*]

terminal, *adj.* **1** beyond saving; extreme.

Tom Bethell's article ["Against Bilingual Education," February] has succeeded in convincing me that the U.S. government is suffering from terminal insanity. *Beryl Lieff Benderly, "Letters," Harper's, April 1979, p 6*

2 ruinous or deadly; fatal.

He [Canadian architect Arthur Erickson] attacked the World Bank specifically, for founding . . . a three-thousand-room hotel development in Bali, "whose impact on that island will be terminal." *Edith Iglauer, "Profiles," The New Yorker, June 4, 1979, p 44*

[1972, figurative sense of the term (OED 1890's) applied to any condition resulting in death]

terminal sequencer, an electronic device which regulates by computer the final countdown before the launching of a rocket.

Then came Launch Control again, reporting that the cut-off was initiated automatically by the terminal sequencer, and that "safing" procedures were now being carried out by the astronauts while Launch Control itself tried to identify the cause of the cut-off. *Graham Chedd, "Launch of the Last Apollo," New Scientist, Dec. 14, 1972, p 645*

[1972]

terminator, *n.* the site on a segment of DNA where the formation of messenger RNA is terminated; sequence of nucleotides that signal the end of transcription.

But to get the gene to work—to be transcribed—certain controlling base sequences had to be added at each end. One end had to have a "promoter" sequence so transcription could start; the other end had to have a "terminator" sequence to stop transcription. Neither the promoter nor terminator sequences were known. *Daniel L. Hartl, "The Man-Made Gene," The World Book Science Annual 1978 (1977), p 249*

[1976]

ter·o·tech·nol·o·gy (,ter ou tek'nəl ə dʒi:), *n.* management and maintenance of the plant of a business or industry; maintenance engineering.

British Leyland won the award this year for applying terotechnology to reducing wear on its 30 miles of conveyor tracks at Longbridge for an estimated £250,000 annual saving. *Barry Ritchie, The Sunday Times (London), Dec. 14, 1975, p 60*

[1970, coined by Anthony Wedgwood Benn as Britain's Labour Minister of Technology, from Greek *tērein* take care of + connecting *-o-* + English *technology*; see BENNERY]

terotechnologist, *n.:* Terotechnologists quote the case of breakdowns of waste heat boilers for 300 tonne oxygen steelmaking vessels. *Israel Berkovitch, New Scientist, April 12, 1973, p 95*

terr, *n. Slang.* (among whites in Zimbabwe-Rhodesia) a black nationalist guerrilla.

As one white farmer who had just returned from 28 days' police reserve duty commented: "Two years ago my fellow reservists were just interested in killing terrs. Now they would go along with a reasonable settlement tomorrow if one could be arranged." *The Times (London), Nov. 10, 1977, p 16*

A short time later, a helicopter rose out of the military garrison in town after reports that 25 "terrs" or Black guerrillas, had been sighted nearby. *"Visitors to Victoria Falls Dwindle to the Foolhardy Few," Athens News (Greece), Nov. 12/13, 1978, p 5*

[1976, shortened from *terrorist*] Also spelled TER. See AF, HOUTIE.

terrain-following radar, a radar system which automatically adjusts the altitude of an aircraft or missile in relation to the topography of the ground over which it is flying, allowing high-speed flight close to the ground.

The Tornado, which can fly at more than twice the speed of sound, is the first RAF aircraft to be equipped with Terrain Following Radar (TFR), which will enable low, high-speed penetration of enemy air space on missions against airfields, fuel dumps and troop concentrations. The aircraft could also be used against surface shipping in support of the Royal Navy. *The Times (London), Aug. 15, 1978, p 2*

[1971]

tertiary recovery, any of various methods for extracting oil or gas when simpler methods have failed.

Oil companies are testing a number of *tertiary recovery* techniques to get at previously unrecoverable reserves. In places where the oil is too thick for waterflooding, it can be thinned by injecting steam into a well so that oil flows more freely. By injecting air into oil-bearing rocks, it is possible to ignite some of the oil, making the rest thin enough for waterflooding. A third method involves the pumping of surfactants into the rock. These compounds, which function like laundry detergents, remove oil droplets that would otherwise remain in the rock. *Jenny Tesar, "Energy," Encyclopedia Science Supplement (Grolier) 1975, p 156*

[1975, called *tertiary* because it is the next measure taken when *secondary recovery* (1953) proves inadequate] Also called ENHANCED RECOVERY.

TESOL ('tes,ɔːl), *n.* acronym for *Teachers of English to Speakers of Other Languages* (an organization formed in the United States in 1966 to improve the teaching of English as a second language).

An initial objective of TESOL had its origin in two circumstances: the revelation that most ESL teachers lacked special preparation and the wide diversity in content and quality to be found in the multiplying graduate programs for ESL teacher preparation. *Harold B. Allen, "English As A Second Language," in Current Trends in Linguistics, Vol. 10, 1973, p 317*

[1966] Compare ESL, ESOL, TEFL, TOEFL.

testicular feminization, a genetic disorder in which a male embryo develops into a sterile female.

In rare cases, known as testicular feminization, the male organs do not develop although the foetus has testes and a male genetic constitution . . . these people are completely unaware of their male biological identity. They are usually as happily married as anyone else and know only that they will never have a child. *Arnold Klopper, Science Journal, June 1970, p 50*

. . . male embryos with what is now rather a famous mutation—the mutation causing a condition known as testicular feminisation. Tfm males, as they are known, develop all the female sex organs as well as rather puny male ones. This has turned out to be because their tissues are unable to respond to the male hormone testosterone. *New Scientist, Jan. 13, 1977, p 78*

[1969]

test-tube baby, a baby conceived outside the womb by removing an egg from the mother, fertilizing it in a laboratory apparatus, and implanting the fertilized egg in the womb to develop normally.

The first "test-tube" baby to be apparently fertilised outside the mother's womb was born on 27 July to a British couple amid a flurry of scientific speculation on how the feat was achieved. *"Baby Brown Is Born in England," New Scientist, Aug. 3, 1978, p 325*

While the birth of the first "test-tube baby," in England last July, as a result of the experiments of Dr. Patrick C. Steptoe and Dr. Robert G. Edwards, has been widely publicized, the birth of the second "test-tube baby" has received little public attention, even in India. *"The Talk of the Town," The New Yorker, Nov. 20, 1978, p 38*

[1974] ▶ This term was formerly used in two other senses: one is that of a baby produced through artificial insemination; the second is a baby conceived and developed in a laboratory apparatus until birth.

Once a "perfect" artificial womb has been created, someone somewhere is going to bring forth a true test tube baby. *Nicholas Panagakos, "Biology of the Future," 1971 Collier's Encyclopedia Year Book, p 3*

The test-tube baby in the new sense of an ovum

fertilized in BAVISTER'S MEDIUM and then placed in the womb, is achieved by EXTERNAL FERTILIZATION (also called IN VITRO FERTILIZATION), and the first proven birth by this means was that of Louise Brown, born in Manchester, England, on July 25, 1978. Announcement of this birth raised BIOETHICAL questions, centering on the process and on the status of test-tube babies.

Because several eggs are fertilized but only one is implanted, the question of what constitutes ABORTION is raised. Related to this is the question of whether a unique human being exists at the moment of external fertilization (see PERSON).

His experiment was condemned as immoral by spokesmen for the church, because as a "test tube baby" it was artificial and because it involved abortion. (Embryologists speak of sacrificing or disposing of un-nidated or unimplanted embryos and of *aborting* nidated or implanted uterine tissue.) It seems strange to call the embryo artificial or unnatural. Such labels could only fit the artifacts used, such things as test tubes and lab (Petri) dishes. *Joseph Fletcher, The Ethics of Genetic Control, 1974, p 65*

The possible harmful effects of physical manipulation of the egg or embryo and the legal status of a test-tube baby produced from one woman's egg subsequently implanted in another's womb (EGG TRANSFER or EMBRYO TRANSFER) are also undetermined.

Guidelines for the production of test-tube babies have been urged by various scientists, especially those who view this as a form of genetic engineering. See RECOMBINANT DNA RESEARCH.

Texas pterosaur, an extinct winged reptile of a previously unknown species, whose fossil bones were discovered in Big Bend National Park in west Texas in 1975.

Sheer size is not the only unusual feature of the Texas pterosaur. Most pterodactyls are thought to have subsisted on a diet of fish, which they snared by gliding over the surface of oceans and lakes, but [Douglas A.] Lawson suggests that the newly discovered creatures were meat eaters that scavenged the flesh of dead dinosaurs. *Peter Gwynne, "Science: Really Big Bird," Newsweek, March 24, 1975, p 80*

[1975]

Tex-Mex, *adj. U.S.* of the Texas-Mexico border country; combining Texan and Mexican elements.

It is a mistake to come to Mexico and not try the local cuisine. It is not the Tex-Mex cooking that one is used to getting in the United States and much of it has no hot chili at all. *Rosa Campos, "Cooking," The News (Mexico City) (Vistas Supplement), July 22, 1973, p 7*

In their diversity, the Hispanics have brought some distinctive flavors to the American banquet: the thumping Tex-Mex music of the Southwest borderlands; the *salsa* dancers of urban discos . . . *Time, Oct. 16, 1978, p 50*

—*n.* a variety of Mexican Spanish incorporating elements of English, spoken near the border of Texas and Mexico.

Born in Laredo, Mann spoke border Spanish—"Tex-Mex"—almost as soon as he spoke English and acquired a lifelong fondness for the neighboring Mexicans and the Latin temperament. *Time, May 6, 1966, p 15*

[1964, shortened from *Texan-Mexican*]

text-to-speech, *adj.* converting typewritten or printed text into speech as an aid to the blind.

Another computerized text-to-speech device is being developed by the Kurzweil Computer Products Company of Cambridge, Mass. It has a tiny camera attached to a computer that turns print images into a singsong type of mechanical speech. *Joseph P. Anderson, "Handicapped," The 1977 World Book Year Book, p 349*

[1976] Compare CORTICAL BRAILLE, OPTACON.

textured vegetable protein, a protein derived from soybeans or other vegetables spun into fibers and flavored and used especially as a meat substitute or additive.

Textured vegetable proteins . . . got their first big start in 1971 when the Department of Agriculture approved their use in the national school-lunch program, which covers some 25 million children. *Harland Manchester, "And a New Way to Trim Your Meat Bill," The Reader's Digest, Oct. 1973, p 119*

The soybean derivatives called textured vegetable proteins ("Now There's 'Meatless Meat,' " Feb. 1974) are being sold in more and more grocery stores. *"Cookbook," Changing Times, May 1974, p 6*

[1968] *Abbreviation:* TVP

Thai stick, a thin twig or stick with a potent Asian variety of marijuana wrapped around it.

A customs and Excise officer, Mr Roderick Marr, said two parcels were opened at the overseas mail office and found to contain photograph albums packed with thai sticks, a form of cannabis. *"Cannabis Sent to Canadian Through Post," The Times (London), Aug. 14, 1976, p 2*

Send us your Thai sticks . . . In the fertile heartlands of our broad nation they will soon flourish as American, the Beautiful! *"Stash—American, the Beautiful," High Times, Jan. 1979, p 85*

[1976, from its being produced especially in *Thai*land] Compare ACAPULCO GOLD, COLOMBIAN GOLD.

than·a·tol·o·gy (ˌθæn əˈtɒl ə dʒiː), *n.* the study of the psychological effects and treatment of approaching death.

There is even an emerging profession for the psychological treatment of the terminally ill. It's called thanatology and is in the human-services curriculum of several colleges. *Muriel Fischer, "Dealing With Death in the Family," The New York Times Magazine, March 13, 1977, p 90*

[1970, from Greek *thánatos* death + *-logy* study of. The earlier sense of this word is "the scientific study of the phenomena of death."] See DEATH.

thanatologist, *n.*: A basic tenet of the Hippocratic oath is preservation of life: yet thanatologists ask doctors also to help the terminal patient and his family to meet his own death. *Peter Gwynne, "Forum: New York View: 'Do Not Go Gentle . . .'," New Scientist, March 2, 1972, p 497*

Thanatologists claim to be experts in using the new tool of D & D (Death and Dying). *Malachi B. Martin, "Death at Sunset," National Review, November 22, 1974, p 1356*

thau·ma·tin (ˈθɔː mə tən), *n.* a very sweet protein derived from the fruit of a tropical African plant.

Robert Cagan of the University of Pennsylvania suggests that the two proteins—called monellin and thaumatin . . . should be termed chemostimulatory proteins because of their direct sensory effect. These proteins, which are at least 30,000 times sweeter than sucrose, could both turn out to be extremely useful tools in research into the taste mechanism. *"Monitor: Sweet Proteins Will Help Researchers," New Scientist, July 12, 1973, p 62*

[1973, from New Latin *Thaumatococcus* danielli, the plant + English *-in*] Compare MIRACULIN.

the·be (ˈθeɪ beɪ), *n.* a monetary unit in Botswana. See the quotation.

The new unit—the pula, which will be divided into 100 thebe—will have the same value, however, as the rand, which ceases to become legal tender in this country as of Aug. 23. *"Botswana Reported Ready to Introduce New Currency," The New York Times, Aug. 15, 1976, p 6*

[1976, probably from the Setswana word]

theme park, an amusement park whose features and attractions are organized around one or several unifying ideas, such as wildlife, fairy tales, or space travel.

The number of Americans who visit the theme parks which now dot the U.S. landscape from coast to coast has soared from about 16 million in 1964 to more than 54 million in 1973 and will reach 73 million by 1976, the industry forecasts. *Sylvia Porter, " 'Theme' Park Vacations," New York Post, May 30, 1974, p 30*

Both locals and the latter-day newcomers . . . can be assured that the Navy land being turned over to the city won't become, as had been feared, a "theme park," à la Disneyland. *Albin Krebs, "Key West: Anyone's Place in the Sun" The New York Times Magazine, Dec. 31, 1978, p 32* [1960]

theology of liberation, variant name of LIBERATION THEOLOGY.

Jesuits are at loggerheads in Latin America over a Christian-Marxist synthesis known as the "theology of liberation." . . . But longtime Political Activist Roger Vekemans, a Belgian Jesuit who has spent years backing Christian social democracy in Latin America (most particularly Chile's former President Frei), decries the theology of liberation as simplistic and totalitarian. *"Religion: The Jesuits' Search for a New Identity," Time, April 23, 1973, p 42*

Alienation is a useful word that no longer belongs exclusively to Marxists; and liberation illuminated by the so-called theology of liberation, adds to our understanding of human relationships at personal, political and religious levels. *Clifford Longley, The Times (London), Jan. 7, 1974, p 12*

[1973]

ther·mal·ing (ˈθɜr mə lɪŋ), *n.* the sport of soaring or hang gliding over rising currents of warm air.

With a Rogallo you can also do another type of soaring, called thermaling, where you circle in chimney-like updrafts of warm air that rise from sun-heated ground. Rogallos have climbed hundreds of feet. In the strong thermals of the Western deserts, they will soon climb thousands. *Wolfgang Langewiesche, "The Flyingest Flying There Is," The Reader's Digest, Feb. 1974, p 89*

[1974, from *thermal* a rising current of warm air + *-ing* (noun suffix)]

thermoluminescent dating or **thermoluminescence dating,** a method of determining the age of an archaeological or geological specimen by measuring the intensity of the light given off by the specimen when heated at a controlled rate.

Forged Hui Hsien Chinese pottery widely bought by collectors and museums 25 years ago has been unmasked by the Oxford Research Laboratory for Archaeology and the History of Art. Thermoluminescent dating established that the pottery was only 30 years old, not 2300 years old as claimed. *"Technology Review: Pots Spent on China Fakes," New Scientist, Aug. 10, 1972, p 296*

[1969] Also called TL DATING. Compare AMINO-ACID DATING, IODINE-XENON DATING, RUBIDIUM-STRONTIUM DATING. See also AGE-DATE.

ther·mol·y·sin (θər'məl ə sən), *n.* a calcium-dependent enzyme that breaks down peptides, found in bacteria which require high temperature for growth.

Complete molecular structures of enzymes are being determined by X-ray crystallography so rapidly now that the publication of a new structure is no longer worthy of comment in itself. But the recent analysis of the structure of thermolysin by a group at the University of Oregon is noteworthy because the enzyme is remarkably stable to heat. *"High-Temperature Enzyme Stabilised by Calcium," New Scientist, Dec. 14, 1972, p 624*

[1972, from *thermo-* heat + *lys-* dissolution + *-in* suffix meaning protein]

thermoregulate, *v.i.* to regulate the body's temperature.

The fact that the deep-body temperature of the fish remained nearly constant over extended periods in both cold water and warm indicates that the bluefin was indeed thermoregulating. *Francis G. Carey, "Fishes With Warm Bodies," Scientific American, Feb. 1973, p 43*

[1971, back formation from *thermoregulation* (1950's) regulation of body temperature]

thermosphere, *n.* the region of the earth's atmosphere in which temperature increases with height. It extends from about 50 miles to about 300 miles above the earth.

The temperature . . . rises in the stratosphere to a maximum at 50 km (the stratopause), decreases again in the mesosphere, coming to a second minimum at about 80-90 km (the mesopause), and then rises to much higher values (800-1200 K) in the thermosphere. *Frederick Kaufman, "Ozone in the Atmosphere," McGraw-Hill Yearbook of Science and Technology 1976, p 14*

[1964, from *thermo-* heat, temperature + atmo*sphere*]

thermospheric, *adj.:* Other thermospheric wind systems appear to be established during magnetic storms when large amounts of energy are deposited in the auroral regions through the precipitation of energetic particles. *J. V. Evans, "The Upper Atmosphere Observatory," Science, May 5, 1972, p 466*

theta wave, a brain wave in the frequency of 4 to 8 cycles per second.

Theta waves are still subject to interpretation, provisionally correlated with creative work, free association: the image-making period just before sleep. *D. Keith Mano, National Review, Sept. 15, 1972, p 1022*

Although they are most prominent in the hippocampus, theta waves are readily recorded from many regions of the brain, including cortex, when rodents and carnivores are alert or aroused, and during the early stages of conditioning. *Philip W. Landfield, et al., Science, Jan. 7, 1972, p 87*

[1970, patterned on *alpha wave, beta wave*]

think-in, *n. Informal.* any conference or symposium.

The Social Democratic and Labour Party is to have a major "think-in" this weekend to prepare the party and its supporters for the White Paper. *Belfast Telegraph, Feb. 23, 1973, p 4*

Between May 31 and June 11, some 2,000 delegates from more than 140 nations will meet in Vancouver for a multimillion-dollar think-in entitled Habitat, or more formally the United Nations Conference on Human Settlements. *"Hooray for Motherhood," Maclean's, May 31, 1976, p 21*

[1972, originally (1965) applied to a university forum or seminar to discuss important political or social issues, formed on the model of *teach-in* (1965)]

third age, the years after middle age; old age.

"We have devised a package deal for elderly people from the Continent," Mr [Peter] Bedford said. "We are attempting to attract some Belgian old age pensioners. In Belgium it is called the third age." *Patrick O'Leary, The Times (London), March 16, 1972, p 13*

[1972, translation of French *troisième âge*] Compare SENIOR CITIZENSHIP.

third ager: When the Third Agers first arrived on campus there was a bit of snickering from the younger students. *"White-Hair College," Time, March 11, 1974, p 75*

third kingdom, a proposed division of living organisms comprising the ARCHAEBACTERIA, as distinguished from the animal and plant kingdoms.

Scientists studying the evolution of primitive organisms reported in late 1977 the existence of a separate form of life that is hard to find in nature. They described it as a "third kingdom" of living material, not plant or animal. The organisms in the third kingdom are composed of ancestral cells that abhor oxygen, digest carbon dioxide, and produce methane. *Richard D. Lyons, "Methanogens," Encyclopedia Science Supplement (Grolier) 1979 (1978), p 68*

[1977]

third-level carrier, *U.S.* an airline that makes short flights between small cities and towns.

Now the CAB is trying a different approach to serve smaller communities: strengthening the nation's 3,200 "third-level" carriers—the air taxis and commuter lines that usually fly smaller planes—Cessnas, Pipers, Beechcraft and the like. *"Aviation: A Wing and a Subsidy," Time, Feb. 28, 1972, p 74*

[1969]

Third World or **third world,** the underdeveloped countries of the world, especially those of Africa, Asia, and Latin America, without regard to their political alignment.

In a keynote address to the Special Session of the UN General Assembly in April, Vice-Premier Teng Hsiao-p'ing declared that in the Chinese view the socialist camp no longer existed. The world was now divided into three. The First World was that of the two superpowers, the Second was that of the other developed countries and the Third was that of the developing countries. China is a socialist country belonging to the Third World. The Third World was described as the motive force propelling history forward in the world today. *Michael Yahuda, "China," The Annual Register of World Events in 1974 (1975), p 318*

Attributive use (often in allusion to the racial composition of peoples in the Third World).

"The law penalized the poor and third-world woman who

469

has no other options than prostitution if they want to pay the rent. The law does not hit the wealthy call girl — just the one on the street who is most deprived." *"A Loitering Law in Seattle Said to Inhibit Prostitutes," The New York Times, April 18, 1976, p 21*

[1968, generalized from the original sense (1965) of a group of underdeveloped countries of Asia and Africa not aligned with the Communist or non-Communist world]

► See the note under DEVELOPING.

threatened, *adj.* (of a wildlife species) facing serious, but not immediate, danger of extinction.

Seven hundred and sixty-one plants were designated as "endangered," meaning their survival was in serious doubt, twelve hundred and thirty-eight were listed as "threatened" and an even one hundred were declared extinct — at least in the wild. *Eugene Kinkead, "Our Footloose Correspondents: The Search for Betula Uber," The New Yorker, Jan. 12, 1976, p 58*

[1976]

3HO ('θri:'eitʃ'ou), *n.* a form of Sikhism (a kind of monotheistic Hinduism including elements of Islam) practiced in North America that sometimes incorporates elements of yoga and vegetarianism, founded by the Indian Sikh Yogi Bhajan in 1969.

The 3HO Sikhs lead a life that combines asceticism and idealism with rigorous exercise and entrepreneurial ventures. *Hubert de Santana, "Religion," Maclean's, April 18, 1977, p 74*

Neighbors are nervous about 3HO's expensive land purchases in the area. Less visible than the cymbal-clanging Hare Krishnas, the 3HO disciples rival them in devotion. Men and women alike follow the Sikh traditions of not cutting their hair and bearing symbolic daggers, combs and bracelets. *Time, Sept. 5, 1977, p 70*

[1971, from the abbreviation of *Happy, Healthy, Holy Organization,* its name]

three-martini lunch, *U.S.* a luncheon deducted as a business expense.

Other reforms that the President proposed would further restrict certain tax shelters for well-off people . . . and cut in half permitted deductions for business meals — an attack on the by now fabled three-martini lunch. *Time, Jan. 30, 1978, p 21*

A small band of us devoted an entire three-martini luncheon to the problem the other day. *Art Buchwald, New York Post, March 22, 1979, p 25*

[1972] ► According to *Safire's Political Dictionary* (William Safire, 1978), the term was first used by Senator George McGovern during the national election campaign of 1972.

threshold, *British.* — *adj.* of or having to do with an agreement in which wage increases depend upon the cost-of-living index reaching a predetermined figure.

The threshold idea, which ties pay to the cost of living and automatically compensates workers when prices rise above an agreed figure, originated with the unions. They suggested it in the National Economic Development Council some two years ago, but the Government was unimpressed. *The Times (London), July 23, 1973, p 1*

From the second quarter of 1974 the rate of increase of money wages accelerated sharply. This was partly due to

"threshold agreements," which permitted addition to wages of £0.40 per week for every 1 percentage point rise of the cost-of-living index above its level of October 1973. *D. A. S. Jackson, "Employment, Wages, and Hours," Britannica Book of the Year 1975, p 271*

— *n.* a threshold agreement.

Thresholds are giving about 10 million workers supplements of up to £2.80 a week and a further two payments would bring the total to £3.60. *John Carvel, The Manchester Guardian Weekly, Oct. 19, 1974, p 4*

[1972]

throm·bos·the·nin (,θrɑm'bɑs θə nin), *n.* a contractile protein found in human blood platelets.

Investigators . . . at the National Institutes of Health in Bethesda, Md., isolated actin and myosinlike proteins from thrombosthenin — a group of contractile proteins in human blood platelets. It is probably involved in coagulation. *Earl A. Evans, "Biochemistry," The World Book Science Annual 1973 (1972), p 276*

[1972, from *thrombo-* blood platelet (from Greek *thrómbos* clot) + *sthen-* strength (from Greek *sthénos*) + *-in* (protein) substance]

throm·box·ane (θrɑm'bɑk,sein), *n.* a hormonelike substance that stimulates the aggregation of blood platelets and the constriction of blood vessels.

A Swedish research team discovered that platelets can convert prostaglandins into previously unknown compounds, called thromboxanes, which not only encourage the platelets to stick to one another but also cause arteries to contract. That combined action can result in thrombosis and therefore needs to be suppressed. The mechanism of that suppression, it turns out, involves another new compound, probably a prostaglandin. *"Science Report: Haematology: Preventing Thrombosis," The Times (London), Oct. 21, 1976, p 16*

[1976, from *thrombo*sis (from Greek *thrómbos* clot) + *oxygen* + *-ane* (chemical suffix)] Compare PROSTACYCLIN. See also ENDOPEROXIDE.

through-deck cruiser, a British lightweight, nuclear-powered aircraft carrier.

The Kiev and her sisters, at about 40,000 tons displacement, fit neatly between the US Navy's carriers of twice the size and the Harrier-equipped 18,000 ton vessels such as the Royal Navy's through-deck cruisers and the US Navy's Guam. *"Technology: Soviet Aircraft Carrier Reveals Its Weapons," New Scientist, Aug. 19, 1976, p 394*

[1970, so called from its having the flat deck of a carrier and the displacement of a cruiser]

throw weight, the maximum weight in megatons which a nuclear missile can deliver on a target.

The U.S. has placed a higher priority on the accuracy of its missiles, while the Soviet Union has emphasized higher firepower or "throw weight." Each side would be free to change that emphasis if it desired. *"The 'Breakthrough' on SALT," Time, Dec. 9, 1974, p 16*

The throw weight and absolute numbers of missiles, parameters which are used in the current public debate, are not directly related to the efficacy, lethality, or reliability of the missiles or of a nuclear arsenal. *Kosta Tsipis, "Physics and Calculus of Countercity and Counterforce Nuclear Attacks," Science, Feb. 7, 1975, p 396*

The powerful throw-weight of the Soviet missiles means that they can carry more warheads. As a result, the explosions they cause would be larger, and they would not have to be aimed so precisely at their targets. *George B. Kistiakowsky, "False Alarm: The Story Behind Salt II," The New York Review of Books, March 22, 1979, p 36*

[1969]

thumb piano, any of various small African musical instruments consisting of a wooden box with tuned metal or wooden strips inserted along it lengthwise that vibrate when played with the thumbs.

Pharaoh Sanders . . . playing a ram's horn. Later, he played cowbells, a reed flute, a contrabass clarinet, marimbas, and an African thumb piano. *"The Talk of the Town," The New Yorker, Aug. 1, 1970, p 23*

He might have added that this instrument is usually called a thumb piano, that its most common African name is zanza, and that you can buy a kit to make one in American novelty shops. *Eliot Elisofon, "A Four-Eyed View of Africa," Natural History, Dec. 1972, p 92*

[1965]

thunderboat, *n.* another name for UNLIMITED HYDROPLANE.

In 1973 unlimited hydroplane championship was not settled until the last race on the U.S. circuit, when an innovative, tail-winged thunderboat nailed down the title. *Jim Martenhoff, "Motor Sports," Britannica Book of the Year 1974, p 494*

[1965, so called from the noise made by its powerful engine]

thy·la·koid ('θɑi lə‚kɔid), *n. Botany.* one of the membranous structures in a chloroplast which contain most of the pigment molecules needed for photosynthesis.

Zooxanthellae possess four conspicuous organelles. The chloroplast is single-lobed and peripheral, and its lamellae exhibit a three-thylakoid arrangement. *Leonard Muscatine, "Symbiosis," McGraw-Hill Yearbook of Science and Technology 1974, p 403*

[1972, from Greek *thýlax, -akos* sack + *-oid* thing resembling]

thy·mo·sin ('θɑi mə sən), *n.* a hormone produced by the thymus gland, believed to be associated with the development of T cells.

Thymosin treatment has raised the T-cell count in more than 75 per cent of the cancer patients receiving it either alone or along with chemical and radiation therapy. *Allan L. Goldstein, "Fine Tuning the Immune System," The World Book Science Annual 1978 (1977), p 298*

[1974, from Greek *thýmos* thymus gland + English *-in* (chemical suffix)]

ticky-tacky, *Especially U.S.* — *n.* cheap or inferior material, especially that used in building rows of uniform small houses.

The real point is, will . . . Watchung Pharmaceutical get those 250 unspoiled acres around Howard's tree farm which have been zoned for a park, there to produce more poppable pills and sprinkle company ticky-tacky over the landscape? *S. K. Oberbeck, "Barren Acres," Review of "Garden State" by Julian Moynahan, Newsweek, July 30, 1973, p 71*

— *adj.* made of ticky-tacky.

A part-time social worker sits in a tent waiting for the victims of bad acid trips to reel in. 'Look, they're young,

they're still free, they really love love and they hate materialism. They've got maybe two years before they join their own little nuclear families and live in ticky-tacky mortgaged houses.' *Tom Mangold, The Listener, Sept. 6, 1973, p 305*

[1964, coined by the American folk-song writer Malvina Reynolds, 1900-1978, probably by reduplication of *tacky, adj.* shabby, dowdy (1880's)]

tight end, an offensive end in American football who lines up close to the tackle.

By way of celebration, a number of Colts crowd into a tavern near the practice field . . . linebacker Ted (The Mad Stork) Hendricks, tight end Tom Mitchell, guard Dan Sullivan, tackle Fred Miller. *Larry L. King, "The Beasts of Baltimore," The Atlantic, Jan. 1972, p 74*

[1967]

tilt, *U.S.* — *v.i.* to tend or incline (toward one side and against another); have a slant or bias.

A widespread belief that the balance of effective nuclear power was tilting against the United States might encourage the Soviets to adopt more adventurous policies — for example, in the Middle East. *Henry Owen, "The Weapons Debate," The Atlantic, June 1972, p 12*

Mr. Nixon disclosed that he "tilted toward" a proposal to bomb several North Korean military airfields in April 1969 to retaliate for the downing of an unarmed American reconnaissance plane. *James M. Naughton, The New York Times, Sept. 4, 1977, p 25*

— *n.* inclination (toward or against); slant; bias.

The contribution to the American language of other cultures has long been acknowledged . . . but it is unscholarly to insist on a "tilt" toward minority contribution to satisfy resentment over past neglect. *William Safire, Review of "All American English" by J. L. Dillard, The New York Times Book Review, May 11, 1975, p 14*

The pro-Soviet tilt of the new rulers in Kabul, the Afghan capital, is already stirring some recriminations in Washington. *Time, Dec. 18, 1978, p 40*

[1972, figurative use of *tilt, v.i.,* to slope, slant (OED 1626)]

time frame, the limits of time for any given situation or event.

The time frame envisaged as necessary for significant change is, as in the Prince Edward Island Plan, fifteen years. *Margaret C. Storrie, "Prognosis for Atlantic Provinces," The Geographical, July 1972, p 679*

This trial, like most trials, has created jargon all of its own. Witnesses speak, for instance not of dates on the calendar as May or June, say, but as "time frames," which was a holdover from the Senate Watergate hearings. *Martin Arnold, "Sears Testimony Studied by Jury," The New York Times, April 28, 1974, p 51*

As I got up to go, I asked Codd how the future looked to him.

"In the current time frame, I look forward to a good year — that is, a better year for law-abiding citizens and a worse year for lawbreakers," he said. *Richard Harris, "A Reporter at Large," The New Yorker, Sept. 26, 1977, p 66*

[1964, originally used in aerospace and computer technology]

timeline, *n.* a schedule detailing the times and sequence of activities of the crew of a space flight.

When at last Carr and Pogue came upon the camera on

the floor of the workshop, they were well behind the time-line, for the ground had allotted only ten minutes to move from one experiment to the next. *Henry S. F. Cooper, Jr., "A Reporter at Large: Life in a Space Station—1," The New Yorker, Aug. 30, 1976, p 59*

[1967]

time-sharing, *n. U.S.* an arrangement in which a person shares the cost of a furnished vacation dwelling by buying a percentage of the unit at a set price based on the time period he wants to live in it each year. *Often used attributively.*

Under time-sharing plans, participants pay anywhere from $800 to $8,000 for bargain-rate accommodations in a certain condominium or vacation resort for a given number of weeks in a particular season each year, usually for at least twelve years and in some cases indefinitely. In exchange for guaranteed occupancy over an extended period, time-sharing resorts offer low prices, luxury suites usually equipped with kitchens, and discounts on the use of entertainment facilities. *"Economy and Business: Holidays on the Cheap," Time, Aug. 30, 1976, p 67*

[1976, apparently influenced by the computer term *time-sharing* (1964), meaning the use by many persons at remote locations of a central computer]

time-share, *n.:* A time-share can be very inexpensive, though, certainly compared to hotel costs in that location. Generally, 1979 prices ran from $5,000 to $9,000 or so for two weeks for however many years you like at a two-bedroom two-bath luxury condominium unit that might cost you $90,000 to purchase. *Ruth Rejnis, Her Home, 1980, p 73*

time-symmetric, *adj.* moving both forward and backward in time.

This finding ... suggests that the universe is not ever-expanding but rather is "time-symmetric" (that is, alternately expanding and contracting). *"Science and the Citizen: Experimental Cosmology," Scientific American, Oct. 1973, p 50*

[1972] Compare ARROW OF TIME.

time warp, an imaginary discontinuity or distortion in the flow of time.

Science-fiction writers, stymied by the laws of physics, turn to such literary devices as time warps to make interstellar travel possible. *Time, Sept. 11, 1972, p 47*

The other dominant subject is science's latest fad (and it may be no more than that)—black holes, the suspected but so far unverified regions of the cosmos that constitute tunnels in space and might even turn out to be the long dreamed-of space and time warps capable of providing instantaneous passage across the universe. *Mark Nichols, "In the Beginning," Maclean's, Aug. 22, 1977, p 56*

[1972] Compare SPACE WARP. See also ARROW OF TIME.

time-space warp: There have been about half a dozen successful books on the Bermuda Triangle, some of them going high in the best-seller lists. Although they all tell basically the same stories, they advocate different solutions: the missing craft have been carried off by unidentified flying objects ... they have encountered a time-space warp and been carried into another dimension. *Graham Massey, "The Case of the Bermuda Triangle," The Listener, Feb. 19, 1976, p 199*

time-warped, *adj.:* Splendidly malicious fables about the exaggerated elaborations of the astronaut Tichy, who meets himself in time-warped multitude and who, as Earth's delegate to United Planets, has a most difficult time explaining

why the human race should be admitted to the organization. *Tom Hutchinson, Review of "The Star Diaries" by Stanislaw Lem, The Times (London), Nov. 11, 1976, p 14*

Ti·o Ta·co ('ti: ou 'tɑ: kou), *U.S. Slang.* (derogatory in use) a Mexican American who adopts the culture and values of white American society.

California's only Mexican-American congressman depends on Anglo suburbs for more than half his support, and in the state legislature the gerrymandering is even more effective; there was in 1971 only one Mexican assemblyman and no state senator. It was a system that placed high premium on the Tio Taco, or Uncle Tom. *John Gregory Dunne, "To Die Standing," The Atlantic, June 1971, p 45*

[1969, from Spanish, literally, Uncle Taco] Compare UNCLE TOMAHAWK.

tipee, *n.* a person who receives inside information on stock market prices.

What about so called "tipees"—people who come by price sensitive information often because of a breakdown in security by a professional adviser or within the company? The CSI feels it is ethically wrong for anyone who receives from an insider information which he believes to be price sensitive and then deals on it. *The Times, (London), Oct. 12, 1978, p 29*

[1968, from *tip* to give secret information to + *-ee*]

t.j. or **T.J.,** abbreviation of TALK JOCKEY.

Some of the new talk jockeys—or t.j.s—still play music, but it is always subordinate to their dialogue with listeners. *"Show Business: The New Talk Jockeys," Time, May 22, 1972, p 76*

[1972, patterned on *D.J.* for disc jockey]

TL dating, short for THERMOLUMINESCENT (or THERMOLUMINESCENCE) DATING.

TL-dating was developed in the 1960s for dating pottery and other fired materials from archaeological sites; it has not been without its difficulties, as with the Glozel forgeries ... but recent results on pottery have generally been archaeologically acceptable. *The Times (London), Nov. 11, 1978, p 3*

[1972]

T lymphocyte, another name for T CELL.

In seeking the answer, Dr. Good found that there are two kinds of mature lymphocytes. One kind is called the T lymphocyte; the other, the B lymphocyte. *The Reader's Digest, Condensed from "The Body is the Hero" by Ronald J. Glasser, Oct. 1976, p 267*

In the mid-1960's, research revealed that the lymphocyte controls the immune defenses and that there are two basic types of lymphocytes, T lymphocytes and B lymphocytes, each controlling different parts of the immune system. *William Stockton, "A New Clue in the Cancer Mystery," The New York Times Magazine, April 2, 1978, p 64*

[1976]

TM, abbreviation of TRANSCENDENTAL MEDITATION.

Although transcendental meditation or TM as it has come to be called, appears to be an effective method of mental relaxation, it probably has no advantages over any other meditative techniques, whether they be zen or yoga or what-have-you. *Joe Graedon, The People's Pharmacy, 1976, p 262*

What still surprises me is that TM, stripped of the mysticism (which is basically what you pay through the nose for), is a suggestion that sitting still and in quiet, and thinking about nice things, is likely to help your blood pressure. *Tim Robinson, New Scientist, Oct. 12, 1978, p xxvi*

[1971]

TMer (‚ti:'em ər), *n. U.S.* an adherent or practitioner of transcendental meditation.

Rather than having a "genuine hunger for religious and mystical experience," I think the TMers, like the revolutionaries you recently featured, are middle-class kids who are having difficulty with the real world. *William S. Greenfield, "Forum," Time, Nov. 3, 1975, p 6*

Sure they keep repeating their mantra—so do insurance salesmen, housewives and millions of other T.M.'ers (though I grant you with less ardor and frequency). Other people say rosary beads. *Judith Wax, "Sharing a Son With Hare Krishna," The New York Times Magazine, May 1, 1977, p 42*

[1972, from TM + -*er*]

T-mycoplasma, *n.* a viruslike microorganism (mycoplasma) that coats and distorts the bodies of sperm cells, possibly causing infertility.

Another possible new approach to birth control arose from research on microorganisms called T-mycoplasmas. . . . These microorganisms can trigger certain cases of reproductive failure among men, apparently by inhibiting the movement of sperm up the female vaginal tract. *Joan Arehart-Treichel, "Medicine," 1977 Collier's Encyclopedia Year Book (1976), p 356*

[1976, perhaps from its resemblance to the letter *T*]

tobaccophobe, *n.* a person who hates tobacco smoke, especially one who opposes smoking in public places and supports the enactment of anti-smoking laws.

While many tobaccophobes maintain that their aim is to "educate" smokers, they have not in the past been noticeably successful—as witness a turn-of-the-century campaign to censor a nursery rhyme because Old King Cole "called for his pipe." *Michael Demarest, "Time Essay: Smoking: Fighting Fire With Ire," Time, Jan. 12, 1976, p 36*

[1975, from *tobacco* + -*phobe* one who hates or has a phobia about (something)]

TOEFL ('tou fəl), *n.* acronym for *Testing of English as a Foreign Language.*

It is of primary importance that all such materials, like all TOEFL materials, take the student's native language (here, dialect) into full account. *J. L. Dillard, Black English, 1972, p 272*

[1962]

toe sock, a sock with a separate place for each toe or for the big toe.

By far the best seller in the socks scene is a style known as the "toe sock" or "wiggler," which fits, glovelike, in between the toes. *"Modern Living: The Sock-O Look," Time, Feb. 3, 1975, p 56*

[1975] Compare TUBE SOCK.

toke, *v.i. U.S. Slang.* to take a puff on a marijuana cigarette.

Bill Buckley says he went "outside the 3-mile limit—I'm a law-and-order advocate, you know"—to toke up, but neglects to mention where he got the stuff. Did he grow it on international waters? . . . I would like to hear his explanation of how he came by the weed legally. *Linda Chapel, Big*

Rapids, Mich., in a Letter to the Editor, Newsweek, Jan. 1, 1973, p 4

[1970, verb use of the noun (1968)]

token economy, a method used in behavior modification to reinforce desirable behavior by rewards of token money that can be exchanged for predetermined items of value, such as food or free time.

The goals of the token economy, as with other contingency management procedures, are to promote behaviors necessary for effective personal functioning, not only in an institutional or school environment, but also in natural settings. *Ralph Barocas and William G. Johnson, "Behavior Modification," McGraw-Hill Yearbook of Science and Technology 1976, p 53*

[1968]

ton, *n. Slang.* a score of 100 points or runs (in various games).

When he started, he averaged 35 points per round. Now he's averaging 60 or more, frequently throws a "ton"—a round of 100 or more points—and can put a dart into a fifty-cent-piece area every time. *Steven Warner, "Nietzsche Would Have Been a Great Dart Player," The Atlantic, Aug. 1973, p 73*

[1973, extended from earlier (chiefly British) slang senses: a speed of 100 miles per hour (1954); a sum of 100 pounds (1940's)]

toot (tu:t), *U.S. and Canadian, Slang.* —*n.* **1** cocaine.

A couple from *Flushing, Queens,* New York, was busted on a Miami street corner in possession of *nine pounds of toot. High Times, Jan. 1979, p 33*

20 little white plastic spoons . . . ringed a brass bowl. Each man dipped a spoon into the white powder and got his toot the same way. *Marcia Kramer, "The $16 Billion Coke Scene," Daily News (New York), Sept. 23, 1979, p 5*

2 a snort of cocaine.

The possibility of a jail sentence is enough to make most of Vancouver's professional people ultra discreet about their use of the drug, while they slink into some of the finer furnished bathrooms of the city for a quick toot. *Judith Timson, "Going Better With Coke," Maclean's, May 2, 1977, p 24*

—*v.t.* to inhale (cocaine) through the nostrils.

The connoisseur's choice. You'll feel better knowing that what you toot is cut with the original Italian Mannite Conoscenti. *Advertisement in High Times, Jan. 1979, p 52*

[1977, origin unknown]

top, *v.t.* **top off,** to fill (a gasoline tank that is nearly full) to the top in order to have as much gas as possible.

The worst is yet to come: by the end of the month, ration coupons will replace the "horror system," which last week allowed hundreds of white Rhodesians to top off their tanks by bribing black filling-station attendants. *Time, Jan. 7, 1966, p 27*

An executive order [gave] the nation's governors the power to require some filling stations to remain open on weekends, to prevent drivers from topping off tanks, and to impose an odd-even day system of gasoline sales. *Jerome Cahill, Daily News (New York), May 30, 1979, p 3*

[1966] See ENERGY CRISIS.

topless radio, *U.S.* radio programming which solicits telephone calls to discuss the caller's sexual

473

problems with the host as part of the broadcast.

No phone-in programme I have heard sounds quite like the master of the Los Angeles air-waves, Bill Ballance. He pioneered what is now known as 'topless radio' in the United States. For five hours every day on station KGBS, he delved into the psyche of Californian women and collected confessional erotica from them. *The Listener, Dec. 5, 1974, p 730*

[1973, from *topless* in the sense of "baring, exposing, revealing" as applied to bare-breasted dancers, etc.] See TALK JOCKEY.

top quark, a quark that may have a mass 13 times that of the proton.

Dr. Samuel Ting of M.I.T., who shared a Nobel Prize for discovery of the J/Psi particle, says that he and other scientists . . . have been working toward collision energies of 40 billion electron volts, more than they expect is needed to detect the top quark. *Walter Sullivan, "New Quarks Stir Debate On Basic Laws of Nature," The New York Times, Feb. 13, 1979, p C2*

[1977] Compare BOTTOM QUARK. See also QUARK.

Topsider, *n.* **1** the trademark for a soft leather or canvas shoe with a low heel and soft rubber sole, designed for casual wear, originally on a boat. *Often used attributively.*

The other uniform seen at Harvard, that of the clubbie . . . is the garb of Topsider moccasins, pastel Shetland sweater, and out-at-the-elbow tweed jacket, part of the new ethnic assertion of the Wasp. *Nelson W. Aldrich, Jr., Harper's, March 1976, p 49*

2 topsider, any similar shoe.

Visors, at $2, make fine accessories to the sporty look, and so do topsiders. *"Good Looks: Wearing the Real McCoy," McCall's, June 1974, p 16*

[1974, trademarked 1937, from *topside* the upper part or deck of a ship + *-er*]

toss, *U.S. Slang. −v.t.* to search (a person), especially for narcotics; frisk.

The dissenters were also worried about "the possibility that a police officer . . . will use a traffic arrest as a pretext to conduct a search." In fact, some do already; if they "toss" the suspect and find nothing, they may not even bother with the traffic arrest. *"The Law: Tossings and Traffic," Time, Dec. 24, 1973, p 74*

−n. an act or instance of tossing; a frisk.

A toss is no funny business, and the risks for a cop are enormous at all times, and for this reason he has mastered some extremely impressive techniques. *Robert Daley, "Police Report on the TV Cop Shows," The New York Times Magazine, Nov. 19, 1972, p 106*

[1972, so called from the manner in which suspects are often handled by the police] Compare PAT-DOWN SEARCH, SKINSEARCH.

total fertility rate, the number of offspring born per woman during a lifetime of childbearing, used as a measure of the fertility of a population.

The total fertility rate of 1.5 births per woman in West Germany is unquestionably the lowest in the world. *Charles F. Westoff, "The Populations of the Developed Countries," Scientific American, Sept. 1974, p 112*

The total fertility rate, an index used by demographers to measure the birth rate in any given year, in fact dropped

from 2.9 children per woman of childbearing age (18 to 40) in 1964 to 2.1 a decade later and 1.9 last year. It's the lowest peacetime rate recorded in French demographic history. *Jean-Marie Dupont, "Declining Birth Rate in France," The Manchester Guardian Weekly (Le Monde section), Feb. 15, 1976, p 12*

[1974] See REPLACEMENT LEVEL.

total history, historical writing that includes many of the significant aspects of human endeavor in a particular time.

The book has been acclaimed as a masterpiece of 'total history'. What does this mean? It is an attempt to depict a society in all its aspects embracing economic, social, cultural, religious and political developments all at once. The nation is too large a subject for successful treatment in this way. And so historians paint on a smaller canvas; but, for that reason, they can show more detail. *Joan Thirsk, Review of "The Peasants of Languedoc" by E. Le Roy Ladurie, translated by John Day, The Listener, Jan. 29, 1976, p 123*

[1972]

Touch-a-Matic, *n. U.S.* a trademark for a type of telephone developed by the Bell System which can dial automatically over 30 telephone numbers stored in an an integrated circuit memory built into the instrument.

One of these was a solid-state memory-equipped instrument called the Touch-a-matic. At the touch of one of 31 buttons, the set immediately called the party whose number had been recorded previously by the user (by dialing it manually after pressing the record button). In addition, one memory slot remembered the last manually dialed call, so that, in case of a busy signal or no answer, the caller could try again by touching button no. 32. *Ernest R. Kretzmer, "Communications," 1975 Britannica Yearbook of Science and the Future (1974), p 215*

[1973, trademarked 1962; perhaps influenced by *Touch-o-matic* (1952)]

touch dancing, dancing in which the partners hold each other, especially ballroom dancing to such music as DISCO, HUSTLE, and SALSA.

A few lessons are more important than ever now that real dancing is back, *touch* dancing—that exciting contact-to-music that brings out feelings no other kind of dancing ever did. *Advertisement in Newsweek, Sept. 24, 1973, p 56*

TV dance programs, such as an updated American Bandstand and Soul Train, now feature teen touch dancing. *Wende Devlin, "Focus on Touch Dancing—Where It's At," Harper's Bazaar, Feb. 1974, p 131*

[1972, so called to distinguish it from rock'n'roll dances in which partners do not touch] Also called BODY DANCING.

► As interest in the "old" form of social dancing was revived, the term *touch dancing* developed to fill the need for a distinction between closely coordinated ballroom dancing and the individual style of rock'n'roll dancing.

This need to remove ambiguity in language is at work when new developments such as the *digital watch* generate more specific terms for older devices such as *analog watch* to describe the common watch with hands.

tour·iste (tu:'ri:st), *n. Canadian Slang.* traveler's diarrhea acquired in French Canada.

The Queen brings her own drinking water, out of concern for *touriste*. *June Callwood, "Liz Windsor Superstar," Maclean's, Sept. 1973, p 72*

[1973, from Canadian French, literally, tourist]

▶ The doublet *turista* (from Spanish) has been applied since about 1959 to this condition when contracted in Mexico. See the note under DELHI BELLY.

tout (taut), *n. Slang.* (in Northern Ireland) an informer.

Corrigan and Williams, who plan to take their campaign throughout Northern Ireland, have also received death threats and obscene letters branding them "touts." *"Northern Ireland: Pied Pipers of Peace," Time, Sept. 6, 1976, p 27*

[1976, probably extended from the earlier slang meaning (OED 1718) "a thieves' scout or watchman," ultimately from the Middle English verb *tuten* to peep]

TOW (tou), *n.* or **TOW missile,** an antitank missile guided to its target by signals sent over a wire connected to the missile during flight.

The U.S. is allowing the export of the remote-controlled TOW, perhaps the world's deadliest antitank weapon, to Israel, South Viet Nam, Lebanon and Jordan. *"The World: The Arms Dealers: Guns For All," Time, March 3, 1975, p 34*

The TOW missile can be used offensively from jeeps or armed cars when accompanying armor and infantry on attack. *Drew Middleton, The New York Times, March 28, 1976, p 1*

[1969, acronym for *t*ube-launched, *o*ptically tracked, *w*ire-guided] See WIRE-GUIDED.

township, *n.* an area in South Africa set aside for blacks and other people not of European origin.

The slightest sign of unrest in the black townships is crushed by swift and vigorous police action. Hundreds of blacks are still languishing in detention without charge (although some have been released) while random police raids in the townships are still a regular occurrence. *Nicholas Ashford, "Confrontation or Compromise? The Question for South Africa in 1977," The Times (London), Dec. 31, 1976, p 14*

WINDHOEK, South-West Africa. Just outside this capital city, shielded from view by a slight rise in the terrain, lies a place called Katutura. In one of the euphemisms of apartheid, it is what is known as a township, although it lacks most of the amenities associated with the term. *John F. Burns, The New York Times, Feb. 15, 1978, p A2*

[1970] Compare HOMELAND.

▶ This term came into widespread use after June 1976, when extensive rioting to protest the proposed compulsory use of Afrikaans as well as English in Bantu schools took place in Soweto, a black township near Johannesburg. *Soweto*, acronym of *So*uth *We*stern *To*wnships, is not of Bantu origin.

tox·i·coid ('tak sə,kɔid), *n.* any poisonous chemical substance.

The process which must be controlled is the voiding of morbid material: anything which will taint, poison, or reduce the fecundity of any member of the food web to the detriment of the marine resource. This includes toxicoids (heavy metals, pesticides), oil, detergents, emulsifiers and hot water. *David Bellamy, New Scientist, April 13, 1972, p 77*

[1972, noun use of adjective (1890's) meaning resembling poison, from Latin *toxicum* poison + English *-oid* resembling]

tox·o·ca·ri·a·sis (,tak sə kə'rai ə sis), *n.* human infection with the larvae of an intestinal worm found in dogs, causing swelling of the liver and, sometimes, damage to the interior of the eyes.

There are also several diseases that are spread throughout any community where dogs and men live close together. The most serious of these, other than rabies, is toxocariasis or visceral larva migrans. *Tony Smith, "Rabies: The Fears and the Reality," The Times (London), June 25, 1976, p 16*

[1970, from New Latin *Toxocara*, the genus of nematode worms whose larvae cause this infection (from Greek *tóxon* bow + *kárā* head) + *-iasis* diseased condition]

toxocaral, *adj.:* Prior to our work in 1973 it was not known that serious toxocaral infections could result from contamination by dogs of soil in public parks. *A. W. Woodruff, The Times (London), Jan. 12, 1978, p 15*

t quark, short for TOP QUARK.

Theory right now envisions six, and to those four it adds a t quark (prosaically called "top," but the more philosophically inclined say "truth") and a b quark ("bottom" or "beauty"). *Science News, June 3, 1978, p 357*

[1977]

track lighting, a means of providing light by an electrified metal strip or track along which light fixtures can be inserted, moved and adjusted to the desired position.

For all their versatility, track-lighting systems do have disadvantages over conventional floor and table lamps. Installation of the track on the ceiling is tricky, and, in most instances, involves hiding the wires from the ceiling to the light switch. Special bulbs are usually required. *Norma Skurka, "On the Track," The New York Times Magazine, Aug. 15, 1976, p 47*

[1972]

track light: Walls and floors are lit with ellipses of color from track lights. *Picture legend, The New York Times Magazine, May 14, 1978, p 74*

tractorcade, *n.* a procession of tractors.

Their [U.S. farmers] immediate aim was attention, and they proved to have a brilliant flair for hokey but effective publicity. Turned-over tractors were parked on highway overpasses, tractorcades drove through the streets of county seats and state capitals, and bright orange strike stickers glowed over the cigar counter of every small-town café. *Anne Nelson, "A Long Row to Hoe," Harper's, May 1978, p 33*

[1977, from *tractor* + *-cade* combining form meaning procession, as in *motorcade*]

Trademarks. ▶ Among the new words that become part of a language are the trademarks of popular products and services. Only those that became widely current during the 1970's (such as ADIDAS) appear in this dictionary.

There is no set pattern for coining trademarks. Every type of word formation has been tried (see COINAGES), although certain affixes (the current *-O-Matic*, as in *Ice-O-Matic*) become fads. The most common trademarks rely on traditional patterns of word formation, such as:

compounding, SKYTRAIN, a simple compound, ASTROTURF (from *Astro*dome + *turf*), INSTAMATIC (from *instan*t + auto*matic*)

blending, SENSURROUND (*sen(s)e* and *(s)urround*), EXERCYCLE (*exer(c)ise* and *(c)ycle*)

derivation, ULTRASUEDE (*ultra-*, meaning beyond, + *suede*), PHOTO-FIT (*photo-* + *fit*).

Some trademarks are of foreign origin or contain foreign elements, as LAETRILE, formed from *l-*mandeloni*trile*, a chemical name which includes the German word *Mandel*, meaning almond. Some trademarks come from proper names (JACUZZI) or represent deliberately altered forms (LITEK, probably from *Light Tech*nology Corp. or *Light Technol*ogy Corp.), or are names formed from obscure or unknown elements, such as KEPONE and KEVLAR.

Trademarks often undergo the changes and processes that affect other words. The trademark TASER shifted in function to become a verb: "to Taser" means to immobilize someone with a Taser. QUAALUDE, a trademark for the sedative drug methaqualone, was so widely used that the name was modified by shortening to QUAD and by clipping to LUDE. Another trademark for the same drug, SOPOR, was altered by analogy to SOAPER or SOPER.

Another, but more unusual feature of trademarks is that some have taken on figurative and transferred senses. MR. CLEAN, the trademark of an all-purpose cleanser, now has the figurative meaning of a highly moral or incorruptible person. The recording company trademark MOTOWN describes a style of popular music typical of many of this company's recordings.

Since the purpose of a trademark is to identify a product or service and to make the name easy to use and remember, it is ironic that the more popular a trademark becomes the more it is in jeopardy. If a term achieves generic use so that it can be applied to all similar products or services it can be lost to its owner. This happened to the former trademarks *aspirin, cellophane, thermos, escalator, kerosene, linoleum*, and, now, GRANOLA. In order to prevent such loss companies vigorously protect their trademarks from infringement, especially from improper use in print. The United States Trademark Association advises owners of registered trademarks to "Capitalize trademarks and use them as adjectives with the generic term of the product." For example, their recommendation would be Cuisinart *food processor*, Pyrex *glassware*, and Sanka *brand coffee*.

Despite these and similar precautions, the most popular (and apt) trademarks tend to be substituted for the generic form by a public oblivious to the niceties of protecting a particular product's name that is registered as linguistic property. Speakers, of course, cannot show that they are saying a trademark without using the term in the adjective position referred to above; writers tend to spell it as they hear it, that is, without a capital or without some

other special characteristic, such as a hyphen, and as a consequence popular written variants appear (*Earth Shoes, earth shoes*). Variant spellings of trademarks that occur frequently are recorded in this dictionary but should not be regarded as indications that the trademark is, or is becoming, a generic term. The law requires owners to protect their trademarks from encroachment. This is a difficult task in a time of mass media and world-wide communication in which monitoring usage becomes an unrealistic requirement. It also implies an ability to control usage, an attitude considered naive in linguistics.

trailable, *adj.* (of a boat) able to be carried on and launched from a trailer pulled by an automobile.

As slip and mooring space become more difficult to find, the trailable boat represents an alternative—it can be dry sailed from a boatyard or moored at home. *Joanne A. Fishman, "North Atlantic Show to Open Thursday," The New York Times, Sept. 5, 1976, Sec. 5, p 11*

[1976, probably alteration of *trailerable*, from *trailer, v.*, transport by a trailer + *-able*]

trank (træŋk), *n. U.S. and Canadian, Informal.* a tranquilizing drug.

The Canadian Medical Association has officially expressed "alarm" about over-prescriptions of minor tranks, and their abuse by consumers. Valium and Librium have become so at home in the Canadian family's medicine chest that they ranked first and third respectively among products that poisoned children under six during 1973. *Sheila Gormely, "Behavior: Tranquilizers: The New, Approved Opiate of the People," Maclean's, March 22, 1976, p 58*

[1972, by shortening and alteration of *tranquilizer*]

tran·nie or **tran·ny** ('træn iː), *n. British Informal.* a transistor radio.

Take a piece of tin foil and rotate it round a really cheap "trannie" turned to a blank part of the dial, volume at maximum. If the foil obstructs a micro-wave source the radio static will become louder. *Christopher Reed, "Phreak Out to Crunch the Bugs," The Manchester Guardian Weekly, Aug. 14, 1977, p 20*

You do better by sticking in London and keeping your ear glued to the tranny. These news programmes they have on all the time are a right godsend and better still there's police radio. *R. G. G. Price, Punch, March 26, 1975, p 523*

[1971, shortening and alteration of *transistor*]

transaction, *n.* (in transactional analysis) any exchange or interaction between persons involving the ego-states of the participants.

Steps of the transaction are shown by drawing arrows from one circle to another. Let us imagine a married couple, John and Barbara. These two adults (but not at the moment, in T. A. vocabulary, Adults) are having fun at a party. The transaction of having fun together involves the Child ego-state on both sides. *Kenneth Lamott, "The Four Possible Life Positions . . . ," The New York Times Magazine, Nov. 19, 1972, p 130*

[1967]

transactional analysis, a method of psychotherapy in which interpersonal relationships are analyzed in terms of confrontations between three ego-states

(Parent, Adult, and Child) whose misplacement in the individual's personality is supposed to be responsible for most neurotic behavior. It was developed by the Canadian-born psychiatrist Eric Berne, 1910-1970.

In the 1960s it was encounter groups. In the 1970s it is transactional analysis, or T.A., the pop-psychological path to happiness charted by Sacramento Psychiatrist Thomas A. Harris in his bestseller *I'm OK—You're OK*. T.A., or close facsimiles of it, is now practiced by some 3,000 psychiatrists, psychologists, social workers and ministers in the U.S. and 14 foreign countries. *"Behavior: T.A.: Doing OK," Time, Aug. 20, 1973, p 44*

Roman Catholics leave the priesthood to marry; and Protestants leave the ministry to conduct encounter groups and workshops in transactional analysis. *William C. Martin, "Texans and God," The Atlantic, March 1975, p 90*

[1967] *Abbreviation:* TA

transactional analyst: "What we have are competing systems of belief. The scream therapist says, 'We are better than the transactional analyst,' who says, 'We are better than the group therapist,' who says, 'We are better than the sex therapist,' and so on." *Salvador Minuchin, quoted by Janet Malcolm, "A Reporter at Large: The One-Way Mirror," The New Yorker, May 15, 1978, p 78*

trans·am·i·nate (træns'æm ə‚neit), *v.t. Chemistry.* to cause the transfer of (an amino group) from one compound to another.

The group that was selectively altered included amino-acids, for example, valine, that are not transaminated or oxidized in myocardium and those such as alanine that can be transaminated and used for energy production. *Kern Wildenthal, Dallas, Tex., "Letters to Nature: Protein Breakdown Inhibited by Insulin to Improve Heart Culture," Nature, Sept. 8, 1972, p 101*

[1972, back formation from *transamination* the reversible transfer of an amino group]

transbus, *n. U.S.* a bus of advanced design with such features as extra length, reduced noise level, and lower floors to facilitate access by the elderly and handicapped.

He [David Duffy] prefers specially constructed vans, which already provide door-to-door service in Dade County for more than 800 people a day, but he expects that the high cost of the transbuses (as much as $50,000 more than a regular bus) will halt the expansion of the special van service. *"The Nation: Helping the Handicapped," Time, Dec. 5, 1977, p 34*

[1973, from *trans-* beyond + *bus,* because the improved design will transcend the quality of service offered by conventional bus service] See KNEELING BUS.

transcendental meditation, a method of meditation that is supposed to help the mind transcend all thought to bring about a blissful state of pure consciousness through complete physical and mental relaxation induced by such techniques as repetition of a secret personal incantation. It was developed by the Hindu guru Maharishi Mahesh Yogi, born about 1911.

Transcendental meditation (TM) has been found to produce definite physiological changes in respiration, brain wave and heart rate. Just exactly how these changes affect behavior is still not clear but psychologists have found personality differences in persons before and after they began using TM. *"Behavioral Sciences: Meditating in Prison," Science News, Sept. 8, 1973, p 152*

It was not long after this startling discovery that Dr. Benson applied the techniques of transcendental meditation to a group of hypertensive patients. By recording their blood pressure weeks before they learned how to meditate, he was able to establish baseline blood pressure levels. *Joe Graedon, The People's Pharmacy, 1976, p 261*

[1967] *Abbreviation:* TM. See SIDDHI.

trans·fect (‚træns'fekt), *v.t.* to cause (bacterial cells infected with nucleic acid of viruses) to produce viruses.

Scientists employed the DNA from an animal virus, vaccinia, to transfect competent cells of B[acillus] subtilis. They obtained evidence for the production of new infective viruses within the cytoplasm of the bacterial cells. *P. Sypherd, "Bacterial Transfection," McGraw-Hill Yearbook of Science and Technology 1968, p 120*

[1968, from *trans-* through + in*fect*]

transfection, *n.:* For certain phage the presence of . . . DNase in recipient cells reduces the efficiency of transfection, which involves introduction of intact purified phage DNA. *Sandip K. Basu and Michio Oishi, "Factor Which Affects the Mode of Genetic Recombination in E. Coli," Nature, Jan. 10, 1975, p 140*

transhistorical, *adj.* transcending the historical; going beyond the boundaries of history or chronology.

Malraux's use of pathetic fallacy, of transhistorical references, and of tableaux bordering on the *précieux* is quite effective when properly controlled. *Stephen E. Bornstein, "Myth, Man and Memoirs: The Case of André Malraux," The American Scholar, Summer 1972, p 458*

[1969]

Trans·kei·an (‚træns'kai ən), *adj.* of or relating to Transkei, a region in southeastern South Africa that in 1976 became the first homeland (of the Xhosa people) to be declared independent by the Republic of South Africa.

Tonight the South African flag will be lowered in Umtata and the Transkeian flag will be raised, but the international community is boycotting the ceremony and has announced there will be no recognition of Transkeian independence any more than of Rhodesian. *The Times (London), Oct. 25, 1976, p 13*

—*n.* a native or inhabitant of Transkei.

Forty-five percent of all Transkeians, and 80% of its adult males, will continue to work "abroad" in South Africa, which is just as well, because there are few jobs at home. *Time, Oct. 11, 1976, p 41*

[1963, from Latin *trāns* across + *Kei* name of a river]

transmodality, *n.* the integration of different modes of transportation.

Movement in containers, bulk and unit loads, and by roll-on/roll-off services can involve one continuous transport process by road, rail, sea, and inland waterway — the word transmodality was coined to describe it — and new facilities and handling equipment were being provided on an increasing scale to cope with it. *Ernest Davies, "Transportation," Britannica Book of the Year 1973, p 687*

[1972]

transnational, *n.* another name for MULTINA-TIONAL.

In these circumstances there is no free market: the transnationals are buying and selling to themselves in a closed circuit. Typically, a raw material is extracted by a transnational in a developing country and sold to the same transnational in an industrialised country, where it is processed, manufactured and distributed. *John Tinker, New Scientist, Sept. 4, 1975, p 529*

[1969, noun use of the adjective, abstracted from *transnational company* (or *corporation*)]

transnationalism, *n.:* Energy relationships, for instance, are being taken out of the hands of multinational companies and becoming the direct concern of governments. . . . Yet the reality of transnationalism, at any rate in the non-Communist world, simply cannot be denied. *Alastair Buchan, "The Search for a New Order: Transnationalism," The Listener, Dec. 20, 1973, p 845*

transpersonal psychology, a method of psycho-therapy that postulates various levels of conscious-ness and is concerned especially with extrasensory perception.

Many humanistic psychologists have gone into transper-sonal psychology, with its emphasis on the suprapersonal or mystical experiences. *T. George Harris, "Era of Conscious Action," Britannica Book of the Year 1973, p 11*

[1972] See ALTERED STATE OF CONSCIOUSNESS.

transuranic, *n.* a chemical element whose atomic number is higher than that of uranium; a trans-uranic element.

The new elements are called transuranic because ura-nium number 92 is the heaviest to occur naturally on earth. There is debate over whether the transuranics can and do exist naturally in the universe outside earth, but from a provincial terrestrial point of view they can truly be called manufactured elements. *"The Newest Element: 106," Science News, Sept. 14, 1974, p 164*

[1969, noun use of the adjective, abstracted from *transuranic element*]

Trek·kie ('trek i:), *n. Especially U.S.* a fan of the science-fiction television series "Star Trek."

"Of course, I didn't know George was a Trekkie when I married him." *Cartoon legend by Jack Ziegler, The New Yorker, Feb. 16, 1976, p 39*

At a cost of $15 million, the movie remake of the late '60s television show will reunite the original cast of the Starship Enterprise, hoping to cash in on the Trekkies craze which has spawned 371 fan clubs, annual conventions, more than 50 books and 431 fan publications. *Jane O'Hara, "People," Maclean's, Jan. 15, 1979, p 35*

[1976] ► This name is not acceptable to fans who generally prefer *Trekker*, according to Patricia Byrd (University of Florida), in "Star Trek Lives: Trekker Slang" (*American Speech*, Spring 1978, pp 54-58). See also ZINE.

TRF or **TRH,** abbreviation of *thyrotropin-releasing factor* (or *hormone*), a hormone produced in the hypothalamus that causes the release of the thyroid-stimulating hormone thyrotropin.

After processing some 270,000 sheep hypothalami they had obtained a 1 mg sample of thyrotropin-releasing factor (TRF), the hormone with which the brain directs the pitu-itary's control of the thyroid gland. Their sample was pure enough to allow two conclusions to be drawn. First, the sheep TRF molecule consisted of three amino acids, glu-tamate, histidine, and proline. *Nicholas Wade, New Scientist, May 4, 1978, p 301*

The first hypothalamic hormone to be discovered is called TRH for thyrotropin-releasing hormone. TRH causes the pituitary gland to release a substance called thyro-tropin, which, in turn, causes the thyroid gland to release thyroid hormone. The research groups headed by Schally and Guillemin discovered TRH virtually simultaneously in 1969. *David Hendin, "The 1977 Nobel Prize Winners in Physiology or Medicine," Encyclopedia Science Supplement (Grolier) 1979 (1978), p 95*

[1970] Compare LRF.

triad, *n.* the strategic nuclear force of the United States, consisting of land-based missiles, sub-marine-launched missiles, and long-range bombers.

The President . . . confirmed the continuing commitment to the three-legged "triad" (air- and sea-launched and land-based strategic missiles) of the American nuclear deter-rent. *Time, March 27, 1978, p 16*

They argue that the triad also provides for "flexible op-tions" in the selection of targets, including "conventional forces, lines of communication, war-supporting industry and targets of increasing hardness: from aircraft runways and nuclear storage sites to command bunkers and ICBM silos." *Philip Morrison and Paul F. Walker, "A New Strategy for Military Spending," Scientific American, Oct. 1978, p 52*

Attributive use.

The so-called "triad composition" of our strategic forces —the distribution of warheads in silos, submarines, and bombers—was designed to reduce the threat of a Soviet first strike aimed at our land-based missiles. *George B. Kistiakowsky, "False Alarm: The Story Behind Salt II," The New York Review of Books, March 22, 1979, p 36*

[1978, specialized use of the sense "group or set of three" (OED 1546)]

triage (tri:'ɑːʒ *or* 'tri: ɑːʒ), *n.* the principle or policy of allocating limited resources, such as food, on the basis of urgency or expediency rather than accord-ing to humanitarian or other moral principles.

In the West, there is increasing talk of triage, a common-sense if callous concept that teaches that when resources are scarce, they must be used where they will do most good. *"What to Do: Costly Choices," Time, Nov. 11, 1974, p 80*

Finally, and most significantly, one cannot talk about triage without addressing its ethical implications. What does it mean to countries too poor to make the "aid list"? And what does it mean to those in affluent societies who are in a position to help? *Natural History, June 1975, p 6*

The term "triage," once used only in military medicine to describe the selection on the battlefield of whom to treat and whom to abandon, now extends beyond even general hospital practice to embrace a wider social predicament: Where and on what basis will an effort be made to save endangered peoples, and where not? *Leonard C. Lewin, "Bioethical Questions," Harper's, Aug. 1978, p 28*

Triage is one thing more: it is *racist*, for triagelike catego-ries follow not only economic but racial lines as well. The upper economic third is composed mainly of the white race, the middle one of the yellow, and the bottom of the brown and black. *Albert J. Fritsch, et al., Environmental Ethics, 1980, p 285*

[1974, extended sense of the World War I military

term for the emergency sorting of wounded on the battlefield, from French, from *trier* to sort] Compare LIFEBOAT ETHIC.

► In the original sense, *triage* meant dividing the wounded into three groups. In the current sense, triage would apportion the world's resources in an analogous order of priority.

Trib·u·nite ('trib yə,nait), *n. British.* one of a group of Labourites holding extreme left-wing views.

The Prime Minister decided that the rebellion had to be put down instantly, if only to prove to the outside world that he still controlled what happened at Westminster, and that his Government was not to be brought down by a mere 37 Tribunites. He called for a vote of confidence and got it after a debate. *James Lewis, "The Week in Britain: Last Troubles with Tribunites?" The Manchester Guardian Weekly, March 21, 1976, p 4*

[1970, from *Tribune (group)*, named after the *Tribune*, the group's weekly journal] Compare MONDAY CLUBBER.

Tri·cap ('trai,kæp), *n.* a division of the United States Army, introduced in 1971, in which tanks, mechanized light infantry, and mobile air support are coordinated to protect one another. *Often used attributively.*

Within the continental U.S., the main active unit was the Strategic Reserve of one Tricap (triple-capable) division, one infantry, one air-mobile, and one airborne division, though most of these units were not at full strength. *Robert J. Ranger, "Defense: United States," Britannica Book of the Year 1974, p 234*

[1971, short for *Tri*ple-*cap*able division]

trickle irrigation, a method of irrigation involving the slow application of water at regulated intervals by small-diameter perforated hoses placed on top of the soil.

The concept, which is now called drip irrigation or trickle irrigation, has gained wide acceptance, proving to be particularly valuable in areas that are arid and have high labor costs. An unforeseen benefit is that the system works well with water that is highly saline, as water in arid regions often is. *Kobe Shoji, "Drip Irrigation," Scientific American, Nov. 1977, p 62*

[1971]

tri·cy·clic (trai'saik lik), *n.* any of a class of antidepressant drugs that prevent the breakdown of serotonin, a chemical transmitter of nerve impulses believed to be involved in depression.

Tricyclics anti-depressants help the people who get to sleep, but wake up at about three, seeing everything as a disaster: their mortgage is going to fall in, they're going to lose their job, their daughter's going to marry the wrong man, their wife's going to leave them. . . . You want to give them tricyclics at night sufficient to stop this early-morning waking, this early-morning panic. *"Depression—Symptoms and Cures," The Listener, Oct. 18, 1973, p 515*

[1972, noun use of the adjective; so called from the drugs being tricyclic compounds (having a three-ringed molecular structure)]

Trident, *n.* **1** a large, nuclear-powered United States submarine, capable of carrying up to twenty-four ballistic missiles.

The rush to develop a fleet of new submarines, called Tridents, is even harder to justify. They are designed to fire missiles with a longer range than those fitted into our present Polaris and Poseidon submarines; consequently the Tridents could roam around a wider area of the ocean and thus make it harder for an enemy to find them. *John Fischer, Harper's, Sept. 1973, p 20*

2 a ballistic missile designed to be carried on and launched from this submarine.

A new submarine-launched ballistic missile (SLBM), the Trident, entered the flight test phase January 18, and by September the navy had launched six more, all of them successfully. Trident is expected to carry ten multiple independently targetable reentry vehicles (MIRV's) to distances of 4,600 to 6,700 miles. *John Rhea, 1978 Collier's Encyclopedia Year Book (1977), p 102*

[1973]

tri·fec·ta (trai'fek tə), *n. U.S.* **1** a form of betting in horse races in which the bettor must pick the first three horses to finish in the exact order in a given race.

The money that is bet on gimmick races like the trifecta is placed in a separate pool from the straight win, place, and show wagering. *Anonymous, "Superfix: How Certain Jockeys Cash in on the Gimmick Races," Daily News (New York), Feb. 6, 1974, p 46*

2 this form of betting used in the game of jai alai.

For the trifecta, more recently introduced, you have to pick teams to win, place and show—in order. It usually pays off in four figures. *Hubert Saal, "The Basques of Bridgeport," The New York Times Magazine, Sept. 19, 1976, p 82*

[1974, from *tri-* + per*fecta* (in which the first two finishers are picked)] Also called TRIPLE. Compare SUPERFECTA.

trif·fid ('trif id), *n.* (in science fiction) a huge walking plant that attacks human beings.

This system has now grown like a menacing forest of triffids to the stage where it threatens to strangle the people who invented it. *Brian Gardner, New Scientist, Aug. 30, 1973, p 513*

[1963, from the name of the imaginary plant in the science-fiction novel *The Day of the Triffids* (1951), by the English writer John Wyndham, 1903-1969, perhaps formed by alteration of *trifid* three-cleft (plant or animal)]

tri·lat·er·al·ism (trai'læt ər ə,liz əm), *n.* a policy of fostering close ties and cooperation among the industrialized countries of North America, Western Europe, and Japan.

Trilateralism . . . deemphasises the Soviet-American confrontation. It talks of greater flexibility in negotiating with the Third World, but just as few concessions. At the same time, it wants closer interaction, and, if possible, a united foreign front by the industrial nations of the non-Communist world. *Jonathan Steele, The Manchester Guardian Weekly, Jan. 30, 1977, p 6*

The United States must widen its relationship beyond western Europe and Japan. The present trilateralism was not enough. That was why the President had visited key countries such as Nigeria, Iran and Saudi Arabia. *The Times (London), July 13, 1978, p 16*

[1977, from the *Trilateral (Commission)*, a group

organized in 1973 to promote such a policy + -*ism*]

trilateralist, *n.:* Among the other Trilateralists, a band of half a hundred elitists from politics, government, business, labor and academia, were Harold Brown . . . Cyrus R. Vance . . . Walter F. Mondale . . . and Zbigniew Brzezinski. *Leonard Silk, "Carter and Key Advisers Among the Trilateralists," The New York Times, Jan. 6, 1977, p 41*

tri·meth·o·prim (trai'meθ ə₁prim), *n.* a chemical substance that in combination with a sulfonamide destroys or inhibits the growth of bacteria. *Formula:* $C_{14}H_{18}N_4O_3$

A remarkably potent combination of two antibiotics — trimethoprim, a folate antagonist, and sulfamethoxazole, a slow-acting sulfonamide — was approved by the FDA. These two drugs act synergistically against a wide variety of organisms, particularly the gram negative bacilli, a common cause of urinary tract infections. This drug combination is also effective against typhoid fever. *Frank P. Mathews, "Medicine," 1975 Collier's Encyclopedia Year Book (1974), p 338*

[1968, from *trimethoxybenzyl-pyrimidine*, part of the chemical name]

tri·mu·on ('trai₁myu: ɑn), *n. Nuclear Physics.* a triplet of muons that are products of the decay of particles governed by the interactions of neutrinos at high energy.

Events with three muons (trimuons) have not yet been observed, even though the efficiency of detection of trimuons is comparable to that for dimuons. *A. K. Mann, "Elementary Particle," McGraw-Hill Yearbook of Science and Technology 1977, p 211*

The new events are rare. Corrected for detection efficiencies the group have found a rate of 3×10^{-3} for dimuons . . . and 1×10^{-4} for trimuons. In their paper (*Physical Review Letters*, vol. 38, p 577) the Barish group speculate that the trimuon rate might be equated with the similar rate (1 in 10^4 events) for another problem phenomenon — the production of *dimuons* in the collision of hadrons with nuclei. Here a fast hadron strikes a nucleus and creates a slow muon pair — just like the neutrino in the trimuon case. *"Monitor: Now Neutrinos Create Trimuons," New Scientist, March 24, 1977, p 697*

[1975, from *tri-* three + *muon*]

triple, *n.* another name for TRIFECTA (def. 1).

For, ah, tax reasons, each bet was placed in the name of a different member of the group. They had hit on a triple (picking the first three horses in the right order), and it was the young woman's turn to collect. *John Leonard, "About New York: OTB or Not OTB," The New York Times, Aug. 21, 1976, p 22*

[1972]

triple-digit, *adj. Especially U.S.* equaling or exceeding a rate of 100 per cent (up to a possible 999 per cent).

Last week the [Israeli] government conceded that the cost of living for April had jumped a shocking 8.7%, more than 100% if projected over the entire year. The admission provoked howls of alarm that the country could be heading toward uncontrollable triple-digit inflation. *"The Rising Cost of Peace," Time, May 28, 1979, p 22*

[1976, patterned on DOUBLE-DIGIT]

trippy, *adj. U.S. and Canadian, Slang.* stupefied, as by the use of narcotics; SPACY.

In my trippy daze, dope was the filter for the movie camera in my mind, the regulator of my psychic jets. *Jay Spencer, "Living on Lithium," Harper's, June 1975, p 9*

The trippy optimism of the '60s lent importance to such things as creativity and communication, which in the '70s have given way to matters of a homelier urgency. *David Livingstone, "Music," Maclean's, Nov. 13, 1978, p 78*

[1975, from *trip* (1966) hallucinatory experience produced by narcotics + -*y* (adj. suffix)]

trippiness, *n.:* Robert Wise directed with tame, impersonal good taste; there's none of the blissful trippiness of being carried in the belly of a zeppelin, and none of the carnival vulgarity of the recent disaster thrillers. *Pauline Kael, "The Current Cinema," Review of "The Hindenburg," The New Yorker, Jan. 19, 1976, p 48*

troop·ie ('tru: pi:), *n. Slang.* a soldier of the lowest rank in Zimbabwe (Rhodesia) and South Africa.

Whether tracking guerrillas by day or setting up ambush positions at night, the "troopies" communicate by hand signals as they search out foot and boot prints, bowed grass, broken camps or other varieties of "terr spoor," army slang for terrorist tracks. *Time, Feb. 27, 1978, p 38*

[1976, probably diminutive from *troop* or *trooper*]

► The term is also reported in the *Dictionary of South African English* (Jean Branford, 1978) with the spelling *troepie* (from Afrikaans and Dutch *troep* troop).

tro·po·col·la·gen (₁trou pou'kɑl ə dʒən), *n.* a protein from which the collagen fibers of connective tissue, bone, etc., are formed.

The implant materials — air, saline, preserved vitreous, hyaluronic acid, and tropocollagen — are used to reform the globe, restore normal tension, and push the detached retina back against the choroid. *Roland I. Pritikin and M. L. Duchon, "Medicine: Eye Diseases," The Americana Annual 1974, p 375*

[1963, from *tropo-* a turning, change (from Greek *trópos*) + *collagen*]

tro·po·nin ('trou pə nin), *n.* a protein in muscle tissue regulated by calcium ions, important in muscle contraction.

Troponin, a protein intimately associated with actin, inhibits the interaction that produces movement if calcium ions are present. As a result of its presence the contraction of muscle becomes sensitive to fluxes of calcium ions and its regulation by the nervous system possible. *Dennis Bray, "How Movements Evolved," New Scientist, Jan. 27, 1972, p 199*

[1968, from *tropo-* turning + -*nin*, perhaps as in *actinin*] Compare ACTININ.

trouble, *n.* **the troubles,** a euphemism for the riots, bombings, and continued violence in Northern Ireland during the 1970's.

Four years ago, when the troubles in Ulster were just becoming serious there were signs of growing nationalism in both Scotland and Wales. *Maurice Latey, "Thoughts on the British Constitution," The Listener, April 28, 1973, p 533*

For the first time since the troubles began six years ago, the British army will actively attempt to seek out and destroy the terrorists. *"Northern Ireland: Down the Road to Hell," Time, Jan. 19, 1976, p 41*

Although nearly everyone in Northern Ireland knows of a

mixed marriage somewhere in his own family, it is assumed that fewer mixed marriages are occurring than before the Troubles, particularly among working-class people, because of the hardening of ghetto frontiers and the greater dangers involved. *Anthony Bailey, "A Reporter At Large," The New Yorker, May 8, 1978, p 56*

[1973, a revival of the phrase used to describe the violence in Ireland during the 1920's, especially the civil war of 1922 between the Irish republicans and the Free State government]

truck, *v.i. U.S. Slang.* to move ahead; go or march forward (especially in the catch phrase of encouragement or approval *keep on truckin').*

One poster taped on the wall at YVP's Los Angeles headquarters on Wilshire Boulevard shows the famous R. Crumb cartoon characters and bears the caption: "Let's Keep On Truckin' . . ." *Steven V. Roberts, "Keep On Truckin' With Nixon," Saturday Review, Oct. 28, 1972, p 12*

Trucking – Walking – using legs to get somewhere.

"To the returning P.O.W.'s: This list may be a little far out for you dudes, a little heavy, but it's what we've been into while you were gone. Dig?" *The New York Times, March 8, 1973, p 39*

[1972, originally (1930's) Black English (especially jazz) slang meaning to go, walk, stroll; phrase probably influenced by the strolling, shuffling dance of the 1930's called *trucking*]

truck cap, *U.S.* a wood and aluminum shelter mounted over the bed of a pickup truck to convert it into a camper.

The truck cap . . . offers a place to get in out of the weather and eliminates the need of pitching a tent at every stop. Since it adds very little weight and bulk to a truck, it is popular with hunters, fishermen, and others who get far off the beaten path. *Norman Strung, "Everybody's Going Camping," The Americana Annual 1972, p 56*

[1972]

truth, *n.* the property of a type of quark called TOP QUARK.

The new quarks will apparently be called "top" and "bottom," the names being meant to suggest properties surpassing those of the up and down quarks found in ordinary matter. If the two new quarks do exist, there must also be two new properties of matter, which some physicists have taken to calling "truth" and "beauty." *"Science and the Citizen," Scientific American, Oct. 1977, p 74*

[1977, named on the models of BEAUTY, CHARM] See QUARK.

tsats·ke ('tsɑts kə), *n.* variant of TCHOTCHKE.

"Décor doesn't add to the glamour of a suit," an owner pointed out. "You're not buying the rugs or the lamps or the tsatskes." *Georgia Dullea, The New York Times, July 12, 1974, p 31*

[1968, from Yiddish]

tsou·ris or **tsu·ris** ('tsɔ: res *or* 'tsu: ris), *n.pl. U.S. Slang.* troubles; woes.

Mary is 50, widowed, loaded, and an alumna of analysis and a veteran of A.A. She has had a bad back, a bad psychoanalytic trip and miscellaneous medical tsouris. But is she downhearted? No! *Review of "My Name Is Mary . . ." by Anita Katzmann, The New York Times Book Review, March 16, 1975, p 31*

Having been with the paper only 25 years, Mr. Suller would not dream of challenging Mr. Novick for supremacy. "I don't feel I can measure up to him," Mr. Suller said, in an interlude between hymns of praise. "That's No. 1. No. 2 is I have enough tsuris of my own." *The New York Times, Feb. 12, 1978, p 48*

[1963, from Yiddish *tsores,* plural of *tsore* trouble, from Hebrew *tsārāh*]

tsu·tsu·mu (tsu:'tsu: mu:), *n.* the Japanese art of wrapping articles in bamboo, paper, etc., so that the packages harmonize with and enhance their contents.

Each of the 300 packages in the show (called "Tsutsumu, The Art of the Japanese Package") was purchased in 1974 in Japan, where an object's wrapping can be as important as the object itself. *Norma Skurka, "The Way of Tsutsumu," The New York Times Magazine, Feb. 9, 1975, p 56*

[1975, from Japanese, bundle, package]

tubal ligation, a form of female sterilization in which the Fallopian tubes are surgically tied into a loop.

Tubal ligation . . . is another form of surgical intervention, far less drastic than hysterectomy. In the tubal ligation operation, the passageway for the ovum to reach the womb after leaving the ovary is blocked. The male sperm is therefore unable to reach the egg, preventing conception. But, like all abdominal surgical procedures, tubal ligation does require hospitalization, and does involve some discomfort. More recent procedures, practiced in the major medical centers of the United States, have greatly simplified the operation. This operation is irreversible. *Estelle Fuchs, The Second Season, 1977, p 154*

The Indian doctors' method was indirectly inspired by Mrs. Gandhi's campaign for forced mass sterilization to check India's overpopulation, when vaginal access was used for tubal ligations for reasons of speed. *"The Talk of the Town," The New Yorker, Nov. 20, 1978, p 39*

[1972] Compare VASOLIGATE.

tube, *n.* **1** *Surfing Slang.* the hollow space formed by the curling of a breaking wave.

Many people refer to plunging waves as "crashers" or "dumpers" because of their ferocity. Hollow plungers are the most challenging waves for surfers because their steepness makes for a very fast ride, and it is often possible for surfers to crouch under the falling crest – to be "locked in the tube." *Steve Lissau, "Ocean Waves," Encyclopedia Science Supplement (Grolier) 1976, p 159*

Shootin' the tube, a surfer threads the eye of a breaker off Little Avalon, northeast of Sydney. *Picture legend, "Sydney," National Geographic Magazine, Feb. 1979, p 235*

See CURL.

2 **go down the tube** (or **tubes**), *U.S. Slang.* to be lost or finished; go down the drain.

Dumping the Vice President simply made no political sense, Nixon aides kept insisting. After all, the President had twice picked Agnew as his running mate. Said one aide: "Let's face it; if Agnew goes down the tube, that rubs off on the old man too." *Time, Oct. 1, 1973, p 15*

One of the Senate's most powerful unknown men, Republican Milton Young, is about to go down the tubes here. *New Times, Oct. 4, 1974, p 11*

"I really think the Supreme Court will realize that they did take the wrong step. The death penalty will be so narrowly defined that it will go down the tubes. But it's going to be a lot of bloody years before that comes to pass." *Millard*

481

Farmer, quoted by William Greider, "The Return of the Death Penalty," The Manchester Guardian Weekly (The Washington Post section), Dec. 12, 1976, p 15

[1964 for def. 1; 1968 for def. 2]

tube sock, a sock shaped like a tube with no heel, but made of fabric that stretches easily so the heel may be shifted to a different area each time the sock is worn, used for sport and casual wear.

Now a young man and woman n turtlenecks and Earth shoes wheel up a grocery cart full of comic books, cotton hats, incense, and tube socks. *John McPhee, "A Reporter at Large," The New Yorker, July 3, 1978, p 52*

[1976] Compare TOE SOCK.

tubing, *n.* the sport of sliding on an automobile inner tube downhill on snow.

But the big rage of the ski year—and the most painful—is a pastime called "tubing." For experts, the idea is to take a running start and then execute a belly-flop onto an ordinary inflated inner tube. The tube is almost impossible to control and it can reach speeds of 40 mph. *"Life Style: Skiing Without Skis," Newsweek, Feb. 3, 1975, p 69*

[1975] ► This is a new application of the sport of *tubing* known since the 1950's, which consists of riding or floating down a stream on an inner tube.

tu·bu·lin ('tu: byə lən), *n.* the protein from which microtubules (cylindrical structures in the cytoplasm of cells) are formed.

Osborn and Weber have for some time been developing methods for studying the . . . network of fibres (microtubules) extending from the nucleus and running through the cytoplasm. These fibres can be isolated and shown to contain one main protein component which has been named tubulin. By purifying tubulin and raising antibodies against it Osborn and Weber have been able to study the distribution of tubulin, and hence of microtubules in whole cells. *"Monitor: Fluorescence Shows That Electron Images Check Out," New Scientist, Nov. 2, 1978, p 356*

[1971, from micro*tubule* + *-in* (chemical suffix)]

tu·mesce (tu:'mes), *v.i., v.t.* to experience or cause to have tumescence of the sexual organ.

Peter Miller was tooling along in his Jaguar XK 150 S on the Hamburg autobahn . . . savoring memories of a glorious night spent tumescing and detumescing with Sigi, a smart stripper with a heart of eighteen-karat gold. *Max Geltman, Review of "The Odessa File" by Frederick Forsyth, National Review, Nov. 24, 1972, p 1311*

I'd never heard, from Athene or the several accounts of fellow-heroes which I'd studied in the past decade, of erections in Elysium, whereas the Olympians seemed as permanently tumesced as the mount they dwelt on. *John Barth, "Perseid: The Hero at Forty Reviews and Revises His Legend," Harper's, Oct. 1972, p 81*

[1972, back formation from *tumescence* or *tumescent*]

tumorigenesis or **tumorogenesis,** *n.* the formation or production of a tumor or tumors.

The mechanism of tumorigenesis or the factors that mediate natural or acquired resistance to MD [Marek's disease] are not well understood. *J. M. Sharma, "Letters to Nature: Resistance to Marek's Disease in Immunologically Deficient Chickens," Nature, Jan. 11, 1974, p 117*

Hot particles produce a disrupted tissue mass and the description of such lesions suggests an incipient tu-

morogenic response. We have proposed that the tumorogenesis involves an injury mediated mechanism. *Arthur Tamplin and Thomas Cochran, New Scientist, May 29, 1975, p 499*

[1973, from *tumor* + connecting *-i-* or *-o-* + *genesis*]

tunnel vision, a very narrow perspective or point of view.

The answer is to expand our tunnel vision beyond the parks themselves to what they are a small fragment of, the nation's total of recreational resources, and to relate these to the nation's total of recreational needs. *Gladwin Hill, "Pristine Preserves or Popcorn Playgrounds?" Saturday Review, Jan. 1, 1972, p 56*

There has been occasional agitation for deliberately reversing the historical trend and substituting steel for aluminum, solely on the grounds that the former is less energy-intensive. Like most single-purpose policies, this one too suffers from the tunnel vision of its perpetrators. *Hans H. Landsberg, "Materials: Some Recent Trends and Issues," Science, Feb. 20, 1976, p 639*

Discussing his analysis of the tunnel vision of some American intellectuals lurching along their fellow-travelling trips with totalitarian socialism, Wolfe remarks with genuine bewilderment: "Some critics called me Fascist for that article. I see myself as a real democrat." *Barbara Amiel, "A Society's Monitor," Maclean's, Nov. 6, 1978, p 6*

[1970, figurative use of the term for an eye disorder characterized by a constricted range of vision]

tunnel-visioned, *adj.:* "The pronouncements of the national commission on prison research illustrate beautifully how well-intentioned desires to reform prisons can lead otherwise intelligent people to destroy properly performed research that scrupulously involves informed consent and full explanation and avoids coercion to the satisfaction of all but the most tunnel-visioned doctrinaire," Lasagna says. *Science News, April 9, 1977, p 230*

tur·bo·lin·er ('tər bou,lai nər), *n.* a high-speed, lightweight passenger train driven by a gas turbine engine built into one or more of the cars.

The new trains to be maintained at Rensselaer are American-built versions of the French turboliners now operated by Amtrak between Chicago and Milwaukee, Chicago and Port Huron, Mich., and Chicago and Detroit. On good track they are capable of 125 miles an hour. *"Ground Is Broken for Unit to Service Trains to Buffalo," The New York Times, June 8, 1976, p 35*

[1970] ► This term was used earlier (1952) to refer to a passenger airplane powered by turboprop engines.

tur·bo·pause ('tər bou,pɔ:z), *n.* a region in which atmospheric turbulence ceases, especially such a region at the base of the thermosphere.

Since the Martian turbopause is at a lower density level than the turbopause on the earth, as a consequence of more efficient stirring by winds, it seems likely that the atmospheric tides on Mars are stronger than those of the earth. *Conway B. Leovy, "The Atmosphere of Mars," Scientific American, July 1977, p 42*

Important to an understanding of the [Venusian] atmosphere is the turbopause, apparently about 144 km above the surface. *Science News, Dec. 23-30, 1978, p 435*

[1967, from *turbulence* + connecting *-o-* + *pause*, as in *magnetopause*]

turf, *n.* territory; domain.

The Irish . . . will give their hearts to any politician ambitious enough to guard his turf properly. *Jane Kramer, "Letter from Ireland," The New Yorker, Feb. 19, 1972, p 56*

Its [The Los Angeles Times'] metropolitan staff of 96 has problems making sense of its turf—4,800 sq. mi. of overlapping municipal governments that constitute a city editor's nightmare. *Time, Jan. 21, 1974, p 59*

For months he has watched impatiently as Congress encroached upon his diplomatic turf. *Newsweek, Jan. 20, 1975, p 29*

[1970, from the earlier (1954) slang sense of a gang's exclusive territory]

turn, *v.* **turn around,** *U.S.* to change for the better; bring from a bad to a good condition.

At Mendocino State Hospital in California . . . children (ages 13-17) with severe behavioral problems (drug abuse, runaways, stealing) are treated in a "family" situation with hospital staff members as surrogate parents. An innovative school program helps "turn youngsters around." *Science News, Feb. 13, 1971, p 108*

In fairness, figuring out what can be done to improve the lot of farmers must seem comfortably simple to most members of Congress compared with the desperate riddle of what, if anything, can be done to turn around the South Bronx. *Andy Logan, "Around City Hall," The New Yorker, Sept. 4, 1978, p 82*

[1968, extended from the basic sense of "to turn the other way; to reverse"]

turnaround time or **turnaround,** *n.* the time needed to complete a task, process, or operation.

The principal determinants of this are "turn-around" time requirements, volume of ECGs, operational efficiency, simplicity, and unit costs. Rapid turn-around time ("real time") is desirable but not required in some applications. *Cesar A. Caceras, "Electrodiagnosis," McGraw-Hill Yearbook of Science and Technology 1972, p 194*

Studies of engineering productivity led one major aerospace company to create a dual scheduling system for batch work: This offers standard service or rapid turnaround (less than two hours) at a slightly higher internal charge. *"What Is Computing Worth?" Advertisement by IBM, Scientific American, Sept. 1978, p 90*

[1972, extended sense of the term (1950's) meaning the time taken to prepare a ship, airplane, etc., to make a return trip]

TV ('ti:'vi:), *n.* *Slang.* a transvestite.

Gradually I learned the swingers' lingo: "TVs" meant transvestites; "toys" meant anything from vibrators to whips; . . . "uncut" meant uncircumcised, and "well-end" an abbreviation of "endowed." *John Hofsess, "Misadventures in the Skin Trade," Maclean's, July 1974, p 25*

[1966]

TVP, 1 abbreviation of TEXTURED VEGETABLE PROTEIN.

The most stunning fact about TVPs is that they are made from beans. And whereas the tradition of mass carnivorousness is new, pulses have formed a key component of great cuisines for thousands of years. *Colin Tudge, "Who Needs Soya?" New Scientist, Feb. 19, 1976, p 403*

2 a trademark for a brand of textured vegetable protein.

Because TVP is a registered trademark it should not be used interchangeably with the generic names textured vegetable protein or textured vegetable product, but used only when it is identified as the trademark of Archer Daniels Midland Company. *R. E. Burket, "The Mail," The Atlantic, April 1975, p 30*

[1968]

two-digit, *adj.* variant of DOUBLE-DIGIT.

"In recent months we've had a two-digit inflation with the rise in consumer price index 10.2 per cent above the year before levels." *Interview of Nat Goldfinger by William J. Lanouette, "Inflation: A View From Labor," The National Observer, June 15, 1974, p 6*

[1974]

ty·lec·to·my (ˌtai'lek tə mi:), *n.* another name for LUMPECTOMY.

For example, at Guy's Hospital in London, a 10-year study of 370 women with breast cancer has been made. Half the women had radical surgery, and the other half had what is termed a tylectomy: removal of the lump and about an inch of surrounding tissue. *Clifton R. Read, "Breast Cancer—the Disease Women Fear Most: Controversy over Surgery," Encyclopedia Science Supplement (Grolier) 1973, p 270*

[1973, from Greek *týlē* lump + English *-ectomy* surgical removal]

Type A, 1 a behavior pattern characterized by tenseness, impatience, and competitive drive, associated with a tendency to develop coronary heart disease. *Often used attributively.*

What is a Type A personality? According to the originators of the theory, a Type A person is highly competitive and aggressive, totally involved in her or his job, and constantly striving for achievement. This kind of behavior is characterized by haste, impatience, restlessness, hyperalertness, hard-driving conscientiousness, and forceful expression. A Type A person will have "hurry sickness"—he or she never seems to have enough time to do all the things that he feels must be accomplished each day. *Joe Graedon, The People's Pharmacy, 1976, p 275*

2 a person exhibiting such a behavior pattern.

We have met some Type A's so severely afflicted that they almost never enjoy a moment of tranquillity. One sees the darting, hateful, belligerent sparks escaping from their eyes even when they are merely asking the time of day. *Meyer Friedman and Roy H. Rosenman, "How to Add Years to Your Life," Maclean's, June 1974, p 82*

[1972, coined by Meyer Friedman and Roy H. Rosenman, American cardiologists]

► *Type A* is often contrasted with an easygoing, relaxed behavior pattern designated as *Type B*:

Type A is an obsessive striver, has an excessive sense of urgency, fights constantly against deadlines and has an extra dose of hostility and aggression. Type B is the opposite. *Kathy Slobogin, "Stress," The New York Times Magazine, Nov. 20, 1977, p 50*

type C virus, variant of C-TYPE VIRUS.

Some human leukemia cells, and possibly other human cells, contain a type C virus that is in a dormant state or is defective—that is, with incomplete genetic information. Also, the virus is related to the tumor viruses isolated from some primates. *Robert C. Gallo, "Tracing a Human Cancer Virus," The World Book Science Annual 1977 (1976), p 300*

[1975]

U

U, a symbol used in Great Britain to designate motion pictures recommended for general audiences. The equivalent U.S. symbol is *G.*

At the Classic, Hendon, a piece from Israel, *The Policeman* (director Ephraim Kishon; U), a comedy about a kind-hearted, butter-fingered Jaffa cop. *Dilys Powell, "Films," The Sunday Times (London), Feb. 10, 1974, p 30*

"Hell!" cried the priest, "What kind of penitent *are* you? Did you at least make love to your wife, see a U film, buy *Reader's Digest?*"

"No," said the confessant, "none of those." *Alan Coren, "Antichrist Superstar," Punch, Jan. 21, 1977, p 80*

[1970, for *Universal* or *Unrestricted Exhibition*]
▶ See the notes under A and G.

UDAG ('yu:,dæg), *n. U.S.* a government program granting federal funds for projects to revitalize and develop poor or older sections of a city.

Most UDAG projects have been initiated by city governments or agencies, but about one-fifth have been proposed by private developers, with lesser numbers proposed by nonprofit corporations, banks or financial institutions, and citizens' groups. *Cushing N. Dolbeare, "Cities," 1980 Collier's Encyclopedia Year Book (1979), p 215*

[1977, acronym for *Urban Development Action Grant*]

u·ja·ma·a (,u: dʒa:'ma: a:), *n.* a form of socialism in Tanzania that develops local cooperatives, collective farming, and self-help projects, based on traditional African concepts of the extended family and kinship responsibility.

Again, the *ujamaa*—literally "family"—cooperative system is a way of coping with a specifically African problem, the fact that the majority of the 14 million people in the vast rural Tanzanian mainland are scattered in small units. *Nicholas Hagger, The Times (London), Oct. 18, 1972, p 16*

Ujamaa means "familyhood," and the purpose is to build upon the old African kinship customs, with handicapped citizens or the unemployed from the city put back into the care of their hometowns. But the system is intended to be so pervasive that even admission into the university is by permission of the local office of TANU. *Edward Hoagland, "At Large in East Africa," Harper's, Aug. 1976, p 67*

Temu argues that *Ujamaa* villages are unique in the world. He says that "capitalist economists acclaim it because of economies of scale. Socialism adds to this the most important dimension of all: That by living together people will not only be able to improve . . . efficiently, but will learn a new style of life . . . living democratically at the village level." *J. T. Mukui, "Running to Keep Pace," Review of "Papers on the Political Economy of Tanzania," edited by Kim, Mabele, and Schultheis, The Weekly Review, May 11, 1979, p 31*

[1962, from Swahili, from *u*-, prefix meaning state or quality of + *jamaa* family (from Arabic *jamā'a* community)]

▶ Introduced by President Julius K. Nyerere, in *Ujamaa: The Basis of African Socialism* (1962), the term avoids negative connotations of *socialism,* and stresses an approach rooted in traditional African tribal concepts.

ULCC, a petroleum supertanker with a capacity of over 400,000 tons.

The incredible ULCC . . . will be able to deliver 3.5 million barrels of oil from a foreign land to an American port in a single journey. *Advertisement by Tenneco Inc., Houston, Tex., Time, Oct. 14, 1974, p 59*

[1973, abbreviation of *ultra-large crude carrier*] Compare VLCC.

ul·cer·o·gen·ic (,əl sər ə'dʒen ik), *adj.* producing an ulcer or ulcers.

By studying a group of such related compounds, he has been able to determine that the ulcerogenic activity of a toxic substance is "mostly but not exclusively" related to a two-carbon group bearing a reactive radical such as cyanide, nitrile, or sulfhydril. *Janet H. Weinberg, "Toxic Surprises from the Plastics Industry," Science News, Sept. 7, 1974, p 155*

[1969, from *ulcer* + connecting *-o-* + *-genic* producing]

ULMS, a ballistic missile with a range of 4500 to 6000 miles, developed to be launched from a submarine.

The ULMS will have a greater range than either Polaris or Poseidon and in its most sophisticated form would need a new class of submarine, the Trident. *Tony Loftas, "Polaris on the Rocks?" New Scientist, Aug. 30, 1973, p 483*

[1970, abbreviation of *underwater long-range missile system*]

Ul·ti·sol ('əl tə,sɔ:l), *n.* (in U.S. soil taxonomy) any of a group of highly weathered and leached yellow-to-red soils found chiefly in old land surfaces of humid tropical or temperate climates (as in the southeastern United States and in Asia).

Oxisols and Ultisols . . . constitute approximately one-third of the world's potentially arable land. Accordingly, they represent a vast resource for expansion of food production in developing countries, and studies on their mineralogical nature will be of aid in development of agronomic techniques suitable to their efficient utilization. *Robert M. Weaver, "Soil," McGraw-Hill Yearbook of Science and Technology 1973, p 379*

[1967, probably from Latin *ulti*mus final, ultimate +

-sol (from Latin *solum* soil)] Compare ALFISOL, ARIDISOL, ENTISOL, HISTOSOL, INCEPTISOL, OXISOL, SPODOSOL, VERTISOL.

ul·tra·di·an (əl'trei di: ən), *adj.* of or relating to biological rhythms or cycles that recur more than once per day.

Every month, *Psychology Today* (circ. 1.1 million) tells Americans all they might want to know about sex, psychosurgery, bio-feedback, insomnia, ultradian rhythms—indeed the whole galaxy of behavioral phenomena, from alienation to Zen. *Time, May 17, 1976, p 78*

The cyclic pattern of biological life, however, does not stop with the obvious 24-hour cycle. Scientists are finding increasing evidence for a 90-minute cycle, named the ultradian rhythm. . . . Ultradian rhythms were first suspected more than 20 years ago when researchers discovered that rapid eye movement or REM sleep occurs in cycles of 90 to 100 minutes. *Science News, April 12, 1975, p 244*

[1974, from *ultra-* beyond + Latin *diēs* day + English *-an*] Compare INFRADIAN.

ultraelementary particle, a constituent of an elementary particle; a subatomic or subnuclear particle.

The subparticles . . . were tentatively named "partons" to avoid identification with the ultraelementary "quark" particles predicted by theory but not yet surely discovered despite eight years of search. *"Physics," The 1971 Compton Yearbook, p 389*

[1969]

ul·tra·fiche ('əl trə,fi:ʃ), *n.* a microfilm card containing highly reduced frames of printed matter.

Ultrafiches of the photochronic microimage process store up to 4,000 pages on a 4in by 6in film and provide complete industrial data compilations on a pocket scale. *L. Andrew Mannheim, The Times (London), Dec. 1, 1972, p II*

In this new process, for example, 1,800 large, highly detailed maps covering a continuous area of 775 square miles are reduced to a single, continuous ultrafiche of standard 4-by-6-inch size. *Lawrence Lessing, "Microfilm Emerges from Its Dusty Corner," Encyclopedia Science Supplement (Grolier) 1973, p 411*

[1971, by shortening from *ultra-* beyond + micro*fiche* (micro) card]

▶ A *microfiche* (1953) and an *ultrafiche* are usually the same size card, but microfiche contains about 100 microfilmed pages of a book, while an ultrafiche may contain several thousand pages.

ul·tra·mi·cro·fiche (,əl trə'mai krə,fi:ʃ), *n.* another name for ULTRAFICHE.

Ultramicrofiche achieves a reduction ratio of more than 200 and puts up to 8,000 pages on a single film, each page so miniaturized that it is barely visible to the naked eye. *Lawrence Lessing, "Microfilm Emerges from its Dusty Corner," Encyclopedia Science Supplement (Grolier) 1973, p 409*

[1969, from *ultra-* beyond + micro*fiche*]

Ul·tra·suède ('əl trə,sweid), *n.* a trademark for a washable fabric that resembles suède, made of polyester and nonfibrous polyurethane.

Halston hasn't forgotten the fabric he helped launch around the world, Ultrasuède. This time, he matches it up exactly to beige (Ultrasuède jacket over scoop-neck dress) or pink jersey. *Bernadine Morris, "Remembering Those Women Who Like Dresses," The New York Times, Jan. 14, 1977, p B4*

One Ultrasuede safari-type beige jacket with pocketless khaki pants worn by a gentleman with a receding hairline and brown horn-rimmed glasses. *"The Talk of the Town," The New Yorker, Sept. 25, 1978, p 35*

[1976, from *ultra-* beyond + *suède*]

ultraviolence, *n.* extreme or unrelenting violence.

The film [*A Clockwork Orange*] showed how a young hoodlum (Malcolm McDowell), homicidal in his employment of "ultraviolence" (a term that immediately entered the language), was subjected to brainwashing by government scientists. *Stuart Byron, "Motion Pictures," 1973 Collier's Encyclopedia Year Book (1972), p 393*

[1972]

ultraviolet astronomy, the study of stars and nebulae in the ultraviolet region of the spectrum, conducted especially by means of orbiting artificial satellites.

Most wavelengths of ultraviolet light cannot get through the earth's atmosphere. So ultraviolet astronomy has to be done from above the atmosphere. Systematic scans of the sky in ultraviolet had to await a satellite. *Ultraviolet Star Catalogue," Science News, June 16, 1973, p 391*

[1971]

u·na·ry ('yu: nə ri:), *adj. Mathematics.* consisting of, using, or applied to only one object or number.

A good way to grasp the essence of a Turing machine is to make one, albeit a trivial one. . . . Eight cells on the paper tape are marked 1111 + 111, signifying the addition of 4 and 3 in the "unary" system in which an integer *n* is symbolized by *n* 1's. *Martin Gardner, "Mathematical Games," Scientific American, June 1971, p 120*

[1971, from Latin *ūnus* one + English *-ary*, patterned on *binary*] Compare SINGULARY.

uncharmed, *adj.* (of a quark) lacking the property of CHARM.

The new particle, designated upsilon [is] three times as heavy as any known uncharmed particle, and one and a half times as heavy as any previously discovered charmed particle. Its lifetime may be less than 10^{-18} seconds. *"Science News of the Week: The Upsilon: The Heaviest Particle Yet," Science News, Feb. 14, 1976, p 100*

Charm . . . becomes manifest only in hadrons that include a charmed quark or antiquark in combination with uncharmed quarks. *Roy F. Schwitters, "Fundamental Particles With Charm," Scientific American, Oct. 1977, p 68*

[1975, from *un-* not + CHARMED]

Uncle Tomahawk, *U.S.* a derogatory name for an American Indian who works within the white establishment or adopts the culture and values of white society.

President Charlie Vigil has a future some place, perhaps working for the B.I.A. If the tribal constitution permitted it, he would prefer to remain in office rather than join the wandering bureaucrats some call Uncle Tomahawks. *Herbert Gold, "How Rich Is a Rich Apache?" The New York Times Magazine, Feb. 13, 1972, p 46*

[1971, blend of *Uncle Tom* a servile black man and *tomahawk* a light axe used by North American Indians] Also called APPLE. Compare TIO TACO.

unconstructed, *adj.* (of clothes) not shaped with interfacings or paddings and therefore pliant or supple in design.

The classic, unconstructed jacket with lapels and one, two, or three buttons can be adapted to many uses, many occasions. *Addis Durning, "The Perfect Leisure Suit Goes to Business with Ease," Daily News (New York), July 26, 1975, p 12*

Today's cotton corselet is soft and unconstructed and is either laced or buttoned. It can be worn to the beach or to parties, and under a shirt jacket it can even go to the office as a replacement for last year's T-shirt or halter. *Patricia Peterson, "Fashion," The New York Times Magazine, Feb. 20, 1977, p 65*

[1973]

undecidability, *n. Mathematics, Logic.* the condition of being impossible either to prove or disprove a sentence or proposition by logical deduction from the axioms of a system.

Kurt Gödel has shown, in his famous undecidability proof, that arithmetic contains theorems that cannot be established inside the deductive system of arithmetic. *Martin Gardner, Scientific American, July 1970, p 119*

There is an account of . . . numerous results concerning degrees of undecidability. *R. L. Goodstein, Review of "Mathematical Logic, with Special Reference to the Natural Numbers" by S. W. P. Steen, Nature, June 16, 1972, p 411*

[1970, from *undecidable, adj.* (OED 1640; in mathematics and logic since the 1950's) + *-ity*]

underabundant, *adj.* less than abundant; not as abundant as should be.

The production and abundance of nitrogen is very sensitively dependent on the availability of these heavier elements in the interstellar medium and should they be underabundant an extreme deficiency of nitrogen is possible. *N. Sanduleak, et al., Cleveland, Ohio, "Letters to Nature: Nitrogen Deficiency in the Small Magellanic Cloud," Nature, May 5, 1972, p 28*

[1971, patterned on *overabundant*]

underboss, *n. U.S. Underworld Slang.* a member of a Mafia family next below the head (capo) in rank.

In the restructured family on which Joe Colombo solidified his hold as boss, another tantalizing figure emerged, Charles (Charlie Lemons) Mineo . . . Mineo has become a unique kind of underboss, one who is virtually inactive. According to some reports he was enjoying the fruits of retirement when Colombo elevated him to the No. 2 spot in the family. *Fred J. Cook, "A Family Business: Hijacking, Bookmaking, Policy, Dice Games, Loan-Sharking and Special Contracts," The New York Times Magazine, June 4, 1972, p 95*

[1972] See DON, GODFATHER.

undercast, *v.t.* 1 to cast (an actor or performer) in a secondary or minor role.

Rossellini deliberately undercasts him, as he does everyone else. Colbert is made to look uninteresting and rather bourgeois. *Penelope Gilliatt, The New Yorker, Aug. 22, 1970, p 59*

Ridderbush, a light-voiced bass-baritone, is an instance of undercasting. *Irving Kolodin, Review of "The Karajan-Vickers-Dernesch Tristan," Saturday Review, Dec. 2, 1972, p 91*

2 to cast (a play, film, etc.) with secondary actors or minor performers.

Porter had done a dull job in the staging, and the play was woefully undercast. James Valentine—who seemed successfully concerned with giving a moderately accurate impersonation of John Gielgud as Jack Worthing—probably had the best of it. *The Times (London), July 9, 1977, p 10*

[1964]

underdogger, *n.* a person who supports the underdog in a fight or contest.

But hopelessness springs eternal on Rhode Island Sound. After three crushing defeats, *Australia's* [a boat] loyal underdoggers were busy recalling all the old familiar whiny excuses, among them the "She can only move in light air" ploy. *"Sport," Time, Oct. 3, 1977, p 54*

"Pagan saints," I said. "That's what I used to specialize in. They seemed right for the age, the best kind of hero, the embattled loser. The angel with the human smell, the innocent, the do-gooder, the outsider, the perfect stranger. I was a great underdogger." *The Times (London), Sept. 2, 1978, p 7*

[1970]

underfund, *v.t.* to fund inadequately; to fail to provide with sufficient funds.

All of these old programs can help at least some institutions carry out at least some of their educational missions. Most of them, however, have been woefully underfunded in recent years, and now they must compete for funds with the costly new higher education programs. *Eric Wentworth, "No Silver Spoon for Higher Education," Saturday Review, July 22, 1972, p 39*

Even after the act's protections were in force, 20,000 [private pension] plans folded. Plans that are integrated with Social Security sometimes pay nothing if Federal payments rise. Fraud steals the resources of some; others are badly underfunded. *Philip Shabecoff, The New York Times, June 25, 1978, Sec. 4, p 3*

[1967]

UNEP ('yu: nep), *n.* acronym for *United Nations Environment Program,* an agency created in 1972 to initiate and coordinate global efforts to protect the earth's environment. It was originally charged with operating the EARTHWATCH system.

Work supported by UNEP, an agency with headquarters in Nairobi, ranges from formation of a world network of information for action against poisonous chemicals to research projects intended to improve living conditions in towns and rural areas. *Pearce Wright, "Cash Delays Halt UN Environment Projects," The Times (London), March 23, 1976, p 7*

[1973]

uneven bars, parallel wooden bars, one about 7½ feet high, the other about 5 feet high, used in women's gymnastic events.

Whether doing backflips on the beam or rocketing herself around the uneven bars, the deceptively frail-looking sprite . . . was so much in her element that the audience had no more fear of her falling than of a fish drowning. *"Sport: Olympics," Time, Aug. 6, 1976, p 47*

[1972]

Unification Church, an evangelistic sect combining Christian and Buddhist elements, founded in South Korea by the Reverend Sun Myung Moon.

The Unification Church . . . moved its headquarters to the United States in the 1960's. It says that it has about 10,000 members in the United States, out of a total of 500,000 worldwide. *"Around the Nation: Unification Church Buys Mansion in Boston," The New York Times, Jan. 5, 1977, p A12*

Parents who attack the Unification Church are called "Satanic." The top secret 120-day training manual instructs members to have contact with parents "before they start to investigate the UC," so that they "feel peaceful . . ." *The Times (London), Dec. 14, 1977, p 5*

[1975] See MOONIE and MOONISM.

Unionism, *n.* the principles and practices of the Unionist Party (the ruling Protestant political party) of Northern Ireland.

The solution was a Protestant alliance with Unionism in the North, to match that between Catholicism and Irish Nationalism. *Anthony Spencer, "Politics and Religion in Ireland," The Listener, Dec. 21, 1972, p 854*

[1969, from *Unionist, adj., n.* (1955)]

UNISIST or **U·ni·sist** ('yu: nə,sist), *n.* a system for international exchange of scientific and technical information, sponsored by the International Council of Scientific Unions and UNESCO.

The object of the system, to be known as UNISIST, would be to help scientists and engineers to get easier access to about 2 million articles published every year in some 70,000 specialized scientific journals. *Leslie Aldous, "The United Nations and Its Specialized Agencies," The Annual Register of World Events in 1971 (1972), p 343*

[1971, acronym for *United Nations Intergovernmental System of Information in Science and Technology*]

UNITA or **U·ni·ta** ('yu: ni ta:), *n.* a guerrilla organization in Angola. See the quotation.

Secretary of State Cyrus Vance . . . defeated a move by President Carter's national security advisor, Zbigniew Brzezinski, proposing the covert sending of arms to UNITA guerrillas fighting in Angola against the Marxist Government of President Agostinho Neto. *"The Week," The Manchester Guardian Weekly, July 2, 1978, p 6*

[1967, from the Portuguese acronym for National Union for the Total Independence of Angola]

u·ni·tard ('yu: nə,tard), *n.* a leotard covering the torso and legs and, usually, the feet.

Red headbands and black eyepatches, track pants, silver lamé jackets and flashing neon lapel pins are the order of the night here. Girls boogie by in the shortest of shorts and one woman, dressed in unitards and a wide gold sash, bounces dull-eyed in the center of the room. *The New York Times, Feb. 2, 1979, p C16*

[1979, from *uni-* one (probably a reference to *one-piece*) + leo*tard*] Also, **unitards.**

▶ This word may have been coined to avoid confusion in the use of *leotard* meaning a garment that covers the torso alone, or *leotards* meaning a garment that covers the legs and lower trunk of the body.

unitarity, *n. Nuclear Physics.* a principle that states, if a particle can decay by several modes, the sum of the fractions taking each mode should add up to one.

For a long time, unsuccessful attempts to discover the radioactive decay of K^0_L (pronounced K-zero-long) mesons into a pair of muons made particle physicists very nervous. Among all the processes particle physicists have to deal with, the decay of K into two muons may seem a small thing to cause consternation, but its nonappearance indicated a possible violation of a fundamental law, the principle of unitarity. *"Physical Sciences: The Muonic Decay of K Mesons," Science News, Feb. 28, 1976, p 130*

[1971, from *unitary* + *-ity*]

Universal Coordinated Time, standard time measured by atomic clocks at several timekeeping stations. It is equivalent to Greenwich Mean Time but corrected periodically to match the earth's rotation.

M. Guinot's Bureau International de l'Heure was empowered to proclaim the addition or subtraction of a second to or from Universal Coordinated Time at the halfway point or the end of any year. Thus the two leap seconds of 1972. Just before the first one was added, on June 30th, atomic time was seven-tenths of a second behind earth time; on December 31st it was lagging by two-tenths of a second. *E. J. Kahn, Jr., "Our Far-Flung Correspondents: The Leap Second," The New Yorker, Aug. 27, 1973, p 56*

[1973] Also called COORDINATED UNIVERSAL TIME.

Universal Product Code, *U.S.* a coded series of lines, spaces, and numbers printed on a package for an optical scanner to identify the product at a store's checkout counter.

The computer system has no need for the usual price markings on packages. The checkout clerk merely moves any packaged product past an electronic scanner at the checkout counter and drops it in the bag. The machine does the rest: It reads a special code on the package (those now familiar bar symbols, called the Universal Product Code), flashes the product's price on a viewer for the shopper to glimpse, prints the product's name and price on the register slip, and, finally, prints the total bill on the receipt. *"Should Congress Act to Keep Prices on Food?" Consumer Reports, Feb. 1976, p 65*

The assumption underlying these laws is the consumer's basic right to information and equity in transactions. Proposed legislation to further safeguard this right included a bill that would require unit and item price disclosure in conjunction with a universal product code. *Edward J. Metzen, "Consumerism," The Americana Annual 1976, p 198*

[1974] *Abbreviation:* UPC. See BAR CODE.

unlib, *adj.* short for UNLIBERATED.

Ms. . . . is *the* feminist magazine, the one with Gloria Steinem, with slick paper, full-color, full-page Chevrolet ads . . . *Ms.* seems to be to women's lib what *Vogue* is to the unlib. *M. J. Sobran, Jr., "Inside Ms.: Of Ms. and Men," National Review, May 24, 1974, p 579*

[1971]

unliberated, *adj.* submitting to a passive or secondary role in society; not liberated.

More likely, dearie, you'll hold down two jobs — 'cause when you get home from that executive job in the sky, there ain't gonna be no unliberated woman left (and certainly no man) to do your grub work. *Mimi Winer, Wayland, Mass., "Letters," Time, March 20, 1972, p 11*

[1971]

unlimited, *n.* short for UNLIMITED HYDROPLANE.

For one thing, unlimiteds, those manta-ray-shaped thunderboats that have hit over 200 mph on straightaways, had been . . . attracting hundreds of thousands of devotees on both sides of the river. *Parton Keese, "Sports: Powerboating; Hydroplanes," 1972 Collier's Encyclopedia Year Book (1971), p 521*

[1965]

unlimited hydroplane, the largest type of hydroplane, powered by an inboard aircraft engine of unlimited displacement.

The national championship series for unlimited hydroplanes consisted of 10 races with $350,000 in purses. *Frank Litsky, "Boating: Powerboats," The 1976 World Book Year Book, p 218*

[1965] Also called THUNDERBOAT.

unsocial hours, *British.* working hours outside the normal or usual times.

The Department of Employment said: "Any supplementary allowance for unsocial hours, overtime or bonuses can under the policy continue to be paid. But the criteria for calculating them cannot be altered. This claim would contravene the policy." *Christopher Thomas, "New Blackout Threat by BBC Journalists," The Times (London), Jan. 24, 1976, p 3*

[1975, so called because the time does not conform to the standard social hours (time spent with family and friends) of most workers]

untogether, *adj. U.S. Slang.* confused; disorganized.

The labels have been stuck so fast for so many years it's hard tearin' 'em away. Lots of ofays still think we all play boogie woogie and shine shoes, but I'll tell you, the most prejudiced, jivest, complex, untogether race in the world is blacks. There are so many divisions, so many gradations of color, that's why it's taken us so long to get anywhere; all those years black, brown, high yeller shovin' each other to get closer to the front of the bus. Survival. Mm-hmm. *Hampton Hawes, "Performing Arts: Where I'm At Now," Harper's, Oct. 1972, p 50*

[1972, from *un-* not + *together,* slang word for composed, organized, stable, free of confusion or anxiety (1970)]

un·wind·ase (ən'waιn,deis), *n. Molecular Biology.* an enzyme that unwinds the double-stranded DNA molecule and aligns the template strands before the DNA polymerase replicates the molecule.

The functions of the products of genes 32 and 43 have, of course, been determined; they specify a DNA unwindase and T4 DNA polymerase. *"Biochemistry: Replicating DNA," Nature, Oct. 6, 1972, p 310*

[1972, from *unwind* + *-ase* enzyme] Also called UNWINDING PROTEIN.

unwinding protein, another name for UNWINDASE.

An interesting class of proteins was discovered by B. Alberts (Princeton) and called unwinding proteins. . . . These proteins serve to denature or unwind the double-stranded DNA molecule. *James Clinton Copeland, "Life Sciences: Molecular Biology," Britannica Book of the Year 1972, p 422*

[1972]

up, *Especially U.S. Slang.—adj.* cheerful; happy; upbeat.

Although Alec Wilder responds to a wide range of styles,

he prefers ballads to up tunes; he prizes suavity and finesse more than drive and vigor. *Walter Clemons, Review of "American Popular Song: The Great Innovators, 1900-1950" by Alec Wilder, The New York Times Book Review, April 23, 1972, p 6*

Your friend has wide personality swings which are a symptom of mental illness. When she's "up" she's friendly. When she's "down" she's cool and distant. *"Ann Landers," The News (Mexico City), April 22, 1973, p 16*

—*v.i.* to take uppers (stimulant drugs).

Amphetamines and barbiturates also have two faces. They are a familiar item in the doctor's armamentarium and, as such, reassuring. And yet excessive "upping" or "downing" can cause severe psychic dislocation, certainly as damaging as any of the effects of LSD. *Norman E. Zinberg and John A. Robertson, Drugs and the Public, 1972, p 49*

[1972] See UPPER.

UPC or **U.P.C.,** *U.S.* abbreviation of UNIVERSAL PRODUCT CODE.

UPC is a series of thin black bars on a label that has ten numbers right below the bars. The first five numbers represent the manufacturer or distributor, and the last five numbers represent the specific product and package which carries that number. *Steward M. Lee, "Consumerism," The Americana Annual 1975, p 196*

An optical scanner attached to the terminal automatically "reads" the name of the product from the U.P.C. printed on its label. Once the computer has identified the item, it scans its memory banks for the correct price and registers the sale—all in less than a second. *Allan J. Mayer, "The Computerized Supermarket," The New York Times Magazine, Feb. 8, 1976, p 54*

[1974]

up-front, *adj. U.S. Informal.* **1** straightforward; open; frank; uninhibited.

The constant identification by the media of the lesbian with the male homosexual movement is a clever device to separate women from each other . . . by the subtle (if unconscious) co-option of the most upfront sexual women (the political lesbians) by the already overwhelmingly recognized sexuality of the male. *Jill Johnston, "Lesbians Are Homosexuals Too," The New York Times Book Review, Feb. 20, 1972, p 12*

All the double-edged kidding and up-front aggressiveness stand in some contrast to the cool, measured and often affectless characters Nicholson has played so well on the screen. *"The Star with the Killer Smile," Time, Aug. 12, 1974, p 47*

But what, several asked, can we hope to learn from Ron Ziegler? "He can't be a worthwhile speaker 'cause he won't be honest and up-front." *John Guaspari, "Disinviting Ron Ziegler," National Review, Feb. 28, 1975, p 224*

2 of or in the forefront; foremost, leading, or important.

Integration has become a back-burner issue, by choice or hard political realism. The up-front concern now is to improve economic and social conditions for blacks in the urban ghettos and the rural backwaters—where most blacks are. *Peter Goldman, "Black Power at Work," Newsweek, Feb. 19, 1973, p 33*

As another up-front New York office building, it is the perfect object for vague aesthetic discussion about architecture with all socially responsible or even utilitarian questions left out. *Nathan Silver, "Architecture: The First Avenue School," Harper's, Jan. 1977, p 91*

3 of or belonging to the management of a business or other organization.

Colson sees his ministry to crowds as a religious duty. "I never liked to give speeches. I was not an up-front guy — that's why I never saw you people of the press. I was a back-room guy." *Gary Wills, " 'Born Again' Politics," The New York Times Magazine, Aug. 1, 1976, p 49*

4 made or coming in advance.

The condominium ... makes possible multimillion-dollar housing communities with expensive amenities requiring heavy "up-front" outlays for heavy-cost investments such as pools, recreational buildings, sewer-treatment plants, and roads. *Carter B. Horsley, " 'Condos' Break the Housing Mold," The New York Times, Feb. 1, 1976, Sec. 8, p 1*

[1967, from the phrase (to be) *up front*] See **up front** under FRONT.

uplink, *n.* transmission of data, signals, etc., from the ground to a spacecraft or satellite. *Often used attributively.*

Problems were uncovered, Mr. Martin said of the simulation, but nothing major. The computer program had to be redesigned to facilitate "uplink commands" to the spacecraft cameras. *John Noble Wilford, "At Viking Control, the First Landings on Mars Are Being Experienced — in Simulation," The New York Times, March 4, 1976, p 32*

—v.t. to transmit from the ground to a spacecraft or satellite.

Deiterich, who felt he was beginning to run out of time, passed to Russell, the GUIDO, some of the reëntry information that would have to be up-linked to the spacecraft computer; however, he asked Russell to hold off sending it, because some of the data might have to be changed. *Henry S. F. Cooper, Jr., "Annals of Exploration: An Accident in Space — II," The New Yorker, Nov. 18, 1972, p 159*

[1969 for noun; 1972 for verb] Compare DOWNLINK.

up-market, *Especially British.* *—adj.* of or for the high-income consumer; of higher grade or quality.

Faced with the need to cut their motoring costs, car owners appear to be choosing a solution which is least painful to the ego as well as to the pocket — to buy a car which is slightly more up-market than they would previously have done, look after it better and keep it longer. *Judith Jackson, The Sunday Times (London), April 13, 1975, p 23*

The object of this growing wrath on the part of many conservative Winnipeggers, for whom caution is almost as precious as a block heater, is an up-market women's clothing store opened last December by 32-year-old psychologist Kimie McIvor. *Cynthia Wine, "Not a Fit Sight for God-Fearing Winnipeg's Eyes," Maclean's, June 27, 1977, p 18*

—adv. in or into the up-market field.

It is possible that Chrysler could still move upmarket, but it will need less conservative management from the US parent. *David Knight, "Comment: Grim Truths of the Car Industry," New Scientist, Jan. 1, 1976, p 2*

Mr Barber was identified with a strategy designed to move Leyland "up market" by concentrating on more profitable specialist cars whereas Turnbull, a life-long "production" man, wanted to see an expansion of the high volume cars produced by the Austin Morris division. *Victor Keegan, "Korea Master," The Manchester Guardian Weekly, Jan. 14, 1979, p 4*

—v.t., v.i. to place or go into a high-income or higher-income consumer market.

Mathew Clark wants to upmarket Noilly Dry French, plugging heavily the drink's provenance compared with that of the Italian Martini and Cinzano (although to be strictly correct, Cinzano Dry comes from France as well). *"Business Diary," The Times (London), Aug. 25, 1972, p 17*

In the United States, the hi-fi industry has breathlessly watched its sales soar ... as customers have upmarketed continuously from monaural to stereo equipment and now to quadraphonic. *"Technology Review: Four-channel Records that Sweet Sound of Success," New Scientist, Jan 11, 1973, p 78*

[1972] Compare DOWN-MARKET, UPSCALE.

upper, *n. U.S. Slang.* something cheering or stimulating; a pleasant experience.

Your story "The Pleasures of Dying" [Dec. 4] was unbelievably absurd. A morbid comment on human curiosity. ... Once you've made the jump, you're gone. Granted, it certainly is a relief to know that State 2 is an upper; but by that time, who cares? *Claudia Sundberg, Toledo, in a Letter to the Editor, Time, Jan. 1, 1973, p K2*

[1971, figurative use of the slang term (1968) for· a stimulant; patterned on *downer* (1970)]

up quark, a type of quark (hypothetical nuclear particle) possessing a charge of $+2/3$ and a spin of $+1/2$

It was possible to distinguish between two types of quarks on the basis of their different masses and electric charges. These were called "up quarks" and "down quarks." The two kinds of quarks were sufficient to construct neutrons and protons. According to this conjecture, everything in the workaday world is made up exclusively of these two kinds of quarks, along with electrons. *Sheldon L. Glashow, "The Hunting of the Quark," Encyclopedia Science Supplement (Grolier) 1977, p 318*

[1976, so called in reference to the upward spin it is supposed to exhibit] Also called U QUARK. See QUARK.

up·scale ('əp₁skeil), *adj. U.S.* in the upper levels of income, education, and social standing; belonging to a higher-than-average economic and social stratum.

Its [Smithsonian magazine] affluent readership constitutes what one magazine-industry spokesman calls "one of the most up-scale demographics in the business." *"The Media: A Life of Its Own," Newsweek, Aug. 27, 1973, p 76*

The size and character — young and "upscale" — of the Python audience inevitably attracted the interest of the commercial networks. *Hendrik Hertzberg, "Onward and Upward With the Arts," The New Yorker, March 29, 1976, p 70*

They said it would be aimed at "educated, sophisticated, active, upscale, career-oriented males 25 to 45 years old," who might need guidance in a world in which "rules of society have completely changed." *Charlotte Evans, "2 Tennesseans Buy Esquire; To Continue Its 'Tradition'," The New York Times, May 1, 1979, p B4*

[1968]

upsilon, *n.* any of a group of extremely heavy, short-lived subatomic particles produced by bombarding beryllium nuclei with high-energy protons.

The existence of upsilon can also be taken to mean that a quark whose existence had been theoretically postulated, but for which there had not been any experimental evidence, does exist. This would bring the number of experimentally observed quarks to five. *Dietrick E. Thomsen, "Physics," 1978 Collier's Encyclopedia Year Book (1977), p 450*

The impact of the upsilon has already been far-reaching. It has prompted searches for other heavy particles in hitherto unexplored ranges of mass, and it has shed light on the inscrutable strong force. This force, which binds quarks together into hadrons and hadrons together into atomic nuclei, is too powerful to investigate by conventional scattering and collision techniques. *Leon M. Lederman, "The Upsilon Particle," Scientific American, Oct. 1978, p 79*

[1977, from the name of the 20th letter of the Greek alphabet] *Symbol:* Y. See QUARK.

upstream, *adj., adv.* of, relating to, or for the discovery, extraction, and transportation of oil to the port of shipment.

The most natural way the oil producers can spend their vast wealth, however, is in developing the industry itself. Huge investment is needed "upstream" . . . Until now most of the oil companies' profits have been upstream. *The Auckland Star (N.Z.), Feb. 10, 1973, p 18*

[1973] Compare DOWNSTREAM.

uptick, *n. U.S.* an upward turn or trend, especially in business; upswing.

A recent uptick in applications, following a massive publicity campaign, apparently persuaded the President that his postwar "act of mercy" was finally working. *"Amnesty: One More Chance," Newsweek, Feb. 10, 1975, p 20*

The biggest uptick in demand came last winter, when consuming nations in both Europe and North America were beset by the worst winter in decades. To meet the clamor for heating oil, refineries processed record amounts of crude oil. *Anthony J. Parisi, "More Fuel This Winter?" The New York Times, Sept. 12, 1977, p 51*

Less cheering was an uptick in the unemployment rate, which had earlier been inching down. *Time, July 18, 1977, p 66*

[1970, extended from the original sense (1957) of a sale of stocks made at a price higher than the immediately preceding one]

upwardly mobile, tending or seeking to rise from a lower to a higher economic or social class.

Not all of them were born and educated in Toronto but they have the Toronto manner. That is, they're clearly recognizable as members of the upwardly mobile, forward marching, Anglophone-Canadian middle class who give that city its predominant tone. *Christina Newman, "Politicizing Pierre," Maclean's, Oct. 1974, p 38*

There are class differences in women's headgear. The upwardly mobile class wears knitted caps or fur hats; the nonmobile, the timeless Slavic shawl, folded in the timeless Slavic manner. *Nika Hazelton, "Impressions of a Short Russian Tour," National Review, Feb. 20, 1976, p 160*

The conclusion was wrong, with few exceptions, for the new black middle class, led by a segment of upwardly mobile young professionals, has opened a double-door exit from the ghetto. *William Brashler, "The Black Middle Class: Making It," The New York Times Magazine, Dec. 3, 1978, p 35*

[1964, from *upward-mobile, adj.* and *upward mobility* (1963)]

u quark, short for UP QUARK.

The proton is a particle with spin 1/2, charge +1, and strangeness O. It can be constructed with two *u* quarks and one *d* quark. *Henry T. Simmons, "Particle Physics: A Realm of Charm, Strangeness, and Symmetry," 1977 Bri-*

tannica Yearbook of Science and the Future (1976), p 157

[1976]

urban anthropology, a branch of cultural anthropology dealing with the subcultures of people living in urban communities.

Urban anthropology . . . focused research on a variety of populations including the urban and rural, migrant labourers, women, the young and the elderly, the ill and the handicapped, as well as all ethnic and racial minorities. *Robert B. Edgerton, "Anthropology," Britannica Book of the Year 1973, p 82*

[1972]

urban homesteading, *U.S.* a federal program sponsoring the reoccupation and renovation of abandoned buildings by tenants who obtain in return an equity ownership in the restored property.

You read all about urban homesteading when local governments began early in the 1970s to sell or offer through a lottery vacant city properties they acquired through transfer from HUD. The houses, many of them tumbledown shells, were sold for token sums, sometimes as little as $1.00 to individuals or families who would make repairs to meet minimum standards before moving in. *Ruth Rejnis, Her Home, 1980, p 22*

[1975, from the *Urban Homestead* Act of 1973] Also shortened to HOMESTEADING. See SWEAT EQUITY.

urban homesteader: Several score "urban homesteaders" have taken title to dilapidated row houses for a dollar each on condition that they restore them and live in them for three years. *Bob Kuttner, "Ethnic Renewal," The New York Times Magazine, May 9, 1976, p 18*

urban ore, discarded tin cans, bottles, and other solid refuse buried in urban landfills, held to be a rich source of raw material.

One can consider MSW [municipal solid waste] as an "urban ore" and follow its assay from location to location and also for a long time period during which its composition may change. These changes may be caused either by the purchasing tastes of the public, which can alter the composition of MSW, or by the choice of disposal techniques, which might concentrate given materials in an area where special beneficiation methods are warranted. *S. L. Blum, "Tapping Resources in Municipal Solid Waste," Science, Feb. 20, 1976, p 671*

[1971]

ur·bi·cide ('ər bə,saɪd), *n.* the destruction of a city, usually by altering its appearance with building projects that destroy existing architecture or disregard land use in surrounding areas.

It does no good to speculate at what point real estate becomes art, or history, or a talisman of place. When it does, it enters the public domain. To destroy it is an act of urbicide. *"Editorial: Empire State," The New York Times, Oct. 15, 1972, Sec. 4, p 14*

[1966, coined by Wolf Von Eckardt, American architectural critic, from *urbi-* (from Latin *urbs* city)+ *-cide* a killing]

Usage. ► Information about usage is often obtainable from the quotation or from the bibliographical reference for the quotation under each definition. This bibliographical information usually gives some frame of reference as to the type of writing (informal, jocular, etc.) in which the word is used. There are questions of usage, however, which quotations themselves cannot answer adequately. Breadth of usage in the English-speaking world, appropriateness in a particular context, etc., are questions better reserved for the label and note in the confined space of a dictionary.

Regional variations. Major regional varieties indicated by our files are marked by speech-area labels, such as *U.S.* UPTICK, *British* CRUISEWAY, *Canadian* HOTLINER, and *Australian* OCKER. Sometimes a regional label is modified by "Especially" to show that usage is not entirely restricted, as in GREENWAY *Especially U.S.*, DEKE *Especially Canadian*, EVENTING *Especially British*. In cases where a regional equivalent exists that is different from standard terminology these are also included, as in ACTION REPLAY (*British*), equivalent to the American INSTANT REPLAY.

Linguistic variations. Questions of usage are also associated with special categories of words, such as the vocabulary of science and technology (see TECHNICAL TERMS), the vocabulary of slang, and the vocabulary that derives from foreign words and phrases (see BORROWINGS). Distinctly foreign words such as FUROR COLLIGENDI, EN VOGUE, and GLEITZEIT, have a language label or identification to distinguish them from words of foreign origin that are regarded as naturalized.

Like technical terms, slang terms come from many fields of activity and diverse groups of speakers. Typically slang comes into the general vocabulary from the usage of the underworld, drug addicts, show business, sports, high-school and college students, the military services, and various ethnic groups. In recent years, many American slang words and expressions have emerged from Black English; see for example BAD and DOZEN. Another source of recent American slang is citizens band radio, whose devotees, known as CBers, have adopted the argot of truckers and added many new terms of their own (see the note under CB). Slang terms are labeled wherever possible to indicate the speech area or sometimes the particular field in which our evidence shows the terms occur. For example:

ACE in *ace out* (U.S. College Slang),
FARM in *buy the farm* (U.S. Military Slang),
OPEN CONTRACT (Underworld Slang).

Social variations. Within the compass of the standard language are degrees of appropriateness and acceptability determined by custom and fashion and how these are applied depends entirely on the social situation or particular context of use.

The intention of labeling social variations is one of description. We seek to complete the description of evidence in our files by making available an evaluation of the circumstances and contexts in which our quotations appear. The usage label is the result of that evaluation, as in the following examples.

merc, *n. Informal.*

jargonaut, *n. Humorous.*

feelgood, *n.* **2** *(used disparagingly)*

gentleperson, *n. U.S. (often used humorously or ironically)*

povertician, *U.S. (derogatory use)*

Usage involving grammar, spelling, pronunciation, etc., may be indicated in the definition itself at the beginning of an entry or in a usage note following, as under ARTICLE, DYNAMITE, and ADOPT.

Changes in usage that are the result of changing social attitudes are discussed in various articles, as those under ABORTION, ALIMONY, DEATH, MARRIAGE, MAN, WOMAN.

use immunity, *U.S. Law.* a form of immunity which protects witnesses compelled to testify from subsequent prosecution based solely on evidence revealed in their testimony.

To get around the Fifth Amendment privilege against self-incrimination, the act gives the government the right to offer "use immunity"—a guarantee that the witness's testimony will not be used against him. *"Justice: The Big Flap Over Immunity," Newsweek, Oct. 29, 1973, p 68*

The Federal law, which was immediately copied by half the states, grants a witness "use" immunity, which blocks prosecutors from the later use of what the witness has specifically testified to. *Tom Goldstein, "On Waiving Immunity," The New York Times, April 15, 1976, p 39*

[1972] Compare IMMUNITY BATH.

U-value, *n. British.* a measure of the resistance to heat flow through a wall, roof, or floor, especially as provided by insulating material. A low U-value corresponds to a high level of insulating effectiveness.

Clearly it is a good idea to exceed the current Regulations. Our improved semi has the following U-values—roof and ceiling 0.40 watts/sq.m/°C; external walls (excluding the windows) 0.51 watts/sq.m/°C; external walls (overall) 0.97 watts/sq.m/°C. These values are all considerably better than the current statutory maxima. *Barrie Jones, "Energy Conservation Begins at Home," New Scientist, Jan. 29, 1976, p 227*

[1963, from British Thermal *U*nit, a unit for measuring heat] Compare R-VALUE.

V

vacancy decontrol, *U.S.* the legal removal of rent control from an apartment or other dwelling unit after it has been vacated.

Another innovation of this period was vacancy decontrol. This was a great victory for the landlords. . . . Vacancy decontrol meant higher rents for new tenants at a time when recession and inflation were hitting people badly, particularly the old and/or poor. *B. Bruce-Briggs, "Rent Control Must Go," The New York Times Magazine, April 18, 1976, p 24*

[1971]

vacuum aspiration, a method of abortion, performed within the first 10 to 12 weeks of pregnancy, in which a specially designed tube is inserted into the uterus to draw out the contents by suction.

Induced abortion is performed on request, usually in very early pregnancy. . . . The procedure is almost always done by vacuum aspiration conducted by nurses, midwives or barefoot doctors and the rate of complications is said to be very low. *"Science and the Citizen," Scientific American, Nov. 1972, p 50*

[1971] Also called SUCTION METHOD, LUNCHTIME ABORTION. Compare MENSTRUAL EXTRACTION, SALINE. See also KARMAN CANNULA.

vacuum cleaner, any of various suction-producing devices. See the quotations.

16 "vacuum cleaners" sucking at an overhead rail lift it [a train] off its supports. Riding on air, the train accelerates to 30 mph in seconds, without a sound; when the current is reversed, it decelerates equally rapidly and silently. *Joseph Gies, "Transportation," 1971 Britannica Yearbook of Science and the Future (1970), p 281*

The vacuum cleaner is actually a hydraulic pump designed to lift as much as 400 tons of material from the sea floor daily. *Richard C. Vetter, "Oceanography," The World Book Science Annual 1972 (1971), p 342*

[1970, transferred sense of the term (OED 1903) meaning a suction device for cleaning carpets, rugs, etc.]

valley of the dolls, a condition of excessive dependence on stimulant and depressant drugs.

Like the Bogart and Garland cults, today's Monroemania has its far-out fringe—the masochists who identify with suffering and the parlor psychoanalysts who hone their Freudian clichés on her Dickensian childhood, failed marriages and miscarriages . . . and her almost preordained plunge into the valley of the dolls. *Harry Waters, "Taking a New Look at MM," Newsweek, Oct. 16, 1972, p 80*

When I asked if she liked him she replied "No—he's beyond the valley of the dolls." *The Bulletin (Sydney, Australia), Aug. 7, 1976 (page not known)*

[1972, from the novel *Valley of the Dolls* (1966) by the American author Jacqueline Susann, 1921-1974] See DOLL.

val·pro·ate (væl'prou eit), *n.* an anticonvulsive drug effective against petit mal. *Formula:* $C_8H_{15}NaO_2$

The drug, valproate, has been available in Europe for a decade. It will benefit more than 560,000 patients a year, the Epilepsy Foundation predicts. *Science News, March 11, 1978, p 151*

[1978, from *val*eric acid + *pro*pyl + *-ate* salt]

vanity plate, *U.S.* an automobile license plate with a distinctive combination of letters or numbers chosen by the purchaser, usually at extra cost.

The Assembly—not without a few hoots and whistles—passed a bill imposing $15 fee for legislators, newsmen and physicians wishing special license plates identifying their work. . . . The bill also would raise the regular $5 charge for non-specialized "vanity plates" to $15. *Ronald Smothers, The New York Times, May 6, 1976, p 21*

[1967]

van·ner ('væn ər), *n. U.S. and Canadian.* an owner or operator of a van or truck.

Semiprofessional vanners go through about a van a year, selling at a tidy profit and starting from scratch again. But it's creativity not profit that motivates the true vanner. *Michael Ryval, "Lifestyles," Maclean's, Dec. 13, 1976, p 72*

Vanners themselves, or at least the zealots, seem as much a cult as a fellowship. They have formed hundreds of societies. Many drive hundreds or even thousands of miles to converge with other vanners at picnicky socials that are held all over the country. *Time, Sept. 5, 1977, p 55*

[1976] ► In the 1800's the term was used for a horse pulling a small van.

vanpool, *U.S.* —*n.* an arrangement in which a group of people share commuting costs by using a large passenger van.

Federal money was made available for as much as 90 percent of the start-up costs of a vanpool, including the purchase or leasing of the vehicle, and the department said that a dozen states had taken advantage of the program. . . . The energy saving in a vanpool was high, officials said, and the projects were operated and coordinated on state levels. *The New York Times, Jan. 17, 1978, p 2*

—*v.i.* to join or take part in a vanpool.

By making commuters aware of the costs of driving alone . . . , it is hoped that more commuters who presently drive alone will carpool or vanpool. *"Rideshare and Save—A Cost Comparison," U.S. Department of Transportation, 1978, p 1*

[1976]

variable life insurance, a form of life insurance in which the face value of the policy varies with an equity index or some other variable factor.

The variable life insurance policy concept has been employed for years in Britain, and such policies have been offered in recent years in Canada. No such policies are now available in the United States. *Robert Metz, "Market Place," The New York Times, Feb. 4, 1976, p 46*

[1972]

variable rate mortgage, *U.S.* a mortgage on which the interest rate rises or falls with the interest rate on the money market.

Variable rate mortgages (VRMs) are in use at savings and loan associations in about a dozen states. The VRM is usually offered at half a percentage point below the going interest rate, but after five years it fluctuates, depending on such factors as the long-term federal bond rate. *Ruth Rejnis, Her Home, 1980, p 25*

[1979] Compare GRADUATED PAYMENT MORTGAGE.

var·i·o·mat·ic (ˌver i: əˈmæt ik), *adj. British.* of or relating to a belt-driven automatic transmission.

Careful design at the planning stage could make optional variations for the disabled cheap to incorporate. . . . variomatic drive (now common in many cars) eliminates the difficulties of changing gear. *Fabian Acker, "Comment: Cost and Compassion," New Scientist, July 22, 1976, p 162*

[1973, from *vari*able + aut*omatic*]

VASCAR or **Vas·car** ('væsˌkɑr), *n.* a trademark for a computer-controlled electronic device for clocking the speed of motorists.

There are 9000 VASCARs currently in use in all but three states. It works on all kinds of roads and in most weather conditions (except when visibility is severely reduced). *New Scientist, Aug. 23, 1973, p 446*

Vascar . . . measures the time a vehicle takes to travel between two "reference points" fixed by the operator. It measures the distance between the points and works out the vehicle's average speed over that distance. *The Times (London), Nov. 22, 1973, p 4*

[1966, acronym for *Visual Average Speed Computer And Recorder*]

vas·o·li·gate (ˌvæs ouˈlɑi geit), *v.t.* to tie off the vasa deferentia or sperm-carrying tubes of (a person or animal) in order to produce sterility; to subject to vasoligation.

They got together three groups of young rats, each containing about thirty animals. One group were vasectomised, the second vasoligated, and the last were controls. *"Monitor: Fresh Anxiety Over the Consequences of Vasectomy," New Scientist, Jan. 25, 1973, p 172*

[1973, back formation from *vasoligation* (1954) surgical ligation of the vasa deferentia] Compare TUBAL LIGATION.

Vaticanologist, *n.* a student of the policies, leaders, and practices of the Vatican and the papacy.

Mr. Hebblethwaite is exceptionally qualified to answer the question. His publishers describe him as "a leading Vaticanologist," and he does appear to know more than most people about the Curia, which he describes as "the most unknown and impenetrable level of ecclesiastical life." *Alec Vidler, The Manchester Guardian Weekly, Dec. 14, 1975, p 27*

As the Cardinals entered their carefully sealed sanctum, most Vaticanologists anticipated a wide-open race but, paradoxically, a relatively brief conclave. *Time, Sept. 4, 1978, p 65*

[1974, from *Vatican* + *-ologist* student of]

VCR, abbreviation of VIDEOCASSETTE RECORDER.

Schools throughout the country are receiving VCRs as fast as they can be imported and some are going into business networks. *Garry Pownall, New Scientist, Feb. 22, 1973, p 446*

Most VCRs have a pause-control button so the viewer can edit out commercials while recording. The tapes are reusable; the VCR simply erases the old program as it records the new one. *Fred Warshofsky, "VCRs—The Biggest Thing Since Television," The Reader's Digest, Feb. 1979, p 142*

[1971]

VDT, abbreviation of *visual display terminal,* a computer terminal with a display screen and a keyboard.

The VDT, a more elaborate device, is changing editing methods. By tapping out a code at the VDT keyboard, an editor can call back any story from computer storage for display on the screen. He can make desired changes by using the keyboard and pressing a button to send the edited story back to the computer, which digests the changes and readies the copy for the photocomposition machine. *John Luter, "Newspapers," 1976 Collier's Encyclopedia Year Book (1975), p 375*

[1975]

VDU, abbreviation of *visual display unit,* any device for displaying data from a computer, tape, etc., on a screen.

The computer programs written last up to two hours. They involve the patient sitting down in front of the screen and answering either yes, no, or "don't understand" to questions displayed on the VDU. All the information captured will be printed out and given to the doctor, who will then question patients more closely on the relevant aspects of their health. *Peter Marsh, New Scientist, Aug. 3, 1978, p 345*

[1972]

veer, *n.* a type of offense in American football, using a variation of the T-formation, in which the quarterback pitches the ball to a running back or runs with it himself.

"We feel we have the personnel to run the veer," says Jordan. "Our quarterbacks are able to read defenses and they can execute the option." *Southeastern Football (Nashville, Tenn.) Pre-Season Ed., 1974, p 20*

[1974, transferred sense of a shift in direction, because the quarterback usually runs laterally before pitching the ball back or running upfield] Compare WISHBONE.

ve·gan·ism ('vi: gəˌniz əm), *n. Especially British.* vegetarianism in which no animals or animal products are used; strict vegetarianism.

It [vegetarianism] would also, if logically carried on as in Veganism, abolish milk and eggs, since farmers could not rear cattle for milk only (what would one do with the bull calves?) or poultry for eggs only. *Doris Davy, Forest Row, Sussex, "'Organic' Food," in a Letter to the Editor, New Scientist, May 4, 1972, p 297*

[1967, from *vegan* (1940's) a strict vegetarian (contraction of *vegetarian*) + *-ism*] See OVO-LACTARIAN.

veganist, *n.*: I like, too, his [John Hawthorn's] swipe at the veganists whose diet in Britain "is a form of slow but certain suicide unless [it] is supplemented with vitamin B12." *Ian Low, Review of "The Biology of Affluence," edited by George Smith and John C. Smyth, New Scientist, Feb. 3, 1972, p 287*

veg·gies or **veg·ies** ('vedʒ i:z), *n.pl. Informal.* vegetables.

The pantry, in Daniel's reading of the Escoffier design, is at the bottom—they're like buck privates. They wash and chop veggies and hand them out at the right time to the right people. *"The Talk of the Town: Behind the Swinging Doors," The New Yorker, March 8, 1976, p 28*

He pushes away his cole slaw. "You should eat it," I say. "No no; can't eat vegies," he says. The suppressed dietician in me notes that he is probably suffering from a vitamin A deficiency. *Margaret Atwood, "Under Glass," Harper's, Feb. 1972, p 80*

[1966, by shortening and alteration of *vegetables*]

vertical divestiture, the disposal of a company's holdings in related operations or businesses whose control allows it to regulate activities in a market or business.

Proponents of the effort call it vertical divestiture, by which they mean forcing the largest oil companies to pick one activity—production or refining or transportation/marketing—and sell off the other parts of the action. As it is today, a company like Exxon is vertically integrated in its operations in such a way that it controls everything from the oil well to the retail pump. *Robert Sherrill, "Breaking up Big Oil," The New York Times Magazine, Oct. 3, 1975, p 15*

[1975] Compare HORIZONTAL DIVESTITURE.

vertical proliferation, increase in the number of nuclear weapons among nations.

Two questions dominate the argument about the threat to mankind from nuclear weapons. One ("vertical proliferation," which can equally well be called upward spread) is the size of the arsenals already possessed by the six countries, including India, which have carried out nuclear tests and especially the size of the American and Russian arsenals. *"Comment," The Manchester Guardian Weekly, Jan. 29, 1978, p 10*

[1976] Compare HORIZONTAL PROLIFERATION.

Ver·ti·sol ('vər tə,sɔːl), *n.* (in U.S. soil taxonomy) any of a group of soils having a large proportion of clay forming deep surface cracks, found in regions with one or more dry seasons.

Similar to Mollisols in losses of nutrient elements during formation are the Aridisols, Inceptisols of cold or dry regions, and Vertisols. If anything, losses from these soils are smaller than from Mollisols. Collectively these broad groups and the Mollisols occupy 40% of the land surface of the Earth. *Roy W. Simonson, "Soil," McGraw-Hill Yearbook of Science and Technology 1972, p 374*

[1972, from *vertical* + *-sol* (from Latin *solum* soil)] Compare ALFISOL, ENTISOL, HISTOSOL, INCEPTISOL, OXISOL, SPODOSOL, ULTISOL.

ves·ti·bu·lec·to·my (,ves tə,byu:'lek tə mi:), *n.* surgical removal of the sensors of equilibrium in the vestibule of the inner ear.

Another mechanism contributing to the remarkable recovery in the coordination of the eye-head movements that occurs within the first two to three months following vestibulectomy entails a "recalibration" of saccadic eye movements with respect to visual input. *Emilio Bizzi, "The Coordination of Eye-Head Movement," Scientific American, Oct. 1974, p 106*

[1974, from *vestibule* + *-ectomy* surgical removal]

vex·il·lol·o·gist (,vek sə'lɑl ə dʒist), *n.* a student of flags.

Vexillology sounds rather like an obscure branch of tropical medicine, which for the vexillologists of the world must be rather vexing. But the almost universal ignorance of the discipline is understandable, since it is so new. Vexillology, the study of flags, has only just fluttered into the dictionaries. *"Flags: Up with Vexillology," Time, Oct. 1, 1973, p 44*

[1973, derivative of *vexillology* (1971) the study of flags, from Latin *vexillum* flag]

V gene, a gene that codes for the variable portion of an immunoglobulin (protein antibody).

An individual mammal can make in its lifetime an astonishing variety of antibodies that differ in amino-acid composition. These differences in structure appear in a variable part of the immunoglobulin molecule, which is otherwise constant. The variable part is under the control of one or only a few V genes. *Arnold W. Ravin, "Molecular Biology," 1976 Britannica Yearbook of Science and the Future (1975), p 343*

[1970, short for *variable gene*]

vib·ri·o·ci·dal (,vib ri: ə'sɑi dəl), *adj.* destroying vibrios (a genus of bacteria, a species of which causes cholera); vibrio-killing.

The vaccine now in use (killed *V. cholerae*) elicits formation of vibriocidal antibody, which reacts with the somatic, or cell-wall, antigen of the organism. In contrast, the antibody produced in response to pure toxin (or pure toxoid) is an antitoxin that inactivates toxin but has no vibriocidal activity. *Mary M. Eichhorn Adams, "Cholera: New Aids in Treatment and Prevention," Science, Feb. 9, 1973, p 554*

[1972, from *vibrio* + *-cidal* destroying, killing (from *-cide* killer, killing + *-al*, adj. suffix)]

vi·car·i·ance (vɑi'ker i: əns), *n.* the geographical separation of similar species of plants or animals by barriers such as mountain ranges and oceans resulting from massive displacements of the earth's crust.

Dr. Niles Eldridge, an American Museum paleontologist, said at the opening session that "the debate here is whether a certain pattern of species distribution was caused by dispersal or vicariance." *Bayard Webster, "New Theory Disputes Old in Geographical Distribution of Species," The New York Times, May 8, 1979, p C2*

[1979, from Latin *vicārius* that takes the place of another (used in the broad sense of being placed in widely separated areas) + English *-ance* (noun suffix)]

victimless, *adj. Especially U.S.* (of legal offenses) not having or involving a victim.

Drug offenses are on the whole "victimless" crimes. Possessing or using a drug is usually a private act. Even drug sales occur in private with other consenting persons. Drug offenses seldom impinge so forcefully on others that they feel impelled to notify the police. *Norman E. Zinberg and*

John A. Robertson, Drugs and the Public, 1972, p 219

"Victimless sex laws," said Marilyn Haft, director of the Sexual Privacy Project of the American Civil Liberties Union, "are just a way of one group imposing their morality upon another group. They are used as a weapon against 'undesirables,' like hippies, homosexuals. Sex is something most people do, but only a select few are prosecuted for." *Anthony Mancini, "The Sex Laws," New York Post, June 21, 1975, p 23*

Over the dissent of one member, a federally financed advisory committee has urged state legislatures to go slow in decriminalizing or legalizing so-called victimless crimes such as gambling, prostitution and pornography. *The New York Times, Dec. 26, 1976, p 39*

[1972] ► A victimless offense is not one where there is no victim *in any sense*, since the person committing the offense (for example, using heroin) is also the victim. Strictly, a victimless crime is one that involves only consenting persons and no complainant claiming to be a victim.

vid·ar·a·bine (vid'ær ə,bin), *n.* another name for ARA-A.

An infectable drug, Vidarabine, that successfully treats herpes simplex virus encephalitis, a rare but often deadly viral infection, was approved for use by the Federal Drug Administration. *Arthur H. Hayes, Jr., "Drugs," The World Book Science Annual 1980 (1979), p 268*

[1977, from Latin *vidēre* to see (because the drug is often used to treat viral infections of the eye) + *arabi*nose + aden*ine*]

video art, a form of art utilizing videotapes to produce abstract or representational works; art that uses or stresses the visual effects of television.

The video art of Nam June Paik, Bruce Nauman, and Vito Acconci provided occasion for thought rather than compelling forms for the eye, but engineers continue to extend the possibilities for richer visual experience. *Victor H. Miesel, "Art," The Americana Annual 1975, p 105*

The video world is much larger than the art world, and people who eventually wind up making video art can have very diverse backgrounds in the medium. Consequently, the term "video art" does not describe any single unified style; it indicates a shared medium. *Joanna Gill, "An Introduction to Video Art," RF Illustrated, March 1976, p 9*

[1972] See VIDEOGRAPHER.

video artist: Mr. Gillette, whose new work is part of a 12-piece cycle with an ecological theme, is one of a growing breed of video artists, for whom the TV screen has become an esthetic medium. Uninterested in commercial television, they produce videotapes that take ingenious advantage of the technology, from crude vignettes shot on site to elaborate productions that call on the full technical resources of a TV studio. *Grace Glueck, The New York Times, April 14, 1975, p 33*

vid·e·o·cas·sette recorder ('vid i: ou kə'set), a machine for recording television programs from a television set onto videotape cassettes.

The video-cassette recorder was introduced [into the mass market] in 1975. It boasted, correctly, that the owner could watch one channel while recording another. *Alistair Cooke, "Focus on the Arts," The 1978 World Book Year Book, p 52*

The introduction of video cassette recorders, which allow us to record television programs we can't be home to

watch, . . . type us as busy, working, afraid-to-miss-anything people. *Suzanne Slesin, "Newest TV Sets Do Something More," The New York Times, May 3, 1979, p C14*

[1971] *Abbreviation:* VCR

videocassette recording: Allied Artists . . . plans to offer videocassette recordings of all future movie releases. *Fred Warshofsky, "VCRs—The Biggest Thing Since Television," The Reader's Digest, Feb. 1979, p 142*

video game, a game played by manipulating points of light on a television screen or other display screen by means of an electronic or computerized control device.

Video games are easily connected into any conventional television set through its antenna lead, enabling the games to take over the screen. Players sit back with a small control board and, by twisting knobs, they can play soccer, hockey or tennis, shoot tanks, race cars or doodle. Some games use semiconductor chips, while more complex units have built-in minicomputers called microprocessors. *John Wark, "Boom and Bust in Video Games?" The New York Times, Dec. 12, 1976, Sec. 3, p 17*

There are two types of video games. The cheaper, "dedicated" type is designed to provide a number of "ball-and-paddle" games—usually tennis or ping-pong, hockey, squash or handball (some models refer to it as jai alai), and a practice game that one person can play alone. A few models also have simple target games. . . . The second type is the programmable video game. It relies on a microprocessor, a small computer-like device, to provide the potential for an almost unlimited variety of games. Some programmable models come with a few games built right in. *"Video Games," Consumer Reports, Nov. 1977, p 630*

[1976] Compare COMPUTER GAME. See also PONG.

vid·e·og·ra·pher (,vid i:'ag rə fər), *n.* a person who produces works of VIDEO ART; a VIDEO ARTIST.

Composer Richard Feliciano collaborated with videographer Stephen Beck in January 1971 on *Point of Inflection*, a highly geometric work in which diamonds re-form as squares, and periodic waves interrupt the screen. *Jonathan Price, "Video Pioneers: From Banality to Beauty: TV as a New Form of Visual Art," Harper's, June 1972, p 90*

[1972, from *video* art + *-grapher*, as in *photographer*]

video-record, *v.t. Especially British.* to record on magnetic tape; to videotape.

The National Archives at Washington DC are video-recording news programmes off the air for preservation, and there are, throughout the world, at least a dozen other archives known to the International Film and Television Council of UNESCO which collect television material. *Clive Coultass, London, "Got It Taped," in a Letter to the Editor, The Listener, Feb. 26, 1976, p 244*

[1971]

Vid·i·font ('vid ə,fant), *n.* a trademark for an electronic device that displays letters and numbers on a television screen by means of a keyboard.

165 people . . . will appear on home screens; twenty-one cameras, 16 of them the full-size "hard" variety, three hand-held, one in a helicopter and one in the Goodyear blimp, five slow-motion "discs" for replays, and a vidifont, a computer-like machine that can instantaneously cough up players' names and statistics. *"The Super Show," Time, Jan. 10, 1977, p 28*

[1972, from *vidi-* visual (ultimately from Latin *vidēre*) + *font* set of type]

viewdata, *n.* any system or network providing computerized information by linking television sets to a computer and displaying the printout on the television screen.

UK Post Office engineers travelled to Darmstadt this week to investigate new German proposals on standardising viewdata characters which could defuse a nasty confrontation between Britain and France. The argument is over a proposed world standard for viewdata, which the various international standards and telecommunication bodies have to decide on in the next few years. *"Germany Heads Off a Viewdata Row," New Scientist, Nov. 16, 1978, p 522*

In education, Viewdata makes possible a sort of two-way *Sesame Street* for handicapped children who need individually paced instruction in the home; in politics, it offers a national poll on issues of the moment; and at income tax time, it can do everything from providing data on laws and procedures to making the calculations and delivering the returns to the revenue department. It even offers an elegant solution to postal paralysis; electronic mail. *David Thomas, Maclean's, Jan. 9, 1978, p 55*

The Federal Communications Commission is working on technical standards for viewdata right now. *Raymond L. Boggs, in a Letter to the Editor, The New York Times Magazine, Sept. 23, 1979, p 110*

[1978] See PRESTEL, TELETEXT.

viewership, *n.* the number of people who watch television or a particular television program; the audience of viewers.

The book will receive not only a wide readership (it is already a selection of the Book-of-the-Month Club) but also a wide viewership. The BBC has filmed *The Age of Uncertainty* as a 13-part TV series. *Time, April 4, 1977, p 85*

Media freaks here may have read that television-viewership in the US declined in 1977, for the first year since the Creation. *Bart Mills, The Listener, June 22, 1978, p 802*

"King," the six-hour special that ended a three-night run on NBC with its concluding episode Tuesday evening, scored nowhere near the viewership of "Roots," the ABC-TV dramatization of a black family's life in the slave era. *The New York Times, Feb. 16, 1978, p 27*

[1958, patterned on *listenership* (1940's)]

vin·cris·tine (vin'kris ti:n), *n.* an alkaloid derived from the periwinkle of Madagascar, used to treat acute leukemia. *Formula:* $C_{46}H_{56}N_4O_{10}$

Vincristine can cause constipation and is usually given in conjunction with a laxative or stool-softener. About half the time, vincristine also causes children to lose their hair temporarily. At the end of this initial four weeks, however, about 90 to 95 percent of children have achieved a state called remission. *Marion Steinmann, The New York Times Magazine, Dec. 10, 1978, p 161*

[1962, from New Latin *Vinca*, the genus name of the periwinkle + Latin *crista* crest + English *-ine*]

Vi·ra·zole ('vai rə,zoul), *n.* a trademark for RIBAVIRIN.

Medical scientists are finding or designing drugs that attack viruses selectively, that is, by largely or even totally sparing the cells that house them. Two of these drugs look especially promising in the treatment of more serious viral diseases, those that strike the body internally. One is Virazole. It has successfully countered flu in both animals and humans. *Science News, Aug. 20, 1977, p 116*

[1972, from *virus* + *azole*]

vir·gin·ia·my·cin (vər,dʒin yə'mɑi sən), *n.* an antibacterial substance derived from a species of streptomyces.

Only three true antibiotics may now be used in animal feeds without prescription. One is virginiamycin which . . . significantly enhances rabbit growth over six- or eight-week periods — and does not depress growth during the first two weeks of feeding. *Colin Tudge, New Scientist, Jan. 6, 1972, p 5*

[1969, from (*Streptomyces*) *virginiae*, the species from which the substance is derived + *-mycin* fungal substance] Compare FLAVOMYCIN.

vi·ro·gene ('vai rə,dʒi:n), *n.* a viral gene, especially one able, under certain conditions, to produce a carcinogenic virus within a normal cell.

Endogenous viruses are postulated to be produced by a gene, known as a virogene, which may be part of the genetic complement of each member of a species. *Thomas H. Maugh II, "Research News: Leukemia: A Second Human Tumor Virus," Science, Jan. 31, 1975: p 336*

Tricks for getting the virogenes to express themselves as infectious viruses in cultured cells were discovered some time ago. But the viruses produced in this way are generally not very good at reproducing themselves in the animal, and seldom cause tumours, although they belong to the C-type cancer-causing group of viruses. *"Monitor," New Scientist, Sept. 14, 1978, p 768*

[1972] See C-TYPE VIRUS.

viroid, *n.* any of a group of infectious particles of RNA, smaller than any known viruses, that have been identified as the cause of various plant diseases.

Named a viroid, the infectious particle causes potato spindle tuber. . . . The discovery may have implications in the elusive nature of some human diseases, such as multiple sclerosis, infectious hepatitis, and some types of cancer. Many plant and animal diseases whose causes have eluded scientists may also be caused by viroids. *Robert B. Rathbone, "U.S. Agricultural Research," The Americana Annual 1972, p 80*

Viroids have been identified by T. O. Diener as the smallest known agents of infectious disease. The molecular weight of viroids is estimated to be as little as $7.5\text{-}8.5 \times 10^4$ daltons, in marked contrast to the conventional plant virus genomes, which have molecular weights of approximately 2×10^6 daltons. *R. K. Horst, "Viroid," McGraw-Hill Yearbook of Science and Technology 1977, p 417*

[1972, coined by Theodor O. Diener of the U.S. Dept. of Agriculture, from *virus* + *-oid* one like]

► In the 1950's this term was used to describe a hypothetical viruslike organism capable of infecting a host cell or mutating into a virus.

virtual, *adj. Nuclear Physics.* being too transient to be detected or observed directly.

Photons serve as the sole mediator of all other electromagnetic interactions: two electrons repel each other by firing photons back and forth. The exchanged photons exist for exceedingly short times and cannot be directly detected. For this reason they are called "virtual." *Frederick V. Murphy and David E. Yount, "Photons as Hadrons," Scientific American, July 1971, p 96*

Most experimental evidence is compatible with the concept that a proton is made up of three quarks (and there may be several additional and virtual quark-antiquark pairs). . . . (A virtual particle is one that is formed and then reabsorbed too quickly to provide direct evidence for its existence.) *Lawrence W. Jones, "Physics: High-Energy Physics," 1975 Britannica Yearbook of Science and the Future (1974), p 310*

[1967]

virtual memory or **virtual storage,** a method of computer programming that permits the temporary transfer of internally stored programs to less expensive external memory devices, such as magnetic disks, making the computer's main memory or storage capacity appear to be much larger.

Virtual memory . . . provided for the efficient transfer of programs between the computer's main memory and auxiliary storage units. It is an exciting idea which hardly anyone in the business has ever been able to carry out effectively. RCA decided to concentrate its energies on developing a virtual memory system which would surpass the most advanced efforts of IBM. *Katharine Davis Fishman, "Programmed for Disaster," The Atlantic, May 1972, p 37*

Virtual storage is a combination of hardware and software that permits a programmer to ignore the physical capacity of the computer's memory; what spills over is kept on a disk or drum and retrieved automatically as needed. *Wallace B. Riley, "Computers," Britannica Book of the Year 1973, p 192*

[1966, *virtual memory;* 1972, *virtual storage*]

visceral learning, the faculty of acquiring control over involuntary bodily processes.

Psychologists were astounded when New York researchers demonstrated that humans and experimental animals could alter their heart rate, apparently at will. The nature of the phenomenon — known as visceral learning — is now being questioned because of data from recent new experiments. *Abraham Black, "Unlearning Visceral Learning," New Scientist, Jan. 31, 1974, p 269*

[1970]

visual, *n.* Often, **visuals,** *pl. Especially U.S.* **1** a photograph, film, videotape, or other visual display.

"Today's children are exposed to extremely well-done visuals — on television and in printed media," the Zaner-Bloser series explains. *Patti Hagan, "Penmanship," The New York Times Magazine, May 23, 1976, p 68*

2 a picture or film for promotion.

So today is farm day in the Carter campaign, and the Presidential candidate, in pursuit of the sort of "visual" that every Presidential candidate seeks, has come to Hans Sieverding's farm. *Elizabeth Drew, "A Reporter in Washington, D.C.: Autumn Notes—I," The New Yorker, Jan. 10, 1977, p 43*

[1970, originally (1950's) used in the plural to refer to the visual or soundless part of a motion picture]

visual artist, a person engaged in any of the visual arts, such as painting, photography, sculpture, and architecture.

The plight of the visual artist is described as deplorable, most having to resort to part-time jobs to supplement meagre earnings. The number and level of bursaries and fellowships should be increased, more artists-in-residence schemes encouraged and more public bodies should employ artists. Visual artists should also be paid for lending their work for exhibition in public and commercial galleries. *The Times (London), Sept. 9, 1977, p 3*

[1974]

visual capture, the dominance of sight over the other senses when visual input conflicts with input perceived by any of the other senses.

A person wearing distorting spectacles tends to rely completely on vision for localising an object in space, even when other stimuli, for example sound from a loudspeaker, provide truer information. Psychologists call this "visual capture" and have assumed that it occurs because most of our spatial information is received through the eyes so the brain is in some way set to respond such that "seeing is believing." *"Monitor: The Eyes Have It," New Scientist, May 6, 1976, p 291*

[1967]

visual literacy, the ability to understand or appreciate things perceived through the sense of sight.

In Nashville, Tennessee, next month, a conference on 'Visual Literacy' is being held — a subject not too remote from the language of dance and the language of sport. *D. A. N. Jones, The Listener, Feb. 26, 1976, p 238*

[1972] See GRAPHICACY, ORACY.

vis·u·o·spa·tial ('vɪʒ u ouˈspei ʃəl), *adj.* relating to or involving the field of vision, especially as it involves the relationships of space and configuration of objects seen.

Psychological testing has repeatedly shown that girls are in general better at verbal skills, whereas boys are better at visuo-spatial skills (such as jigsaw puzzles). *"Science Report: Psychology: Sex Differences," The Times (London), May 5, 1976, p 18*

About 60 percent of left-handed individuals have language functions in the left hemisphere and visuospatial functions in the right (the same as right-handed individuals). *"Hooked Handedness and the Brain," Science News, Oct. 16, 1976, p 247*

[1975] Compare SPATIO-PERCEPTUAL.

vitamin B$_{17}$, another name for LAETRILE.

The promoters of Laetrile are a tough bunch. They have the temerity to call their stuff Vitamin B-17 and, even after all these years, are presenting full-page ads in an assortment of underground magazines. *Ray N. Lawson, Montreal, Canada, in a Letter to the Editor, Maclean's, Feb. 23, 1976, p 8*

Still a third assertion by Laetrile proponents is that Laetrile is a vitamin — vitamin B$_{17}$ — and thus a nutritional substance rather than a drug. . . . In contrast [Thomas H.] Jukes declares that Laetrile has "not the slightest resemblance to a vitamin. The crucial property of a vitamin is that its absence from the diet produces a specific deficiency disease in vertebrate animals. The cyanogenetic glycosides do not have this property." *Science News, Aug. 6, 1977, p 94*

[1976]

VLA, a system of radio telescopes coordinated to function as a unit in the U.S. National Radio Astronomy Observatory.

The VLA will consist of 27 radio reflectors, each one a fully steerable dish 82 feet in diameter. Arranged in a 39-mile-long, Y-shaped pattern, it will be built on the Plains of San Agustin, west of Socorro, N. Mex. *Stephen P. Maran, "Astronomy," The New World Book Science Annual 1973 (1972), p 269*

[1972, abbreviation of *Very Large Array*]

VLBI, a method used in radio astronomy for measuring signals from a radio source by matching tape recordings of the signals received simultaneously at widely separated radio telescopes.

VLBI ... gives a signal that can discern finer detail in the source than any single telescope could. *"Long Baseline Sizes Up Two Small Radio Objects," Science News, April 14, 1973, p 239*

[1971, abbreviation of *very long baseline interferometry*] Compare APERTURE SYNTHESIS.

VLCC, a petroleum supertanker with a capacity of over 300,000 tons.

The present boom in ordering of VLCCs ... has consolidated the position of 300,000 ton vessels, so that ships of this size can no longer be regarded as outside freaks. *The Times (London), July 17, 1973, p IV*

[1968, abbreviation of *very large crude carrier*] Compare ULCC.

VLDL, a lipoprotein containing a very large proportion of lipids to protein, thought to carry most cholesterol from the liver to the tissues.

VLDLs ... are primarily responsible for transporting triglycerides, which result from dietary excesses of carbohydrates and calories, from the liver to the fatty deposits throughout the body. *Jane E. Brody, "Chemical Carriers of Cholesterol Put Light on Heart-Attack Puzzle," The New York Times, Jan. 18, 1977, p 13*

[1977, abbreviation of *very low-density lipoprotein*] Compare HDL and LDL.

VLSI, a microminiaturization technique for fabricating hundreds of thousands of integrated circuits as a unit on a single silicon chip.

Many experts believe that VLSI will make it possible, perhaps within five years, to compress the number-handling prowess of a modern, large computer into a single part about the size of a match head. ... In addition, products already given some electronic intelligence by LSI chips — ovens, clocks, traffic lights, to name a few — will become smarter with VLSI. Thus, the electric office typewriter, which became the electronic typewriter with the addition of a few memory chips, could be transformed by a superchip into a complete word-processing system allowing a user to edit substantial quantities of text before putting the final version on paper. *Richard Shaffer, "The Superchip," The Wall Street Journal, April 27, 1979, p 1*

[1976, abbreviation of *very large scale integration*]

vol·can·i·clas·tic (val͵kæn ə'klæs tik), *adj.* consisting of volcanic fragments or sediments.

The only close-up of an outcrop of welded tuff (plate 168A) is a highly atypical example. A geologist who seeks guidance in distinguishing between the various kinds of volcaniclastic rock will be disappointed. *G. P. L. Walker,*

"Book Review: Volcanology," Review of "Volcanic Landforms and Surface Features," edited by Jack Green and Nicholas M. Short, Nature, Aug. 4, 1972, p 294

— *n.* a volcaniclastic rock.

The major detrital sources were nearby granitic batholiths and andesitic lava flows, all of late Mesozoic age, rhyolitic volcaniclastics of Cenozoic age, and uplifted sedimentary rocks of all ages. *Michael McLane, "Sandstone: Secular Trends in Lithology in Southwestern Montana," Science, Nov. 3, 1972, p 503*

[1972, blend of *volcanic* and *clastic*]

vol·can·o·gen·ic (͵val kə nə'dʒen ik), *adj.* originating in or produced by volcanoes.

In the Indian Ocean gaps in the sedimentary record have been encountered in a broad spectrum of terrigenous, pelagic, biogenic and volcanogenic sediments encompassing late Mesozoic and Cainozoic time. *Thomas A. Davies, et al., "Unconformities in the Sediments of the Indian Ocean," Nature, Jan. 3, 1975, p 15*

[1968, from *volcano* + *-genic* produced by]

von Wil·le·brand's disease (fɔːn 'vil ə͵braːnts; *Anglicized* van 'wil ə͵brændz), a hemophilic disorder of men and women characterized by lengthy bleeding caused by the deficiency of a clotting factor.

Question: What is Von Willebrand's disease? Answer: An inherited disorder of the blood, involving faulty clotting. Unlike hemophilia, it occurs in women as well as men. Ease of bruising and bleeding, such as from the bowel, and excessive menstruation are features. *The Province (Vancouver), June 2, 1973, p 54*

[1964, named after Everard A. *von Willebrand,* 1892-1949?, a German-born Finnish physician, who first described it]

voucher plan or **voucher system,** *U.S.* a system for allotting tax revenues in the form of redeemable certificates which a parent can apply as tuition in a private school.

On the national level the alternative receiving the most attention was the voucher plan, which would permit parents to decide whether they wanted to send a child to the public schools or to some private or church school. *Kenneth G. Gehret and Leonard Ralph Buckley, "Education," Britannica Book of the Year 1972, p 271*

A voucher system, he [John E. Coons] contends, would improve education by eliminating the monopoly that the public schools now have, in a system ... in which the rich get choice and deductions, and the poor get sent. *Robert Lindsey, "Education: Men Behind Voucher Debate," The New York Times, Dec. 4, 1979, p C5*

[1970]

W

walk, *n.* the slow orbiting of a spacecraft around a heavenly body.

The three drifting "walks" by the orbiters have been particularly valuable to the radio team in refining the shape of the Martian gravitational field. *"Viking: Riches in a Radio Beam," Science News, Nov. 20, 1976, p 326*

—*v.i.* to follow a slow orbit.

Because the pathway of Viking 2 "walks" around the planet every nine days or so, it can study different regions at different times of day. *"Rocket Firing Helps Viking 2 Adjust Orbit for Landing Photos," The New York Times, Aug. 10, 1976, p 12*

[1976]

Walk, *n.* a dance usually done by several people in a line to disco music. It is characterized by steps similar to walking but also includes kicks and turns.

The new Walk, just to make things difficult, is an anathema to all this talk of returning romanticism, because you do it alone, without touching. You needn't even look at the person next to you. It does have style though, and it's friendly; you can hardly be a wallflower if you can Walk. Perhaps . . . the Walk is "a copout for people who can't Hustle." *Joyce Purnick, "Just Get Out There and Dance," New York Post, Dec. 27, 1975, p 23*

—*v.i.* to dance the Walk.

There is no shortage here of glittering clubs in which to hustle, walk, bump or samba the night away. *Shawn G. Kennedy, "The New Discotheque Scene," The New York Times, Jan. 3, 1976, p 10*

[1975]

walking machine, a mechanical device attached to a person to serve as an extension or enlargement of his body, enabling him to climb large obstacles, carry heavy objects, etc.

A four-legged "walking machine" mimics and amplifies the movements of its human operator. The right front leg of the machine is controlled by the operator's right arm, the left front leg by his left arm, the right rear leg by his right leg, and the left rear leg by his left leg. *John McCarthy, "Mechanical Servants for Mankind," 1973 Britannica Yearbook of Science and the Future (1972), p 102*

[1971]

wall, *n.* **off the wall,** *U.S. Slang.* unconventional; unusual; out of the ordinary.

It's been suggested that when Kiss [a rock group] began, some of the boys didn't even know how to play instruments. "That is absolutely not true," says Delaney. "Kiss was so off the wall the rock critics didn't know what to say, so they dumped on them, talking about their 'three-chord knee-jerk' music and stuff like that." *Colette Dowling, "An Out-*rage Called Kiss," The New York Times Magazine, June 19, 1977, p 69*

"Our meetings on the Guild business were right off the wall," he said to me afterward. "Murdoch had his hit list, and he was highly emotional about it." *A. H. Raskin, "A Reporter at Large," The New Yorker, Jan. 22, 1979, p 56*

[1974] See OFF-THE-WALL.

wall·bang·er ('wɔ:l,bæŋ ər), *n. U.S.* a cocktail consisting of vodka or gin with orange juice, and sometimes with rose hip tea or cinnamon.

"A wallbanger is . . . much the same as what they call an orange blossom, but the name of a wallbanger goes down better with the men when they're at a function. The vodka gives you a lift, you know." *Penelope Gilliatt, "Catering," The New Yorker, Sept. 30, 1972, p 41*

[1972]

wallposter, *n.* a bulletin or newspaper written in large characters and containing political propaganda or information, posted on walls in public places in China.

Wallposters have appeared at Shanghai University criticising senior Vice-Premier Teng Hsiao-ping as "China's new Khrushchev." *"The Week," The Manchester Guardian Weekly, Feb. 22, 1976, p 6*

[1967, translation of Chinese (Pinyin) *dazubao* big-character poster] Also called DAZIBAO.

▶ Observers of affairs in China believe that wallposters appearing in major cities reflect current political trends and serve as a barometer of dissent, because wallposters deviating too far from the Communist Party line are taken down.

warehouse, *U.S. (used disparagingly).* —*n.* any large and impersonal public facility for the care of the mentally ill, the aged, the poor, etc.

But for most of Willowbrook's residents, the institution is a warehouse, a place capable of providing only shelter and the barest essentials, for those whose families are either unwilling or unable to care for them. *"Human Warehouse," Time, Feb. 14, 1972, p 67*

We ought to protect our families from the emotional and material burden of such diseased individuals, and from the misery of their simply "existing" (not *living*) in a nearby "warehouse" or public institution. *Joseph Fletcher, The Ethics of Genetic Control, 1974, p 157*

Subsidized public housing has been anathema to the emigrees who now live in the suburbs, where the very mention conjures specters of high-rise "human warehouses" like those that have been erected in ghetto areas. *"U.S. Residential Patterns: Still Separate and Unequal," The New York Times, April 25, 1976, Sec. 4, p 1*

warehouse

—*v.t.* to commit to a place of this kind.

The current federal lawsuit against Partlow State School and Hospital may become a landmark decision in America as the country continues its "trend away from large custodial institutions where people are warehoused and where they are denied the opportunity to develop their full potential," Dr. Philip Roos said here Monday. *Paul Davis, The Tuscaloosa News (Alabama), Feb. 22, 1972, p 1*

California has pioneered the concept of treating the mentally ill with an expanded system of community mental health programs. . . . This year it is more than $140 million and California's shift from the "warehousing of the mentally ill" in large state mental institutions has become a model for the nation. *Ronald Reagan, "The Taxpayers Revolt: Reflections on the Failure of Proposition #1," National Review, Dec. 7, 1973, p 1259*

[1970]

warfighting, *n.* combat between ballistic missiles; warfare conducted by using missiles to attack or intercept enemy missiles. *Often used attributively.*

He [General Brown] agreed that the American-Soviet balance currently remained in "rough equivalence." But he was alarmed at the Soviet trend. His formal report declared: "I now believe the Soviets are striving to achieve warfighting capabilities which, if war occurred, could leave them in the better relative position." *Fred Emery, "Review of US Defence Planned," The Times (London), Jan. 26, 1977, p 6*

[1972, probably from *warhead* + *fighting*]

Washingtonologist, *n.* a student of the policies, leaders, and practices of the United States government.

One of the rules of Kremlinology is that if two contradictory views are expressed in the Soviet press, then the Kremlin itself is probably divided on the issue. This impression is strengthened by some of the questions which the Kremlin's own Washingtonologists have lately been asking. *Victor Zorza, The Manchester Guardian Weekly, Sept. 19, 1976, p 8*

[1974, from *Washington*, D.C. + *-ologist* student of]

WASP·y or **Wasp·y** ('wɑs piː), *adj.* of, belonging to, or characteristic of white Anglo-Saxon Protestants as a group.

In one historic suburb an open-admissions class . . . ends up anyway with the same sort of membership as Mrs. Exeter's—"kind of WASPy but fun." Why should this be? One might as well ask why Irishmen join the Hibernian Society or Italians the Knights of Columbus. Art Buchwald, perceptive sociologist, has observed that WASP's now form just another ethnic group. *Jane Davison, The New York Times Magazine, Dec. 19, 1976, p 96*

Lydia Kingswell Commander regards "the ballot as the best cure for race-suicide." Women's Suffrage washes whiter and Waspier. *"Votes for Women," Review of "Woman Suffrage: Arguments and Results, 1910-1911," The Times Literary Supplement, Feb. 18, 1972, p 180*

[1968, from *WASP* or *Wasp* a white Anglo-Saxon Protestant (especially of the United States) + *-y* (adj. suffix)]

wasteplex, *n.* an industrial complex for recycling wastes.

The laboratory will analyze the raw materials entering the area and the refuse leaving it. Then "wasteplexes"—recycling centres feeding city wastes back to cities as new

raw materials—will be designed specifically for local needs. *"Consigning Rubbish to the Dustbin of History," New Scientist, March 7, 1974, p 614*

[1974, from *waste* + com*plex*]

-watcher, a combining form meaning "a habitual observer of _____; a close follower of the activities of _____." The form became widespread during the 1970's, probably influenced by the political term *China-watcher* (1966), which may have been adapted from *bird watcher* (OEDS 1905). Some recent uses appear below:

celebrity-watcher: The men accompanying the women who were lovely escorted them as in a ballet. . . . It was a celebrity-watchers' paradise. *"The Talk of the Town," The New Yorker, Dec. 20, 1976, p 29*

court-watcher: Some court-watchers are expecting a reversal by "Nixon's Court," if only because of a series of recent retreats from the liberalism of the years under the now retired chief justice Earl Warren. *Robert Lewis, Maclean's, April 19, 1976, p 18*

Kremlin-watcher: One of the senior Kremlin-watchers in Moscow puts it flatly, and puts it best: "Brezhnev runs the show." *Time, Jan. 22, 1979, p 20*

NASA-watcher: NASA said it was making the cuts now—only a month in advance of the President's 1974 budget proposal "to save the maximum amount of money." This, NASA-watchers took as an ill omen for the 1974 budget. *Science News, Jan. 13, 1973, p 20*

Nixon-watcher: The Nixon-watchers, however, would construe Kissinger's return to Cambridge as a potential calamity. *Peter Lisagor, "Life Without Kissinger," New York Post, Dec. 20, 1971, p 40*

Peking-watcher: To be a real "Peking-watcher," do not wear bright Western clothes; try to dress Chinese-style, in dark blues or whites. *B. Michael Frolic, "Wide-Eyed in Peking: A Diplomat's Diary," The New York Times Magazine, Jan. 11, 1976, p 21*

Washington-watcher: The Soviet leaders would hardly have taken such a calculated risk in Angola without first consulting Mr Arbatov and his Washington-watchers on probable United States reaction. *Edmund Stevens, The Times (London), March 23, 1976, p 14*

winewatcher: To anyone who is not a winewatcher, that may not seem as wondrous an event as man's first walk on the moon or the invention of sugarless gum, but it capped a fifty-year campaign undertaken by Baron Philippe de Rothschild to correct the injustice done nearly 120 years ago. *Horace Sutton, "At the Source Bordelaise," Saturday Review, Nov. 20, 1973, p 45*

[1966]

watchlist, *n. U.S.* a list of items that require close scrutiny or surveillance.

Combining bank supervision in one agency was an idea that developed from the well-publicized "problem bank" situation. Many institutions had gotten into difficulty during the recession from bad loans, particularly those involving real estate. The so-called watchlists maintained by the Federal Reserve Board, the Comptroller of the Currency, the Federal Deposit Insurance Corporation, and the Federal Home Loan Bank Board swelled to or approached record levels. *Robert D. Hershey, Jr., "Banking," The Americana Annual 1977, p 114*

[1973]

Watergate, *n.* **1** a major political scandal in the administration of President Richard M. Nixon, including attempts to conceal illegal activities of the participants. *Often used attributively.*

So many other crimes and malpractices came to light that the word Watergate became a generic term for the many abuses of power that made up this complex and explosive political scandal. *James Bishop, "The United States of America," The Annual Register of World Events in 1973 (1974), p 61*

Napoleon had his Waterloo and Nixon had his Watergate. *Barbara Trecker, New York Post, May 22, 1974, p 80*

"The Republicans are lambasting us, calling the scandal here another Watergate," Mr. Madden declared in a voice choked with emotion. "It's political strategy to use this issue to take the public's mind off Watergate." *Richard D. Lyons, "House Reforms Approved by Democrats After Fight," The New York Times, June 24, 1976, p 1*

2 any scandal, especially one that involves an attempt to conceal damaging information or illegal activities.

Do we need a dental Watergate? The worldwide evidence for and against fluoridation is now in. *Advertisement by Stein and Day for the Book "The Fluoride Question" by Anne-Lise Gotzsche, The New York Times Book Review, April 27, 1975, p 29*

If the jockeys really did know something in advance, we'd have a horse-racing Watergate. *Roger Kahn, "Angel Cordero's Luck," Esquire, June 1976, p 11*

"Hell, he [Lazarus] didn't dig up anything. Everything he found out about us, I gave him. We have nothing to hide. ... But he figured he could make a Watergate and get himself promoted to Chicago." *Fred Frazier, quoted in Columbia Journalism Review, July/Aug. 1976, p 35*

The pro-laetrile movement responds in like fashion, accusing the US medical establishment of a cover-up. "It's a medical Watergate," said one. "The laetrile issue will destroy the American Cancer Society—they're very afraid, the American Cancer people," says another. *Jon Trux, M. Murphy-Ferris and Lee Torrey, New Scientist, June 30, 1977, p 766*

The easiest refuge in dull times is to hype a story—to make every major or minor shenanigan a Watergate (as in Koreagate, Lancegate and Hollywoodgate). *Time, June 12, 1978, p 102*

—*v.t.* to involve in scandal; charge with wrongdoings.

"Why are they Watergating her [Marilyn Monroe]?" he [Dr. Ralph Greenson] asks. "Why can't they let her rest in peace. She was a bedeviled, fatherless young woman, torn between being a waif one minute and a princess the next. How could she have been murdered? I think Mailer is all wrong." *Week-End Star (Kingston, Jamaica), Sept. 21, 1973, p 27*

[1973, from the *Watergate*, a building in Washington, D.C., where the Democratic National Committee had headquarters. An attempt to break into and take documents from the headquarters by men associated with reelection efforts of President Nixon led to an investigation and a scandal.]

▶ The Watergate affair left a strong imprint on the language of the 1970's. The word spawned various coinages and the combining form *-gate*, used to denote scandal or corruption (see the entry -GATE), especially in the term *Koreagate*. The following quotations illustrate some of the derivatives:

Watergateana, *n.:* In all the immense outpouring of Watergateana, quite a lot of which has washed eastward across the Atlantic, it has been next to impossible to form any clear notion of what actually happened. *Malcolm Muggeridge, Esquire, Sept. 1974, p 58*

Watergater, *n.:* Having sentenced 17 Watergaters to prison terms, Sirica was ruling on petitions for leniency from the only ones who are still imprisoned. *Time, Oct. 17, 1977, p 19*

Watergatese, *n.:* Translations of a famous passage of Churchill's not into Basic English but into Watergatese: At no previous point of time in a conflict situation personnelwise has global indebtedness to an occupational minority group been operative in the same ball-court. *Philip Howard, The Times (London), Sept. 26, 1973, p 14*

Watergatish, *adj.:* Everything the ministers of the Nine say in their meetings is recorded on tape—recorded twice, in fact, because the actual words are recorded, and the French translation of them. Even more 'Watergatish' is the fact that these tapes are never made public; they are only there in case there is a legal disagreement. *John Simpson, "No Records in Brussels," The Listener, Jan. 29, 1976, p 100*

Watergatism, *n.:* It has been reported but never confirmed that it was Connally who helped devise that May strategy. His critics say he was knowingly helping Nixon "stonewall it," to use a Watergatism. *James P. Sterba, "The Return of John Connally," The New York Times Magazine, Aug. 8, 1976, p 49*

Watergatologist, *n.:* Hawkeyed Watergatologists will note a new fact in the film of *All the President's Men* which is not in the book. So far the sleuths of the American press have missed it, and Mr Woodward confirmed it to me. *Fred Emery, The Times (London), May 4, 1976, p 6*

In addition, the Watergate affair generated or revived such terms and new meanings as CREEP, ENEMIES LIST, PLUMBER, POINT IN TIME, SMOKING GUN, STONEWALL, and *twist in the* WIND.

water hole or **waterhole,** *n.* a part of the electromagnetic spectrum that is comparatively free of radio noise, considered as the most likely frequency band to be used by extraterrestrial beings trying to make contact with earth.

Between the hydrogen and hydroxyl (OH) bands, for example, lies the "water hole," the emission frequency of H_2O, which is not only a basic constituent of life as even most exobiologists can envision it, but also offers a frequency less drowned in deep-space static, or "sky noise." *"Science News of the Week: Six Searches for Extraterrestrial Civilizations," Science News, Feb. 28, 1976, p 132*

The waterhole is freer from radio noise than any other band, and aliens, presumably, would broadcast on it for just that reason. However, portions of the band are now available by international agreement, for satellite communications. The United States Air Force, for example plans to orbit 24 navigation satellites, broadcasting in the waterhole, over the next eight years; other navigation and communications satellite systems also have their eyes on it. *Tom Ferrell and Virginia Adams, The New York Times, Sept. 4, 1977, Sec. 4, p 7*

[1976, so called because interstellar hydrogen and oxygen (the elements forming water) radiate on this band of frequencies] See SETI.

wave power, energy derived from the motion of waves and converted or put to useful work. Recent inventions utilizing wave power are the RUSSELL RECTIFIER and the SALTER DUCK.

wave-powered

The new solar-power programme came after similar research commitments on wave power and on geothermal energy, and other alternative sources of energy were being examined. *Kenneth Owen, The Times (London), Feb. 18, 1977, p 2*

Says Alexander Eadie, Britain's Under Secretary for Energy: "Wave power is not just a boffin's pipe-dream. It is a credible proposition." The British government has doubled spending on wave-power research this year, to $5.5 million, and the Japanese have committed $5 million over the next two years. They are betting that these investments could pay off in decades ahead. Oil wells may dry up but waves will never cease to roll. *Time, Oct. 16, 1978, p 92*

[1974]

wave-powered, *adj.:* Wave-powered buoys and small lighthouses have been used in the past, but tapping Japan's sea potential in a big way is just beginning. *Science News, June 24, 1978, p 402*

weath·er·ize ('weð ər,aiz), *v.t. U.S.* to provide (a dwelling) with new or improved insulation or other materials and devices to keep heating and cooling costs down.

Last year Mr. Ballou, who . . . lives on Social Security and Supplemental Security Income, spent about one-third of his income for heat. His house is not weatherized and already he's noticed a difference. *"Operation Open City Helps the Poor Weatherize Their Homes and Apartments and Prevent Wasting of Fuel," The New York Times, Nov. 7, 1976, p 55*

[1976, from *weather* + *-ize;* patterned on *winterize*]

weatherization, *n.:* Criteria for Retrofit Materials and Products for Weatherization of Residences. This booklet identifies and lists criteria for materials and products considered eligible under the Department of Energy Weatherization Assistance Program. The materials included are insulation and vapor barriers, storm windows and doors, caulking and weatherstripping, clock thermostats, replacement windows, and replacement glazing. *Selected U.S. Government Publications Jan. 1979, Vol. 8, No. 1, p 11*

► *Weatherize* was occasionally used in the past in the restricted sense (applied to cloth) "to make weatherproof." The new use gained currency as an energy-conservation measure to counteract the shortage and rising cost of fuel.

wedge, *n.* a woman's short hairdo that falls over the forehead and forms a triangle in the back.

There are many variations on the new wedge. Stylists at the Paul McGregor shops in New York and Los Angeles have shaped the back of the cut into three inverted pyramids. *"Modern Living: The Dorothy Do," Time, April 19, 1976, p 69*

[1976]

weeny-bopper, *n. Slang.* a preadolescent boy or girl who follows the latest fashions and fads in dress, music, etc.

Pop, which is almost as changeable as the weather, is suddenly bathed in sunshine. Two groups of young Americans, the Osmonds and the Jackson Five, have brought the Weenyboppers out in strength. It is all happening. *Week-End Star (Kingston, Jamaica), July 20, 1973, p 22*

My fairly concentrated listening so far shows a pattern of middle-of-the-road pop during the day: screaming weeny-bopper pop at night; and then, after midnight, a succession of those meandering songs sung *sotto voce* by breathy

young ladies. *The Listener, Nov. 7, 1974, p 644*

[1973, from *weeny* very small + *-bopper,* as in *teeny-bopper* (1967)]

Weinberg-Salam theory or **model,** *Physics.* a theory uniting weak and electromagnetic interactions and predicting the existence of the neutral current.

The Weinberg-Salam theory . . . hypothesized that electromagnetism and the weak force are facets of the same phenomenon and predicted that both would be found to behave in the same way, in that a neutral current, analogous to electromagnetic currents, would be detected in reactions involving the weak force. *Caroline G. Dudley, "Nobel Prizes: Physics," 1980 Collier's Encyclopedia Year Book (1979), p 398*

The modern unified field theory, often called the Weinberg-Salam model . . . begins with the weak and electromagnetic interactions. An experiment recently done at the Stanford Linear Accelerator Center has confirmed some key predictions of the Weinberg-Salam model, suggesting that there are not four forces in nature but three: gravity, the strong interaction and the one for which there is no name yet, the weak interaction *cum* electromagnetism. *Science News, July 8, 1978, p 20*

[1976, named after Steven *Weinberg,* born 1933, an American physicist, and Abdus *Salam,* born 1926, a Pakistani physicist, who independently developed the theory in the 1960's] See GAUGE THEORY, HIGGS MESON.

welfare hotel, a hotel in which people on welfare are housed, usually until permanent quarters are found for them.

A year ago, conditions in the welfare hotels were a scandal. *Michael Leapman, "Meanwhile, Back at the Great Northern," The Times (London), March 7, 1972, p 6*

Few Outsiders venture into welfare hotels. Mothers picking up their children at P.S. 75 across the street steer clear of the hotel's entrance. Pedestrians pass hurriedly by. *Peter Koenig, The New York Times Magazine, May 21, 1978, p 17*

[1971] Compare S.R.O. HOTEL.

welfarite, *n. U.S. (used disparagingly)* a person supported by public welfare; person on relief.

(The doctor who had written the report specialized in welfarites and mentioned that this patient would be coming to him for a substantial amount of treatment.) The welfare department, fearing legal suits if they made the man work and it turned out that he really was ill, decided to classify him unemployable. *Clayton Thomas, "The New York Picture: The Welfare Dollar Goes 'Round and 'Round," National Review, Jan. 18, 1974, p 78*

[1974]

Wer·ner's syndrome ('wər nərz *or* 'ver nərz), an inherited disorder characterized by premature aging, dwarfism, and impairment in glandular function.

The problem is being tackled by research on people suffering from Werner's syndrome, a rare inherited disease which causes premature senility. Cells from these people have a very short life-span, dividing only about ten times outside the body — supporting the view that the aging of cells leads to the aging of organisms. *"Science Report," The Times (London), Oct. 25, 1974, p 18*

The variability of the expression of ageing also leads to the question of whether Werner's syndrome patients are simply the few at the tail end of the distribution of rates of ageing within the population at large. This would imply that these individuals did not suffer from a particular disease but possessed a fortuitously high genetic predisposition to faster ageing. A careful analysis of the families of affected individuals revealed that this was not the case. *"A Pathological Race Through Life," New Scientist, April 21, 1977, p 122*

[1972, named after C. *Werner*, a 20th-century German physician]

West Banker, a native or inhabitant of the West Bank of the Jordan River, formerly a part of Palestine.

Israelis point out that West Bankers choose their own mayors. The West Bank's standard of living has improved dramatically, and more than 40,000 Palestinians work in Israel. As might be expected, there are differing opinions between Israelis and West Bankers on what the occupation has meant economically to the region. Foreign economists conclude that both sides benefit, though Israel comes out ahead. *Time, June 19, 1978, p 39*

[1968]

wet-dog shakes, *Slang.* violent trembling during withdrawal from drug or alcohol addiction.

The effects of these very similar chemicals can be quite different. (What they all do, however, greatly to the amazement of Bloom and his collaborators, is to produce . . . the "wet-dog shakes" characteristic of morphine *withdrawal*—quite unexpected in a drug which is supposed to imitate morphine.) *"Monitor: Schizophrenia Linked With Opiates," New Scientist, Nov. 11, 1976, p 332*

After only three days of . . . treatment the teetotaling rats began switching to the sauce. Indeed, after a while the rodents became so addicted that they exhibited all the symptoms of alcoholism, including a rodent version of delirium tremens (DTs) characterized by whisker-twitching, jerking movements and "wet-dog" shakes. *Time, May 9, 1977, p 56*

[1973]

wet leasing, the renting of aircraft complete with crews and engineering and other support services.

This practice of "wet leasing" is popular in the airline industry because it allows operators to avoid the enormous capital costs involved in buying new aircraft at a time when traffic is fluctuating. *Arthur Reed, "British Share in Growing Move to Lease Airliners," The Times (London), Jan. 6, 1976, p 14*

[1976, from *wet* in contrast to *dry*, meaning bare, without accessories]

wet thumb, ability or success in raising fish in aquariums, fish farms, etc.

Possession of a "wet thumb" is still the most important attribute for any fish keeper, be he professional fish culturist or pet fish fancier. *James W. Atz, "The Supersensitivity of Fishes," Natural History, Nov. 1972, p 60*

[1972, patterned on *green thumb* (1943)] Compare BROWN THUMB.

white-collar criminal, a person in a business or profession who breaks the law in the course of his occupation, as by committing embezzlement or fraud, or engaging in tax evasion, bribery, patent infringement, misrepresentation in advertising, and the like.

Strong disapproval of lenient sentences for white-collar criminals has been voiced by a top Federal prosecutor, who said that substantial prison terms could deter businessmen from committing crimes. *Arnold H. Lubasch, "Leniency Decried in Business Crime," The New York Times, Aug. 1, 1976, p 25*

The percentage of prisoners who are nonviolent felons — burglars, auto thieves, and larcenists — has declined, as has the percentage who are "white-collar" criminals (embezzlers, forgers, and defrauders). *James Q. Wilson, "Changing Criminal Sentences," Harper's, Nov. 1977, p 20*

[1972, derived from *white-collar crime* (1952), a term coined by the American criminologist Edwin H. Sutherland and popularized in his book *White Collar Crime* (1949)]

White English, English as spoken by white Americans in contrast to Black English.

Intonation patterns of Black English were studied and compared with those occurring in White English and formal Black English. It was found that: (1) the Black English corpus was characterized by a wider pitch range, extending into higher pitch levels than either the White vernacular or the formal Black English of the adult information. *Newsletter of the American Dialect Society, Vol. 6, No. 3, Nov. 1974, p 44*

[1974]

white flight, *U.S.* the movement of urban whites, especially middle-class whites, to the suburbs to avoid consequences of living in a city, such as increased danger from a high rate of crime, racial integration, high taxation, etc.

Previous studies of this so-called "white flight" phenomenon have been criticized for not taking into account the type of desegregation involved and for ignoring other factors that might have induced white families to leave the central city anyway. Armor tries to correct these deficiencies by comparing white flight under court-ordered busing to that under voluntary integration plans, and by trying to estimate what demographic changes would have occurred if no desegregation plans had been implemented. *Science News, Sept. 23, 1978, p 216*

[1976]

white hole, a hypothetical source of matter and energy.

Recent speculation suggests that matter in our universe is disappearing into the fantastic gravitational wells of black holes, only to appear in other universes through what appear to be "white holes." Our white holes may be the quasars, whose prodigious energies we are currently at a loss to explain. *John P. Wiley, Jr., "At the Creation," Natural History, April 1972, p 44*

Asimov . . . suggests that a network of black holes interlacing the universe may have, through all eternity, been sucking matter in at one end and expelling it through "white holes" at the other end to "create a closed circuit, sending matter back into a more contracted past to begin expansion all over" again — an idea that sounds suspiciously like a new version of Hoyle's discredited Steady State and brings the complex and confusing debate over the origins and future of the universe neatly full circle. *Mark Nichols, "In the Beginning," Maclean's, Aug. 22, 1977, p 59*

white market

[1971, patterned on *black hole* (1968), which engulfs matter and energy] See WORMHOLE.

white market, legal or officially sanctioned trade in ration coupons, etc., to discourage illegal transactions or the emergence of a black market.

Even if the pinch were eased by permitting a "white market" on which coupons could be legally sold, the Federal Energy Agency calculated that the price of the coupons would be 80 cents to $1.25 a gallon—an inflationary factor even worse than the President's proposed taxes. *"Is Rationing the Answer," Newsweek, Feb. 3, 1975, p 16*

The Administration presented a new proposal for standby gasoline rationing that . . . would permit motorists to sell their rationing coupons to others in a "white market." *The New York Times, Dec. 9, 1979, p 1E*

[1972] ► This is a revival of a term used in the period 1946-48 in the sense of the legal market in currencies existing at that time in Europe.

white meter, *British.* an electric meter that registers off-peak consumption of electricity.

The consumer has to compare white meter costs himself, *Which?* says. A typical family in the North-east using 1,050 units a quarter and paying 10.67 on the standard domestic tariff, would have to use well over 300 units at night to benefit from going onto the white meter, it claims. *The Times (London), Oct. 11, 1973, p 6*

[1972, so called from its color, to distinguish it from the ordinary gray meter]

white tea commune, a commune in China which is impoverished because of its poor agricultural resources or its distance from city markets.

One may legitimately ask how long peasants in "white tea" communes will accept the idea of "learning from Tachia" (the model "self-reliance" brigade) as it becomes clear that nothing except direct Government help will lift the poorer units to the level of the richer? *Martin Woollacott, "China's Gross Inequalities," The Manchester Guardian Weekly, Nov. 28, 1976, p 7*

[1976, so called from the commune's drinking of hot water instead of real tea]

wholefood, *n. British.* any food grown organically and prepared without artificial additives or preservatives.

Those attending the festival will live in a geodesic domed village, enjoying solar heated showers, eat wholefoods prepared at a vegetarian kitchen, and take part in discussions. *The Times (London), Aug. 23, 1977, p 12*

[1965]

why·dun·it (ˌhwaiˈdənˌit), *n.* a mystery novel, play, or motion picture which deals primarily with the motivation for the crime.

Psychological whydunnit, with Dame Peggy Ashcroft wonderfully piteous as the naughty butcher. *"Week Ahead," Theatre," The Manchester Guardian Weekly, Aug. 7, 1971, p 19*

Connery takes over the interrogation and in the process beats the man to death. This much we know almost from the beginning, so the film is less of a whodunit than a whydunit. *Richard Schickel, "Cinema: Offencive," Review of "The Offence," Time, June 4, 1973, p 99*

[1971, patterned on *whodunit* (1930)]

504

Wic·ca or **wic·ca** (ˈwik ə), *n.* the practice or cult of witchcraft.

Witches call their religion Wicca, from the Anglo-Saxon word meaning wisdom, which is the root of such words as witch, wizard and wicked. They practice a rite similar in form to Baptism in which infants are accepted into the faith. *Sunday Post-Herald (Hongkong), July 22, 1973, p 22*

The ancient rites of the *wicca,* as witchcraft is known to its serious practitioners, were practiced in 1971 with no one knows what degree of success by no one knows how many witches in the United States. *Constance Urdang, "Witchcraft," 1972 Collier's Encyclopedia Year Book (1971), p 10*

[1970, from Old English *wicca* (masculine) wizard]

Wiccadom, *n.:* The most important fertility rites in all Wiccadom occur in spring. It is the time to worship fervently in the coven of one's choice. *Time, April 27, 1970, p 98*

Wiccan, *adj.:* Witches do not . . . torture animals or kill them for pleasure. Such perverted practices are the antithesis of all Wiccan teachings. *V. R. Gulevich, Brooklyn, in a Letter to the Editor, New York Post, Aug. 22, 1979, p 26*

wide-body, *adj.* having a wide fuselage.

Many people are forced, despite their continual distress from aircraft noise, to remain living near Heathrow Airport because of employment or economic factors, and the prospect of improving their lot by retrofitting of noisy aircraft, and the introduction of quieter wide-body turbo-fan aircraft is unfortunately not only still remote, but totally inadequate. *The Times (London), May 3, 1973, p 18*

The new planes are needed to modernize the United Fleet, largest in the free world, to improve fuel efficiency and to expand operation of wide body jets. *"We Don't Want to Hear About It Department," The New Yorker, Dec. 11, 1978, p 120*

[1972]

wide receiver, a pass receiver in American football who stands a few yards to the side of the rest of the team to enable him to get quickly downfield without having to run through the opposing team's line.

Holtz lost his five best running backs through defections, trades and retirement. He lost his best wide receiver and his best defensive lineman through injuries. *William Barry Furlong, "Secrets of a Turnaround Coach," The New York Times Magazine, Dec. 12, 1976, p 65*

[1968]

widow's mandate, *U.S.* the election or appointment of a widow to the political office held by her husband, usually to complete his unexpired term.

Among the widows who were elected to office on the basis of "widow's mandate" were many who developed distinct political reputation and won terms in their own right. *"The Women of Congress," The New York Times, Aug. 27, 1976, p B4*

[1976]

wiggle seat, a lie detector fitted into a chair to measure physiological changes and movement of the occupant.

In addition to the 50-year-old polygraph, which measured blood pressure, respiration rate, and galvanic skin response, several new lie detectors are now available. These include the "wiggle seat," which registers body temperature and minute muscle movements; a device which records changes in the size of the pupil of the eye; and the Psychological Stress Evaluator. *Steve Aaronson, "Technology," Encyclopedia Science Supplement (Grolier) 1976, p 345*

[1976]

wild-card, *adj. U.S.* (of a sports team) qualifying for championship play-offs by winning an arbitrary play-off among second-place teams or by winning the most games among teams that did not qualify for play-offs.

The Cowboys locked up the National Conference's "wild card" slot Saturday as they defeated the East Division champion Washington Redskins 34-24. *Bruce Lowitt, The Tuscaloosa News (Alabama), Dec. 10, 1972, p 8B*

This would entail the establishment of three geographical divisions within each league, and a playoff season that would stretch over several weeks, involving three regional winners in each league plus a "wild card" team. *Roger Angell, "The Sporting Scene," The New Yorker, Nov. 20, 1978, p 57*

[1972, so called from the supposed resemblance of such a team to a *wild card*, a playing card of arbitrary denomination]

wild white, a virus related to the smallpox virus, isolated from the tissues of chimpanzees and monkeys.

There is one entirely compelling argument in favour of conserving the smallpox virus. . . . First, smallpox virus will be required in studying the antigenic relationships between it and monkeypox, "wild white," and other viruses that have come to light increasingly with the progress of smallpox eradication. This analysis is not only of basic biological interest; it could also prove of enormous practical importance if any of these smallpox-related viruses were to pose a major health problem. *Bernard Dixon, "Smallpox-Imminent Extinction, and an Unresolved Dilemma," New Scientist, Feb. 26, 1976, p 432*

[1976]

Wilson cycle, the pattern of appearance and disappearance of oceans in geologic time.

The sites of old hot spots have proved readily recognizable, and during 1974 it was shown that hot spots have formed a distinctive feature of the Wilson cycle throughout the last 2,000,000,000 years. *Kevin Burke and W. S. F. Kidd, "Earth, Heat Flow In," McGraw-Hill Yearbook of Science and Technology 1975, p 168*

[1975, named after John Tuzo *Wilson*, born 1908, a Canadian geologist]

wimp, *n. U.S. and Canadian Slang.* an unathletic or unaggressive person, often considered a weakling or sissy.

The sensitive, unathletic kid refused to stifle his artistic instincts. He served as president of the Art Association ("Twenty of us little wimps reading *Artforum*," says Wheelwright). *Time, Feb. 9, 1976, p 60*

Part of being a wimp is feeling sorry for yourself. . . . Every student encounter in this teleplay is sticky with wimps' self-pity. Strange. The law students I remember were cannibal barracudas ever ready to devour the flesh of their fellows. *William Casselman, "Where Are the Males of Yesteryear?" Maclean's, Oct. 9, 1978, p 69*

[1959, 1971, probably short for *Wimpy*, a fat charac-

ter forever eating in the comic strip "Popeye," created in 1929 by Elzie C. Segar, 1894-1938]

WIN[1], *n., v. U.S.* acronym for *Whip Inflation Now*, a slogan promoted under the administration of President Gerald R. Ford (1974-76).

Newspapers, magazines, radio, and television gave all kinds of suggestions on how to WIN and how to shop more prudently. *Stewart M. Lee, "Consumerism," The Americana Annual 1975, p 195*

Richard Nixon tried mandatory wage-price controls, Gerald Ford tried the WIN button, Jimmy Carter tried voluntary guidelines. *"The Limits of Power," Newsweek, Nov. 19, 1979, p 89*

[1974]

WIN[2], *n. U.S.* acronym for *Work Incentive*, a federal program designed to provide jobs for people on welfare, instituted by a 1967 amendment to the Social Security Act.

WIN has provided educational and job training for welfare recipients with the aim of preparing them to compete in the private sector. *Michael Harrington, "Government Should Be the Employer of First Resort," The New York Times Magazine, March 26, 1972, p 44*

The number of "slots" WIN was able to offer for training was always exceeded by the number of persons voluntarily seeking training. *Daniel P. Moynihan, "Annals of Politics: Income by Right — II," The New Yorker, Jan. 20, 1973, p 67*

[1970]

wind, *n.* **twist in the wind,** to experience great uncertainty or endure painful suspense.

There were those who felt that for one who had sat on the ducking stool, and been tarred and feathered in addition, I had suffered enough. But the inquisitors thought otherwise. For ten months I was left hanging there, twisting in the wind. *Herbert L. Porter, "My Little White Lie," Harper's, Oct. 1974, p 76*

Everybody, or a lot of the press, has taken it that, in fact, the Government was jolly well making you wait for the money; it was keeping you twisting in the wind, I think is the phrase. *Michael Swann, in an Interview with William Hardcastle, The Listener, Feb. 13, 1975, p 201*

[1974] ► The expression *twist (slowly) in the wind* became current during the Watergate affair (1972-74). In *Safire's Political Dictionary* (William Safire, 1978), the origin of the phrase is attributed to John Ehrlichman.

windsurfing, *n.* the sport of riding a surfboard equipped with a mast and sail.

For recreation, she likes windsurfing and tennis, though windsurfing is something more than a pastime since she teaches this burgeoning sport. It involves standing on a surf board and allowing a hand-held sail, once laboriously hauled from the water by strength of arm, to propel the craft along. It requires exceptional balance, too, which no doubt stands Miss Bader in good stead on the snow. *The Times (London), Dec. 8, 1977, p 9*

[1972]

windsurfer, *n.:* From Nov. 15 to 20 in the Bahamas, 400 or so windsurfers will be . . . participating in the 1976 World Championships of Windsurfing. *John Brannon Albright, "Notes: Windsurfing Championships," The New York Times, Oct. 31, 1976, Sec. 10, p 5*

You can't imagine a simpler craft than a Windsurfer. There is no rudder and no ropes: the mast is supported and controlled by the sailor, and the 'boat' is steered by moving the body. *The Sunday Times Magazine (London), Dec. 21, 1975, p 3*

wire-guided, *adj.* guided to a target by electrical impulses transmitted through a wire connecting the weapon and the operator.

More than 130 Israeli tanks had been killed by Russian-made Sagger antitank missiles: 25-pound wire-guided rockets carried by lightly armored vehicles, widely deployed since 1965 by the Warsaw Pact forces and others. *Philip Morrison and Paul F. Walker, "A New Strategy for Military Spending," Scientific American, Oct. 1978, p 57*

[1963] See TOW.

wireman, *n.* *U.S.* an expert in wiretapping.

Dusk [in Washington, D.C.] delivers a sense of impending *Walpurgisnacht*, and the reason is clear: never before have there been so many "spooks" abroad in the land, so many spies and counterspies, clandestine analysts, secret movers, shakers, agents, operatives, wiremen, and gumshoes. *Jim Hougan, "A Surfeit of Spies," Harper's, Dec. 1974, p 51*

Among the practitioners of his craft, Frank Chin, 48, was a pro. He had been one of the most sought-after "wiremen," or electronic eavesdroppers, in the East, supplying bugging and recording devices to clients on both sides of the law. *Time, Feb. 21, 1977, p 19*

[1973, from *wiretap* + *man*]

wishbone, *n.* or **wishbone T,** an offensive formation in American football, a variant of the T-formation, in which the fullback is lined up ahead of the two halfbacks in an alignment resembling a wishbone. *Often used attributively.*

The Sugar Bowl wasn't a complete artistic triumph, as Clements arched high, floating passes and hoped for the best, and Alabama's incredibly fast wishbone attack also proved somewhat erratic. *Newsweek, Jan. 14, 1974, p 70*

Penn stands last in the league on defense, a phase of the game in which Princeton excels, but Penn's wishbone offense has ground out 1,118 yards in four league games, far better than any other team. *Deane McGowen, The New York Times, Oct. 28, 1977, p A20*

[1970] Compare VEER.

Wis·kott·Al·drich syndrome ('wis,kɑt'ɔ:l,dritʃ), a genetic disorder characterized especially by a decrease in white blood cells and platelets, chronic eczema, and recurrent infections.

Fifteen-month-old Tony Olivo of Dallas was reported to have spent his entire short life in a special germ-free room in a hospital; he had been born a victim of the Wiskott-Aldrich syndrome: having virtually no resistance to any infection, he could not survive outside a sterile environment. Now he was being taken to the Boston Children's Hospital Center for an elaborate new treatment—a bone-marrow transplant—that it was hoped would correct his condition. *Leonard C. Lewin, "Bioethical Questions," Harper's, Aug. 1978, p 21*

[1968, named fter R. A. *Aldrich*, a 20th-century American pediatrician; origin of the name *Wiskott* is unknown]

witch's cradle or **witches' cradle,** a metal platform or cage, suspended several inches above the ground, on which a subject of parapsychological experiments is placed in a darkened, soundproof room to induce in him various altered states of consciousness.

The "witch's cradle," or suspended sensory isolation cradle, is one prop they use to produce an ASC [altered state of consciousness]. *Robert J. Trotter, "ESP and ASC," Science News, Nov. 10, 1973, p 300*

ESP scores also appear to be enhanced when extraneous sensory input is reduced. Experiments supporting this point have been done with subjects strapped into a "witches' cradle," in which sight and sound are blocked off as one swings slowly through the air in a metal frame. *Stanley Krippner, "Parapsychology," Britannica Book of the Year 1975, p 77*

[1973, probably named after an old, cradlelike device into which suspected witches were strapped to punish or isolate them]

woman, *n.* ► The movement to eliminate sexism in language led during the 1970's to an increasing avoidance of words and phrases that refer to women in a patronizing way (as in "the little woman") or in disparaging stereotypes ("women drivers") or in needless typing by sex ("a woman author"). Also regarded as sexist and proscribed by many of the new style guides of publishing houses, newspapers, and magazines, were indirect references to women from a masculine standpoint (as in "the fair sex," "the female of the species," "the better half") as well as the use of descriptive terms that stress the appearance of women ("attractive blonde"), their marital status ("recent divorcée"), their sex role ("busy housewife and mother"), and their femaleness ("young usherette," "famous aviatrix," "funny comedienne").

Similar guidelines have been issued and popularized to deal with the use of *man* in various contexts, especially when it is used in the generic sense of "any human being or person" (see MAN).

One widespread approach toward equalizing the sexes in language has been the use of *person* as a neutral designation that includes both sexes (see PERSON).

Another tendency has been to replace or supplement the word *man* with *woman* in phrases or contexts dealing with members of the female sex.

In the quotations below, *woman* is used to replace or supplement *man* in words and phrases in which *man* is ambiguous (i.e., it may mean either "a male" or "a human being"). The derivation of each example is given in brackets next to the boldface heading.

one's own woman [replacement of idiom *one's own man*]: Thank heaven I have graduated from the "girl who cain't say no." I'm my own woman now. I don't belong to the party, nor the people. *Judy La Marsh, "I'm the Girl Who Learned to Say No," Maclean's, July 1974, p 4*

woman, *v.t.* [supplement of *man*, *v.t.*, to operate]: Mrs. Prior is one of about a hundred girls and men who man and woman the Vauxhall Directory Inquiry Bureau around the clock. *Philip Howard, "London: Telephones," The Times (London), Nov. 15, 1972, p 6*

Womanagement, *n.* [blend of *woman* and *management,* though the latter derives from Latin *manus* hand, not *man*]: Recently, I went to the Western Electric Corporate Education Center in Hopewell, N.J. (a Bell System training center), to observe a group participating in a three-day Womanagement workshop. It was the second day and the women were about to play "Alice in Corporation-land," a power strategy game George Peabody had adapted for Womanagement from "Powerplay," a game he invented with another management consultant. *Gwyneth Cravens, "How Ma Bell is Training Women for Management," The New York Times Magazine, May 29, 1977, p 13*

womanfully, *adv.* [replacement of *manfully, adv.*]: She has struggled womanfully to avoid allowing her prose to slide into the mire of lunar jargon. *Robert Thompson, Review of "Lunar Mineralogy" by Judith W. Frondel, New Scientist, Jan. 29, 1976, p 243*

woman-hour, *n.* [supplement of *man-hour*]: An eminently do-it-yourself proposition, the intermittent man and woman-hours between basket-making and baking amounted to perhaps 6 or 7 people-weeks. *New Scientist, Sept. 19, 1974, p 712*

woman in the street [replacement of *man in the street* the average person]: I treasure the letter as a living example of this happy breed which produces government departments with the time and manpower to explain at such length to a mere woman-in-the-street why private enterprise cannot stock its shops properly. *Carolyn Bryn-Jones, The Times (London), Oct. 4, 1972, p 11*

woman-year, *n.* [replacement of *man-year*]: Among women who give up the pill there is no increase in the number of abnormal babies born but there is an abortion rate of 21 per cent. The pill's failure rate as a contraceptive is miniscule—0.34 per hundred woman-years. *John Cunningham, "Clean Bill of Health for the Pill," The Manchester Guardian Weekly, May 25, 1974, p 8*

womb-envy, *n.* a supposed masculine envy of the female capacity to give birth.

In these men one saw a real womb-envy, a feeling that their women, however they treated them, had a direct line to the Lord through their wombs. I did, for a moment, envy the women the envy of their men, understanding the simplistic male celebration of procreation. *Anne Taylor Fleming, "That Week in Houston," The New York Times Magazine, Dec. 25, 1977, p 13*

[1972, patterned on *penis envy* (a Freudian term)]

womb-to-tomb, *adj. U.S. Informal.* from birth to death; spanning a lifetime.

He [Donald T. Regan] thinks more than 40 million Americans will own stock before the end of the seventies. "And we'll be closer to the idea of a brokerage office providing womb-to-tomb financial coverage for its clients." *Murray Teigh Bloom, "Why Merrill Lynch Is Bullish About Merrill Lynch," The New York Times Magazine, May 21, 1972, p 78*

His principal monument is Britain's National Health Service, still the model of womb-to-tomb medical care. *Michael Demarest, "Books," Review of "Aneurin Bevan: A Biography, Vol. II, 1945-1960" by Michael Foot, Time, Jan. 28, 1974, p K6*

Along with work and community involvement we need "life-cycle education"—a womb-to-tomb activity covering the human life span. *Maggie Kuhn, "New Life for the Elderly: Liberation from 'Ageism'," in The New Old: Struggling for Decent Aging, 1978, p 301*

[1972, from the phrase *from womb to tomb;* cf. *cradle-to-grave* (OEDS 1943)]

▶ Strictly, *womb-to-tomb* medical care includes prenatal care of the mother-to-be as well as monitoring the fetus before its birth.

women's movement or **Women's Movement,** the Women's Liberation Movement.

Because of the women's movement, men must now take seriously inquiries about the female condition, and women must also. In the long run, this may be even more important. Changes in attitude and changes in law go hand in hand. *Norma Rosen, in "American Scholar Forum: Women on Women," The American Scholar, Autumn 1972, p 621*

Before the Women's Movement you either, if you were married, popped pills which your sympathetic shrink prescribed (for anxiety about "frigidity") . . . or, if unmarried, got involved in work and periodically swore off men in a fit of disgust and self-reproach. *Myrna Kostash, "Courting Sappho: If I Only Could, I Surely Would," Maclean's, Nov. 1974, p 19*

By 1979, pornography had done what a million abortions a year had done: it had given the "women's movement" doubts about the dogma that sexual mores are none of the law's business. *George F. Will, "The Illusion of Progress," Newsweek, Nov. 19, 1979, p 59*

[1972] Also called the MOVEMENT.

women's studies, a program of courses dealing with the role of women in history and culture.

In the classroom, many women think less of competing with men than of learning about themselves. "Women's studies" was nearly unknown before 1970; now 78 institutions have complete women's studies programs, and some 2,000 courses are offered on another 500 campuses. *"The New Campus Rebels: Women," Newsweek, Dec. 10, 1973, p 124*

[1972]

Woodstock, *n.* an American rock-music festival where thousands of young people converged in August, 1969. *Often used attributively.*

The film of the Off Broadway smash called "Godspell" is a version of the Gospels designed to be read as show-biz literature by the Woodstock generation. *Penelope Gilliatt, "The Current Cinema," The New Yorker, April 7, 1973, p 134*

The most exciting part of the Second World Black and African Festival of Arts and Culture is . . . the nightly parties and jam sessions taking place at Festac Village, a barracks-style housing development for 22,000 people six miles out of town that has become an African Woodstock. *John Darnton, "African Woodstock Overshadows Festival," The New York Times, Jan. 29, 1977, p 6*

[1970, so called because the festival was originally to be held in *Woodstock,* N.Y.]

Woodstockian, *adj.:* This summer Miami will be swamped with conventioneers grappling with the dilemma of picking a candidate and finding a place in the sun. . . . During that time, Miami will affect a Woodstockian aura. *Barbara Gordon, "Everyone Should Have a Summer of '72," Saturday Review, May 20, 1972, p 24*

Woodstock Nation: High days for the Woodstock Nation, when . . . a generation of youth could skip the work force and join a children's crusade that rejected materialism and set forth to the East, seeking experience, drugs, ultimate truth and gurus in India. *Adam Smith, "East, West," The New York Times Book Review, Dec. 9, 1979, p 12*

woofing or **woofin',** *n. U.S. Slang.* an aggressive or

507

emphatic way of asserting oneself verbally and by stance or gesture, especially to intimidate another person.

Woofing is a style of bragging and boasting about how "bad" one is and is sometimes used by males and females when rapping to each other. This would be a sincere self-image, and the attitude is very emphatic, as "I'm bad and I know I'm bad!" ["Bad" means excellent.] *Benjamin G. Cooke, "Nonverbal Communication Among Afro-Americans," in Rappin' and Stylin' Out, 1972, p 45*

In colleges, woofin' is usually used for personal or group gain. In some rare cases, woofin' has actually been used to procure an undergraduate degree in mostly independent study.

Assuredly, some of the woofin' has been precipitated by Whites trying to hustle Blacks out of goods and materials which have been promised or which are rightfully theirs. *Herbert L. Foster, "Don't Be Put On! Learn About the Games Kids Play," Today's Education, Sept./Oct. 1975, p 54*

[1972, perhaps from *woof* to bark like a dog] Compare the DOZENS, SHUCKING AND JIVING, SIGNIFYING, SOUNDING.

word, *n.* any of the three-letter combinations (such as UGA for the sequence uracil-guanine-adenine) that represent the nucleotide triplets or codons in the genetic code.

The genetic code, which is the same for all living beings from viruses to men, is written in three-letter "words" (codons) made of different combinations of the four chemical building blocks that make DNA. Each codon specifies one of the 20 amino acids that go into the making of protein chains. *Nature-Times News Service, "Science Report: Molecular Biology: Genetic Clues," The Times (London), Nov. 6, 1976, p 16*

In two regions of phiX174, a stretch of DNA codes for two completely different proteins. The overlapping genes begin at different "start" signals so they group nucleotide "letters" into different three-letter "words" and thus code for different amino acid parts of a protein. *Julie Miller, "Biology," Encyclopedia Science Supplement (Grolier) 1979 (1978), p 67*

[1968, probably short for CODE WORD (def. 2)] Compare SYNONYM. See also EXPRESSION, SENTENCE.

word processing, the use of high-speed, computerized typewriters and other office equipment to produce letters, reports, memoranda, etc.

The vague, catch-all term, "word processing," describes the use of a computer's ability to store and process electronic information in composing and producing the paperwork of an office: letters, contracts, reports, statistical tables and the like. *Victor K. McElheny, "Redactron Unit of Burroughs is Applying Powers of the Computer to Processing Words in Offices," The New York Times, Jan. 1, 1977, p 21*

Word processing can already be seen to be at the forefront of the next revolution in the office which can be expected to make an important contribution to improved productivity. The keyboard of the word-processing typewriter, which has already made its appearance in some of the most modern offices, is standard but typing on it produces not only a paper copy but also a magnetic recording which can be automatically searched and edited. *The Times (London), Sept. 12, 1977, p 5*

[1974] *Abbreviation:* WP.

word processor: Word processors call up documents, page by page and line by line, on cathode ray screens for editing. They print out finished versions automatically or send them via telephone lines to distant points. Similar systems are penetrating the newspaper business rapidly. *Victor K. McElheny, The New York Times, Jan. 1, 1977, p 22*

The name "word processor" can be confusing. Basically it is any machine that handles paperwork electronically—at its simplest this embraces typing, data recording, dictating and transcribing, etc. The most straightforward word processor is an automatic typewriter of the type that first appeared in the early 1960s. *"Automation Enters the Office Block," New Scientist, June 15, 1978, p 747*

workaholism, *n.* an uncontrollable need to work constantly.

The story goes that *he* was conservative and inclined to workaholism, while *she* converted from Bendel's to the barricades. *Erica Abeel, New York Magazine, Nov. 4, 1974, p 50*

What causes workaholism? Obvious prerequisites are energy, optimism and drive. Competition, leading toward dominance, is the pattern that usually results. The workaholic's ultimate goal is not money and not even power—it is simply to be No. 1. *Marilyn M. Machlowitz, "Working the 100-Hour Week—and Loving It," The New York Times, Oct. 3, 1976, Sec. 3, p 3*

Many officers have left First Chicago because Abboud has a short fuse—befitting a man who is 5 ft. 6 in. and expects everybody to share his own I-made-it-the-hard-way workaholism. *Time, Aug. 21, 1978, p 58*

[1971, from *workaholic* a person having an uncontrollable need to work + *-ism;* coined by Wayne Oates, American pastoral counselor. See -AHOLIC.]

workaround, *n. Aerospace.* an alternative method available in the event a plan or mechanism fails to work as expected. *Often used attributively.*

Finally, at 12.15 am, Launch Control announced that everyone was happy with the "workaround" solution devised at Huntsville and the count was resumed at 12.25. *Graham Chedd, "Launch of the Last Apollo," New Scientist, Dec. 14, 1972, p 645*

"We may never have dreamed that an oxygen bottle would blow and the sort of damage that one did, but we designed and built the total spacecraft in such a way that there were always 'workarounds'—different ways of getting around a problem—so that we wouldn't be left hanging by our thumbs if something unexpected did crop up." *Don G. Meigham, "How Safe Is Safe Enough?" The New York Times Magazine, June 20, 1976, p 46*

[1972, from the verb phrase *work around* (a problem, etc.)]

worker-director, *n. Especially British.* an employee selected to serve on the board of directors of the company for which he works.

The worker-directors, who will continue to do their own jobs, will participate in a four-tier system of management. On the main board will be the chairman, Sir Brian Morton, five executive directors and the five employee representatives. *Paul Routlege, "State-Owned Shipyard to Get Workers on Board," The Times (London), April 1, 1976, p 1*

In Britain, action was never taken on a 1977 government recommendation to require worker directors in all companies with more than 2,000 employees. *"When Workers Sit on the Company Board," U.S. News and World Report, Nov. 19, 1979, p 85*

[1970]

worker participation or **workers' participation,** a system in which employees take part in the management of the company they work for, as by helping to formulate policies dealing with production and workers' benefits.

Worker participation is a catch-all description of widely varied efforts all over Europe to give employees a greater say in how they do their jobs and how their companies are run. At the extreme, it means wresting all control of industry from the stockholders and turning it over to the workers. *Peter T. Kilborn, "Norway Workers Make Own Rules," The New York Times, Sept. 9, 1976, p 57*

I believe that worker-participation will be accepted as an essential part of the proper management of industry throughout Europe and beyond Europe before very long. *Jack Jones, The Times (London), Sept. 10, 1976, p 4*

When he regained his hold on the nation's political and administrative machinery, Teng slashed program after program initiated by Mao. Worker participation in management of factories was eroding any sense of production discipline; ideological controls were hampering the work of research scientists. *Harold Ellithorpe, "The World," Maclean's, Aug. 8, 1977, p 43*

[1971] Also called COMANAGEMENT, COSUPER-VISION. See MITBESTIMMUNG.

work ethic, a set of values that stresses the virtuous aspects of hard work, diligence, and industry.

From the first, it was understood that a guaranteed income could come about only if it was accompanied by some assurance that the nation was not abandoning what is, in truth, a potent and deeply believed "work ethic." *Daniel P. Moynihan, "Annals of Politics: Income by Right—II," The New Yorker, Jan. 20, 1973, p 72*

Because of these values, which include a religious respect for the work ethic, welfare comes under savage criticism in New Brunswick. Welfare "bums," "freeloaders," and "chiselers" are favorite targets for the writers of letters to the editor. *Alden Nowlan, "Welfare Without Tears," Maclean's, July 1974, p 54*

As the 1970s began, every American institution had been or was going through a period of extreme trial and testing. One institution that seemed in particular peril from these political, economic, and social upheavals was the work ethic, foundation stone of the American industrial system. *A. H. Raskin, "The Job in Your Future," The 1978 World Book Year Book, p 143*

[1968] ► Before the late 1960's, *work ethic* was the set of attitudes of workers toward their work. In the current sense, the term is generally synonymous with *Protestant ethic* and the two phrases are often combined in the *Protestant work ethic.*

work island. See the quotation for the meaning.

Other labor innovations that have been hailed in Germany and Scandinavia . . . include "flextime," whereby workers set their own hours, usually within specified limits, and assembly lines are replaced by "work islands"—autonomous groups of workers assigned to work together on an entire section of a project. *"Labor Is Refocusing on Goals," The New York Times, Jan. 25, 1976, Sec. 3, p 44*

[1976]

workover, *n.* a maintenance procedure on an oil rig to repair or replace dull or fouled equipment by forcing oil back into its underground reservoir and sealing the well.

One of the prime reasons for deciding to recover the platform was that corrosion in the steel tubing of the well system itself had meant that the whole structure needed a "workover"—offshore terminology for a major refit. *John Stansell, "Getting to the Bottom of a North Sea Secret," New Scientist, Dec. 14, 1978, p 842*

[1977, noun use of the verb phrase *work over* to subject to thorough treatment]

work-release, *adj.* of or designed for the part-time release of prisoners to permit them to engage in normal work or continue in their regular jobs.

The defendants . . . will be eligible for "work-release" programs. That means they could report to their offices by day but would have to spend their nights locked up. *"Crime: Jail for Box Bosses?" Time, Dec. 13, 1976, p 65*

[1967]

work-to-contract, *n. British.* a form of job slowdown in which employees refuse to fulfill any tasks except those specified in their contract.

So the question . . . is whether the Government feels able to approve an award to hospital doctors who, by their work-to-contract, are causing delays in admission and limiting the number of patients treated. *John Cunningham, "Doctors Seek Rises of 40 Per Cent," The Manchester Guardian Weekly, April 5, 1975, p 4*

[1970, patterned on WORK-TO-RULE]

work-to-rule, *n. Especially British and Canadian.* a job action marked by vigorous observance and literal interpretation of every regulation for a job. It is often used by workers as a form of protest or to force concessions from management. *Often used attributively.*

Hospital consultants began a work-to-rule on 2 January, in protest against the new contract they had been offered. *H. V. Hodson, "United Kingdom," The Annual Register of World Events in 1975 (1976), p 37*

Following last month's nine-day air strike over the issue, French-speaking controllers in Quebec mounted a two-day work-to-rule campaign. *Janet Mackenzie and Julianne Lebreche, "English Only Spoken Here—With Near-Calamitous Results," Maclean's, July 1976, p 19*

The work-to-rules and go-slows by Spanish air traffic controllers have already led to an admission by the Ministry of Aviation in Madrid that there were "technical difficulties and difficulties in some equipment" at some of the country's civil airports. *Peter Chippindale, The Manchester Guardian Weekly, April 3, 1977, p 6*

[1962, from the verb phrase *work to rule*]

workwear, *n.* **1** clothes made for workers; working clothes.

The replacement of cotton by Terylene workwear was found to reduce considerably the amount of dust which entered the workers' breathing zone. *Margaret Hamilton, New Scientist, Jan. 15, 1970, p 122*

2 a style of clothing fashioned after working clothes.

Blue jeans continued to be the most popular single fashion garment, and denim skirts, coats, tunics and overblouses were introduced, often designed as Chinese 'workwear', a new term introduced to describe loose garments fastened with strings or toggles. *Anne Price, "Fashion," The Annual Register of World Events in 1975 (1976), p 418*

[1970]

wormery, *n.* a place for breeding worms, especially to be sold as fishing bait.

The Manitoba Department of Agriculture has lent Main $10,000 to expand his wormery into a large-scale business with 100 work pits and 7.5 million wriggling workmen. *Rosalie Woloski, Maclean's, Feb. 9, 1976, p 48*

[1976, patterned on *fishery*]

wormhole, *n.* a hypothetical passageway in space connecting a black hole and a white hole.

Perhaps because of a philosophical or psychological reluctance to accept the finality of black holes, some scientists speculate that matter going down these drains may not always be destroyed. On the contrary, under special circumstances the matter might be conducted by a rapidly rotating black hole through space and time via passages dubbed wormholes. It would reemerge in a different part of the universe or perhaps in another universe entirely. *Time, Sept. 4, 1978, p 54*

Particularly appealing to science-fiction writers is the concept of "wormholes," which tunnel through the contorted space-time geometry of black holes into other universes — or emerge into our own universe at some other time and place. If a star went through such a wormhole it might, according to one hypothesis, burst forth far away, in space-time dimensions, radiating intense energy. *Walter Sullivan, Black Holes, 1979, p 197*

[1978, figurative use of the noun meaning the thin burrow of a worm] See EVENT HORIZON, SINGULARITY, WHITE HOLE.

worst-case, *adj.* designed to include or provide for the most unfavorable conditions or circumstances possible.

Another important change in the guidelines would . . . allow experiments currently prohibited, such as the transfer of genes for biosynthesis of potent toxins. Almost all the witnesses favored such a policy because it would allow "worst case" experiments, intended to evaluate whether organisms containing recombinant DNA could actually be harmful. *"Gene Rules: Violation and Revisions," Science News, Dec. 24 and 31, 1977, p 420*

Think about it for a minute: In a limited war, with the wind blowing south, one in every 11 Canadians could be killed or injured. In a worst-case scenario with a stiff breeze driving the fallout on to Canada instead of away, half the population could be lost in a day. *William Lowther, "Russia Is Shifting the Balance of Terror," Maclean's, May 29, 1978, p 22*

San Francisco Mayor George Moscone was studying a worst-case budget: the $84.9 million to operate city buses,

trolleys and cable cars would be more than halved, the street-cleaning fund would drop from $783,000 to $90,000, and the city's human rights commission (scheduled to spend $332,101) would get no money at all. *Time, June 19, 1978, p 14*

Also included in the Sandia study was a "worst case" projection that a massive accident or act of sabotage that succeeded in breaching the cask of a shipment of elements carried by truck in mid-city could afflict more than 3,300 New Yorkers with fatal radiation doses or radiation-induced fatal cancers. (An even worse worst-case projection would involve rail shipments). *Fred C. Shapiro, "Our Local Correspondents," The New Yorker, Nov. 13, 1978, p 146*

[1967, originally used in military planning] Compare BEST-CASE.

WP, abbreviation of WORD PROCESSING.

Although a latecomer in the WP marketplace, Xerox is not holding back on training of its WP customers at the well-equipped facilities in Dallas. *"News Front: Xerox Begins Customer Training Courses," Word Processing World, May-June 1975, p 6*

The basic hardware in WP systems is the typewriter with a memory. Text which is stored on discs, tapes or cards can be reproduced quickly and stored information can easily be edited and revised. Like the development of the computer, WP combines a specific type of technology and an economic requirement for the best use of the technology. *The Times (London), Oct. 2, 1978, p III*

[1974]

wristwrestling, *n.* a variety of Indian wrestling in which the contenders lock right thumbs instead of hands in trying to force down each other's arm.

It seems perfectly natural for a wristwrestling championship to be held in Timmins, wristwrestling being a backwoods barroom sport and Timmins being a backwoods barroom mining town in Northern Ontario. No dazzling footwork here; you put his arm down or he puts yours down. Brawn, pure brawn. Timmins has hosted the World Wristwrestling Championships for eight years. *Martin O'Malley, "Sports," Maclean's, June 12, 1978, p 62*

[1976]

wu shu ('wu: 'ʃu:), the Chinese martial arts.

With a history going back more than 2,000 years, "Wu shu" — meaning "traditional Chinese sports" — was once the pastime of exclusive sects organized into elaborate hierarchies of masters and disciples. *Newsweek, July 15, 1974, p 52*

[1974, from Chinese] See KUNG FU.

X

X, a symbol meaning "not for children; restricted to adults."

If county Board of Legislators Chairman Andrew O'Rourke has his way, Westchester "head shops" will be rated "X"—for adults only. O'Rourke . . . is launching a campaign to either outlaw or restrict to adults the sale of rolling paper, cocaine spoons, and other drug-related paraphernalia. *Bill Falk, Metro (Westchester, N.Y.), May 2, 1979, p A9*

[1970, originally (1950's) applied to motion pictures] See X-RATED.

xan·than ('zæn thən), *n.* or **xanthan gum,** a water-soluble gum made from polysaccharides produced by certain bacteria in sugar solutions. It is used as a thickener and stabilizer especially in the food industry, medicine, and pharmacy.

A new gum called xanthan was developed on a commercial scale in 1974. In the food industry it serves as an emulsion stabilizer in salad dressings and enhances certain starch products. When xanthan is used in gluten-free bread dough, it is possible to enrich the product with soybean protein, thereby greatly increasing the nutritional qualities of the bread. *J. R. Porter, "Microbiology," The Americana Annual 1975, p 382*

A thickener called xanthan gum is being used with detergents to help free oil that clings to underground rock formations and resists recovery by conventional methods. Once injected into a well, the thickener restricts the detergent to where it will do the most good, keeping it from running all over the place. *Advertisement by Mobil Corporation, The New York Times Magazine, Feb. 6, 1977, p 41*

[1970, from *Xanth(omonas campestris)* a species of bacteria cultivated to produce this gum + *-an* (chemical suffix)]

X-C skiing, *U.S. and Canadian.* cross-country skiing; skiing across the countryside.

Appreciated the rundown (Travel Notes, Dec. 12) of spectator-participant events for the cross-country ski enthusiast. Finally, X-C skiing is being appreciated for the "total" sport it has become with multitudes of adherents. *Betsy Palmedo-Thompson, Princeton, N.J., "Cross-Country Skiing," in a Letter to the Editor, The New York Times, Jan. 2, 1977, Sec. 10, p 11*

[1976, *X-C* from *X* (for *cross*) + *C*, abbreviation of *country*] Compare SKI TOURING.

xen·o·bi·ot·ic (ˌzen ou bai'ɑt ik), *n.* a foreign substance capable of harming or affecting a living organism.

Groups of exposed women (smokers) and controls (nonsmokers) were readily available. "Nicotine can be a model for other xenobiotics—for a broad spectrum of foreign substances," Castagnoli explains. In other experiments, Petrakis and colleagues observed barbiturates and foreign fatty acids secreted into breast fluids. *Science News, Jan. 21, 1978, p 39*

[1972, from *xeno-* foreign + *-biotic* relating to life]

xenocurrency, *n.* currency circulating outside its country of origin.

International bankers are adding a new word to their jargon: "xenocurrency." West German Chancellor Helmut Schmidt and U.S. Treasury Secretary G. William Miller jointly proposed the term—"xeno" comes from the Greek for "foreign"—to supplant "Eurodollars" and "Eurocurrency." . . . Schmidt and Miller made a point of referring to "xenocurrency" markets [and] argued that Eurodollars and Eurocurrency are misnomers when applied to the billions of dollars and marks now circulating in Hong Kong, Singapore, the Bahamas and other non-European money markets. *"Periscope: Coining a New Word for Money," Newsweek, Oct. 15, 1979, p 37*

[1979, from *xeno-* foreign + *currency*] See ASIADOLLAR.

xen·o·ge·ne·ic (ˌzen ou dʒə'ni: ik), *adj.* (of transplanted tissues) deriving from an organism of a different species.

We strongly suggest that this assay can be used as an accurate *in vivo* test to detect immunological cross-reactivity between common antigens of a variety of tumour and foetal-cell inocula, even in xenogeneic systems, because syngeneic foetal liver cells are always the test-cell dose. *F. A. Salinas, et al., Oak Ridge, Tenn., "Letters to Nature: Immunological Cross-Reactivity of Antigens Common to Tumour and Foetal Cells," Nature, Nov. 3, 1972, p 42*

The survival of these grafts, as compared with similar grafts on females inoculated with female rat lymph node cells, indicated whether the xenogeneic male cell inoculum had sensitized the recipients with respect to H-Y antigen. *Willys K. Silvers and Sen-Liang Yang, "Male Specific Antigen: Homology in Mice and Rats," Science, Aug. 10, 1973, p 571*

[1972, from *xeno-* foreign + *-geneic*, as in *syngeneic* of the same origin] Compare ALLOGENEIC.

xerography, *n.* a xerographic process used in medicine for producing an image of internal parts of the body on a sheet of opaque, plastic-coated paper.

Simple X-ray procedures are often helpful in finding breast cancer. So is a new technique called xerography, which uses a charged electric plate and a photoelectric system to build an image on paper. *Irwin J. Polk, "Medicine," The Americana Annual 1975, p 371*

[1968, extended sense of the term for a dry photographic printing process (1948)]

xeroradiograph, *v.t.* to make an X-ray picture of by using an electrically charged metal plate; to photograph or record by means of xeroradiography.

After X-raying and xeroradiographing the mummy, the pathologists cut the stiff wrapping lengthwise, to open up the specimen like a violin case. *Peter Gwynne, "New York View: Doctors Learn from Mummies," New Scientist, April 19, 1973, p 169*

[1973, verb use of the noun (1957) meaning an X-ray picture made by *xeroradiography* (1954)]

X-o·gen ('ek sə dʒən), *n.* an interstellar molecule detected through radio emissions from several galactic sources.

X-ogen was first noticed about three years ago. The latest report on the subject . . . shows that it is found in at least eight locations in the sky: W3(OH), Orion, Sagittarius A, W51, W3(companion), NGC 2024, NGC 6334N and K3-50. *Dietrick E. Thomsen, "Astronomy's Mystery Molecule," Science News, April 27, 1973, p 258*

Chemists at Monash University in Melbourne, Australia, check the microwave spectrum of a compound they produced that helped to identify the spectrum of "X-ogen" – a strange interstellar molecule that could not be found in spectral catalogs. The peaks on the left that matched the interstellar spectrum were produced by the highly reactive HNC radical, which survives uncombined on earth for only a fraction of a second. *Picture legend, "Astronomy," The World Book Science Annual 1978 (1977), p 242*

[1970, coined by the American astronomers David Buhl and Lewis Snyder from *X* for unknown (from the uncertainty of its structure until 1976) + *-ogen* as in *hydrogen* and *nitrogen*] Compare Y-OGEN.

X-rated, *adj.* **1a** that is sexually explicit or prurient.

"Phaedra" (1962), which has also been revived, is still being taken more seriously than it deserves to be. It's Graham's X-rated treatment of Euripides; Noguchi provided the peep-show scenery. *Arlene Croce, "Dancing," The New Yorker, June 13, 1977, p 104*

In production, the saddening tendency of past years continued, with renewed efforts to goad the lagging cinemagoer with sexual stimulation through screen voyeurism. The mass production of indifferent or plainly bad X-rated films persisted, notably in Japan, West Germany, Italy and America. *Roger Manvell, "The Cinema," The Annual Register of World Events in 1973 (1974), p 436*

b featuring nude performers or performances, as in a burlesque show.

BUMP AND GRIND REVUE: The Colonial Tavern . . . Hot Tamale and her breathtaking Fire Dance accompanied by X-rated live shows. Exotic dancers perform noon to 1 a.m. *Advertisement in the Globe and Mail (Toronto), March 29, 1979, p 16*

2 vulgar; obscene.

His communicators at the same time kept insisting improbably that the transcripts actually clear the President of any crime more grievous than using X-rated language and thinking unsavory thoughts. *Newsweek, May 20, 1974, p 23*

[1970, from the symbol *X*, used in the United States and Great Britain since the 1950's to rate motion pictures dealing with subjects or using language suitable only for adults] Compare ADULT.

X-ray burst, one of the periodic bursts emitted by an X-ray burster.

The cooperative observations are being arranged as a result of the first detection of light bursts coincident with X-ray bursts by the 150-centimeter telescope at the Cerro Tololo Inter-American Observatory in Chile on June 2. The source was MXB1735-44. Two optical bursts were recorded. There are no X-ray data for the time of the first burst, but SAS 3 recorded an X-ray burst coincident with the second. *Science News, June 24, 1978, p 405*

[1976] Compare GAMMA-RAY BURST.

X-ray burster, a celestial body that is the source of powerful periodic bursts of X rays.

The new X-ray bursters, as they are being colloquially called, flare up and die again in only a few seconds, which has so far made them more difficult to detect. "X-ray bursts are going to be the big story of 1976," predicted Leicester University's Professor Ken Pounds. *Ian Ridpath, "Monitor: New X-ray Bursts Sources Discovered," New Scientist, March 25, 1976, p 676*

More recently the X-ray telescopes aboard satellites have discovered more than 30 X-ray "bursters": a special kind of X-ray star that emits brief but brilliant bursts of X rays lasting up to several seconds. In some cases the bursts repeat at fairly regular intervals measured in hours or days. *George W. Clark, "X-Ray Stars in Globular Clusters," Scientific American, Oct. 1977, p 42*

[1976] Also shortened to BURSTER.

X-ray laser, a device similar in function to a laser, which amplifies X-rays by stimulated emission to produce a beam of great penetrating power.

A carbon-dioxide laser scalpel among the exhibits at the Science Museum; lasers as playing heads for video discs are on the horizon; X-ray lasers in the future will make possible true X-ray holograms. *Kenneth Owen, The Times (London), Nov. 4, 1977, p 21*

During the year development of an X-ray laser, which would have particular application to crystallography and medical holography, progressed along two separate routes. *S. B. Palmer, "Physics," Britannica Book of the Year 1978, p 584*

[1967] Compare GAMMA-RAY LASER.

Y

Y, symbol for UPSILON.

Designated upsilon (Y), the new particle points to the existence of a fifth quark, one more massive than any of the others. . . . Its existence appears to be a mixed blessing for the quark hypothesis. *Leon M. Lederman, "The Upsilon Particle," Scientific American, Oct. 1978, p 22*

[1977, from the Greek letter upsilon]

yachtie₁ *n. Informal.* a person who owns or sails a boat, especially a yacht.

"Dunnie's a yachtie, he lives up on the cliff, and he's a rich guy who hasn't worked a day in his life," says a restaurant owner. "He was the wrong one to sell us a bill of goods." *J. Anthony Lukas, "The Developers Are Coming, The Developers Are Coming," Saturday Review, Oct. 21, 1972, p 62*

Less familiar, because less conspicuous, are the ones who do it by sea — shoals of them, from Mr Saunders's account, bumming around the world in little boats. There is even a word for them: yachties. *Denis Thomas, "Yachties," Review of "The Walkabouts" by Mike Saunders, The Listener, Feb. 13, 1975, p 221*

[1972, from *yacht* + *-ie* (diminutive suffix)]

yak·ow ('yæk au), *n.* any of a breed of beef cattle developed in Great Britain by crossbreeding yaks and Highland cows.

Roast Yakow could be Britain's answer to American beefalo — offering cheaper, leaner Sunday joints. But whereas the Beefalo (a cross between the American Buffalo and a beef cow) has been bred to produce meat from warm grassland, the Yakow should be better adapted to our cool wet higher land. *Graham Rose, "Enter the Yakow," The Sunday Times (London), Nov. 23, 1975, p 15*

Baby Yakow, a cross between a yak and a Highland cow, was bred to flourish in the uplands of Great Britain and eventually provide inexpensive meat to residents of the U.K. *Picture legend, "Agriculture," 1978 Britannica Yearbook of Science and the Future (1977), p 315*

[1975, blend of *yak* and *cow*]

ya·ku·za ('ya: ku‚za:), *n. sing.* or *pl.* a Japanese hoodlum or gangster.

The yakuza are Japanese mobsters, and one of the items in their "code" is that you can show penitence for an offense against the mob chieftain by slicing off your little finger and presenting it to him. Robert Mitchum plays an American private eye who goes to Japan to rescue an American girl kidnapped by yakuza; he enlists the aid of a "retired" yakuza, a master-teacher of swordsmanship (Takakura Ken), and they fight side by side, the gun and the sword. *"Goings On About Town," The New Yorker, Feb. 23, 1976, p 25*

[1970, from Japanese, literally, good-for-nothing] Compare YAMAGUCHI-GUMI.

Ya·ma·gu·chi-gu·mi (‚ya: mɑ:'gu: tʃi:'gu: mi:), *n.* a large organization of criminals in Japan.

Yamaguchi-gumi is a veritable army of 10,000 men. Under the command of Japan's top mobster, Kazuo Taoka, 60, police say that Yamaguchi-gumi has become a criminal conglomerate that controls more than 50 corporations, ranging from restaurants and bars to trucking companies and talent agencies. *"Japan: The Mob Muscles In," Time, Feb. 26, 1973, p 31*

"We are linked by a spiritual bond," says Oda, unabashedly reiterating the precept of public and personal honor inculcated among the Yamaguchi's 11,000 members, unquestionably the largest, most tightly knit band of gamblers, extortionists, pimps and general hoodlums-about-town in modern times. *Donald Kirk, "Crime, Politics and Finger Chopping," The New York Times Magazine, Dec. 12, 1976, p 61*

[1973, from Japanese, literally, Yamaguchi-gang, from Harukichi *Yamaguchi*, the organization's original leader + *-gumi* gang] Also, **Yamaguchi.** Compare YAKUZA.

Ya·no·ma·ma (‚ya: nou mɑ:'mɑ:) or **Ya·no·ma·mo** (‚ya: nou mɑ:'mou), *n.* a member of a primitive, warlike people of northern Brazil and southern Venezuela, who have been the subject of numerous studies since contact was established with them in the late 1960's. *Often used attributively.*

As the Yanomama population grew and new villages were founded, the blood protein differences and linguistic differences between Yanomama groups grew at about the same rate, indicating that biological and cultural change rates correspond closely. *Fred Plog, "Anthropology," The 1975 World Book Year Book, p 197*

Among the Yanomamo tribes population is controlled by warfare, feuding and infanticide. *"Science Report," The Times (London), Nov. 1, 1972, p 10*

[1967] Compare ACHÉ and TASADAY.

yard sale, *U.S.* a sale of old or used household belongings, held on the front or back yard or lawn of a house.

A man never realizes how ruthless a wife can be until she holds a yard sale. Nothing is sacred. A set of Hardy Boys in mint condition, a Turkish water pipe, a rowing machine. . . . She said the whole point of a yard sale was to get rid of stuff. *Will Stanton, "At Yard Sales, Everything Goes," The Reader's Digest, May 1979, p 150*

[1976] Compare GARAGE SALE.

YAVIS, *n. U.S.* acronym for *Young, Attractive, Verbal, Intelligent, and Successful.*

From its inception, psychoanalysis has been plagued by an elitist image. . . . Analysts say that the treatment works

513

yecch

best for the YAVIS. *"Behavior: Psychiatry on the Couch," Time, April 2, 1979, p 79*

[1976]

yecch (yək), *interj. Especially U.S. Slang.* an exclamation of strong distaste or disgust.

"And lunches. We have terrible lunches. Yecch!" *"Education: New Faces for Old," Time, Feb. 14, 1972, p 45*

"You ask a guy today how the economy will be in three weeks and he'll say 'Yecch!' " a Ford official said last week. *Tom Nicholson, et al., "Business and Finance: Selling Cars Without Rebates," Newsweek, March 24, 1975, p 72*

Laughingly, she offers a snatch of typical dinnertime family conversation: "I would say things like, 'Oh, today I saw a man who had 10 noses and, yech, he was really ugly and he was throwing up all over the place,' and my parents would say, 'Not at the table, Phoebe' . . ." *Phoebe Snow, quoted by Stephen E. Rubin, "Forecast: SNOW," The New York Times Magazine, Feb. 15, 1976, p 47*

[1972, perhaps imitative of the sound of retching] Also spelled YUCK.

yecch·y ('yək i:), *adj. Especially U.S. Slang.* variant of YUCKY.

The disgusted "yecchy," with its comic-strip origins, fades, but the equally disgusted *gross* (ugly, objectionable, and sometimes used admiringly) shows staying power. *William Safire, "Vogue Words Are Trific, Right?" The New York Times Magazine, March 21, 1976, p 111*

[1973]

yellow card, *Soccer.* a card of a yellow color raised by a referee as a warning to a player who has violated a rule.

Den Haag were, understandably, bitterly disappointed and their frustration was shown in the cautions administered to Mansveld for arguing and Kila for a foul on Robson. Jennings was also shown the yellow card, for kicking the ball away after yet another offside decision. *Norman de Mesquita, The Times (London), March 18, 1976, p 19*

[1976]

yellow flu, *U.S.* an organized absence of students from schools to which they are bused, on the pretext of sickness but actually as a protest against compulsory BUSING.

The Community had reacted strongly to an earlier plan which required busing between the suburbs and the central city. . . . In an allusion to the buses that transport students, two groups called for an epidemic of "yellow flu," but absenteeism was only slightly greater last week than what is considered normal for the first week of a new school term. *Caroline Rand Herron and R. V. Denenberg, "The Nation: In Summary," The New York Times, Feb. 1, 1976, Sec. 4, p 2*

[1976, so called from the yellow color of school buses] Compare BLUE FLU.

Yellow Pages, *U.S.* a classified directory of businesses, services, professions, or products in any field.

A "Yellow Pages" of technology is how Control Data Corp. describes Technotec, its computer-based technology-exchange service. Users interested in a particular technology need only search, for an average charge of $8 or $10, the listings stored in a $1 billion computer network via a Telex, . . . telephone or computer-terminal connection. *Science News, Sept. 3, 1977, p 152*

[1966, transferred sense of the popular term for the classified directory of a telephone book, usually printed on pages of a yellow color]

Yerkish, *n.* an artificial language in which geometric symbols represent words, designed for communication between chimpanzees and humans. *Also used attributively.*

In order to teach Lana to communicate, a special language, Yerkish, had to be designed. It is made up of nine simple geometric figures that can be superimposed on each other to form lexigrams that stand for various concepts. The lexigrams are displayed on a typewriter-like computer keyboard that Lana has learned to use to type out grammatically correct requests for food and entertainment. A possible 256 lexigrams can be handled by the present computer system. *Robert J. Trotter, "I Talk to the Animals," Science News, June 2, 1973, p 360*

A parrot that asks for a cracker is only mimicking a human or another parrot. But a chimpanzee who can "speak" in Ameslan (American sign language) or Yerkish by striking combinations on a keyboard of color-coded symbols seems to be creating syntax, a property of human language. It is not the voice but the process that is critical. *"Books: Return to the Planet of the Apes," Review of "Look Who's Talking!" by Emily Hahn, Time, June 26, 1978, p 75*

[1973, coined by the American psychologist Duane M. Rumbaugh from *Yerkes* Regional Primate Center, Georgia (named after Robert M. Yerkes, 1876-1956, American primatologist), where the language was devised and applied + *-ish*, as in *English*]

yer·sin·i·o·sis (yər,sin i:'o sis), *n.* an intestinal disease with symptoms resembling those of appendicitis, caused by a highly contagious type of bacteria.

Surgeons also performed three or four emergency appendectomies on children at City Hospital in nearby Rome, according to a hospital pathologist who declined to be identified. He said the hospital's laboratory later isolated yersiniosis bacteria in the patients' stools. *"12 Undergo Appendicitis Operation for Ailment Calling for Antibiotics," The New York Times, Oct. 21, 1976, p 35*

[1976, from New Latin *Yersinia*, the genus name of the bacteria (from Alexandre *Yersin*, 1863-1943, Swiss bacteriologist) + *-osis* diseased condition]

Yinglish, *n.* English containing many Yiddish words and expressions.

Relying not on my memory alone (that is, my memory of grandparents' and parents' conversations in English, Yiddish, and Yinglish) but also on Leo Rosten's *The Joys of Yiddish*, I present the following old joke as explanation: "The schlemozzle is the guy who the schlemiel spills the soup on." *Frima Botnick Braswell, Storrs, Conn., in a Letter to the Editor, Saturday Review, Sept. 9, 1972, p 27*

[1967, blend of *Yiddish* and *English*]

► This word was popularized by the American writer Leo Rosten in his book *The Joys of Yiddish* (1968), where he used it primarily to designate Yiddish words, such as *bagel* and *chutzpah*, that have become part of colloquial English. In the sense of "a Yiddish-English mixture" the term was occasionally used in the 1950's, as in the title of an article by H. J. Gans in *American Quarterly,* 21 (1953): "The 'Yinglish' Music of Mickey Katz." The coinage of this word apparently preceded the parallel terms *Spanglish, Japlish,* and *Hinglish,* all hybrids of English with another language.

Y·o·gen ('waɪ ə dʒən), *n.* an unidentified interstellar molecule detected through radio emission in the region of the constellation Sagittarius.

The $H^{13}C^{16}O^+$ line in Sagittarius B2 is contaminated with yet another new molecule nearly overlapping in frequency. ... Thus no sooner is the X-ogen mystery laid to rest than Y-ogen springs up to fox radio astronomers. Will Y-ogen prove as elusive? *"Monitor: Elusive Interstellar Molecule Tracked Down at Last," New Scientist, Oct. 28, 1976, p 212*

[1976, patterned on X-OGEN]

yo·ko·zu·na (,you kə'zu: nə), *n.* a grand champion sumo wrestler; a wrestler of the highest rank in sumo.

To be yokozuna in Japan is to be a Babe Ruth or Willie Mays, and here, as almost everywhere, fame brings fortune. *Richard Halloran, "Notes of a Sumo Wrestling Fan," The New York Times, Jan. 6, 1974, Sec. 10, p 1*

[1966, from Japanese] Compare OZEKI. See also BASHO.

yor·dim (yɔr'di:m), *n.pl.* Israeli citizens who emigrate to another country, especially the United States.

Those who stay call those who leave *yordim* (from the Hebrew verb meaning to descend) and look down on them as deserters. ... Some of the *yordim* reply that they have left for one reason only: greater opportunity. *"Israel: A Troubling Reverse Exodus," Time, Jan. 12, 1976, p 24*

[1966, from Hebrew, literally, those who descend, patterned on *olim* immigrants to Israel, (literally) those who ascend] Compare CHOZRIM.

youthcult, *n.* the values and mores of youth viewed as a distinctive culture. *Often used attributively.*

Clifford Adelman, who has taught at CCNY and Yale, "wished to verify the extent to which the equation of the youthcult with the multifarious spirits of counter culture and counter politics was justified." *Norman Schreiber, Review of "Generations: A Collage on Youthcult" by Clifford Adelman, Saturday Review, Sept. 2, 1972, p 58*

Given the age of most people attending movies this silly, youthcult corruption of the story of Francis of Assisi, with songs by Donovan, may prove to be as likeable with the young as *Lost Horizon* is with the geriatric set. *John Hofsess, "Films," Review of "Brother Sun, Sister Moon," Maclean's, June 1973, p 90*

[1968, contraction of *youth culture* on the pattern of *masscult, midcult* (1960)]

YSO, abbreviation of *young stellar object*, a protostar, especially a faint star with a high degree of irregularity in its emission spectrum.

The most logical regions to search for YSOs were the dark interstellar clouds. Before the late 1960s, searches of stellar birthplaces could only be made at optical wavelengths. Three major classes of YSOs were isolated from such searches. *Stephen E. Strom, "The Formation of Stars," 1977 Britannica Yearbook of Science and the Future (1976), p 78*

[1976]

yuck or **yuk,** *interj. Especially U.S. Slang.* variant of YECCH.

In one seminar I attended, a personnel-placement specialist ... tried to demonstrate how perspectives have to be broadened by asking one young woman in the audience how she would react to the name of the Chase Manhattan Bank. "You'd say it sounds awful, wouldn't you?" he said. "Yuck! Who wants to work in a bank!" *Calvin Trillin, "U.S. Journal: Manhattan," The New Yorker, March 7, 1977, p 90*

Expand your thinking about meats. Too many people say 'yuk' to liver because they have never tasted it cooked well. Kidneys and liver combine beautifully with wine and spices. *Meredith Chaplin, "Save that Vitamin Before you Cook!" New York Post, Jan. 23, 1979, p 24*

[1972]

yucky or **yukky,** *adj. Especially U.S. Slang.* disgusting; repugnant; repulsive.

"Mmmm," purred an ecstatic Zero Mostel, dipping his tongue into a lemon meringue pie topped with whipped cream. Then his face congealed in horror: "I never eat this glop," he growled. Picky-Eater Mostel was not indulging a fad: he was acting first "yummy" and then "yucky" for Poet/Novelist George Mendoza's *The Sesame Street Book of Opposites*, a picture book. *"People," Time, Jan. 21, 1974, p 42*

"It's a nice street, there's a good community spirit and I like the mixture of old and new residents. But from an architectural point of view, it's yukky." *Maureen Walker, "Our Street," The Sunday Times (London), March 30, 1975, p 41*

About all Desiree can bring herself to say about her diabetes is that the urine tests are "yukky." *William Stockton, "The Healy Sisters—Clues to Diabetes," The New York Times Magazine, June 12, 1977, p 103*

[1972] Also spelled YECCHY.

yu·sho ('yu: ʃou), *n.* a diseased condition caused by ingestion of polychlorinated biphenyl (PCB), characterized by skin eruptions, swollen eyelids, swelling of joints, palsy, etc. *Often used attributively.*

Even today, almost nine years after eating tiny quantities of PCB's—and long after all traces have passed from their bodies—the symptoms of many *Yusho* victims persist. Recently, a Japanese researcher told a cancer conference at Cold Spring Harbor that the incidence of liver cancer among Yusho patients now appears to be as high as 15 times the normal rate. *Peter Hellman, "For the Hudson Bad News and Good," The New York Times Magazine, Oct. 24, 1976, p 26*

[1973, from Japanese *yushō*, literally, oil disease (from *yu* oil + *shō* disease), so called from its occurrence in Japan in 1968 among thousands of people who consumed rice oil that had been accidentally contaminated with PCB]

Z

zai·kai ('zɑi,kɑi), *n.* commercial groups or financial circles of Japan.

Only now, as industry and business come to be seen as major suspects for rocketing prices and rampant pollution, has a wider spectrum of Japanese begun to scrutinize the *zaikai* and how it works. *The Times (London), July 10, 1973, p IX*

The party, moreover, is receiving the open support of the great zaikai (conglomerates) for the first time. Some firms, including Mitsubishi, Hitachi and Toyota, are "sponsoring" their own candidates. *Time, July 8, 1974, p 27*

Some top *zaikai* (business community) leaders have sought to explain Lockheed not as a product of a corrupt system but as an aberration caused by overly ambitious, vulgar and greedy men. *Jerome Alan Cohen, "Japan's Watergate: Made in U.S.A.," The New York Times Magazine, Nov. 21, 1976, p 112*

[1970, from Japanese, from *zai* money, wealth + *-kai* community, world, domain]

Zam·bo·ni (zæm'bou ni:), *n.* the trademark for a small tractorlike vehicle used to smooth the surface of ice-skating or ice-hockey rinks.

The basketball court, the Zamboni ice-making machine and other gear normally stored in the building, will be taken out, and, according to Deputy Mayor Stanley M. Friedman, will be stored free in city warehouses. *Maurice Carroll, "After Circus With Elephants, Garden Will Get One With Donkeys," The New York Times, Feb. 16, 1976, p 30*

—*v.t.* to smooth (ice) with such a vehicle.

At the conclusion of each skating session, a crew of a half-dozen city employees—all of them skating guards at Lasker—take to the ice and skim the worn surface with broad-bladed shovels.... Following that, the ice receives a light spray of hot water, which leaves the surface almost as slick as if it had been mechanically Zambonied. *"The Talk of the Town," The New Yorker, Feb. 6, 1978, p 25*

[1976, from the name of its inventor]

ZANU ('zɑ: nu:), *n.* acronym for *Zimbabwe African National Union*, a black nationalist guerrilla organization formed in Zimbabwe (Rhodesia) in 1963.

Serious problems developed as a result between the estimated 12,000 ZANU guerrillas and the local population, who often were forced to yield their crops and cattle to the insurgents. The Mozambique peasantry made little secret of their distaste for ZANU, a feeling which was reflected by several Frelimo officials who also had a poor opinion of the discipline and politicisation of their guerrilla guests. *The Manchester Guardian Weekly, Jan. 1, 1979, p 11*

[1964] Compare ZAPU. See also PATRIOTIC FRONT.

Za·pa·ta mustache (zə'pæ tə), a mustache that slants sharply down on each side.

Lip gloss, hair spray, three-tone streaks, cocoa-butter tans, insecure Zapata mustaches and wine red crushed velvet tuxedos: the women looked like tennis club matrons and their escorts like croupiers. *Robert Hughes, "The Day for Night Stars," Time, April 12, 1976, p 61*

There were now several storyboards in the room, presided over by a string bean of a man with a Zapata mustache. *John Culhane, "The Old Disney Magic," The New York Times Magazine, Aug. 1, 1976, p 36*

[1968, named after the Mexican revolutionist Emiliano *Zapata, c*1880-1919, probably from his portrayal in the motion picture *Viva Zapata!* (1952) by the American actor Marlon Brando]

zapper, *n. U.S.* **1** a device for directing microwave or other radiation against a target, especially insects, weeds, and other pests.

One particularly promising application, making use of small portable zappers, is for greenhouses and other horticultural enterprises. *"Science and the Citizen: Zap!" Scientific American, Sept. 1973, p 74*

Although various alternatives are promising, there is no magic 'insect zapper' . . . to replace chemical poisons in the near future. *Colin Norman, "Alternative Technologies Urged in Pesticide Report," Nature, Feb. 12, 1976, p 441*

2 *Figurative use.* **a** a forceful attacker or critic.

The [Alice Cooper] group was so weird that it naturally came to the attention of that master zapper of the Establishment Frank Zappa, who released Alice's first LP (*Pretties for You*) on his own Straight label. *"Show Business," Time, May 28, 1973, p 83*

b a forceful attack or criticism.

He [Mr. Rockefeller] titillated his audience with such zappers as: "Today, New York City has neither an effective, citywide, oldline political organization . . . nor does it have true community or neighborhood elective government with the power to be either responsive to the people or accountable to them in meeting their needs." *William E. Farrell, The New York Times, Jan. 23, 1972, Sec. 4, p 3*

[1972, from *zap* attack, kill + *-er*]

zap pit, a microscopic depression on the surface of lunar rocks, caused by the impact of micrometeorites, particles of cosmic dust, etc.

Measurements of micrometeorite impact pits ("zap" pits) on surfaces dated by particle track techniques have led to the suggestion that the present flux of micrometeorites is about tenfold higher than the average value during the last several million years. *Robert M. Walker, "Particle Track Etching," McGraw-Hill Yearbook of Science and Technology 1974, p 327*

[1973, from *zap* interjection used to indicate a sudden blow or impact]

zappy, *adj. Informal.* full of vitality; forceful; zippy.

The style is De Vries's customarily zappy, pun-a-minute stuff. *Valentine Cunningham, "Books: Zappy," Review of "Forever Painting" by Peter de Vries, The Listener, Sept. 13, 1973, p 352*

The method: Zappy brochures, massive repetitive mailings, fund-raising kaffeeklatches. *Sandra Peredo, Maclean's, Jan. 10, 1977, p 54*

[1973, from *zap* force, vitality + *-y* (adj. suffix)]

ZAPU ('zɑ: pu:), *n.* acronym for *Zimbabwe African People's Union,* a black nationalist guerrilla organization formed in Zimbabwe (Rhodesia) in 1961.

The slogans shouted at the meeting described what is on the minds of ZAPU officials and all nationalist politicians these days. First the speaker shouts, "Z," and the thunderous reply is "Zimbabwe," the nationalist name for Rhodesia. Next, he cries out, "ZAPU," and the refrain is Puza, a rearrangement of the group's initials. Finally, the climax comes: "Nkomo," bellows the speaker. "P-O-W-E-R," roars back the crowd. *David B. Ottaway, "The Twilight of Rhodesia," The Manchester Guardian Weekly (The Washington Post section), July 30, 1978, p 17*

[1961] Compare ZANU. See also PATRIOTIC FRONT.

za·zen ('zɑ:,zen), *n.* meditation as practiced in Zen Buddhism, especially mystical contemplation of one's navel.

During *zazen,* the period for "just sitting," brown-robed members of the *zendo* and newcomers in street clothes sit on the cushions in a full lotus position—right foot on left thigh, left foot on right thigh, knees touching cushion—if possible. Otherwise they sit in some only slightly less taxing Zen position or approximation thereof. *Lindsay Miller, "The American Way of Zen," New York Post, June 12, 1976, p 23*

[1964, from Japanese, literally, sitting Zen] Compare SESSHIN.

ZBB or **Z.B.B.,** abbreviation of ZERO-BASED BUDGETING.

ZBB is just the latest of many management science ideas to sweep through business and government. Perhaps their ultimate value is that in the name of novelty they prod organizations to do what common sense would dictate anyway. *Roberta Walker, Maclean's, May 30, 1977, p 51*

Z.B.B., as it is widely known, calls for the justification of all spending in relation to priorities and has already come into use at more than 100 companies. *Robert J. Cole, "Management," The New York Times, Aug. 27, 1976, p D1*

[1976]

Z disk or **Z disc,** a thin, dark disk of fibrous protein that passes through striated muscle fiber and marks the boundaries of contiguous contractile units.

Skeletal muscles contract by way of thick protein rods sliding between thin rods. The muscle is given strength, and its speed of contraction increased, by intermittent cross-walls known as Z discs. These appear as narrow stripes under the microscope—one reason why skeletal muscle is often called "striped" muscle. But because of those Z-discs, contraction is limited; the contracted length of a skeletal muscle is only 40 per cent of the extended length. *"How a Chameleon Tucks Away Its Tongue," New Scientist, May 31, 1973, p 533*

[1972, translation of German *Z-Scheibe,* abbreviated form of *Zwischenscheibe* intermediate disk]

ze·a·tin ('zi: ə tin), *n.* a naturally occurring plant hormone that stimulates cell division (cytokinin), originally isolated from young maize kernels.

Zeatin, dihydrozeatin (zeatin's counterpart with the saturated double bond) and the ribosides of these compounds have been isolated from extracts of plant tissues. *J. P. Helgeson and C. D. Upper, "Plant Hormone," McGraw-Hill Yearbook of Science and Technology 1970, p 302*

[1964, coined by D. S. Letham, researcher for the New Zealand Department of Scientific and Industrial Research, from New Latin *Zea (mays)* the maize plant + English kine*tin* a synthetic type of cytokinin]

zebra, *n. U.S. Slang.* a referee, linesman, or other official in a football game.

This year's Super Bowl zebras will, as always, be an all-star cast, chosen by N.F.L. [National Football League] Supervisor of Officials Art McNally and his staff after watching game films and grading performances. *"Now for the Zebras . . . ," Time, Jan. 16, 1978, p ,70*

[1978, from the striped shirts worn by officials]

ze·donk ('zi:,dɑŋk or 'zi:,dɔŋk), *n.* the offspring of a male zebra and a female donkey.

Melbourne, Australia—A local donkey breeding farm claims to have mated a zebra with a donkey and produced a zedonk named Zarebba. . . . Mrs. Finnigan said she knows of only three zedonks in the world, two in England and one in Canada. "The two in England don't have the same markings and look more like donkeys," she said. *"Aussie Zedonk Is Fair Dinkum," New York Post, Sept. 3, 1976, p 4*

[1971, from *zebra* + *donk*ey]

ZEG or **Z.E.G.,** abbreviation of ZERO ECONOMIC GROWTH.

A third view is that there is very little relationship between Z.P.G. [zero population growth] and Z.E.G. Sociologist Lincoln Day believes that "there is nothing in a stationary population itself that would inevitably be productive of any particular economic change or condition." *Time, Sept. 16, 1974, p 63*

[1972]

zek, *n.* an inmate of a Soviet prison or forced labor camp.

In a system based on mistrust and espionage, they . . . intrigued among themselves, but were united against the rabble. The newly arrived zek soon learned, as in an army, to hide his skills and watch his chance. *New Statesman, Dec. 5, 1975, p 716*

And didn't his author work gratefully too in the same *sharashka,* or Island of Paradise, as the zeks called these "soft" research camps, and admit, in Gulag II, to a common guilt in thus aiding the system? *W. L. Webb, Review of "No Jail Without Thought" by Lev Kopelev, The Manchester Guardian Weekly, June 26, 1977, p 22*

A web of concentration camps had developed around Rubtsovsk, and shifts of prisoners, or *zeks,* as the Russians called them, were trucked in to keep the industries going 24 hours a day. *John Barron, "MiG Pilot," The Reader's Digest, Jan. 1980, p 192*

[1964, from Russian prison slang, probably from the pronunciation of *z/k,* abbreviation of Russian *zaklyuchennyi* prisoner; popularized by the Russian author Aleksandr Solzhenitsyn, born 1918] See GULAG.

zendo, *n.* a Zen Buddhist center for meditation and study.

We gather in silence outside the zendo and do our best, with various forms of yoga and calisthenics, to stretch out our backs and legs. *Lawrence Shainberg, "The Violence of 'Just Sitting'," The New York Times Magazine, Oct. 10, 1976, p 64*

[1968, from Japanese *zendō*] See ZAZEN.

zero-based budgeting or **zero-base budgeting,** *U.S. and Canadian.* a method of preparing a budget by reviewing the basis of all expenditures of a department, agency, etc., rather than calculating the necessary percentage of increase or decrease in spending from the budget of the previous year.

Brown . . . makes fun of Carter's suggestions for reorganizing the executive branch and proceeding on zero-based budgeting—requiring each agency to defend its budget from scratch, rather than its increments—as solutions to the problems of government. *Elizabeth Drew, "A Reporter in Washington, D.C.," The New Yorker, Sept. 13, 1976, p 68*

Broadly, the burden of Joe Clark's message is that the heady days of strong central direction and mystery on the Rideau are over. He has borrowed a page from Jimmy Carter's playbook—along with zero-based budgeting—and mounted a thinly veiled anti-Ottawa campaign. *Robert Lewis, Maclean's, Oct. 30, 1978, p 22*

In Georgia Mr. McIntyre pushed zero-base budgeting, a tougher justification process for money than the budget office is now applying to the more than 100 Federal agencies. *Clyde H. Farnsworth, "The Budget Office Carries On," The New York Times, Sept. 7, 1977, p 48*

[1976 for *zero-based*; 1970 for *zero-base*] *Abbreviation:* ZBB.

zero economic growth, a condition in which a nation's per capita income shows no appreciable increase.

There is a real crisis . . . in the shape of the looming recession, and the prospect of zero economic growth next year. That will mean a double crunch, political and economic; the first duty will be survival once again. *Phillip Whitehead, The Listener, Dec. 27, 1973, p 871*

[1965] *Abbreviation:* ZEG.

zero growth, 1 short for *zero population growth* (the condition in which the size of a population remains constant).

The possibility of zero growth in the population of the United States has stimulated some recent investigations of the implications of alternative paths to that condition, based on projections of the population as a whole. *Ernest B. Attah, "Racial Aspects of Zero Population Growth," Science, June 15, 1973, p 1143*

Several European countries—Austria, East and West Germany and Luxembourg—have already gone beyond zero growth: they have more deaths than births each year. The United Kingdom is right at the balance point, with births and deaths about equal. If current trends in fertility continue, Belgium, Czechoslovakia, Denmark, Hungary, Norway and Sweden will reach or fall below zero growth in a few years. *Charles F. Westoff, "Marriage and Fertility in the Developed Countries," Scientific American, Dec. 1978, p 51*

2 short for ZERO ECONOMIC GROWTH.

In 1965, the Oxford undergraduate economics exam asked, "Can economies have simultaneously zero growth,

rapid inflation, substantial unemployment, and a balance of payments deficit?" The acceptable answer back then was that this combination could occur only in an underdeveloped country. *Daniel Yergin, "Reports and Comment: Britain," The Atlantic, Jan. 1976, p 4*

3 a policy of preventing expansion or development.

This community of 1,500 [Bolinas] is not an incorporated township, but power to stop new construction is wielded through the five-man water board of the Public Utility District, a majority of which is dedicated to zero growth. They keep out developers by refusing to issue new water meters. *Ted Morgan, "The Good Life," The New York Times Magazine, July 4, 1976, p 73*

[1967 for defs. 1, 3; 1965 for def. 2]

zero-rate, *v.t. British.* to exempt from payment of a value-added tax.

Value Added Tax would be levied at 10 per cent. Food, other than pet foods, would be zero-rated: so would children's clothes and shoes. *William Hardcastle, "Britain's Week," The Listener, March 8, 1973, p 295*

The structure of the value added tax, which zero-rates half—the most important half—of family expenditure, can be shown to be in many respects progressive rather than regressive. *Peter Jenkins, The Manchester Guardian Weekly, Dec. 12, 1976, p 3*

[1972] See ADDED VALUE.

zero-rating, *n.:* There would also probably be fewer anomalies between items which were zero-rated and items which were positively rated, because the broad blocks of expenditure which had been relieved by zero-rating were clearly defined. *The Times (London), May 11, 1972, p 10*

zero tillage, another name for NO-TILLAGE.

Zero tillage, a technique for growing crops, enables grain farmers to reduce fuel consumption by 50 percent while protecting the soil from erosion, according to Elmer Stobbe, a plant scientist. . . . Zero tillage, which means no cultivation, involves seeding directly into untilled soil with minimum disturbance of the soil. *Daly deGagne, " 'Zero Tillage' Cuts Energy Use," The New York Times, Aug. 14, 1979, p C3*

[1977]

zetz, *U.S. Slang. Often figurative in use.* —*n.* a punch, blow, or slap.

The actor had come to tape "The Phil Donahue Show," to talk about his new movie, "The Big Fix," and maybe even to get a little zetz going with Donahue, whose political barbs during interviews had impressed him. *Cameron Crowe, "The Rolling Stone Interview: Richard Dreyfuss," Rolling Stone, Jan. 11, 1979, p 85*

—*v.t.* to strike, throw, or deliver.

We said we hadn't quite got his last remark. "That's glyph for 'Mein Gott im Himmel,' " he said. "I like to zetz in a little glyph now and then." *"The Talk of the Town," The New Yorker, Dec. 25, 1978, p 21*

[1968, from Yiddish *zets*, ultimately from *zetsn* to set, put]

zills (zilz), *n.pl.* a pair of round metal pieces attached by loops to the thumb and second finger and struck together for percussion and rhythm in belly dancing.

As the mid-eastern music starts to wail . . . the dancers begin to acquire some semblance of the right movement while finger cymbals (called zills) start tinkling out a dance rhythm. *Ursula Mahoney, "Belly Dancing," The New York Times, Nov. 24, 1974, p 39*

[1973, perhaps from an Arabic word related to ṣalil rattle, jingling, clatter]

Zim·ba·bwe (zim'bɑ:b wei), *n.* the name given to Rhodesia by African nationalists, adopted as the official name in 1979.

The political declaration expressed support and encouragement of the independence movements of Namibia (South-West Africa), Zimbabwe (Rhodesia), and Azania (South Africa); it harshly condemned South Africa's creation of alleged independent tribal states called Bantustans. *Robert Shaplen, "Letter from Sri Lanka," The New Yorker, Sept. 13, 1976, p 138*

Attributive use.

A U.N. peace-keeping force would guarantee a truce until the creation of a unified Zimbabwe army, composed of guerrillas and "acceptable elements" of the Rhodesian armed forces. *Time, Oct. 9, 1978, p 56*

[1961, from Shona (a Bantu language) *zimbabwe* dwellings of stone] See ZANU, ZAPU.

Zimbabwean or **Zimbabwian**, *adj., n.:* Once the Namibians and Zimbabweans have got their independence, the great black majority in South Africa is going to move to change the Republic into the state of Azania. *Andrew Faulds, The Times (London), May 4, 1976, p 12*

A guerrilla war would radicalize the Zimbabwean situation in the manner of Angola and Mozambique. *Basil Davidson, "The Aftermath of Angola," Britannica Book of the Year 1977, p 10*

Zimbabwe Rhodesia or **Zimbabwe-Rhodesia**, *n.* the name often given to Zimbabwe under the biracial interim government established in 1979.

Wars known only from newspaper accounts seem quite unreal, especially guerrilla wars of the kind that went on for seven years—until the ceasefire that took effect in December—in what is now called Zimbabwe-Rhodesia. *Roger Wilkins, "Our Far-Flung Correspondents: Transition," The New Yorker, Feb. 11, 1980, p 66*

But the lordly Governor of Britain's last African colony has little cause for buoyancy these days. He bears responsibility for running "free and fair" elections to Zimbabwe Rhodesia's new, 100-member House of Assembly. *Time, Feb. 4, 1980, p 45*

[1979]

Zimbabwe Rhodesian or **Zimbabwe-Rhodesian**, *adj.:* Zimbabwe Rhodesian officials here are keeping a close eye on developments at the Commonwealth conference just across the border in Zambia. *Tony Hawkins, "Zimbabwe Rhodesia Keeps Keen Ear on Lusaka Talks," The Christian Science Monitor, Aug. 1, 1979, p 11*

zine (zi:n), *n. U.S.* a magazine or newsletter produced by a science-fiction fan or group of fans.

Devra Langsam, one of our hard-working crew, was editor of *Spockanalia,* the very first "Star Trek" zine and still one of the best. *Joan Winston, The Making of the Trek Conventions, 1977, p 19*

[1965, short for *fanzine* (1951), from *fan* + maga*zine*]
▶ This form is frequently used by science-fiction fans to create nonce compounds such as *newszine, letterzine, book-a-zine.* For other examples, see "Star Trek Lives: Trekker Slang," by Patricia Byrd, in *American Speech,* Spring 1978, pp 52-54.

zip, *U.S. Slang. —n.* zero; nothing (often referring to a score in sports).

"Here are your facts," he said. "I think I've got everything here. Armed robbery. Zip to ten. Second offense. That's you, isn't it?" *John Cheever, Falconer, 1975, p 67*

In that span, folks, the Milwaukee Bucks did not score a basket. None. Zip. Zero. *New York Post, Feb. 11, 1976, p 88*

Score at the end of the first half of the first inning: 26 to zip. *Jay Cocks, "Cinema: Left-Field Hit," Review of "The Bad News Bears," Time, April 26, 1976, p 45*

A reliance on black culture, they say . . . may make you feel good, and it may be something you feel in your bones and on weekends and when the beat thumps, but it goes for zip in the real world. *William Brashler, "The Black Middle Class: Making It," The New York Times Magazine, Dec. 3, 1978, p 150*

—v.t. to beat (a team) without allowing it to score; shut out.

The Adams Division leaders zipped Los Angeles, 4-0. *Picture legend, "The King is Dead," Daily News (New York), Jan. 16, 1976, p 82*

"By God, the Broncos went out and beat the hell out of them, then the next week, went and zipped Cleveland." *Time, Jan. 16, 1978, p 66*

[1975, of uncertain origin]

zit, *n. U.S. Slang.* **1** a pimple.

The characters in the commercial are usually a young girl talking breathlessly about "blemishes" to a friend, or a girl and her brother "telling it like it is" by referring to their affliction as "zits." *Mopsy Strange Kennedy, "Acne Has No Respect for Age," The New York Times Magazine, April 15, 1979, p 69*

2 *Transferred use.*

One splendid effort in 1971 featured districts that looked like giant chickens . . . and districts with remarkable pimples in their boundary lines, zits that popped up to include the home of one liberal incumbent in the district of another liberal incumbent. *Molly Ivins, The Atlantic, March 1975, p 51*

[1975, of uncertain origin]

zizzy, *adj. Slang.* **1** showy in dress or manner.

My wife said I should wear a dark suit but I did risk a particularly zizzy tie. Everyone else seemed to be in deepest mourning. *Alec Guinness, The Times (London), Oct. 4, 1976, p 7*

2 that is boisterous and often clownish.

You have to let this Mel Brooks comedy do everything for you, because that's the only way it works. If you accept the silly, zizzy obviousness, it can make you laugh helplessly. *"Goings On About Town: In Brief," The New Yorker, May 17, 1976, p 27*

[1968, from *zizz* humming sound (as of a bee), buzz + -y (adj. suffix)]

Zollinger-Ellison syndrome, a condition of excessive secretion and hyperacidity of gastric juices resulting in the formation of peptic ulcers and tumors in cells of the pancreas.

The F.D.A.'s approval was . . . limited to the prescribing of Tagamet for up to eight-week treatments of duodenal ulcers and possibly longer periods for treatments of one of a complex of diseases known collectively by the forbidding eponym of Zollinger-Ellison syndrome. *Gilbert Cant, "Worrying About Ulcers," The New York Times Magazine, Nov. 6, 1977, p 76*

[1969, named after R. M. *Zollinger* and E. H. *Ellison,* American surgeons who first described it]

zoo, *n. Slang.* the large number and variety of nuclear particles discovered or proposed as a result of research in high-energy physics.

The large "zoo" of subatomic particles, as physicists call it, includes an even stranger will-o'-the-wisp called the neutrino: a virtually massless and chargeless bundle of energy. *"Science: Messages by Muons," Time, Aug. 14, 1972, p 74*

No one has yet seen a quark on its own — but the relevant categories of particles in the high energy physics zoo can now be fairly easily labelled by the number and type of quarks that make them up. *Ros Herman, New Scientist, Sept. 21, 1978, p 838*

[1974, from a comparison to animals in a zoo]

zoo plane, *U.S.* a plane carrying members of the news media assigned to follow a candidate during a campaign.

The atmosphere on the Zoo Plane became crazier and crazier as the atmosphere on the Dakota Queen became more reserved and somber. The kinkier members of the press tended to drift onto the Zoo Plane. The atmosphere was more comfortable. There were tremendous amounts of cocaine, for instance. . . . What happened was that the press took over the Zoo Plane — totally. *Hunter S. Thompson, Fear and Loathing: On the Campaign Trail '72, 1973, p 424*

[1972]

zo·o·se·mi·ot·ics (ˌzou əˌsi: mi:'at iks), *n.* the study of communication between animals.

In a collection of papers written by various experts in the field of . . . "zoosemiotics" — in other words, animal communication — each writer tries valiantly to define what he means by the term, and, if no two of them actually agree on a definition, at least they provide a most stimulating lot of theories. *Emily Hahn, "A Reporter At Large: Getting Through to Others," The New Yorker, April 17, 1978, p 78*

[1965, coined by the American linguist Thomas A. Sebeok, born 1920, from *zoo-* combining form meaning animal + *semiotics* study of signs and symbols]

zo·o·tox·in (ˌzou ə'tak sən), *n.* any of various poisons produced by animals.

Zootoxins can be divided into: (1) oral poisons, those poisonous when eaten; (2) parenteral poisons or venoms . . . and (3) crinotoxins. *Bruce W. Halstead, "Biotoxins: The Poisons of Life," 1977 Britannica Yearbook of Science and the Future (1976), p 229*

[1976]

Z-therapy, *n.* a form of psychotherapy in which the patient is held down by a group of people, interrogated sharply, and compelled by rough prodding or tickling to release pent-up emotions supposedly leading to a catharsis.

The controversial 'Z therapy' . . . may benefit nonpsychotic children who have severe antisocial personality disorders, Dr. Foster W. Cline said at the annual meeting of the American Association for the Advancement of Science. . . . 'Z therapy' is based on the assumption that children who are unable to love because they were unloved must have love forced on them before they can develop other loving attachments. *Thomas Szasz, The Myth of Psychotherapy, 1979, p 206, quoting Clinical Psychiatry News (June, 1977), p 50*

[1973, from Robert W. *Zaslow,* an American psychologist, who developed it + *therapy*]

Zug·un·ru·he ('tsu:k u:nˌru: ə; *Anglicized* 'zu:gənˌru: *or* -ˌru: ə), *n.* the migratory drive in animals, especially birds.

The behavior of the four groups was studied in terms of signs of *Zugunruhe,* or migratory urge, as shown by night activity and by the molt of feathers (which normally occurs during the winter after migration to the wintering area). *Eric T. Pengelley and Sally J. Asmundson, "Annual Biological Clocks," Scientific American, April 1971, p 76*

There have been several reports in the literature of extraretinally mediated effects of light on avian circadian and reproductive cycles, for example, *Zugunruhe,* fat deposition, and testicular growth. *Marshall Stephen Harth and Marieta Barrow Heaton, "Nonvisual Photic Responsiveness in Newly Hatched Pigeons (Columbia livia)," Science, May 18, 1973, p 753*

[1967, from German, from *Zug* travel + *Unruhe* unrest]

Zulu, *n.* the aeronautical name for Greenwich Mean Time.

On the walls, digital clocks told the time at Greenwich, England — Zulu it is called — at major radar stations. *The New York Times, Jan. 29, 1978, p 8*

At 1750 hours Zulu, about three in the afternoon local time, the *Double Eagle II* climbed to 10,000 feet, but it was still difficult to maintain altitude. *Charles McCarthy, "Book Section: Double Eagle," The Reader's Digest, Nov. 1979, p 283*

[1963, from the present radio code name for the letter *z* (replacing the older name *Zebra,* as in *Zebra time* and *Z Time*) to represent *zero* degrees, the longitude at Greenwich, England]

Zwicky galaxy or **Zwicky object,** any of a group of compact galaxies whose luminosity is concentrated in a small area.

Along with a small army of research students he has . . . circulated several lists of compact galaxies (now called Zwicky galaxies). *"Feedback: Astronomical Gold Medalist," New Scientist, March 2, 1972, p 501*

[E. E.] Khachikyan says that it is now clear that the Markarian galaxies, under their broad umbrella of excess ultraviolet, contain many different types: Seyferts, Zwicky objects, . . . many giant galaxies, many dwarf galaxies, distant galaxies and close galaxies; even quasars might be numbered among them. *Dietrick E. Thomsen, Science News, Aug. 18-25, 1973, p 117*

[1969, named for Fritz *Zwicky,* 1898-1974, a Bulgarian-born American astronomer and inventor, who catalogued them]

zy·mo·gram ('zɑi məˌgræm), *n.* a diagram or other representation of the different molecular forms of an enzyme, obtained by electrophoresis.

Most varieties have consistent patterns of isozymes (variants of the esterase enzymes). . . . The isozyme distribution can be summarised in a zymogram, which provides the basis for identifying the variety of the seedling. But the identification is not a "finger-printing" — some varieties cannot be distinguished from each other. *"How to Tell One Seed from Another," New Scientist, April 4, 1974, p 26*

[1964, from *zymo-* combining form meaning enzyme + *-gram* something drawn]